B L A C K S E A
P9-DSZ-569
Ephesus
Antioch
Damascus
N
S E A
Jerusalem
Alexandria
E LOWENSTEIN

THE INTERPRETER'S BIBLE

THE INTERPRETER'S BIBLE

IN TWELVE VOLUMES

VOLUME

I. General Articles on the Bible; General Articles on the Old Testament; Genesis; Exodus

II. Leviticus; Numbers; Deuteronomy; Joshua; Judges; Ruth; Samuel

III. Kings; Chronicles; Ezra; Nehemiah; Esther; Job

IV. Psalms; Proverbs

V. Ecclesiastes; Song of Songs; Isaiah; Jeremiah

VI. Lamentations; Ezekiel; Daniel; Hosea; Joel; Amos; Obadiah; Jonah; Micah; Nahum; Habakkuk; Zephaniah; Haggai; Zechariah; Malachi

VII. General Articles on the New Testament; Matthew; Mark

VIII. Luke; John

IX. Acts; Romans

X. Corinthians; Galatians; Ephesians

XI. Philippians; Colossians; Thessalonians; Timothy; Titus; Philemon; Hebrews

XII. James; Peter; John; Jude; Revelation; General Articles; Indexes

VOLUME IX

THE ACTS
OF THE APOSTLES

THE EPISTLE TO THE
ROMANS

EDITORIAL BOARD

GEORGE ARTHUR BUTTRICK
Commentary Editor

WALTER RUSSELL BOWIE
Associate Editor of Exposition

PAUL SCHERER
Associate Editor of Exposition

JOHN KNOX
Associate Editor of New Testament Introduction and Exegesis

SAMUEL TERRIEN
Associate Editor of Old Testament Introduction and Exegesis

NOLAN B. HARMON
Editor, Abingdon Press

THE INTERPRETER'S BIBLE

The Holy Scriptures

IN THE KING JAMES AND REVISED STANDARD VERSIONS
WITH GENERAL ARTICLES AND
INTRODUCTION, EXEGESIS, EXPOSITION
FOR EACH BOOK OF THE BIBLE

IN TWELVE VOLUMES

VOLUME
IX

Ἐν ἀρχῇ ἦν ὁ λόγος

Abingdon
NASHVILLE

Copyright 1954 by Pierce and Washabaugh in the United States of America. Copyright secured in all countries of the International Copyright Union. Published simultaneously in the United States, the Dominion of Canada, and Great Britain. All rights reserved. No part of the text may be reproduced in any manner whatsoever without written permission of the publishers, except brief quotations embodied in critical articles or reviews.
For information, address Abingdon,
Nashville, Tennessee.

ISBN-0-687-19215-3

Library of Congress Catalog Card Number: 51-12276

The text of the Revised Standard Version of the Bible (RSV) and quotations therefrom are copyright 1946, 1952 by Division of Christian Education of the National Council of the Churches of Christ in the United States of America. Scripture quotations designated "ASV" are from the American Standard Version of the Revised Bible, copyright renewed 1929 by the International Council of Religious Education. Those designated "Moffatt" are from *The Bible, A New Translation*, by James Moffatt, copyright in the United States, 1935, by Harper & Brothers, New York; copyright in countries of the International Copyright Union by Hodder & Stoughton, Ltd., London. Those designated "Amer. Trans." or "Goodspeed" are from *The Complete Bible, An American Translation*, by J. M. Powis Smith and Edgar J. Goodspeed, copyright 1939 by the University of Chicago.

Thirty-seventh Printing 1982

MANUFACTURED BY THE PARTHENON
PRESS AT NASHVILLE, TENNESSEE,
UNITED STATES OF AMERICA

ABBREVIATIONS AND EXPLANATIONS

Abbreviations

Canonical books and bibliographical terms are abbreviated according to common usage

Amer. Trans. — *The Bible, An American Translation,* Old Testament, ed. J. M. P. Smith
Apoc.—Apocrypha
Aq.—Aquila
ASV—American Standard Version (1901)
Barn.—Epistle of Barnabas
Clem.—Clement
C.T.—Consonantal Text
Did.—Didache
Ecclus.—Ecclesiasticus
ERV—English Revised Version (1881-85)
Exeg.—Exegesis
Expos.—Exposition
Goodspeed—*The Bible, An American Translation,* New Testament and Apocrypha, tr. Edgar J. Goodspeed
Herm. Vis., etc.—The Shepherd of Hermas: Visions, Mandates, Similitudes
Ign. Eph., etc.—Epistles of Ignatius to the Ephesians, Magnesians, Trallians, Romans, Philadelphians, Smyrnaeans, and Polycarp
KJV—King James Version (1611)
LXX—Septuagint
Macc.—Maccabees
Moffatt—*The Bible, A New Translation,* by James Moffatt
M.T.—Masoretic Text
N.T.—New Testament
O.T.—Old Testament
Polyc. Phil.—Epistle of Polycarp to the Philippians
Pseudep.—Pseudepigrapha
Pss. Sol.—Psalms of Solomon
RSV—Revised Standard Version (1946-52)
Samar.—Samaritan recension
Symm.—Symmachus
Targ.—Targum
Test. Reuben, etc.—Testament of Reuben, and others of the Twelve Patriarchs
Theod.—Theodotion
Tob.—Tobit
Vulg.—Vulgate
Weymouth—*The New Testament in Modern Speech,* by Richard Francis Weymouth
Wisd. Sol.—Wisdom of Solomon

Quotations and References

Boldface type in Exegesis and Exposition indicates a quotation from either the King James or the Revised Standard Version of the passage under discussion. The two versions are distinguished only when attention is called to a difference between them. Readings of other versions are not in boldface type and are regularly identified.

In scripture references a letter (*a, b,* etc.) appended to a verse number indicates a clause within the verse; an additional Greek letter indicates a subdivision within the clause. When no book is named, the book under discussion is understood.

Arabic numbers connected by colons, as in scripture references, indicate chapters and verses in deuterocanonical and noncanonical works. For other ancient writings roman numbers indicate major divisions, arabic numbers subdivisions, these being connected by periods. For modern works a roman number and an arabic number connected by a comma indicate volume and page. Bibliographical data on a contemporary work cited by a writer may be found by consulting the first reference to the work by that writer (or the bibliography, if the writer has included one).

Greek Transliterations

α = a	ε = e	ι = i	ν = n	ρ = r	φ = ph
β = b	ζ = z	κ = k	ξ = x	σ(ς) = s	χ = ch
γ = g	η = ē	λ = l	ο = o	τ = t	ψ = ps
δ = d	θ = th	μ = m	π = p	υ = u, y	ω = ō

Hebrew and Aramaic Transliterations

I. HEBREW ALPHABET

א = ʾ	ה = h	ט = ṭ	מ(ם) = m	פ(ף) = p, ph	שׁ = s, sh
ב = b, bh	ו = w	י = y	נ(ן) = n	צ(ץ) = ç	ת = t, th
ג = g, gh	ז = z	כ(ך) = k, kh	ס = ş	ק = q	
ד = d, dh	ח = ḥ	ל = l	ע = ʿ	ר = r	

II. MASORETIC POINTING

Pure-long	Tone-long	Short	Composite *shᵉwa*
◌ָ = â	◌ָ = ā	◌ַ = a	◌ֲ = ª
◌ֵ = ê	◌ֵ = ē	◌ֶ = e	◌ֱ = ᵉ
◌ִ *or* ◌ִי = î		◌ִ = i	
וֹ *or* ◌ֹ = ô	◌ֹ = ō	◌ָ = o	◌ֳ = ᵒ
וּ = û		◌ֻ = u	

Note: (*a*) The *páthaḥ* furtive is transliterated as a *ḥaṭeph-páthaḥ.* (*b*) The simple *shᵉwa,* when vocal, is transliterated ᵉ. (*c*) The tonic accent, which is indicated only when it occurs on a syllable other than the last, is transliterated by an acute accent over the vowel.

TABLE OF CONTENTS

VOLUME IX

THE ACTS OF THE APOSTLES

THE EPISTLE TO THE ROMANS

MAPS

THE ACTS OF THE APOSTLES

Introduction and Exegesis by G. H. C. Macgregor

Exposition by Theodore P. Ferris

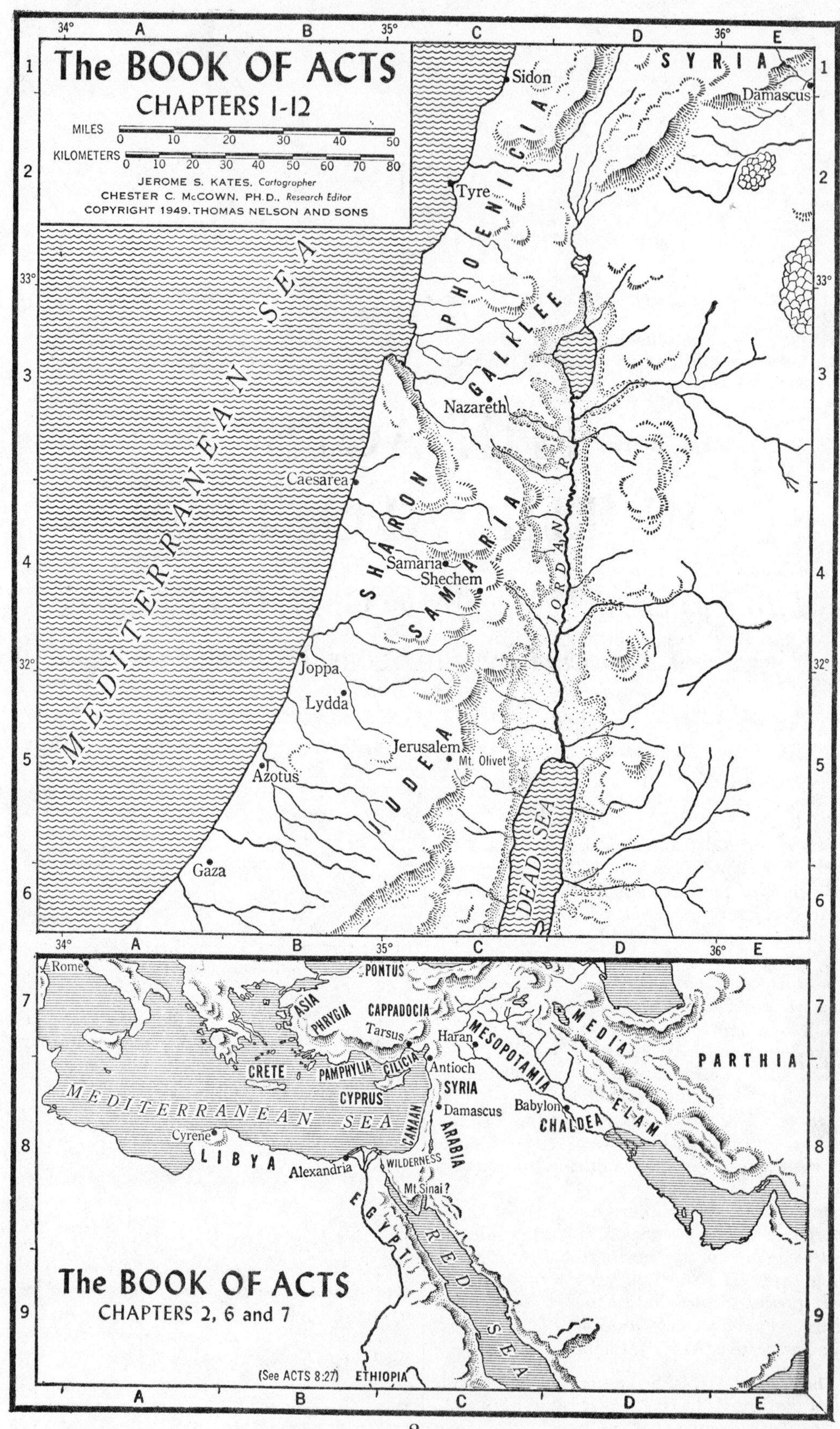

The BOOK OF ACTS
CHAPTERS 1-12
MILES
0 10 20 30 40 50
KILOMETERS
0 10 20 30 40 50 60 70 80
JEROME S. KATES, Cartographer
CHESTER C. McCOWN, PH.D., Research Editor
COPYRIGHT 1949. THOMAS NELSON AND SONS
34°
35°
36°
33°
32°
A
B
C
D
E
1
2
3
4
5
6
MEDITERRANEAN SEA
SYRIA
Sidon
Damascus
PHOENICIA
Tyre
GALILEE
Nazareth
Caesarea
SHARON
SAMARIA
Samaria
Shechem
JORDAN R.
Joppa
Lydda
Jerusalem
Mt. Olivet
JUDEA
Azotus
Gaza
DEAD SEA
7
8
9
Rome
PONTUS
ASIA
PHRYGIA
CAPPADOCIA
Tarsus
Haran
MESOPOTAMIA
MEDIA
PARTHIA
CRETE
PAMPHYLIA
CILICIA
Antioch
SYRIA
CYPRUS
MEDITERRANEAN SEA
CANAAN
Damascus
Babylon
CHALDEA
ELAM
Cyrene
LIBYA
Alexandria
ARABIA
WILDERNESS
Mt. Sinai?
EGYPT
RED SEA
The BOOK OF ACTS
CHAPTERS 2, 6 and 7
(See ACTS 8:27)
ETHIOPIA

ACTS

INTRODUCTION

It might well be claimed for "Luke"—the name is used without prejudging the problem of authorship—that he is the most important of all the New Testament writers. His two-volume work, most conveniently known as "Luke-Acts," is the longest contribution made by any one author. It comprises rather more than one quarter of the entire New Testament, and exceeds in bulk both the Pauline corpus of thirteen letters and the five writings—Gospel, epistles, and Revelation—traditionally ascribed to "John."

But in terms of content Luke's work is even more important. The Third Gospel is much the richest of the three Synoptics. It contains a great deal more material peculiar to itself—including a number of the best-loved parables and most of our information concerning the postresurrection days—than does either Matthew or Mark. The loss of no other one book would have deprived us of so much information about Jesus and his teaching.

The book of Acts is at least of equal importance, for no parallel narrative of the beginnings of Christianity has survived. True, by reading between the lines, we can deduce from the Pauline epistles much valuable information concerning the missionary work of the great apostle and his companions. But many of Paul's references to the events of his life would be quite obscure to us but for the light thrown upon them by Acts. Luke's continuous narrative provides the indispensable framework wherein Paul's passing allusions fall into their true perspective. As H. J. Cadbury has said:

> The Book of Acts is the keystone linking the two major portions of the New Testament, the "Gospel" and the "Apostle," as the early Christians called them, . . . the only bridge we have across the seemingly impassable gulf that separates Jesus from Paul, Christ from Christianity, the gospel of Jesus from the gospel\about Jesus.[1]

I. Luke-Acts: Its Unity and Common Authorship

It is of the utmost importance to visualize the Third Gospel and the book of Acts as two parts of a single whole. Scholarship has been greatly handicapped by their conventional treatment in introductions and commentaries as separate books, and a commentary which will deal with the whole of Luke's work as a single unit is still greatly to be desired. Amidst the sharpest division of opinion concerning many of the critical problems of Acts, modern scholars are almost unanimous that Luke and Acts have a common author. Even among radicals, Norden and Loisy (see pp. 14, 20) stand almost alone in attributing to the author of the Third Gospel, not the whole of Acts, but only its principal source—the travel diary. Apart altogether from the witness of tradition, the linguistic evidence (see pp. 7-8) seems conclusive that however diverse the sources of his information, one ultimate editor has left his own hallmark upon the whole of his varied materials from the beginning of Luke to the end of Acts. For conservative and radical scholars alike to accept or deny the "Lukan" authorship of Acts means the acceptance or denial of the "Lukan" authorship of the Gospel.

A study of the major interests of the two books (see Intro. to Luke's Gospel, Vol. VIII)

[1] *The Making of Luke-Acts* (New York: The Macmillan Co., 1927), p. 2.

confirms the impression of unity of authorship. Both regard Christianity as the new universal religion that recognizes no limitations of race (Luke 2:32; 4:23-27; 10:29-37; 17:15-18—and note the omission of the material of Matt. 7:6; 10:5-6; 15:21-28; 18:17—Acts 10:34-35; 13:46-47; 17:26-28; 28:28). Both continually emphasize the power of the Holy Spirit at work, first in the ministry of Jesus himself, and subsequently in the apostolic missions (Luke 1:15, 35; 2:25-27; 3:22; 4:1, 18; 10:21; 24:49; Acts 1:2, 8; 2:1-4, 38; 8:14-17, 29, 39; 10:44-47; 13:2, 4, 9; 15:28; 16:7; 19:1-7; etc.). Both show a marked sympathy for the poor (Luke 3:11; 4:18; 6:20; 16:22; Acts 2:44-45; 4:34-35; 9:36, 39), a certain antipathy to the rich (Luke 1:53; 6:24; 12:13-21; 16:14, 19 ff.; Acts 8:18-24), and stress the duty of the proper stewardship of wealth (Luke 12:42-48; 16:1-13; 19:12-27; Acts 4:36-37; 5:1-11; 20:35). Both seem specially interested in the part played by women in the Christian community (Luke 1:39-56; 2:36-38; 7:37-38; 23:27-29; 24:10; Acts 5:1 ff.; 9:36 ff.; 12:12-13; 16:13-15, 16-18; 18:2; 24:24; 25:13). Both give much attention to such subjects as prayer (Luke 11:5-13; 18:1-5, 9-14; 22:39-46—and note the references to Jesus at prayer, not in Mark, in Luke 3:21; 6:12; 9:28-29; 11:1—Acts 1:24-25; 2:42; 4:31; 6:6; 10:2, 9; 12:12; 13:3; 16:25; 21:5), "grace" or "favor" (the word χάρις, which is used by neither Mark nor Matthew, occurs nine times in Luke and seventeen times in Acts), and the forgiveness of sins (Luke 1:77; 7:47; 11:4; 15:11-32; 24:47; Acts 2:38; 5:31; 10:43; 13:38; 26:18). We even have hints in the Gospel of what we shall find to be one of the main postulates of Acts—that Christianity is not to be considered a subversive sect, but on the contrary was in general regarded with favor by the Roman authorities, who but for the inveterate hatred of the Jews would have refused to condemn either Jesus or his apostles (Luke 20:20-26; 23:4, 13-16, 20-22, 47; Acts 13:7, 12; 16:35-40; 18:12-17; 19:31, 37; 23:26-30; 24:23; 25:25-27; 26:30-32; 27:43; 28:30-31).

But not only have Luke and Acts a common author; they are two parts of one continuous work. Nor should we think of Acts as a mere "sequel" to the Gospel, written it may be years later as an afterthought. The second volume was almost certainly part of the author's original plan for a two-volume work. Indeed it has been conjectured that he orginally intended to write a third volume, and that only so can the abrupt ending of Acts be satisfactorily explained (see Exeg. at end of ch. 28). However that may be, that Luke planned at least two volumes seems conclusively proved by the twin prefaces (see below, p. 20 and Exeg. on 1:1). Both volumes are addressed to the same Theophilus. The opening verses of Luke appear to be a general *prooimion* covering both volumes, for the words "the things which have been accomplished among us" (Luke 1:1) obviously have reference not only to the contents of the Gospel, but to the whole story of the birth and growth of Christianity, which is the theme of both books. Similarly the preface of Acts is a conventional *proekthesis,* which refers to "the first book" (Acts 1:1), or "volume one," as we should say, and picks up the thread of events where it was there broken off. The Gospel ends with Jesus' assurance that he will "send the promise of my Father upon you," with his command to "stay in the city, until you are clothed with power from on high," and with the briefest possible account of how "he parted from them." Acts opens with a reminder of this promise and command, a picture of the disciples waiting at Jerusalem for its fulfillment, a fuller account of the Ascension, and a vivid description of the fulfillment of the promise by the gift of the Spirit at Pentecost. Just as volume one looked forward to volume two, so does volume two look back to volume one. Both are parts of a single planned whole.

The unity and common authorship of Luke and Acts being thus assumed, how are we to explain the early separation of the two books in the arrangement of the New Testament writings? The first volume corresponded in character and contents with other outlines of Jesus' life and teaching, and together with the three other "Gospels" it passed into the New Testament canon as one of a clearly defined group of four which, with certain variations in order, were also transmitted together. The second volume, the Acts, appeared to belong to a different category of writings. It too had a number of close relatives in early Christian literature, memorabilia about the apostles, but alone in this class of writings it won a place in the canon. It thus became separated from its companion volume, and its place in the order of the New Testament books varies according as it is related more closely to the Catholic epistles or to the Pauline epistles.

> The book was canonised first of all as a supplement to the catholic epistles,—to make up for the fact that many of the apostles had left no writings behind them,—and, in the second place, as a link between the Pauline and the catholic epistles, by way of documentary proof that Paul and the twelve were at one.[2]

The most ancient tradition seems to have closely associated Acts with the Catholic epistles,

[2] Johann Leipoldt, *Geschichte des Neutestamentliche Kanons* (Leipzig: J. C. Hinrichs, 1907-8), I, 205, tr. in James Moffatt, *Introduction to the Literature of the New*

and we have the order: Gospels, Acts, Catholic epistles, Pauline epistles. This is the order of the codices A, B, and C, of the Fathers Athanasius and Cyril of Jerusalem; and among modern editors Tischendorff, Westcott and Hort, and von Soden have adopted it. A rarer order, but one which still associates Acts with the Catholic epistles, is: Gospels, Pauline epistles, Acts, Catholic epistles. This is the order in Codex Sinaiticus, and it is also attested by Epiphanius and Jerome. Sometimes, on the other hand, Acts is associated more closely with the Pauline epistles, so that we have the order: Gospels, Acts, Pauline epistles, Catholic epistles. This order is found in none of the more ancient manuscripts, but it is attested among other authorities by the Muratorian Canon, Eusebius, and the Codex Amiatinus of the Vulgate. Most of the early editors—Erasmus, Stephanus, Théodore de Bèze, the Elzeviri—followed it, so that it became the recognized order in the Textus Receptus and consequently in nearly all modern translations.

What title, if any, the author gave to his two-volume work, we do not know. Ancient writers commonly entitled their books "Concerning So-and-So," or used the name of their patron: in Luke's case the title would be, if dedicated in Latin, *Ad Theophilum.* Only after the separation of the two volumes would the title Acts (πράξεις) of the Apostles be applied to the second. The word πράξεις had previously been used as a book title, as, for example, by Callisthenes, a contemporary of Alexander the Great, who wrote *The Acts of Alexander.* The title Acts of the Apostles does not correspond particularly well with the contents of the book, which has nothing to say about any of the original "apostles" save Peter and John. It probably reflects the point of view of the second-century church for which Peter and Paul were the "apostles" par excellence. But πράξεις was a simple and natural word to employ as a title, and it was probably not originally intended to indicate any formal literary classification. Nevertheless once it had been applied to the canonical "Acts," the latter became in fact the prototype of a succession of apocryphal "Acts" which, however inferior in quality, were felt to belong to the same literary genre.

II. Luke-Acts: The Witness of Tradition

Tradition is unanimous in ascribing both the Third Gospel and Acts to Luke, but it is not till the latter part of the second century that Acts is expressly quoted as his work. The writings of the Apostolic Fathers contain what may well be echoes of Acts, but they are never so precise as to demand direct dependence. Clement of Rome, for example, speaks of "giving more willingly than receiving,"[3] which recalls the words of Jesus quoted in Acts 20:35, "It is more blessed to give than to receive," but is hardly a direct quotation. Similarly the fact that in the same epistle Ps. 89:20 and I Sam. 13:14 are combined in the same manner as in Acts 13:22 may indicate no more than that both writers are dependent on the same collection of "testimonies," or messianic proof texts.

In Did. 4:8 we have the words, "Thou shalt share everything in common with thy brother, and thou shalt not say that it belongs to thee personally," which again reads like an echo of Acts 4:32, but is not close enough to be regarded as an actual quotation.[4] Similarly Barnabas, Ignatius, Polycarp, and Hermas all contain phrases which are more or less closely reminiscent of Acts and create a presumption, which however falls short of certainty, that they were familiar with Luke's work.[5]

In the last quarter of the second century the evidence becomes perfectly definite. In the Western church Irenaeus regards Acts as holy Scripture and cites it as *Lucae de apostolis testificatio.*[6] The Muratorian Canon is still more explicit: "The Acts of all the Apostles are written in a single book. Luke compiled for 'most excellent Theophilus' everything that happened in detail in his presence . . ."—a statement evidently intended to exclude from the canon the various apocryphal "Acts." Similarly Tertullian in the church of Africa speaks of Acts as a "commentary of Luke," and in Alexandria Clement[7] recognizes it as an authentic Lukan writing.

Thereafter the testimony of tradition regarding Acts no less than the Third Gospel is so unanimous that it is unnecessary to cite witnesses. As Moffatt puts it: "What helped eventually to popularise [Acts] and to win canonical prestige was its ecclesiastical emphasis on the apostles and Paul as leaders of the catholic church—a trait which became particularly grateful in the controversy with Marcion."[8]

Testament (New York: Charles Scribner's Sons, 1923), p. 314.

[3] I Clem. 2:1.

[4] Cf. also Did. 1:2, πάντα δὲ ὅσα ἐὰν θελήσῃς μὴ γίνεσθαι σοι, καὶ σὺ ἄλλῳ μὴ ποίει with the Western addition in Acts 15:20, καὶ ὅσα μὴ θέλετε ἑαυτοὶς γίνεσθαι, ἑτέρῳ μὴ ποιεῖν.

[5] Cf. Barn. 7:2 with Acts 10:42; Barn. 4-14; 5:8 (τέρατα καὶ σημεῖα) with Acts *passim;* Ign. Magn. 5:1 with Acts 1:25; Ign. Smyrn. 3:3 with Acts 10:41; Polyc. Phil. 1:2 with Acts 2:24; Herm. Vis. IV. 2. 4 with Acts 4:12; Mand. IV. 3. 4 with Acts 1:24.

[6] *Against Heresies* III. 13. 3; cf. also III. 14. 1 ff.

[7] Tertullian *On Fasting* 10; Clement *Miscellanies* V. 12.

[8] *Intro. to Literature of N.T.*, p. 314.

III. Luke the Physician in the New Testament and in Tradition

Apart from what we can deduce from Acts, on the assumption that it, or at least the diary source, is to be ascribed to him, the New Testament tells us little of Luke. In Col. 4:14 Paul calls him "the beloved physician," and he is mentioned as if in Paul's company along with Aristarchus, Mark, Jesus Justus, Epaphras, and Demas. The first three are called "the only men of the circumcision among my fellow workers" (Col. 4:11), whence it may be deduced that Luke was a Gentile by origin. The same names, except that of Justus, are mentioned in Philem. 24 and are called by Paul "my fellow workers." In II Tim. 4:10-11 Luke is again mentioned alongside Demas, which suggests some possible relationship between them. But "Demas . . . has deserted me . . . ; Luke alone is with me." Doubt as to the authenticity of the Pastorals lessens the value of this allusion.

Efforts have been made to find references to Luke elsewhere in the New Testament. Theophylact and Gregory the Great wished to identify him with the unnamed companion of Cleopas on the road to Emmaus (Luke 24:13 ff.); but this is pure speculation. Tradition numbered him among "the seventy" (Luke 10:1), but this is most improbable if he was of pagan origin. An allusion to him has been supposed in "the brother, whose praise is in the gospel throughout all the churches" (II Cor. 8:18 KJV), who was sent by Paul with Titus to Corinth. But the correct translation is "the brother who is famous among all the churches for his preaching of the gospel" (RSV); and to see in a letter written as early as II Corinthians, as do Origen and Jerome,[9] an allusion to Luke's Gospel is of course an anachronism. Luke has been identified also with one or other Lucius mentioned in Acts 13:1 (see Exeg., *ad loc.*) and Rom. 16:21 on the supposition that the Greek form Loukas is an intimate abbreviated form of Loukios, which inscriptions show was used in the vernacular koine for the Latin Lucius. Finally the attempt to identify Luke with Silvanus (Silas)—on the ground presumably that the Latin term *lucus* is a synonym for *silva*—can only be pronounced with Alfred Plummer "a caricature of critical ingenuity."

Later traditions outside the New Testament have little if any historical value. In some lists of apostles Luke is given a place beside Paul and Mark to the exclusion of Philip, Thaddaeus, and James the son of Alphaeus. He is said variously to have conducted missions in Italy, Greece, Dalmatia, Gaul, Bithynia, Africa—in fact over all the known world. One legend makes him a notable painter. In others he appears as bishop either of Alexandria or Laodicea. Traditions about his death are equally conflicting. Sometimes he dies a natural death, both at Thebes in Boeotia and at Ephesus; sometimes he suffers a martyr's death, either by decapitation at Alexandria or in a mass slaughter with "169 brothers" at Rome. His relics were allegedly transferred to Constantinople in A.D. 357 with those of Andrew and Timothy.[10]

The one tradition which is so ancient and widespread as to appear likely to have some substance is that Luke hailed from Antioch in Syria. Eusebius expressly describes him as "being by birth of those from Antioch and by profession a physician," and his statement reappears in Jerome who speaks of "Luke the physician, an Antiochian."[11] The Western text after Acts 11:27 reads: "And there was great rejoicing; and when *we* were gathered together one of them stood up and said . . ."—as if Luke himself were present. Even though this is only a Western addition, it may witness to the early belief that Luke was associated with the church at Antioch during the first stay there of Paul and Barnabas. Harnack[12] has attempted with some success to show from the internal evidence of Acts its author's special interest in Antioch. On the other hand it is possible that the tradition merely grew out of a false Western reading which, by introducing a "we" at Antioch in Acts 11:27, invited the deduction that this was Luke's place of residence. It has even been plausibly suggested that Luke's alleged Antiochene origin is a deduction from that of Theophilus. The title "most excellent" indicates a man of rank. The romance called the *Clementine Recognitions*[13] pictures Theophilus as a wealthy resident of Antioch. Later Christian writers transformed him into a bishop, and finally confounded him with the famous apologist at the end of the second century, Bishop Theophilus of Antioch. Has Luke simply been assigned to the same city as his patron? Nevertheless only one other city seriously rivals Antioch as Luke's possible birthplace. Ramsay, following Renan, claims the honor for Philippi, arguing that the "man of Macedonia" (16:9) whom Paul saw in a vision at Troas, was in fact Luke, who had visited Paul to plead the claims of his own city to hear the gospel. The first authentic "we-

[9] Origen *Hom. 1 in Lucam;* Jerome *On Famous Men* 7.

[10] For these legends see Theodor Schermann, *Prophetenund Apostellegenden* (Leipzig: J. C. Hinrichs, 1907).

[11] Eusebius *Church History* III. 4. 7; Jerome *On Famous Men* 7.

[12] *Luke the Physician,* tr. J. R. Wilkinson (London: Williams & Norgate, 1907), pp. 20-24.

[13] X. 1.

passage" begins in the very next verse, and Paul makes his way directly to Philippi. Luke's native pride is evidenced in 16:12, where he calls Philippi "the leading city of the district of Macedonia." S. C. Carpenter ingeniously suggests that "the two views [as to Luke's place of origin] may perhaps be combined by supposing that he was an Antiochene who was in medical practice at Philippi."[14] To the much-debated question when Luke became a Christian, many possible answers have been suggested. Was it at Antioch when Paul came there with Barnabas? Or at Troas, when according to Ramsay, he met Paul for the first time? Or at Antioch in Galatia, when, as Rackham suggests, Paul may have called him in to attend him? Harnack's conclusion is the wisest: "We have no knowledge when and by whose influence he became a Christian, nor whether he had previously come into sympathetic touch with the Judaism of the Dispersion; only one thing is certain—that he had never been in Jerusalem or Palestine."[15]

IV. Luke-Acts: Its Style, Vocabulary, and Literary Character

The author of Luke-Acts is an accomplished and versatile literary artist, and his style is very supple and varied. As is evident from a study of the Synoptic parallels, he does not hesitate to polish and embellish the language of his Marcan source to a much greater extent than does Matthew. In Acts some of his narratives—the gift of the Spirit at Pentecost, the story of Philip the evangelist, the conversion of Cornelius—are written in an archaic, redundant style which is characteristically Hebraic; while others, such as the account of Paul's appearance before the Areopagus, are so wholly Greek in color and outlook as to suggest that they could be written only by a pure Hellene. The truth is that the book is written, not in one style, but in several; and this can be explained, not merely by the use of varied sources, but by the author's practice of skillfully adapting his style to suit the atmosphere of the situation which he is describing. As J. H. Moulton has said, "He steeps his style in Biblical phraseology, drawn from the Greek Old Testament, so long as his narrative moves in Palestinian circles, where the speakers use Greek that obviously represents a foreign idiom," whereas he "instinctively departs from that style when his subject takes him away from the Biblical land and people."[16] As Cadbury has pointed out, it is sometimes difficult to decide whether imitation is conscious or unconscious. The "biblical flavor" of writers like Bunyan and Lincoln was unconscious; but Luke belonged to an age in which imitative style was not uncommon, so that it is likely enough that some of the more obvious Semitisms, especially in the speeches of Acts, are deliberate biblical imitation. Note too the Hebrew prepositional use of parts of the body: "to the face of" (before), "from the face of" (away from), "on the face of" (upon), "by the hand of," "by the mouth of." Nor, one feels, would any Greek man of letters, as was Luke, use except by way of imitation such characteristic Semitic parallelisms as "in the gall of bitterness and in the bond of iniquity" (8:23) or "that they may turn from darkness to light and from the power of Satan to God" (26:18).[17]

In a series of elaborate linguistic studies Harnack and in particular J. C. Hawkins[18] claim with justice to have proved a unity of style between the Third Gospel and Acts. There are undoubtedly more affinities of vocabulary between these two books than between any other two New Testament writings. There are, for example, seventeen words found both in Acts and Matthew but nowhere else in the New Testament; fourteen words found only in Acts and Mark; thirteen only in Acts and John; but no fewer than fifty-eight found only in Acts and Luke. By similar methods of analysis the linguistic unity of the whole book of Acts can be demonstrated, for the characteristic "Lukan" expressions occur in all sections—in the early chapters as well as in the diary source. This would seem to suggest either that the writer of the diary is the author of the whole book, which is the traditional view; or that the author of the book as a whole has imposed his own style on someone else's diary; or even conversely that a later editor has assimilated his own style to that of the Lukan diary source which he is incorporating. Of the three alternatives the first appears much the most probable. The third alternative seems very unnatural, though Maurice Goguel pleads in its favor that Harnack's statistics show the "we-sections" to be "not only Lukan but hyper-Lukan." They are the fountainhead of the Lukan style, which is more diluted throughout the rest of the book.[19]

Much weight has also been put on the linguistic argument that the author of Luke-Acts

[14] *Christianity According to S. Luke* (London: Society for Promoting Christian Knowledge, 1919), p. 20.

[15] *Luke the Physician,* p. 146.

[16] *A Grammar of New Testament Greek* (Edinburgh: T. & T. Clark, 1919), II, 7-8.

[17] See Cadbury, *Making of Luke-Acts,* pp. 122-23.

[18] Harnack, *Luke the Physician,* ch. ii; Hawkins, *Horae Synopticae* (2nd ed.; Oxford: Clarendon Press, 1909), pp. 174-93.

[19] *Introduction au Nouveau Testament,* "Le Livre des Actes" (Paris: Ernest Leroux, 1922), III, 138, 141-42.

is a physician.[20] It is questionable whether this line of research would ever have suggested itself were it not stated in Col. 4:14 that Luke the companion of Paul was a physician: it would therefore be strong confirmation of the traditional theory of authorship if it could be proved that the author's language is characterized by technical medical terms. There are in fact numerous points of contact between the vocabulary of Luke and that of Greek medical writers such as Hippocrates (*ca.* 460 B.C.) and Galen (*ca.* A.D. 130), and technical terms are more numerous and more precise in the stories of healing in Luke-Acts than in the other Gospels. But more recent work, particularly that of H. J. Cadbury,[21] has largely undermined the purely linguistic argument. Of the 400 supposed medical terms listed by Hobart 360 are found in the Septuagint; other nonmedical authors, such as Philo and Lucian, supply as many "medical terms" as does Luke. Practically all Luke's alleged technical terms are used also by nonmedical writers; both Plutarch and Lucian use 90 per cent of them; if Josephus and the Septuagint are taken together, no less than 390 out of the 400 can be paralleled. The truth seems to be that the language of Greek doctors was not highly specialized, and that the use made by Luke of so-called technical terms does not exceed what might be expected of any writer of wide general culture. It would indeed be equally easy to prove from the number of nautical terms used in ch. 27 that Luke was a sailor, or that he was a lawyer from the considerable number of legal expressions used in the closing chapters.

The fallacy of most of the linguistic statistics must be admitted. But the argument is not one from language only but also from medical interest, and it is indubitable that the whole of Luke-Acts shows this to a remarkable degree. In the Gospel, to a greater extent than in any of the others, attention is focused on the healing and care of the sick. Luke alone tells the parable of the good Samaritan. For him Jesus' cures are a signal proof of his messiahship (Luke 7:18-23). In Acts great emphasis is laid on the numerous cures wrought by the apostles in general at Jerusalem (5:12-16) and by Paul at Ephesus (19:11). Such cures are proof that the power of Jesus himself is still at work (3:12-13; 4:7-10). Harnack indeed rightly calls attention to Luke's disposition to see in miracles of healing the chief function of the mighty forces of the new religion. When we recall such vivid descriptions of healing as Luke 4:38-41 or Acts 3:1-10—or note how tactfully Luke 8:43 modifies Mark 5:26 in the interest of the good name of the medical profession!—the impression is cumulative that the author may well have been a doctor. This would probably be generally admitted by scholars were there not other reasons—some of them undoubtedly strong—which have prejudiced them against the traditional view that the author is Luke the physician. But as Windisch, himself an opponent of the traditional view, confesses: "We cannot demand unconditionally that the medical calling of an author should appear in an evangelic and apostolic history. If, however, we do find traces of such a professional education, we appear to have an unexpectedly brilliant confirmation of the tradition." [22]

Finally it may be asked under what literary genre Luke-Acts should be classified stylistically. The truth is that it belongs, strictly speaking, to none of the recognized literary types of antiquity. The Gospels appear at first sight to fall under the category of "biography" alongside, for example, Plutarch's *Parallel Lives,* Suetonius' *Lives of the Caesars,* Tacitus' *Agricola.* An even closer parallel might seem to be provided by memorabilia, such as Xenophon's *Recollections of Socrates* or Philostratus' *Life of Apollonius of Tyana.* But it is of the nature of memorabilia that the author should claim to be present at the events he records, and this, apart from the diary source, the author of Luke-Acts does not. Moreover Cadbury[23] well remarks that, quite apart from their admitted apologetic and religious purpose, the factor distinguishing the Gospels from ancient literary "biography" or "memoirs" is their "popular" character—not in the sense that they are written for plain folk in a popular style, but rather in the sense that they grew out of the common popular life of the church. The material is the spontaneous creation of the Christian community, and the final recorder is content to set it down much as it came to him. Though Luke's Gospel has more claim to be literature than have Matthew and Mark, it is still "popular" in this sense. And this is just as true of Luke's second volume. Still less can it be classified as biography, for though full of biographical interest, it makes no attempt to trace the full career of the principal characters—Peter, Stephen, Philip, Paul—who pass across the pages more like the actors in a drama than the subjects of a formal biography. For Acts "his-

[20] W. K. Hobart, *The Medical Language of St. Luke* (Dublin: Hodges, Figgis & Co., 1882); Harnack, *Luke the Physician.*

[21] *The Style and Literary Method of Luke* (Cambridge: Harvard University Press, 1920), pp. 39-72, and "Lexical Notes on Luke-Acts," *The Journal of Biblical Literature,* XLV (1926), pp. 190-209.

[22] *The Beginnings of Christianity,* ed. F. J. Foakes Jackson and Kirsopp Lake (London: Macmillan & Co., 1920-33), II, 315-16.

[23] *The Making of Luke-Acts,* pp. 130-31.

tory" might appear to be a more apt classification; and indeed it has many points of contact with typical histories of antiquity—the working up of earlier sources, the introduction of speeches, the use of a series of outstanding names as a thread on which to carry forward the continuous narrative. But once again, only with many reservations can Acts be classified as formal history. The narrative is too disjointed, and too noticeably lacking in balance and proportion;[24] the gaps in the story of the church's growth are too obvious; the selection of the material is determined too clearly by motives which are not primarily historical. Once again Luke appears as a transmitter of popular Christian tradition rather than as a formal littérateur. This of course is not to deny that his book contains a vast amount of valuable and reliable history. But it does mean that other motives than that of pure historical research lie behind his writing, and that we can understand his book only as we appreciate that fact.

V. The Greek Text of Acts

The problem presented by the text of Acts is unique in the New Testament. The manuscripts have preserved two types of text, and the divergent readings in this or that family are so general and consistent as to suggest to some scholars that we have to do, not merely with a large number of independent variants, but rather with two separate recensions of the original text. The "Neutral" text as given in most modern critical editions is based on our oldest uncials—Vaticanus, Sinaiticus, Alexandrinus—supported by the Vulgate Latin, the Peshitta Syriac, and the Greek fathers such as Clement of Alexandria, Origen, and Chrysostom. The "Western" text, which in Acts differs much more widely from the "Neutral" than in other New Testament books, derives chiefly from Codex Bezae (D) and Codex Laudianus, supported by the Old Latin, certain Syriac authorities, in particular the margin of the Harclean Syriac, Irenaeus, and the Latin fathers such as Tertullian, Cyprian, and Augustine. The regular occurrence of the same variant (for example, the important variants in the text of the "apostolic decrees" in ch. 15) in all the manuscripts of a Western type has led to the theory that they must all come from a common source, and that we are dealing, not with a collection of more or less fortuitous variants, but with a separate edition of the original text.

[24] Contrast, for example, the disproportionate space given to the conversion of Cornelius (10:1–11:18) or to Paul's appearances before his various judges (chs. 22–26) with the paucity of information about his three years' ministry at Ephesus (ch. 19) or his last visit to Greece (20:1-3).

The most important development of this theory is that of Friedrich Wilhelm Blass. Following up the work of Bornemann[25] and of Paul de Lagarde,[26] both of whom gave preference to the Western text, Blass[27] propounded the hypothesis that Luke had in fact issued two editions of Acts. Having composed the book at the end of the two years of Paul's imprisonment at Rome, Luke carefully revised it and sent a copy of the revision to Theophilus at Antioch. This copy was the prototype of the Neutral recension (Blass's α text). Luke then handed over his original draft to the Christians of Rome, and this in turn became the source of the Western or Roman recension (Blass's β text). Curiously, while in Acts the Western readings are uniformly longer than the Neutral, in the Gospel the reverse is usually the case. This Blass explained by the converse theory that in the case of the Gospel the original draft, written before Luke arrived in Rome, lies behind the Neutral text, while the Western text has its origin in a revised edition which Luke specially made for the Roman church.

There would seem to be three tenable views concerning the relationship to each other of the two types of text: (*a*) The view of Blass, which though ingenious has found little support, that Luke did in fact himself issue two editions. (*b*) The view that the Western text is nearer the original, the Neutral representing a later scholarly revision. Though the tendency today is certainly to pay greater respect to Western readings, and the priority of the Western text has been urged with great cogency by A. C. Clark,[28] this view has not yet found general acceptance. Matthew Black, an Aramaic expert, has emphasized the value of the text of the Bezan Codex and holds that "D represents the Aramaic background of the Synoptic tradition more faithfully than do non-Western manuscripts."[29] (*c*) The view that the Neutral text is most nearly primitive, while the Western readings are merely the corrections, paraphrases, and expansions of successive scribes, or are possibly in part at least due to a later redaction of the Lukan text, as is argued by Harnack and more recently by J. H. Ropes.[30]

The more interesting Western variations are noted throughout the commentary. A study of them in detail seems, generally speaking, to con-

[25] *Acta Apostolorum ad Codicis Cantabrigiensis Fidem* (London: 1848).

[26] *De Novo Testamento ad Versionum Orientalium Fidem Edendo* (Berlin: 1857).

[27] *Die zweifache Textüberlieferung in der Apostelgeschichte, Studien und Kritiken* (1894), pp. 86-119.

[28] *The Acts of the Apostles* (Oxford: Clarendon Press, 1933).

[29] *An Aramaic Approach to the Gospels and Acts* (Oxford: Clarendon Press, 1946), p. 212.

[30] *Beginnings of Christianity,* Vol. III.

firm the priority of the shorter Neutral text. Some of the Western variations are evidently designed to bring the text into line with some parallel passage: for example, the Western expansion of 9:5-6 (cf. KJV with RSV) is evidently based on 22:10 and 26:14; and the addition in 13:33 of the words "Ask of me and I shall give thee the Gentiles for thine inheritance and the uttermost parts of the earth for thy possession" merely completes the quotation from Ps. 2:7-8. In 18:27 the Western addition that "some Corinthians urged him [Apollos] to go with them to their country" can perhaps be explained by reference to I Cor. 16:12. Other additions aim at giving greater precision to circumstances of time (1:5, "at Pentecost"; 5:21, "rising up early"), or of place (12:1, "some who belonged to the church in Judea"; 12:20, "they came to him in a body from both the cities"). Others again appear to be purely stylistic and due to a scribe or editor who, as Adolf Jülicher says, "occasionally even altered from the mere joy of altering."[31] See 2:37 and especially 19:14, where in both passages, particularly the second, the text is greatly expanded without anything essentially new being said. If it is the Neutral scribe who is responsible for a later abbreviation of such passages, it is difficult to understand how his zeal for abridgment could have spared him room for three accounts of Paul's conversion and all the redundancies of the story of Cornelius.

When the Western variant is not merely stylistic but factual, it is again usually most easily explained as an expansion of an originally shorter text. In the Western text of 5:39, where Gamaliel says, "You will not be able to overthrow them, neither you nor emperors nor tyrants," we see reflected the church's later experience of state persecution. The confession of faith in 8:37 (KJV) is evidently added under the influence of later baptismal practice. For the very important variants in the text of the apostolic decrees in 15:20, 29 see Exeg., *ad loc.*, where again the Neutral text is preferred.

It is true that certain Western readings leave the impression that they are based on good authority. Such are the first occurrence of a "we" in 11:28, the mention of the "seven steps" in 12:10, of Trogyllium in 20:15 and of Myra in 21:1, the remark in 28:16 that "the centurion delivered the prisoners to the stratopedarch." But even in these cases, if the readings were indeed original, it is difficult to understand why such vivid details should have been deliberately excised at a later editing, whether by the author, by a subsequent redactor, or by a mere scribe. The conclusion is that while certain individual Western readings may have some claim to originality on their own merit, the Western text as a whole is almost certainly secondary, and has probably resulted, except perhaps in the case of certain key passages such as the apostolic decrees, from a fortuitous accumulation of scribal alterations, paraphrases, and expansions, rather than from a systematic redaction of the entire Lukan text.

[31] *An Introduction to the New Testament*, tr. Janet Penrose Ward (London: Smith, Elder & Co., 1904), p. 455.

VI. Acts: Its Literary Contacts

A. With the Pauline Epistles.—The Pauline epistles can, generally speaking, be fitted so well into the biographical framework provided by Acts that it is natural to ask whether the author has not used the epistles as one of his sources. The question can be answered only after considering, first, passages where there may be such close agreement as to suggest that Acts is drawing upon the epistles; and, second, passages in Acts which show disagreement with or omission of important data given in the epistles. Most modern scholars pronounce against the theory that our author is dependent upon the epistles.

With regard to agreements between Acts and the epistles, in order to prove dependence it would be necessary either to show that Luke could have obtained his facts only from the epistles, or to produce actual verbal echoes—passages where Luke not only tells the same facts, but tells them in the same words. Both these tests in fact fail. We know that Luke had at his disposal excellent sources of knowledge quite apart from the epistles. As for verbal accords, they are virtually nonexistent. On the other hand if Luke knew the epistles, it is difficult to understand why he has so often passed over in silence events of crucial importance for Paul and omitted so many of the vivid details with which the epistles might have furnished him. Moreover there are sections of Acts where the author's picture of Paul so far contradicts the impression left by the epistles that, if he knew and used the epistles, we should have to conclude that he has not only falsified his narrative, but has done so deliberately in the interests of a "tendency"—the position of the Tübingen school, which is no longer generally held.

So far as the general outline of Paul's life is concerned, the hypothesis that our author used the epistles is quite superfluous. A detailed study of the individual epistles confirms this conclusion. Only two passages in Acts have any claim to be considered verbal echoes of Paul. The closest is in Acts 9:21, where "Is not this the man who made havoc (πορθήσας) in Jerusalem of those who called on this name?" reads like a reminiscence of Gal. 1:13, "I persecuted the church of God violently and tried to destroy (ἐπόρθουν) it." Again Acts 14:15, "That you should turn from these vain things to a living God," might seem to be an echo of I Thess. 1:9, "How you turned to God from idols, to serve a living and true God"; but this is language that might well be used by any writer describing the conversion of pagans to the faith.

A brief glance at Paul's four chief letters leads to the same conclusion: [32]

1. Romans.—The author of Acts, one of whose chief aims was to illustrate the expansion of Christianity from Jerusalem all over the world, says nothing about Paul's preaching "as far round as Illyricum" (Rom. 15:19). He gives no sign that in Paul's own mind Rome was not the final goal of his labors, but rather a starting point for a new stage, as Paul hints when he writes, "I hope to see you in passing as I go to Spain" (Rom. 15:24). Nor does he hint that when Paul arrived in Rome, there was already in existence there a large church to which Paul had written his most important letter.

2. I and II Corinthians.—Our author omits a great many details which we should expect to be mentioned had he known the letters. No mention is made of such names as Stephanas, Fortunatus, Gaius, Achaicus. There is no account of the rival factions at Corinth (I Cor. 1:10 ff.) nor of the trouble with reference to the Lord's Supper (I Cor. 11:17 ff.). With reference to Paul's ministry at Ephesus, where I Corinthians was written, a number of intriguing allusions are completely ignored in Acts, e.g., "What do I gain if, humanly speaking, I fought with beasts at Ephesus?" (I Cor. 15:32) and "We were so utterly, unbearably crushed that we despaired of life itself" (II Cor. 1:8). If Luke had read the letters, it is difficult to believe that he would not have turned these vivid allusions to account for his own narrative.[33]

3. Galatians.—It is with reference to this epistle that the most striking discrepancies occur. The account of Paul's activities after his conversion and on the occasion of his visits to Jerusalem to confer with the apostles leaves a very different impression according as we read it in Acts 9:20-29; 11:29-30; 15:1-29 or in Gal. 1:15–2:10. For a full discussion of the resulting problems see Exeg., *ad loc.* It is possible to explain the apparent lack of harmony if the author of Acts was not familiar with Galatians. If he did know the facts as Paul tells them, no explanation is possible without calling in question the good faith of our author, and assuming that he has been distorting his facts in the interests of a theory—a point of view which scholarship has outgrown.

We may conclude, then, that our author did not directly use the Pauline epistles as a source of information. Three important consequences follow: (*a*) If the witness of Acts is thus independent of the epistles, and yet is in so many details confirmed by the epistles, then it acquires all the more historical trustworthiness. When there are points of contact between Acts and the epistles, the agreements are far more numerous and important than the disagreements. Therefore, when Luke gives facts which we cannot check by reference to the epistles, we may have a corresponding confidence in them. (*b*) Acts must have been written at a comparatively early date, when as yet the Pauline epistles had not been collected and broadcast so that they would automatically be at the disposal of an author as an easily accessible source of information and one to be consulted as a matter of course. As I Clement already seems to show a knowledge of at least Romans and I Corinthians, a date for Acts later than about 95 is most improbable. (*c*) The probability of the traditional authorship of Luke is strengthened. A later comer, not being an eyewitness, would have searched for all possible sources of information, and would almost certainly have discovered the epistles and have fully used them, especially to lend verisimilitude to the speeches which he puts in Paul's mouth. Luke, it may be argued, felt less need for such written sources because he relied either on his own recollections or on the firsthand verbal accounts of other eyewitnesses.

B. With the Works of Josephus.—Elaborate linguistic tests indicate a certain affinity between the vocabulary of Luke and Josephus, and there are also various points of contact in the facts recorded. But this might well prove nothing more than that the two writers are near contemporaries and both engaged in writing Jewish history. A number of scholars, however, believe that Luke knew and is occasionally dependent on Josephus.[34] The passage on which most stress has been laid is the allusion in 5:36-37 in the speech of Gamaliel to the rebellions of Theudas and of Judas the Galilean. Luke is guilty here of a gross anachronism which, it is argued, could be explained by a

[32] For Philippians see on 16:11, and for I and II Thessalonians on 17:1.

[33] See also with reference to the Corinthian mission Exeg. on 18:1-17, and with reference to the Ephesian mission Exeg. on 19:1-41.

[34] The fullest treatment is by Max Krenkel, *Josephus und Lukas* (Leipzig: H. Haessel, 1894)—an outstanding example of perverse ingenuity applied to New Testament scholarship.

misunderstanding of Josephus (see Exeg., *ad loc.*). But the passage in Josephus is so explicit that, had Luke referred to it, he could hardly have misread it as alleged. Another case of careless reading of Josephus by Luke has been suspected in Luke 3:1, where Lysanias is stated to have been the tetrarch of Abilene about A.D. 28, whereas the only Lysanias known to have held this rule died in 36 B.C.[35] Josephus, however, when relating how in A.D. 53 Agrippa II obtained Abilene, adds that this "had been" the tetrarchy of Lysanias.[36] Other possible echoes have been suspected in Acts 21:38 and 25:11, on which see Exeg., *ad loc.* These examples of Lukan mistakes which may possibly be explained by reference to Josephus are certainly plausible; but even those who accept this evidence must admit that "they fall just short of demonstration." [37] They have force only if we are prepared to attribute gross carelessness to a writer who, when it is possible to test him, usually proves to be remarkably accurate in small details. It is at least equally probable that he had no knowledge of Josephus, and that the points of contact, such as they are, may be due to both of them having used a common source.[38] The conclusion that Luke is independent of Josephus, like that already reached concerning his nonuse of the Pauline epistles, is of great importance for the dating of Luke-Acts; for if Luke used Josephus, the date must be at the very end of the first century at the earliest, Josephus' *Antiquities* being dated about A.D. 93.

VII. The Criticism of Acts

"No other book," wrote Harnack, "has suffered so much from critics as the Acts of the Apostles. . . . All the mistakes which have been made in New Testament criticism have been focussed into the criticism of the Acts of the Apostles." [39] It is true also that conclusions reached by a critic concerning the composition and historical value of Acts are likely to determine his views on the whole process of development, not only of the New Testament literature, but of primitive Christianity itself. Acts is thus the key book in the study of the New Testament, and to trace the successive theories held concerning it is to review the chief problems not only of the book itself but of the beginnings of Christianity. In particular such a review is valuable because each stage in the history of criticism has tended to isolate and set in a clear light one special aspect of our author's purpose in writing his book.

Until about the middle of the nineteenth century the book was considered to have a straightforward historical motive. According to Hugo Grotius (1644) it was to provide a biography of the two leading apostles; according to Griesbach (1798) to offer a defense for Paul's conduct of his ministry; according to Eichhorn (1824) to tell the story of the spread of Christianity from Jerusalem and Antioch to Rome. With Schneckenburger (1841) we meet for the first time the view that the author's motive is not primarily historical; he writes in the interest of a particular "tendency" and to serve certain apologetic purposes. These are in the main two: (*a*) To conciliate as far as possible the prejudice of Jewish Christians against Paul. This he does by stressing the unity and solidarity of the Petrine and Pauline wings of the church, and by exaggerating the parallelism between the careers of the two apostles. (*b*) A subsidiary political motive—to prove that there had never been any real cause of conflict between the growing Christian church and the Roman authorities. While stressing the controversial aims of the author, Schneckenburger maintained that Luke's facts, generally speaking, were reliable, and that he did not seriously falsify history in the interests of his apologetic.

It was the Tübingen school, under the leadership of F. C. Baur, which first seriously argued that the author's apologetic aims have entirely vitiated the historical trustworthiness of his book, and that he cannot have been a contemporary of Paul: "For a writer so large a part of whose account has so little the character of historical objectivity, and who sets the events in such a perspective as to show a definite purpose and tendency, must have been some distance from the facts he records, and can have written only under conditions dominated by interests other than those that can be assumed for the time of the Apostle." [40] Baur reconstructed early Christian history according to the Hegelian presupposition of a thesis and an antithesis resolving themselves after conflict in a synthesis. Acts belongs to a group of irenical writings designed to reconcile the two rival wings of the church, the Jewish Christians and the Paulinists. It must be dated at least as late as the middle of the second century.

The classic presentation of the Tübingen theories of history as applied to Acts is the

[35] See, however, J. M. Creed, *The Gospel According to St. Luke* (London: Macmillan & Co., 1930), pp. 307 ff. for the possibility that there was a second Lysanias in the reign of Tiberius.

[36] *Antiquities* XX. 7. 1.

[37] *Beginnings of Christianity,* II, 357.

[38] It has been suggested, for example, that in the last seven books of the *Antiquities* Josephus may have made use of a history of Herod and that Luke too may have known this source. See Goguel, *Introduction au N.T.*, III, 129.

[39] *Luke the Physician,* p. 122.

[40] *Der Apostel Paulus* (1845), p. 12; tr. in *Beginnings of Christianity,* II, 372.

work of Eduard Zeller.[41] Acts as history is thoroughly untrustworthy, its mode of composition and its contents being controlled solely by its apologetic purpose, which is to reconcile Jewish Christians and Paulinists. The author so rewrites history as to justify Paulinism and yet at the same time to conciliate its opponents by abandoning its more extreme claims. Thus he sacrifices Paul's originality by claiming for Peter the honor of converting the first Gentile in the person of Cornelius; while conversely he pictures Paul as beginning every mission by preaching to Jews. Zeller throughout grotesquely overstresses the parallelism between the two great apostles, holding that the author of Acts deliberately pictures Paul as Petrine and Peter as Pauline as possible. The book is consciously planned as a mediating work written from the point of view of a follower of Paul but addressed to members of both parties: "The work is the peace proposal of a Paulinist who wishes to purchase the recognition of Gentile Christianity from Jewish Christians by concessions to Judaism and in this sense desires to influence both parties." [42]

A new point of view appears with F. C. Overbeck.[43] His criticism of Acts is no less drastic than Zeller's. The purpose of the book is definitely apologetic rather than historical. The events are still held to have been set in perspective by one who is remote from his subject. But the reason given for the painting of such a picture is different. The author did not deliberately misconstrue history in order to create a false impression of harmony and so reconcile the two wings of the church. The church of his day had already outlived the conflict between Judaizers and Paulinists and was indeed unconscious that there had ever been such disharmony; and Acts represents the resulting viewpoint of such a church, where the "synthesis" had already been achieved. As H. J. Holtzmann puts it: "Where, according to the Tübingen criticism, the author of Acts *would* not see, according to the newer interpretation he *could* not see." [44] This still implies a late date for Acts. But the charge of deliberate falsification in the interests of a tendency is dropped; and here is the marked difference between the attitude of the Tübingen school and even the most radical criticism of the present day.

The work of Otto Pfleiderer and August Sabatier [45] is on similar lines. But the results of nineteenth-century criticism in reaction against the Tübingen school may best be summed up by reference to the work of Edouard Reuss, of whom Goguel writes that he has done more than any other critic of his day to disentangle exegetical science from the a priori dogmatism of conservatism on the one hand and the presuppositions of a philosophical system on the other hand.[46] Acts cannot be considered a book of pure history, for certain facts have been chosen and arranged in order to combat the prejudice against Paul, and to render Paulinism, and particularly its universalism, more acceptable in Jewish eyes. But there has been no systematic and conscious distortion of history. This indeed was the position reached by criticism by the end of the century. Acts may present an apology for Paul from the point of view of a disciple. His portrait may be well intentioned rather than strictly accurate. But any such apologetic inexactitudes—as compared with the epistles—are not conscious and deliberate perversions of the truth. If ever the trustworthiness of our author is in question, we should indict not his good faith but the exactness of his sources and his own power of insight into events and conditions which, in part at least, he knew only at secondhand.

The work of British and American scholars during the same period invites less full notice, for it pursues the even tenor of its safe conservative way and raises few controversial issues. The one exception is the two volumes published anonymously in 1874 by W. R. Cassells under the title *Supernatural Religion* in which he popularized Baur's theories. He was at once challenged by J. B. Lightfoot, whose series of Pauline commentaries, and particularly the dissertations appended to that on Galatians, present the reply of English-speaking scholarship to the Tübingen school.

The criticism of the first quarter of the present century may be illustrated by a few typical names. According to Jülicher, who carried on the critical tradition of Overbeck, what the

[41] *The Acts of the Apostles*, tr. Joseph Dare (London: Williams & Norgate, 1875-76).

[42] *Ibid.*, p. 363; quoted in *Beginnings of Christianity*, II, 376. For a most damaging criticism of the whole Tübingen position see B. H. Streeter, *The Four Gospels* (London: Macmillan & Co., 1924), pp. 542 ff. History written thus in accordance with a priori philosophical presuppositions "is not history at all. It is dogma disguised as history; it is 'tendency-writing' of a far more misleading character than anything produced by the apologetic or theological bias of the writers whose view of history the critic professes to correct. . . . The discussion is still haunted by the ghost of F. C. Baur; it is time the ghost was laid."

[43] *Kurze Erklärung der Apostelgeschichte* (4th ed.; Leipzig: S. Hirzel, 1870). An English translation of the Introduction of this work appears in Vol. I of Zeller, *op. cit.*

[44] *Hand-commentar zum Neuen Testament* (Freiburg: J. C. B. Mohr, 1892), I, 308.

[45] Pfleiderer, *Das Urchristentum* (Berlin: Georg Reimer, 1887). Sabatier, "Actes des Apôtres" in *Encyclopédie des Sciences Religieuses* (Paris: Sandoz & Fischbacher, 1877).

[46] Goguel, *Introduction au N.T.*, III, 48.

author "intended to write was a *History of the Power of God in the Apostles*," [47] and in so doing he projects into the apostolic age the conditions and characteristics of the Christian community in his own day. But he does so in good faith, not because he is deliberately overcoloring his picture, but because he wrote too long after the events and possessed sources too fragmentary to enable him to complete a wholly satisfactory history.

The work of Johannes Weiss is interesting as emphasizing once again the political aim of the author of Acts. His chief purpose is neither historical nor religious but rather to promote the interests of the church by conciliating the Roman authorities. "I can understand the Acts only as an apology for the Christian religion addressed to the heathen and directed against the accusations of the Jews, which shows how it happened that Judaism had been supplanted in its world-mission by Christianity." [48] The author thus answers the charge that Christians being apostates from Judaism are adherents of a *religio illicita* and a menace to the state. The American scholar A. C. McGiffert in his invaluable *History of Christianity in the Apostolic Age* traces throughout Acts the same political apologetic purpose.

The French scholar Alfred Loisy [49] is almost unique in considering the author of the Gospel and the final editor of Acts to be two separate persons. Luke (the *auctor ad Theophilum*) is the author of the Gospel, but only of the most reliable source of Acts, which the final editor has distorted and mutilated. Loisy allows that Luke's original work had the highest historical value; but this admission amounts to little, for he ascribes to this original source the fewest possible passages. All the rest of Luke's work has disappeared beneath the hand of a later redactor who has effaced everything that contradicted his leading thesis, inspired by a purely apologetic preoccupation—the fundamental identity of Christianity with Judaism. The ingenuity of Loisy's criticism is matched only by its perversity, and Acts is reduced to something little better than a disfigured and dismembered corpse! Maurice Goguel [50] is much under the influence of Loisy, but he treats the material with a great deal more sanity and balance, and his book is one of the most interesting modern radical discussions.

The leader of the "conservative reaction" in Germany was Adolf Harnack.[51] He reasserted over against current criticism the Lukan authorship of the whole book, which he held was written not later than 63 or 64, at the end of the two years spent with Paul while the latter was in captivity at Rome. The central idea of Acts, according to Harnack, is one that links it up with the Third Gospel, of which it is the continuation—the power of Jesus Christ himself expressing itself anew through the apostles, so that their missions may be considered an actual prolongation of the ministry of Jesus. In spite of frequent inaccuracy and carelessness Acts must be ranked as a historical authority very much higher than is allowed by most contemporary critics, though Harnack remains critical and is far from according it his complete confidence. He concedes that the defense of Paul against Jewish accusations is a secondary aim of the work; but he denies any political apologetic motive.

In England this rehabilitation of Acts had already been carried a stage farther by the work of Sir William M. Ramsay.[52] Basing his work on firsthand archaeological research about which W. Sanday declared that "Professor Ramsay's explorations in Asia Minor are among the three or four best things done by Englishmen in the field of scientific scholarship in this generation," [53] Ramsay concluded that Luke, the companion of Paul, is the author of the entire book and that his accuracy, even in small matters of local popular custom and official practice, has been proved by archaeology to merit complete confidence. These conservative findings seemed to be further confirmed by C. H. Turner in his essay on "Chronology" in Hastings' *Dictionary of the Bible;* by Sir John Hawkins, who sought to prove by linguistic evidence that the author of the "we-sections" is also the author of the whole book; and by later writers such as B. H. Streeter and A. H. McNeile.[54] Indeed, for English-speaking scholarship at least, the work of these scholars might seem to have re-established the Lukan authorship and historical trustworthiness of Acts, had not the great five-volume work edited by F. J. Foakes Jackson and Kirsopp Lake under the

[47] *Introduction to N.T.*, p. 439.

[48] *Über die Absicht und den literischen Character der Apostelgeschichte* (1897), p. 56; tr. in *Beginnings of Christianity*, II, 388-89. This thesis is illustrated *passim* in Johannes Weiss, *History of Primitive Christianity*, ed. F. C. Grant (New York: Wilson-Erickson, 1937), Vol. I.

[49] *Les Actes des Apôtres* (Paris: Émile Nourry, 1920).

[50] *Introduction au N.T.*, Vol. III.

[51] *Luke the Physician; The Acts of the Apostles* (tr. J. R. Wilkinson; London: Williams & Norgate, 1909); *The Date of the Acts and the Synoptic Gospels* (tr. J. R. Wilkinson; London: Williams & Norgate, 1908).

[52] *The Historical Geography of Asia Minor* (London: John Murray, 1890); *The Church in the Roman Empire* (New York: G. P. Putnam's Sons, 1893); *St. Paul the Traveller and the Roman Citizen* (London: Hodder & Stoughton, 1895).

[53] "Professor Ramsay on the Geography of Asia Minor," *Expositor*, Ser. IV, No. 3 (1891), pp. 232 ff.

[54] Hawkins, *Horae Synopticae*, pp. 182 ff.; Streeter, *Four Gospels*, pp. 531 ff.; McNeile, *Introduction to the New Testament* (Oxford: Clarendon Press, 1927).

title *The Beginnings of Christianity* (1920-33) once again thrown the whole problem into the melting pot. The point of view of the editors may be stated in Windisch's summary: "The chief positions maintained to-day are: (1) The separation of the 'we' source, which was the work of a companion of Paul, probably Luke, from the other material which the actual author of Acts has combined with it. (2) The demonstration that the author of Acts was unfamiliar with the general trend of primitive Christianity . . . and represents, contrary to the historical facts, the original Apostles as initiating the missions to the Gentiles. (3) The demonstration that the author of Acts is ignorant of the peculiar character of Paul, obliterates his anti-Judaism, leaves unnoticed . . . experiences that were decisive for him . . . not so much because he has some special purpose in mind as because he is naïvely of the opinion that complete harmony prevailed between Paul and the original Apostles." [55]

The critical controversy concerning Acts is thus still *sub judice.* But on the Continent one important work at least shows a healthy reaction from the more extreme criticism. Eduard Meyer [56] in his three-volume work on the beginnings of Christianity defends Luke from what he considers the arbitrary methods of theologians! He has the right to be treated with the same respect as Polybius or Livy. His statements must be carefully examined, but unless there is good reason to the contrary we must accept them as we would those of any other historian. Even the first part of Acts, for the events of which Luke himself was not an eyewitness, is largely derived from materials supplied, if not by Paul himself, then by other eyewitnesses, in particular John Mark. Even when there is conflict with the Pauline epistles, Luke must sometimes be preferred. On theological grounds it has been judged that Paul must always be right. But historically speaking —well, what sort of a portrait could be painted on the basis of preferring, let us say, Napoleon's ideal picture of himself to that drawn by an intelligent onlooker? Meyer's conclusions in general concerning the character of Acts are refreshingly constructive.

The study of the criticism of the past one hundred years shows that four main aims have been attributed to the author of Acts: (*a*) A historical aim—to describe the expansion of Christianity in widening circles from Jerusalem to Rome. (*b*) A religious aim—to demonstrate the power of the Spirit in the work of the apostles. (*c*) An apologetic aim—to commend the Pauline mission and to minimize the divisions within the Christian community. (*d*) A political aim—to commend the Christian church to the contemporary Roman authorities. But on one important point critics generally are agreed. Though our author's treatment of events may not always be completely well informed or intelligent, there has been no deliberate falsification of history in the interests of a "tendency." Though Luke's accuracy may sometimes be challenged, there is at least no question concerning his good faith.

VIII. The Sources and Composition of Acts

It has been customary to divide the book of Acts into two parts, the first devoted to Peter and the church at Jerusalem, and the second to Paul and his missions. But this distinction between the two halves is by no means absolute. The conversion of Paul in ch. 9 is intruded into the first part, while the account of the council at Jerusalem is given in ch. 15, after the story of Paul's first missionary journey. The two parts of the book thus overlap, and probably the author had in mind no such division, nor indeed any clear-cut literary plan. His book is better analyzed according to the sources he has used. C. H. Turner, however, has divided the book into what he calls "six panels, each labelled with a general summary of progress. . . . Of these six sections the protagonist in the first three is St. Peter, in the last three St. Paul; and the two halves into which the book thus naturally falls make almost equal divisions at the middle of the whole period covered." The six panels are as follows: [57]

(*a*) The church in Jerusalem and Peter's preaching. Summary in 6:7, "And the word of God increased; and the number of the disciples multiplied greatly in Jerusalem."

(*b*) The expansion of the church through Palestine. Summary in 9:31, "So the church throughout all Judea and Galilee and Samaria had peace and was built up."

(*c*) The expansion of the church to Antioch, etc. Summary in 12:24, "But the word of God grew and multiplied."

(*d*) The expansion of the church to Asia Minor and Galatia. Summary in 16:5, "So the churches were strengthened in the faith, and they increased in numbers daily."

(*e*) The expansion of the church to Europe. Summary in 19:20, "So the word of the Lord grew and prevailed mightily."

(*f*) The expansion of the church to Rome. Summary in 28:31, "Preaching the kingdom of

[55] London: Macmillan & Co.; New York: The Macmillan Co., 1920-33, II, 301.

[56] *Ursprung und Anfänge des Christentums* (Berlin: J. G. Cotta, 1921-23).

[57] Article "Chronology of the New Testament," *Dictionary of the Bible,* ed. James Hastings (New York: Charles Scribner's Sons, 1898), I, 421.

God and teaching about the Lord Jesus Christ quite openly and unhindered."

This analysis may be quite usefully accepted, though it may be noted that there appear to be two other similar "summaries" in 2:47, "The Lord added to their number day by day those who were being saved"; and 11:21, "And the hand of the Lord was with them, and a great number that believed turned to the Lord."

The source criticism of Acts finds its starting point at the bisection of the book at either 15:35 or 16:5. The material then resolves itself into three constituents:

(*a*) The first fifteen chapters which, for the moment, may be treated as a unity, but must be analyzed later.

(*b*) The so-called "we-sections"—extracts from a diary written in the first person plural which are found inserted at intervals in chs. 16 onward.

(*c*) The long sections of narrative in chs. 16 onward which link together the "we-sections," and in which the latter are embedded. In these intervening sections Paul is still the chief subject, but the first person is not used.

The stages in the growth of the book as we now have it may therefore be outlined thus:

(*a*) Someone, presumably a companion of Paul, composed a travel diary covering the periods during which he was in the apostle's company.

(*b*) Someone filled out this diary by adding the intervening narrative of Paul's labors by which the separate "we-sections" are now linked up. But was this done by the diarist himself, or by someone else?

(*c*) Someone connected up this Paul-narrative with the earlier Peter-narrative in the first half of the book. Once again, was this final compiler the diarist, or the author—if he was a separate individual—of the intervening narrative, or even a third editor distinct from both?

In other words, if for the moment we may assume that the "we-sections" at least are written by an eyewitness, the problem may be thus defined: May all three of these stages in the growth of Acts be attributed to this eyewitness? Or are we to regard him as the author only of the Paul-narrative? Or, as a third alternative, must we think of him merely as the writer of a diary from which the "we-sections" are extracts?

We begin, then, with the "we-sections." When strictly delimited by reference to the use of the first person, they are as follows: 16:10-17; 20:5-15; 21:1-18; 27:1–28:16. But the actual extracts from the diary may well include additional verses. It is, for example, hard to believe that the first extract did not also comprise the material at least up to 16:24, if not to vs. 40; the third might well run on to the end of ch. 21; and it is at least arguable whether the second and the third are not in fact one single extract containing the intervening material—Paul's interview with the Ephesian elders.

The use of the pronoun "we" seems adequate proof that we have to do with extracts from a genuine diary, and few scholars would now deny that the origin of the "we-sections" is the actual diary of a fellow traveler of Paul. As Windisch, the champion of "the case against the tradition," frankly admits: "The effort has been made to explain the 'we' as a literary fiction on the part of the author, but the simplicity and comprehensibility of the 'we' narratives in contradistinction to all the others is, in my opinion, a sufficient proof of their genuineness." [58]

But what of the remainder of the Paul-narrative, the material in which the "we-sections" are embedded? We have already noted that the latter, as most strictly defined, may have to be extended to include passages in which the "we" does not actually occur. Indeed they may well be but fragments of a much more extended travel document, only part of which was written in the first person. Numerous literary parallels may be quoted to illustrate the habit of combining in a single document passages written now in the first person, now in the third.[59] Such was the form frequently taken by the reports of provincial governors, the dispatches of military leaders, the narratives of travelers—the first person being used to show that the author was actually present at the events being narrated. In the books of Ezra and Nehemiah we have a combination of the use of the first and third person; and the same is true of Philostratus' *Life of Apollonius of Tyana,* which is based in part on the personal memoirs of his disciple Damis. But the last example shows that the author of the memoirs need not necessarily be the compiler also of the book as a whole.

In the case of Acts, then, may we assign the whole of the second part to the diarist? When he uses the first person, does he do so simply to indicate the events of which he was an actual witness? Here at least the evidence of style and language would seem to give an affirmative answer. As the editors of *The Beginnings of Christianity* write: "In general it may be said that whereas there is some difference in style between Acts i.-xv. and the second part of the

[58] *Beginnings of Christianity,* II, 304.

[59] See Eduard Norden, *Agnostos Theos* (Leipzig: B. G. Teubner, 1913), pp. 313-14; Cadbury, *Making of Luke-Acts,* pp. 144-46.

book, there is none between the 'we' sections and the narrative in which they are embedded." [60] Nor do the contents of those parts of chs. 16–28 which are outside the "we-sections" present any insuperable difficulties to the assumption that the diarist is the source of the whole. Generally speaking any lack of verisimilitude in the narrative is sufficiently explained by the supposition that the author was not actually present. Indeed it may be said that the decision as to the origin of that part of the Paul-narrative which lies between the "we-sections" will depend on whether or not the diarist may also be considered to be the compiler of the first half of the book. If it is considered necessary to assume a final compiler other than the diarist, then it becomes natural enough to assign to such an editor also the material in chs. 16–28 which is outside the "we-sections." Otherwise—if the second part of the book can be approached with a judgment unbiased by difficulties suggested by the first part—there seems no sufficient reason for questioning the unity of chs. 16–28 and the assignment of the whole of the second half of Acts to the author of the diary source. The problem thus resolves itself to this: Can we hold that the hand which wrote the diary is also the hand which compiled the book as a whole? Or must we call in another editor by no means so near the events or so familiar with the facts? The traditional view that the diarist is also the compiler of the whole book has much to commend it.

In the first place this is much the most natural explanation of the retention of the "we" after the diary sections had been incorporated. What is more natural than to suppose that when a "we" appears without any explanation, the compiler is indicating that in this particular part of his story he himself had a personal share? True, it may be argued that, with a naïveté permitted by ancient literary ethics, the compiler has retained the "we" of another man's diary with the deliberate intention of proving that he has fulfilled his claim, made in the preface, to give the evidence of eyewitnesses. But if this was his motive, it is difficult to believe that he would have contented himself with such a frugal use of the first person. As S. C. Carpenter says aptly, "If he had wanted to pretend he would have been clever enough to do it more efficiently." [61] One feels rather that if some later editor has in fact worked over the diary source, the retention of the "we" would be a piece of negligence quite out of keeping with the literary polish of the book. The view that the compiler is identical with the diarist, and retains the "we" to show that he was present during the events being narrated at the moment, is much the simplest and most satisfying explanation of the many proposed.

Again, this view is confirmed by the community of thought and standpoint between the "we-sections" and the whole of the rest of Acts, and by Harnack's and Hawkins' linguistic proof that the diarist is also the author both of Luke's Gospel and of both halves of Acts. Attempts have been made to shake this argument from language, in particular by the editors of *The Beginnings of Christianity,* and it is always possible to argue that the later compiler created a literary unity by revising all his sources, including the diary sections, to conform to his own style and language. But would such a consummate literary harmonist have retained the "we"? On the whole it must be said that the argument for unity based on style and language still holds good, and the rejection of this simple explanation of the relation of the "we-sections" to the rest of the book is part of the price which has to be paid when, for reasons of historical criticism, the first part of Acts and in particular ch. 15 is regarded as the work of a post-apostolic writer. This question, which is indeed the crux of the whole problem, is discussed below in the section on "The Authorship of Luke-Acts."

It remains to indicate the possible sources of chs. 1–15. If it is granted that the book as a whole was compiled by a companion of Paul, then an obvious source of information was ready to hand in Paul himself or other companions of Paul. Oral information would certainly be forthcoming also from persons themselves present at the events recorded in the earlier chapters, with whom the editor may be supposed later to have come into contact—Mark, Philip, James the brother of our Lord, possibly Peter himself. The names of many such possible informants can be collected from Acts and the epistles and need not be catalogued here.

But had the author also at his disposal for the earlier period written sources? It seems clear that he draws on several separate local traditions. But were they preserved only orally or in written documents? Whatever the answer, it is at least certain that the first half of the book bears upon itself, just as clearly as the second half, the stamp of one hand. If several sources have been incorporated, they have been very thoroughly assimilated. "Although there is a *prima facie* probability for the use of written sources in Acts, . . . the writer wrote too well to allow us to distinguish with certainty either the boundaries of his sources or the ex-

[60] II, 158.
[61] *Christianity According to S. Luke,* p. 14.

tent of his own editorial work."[62] Harnack's analysis of the first half of Acts is as satisfactory as any and will serve as an example of the saner type of source criticism. Reviewing the contents of the chapters in relation to the persons and places which are central in each section, Harnack thinks that he can disentangle three main sources. The first chapters are concerned mainly with events at Jerusalem in which Peter, or Peter and John, are the central figures. The interest is then transferred to Caesarea, with Peter, or Peter and Philip, in the foreground. Finally the center of movement becomes Antioch and the leading figures Barnabas and Paul. Corresponding with these three blocks of material Harnack traces three main sources: (*a*) a Jerusalem source comprising the first five chapters; (*b*) a Jerusalem-Caesarean source of which the nucleus is 8:5-40; (*c*) an Antiochene source having its nucleus in 11:19-30. Using as clues various peculiarities of outlook and phraseology, Harnack then attaches the remaining sections of the first fifteen chapters to one or other of these three nucleuses, with the exception of 9:1-30 (the conversion of Paul), for which he postulates a special Pauline source akin either to the Antiochene or Jerusalem-Caesarean tradition. Finally, on the evidence of certain "doublets," which appear to give two versions of the same story, and of slight differences of outlook between chs. 2 and 3, Harnack concludes that the Jerusalem section is itself composite. He therefore postulates two Jerusalem sources, a superior source comprising ch. 3, which he calls "Jerusalem Source A," and an inferior source, of which the nucleus is ch. 2, which he calls "Jerusalem Source B." Jerusalem Source A, he thinks, may be identical with the Jerusalem-Caesarean source. The editors of *The Beginnings of Christianity* suggest that Jerusalem Source A may be a continuation of the Marcan source which is one of the main strands of the Third Gospel, while Jerusalem Source B may continue the special "Lukan" Jerusalem tradition followed in Luke 24.[63]

Harnack's analysis of the first half of Acts is then as follows:[64]

Jerusalem Source A: 3:1–5:16 (Peter's healing and preaching; the first clash with Judaism; life within the community).

Jerusalem Source B: 1:6–2:47 (the Ascension; the filling up of the number of the twelve; the gift of the Spirit at Pentecost; Peter's speech; the results of Pentecost; the beginnings of communal life); 5:17-42 (the second clash with Judaism).

[62] *Beginnings of Christianity,* II, 133.
[63] II, 139, 145-46.
[64] *The Acts of the Apostles,* pp. 162-202.

Jerusalem-Caesarean source: 8:5-40 (the story of Philip); 9:31–11:18 (Peter's preliminary mission; the conversion of Cornelius); 12:1-24 (the persecution under Herod).

Pauline source: 9:1-30 (the conversion of Saul).

Antiochene source: 6:1–8:4 (the appointment of the seven; the story of Stephen); 11:19-30 (the foundation of the church at Antioch); 12:25–15:35 (the commissioning of Barnabas and Saul; the mission to Cyprus; the mission to Galatia; the trouble at Antioch and Jerusalem; the council at Jerusalem; Paul and Barnabas at Antioch).

This analysis draws attention to certain blocks of material which may be held to represent separate local traditions. But it cannot be conclusively proved that all or any of these sources existed as written documents, unless indeed C. C. Torrey[65] is right in his theory that the whole of chs. 1–15 is a careful translation—by the writer of the "we-sections"—of an Aramaic document written by a Christian of Jerusalem as early as A.D. 49-50. Torrey postulates only one uniform Aramaic document, not like Harnack a threefold or fourfold tradition. Its writer's chief interest was in the universal mission of Christianity, and he was concerned to show "how Antioch became the first great Gentile center of Christianity." Torrey's chief evidence is a series of passages in which very obscure Greek becomes intelligible when treated as a mistranslation (often through the confusion of two similar Aramaic words) of an original Aramaic. Good examples are 2:47 and 3:16 on which see Exeg., *ad loc.* Unfortunately Aramaic experts seldom agree, and Matthew Black[66] rejects as linguistically unsound some of Torrey's most striking examples, notably 2:47. He does not believe that either in the Gospels or Acts we have direct translation from Aramaic, but he concedes that the evangelists may have used an Aramaic sayings-source for the words of Jesus, and that in Acts Aramaic sources may underlie the speeches of Peter and Stephen. Nevertheless the series of doublets in chs. 2–5[67] creates a strong presumption in favor of parallel written sources; and any source that originated in Jerusalem would naturally be written in Aramaic. Torrey's work, at any rate on its linguistic side, combines well with Harnack's, and it probably justifies a cautious acceptance of the hypothesis that for the first part of his book our author used at least three written sources, and that the Jerusalem source at any rate was in Aramaic.

[65] *The Composition and Date of Acts* (Cambridge: Harvard University Press, 1916).
[66] *Aramaic Approach to Gospels and Acts,* pp. 8-12.
[67] See Exeg. on 4:23–5:16.

IX. *The Authorship of Luke-Acts*

Thus far we have called our author "Luke" only for convenience without prejudice to the problem of authorship. But tradition, as we have seen, is unanimous in ascribing both the Third Gospel and Acts to "Luke the beloved physician," the companion of Paul. There is a strong presumption that the tradition is true. Luke was not an apostle, nor was he even a prominent figure in the apostolic age; and if the Gospel and Acts had not from the very first been indubitably associated with him, there seems no reason why tradition should have selected him as the author.

Once again the "we-sections" are our starting point. Once admit that the diarist was a companion of Paul, and there is no reason why, in the face of tradition, we should prefer some other of Paul's fellow travelers. The evidence of the Pauline epistles tallies. By a process of elimination, into which it is needless to enter, it can be shown that among Paul's companions —Silas, Timothy, Titus, Epaphroditus—no rival claimant can be found who is known to have been present with Paul on every occasion when the first person is used in Acts. We can accept this as confirmation of the tradition without agreeing with Cadbury[68] that it is probable that second-century Christians "discovered" an author for Luke-Acts by the same critical process! The Lukan authorship of the diary source is indeed generally admitted even by extreme critics. "The author [of the book as a whole] was not Luke; but he used as a source a diary of Luke's."[69]

As we have seen, there seems no point in distinguishing a hypothetical editor of the Paul-narrative, who incorporated a Lukan diary, from an equally hypothetical editor of the whole book. There is no trace whatever of such a third hand; and the decision must lie between the Lukan authorship of the diary fragments alone (with the possible addition of some immediately adjacent material) and the Lukan authorship of Luke-Acts as a whole.

The crux of the problem of authorship is thus the question whether the general character of Acts as a whole is such as to permit us to ascribe it to a companion of Paul. Are the discrepancies between Acts and the epistles so serious that we must assume Acts to be the work of one who had not personally known Paul? Those who make this assumption base their argument for the post-apostolic origin of Acts mainly on two considerations. First, the author, it is alleged, was ignorant of the manner in which primitive Christianity developed; he does not understand the meaning of "speaking with tongues" at Pentecost; he invests the original apostles with an authority they never possessed; and in particular he represents them, contrary to the facts, as initiating missions to the Gentiles. Second, he presents us with a picture of Paul which clashes with the apostle's self-portrait in his own epistles; he tones down Paul's anti-Jewish bias, omits all reference to controversies which for Paul himself were decisive, and thus leaves a quite false impression of complete harmony between Paul and the original apostles.

The key passages are the story of Pentecost (2:1-13); the account of Paul's doings after his conversion (9:20-30); the conversion of Cornelius (10:1–11:18); the account of the council at Jerusalem (15:6-29); the circumcision of Timothy (16:1-3); the omission of important events during the ministry at Ephesus (ch. 19); Paul's participation in the ritual of a vow (20:17-26); Paul's defense before the Sanhedrin (23:1-10). All these passages raise real difficulties; they demand a close comparison of Acts with the epistles and can be dealt with adequately only in their context. They are all fully discussed in this commentary. Here only a few general considerations may be suggested by way of meeting the objections to Lukan authorship.

(*a*) Harnack has cogently argued that the apparently exaggerated importance attached to the original apostles, and the Jewish-Christian coloring of the story and many of the speeches, may well be due to the fact that Luke, a converted Gentile, held the Old Testament, the revealed Jewish religion, and the first witnesses to the Christian faith in very high respect. As for the Jewish-Christian garb in which Paul himself appears, it is easy to show from the epistles that on the whole it corresponds to the historical truth. So far as his own religion and his attitude to the law were concerned, Paul to the end remained a genuine Jewish Christian.

(*b*) Paul in his epistles is often engaged in controversy and writes as a partisan. Therefore it is possible that the account in Acts of an incident told from the viewpoint of a less biased onlooker may be worthy of consideration even if it conflicts with Paul's own account. When we remember how vigorous are Paul's polemics in his letters, yet how willing he shows himself in personal practice to go great lengths on the way of compromise and accommodation—"I have become all things to all men, that I might by all means save some" (I Cor. 9:22)—we shall realize how much room there is for apparent inconsistency between his own partisan writing in Galatians

[68] *Making of Luke-Acts,* pp. 351-52.

[69] Windisch in *Beginnings of Christianity,* II, 342.

and what may be the perfectly sincere account of his actions written in Acts by a companion who, we recall, had not access to his letters.

(*c*) As for Luke himself, we must not measure by too rigid a standard the opinions of which even a companion of Paul might have been capable, nor the extent to which he might diverge from the interpretation which Paul himself might put upon a particular situation. When some statement in Acts about Peter or Paul appears to us unlikely to be correct, it does not follow that Luke, finding it perhaps in some source, would have been able to recognize it as such, and would therefore have been incapable of accepting it as true. Harnack justifiably says that Acts "has been forced to suffer because critics were still influenced by a strange survival of the old veneration for an apostolic man, and without any justification have made the highest demands of a companion of St. Paul—he must thoroughly understand St. Paul, he must be of congenial disposition and free from prejudice, he must be absolutely trustworthy and his memory must never fail!" [70] It is really no argument to say that such-and-such a speech or course of action is un-Pauline and could not therefore have been recorded by Luke the friend of Paul. As Moffatt well says of Luke, "One of the most assured results of recent research is that he was not a Paulinist masquerading as a historian." [71]

If we are persuaded that the discrepancy between Acts and the Pauline epistles is not such as to rule out the possibility of Lukan authorship, the corroborative evidence of the two prefaces may then be allowed its full weight. Critics of all shades of opinion admit that the prefaces prove the Third Gospel and the Acts to be by the same author, and few would question the Lukan authorship of the Gospel, if the latter were alone in question. "If the Gospel," writes Johannes Weiss, "were the only writing ascribed to his authorship, we should probably raise no objection against the record of ancient tradition; for we have no sufficient reason for asserting that a disciple of Paul could not have composed this work." [72] Yet radical critics are compelled to reject the Lukan authorship of the Gospel because they have first rejected it in the case of Acts, and Weiss therefore concludes that "the Lukan writings as a whole are the work of a man of the post-apostolic generation." A safer canon would seem to be that laid down by Streeter: "The burden of proof is on those who would assert the traditional authorship of Matthew and John and on those who would deny it in the case of Mark and Luke." [73] In view of the tendency, so marked in the early church, to ascribe New Testament books to apostolic names, this seems a wholly reasonable conclusion. And with the Lukan authorship of the Gospel there follows, on grounds of tradition, linguistic usage, community of thought and doctrinal outlook, the Lukan authorship of Acts.

To sum up the question of authorship there seem to be three alternatives: (*a*) Luke is the *auctor ad Theophilum,* the writer both of the Third Gospel and of the whole of Acts. In the composition of the latter he made use of his own diary, and also, especially in the first part, of several early sources, and, especially in the second part, of various cycles of tradition gathered chiefly orally.

(*b*) Luke is the original *auctor ad Theophilum* and may be considered to be the author of the Gospel practically as we now have it. But his original sketch of Acts, of which the diary is the kernel, has been drastically altered and surcharged by another and final redactor working at some distance from the events and with an end largely apologetic. His history can be trusted only so far as we can probe behind it to the original Lukan source. This is the viewpoint of Loisy's commentary, but it is not that of most modern radical critics, who adopt the third alternative.

(*c*) Luke is the author only of the "we-sections" and (according to some) possibly also of the passages which provide their immediate setting. But Luke is not, and never was, the *auctor ad Theophilum.* The latter, who consequently is the author also of the Third Gospel, is a later editor who has used the Lukan material merely as the most reliable of his sources, and has combined it more or less happily with diverse traditions both written and oral, all of which he has to some extent modified with apologetic aims in view.

General considerations of external evidence, and even linguistic and literary considerations, cannot solve the problem. A decision depends mainly on considerations of historical criticism and particularly on the question whether the picture of Paul in Acts and in the epistles respectively can be harmonized sufficiently to justify the conclusion that Acts was written by a companion of Paul. The answer reached in this commentary is a somewhat cautious "Yes." We are therefore prepared provisionally to adopt hypothesis (*a*). Hypothesis (*b*) is attractive only because it would enable us to maintain the Lukan authorship of the Third Gospel, while rejecting it in the case of Acts. Otherwise hypothesis (*b*) has little to commend it and,

[70] *Luke the Physician,* p. 122.

[71] *Intro. to Literature of N.T.,* p. 281.

[72] *Die Schriften des Neuen Testament* (Göttingen: Vandenhoeck & Ruprecht, 1906), p. 378.

[73] *Four Gospels,* p. 562.

failing hypothesis (*a*), we should be driven back on hypothesis (*c*), one of the strongest objections to which is that it carries with it the denial of the Lukan authorship of the Gospel, which, apart from doubts about Acts, would admittedly never be questioned.

X. The Date and Place of Origin of Luke-Acts

Most of the data for determining the date of Luke-Acts must be derived from the second volume. Very varied opinions have been held by scholars, the dates suggested covering a period of close to one hundred years. The extreme limits are A.D. 60, or perhaps a little before it, the earliest date at which Paul can have reached Rome, and A.D. 150, when Marcion made definite use of the Gospel. Three possible opinions concerning a date must be considered.

(*a*) A date in the first half of the second century, whether we set the limits as 110-25 with such scholars as Overbeck, or 125-50 with the radical Dutch school of van Manen. But any date later than about A.D. 100 seems quite unnecessary, unless we are convinced by our general study of the book that the author's picture of apostolic times is so completely out of touch with reality as to demand a second-century date. The judgment reached in this commentary is that this is not the case.

(*b*) A very early date, probably 63-64, the second volume being completed at the close of the two years spent with Paul at Rome. This was Harnack's view, at least in his latest pronouncements. In its favor it is urged: (i) Only so can we explain the abrupt ending of Acts with no mention either of Paul's death or of his release. (ii) The statement in Acts 20:25, 38 that the Ephesian elders would not see Paul's face again is most improbable if the author had known that Paul, as is proved by the Pastorals, did in fact return to Ephesus. (iii) If written later, Acts must have shown knowledge that Paul visited Spain (Rom. 15:24, 28). For a reply to these three arguments see Exeg. at the end of ch. 28. (iv) There is no trace in Luke-Acts of any recollection of the persecution under Nero, nor is the reference, if any, to the fall of Jerusalem as explicit as might be expected from one writing after that catastrophe.

(*c*) A date between 80 and 90 seems much the most probable. The two considerations which fix the *terminus a quo* and the *terminus ad quem* are the use of Mark by the author of the Third Gospel, and the nonuse by the author of Acts of the Pauline epistles. To date Luke-Acts as early as does Harnack would throw back the composition of Mark to a date not much later than 55 which, though perhaps not quite impossibly early, is earlier than most scholars are ready to accept. On the other hand a date much later than 90 makes it increasingly difficult to understand the author's failure to use the Pauline epistles, of the existence of which in collected form at Rome by about 95 the First Epistle of Clement is generally believed to afford evidence. Clement moreover quite probably had a knowledge of Acts itself. Luke-Acts furthermore shows no such traces of the beginnings of the Gnostic and Docetic controversy (save perhaps 20:29-30?) as do the Johannine Gospel and epistles, which were probably written about the turn of the century. The author too can surely not have had any experience of the general persecution of Christians, or he would hardly have emphasized so consistently the moderation of Roman officials. All these points are in favor of a date not later than 90.

Such a middle date fits in best also with the data provided by the Gospel. The latter was unquestionably written after the fall of Jerusalem in 70. Luke 19:43-44 and 21:20-24 strongly suggest that the author was aware that Jesus' prediction about the destruction of Jerusalem had been fulfilled. Particularly significant is the way in which, in the second passage, Luke, who has been following Mark closely, suddenly begins to modify the language, so that the symbol of the Antichrist—"the desolating sacrilege set up where it ought not to be" (Mark 13:14)—becomes a picture of "Jerusalem surrounded by armies." As Streeter says, "Seeing that in A.D. 70 the appearance of the Anti-Christ did *not* take place, but the things which Luke mentions *did,* the alteration is most reasonably explained as due to the author's knowledge of these facts." [74] Even so, a date later than about 75 is not demanded for the Gospel. It is probable, however, that Luke's second volume followed the first after no very long interval, and Acts seems to require a somewhat later date. The divergence from the Pauline epistles, and some passages where Luke's knowledge of the facts seems somewhat vague (very difficult to explain if, as Harnack urges, Luke was writing while he was still in Paul's company and could refer to him), become much more understandable if he is writing some twenty years after Paul's death. Other features in Acts also seem to demand a longer lapse of time: the underlying conception of the world-wide mission of Christianity—what we may call the "ecumenicity" of Acts—the idealization of the primitive church in the early chapters, the picture drawn of church order and church government. On the other hand if Acts was written by a companion of Paul, each year later than 85 becomes increasingly improbable.

[74] *Ibid.*, p. 540.

Indeed a later date is necessary only if it is proved that Luke is dependent on Josephus, in which case, as the *Antiquities* is dated about 93, Acts can hardly have been written much before the end of the century. But we have already judged Luke's use of Josephus to be not proved. Our conclusion would be that Luke's Gospel was written about 80 and Acts about 85.

The place of origin of Luke-Acts is quite uncertain. Tradition, at least since the time of Jerome, has assigned Acts to Rome, and this still remains much the most probable theory, at any rate as regards Acts, if not the Gospel also. But admittedly the origin of this tradition seems to lie in the belief that Luke completed his literary work while he was Paul's companion during his captivity at Rome. In favor of Rome too is this further consideration: the author is much preoccupied, first, with tracing the expansion of the church from Jerusalem to Rome until it became a truly "catholic" community, and second, with stressing the favorable attitude of the Roman authorities to the first missionaries. His book is likely therefore to have close associations with the city which was both the seat of Roman government and also the place where ecclesiastical organization most rapidly took definite shape. Streeter, who argues that "the Lucan writings were primarily written to present the case for Christianity to certain members of the Roman aristocracy," makes out a strong case for Rome, and thinks that "everything points to Rome as the Church for which the Acts was written." [75] Less probable suggestions are Antioch, on account of the persistent tradition that this was Luke's own city, and because one of his important sources for the first part of Acts seems to have originated there; or Ephesus, because of the writer's apparent interest in this church as shown by 18:24-26; 19; 20:17-38.

If Acts was written from Rome, it may well be that the Gospel was written from there also. The Marcionite prologue, it is true, states that Luke wrote his Gospel in Achaia, and Streeter tentatively suggests Corinth, with the probability that "Proto-Luke" had already been compiled at Caesarea as early as A.D. 60. But the statement of the prologue may be merely an inference from the fact that "the brother, whose praise is in the gospel" (II Cor. 8:18), whom tradition identified with Luke, is mentioned in a letter to "the saints who are in the whole of Achaia" (II Cor. 1:1). There is some slight evidence that the writing of Acts did not quite immediately follow that of the Gospel: the discrepancy concerning the day of the Ascension; certain linguistic differences noted by Hawkins; [76] the different nature of the problems presented by the text of the Gospel and Acts respectively; all these points might be more easily explained on the assumption that at least five years elapsed between the writing of the two volumes. If this is so, the Gospel may have been written elsewhere than Acts. But we are entirely without definite evidence; and on the whole Rome remains the most probable place of origin for both volumes.

XI. Outline of Contents

- I. From Jerusalem to Antioch (1:1–12:25)
  - A. Days of expectation (1:1-26)
    - 1. Introductory preface (1:1-5)
    - 2. The Ascension (1:6-11)
    - 3. Filling up of the number of the twelve (1:12-26)
  - B. Birth of the church (2:1-47)
    - 1. Gift of the Spirit (2:1-13)
    - 2. Peter's speech (2:14-36)
    - 3. Results of Pentecost (2:37-41)
    - 4. Beginnings of communal life (2:42-47)
  - C. The church at Jerusalem (3:1–5:42)
    - 1. Peter's healing and preaching (3:1-26)
    - 2. First clash with Judaism (4:1-22)
    - 3. Life within the community (4:23–5:16)
      - *a*) New outpouring of the Spirit (4:23-31)
      - *b*) Sharing of goods (4:32–5:10)
      - *c*) Summary (5:11-16)
    - 4. Second clash with Judaism (5:17-42)
  - D. Beginnings of Hellenistic Christianity (6:1–8:40)
    - 1. Appointment of the seven (6:1-7)
    - 2. Story of Stephen (6:8–8:3)
    - 3. Story of Philip (8:4-40)
      - *a*) The mission to Samaria (8:4-13)
      - *b*) The apostles' confirmatory visit (8:14-25)
      - *c*) Philip and the Ethiopian eunuch (8:26-40)
  - E. Conversion of Saul (9:1-31)
    - 1. The conversion itself (9:1-19)
    - 2. The immediate aftermath (9:20-31)
  - F. The first missions to Gentiles (9:32–11:30)
    - 1. Peter's preliminary mission (9:32-43)
    - 2. Conversion of Cornelius (10:1–11:18)
    - 3. Early history of the church at Antioch (11:19-30)
      - *a*) Foundation of the church (11:19-21)
      - *b*) Visit of Barnabas (11:22-24)
      - *c*) Paul comes to Antioch (11:25-26)
      - *d*) Visit to Jerusalem at the time of the famine (11:27-30)
  - G. Persecution under Herod (12:1-25)
- II. From Antioch to Rome (13:1–28:31)
  - A. First mission of Barnabas and Paul to the Gentiles (13:1–14:28)
    - 1. Commissioning of Barnabas and Paul (13:1-3)
    - 2. Mission to Cyprus (13:4-12)
    - 3. Mission to Galatia (13:13–14:28)
      - *a*) From Paphos to Perga (13:13)

[75] *Ibid.*, pp. 531 ff.

[76] *Horae Synopticae*, pp. 177 ff.

b) At Pisidian Antioch (13:14-52)
c) At Iconium and Lystra (14:1-18)
(1) At Iconium (14:1-7)
(2) At Lystra (14:8-18)
d) Return to Antioch (14:19-28)
B. Controversy concerning Gentile freedom (15:1-41)
1. Trouble at Antioch and Jerusalem (15:1-5)
2. Council at Jerusalem (15:6-29)
3. Paul and Barnabas at Antioch (15:30-41)
C. Mission of Paul to Europe (16:1–18:17)
1. Through Galatia and Asia (16:1-10)
a) Timothy joins the apostle (16:1-5)
b) To Troas (16:6-10)
2. In Macedonia (16:11–17:15)
a) Philippi (16:11-40)
(1) The church is established (16:11-15)
(2) Opposition and imprisonment (16:16-24)
(3) The miraculous deliverance (16:25-40)
b) Thessalonica (17:1-9)
c) Beroea (17:10-15)
3. In Achaia (17:16–18:17)
a) Athens (17:16-34)
b) Corinth (18:1-17)
D. Mission of Paul to Asia (18:18–19:41)
1. Preliminary tour of confirmation (18:18-23)
2. Apollos at Ephesus (18:24-28)
3. Paul at Ephesus (19:1-41)
a) Paul's return and his ministry in Asia (19:1-12)
b) Paul and the exorcists (19:13-20)
c) Paul's future plans (19:21-22)
d) The riot at Ephesus (19:23-41)
E. Paul's final visit to Macedonia and Achaia (20:1-4)
F. Return to Jerusalem (20:5–21:26)
1. From Philippi to Miletus (20:5-16)
2. Paul's defense to the elders of Ephesus (20:17-38)
3. From Miletus to Caesarea (21:1-14)
4. Paul with the Jerusalem church (21:15-26)
G. Paul the prisoner (21:27–28:31)
1. Paul's arrest and defense (21:27–22:29)
2. Paul before the Sanhedrin (22:30–23:11)
3. Paul's transference to Caesarea (23:12-35)
4. Paul at Caesarea (24:1–26:32)
a) Paul and Felix (24:1-27)
b) Paul and Festus (25:1-27)
(1) Paul before Festus (25:1-12)
(2) Festus consults with Agrippa (25:13-27)
c) Paul's defense before Agrippa (26:1-32)
5. Voyage to Rome (27:1–28:16)
6. Paul at Rome (28:17-31)

XII. Selected Bibliography

CADBURY, HENRY J. *The Making of Luke-Acts.* New York: The Macmillan Co., 1927.

HARNACK, ADOLF VON. *The Acts of the Apostles,* tr. J. R. Wilkinson. London: Williams & Norgate, 1909.

———. *Luke the Physician,* tr. J. R. Wilkinson. London: Williams & Norgate, 1907.

JACKSON, F. J. FOAKES, and LAKE, KIRSOPP, eds. *The Beginnings of Christianity.* London: Macmillan & Co., 1920-33.

MEYER, EDUARD. *Ursprung und Anfänge des Christentums.* Stuttgart: J. G. Cotta, 1921.

RAMSAY, W. M. *St. Paul the Traveller and the Roman Citizen.* London: Hodder & Stoughton, 1896.

WEISS, JOHANNES. *The History of Primitive Christianity,* ed. F. C. Grant. New York. Wilson-Erickson, 1937.

ACTS

TEXT, EXEGESIS, AND EXPOSITION

I. FROM JERUSALEM TO ANTIOCH (1:1–12:25)

A. DAYS OF EXPECTATION (1:1-26)

1. INTRODUCTORY PREFACE (1:1-5)

The introductory verses, both of his Gospel and of Acts, stamp Luke as a typical man of letters of his day. Such prefaces were used neither by ancient Greek nor ancient Semitic writers, but came into fashion in the Hellenistic age among both Greeks and Romans. They usually followed conventional lines. References would be made to earlier writers on the same subject—often with unflattering comparisons with the author's own work—claims put forward to special knowledge, and an explanation given

1 The former treatise have I made, O Theophilus, of all that Jesus began both to do and teach,

1 In the first book, O The-oph'i-lus, I have dealt with all that Jesus began to

of the author's purpose in writing. When the work was divided into several *logoi* or books, the whole work began with a general preface or *prooimion* setting forth the author's method and aim. This we have at the beginning of Luke's Gospel. At the beginning of each subsequent volume came a subsidiary preface or *proekthesis* linking this volume with the preceding one and noting the stage reached in the work. This we have here; and the natural deduction is that the two books are by the same author. A good example of the *proekthesis* is found at the beginning of the fourth book of Polybius' *Histories:* "In the preceding book, after pointing out the causes of the second war between Rome and Carthage, I described the invasion of Italy by Hannibal. . . . I shall now give an account of the contemporary events in Greece. . . ." True, the *proekthesis* of Acts is incomplete: we have a summary of the first *logos,* but not the usual sketch of the contents of the second. This suggests to some critics that the preface has been mutilated by a later editor, who at the same time has introduced a second and discordant account of the Ascension, an incident already narrated in the Gospel, and alluded to in vs. 2—**until the day when he was taken up.** It is surely better to recognize that Luke is not slavishly bound by literary convention, and that the opening sentence is in fact balanced by the whole succeeding narrative.

1:1. There is no reliable tradition about **Theophilus,** and it has even been suggested that the name, "lover of God," means merely "Christian reader." But the title "most excellent" (Luke 1:3) suggests a real person. It is thrice used in Acts (23:26; 24:3; 26:25), always of persons of high official rank. B. H. Streeter (*The Four Gospels* [New York: The Macmillan Co., 1925], p. 539) suggests that Theophilus may have been the secret Christian name of Flavius Clemens, cousin and heir of Domitian. His wife Domitilla was secretly an adherent of the church, and he himself at least an inquirer. He was put to death by Domitian in A.D. 96. Acts would thus be the first of those "apologies" addressed by the church to prominent members of the Imperial House. The Clementine Recognitions speaks of Theophilus as a wealthy resident of Antioch, the probable birthplace of Luke. Later Christian writers transform him into a bishop, and finally confound him with the apologist of the same name at the end of the second century, Bishop Theophilus of Antioch. **First** (πρῶτον, not πρότερον) in the Greek of Luke's day need not imply that the author had written, or intended to write, more than two books in the present series. **Began to do** in Semitic idiom means little more than "did." The first book narrates Jesus' activities "from the beginning" (Luke 1:2) till the Ascension. The idea that Acts narrates what the ascended Christ *continued* to do is true, but too subtle.

1:1-14. ***The Ascension of Jesus.***—Preaching on the Ascension encounters certain obstacles which may in turn be used as opportunities. The first obstacle is the resistance of the average layman to Christian doctrine. In spite of the rising tide of "neo-orthodoxy" among the clergy, there are still a great many laymen who are interested in Christianity as a way of life, but not at all interested in its framework of faith. They believe that they can keep the Christian standards of moral conduct and give up the Christian articles of faith. The Ascension, being one of those articles, does not concern them. They want to know the things Jesus said, not the things that were said about him. Now the Ascension is definitely something that people have said about Jesus; they said it from the earliest days of the Christian fellowship; of all who said it, the writer of the Acts of the Apostles said it most explicitly and concretely. And the opportunity of the interpreter is to say it again, and to say it in such language and with such reference to life that the listener will see that it is far more than a part of a dispensable superstructure and that, like all doctrine, it has to do with life, grows out of it, refers to it, and is judged by it.

Thus the interpreter's opportunity in general is to show the people what Christian doctrine really is. Specifically here it is to show what the faithful followers of Jesus were trying to say about him when they said that he as-

2 Until the day in which he was taken up, after that he through the Holy Ghost had given commandments unto the apostles whom he had chosen:

do and teach, 2 until the day when he was taken up, after he had given commandment through the Holy Spirit to the apos-

2. The order of the Greek words shows that **through the Holy Spirit** should be taken with **given commandment** rather than with **had chosen.** The text here is doubtful; and **after he had given commandment,** without any explanatory object, is left curiously vague. Possibly διά ("through") is here used to translate an Aramaic preposition meaning "in the case of," and the original sense may have been "when he had given commandment concerning the Holy Spirit"—a reference forward to vss. 4-5.

cended into heaven and sat on the right hand of God. For such instruction, the first fourteen verses of the first chapter of the Acts may be taken as the background.

A doctrine begins with a significant event from which people draw a general conclusion. Just as people cannot escape the impact of events, so they cannot escape drawing conclusions which attempt to explain the experience, relate it to the rest of experience, and communicate it to future generations by expressing it in an intelligible form.

For example, a small group of men set out to sea. There is nothing unusual about that, and the event would arouse only a local and passing interest. But a particular crew kept on going and going and, without changing their direction, finally came back to the place they started from. Hardly knowing what they were doing, they had circumnavigated the globe. That was an event that made men stop and think. Obviously it had more than a local significance. It had world-wide implications and eventually cosmic repercussions. From it men drew the conclusion that the earth was not a plane but a globe; and thenceforth the fact that the earth is round has been a dogma of geography.

It is worth while to notice that the conclusion drawn from the event was more like an act of faith than anything else. The fact that the earth, despite all appearances to the contrary, was round, was not an easy thing to demonstrate in the fifteenth century. There were only a handful of men who were actual witnesses to the fact that the ship had encircled the globe. Nevertheless there were some who drew the conclusion without hesitation and dared to venture into the unknown, proceeding upon its basic assumption that the earth is round, not flat. They discovered continents, confirmed the guesses of astronomers and geographers, and added their testimony to what other men were discovering in different but related fields, each new fact confirming and substantiating the original conclusion. Ultimately our knowledge of the solar system emerged.

Christian doctrine grows in essentially the same way. It begins with an event from which general conclusions are drawn and on which men, in faith, are willing to base their lives. The doctrine of the Ascension is an illustration of this principle. The event is the disappearance of Jesus, in itself a neutral if not a negative event. Every man disappears sooner or later. Yet the disappearance of Jesus was different. In the first place he was different. His life had something that other human lives do not have; he did something that no one else has ever done. Men recognized that from the beginning, though they found it difficult to define precisely what it was. Furthermore, after he died he reappeared to his friends. The form of his reappearance cannot be accurately defined, neither can the fact of it be denied. And after his final disappearance, so to speak, his influence was stronger than ever. His presence was even more vividly felt than it had been before. His power continued to make itself felt through the fellowship of those who had been and were to be his followers.

So much for the experience of Jesus' followers. What conclusion were they to draw from it? Draw one they must, not because they were academic people with nothing else to do but sit around a table and formulate theories about the universe, but because they were human beings with minds through which God could speak to them in the language of events. The conclusion they drew was this: Jesus had ascended into heaven and was sitting at the right hand of God! What a bold leap from fact to faith! A humble, Jewish peasant on the throne of God! A ruling Christ to whom all the reigning Caesars must ultimately yield! That was their conclusion and that became the doctrine of the Christian church.

Like the conclusion that the navigators drew, it began with a fact but reached far beyond all demonstrable fact into the realms of faith. The first Christians believed that there could be no two ways about Jesus. Jesus, they said, is not buried in the ground, nor stored away in the archives of history, nor lost in the shades

3 To whom also he showed himself alive after his passion by many infallible proofs, being seen of them forty days, and speaking of the things pertaining to the kingdom of God:

tles whom he had chosen. 3 To them he presented himself alive after his passion by many proofs, appearing to them during forty days, and speaking of the kingdom of

3. The Greek word for **appearing to them** occurs only here in the N.T., but is used in the LXX in Num. 14:14 of Yahweh's self-manifestation in the wilderness. These appearances occurred **during forty days**—a number traditional in sacred history (Exod. 34:28; I Kings 19:8; Matt. 4:2). In Luke's Gospel there is nothing to indicate that the Ascension did not take place on the same day as the Resurrection—a view perhaps shared by Paul who seems to regard the two as synonymous. The acceptance of the longer

of oblivion, nor held, like a fading image, in the human memory. Jesus is where God is—in heaven, where neither time nor space can set any limits whatsoever upon him and upon his manifested power.

Such a conclusion cannot be proved. Even if we should discover authentic photographs of Jesus rising aloft into the clouds, it would prove nothing. Yet men and women who dare to act upon the conclusion, and live as though Jesus were master of all things, find the conclusion confirmed and substantiated by one experience after another.

The interpreter must also face the obstacle of language. He must help others get through what may be the unfamiliar language of a doctrine to its meaning. That we have already considered. But in the case of the Ascension the language is doubly difficult because it is completely foreign to us. It is pre-Copernican. Whatever the word "heaven" may mean to the average listener today, it certainly does not mean what it meant to the average man of the first century. The interpreter's task is to translate it.

It should be noted and pointed out to all who listen, perhaps, that this situation is not peculiar to theology. It is found, for instance, in the theater. *Hamlet* appeals to audiences of every generation because it searches the deepest places of the human soul. But the role that the ghost plays must first be translated to a modern audience which does not think or feel in terms of ghosts. Once that translation is made, the play is as vital as it was in Elizabethan England.

How then shall we translate the word "heaven," and in what terms can we transcribe the picture of Jesus ascending thitherward to sit at God's right hand? At least two factors must be included in the translation.

(*a*) The universality of Jesus. It was soon evident that Jesus spoke a universal language. Not everyone can understand Plato, and only a few can understand Einstein. But everyone can understand Jesus—everyone who wants to. When he stretched out his hand to heal a leper, breaking through all conventions, restrictions, and natural repulsions, everybody knew what it meant. When Jesus told a story about a father's broken heart, everybody understood. When, dying on the Cross, he asked God to pardon his enemies, no one needed a dictionary or a commentary to know what he meant. Whether one is a Jew of the first century or a Chinese of the twentieth, whether he lives in the country or a city, whether he is rich or poor, learned or ignorant, a success or a failure, he can understand Jesus, for Jesus is translatable into every tongue known to man. Time and space do not count. The Sermon on the Mount is not worn by the passing of time, nor is the light of the Transfiguration dimmed by ten thousand miles of space. Jesus is, so to speak, in heaven and, like the stars, he shines as brightly now as he did two thousand years ago, as brightly in the southern skies as he does over the North Pole.

(*b*) The centrality of Jesus. Not only did Jesus speak a universal language, but his word was universal law. Increasingly men became aware of the fact that his teaching was more than wise counsel and advice. More and more they realized that the words of Jesus made articulate the laws by which the universe operates. Indeed all the experience of our troubled times confirms this assumption of the early church. There is something in the universe that will not tolerate cruelty, pride, hypocrisy, selfishness, materialism. Over and over again men have played for power, have had their temporary and devastating day, and finally have been ruled out of order. Jesus is master not only of those who freely accept him; he is master also of those who ignore or deny him. We are called upon, therefore, not only to love Jesus, but also to obey him, for he is the articulate expression of the will of God. In other words he is "in heaven"—where God rules, and he himself is at God's right hand, the hand by which he puts into operation his will.

4 And, being assembled together with *them,* commanded them that they should not depart from Jerusalem, but wait for the promise of the Father, which, *saith he,* ye have heard of me.

5 For John truly baptized with water; but ye shall be baptized with the Holy Ghost not many days hence.

God. 4 And while staying[a] with them he charged them not to depart from Jerusalem, but to wait for the promise of the Father, which, he said, "you heard from me, 5 for John baptized with water, but before many days you shall be baptized with the Holy Spirit."

[a] Or *eating.*

period by church tradition was probably due to the desire to make room for the imparting of secret instruction to the inner circle of his disciples by the risen Jesus, in particular concerning **the kingdom of God.** The **kingdom** in Acts is much more closely identified with the church than is the case in the Synoptic Gospels, though nowhere in Acts is the earlier eschatological meaning excluded by the context (see 8:12; 14:22; 19:8; 20:25; 28:23, 31).

4. **While staying with them** is the translation of a difficult Greek word (συναλιζόμενος) variously taken as meaning (*a*) **being assembled together**—a rare word from the root ἁλής, "crowded"; (*b*) "eating salt together"—presumably with reference to Luke 24:42; (*c*) "lodging together"—a spelling variant of συναυλιζόμενος, and on the whole the most probable rendering. The word might even mean "camping with them in the open"—it is a military term, to "bivouac" —as according to Luke 21:37, he had done during the week before the Crucifixion. The disciples are charged **not to depart from Jerusalem**—the suggestion being that it had been their intention to do so. Is Luke deliberately contradicting the variant "Galilean tradition," according to which Jesus' first appearances took place at a distance from Jerusalem? According to our author, it is in Jerusalem that they are to **wait for the promise of the Father,** i.e., for the gift of the Holy Spirit. This promise, says Jesus, **you heard from me** (in Luke 24:49), and to its fulfillment at Pentecost Peter makes reference in 2:33. For the promise of the Spirit see also Gal 3:14; Eph. 1:13.

5. Here, as also in 11:16, Luke puts on Jesus' lips words elsewhere ascribed, not to Jesus, but to John the Baptist (Mark 1:8; Luke 3:16). The idea, evidently here present, that this promise was fulfilled, quite apart from any specifically Christian baptismal rite, by the gift of the Holy Spirit at Pentecost, is genuinely primitive. Later the words were understood as referring to a Christian baptism with water which differed from John's baptism, not because it was Spirit-baptism rather than water-baptism, but because though still water-baptism it also bestowed the Spirit, as John's baptism did not (see on 19:1-6 and a fuller note on 2:37-41).

Howard Chandler Robbins has made the most satisfactory translation in the more flexible, imaginative form of poetry.

And have the bright immensities
  Received our risen Lord,
Where light-years frame the Pleiades
  And point Orion's sword?

Do flaming suns his footsteps trace
  Through corridors sublime,
The Lord of interstellar space
  And Conqueror of time? [1]

Single verses within this passage suggest themes which are secondary to the main theme itself.

[1] By permission of the publisher, Morehouse-Gorham Co., New York.

4. ***Commanded Them That They Should Not Depart from Jerusalem, but Wait.***—There are times when the hardest thing in the world is to do nothing, yet there are times when that is the only thing to do. There are some things we can work for; there are other things we can only wait for. We can work for a living; we can only wait for the spring. Life is a composition of activity and passivity. We have become experts in activity and are only novices in passivity. Yet in religion there is a primary place for passivity. It is the mood in which the soul is receptive to power from outside, responsive to intimations from above. A man who waits upon God is like a man waiting for the sun, expectant, ready to obey his bidding. The active and the passive mood in religion is a theme suggested by this text.

6 When they therefore were come together, they asked of him, saying, Lord, wilt thou at this time restore again the kingdom to Israel?

6 So when they had come together, they asked him, "Lord, will you at this time

2. The Ascension (1:6-11)

For the first Christians the two cardinal events after the Crucifixion were the Resurrection and the gift of the Holy Spirit at Pentecost. The Ascension holds a peculiar middle position. There is little reference to it in the earliest Christian teaching, and it was probably not felt to mark so complete a break in Jesus' earthly fellowship with his disciples as it is now often regarded as doing. Paul, for example, in I Cor. 15, enumerates the resurrection "appearances" without any reference to the Ascension, and evidently felt no radical difference between the appearances to the eleven before the Ascension and that to himself later on the Damascus road. For Paul the risen Christ, even when he appeared to the eleven, was already clothed in a "spiritual" or "glorified" body; and the Ascension, as symbolical of his passage to heaven, was in fact identical with the Resurrection. But with the growth of the tradition of the "forty days," the Resurrection implied first a temporary renewal of earthly intercourse with the disciples, followed by the Ascension as a separate event. Acts gives us the only explicit account of the Ascension in the N.T., apart from the Marcan appendix (Mark 16:19), for Luke 24:51-52 is textually suspect and the best texts bracket the words "and carried up into heaven" (KJV). Yet the exaltation of Jesus at the right hand of God quickly became an integral part of the earliest Christian creed; and this, given ancient cosmic ideas, presupposes an "ascension." Such a happening would also help to explain the cessation of appearances of the risen Jesus. But the silence of Matthew and Mark, apart from the appendix, suggests that the Ascension, as an event separate from the Resurrection, had no place in the most primitive tradition.

6. The disciples are pictured as misunderstanding the meaning of the "promise" (vs. 4). They still connect it with the expected restoration of the national theocracy and therefore ask, **Lord, will you at this time restore the kingdom to Israel?** It is quite likely that the disciples' earliest expectations would in fact take this line. They would be looking for the personal return of Jesus as the herald of the kingdom. In the Gospels Jesus speaks much of the coming of the kingdom, but little of the Holy Spirit. But by the time Acts was written the church had realized that the truest return of Jesus was in the manifest power of the Holy Spirit.

6-8. ***Lord, Wilt Thou at This Time Restore Again the Kingdom to Israel?***—It is interesting to notice that Jesus did not answer the question; he corrected it. **It is not for you to know the times or the seasons, which the Father hath put in his own power. But ye shall receive power . . . and ye shall be witnesses unto me.** He shifted the emphasis from speculation about the future to demonstration in the present. When times are hard, it is always a temptation to some people to dream about the future, and to project into the future all the things they long for, yet lack in the present. So the Jews dreamed about the kingdom. So we speculate about the future—the next war, the atomic bomb, the future of democracy, the survival of the church. Jesus was of a different mind. "Be witnesses unto me," he said. "Begin now. Let the world see a demonstration of what the power of God can do when it works through the fellowship of those who trust in him." He would say the same to us. Stop speculating about the future and begin to show people what democracy can be when Christians respect their fellow men because they are children of God.

Furthermore, he shifted the emphasis from the restoration of the past to the transformation of the present. Some people, when times are hard, take refuge in the past. They hark back to "the good old days." The disciples were doing just that when they asked for the restoration of a kingdom that was like the echo of David's day. There is no way back, the answer of Jesus implied; history is a stream of events and it moves forward; you cannot set the clock back. Our task, according to Jesus, is to transform the present by witnessing to him. We cannot restore the medieval guilds; we can only transform modern industry by taking the selfishness out of it. We cannot restore the golden days of

7 And he said unto them, It is not for you to know the times or the seasons, which the Father hath put in his own power.

8 But ye shall receive power, after that the Holy Ghost is come upon you: and ye shall be witnesses unto me both in Jerusalem, and in all Judea, and in Samaria, and unto the uttermost part of the earth.

9 And when he had spoken these things, while they beheld, he was taken up; and a cloud received him out of their sight.

10 And while they looked steadfastly toward heaven as he went up, behold, two men stood by them in white apparel;

restore the kingdom to Israel?" 7 He said
to them, "It is not for you to know times
or seasons which the Father has fixed by
his own authority. 8 But you shall receive
power when the Holy Spirit has come upon
you; and you shall be my witnesses in
Jerusalem and in all Judea and Sa-ma'ri-a
and to the end of the earth." 9 And when
he had said this, as they were looking on,
he was lifted up, and a cloud took him out
of their sight. 10 And while they were gazing into heaven as he went, behold, two

7-8. The Western text here reads "no one can know," which makes the parallel closer with Mark 13:32, a verse which Luke omits in his Gospel. It has been noted that Acts not infrequently thus compensates for an omission of Marcan material from Luke's Gospel (cf. 5:15; 6:13; 12:4). **Power** implies the ability to work miracles, and such ability, according to contemporary ideas, was the chief evidence expected of **witnesses** of Jesus. Mark 16:17-18 reads like a later elaboration of this promise, which is itself the Lukan form of the universal commission in Matt. 28:19, "Go therefore and make disciples of all nations" (RSV). The widening circle—**Jerusalem . . . Judea . . . Samaria . . . the end of the earth**—suggests the plan of Acts. Note again how in place of the promise in Matt. 28:20, that Jesus in person will be "with you always," we have here a promise of the Spirit. If Jesus had in actual fact commanded such a universal Gentile mission, would the apostles have shown the hesitation which is so evident in the first half of Acts? (See on Matt. 28:20, Vol. VII.)

9. A cloud took him out of their sight may be understood metaphorically; but the spiritual reality could not be better conveyed pictorially to Luke's readers. Daniel speaks of one like a Son of man who "came with the clouds of heaven" (Dan. 7:13); in the O.T. the incomprehensibleness of Yahweh is represented by the cloud that hides him from view; now Jesus is received into the same cloud of the Shekinah or divine glory.

10-11. In the message of the men **in white robes,** the garb of angels (Mark 16:5),

peace and prosperity and national security; we can transform the days we have now by witnessing to him, by taking the selfishness out of the existing political systems so that they may be used by God for his purposes.

9. ***A Cloud Received Him out of Their Sight.***—At the very moment that we want Jesus to be most vivid something obscures him. This verse suggests a sermon on the theme "The Absence of Christ." A companion text from John's Gospel balances the negative tone of this one from the Acts: "It is expedient for you that I go away" (John 16:7). All things come and go in life. Jesus came and went. Sometimes there is an unrecognized good in the going. A parent takes a small boy to camp and goes home without him. "A cloud received him" out of the child's sight. But his going was for the child's good; the child must learn how to live with his contemporaries, how to carry his own load, how to play and how to get along without the constant oversight of his parents. There are times when God disappears to put us on our own. He wants persons, not puppets. And yet there is a sense in which Jesus did not go away at all. Whereas he had once dwelt among them, he now dwelt within them! In some ways he was more real than he was before. They could reach him wherever they were, in the Jewish courtroom or the Roman arena. So in one sense, at least, Jesus was never more present than when he was absent! It is true of the great relationships of life that they one day reach that realm where there is neither time nor space, and though the happy intercourse of earthly existence may cease, yet there is an even deeper and more abiding relationship as between two sounds blended into a single chord. May that not be something of what the Bible means by heaven?

10-11. ***They Looked Steadfastly Toward Heaven.***—The heavens always fascinate people. Some are looking for stars, some for airplanes, some for new moons. The early Christians

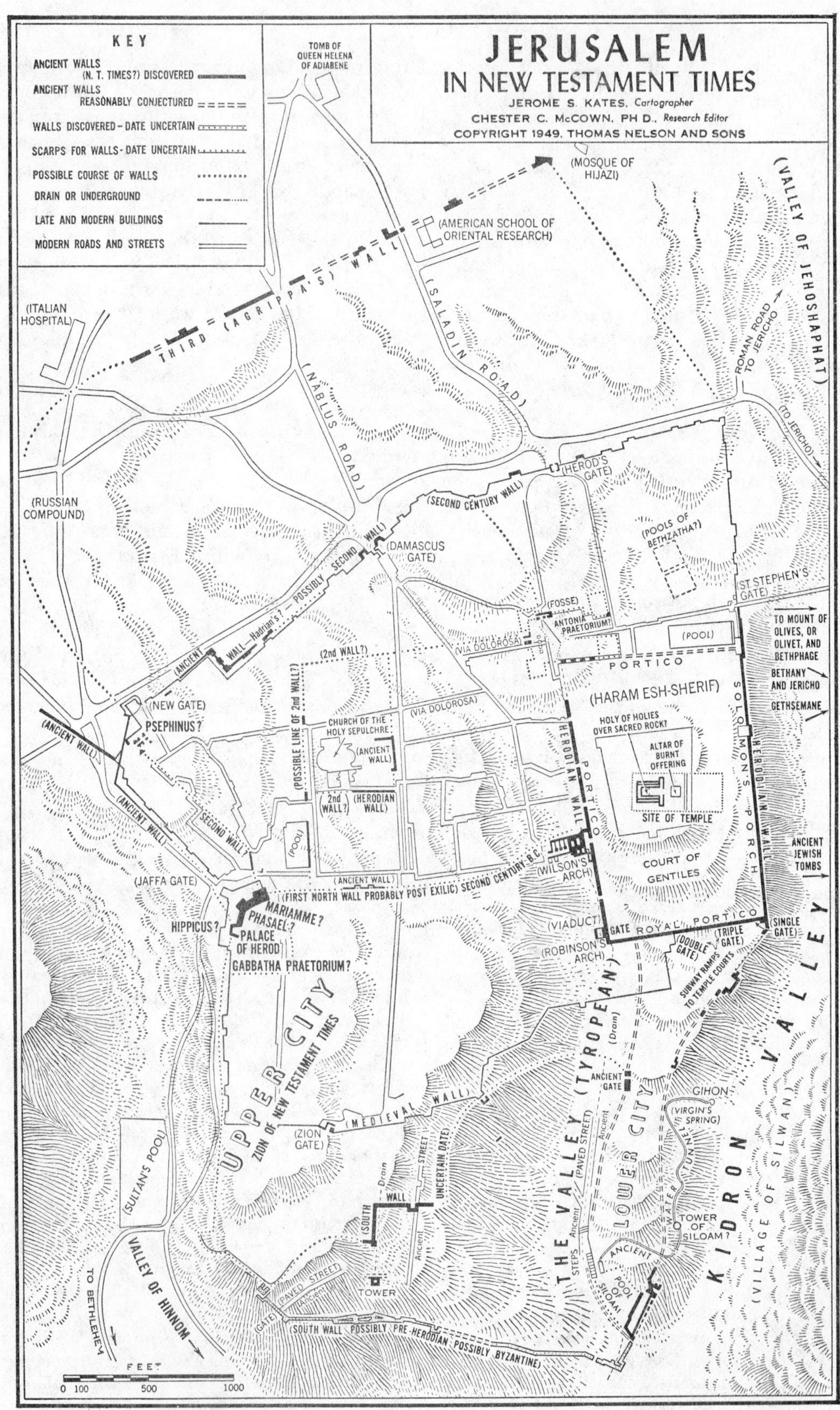
JERUSALEM
IN NEW TESTAMENT TIMES
JEROME S. KATES, Cartographer
CHESTER C. McCOWN, PH D., Research Editor
COPYRIGHT 1949, THOMAS NELSON AND SONS
KEY
ANCIENT WALLS (N. T. TIMES?) DISCOVERED
ANCIENT WALLS REASONABLY CONJECTURED
WALLS DISCOVERED - DATE UNCERTAIN
SCARPS FOR WALLS - DATE UNCERTAIN
POSSIBLE COURSE OF WALLS
DRAIN OR UNDERGROUND
LATE AND MODERN BUILDINGS
MODERN ROADS AND STREETS
TOMB OF QUEEN HELENA OF ADIABENE
(MOSQUE OF HIJAZI)
(AMERICAN SCHOOL OF ORIENTAL RESEARCH)
THIRD (AGRIPPA'S) WALL
(ITALIAN HOSPITAL)
(SALADIN ROAD)
(NABLUS ROAD)
(VALLEY OF JEHOSHAPHAT)
ROMAN ROAD TO JERICHO
(TO JERICHO)
(HEROD'S GATE)
(SECOND CENTURY WALL)
(RUSSIAN COMPOUND)
(DAMASCUS GATE)
POSSIBLY SECOND WALL
(POOLS OF BETHZATHA?)
ST STEPHEN'S GATE
(FOSSE)
ANTONIA PRAETORIUM?
(POOL)
TO MOUNT OF OLIVES, OR OLIVET, AND BETHPHAGE
BETHANY AND JERICHO
GETHSEMANE
(ANCIENT) WALL—Hadrian's?
(VIA DOLOROSA)
(2nd WALL?)
PORTICO
(HARAM ESH-SHERIF)
HOLY OF HOLIES OVER SACRED ROCK?
ALTAR OF BURNT OFFERING
SITE OF TEMPLE
COURT OF GENTILES
(NEW GATE)
PSEPHINUS?
(ANCIENT WALL)
CHURCH OF THE HOLY SEPULCHRE
(ANCIENT WALL)
(POSSIBLE LINE OF 2nd WALL?)
2nd WALL?
(HERODIAN WALL)
SECOND WALL?
(POOL)
HERODIAN WALL
PORTICO
SOLOMON'S PORCH
HERODIAN WALL
ANCIENT JEWISH TOMBS
(WILSON'S ARCH)
(JAFFA GATE)
(ANCIENT WALL)
(FIRST NORTH WALL PROBABLY POST EXILIC) SECOND CENTURY B.C.
MARIAMME?
PHASAEL?
HIPPICUS?
PALACE OF HEROD
GABBATHA PRAETORIUM?
(VIADUCT)
GATE
ROYAL PORTICO
(SINGLE GATE)
(TRIPLE GATE)
(DOUBLE GATE)
(ROBINSON'S ARCH)
SUBWAY RAMPS TO TEMPLE COURTS
(TYROPEAN)
(Drain)
UPPER CITY
ZION OF NEW TESTAMENT TIMES
ANCIENT GATE
KIDRON VALLEY
GIHON
(VIRGIN'S SPRING)
(MEDIEVAL WALL)
(ZION GATE)
LOWER CITY
THE VALLEY
(PAVED STREET)
Ancient
WATER TUNNEL
(SULTAN'S POOL)
Drain
STREET
UNCERTAIN DATE
WALL
(SOUTH
TOWER OF SILOAM?
(VILLAGE OF SILWAN)
STEPS
ANCIENT POOL OF SILOAM
TOWER
(PAVED STREET)
(GATE)
VALLEY OF HINNOM
TO BETHLEHEM
SOUTH WALL POSSIBLY PRE-HERODIAN POSSIBLY BYZANTINE
FEET
0 100 500 1000

11 Which also said, Ye men of Galilee,
why stand ye gazing up into heaven? this
same Jesus, which is taken up from you
into heaven, shall so come in like manner
as ye have seen him go into heaven.
12 Then returned they unto Jerusalem

men stood by them in white robes, 11 and
said, "Men of Galilee, why do you stand
looking into heaven? This Jesus, who was
taken up from you into heaven, will come
in the same way as you saw him go into
heaven."
12 Then they returned to Jerusalem

---

the belief in Christ's personal return, which is one of the central tenets of the earliest creed, is set in the very forefront of Acts.

3. Filling Up of the Number of the Twelve (1:12-26)

The first act of the new community was to appoint one of their number to take the place of the traitor Judas. The filling up of the number of the twelve was evidently considered of great importance. This is the more remarkable in that the twelve as such play a small part in the rest of the book, only three of them being again mentioned (Peter, James, and John), and Matthias never at all. At their original appointment the number twelve certainly had a symbolic reference to the twelve tribes, and in some ancient lists a tribe is assigned to each apostle. In the kingdom the twelve are to "sit on thrones judging the twelve tribes of Israel" (Luke 22:30). The disciples presumably wished to preserve this national symbolism by keeping the number intact. It is interesting that later no successor was appointed to James, possibly because it was felt that the martyr, unlike the traitor, would still judge the tribe allotted to him. At this time the disciples anticipated neither an apostolate to the Gentiles, which would deprive the symbol of its significance, nor such a long delay of the Parousia as would make it impossible to keep the number twelve intact.

What was the significance attached to the twelve in the most primitive tradition? Apparently they held no "official" position, nor were they commissioned with authority

---

looked toward heaven because they believed Jesus was there. Though their sight may have been inaccurate according to our standards, their insight was indubitably sound. They knew where Jesus was. They knew that all good things go up, never down. Prayer was good and prayers went up like smoke rising from bowls of incense. Jesus was good—radically and wonderfully good. When he no longer went about his accustomed ways, they knew that he had gone up, that he had ascended, because he was supremely good. Likewise, in their drawings of the universe all living things went upward, not downward. Men and women lived on the ground floor of a rather neatly arranged universe. In the damp shadows of the cellar lived the spirits of those who had departed this earthly life. But up above, in the fine open spaces of the heavens, God lived. Jesus, so intensely alive, so everlastingly present, could be in no other place than that where life was uninhibited, vitality inexhaustible, and power limited only by love.

These men were right also in knowing that Jesus would come back. "This Jesus who has been taken from you into heaven will come back" (vs. 11 Moffatt). They knew he would come back because he told them he would. They believed what he said. Truth always comes back. In fact, truth never goes away; it is men who forsake truth. The dark night that came over central Europe during the fifth century put out the lights of Greek philosophy. Eight hundred years later Thomas Aquinas, poking in the embers of an old fire, found the flame. Through him Plato and Aristotle came back. Men have tried hard and tried persistently to eliminate human freedom from the earth. Alexander tried it. So did the Caesars; so did the Huns; so did Napoleon; so have we. But again and again freedom has come back, stronger and more able. From the Cross to the campaigns of modern barbarism men have tried to subtract Christ from human existence. Yet in some unexpected and undreamed of way the Christ comes back.

One mistake, however, these early Christian men made. They thought that he would come back the same way he went. They watched the skies for his return. They forgot, or perhaps they never knew, that things seldom come back the way they go. History never repeats itself—quite. When Aristotle came back through Aquinas, it was not exactly the same man who tutored Alexander. The people we love always come back to us, but seldom do they come in

from the mount called Olivet, which is
from Jerusalem a sabbath day's journey.
13 And when they were come in, they
went up into an upper room, where abode
both Peter, and James, and John, and Andrew, Philip, and Thomas, Bartholomew,
and Matthew, James *the son* of Alpheus,
and Simon Zelotes, and Judas *the brother*
of James.
14 These all continued with one accord
in prayer and supplication, with the

from the mount called Olivet, which is
near Jerusalem, a sabbath day's journey
away; 13 and when they had entered, they
went up to the upper room, where they were
staying, Peter and John and James and
Andrew, Philip and Thomas, Bartholomew
and Matthew, James the son of Alphaeus
and Simon the Zealot and Judas the son of
James. 14 All these with one accord devoted themselves to prayer, together with

---

to govern the whole church. It was not the twelve as a "college" who headed the Jerusalem church, but certain individuals—Peter, and John, and later James the Lord's brother. Matthias is here appointed, not as an office-bearer, but as **a witness to his resurrection** (vs. 22). An "apostle" was a *shelîaḥ*—the Aramaic word for one "sent out" by Jesus, of which "apostle" is the Greek translation (cf. Luke 6:13, "whom he named apostles"). The title was perhaps originally confined to the twelve. But very quickly it was extended to others like Paul and Barnabas, who worked as traveling missionaries without necessarily holding any "official" position in the churches. Indeed, even in the case of the twelve we have a hint here that they were "apostles" primarily as missionaries. They have been commanded to wait in Jerusalem (vs. 4), not permanently as resident officials, but until they "receive power" to become "witnesses."

But a later conception of the significance of the twelve soon becomes apparent in Acts. Already they are beginning to be thought of as constituting an "apostolic college" which remained in being for some years at Jerusalem, had in its hands the first organization of the church, and provided the official heads, not only of local congregations, but of the church at large (cf. 6:2; 8:14; 11:1; and vs. 20, **his office let another take**). But such a conception is out of accord with the facts even as they appear in Acts, and will not square with what we know from Paul's epistles concerning the Jerusalem church.

12-13. The disciples then **returned to Jerusalem** in expectation that Jesus was about to appear as the triumphant Messiah. The list of the eleven agrees with that in Luke's Gospel (Luke 6:14-16), save that John now ranks next to Peter, as throughout the following narrative, while Thomas is coupled with Philip, perhaps because both are prominent in the resurrection stories. The eleven are regarded as the nucleus of the new community, and they have their rendezvous in the **upper room,** probably the scene of the Last Supper (Luke 22:12), and perhaps in the house of Mary the mother of Mark (12:12).

14. Devoted themselves to prayer: Probably in the temple, where it was expected that the Messiah would appear (Mal. 3:1). But the Greek may mean "attended the

---

exactly the same way that they left us. In the glance of a young daughter's eye, a wife lost early may come back to her husband. Across a page of poetry years after, a friend comes back to his comrade.

Those, therefore, who have watched the sky for Jesus have been disappointed, and so will they always be. He will never come that way. He will come in the need of this dreadful hour. He will stand crucified above the debris of our wrecked cathedrals, pointing to our shame and promising his help. He will come in the closed rooms of our secret lives to quiet our hurried breathing and steady our rapid pulse. With him will come all good and true things. Not just as they left will they return, but purer, stronger, and more real.

14. *These All Continued with One Accord in Prayer and Supplication.*—For a great many people religion is an occasional thing, something to enjoy on great festivals, something to rely on in time of danger. But real religion is more than an emergency measure. It is continual. It sets the pattern of man's daily thought and practice. Like regular meals, it silently stocks the storehouses of his spirit with power. It works by the law of accumulated reserves. Tracks are laid, patterns formed, habits established. Like the continual presence of the masterworks of art, it cures the heart of second-

women, and Mary the mother of Jesus, and with his brethren.

15 ¶ And in those days Peter stood up in the midst of the disciples, and said, (the number of names together were about a hundred and twenty,)

16 Men *and* brethren, this Scripture must needs have been fulfilled, which the Holy Ghost by the mouth of David spake before concerning Judas, which was guide to them that took Jesus.

the women and Mary the mother of Jesus, and with his brothers.

15 In those days Peter stood up among the brethren (the company of persons was in all about a hundred and twenty), and said, 16 "Brethren, the scripture had to be fulfilled, which the Holy Spirit spoke beforehand by the mouth of David, concerning Judas who was guide to those who

place of prayer," i.e., the synagogue (cf. 16:13, 16). But the similar phrase in 2:42 seems rather to mean "attended the service of prayer," presumably in the temple. **With the women** may be purely general—"with their wives," rather than a reference to "the women" mentioned in Luke 8:2; 24:10.

15. It is noteworthy that from the first, Peter, in spite of his cowardly denial, takes the leadership. The obvious explanation of this rapid recovery of authority is that it was to Peter that the risen Lord first appeared (Luke 24:34; I Cor. 15:5), and that his sturdy faith had rallied the others from despair. Jesus' words that "upon this rock" he would build his church (Matt. 16:18) had found literal fulfillment.

How much of the content of these first speeches in Acts rests on an earlier tradition is debatable. Attention has often been called to the primitive Christology of the sermons attributed to Peter. But generally speaking there is doctrinally no essential difference between Peter's speeches and Paul's. Nor should we look for it; for Luke can hardly have had any idea of an "evolution of theology." No doubt he sometimes skillfully adapts thought and language both to the occasion and to the speaker. The present speech certainly reflects a primitive stage of Christian thought, such as might be expected in Peter's teaching. If vss. 17-19 are regarded as an insertion of the author, there remains nothing that might not fittingly have been said by Peter. But on the whole it is safer to assume that the theology underlying the speeches is neither Peter's nor Paul's, but Luke's own—the average point of view of the Gentile Christianity of Antioch.

In all, ἐπὶ τὸ αὐτό: see note on 2:47. **A hundred and twenty:** Is it a coincidence that the tract Sanhedrin (1:6) states that the number of officers in a community (here the twelve) shall be one tenth of the membership?

16. The scripture had to be fulfilled, i.e., presumably that freely quoted in vs. 20 (Pss. 69:25; 109:8). The tense in the Greek implies that the prophecy had already been fulfilled.

rate satisfactions. It is hard for a man brought up on the music of Bach to be completely satisfied with the tunes of tin-pan alley. It is hard for a person who has been raised in the company of Jesus to be satisfied with chiselers and compromisers. Above all, this continual religion gives a man a working knowledge of the ways of God. We know the ways of the world all too well. The ways of God are not easy. They must be studied with more care than a man studies the circuit of the stars. Not all meals are exciting. Sometimes nothing happens aside from the fact that we are fed. But out of that regular, routine feeding there rises now and then a meal that is unforgettable, at which friends and family are drawn together in the closest circle of joy and peace. So continual religion is not always emotionally rewarding. It is not always a matter of following a star; sometimes it is no more than the footprints left in the dust. Yet the occasional flights of the spirit, to which we all look forward, come only after we have patiently leveled a runway from which we can take off to higher regions.

15-26. ***The Choice of Matthias.***—At first glance this passage does not appear to be a fertile field for the expositor. If he wishes to speak on the ministry, there are far greater passages in the epistles of Paul. If he wishes to search the character of Judas, there are passages in the Gospels which are far more illuminating. Yet there are themes suggested by this passage that an interpreter will not overlook. The very fact that from the glory of the Ascension we

17 For he was numbered with us, and had obtained part of this ministry.

18 Now this man purchased a field with the reward of iniquity; and falling headlong, he burst asunder in the midst, and all his bowels gushed out.

19 And it was known unto all the dwellers at Jerusalem; insomuch as that field is called, in their proper tongue, Aceldama, that is to say, The field of blood.

20 For it is written in the book of Psalms, Let his habitation be desolate, and let no man dwell therein: and, His bishopric let another take.

arrested Jesus. 17 For he was numbered
among us, and was allotted his share in
this ministry. 18 (Now this man bought a
field with the reward of his wickedness;
and falling headlong[b] he burst open in the
middle and all his bowels gushed out.
19 And it became known to all the inhabitants of Jerusalem, so that the field
was called in their language A-kel'da-ma,
that is, Field of Blood.) 20 For it is written
in the book of Psalms,

'Let his habitation become desolate,
and let there be no one to live in it';

and

'His office let another take.'

[b] Or *swelling up.*

18-20. A field: or perhaps better "a farm" or "estate" in the country. **Reward of his wickedness:** Or, by a common Semitic idiom (cf. Luke 16:8-9; 18:6; II Pet. 2:15), simply "with his unjust reward." There are three traditions concerning the death of Judas: (*a*) the account here in Acts; (*b*) Matt. 27:3-10, according to which he hanged himself; (*c*) the story preserved by Papias that, on account of a loathsome disease, he suffered from excessive swelling (πρησθείς) and was crushed by a wagon in a narrow place where it could normally have passed him (see J. A. Cramer, *Catenae in Evangelia S. Matthaei et S. Marci* [Oxford: Typographeo Academico, 1844], on Matt. 27). It has been suggested that Papias is really dependent on the same tradition as Acts, and that the somewhat strange phrase πρηνὴς γενόμενος, **falling headlong,** is an obscure medical term with the same meaning as πρησθείς (see *The Beginnings of Christianity,* ed. F. J. Foakes Jackson and Kirsopp Lake [London: Macmillan & Co., 1933], V, 22-30). **His habitation** is presumably the estate Judas had bought, while **his office** is his commission as apostle.

are pitched into the problems of administration suggests the theme for a sermon. Life is a strange mixture of rapture and routine, and we cannot have one without the other. No one knows that better than the preacher himself. How many good people want to spare him the burdens of parish administration and how well he knows that, though there is the constant danger of being swallowed up by minor matters of administration, yet it is out of that very convergence of the things of the spirit with the hard, resistant facts of organization that many of his sermons spring. Religion can never be all light and no hard labor. Good government by itself will never make a happy home or a prosperous nation, but surely no family will be happy and no nation prosperous that is not well ordered. The same is true with the church. Organization can be a strait jacket in which the spirit of Christ is paralyzed, but the spirit without any framework whatsoever can be like the wind with no sails to catch it.

The need of a ministry might be another theme, following close upon the one just considered. The story in these verses is repeated over and over again. First, the place left vacant. Not always by default; sometimes by death or disability. Tragic it is when the place is made vacant as this one was. Judas stands forever as one of the lost leaders of Christendom. There have been many others. Second, Peter takes the lead. How many times a man rises to meet a situation! Too often, indeed, for us to think it nothing but chance. **Peter stood up**; yes, and stood out, head and shoulders above the others, to take the lead. So stood Francis of Assisi, Luther, Wesley, Fox. So we pray someone will rise up to speak for Christendom; to take the place of a man like William Temple; to arouse the Christian conscience, to set forth Christian thought in language that is simple and clear, to lead the way to Christian action. Granted that the church is in a seriously weakened condition, how much of the fault can be traced to poor leadership? When the best men take the lead in the church, they are not left entirely without a following. Third, the one requirement—firsthand knowledge of Jesus as he **went in and out among us.** The burden of their message was the Resurrection, but the basis of it, and that without which it meant nothing, was personal acquaintance with the Lord Jesus.

21 Wherefore of these men which have companied with us all the time that the Lord Jesus went in and out among us,

22 Beginning from the baptism of John, unto that same day that he was taken up from us, must one be ordained to be a witness with us of his resurrection.

23 And they appointed two, Joseph called Barsabas, who was surnamed Justus, and Matthias.

24 And they prayed, and said, Thou, Lord, which knowest the hearts of all *men*, show whether of these two thou hast chosen,

25 That he may take part of this ministry and apostleship, from which Judas by transgression fell, that he might go to his own place.

26 And they gave forth their lots; and the lot fell upon Matthias; and he was numbered with the eleven apostles.

21 So one of the men who have accompanied
us during all the time that the Lord Jesus
went in and out among us, 22 beginning
from the baptism of John until the day
when he was taken up from us — one of
these men must become with us a witness
to his resurrection." 23 And they put forward two, Joseph called Bar'sab-bas, who
was surnamed Justus, and Mat-thi'as.
24 And they prayed and said, "Lord, who
knowest the hearts of all men, show which
one of these two thou hast chosen 25 to take
the place in this ministry and apostleship
from which Judas turned aside, to go to his
own place." 26 And they cast lots for them,
and the lot fell on Mat-thi'as; and he was
enrolled with the eleven apostles.

21-23. The baptism of John: The more natural meaning would be "from Jesus' baptism by John till his ascension"; but the parallel in 10:37 suggests "from the time when John was baptizing" (cf. 13:24). **They put forward:** According to the Western text it is Peter, and not the community, who makes the nomination. Of **Joseph called Barsabbas** (to be distinguished from Judas Barsabbas in 15:22) all that we know is that Eusebius numbers him, like Matthias, among the seventy, while Papias is said to have related that, according to Jesus' promise in Mark 16:18, he drank poison and came to no harm. **Matthias** means the "gift of Yahweh"; about him also there is no trustworthy tradition. He was later constantly confused with Matthew; Clement of Alexandria identifies him with Zacchaeus, and the Clementine Recognitions with Barnabas.

24. Lord, who knowest the hearts would more naturally refer to God. But the word for **chosen** is the same as that used in vs. 2 of the original choice by Jesus of the apostles (Luke 6:13), and this would seem to indicate that the prayer is addressed to Jesus.

26. Cast lots: The story strikes a very primitive O.T. note. There is no mention yet of ordination by the laying on of hands. The method of "casting lots" would be to put stones with names written on them into a vessel and shake it until one fell out. But the natural verb would be ἔβαλον, not ἔδωκαν, and it is just possible that the phrase here means "gave their votes."

No substitute has ever been found for that first basic requirement. A man must first be a witness to the Christian way of life before he can presume to speak of the Christian explanation about life. He must be the companion of him who went about doing good before he can be the champion of him who is alive forevermore. Nothing gives us confidence in the sanity of the first Christians more than this: that in spite of the spectacle of the Resurrection with its promise of power and glory, the emphasis was placed from the very beginning on the life of service and suffering. "No cross, no crown." The Christians appreciated that from the beginning. Fourth, the ultimate choice was God's. Crudely, it may seem to us, is the sense of divine choice expressed; **and the lot fell upon Matthias.** We still use, however, the same figure of speech to express the sense of being called to do something; "It is my lot to do it." Life is made up of choices and compulsions. Simon was compelled to bear Jesus' cross. Some men are drafted into service. Burdens are laid upon us and we have no choice but to carry them. So it is the lot of some men to bear the burdens and share the joys of leadership in the Christian community. It is not so much a question of their choice as it is that they have no other choice. Their talent, their situation, their opportunities, their temperament and nature, their

2 And when the day of Pentecost was fully come, they were all with one accord in one place.

2 When the day of Pentecost had come, they were all together in one place.

B. Birth of the Church (2:1-47)

In 2:1-40 we have, according to Harnack, the first of several sections derived from Jerusalem Source B (see Intro., p. 18 and note on p. 69). Vss. 41-47 are more probably a summary by Luke himself. The story of Pentecost falls into four parts: a description of the descent of the Spirit and the accompanying phenomena (vss. 1-13); an explanatory speech by Peter (vss. 14-36); a description of the effects produced (vss. 37-41); and an account of the beginnings of communal life (vss. 42-47).

1. Gift of the Spirit (2:1-13)

The conviction that shortly after the Resurrection the Christian community "received the Holy Spirit" is a constant factor in N.T. writings; but there appear to have been more than one tradition concerning the time and circumstances of the gift. In the Fourth Gospel the Spirit is bestowed by Jesus himself on the day of Resurrection: "He breathed on them, and said to them, 'Receive the Holy Spirit' " (John 20:22). According to Acts, the Spirit descended on the day of Pentecost, fifty days after the Resurrection. But both traditions bear witness to the fact that, as a result of the Resurrection, the disciples became conscious of a new inward power which completely transformed their whole outlook; and this they attributed to the possession by the Spirit of God. It is indeed this new sense of power that is the significant factor in the experience of Pentecost. For Pentecost can hardly have been the first occasion when the little community felt the presence of the Holy Spirit; it must have been through the Spirit's enlightening influence that they had already reached the conviction that Jesus had risen. But now they became conscious of the Spirit as *power*—in accordance with the promise of 1:8—wherein they might go forth to their work of witness-bearing. Accordingly the great central fact of the day was not that on it the Spirit was given for the first time, but that it marked the beginning of their active missionary work (cf. 4:31).

But this is not the conception of our author, for whom Pentecost does mark the first descent of the Holy Spirit. The accompanying miraculous phenomena are set forth as evidence that this was a completely new and strange gift, marking the birthday of a new

---

inheritance—all these things converge upon them to press them into a certain channel. Such is the call to the ministry of the church. Given the one requirement—personal association with Jesus—everything else conspires to give a man no other choice than the ministry of God. Wise is the man who accepts the lot when it falls upon him, and woe to the man who, when the lot falls, refuses to be numbered with the apostles.

2:1-47. *The Meaning of the Spirit.*—This chapter of the Acts of the Apostles introduces the second main theme of the book—the Spirit. It is important to realize that in the Acts we do not find the mind of man working out an idea or concept of the Spirit, but rather the Spirit working upon the mind and life of man. This theme as it is set forth in the Acts is enriched for us by all that succeeding generations have thought and felt about the Spirit, but the unique value of this chapter as a starting point for thought is in its closeness to a mighty experience before the theorizing mind of man had time to dull its brightness.

> The Spirit of God in the Old Testament is a phrase for the vital energy of the divine nature, and is regarded as the creative and vitalizing force of the world, and as the source, in men, of abnormal skill or strength or wisdom, of prophetic ecstasy or inspiration, and of moral purity. . . . This energy they [the early Christian fellowship] ascribed to the continuous living activity of Jesus, and called by the name "holy spirit", which was thus the link between the Messianic community and its Head. The basis, let us note, was a fact of experience; the enthusiasm was actually there and became theirs; and the phrase "holy spirit" was their interpretation of the fact.[2]

1-13. *The Story of Pentecost.*—From this historical reflection we can see how the Spirit worked one of his mightiest acts. We might call

[2] A. W. F. Blunt, *The Acts of the Apostles* (Oxford: Clarendon Press, 1926; "The Clarendon Bible"), p. 144. Used by permission.

2 And suddenly there came a sound from heaven as of a rushing mighty wind, and it filled all the house where they were sitting.

2 And suddenly a sound came from heaven like the rush of a mighty wind, and it filled all the house where they were sitting.

---

community. Even the gift of "speaking with tongues," apparently a common enough experience in the later Pauline churches, is described as if it were something abnormal and unique, and is given quite another significance than it has in the epistles. There this glossolalia quite clearly means the outpouring of inarticulate sounds under the stress of an overpowering religious emotion, a phenomenon to which there are many parallels in the history of all religious revivals down to our own day. It was evidently regarded as a supreme proof of possession by the divine Spirit and as such was earnestly coveted. But it is a gift to which Paul gives no very high place in his list of *charismata* (see I Cor. 12:4-11 and ch. 14 throughout), because it did not edify unbelievers, tended to disorder, and could be easily counterfeited. It is among the "childish things" which are to be put away while we "earnestly desire the higher gifts" (I Cor. 13:11; 12:31).

The "speaking with tongues" at Pentecost was almost certainly the same common phenomenon, and not something unique as is suggested by Luke, who undoubtedly intends us to understand that the disciples were miraculously endowed with the power to speak foreign languages. But this idea is quite inconsistent with the evidence elsewhere, even of Acts itself. There is, of course, no hint elsewhere that the apostles ever made use of such a gift in their missionary labors; nor would it have been necessary in a world where the Greek Koine was almost universally understood. In 10:46 and 19:6 glossolalia is mentioned in the true Pauline sense with no hint of misunderstanding. Even in the present context the impression produced is that **they are filled with new wine,** which exactly suits the known phenomena, but not Luke's conception. In the following speech Peter draws a comparison with the expected messianic outpouring of the Spirit foretold by Joel, and makes no reference to foreign tongues, even in his defense against the charge of drunkenness. We must probably assume that the glamour surrounding the birth of the church has, either for Luke or for the compiler of his source, invested even familiar occurrences with unique marvel and mystery, so that to add to the wonders of "wind" and "fire" he creates a similar unique miracle out of the everyday phenomena with which the church of his day was familiar.

2:1. Pentecost is the Hellenistic name for the Hebrew feast of Weeks, the institution of which is described in Lev. 23:15-21. **They were all together:** Either all the Christians (the 120 of 1:15?); or all the apostles, if it is held that vs. 4 implies that it was upon the apostles only that the Spirit fell.

---

it "the divine disturbance." Whenever you see a crowd you look for a disturbance. So if you had seen a crowd gathering in Jerusalem nineteen hundred years ago, you might have expected a disturbance. You would have found a small group of the followers of Jesus. You would have recognized instantly that they were on fire. They were talking, but they were talking in a very unusual way. Their passionate conviction conveyed the power of their message even to men who did not understand their language. They were unusually fearless. They stood up and said what they wanted to say, even though they knew that their words might mean death. And above all they were amazingly effective. People listened to them, and were moved by them, and were amazed as they heard them tell the wondrous works of God. The event is described by the writer of Acts in a single sentence, **And they were all filled with the Holy Spirit and began to speak in other tongues, as the Spirit gave them utterance.**

One of the problems that such a passage presents to the modern interpreter is this: Modern biblical scholarship has proved beyond a doubt that the record as we have it is not always an accurate description of what actually happened, but is a compilation of what happened plus the presumptions, reflection, and judgment of the next generation. For instance, it is agreed by most scholars that the "speaking in tongues" referred to in this passage originally had nothing whatever to do with speaking a foreign language. Rather it had to do with a kind of religious ecstasy which exceeded the bounds of rationality and was described and

3 And there appeared unto them cloven tongues like as of fire, and it sat upon each of them.
4 And they were all filled with the Holy Ghost, and began to speak with other tongues, as the Spirit gave them utterance.
5 And there were dwelling at Jerusalem Jews, devout men, out of every nation under heaven.

3 And there appeared to them tongues as of fire, distributed and resting on each
one of them. 4 And they were all filled with the Holy Spirit and began to speak in other tongues, as the Spirit gave them utterance.
5 Now there were dwelling in Jerusalem Jews, devout men from every nation under

---

3. The **tongues . . . of fire** are **distributed** so that one rests on each disciple. The promise of baptism "with the Holy Spirit and with fire" is fulfilled (Luke 3:16). The word **tongues** is chosen probably to suit the glossolalia that follows; and if the twelve only are involved, the suggestion may be that each apostle spoke one of the languages.

5. There is some textual evidence for the omission of the word **Jews.** It is omitted by Codex Sinaiticus, and the fact that in vs. 10 **Jews and proselytes** are treated as merely component parts of the crowd suggests that it is not wholly composed of Jews.

---

deplored by Paul. In other words, in the original experience which the writer of Acts is describing, "speaking in tongues" refers to the tremendous excitement and fervor of the occasion, and a later generation which was impressed by the spontaneous expansion and translatability of Christianity used it as a prophetic foretaste of that event. The interpreter is confronted here, as in so many other places in the Bible, with the question of how much he will defer to these facts that have been revealed by the scholars and how much he will follow the text as it is.

No one can lay down general rules for another on a subject such as this. Here, however, is a suggested policy. First, know as much as you can about the passage under consideration. Know all the theories that have been advanced by biblical scholars. Second, take the text as it stands, not only as a product of historical creation, but also as the total production of the literary and religious mind of a community. When the fruits of scholarship throw light on the total subject, use them. Never deny or violate them. In this particular case it would seem perfectly valid to preach or teach the pentecostal experience as a unifying experience which transcended all barriers of nationality and language. It may not have done so immediately, at the hour which is at the heart of this account. Yet even at that hour such universality was already implicit, and as the successive hours unfolded themselves it became more and more explicit.

Along that line one might begin by recognizing that we live in a world in which the forces that divide us threaten to destroy us. Nations are divided by rival systems of politics and economics; groups within nations are divided by class consciousness and conflict; families are increasingly divided by divorce; and individuals are virtually split in two. Our only hope is to discover and to develop stronger forces than these that can draw us together in some kind of a working, if not perfect, harmony. That hope on many occasions is dim, and at times almost extinct.

But of all people in the world Christians have the most reason to be hopeful, for the story of Pentecost is the story of forces drawing people together in a kind of unity that empowered them to resist the forces that were destroying them. To remember Pentecost is to revive our hope and to reproduce Pentecost now would be to fulfill that hope. The question therefore is: Is Pentecost reproducible?

There are two things that invariably draw men together: a common danger and a common devotion. Danger drives them together. Devotion draws them together voluntarily, and therefore those who do not have the will are left out.

Christians are people who are drawn together by a common devotion. **They were all with one accord in one place.** They were a group of people who probably had nothing else in common save this one thing: they loved Jesus. They were all there, their differences overcome, for the simple reason that they adored him. Christians have been drawn together for the same reason ever since. Even now! Congregations are drawn together every Sunday, in spite of their differences, because men and women remember Jesus. There is something about the everlasting Christ that draws men together.

We, then, as Christians are united with every other Christian on the face of the globe, not only on that lower level of life's basic necessities, but also on the higher and more significant level to which men aspire and toward

6 Now when this was noised abroad, the multitude came together, and were confounded, because that every man heard them speak in his own language.

7 And they were all amazed and marveled, saying one to another, Behold, are not all these which speak Galileans?

8 And how hear we every man in our own tongue, wherein we were born?

heaven.
6 And at this sound the multitude
came together, and they were bewildered,
because each one heard them speaking in
his own language.
7 And they were amazed
and wondered, saying, "Are not all these
who are speaking Galileans?
8 And how is
it that we hear, each of us in his own na-

It would then follow that the crowd at Pentecost represents the whole world, Jewish and heathen alike, and Luke presumably considers this as the beginning of the world-wide mission entrusted to the disciples in 1:8.

6. The **multitude** here apparently means the whole company of **devout men** just mentioned, rather than the entire Christian community or the general populace. There are undoubtedly signs of confusion in the language, due possibly to the author's having written up the earlier source—perhaps transferring the scene from **the house** to the open air, and converting the glossolalia into the novel phenomenon of speaking in

---

which they are drawn by Jesus Christ. When men are united in that kind of fellowship, they all share, to varying degrees, the same experience. **And they were all filled with the Holy Spirit.** There is nothing exclusive or discriminating in that kind of communication. The tongues of flame rested on each of them. Furthermore, such a happening as that takes a man up to the highest plane of shared experience. We are interested to note in the story of Pentecost that everyone understood what the others were saying. That is not a problem in linguistics. They understood each other because they were all talking about the same thing, the wondrous things of God. These were the basic things, the first and surest realities of all life. It is undeniable that when we talk about the things that are basic in existence, everybody understands us. Love and loyalty, need and failure, sin and salvation, hope and freedom—these things are common to all men regardless of race or nationality. How tragic it is that too often Christians waste their opportunities by talking about lesser things, things important but secondary, like liturgies, ceremonies, rituals, vestments, orders of government and local customs. No wonder people do not understand us! Christians are not united, by and large, by their liturgies or by the way they build and manage their churches. They are drawn together and held together by life's common denominators—God, sin, death, Christ, sacrifice, love.

On that level men begin to live a common life. In the beginning Christians lived together and "had all things common." It was a bold experiment which apparently did not succeed. It probably will never work. But let this be said, that the Christian movement will never again be on fire until all that is implied in its common devotion, experience, and language is expressed in some kind of common life in which men recognize that all they have comes from God, belongs to God, and as such must be shared with all the members of his family. Allowing for all its weakness, it can be proudly claimed that in spite of World War II, the common life of the Christian church did not completely break down. Christians in the United States were concerned about Christians in Germany and Japan, and when the war was over, it was the Christians who took the first step toward reconciliation. At this very moment Christianity has the strongest potential for unity that exists in the world today: a common devotion, a common experience, a common language, and a common life.

An illustration may help to make this pentecostal phenomenon clearer to the modern man. Thousands of people go to an outdoor symphony concert. They represent every conceivable nationality, political party, religious conviction, temperamental variation, and personal taste. They are drawn together by a common devotion to music. If the concert, as often happens, is a great one, the whole audience is electrified by it. Those who are better prepared will obviously reap a greater harvest, but even the casual listener will be caught by the spell. They will all share to some degree the same experience. When the concert is over, they will leave silently, moved by an experience too great for words, raised, for the time being, to one of life's supreme levels of emotion. When the spell has passed, they will want everyone they know to have the opportunity to share in an experience like that. They will want everyone to hear the music and they will be drawn together in

9 Parthians, and Medes, and Elamites, and the dwellers of Mesopotamia, and in Judea, and Cappadocia, in Pontus, and Asia,
10 Phrygia, and Pamphylia, in Egypt, and in the parts of Libya about Cyrene, and strangers of Rome, Jews and proselytes,

tive language? 9 Par'thi-ans and Medes and
E'lam-ites and residents of Mes-o-po-ta'mi-a,
Judea and Cap-pa-do'ci-a, Pontus and Asia,
10 Phryg'i-a and Pam-phyl'i-a, Egypt and the
parts of Libya belonging to Cy-re'ne, and
visitors from Rome, both Jews and prose-

---

foreign languages. As Lake says: "The facts would be adequately covered if it were supposed that the original source ran 'and they were all filled with the Holy Spirit and began to speak with tongues, as the Spirit gave them utterance, and when this voice arose the populace came together, and they were all astonished and perplexed, one saying to another, "What does this mean?" But others jeered and said, "They are full of sweet wine"'" (*Beginnings of Christianity,* ed. F. J. Foakes Jackson and Kirsopp Lake [London: Macmillan & Co., 1920-33], V, 119).

9-11. The list of people is intended to cover **every nation under heaven** (vs. 5). **Parthians and Medes and Elamites** represent Eastern races outside the Roman Empire.

---

that great fellowship of those who love and serve music. Something like that was the pentecostal experience.

Another treatment of the Pentecost story might follow a different course. Its purpose would be to make people feel the reality and the power of the unseen, the spiritual; to offset the overemphasis on the material things of life. It might well begin by pointing out that everybody knows that there are times when a man outdoes himself. A young football player, for instance, in the last two minutes of the game, with the score against his team, makes a touchdown. He runs faster than his legs can carry him, and farther than he ever dreamed of running. When he comes out, the coach says to him, "I didn't know you had it in you." He replies, "I didn't. I was picked up and carried by something outside myself." That is the experience that men have when they completely outreach and outdo themselves.

From such a simple experience it is easy to take the next step and see that it was an experience something like that which the first Christians had. Everybody knew that Peter, for example, was no orator, yet he stood up in front of the crowd and when he began to speak, they all listened. He spoke with boldness and with power. If anyone had said to Peter, "I didn't know you had it in you," he surely would have said, "I didn't. It was the Spirit of the Lord Jesus that gave me utterance." Likewise, no one looked for anything extraordinary from Stephen, and yet he too stood up and spoke his mind, and when he was stoned, he prayed for those who were killing him in such a moving way that men have repeated the prayer ever since. He did not have it in him; it was the Spirit that gave him utterance.

Facts such as these remind us that men and women like ourselves can be the channel for the Spirit of God. Sometimes it is a thing like the group spirit that takes hold of us and gives us the power to score. Sometimes it is more like a passion, and there are times when it is as though the Spirit of Jesus comes to us and moves through us as through a channel.

These undeniable facts have great implications which we do not always appreciate. We become more and more preoccupied with the material world. It is only natural that we should. The scientists have drawn the most accurate charts of it. They have analyzed its laws; they have released undreamed of power and treasure, and things that were hidden for centuries they have revealed. And yet, preoccupied as we are with this world, we are increasingly disillusioned by it. Its laws of cause and effect can be rigid, inflexible things that grind our dreams to powder. This world that is so transient and unfinished, that can be so cruel and heartless, wonderful as it is in many ways, if it were all, would leave us as men without hope. But it is not all. The Pentecost story reminds us that there is something beside what we see; "Simon Peter, fisherman" does not tell the whole story. That something else beside we call the spirit. It is free, not bound; flexible, not fixed; creative, not cruel; personal, not impersonal. Every now and again it breaks through into this world of flesh and matter in an incredibly wonderful way. Into a degenerate Roman world, where there seemed to be no hope for any good future, came a mighty rushing wind, and flames of fire, like a directive from on high. All the things men thought were fixed forever changed, and a free, life-renewing Spirit invaded this world from outside.

11 Cretes and Arabians, we do hear them
speak in our tongues the wonderful works
of God.
12 And they were all amazed, and were
in doubt, saying one to another, What
meaneth this?
13 Others mocking said, These men are
full of new wine.
14 ¶ But Peter, standing up with the
eleven, lifted up his voice, and said unto
them, Ye men of Judea, and all *ye* that

lytes, 11 Cre'tans and Arabians, we hear
them telling in our own tongues the mighty
works of God." 12 And all were amazed and
perplexed, saying to one another, "What
does this mean?" 13 But others mocking
said, "They are filled with new wine."
14 But Peter, standing with the eleven,
lifted up his voice and addressed them,

Then come the **residents of** the districts around the eastern Mediterranean, followed by **visitors from Rome** (i.e., temporarily resident in Jerusalem), and **Cretans and Arabians,** who perhaps represent the two extremes of West and Southeast. But the classification may be one of language rather than geography, **Judea** perhaps meaning Aramaic-speaking Palestine and Syria.

2. Peter's Speech (2:14-36)

Peter's speech at Pentecost appears to be derived from a very primitive tradition concerning, if not his own teaching, at any rate that of the earliest community. The Christology is very elementary, and there is little trace of Pauline ideas which must have been current in the environment in which Luke wrote. For example, any reference to faith as a necessary condition of sharing in the blessings of the messianic age is noticeably absent. Only once in these early speeches does Peter mention it: in 3:16, where it is stated to be the ground of the healing of the lame man—a close resemblance to the view of faith characteristic of the Synoptic Gospels. As Christianity for Luke and his contemporaries was above all the proclamation of salvation through faith in Jesus Christ, the absence of such ideas in the early Petrine speeches argues strongly for the use of primitive documentary sources.

In this speech numerous parallels have been traced with the thought and language of I Peter. **Foreknowledge** occurs in the N.T. only here (vs. 23) and in I Pet. 1:2. The following ideas are prominent both here and in the epistle: that Christ is Lord (vs. 36; I Pet. 3:15); his rejection by his own (vs. 23; I Pet. 2:4, 7); his ascension and session at the right hand of God (vs. 33; I Pet. 3:22); the promised gift of the Spirit (vs. 33; I Pet. 1:12; 4:14); the glory that follows upon suffering (vs. 36; I Pet. 1:11; 4:12-14); salvation and baptism (vs. 38; I Pet. 3:21). E. G. Selwyn (*The First Epistle of St. Peter* [London: Macmillan & Co., 1946], p. 12) has suggested that the echoes of I Peter which are

We know that we need the power of the same Spirit. We know that nothing can change this world but some such intrusion by a power greater than anything the world itself contains. It is the particular task of the church to present opportunities for the Spirit to break through. If a church ties itself up with great wealth, becomes involved in vested interests so that it must compromise its principles, we know that the spirit will never break through that church. We know that the Spirit cannot break through flesh that has been perpetually indulged and pampered. Neither can it break through traditions that have become so fixed that they are like a coat of mail encasing a body. Nor can it break through the church that has become comfortable, settled in its own beautiful building, forgetting the heart-rending needs of the world, well fed and unconcerned.

Sometimes when we travel by plane, as we approach the airport, the message is brought to us that we cannot land because there is a ground fog. How many churches are there today over which the ground fog is so dense that the Spirit of God can never make a landing there. That is a challenge and a solemn charge to all church members. On Pentecost we should ask ourselves this question: In a world in which it is possible for the Spirit to work such mighty acts, what is preventing it now? What is there in us that is blocking it?

14-40. *Peter's First Sermon.*—The speeches in the first part of the Acts are probably not verbatim reports of what actually was said.

dwell at Jerusalem, be this known unto you, and hearken to my words:

"Men of Judea and all who dwell in Jerusalem, let this be known to you, and give

---

heard in Acts may be due partly to the fact that Silvanus, who was the joint author with Peter of the epistle (I Pet. 5:12), was also a friend and companion of Luke.

The speech may be said to be the earliest Christian apology. The first aim of the Christian preacher was to show to his fellow countrymen that Jesus was the promised Messiah. The Crucifixion seemed to have given the lie to Jesus' claims to be the revealer of God, and till this impression was dispelled all preaching of the Christian message was futile. Hence the defense of the gospel rather than its exposition is the need of the hour, and the stress is not so much on the content of the gospel as on the evidence of its truth. To judge by these early sermons the first preachers contented themselves with the demonstration of the messiahship, and did not ask what the messiahship involved for Jesus himself. There is no reason to suppose that at first their idea of messiahship differed greatly from that of their fellow Jews. It was only when the original messianic expectations had somewhat waned that Christians began to fill in or add to the picture with its original Jewish content, probably by drawing on their recollection of Jesus' own words, the full meaning of which they had at the time missed. Only when it dawned upon them that Jesus' work was something more than the founding of a national messianic kingdom did they begin to speculate upon the person of Jesus himself. Hence the complete absence here of any developed Christology.

The supreme argument for the messiahship was the Resurrection, for it effaced the impression left by a disgraceful death, proved that Jesus was no impostor, and vindicated all his claims. Hence the effort, so well illustrated in this speech, to show that such a resurrection, though no part of common messianic expectation, had nevertheless been foretold in Scripture. To a Jewish audience no other argument would be necessary; that an event had been prophesied was sufficient reason for believing in its truth and its

---

They are samples of the kind of thing that was said. Peter's first word is a rebuke to the cynic's interpretation of Pentecost: "These men are full of new wine." So the appearance of new ideas and new life is invariably greeted. The leaders of a new movement are called crackpots by those who are fearful of change. It is well to remember a remark of John Haynes Holmes to the effect that it is the cracked people who let the light through. Every inventor, every discoverer, every man who has made significant advances in human life has had his share of popular scorn. Thank God for the Peters who are prepared to stand up and point out to the people that these things are the work of God, and that through these sensitive people God is pouring out his Spirit upon all men.

Peter proceeds to preach Jesus. The manner and the method are not congenial to the modern preacher or to the modern congregation. We do not rest our claims for Jesus supremely on O.T. authority. We can, however, show that the past experience of the race points toward Jesus. He is the fulfillment of its greatest need and the flowering of its greatest possibilities. Nowhere outside the O.T. will we find more sure and authentic indication of this fact. The important consideration for the modern teacher is not so much the method by which the first evangelists preached Christ as it is the fact that they did it and that in that preaching was their power.

There is a general pattern which all the early speeches in the Acts follow. Five points are set forth with utmost clarity, though not always in the same order, and with occasional omissions. They suggest a pattern for interpreters today. (*a*) *What Jesus did.* By the power of God he did **miracles and wonders and signs.** In other words he did the impossible. He brought life where it seemed that only death could reign. (*b*) *What you did.* **Him . . . ye have taken, and by wicked hands have crucified and slain.** How could human perversity be set forth with more appalling clarity: the best that man can conceive despoiled by the worst to which man can stoop? (*c*) *What God did.* **Whom God hath raised up, having loosed the pains of death.** God did not intervene in man's malicious plans for crucifixion. He did not prevent the Cross in order to spare his innocent Son and thereby relieve the rest of the human family from their moral responsibilities and from the consequences of their moral action. But he wondrously reversed the verdict and changed the Cross from the seal of death to the sign of salvation and the entrance to life. (*d*) *What we*

15 For these are not drunken, as ye suppose, seeing it is *but* the third hour of the day.

16 But this is that which was spoken by the prophet Joel;

17 And it shall come to pass in the last days, saith God, I will pour out of my Spirit upon all flesh: and your sons and your daughters shall prophesy, and your young men shall see visions, and your old men shall dream dreams:

ear to my words. 15 For these men are not
drunk, as you suppose, since it is only the
third hour of the day; 16 but this is what
was spoken by the prophet Joel:
17 'And in the last days it shall be, God
declares,
that I will pour out my Spirit upon all
flesh,
and your sons and your daughters
shall prophesy,
and your young men shall see visions,
and your old men shall dream dreams;

---

divine significance. So Peter (vss. 25-28) appeals to Ps. 16 and claims that it foretells the resurrection of the Messiah. This would both make Jesus' resurrection credible and be convincing proof that he was Christ. Peter argues also (vss. 32-35) that the Messiah must be exalted to the right hand of God, and Jesus' ascension becomes yet further proof of his claims. Such an exaltation is evidenced by the outpouring of the Holy Spirit, which in turn is a final proof, after Joel, that the messianic age has arrived; for the gift of the Spirit is the work of the glorified Jesus and shows him to be **Lord and Christ** (vs. 36).

The view taken of Jesus' death is also very primitive. The Cross is an obstacle to faith, to be overcome by stressing the Resurrection; it has not become a central doctrine of the faith. The conception of a suffering Messiah was completely strange to contemporary Judaism, and there is little sign that the disciples saw at first in Jesus' death, as did Jesus himself, any positive contribution to the advancement of the kingdom of God. Such a development of thought may well have taken place before Paul, for one of the truths that Paul "received" was that "Christ died for our sins in accordance with the scriptures" (I Cor. 15:3). But there is little trace of such a thought in these earliest days, and its absence here seems again to confirm the authenticity of the primitive tradition underlying the speech.

15-17. The third hour: about 9 A.M., the hour of morning prayer, before which a Jew would not customarily eat. **The prophet** is Joel 2:28-32. The Western text omits the name and also makes several alterations in the quotation to suit it to the occasion more exactly, and to suggest that the promise was made to **all flesh** and not only to the Jews: e.g., "*your* sons and daughters" becomes "*their* sons and daughters," and the "my" is omitted before "menservants and maidservants" (cf. the similar omission of "Jews" in vs. 5).

---

are doing now. **Whereof we all are witnesses.** Peter was speaking for the small group who had resisted the wave of popular indifference and who had recognized the glory of God in the face of Jesus Christ. Those in that group were now continuing to exercise the power that Jesus had exercised. They were the agents of life. They were the new shoots that had newly appeared around the dead stump, and everything they did and said was witness to what God had done in Christ. (*e*) *What you can do.* In this particular sermon this point makes an epilogue. After Peter had finished the address, **they were pricked in their heart, and said unto Peter and to the rest of the apostles, Men and brethren, what shall we do?** Peter's answer was plain and precise. **Repent, and be baptized every one of you in the name of Jesus Christ.**

It is at exactly this point that much contemporary preaching falls down. The proposition is set forth, the movement is described, but when serious-minded people ask, "How do I start? What do I do to become a Christian?" they are left with vague and general platitudes. We shall consider this in more detail when we come to the question of the jailer in ch. 16. It is enough now to point out that the first Christians were specific about ways and means. The steps to be taken were definite and well marked. **Repent, and be baptized.**

Peter left his congregation with the words, **Save yourselves from this untoward generation** (KJV), or as we more often hear it, **Save yourselves from this crooked generation** (RSV). That single line raises one of the most important questions that contemporary Christianity has

18 And on my servants and on my hand-
maidens I will pour out in those days of
my Spirit; and they shall prophesy:
19 And I will show wonders in heaven
above, and signs in the earth beneath;
blood, and fire, and vapor of smoke:
20 The sun shall be turned into darkness, and the moon into blood, before that
great and notable day of the Lord come:
21 And it shall come to pass, *that* whosoever shall call on the name of the Lord
shall be saved.

18 yea, and on my menservants and my maidservants in those days
I will pour out my Spirit, and they shall prophesy.
19 And I will show wonders in the heaven above
and signs on the earth beneath,
blood, and fire, and vapor of smoke;
20 the sun shall be turned into darkness
and the moon into blood,
before the day of the Lord comes,
the great and manifest day.
21 And it shall be that whoever calls on the name of the Lord shall be saved.'

18-21. Do the words **and they shall prophesy** indicate that Luke thought that the "speaking with tongues" was such prophecy? In I Cor. 12:10 Paul of course clearly distinguishes between "prophecy" and glossolalia as he knew it. **Blood, and fire, and vapor of smoke:** omitted by the Western text, again presumably to make the quotation suit the circumstances. The **manifest day** is in the Hebrew original the "terrible day"; but owing to the confusion of similar Hebrew roots meaning respectively "fear" and "see," the LXX translation is ἐπιφανής, which may here mean "conspicuous" in the sense of **notable** (KJV) or "splendid." **The Lord** in Joel is of course Yahweh; but in Luke's thought the title, as in vss. 34-36, is transferred to Jesus as Messiah.

to face. What is the relationship between the church and the generation or the civilization in which it lives? This question cannot be answered out of a book, even the book of the Acts of the Apostles. Indeed, it is not specifically dealt with in the Acts. Rather the story that the Acts unfolds is one answer to the question. It is worth serious thought. The greatest Christian minds of our time are working upon it. A book like *What Is Christian Civilization?* by John Baillie is a sample of that work at its best. Arnold J. Toynbee's *A Study of History,* while not a direct answer to the question, is filled with illuminating suggestions. How can the preacher introduce his rather reluctant congregation to these urgent and disturbing considerations?

He can begin by pointing out that among the questions that perplex all thoughtful Christians, this is question number one: The world is on the brink of disaster. What can Christians do about it? Can they do anything about it? Must they be content to sit on the side lines and watch it go? Is their only alternative to withdraw from the world and live in such spiritual seclusion as is possible to obtain? Or can they do something about it? Can they prevent the disaster? And if they can do anything about it, exactly what is it that they can do? There is no simple answer to questions like these. There is, however, the possibility of turning back the pages of history and finding in another historical situation, comparable to our own, suggestions that may point the way to our solutions. We do so knowing full well that there are no perfect parallels in history. There are only situations sufficiently similar so that the solutions found in an earlier time may suggest possible solutions for our time.

Look, therefore, at the picture of Palestine as it was seen through the eyes of a Christian a generation after the Crucifixion. To such a man, observing the scene of current history, it was clear as daylight that he was living at the end of an era. Greece had already gone. The glory of Platonism had faded into the lesser glory of Neoplatonism. Jerusalem was as good as gone. The Jews had made a contribution of inestimable worth to the world, namely, the gift of ethical monotheism. Their prophets stand like mountain peaks in the land of spiritual development and discernment. But they had rejected their greatest Son and missed their most pregnant opportunity. They were hoping against hope that they could hold out against Roman power. In A.D. 70 they met their inevitable doom and brought to an end their life as a nation. Rome, on the other hand, had risen with a glory all its own. It had made contributions to government and law. It had provided the Mediterranean world with a unified life and culture symbolized by the roads which,

22 Ye men of Israel, hear these words;
Jesus of Nazareth, a man approved of God
among you by miracles and wonders and
signs, which God did by him in the midst
of you, as ye yourselves also know:
23 Him, being delivered by the deter-
minate counsel and foreknowledge of God,
ye have taken, and by wicked hands have
crucified and slain:
24 Whom God hath raised up, having
loosed the pains of death: because it was
not possible that he should be holden of
it.

22 "Men of Israel, hear these words:
Jesus of Nazareth, a man attested to you
by God with mighty works and wonders
and signs which God did through him in
your midst, as you yourselves know — 23 this
Jesus, delivered up according to the definite
plan and foreknowledge of God, you crucified and killed by the hands of lawless
men. 24 But God raised him up, having
loosed the pangs of death, because it was
not possible for him to be held by it.

---

22. **Jesus of Nazareth:** literally "the Nazoraean." Two forms of the word are found in the N.T.: Ναζωραῖος (regularly in Acts), and Ναζαρηνός (in Mark and Luke 4:34; 24:19). In spite of the attempt, based on Matt. 2:23, to make the words the name of a religious sect, there seems to be no decisive philological argument against deriving both forms of the adjective from the name of the town Nazareth (see on 24:5; also G. F. Moore in *Beginnings of Christianity,* I, 429). **Attested:** The Greek is ἀποδεδειγμένον, which would mean, as frequently in contemporary papyri, *designatus,* proclaimed or appointed to office. Jesus is the "elected Messiah," and was actual Messiah here on earth. The Western text reads δεδοκιμασμένον—translated *destinatum* by Tertullian—which would suggest rather that Jesus was "Messiah-elect," and entered on his actual messiahship only at his ascension.

23-24. A hint, in spite of what was said above, that even thus early the Cross is seen to be part of the **definite plan** of God for salvation. **Lawless men** may mean either "wicked men" or merely those "outside the law," i.e., the heathen. **Pangs** (ὠδῖνας) is also used in the LXX to translate a Hebrew word really meaning "cords" or "bands" (e.g., Ps. 18:4-5). Hence perhaps the somewhat strange expression **loosed the pangs,** a phrase which actually occurs in the LXX of Job 39:2.

---

like a net, held the civilized world together. It had been like an eagle, its power and majesty like the spread of an eagle's wings. It was becoming a vulture. It was losing its soul. Its power was going to its head. It had within its material prosperity the seed of decay. Within a century or two it would be virtually gone. It was the end of an era and, to the imaginative and dramatic mind of a Jewish Christian, it was the veritable end of the world.

The Christians had a strategy for the situation and Peter, their first spokesman, put it in brief, precise language when he said **Save yourselves from this crooked generation.** A modern congregation would undoubtedly have expected him to say, "Save this crooked generation," but he did not. His strategy was different. We might paraphrase his plan for action in some such way as this: As he saw the situation, it was as though a house were on fire. The flames were licking the very pinnacles of its roof, and Peter, speaking for the Christians, said: "The fire has gone too far to be extinguished. The house cannot be saved. Let it go. The people in the house, however, can be saved. Get them out of it. Get them into a new order of society that God has established among us. Jesus, who was crucified and is now alive, is the center of it. When a man becomes a part of it he is changed from a self-centered, self-seeking human being into a self-forgetting one, from one who is anxious and fearful into one who is full of courage and hope. That order of society," Peter went on to say, "has its roots in reality. It is independent of anything that can happen in the political arena of international events, and it reaches clear beyond the horizon and over it to where death has no dominion whatsoever."

The Christians acted, for better or worse, on that strategy. Of course they continued to live in the world. They had to go through all the vicissitudes of the decline and fall of the Roman Empire. They had to submit themselves to the ignominy of slavery and they were forced to endure the sight of idolatry and emperor worship. But they lived in a new world. Indeed, they were a new world. They did not hesitate to let the old life go. It was an era beyond repair. They let it go. They kept the kingdom. They laid hold on Christ. They cultivated the

25 For David speaketh concerning him, I foresaw the Lord always before my face; for he is on my right hand, that I should not be moved:
26 Therefore did my heart rejoice, and my tongue was glad; moreover also my flesh shall rest in hope:
27 Because thou wilt not leave my soul in hell, neither wilt thou suffer thine Holy One to see corruption.
28 Thou hast made known to me the ways of life; thou shalt make me full of joy with thy countenance.

25 For David says concerning him,
'I saw the Lord always before me,
for he is at my right hand that I may not be shaken;
26 therefore my heart was glad, and my tongue rejoiced;
moreover my flesh will dwell in hope.
27 For thou wilt not abandon my soul to Hades,
nor let thy Holy One see corruption.
28 Thou hast made known to me the ways of life;
thou wilt make me full of gladness with thy presence.'

25-28. Accurately quoted from Ps. 16:8-11 in the LXX which, as here, has **my tongue rejoiced** in place of the Hebrew "my glory rejoices." Curiously enough the latter phrase is the very one on the basis of which the Midrash gives the psalm a messianic interpretation. Elsewhere in rabbinical literature the psalm is not applied to the Messiah. **My flesh will dwell in hope:** The Hebrew has "shall dwell safely," i.e., with God's help the psalmist need have no fear of death. But for Luke the LXX variant **in hope** gives to the quotation its main point: Peter's whole argument is that this hope was not fulfilled in the person of David, but only in Jesus' resurrection.

---

inner life of the new order in which all men were the sons of God. Life was released through them, the risen life and power of Jesus. It spread abroad into the world. It was as though the waters of life had been held back, gathered together in one place by the building of a dam. Gradually the waters rose. Finally they spilled over the dam in an excess of vitality and joy, running down into every valley of life, fertilizing it, redeeming it from its drought. They were not deliberately concerned with the world at all. They were concerned with Christ and his kingdom. There is not a single mention in the Acts of any significant Christian reform party. They made no protest against the social evil of slavery, and the only thing they could do about emperor worship was to refuse to conform. And yet when Rome fell, they were the ones who held in their hand the seeds of a new world. They saved the world by indirection. The surplus of their spiritual life was so great that it built hospitals for the sick, schools for the ignorant, and cathedrals for the glory of God.

Johannes Weiss in his *History of Primitive Christianity* makes this comment upon their achievement. "Truly, in the midst of a gloomy, hopeless, 'crooked and perverse' generation, here is a group of inspired, courageous men, reliant upon their God; in the midst of a nation moving on to destruction, a new people, with a future!" [3]

[3] New York: Wilson-Erickson, 1937, I, 41.

Look at the picture today. We too are conscious of living at the end of an era. We too are living in what might be called "a crooked generation." Mark this: When a generation is branded as a crooked one, it does not mean that everything in it is crooked, nor does it mean that every person in it is a crook. What it means is that the direction of that generation is crooked, and that in general it is moving toward death and not toward life.

Some unperceiving folk still require documentary evidence. Look at our political systems. We cannot live without political order and government. Some political systems have produced magnificent results, especially democracy. And yet those very systems have not been able so to order the life of men as to avoid two total global wars within twenty-five years. There is something crooked about that. Again, look at the relations between capital and labor, with the tension between them which seems often to be increasing. There is something wrong about that. Look at science. With all its glorious achievements—the glory of which no sane man wishes to minimize—it is now in the position of offering mankind the means whereby he may destroy himself. Look at the arts. Everyone who is intelligent has a high regard for the sincerity of the modern artist, and yet when you see that the prevailing mood of modern art is what we might call the cult of dissonance, the ugly, the obscure, and the purely private, it is hard to deny that there is something crooked there.

29 Men *and* brethren, let me freely speak unto you of the patriarch David, that he is both dead and buried, and his sepulchre is with us unto this day.

30 Therefore being a prophet, and knowing that God had sworn with an oath to him, that of the fruit of his loins, according to the flesh, he would raise up Christ to sit on his throne;

31 He, seeing this before, spake of the resurrection of Christ, that his soul was not left in hell, neither his flesh did see corruption.

32 This Jesus hath God raised up, whereof we all are witnesses.

33 Therefore being by the right hand of God exalted, and having received of the Father the promise of the Holy Ghost, he hath shed forth this, which ye now see and hear.

34 For David is not ascended into the heavens: but he saith himself, The LORD said unto my Lord, Sit thou on my right hand,

35 Until I make thy foes thy footstool.

29 "Brethren, I may say to you confidently of the patriarch David that he both
died and was buried, and his tomb is with
us to this day. 30 Being therefore a prophet,
and knowing that God had sworn with
an oath to him that he would set one of
his descendants upon his throne, 31 he foresaw and spoke of the resurrection of the
Christ, that he was not abandoned to
Hades, nor did his flesh see corruption.
32 This Jesus God raised up, and of that
we all are witnesses. 33 Being therefore exalted at the right hand of God, and having
received from the Father the promise of
the Holy Spirit, he has poured out this
which you see and hear. 34 For David did
not ascend into the heavens; but he himself says,
'The Lord said to my Lord, Sit at my
right hand,
35 till I make thy enemies a stool for thy
feet.'

29-30. The site of David's **tomb** is uncertain, but it was probably on the southeastern hill. It is only since the Crusades that it has been located on "Mount Zion" (southwestern hill). **That he would set** (RSV) is a more accurate translation than **would raise up Christ to sit** (KJV), and better suits the original in Ps. 132:11: "Of the fruit of thy body will I set upon thy throne."

32-33. Of that (i.e., the Resurrection) rather than "of whom" (i.e., Christ) suits better 1:22, where the function of an apostle is to be "a witness of his resurrection." Vs. 34 supports the translation **at the right hand of God** (RSV), rather than **by the right hand** (KJV), in spite of a curious Midrash on Ps. 118:16, which states that "the right hand of the Lord exalts."

34. Since the psalm quoted (110:1) cannot refer to David, who did not ascend to the heavens, it must refer to the Messiah; and Jesus in virtue of his ascension is proved to be that Messiah and also to have the right to the supreme divine title **Lord.** For a similar confession by Paul see I Cor. 12:3; Rom. 10:9; Phil. 2:11; and for Jesus' own treatment of the same verse from Ps. 110 see Mark 12:35 and parallels.

Look at the schools. There are more of them than ever before in human history, and at the same time more illiterate, untrained people than we dare to think. Look at the family and the home. We know that there are times when divorce seems to be the only alternative, but the increasing and alarming divorce rate is certainly an undeniable sign that there is something crooked somewhere in our home life. Look at the youth who went off to fight a war which they did not want. While they were about their bloody business and were drawn together with their fellow men in a common undertaking, a kind of meaning was imposed upon their lives. But at the end the prevailing mood is one of meaninglessness: nothing to do that counts much, no incentive to do it, no use in the world or for the world. Days drag out in a pretended spirit of gaiety of which the sterility and joylessness of the cocktail party is the sad symbol.

Before attempting to state the solution to our problem, we should recall the warning that there are no perfect parallels in history. It would be dangerous, therefore, for us to take the early Christian solution and apply it item by item to our own situation. There are significant differences in the two situations. The most obvious

36 Therefore let all the house of Israel know assuredly, that God hath made that same Jesus, whom ye have crucified, both Lord and Christ.

37 ¶ Now when they heard *this,* they were pricked in their heart, and said unto Peter and to the rest of the apostles, Men *and* brethren, what shall we do?

36 Let all the house of Israel therefore know assuredly that God has made him both Lord and Christ, this Jesus whom you crucified."

37 Now when they heard this they were cut to the heart, and said to Peter and the rest of the apostles, "Brethren, what shall

3. Results of Pentecost (2:37-41)

Vss. 37-41 describe the immediate results of Pentecost and of Peter's speech, and summarize the requirements for membership in the new community. Special emphasis is given first to the need for *repentance,* which in the most primitive preaching means primarily repentance for the failure to recognize Jesus as the Messiah and for the consequent crime of the Crucifixion (cf. 3:17-19). If there is any more general idea of the necessity for repentance as a condition of God's blessing, this too is purely a Jewish conception. There is as yet no trace of the specifically Christian idea that every man is a sinner, and that repentance, as contrasted with the keeping of the law, is a universal precondition of salvation. Second, closely linked with repentance is *baptism.* Here too there is nothing essentially novel, for baptism as such was in line with Jewish rites of purification for the admission of proselytes, and John the Baptist—a great Jewish prophet, quite apart from his intimate connection with Jesus—had already associated baptism with repentance (Mark 1:4). But throughout Acts the conception of the significance of baptism, and in turn of its relationship to the gift of the Holy Spirit, varies to such an extent that we can only assume that several traditions have been inconsistently combined. There is no evidence that Jesus himself ever baptized—except in John 3:22, corrected in 4:2. The earliest idea seems to have been that the Christian equivalent of John's baptism was not a similar water-baptism, but rather a baptism with the Holy Spirit such as is pictured at Pentecost (see on 1:5). Later the distinction between Christian baptism and John's baptism—both alike being with water—was held to be that the former bestowed the Spirit as the latter did not (cf. 19:1-7). Similarly there is no consistent view of the part played by baptism in the gift of the Spirit. Perhaps in the beginning the Spirit is given before there is any question of baptism, which is added rather as a seal upon a gift already bestowed; so in the case of Cornelius (10:44-48). Later, baptism is regarded as a necessary condition of entrance into the community and an opportunity for public confession, but the gift of the Spirit is still distinct from it. So in 8:12-17 Samaritans are baptized, but they do not receive the Spirit until Peter and

of them is the fact that Christianity is not now a small, struggling minority group. At least on paper it is far more than a remnant, and in the Western world it is coextensive with the civilization it has helped to create. It has become practically, at least in theory and often in fact, coincidental with culture and civilization. There is some reason to believe and to hope that it can exert an effective influence upon the life of that civilization from its present position within it, as over against its first-century position outside it. Also, our problem is on a vastly greater scale. We have a world to deal with instead of a Mediterranean basin. But some clues may be gleaned from the records of an earlier and more inflamed Christian generation.

Some of us are prepared to say with Peter that Christianity cannot arrest the world's destruction. Things have gone too far. Civilization is reaping the bitter harvest of its own sowing. The pride that raised its head in the dawn of the Renaissance is now about to fall in the twilight of its own disillusionment. There are inexorable laws of God that are working themselves out. If the system of our civilization cannot be saved, perhaps it can be reformed. Undoubtedly it can be, and Christians are always working to that end. But reform by itself is not enough. The Christian contribution is not a reformed system but reborn men. In other words the Christian's task is to keep alive that order of society which has had its ups and downs in history, but which is centered in the activity of God coming into the life of man in the character of Jesus Christ. That society is necessarily in the world. The Lord and Master

38 Then Peter said unto them, Repent, and be baptized every one of you in the name of Jesus Christ for the remission of sins, and ye shall receive the gift of the Holy Ghost.

39 For the promise is unto you, and to your children, and to all that are afar off, *even* as many as the Lord our God shall call.

40 And with many other words did he testify and exhort, saying, Save yourselves from this untoward generation.

we do?" 38 And Peter said to them, "Repent, and be baptized every one of you in
the name of Jesus Christ for the forgiveness
of your sins; and you shall receive the gift
of the Holy Spirit. 39 For the promise is to
you and to your children and to all that
are far off, every one whom the Lord our
God calls to him." 40 And he testified with
many other words and exhorted them, saying, "Save yourselves from this crooked

---

John, dispatched from Jerusalem for that very purpose, lay apostolic hands upon them. And finally the stage is reached when baptism with the Spirit becomes the direct consequence of baptism with water, so that Christian baptism becomes the essential condition of Christian spiritual experience (19:5-6). Although the present narrative is in general so primitive, 2:38 seems to reflect this final stage of development.

It has been suggested that baptism may have been adopted by the Christian community only as part of the Hellenistic mission which followed the appointment of the seven (6:1-6). It seems much more likely that with the beginnings of organization the fitness and indeed necessity of some such initiatory rite would be recognized, and baptism, at first simply as a rite of incorporation into the fellowship of those who professed "the name of Christ" and awaited his Parousia, would readily be adapted from the practice by which his forerunner had symbolized repentance in preparation for the coming kingdom. All that was necessary was the addition of the distinctively Christian formula **in the name of Jesus Christ.** This phrase (cf. 8:16; 10:48; 19:5) sometimes means "with the authority of" (e.g., Mark 9:38-39), but as a primitive baptismal formula the invocation of the name implies primarily recognition of Jesus as "Lord and Christ." There is as yet no trace of the trinitarian formula of Matt. 28:19, which is not to be taken as part of Jesus' original commission, but comes from later liturgical use.

38-40. Does our author hold that baptism not only confers the gift of the Holy Spirit but also conveys **the forgiveness of your sins?** Probably this latter thought should be linked up as closely with **repent** as with **be baptized,** for the ideas of repentance and forgiveness are constantly associated in Luke-Acts (Luke 3:3; 24:47; Acts 5:31). **Far off** may refer either to space or time, and mean either "to those who live far away" (for which cf. Isa. 57:19, quoted in Eph. 2:17; Acts 22:21), or "to you and to your children and to your distant descendants." **Crooked generation:** a proverbial phrase drawn from Deut. 32:5; Ps. 78:8.

---

of it loves the world. Yet it is independent of the world, having at its heart a life of its own by which men and women are enabled to transcend the misfortunes of life and to resist the influences which are currently degrading life.

When men go duckhunting, they do not aim at the duck, for the duck is on the wing. They aim just ahead of the duck and if their calculations are accurate, they hit it. Since the beginning of the Renaissance we have been aiming at the world, the material world. We have concentrated every ounce of our energy and talent upon it. We have either ignored or forgotten the fact that there is any other world. We are now scarcely able to believe the fact that this world is nearer destruction than ever before in its history. We aimed at the world and we did not hit it. Perhaps we shall learn before it is too late to aim ahead at some shining, infinite thing, and aiming in such wise we may hit the world, and indirectly, as did the early Christians, wound it with none other than the saving blood of Christ himself.

People will always be likely to misunderstand such a message. They must be reassured over and over again that it does not mean that Christianity has no interest in or anything to do with the world. To say that would be to betray everything in the Gospels. Perhaps a line from Paul's letter to the Philippians will make the meaning clear. After he had given his people certain moral directions, he went on

41 ¶ Then they that gladly received his word were baptized: and the same day there were added *unto them* about three thousand souls.
42 And they continued steadfastly in the

generation." 41 So those who received his word were baptized, and there were added that day about three thousand souls. 42 And they devoted themselves to the apostles'

41. So (μὲν οὖν) is a regular formula in Acts summarizing what has just preceded and looking forward to a new section (cf. 1:6; 5:41; 8:25; 9:31; 11:19; 12:5; 13:4; 15:3, 30; 16:5). If Harnack's source division is accepted, it here marks the end of the first section extracted by Luke from Jerusalem Source B. **Three thousand souls:** The use of ψυχή, "soul," in the sense of an "individual," comes from the LXX, where it is used to translate the Hebrew *néphesh,* which has the same meaning.

4. Beginnings of Communal Life (2:42-47)

The paragraph seems to be composite; vss. 42 and 46 read like two parallel summaries, and may be doublets. Possibly vss. 42 and 43 are Luke's summarizing link by which he joins his account of Pentecost with a more ancient fragment, vss. 44-47, describing the life of the primitive community. Four characteristic features of the early church are emphasized. First, concern with **the apostles' teaching**—chiefly, it may be supposed, their personal recollections of Jesus and his teaching. It would not be long before a comparatively fixed body of such teaching would take shape. Thus Paul speaks of the "standard of teaching" (Rom. 6:17) and the "pattern of the sound words" (II Tim. 1:13). Out of this would be formed the tradition which ultimately was reduced to writing in the *logia,* to which on one theory Papias refers, and which may supply the Q material in Matthew and Luke. Such "teaching" would no doubt also include renewed study of the O.T., especially such passages as appeared to foretell Jesus as the Christ—the *testimonia,* or "proof texts," of later days.

Second, **fellowship** (κοινωνία)—first perhaps with the apostles, but also with reference to the wider fellowship of all believers. It is Paul's favorite word to describe the unity of believers with each other and with their Lord. In I Cor. 1:9 ("called into the fellowship of his Son") it seems almost to take on the concrete sense of "the body of believers." Its equivalent in Aramaic (*ḥabhûrā'*) seems to have been in common use to describe a group of companions who shared a common life, particularly those who united to celebrate a common Passover meal. Thus there may possibly be a reference here to the tablefellowship which becomes more explicit in the **breaking of bread.** Again, this **fellowship** found practical expression in experiments in Christian communism (vss. 44-45; for a fuller discussion see on 4:32-37). The original *ḥabhûrā'* of Jesus had shared a common life (cf. John 13:29), and the communism of Jerusalem was simply a continuation of that practice. The word κοινωνία sometimes has the sense almost of "almsgiving" or "relief" (cf. Rom. 15:26, "to make some contribution for the poor"). What is in view here is clearly not absolute communism, but a sharing of goods for the benefit of those in need. Nevertheless the motive was probably not mere charity, but the recognition that the claims of the Christian family are superior to those of the individual, and that

to write this: "That ye may be blameless and harmless, the sons of God, without rebuke, in the midst of a crooked and perverse nation, among whom ye shine as lights in the world; holding forth the word of life" (Phil. 2:15-16*a*). They kept their eyes fixed on the light that is in Christ, not on the darkness of the world, and quite unwittingly the light began to shine in them and from them, and penetrate the darkest corners of the world which was going to pieces.

41-47. ***The Life of the New Community.***—It has been said that many intellectuals are now accepting Christianity as an *explanation* of life, but they are not yet prepared to accept it as a *way* of life. It is clear from a passage such as vss. 41-47 that Christianity has always been a way of life, a way from which certain explanations and inferences about life were inevitably drawn. In days like these, especially, people are looking for explanations. In many cases they find the Christian explanations more satisfac-

apostles' doctrine and fellowship, and in breaking of bread, and in prayers.

teaching and fellowship, to the breaking of bread and the prayers.

brethren must have their share, not only because they are needy, but because they are brethren. No doubt the vivid expectation of the Parousia and the consequent undervaluing of possessions made this "communism" easier, but it does not explain it.

Third, we have mention of the **breaking of bread,** picked up in vs. 46 by the words **breaking bread in their homes.** The association of this in vs. 42 with **teaching** and **prayers** shows that it has a religious significance, and immediately following the reference to **fellowship** it appears as the peculiar symbol of that fellowship. For this same word κοινωνία is, of course, the word used of the "communion of the blood of Christ" and the "communion of the body of Christ" at the Lord's Supper (I Cor. 10:16), which is the central pledge and symbol of a common life and a common faith. At the same time the close conjunction in vs. 46 of **breaking bread** and **they partook of food** proves that the former, though already of religious significance, was still part of a regular nourishing meal. It may be indeed that the poorer members of the community found in it their chief means of subsistence. It was only later that the Eucharist became differentiated from the agape. The exact phrase **breaking of bread** occurs only in vs. 42 and in Luke 24:35; but the verbal phrase "to break bread" occurs also in Luke 24:30; Acts 2:46; 20:7-11; 27:35; and in connection with the feeding of the multitude, and the institution of the Lord's Supper. The phrase springs from the Jewish custom of beginning a meal with the prayer, "Blessed be thou, O Lord our God, that thou didst make bread to be on earth," followed by a ceremonial breaking of bread. In vs. 46 **breaking bread in their homes** seems to be contrasted with **attending the temple together.** Regular attendance at the public worship of the temple would mark the disciples as still being loyal Jews. It was the common religious meal in their own homes that provided them with the opportunity for distinctively Christian fellowship and worship.

Fourth, **they devoted themselves to . . . the prayers.** So far as public worship is in view this would still be through **attending the temple together,** and in the regular meetings of the Jewish synagogue. As yet there was no idea of establishing separate places of public worship. But once again the specifically Christian side of this devotional life would find expression in family gatherings for prayer, and in daily intercourse in the homes of members of the new community. Christian public worship, when it did take shape, closely followed Jewish models, as is seen by a comparison of the prayers of the Didache with the Jewish liturgy. But meantime the emphasis would be on domestic family worship and private prayers at home (see references in 1:24; 4:23-30; 12:12).

tory than any others. The Christian doctrine of original sin, for instance, seems a much better explanation of the facts than the nineteenth-century doctrine of human perfectibility. The danger to which these people are constantly exposed is the danger of assuming that the Christian explanations make sense apart from the Christian way of life. It is far more difficult to practice the way than to accept the explanation.

For one thing it means living in close association with other Christians. **And all that believed were together.** No intellectual snobbery here! No social superiority, no racial intolerance, no temperamental privileges here! They were all together, bound into a fellowship by the same ideas (the apostles' teaching), by the same practices (the breaking of bread), by the same religious habits (prayers), and by the same economic rights and responsibilities (**and sold their possessions and goods, and parted them to all men, as every man had need).**

All this was done with joy and gladness. There was nothing drab or grim about it. They **did eat their meat with gladness.** No wonder, for there is nothing that gives greater joy to a man than the sense of belonging to a community the life of which he shares. Scores of men, drafted into military service, find for the first time in their lives, even under the pressure of combat, the joy of living in close association with those whose lives are bound up with theirs. How much more the joy of a man who lives as a member of the community that centers in Christ Jesus!

Yet few would deny that the Christian community has gradually lost its identity as it has merged into the total community of a semi-

43 And fear came upon every soul: and many wonders and signs were done by the apostles.

44 And all that believed were together, and had all things common;

45 And sold their possessions and goods, and parted them to all *men*, as every man had need.

46 And they, continuing daily with one accord in the temple, and breaking bread from house to house, did eat their meat with gladness and singleness of heart,

47 Praising God, and having favor with all the people. And the Lord added to the church daily such as should be saved.

43 And fear came upon every soul; and
many wonders and signs were done through
the apostles. 44 And all who believed were
together and had all things in common;
45 and they sold their possessions and goods
and distributed them to all, as any had
need. 46 And day by day, attending the
temple together and breaking bread in their
homes, they partook of food with glad and
generous hearts, 47 praising God and having favor with all the people. And the
Lord added to their number day by day
those who were being saved.

43-44. The mention of **fear** at this point appears strange; but it suits the context exactly in 5:5; 5:11, where this "summary" reappears (see on 4:23–5:16 for the theory of possible "doublets") . **Wonders and signs** is a common O.T. description of miracles. It is frequent in the first half of Acts with its marked Aramaic background, but does not occur in the second half. Paul uses it in Rom. 15:19; II Cor. 12:12; II Thess. 2:9.

45-46. The tense of the verb **sold** is imperfect, "used to sell," not in one great sale, but occasionally as the need arose. **Possessions and goods** are properly "real estate" and "private possessions"; the meaning probably is that they sold the former and divided the proceeds, while they **distributed** the latter. **In their homes** may mean (*a*) merely "at home," in contrast with **attending the temple,** or (*b*) **from house to house** or "in separate houses," implying a possible contrast with the preceding **together.**

47. The phrase translated **to their number** (ἐπὶ τὸ αὐτό) has given much difficulty, as is evidenced by the confusion in the text. Usually it seems to mean "together" (Luke 17:35; Acts 1:15; 2:1; 2:44; 4:26) ; but here it is so awkward that Torrey suggests the mistranslation of an Aramaic adverbial compound meaning "exceedingly." The word has this meaning only in the Judean dialect, of which Luke may well have been ignorant, and is also regularly put at the end of a clause, as here. The Western text tried to solve the puzzle by adding ἐν τῇ ἐκκλησίᾳ, and the omission of the ἐν gave us the KJV translation **added to the church.** Lake and Cadbury (*Beginnings of Christianity,* IV, 30) point out that in the papyri ἐπὶ τὸ αὐτὸ is used in financial statements as being "in total," and wonder whether a number should follow it here as in 1:15. **Saved** is an echo of Peter's quotation (vs. 21) of Joel 2:32.

Christian civilization. How can that identity be recovered? First, by strengthening the teaching. People are drawn together by the things that they believe in common. Too often modern Christians do not know what they believe, and what they do believe is little more than the popular notions of the day tinged with Christian emotion. Second, by strengthening the fellowship. The church should be the center of a community life in which the lonely find friends, the sinful find understanding and forgiveness, the believers find the support of those who believe the same things. Third, by strengthening the ritual, not as a matter of routine practice, but as habitual acts in which people are drawn together in the way that the family is drawn together around the dining-room table. Fourth, by strengthening the prayer life. People who remember each other in their prayers can survive the separations which otherwise might destroy their unity. People who pray together, people who keep the Lord's Day in the same way, achieve a unity of the spirit in spite of the fact that they work for different concerns, in different parts of the city, and under different circumstances. And finally, by strengthening the ties of economic responsibility. No Christians ever had a greater opportunity of assuming responsibility for their fellow Christians in need. While we live in relative plenty, our Christian brethren in other parts of the world are living on the edge of economic destruction. Clothing and food are sent across the sea from one Christian to another. Let them go faster

3 Now Peter and John went up together into the temple at the hour of prayer, *being* the ninth *hour.*

3 Now Peter and John were going up to the temple at the hour of prayer, the

C. The Church at Jerusalem (3:1–5:42)

1. Peter's Healing and Preaching (3:1-26)

Some scholars believe that 3:1–5:16 is a "doublet" of ch. 2, *plus* 5:17-42, and represents an earlier and more reliable tradition about "the birth of the church." For a fuller discussion see pp. 69-70, 72-73; on this theory 4:31 would be the simplest and most primitive version of the Pentecost story.

Peter's healing of a lame man and his provocative speech which follows lead to the first serious clash with the Jewish authorities. The account of the healing should be compared with that by Paul of a lame man at Lystra (14:8-11)—one of the best illustrations of the alleged parallelism between the two halves of Acts. According to our author, the power to work miracles was the supreme proof that the apostles had inherited the mission and authority of their Master. In Acts, as in the Gospels, we note a twofold attitude to miracles: (*a*) faith is necessary in order that a miracle may be worked (vs. 16; 14:9); (*b*) conversely, miracle is the supreme way of awakening faith (4:16, 21-22). The presence of a miraculous element in the narrative must therefore not be regarded as evidence either against the Lukan authorship or against the writer's dependence on a quite primitive tradition. There can be no question that the first Christians lived in daily expectation of "miracles," and may therefore well have experienced them; and Luke is just as likely as any alleged later editor to record miracles in full good faith.

Peter's speech follows very much the same lines as his first one. Again the language is strongly messianic; and we have the same emphasis on the rejection of Jesus by his own people, on his rehabilitation as Christ through the Resurrection, and on the consequent need of repentance if the blessings of the messianic era are to be enjoyed. It is again alleged that this speech, like the first, is full of ideas which can be paralleled in I Peter; e.g., vss. 20-21 are compared with I Pet. 1:10-11. But the ideas are all such as were common to primitive Christianity in general, and the parallelism is hardly sufficient to prove conclusively either the Petrine origin of the speech or the Petrine authorship of the First Epistle of Peter. This speech possibly reflects an even more primitive viewpoint than that in ch. 2 (as being derived from the better of the two sources?). Here the return of Jesus is the chief hope and central message (vs. 20); there the central place is given to the gift of the Spirit, the bestowal of which is the chief work of the ascended Jesus. This speech is also written in much less polished Greek than most of Acts, which may indicate a translation from an Aramaic source.

3:1. John, generally assumed to be the son of Zebedee, is, as in the Gospels, closely associated with Peter; but in Acts he takes a quite subordinate position (see 8:14 ff.)—

and in greater quantity. Funds are raised in one country to relieve the necessities of those in another. Let them be raised with greater speed and generosity. In our own cities the need of the brethren is always present. Let each be responsible for at least one other in distress. L. P. Jacks defined the church as "the union of those who love for the sake of those who suffer."

When these things have been done, joy and gladness will once again radiate from the Christian community.

3:1-11. ***Healing of the Lame Man.***—Peter and John were going about their regular religious routine. They were going up to the temple. They were stopped on their way by a lame man who asked them for money. Peter looked at him and said, **Silver and gold have I none; but such as I have give I thee: In the name of Jesus Christ of Nazareth rise up and walk.** And Peter took him by the right hand and the lame man went into the temple with them, **walking, and leaping, and praising God.**

Peter saw someone who was a cripple. There was no particular reason why he should see him. Beggars have a way of lingering around temple gates to touch the hearts of the people at their most vulnerable point. Peter had nothing to gain, certainly, by taking notice of this man who had been lame for forty years. But

2 And a certain man lame from his
mother's womb was carried, whom they
laid daily at the gate of the temple which
is called Beautiful, to ask alms of them
that entered into the temple;
3 Who, seeing Peter and John about to
go into the temple, asked an alms.

ninth hour.
2 And a man lame from birth
was being carried, whom they laid daily
at that gate of the temple which is called
Beautiful to ask alms of those who entered
the temple.
3 Seeing Peter and John about
to go into the temple, he asked for alms.

---

which is strange if he was really so prominent a figure in the early church as tradition asserts. If, as some hold, the source from which this section comes (Jerusalem Source A) is a continuation of the original Marcan narrative, Lake's suggestion would be attractive —that the **John** who accompanied Peter was not the apostle but John Mark, who was traditionally "the interpreter of Peter" (so Papias; Eusebius *Church History* III. 39). This would certainly better explain his lack of prominence.

2. The **gate . . . Beautiful** of the temple is usually identified with either (*a*) the Shushan Gate, which was the eastern external gate to the temple area. This would be on the outside of "the portico called Solomon's" (vs. 11), and would better suit our ("Neutral") text, according to which the apostles "entered the temple" (vs. 8), or rather the temple area, presumably through the "Beautiful Gate," and inside it were surrounded by a crowd in Solomon's Portico, which was a colonnade, probably on the east side of the temple area. Or (*b*) the gate in question is the Nicanor Gate, the eastern gate of the temple buildings proper, the special magnificence of which is described both in the Mishnah and by Josephus. This suits the Western text which reads: "When Peter and John *were going out,* he went with them, holding on to them, and they [the people] stood astonished in the portico called Solomon's"; this would seem to indicate that the "Beautiful Gate" was farther in than Solomon's Portico. Lake and Cadbury suggest that the reason why the apostles entered from the east, rather than by the usual great southern entrance, may have been that they were still coming in daily from the Bethany district. True, 1:13 seems to regard the upper room in Jerusalem as their home; but, if Harnack's source analysis is true, that verse comes from Jerusalem Source B, while the present passage belongs to Jerusalem Source A.

Peter was not so exclusively intent upon what he was about as to pass a man in misery. Christians are those who can be expected to be conscious of the cripples around their doors. Those unfortunate individuals may have been crushed by the hard march of events. Some of them have suffered great losses, others are carrying burdens too heavy for a single man to bear. Not only individuals catch the eye of the Christian, but the whole world seems to be going on crutches, and the Christian should be more aware of it than anyone else. Crippled by fear, paralyzed by hate, the old world looks as though it had flung itself on the temple doorstep to beg for alms.

Peter had something that would not keep. Some things will keep—like stones and diamonds. Some things can be preserved and pickled. But the real things in life cannot be kept. Try to keep love and watch it turn to lust. Try to keep peace to yourself and see it degenerate into passivity. Try to keep money and watch it change into mammon. Try to keep beauty and you become a mummy. Keep a vision and you become a visionary. Try to keep Christ and you become a bigot. Peter could not keep the precious gift of life in Christ. He could only give it away. Like Peter, everyone has something that will not keep. To everyone life at some time or other communicates one of its secrets. To one it is the secret of beauty, to another the secret of endurance, to another the secret of sight beyond the rim of time and space. These things will not keep. They must be given away.

Peter gave something that was not asked. The lame man asked for money. Peter gave him walking, leaping, and praising. So children ask for toys. Give them toys, but, parents, give them time also. Workmen ask for relief. Give them redemption; that is what they really need. That means respect and consideration over and above wages. The city asks for money. Can we not give it more than that? It needs moral and spiritual energy. Enough of that is wasted every day to revitalize great areas of the country. God asks for obedience. Surely we can give him more than that. We can give him our minds and imaginations, our hands and voices, our wills and our desires.

4 And Peter, fastening his eyes upon him with John, said, Look on us.

5 And he gave heed unto them, expecting to receive something of them.

6 Then Peter said, Silver and gold have I none; but such as I have give I thee: In the name of Jesus Christ of Nazareth rise up and walk.

7 And he took him by the right hand, and lifted *him* up: and immediately his feet and ankle bones received strength.

4 And Peter directed his gaze at him, with
John, and said, "Look at us." 5 And he
fixed his attention upon them, expecting
to receive something from them. 6 But
Peter said, "I have no silver and gold, but
I give you what I have; in the name of
Jesus Christ of Nazareth, walk." 7 And he
took him by the right hand and raised him
up; and immediately his feet and ankles

6-7. In the name: The use of "the name" in religious formulas and practice springs from the identification of a name with the person to whom the name belongs and the belief that the qualities and powers of that person are inherent in his "name," so that by invoking the "name" his power and authority are called into operation. For the use of "the name" in the N.T. see Mark 9:38 ff.; Matt. 7:22; Luke 10:17; Phil. 2:9-11, and the common baptismal formula (e.g., I Cor. 6:11); for Acts in particular see 2:38; 3:16; 4:12; 5:41; 9:14; 16:18; 19:13. Note that while others work miracles in the power of "the name," Jesus does so by his own "authority" (Mark 1:27). Vs. 7 is a favorite passage with those who seek proof from his technical language that the author of Acts was a medical man.

There once was a time when God saw the world lying like a cripple on the doorstep of heaven. God had something that he could not keep. That was his own life and love. The beggar asked only for alms and a cooling drink, but God gave him a Baby to love, a Man to follow, a Life to adore, a Spirit to dwell in his own wretched, crippled body and make him walk, and leap, and praise again.

Along some such lines as these this passage may be used allegorically as the basis for exposition. But generally it is wiser to approach more directly the subject with which the passage deals. In this case the subject is the relationship between Christian faith and disease. It cannot be denied that among the first fruits of the Spirit working in the first Christian fellowship none was more notable than the healing of the sick.

The battle against disease is one from which there are no exemptions. Some people are drafted for lifelong struggles against chronic ailments, permanent handicaps, and native disabilities. Others, more fortunate, have only occasional engagements with the enemy. The question is: What part does the Christian religion play in the battle against disease?

In answer to this question there are two extreme views. According to the first view, religion plays the whole part in the battle against disease, and the chief exponents of that view in our time are the Christian Scientists. They believe that God is good; that disease is evil; therefore God cannot and did not make disease, and disease, therefore, has no legitimate part in his universe and hence no reality. Man makes disease, they believe, by his imperfect and impure thinking, and man can therefore destroy disease by correcting his thinking and purifying his belief. According to this view, the doctor has no place at all, for disease can be fought *only* by spiritual weapons.

At the other extreme there are those who believe that religion plays no part in the battle against disease, and most Christians in practice hold that point of view. They may pray when they are sick, and there are exceptional examples of Christians who depend upon spiritual reserves in time of illness, but by and large, most of us, tacitly at any rate, hold the view that religion plays no direct part in the battle against disease. In our pattern of life the doctor and the minister work together, but in parallel lines. Each has his own limited sphere of influence and, if there is any overlapping, it is far more likely that the doctor assumes the role of spiritual counselor than the other way around.

There is, however, a third point of view—that which we find so clearly expressed in the N.T., in the Gospels and in the Acts of the Apostles. That point of view is never set forth in a theoretical way because Jesus was not a theorizing person. It is expressed in action. Four facts emerge from the action of Jesus, both in his own ministry in Galilee and in the ministry of the Spirit working within and through the group that followed him after the Resurrection and Ascension.

The first fact is that Jesus indisputably made sick people well. "Now when the sun was

8 And he leaping up stood, and walked,
and entered with them into the temple,
walking, and leaping, and praising God.
9 And all the people saw him walking
and praising God:
10 And they knew that it was he which
sat for alms at the Beautiful gate of the
temple: and they were filled with wonder
and amazement at that which had happened unto him.
11 And as the lame man which was
healed held Peter and John, all the people
ran together unto them in the porch that
is called Solomon's, greatly wondering.

were made strong. **8** And leaping up he
stood and walked and entered the temple
with them, walking and leaping and praising God. **9** And all the people saw him
walking and praising God, **10** and recognized him as the one who sat for alms at
the Beautiful Gate of the temple; and
they were filled with wonder and amazement at what had happened to him.
11 While he clung to Peter and John,
all the people ran together to them in the

---

setting, all they that had any sick . . . brought them unto him; and he laid his hands on every one of them, and healed them" (Luke 4:40). That healing continued with increasing vigor, even though the time came when Jesus himself was no longer present as an earthly figure. The book of the Acts gives ample evidence of that. Second, he often made people well before he made them good. That may be a shock to us who have put an almost exclusively moral emphasis on religion. "And whithersoever he entered, into villages, or cities, or country, they laid the sick in the streets, . . . and as many as touched him were made whole" (Mark 6:56). And that happened apparently even before he had had an opportunity to preach to them about the moral demands of God. All through the first part of the Acts it is the amazing physical reconversion of men rather than a moral one that is set forth as the compelling sign that God was at work in the fellowship. Third, when he gave his credentials to those who came from John the Baptist to ask if he were the Messiah or not, notice the order in which he listed them. "The blind receive their sight, and the lame walk, the lepers are cleansed, and the deaf hear, . . . and the poor have the gospel preached to them" (Matt. 11:5). Finally, when he sent out his disciples, he gave them order to do the selfsame thing. According to Luke, he sent them forth with this charge: "And he sent them to preach the kingdom of God, and *to heal the sick*" (Luke 9:2). It is difficult to get around those facts, and if we put any confidence at all in the picture of Jesus as it comes from the Synoptic Gospels, we have the picture of one who made a strong impression upon the people of his own time as one who could and did make sick people well. He did not proceed to theorize about it or to philosophize about the nature of reality. He did not say that disease is unreal, nor that it is always curable. He did not cure everyone. He accepted disease as a fact and brought to bear upon it all the spiritual energy that he could muster.

Current experience and practice confirm the N.T. point of view. One of the cardinal facts that current experience has discovered is this: Man is all of a piece, not a collection of parts. One of the results of our analytical study of man is that we have divided him into three equal parts—body, mind, and spirit. That is a useful analysis, but it can be a misleading one. We have often treated man as though he moved along three parallel lines, body, mind, and spirit, rather than in mesh, as a unit; not a collection of parts, but a trinity, three parts in one person. It is hard to believe that we have gone so far off the track, for the simplest experience shows us that those three parts of our nature are all tied up together. For instance, when you have a splitting headache, you are not likely to think clearly. And when you are suffering a severe sinus pain, your disposition may not be as sweet as it otherwise would be. Likewise, when your mind is harassed by doubts and anxieties, your body soon shows the strain and you complain that you cannot sleep. In other words man's tormented body is more than once a sign of a twisted spirit. For man is a trinity of interrelated parts, body, mind, and spirit, these three.

But the greatest of these is spirit. That is the second fact that current experience is confirming. All experience of everyday life confirms the insight that in the long run, allowing the body its sphere of influence, a man's spirit has the upper hand. A boy was being chased by a ferocious animal and in his fear—which is a spiritual, not a physical incitement—he scaled a fence which he not only had never been able to scale before, but which even as a grown man he could never scale again.

The spirit, we go on to say in confirming what the N.T. so magnificently affirmed, is like a river, not a reservoir. The spirit—that is,

12 ¶ And when Peter saw *it,* he answered unto the people, Ye men of Israel, why marvel ye at this? or why look ye so earnestly on us, as though by our own power or holiness we had made this man to walk?

13 The God of Abraham, and of Isaac, and of Jacob, the God of our fathers, hath glorified his Son Jesus; whom ye delivered up, and denied him in the presence of Pilate, when he was determined to let *him* go.

portico called Solomon's, astounded. 12 And
when Peter saw it he addressed the people,
"Men of Israel, why do you wonder at
this, or why do you stare at us, as though
by our own power or piety we had made
him walk? 13 The God of Abraham and
of Isaac and of Jacob, the God of our
fathers, glorified his servant[b] Jesus, whom
you delivered up and denied in the presence of Pilate, when he had decided to re-

[b] Or *child.*

13. The words **glorified his servant Jesus** read like an echo of Isa. 52:13, whence it has been deduced that Peter and the early Jerusalem community already identified Jesus with the "righteous servant" of Second Isaiah (see also 4:27-30). The word **servant** (παῖς) is ambiguous in the Greek, and may mean either "child" or "servant"; there is no such ambiguity in the Hebrew, and from this it has been argued that its use as a title for Jesus is more likely to have begun among Greek-speaking Christians. The only passage in Acts which quite clearly identifies Jesus with "the servant" of Isaiah is 8:32, which, according to Harnack, comes from a source connected with Caesarea, and would reflect

the invisible, instinctive, emotional drives that inform the human spirit—is not like something that you can contain in a receptacle. It is like something that flows through a channel. If it is like a river, then like a river it must flow. When it ceases to flow it becomes stagnant, and when it becomes stagnant, it becomes poisoned. One of the reasons why people get sick is that the flow of their spiritual energy is blocked, either at the source or at the mouth. If it is blocked at the mouth, the energy that should be expended in self-forgetful activity is held back in a fearful effort to conserve it. When a man's energies are so dammed up within him that he is continually obsessed with himself, no wonder that his body stalls. He is fatigued not because he is exhausted, but because he is stagnant!

Other people are blocked more seriously at the source. They do not really trust God. No one who does not trust God can be vigorously well physically. He may express that trust in the familiar language of religion, or he may not. Two things are the sign of his trust: He does not fear the past once it is done, nor does he dread the future, however uncertain it may be. He is able to say to himself, "God will keep me through everything; not protecting me from all the strains of life, nor insuring me against all disaster; but he will keep me; he will never let me go; and there is nothing that can happen to me that I am afraid of."

When a man's life is open so that the spiritual energies can flow through it, then, as the poisons that flow into a river do not corrupt it but are carried off by the moving stream into the sea, so the disease that threatens us every moment is overcome by the vitality of our inner strength. Christianity does not promise perfect health. What it does promise is this: With that confidence in the Source of Life, that openness toward God which eliminates fear and frenzy and breaks through the barriers of distrust and doubt, a man will have at his disposal God's power and God's weapons and all the purity that comes from him to meet the enemy and triumph over it.

It is quite apparent that what has been said is a far more self-conscious, analytical account of healing than we find in the story of the healing of the lame man. The healing stories in Acts are told as signs and indications that the power of God was at work in the world. The cures were instantaneous. They were incontrovertible. Allowing for the possibility that legend played its part, yet it is entirely within the range of possibility that such extraordinary results proceeded from such an extraordinary demonstration of spiritual power. By and large, however, the Spirit of God does not operate in that sudden way now. The task of the interpreter is to show that the same Spirit, exercising the same power, does operate through channels of his own choosing to produce essentially the same results.

12-26. *Peter's Second Sermon.*—Like all great preaching, Peter's sermon was drawn out of him by a situation. It was the wonder of the people that made Peter speak. They had seen the lame man healed. They wanted to know what it was all about. They wanted someone to interpret the facts. The first thing that Peter

14 But ye denied the Holy One and the Just, and desired a murderer to be granted unto you;

15 And killed the Prince of life, whom God hath raised from the dead; whereof we are witnesses.

lease him. 14 But you denied the Holy and Righteous One, and asked for a murderer to be granted to you, 15 and killed the Author of life, whom God raised from the

---

the view of the Hellenistic-Jewish circle to which Philip belonged. But if Jesus himself, as seems highly probable, identified himself with the servant (cf. Luke 4:17 ff.; Mark 10:45), there seems no good reason why Peter and the earliest disciples should not have bestowed the title upon him. The servant was **glorified** first by the sign just performed in his name, but chiefly through the Resurrection (vs. 15).

14-15. The Holy and Righteous One likewise seems an echo of Isa. 53:11. The "Just One" is again used as a title for Jesus in 22:14. The only evidence that it was a Jewish title of the Messiah is in Enoch 38:2. Wisd. Sol. 2 speaks of the persecution of the "righteous one" by the wicked, but without any messianic reference. But it was evidently one of the earliest titles given to Jesus. Have we an echo of it in Matt. 27:19; Luke 23:47; Jas. 5:6; I Pet. 3:18? And was the title passed on to James the Lord's brother, who was also called "the Just"? (See also 7:52; 22:14.) **The Author of life:** Except in Acts, the word (ἀρχηγός) occurs in the N.T. only in Heb. 2:10; 12:2, and in both those passages means, as here, "originator" rather than "captain," which, however, seems to be the meaning in Acts 5:31. Bengel remarks on the *magnificum antitheton* which calls Barabbas **a murderer** and Jesus **the Author of life.**

---

did was to refuse to take the credit for the cure. Neither he nor John were to be credited with it. It was the power of Jesus that healed the man, the same Jesus whom the people had rejected and slain, the same Jesus whom God had raised from the dead and whose Spirit was now present among them.

The rest of the sermon follows in general the pattern set forth in the exposition of ch. 2. It raises once again in the mind of the preacher the question: How shall I preach Jesus to the people of my own day? Peter did it in the familiar terms of O.T. prophecy and messianic expectation. For most contemporary people Peter speaks an altogether unfamiliar and strange language. If they are to understand the gospel and appreciate the meaning of Jesus in anything like the fullness of the Christian faith, it must be set forth in their own terms and against the background of their own times. If Jesus is eternal, not local and temporary, he will remain though the background change.

The attempt to express the eternal truth of the meaning of Jesus in a changed time may be made in many different ways with varying degrees of success, sometimes with none at all. One way, at least, can begin with the recognition that the two most significant events in human history are the birth of Jesus and the atomic bomb. In many ways they are not comparable. One is an event in creation and the other in destruction. And yet, different as they are in character, set side by side there is a sense in which the more recent event illuminates the earlier one. Four observations may help to project that illumination into the midst of a "wondering" inquirer.

(*a*) The atomic bomb is a fact. It is not a physicist's hope; it is not a chemist's dream. It went off at 8:15 A.M. Japanese time, August 6, 1945. It is something done. That is where we begin with Jesus. The birth, life, and death of Jesus are facts of recorded history. The whole reality of that career is not a myth; it is not a pious hope or a dream. It is something that happened when Caesar Augustus was emperor, when Pontius Pilate was governor of Judea. It can be dated; it can be timed. To be sure, we may not know quite so much about that fact as we thought we did when we read the Gospels with no critical judgment whatever. We realize now that the gospel records, like all other historical records, are more like reflections of the truth than direct reproductions of it. And yet we know enough to have an unmistakable impression. There upon the conscience of mankind, in the gallery of human history, is the fact of Jesus, recognized by everyone save a few eccentrics.

(*b*) The atomic bomb is not a fact by itself alone. If you are discussing or evaluating the significance of the atomic bomb, you cannot do so if you isolate it and treat it as though it were an exhibit in a laboratory. You cannot

16 And his name, through faith in his name, hath made this man strong, whom ye see and know: yea, the faith which is by him hath given him this perfect soundness in the presence of you all.

17 And now, brethren, I wot that through ignorance ye did *it,* as *did* also your rulers.

18 But those things, which God before had showed by the mouth of all his prophets, that Christ should suffer, he hath so fulfilled.

19 ¶ Repent ye therefore, and be converted, that your sins may be blotted out, when the times of refreshing shall come from the presence of the Lord;

dead. To this we are witnesses. 16 And his
name, by faith in his name, has made this
man strong whom you see and know; and
the faith which is through Jesus[c] has given
the man this perfect health in the presence
of you all.
17 "And now, brethren, I know that you
acted in ignorance, as did also your rulers.
18 But what God foretold by the mouth of
all the prophets, that his Christ should
suffer, he thus fulfilled. 19 Repent therefore, and turn again, that your sins may
be blotted out, that times of refreshing may

[c] Greek *him.*

---

16. The language here is intolerably awkward, and the text must surely be confused. Torrey (*The Composition & Date of Acts* [Cambridge: Harvard University Press, 1916]) suggests that an original Aramaic phrase meaning "[God] made him strong" has been misread and mistranslated as if it were another phrase meaning "his name has strengthened." This is perhaps his most ingenious and convincing proof from mistranslation of the existence of an Aramaic original. Alternatively, Burkitt alters the punctuation to read: "To this we are witnesses, and to faith in his name; this man . . . did his name make strong" (*Journal of Theological Studies,* XX [1919], 320 ff.). The **faith** in question is either the lame man's or, perhaps more probably, the apostles' faith in Jesus which enables them to work miracles in his name (cf. vs. 6).

17. Note I Cor. 2:8: However, there "the rulers of this age" are probably to be understood, not as the civil authorities, but as the demonic "principalities and powers."

18-19. Strictly speaking, **the prophets** neither in the original passages nor in Jewish interpretation of them **foretold . . . that his Christ should suffer;** for even the suffering Servant prophecies were never interpreted messianically. But Christian interpretation soon came to apply to Christ all references to suffering both in the Psalms and the Prophets. Lake and Cadbury remark that "the assumption . . . that the Christian interpretation was recognized and accepted by Jews in Jerusalem is difficult to reconcile with the view that the speech is authentic" (*Beginnings of Christianity,* IV, 37; see also on 17:3; 26:23). The context shows that by **times of refreshing** is meant the coming of the messianic age, though the Greek word appears never to be technically so used in Jewish writings.

---

talk about the atomic bomb and leave out Hiroshima. The fact of the atomic bomb is the bomb itself, plus what it did, and any discussion of the fact must include both things. So when we turn to Jesus, we cannot make any evaluation of him by taking out a single leaf from the Gospels, a few choice paragraphs from the Sermon on the Mount, or one or two stories that happen to strike our fancy. We cannot discuss him as a fact all by himself. The fact we are considering is Jesus, his life and death, plus the people of Palestine into whose life he was born and to whom he brought eternal life. Just as absurd would it be to write a study of Hitler without mentioning Nazi Germany.

When we look at it from this point of view, what did Jesus do? With the N.T. as a guide, it is not difficult to discover that Jesus set people free. He was a liberator. He set them free from an abnormal sense of guilt, from a gnawing sense of insecurity, from a despair that was rotting away their lives, from the fear of death, from meaningless suffering, and from the grappling power of sin itself. In any account of the fact of Jesus it must be the life of Jesus *plus* the liberation, the love *plus* the power of that love to set men free. No wonder people fell down and worshiped him when they saw the prison doors open! No wonder they cried out to their comrades, "Stand fast therefore in the liberty wherewith Christ hath made us free" (Gal. 5:1).

20 And he shall send Jesus Christ, which before was preached unto you:

21 Whom the heaven must receive until the times of restitution of all things, which God hath spoken by the mouth of all his holy prophets since the world began.

22 For Moses truly said unto the fathers, A Prophet shall the Lord your God raise up unto you of your brethren, like unto me; him shall ye hear in all things whatsoever he shall say unto you.

23 And it shall come to pass, *that* every soul, which will not hear that Prophet, shall be destroyed from among the people.

24 Yea, and all the prophets from Samuel and those that follow after, as many as have spoken, have likewise foretold of these days.

25 Ye are the children of the prophets, and of the covenant which God made with our fathers, saying unto Abraham, And in thy seed shall all the kindreds of the earth be blessed.

come from the presence of the Lord, 20 and
that he may send the Christ appointed for
you, Jesus, 21 whom heaven must receive
until the time for establishing all that
God spoke by the mouth of his holy prophets from of old. 22 Moses said, 'The Lord
God will raise up for you a prophet from
your brethren as he raised me up. You shall
listen to him in whatever he tells you.
23 And it shall be that every soul that does
not listen to that prophet shall be destroyed
from the people.' 24 And all the prophets
who have spoken, from Samuel and those
who came afterwards, also proclaimed these
days. 25 You are the sons of the prophets
and of the covenant which God gave to
your fathers, saying to Abraham, 'And in
your posterity shall all the families of the

21-23. The time for establishing: The Greek word ought properly to mean "restoration"; but "in relation to prophecy it may mean the establishment of what was predicted rather than the restoration of an earlier condition" (*ibid.* IV, 38). The quotation in vss. 22-23 is a combination of Deut. 18:15 and Lev. 23:29, possibly taken from some collection of *testimonia* or proof texts, where they were already run together. The Jews distinguished this **prophet** from the Messiah (see John 1:20-21; 7:40-41), but Christian interpretation, as here and in 7:37, united them in the person of Jesus.

25. Note Gen. 12:3; 22:18, and the use made by Paul of the latter verse in Gal. 3:16.

(*c*) The atomic bomb reveals the nature of existence as no other bomb has ever revealed it. In other words scientists knew from the beginning that the atomic bomb is not just another bomb. It is not simply another bomb that can destroy more property more thoroughly. It is different from every other bomb in that it releases and reveals the nature of atomic energy. After that bomb went off, the whole universe was differently understood by the mind of man. The power was always there, the reality was the same, but the event of the bomb released and revealed the power as it had never been released or revealed before. So we may say that the atomic age began with the atomic bomb.

That illuminates what Christians have always felt about Jesus. They have always said, in one way or another, that Jesus is not just another man. He is not simply another human being, a little better than the rest. After the life and death of Jesus, the whole universe looked different. It was the revelation and release of a new energy in the universe. It was the energy of the love of God. The energy had been there, but the life of Jesus let it loose, so to speak. From the beginning people sensed the fact that Jesus began a new era. Time divided upon him. They began to explain his relationship with God and his place in the total human picture in terms of the Messiah. He was the Liberator. They went even further and used the blood relationship of father and son. He was the Son. Paul, in his letter to the Colossians, went so far as to write, "For in him dwelleth all the fulness of the Godhead bodily" (Col. 2:9).

(*d*) The people who really appreciate the atomic bomb are the ones who saw it go off. Everyone knows that the bomb did go off, that there is something new and different about it, something to be alarmed about. But you have to see it to grasp the full significance of it. It is the scientists who made it, who saw it go off, and who saw the devastation that it caused, who speak of it in the surest terms. It is the same with Jesus. A man can read about him in the Bible, talk about him, theorize about

26 Unto you first God, having raised up his Son Jesus, sent him to bless you, in turning away every one of you from his iniquities.

4 And as they spake unto the people, the priests, and the captain of the temple, and the Sadducees, came upon them,

earth be blessed.' 26 God, having raised up his servant,[b] sent him to you first, to bless you in turning every one of you from your wickedness."

4 And as they were speaking to the people, the priests and the captain of the temple and the Sad'du-cees came upon

[b] Or *child.*

26. **Having raised up** apparently echoes the quotation in vs. 22, and means "caused to appear," with reference to Jesus' ministry. But the Greek word is used regularly of the Resurrection, and 4:2 (as well as 26:22-23, where many of the same ideas as here reappear) suggests that here too the reference may be to the Resurrection: in Pentecost and the miracle of healing God has **sent** the risen Jesus on a new ministry. In that case should **first** be taken as an adjective agreeing with **his servant,** as in 26:23, where Christ is "the first to rise from the dead," and in Col. 1:18 where he is "the first-born from the dead"?

2. First Clash with Judaism (4:1-22)

According to vs. 4, the number of persons belonging to the new Christian community had now risen to **about five thousand.** Such a statement some scholars feel "defies every resemblance to truth" (Maurice Goguel, *Introduction au Nouveau Testament,* "Le Livre des Actes" [Paris: Ernest Leroux, 1922], III, 179). It is true that the verse reads like an editorial summary, so that the figure may not have stood in the source. On the other hand, though most of these notes about the growth of numbers are very vague (see 2:47; 5:14; 6:1; 9:31), and almost certainly editorial, in other cases specific numbers are given (so 1:15—"about a hundred and twenty"; 2:41—"about three thousand"; 4:4—"about five thousand"), which suggests the possibility that in these cases Luke may be quoting from his sources, and that the figures are not merely the result of his own idealization of early history. In any case the growth of the community was evidently extremely rapid; and it was probably alarm at this that prompted the authorities to take action. Hitherto they had not thought it worth while to do so; that the Christians were still proclaiming a gibbeted malefactor as Messiah merely stamped them as deluded fanatics; and that they never questioned the validity of the Jewish law, and were in no sense revolutionaries against either church or state, would disarm suspicion. This would be the situation until the steady increase of their numbers attracted hostile attention.

It is significant that it was not the Pharisees who first took action, but **the priests and the captain of the temple and the Sadducees.** Although Judea had been a Roman province under a procurator since A.D. 6, external affairs were left to the Jewish authorities in the persons of the high priest and the seventy members of the Sanhedrin drawn from the **rulers,** or actual holders of political office, the **elders,** who owed their position not to office but to blood or wealth or religious prestige, and the **scribes** or teachers of the law. But political power was concentrated in the hands of "the high priest . . . and all who were with him, that is, the party of the Sadducees" (5:17). Theologically the

him, but he never appreciates Jesus' real meaning until he sees him explode, so to speak, in a human life with the power of a new affection. If it happens to be his own life, so much the better. When that happens, Jesus is no longer a matter of experiment or argument, and the generalizations of theology become the intimate possessions of personal experience. It is when a man suddenly sees that all that he adores in God is in Jesus and finds in Jesus all that he needs in God, that the truth proclaimed by Peter, Paul, and all the others through the ages, makes sense.

4:1-4. ***Peter and John Get into Trouble.***—New ideas always make enemies. The world is round; the earth travels around the sun; all men are created equal; government of the people, by the people, for the people; this is one world—ideas like these always make enemies and always get their promoters into trouble.

2 Being grieved that they taught the people, and preached through Jesus the resurrection from the dead.

them, 2 annoyed because they were teaching the people and proclaiming in Jesus

---

hierarchical aristocracy represented a rationalistic and skeptical tendency; for example they denied the resurrection and the existence of spirits (23:8). But their religious views were subordinated to policy. Their one aim was to maintain their own ascendancy and to prevent this being endangered by any popular restlessness that might provoke the Romans to place restrictions on local self-government (cf. especially John 11:48). Hence their suspicion of any undue religious enthusiasm, especially of the messianic order such as was being manifested by the new Christian sect. Thus Luke is undoubtedly right in representing the first opposition as coming from the Sadducees rather than from the Pharisees, who would have had no reason for proceeding against such consistent Jews. The apostles almost certainly were arrested, not as teachers of false doctrine, but as potential disturbers of the public peace. For Luke is probably wrong in the reason which he gives for the hostility of the Sadducees—**because they were . . . proclaiming in Jesus the resurrection from the dead.** The Sadducees were tolerant to a fault, and never sought to silence those who merely differed from them theologically. But for Luke it is a postulate that the Sadducees "say that there is no resurrection" (Luke 20:27; Acts 23:8),

---

Men habitually fear the thing that frees them. They prefer the known and familiar, uncomfortable and handicapping as it may be, to the unknown and strange, even though it may mean their eventual liberation. The average man lacks both the imagination to perceive and the courage to risk the unpopularity of a new idea.

But there are always a few who respond. Peter and John belong to that small company. They had a new idea. It was the idea that Jesus was the Messiah; that the future to which the Jews had looked, and for which they had longed for so many desperate generations, was now upon them; that the new age had already begun; that Jesus was the heart and center of it; and that life must be lived not in the old terms of death and the law, but in the new terms of life and love in Christ. They not only had the idea in their minds, but they also had it on their tongues. They talked about it constantly.

But so long as an idea is only talked about it does little harm. When it once begins to demonstrate itself in action, then the real trouble begins. Nobody cares very much when people talk about world government, but when they begin to take action, and that action threatens one of our coveted national prerogatives, then the trouble begins. In the middle of the nineteenth century no one minded when men talked against slavery, but when those same men took steps to set the slaves free, they found opposition that was not easily overcome.

Most of our current Christianity is talk. It seldom gets us into trouble. But on those rare occasions when the talk issues in action, we find the story of Peter and John repeated. In war time a conscientious Christian pacifist does not stir up much trouble by talking about pacifism, but once he starts to raise money for conscientious objectors, or defends their rights as citizens, that is a different matter. Christians can talk about social justice from now until doomsday and live peaceful and untroubled lives. Once they begin, however, to promote legislation which will make that justice effective, then they run into a stone wall of opposition. It is all right to talk about the atomic age, but to do anything about it that will interfere with the normal course of our day-to-day existence is quite a different story.

The very fact that Christians now get into so little trouble on account of their religion makes us wonder how much of it is talk and talk alone, and how much is talk demonstrated in action. For the world has not changed much in this regard. New ideas always make enemies and the men who promote them invariably get into trouble.

In the case of Peter and John it did a great deal more than talk. They healed a lame man in the presence of hundreds of people on the very threshold of the temple. They had talked about the Pioneer of life whom the people had crucified; they had claimed that God had raised him from the dead, and that in him there was life. "Good talk, but harmless," the unimaginative listeners might have said. They could say it no longer. New life? Here it was, right in front of them, on the doorstep of established religion. Inside the temple the old rites and ceremonies were being fastidiously performed. Outside the temple life was being renewed. No wonder the people were thrilled and the authorities were terrified. So Peter and John were

3 And they laid hands on them, and put *them* in hold unto the next day: for it was now eventide.

the resurrection from the dead. 3 And they arrested them and put them in custody until the morrow, for it was already eve-

---

and it may well be that he ignores the real reason because of his concern throughout the book to demonstrate that the Christians were never politically suspect in the eyes of the Roman authorities.

On the ground that the account of the arrest is so vague, and that so little is said of any definite charge, some scholars (e.g., Loisy) think that the disciples were merely warned, and that no formal proceedings can have been taken before the Sanhedrin. But for Luke at least the trial provides the dramatic climax to which the story of the cure is introductory. A few weeks before, Jesus himself had been arraigned before the same court; he had warned his disciples that "they will deliver you up to councils" (Mark 13:9); and here is the fulfillment of the prophecy.

---

put in jail. It was the only thing that the representatives of the old order could do.

Nowhere is there a more vivid contrast between official religion and real religion. Official religion was encased in a magnificent building, fortified by its roof and walls, protected by its porticoes. Real religion was out on the steps where men and women were struggling with the problems and pains of a day-to-day existence. Over and over again that has happened. While the established Church of England pursued its quiet life within the gray stone walls of Gothic buildings, John Wesley and his company were outdoors where people were fighting for a living, children struggling for an education, people thirsting for the love of God as plants stretch toward the light of the sun. Jesus himself was forced out of the synagogues and preached in the open air.

Does this mean that all our churches ought to be torn down? Obviously not! It does mean that religion is always in danger of becoming a purely indoor affair, divorced from the life of the people, uninterested in anything except its own precious routine of rite and ceremony. When that happens, religion must be turned out of doors. The way to fill the churches is to get people out of the churches. In other words the way to strengthen the life of the church is to get Christianity on the street. Not in the sense of street corner preaching, however effective some may feel that to be, but in the sense of bringing Christianity to bear upon the problems with which men and women are laboring. Let the idea demonstrate itself in action. Let the world see a few resurrected individuals! It may get some people in trouble, but it will give the church new life. This is one of the times in the history of Christianity when it needs to get out of doors lest it be smothered to death in its own dark, stuffy buildings.

Notice too how official religion is moved by fear. Peter and John, and the new idea they were expressing, were trespassing on property that did not belong to them. It belonged to the wealthy and entrenched hierarchy of the temple. With all their wealth and accumulated power, you might have expected the temple authorities to be fearless. Not so. Nor is it ever so with those in whom authority has lodged for so many generations that it becomes a kind of guaranteed right not to be taken away. It was Peter and John who were fearless. They who had nothing to lose and everything to gain were the ones who were willing to risk their lives on behalf of the new idea. Official religion always has property to consider, prerogatives and privileges to guard. It is afraid to act decisively lest powerful allies be offended on the one hand and incomes be reduced on the other. Large city churches in the United States are exposed to that fear constantly. They possess large endowments that are tied up in city real estate that in turn is closely related to city politics. Dare they cut off the hand that feeds them? They have one or two large contributors who carry the financial burden. Dare they propose ideas and policies of which those wealthy patrons disapprove? Is it not a question of keeping the doors open? When that time arrives, is it not the time to get out of doors? If the property means the sacrifice of the life, then let the property go. Silver and gold Peter and John did not have, but they had the life and the power. We, in our timid hearts, cling to the silver and the gold in order to ensure the life and the power. Alas for our folly! History warns us that it is always the other way round. It is the life and the power that ensure whatever material accessories we may think desirable.

How far dare Christianity trespass into the sacred precincts of established thought and practice? Will it dare trespass into the domain of economic relationships between human beings? Will it dare trespass into the region of

4 Howbeit many of them which heard
the word believed; and the number of the
men was about five thousand.
5 ¶ And it came to pass on the morrow,
that their rulers, and elders, and scribes,

ning. 4 But many of those who heard the
word believed; and the number of the
men came to about five thousand.
5 On the morrow their rulers and elders
and scribes were gathered together in Jeru-

4:1-2. The captain of the temple is either (*a*) the *ṣāghān* who held rank next to the high priest and was his chief executive officer; he is called "captain" in the LXX; or (*b*) a lesser official in charge of the temple guard, to whom Josephus gives the same title. **Proclaiming in Jesus the resurrection,** i.e., in Jesus they found proof of the doctrine denied by the Sadducees.

5-6. The **rulers** are presumably the office-holding **priests** of vs. 1. Compare the usual collocation, as here, with **elders and scribes** of "chief priests" in Luke 9:22; 20:1; etc., the latter being not only those who had actually held office as high priest, but also their priestly relatives—**all who were of the high-priestly family. Annas** had been high priest from A.D. 6 to 14, but as five of his sons and his son-in-law Caiaphas (now the legal high priest) had followed him in the office, he was still the power behind the throne

---

political relationships between nations? Will it dare trespass into the hidden areas of personal life, its motivations and desires? If it does, it will get into trouble. But if, on the doorstep of established religion, it can demonstrate its power to make men new creatures, its trouble will be like a blood-red banner signifying victory.

In these verses in ch. 4 we find the old story of resistance to a new idea, and we are warned that the most stubborn resistance can be presented in the very ranks of official religion in which we are enrolled.

5-12. ***A Question and Answer.***—In the morning the authorities proceeded to examine Peter and John. Their first question was, **By what power or by what name did you do this?** The fact that they had healed the lame man could not be questioned because everyone had seen it happen. The fact that it was a good thing could not seriously be questioned by Jews who were taught to do good to their fellow Jews. The only way left open to the authorities was the cheap but ever-present way of discrediting the deed by throwing suspicion upon the source of its origin. It was an old trick. The opponents of Jesus had tried it before. They could not deny that he cast out devils and that a devil-free man was better than a devil-possessed man, but they could throw suspicion upon Jesus himself by saying that he did what he did by joining forces with the devil.

Such is the defensive action of officialdom. It distracts the attention from the deed that has been done to the reason for which, and the authority by which, it was done. There is always activity on the doorstep of the temple of religion. Unofficial groups perform miracles of renewed life. They challenge the conscience of established religion, and that established religion too often replies by questioning their authority. The Salvation Army went out into the streets of London without the authority of apostolic orders in the sense in which the Church of England understands it. But the Salvation Army saved souls. How vain would it be for the Established Church to question the authority by which this miracle was performed! This is not to say that the question is at all times out of order; it has its necessary and rightful place. When it is completely out of order is when it is used as a screen behind which the barren representatives of authority hide as they strive to discredit the deeds of those who have unmistakably the authority of the Spirit of God.

The answer to the question that the authorities asked was given by Peter. Peter came to be the most articulate spokesman for the group. It is interesting, at this point, to note the growth and development of Peter. He comes upon the scene of the N.T. a young man earning his living by catching and selling fish. His horizons do not extend much beyond the Sea of Galilee, out of which his livelihood comes. There is no indication that his interests reach much farther than the little rural province in which his life is tucked away and the concerns of the daily round from which no workman can escape. As the story proceeds, Peter's place in the affection of Jesus grows. He is one of the inner circle and, along with James and John, he is allowed into the most intimate recesses of his Master's life. He is the first to see that Jesus is more than a good friend and a great man. He associates him with the new age itself. In the Garden of Gethsemane, however, his eyes are heavy with sleep. At the time of the trial his eyes are wet with the tears that he shed for his denial. Now look at him: **Peter,**

6 And Annas the high priest, and Caiaphas, and John, and Alexander, and as
many as were of the kindred of the high
priest, were gathered together at Jerusalem.
7 And when they had set them in the
midst, they asked, By what power, or by
what name, have ye done this?

salem, [6]with Annas the high priest and
Ca'ia-phas and John and Alexander, and all
who were of the high-priestly family. **7** And
when they had set them in the midst, they
inquired, "By what power or by what

(cf. John 18:13). Did Luke believe that Annas and Caiaphas both held office at the same time, as seems implied by the words "in the high-priesthood of Annas and Caiaphas" (Luke 3:2)? For **John** Codex Bezae (D) reads "Jonathan"; if this is correct, he may be the son of Annas who succeeded Caiaphas as high priest in A.D. 36. Of **Alexander** we know nothing.

---

filled with the Holy Spirit. Peter, speaking with an eloquence that commanded the attention not only of the crowd, but also of the authorities, outreaches the limits of his own abilities. Filled with the power of something greater than and beyond himself, he stands up—one can almost feel his height as he proudly rises to speak—before the high and mighty and in simple, sincere, and unambiguous language answers their question in such a way as to shame them for all time.

This speech of Peter's follows very much the same pattern as that of the two we have already discussed. This speech, however, has one new element. Peter concludes the speech by saying this: "There is no salvation by anyone else, nor even a second Name under heaven appointed for us men and our salvation" (Moffatt). In other words Peter went so far as to say not only that Jesus saves, but that *only* Jesus saves. He claimed for Jesus an exclusive and absolute position as the Savior of the world. Before the modern interpreter tackles that claim, he must make it clear what salvation means in the first place. Each generation describes and experiences salvation in its own terms. The thing itself does not change, but the language and the pictures do change. This much is certain: Salvation cannot be presented to a modern enquirer in terms of flaming fire from which a man is either graciously delivered or to which he is heartlessly condemned at the hour of his death. It is fair to say that something like that is the popular notion of salvation in the minds of by far the larger number of people, particularly the religiously uninformed. It is also fair to say that the popular impression is supported by popular hymns that have captured the fancy of earnest, yet simple-minded people; that it is further supported by the medieval art and poetry of Christianity; that it is implied by some passages in Scripture; but that in the life and ministry of Jesus, taking it as a whole, such a limited idea of salvation finds no support whatsoever. The task of the preacher, once again, is to get behind the pictures and see what they mean; to understand the imagery and interpret its meaning.

Daniel Webster once said that he would not give a silver dollar for all of Oregon. Why? There was plenty of land, but there was no water. The streams, flooding their banks in the spring, ran dry in summer and left the land a desert. In later years a dam was built. When the winter snows melt, the water is held in store; canals carry it to the land, and the land is once more fertile. Over twenty million acres of land have been reclaimed and more than a million people are living on the fruit of that once sterile soil.

The reclaimed land is a parable which tells the story of salvation to a modern congregation. There are thousands of people who have flesh and blood enough and years enough, but for some reason they have been cut off from the mainspring of life. It is not so much that they are worse sinners than the rest of us, as it is that they are detached from the nerve center. They are like wasteland; they have no contact with the mountain springs and lakes. Some of them are in the service of demons—demons in modern dress, to be sure, but demons nonetheless. They are possessed by obsessions, neuroses, inhibitions, fears, and fancies. They pay tribute to machines and sell their souls for a moment's pleasure. They may not believe in heaven or hell, yet they cannot mistake the atmosphere of either. Heaven or hell is not a question of temperature; it is a question of being in touch or out of touch with the invigorating life of God. And they are out of touch. In words that some think old fashioned, they are lost souls. Their question is: How can I reclaim my life so that it can function and produce as God intended it to function and produce? To them salvation means something real. It means deliverance from a drought which is sterilizing

8 Then Peter, filled with the Holy Ghost, said unto them, Ye rulers of the people, and elders of Israel,

9 If we this day be examined of the good deed done to the impotent man, by what means he is made whole;

name did you do this?" 8 Then Peter, filled
with the Holy Spirit, said to them, "Rulers
of the people and elders, 9 if we are being
examined today concerning a good deed
done to a cripple, by what means this man

8-9. Filled with the Holy Spirit: Another very primitive touch, the action of the Spirit, as often in the O.T., being still regarded as intermittent (e.g., I Sam. 19:20, 23; Judg. 11:29; 15:14; see on 4:31). **By what means this man has been healed:** The Greek word for **healed** is the same as that for "saved" (vs. 12), but the play on the word cannot be reproduced in English.

---

their life. If the Middle Ages thought of hell in terms of heat, we may well think of it in terms of drought. Remembering the references in the Gospels to Jesus as the "living water" we need not fear the charge of being unscriptural. This one fact, however, must be constantly emphasized: It is not a drought to which a man is consigned after death as a punishment for the mistakes he made during his life, but rather it is a drought that overtakes a man during his life, drying up his resources and his energies, caused by some block between himself and God, and relieved only when that block is removed.

Peter goes on to say, according to our imagery, that the only person who can remove it is Jesus Christ. Right there the well-educated person begins to protest. He has read a great deal about other religions. He knows that the religions of the East have their literature and culture; that they have produced great characters and noble lives. It offends him, as it did not offend his forefathers, when an exclusive claim such as Peter's is made for Christianity. He wants to be fair and tolerant to all people. It goes against the grain of his training and habit of thought to hear the words, **There is salvation in no one else.** It sounds pretentious. Furthermore it sounds inaccurate.

In the first place we must dispel the popular notion that one religion is as good as another. One religion is not as good as another. The practice of child sacrifice in primitive religion is not as good as the care and love for children in Christianity. Nor is the caste system in Hinduism as good as the doctrine of human dignity in Christianity. If there is any such thing as objective truth, such things as these belong in that realm. They are not matters of opinion but of truth. Science is not a matter of opinion; it is a matter of truth. A man has no choice whether he accepts the law of gravity or not. It is no less valid in the United States than it is in China. His opinions about it may be right or wrong, but the truth stands, regardless of what he thinks about it. Religion is concerned with truth, not opinion; that which is, not that which men think about it. It is not merely a matter of what appeals to a man; it is a matter of what claims a man. The truth that two and two makes four does not always appeal to everyone, but it claims everyone. The truth that is in Jesus may not appeal to everyone, may not be accepted by everyone, but that does not say that it does not claim everyone, simply because it is the truth!

We must go on to show what that truth is which has become objectively real and universally binding in Jesus. No one setting forth can pretend to reach any such goal as that. It is the task of an interpreter's lifetime. But at one particular time of that life he might set it down in words something like these.

Jesus began with the family. The family is a network of relationships and responsibilities. At its best it is a sample in miniature of a man's relationships with the whole of life and it is a clue to the meaning of life. Take the child's relationship with the father. On the child's part it is trust, and on the father's it is love, a love that never indulges, yet never lets go. Project that to the scale of the universe and you find the right relationship between a man and God. The children in the family do not always like each other, but they respect each other and try to help and understand each other because they belong to the same family, and more especially to the same parents. Project that to a world-wide scale and you see the right relationship between all men on the basis of their common humanity and sonship. Black sheep in the family are not condoned, neither are they cast off. They are loved in spite of their failure. Within the family there is an easy and natural intercourse between the father and the children. He cannot always give the children what they want, but he is always interested in knowing what they want, and when he can give it to them, he does so gladly, and when he cannot, he withholds it for a good reason. Project that family intercourse to cosmic pro-

10 Be it known unto you all, and to all the people of Israel, that by the name of Jesus Christ of Nazareth, whom ye crucified, whom God raised from the dead, *even* by him doth this man stand here before you whole.

11 This is the stone which was set at nought of you builders, which is become the head of the corner.

has been healed, 10 be it known to you all, and to all the people of Israel, that by the name of Jesus Christ of Nazareth, whom you crucified, whom God raised from the dead, by him this man is standing before you well. 11 This is the stone which was rejected by you builders, but which has

---

11. **This is the stone** refers of course to Jesus. The quotation is from Ps. 118:22. In Luke 20:17 (following Mark 12:10) it is quoted verbatim from the LXX; but here we have a free paraphrase from the original Hebrew, again perhaps from some collection of *testimonia* (see on 3:22). **The head of the corner** may be either (*a*) a stone in the foundation, which suits the reference in Isa. 28:16 (quoted in Rom. 9:33) and in Eph. 2:20; or (*b*) a stone at the top of a corner, binding the walls together where they meet, which better suits the word **head.** (See also I Pet. 2:7.)

---

portions and it becomes the pattern of Christian prayer. Again, the ties that bind a family together are not broken by death. The parents never cease to love and care, and life is held in that love and care in spite of all external circumstances. So the life of the great human family is held in the love of God the Father. The closer we are to him, the closer we are to each other, whether in life or in death. The Father's love prevails over death.

In short, Jesus acted on the assumption that life on the cosmic scale is life on the family scale magnified to the degree of infinity, and that the relationships that prevail in the lesser realm are a clue to the ones that prevail in the greater. He then set about to reveal those relationships as they truly exist, and by his life, and more especially by his death, restore the broken relationships of humanity, the relationship of man with God and the relationship of man with his fellow man.

The Christian claim, therefore, rests on two facts. First, humanity is the family of God and the only way to live a full life as a human being is to live as a member of that family. Second, Jesus not only reveals the relationships which exist between man and God, and between man and man as they are not elsewhere revealed, but he also restores those relationships as no one else can restore them.

The question is this: Is that claim true or false? Certainly the development of world events seems to prove beyond the shadow of doubt that the family principles are the only principles which will save this world from complete destruction, and there is ample evidence to show that in Jesus humanity, as well as God, is incarnate.

A pilot came back from overseas during World War II. He had been shot down over Germany and spent nine months in a German prison camp. He was telling his experiences to a friend. He told how in his days of training he was instructed in the use of a parachute but he never actually used one. He was never given an opportunity to bail out. Then the time came, in combat over Germany, surrounded by many enemy fighter planes, when his own plane was struck and it burst into flames. "Then," he said, "I knew that I had to jump. I could not pull the string at once because I was surrounded by enemy planes and I had to fall, waiting until I fell into the clouds before pulling the cord." His friend said in amazement, "I don't see how you could do it, never having done it before." "I could do it," he said, "because I knew it was my only chance."

That suggests the mood of the early Christians. When Peter stood up to address the opponents of Christianity, he held up before them the Lord Christ whom they had nailed to a tree and whom God had raised from the dead. As he presented that Christ in his risen power and glory, he added the ominous words, "He is your only chance." Or in Peter's own words, **There is salvation in no one else.** It is more and more evident that E. Stanley Jones was correct when he narrowed the choice to "Christ or chaos." From the point of view of personal and individual religion it may not be easy to demonstrate this to a modern congregation. They know a good Hindu or a good Jew whose life has been reclaimed by some other agent. But with regard to humanity as a whole is it not becoming more and more self-evident that we either live as a family or die? And is it not becoming clearer each day that in Jesus man finds not only his God but himself?

This passage contains in itself the seed for

12 Neither is there salvation in any other: for there is none other name under heaven given among men, whereby we must be saved.

13 ¶ Now when they saw the boldness of Peter and John, and perceived that they were unlearned and ignorant men, they marveled; and they took knowledge of them, that they had been with Jesus.

14 And beholding the man which was healed standing with them, they could say nothing against it.

15 But when they had commanded them to go aside out of the council, they conferred among themselves,

16 Saying, What shall we do to these men? for that indeed a notable miracle hath been done by them *is* manifest to all them that dwell in Jerusalem; and we cannot deny *it*.

17 But that it spread no further among the people, let us straitly threaten them, that they speak henceforth to no man in this name.

become the head of the corner. 12 And there
is salvation in no one else, for there is no
other name under heaven given among men
by which we must be saved."
13 Now when they saw the boldness of
Peter and John, and perceived that they
were uneducated, common men, they wondered; and they recognized that they had
been with Jesus. 14 But seeing the man that
had been healed standing beside them, they
had nothing to say in opposition. 15 But
when they had commanded them to go
aside out of the council, they conferred
with one another, 16 saying, "What shall
we do with these men? For that a notable
sign has been performed through them is
manifest to all the inhabitants of Jerusalem, and we cannot deny it. 17 But in order
that it may spread no further among the
people, let us warn them to speak no more

---

13. Uneducated, common men (ἀγράμματόι . . . ἰδιῶται): The first word means properly "unable to write," but here probably implies that they had not been educated in the rabbinical schools. The ἰδιώτης is properly the layman as opposed to the professional in any field. The implication is that the apostles belong to the Amhaarez, the "people of the land," of whom the Pharisees say in John 7:49 that "this crowd, who do not know the law, are accursed." **They recognized that they had been with Jesus:** Does this imply that up to this point the authorities had not actually associated the apostles with Jesus? Possibly so; and the longer Western text makes this even more evident. But Luke may

---

a missionary message, for the implication is unmistakable that Christianity is a global religion. It might well deal with two points: (*a*) the desirability of a global religion, and (*b*) the possibility of a global religion. The minds of the people are far better prepared than they were twenty years ago for such a sermon. On Friday, October 13, 1944, an editorial in the *New York Times* included these lines:

> Our advancing troops always know when they are nearing one of these mission stations, because the natives are friendly and trustful. There, some selfless man, serene in the face of death, has pursued his task of spreading education, loyalty, cleanliness, and Christian principles among flocks once turbulent and discontent. They are forerunners of the many who must soon take up the work of rehabilitation of the submerged populations who have lived through the storm sweeping Asia. They have cut a pathway of grace through the wilderness. Their weary hands need sustaining now more than ever.

13-31. *Counterattack of the Authorities.*—There were two things the authorities could not get away from. (*a*) The undeniable influence of Christ in the lives of these men. They were men of no extraordinary powers, little education, and no prestige. Yet they were bold to speak, and as they spoke it became clear that their power came from Jesus. They had been with him and had caught from him something of his own faith. They shared in his courage, and through them his love and power spread into the circles of wretched humanity. Observers could not get away from the fact that these men were carrying on the work of him who they thought was dead and buried. (*b*) Neither could they get away from the undeniable evidence. There was the lame man standing right in front of them. They were not dealing with a theory which could be abstractly denied, nor with a proposition or claim that could be conquered by a battle of wits. They were dealing with a deed, something

18 And they called them, and commanded them not to speak at all nor teach in the name of Jesus.

19 But Peter and John answered and said unto them, Whether it be right in the sight of God to hearken unto you more than unto God, judge ye.

20 For we cannot but speak the things which we have seen and heard.

21 So when they had further threatened them, they let them go, finding nothing how they might punish them, because of the people: for all *men* glorified God for that which was done.

22 For the man was above forty years old, on whom this miracle of healing was showed.

23 ¶ And being let go, they went to their

to any one in this name." 18 So they called
them and charged them not to speak or
teach at all in the name of Jesus. 19 But
Peter and John answered them, "Whether
it is right in the sight of God to listen to
you rather than to God, you must judge;
20 for we cannot but speak of what we
have seen and heard." 21 And when they
had further threatened them, they let them
go, finding no way to punish them, because
of the people; for all men praised God for
what had happened. 22 For the man on
whom this sign of healing was performed
was more than forty years old.
23 When they were released they went

mean rather that the authorities, already knowing that they were followers of Jesus, now put two and two together and deduced that it was just because they were Christians that they possessed such marvelous powers.

19. So Socrates, in Plato *Apology* 29. D: "I shall obey God rather than you."

21. Because of the people: The Pharisees, not the Sadducees, were the party in favor with the people, and the Sadducees had therefore carefully to watch public opinion (cf. 5:26; Matt. 21:26; 26:5).

3. Life Within the Community (4:23–5:16)

The key verse of this section is 4:31, describing a new outpouring of the Holy Spirit. This reads so like a repetition of the Pentecost experience that it is convenient at this point to call attention to the remarkable parallelism between the two blocks of material represented by (*a*) 2:1-47 *plus* 5:17-42, and (*b*) 3:1–5:16, corresponding respectively to Harnack's two sources, Jerusalem Source B and Jerusalem Source A. The "doublets" may be set in parallel columns, the passages attributed by Harnack to Jerusalem Source A being in boldface type. If it is conceded that we have in fact two parallel accounts of the same series of events, which the author has set down consecutively, there is a general inclination to prefer that derived from Jerusalem Source A as being a simpler and therefore more authentic account of the church's infancy. The series of parallels is certainly most striking, and in particular the duplication of "summaries of progress" is somewhat suspicious (cf. 2:43*a* with 5:5*b*; 2:43*b* with 5:12*a*; 2:46*a* with 5:12*b*; 2:47*a* with 5:13*b*; 2:47*b* with 5:14). It is of course not impossible that events did thus repeat themselves. If, on the other hand, we accept the theory of two accounts of the same series of

that had been done. They could not get around it. They could not even say that it was bad. The undeniable evidence of religion is always like that. It is a life that has been changed, a fearful man who has been given confidence, a lost soul that has been rescued from destruction. It is something done in the community, a school built, a hospital endowed, a rescue party sent out, a home for children established. These are the things that no one can deny. They are the proof of the pudding.

In the face of such facts the authorities were driven to a last resort. They forbade the men to talk about Jesus. They might as well have commanded the tides of the sea to stand still. **We cannot but speak the things which we have seen and heard.** The compulsion to preach is the first prerequisite of good preaching. A man talks about the weather because he has nothing else to talk about. He talks about Jesus because nothing else is worth talking about. That kind of compulsion comes only to those who have felt the power of Christ at first hand. Like men released from prison after all hope

own company, and reported all that the chief priests and elders had said unto them.	to their friends and reported what the chief priests and the elders had said to them.

happenings, then the very closeness of the parallelism, quite unconsciously reproduced by our author, is surely a proof of the historicity of the sequence of events.

2:1-13	Outpouring of the Spirit.	**4:31*a***	Outpouring of the Spirit.
2:14-21	Peter's speech at Pentecost.	**4:31*b***	"They . . . spoke the word of God with boldness."
2:42-47	Summary: the communal life of the church.	**4:32-35**	Summary: the communal life of the church.
		4:36–5:11	Two examples of communism: Barnabas, Ananias.
2:43*a*	"Fear came upon every soul."	**5:5*b***	"Great fear came upon all who heard it."
		5:11	"Great fear came upon the whole church."
2:43*b*	"Many wonders and signs were done through the apostles."	**5:12*a***	"Many signs and wonders were done . . . by the hands of the apostles."
3:1-11	Healing of the lame man.	**5:12*b*-16**	Typical healings.
3:12-26	Peter's speech in Solomon's Portico.	5:12*b*	"They were all together in Solomon's Portico."
4:1-7	Arrest of the apostles.	5:17-18	Arrest of the apostles.
4:4	"Many of those who heard the word believed."	5:19-28	The apostles escape and preach the word (vs. 20).
4:8-12	Peter's speech to his accusers.	5:29-32	Peter's speech to his accusers.
4:13-17	The council deliberates.	5:33-39	The council deliberates (Gamaliel).
4:18-22	The apostles are warned and freed.	5:40	The apostles are warned and freed.
4:23-30	The community rejoices.	5:41-42	"Rejoicing that they were counted worthy to suffer."

The passages 2:42-47 and 4:32-35 may either be ascribed to Jerusalem Source B and Jerusalem Source A respectively, or may be regarded as editorial summaries not derived from either source. The passage 4:36–5:11 is not regarded by Lake as part of Jerusalem Source A, on the ground that logically 5:12 ff. is a continuation of 4:31, so that all the intervening verses (and not merely 4:32-35) must be an intrusion from elsewhere (see *Beginnings of Christianity,* V, 142). But 5:12*b*-16 provides the same prelude to the arrest of the disciples in 5:17-18 as does the healing of the lame man to their arrest in 4:1 ff. It is tempting therefore to transfer 5:12*b*-16 to Jerusalem Source B, to which the sequel belongs, or to suppose that the verses are Luke's own composition. Vs. 12*a* should surely be combined with vs. 11 to form a summary conclusion to Jerusalem Source A parallel to 2:43, which provides an exactly similar conclusion to Jerusalem Source B. The two sets of doublets would then be complete; and if ch. 2 were transposed to follow ch. 5, we should have from Jerusalem Source B a complete narrative parallel in detail to that from Jerusalem Source A in 3:1–5:12*a*. Whereas, with ch. 2 in its present position, there is nothing to lead up to Pentecost, we might now assume that in both sources the first outpouring of the Spirit followed the first public appearance of the apostles as miraculous healers and their first encounter with the Jewish authorities. The result of the gift of the Spirit shows itself in a new boldness in witness-bearing in the face of persecution, thereby illustrating the fulfillment of the promise given by Jesus (Luke 12:11-12).

a) New Outpouring of the Spirit (4:23-31)

The prayer of thanksgiving (vss. 24-30) is a lyric comparable with the songs and prayers of Luke's nativity story. It is quite in the style of the O.T. to insert such lyrics in the middle of narrative, good examples being the prayer of Jonah "out of the fish's

24 And when they heard that, they lifted up their voice to God with one accord, and said, Lord, thou *art* God, which hast made heaven, and earth, and the sea, and all that in them is;

25 Who by the mouth of thy servant David hast said, Why did the heathen rage, and the people imagine vain things?

24 And when they heard it, they lifted their voices together to God and said, "Sovereign Lord, who didst make the heaven and the earth and the sea and everything in them,
25 who by the mouth of our father David, thy servant,[b] didst say by the Holy Spirit,

'Why did the Gentiles rage,
and the peoples imagine vain things?

[b] Or *child*.

---

belly" (Jonah 2), and the song of the three children "in the burning fiery furnace" (Dan. 3, in the Greek). Luke here with great skill reproduces the O.T. flavor, and if, as seems likely, the lyric is his own composition, it illustrates how well he conforms to the conventions of his twofold literary inheritance—Greek in the case of the speeches, Hebrew in this characteristically Hebraic section.

Immediately after the prayer of thanksgiving **they were all filled with the Holy Spirit** (vs. 31). Acts is particularly full of references to the activity of the Spirit. Men are variously spoken of as in it, under it, filled with it, baptized with it, anointed with it, instructed by it. They speak through it, or it through them. Sometimes it is called the Spirit of the Lord, or the Spirit of Jesus, and is in fact almost indistinguishable from the risen Jesus himself. All this is of course not peculiar to Luke, whose special outlook is shown (*a*) in his emphasis on the materiality of the Spirit: at Jesus' baptism it descends "in bodily form, as a dove" (Luke 3:22); Jesus casts out devils "by the finger of God" (Luke 11:20; Matt. 12:28 has "by the Spirit of God"); at Pentecost we have the actual sound of "wind" and the tongues of "fire"; and the idea of "filling" and "pouring," almost as of some kind of material fluid, is especially frequent. Is Luke showing the characteristic interest of the physician in the tangible and corporeal? (*b*) Noticeable too is the definiteness with which Luke marks the arrival of the Spirit; there are outstanding moments when the Spirit manifests itself quite apart from the normal spiritual experience of Christians. Here Luke certainly reflects a point of view much more primitive than Paul's. For Paul the Spirit is the active moving power in normal Christian living; the life of every true Christian is "spiritual" in the fullest sense. But the primitive view saw the highest expression of the Spirit's activity, not in the everyday faith and piety of the common disciple, but in the abnormal and unusual in character, word, or work. To see visions, speak with tongues, preach with more than ordinary power was a proof of possession by the Spirit, of which the ordinary disciple was expected to show no striking evidence. Thus the community as a whole could be "filled with the Spirit" only on special ecstatic occasions such as the present. Nevertheless in the case of some saints such possession by the Spirit, attainable by others only spasmodically, was regarded as habitual and characteristic, and they are called men "full of the Spirit" (6:3). Stephen (6:5) and Barnabas (11:24) are specifically so called. Such were men whose religious power was so pre-eminent that only the permanent indwelling of the Spirit of God could account for it. It was not the least of Paul's achievements that he transcended this somewhat artificial distinction between the man whose religious fervor manifested itself in striking outward effects, and the saint in whom the Spirit expressed itself in the depth of his personal devotional life. (On the Spirit in the primitive church see also article "The Gospel in the New Testament," in Vol. VII of this work, especially pp. 8-10.)

24. The only other place where Luke uses the title **Sovereign Lord** (δεσπότης) of God is Luke 2:29, where also the word "slave" (δοῦλος, the word translated "servants" in vs. 29) is used in antithesis. Is a similar antithesis implied by the use in vs. 27 of the phrase "thy holy servant [παῖδα] Jesus"—our Lord being thus identified with the "servant of Yahweh" of Isa. 52:13, etc.? (See on 3:13.)

25. Though the RSV probably gives the intended sense, the Greek here is "an incoherent jumble of words" (Torrey). The text is almost certainly corrupt, though

26 The kings of the earth stood up, and the rulers were gathered together against the Lord, and against his Christ.

27 For of a truth against thy holy child Jesus, whom thou hast anointed, both Herod, and Pontius Pilate, with the Gentiles, and the people of Israel, were gathered together,

28 For to do whatsoever thy hand and thy counsel determined before to be done.

29 And now, Lord, behold their threatenings: and grant unto thy servants, that with all boldness they may speak thy word,

30 By stretching forth thine hand to heal; and that signs and wonders may be done by the name of thy holy child Jesus.

31 ¶ And when they had prayed, the place was shaken where they were assembled together; and they were all filled with the Holy Ghost, and they spake the word of God with boldness.

32 And the multitude of them that believed were of one heart and of one soul:

26 The kings of the earth set themselves
in array,
and the rulers were gathered together,
against the Lord and against his
Anointed'[d] —
27 for truly in this city there were gathered
together against thy holy servant[b] Jesus,
whom thou didst anoint, both Herod and
Pontius Pilate, with the Gentiles and the
peoples of Israel, 28 to do whatever thy
hand and thy plan had predestined to take
place. 29 And now, Lord, look upon their
threats, and grant to thy servants[e] to speak
thy word with all boldness, 30 while thou
stretchest out thy hand to heal, and signs
and wonders are performed through the
name of thy holy servant[b] Jesus." 31 And
when they had prayed, the place in which
they were gathered together was shaken;
and they were all filled with the Holy Spirit
and spoke the word of God with boldness.
32 Now the company of those who be-

[b] Or *child*.
[d] Or *Christ*.
[e] Or *slaves*.

Torrey suspects a mistranslation of an original Aramaic sentence meaning, "That which our father, thy servant David, said by command of the Holy Spirit." The quotation is from Ps. 2:1-2.

27. **Whom thou didst anoint,** i.e., "make Christ," "make Messiah." Did Luke think of this anointing as taking place at Jesus' baptism? **Herod** represents "the kings" of the quotation, and **Pontius Pilate** represents "the rulers."

31. An earthquake would be considered an outward sign of divine activity, and it is the only one of the four signs in the divine manifestation to Elijah (I Kings 19:11-12) which was not reproduced in the account of Pentecost in ch. 2. **Boldness,** as illustrated in vs. 8 above, is the result of the possession of the Spirit. The phrase almost means "without inhibition"; cf. its use of Jesus in Mark 8:32 ("he said this plainly"), and for the thought in general cf. Luke 12:11-12.

b) THE SHARING OF GOODS (4:32–5:10)

Immediately after the notice of the outpouring of the Spirit there follows once again (as in 2:42-47 after the story of Pentecost) a summary giving a little tableau of life

had gone, they cannot refrain from telling others about it, especially others who themselves are imprisoned.

When the men went back to their friends they burst out in a hymn of praise and thanksgiving, ending with the petition that they be given the power, not to keep still, but to speak out with even greater boldness than before. Their prayers were answered. The whole building seemed to shake, as if a power too great to be contained was shaking itself loose. And the men went out and spoke the word of God with boldness.

Johannes Weiss writes in his *History of Primitive Christianity:*

> A tempestuous enthusiasm, an overwhelming intensity of feeling, an immediate awareness of the presence of God, an incomparable sense of power and an irresistible control over the will and inner spirit and even the physical condition of other men—these are ineradicable features of historic early Christianity.[4]

32-37. ***The Life of the Community.***—Once again the corporate life of the community is

[4] Vol. I, pp. 42-43.

within the primitive community. Those who regard the two summaries as doublets are inclined to give priority to the present passage. In both stress is laid upon the apostles' teaching and upon the community of goods, practiced not as a compulsory system but as a voluntary means of meeting the common need.

The two illustrations given of "communism"—the cases of Barnabas and Ananias—show that there can have been no absolute or even general rule. The special liberality of Barnabas had no reason to be mentioned if vs. 32 is to be taken with strict literalness. Similarly 5:4 makes it clear that Ananias was perfectly at liberty to keep his possessions if he so wished. His sin was not that he withheld part of his goods, but that he lied **to the Holy Spirit** (5:3) by retaining part of the proceeds of the sale, and thereby pretending to be more generous than in fact he was. Whatever may have been the extent of this "communistic" experiment at Jerusalem, it appears very soon to have broken down, first, perhaps on account of the dissension between "Hellenists" and "Hebrews" (6:1), and second, because the administrators who had been appointed as a result of the dispute had been driven from the city by the Jews. Probably also the eager expectation of the Parousia led to improvidence for the future, so that the Jerusalem community was always poor. Accordingly we find the selling of local possessions superseded by the sending of alms to the mother church by the richer daughter churches. Antioch sent relief by Barnabas and Paul (11:30); Paul was asked "to remember the poor," presumably of Jerusalem (Gal. 2:10); and later he brought a contribution from the Gentile churches (Rom. 15:25 ff.; II Cor. 8:1 ff.).

Barnabas is here mentioned for the first time. For a considerable period, until Paul later took the leadership, he must have been the most prominent figure in Hellenistic Jewish-Christian circles. In the calendar of the Anglican church he is given the title of "apostle," and is the only saint outside the twelve, except Paul and the evangelists, to be honored with a red-letter day. By birth he was a Cypriote; but he probably had connections with Jerusalem, for John Mark was his cousin. Originally named Joseph, he received the surname "Barnabas" possibly to mark his admission to the function of prophet or teacher—if we accept the traditional derivation of the name from *bar-nᵉbhû'āh,* "son of prophecy." This might also give the meaning "Son of exhortation" (ASV). Alternatively, an Aramaic derivation from *bar-nᵉwaḥâ'* ("rest" or "refreshment") would give "son of consolation" (KJV). Luke's Greek (υἱὸς παρακλήσεως) might at a stretch bear either meaning. A "paraclete" is properly a person called in to one's side to help; hence in I John 2:1 it is translated "advocate"; in John 14:16 it is used of the Holy Spirit and is translated "Comforter" (KJV) or "Counselor" (RSV). Here a good translation is **Son of encouragement,** which includes both ideas. In Acts Barnabas lives up to his name

---

emphasized. We have already considered it in some detail in Expos., 2:41-47, but in this passage a new note is added. It is the close association between the apostles' witness to the resurrection of Jesus and the life of the community. It is as though the community itself were the demonstration of that Resurrection, like the corona of the sun. In the group the new power was at work, like sun streaming through breaking clouds, not only to heal the sick but to transform self-centered individuals into self-sacrificing members of a society. It is important to notice this moral and spiritual change in the life of believers.

Every church is, at least potentially, a resurrection center. Into it come people who have been primarily concerned with their own affairs. By it their horizons are broadened. They come to know and feel the needs of other people. They share what they have with those who have less or nothing at all. Their own burdens are eased as the shoulders of their fellow men assume part of the weight. As a result, their own lives begin to throb with a new life beside which their old life seems a narrow and useless existence.

There are two poles in human life: the individual and the group. It has been the function of the church since the earliest days of its existence to help the individual find himself. In the current situation, with the sense of belonging to a community greatly reduced, it is the function of the church to help the individual find himself by incorporating him into the life of the Christian community. Abraham, according to the writer of the Epistle to the Hebrews, was looking for a city. In the same way the church today is looking for a com-

neither said any *of them* that aught of the things which he possessed was his own; but they had all things common.

33 And with great power gave the apostles witness of the resurrection of the Lord Jesus: and great grace was upon them all.

34 Neither was there any among them that lacked: for as many as were possessors of lands or houses sold them, and brought the prices of the things that were sold,

lieved were of one heart and soul, and no one said that any of the things which he possessed was his own, but they had everything in common. 33 And with great power the apostles gave their testimony to the resurrection of the Lord Jesus, and great grace was upon them all. 34 There was not a needy person among them, for as many as were possessors of lands or houses sold them, and brought the proceeds of what

(see e.g., 11:23 ff.). Adolf Deissmann (*Bible Studies* [Edinburgh: T. & T. Clark, 1901], pp. 307-10) and others prefer a derivation from *Nebo,* apparently a heathen demon-god, in which case Luke's translation seems quite arbitrary, though curiously, as Lake and Cadbury note, it would fit Manaen, who appears with Barnabas in 13:1. Can there have been some confusion? A similar problem arises in connection with the meaning of the name Elymas in 13:8.

For the extreme punishment meted out to Ananias and Sapphira we may compare Paul's words in I Cor. 5:5, "You are to deliver this man to Satan for the destruction of the flesh, that his spirit may be saved in the day of the Lord Jesus." Some may prefer to believe that the account has been somewhat "written up": the coincidence of the sudden death of the guilty pair was put down to a direct visitation of the Spirit—cf. **lie to the Holy Spirit** (5:3); **tempt the Spirit of the Lord** (5:9)—and the actual agency of Peter in causing the deaths was introduced later. But more important than the accuracy of the story in detail is the light it throws on the ideas of the primitive community—the constant oversight of the Spirit whom none can deceive; the odiousness of hypocrisy, which Jesus had treated as the chief of all sins; the love of money as the root of all evil. Indeed, greed for gain or trust in the power of money lies behind most of the sins or failures recorded in Acts: Judas' betrayal (1:18), the sin of Simon (8:18), the opposition of the "owners" of the mediumistic slave girl at Philippi (16:16 ff.) and of the silversmiths at Ephesus (19:23 ff.), and even the procrastination of Felix (24:26). The sin of Ananias was that he tried "to make the best of both worlds."

32. The company of those who believed means the whole body of Christians and is practically synonymous with "the church" (cf. 6:2, 5; 15:12, 30).

munity in which men can live together cooperatively and creatively.

Some people are still on the lookout for a castle. They are searching for some impregnable fortress where they may pursue their private ways with little or no concern for the rest of mankind. All of us have a recurring desire for a one-room castle. In too many cases that desire has been fulfilled; we live in one-room castles, soundproof, loveproof. We are now realizing that insulated units of humanity finally break down into lonely fragments of forlorn life. We begin to look for a community where private enterprise will be redeemed by a concern for public benefit. The church will not and should not presume to dictate the legal and economic ways and means by which this society will be organized, but the church can and must affirm the underlying principles which govern sound community life. The precious privilege of individual initiative must be guarded at all costs. The right of private property is to many of us the necessary and natural stimulation to the exercise of that privilege. But where private enterprise exploits the life and talents of the people, where it monopolizes the fruits of the earth which are meant to be shared by all men, and where it makes its way without regard for the welfare of the people at large, it must be checked either by the free consent of those concerned or by the legislated will of the people. The incentive for such a self-imposed discipline is to be found where the first Christians found it, in Jesus; and the power to practice the discipline is the power of the living Christ.

Other people are looking for a camp. There is enough of the nomad in every man to lure him to the vagabond life of those who are continually on the move. No stakes, no roots, no permanent alliances or responsibilities. We have given wide and generous reign to that

35 And laid *them* down at the apostles' feet: and distribution was made unto every man according as he had need.

36 And Joses, who by the apostles was surnamed Barnabas, (which is, being interpreted, The son of consolation,) a Levite, *and* of the country of Cyprus,

37 Having land, sold *it*, and brought the money, and laid *it* at the apostles' feet.

5 But a certain man named Ananias, with Sapphira his wife, sold a possession,

2 And kept back *part* of the price, his wife also being privy *to it*, and brought a certain part, and laid *it* at the apostles' feet.

was sold 35 and laid it at the apostles' feet;
and distribution was made to each as any
had need. 36 Thus Joseph who was surnamed by the apostles Barnabas (which
means, Son of encouragement), a Levite,
a native of Cyprus, 37 sold a field which
belonged to him, and brought the money
and laid it at the apostles' feet.

5 But a man named An-a-ni'as with his
wife Sap-phi'ra sold a piece of property,
2 and with his wife's knowledge he kept
back some of the proceeds, and brought
only a part and laid it at the apostles' feet.

---

35. **Laid it at the apostles' feet** may reflect an old legal convention by which property was transferred by placing it at or under the feet of the recipient.

5:1-2. Ananias, not an uncommon name (9:10; 23:2), means "Yahweh is gracious." **Sapphira** means "beautiful." **Kept back some of the proceeds:** The Greek verb is somewhat obscure, but is regularly used of appropriating something that is held in trust; the implication is that the proceeds of the sale, having already been dedicated to the community, were no longer at Ananias' own disposal. Lake and Cadbury well translate: "embezzled part of the price." The word is used in Josh. 7:1 of Achan who "took of the accursed thing," i.e., "retained part of the consecrated spoil." The word may well have been chosen with that story in view, for the enormity of Ananias' sin, like Achan's, was that through it sin entered into the community.

---

impulse. We have in many instances cut ourselves off from the mainland of culture and tradition. We have "gone west" to avoid public responsibility; we have left home and gone to "the city," where no one will know us and we can do what we please. The church will work to re-establish the bonds which bind us to the past and the roots which tie us to reality. The moral seriousness of the Hebrews, the beauty and form of the Greeks, the science and art of the Europeans—all these shall be recovered and, like anchors, keep our community from drifting. But ever within this larger community will be the company of the faithful who are held together by their relationship to Christ.

Some people unfortunately are looking for a cloister. Religion, according to their understanding, is a personal matter and scorns to rub shoulders with the common crowd. Let such a person remember this: Without the community there would be no sanctuary, no men of spiritual genius; for the great ones have been lifted, as it were, on the shoulders of the group, articulating, refining, and propelling the unexpressed intimations of the less gifted members of the group. Let him remember this: A man is saved not by his achievements alone, but by his associations also. What a man belongs to will in more instances than one be the saving factor in his life. If Christianity expects to exert an influence on this chaotic world, it will never do it through unrelated, though well-meaning individuals. It will do it through the community that is dedicated to a divine commission.

5:1-11. ***Trouble Within the Community.***—Every family has its black sheep. The church is no exception. Even within the small group of hand-picked, carefully chosen disciples, there was one black sheep. Even in the first days of the church, when its life was fresh and pure, there were two black sheep, Ananias and Sapphira, by name. There may have been more; we are not told. But we are grateful to the author who was frank enough to release the story of these two. For one thing it increases our confidence in him as a writer of history. He was an ardent admirer of the church, and in his enthusiasm he might have held back a story that would discredit it. He chose, however, the way of his predecessors and the tradition of Jewish scripture: he told all the facts.

For another thing, we, who find so many black sheep in the Christian society of our day, have at least this much encouragement, that they have always been there, that they are not a sign of total decay and disintegration. Apparently as it takes all kinds of people to

3 But Peter said, Ananias, why hath Satan filled thine heart to lie to the Holy Ghost, and to keep back *part* of the price of the land?

4 While it remained, was it not thine own? and after it was sold, was it not in thine own power? why hast thou conceived this thing in thine heart? thou hast not lied unto men, but unto God.

5 And Ananias hearing these words fell down, and gave up the ghost: and great fear came on all them that heard these things.

3 But Peter said, "An-a-ni'as, why has Satan filled your heart to lie to the Holy Spirit and to keep back part of the proceeds of the land? 4 While it remained unsold, did it not remain your own? And after it was sold, was it not at your disposal? How is it that you have contrived this deed in your heart? You have not lied to men but to God." 5 When An-a-ni'as heard these words, he fell down and died. And great fear came

---

3. Lie to [or "cheat"] **the Holy Spirit:** The essential "sin against the Holy Spirit" is always to confound evil with good. In Mark 3:29 to ascribe Jesus' good deeds to the Devil's agency is to "blaspheme the Holy Spirit"; here the **lie to the Holy Spirit** is for a miserly man to pose as generous—a piece of willful hypocrisy. Note that this "lie to the Spirit" is equivalent to lying to God (vs. 4), and to tempting the Spirit of the Lord (vs. 9).

---

make a world, it takes all kinds to make a church. It was so from the very beginning.

In this particular case the black sheep seem blacker than usual because of the fact that they stand so close to Barnabas (4:36-37). Barnabas had just been introduced by the writer of the Acts. He was generous, holding back nothing, clear and clean all the way through. Standing beside him, the calculating Ananias and Sapphira look even blacker than they otherwise might. It is when sin is thrown against the background of real goodness that its evil is unmasked. Pilate, Judas, Caiaphas, the soldiers, and all the rest who carried out the details of the Crucifixion show themselves in their real colors because behind them stands the vivid contrast of Jesus. Without that background, what they did might easily pass as one of the expedients of political action.

One of the reasons why black sheep are less conspicuous in the church today than they were in the days when the Acts was written may be that the average degree of whiteness is less intense. When most of the sheep are a dirty gray, the black ones have an easier time of it. When ninety-nine are honest, it is hard for the one hundredth to chisel without notoriety.

What is to be said about this unfortunate couple could well be divided into four parts.

(a) *What the couple did.* As nearly as we can discover from the story as it is reported to us, the couple sold a piece of property. They did it of their own free will; at this point there were no communistic compulsions in the Christian fellowship, none but the compulsion of a man's own desire to share his property in order to help others who had need of it. They contributed part of what they received for the property to the Christian church, and part they held back. It was not so much that they lied; they cheated. They did not play the game. In the eyes of the public they were generous givers. In the eyes of God they were hypocrites.

People have always been tempted to live behind deceptive façades. They have thought that so long as the front windows were clean, it did not matter much about the back ones. This was the sin that in the eyes of Jesus was the most loathsome of all—the sin of appearing to be something that you are not. This couple wanted to appear to be zealous supporters of the church, but in reality they were supporters of themselves. The implication is that had they gone ahead and lived a self-centered existence without pretending anything else, they might have escaped the final penalty. It was their cheating that was their undoing. When the figures in the showcase do not match the figures in the private vaults, there will be trouble.

(b) *What they did to themselves.* The writer of the Acts does not linger in sentimental sympathy over the end of these people. They both dropped dead. It is neither possible nor necessary to describe in detail the why and the wherefore of this terrible ending. It is enough to note that there is nothing in the story to indicate that Peter killed either of them. The sense of their own guilt, coming upon them with the force of a shock that was fatal, is enough to explain the event. It seems to the modern reader like a cruel fate. It offends the temper of tolerance which we have cultivated in the Christian community. It seems to some to deny the mercy of God and to violate the spirit of lovingkindness which Jesus himself displayed.

6 And the young men arose, wound him
up, and carried *him* out, and buried *him*.
7 And it was about the space of three
hours after, when his wife, not knowing
what was done, came in.
8 And Peter answered unto her, Tell me
whether ye sold the land for so much? And
she said, Yea, for so much.

upon all who heard of it. 6 The young men
rose and wrapped him up and carried him
out and buried him.
7 After an interval of about three hours
his wife came in, not knowing what had
happened. 8 And Peter said to her, "Tell me
whether you sold the land for so much."

---

6. The young men: Literally "the younger men," possibly in distinction from the "elders"; but it is questionable whether even the latter yet existed as officials, and most unlikely that "the younger men" were an official "body of men devoted to such offices as burying" (Rackham). In vs. 10 they are called simply "young men," the Greek word having no such official flavor.

Regardless of the exact manner in which they met their death, it is good for the modern Christian to remember that there has been from the beginning an austerity at the heart of Christian love. We have been inclined to leave out that note. We have purged the Gospels of their severity. We have flung wide the door that was shut, and thrown a bridge across the gulf that was fixed. We have canonized the sheep and forgotten the goats and explained away their fearful fate. Life is not like that, however, nor is Christianity when the facts are properly regarded. There are severities in life which are inescapable. There are some things that you cannot do and live. There are penalties that must be paid.

In view of these considerations it is fair to say that whatever happened to this couple, they brought it upon themselves. They cut themselves off from the group when they violated their own relationship with that group. Whether they died or continued to live, it would have been as members torn asunder from the body. Members of a family who do not play the game may continue to dwell in the same house, but their relationship with the family is broken. So it is with a citizen who refuses to play the game, a student in a school, a man in an office, a member of a church.

(*c*) *What they did to the church.* The writer of the Acts does not tell us what harm this couple did to the church. Surely they did not do it any good. One of the most impressive things about this small group was the spirit that existed within it among the members. They were interested in each other; they were loyal to each other; they took care of one another. As much as the preaching, it was this spirit of fellowship that swept people off their feet. "See how they love one another!" they said. That was the final test.

It is permissible for us to wonder how many people Ananias and his wife kept out of that first Christian fellowship. How many people might there have been who, when they heard about the couple who cheated, said to themselves, "If that is the best that these Christians can do, it is not for me"? There is no answer to that question, but when we bring the question down to our times, it loses some of its theoretical abstractness. Think of some of the people that make up the church today. The men in business who make no pretense even to acknowledge the Christian ethical ideal in their business, let alone practice it; the couples who make little or no effort to maintain the dignity and sanctity of their marriage vows; the individuals who at least seem to make no consistent effort to control their tempers, or bridle their tongues, or soften their judgments; the people who make racial discriminations without thinking twice, refusing to sit next to a Negro, or to live in the same hotel with a Jew; the people who reap large incomes, either inherited or earned, and yet are blind to the injustice that prevails in groups like migrant farmers. What do these people do to themselves? They cut themselves off from the real life of the Christian community. But the important question is; What do they do to the church? They cast upon it the shadow of hypocrisy. They confirm the suspicions of the cynical and alienate the loyalty of the young. If it were only a question of their own fate, it would be bad enough, but when it involves as it does the fate of the Christian community, the blackness of the black sheep is even blacker.

(*d*) *What shall the church do with them?* The presence of black sheep within the church has always embarrassed the church. It has raised the question: What shall be done with them? Shall we overlook their sin and keep them in the fold, or shall we cast them out? At different times during the history of the church the policy has been different. There have been movements and sects that have adopted the pol-

9 Then Peter said unto her, How is it
that ye have agreed together to tempt the
Spirit of the Lord? behold, the feet of them
which have buried thy husband *are* at the
door, and shall carry thee out.
10 Then fell she down straightway at
his feet, and yielded up the ghost: and the
young men came in, and found her dead,
and, carrying *her* forth, buried *her* by her
husband.
11 And great fear came upon all the
church, and upon as many as heard these
things.

And she said, "Yes, for so much." 9 But
Peter said to her, "How is it that you have
agreed together to tempt the Spirit of the
Lord? Hark, the feet of those that have
buried your husband are at the door, and
they will carry you out." 10 Immediately
she fell down at his feet and died. When
the young men came in they found her
dead, and they carried her out and buried
her beside her husband. 11 And great fear
came upon the whole church, and upon all
who heard of these things.

---

9. To tempt the Spirit of the Lord: The primitive idea of seeing how far one can go without provoking retaliation; cf. the common O.T. phrase of "tempt the Lord" (e.g., Exod. 17:2), and notice how, as in I Cor. 10:9, the idea, and indeed the very title "Lord," is transferred from God to Christ.

c) Summary (5:11-16)

Vss. 11-12*a* probably go together to form a summary conclusion to Jerusalem Source A parallel to 2:43, which provides an exactly similar conclusion to Jerusalem Source B. In the following verses (12*b*-16) the idea of **signs and wonders** is developed into a generalizing summary which provides a fitting climax to the whole section. This was probably composed by Luke himself. Or did he take over these verses also from one or other of his sources? (See Exeg., above on p. 70.)

11. The word **church** (ἐκκλησία) is here used for the first time as a name for the Christian community. At first any such name would be unnecessary, for Christians were still within the Jewish community, though marked out as "those who called on this name" (i.e., of Jesus; 9:21). Then vague phrases like "the Way" (9:2), "this Life" (5:20), "this salvation" (13:26) were perhaps used. The Christians, as a sect within Judaism, were probably called "Nazarenes," and their synagogue in Aramaic would be "the *Kenîshta'* [Hebrew *Keneṣeth*] of the Nazarenes." Among themselves they were known as "saints" or "brothers," the name "Christian" being regarded as a mere nickname (11:26) and not used till well on in the second century. As the rift with Judaism widened, "the church" was accepted as a distinctive title. The usage has its roots in the LXX, where ἐκκλησία (*ecclēsia*) is one of two words used to describe the "congregation" or "assembly" of Israel, the other being συναγωγή, "synagogue." The Hebrew words used to describe the people assembled for acts of public worship, deliberation, and judgment are *'ēdhāh* (ASV "congregation") and *qāhāl* (ASV "assembly"). Both words seem sometimes to be used in exactly the same sense; but the distinction is that *'ēdhāh* can denote all Israelites as a community, while *qāhāl* is rather the "assembly" called for a specific purpose. In the LXX the distinction becomes clearer: συναγωγή is often used to translate both Hebrew words in the more general sense. But there was ready at hand another Greek word ἐκκλησία, with the technical sense of a specially convoked public assembly "called

---

icy of puritanism. They would have none of these black sheep in their fold. Out with them! To them the church was a congregation of saints, not a haven for sinners.

In Matthew's Gospel it is clearly indicated that this problem perplexed the church from the earliest days. The parable of the wheat and the tares is an attempt to answer it. Whether the parable comes from Jesus himself, or whether it is the judgment of his early followers, need not be settled here. It is enough to say that it clearly reflects the temper and judgment of Jesus. In a field in which there are inevitably both wheat and weeds, let the weeds alone, lest in pulling them up you disturb the roots of the wheat. God will separate them when the harvest comes. In other words, in a church in which there are inevitably both

12 ¶ And by the hands of the apostles were many signs and wonders wrought among the people; (and they were all with one accord in Solomon's porch.

13 And of the rest durst no man join himself to them: but the people magnified them.

14 And believers were the more added to the Lord, multitudes both of men and women;)

12 Now many signs and wonders were done among the people by the hands of
the apostles. And they were all together
in Solomon's Portico. 13 None of the rest
dared join them, but the people held them
in high honor. 14 And more than ever believers were added to the Lord, multitudes

out" by trumpet or otherwise. When the *qāhāl* in question is a formal assembly for solemn religious purposes (e.g., on Sinai, Ebal, and Gerizim, at the dedication of the temple, or at Hezekiah's and Josiah's Passovers), the regular LXX translation is ἐκκλησία. Hence Israel as God's "called" community might be spoken of as "the *ecclēsia,* or church, of the Lord," and the use of the word by the Christians certainly implies the claim that they, rather than the Jews, were the true "people of God." The Jews appear to have preferred to use συναγωγή in the same sense; e.g., Ps. 74:2 in the LXX runs, "Remember thy *synagogue* which thou hast purchased and redeemed of old"—for which Paul significantly substitutes "church" when he echoes the verse (Acts 20:28). In short the Christians appropriated the word ἐκκλησία; over against the Jewish "synagogue" stands the Christian "church." As in the Pauline epistles, the use of the word "church" in Acts is threefold: (*a*) The whole church as a religious community; 20:28 comes nearest to this "catholic" use; cf. also 5:11; 9:31; I Cor. 10:32. (*b*) The local Christian body: e.g., 13:1, "the church at Antioch," or 11:26, where the local community at the same place is called "the church"; so both in Paul and Acts we have "the churches" with reference to the local bodies; this is much the most common usage. (*c*) The original use with reference to the people in actual assembly. So throughout I Cor. 14 ἐν ἐκκλησίᾳ almost means, as we would say, "in church," and in 14:23 κατ' ἐκκλησίαν may mean "at church," just as in 2:46 κατ' οἶκον means "at home." An extension of this usage would be the application of the word to the church building, as with the word "synagogue." A possible, but unlikely, example might be I Cor. 11:22, where οἰκίας (homes) and ἐκκλησίας (church building?) may be in antithesis.

12*b*-14. These verses are very obscure. The **all** who were **together in Solomon's Portico** are presumably the apostles and their immediate following, or possibly the whole Christian community, in which case **the rest** will be other interested spectators who still hesitated to identify themselves thus publicly with the Christians, even though **the people** in general **held them in high honor.** But vs. 14 seems a contradiction unless we suppose that **dared join them** means not merely to join the community but to

saints and sinners, let the sinners alone; do not try to weed them out, excommunicate them, ostracize them, brand them with a red letter. In the first place it would be a difficult procedure, for who is to determine who the black sheep are? Undoubtedly some are blacker than others, but are there any who in some secret place have no patch of blackness? Who can read the inner secrets of the heart? God alone can do that. Therefore let God do the work of separation.

Does this mean that the church is to lose its moral standards? Decidedly not. Before God all its members confess their sins. Toward him they all strive. From him they all derive their strength. In his presence they all share their mistakes and receive the confirmation of forgiveness, not only from God, but from the group. Strengthened by the fellowship, they go out after the black sheep as Jesus went out after the one that was lost.

12-16. ***The Apostles Grow in Power.***—In this description of the continued and increasing activity of the apostles there are two items which are especially important. The first is vs. 13: **And of the rest durst no man join himself to them.** (But see Exeg.) The danger of being a Christian! There were real dangers then, the danger of being put in jail, perhaps killed. There have been dangers in succeeding generations. The Christians in Germany during World War II were exposed to the danger of the concentra-

15 Insomuch that they brought forth the
sick into the streets, and laid *them* on beds
and couches, that at the least the shadow
of Peter passing by might overshadow some
of them.

16 There came also a multitude *out* of
the cities round about unto Jerusalem,
bringing sick folks, and them which were
vexed with unclean spirits: and they were
healed every one.

both of men and women, **15** so that they
even carried out the sick into the streets,
and laid them on beds and pallets, that as
Peter came by at least his shadow might
fall on some of them. **16** The people also
gathered from the towns around Jerusalem,
bringing the sick and those afflicted with
unclean spirits, and they were all healed.

---

co-operate in courageous public witness. It is suggested that **join them** (κολλᾶσθαι, "be cemented to") is a mistranslation of an Aramaic word meaning "interfere with."

15-16. So that: The connection is obviously with 12*a* rather than with the immediately preceding words, which suggests that the obscure intervening sentences may be a misplaced editorial summary. Note the close parallel between vss. 15-16 and Mark 6:56, which is part of a Marcan section omitted by Luke's Gospel (see on 1:7). For the healing power of Peter's shadow compare the faith in Paul's "handkerchiefs" (19:12).

---

tion camp. But in the United States there has seemed to be no great danger. Whether that state of affairs is due to the fact that the authorities now welcome Christianity, or whether it is due to the fact that Christians are no longer dangerous, is open to question. Most honest Christians would choose the latter explanation, and while they may rejoice that Christianity is no longer persecuted but accepted as the basis of our civilization, they regret that Christians have so merged themselves with the practices and standards of the secular world that they have ceased to be dangerous. Herod need no longer be "troubled."

There is, however, another kind of danger to which Christians are now exposed. It is the danger of being different. It is the danger so well known to the child whose parents insist that he wear clothes that are different from those of his friends. The Christian thinks differently about life and about the universe than does his materialist friend. He behaves differently toward Negroes and Jews, toward criminals and refugees. He has a different value for money. He goes to church, prays, gives more than he can afford, takes offense without revenge. All these things make him different, and the danger to which he is exposed is not the danger of the cell or the block; it is the danger of the laugh. He breaks the pattern of the gang and becomes the laughingstock of his crowd. That is bitter punishment, even for a man.

It should be said, however, that this text is not a strong one to stand on, at least from a critical point of view. Commentators do not agree on the meaning of the passage as a whole, and so we might be wise to pass by it and find the biblical ground for this theme elsewhere.

The second verse in this passage which attracts the eye is vs. 15: **They even carried out the sick into the streets, and laid them on beds and pallets, that as Peter came by at least his shadow might fall on some of them.** On its lowest level this is superstition. Undoubtedly there was a superstitious element involved in the popularity of Peter and the faith people had in his shadow. Yet without surrendering completely to sentimentalism, there is a real sense in which this sentence tells something about the unconscious and far-reaching influence of a man who is filled with the power of God. It describes another stage of the development of Peter. A man's influence is in direct proportion to his dedication. His radius increases as his center moves nearer to him who is the real center.

There are doctors who make you feel better just by being there. They radiate confidence. There are some people who, being near in time of trouble, take the sting out of grief. To look at some men is enough to turn you away from something cheap and vulgar. What is it that these people have? They have quietness and confidence. They are not proud, for they know that by themselves they can do nothing. Yet they are never fearful, for they know that they can do all things through him who strengthens them. They are channels of spiritual energy from which all the blocks have been removed. It is not a matter of education; Peter had none. It is not a matter of talent or genius; Peter had little of either. It is not a moral achievement; Peter had little to boast of when his record was examined. It is not a matter of power or prestige; Peter was a workingman just out of jail. It is a matter rather of association and contact. Peter was in contact with a source of unlimited vitality. He cleared the way for it and let

17 ¶ Then the high priest rose up, and all they that were with him, (which is the sect of the Sadducees,) and were filled with indignation,

17 But the high priest rose up and all who were with him, that is, the party of the Sad′du-cees, and filled with jealousy

4. Second Clash with Judaism (5:17-42)

The second encounter of the apostles with the Sanhedrin is very much like that recorded in 4:1-22, and, as we have seen, there is some reason for regarding the two accounts as "doublets." There is also a close resemblance to the account of Peter's escape from prison in 12:6-11, though the present narrative has none of the vivid circumstantial details of the later story. If we are dealing with doublets, then we should recall that the present account is, according to Harnack, from Jerusalem Source B, the less satisfactory of the two parallel Jerusalem sources. It is perhaps significant that the section contains what appears to be the worst historical error in Acts. In 5:36 Gamaliel refers to a rebellion of Theudas which, according to Josephus (*Antiquities* XX. 5), took place ten or twelve years after the time when he is speaking. He also makes it appear that Theudas rebelled at an earlier date than Judas, who in fact led a revolt in A.D. 6-8. This notorious anachronism has been made the basis for the argument that the author of Acts had read Josephus' *Antiquities;* for the latter, after narrating the rebellion of Theudas, goes on to tell of the subsequent execution of the sons of Judas. The two names thus occur in reverse order, and it is suggested that Luke's anachronism is due to a careless reading of Josephus. The importance of this is that it would necessitate a later date for Acts, as Josephus did not publish his *Antiquities* till about A.D. 93. Two other passages are quoted as proving Luke's dependence on Josephus—Luke 3:1; Acts 21:38. But it must be granted that all three passages "fall just short of demonstration," and in the case of the present passage "there is always the possibility that Luke and Josephus were using a common source in which the events were arranged in the order given by Josephus" (*Beginnings of Christianity,* II, 357). There is in fact no need to assume any acquaintance on Luke's part with the works of Josephus.

The historicity of Gamaliel's intervention has been commonly denied by radical critics, on account both of the anachronism in his speech and of the general line that he is alleged to have taken. But Gamaliel belonged to the more liberal school of Hillel, as opposed to the more rigid followers of Shammai; and it is quite likely that he may have counseled moderation for reasons of conviction as well as of policy. As a Pharisee he may well have had a bias in favor of the Christians as loyal observers of the law over against their Sadducean persecutors; and as a coolheaded statesman he may have believed that firm control would accomplish more than harsh repression, which might provoke a popular outbreak in support of a respected sect. It is entirely credible that Gamaliel, as indeed any other member of the Sanhedrin, may have taken up the attitude indicated by Luke. The Christians were in fact for some considerable time treated with just the kind of toleration that Gamaliel urged.

17. The party of the Sadducees: The Greek is ἡ οὖσα αἵρεσις—an odd use of the participle, for which cf. 13:1. Lake and Cadbury suspect a semitechnical usage, for which

it flow! Like a river it carried away the silt and debris, and like a river it made many a desert blossom like the rose.

17-26. ***The Prisoners Escape.***—This is the story of an escape. The Bible is filled with such stories. Indeed it might be called the story of one escape after another—Moses escapes from Pharaoh, Jeremiah escapes from the bottom of a well, Daniel escapes from the lion's den, Jesus escapes from the angry people of Nazareth, Paul and Silas escape from prison—so runs the story. It is the story of man's narrow escape from sin.

First, notice how the escape came about. It was not the accomplishment of the prisoners. They made no tunnels, picked no locks, bored no holes; they made no attempt to escape. **An angel of the Lord opened the prison doors.** Angels are not altogether familiar figures to contemporary audiences. They suggest something unreal and far-fetched. Such was not their original connotation. They were agents who

18 And laid their hands on the apostles, and put them in the common prison.

19 But the angel of the Lord by night opened the prison doors, and brought them forth, and said,

20 Go, stand and speak in the temple to the people all the words of this life.

18 they arrested the apostles and put them
in the common prison. 19 But at night an
angel of the Lord opened the prison doors
and brought them out and said, 20 "Go and
stand in the temple and speak to the peo-

---

there is some evidence in the papyri, of a participle "referring to what was existent at the place mentioned or the time mentioned, for which our English equivalent would be 'local' and 'current' respectively" (*Beginnings of Christianity,* IV, 56). Here the meaning would be "the local party of the Sadducees." Would this explain the famous crux in Eph. 1:1, which might be translated "to the local saints and believers in Christ Jesus"?

19-20. An angel sometimes appears in the O.T. as a quite impersonal agent of God's purpose, as when, e.g., "an angel" (pestilence) smites Sennacherib's army (II Kings 19:35; cf. II Sam. 24:16) or protects Daniel from the lions (Dan. 6:22). Here some providential intervention is suggested, perhaps the connivance of a jailer or the help of a friend (see also 8:26; 12:7, 23). **This Life:** a unique expression, perhaps like "the Way," used by Christians to describe their gospel.

---

carried out the will of God. What they indicate in a passage like this is the conviction that this remarkable escape was not a matter of chance or luck. It was a part of God's plan. Whether it was carried out by the ingenuity of a fellow Christian, or whether it was the result of the accidental failure of a lock, is beside the point. To the Christian mind of that day and of this there are no pure accidents. An escape like this one could not fairly be described as a circumstance of good luck. It was part of God's strategy.

More important than the identification of the angel is the assignment that the angel gave to the released prisoners: **Go and stand in the temple and speak to the people all the words of this Life.** No mean assignment, to go directly back to the place where the opposition was the hottest and begin once again with the same story. Christian preachers have seldom failed to speak, but they have not always had the courage or the wits to speak in the right places. It is one thing to talk about social injustice in a Christian pulpit where all the sentiment is in its favor, and quite another thing to talk about it in clubs and public meetings where the consequences of it are anathema.

This assignment of the mysterious angel might well be the assignment given to every Christian minister at the time of his ordination. It centers the attention, in the first place, upon the real center—the new life that is in Christ. That includes, of course, the life of Jesus himself, its amazing resources of energy, redoubled by his resurrection, and released to all men at all times by his ascension. It includes also the life as it becomes the life of individuals knit together in him. It is the life that is not disturbed by threats of disease and physical disaster. It is the life that is forever renewable, not yielding to defeat, or compromising with inferiority. It is the life for which all people are yearning, even though they do not know it.

What are the prisoners told to do about this life—argue about it, speculate about it, exhort the people to accept it? No. They are told to tell the people all about it—describe it, picture it, explain it, proclaim it. In that assignment is found one of the secrets of great Christian preaching and teaching. It is always a disclosure of some aspect of the reality of God in reference to some need or condition of man. It is a statement of fact, not a speculation about a fact. It is in the indicative mood, not the imperative mood of exhortation, or the subjunctive mood of condition. It is the unveiling of something unutterably great, the revelation of something that cannot be hidden.

In this lies the great strength of the religion of the Bible. It is religion in the indicative mood. "In the beginning God created the heaven and the earth" (Gen. 1:1); "The LORD *is* my light and my salvation" (Ps. 27:1); "Behold, all souls *are* mine" (Ezek. 18:4); "He that loseth his life . . . shall find it" (Matt. 10:39); "I am the way" (John 14:6); "And now abideth faith, hope, charity, these three" (I Cor. 13:13). There are, to be sure, commands and exhortations in the Bible. "Go, and do thou likewise" (Luke 10:37) is one of the famous ones. But it must be remembered that that moral exhortation is one line that comes at the end of a story written in the indicative, "A certain man went down from Jerusalem to Jericho, and fell among thieves" (Luke 10:30). If, after hear-

21 And when they heard *that,* they entered into the temple early in the morning,
and taught. But the high priest came, and
they that were with him, and called the
council together, and all the senate of the
children of Israel, and sent to the prison
to have them brought.
22 But when the officers came, and
found them not in the prison, they returned, and told,
23 Saying, The prison truly found we
shut with all safety, and the keepers standing without before the doors: but when
we had opened, we found no man within.
24 Now when the high priest and the
captain of the temple and the chief priests
heard these things, they doubted of them
whereunto this would grow.
25 Then came one and told them, saying, Behold, the men whom ye put in prison
are standing in the temple, and teaching
the people.
26 Then went the captain with the officers, and brought them without violence:
for they feared the people, lest they should
have been stoned.
27 And when they had brought them,
they set *them* before the council: and the
high priest asked them,

ple all the words of this Life." 21 And when
they heard this, they entered the temple
at daybreak and taught.
Now the high priest came and those who
were with him and called together the
council and all the senate of Israel, and sent
to the prison to have them brought. 22 But
when the officers came, they did not find
them in the prison, and they returned and
reported, 23 "We found the prison securely
locked and the sentries standing at the
doors, but when we opened it we found no
one inside." 24 Now when the captain of
the temple and the chief priests heard these
words, they were much perplexed about
them, wondering what this would come to.
25 And some one came and told them,
"The men whom you put in prison are
standing in the temple and teaching the
people." 26 Then the captain with the
officers went and brought them, but without violence, for they were afraid of being
stoned by the people.
27 And when they had brought them,
they set them before the council. And the

---

21. **The council and all the senate** are one and the same body, the Jewish Sanhedrin. **Senate** is an older name which well suits the archaic language, **the senate of the children of Israel.** It is, however, just possible that Luke thought that there was a deliberative body of "elders" in addition to the "council" or "Sanhedrin" as the judicial body.

---

ing it, men were inclined to be more inclusive in their neighborliness, they were so moved not by the one imperative line at the end, but by the revelation of true neighborliness that the story set forth.

Preachers cannot afford to overlook this. One of the reasons why contemporary preaching is so far below par is that so much of it has deteriorated into moral nagging. Most sermons are primarily concerned with telling people what they ought to do, rather than with telling them who God is and who they are. Preachers have sold their birthright as town crier, and degenerated into petty officers of the Watch and Ward Society. Not only do they forego their succession in the biblical line of the prophets when they descend to incessant exhortation; they lose whatever effectiveness they might have. For it is a well-known and observed fact that you cannot make a man good by telling him that he ought to be good. The fact is that the more you tell him, the more he is determined to resist it. The only way you can make a man good is by holding something before him which in its irresistible goodness draws him as the beauty of the rising sun draws all men to itself.

A piano recital by a great artist is not an attempt to make people like music by telling them they ought to. It is a performance of great music which, falling upon ears that are open to it, becomes a standard by which all poor, vulgar music is judged, and an ideal toward which the listener henceforth strives with more unceasing effort.

What would happen to most sermons if every subjunctive and imperative were crossed out, every "let us" and "must" eliminated? In many cases there would not be a great deal left. There are times, of course, when specific application of principles to actual situations must be made, and the preacher is often in a

28 Saying, Did not we straitly command you that ye should not teach in this name? and, behold, ye have filled Jerusalem with your doctrine, and intend to bring this man's blood upon us.

29 ¶ Then Peter and the *other* apostles answered and said, We ought to obey God rather than men.

30 The God of our fathers raised up Jesus, whom ye slew and hanged on a tree.

high priest questioned them, 28 saying, "We
strictly charged you not to teach in this
name, yet here you have filled Jerusalem
with your teaching and you intend to bring
this man's blood upon us." 29 But Peter
and the apostles answered, "We must obey
God rather than men. 30 The God of our
fathers raised Jesus whom you killed by

28-29. We strictly charged: i.e., referring to 4:18, as **we must obey God** repeats 4:19. Rackham well compares Antigone's words in Sophocles' tragedy (*Antigone* 453-55; tr. E. H. Plumptre):

> Nor did I deem thy edicts strong enough,
> That thou, a mortal man, should'st over-pass
> The unwritten laws of God that know not change.

30-32. The gist of Peter's speech is exactly the same as in the parallel in 4:8 ff.: the Jews are responsible for the crime of crucifying one whom God has vindicated by raising him from the dead and exalting him to the highest honor. **Killed:** The unusual Greek word has perhaps a semislang flavor, for which cf. 26:21; Lake and Cadbury translate "did

---

position to stir the consciences of his people. But the conscience must be awakened before it can be stirred into action, and it is the revelation of some incontrovertible and powerful fact which, like the rising sun, alone has the power to awaken.

29-32. ***Peter Speaks Again.***—Peter, like most preachers, had one sermon; the variations were different, but the theme was forever the same—Jesus is Lord. This particular time when he preached the sermon, he introduced it with a striking line, **We must obey God rather than men.** There are some things that men do because they want to, or because they like to, but there are other things that they do because they must. Life is a mixture of choices and compulsions, and of the compulsions there are two sorts. There is the compulsion that a man is unable to resist, like the muzzle of a gun at his back; and there is the compulsion that he is unwilling to resist, like the compulsion of the dawn. The moral compulsions of life, like the one that fell upon Peter and his companions, belong to the second group, the compulsions without guns.

A great many times we are able to obey man and God at the same time; at least there is no conflict in our loyalty. When we pay our bills, for instance, we are obeying the laws of man, and at the same time we are obeying the moral laws of God. When we obey the orders of a superior in business, the chances are good that we can do so without violating any divine order. The trouble comes when men tell us to do one thing and God tells us to do the opposite. Then what? That is what happened in Peter's case. Men said, "Keep still." God said, "Speak out." Peter could not do both; he had to choose one or the other. He chose to do what God said, regardless of the consequences.

Such a conflict in loyalties is one of the most testing and straining experiences that can come to a man. A doctor, for example, is offered a partnership in a large, rich practice. It will take him away from the simple people whom he has served and who have trusted him. It will put money in his pockets, but seldom any joy in his heart. His ambitious wife says, "Take it." God, the God who speaks through his conscience, his sense of values, his appreciation of human life and its need, that God says, "Let it alone." He is loyal to the wife he loves and he is loyal to the God he knows, but he cannot obey them both. Or consider a man who is engaged as a teacher in a college. He is loyal to the college and the officers who operate it. He is also loyal to the subject which he teaches. He honors its integrity and dignity. When the officers of the college request him to adapt his course to fit some particular political preference, to do which would be to violate the truth as he understands it, he is torn between two conflicting loyalties. The college says one thing; God says another.

In dealing with such conflicts it must be understood that in many cases they are more complicated than they appear. They often involve not two loyalties, but a whole chain of

31 Him hath God exalted with his right
hand *to be* a Prince and a Saviour, for to
give repentance to Israel, and forgiveness
of sins.
32 And we are his witnesses of these
things; and *so is* also the Holy Ghost, whom
God hath given to them that obey him.

hanging him on a tree. 31 God exalted him
at his right hand as Leader and Savior, to
give repentance to Israel and forgiveness
of sins. 32 And we are witnesses to these
things, and so is the Holy Spirit whom God
has given to those who obey him."

away with." **Hanging him on a tree;** cf. Deut. 21:22 and see on 10:39. **Leader:** The same word translated in 3:15 as "the Author of life." **To these things:** Literally "words," probably one of Luke's deliberate Hebraisms, based on the similar use of the Hebrew word *dābhār;* cf. 10:37. **So is the Holy Spirit,** i.e., as demonstrated by the deeds of the apostles.

loyalties. For instance the college professor has a wife and children. If he refuses to comply with the request of the authorities, he will probably lose his job. If he were the only person involved, he would gladly make the sacrifice. But what about the children? Has he any right to make them suffer and pay the price of his compulsions? What about the students in the college who look to him for leadership and will be left high and dry if he is removed? All these questions, and many more, bear upon the issue, and an expositor must give clear evidence that he appreciates them before he insists upon a plan of high-minded action.

One of the things for a man to remember when he finds himself caught in a vise of conflicting loyalties is that he is not the first to be there. It is the price men pay for their moral nature and the noblest men have paid the highest price. Beasts go through no such torment. Jesus paid the highest of all. He was a Palestinian Jew. He loved the land and the people. But when the leaders of the people refused to face facts, when they hid behind the skirts of their own privilege, when they rallied around the banners of national pride and personal glory, he had to make a choice. The people said, "Be one of us." God said, "Be my Son." Jesus obeyed God, not men.

In the trying days of World War II Martin Niemöller faced the same conflict. The Nazi government told him to preach one thing, and God told him to preach another. Eight years in a prison camp was the price he paid for obeying God rather than man. Not many of us will measure up to that, nor will we necessarily be called upon to do so. Our conflicting compulsions will be less spectacular, but not thereby any the less significant.

It is good also for a man to remember the particular status in which being a Christian places him. He is something like a colonist. A colony is a group of people who live in a community to which they do not altogether belong. They speak the language of the community, obey its laws, pay its rents and taxes, enjoy its rights and privileges, but their ultimate loyalty is always somewhere outside it, back home. So Christians live in this world community. They take their part and place, they pay their dues, they reap their harvest of rewards, but they never altogether and completely belong here. They have a loyalty outside that is above and beyond every local loyalty.

A Christian therefore cannot pledge his ultimate allegiance to the flag because above the flag is the cross of Christ, and the flag and the nation for which it stands must in the last analysis be judged by the cross of Christ and by the principles for which he died. He cannot commit himself without reservation to a political party, for the party allegiance always stands second to the Christian allegiance.

Such a position would be difficult indeed were it not for the fact that the colonist can rely on outside supplies. He is not entirely dependent upon the resources of the community. Help is always coming from home. Likewise Christians can rely on fresh supplies from outside sources. Help is always coming from Home. Find the man who has faced his conflicting compulsions squarely; find the man who has been willing to obey God rather than men, no matter what the cost, and you will find a man who has been wonderfully strengthened for the deed. Let the Nazi government lock the Lutheran pastor in a cell, cut him off from the people and from his church. They could stop all commerce between him and the outside world, but they could not stop the flow of supplies that came in from outside. He had a Bible with him and as he read to the prisoners walking above his window, out of sight but not out of hearing, fresh supplies of God's power and joy poured in from Home. Whenever a man has set out to obey God, even though it meant disobeying men and women whom he had every natural inclination to please, God has kept him and his family somehow—from death or in death.

33 ¶ When they heard *that,* they were cut *to the heart,* and took counsel to slay them.

34 Then stood there up one in the council, a Pharisee, named Gamaliel, a doctor of the law, had in reputation among all the people, and commanded to put the apostles forth a little space;

35 And said unto them, Ye men of Israel, take heed to yourselves what ye intend to do as touching these men.

36 For before these days rose up Theudas, boasting himself to be somebody; to whom a number of men, about four hundred, joined themselves: who was slain; and all, as many as obeyed him, were scattered, and brought to nought.

37 After this man rose up Judas of Galilee in the days of the taxing, and drew away much people after him: he also perished; and all, *even* as many as obeyed him, were dispersed.

33 When they heard this they were enraged and wanted to kill them. 34 But a
Pharisee in the council named Ga-ma'li-el,
a teacher of the law, held in honor by all
the people, stood up and ordered the men
to be put outside for a while. 35 And he
said to them, "Men of Israel, take care
what you do with these men. 36 For before
these days Theu'das arose, giving himself
out to be somebody, and a number of men,
about four hundred, joined him; but he
was slain and all who followed him were
dispersed and came to nothing. 37 After him
Judas the Galilean arose in the days of
the census and drew away some of the people after him; he also perished, and all

34. **Gamaliel:** The first of the famous rabbis of that name, he was a descendant of Hillel and is named in the traditional list as one of the successive "presidents of the council." His reputation is later attested by the saying, "Since Rabban Gamaliel the elder died, there has been no more reverence for the law" (quoted in Emil Schürer, *A History of the Jewish People in the Time of Jesus Christ* [New York: Charles Scribner's Sons, 1891], Div. II, Vol. I, p. 364). According to 22:3, he was Paul's teacher.

36-37. **Theudas:** There is no evidence of any Theudas other than the rebel mentioned by Josephus as having risen some years later than Gamaliel's speech. The argument is that if Jesus is, like Theudas and Judas, a mere impostor, his cause will as

33-42. ***Gamaliel Intercedes.***—A series of expositions might be written on the minor characters in the Acts of the Apostles. In such a series Gamaliel would occupy a prominent place. To call him a minor character is to say that a man's greatness is finally measured by the company that he keeps. Gamaliel, measured by the group of lawyers with whom he associated, is a giant. Measured by Peter and Paul, Stephen and Barnabas, and by the movement of which they were the spearhead, he is a minor character. He belonged to the wrong group. It behooves men and women to watch not only their personal development and cultivation, but also the company in which they travel. Gamaliel and Peter, think of the contrast! Gamaliel clearly more highly educated than Peter, more cultivated, more talented. And yet Peter is the torch that burns through the years and Gamaliel the glow of a dying ember. Gamaliel was moving with the current that had run its course. Peter was moving with the rushing stream of a new life!

Gamaliel, however, is not to be overlooked, nor is his contribution to the occasion to be minimized. He is a personification of the elder statesman. His counsel is one of wise restraint. Do nothing for the time being. Wait. See what happens. If the movement is bad, God will destroy it; if it is good, no one will be able to destroy it. He is a perfect instance of the moderating influence of the judicial mind.

Gamaliel and his kind might be called the well-balanced people. They see both sides of a situation. They are able to stand apart from it and look at it with dispassion. They have an inner serenity that quiets many a troubled sea. They know how to wait. They have a deep-rooted trust in the way things work out. They are not hotheaded, nor are they apathetic. They care, but they care quietly and soberly. How many a family quarrel has been stopped by the one who wanted to wait and see how things work out!

There are times when such a policy looks very much like appeasement. It often is the easiest way out—to do nothing. But there are other times when it is the only thing to do,

38 And now I say unto you, Refrain from these men, and let them alone: for if this counsel or this work be of men, it will come to nought:

39 But if it be of God, ye cannot overthrow it; lest haply ye be found even to fight against God.

40 And to him they agreed: and when they had called the apostles, and beaten *them,* they commanded that they should not speak in the name of Jesus, and let them go.

41 ¶ And they departed from the presence of the council, rejoicing that they were counted worthy to suffer shame for his name.

42 And daily in the temple, and in every house, they ceased not to teach and preach Jesus Christ.

6 And in those days, when the number of the disciples was multiplied, there arose a murmuring of the Grecians against

who followed him were scattered. 38 So in
the present case I tell you, keep away from
these men and let them alone; for if this
plan or this undertaking is of men, it will
fail; 39 but if it is of God, you will not be
able to overthrow them. You might even
be found opposing God!"
40 So they took his advice, and when
they had called in the apostles, they beat
them and charged them not to speak in
the name of Jesus, and let them go. 41 Then
they left the presence of the council, rejoicing that they were counted worthy to
suffer dishonor for the name. 42 And every
day in the temple and at home they did
not cease teaching and preaching Jesus as
the Christ.

6 Now in these days when the disciples
were increasing in number, the Hellen-

---

speedily collapse. The **census** in question in connection with Judas is that made by Quirinius in A.D. 6, and is not that of Luke 2:1, though there is a question that Luke may have confused them. **Judas,** according to Josephus (*Jewish War* II. 8. 1), was the leader of a much more serious uprising than is here implied and his followers, so far from being completely exterminated, became the origin of the "Zealots," who in turn were largely responsible for the movement which eventually led to the great rebellion and the fall of Jerusalem in A.D. 70.

41-42. For the phrase **the name,** without qualification, cf. the Greek of III John 7. **Jesus as the Christ:** Alternatively, we may have here the use of the double name—"telling the good news of Christ Jesus."

D. The Beginnings of Hellenistic Christianity (6:1–8:40)

1. Appointment of the Seven (6:1-7)

At this point a new factor enters into the history of the church—the growth of a Hellenistic as distinct from a purely Hebrew Christianity. There are indications, too, that Luke begins here to draw upon a new source. There is a definite break with what

---

for the simple reason that God has not yet made his will clear. Some people are ready to condemn a movement when it has hardly begun. Some were ready to bury the New Deal before it had been born. The Gamaliels, on the other hand, said, "Give it a chance. Wait and see what happens. It may be the way out. If it is not, it will soon collapse. If it is, we had better be on the right side."

Gamaliel and Peter represent two contrasting temperaments. Peter is hotheaded, ready to plunge into action, impatient with the cool philosophy of thought, blind to everything except the gospel. Gamaliel, on the other hand, is restrained, moderate, slow to act, circumspect, balancing one view against another, seeing all sides of the question, tolerant, fair, honest. The truth is that we need both temperaments in a world like ours. The Peters get things done, while the Gamaliels see to it that certain things are not done. The Peters are the leaders of great movements, while the Gamaliels pave the way for the greater ones to travel.

Within the individual there is room for both accents. Wise is the man who understands himself well enough to know whether he is a Peter or a Gamaliel, and then is humble enough to make friends with his opposite.

6:1–7:60. ***The First Martyr.***—Peter and John got in trouble again and again. Stephen lost his life. He is the first Christian martyr. His story is the story of thousands who have cared

the Hebrews, because their widows were neglected in the daily ministration.

ists murmured against the Hebrews because their widows were neglected in the daily

precedes. **The daily distribution,** though not previously alluded to, is referred to as if familiar, presumably because it has been mentioned earlier in the source; and the whole passage rests upon a fundamental distinction between "Hebrew" and "Hellenist" Christians that has not previously been drawn but now is taken for granted without explanation. Harnack in his analysis calls this the "Antiochene" source, and believes that it originated from a locality where there was special interest in the development of Hellenistic Christianity. He traces this source in 6:1–8:4, with which he links up 11:19-30—the first spread of Christianity to Antioch and district—and 12:25–15:35—Paul's mission from Antioch on his first tour and his return to Antioch. It is interesting, as evidence that this is an Antioch rather than a Jerusalem source, that none of Torrey's examples of possible mistranslation from Aramaic occur in these sections. Torrey claims an Aramaic origin for the whole of the first part of Acts; but his evidence is much weaker here than elsewhere.

The **Hellenists** (RSV) or **Grecians** (KJV) in Acts have always been regarded as Greek-speaking *Jews* in contrast with the "Hellenes," who are *Greeks* by race and upbringing. This interpretation, though almost certainly right, depends entirely upon the context and not on the intrinsic meaning of the word, which signifies simply "one who Grecizes" either in language or in habits. Here the **Hellenists** are contrasted with the **Hebrews;** and as the latter word refers to race rather than to language, the Hellenists here (if they are in fact Jews) are perhaps not "Greek-speaking Jews," but rather Jews who adopted Greek customs in contrast with the more conservative Hebrews. Cadbury (*Beginnings of Christianity,* V, 59 ff.) in an important note argues that the word "Hellenists" refers not to Jews but to Gentiles, and is simply an alternative for "Hellenes." He points out that the other two passages in which "Hellenists" are mentioned are (*a*) 9:29, where there is nothing to indicate who is meant, and (*b*) 11:20, where the context makes it plain that pure Gentile Greeks are in view, and the best-attested reading is undoubtedly "Hellenists" (Ἑλληνιστάς with ℵ B), though most editors adopt "Greeks" (Ἕλληνες with $\aleph^2$ A D). His conclusion is that the word "Hellenists" really refers to Gentile Greeks; Luke loves verbal variations, and while in the latter half of the book "Hellenes" or "Greeks" is used, in the first twelve chapters only "Hellenists" is found. But in the present passage the insuperable obstacle to Cadbury's view would be so early a mention of Gentile Christians without any comment on this innovation. Our author gives so much attention to the case of Cornelius, as the first Gentile conversion and a turning point in Christian missions, that it is very hard to believe that, as Cadbury himself puts it, he could "introduce a reference to Gentile Christians so early in his story and so casually."

6:1-3. The daily distribution: This may be a reference to the public assistance given by means of the agape or common religious meal. The case of **widows** without legal

less about life itself than they have cared about Christ. In days like these, when Christianity is no longer part of man's inherited pattern, and when the opposition to it is not only implied but also increasingly expressed, the figure of Stephen is one around which people are ready to rally.

1-6. ***How He Got His Start.***—Stephen was drawn out of the crowd to meet an emergency which had arisen in the Christian community. As the community grew, new situations which had not been anticipated developed. All growing things do likewise—plants, children, institutions. In this case it was a question of administering relief. Christians, as well as their Jewish forebears, took their social responsibilities seriously, and the need of an individual was the responsibility of the group. As the size of the group increased and the work of the preaching and teaching ministry expanded, the relief work was neglected. Complaints were sent in by the overlooked widows. The clergy have never since been free of complaint. Yet while many complaints are little more than bids for attention and sympathy, some are like the goads which start things moving. Blessed are these widows whose complaints started Stephen moving on his valiant way!

2 Then the twelve called the multitude of the disciples *unto them,* and said, It is not reason that we should leave the word of God, and serve tables.

3 Wherefore, brethren, look ye out among you seven men of honest report, full of the Holy Ghost and wisdom, whom we may appoint over this business.

4 But we will give ourselves continually to prayer, and to the ministry of the word.

5 ¶ And the saying pleased the whole multitude: and they chose Stephen, a man full of faith and of the Holy Ghost, and Philip, and Prochorus, and Nicanor, and Timon, and Parmenas, and Nicolas a proselyte of Antioch;

distribution. 2 And the twelve summoned
the body of the disciples and said, "It is
not right that we should give up preaching
the word of God to serve tables. 3 Therefore,
brethren, pick out from among you seven
men of good repute, full of the Spirit and
of wisdom, whom we may appoint to this
duty. 4 But we will devote ourselves to
prayer and to the ministry of the word."
5 And what they said pleased the whole
multitude, and they chose Stephen, a man
full of faith and of the Holy Spirit, and
Philip, and Proch'o-rus, and Ni-ca'nor, and
Timon, and Par'me-nas, and Nic-o-la'us, a

---

protection was particularly hard, and the church quickly copied the Jewish custom of providing funds for their relief. Later the "widows" appear to have been a recognized body with their names on a roll (I Tim. 5:9). **Tables** is usually understood as referring to dining tables; but it is possible that the money-changer's table is meant, with reference to the general financial administration of the community. **Pick out from among you:** It is the congregation which makes the selection, while the apostles set them apart. Curiously Codex Vaticanus (B) reads, "Let *us* choose, brethren, seven men from among you," which may imply, though not necessarily, that the apostles made the selection also.

5. Of **Prochorus, Nicanor, Timon,** and **Parmenas** we know nothing but legend, save that Prochorus is traditionally the writer of the Prochoran Acts of John, and, according to Byzantine art, John dictated the Fourth Gospel to him. **Nicolaus** was traditionally the founder of the heretical sect of the Nicolaitans found at Ephesus and Pergamum (Rev. 2:6, 15). **Antioch** is here mentioned for the first time, and perhaps indicates the interest of the source-compiler in that city.

For Stephen was one of the seven appointed to do this particular work. Here is the beginning of a specialized ministry to perform specific functions. It is the way things develop. They do not spring full grown from the brow of a god. They begin like a seed and then they grow. New situations call forth new devices, new provisions, new organizations, new methods, and above all, new men. Stephen was one of those men.

That is the way that most men who live significant lives get their start. They step forth out of the crowd to deal with an unexpected situation. Lincoln did not push his way to the White House. He was drawn there by events to which he responded positively. Lesser men have done the same thing only in a less spectacular way. They have not sat down and brooded over the question, "What shall I do with my life?" They have felt some claim laid upon them and they have responded to that. It may have been some hidden thing which the public will never know, like the bearing of some family burden. Yet there it is, unexpected, undesired, but claiming a man, and as he rises to meet it something new in him is born. In one sense every man is a man of his times. The times do not make the man, but like the prompter, they give him his cue.

Of course there is the other side of the picture. The man must have in himself the raw material which will meet the situation. Stephen evidently had it in abundance. He was a young man **full of faith and of the Holy Spirit.** He met the requirements of the office which provided for **men of good repute, full of the Spirit and of wisdom.** And above all, he shows later on how closely he had followed the Master's life; so closely that his trial and death bring back memories of the trial and death of Jesus. It was not only an external pattern and form that was imitated; it was the spirit of Jesus—the spirit of forgiveness and trust—that was re-created.

So Stephen got his start. A young man of unusual gifts and talents, he responded to the pressure of God's purpose moving through the events of his day. The growing church faced new and growing opportunities. Men were needed. Stephen was such a man.

6 Whom they set before the apostles: and when they had prayed, they laid *their* hands on them.

proselyte of Antioch. 6 These they set before the apostles, and they prayed and laid their hands upon them.

---

6. Laid their hands upon them: The "laying on of hands" usually symbolizes the bestowal of the Holy Spirit, which at the very beginning seems to have been connected with this rite rather than with baptism (see 19:5-6 and on 8:17). The rite is taken over from the O.T., where it symbolizes the establishment of some vital connection between two persons, and the transference of some power or responsibility from the one to the other. Thus Moses, when appointing Joshua his successor, laid his hands on him, by which act he "put some of his honor upon him" (Num. 27:23, 20). So the apostles in Acts frequently do in healing, confirming, and ordaining. Here the bestowal of some special *charisma* is not necessarily implied, for the seven were already men **full of the Spirit** (vs. 3). The rite is the formal sign of appointment to office, as it was in the admission of new members of the Sanhedrin. It would be dangerous, as does Rackham, to base on this verse a full doctrine of apostolic succession. More truly, says Chrysostom, "The hand of man is laid on, but all is the work of God; and it is his hand that touches the head of the candidate, if he is rightly ordained."

The question why the seven were appointed, and what was their function, raises a somewhat difficult problem. Evidently a certain tension had arisen between the "Hebrew" Jews of Jerusalem and the "Hellenists" who had returned to the capital after a period of residence abroad. Possibly the latter felt that they were being treated with unfair discrimination as outsiders. If such was the case, the reason would probably be mere local prejudice rather than any suspicion of their religious orthodoxy. For, as evidence of the Hellenists' loyalty to Jewish law and worship, it is noteworthy that the attack upon Stephen was instigated, not by Palestinian, but by Hellenist Jews. All the seven have Greek names, and they were evidently appointed in some way to safeguard the interests of the Hellenists. But what were their functions? There are three possible views: (*a*) They have traditionally been regarded as the first "deacons." Luke implies that they were to be responsible for the fair distribution of alms. He does not actually call them "deacons" (διάκονοι); but in connection with them he uses the abstract noun "distribution" (literally **ministration** or "service"; διακονία) and the verb "serve" (διακονεῖν); and as by the time that Luke wrote there did in fact exist an order with the name of deacons, the use of these cognate words at least suggests that Luke considers the seven to be deacons. The difficulty is that nowhere in the N.T. are any of the seven referred to as such; nor is there any evidence that there ever were in Jerusalem deacons with functions like those of the deacons whom we meet toward the end of the first century. Whereas, according to Luke, the seven were appointed to be in charge of financial administration, the deacon, as we know him from Phil. 1:1; I Tim. 3:8 ff.; the Didache; and Clement, is commonly mentioned alongside the bishop, and appears to have been his assistant generally in the conduct of the Eucharist, and the ordering of discipline, as well as in the organization of alms. (*b*) It has been suggested that the seven were the first "elders" of the Jerusalem church. Later in Acts "apostles and elders" are mentioned as the important personages, and in 11:30 it is stated that Antioch sent alms to "the elders," as if the latter had charge of the duties entrusted here to the seven. But it is most unlikely that as early as this "elders" would be officially "appointed" and "ordained." Rather would they naturally assume leadership in virtue of personal prestige and larger experience in the faith. Nor can we explain why all the first elders at Jerusalem should be Hellenists. (*c*) It is noticeable that the seven comport themselves not as administrators but as missionaries, and Stephen and Philip in particular at once assume an almost apostolic prominence in aggressive evangelism. Hence it is perhaps more likely that the seven were, as Chrysostom says, "neither presbyters nor deacons," but rather held a unique office parallel to the apostolate. The motive for their appointment lay in a Hebrew-Hellenist disharmony which the matter of practical administration merely brought to a head.

7 And the word of God increased; and
the number of the disciples multiplied in
Jerusalem greatly; and a great company
of the priests were obedient to the faith.
8 And Stephen, full of faith and power,
did great wonders and miracles among the
people.

7 And the word of God increased; and
the number of the disciples multiplied
greatly in Jerusalem, and a great many of
the priests were obedient to the faith.
8 And Stephen, full of grace and power,
did great wonders and signs among the

Probably the Hellenists were discovering that their own view of the gospel was not quite that of the Palestinian brethren, and they wished apostles of their own who would represent it. Thus the title "the seven" corresponds to the title "the twelve," and the names of the seven are given in full like those of the apostles. The distinction between the seven and the twelve was one of sphere rather than of function. The seven were to be for the Hellenists exactly what the twelve were for the Hebrews. If Luke has obscured this, has put all the emphasis on the minor question of the "distribution," and made it to appear that the seven were intended to be mere administrators subordinate to the twelve, it is perhaps because he habitually tends to minimize any cleavage between the more Judaistic and the more liberal elements in the church.

7. **Multiplied greatly** (σφόδρα): According to Torrey, this represents the same Aramaic word (*laḥ^{a}dhā*), correctly translated here, as was incorrectly translated by ἐπὶ τὸ αὐτὸ in 2:47. We have in this note the only trace in Acts of any interest in Christianity on the part of the **priests.**

2. Story of Stephen (6:8–8:3)

Some editors have detected a certain incoherence in the telling of the story of Stephen. The connection between the **wonders and signs** in vs. 8 and the disputation that follows in vs. 9 is not very clear; it looks as if the source rather may have told how Stephen carried his aggressive missionary message into the Hellenistic synagogues and thus aroused an acrimonious debate which resulted in his arrest. Furthermore there are curious repetitions in the narrative: (*a*) The charge against Stephen is twice stated, the substance of vss. 9-11 being repeated in vss. 12-14; (*b*) the stoning of Stephen is also described twice, in 7:54-58*a* and in 7:58*b*-60. These doublets suggest that the story may be derived from two sources, possibly reflecting two variant traditions, which have been somewhat infelicitously combined. According to one (6:9-11 *plus* 7:54-58*a*) Stephen was summarily lynched by an angry mob; according to the other (6:12–7:53, *plus* 7:58*b*-60) he was tried, possibly somewhat informally, and executed by the Sanhedrin. Lake points out that one can pass from 6:8-11 to 7:54 ff. without being conscious of any break in the narrative. He is inclined to think that the whole speech, which bears very little relation to the charges brought against Stephen, is a free composition by the author—who considers that Stephen's death was due to the Sanhedrin—inserted into an earlier narrative which related that he was stoned by a mob (*Beginnings of Christianity,* II, 149-50). Even without accepting any such theory of "doublets," it may be admitted that the speech looks like an insertion. Note that the ecstasy of 6:15 reappears in 7:55. If the latter verse is read to follow immediately after 7:1, Stephen's only answer to the high priest, like Jesus', would be a reference to a theophany of the glorified Christ (Mark 14:62)—a most suggestive and impressive parallel. One cannot but wonder whether the story was not told thus in Luke's original source. Quite apart from the acceptance of any one of the

---

8. ***How He Developed.***—Commentators do not agree on the exact state of affairs which existed in the early ministry of the church as it is described in this chapter. Whether or not the seven who were elected to administer relief were expected to confine themselves to that ministry while the disciples did the preaching and praying, we do not know. (See Exeg. on vs. 6.) At any rate, Stephen, according to the account in the Acts, did not spend all his time distributing relief funds. In fact that aspect of his ministry is never again mentioned. Rather he is described as an eloquent teacher and wonder-worker. **Stephen, full of grace and power, did**

complicated theories of source reconstruction, the problem of how and why Stephen was put to death remains, and is discussed below.

Concerning the authenticity of Stephen's speech, it is particularly difficult to reach a clear judgment. At first sight it appears largely irrelevant. No direct answer is made to the charges brought against him. Instead, a lengthy narrative of God's gracious dealings with Israel is followed by illustrations of the ingratitude with which Israel requited God's goodness. But this criticism of the old economy is not balanced by a single word about the new Christian economy which is to supplant it; nor is there any mention of the name of Jesus Christ. The conclusion in vss. 51 ff. is singularly surprising and abrupt. Why should Stephen find the climax of his people's history in the building of Solomon's temple? And having done so, why does he abruptly launch into invective without any attempt to give a reasoned answer to his accusers? It is easy to say that "he was cut short and his defense left incomplete" (Rackham). If he really made so irrelevant a speech, the wonder rather is how the court could have allowed him to run on so long. Moreover, though the speech professes to be a summary of O.T. history, there are a surprising number of variations from and of additions to the O.T. record. Hence most modern editors are unable to accept the speech as Stephen's own. On the other hand Lake and Cadbury comment: "The absence of any allusion to the Judaistic controversy seems to exclude any theory which would make the speech the composition of one who had lived through that controversy in the company of Paul, and was writing with a view to the situation of the Christian Church of the period. . . . The general character of the speech seems to fit in very well with the theory that it represents either a good tradition as to what Stephen really did say, or at least what a very early Christian, not of the Pauline school, would have wished him to say. All observation shows that religious or political pioneers when brought into court never attempt to rebut the accusations brought against them, but use the opportunity for making a partisan address" (*The Beginnings of Christianity,* ed. F. J. Foakes Jackson and Kirsopp Lake [London: Macmillan & Co.; New York: The Macmillan Co., 1920-33], IV, 69-70).

Had Stephen lived he would have ranked with the greatest of the apostles. His career can hardly have lasted more than a few months, or even weeks, and he is the ideal type of man who "being made perfect in a little while fulfills long years" (Wisd. Sol. 4:13). Of his origin we know nothing, save that he was probably a Hellenistic Jew from abroad —possibly from Cyrene or Alexandria, if the name of the synagogue in which he was attacked provides any clue. It has been noted that there is a slight flavor of Alexandrian culture in his speech; e.g., the word "wisdom" occurs four times and nowhere else in Acts; and men from Cyrene were of course also prominent in the early community— Simon who carried the cross (Mark 15:21), and Lucius the prophet of Antioch (13:1). Stephen's significance is that his preaching in the Hellenistic synagogues made it evident that Christianity was something more than just a new Jewish sect, and that its spread would involve danger to the law of Moses. He drove in the first wedge between Judaism and Christianity and made possible the emergence of a distinctively Christian church. Hence the attack upon him by his fellow Hellenist Jews. The accusation must have had some basis in fact; but 6:13 is almost certainly a misrepresentation. Had this been a true charge, Stephen must have earned the disapproval of the Christian community itself,

---

great wonders . . . among the people. Without doing violence to the facts as they are set forth in the Acts, it is fair to find here the development of a man's powers. He rose to meet a situation. He met it and went miles beyond it. The situation was only the prick of circumstance to start him going. When he had done the task for which he was specifically chosen, he did not assume that he had finished. He had only begun. The emergency is often only the door through which a man steps onto a way that leads out and over the horizon.

Jesus began as a teacher in the local synagogue. He ended as the Savior of the world. Stephen began as a server of tables. He ended as the first Christian martyr and the type of all who were to follow. Paul began as a man struck blind on the Damascus road. He ended as the man who turned the world upside down. Wesley began as a single convert who saw the

9 ¶ Then there arose certain of the synagogue, which is called *the synagogue* of the

people. 9 Then some of those who belonged
to the synagogue of the Freedmen (as it

---

which was still wholly loyal to the Jewish faith, and of this there is no trace. Even if we accept the speech as authentic, it would be a mistake to interpret even vss. 48-50 as an attack on the whole temple system as such. The sting of the speech is not in vss. 48-50 but in vss. 51-53, and Stephen's main point is that the real violators of God's law are not the Christians but their accusers and the unconverted Jews in general. Hence the force of vss. 48-50 is not so much that God is to be worshiped only in spirit and that temple worship should be abolished; it is rather that mere external worship is not enough if the hearts of the worshipers are turned away to other gods. Stephen is repeating a thought constantly voiced by the prophets, not launching a new Gentile-Christian anti-Jewish polemic. Probably Stephen was arrested, not because of any definite attack on the law and the temple, but because he represented a more liberal type of Judaism, which emphasized the moral rather than the ceremonial side of the law, perhaps combined with a more spiritual interpretation of the messianic expectations, which may have seemed to belittle national and political hopes. Though Stephen is rightly considered a forerunner of Paul, it is only in this somewhat limited sense that we can think of him as anticipating Paul's assertion of a distinctively free, Gentile Christianity.

As to how, as a matter of history, Stephen's death was brought about, there is a good deal to suggest that Luke's source may have described the martyrdom as an act of mob violence. But the account as edited by Luke implies that he was officially tried and condemned by the Sanhedrin; and in particular the reference to "witnesses" points to a regular execution. On the other hand it is perhaps unlikely that during the Roman dominion in Jerusalem the Sanhedrin could have carried through such a summary trial and execution. It is possible that Stephen really was tried before the Sanhedrin, which had no intention of exceeding its powers by inflicting the death penalty, and that the mob intervened and lynched him. But it is worth remembering that the insertion of a trial scene, whereby the blame for judicial murder would be cast upon the Jewish authorities rather than on the people or the Romans, would be quite in keeping with our author's point of view.

The persecution which followed Stephen's death made more clear the growing cleavage between the two sections within the Christian community. The apostles and the native Christians were apparently permitted to remain in Jerusalem; the followers of Stephen were driven in all directions, many no doubt returning to their former homes, and thereby sowing the first seeds of a wider mission. How long the persecution lasted we do not know. Three years after Paul's conversion (Gal. 1:18) Peter and James, and presumably other Jewish Christians, were still in the city; and a few years later the community was numerous enough to give Herod Agrippa the opportunity to curry favor with the Jews by executing James and imprisoning Peter (12:1 ff.). But Luke records this as something exceptional and in contrast to a general toleration.

9. Better translated: "Some of the members of the synagogue which is called that of the Libertines, both Cyrenians and Alexandrians." Jews who were **Libertines,** or **Freed-**

---

light of God in Christ. He ended as the man who took the world for his parish.

It is not only a man's beginning that is important. It is his development that counts in the end. How many people there are who have the gumption to meet one situation, but then quit! Stephen might have been faithful serving tables as long as he lived, but with Stephen, as with all great men and women, one thing led to another, and the more menial task was an opportunity to perform a more glorious one.

9-11. ***He Ran into Opposition.*** Stephen was not satisfied to do nothing but relieve the necessities of the poor. He soon became well known as a debater for Christ. The synagogues were the customary places for men to argue the questions involved in the Jewish law. Stephen carried on the argument in the same place but for a very different cause. It was inevitable that he should meet opposition. It was the same sort of opposition that Peter and John and their colleagues had met already. It was the same opposition that men like Francis of Assisi

Libertines, and Cyrenians, and Alexandrians, and of them of Cilicia and of Asia,
disputing with Stephen.
10 And they were not able to resist the
wisdom and the spirit by which he spake.
11 Then they suborned men, which said,
We have heard him speak blasphemous
words against Moses, and *against* God.
12 And they stirred up the people, and
the elders, and the scribes, and came upon

was called), and of the Cy-re'ni-ans, and of
the Alexandrians, and of those from Ci-
li'cia and Asia, arose and disputed with
Stephen. 10 But they could not withstand
the wisdom and the Spirit with which he
spoke. 11 Then they secretly instigated men,
who said, "We have heard him speak blasphemous words against Moses and God."
12 And they stirred up the people and the

---

men, had their own synagogue, and in this particular case both **Cyrenians** and **Alexandrians** were included in the membership. **Those from Cilicia and Asia** are mentioned as a separate group. An alternative is to read "Libyans" instead of "Libertines"—these "Libyans" then being defined as "Cyrenians and Alexandrians."

11. Secretly instigated: The Greek word gives the suggestion of a frame-up. **Blasphemous words:** "Blasphemy" in the technical sense according to rabbinical law required

---

and Luther, and their spiritual descendants, have always met. From time to time it is worth while to examine that opposition, and to examine our own lives and the life of our society in the light of it.

Stephen ran into two obstacles, nationalism and traditionalism. He was accused of blaspheming Moses; that was an offense against nationalism. He was also accused of blaspheming God; that was an offense against religious traditionalism. The combined offense was serious enough to put him to death.

While the sermon which he preached in his own defense (7:1-53) is not particularly fertile ground for the modern preacher, and therefore its temporary omission from the story of Stephen is recommended, nevertheless the sermon will give the preacher a more explicit description of Stephen's case. He attacked two precious things: the Holy Land and the temple. God had not confined his actions to a patch of holy ground. He had dealt with the patriarchs in Haran, Egypt, and Midian. And as far as the temple was concerned, the O.T. itself showed that the tabernacle antedated it and was built by divine instruction. Stephen, in other words, was trying to cut Christianity loose from its national swaddling clothes. He saw that Christianity was bigger than any nation and that Judaism could not contain it. But in making such claims he ran straight into the sorest spots imaginable. People cling to their national shrines and monuments as though they were life itself.

Increasing numbers of people are convinced that the time has come when, in order to prevent war, each nation must surrender some part of its sovereignty so that a government of the world can be established. "But what about our Constitution?" cries the nationalist. "What about our government buildings in Washington?" Flags wave and patriotism surges to one of its highest peaks as the nationalists rally to defend their precious possessions. They, like the opponents of Stephen, cannot see that while the treasures of our national life are to be guarded and prized, they are, after all, but the expression and the instrument of something greater, a life that is moving, like a stream rushing toward the sea. It must adapt to new conditions and circumstances. It is not the form that is precious, but the life to which the form gives shape. It is not the Constitution itself that is ultimately valuable, but the spirit of the Constitution that is to be preserved at all costs. And that spirit may, under new circumstances, rise up and break through the Constitution. In that case, when and if it comes, the shell must be shed that the life may expand. The opponents of Stephen, as the opponents of Jesus, and the opponents of all the agents of change, are those who keep the shell and lose the life. Stephen was one of those who knew that the time had come for the shell to be broken.

The conservatives opposed Stephen on religious grounds. He was accused of blaspheming not only Moses, but also God himself. He struck not only at the roots of the national tree but also at the roots of the religious tree as well. Not only was the Holy Land dispensable, but also the temple. God could conceivably get along without either. That was a shock too great to be borne. Traditionalism in religion can be as stubborn an opponent to change as nationalism in politics. To feel the frenzy of this opposition to Stephen we pass to the next passage.

12-14. *The Opposition Reaches Its Climax.*—"This fellow is never done talking against this

him, and caught him, and brought *him* to the council,
13 And set up false witnesses, which said, This man ceaseth not to speak blasphemous words against this holy place, and the law:
14 For we have heard him say, that this Jesus of Nazareth shall destroy this place, and shall change the customs which Moses delivered us.

elders and the scribes, and they came upon him and seized him and brought him before
the council, 13 and set up false witnesses
who said, "This man never ceases to speak words against this holy place and the law;
14 for we have heard him say that this Jesus of Nazareth will destroy this place, and will change the customs which Moses deliv-

---

the use of God's name. But the word can be used of scurrilous language apart from any technical religious offense.

14. An obvious echo of the charge brought against Jesus himself (Mark 14:58).

---

holy Place and the Law! Why, we have heard him say that Jesus the Nazarene will destroy this Place and change the customs handed down to us by Moses!" (Moffatt.) That tested their endurance beyond its strength. Change the customs handed down by Moses? Never!

It is clear from this opposition to Stephen that the young man had caught the spirit of his Master. Jesus, from the beginning, assumed that the truth was continually and everlastingly revealing itself. He knew that truth was not a deposit, but a growing discovery made possible by the ever-increasing self-disclosure of God to men. He had seen too much of a system for him to have faith in systems as such, even in good ones. When he began his ministry, he found an elaborate system, developed through centuries of experience, for the purpose of saving men and women from the powers that threaten their existence. It was a system of law and ceremony. The law in itself was essentially good, and the ceremony in itself was a true representation and dramatization of the Jewish idea of sacrifice. But he soon recognized that the system had run away with things. Instead of saving men it was enslaving them; and instead of making them good it was simply making them dull. He breathed into that stuffy system a spirit. He took the laws about the sabbath and made them serve the spirit of reverence for the Lord of Hosts and the spirit of compassion for the needs of humanity. He took the law concerning moral behavior and made it serve the spirit of human sympathy and understanding. He did not discard discipline; he enlisted it in the service of the spirit.

Jesus, and Stephen following in his train, displayed the essential characteristics of a liberal mind. A spirit from within him challenged the system outside him, and when the system was past the point of flexibility by which it could adapt itself to the valid needs of men, the system had to be either revised or relinquished. Thus he chose the dangerous path of the innovator.

Shakespeare chose the same path. He inherited a system by which dramas were constructed according to universally accepted unities. His imaginative and creative spirit could not confine itself within so narrow a domain, and its constructive vitality completely overrode the system, leaving the unities for the dusty halls of the academicians. The conservative is the man who conserves the values of the past: the liberal is the man who introduces the possibilities of the future.

Jesus, knowing these things, did not promise to leave his disciples a book of rules which would tell them what to do in every conceivable situation. Neither did he promise to leave them a code of laws, nor a final court of authority. He promised to give them a spirit—the Spirit of Truth—and that spirit would guide them into all truth. He took for granted that situations would arise which neither he nor they could foresee. No lawbook would be sufficient. He did not go around the law; he went above it to something infinitely higher, to the reality of God himself to which each human being must respond in each new situation with all the vigor and spontaneity of which he is capable. No wonder from the beginning Jesus was accused of destroying the temple. In a sense, at least, he did that very thing. And in the same sense Stephen, his follower, was doing the same thing.

The church has always been in danger of forfeiting this invaluable bequest of Jesus. A system is so much safer than a spirit; it is more definite, more certain. Put a man on an assembly belt of an ironclad system and, provided no major catastrophes shake him off, he is safely and surely on the way to salvation, with all directions given. Endow him with a spirit, and tell him to surrender his mind and soul to it, to be ready for every new intimation and every fresh advance; tell him that he

15 And all that sat in the council, looking steadfastly on him, saw his face as it had been the face of an angel.

ered to us." 15 And gazing at him, all who sat in the council saw that his face was like the face of an angel.

---

does not yet know all truth, that he may have to make revisions and corrections in what he already believes; tell him these things and you lead him into dangerous ways. Tell him anything else and you lead him into the way of certain and final death.

It seems that Jesus did everything he could to ensure the flexibility of Christianity within certain definite convictions and beliefs. It also seems that at times the church has done everything it could to freeze Christianity. No one wants frozen assets in business. Neither does anyone want the delicate things of the spirit packed on dry ice. Jesus promised the Spirit of truth. That is what we want. Let us not be afraid of it.

Stephen was not afraid of it, and though he may not have appreciated it in its fullness, or even to the degree which his successor, Paul, appreciated it, here he stands on the threshold of Christian history, as one who caught the meaning of Jesus and, at the risk of his life, proclaimed to all that it is not the land, nor the law, nor the temple that saves. These are but the instruments of salvation. From time to time they change to suit the changing needs of God. God is the same and he is the Savior, revealing himself in ever-new forms to the eyes that are open to perceive him.

15. ***How He Was Transfigured.***—"Then all who were seated in the Sanhedrin fixed their eyes on him, and saw that his face shone like the face of an angel" (Moffatt). It is as though the light that shone from Stephen's face was the reflected light of his Master's transfigured countenance. We are familiar with the fact that surroundings may be so altered as to become transfigured. At any moment, without warning, a common bush may be aflame with an unearthly fire. A piece of familiar music may suddenly come alive under the touch of a master performer. A Robert Browning may cross your path and put away all the shadows of your life by the brightness of his being. Such is the wonder of our world that at the touch of some wizard's wand dull things grow brilliant, clouds have a rim of gold, the sour turns sweet, and familiar things are adorable.

Even more significant is the fact that men themselves are transfigured. "The fashion of his countenance was altered" (Luke 9:29) we read of Jesus. "Moses wist not that the skin of his face shone" (Exod. 34:29) we read of Moses. And now we read that Stephen's face "shone like the face of an angel" (Moffatt).

There are two principles by which this personal transfiguration takes place. First, we catch the light of the things we live with. For example Madame Curie began life beset by innumerable hardships, yet endowed with an insatiable thirst for truth. She did not have the natural charm and beauty that some young girls are blessed with, but as she lived and struggled she became beautiful. Her daughter writes of her:

> These struggles and victories had transformed her physically; they had given her a new face. It is impossible to look unmoved at a photograph of Marie Curie taken a little after her thirtieth year. The solid and rather thickset girl had become an ethereal creature.[5]

She had caught the light of the things she lived with.

In much the same way Jesus lived with luminous things. He passed hour after hour in the presence of the Father of Lights. It is little wonder, then, that at one dramatic moment "the fashion of his countenance was altered, and his raiment was white and glistering" (Luke 9:29). He had caught the light of the things he lived with. He was transfigured.

It is embarrassing for us to enumerate the things we live with. Stocks and bonds, breakfast dishes and table menus; motion pictures and radios; social life that is seldom more than a mechanical routine. To say the least, these are not things that communicate light. Yet in those rare moments when we take our company with things that shine, we too marvelously catch the light, and the fashion of our countenance is ever so slightly altered.

The second principle is that we reflect the light we catch. As "the soul is dyed the color of its leisure hours," so a man's environment is dyed the color of his inner life. If our inner life is a mass of merging shadows, those shadows are projected into the world around us until they finally hide the sun. If our inner life is illuminated by a light caught from the perpetual Light, that light is thrown upon the world we live in until even a cross is circled with glory. If the fashion of our countenance is a twisted pattern of gloom mingled with resentment, the burden we are bearing will not only be heavy but unbearable. If the fashion of our countenance is altered so that it becomes the image of bravery and beauty, the burdens

[5] Eve Curie, *Madame Curie* (New York: Doubleday, Doran & Co., 1937), p. 151.

7 Then said the high priest, Are these things so?

2 And he said, Men, brethren, and fathers, hearken; The God of glory appeared unto our father Abraham, when he was in Mesopotamia, before he dwelt in Charran,

3 And said unto him, Get thee out of thy country, and from thy kindred, and come into the land which I shall show thee.

4 Then came he out of the land of the Chaldeans, and dwelt in Charran: and from thence, when his father was dead, he removed him into this land, wherein ye now dwell.

5 And he gave him none inheritance in it, no, not *so much as* to set his foot on: yet he promised that he would give it to him for a possession, and to his seed after him, when *as yet* he had no child.

6 And God spake on this wise, That his seed should sojourn in a strange land; and that they should bring them into bondage, and entreat *them* evil four hundred years.

7 And the high priest said, "Is this so?"
2 And Stephen said:
"Brethren and fathers, hear me. The
God of glory appeared to our father Abraham, when he was in Mes-o-po-ta'mi-a, before he lived in Haran, 3 and said to him,
'Depart from your land and from your kindred and go into the land which I will
show you.' 4 Then he departed from the
land of the Chal-de'ans, and lived in Haran. And after his father died, God removed him from there into this land in
which you are now living; 5 yet he gave
him no inheritance in it, not even a foot's
length, but promised to give it to him in
possession and to his posterity after him,
though he had no child. 6 And God spoke
to this effect, that his posterity would be
aliens in a land belonging to others, who
would enslave them and ill-treat them

7:2. Before he lived in Haran: According to Gen. 11:27–12:5, God's promise to Abraham was made after he had already moved to Haran. But both Philo and Josephus support Stephen's version. There are in the speech a number of variations from the story as told in the Pentateuch, some of which are due to the influence of the LXX and others apparently to the persistence of varying traditions. (On the speech see also pp. 91-93.)

4-5. After his father died: According to the reckoning of Gen. 11:26, 32; 12:4, Terah must still have been living when the move was made from Haran. **A foot's length:** An echo of Deut. 2:5, where, however, the reference is to Mount Seir.

---

will somehow be altered into things bravely and beautiful borne.

If a photograph is dull and uninteresting, it may be that the landscape was dull and lacking in interest. But it may be far more likely that the camera needed a new lens or a different exposure. The same is true of us. When the bushes along the way are dull and never a one flames with glory, it may be that there is something wrong with the bush. Far more likely it is that the light in us has gone out. It is our own transfiguration for which we pray, for in the reflection of that light the whole world looks different.

So Stephen caught a passing ray of the light that streamed from the countenance of Jesus, and as he reflected it into the small circle of his world, even the dull eyes of the Sanhedrin were not blind to it.

7:1-53. ***The Speech Stephen Made.***—As the Exeg. has pointed out, the long speech of Stephen recorded here breaks the unity of the picture of Stephen himself. To see that picture in all its vividness and to follow the whole scene of the trial of Stephen to its tragic end, the reader may well pass over the speech and read the last seven verses of this chapter in immediate sequence to ch. 6.

Returning then to the speech itself, one finds that for the general purposes of exposition there is not much in it that can be profitably used. Most of it is a rehearsal of Jewish history and is more satisfactorily set down in the O.T. itself. But two verses are especially suggestive, namely vss. 47-48.

But Solomon built him a house. It is our nature to protect and preserve whatever we conceive to be of great value. What would painting be without a museum where paintings can be carefully hung? What would music be without a hall where music can be magnificently performed? What would education be without a schoolhouse? What would a family be without a home? Indeed, what would religion be

7 And the nation to whom they shall be in bondage will I judge, said God: and after that shall they come forth, and serve me in this place.

8 And he gave him the covenant of circumcision: and so *Abraham* begat Isaac, and circumcised him the eighth day; and Isaac *begat* Jacob; and Jacob *begat* the twelve patriarchs.

9 And the patriarchs, moved with envy, sold Joseph into Egypt: but God was with him,

10 And delivered him out of all his afflictions, and gave him favor and wisdom in the sight of Pharaoh king of Egypt; and he made him governor over Egypt and all his house.

11 Now there came a dearth over all the land of Egypt and Chanaan, and great affliction: and our fathers found no sustenance.

12 But when Jacob heard that there was corn in Egypt, he sent out our fathers first.

13 And at the second *time* Joseph was made known to his brethren; and Joseph's kindred was made known unto Pharaoh.

14 Then sent Joseph, and called his father Jacob to *him,* and all his kindred, threescore and fifteen souls.

15 So Jacob went down into Egypt, and died, he, and our fathers,

16 And were carried over into Sychem, and laid in the sepulchre that Abraham bought for a sum of money of the sons of Emmor, *the father* of Sychem.

17 But when the time of the promise drew nigh, which God had sworn to Abraham, the people grew and multiplied in Egypt,

18 Till another king arose, which knew not Joseph.

19 The same dealt subtilely with our kindred, and evil entreated our fathers, so

four hundred years. 7 'But I will judge the
nation which they serve,' said God, 'and
after that they shall come out and worship
me in this place.' 8 And he gave him the
covenant of circumcision. And so Abraham
became the father of Isaac, and circumcised him on the eighth day; and Isaac became the father of Jacob, and Jacob of
the twelve patriarchs.

9 "And the patriarchs, jealous of Joseph,
sold him into Egypt; but God was with
him, 10 and rescued him out of all his afflictions, and gave him favor and wisdom
before Pharaoh, king of Egypt, who made
him governor over Egypt and over all his
household. 11 Now there came a famine
throughout all Egypt and Canaan, and
great affliction, and our fathers could find
no food. 12 But when Jacob heard that
there was grain in Egypt, he sent forth our
fathers the first time. 13 And at the second
visit Joseph made himself known to his
brothers, and Joseph's family became
known to Pharaoh. 14 And Joseph sent and
called to him Jacob his father and all his
kindred, seventy-five souls; 15 and Jacob
went down into Egypt. And he died, himself and our fathers, 16 and they were carried back to She'chem and laid in the tomb
that Abraham had bought for a sum of
silver from the sons of Hamor in She'chem.

17 "But as the time of the promise drew
near, which God had granted to Abraham,
the people grew and multiplied in Egypt
18 till there arose over Egypt another king
who had not known Joseph. 19 He dealt

---

7. In this place: An echo of Exod. 3:12, where similarly the reference is not to Canaan but to Mount Sinai. According to Stephen, the promise is not only that they shall inherit the land, but, even more, that they shall have free opportunity of worship; cf. Luke 1:73, "The oath . . . that we . . . might serve him without fear."

14. Seventy-five souls: So the LXX in Gen. 46:27; Exod. 1:5, whereas the original Hebrew has "seventy."

16. Again tradition varies, for according to Josh. 24:32, it was Joseph alone who was buried at Shechem, while according to Gen. 50:13, Jacob—and his other sons? (cf. Josephus *Antiquities* II. 8. 2)—was buried at Hebron.

19. Dealt craftily with: An unusual Greek word well translated "exploited" by Lake and Cadbury; cf. Exod. 1:10, "let us deal wisely with them."

that they cast out their young children, to the end they might not live.

20 In which time Moses was born, and was exceeding fair, and nourished up in his father's house three months:

21 And when he was cast out, Pharaoh's daughter took him up, and nourished him for her own son.

22 And Moses was learned in all the wisdom of the Egyptians, and was mighty in words and in deeds.

23 And when he was full forty years old, it came into his heart to visit his brethren the children of Israel.

24 And seeing one *of them* suffer wrong, he defended *him,* and avenged him that was oppressed, and smote the Egyptian:

25 For he supposed his brethren would have understood how that God by his hand would deliver them; but they understood not.

26 And the next day he showed himself unto them as they strove, and would have set them at one again, saying, Sirs, ye are brethren; why do ye wrong one to another?

27 But he that did his neighbor wrong thrust him away, saying, Who made thee a ruler and a judge over us?

28 Wilt thou kill me, as thou didst the Egyptian yesterday?

29 Then fled Moses at this saying, and was a stranger in the land of Madian, where he begat two sons.

craftily with our race and forced our fathers to expose their infants, that they
might not be kept alive. 20 At this time
Moses was born, and was beautiful before
God. And he was brought up for three
months in his father's house; 21 and when
he was exposed, Pharaoh's daughter
adopted him and brought him up as her
own son. 22 And Moses was instructed in
all the wisdom of the Egyptians, and he
was mighty in his words and deeds.

23 "When he was forty years old, it came
into his heart to visit his brethren, the
sons of Israel. 24 And seeing one of them
being wronged, he defended the oppressed
man and avenged him by striking the Egyptian. 25 He supposed that his brethren understood that God was giving them deliverance by his hand, but they did not
understand. 26 And on the following day he
appeared to them as they were quarreling
and would have reconciled them, saying,
'Men, you are brethren, why do you wrong
each other?' 27 But the man who was wrong-
ing his neighbor thrust him aside, saying,
'Who made you a ruler and a judge over
us? 28 Do you want to kill me as you killed
the Egyptian yesterday?' 29 At this retort
Moses fled, and became an exile in the land
of Midian, where he became the father of
two sons.

---

20. **Beautiful before God,** i.e., even by God's standards—equivalent to a strong superlative (cf. Gen. 10:9). In modern Greek θεο–, prefixed to adjectives, gives them this superlative force.

22. This is not mentioned in the O.T. but is stressed by Philo (*Moses* I. 5).

25. This statement is not supported by any O.T. passage and seems prompted by the desire to draw a parallel between Moses and Jesus, and to illustrate the proverb that "no prophet is acceptable in his own country"; cf. Luke 4:24 ff., where two illustrations are given from the O.T.

---

without a house in which men and women, for the time being, can preoccupy themselves with God without interference or distraction?

Necessary as houses are, they are often dangerous. The art museum can degenerate into a cut and dried academy. The government buildings can become vaults where moribund forms are preserved and new ideas are frozen to death. The church can easily become a monument to something that is long since dead and gone. It was that danger that Stephen recognized in the religion of his day. Jesus had seen it and died because of it. The life of Judaism was doomed unless it too could see it and be saved. Stephen put it in positive language: **Yet the Most High does not dwell in houses made with hands.**

God is a spirit, and while houses and institutions, systems and forms may catch that spirit, be possessed by it, carried by it, and animated by it, they can never contain or confine it. And when they presume to do so, two things invariably happen. First, God is robbed of his universality and limited to prescribed

30 And when forty years were expired, there appeared to him in the wilderness of mount Sina an angel of the Lord in a flame of fire in a bush.

31 When Moses saw *it,* he wondered at the sight: and as he drew near to behold *it,* the voice of the Lord came unto him,

32 *Saying,* I *am* the God of thy fathers, the God of Abraham, and the God of Isaac, and the God of Jacob. Then Moses trembled, and durst not behold.

33 Then said the Lord to him, Put off thy shoes from thy feet: for the place where thou standest is holy ground.

34 I have seen, I have seen the affliction of my people which is in Egypt, and I have heard their groaning, and am come down to deliver them. And now come, I will send thee into Egypt.

35 This Moses whom they refused, saying, Who made thee a ruler and a judge? the same did God send *to be* a ruler and a deliverer by the hand of the angel which appeared to him in the bush.

36 He brought them out, after that he had showed wonders and signs in the land of Egypt, and in the Red sea, and in the wilderness forty years.

37 ¶ This is that Moses, which said unto the children of Israel, A Prophet shall the Lord your God raise up unto you of your brethren, like unto me; him shall ye hear.

38 This is he, that was in the church in the wilderness with the angel which spake to him in the mount Sina, and *with* our fathers: who received the lively oracles to give unto us:

30 "Now when forty years had passed,
an angel appeared to him in the wilderness
of Mount Sinai, in a flame of fire in a
bush. 31 When Moses saw it he wondered at the sight; and as he drew near to
look, the voice of the Lord came, 32 'I am
the God of your fathers, the God of Abraham and of Isaac and of Jacob.' And Moses
trembled and did not dare to look. 33 And
the Lord said to him, 'Take off the shoes
from your feet, for the place where you
are standing is holy ground. 34 I have surely
seen the ill-treatment of my people that are
in Egypt and heard their groaning, and I
have come down to deliver them. And now
come, I will send you to Egypt.'

35 "This Moses whom they refused, saying, 'Who made you a ruler and a judge?'
God sent as both ruler and deliverer by
the hand of the angel that appeared to him
in the bush. 36 He led them out, having
performed wonders and signs in Egypt
and at the Red Sea, and in the wilderness for forty years. 37 This is the Moses
who said to the Israelites, 'God will raise
up for you a prophet from your brethren
as he raised me up.' 38 This is he who was
in the congregation in the wilderness with
the angel who spoke to him at Mount Sinai,
and with our fathers; and he received living

---

30. Mount Sinai: According to Exod. 3:1, Horeb. The relation between the two mountains is something of a puzzle, and later tradition identified them.

35. Deliverer or "redeemer": This word is never applied to Moses in the LXX, and once again the motive here seems to be to compare Moses with Jesus, who in Luke 24:21 is described as "the one to redeem Israel."

37-38. A prophet: See on 3:22. **In the congregation** is an echo of the LXX phrase "the day of the assembly," i.e., the day on which the people assembled to receive the law (Deut. 9:10; 18:16). The **angel** as a mediator is a later tradition added to the original account, in which Yahweh himself gives the law to Moses (see on vs. 53). For **living**

---

areas. He then becomes the private property of the group that owns the building. Jews who localized the Spirit of God in a land, a law, and a temple soon came to believe that God belonged to them and that, outside the boundaries which they had set for him, he was less accessible, less able to achieve his purpose. Spirit is something like the wind: you can catch it, but you cannot hold it. The wind can blow through a room, but close the windows and try to keep the wind and its freshness disappears and its power vanishes. So God's Spirit can dwell in a

39 To whom our fathers would not obey, but thrust *him* from them, and in their hearts turned back again into Egypt,

40 Saying unto Aaron, Make us gods to go before us: for *as for* this Moses, which brought us out of the land of Egypt, we wot not what is become of him.

41 And they made a calf in those days, and offered sacrifice unto the idol, and rejoiced in the works of their own hands.

42 Then God turned, and gave them up to worship the host of heaven; as it is written in the book of the prophets, O ye house of Israel, have ye offered to me slain beasts and sacrifices *by the space of* forty years in the wilderness?

43 Yea, ye took up the tabernacle of Moloch, and the star of your god Remphan, figures which ye made to worship them: and I will carry you away beyond Babylon.

oracles to give to us. **39** Our fathers refused
to obey him, but thrust him aside, and in
their hearts they turned to Egypt, **40** saying
to Aaron, 'Make for us gods to go before
us; as for this Moses who led us out from
the land of Egypt, we do not know what
has become of him.' **41** And they made a
calf in those days, and offered a sacrifice to
the idol and rejoiced in the works of their
hands. **42** But God turned and gave them
over to worship the host of heaven, as it
is written in the book of the prophets:

'Did you offer to me slain beasts and
sacrifices,
forty years in the wilderness, O house
of Israel?

43 And you took up the tent of Moloch,
and the star of the god Rephan,
the figures which you made to worship;
and I will remove you beyond Babylon.'

---

oracles cf. Ezek. 20:11, "I gave them my statutes . . . which if a man do, he shall even live in them."

42-43. For the distinctively Jewish idea that God punishes sinners by giving them over to even worse sin, cf. Rom. 1:24, 26, 28. **The book of the prophets** means the Book of the Twelve or minor prophets, which was one of the books into which the Prophets, or second part of O.T. canon, was divided. The quotation is from the LXX of Amos 5:25-27, but Stephen changes the point. Amos is arguing that whereas no sacrifices were required in the wilderness, the people had later turned to idolatrous sacrifices. Stephen uses the passage as a proof that even in the wilderness Israel rejected God for idols. There are several variations from the Hebrew in the LXX version which Stephen follows. **Rephan** is read for "Chiun"; and whereas the Hebrew has "ye have carried Sikkuth your king," the LXX took "Sikkuth" to mean **tent** (σκηνή) and "your king" (Hebrew *mĕlekh*) to mean the god **Moloch.** Stephen also puts **Babylon** in the place of "Damascus" (both Hebrew and LXX). The important point is that, if we had here a transcript of what Stephen actually said, the text would hardly be likely to follow the LXX in the changes made from the Hebrew. But if the speech was written in Greek by the author of Acts, the facts become intelligible. If it is held, as is argued by the champions of the theory of an Aramaic original, that the translator always brought the O.T. references into line with the LXX, why did he allow **Babylon** to stand in place of "Damascus"?

---

house and fill it with his power, but once the windows are closed the heavenly Spirit no longer has the power and the presence eventually departs.

The second thing that happens is this: the men involved in such systems lose their capacity to perceive the presence of God. Their eyes are fixed in a fearful stare and their minds no longer have the power to imagine undreamed of things. Hence, when prophetic spirits appear on the scene, they are afraid of them. They stone them, crucify them. The house that they built for protection becomes their prison. Because they are afraid that they may lose it, they suspect everyone who enjoys life outside the house and seek to destroy those who wish to alter it.

This situation is not peculiar to religion. For example, democracy is a spirit which prevails in a group of people who wish to live together on the basis of equally shared rights and responsibilities. It implies that people trust and respect each other, and that each man sees in every other man something to be treated with care. Yet democracy, being a spirit, must build itself a house. It must have a constitution, con-

44 Our fathers had the tabernacle of witness in the wilderness, as he had appointed, speaking unto Moses, that he should make it according to the fashion that he had seen.

45 Which also our fathers that came after brought in with Jesus into the possession of the Gentiles, whom God drave out before the face of our fathers, unto the days of David;

46 Who found favor before God, and desired to find a tabernacle for the God of Jacob.

47 But Solomon built him a house.

48 Howbeit the Most High dwelleth not in temples made with hands; as saith the prophet,

49 Heaven *is* my throne, and earth *is* my footstool: what house will ye build me? saith the Lord: or what *is* the place of my rest?

50 Hath not my hand made all these things?

51 ¶ Ye stiffnecked and uncircumcised in heart and ears, ye do always resist the Holy Ghost: as your fathers *did,* so *do* ye.

44 "Our fathers had the tent of witness
in the wilderness, even as he who spoke
to Moses directed him to make it, according to the pattern that he had seen. 45 Our
fathers in turn brought it in with Joshua
when they dispossessed the nations which
God thrust out before our fathers. So it
was until the days of David, 46 who found
favor in the sight of God and asked leave to
find a habitation for the God of Jacob.
47 But it was Solomon who built a house
for him. 48 Yet the Most High does not
dwell in houses made with hands; as the
prophet says,

49 'Heaven is my throne,
and earth my footstool.
What house will you build for me,
says the Lord,
or what is the place of my rest?
50 Did not my hand make all these
things?'

51 "You stiff-necked people, uncircumcised in heart and ears, you always resist the Holy Spirit. As your fathers did, so do you.

---

46. Much the best-attested reading is "for the house of Jacob" (οἴκῳ with ℵ B D), though most editors prefer **God of Jacob** in line with Ps. 132:1-5. But the temple was for the use of the assembled people as well as of Yahweh, and "house" may well be correct.

48. The force of the Greek is: "It is not the Most High who dwells in houses made with hands"—with the implication that the heathen gods do dwell in such houses. **The Most High** (Ὕψιστος) is the LXX rendering of *'Elyôn,* which in the O.T. is the name used by non-Israelites who reverence the God of Israel. **The prophet** is Isaiah (66:1-2), again quoted from the LXX.

51-53. The Holy Spirit: Here, as often in rabbinical writings, with reference to the spirit of prophecy; or possibly Isa. 63:10—"they . . . vexed his Holy Spirit"—is in mind.

---

gress, laws, supreme court, bill of rights, and all the other necessary implements. Once the house is built there is always the danger that some people will identify the house with the spirit itself, that they will persecute anyone who threatens to make alterations in the supreme court, or in any other room of the house, for the simple reason that they mistake the system for the spirit. The system is necessary, but it must be a system through which the spirit can move freely. It must be able to adapt itself to new and changing conditions, and to revise itself when necessary. The democratic spirit has built itself a house in Great Britain and another house in the United States. The houses created by these two nations are quite different in character, yet the spirit is essentially the same.

Religion is forever exposed to this same confusion. The spirit must be housed in a system. Early Christianity soon learned that it must have an ordered ministry, a planned liturgy, a canon of scripture, a pattern of creedal belief. Otherwise the spirit of Christianity would have been like the waters of a river without a channel. Yet once the system was made, the house built, the old danger is always present; namely, the danger that men should suppose God's Spirit to be permanently housed, those outside the house to be somehow totally apart from God, and the supreme necessity to be to preserve the house at all costs. Whenever and wherever

52 Which of the prophets have not your
fathers persecuted? and they have slain
them which showed before of the coming
of the Just One; of whom ye have been
now the betrayers and murderers:
53 Who have received the law by the
disposition of angels, and have not kept *it*.
54 ¶ When they heard these things,
they were cut to the heart, and they
gnashed on him with *their* teeth.
55 But he, being full of the Holy Ghost,
looked up steadfastly into heaven, and saw
the glory of God, and Jesus standing on the
right hand of God,

52 Which of the prophets did not your fathers persecute? And they killed those who
announced beforehand the coming of the
Righteous One, whom you have now betrayed and murdered, 53 you who received
the law as delivered by angels and did not
keep it."
54 Now when they heard these things
they were enraged, and they ground their
teeth against him. 55 But he, full of the
Holy Spirit, gazed into heaven and saw the
glory of God, and Jesus standing at the

They killed: Historically there is no support for this statement, but in legendary tradition nearly every prophet became a martyr. For **the Righteous One** see on 3:14. **As delivered by angels:** The phrase presents us with one of the very few verbal echoes between Acts and the epistles of Paul, who in Gal. 3:19 speaks of the law as being "ordained by angels" (cf. 9:21 for another such possible echo).

55-56. Jesus standing, instead of the usual "seated," seems to suggest that our Lord is about to welcome Stephen into the immediate presence without an intermediate period

---

this has happened, Christianity has not only betrayed its Lord who himself was caught and killed by such a system, but it has lost its power to save the souls of men.

55-56. *How the Heavens Opened.*—**I see the heavens opened,** cried Stephen, **and the Son of man standing at the right hand of God.** Here, after the interruption of the speech, we come to the climax of the story of Stephen, as he saw his vision of the exalted Christ. To the writer of the Acts such an experience as this was a supernatural one. It does not follow, however, that the writer would insist upon our literal translation of the experience. Most people have had no such experience, probably never will have. Is this episode in the life of Stephen, therefore, entirely foreign to them? Not at all, if we understand the real meaning that lies behind the picture.

Sooner or later everyone goes through a time when life seems to be closing in upon him. Prices are going up and income is going down; responsibilities are increasing and physical strength is waning; friends disappoint and circumstances seem to be weighted on the side of the opposition; the doors of opportunity quietly close and the lights on the horizon go out one by one; war ruins our chances for an education and the threat of war takes the joy out of trying to get one; families are fretful and impatient; the crowd is heartless. Then suddenly something happens that clears the air. It may be an event that takes place outside, or it may be something that happens within the secret places of a man's being. Whatever it may be, it is as though the clouds broke, the heavens opened. In spite of handicaps and obstacles, the man is sure of his ground; he can see his way clearly; he is ready to go on. It is the reassurance that God is good and that by his power a man can do all things.

Something like that happened to Stephen. The people were tracking him down the way hounds hunt a fox. They were more like a pack of animals than a group of men as they stood there in front of him. Their fears and jealousy reduced them to savagery. They were ready to rush on him and lash the life right out of him. Imagine what must have gone through Stephen's mind: Are these the men for whom Jesus died? These brutes, these prejudiced, bigoted, inflammable creatures—are they the children of God? Is there any love of God in them? Can their passions ever be tamed? Can the mob spirit in them ever be brought under control? Are they worth the price?

And then the heavens opened. He saw Jesus at the right hand of God. It was the reassurance that he needed. Love still reigned. Love still mattered. God still cared. Man still had a chance. Jesus still came first. That was all he needed. Knowing those things, nothing else mattered and he went his way like a son of God.

To say that such an experience is a common occurrence is by no means to cheapen it or minimize its importance. It does not always occur on the same scale, but according to varying dimensions it happens over and over again. It is most

56 And said, Behold, I see the heavens
opened, and the Son of man standing on
the right hand of God.
57 Then they cried out with a loud voice,
and stopped their ears, and ran upon him
with one accord,
58 And cast *him* out of the city, and
stoned *him:* and the witnesses laid down
their clothes at a young man's feet, whose
name was Saul.
59 And they stoned Stephen, calling
upon *God,* and saying, Lord Jesus, receive
my spirit.

right hand of God; 56 and he said, "Behold,
I see the heavens opened, and the Son of
man standing at the right hand of God."
57 But they cried out with a loud voice
and stopped their ears and rushed together
upon him. 58 Then they cast him out of
the city and stoned him; and the witnesses
laid down their garments at the feet of a
young man named Saul. 59 And as they
were stoning Stephen, he prayed, "Lord

---

of waiting for judgment or resurrection. The parallels of the story of Dives and Lazarus (Luke 16:22) and of the promise made to the penitent thief (Luke 23:43) suggest that this is characteristic Lukan eschatology. **Son of man:** The only place outside the Gospels where the title is given to Jesus. There seems to be an echo of Jesus' own words in Luke 22:69, "But from now on the Son of man shall be seated at the right hand of the power of God."

57-58. The Western text of vs. 57 probably read, "then the people cried out"—perhaps because the copyist regarded the execution as a mob lynching. **Cast him out** again suggests a lynching, whereas the mention of **witnesses** suits better an official execution; their duty was to throw the first stones (Deut. 17:7). **A young man named Saul:** This reads like a "genuine Pauline reminiscence" and "probably turns the scale in favour of the view that Stephen was actually executed rather than lynched" (*Beginnings of Christianity,* IV, 85)—though it is by no means clear that this is Luke's own view. How keenly Luke, if not Paul himself, felt the latter's responsibility is shown by the way he harks back to the subject in Paul's speech to the crowd at Jerusalem (22:20).

59-60. Stephen's last words echo those of Jesus as recorded by Luke: "Father, into thy hands I commit my spirit!" and "Father, forgive them; for they know not what they do"

---

likely to take the same form: the recollection of someone once known and loved now brought to vivid remembrance. One person, when life begins to press and the air is hard to breathe, sees her father and hears his voice. The pressure lifts; the air clears; the heavens open. Another person who often finds life closing in upon him goes to the Lincoln Memorial and stands in silence in the presence of the great seated figure. He hears the words of the second inaugural address; he remembers the scorn and contempt which was heaped upon the man of many sorrows; he sees him go his quiet way unmindful of the danger that surrounded him and finally overtook him. It is as though clouds had been swept away and the heavens split in two. In a world where such a man could occur nothing is too great to expect and nothing too hard to endure.

Instances like these are, of course, only shadows of the greater thing. It is the vision of Jesus which truly clears the skies. It is the remembrance of him which fortifies our drooping spirits. He was serene when everyone else was beside himself; he was forgiving when everyone else was vindictive; he prayed when the whole world around him was in tumult; he loved when he saw nothing but hate; he trusted when everyone was against him; he kept on hoping when there seemed nothing left to keep hope alive. When life closed in on him, it seemed as though his figure stretched itself until, like an arrow, it cleaved the sky in two, and through that opening light has been forever after streaming.

"The heavens opened"; in other words, such experiences of reassurance cannot be brought about by man's ingenuity. They happen. They cannot be predicted or artificially produced. The best that a man can do is to stand as close as possible to the place where the heaven is most likely to open, namely, where the figure of Jesus parts the clouds in two.

59, 60. ***How He Prayed.***—Stephen prayed for himself and for his murderers. **Lord Jesus, receive my spirit,** and **Lord, do not hold this sin against them.** The most natural thing for a man to do when his life is in danger is to pray. Men who have never prayed before in their lives pray when the ship begins to sink. It is a

60 And he kneeled down, and cried with
a loud voice, Lord, lay not this sin to
their charge. And when he had said this,
he fell asleep.

Jesus, receive my spirit." **60** And he knelt
down and cried with a loud voice, "Lord, do
not hold this sin against them." And when

(Luke 23:46, 34). If we could be sure that these are Stephen's exact words, the occurrence of the title **Lord** with reference to Jesus would prove that this use of κύριος (or the Aramaic *mar*) began at Jerusalem and not later among the Hellenistic churches. But Luke has a fondness for this title, and historical deductions would be dangerous.

prayer of desperation. Stephen's prayer was different.

First, the prayer for himself was not a request for deliverance, but an affirmation of trust. Though it is in the form of a petition, it is not difficult to see that the petition rests upon a profound trust in Jesus. Not "Lord, save my life," but "Lord, receive my spirit." It is a prayer that looks forward, not backward. There is no fear in it, only faith. It assumes that whatever happens, Jesus will be there and that he will be adequate to any emergency.

How much more adequate is this prayer of Stephen's than the prayers that most men say when they are in trouble. Lord, get me out of this; make me well; give me back my money; bring back my child; save me from this illness; spare me from that pain. So run our endless prayers of petition. Not so with Stephen. All he asked was that Jesus should keep his spirit, that through his present trial Jesus should steady him, and that when he had once crossed the dividing line between life and death Jesus should be there and that he should be with him. Underneath it all was the assurance that he would be there, and because of this all would be well.

When life is hard for us and things are going against us, we have one supreme need—that Jesus will keep our spirit; keep it free from fear, keep it from turning sour, keep it from clinging to frail rafts of flesh that must ultimately go down, keep it clean, unsoiled by personal resentments and bitterness.

Men were successful in stoning Stephen, but they never succeeded in staining him, for his spirit was in the keeping of Jesus, beyond the reach of their most determined efforts to kill it.

Stephen's prayer was different from most prayers in another way. He prayed for the people who were killing him. When a man is having a hard time of it, he is likely to forget everybody else but himself. He is often blind to the fact that every bad situation is bad for somebody beside himself. The situation that was so bad for Stephen was equally bad, though in a different way, for the men who were guilty of his murder. Think what it does to a man to lynch another man! Stephen's extremity did not blind him to the fact that there were others beside himself involved in this outrageous deed.

But if a man in trouble does think of other people beside himself, they are most likely to be the people he loves. "Lord, take care of my family, watch over my children, remember my friends, help those who have counted on me." It is easy and natural to say that; it is good to do it. But Stephen went further than that: he thought of the people who were responsible for his death, his mortal enemies. **Lord, do not hold this sin against them.**

What a light that prayer throws on the nature of man. It makes it clear in the first place that it is possible for a man to bring the most powerful passions of self-preservation and hate under the sovereign rule of his spirit. It is natural for a man to hit back when he is struck; if he cannot hit back with his fist, then he can lash with his tongue and vilify with his mind. It is supernatural for a man not to hit back but to take it, and to take it as an opportunity to show the greatness of the human heart and spirit. Jesus performed this supernatural feat; he forgave his enemies. Stephen, following in his Master's spirit, performed the same feat. Over and over again it has been done by nameless heroes of the spirit.

This prayer also makes it evident that it is possible to distinguish between the deed and the doer, the sin and the sinner. What they did was wrong. It could never be called right. And yet they themselves might be made right and set right. The deed is done; it cannot be undone. The doer is not done: he is alive; he can be changed. Therefore do not hold the deed against him for that would mean that the door to the future had closed in his face. That is part, at least, of what forgiveness means.

The spirit of forgiveness to which Stephen's last words give unforgettable form is a spirit that cannot be reserved for great emergencies. It is impossible to imagine Stephen as a hard, unyielding, grudging young man a week before he was stoned. If he had been, the stoning would have stripped the skeleton bare. When a man is really up against it, the best and the worst in him are revealed. The crises in a man's life indicate most accurately the level of his char-

8 And Saul was consenting unto his death. And at that time there was a great persecution against the church which was at Jerusalem; and they were all scattered abroad throughout the regions of Judea and Samaria, except the apostles.

he had said this, he fell asleep. 1 And
8 Saul was consenting to his death.

And on that day a great persecution arose against the church in Jerusalem; and they were all scattered throughout the region of Judea and Sa-ma'ri-a, except the

8:1. Saul was consenting: For the Greek word cf. Luke 11:48. Saul was not necessarily an actual member of the Sanhedrin that condemned Stephen. But as a member of the Cilician synagogue he may have taken part in the original dispute, and Luke suggests that the moral consent he gave to the execution carried with it as much responsibility as the actual doing of the deed.

acter. A man whose spirit is pinched all his life is likely to be only the more pinched when life pushes him into a corner. Whereas the man whose spirit has been broad and generous day in and day out, will be generous under the most trying and embarrassing circumstances. Generosity has become the standard pitch of his spirit.

Stephen's prayer of forgiveness was simply the expression of his attitude toward men at all times. It is not enough for us to cultivate the habit of saying the right things in our prayers. We must train ourselves in habitual patterns of thought and attitude. We all deal with people whose interests and purposes do not coincide with our own. We collide with them. In our own eyes they are wrong. And yet if we hold it against them, the poison spreads, the communications between ourselves and them are cut off, the future is blocked. If such an attitude of mind becomes habitual, it will gradually paralyze our own spirit and we shall perish like seeds without moisture.

Rather will we cultivate the enlargement of mind and spirit which overflows the barriers between us, overlooks the differences, overrides the deeds done against us in the interest of a future that is unhampered by preserved animosities and cherished grievances. So the prayer of forgiveness becomes the pattern of a forgiving life.

8:1. ***Saul's First Appearance.***—The first three references to the chief character of the Acts are significant. Saul first appears as a silent witness to the death of Stephen (7:58), to which he then gives his full consent (vs. 1), and after that proceeds to participate actively in the campaign against the Christians (vs. 3). Those three steps represent the normal course of evil in a man's life. First, the man is a silent witness; then a consenting spectator; and finally an active participant. The difficulty of changing the course and arresting the progress of evil becomes greater at each step of the way. Take, for example, the growing evil of broken homes. A young person begins by seeing divorce, witnessing its procedure, being indirectly involved in its results. Soon he takes what he has witnessed for granted; he gives consent to it as a necessary and perhaps even good measure, with only the old-fashioned conventions against it and some new psychiatry for it. Then it is not a great step to take part in it and work for its promotion. That is the way evil grows in a man.

Yet as the opposite of this, one remembers the shining fact of another man's goodness which was beginning to be at work in Saul. It is nowhere stated in so many words, but the conclusion is a difficult one to avoid. The spectacle of Stephen being stoned to death, yet not losing his faith or courage but abounding more and more in spiritual power, was one if not the first of the strongest influences which finally changed Saul into Paul.

So the influence of one man spreads, not like a chain, link to link in an unbroken succession, but like a fire, spark to spark, leaping from life to life, across continents, from century to century. Stephen caught it from his Master, passed it on to Paul; from Paul it has spread to men and women in every corner of the world. Stephen had no idea of the influence his brave death was to have on the future of the world. Men seldom do. Human influence that can be calculated and predicted can usually be discounted. As far as Stephen ever knew, he lost his young life for nothing and his memory would disappear with his generation. Not so! His name is still alive. It speaks for the heroic spirit in man, the willingness to suffer without the hope of gain, and to witness to the truth in spite of the consequences. The influence of that spirit is the surplus of its abundant life which, without conscious effort, overflows into the lives of other people.

We cannot but be struck by the disproportion between the duration of a man's life and the duration of his influence on future generations. Every one of us leaves a trail either modest or brilliant, and this conviction should make itself felt in all the acts of our lives. . . . The wakes of Moses,

2 And devout men carried Stephen *to his burial,* and made great lamentation over him.

3 As for Saul, he made havoc of the church, entering into every house, and haling men and women committed *them* to prison.

4 Therefore they that were scattered abroad went every where preaching the word.

apostles. 2 Devout men buried Stephen, and made great lamentation over him. 3 But Saul laid waste the church, and entering house after house, he dragged off men and women and committed them to prison.

4 Now those who were scattered went

2. The **devout men** would be Jews rather than Christians, for the law prescribed the burial of executed criminals (Deut. 21:22-23). As apparently no **lamentation** or wake was permitted after a legal execution, is this another hint of an irregular lynching?

3. Saul laid waste the church: But did he in fact have a part in this particular persecution? Though he confesses several times that he had persecuted the Christians (Gal. 1:13, 23; I Cor. 15:9; Phil. 3:6), it is nowhere stated that he did so in Jerusalem, and from Galatians it would seem that Damascus was the center of his persecuting activity.

3. Story of Philip (8:4-40)

a) The Mission to Samaria (8:4-13)

According to Harnack, 8:4-40 belongs to a source in which interest is divided between Jerusalem and Caesarea; he calls it the "Jerusalem-Caesarean" source and finds its continuation in 9:32–11:18 and 12:1-24. The present section, however, appears to be composite, as, inserted in the story of Philip, we have a paragraph dealing with Peter's visit to Samaria and his encounter with Simon Magus. This "Petrine" interlude may possibly be derived from Jerusalem Source A.

R. B. Rackham well notes that "this chapter is thoroughly Old Testament in its spirit and language, and . . . we could imagine that we are reading of a second Elijah or Elisha. . . . Like an Old Testament prophet [Philip] wanders about, with sudden and spontaneous movements under the immediate impulse of the Spirit" (*The Acts of the Apostles* [London: Methuen & Co., 1901; "The Westminster Commentary"], p. 112). Philip is the typical Christian "prophet" and "evangelist." His mission to Samaria is chiefly important as marking the first definite initiative into non-Jewish territory, and was naturally enough undertaken by one who was himself a "Hellenist" and therefore, though no doubt as loyal a Jew as his fellows, would feel a deeper interest in the outside world.

of Buddha, of Confucius, of Lao Tse, of Christ, probably exert a greater influence over humanity today than when these men were pondering over its fate and happiness.[6]

4. ***The Church Grows.***—As a result of Stephen's life and death, things in Jerusalem came to a head. It was clearly seen that Christianity could not bloom as a branch of Judaism. They were plants from the same stock, but they were different plants. The Christians were driven out of Jerusalem; they **were scattered abroad.** There are two things to notice about that dispersal.

(*a*) It was something that the people would not have chosen. No one likes to be dispossessed or evicted. It must have appeared at the time to be pure disaster. And yet it was that very disaster that was to be the dispersal of the seed. The Christians fled to the coastal towns and ultimately to Rome. It was like the bursting of the seed pod. How often it happens that history moves forward by steps that seem to us to be steps toward destruction and defeat. The most painful event in a man's life may be the means for releasing hitherto unknown talents and powers. Had the Christians been cooped up in Jerusalem they would have enjoyed a comfortable and happy life. Once they were scattered abroad, they faced all the dangers of a homeless people, but they carried with them the seed of a new life that was meant for the whole world.

(*b*) Once they were scattered, they **went about preaching the word.** In other words,

[6] Lecomte du Noüy, *Human Destiny* (New York: Longmans, Green & Co., 1947), pp. 254-55.

5 Then Philip went down to the city of
Samaria, and preached Christ unto them.
6 And the people with one accord gave
heed unto those things which Philip spake,
hearing and seeing the miracles which he
did.
7 For unclean spirits, crying with loud
voice, came out of many that were possessed
with them: and many taken with palsies,
and that were lame, were healed.
8 And there was great joy in that city.

about preaching the word. 5 Philip went
down to a city of Sa-ma'ri-a, and proclaimed
to them the Christ. 6 And the multitudes
with one accord gave heed to what was said
by Philip, when they heard him and saw
the signs which he did. 7 For unclean spirits
came out of many who were possessed,
crying with a loud voice; and many who
were paralyzed or lame were healed. 8 So
there was much joy in that city.

For the Samaritans formed a halfway house between Judaism and the Gentile world proper. They were a heterogeneous people of mixed Israelitish and heathen blood. But their religion was genuinely Israelitish; they worshiped Yahweh, kept the sabbath, practiced circumcision. But their holy city was Gerizim, and of the Jewish scripture canon they accepted only the Pentateuch. Though hated and despised by their Jewish neighbors, they were not put upon a level with the heathen; their observance of the law was regarded as very defective, but they were not looked upon as complete aliens; and social intercourse with them, though not frequent, was pronounced by the rabbis to be permissible (John 4:9 must not be taken too literally). Thus Philip's new move involved no definite breach of Jewish law. But it revealed a concern for the Samaritans that no ordinary Jew would feel, and to that extent it marked an advance on the spirit of Judaism in general and an approach to Jesus' own broader sympathy. It is no doubt chiefly for this reason that Luke records the visit.

5. A city of Samaria, the Western text reading, seems preferable to "the city of Samaria" (KJV), for in the N.T. "Samaria" always refers to the territory rather than the capital city Sebaste, and "the city *of* Samaria," meaning "called Samaria," is an English and not a Greek idiom. Lake and Cadbury guess that the town in question is Gitta, with which Justin Martyr connects Simon Magus.

---

they used their extremity as an opportunity. If they could not preach Christ in Jerusalem, they would preach him in some other place. The main thing was to tell the world about him. What happened to them in the process was relatively unimportant. Such behavior is the unmistakable sign of maturity. When a man has one major objective and pursues it wherever and however and in whatever form or shape the circumstances allow, the chances are good that he has reached spiritual maturity. If that objective is, in some form or other, to do the will of God, then his maturity is complete. A man can follow that aim no matter what happens. He can want above all things to do God's will whether he is sick or well, rich or poor, happy or sad. If he cannot do it in one way, he will do it in another.

5-8. *Philip's Ministry in Samaria.*—The exact town to which Philip went is not known. The important thing is that it was a town out of bounds as far as Christianity was then known. Up to this point, Christian preaching had been confined to Jerusalem. But Christianity, by its very nature, refuses to be circumscribed by any geographical area. There is in Christian men and women the compulsion to carry the Christian gospel to the place that has never known it. Like nature, Christianity abhors a vacuum. If it exists on one side of the railroad tracks, it will not rest until it is carried to the other side. If it originates in the East, it will not be content until it spreads to the West. If it has its beginning among simple people, it will not cease until it has captured the minds and hearts of the intellectuals. If it is in the heads of the ruling classes, it must also become the possession of the rank and file. As far as the record in the Acts is concerned, the ministry of Philip is Christianity's first venture outside the local precincts of Jerusalem. It marks a new stage in the history of the gospel.

Philip's ministry in Samaria, as far as it is described in the Acts, consisted of preaching and performing miracles. About the preaching we know only one thing—the burden of the preaching was Christ. The miracles were the result of that preaching. They were the release of a new life among the people. They were the result of God's power brought to bear through Christ upon the lives of men and women. Two sorts of miracles are indicated; first, the healing

9 But there was a certain man, called Simon, which beforetime in the same city used sorcery, and bewitched the people of Samaria, giving out that himself was some great one:

10 To whom they all gave heed, from the least to the greatest, saying, This man is the great power of God.

11 And to him they had regard, because that of long time he had bewitched them with sorceries.

12 But when they believed Philip preaching the things concerning the kingdom of God, and the name of Jesus Christ, they were baptized, both men and women.

9 But there was a man named Simon
who had previously practiced magic in the
city and amazed the nation of Sa-ma'ri-a,
saying that he himself was somebody great.
10 They all gave heed to him, from the
least to the greatest, saying, "This man is
that power of God which is called Great."
11 And they gave heed to him, because for
a long time he had amazed them with his
magic. 12 But when they believed Philip
as he preached good news about the kingdom of God and the name of Jesus Christ,
they were baptized, both men and women.

9-10. For **Simon** see on 8:14-25. With **somebody great** cf. Theudas' claim in 5:36 "to be somebody," and Luke 1:32, "He will be great, and will be called the Son of the Most High." Simon, like Theudas, evidently had messianic ambitions. **That power of God which is called Great:** The sentence is awkward, and the Greek may be a mistranslation of an Aramaic phrase meaning "this is the power of the God who is called Great"—**Great** being a title used by foreigners of the God of the Jews. **Power** is a Jewish reverential substitute for "God" (cf. Mark 14:62, "sitting at the right hand of Power," where Luke in his parallel [Luke 22:69] adds, as here, the explanatory words "of God").

12. The kingdom of God and the name of Jesus Christ: Implying, perhaps in contrast to Simon's false claim, that it was only through Jesus, the true Christ, that the messianic kingdom would come. Lake and Cadbury note that "the usage of Acts suggests . . . that Kingdom of God here means the Church—the society of believers in Jesus, who through his representatives, using the power of his name, receive the Holy Spirit which cleanses and saves" (*Beginnings of Christianity,* IV, 91).

of nervous and psychological disorders with all the moral and spiritual implications that such disorders inevitably suggest; and second, the healing of the bodies of those who were suffering from organic disorders. However we may evaluate these miracles, and whether or not they are today the accompaniment of Christian preaching, it is fair to say at least this much, that wherever the gospel of Christ is truly preached the lives of men and women are transformed, fears are removed, inhibitions cleared away, selfishness brought under control, and physical disorders modified by spiritual growth.

The response to Philip's preaching was immediate. Crowds followed him wherever he went. They listened to him and looked at him. They heard what he had to say and they watched what he did. Such a response indicates once again the fullness of Philip's ministry. A ministry in which there is something to listen to and nothing to look at is an incomplete one. Preaching by itself is powerless. Preaching that is great preaching will prove itself by the results which it produces in the lives of the people who hear it.

As a consequence of Philip's ministry, **there was much joy in that city.** We are often likely to think that the arrival of a Christian missionary in a non-Christian community is like the gathering of storm clouds. Some people think that Christianity is a depressing thing, a combination of unwelcome disciplines and unnecessary restraints which a person reluctantly accepts because he dares not do otherwise. Quite the contrary is true, however, wherever real Christianity is concerned. It always brings joy, for it is comparable to releasing a man from prison. Whatever discipline is involved is accepted gladly as a means by which real freedom is attained. One of the best tests that can be suggested for a Christian church in a community is this: Are the people rejoicing because it is there? If they are not, then that church might well re-examine its life and character.

9-25. *The Story of Simon the Charlatan.*— Simon is one of the minor characters in the book of the Acts. He interests us not only because of the role he plays in this particular book, but also because he keeps turning up over and over again in the history of religion.

13 Then Simon himself believed also: and when he was baptized, he continued with Philip, and wondered, beholding the miracles and signs which were done.

14 Now when the apostles which were at Jerusalem heard that Samaria had re-

13 Even Simon himself believed, and after being baptized he continued with Philip. And seeing signs and great miracles performed, he was amazed.

14 Now when the apostles at Jerusalem

---

b) THE APOSTLES' CONFIRMATORY VISIT (8:14-25)

This paragraph reads like the account of an episcopal tour of confirmation. Peter and John, like Barnabas on a later occasion (11:22), are sent to investigate a new development in missionary work, to bestow on the converts by the laying on of apostolic hands a grace which presumably Philip could not bestow, and to give to the new Samaritan church the apostolic sanction which was necessary for its regular organization. All this seems to reflect the point of view of a later age when ecclesiasticism had become much more self-conscious. This comes out in three ways: (*a*) Our author thinks of authority as being centralized in the hands of an apostolic college without whose imprimatur no undertaking was valid. But this is almost certainly to misread history (see on 1:12). No doubt Peter and John did visit Samaria; but the idea that they went as an official delegation to do something that Philip could not do betrays later conceptions. It is very questionable whether the apostles ever constituted an official board with oversight over the whole church in its various local divisions. As A. C. McGiffert says: "It is widely said that the bishops were the successors of the apostles. It would perhaps be as near the truth to say that the apostles were the successors of the bishops! For the official character that has been ascribed to the apostles since the second century was the result of carrying back to them the official character of the bishops" (*A History of Christianity in the Apostolic Age* [New York: Charles Scribner's Sons, 1896], p. 97 n.). (*b*) We have here too the suggestion that the Holy Spirit could be conveyed to converts by the mediation of apostles and no others. Luke evidently supposes that Peter and John exercised a peculiar function not possessed by Philip. But such an association of the gift of the Spirit with a particular office or class of men is foreign to the ideas of the early apostolic age, as is shown by Luke himself in other passages—e.g., in 9:17 Ananias, an ordinary disciple, lays his hands on Paul in order that he may receive the Holy Spirit; and in 2:4 no human agent at all is in view. In 2:33 Peter says that the exalted Jesus has poured forth his Spirit, and there is no suggestion that he, as an apostle, can alone mediate the gift. (*c*) Still less does the tying up of the gift of the Spirit with some specific rite such as baptism or the laying on of hands belong to these earliest months (see also on 6:6). The truly primitive point of view is reflected even by Luke, not only in the passages already referred to, but also in 10:44, 11:15 ff., where it is clearly stated that the Spirit fell on Cornelius and his fellows while Peter was still speaking, and before they were baptized. The evident possession by them of the Christian experience, the fact that they had already "received the Holy Spirit," was precisely the reason urged by Peter that they should then receive baptism—not something which followed the performance of the rite.

Simon, as his traditional name "the Magus" shows, is the typical wonder-working false prophet, and acts as foil to the typical Christian prophet, Philip. The picture suggested by vss. 9-13 of a competition in wonder-working reminds us of Moses' encounter with the magicians of Egypt, or St. Patrick and St. Columba in rivalry with the druids. The decay of orthodox pagan religion had created a keen demand for teachers who by esoteric knowledge of the occult could open up the way to God. The current intermixture of Greek philosophy and Eastern mysticism had given a very varied hue to their pretensions, and the whole Mediterranean world abounded with seers, astrologers, spiritualists, exorcists, and miracle-workers. Some of them were no doubt sincere and able men, as for example Apollonius of Tyana, whose biography by Philostratus rivaled the Gospels in popularity. But the temptation to gain through quackery must have been

ceived the word of God, they sent unto them Peter and John:
15 Who, when they were come down, prayed for them, that they might receive the Holy Ghost:

heard that Sa-ma'ri-a had received the word of God, they sent to them Peter and John,
15 who came down and prayed for them that they might receive the Holy Spirit;

too strong for most, and the majority were certainly charlatans. From the references in Acts, Justin Martyr, and Irenaeus, there seems little doubt that Simon claimed to be Messiah, and instituted in Samaria a movement that was intended to rival Christianity. With his messianic pretensions he seems to have combined Gnostic speculations, including the common conception of a hierarchy of divine emanations or "powers," serving as mediators between God and man, of which he claimed himself to be the chief—"that power of God which is called Great." Justin Martyr tells us that in the reign of Claudius, Simon went to Rome where the senate honored him "with a statue erected upon the Tiber between the two bridges, with the Latin inscription, *Simoni Deo Sancto,* 'To Simon the Holy God' " (I Apology 26:2). This incredible statement has been explained by the discovery on an island in the Tiber, called "between the two bridges," of an altar inscribed *"Semoni Sanco Deo"*—Semo Sancus being an ancient Sabine deity! As Streeter says, "Justin's veracity . . . is completely vindicated, somewhat at the expense of his intelligence" (*The Primitive Church* [New York: The Macmillan Co., 1929], p. 13). Besides giving his name to the sin of "simony" or the use of money to attain spiritual ends, Simon came to be regarded in Christian tradition as the father of all heresy. In Justin's day, about one hundred years later, there were heretics called "Simonians." In the Pseudo-Clementine literature of the third century Simon appears as the foremost opponent of Peter in debate in various cities, and in the next century legend is busy with his end. Denounced by Peter at Rome, he seeks to rehabilitate himself by a superlative feat of magic and offers to fly. The experiment has fatal results!

14. John: If, as is probable, this is the son of Zebedee—who had once wished to call down fire on a Samaritan town! (Luke 9:54)—this is the last time he is mentioned in Acts. But it is just possible that the reference is to John Mark (12:25; 15:37), who in 13:13 is called simply "John."

He is a magician. Magic is man's attempt to change the natural course of events for his own benefit. It is the imposition of man's will upon a higher will. In Simon's case, as in every other case, it is self-centered. His feats of magic glorified himself. By them he bewitched the people, dazzled them. He had a large following, as charlatans often do. There is a deep-seated desire in human beings to control the mysterious forces that govern life, and by exercising that control to bend the will of the gods to their own favor. It is the natural desire in us all to make things easy, rather than to become great. Anyone who can even pretend to bring this about is assured of a large if fickle following. The desire is so strong in people that they are blind to the quackery of the men who work their tricks before their eyes.

With the arrival of Philip, however, Simon found things quite different, for Philip performed miracles. There is a great difference between magic and miracles. Whereas magic is man's attempt to control and alter the natural course of events for his own benefit, a miracle is God's use of his own laws in extraordinary ways to bring to pass his own purposes. In magic we find the imposition of one will upon another, whereas in a miracle it is the surrender of the lesser to the greater will in order that the will of God may work through the will of his servant. Philip was glorifying not himself but God. It is encouraging to notice the fact that while people are seduced by quacks, nevertheless they still have the capacity to respond to the real thing when it appears. When Philip came on the scene, they recognized his superiority, and Simon's trade fell off considerably. Simon himself was converted. He saw in Philip's power a power that was superior to his own, and he made the mistake of thinking that he could manipulate this power as he had previously manipulated the magician's power. He offered to pay for the power, indicating that his conversion, like many conversions, was not a real one, that his point of view was still a selfish one, and that he was attempting to use religion in his own interest.

There are always people who are looking for magic rather than miracle. They pray in

16 (For as yet he was fallen upon none
of them: only they were baptized in the
name of the Lord Jesus.)

17 Then laid they *their* hands on them,
and they received the Holy Ghost.

18 And when Simon saw that through
laying on of the apostles' hands the Holy
Ghost was given, he offered them money,

19 Saying, Give me also this power, that
on whomsoever I lay hands, he may receive the Holy Ghost.

20 But Peter said unto him, Thy money
perish with thee, because thou hast thought
that the gift of God may be purchased
with money.

21 Thou hast neither part nor lot in
this matter: for thy heart is not right in
the sight of God.

22 Repent therefore of this thy wickedness, and pray God, if perhaps the thought
of thine heart may be forgiven thee.

23 For I perceive that thou art in the
gall of bitterness, and *in* the bond of iniquity.

24 Then answered Simon, and said, Pray
ye to the Lord for me, that none of these
things which ye have spoken come upon
me.

25 And they, when they had testified and
preached the word of the Lord, returned
to Jerusalem, and preached the gospel in
many villages of the Samaritans.

16 for it had not yet fallen on any of them,
but they had only been baptized in the
name of the Lord Jesus. 17 Then they laid
their hands on them and they received the
Holy Spirit. 18 Now when Simon saw that
the Spirit was given through the laying on
of the apostles' hands, he offered them
money, 19 saying, "Give me also this power,
that any one on whom I lay my hands may
receive the Holy Spirit." 20 But Peter said
to him, "Your silver perish with you, because you thought you could obtain the
gift of God with money! 21 You have neither part nor lot in this matter, for your
heart is not right before God. 22 Repent
therefore of this wickedness of yours, and
pray to the Lord that, if possible, the intent of your heart may be forgiven you.
23 For I see that you are in the gall of bitterness and in the bond of iniquity." 24 And
Simon answered, "Pray for me to the Lord,
that nothing of what you have said may
come upon me."

25 Now when they had testified and
spoken the word of the Lord, they returned to Jerusalem, preaching the gospel
to many villages of the Samaritans.

16-17. Here it is not baptism but the laying on of hands that bestows the Spirit. In 19:1 ff. certain Christians at Ephesus, who had not received the Holy Spirit as a result of the "baptism of John," are "baptized in the name of the Lord Jesus," and forthwith "when Paul had laid his hands upon them, the Holy Spirit came on them." The two passages taken together suggest that "the baptism of the early church was a conflation of the water-baptism of John with the Christian baptism which was the gift of the Spirit," and that "possibly the 'laying on of hands' was the specifically Christian element in baptism" (*Beginnings of Christianity,* IV, 93). See also on 2:37.

20. Gift: The Greek word means a free gift that cannot be bought.

22-24. If possible: the question being, of course, Simon's repentance. **In the gall of bitterness:** An echo of Deut. 29:18, where the first phrase relates to idolatry. The ERV mg. has "thou wilt become gall of bitterness"—i.e., Simon's sin will be a root of bitter dispute in the church. **Bond of iniquity** is from Isa. 58:6. Simon is held fast by the chain of his sin. The Western text ends vividly, "and he ceased not weeping greatly."

---

order to make God do what they want him to do, whereas true prayer is the surrender of the will of man to the will of God so that man will do what God wants him to do. There is always the temptation to use the sacraments of the church as magic rather than miracle, as techniques by which we control the forces that are greater than ourselves, rather than the means by which we become channels for those forces. Likewise there are always people who think that they can use religion for their own purposes. A man cannot buy religion any more than he can buy love. Religion, like love, is an end in itself. It cannot be sought in order to

26 And the angel of the Lord spake unto Philip, saying, Arise, and go toward the south, unto the way that goeth down from Jerusalem unto Gaza, which is desert.

26 But an angel of the Lord said to Philip, "Rise and go toward the south[f] to the road that goes down from Jesusalem

[f] Or *at noon*.

---

c) Philip and the Ethiopian Eunuch (8:26-40)

The story of Philip and the Ethiopian eunuch is most vividly told, very much in the style of a narrative from the books of Samuel or Kings. Was the eunuch a Jew or a Gentile? Eusebius refers to him as the first Gentile to embrace Christianity; so this Ethiopian has sometimes been regarded as an uncircumcised heathen, and his baptism as the first departure from the principle that Christianity was only for Jews, either native or proselyte. But there is nothing in the story to suggest any such far-reaching innovation. The fact that the Ethiopian was a pilgrim returning from Jerusalem, and that he was reading Isaiah, indicates that already he was at least a Jewish proselyte. Luke quite evidently regards not his case, but that of Cornelius, as the first admission of an uncircumcised Gentile. The stress laid on all the details of Cornelius' case, on the scruples that Peter found so hard to overcome, and on the controversy which the incident precipitated at Jerusalem—all this proves that Luke is describing what he considers to be the first case of the baptism of a heathen. He can hardly have thought of it as a mere repetition of the present event. The conversion of the Ethiopian is significant, not as introducing a new principle, but as an illustration of how far afield the gospel was already spreading. The most important feature of the story is the emergence for the first time of the great suffering servant passage in Isa. 53 as a specifically quoted text for Christian apologetic. If we can believe that the story rests on authentic tradition, this is of the greatest possible significance.

Vss. 26-40 contain a number of echoes of the story of Elijah (cf. I Kings 18:12; II Kings 2:16-17) which, combined with the echoes of Zephaniah noted below (on 8:26), have suggested to some scholars that the whole story may have been built up out of reminiscences extracted from the O.T. This appears a fantastic explanation of what is much more probably a perfectly natural coloring of the narrative by O.T. language.

26. An angel: Compare this verse with vss. 29 and 39, and note the interesting interchange between "angel" and "spirit." Cf. also 10:3 with 10:19, and see 23:8. **Toward the**

---

make him well, or to make him happy, or prosperous. It can be sought only for itself; but once found, it overflows in by-products of health and happiness and prosperity. It cannot be manipulated or controlled by man's personal desire. Those who pretend to such controls are charlatans. They often have a large following and the only thing that can stop them is the truth.

26-40. ***Philip Takes the Desert Route.***—One of the questions that is most often asked is this: How can we spread the Christian life from one person to another? How can we extend and promote the Christian movement? Americans are expert promoters. And yet when we look at the church, we know that it has lost this particular quality of the power to extend itself. Young people grow up to maturity and make their own decisions, apparently with little if any interest in the Christian movement. Well-living, intelligent men and women may have scant concern for the church, do nothing about it, contribute nothing to it, gain nothing from it. Outside the immediate circle of our relatives and friends is the world, the masses of men and women who are completely untouched by this resurrection movement. The question is: How can we make the movement move?

There is a clue in this story in the book of the Acts. Philip was one of the enthusiastic Christians, on fire with the life and message of Jesus. He was directed by God to leave Jerusalem and to go southward by the desert route. As he traveled southward, he overtook a man journeying by chariot. He had the impulse to draw up beside him, and he saw that he was reading. It was a page from Jewish scripture, from the prophet Isaiah. Philip looked at him and said, "Do you understand what you are reading?" The man said, "Not at all. Get up here and sit beside me and tell me what it is all about." Philip climbed up into the chariot and **opened his mouth, and began at the same Scripture, and preached unto him Jesus.**

Let us first consider what Philip found. The man he overtook was what might be called a

27 And he arose and went: and, behold,
a man of Ethiopia, a eunuch of great authority under Candace queen of the Ethiopians, who had the charge of all her treasure, and had come to Jerusalem for to
worship,
28 Was returning, and sitting in his
chariot read Esaias the prophet.
29 Then the Spirit said unto Philip, Go
near, and join thyself to this chariot.

to Gaza." This is a desert road. 27 And he
rose and went. And behold, an Ethiopian,
a eunuch, a minister of Can-da'ce, the
queen of the Ethiopians, in charge of all
her treasure, had come to Jerusalem to worship 28 and was returning; seated in his
chariot, he was reading the prophet Isaiah.
29 And the Spirit said to Philip, "Go up

---

south: This seems the most natural translation; but in the LXX the Greek word always means "midday," and it is possible that we ought here to translate "about noon" (cf. Zeph. 2:4; RSV mg.). Several curious verbal echoes of the LXX of Zephaniah occur in the narrative, including the use of this word and the mention of Ethiopia, Gaza, and Azotus (cf. this verse with Zeph. 2:4; vs. 27 with Zeph. 2:11-12; 3:10; vs. 39 with Zeph. 3:4). **This is a desert road:** Perhaps more probably "this place [i.e., Gaza] is deserted." Old Gaza, about two miles from the sea, had been destroyed by Alexander and was at this time "deserted." New Gaza, on the coast, was not destroyed till A.D. 66. The clause reads like an editorial note.

27. An Ethiopian: The Ethiopians were the Nubian race dwelling in the Nile region south of Egypt proper. It is only in modern times that they have been confused with the Abyssinians, who ethnologically and linguistically are Semitic. **A eunuch:** As such he would be excluded by the law from the "assembly of the Lord"; but for the more charitable prophetic attitude see Isa. 56:3 ff. **To worship** (προσκυνήσων), or "on a pilgrimage." Προσκυνητής is the regular modern Greek word for a "pilgrim" (cf. 24:11).

---

secretary of the treasury of a North African state which the Bible calls "Ethiopia," but probably not the state we know as Ethiopia. He was a man of property and prominence. He had come from North Africa to Jerusalem, for Jerusalem was known far and wide as the place where men of the spirit explored those realms of unseen things that were not always found in the more material cultures of the West. He had come to Jerusalem to worship. Whether he was a Jew or not, we do not know. While there he found, perhaps for the first time, the Jewish scripture. (But see Exeg.) He was reading the magnificent fifty-third chapter of the book of the prophet Isaiah, in which the prophet described the suffering of the innocent servant led like a lamb to the slaughter. When Philip asked him if he understood it, he said, "No, not exactly." How could he unless someone interpreted it to him?

What Philip found was this: He found a man who was seeking something, diligently, sincerely, earnestly, not self-satisfied, reaching out for something more than he had ever known before, and yet a man not understanding what it all meant. That was Philip's great opportunity. Without pressing the parallel too far, contemporary opportunity is somewhat comparable. For the bubble of prewar pride has been pricked. None of us is quite so sure of himself as he once was. No one in the present world can be confident in his own powers or in the powers of his fellow men alone to make the world go right. There are individuals who are discouraged; there are a great many people asking questions. But we have not yet gone far enough downgrade; there have not been enough disappointments; governments have not failed us often enough for disillusionment to set in altogether. This generation is in quest of something. They want to know what it is all about. They want to know the meaning of suffering and of the tragedy and the failure of mankind; and they want to do something toward the prevention of any such catastrophe again. They have a listening ear. There are some who are so preoccupied with frivolities that they will not hear, but by and large the representatives of the Christian movement today have an ear that is more ready to listen than any Christians have had in many a generation. That is what Philip found; that is what we find—a receptive frame of mind.

There are just two ways to spread anything in which you are greatly interested. The first is to live it yourself, and the other is to talk about it. There is no substitute for the first. The way to make anyone realize the value of something you care very much about is to show it forth in your own life. The way to attract

30 And Philip ran thither to *him*, and heard him read the prophet Esaias, and said, Understandest thou what thou readest?

31 And he said, How can I, except some man should guide me? And he desired Philip that he would come up and sit with him.

32 The place of the Scripture which he read was this, He was led as a sheep to the slaughter; and like a lamb dumb before his shearer, so opened he not his mouth:

33 In his humiliation his judgment was taken away: and who shall declare his generation? for his life is taken from the earth.

and join this chariot." 30 So Philip ran to
him, and heard him reading Isaiah the
prophet, and asked, "Do you understand
what you are reading?" 31 And he said,
"How can I, unless some one guides me?"
And he invited Philip to come up and sit
with him. 32 Now the passage of the scripture which he was reading was this:
"As a sheep led to the slaughter
or a lamb before its shearer is dumb,
so he opens not his mouth.
33 In his humiliation justice was denied
him.
Who can describe his generation?
For his life is taken up from the earth."

32-33. The quotation is from the LXX of Isa. 53:7-8 and is important as the first definite application of the passage to Jesus as the suffering Servant. Have we a clue to anything characteristic of Luke's view of Christ's death in the fact that the quotation, as here employed, avoids Isaiah's several references to bearing the sins of others, while Luke also omits both Mark's "give his life as a ransom for many" (cf. Luke 22:27 with Mark 10:45), and also—in the shorter Western text—his reference to the "blood of the covenant, which is poured out for many" (cf. Luke 22:19 with Mark 14:24)? Of vs. 33, Lake and Cadbury say: "The meaning of the original is apparently as obscure to Hebrew scholars as are these Greek words. . . . The truth seems to be that the translators did not know what the meaning of the Hebrew was, and gave a literal but unintelligible rendering" (*Beginnings of Christianity,* IV, 97). But see on 13:36.

---

someone to a cause which you think is worth everything in life is to demonstrate it yourself. One way to spread the Christian movement is for Christians to live it. But that is not the only way. We spread things not only by living them, but also by talking about them, by passing the word on and passing the fire from one person to another by persuasion. To be sure, one of the things that made the great abolition movement in the United States spread was the fact that Abraham Lincoln lived it. He was possessed by the idea of the emancipation of humanity. But that by itself would not have been enough. Lincoln not only lived it; he talked about it again and again, in the Cooper Union address, the Lincoln-Douglas debates, in the inaugural addresses, and in speeches before Congress. He talked about it wherever he went, and so the movement spread by the power of his example and by the power of his persuasion.

Apparently that is what happened in the early days of Christianity. The early Christians drew other people to them because they had something that other people recognized as supremely worth while. In the second century Tertullian wrote, "See how these Christians love one another." That is the real reason why the movement spread. But they also talked about it, and the interesting thing is that when Philip climbed up into the chariot with his friend from Ethiopia, he **opened his mouth.** When people saw the early Christians they cried, "Look at them!" And that exclamation was followed by "Listen to them!"

We have been relying chiefly on the first means to spread the movement, by living it, by being it, by shining, and sometimes we are terribly discouraged. We have been shining now, dimly perhaps, some more than others, but as brightly as we can, for a long time and no one seems to be greatly attracted by our light. We have gone on living quietly, being the thing that we believe in, and yet there seems to be no irresistible magnetic force about us. Our children are not attracted by it many times. Our friends are not interested and the world passes it by. We have never opened our mouths about it. There is a strange kind of reticence that has settled upon the Christian movement like a fog bank, and it does not seem likely that the movement will ever really move until that fog lifts. Have you ever talked to one of your contemporaries about the Christian religion? Have you ever sat down with a college classmate and opened your mouth and talked to him about the things that concern him more than anything else in the world? We say that we respect the liberty and the rights of

34 And the eunuch answered Philip, and said, I pray thee, of whom speaketh the prophet this? of himself, or of some other man?

35 Then Philip opened his mouth, and began at the same Scripture, and preached unto him Jesus.

36 And as they went on *their* way, they came unto a certain water: and the eunuch said, See, *here is* water; what doth hinder me to be baptized?

37 And Philip said, If thou believest with all thine heart, thou mayest. And he answered and said, I believe that Jesus Christ is the Son of God.

38 And he commanded the chariot to stand still: and they went down both into the water, both Philip and the eunuch; and he baptized him.

34 And the eunuch said to Philip, "About
whom, pray, does the prophet say this,
about himself or about some one else?"
35 Then Philip opened his mouth, and
beginning with this scripture he told him
the good news of Jesus. 36 And as they
went along the road they came to some
water, and the eunuch said, "See, here is
water! What is to prevent my being baptized?"[g] 38 And he commanded the chariot
to stop, and they both went down into the
water, Philip and the eunuch, and he bap-

[g] Other ancient authorities add all or most of verse 37, *And Philip said, "If you believe with all your heart, you may." And he replied, "I believe that Jesus Christ is the Son of God."*

36. After the words **What is to prevent my being baptized?** the Western text adds, "And Philip said, 'If you believe with all your heart, you may.' And he replied, 'I believe that Jesus Christ is the Son of God.' " (RSV mg.; vs. 37 in KJV.) This probably represents the earliest form of the baptismal creed; and it is noticeable that it is an expansion, not of the trinitarian formula, but of the primitive formula "in the name of Jesus Christ."

people to think for themselves, and so we do. But there is something strange about reticence when it goes that far and when it comes into the realm of things that presumably we care so much about.

We have already seen what Philip found and what he did—he **opened his mouth.** Finally, what did Philip say? He **preached unto him Jesus.** It would be interesting if we could read that account in modern English, i.e., taken out of a modern situation. We would assume that when we got into conversation in the chariot with a stranger, we would have to make some talk first to establish a point of contact. We would ask him about his family, what class he was in at college, what club he belonged to, what his business was. Not so with Philip. He began from the scripture, where he was, and preached unto him Jesus, right then and there, not beating around the bush. He went straight to the things which concerned him most. We are not only not sure how to do that; we are not at all sure that we want to do it.

In the last part of the nineteenth century, on the streets of Chicago, an older man approached a younger man who was a stranger to him and said to him, "Are you a Christian?" The younger man said, "It is none of your business." The older man said, "Yes, it is." Said the younger, "Then you must be Dwight L. Moody." He was. Moody had the capacity not only to live the Christian religion but to talk about it, and to talk about it with anybody and everybody everywhere he went, and by talking he spread it.

Yet when we try to duplicate that, to transcribe it into our way of living, we are likely to produce something like this, found in one of Thornton Wilder's novels. It grew out of the doggerel verse that he found for children in a Middle Western schoolbook.

> George Brush is my name;
> America's my nation;
> Ludington's my dwelling place
> And heaven's my destination.[7]

George Brush was an upstanding young man. He was graduated from a Baptist college and was converted. He went about the country selling textbooks. He made it his business to talk to everyone he met about Christ. With an earnestness that seems to us a trifle artificial and forced, he went up to a typical Middle Western businessman in a smoking car and said, "Brother, can I talk to you about the most important thing in life?" The man looked at him and said, "Say, if it's insurance, I've got all I

[7] *Heaven's My Destination* (New York: Harper & Bros., 1935), title-page. Used by permission.

39 And when they were come up out of
the water, the Spirit of the Lord caught
away Philip, that the eunuch saw him no
more: and he went on his way rejoicing.
40 But Philip was found at Azotus: and
passing through he preached in all the
cities, till he came to Caesarea.

9 And Saul, yet breathing out threatenings and slaughter against the disciples of the Lord, went unto the high
priest,

tized him. **39** And when they came up out
of the water, the Spirit of the Lord caught
up Philip; and the eunuch saw him no
more, and went on his way rejoicing. **40** But
Philip was found at A-zo′tus, and passing
on he preached the gospel to all the towns
till he came to Caes-a-re′a.

9 But Saul, still breathing threats and
murder against the disciples of the Lord,

---

39. The Spirit of the Lord: cf. II Kings 2:16. In Acts the phrase is used only here; but cf. 16:7, "the Spirit of Jesus," which is probably the meaning here, the title "Lord" being transferred as usual from Yahweh to Christ. No gift of the Spirit is said to follow baptism, unless we read with the Western text, "The Holy Spirit fell on the eunuch, but the angel of the Lord caught away Philip."

40. Azotus is the O.T. Ashdod. Among **all the towns** visited may have been **Lydda** and **Joppa**, where Peter, in 9:32, may have followed up and confirmed Philip's work, just as he had previously done in Samaria. **Caesarea** was the headquarters of the Roman procurators of Judea. Apparently it was Philip's home, for in 21:8 he is still resident there.

E. Conversion of Saul (9:1-31)

This section is clearly the continuation of 8:3 and may come from the same Antiochene source. Harnack, however, assigns it to a special "Pauline source," while Lake thinks that ch. 9, which by giving prominence to Ananias seems to belittle the inde-

---

want. If it's oil wells, I don't touch 'em. And if it's religion, I'm saved." That was the end of the conversation. I cite that for the problem that it raises. It does not work very well, and we shy away from that kind of talk.

Another incident is far more congenial to us. A young Presbyterian minister was in charge of a large church in a great industrial city. The most active and generous person of the church was a woman. She was married to one of the most prominent and wealthy men of the community. He never came to church, he did nothing for it, he gave nothing to it. And as the years went on, that man was on the conscience of the young minister. And he said to himself, "I have got to do something about that man." So, after long deliberation, he finally made an appointment with him. He was an older man, austere, sitting behind a great desk in his office. The young man sat in front of him and proceeded with his story. In very simple terms he set before him the Christian proposition and he said, "I think you ought to do something about this one way or the other." And when he finished, there was dead silence. The man never spoke, never moved. So the young man gathered himself together and went over his story again, amplifying it a little. When he finished, still there was silence. At that point he wished he had never undertaken that particular mission, but he drew himself up once again and rehearsed his story. And when he finished, there was not a sound. And finally, while he wished for a way out of the room, the man reached for a pad and wrote something on it. He passed it to the young man and this was what he had written: "I am so deeply moved that I cannot speak." It was the first time that an adult, in a frank, straightforward way, had ever set before him the Christian gospel, and he became a member of the church and one of the great Christian leaders in that city.

The story of Philip ends with both men descending from the chariot and Philip baptizing his new friend in the name of Jesus: **And they went down both into the water, both Philip and the eunuch; and he baptized him.** It may not always work out that way. In many cases it will not. The point is that talk by itself certainly is empty, but when straight, honest talk is supported by character and directed by intelligent understanding, it is one of the most powerful weapons in the world.

9:1-9. ***The Conversion of Paul.***—Along the road from Jerusalem to Damascus moves a man with a purpose. Suddenly a great light shines from heaven and a voice speaks. The man is stunned and blinded by the light and rises to his feet to finish his journey. His purpose, so

pendence of Paul's apostleship, possibly "partially represents the tradition of Jerusalem as to the conversion of Paul" (*Beginnings of Christianity,* II, 153).

Saul was a native of Tarsus (21:39), a city important both as a commercial center and as the seat of a famous university. He was of pure Israelite descent and proud of it (II Cor. 11:22; Phil. 3:4-6). At the same time he was by birth a Roman citizen (22:28); and as Tarsus did not possess the *civitas,* the probability is that his father had obtained the citizenship as a freedman client of some Roman family, possibly the Aemilian house of which "Paul," adopted by Saul as his second name, was a cognomen. The family would be of some distinction and probably fairly well-to-do. By education and upbringing Saul would certainly be bilingual. It is likely that he was first educated at the university in Tarsus, but it is doubtful whether he would be allowed to absorb much purely Greek culture; for later he was sent to study at Jerusalem in the schools of the rabbis, about whom Josephus says that "the only wisdom they prize is a knowledge of our laws and the correct interpretation of the Scriptures." Definite allusions by Paul to classical writers are found only in the speeches of Acts and in passages in the epistles of doubtful authenticity (e.g., Acts 17:28; Tit. 1:12). In Jerusalem his chief mentor was Gamaliel, by whom he was "educated according to the strict manner of the law" (22:3), though, to judge by Gamaliel's attitude to the Christians in 5:34 ff., the teacher can have been marked by little of his pupil's fanaticism. Saul, like Stephen, should probably be ranked as a "Hellenist" Jew, for the accusers of Stephen appear to have been chiefly

---

dramatically interrupted, is completely and forever abandoned, and the man is a different man from head to foot.

Such are the bare facts of one of the most decisive encounters that ever took place. The man was Paul the apostle. The light and the voice were the manifestations of the risen Christ. The purpose abandoned was the extinction of the Christian church, and the life task undertaken was to preach the unsearchable riches of Christ.

In expounding the conversion of Paul, the modern interpreter must overleap two hurdles which stand in the way of modern man's understanding of the event. The first is its suddenness. Trained in the modern scientific school of thought, and breathing the atmosphere that the scientists have created, modern men are indoctrinated with the idea of gradual growth. One thing leads to another as surely as one link in a chain leads to another link. It is impossible for the modern man to think in terms of the purely miraculous. For him plants do not bloom overnight, nor does Venus arise full grown out of the sea. Nor do stubborn men suddenly change their character. In helping the modern churchman to get over this particular hurdle, the preacher can point out that the encounter between Paul and Christ did not come like a bolt from the blue. By and large, things do not happen in life without due preparation, either open or secret. Paul, for instance, had something to begin with. He had a serious desire to make the most of life. He was neither a waster nor an idler. Though he may never have seen Jesus, he had nevertheless seen him as he was reflected in the lives of his followers. There was at least a faint tracery of his likeness in the back of Paul's mind. Another item in the preparation for Paul's conversion is the fact that Paul was divided, torn between the demands of the law and of his own conscience; between what he wanted to do and what he actually did; between the stern religion of his fathers and the winsome, liberating religion of Jesus. As a young man, Paul was like an orchestra in which every section is playing a different tune. While the change that took place in Paul was a radical one, it reached far back into the recesses of his inner life. The actual explosion was sudden but there was a long fuse burning under the surface which had been lighted years before, and gradually the flame crept nearer and nearer to the explosive center.

At least so much preparation would seem to be required before an encounter with Christ is likely to take place. At least a man must have a sincere desire to make something out of his life. At least he must know something of Jesus so that he will recognize him when he sees him, and above all, the perils of a divided life must be sufficiently dangerous in his eyes to make him be constantly on the lookout for anything that will bring all the sections of the orchestra of his personality into a unison of a single grand theme.

The second hurdle for interpreters today is the supernatural nature of the experience that Paul had on the Damascus road. Visions and voices are suspect by men and women today, and people who see them and hear them are even more open to suspicion. People still ask whether Paul really met anyone on the road to Damascus, whether it was a real encounter or

"Hellenists," and if we are right in identifying Saul closely with them as a member of the synagogue of "those from Cilicia and Asia" (6:9), the inference is that he too belonged to the same class. But he was certainly an "orthodox" rather than a "liberal" Hellenist. His dual character as a Jew speaking the language of Jerusalem and a Roman citizen speaking fluent Greek perfectly fitted him to act as the great missionary mediator between Israel and the empire.

1. The Conversion Itself (9:1-19)

After Stephen's death Saul set out to instigate persecution at Damascus, and on the way occurred the event which changed him suddenly from the fiercest enemy of the faith to its foremost apostle. Paul refers four times in his epistles to his conversion experience (Gal. 1:15-16; I Cor. 9:1; 15:8; II Cor. 4:6). From these passages it is clear that he was convinced that the vision had a truly objective reality. He had "seen Jesus our Lord" (I Cor. 9:1) just as truly as had the original disciples. There was for Paul no distinction in kind between the appearance of Christ to himself at his conversion and the appearances to the eleven before the Ascension. Yet at the same time he thought of the vision as an inward revelation. God had been pleased "to reveal his Son in me" (Gal. 1:15).

---

whether it cannot all be explained in terms of the conflict going on inside Paul. The evidence seems to point the other way. The contemporaries of Paul obviously thought that it was a real encounter, for they included no less than four accounts of it in the slim volume called the N.T. Paul himself evidently relied on it as fact, for on two occasions when he was fighting for his life, once in the temple and once before the king, he turned to the major experience of his life as the clue to it all and for the justification of everything that he had done. Our own experience goes far to confirm what Paul believed to be true. There are times when a claim lays hold of us in such an unmistakable way that we can describe it only in terms of concrete reality—lights and voices. It speaks to us in words that are undeniable, and by the purity of its brightness it blinds us to everything but itself. It is a real encounter, after which we are a different person. The actual form of it does not matter so much as the content which we ourselves find within the form, and its consequences in our own life.

Paul stands, therefore, as one of the primary examples of the twice-born man. The religious history of his life could not be fairly represented by a graph. It would take something more than a birth certificate to indicate his real and true biography. For there came a day when he traveled toward Damascus, about noon, when suddenly without warning, **there shined round about him a light from heaven.** In a single flash that light illuminated not only the dome of heaven but the whole earth and the way of man as well. In its brightness some of the most crucial differences of life are made surprisingly clear. In an age when the twice-born man is less familiar than the once-born man, it is necessary from time to time to point out some of the implications that stream from the fact that there are men like Paul who have been changed overnight.

In the first place twice-born men make it clear that there can be a dividing line in a man's life, a real before and after; that a man need not be the same kind of person forever and ever. Paul's life was virtually bisected by the Damascus road. Before it he was a persecutor of Christianity; after it he was its most passionate propagator. Before it his life was increasingly crippled by a growing sense of guilt; after it his life was crowned with the glory that he found in Christ. On all sides we hear it said that once a man's life has been set, no radical change can be made in it. No more than a leopard can change his spots can a man change the original cut of his life. Against that the voices of all the twice-born men cry out. They tell their own story and say, "Look at me—before and after!" True, a man cannot satisfactorily change the course of his life so long as the center remains the same. The world will stagger back and forth between war and peace so long as it swings from the center of national self-interest. So will a man alternate between resolution and remorse until his life is reorganized around a new center. But in Paul's character the center was changed from Paul to Christ, and how wonderfully different was the course of Paul's life thereafter!

The twice-born man also makes clear the difference between seeing and believing. To see a thing a man needs only to stand still and look. To believe a thing a man must surrender himself to it, welcome it, feel it, commit himself to it. Paul had always been a religious man, but his religion had been the religion of his

He had had the first of those mystical experiences in which he held communion with the indwelling Christ.

There are three accounts in Acts of Saul's conversion—the present passage; 22:4 ff., in Paul's speech to the crowd at Jerusalem; 26:12 ff., in Paul's defense before Agrippa. In the descriptions of the vision there are minor discrepancies. In 9:7 Saul's companions "stood speechless, hearing the voice but seeing no one"; in 22:9 they "saw the light but did not hear the voice"; while in 26:13-14 there was "a light from heaven, brighter than the sun, shining round me and those who journeyed with me," but apparently Saul alone "heard a voice." Much more important is the divergence as to how the call to the apostleship of the Gentiles was given to Saul. In 26:16 ff. the commission is given directly to Saul by the risen Christ himself; in 22:21 it is connected with a later vision during a trance in the temple; while in ch. 9 no definite call is given to Saul himself, who is merely told to go to Damascus, where he will receive instructions (vs. 6), while the announcement about Saul's promised mission is made, not to Saul, but to Ananias (vs. 15). In spite of these discrepancies the verbal agreements between the three accounts are such that they are generally considered to be interdependent. Perhaps that in ch. 26, which can be harmonized more easily with Paul's own account in Galatians, approximates most nearly the story in Luke's source, and constitutes the original out of which he has built up the other two accounts in chs. 9 and 22. The most important addition in chs. 9 and 22 is the part played by Ananias. Paul makes no reference to him in Galatians, and his part as intermediary is very difficult to reconcile with Paul's claim that he was an apostle "not from men nor through man, but through Jesus Christ" (Gal. 1:1). As Lake remarks, "The story of Ananias, as told in Acts ix, seems to be exactly the kind of story against which Paul protests in his epistles" (*Beginnings of Christianity,* II, 153). Yet a fair case can be made for the substantial truth of Luke's account. Though he may possibly have attributed too much importance to Ananias in Saul's

---

fathers. He had seen it and understood it, but it is fair for us to wonder how much he really believed it. Not until he saw God in Christ did he feel it all through him, did he know it for himself, and live it as naturally as he breathed. There are people in every church who see, but seeing, do not believe. They have been brought up in the church; they have heard the prayers all their lives; they have seen the bread broken at the altar, but they have never known. Like a man who sees another man swim, understands the principle of it, and could himself go through all the motions, yet who never dares surrender himself to the buoyancy of the water, these people see the whole thing in principle but never feel the everlasting arms underneath them. Jesus commended those who do not see, yet believe. He made allowance for Thomas who, once he saw, believed. We can but wonder what he would have said about the unfulfilled spirits of those who see and still do not believe. No, seeing is not always believing. There is a difference between them, as there is between night and day, and sometimes a man has to be shown over and over again before he feels with his whole being what he has hitherto perceived in his mind.

Some people may ask why it was so long before Paul saw the light, why he held out against Jesus so stubbornly. There are two factors which might have blinded Paul to Christ. First, his predisposition in favor of Judaism. By birth, by training, and by habit he was predisposed to religion by restraint. When we remember how the predisposition of the North in favor of Lincoln blinded them for years to the greatness of Lee, we can begin to appreciate Paul's situation. Today we are predisposed to the impersonal and material in life. By training and by habit we instinctively trust the things that are tangible and turn to the things that are commercially useful. No wonder our eyes are closed to Jesus. His spirit is too subtle for our understanding. The poetry of his mind is too quick for the sluggishness of our brains.

But there was another factor that blinded Paul to Christ—his preconception of Jesus. From Paul's legal point of view Jesus was a moral anarchist, and Paul's mind was made up from the beginning that Jesus was the archenemy of Jewish religion. How our preconceptions blind us to reality! Think for how many centuries our preconception of the earth as flat blinded us to the circular glory of the globe. Scores of mature men and women never really see Jesus because of a childhood preconception of him—above the bright blue sky, a tender shepherd, choirs of angels hovering about him. Others never see him because their undigested

2 And desired of him letters to Damascus to the synagogues, that if he found any of this way, whether they were men or women, he might bring them bound unto Jerusalem.

3 And as he journeyed, he came near Damascus: and suddenly there shined round about him a light from heaven:

went to the high priest 2 and asked him for letters to the synagogues at Damascus, so that if he found any belonging to the Way, men or women, he might bring them bound to Jerusalem. 3 Now as he journeyed he approached Damascus, and suddenly a

---

conversion, the latter, on the other hand, in Galatians may well have been tempted to exaggerate his independence of all human instruction, as his chief concern there is to prove that his gospel as preached to the Gentiles is his very own. In the heat of this defense of his independence he may have underestimated the part played by Ananias, apart from whose counsel his conversion might never have been confirmed.

9:2. According to I Macc. 15:15, the Romans had granted to the high priest the right of extraditing to Jerusalem Jewish malefactors who had fled abroad. This would cover the case of Christians from Jerusalem who had taken refuge in Damascus, and the reference here is probably to such rather than to residents of Damascus. **The Way** was apparently one of the earliest names in Greek for the primitive Christian community

---

theology puts an opaque screen between their mind and his. They have a notion of what the divinity of Christ means that might conceivably stand by them in the playroom, but hardly anywhere else. They have picked up every ill-considered judgment about him, every stray comment, and collected them all without discrimination. When they come face to face with the real Christ, no wonder they rarely recognize him.

These two factors were overcome in Paul's case by two unanswerable arguments. The first was the death of Stephen. Paul saw a young man die, and he heard him as he died ask forgiveness for the raging mob. Paul did not speak of it at the time, but it left an indelible impression upon his sensitive mind. There never has been any argument for the Christian life that can take the place of the Christ-possessed man. Even when people are blinded to Christ by their predispositions and preconceptions, let some man or woman show unmistakable signs of Christian character and the scales will fall from their eyes. Not in every case, of course, for in the last analysis it all rests on the second unanswerable argument that came to Paul—the light dawning upon his own consciousness. There is only one experience in life that is absolutely authentic and that is to see and feel the real thing. It dawned upon Paul that Jesus was the truth. All the unmanageable pieces of the puzzle fell miraculously into place. He had been looking at Jesus, but now he saw him. Jesus took hold of him and never let him go. More and more, little by little, men of our day are seeing the same thing in their own idiom and according to their own pattern of thought. It is dawning upon man that this is one world, that it lives by God's power and that it is a family, that in Christ the family finds its healing principle and power, and that "we must love one another or die." That is the modern road to Damascus, and those who travel it sincerely are beginning to walk in newness of life.

2. *Any of This Way.*—This is the first instance in which Christianity is referred to as **the Way.** The phrase calls for comment. Christianity is a combination of two things: an interpretation of life and a way of life. Human beings are not satisfied to live a day-to-day existence; they crave explanations. They want to know the why and wherefore of existence. They are not satisfied to be told that the sun rises in the east and sets in the west. They want to know why it behaves in such a manner. Various explanations of life have been given by religions and systems of philosophy. The Christian explanation is one of many. It explains life in terms of creative purpose. It explains evil in terms of the necessary conditions under which men live with a limited freedom and develop a moral nature. It explains man as a creature of God and a fine blend of dust and divinity, neither animal nor angel but a mixture of both. It explains suffering as an opportunity to bear the pain of the world and to grow more deeply into the knowledge of God.

But explanations alone are not enough. Scientific explanations of the universe in terms of cause and effect are valuable, but without the scientific way of experiment, trial and error, testing and proving, those explanations would be useless. So Christianity is in addition to an explanation of life a way of life. It is the way men approach the mystery of the unknown.

4 And he fell to the earth, and heard a voice saying unto him, Saul, Saul, why persecutest thou me?

5 And he said, Who art thou, Lord? And the Lord said, I am Jesus whom thou persecutest: *it is* hard for thee to kick against the pricks.

6 And he trembling and astonished said, Lord, what wilt thou have me to do? And the Lord *said* unto him, Arise, and go into the city, and it shall be told thee what thou must do.

7 And the men which journeyed with him stood speechless, hearing a voice, but seeing no man.

8 And Saul arose from the earth; and when his eyes were opened, he saw no man: but they led him by the hand, and brought *him* into Damascus.

9 And he was three days without sight, and neither did eat nor drink.

10 ¶ And there was a certain disciple at Damascus, named Ananias; and to him

light from heaven flashed about him. 4 And
he fell to the ground and heard a voice
saying to him, "Saul, Saul, why do you persecute me?" 5 And he said, "Who are you,
Lord?" And he said, "I am Jesus, whom
you are persecuting; 6 but rise and enter
the city, and you will be told what you are
to do." 7 The men who were traveling
with him stood speechless, hearing the
voice but seeing no one. 8 Saul arose from
the ground; and when his eyes were opened,
he could see nothing; so they led him by
the hand and brought him into Damascus.
9 And for three days he was without sight,
and neither ate nor drank.

10 Now there was a disciple at Damascus

(cf. "this Life," 5:20); it occurs six times in Acts, curiously always in passages relating to Paul (9:2; 19:9, 23; 22:4; 24:14, 22). Lake and Cadbury argue that there is no evidence that it represents an Aramaic name, though in rabbinical literature *dérekh* ("way") is used in the sense of "customs" or "manner of life." Perhaps the word suggests that to their opponents the new Christian "heresy" appeared as a matter of practice rather than of opinion.

4. Saul: Here Σαούλ, the Semitic spelling, which is found only here, in vs. 17 below, and in the parallel passages in 22:7 and 26:14 (also in 13:21 of King Saul). According to 26:14, the voice was "in the Hebrew language." Elsewhere the Greek spelling Σαῦλος is used (cf. 9:1; etc.).

10-11. A disciple . . . Ananias: In 22:12—significantly in a speech to the Jews—Ananias is called "a devout man according to the law"; but he may well have been a

It is the particular way in which men manage their bodies, neither indulging them nor stifling them, but using them as instruments of the spirit. It is the way men treat other people, not as pieces of property but as persons. It is the way men take trouble, not resenting it, or merely enduring it, but accepting it as an opportunity to share the suffering of Christ. It is the way men meet death, neither anticipating it nor dreading it, but going toward it as men setting out on a great adventure. The important thing to remember is that the explanation and the way go together. One cannot have the way without the explanation. It is hopeless for a man to try to live the Christian way of life unless he holds fast to the principles that undergird that way. On the other hand a man cannot enjoy the Christian explanation of life and refuse to accept it as the way of life. Many people in these days are being driven to accept Christianity as the explanation of life because there is no other explanation that fits the terrible facts of our time. Some of those same people, however, are loath to accept Christianity as a way of life. Not until they have done that will their Christianity bear any resemblance to the Christianity that we find in the Acts.

10-19. ***The Part that Ananias Played.***—One is likely to overlook the figure of Ananias and to lose him in the shadow cast by Paul. And yet Ananias played his part in the story of Paul. It is not a part that can be disregarded. He was in a sense the connecting link between the overpowering experience on the Damascus road and the missionary journeys to Asia Minor, Greece, and Rome. In fact, according to the account in this chapter—and in ch. 22—Ananias

said the Lord in a vision, Ananias. And he said, Behold, I *am here,* Lord.

11 And the Lord *said* unto him, Arise, and go into the street which is called Straight, and inquire in the house of Judas for *one* called Saul, of Tarsus: for, behold, he prayeth,

12 And hath seen in a vision a man named Ananias coming in, and putting *his* hand on him, that he might receive his sight.

13 Then Ananias answered, Lord, I have heard by many of this man, how much evil he hath done to thy saints at Jerusalem:

14 And here he hath authority from the chief priests to bind all that call on thy name.

named An-a-ni'as. The Lord said to him
in a vision, "An-a-ni'as." And he said,
"Here I am, Lord." 11 And the Lord said
to him, "Rise and go to the street called
Straight, and inquire in the house of Judas
for a man of Tarsus named Saul; for behold, he is praying, 12 and he has seen a
man named An-a-ni'as come in and lay his
hands on him so that he might regain his
sight." 13 But An-a-ni'as answered, "Lord, I
have heard from many about this man, how
much evil he has done to thy saints at
Jerusalem; 14 and here he has authority
from the chief priests to bind all who call

Christian "disciple" as well as a loyal Jew, as indeed seems implied by 22:14. If so, he may have been either one of the refugees from Jerusalem, or one of a group of Damascus Jews who had already become Christians. **In the house of Judas:** For the precise directions cf. 10:6—also in a vision. Is this evidence of a firsthand tradition? Or should we say with Lake and Cadbury that "part of the miraculous motif in such visions is the divine communication of details"?

13. **Saints:** The common word in Paul's letters for "Christians," but in Acts used only in this chapter (vss. 13, 32, 41) and in the parallel in 26:10.

---

was the interpreter of the experience. He it was who translated the blinding light into explicit directions and duties.

Seen in this light, the part that Ananias played is by no means an insignificant part. He was the lesser man in terms of world-wide significance. How many times the lesser man has been responsible for launching the greater man! And in the long run who is to say which is lesser and which is greater? In the total pattern the Ananiases are as indispensable as the Pauls. The country doctor who starts an Osler or a Grenfell on his meteoric career; the village parson who launches a Dwight L. Moody or an F. W. Robertson; the schoolteacher who puts the idea of teaching into the head of a Bliss Perry or a Charles W. Eliot—who can say that their roles are not important? They are vital links in the chain by which God brings his purposes to pass.

The part that Ananias played is even more important when it is considered in its interpretative role. The experience that Paul had on the Damascus road was a blinding one. A man cannot be turned upside down and inside out without serious consequences. The danger was that he might be permanently blinded; that his mind be completely dazed; and that the experience produce nothing beyond bewilderment. That is where Ananias is needed, always. He reduced the whole experience, without losing or sacrificing its profound and radical character, into terms of mission and duty. How often men need just such an interpretation of their experiences! Men whose whole outlook has been completely changed by war, and whose point of view has shifted from science to religion, need someone to interpret their experience and to translate it into definite plans and policies for immediate action. That is the meaning, at least in part, of the words **and immediately something like scales fell from his eyes and he regained his sight.** Just as the sun itself is too bright for a man to look at, and must be seen as it is reflected from earthly surfaces, so the vision of Christ himself was so bright as to blind Paul, and not until he saw that vision reflected from the paths of duty and sacrifice did the scales fall from his eyes.

Ananias, in describing the mission of Paul, used unforgettable words: **He is a chosen vessel unto me.** Those are the words that God put into the mind of Ananias, and they are perhaps the most adequate description of the Christian witness. A vessel is made to contain something. It is of no importance in itself. A milk pitcher is of no value without the milk. And yet it is of incomparable value because without it that

15 But the Lord said unto him, Go thy way: for he is a chosen vessel unto me, to bear my name before the Gentiles, and kings, and the children of Israel:

16 For I will show him how great things he must suffer for my name's sake.

17 And Ananias went his way, and entered into the house; and putting his hands on him said, Brother Saul, the Lord, *even* Jesus, that appeared unto thee in the way as thou camest, hath sent me, that thou mightest receive thy sight, and be filled with the Holy Ghost.

18 And immediately there fell from his eyes as it had been scales: and he received sight forthwith, and arose, and was baptized.

upon thy name." **15** But the Lord said to
him, "Go, for he is a chosen instrument of
mine to carry my name before the Gentiles
and kings and the sons of Israel; **16** for I
will show him how much he must suffer
for the sake of my name." **17** So An-a-ni'as
departed and entered the house. And laying his hands on him he said, "Brother
Saul, the Lord Jesus who appeared to you
on the road by which you came, has sent
me that you may regain your sight and be
filled with the Holy Spirit." **18** And immediately something like scales fell from his
eyes and he regained his sight. Then he

---

15. Chosen instrument (σκεῦος ἐκλογῆς): cf. Rom. 9:22, "vessels of wrath" (σκεύη ὀργῆς).

17. Brother Saul practically means "fellow Christian," and again reminds one that Ananias was a Christian. **The Lord Jesus:** Note again (cf. on vs. 10) how in Paul's speech to the Jews in 22:14 Ananias speaks in the language of a good Jew. He comes to Saul with a message from "the God of our fathers," and Jesus is called, not "Lord," but "the Just One." As this was probably the earliest title given to Jesus, it may be that the account in ch. 22 has been less extensively edited than the parallel version in ch. 9.

18. Something like scales: Not necessarily anything physical, but a vivid way of describing the sense of returning sight. **Regained his sight . . . was baptized.** It is interesting that baptism itself is often called φωτισμός—"illumination." Thus is fulfilled the promise of the previous verse that Saul should "regain [his] sight and be filled with the Holy Spirit." The gift of the Spirit is brought into the closest connection with baptism.

---

which it contains would be lost. Without the pitcher the milk would be spilt. If the milk is to be used for the nourishment of men, it must be gathered together, and it is the pitcher that does just that. The Christian minister shares in this paradox of supreme importance and no importance. He is not important in himself. Yet because the word and power of God, if these are to be made available to men, must be gathered together in one place, he is of supreme importance; he is the gathering point, the place where the energies of God are concentrated for the nourishment of men. Paul himself was of no importance, and yet without him God in Christ would have lacked a powerful voice and a highly tuned instrument by which he could speak to the Roman world.

The vessel is a chosen one, carefully selected for its suitability. It is easy for us to see that as we look backward across the centuries. Who was better fitted than Paul for the task? We see that God selected him as surely as nature selects by her own processes the forms of life which are intended to survive. So every disciple feels. If not at the beginning of his work, yet as it progresses through the years, he feels that through events and experiences, through his own talents and abilities, through the needs and circumstances of his day and age, God has chosen him to be the vessel which shall bring to the people something of his power and love. Let him remember that his personality and talents, however great they may be, are of no value whatever in themselves, and that they become valuable only as they are used to contain and convey something of infinite worth.

One cannot forget in this connection Paul's own reference to his ministry in terms of "earthen vessels" (II Cor. 4:7). No one was more conscious than he of the imperfection of the vessel. He had physical handicaps and spiritual weaknesses. No one need tell a minister of the gospel about that! How well he knows his own failures and shortcomings! How often he realizes the dangers that lurk even in this strength! There is the danger of using whatever eloquence he has to exploit the emotions of the people and glorify himself. There is the temptation to use his own physical weakness as an excuse for

19 And when he had received meat, he was strengthened. Then was Saul certain days with the disciples which were at Damascus.

20 And straightway he preached Christ in the synagogues, that he is the Son of God.

rose and was baptized, 19 and took food and was strengthened.

For several days he was with the disciples at Damascus. 20 And in the synagogues immediately he proclaimed Jesus, saying, "He

2. The Immediate Aftermath (9:20-31)

For the events following Saul's conversion, Acts must be checked by the apostle's own account in Gal. 1:15-24. There are a number of perplexing discrepancies:

(*a*) Paul states that immediately after his conversion he "went away into Arabia" (Gal. 1:17). Acts says nothing of this and states that **in the synagogues immediately he proclaimed Jesus.** Here it must be confessed that Luke's account is both historically and psychologically improbable. If the Jewish authorities in Damascus indeed had authority to hand over Christians to an emissary from Jerusalem, they would hardly have allowed that emissary, turned renegade, to preach the faith he came to persecute. Paul himself, too, is much more likely to have sought a quiet breathing space in "Arabia." Like Augustine after his conversion, he went into retreat and "found rest in God from the turmoil of the world."

(*b*) A more important problem is how to reconcile the two accounts of Paul's first visit to Jerusalem. The following difficulties emerge: (i) Whereas Paul says that it was "after three years" that he went up to Jerusalem, Luke compresses this period and writes **when many days had passed**—ἱκαναί, "an adequate number"—not suggesting any very long period. (ii) Luke states that Paul **attempted to join the disciples** and that, failing a welcome, **Barnabas took him, and brought him to the apostles.** In Galatians Paul states on his oath that he saw none of the apostles save Peter and James the Lord's brother, and that he was in Jerusalem for only fifteen days, and then incognito, being "still not known by sight to the churches of Christ in Judea" (Gal. 1:22). Nothing is said of the fact that Barnabas introduced him. (iii) Luke pictures Paul at Jerusalem **preaching boldly in the name of the Lord**—a course which, as in Damascus, is not only historically and psychologically unlikely, but also obviously contradicts the impression left by Galatians.

(*c*) As to Paul's subsequent movements, Acts takes him by way of Caesarea to Tarsus in Cilicia, and in Gal. 1:21 Paul says "I went into the regions of Syria and Cilicia." After this we find him in the company of Barnabas at Antioch, whence Barnabas had gone to bring Paul from Tarsus (11:25-26). If the "fourteen years" of Gal 2:1 is correct, Paul must have spent a very considerable period of time, presumably at Tarsus, about which we know nothing, before Barnabas chose him as his colleague at Antioch.

spiritual shortcomings and to take the way of the prima donna. And yet, says Paul, this very fact of the imperfection of the vessel is all a part of God's plan. For if it were not for the earthenness of our vessel, we should be led to think that the ministry is the result of our own power and to the glory of our own name. The fact that God can and does use these imperfect instruments, not only in spite of their imperfections, but also at times because of them, is the one sure reminder that it is not the vessel that counts but the precious contents which it holds. The vessel cracks, leaks, and sometimes breaks. Then it is that the minister is saved from pride and finds in his own weakness the tie that binds him to suffering humanity. Paul suffered from a physical handicap that seemed at first to retard his work. He was not an eloquent speaker. It was in these very infirmities that he finally found his real strength.

20-31. ***Saul's First Obstacle.***—Saul's first obstacle was his own past. The general public held his past against him. The Jews in Damascus listened to him preach that Jesus is the Son of God, and they did not believe what he said because they could not forget what he had done. Just a few days earlier he had been the Christians' most dangerous enemy. Such a complete change of heart they could not understand, nor could they accept it at its face value. After all, leopards do not change their spots, nor do men and women change completely overnight. That is the way of reasoning along which they traveled. They felt so strongly about it that they tried to do away with him, but Saul had a few faithful friends who managed to

21 But all that heard *him* were amazed, and said; Is not this he that destroyed them which called on this name in Jerusalem, and came hither for that intent, that he might bring them bound unto the chief priests?

is the Son of God." 21 And all who heard him were amazed, and said, "Is not this the man who made havoc in Jerusalem of those who called on this name? And he has come here for this purpose, to bring them bound

Again Paul, intent upon emphasizing his independence, says nothing about his association with Barnabas during this period. But Gal. 2:13 mentions the presence of Barnabas at Antioch, and it is entirely likely that, as Acts 11:26 states, they worked for a year together there before the "famine visit" to Jerusalem (11:30), and their subsequent setting out from Antioch on the first tour (13:4). For the chronology see on 11:30.

Where there is divergence, the Galatian epistle, as our primary authority, must generally speaking be preferred to Acts. The discrepancies suggest that for the early period of Paul's career Luke had no detailed knowledge of events, and filled in his picture in somewhat general terms. It may be that the circumstances of a later visit to Jerusalem have been incorrectly assigned to this first one. We must remember, however, that in Galatians Paul is particularly concerned to stress the immediacy and independence of his apostleship, while Luke throughout wishes to suggest that from the very first there was concord between Paul and the twelve. It is likely that both accounts, but especially Luke's, are unconsciously colored by the respective ends they have in view.

20. Son of God, as a title of Jesus, is used only here in Acts, and significantly it appears here on the lips of Paul, who frequently uses it in his epistles. It was commonly used by the Jews of Messiah (Pss. 2:7; 89:26); and Peter (Matt. 16:16) acknowledges Jesus as "the Christ, the Son of the living God." Here the force of the phrase is still mainly messianic; and it does not, of course, yet convey the full idea that Jesus is "God the Son" in the sense, e.g., of the Nicene Creed.

21. Made havoc: In Gal. 1:13 Paul uses the same Greek word to describe his persecution of the church—"perhaps the nearest approach that there is to verbal evidence of literary dependence of Acts on the Pauline Epistles" (Lake and Cadbury, *Beginnings of Christianity,* IV, 105; cf. 7:53).

get him safely out of the city. His first attempt to preach was a dismal failure. No one would believe him because his own past was against him.

From Damascus he went to Jerusalem. (But see Exeg.) Did he find the disciples waiting for him with open arms? Not at all! They too had memories. They had not forgotten the death of Stephen, and they remembered the consenting figure on the fringe of the crowd at whose feet the persecutors laid their clothes. Saul tried to join the disciples but they closed their doors. They were afraid of him. They had every reason to believe that he was a wolf in sheep's clothing. They could not believe, in the light of what had happened, that he was really a disciple. His record was against him.

We might expect the Hellenists to be more sympathetic with him. They shared his wider and more cosmopolitan background of culture, but they, like the Jews in Damascus, made plans to get rid of him, and he escaped only by the skin of his teeth. He went back to Tarsus, his own home town, with little or nothing to show as a record of achievement. It is the same story today. Whenever a radical change takes place in a man's life, his major obstacle is his own past. People cannot forget what he once was. They suspect that he will continue to be as he always has been. They have been disappointed too often. Too many times people have said they were going to turn over a new leaf—and the new leaf looked just like the old one. The patterns of a lifetime are not quickly and radically altered, and most people look with suspicion upon anyone who is trying to be a new and different creature. In many cases they never give him a fair chance.

The important thing for Christians to remember is that occasionally the life is a new one. There are people like Saul. They become new creatures. Woe to the man who stands in their way and because of past performance refuses to allow them the right to change! Far better is it to take a chance with a man and lose than to lose a man because you refuse to give him a chance! To take an extreme case: A man has just completed a jail sentence. He says that he intends to lead a new life and he gives every evidence that he means what he

22 But Saul increased the more in
strength, and confounded the Jews which
dwelt at Damascus, proving that this is
very Christ.
23 ¶ And after that many days were
fulfilled, the Jews took counsel to kill him:
24 But their laying wait was known of
Saul. And they watched the gates day and
night to kill him.
25 Then the disciples took him by night,
and let *him* down by the wall in a basket.
26 And when Saul was come to Jerusalem,
he assayed to join himself to the
disciples: but they were all afraid of him,
and believed not that he was a disciple.
27 But Barnabas took him, and brought
him to the apostles, and declared unto
them how he had seen the Lord in the way,
and that he had spoken to him, and how
he had preached boldly at Damascus in the
name of Jesus.

before the chief priests." 22 But Saul increased all the more in strength, and confounded the Jews who lived in Damascus
by proving that Jesus was the Christ.
23 When many days had passed, the Jews
plotted to kill him, 24 but their plot became known to Saul. They were watching
the gates day and night, to kill him; 25 but
his disciples took him by night and let him
down over the wall, lowering him in a
basket.
26 And when he had come to Jerusalem
he attempted to join the disciples; and
they were all afraid of him, for they did
not believe that he was a disciple. 27 But
Barnabas took him, and brought him to
the apostles, and declared to them how on
the road he had seen the Lord, who spoke
to him, and how at Damascus he had
preached boldly in the name of Jesus.

23-25. Paul's own account of this incident in II Cor. 11:32 ff. suggests that he was trying to elude, not a plot against him by the Jews within the city, but the watchfulness of "the ethnarch of King Aretas"—the Nabatean Arab king of Petra—who was presumably "guarding the city" to catch Paul as he came out. Are we to suppose that the Jews had enlisted the help of Aretas against Paul? In that case the ethnarch may have been his representative or consul within the city. Or was Aretas himself hostile to Paul, on account perhaps of his activities in "Arabia"?

---

says. How does the Christian community treat him? Just about the way the Jews in Damascus treated Saul. They would rather play safe. Common sense is on their side, and all the twice-born men of history are aligned against them. Indeed it looked for a time as if Saul's new life was nipped in the bud at the very start. And then the story takes a turn for the better. **Barnabas took him, and brought him to the apostles.**

Every word in the Acts about Barnabas indicates that he was a broad-gauged man. His first appearance on the scene is when he sold his farm to give the proceeds to the disciples to make it possible for them to carry on their work. It is not surprising, therefore, that he was willing to take a risk with a man like Saul. Perhaps he had more trust in human nature than the rest of the people; perhaps he was more adventurous by nature; or perhaps he believed in God more than the rest. Whatever the reason might have been does not matter much now. What does matter supremely is that there was a Barnabas who got hold of Saul at a time when his spirit must have been in the depths. After all the agony of his preconversion disquietude, after the shattering experience on the road to Damascus, after the pain of adjustment to an entirely new life, the followers of Jesus himself refused to receive him, to believe him, to give him a chance! What a disillusioning experience that must have been! And then came Barnabas. He saved the day for Saul, and from that time on Saul mingled freely with the disciples. We need more people like Barnabas. They are the people who are willing to gamble on a man. They are prepared for disappointment after disappointment. They are kept going by the thought that out of many disappointments there may be at least one who turns over a new leaf.

Take one splendid example. In the year 1878, in the city of Manchester, England, a young Roman Catholic boy at the age of nineteen was refused admission to the priesthood of the Roman Catholic Church on the grounds of excessive nervous timidity and indolence. There was failure number one. His father was a physician and persuaded him to study medicine, which he did indifferently for six years. He lived with his family during those years and deceived them into believing that he was seriously studying medicine when really his major interest was in literature and books. At

28 And he was with them coming in and
going out at Jerusalem.
29 And he spake boldly in the name of
the Lord Jesus, and disputed against the
Grecians: but they went about to slay him.
30 *Which* when the brethren knew, they
brought him down to Caesarea, and sent
him forth to Tarsus.
31 Then had the churches rest throughout all Judea and Galilee and Samaria,

28 So he went in and out among them at
Jerusalem, 29 preaching boldly in the name
of the Lord. And he spoke and disputed
against the Hellenists; but they were seeking to kill him. 30 And when the brethren
knew it, they brought him down to Caes-
a-re'a, and sent him off to Tarsus.
31 So the church throughout all Judea
and Galilee and Sa-ma'ri-a had peace and

---

30. To Tarsus: Presumably by sea, though Gal. 1:21 ("I went into the regions of Syria and Cilicia") is thought by some to imply a route overland through Syria.

31. Another characteristic summary. The Western text is here defective, but the Antiochene text, which often preserves the Western reading, has "churches" in place of "church." If **church** is the correct reading, this is the best example in Acts of the catholic meaning of the word (see on 5:11). **Walking** (πορευομένη): Torrey suggests that this may represent the idiomatic use of the Hebrew *hālakh* ("walk"), which indicates that

---

one period of that career he was persuaded by some of the family to enlist in the army. That, it was believed, might do him good physically. After a few months he failed to pass the physical examination. That was failure number two. After two years studying medicine, his mother, shortly before her untimely death, knowing his delight in English prose, with every good intention, but ill-advisedly, gave him a copy of De Quincey's *Confessions of an English Opium Eater.* The spell of that magnificent prose, together with his restlessness and the instability of his whole nervous system, coupled with all the failures that had so far accumulated against him, led him to become himself an opium eater. At the end of six years he left home and went to London. The story of those weeks and months in London is the story of degradation. He went from bad to worse, if anybody ever did. He went down and down from the pavement, to the street, to the gutter. He made what little money he could by selling matches, by hailing cabs for people. He spent what he had to for food to keep himself going, with some left over for drugs. There he was with only a flicker of his original desire to make great literature.

Nevertheless, one day, standing under a lamppost, the only light he could find, scribbling on a dirty piece of paper, he wrote out an essay that had been in his mind for a long time; he called it "Paganism," and added to it one or two religious poems that he had written several years before, and put it in a mailbox, addressed to Wilfrid Meynell, the editor of *Merrie England.* Meynell was one of the great Roman Catholic editors of his day and the husband of Alice Meynell, one of the great Catholic poets of all days. The envelope had upon it the return address, "The Post Office, Charing Cross." But the envelope was so dirty when the editor received it that he stuck it in a pigeonhole and thought nothing more about it for six months. Then when he was cleaning out his desk, he found the dirty paper and read the essay and the poems and had, like Barnabas, the discernment to see in the poems something that was potentially great. He could not trace the man who wrote it for he was no longer in the vicinity of Charing Cross, and his letter seeking for information came back marked "Dead Letter." He published the poem, and the author happened to see it. One day there came a knock on Meynell's door and a young man in rags, with shoes that were hardly soles to cover his feet, stood before him. And he said, "I am the man who wrote the poem 'The Passion of Mary' which you published in *Merrie England.*" Meynell took the young man with all that record against him, failure in school, failure in the army and in a profession, failure with people, failure to hold a job, failure to master himself—Meynell got hold of him. He took him into his own home. Under the influence of Alice and Wilfrid Meynell he renounced opium; he then went to a Roman Catholic priory for a year, where he ordered his own life and brought his body under subjection. He came out and presented himself to the world as Francis Thompson, the writer of one of the greatest single religious poems of our time, "The Hound of Heaven."

The story of Christianity is the story of Barnabas and Saul, raised to its highest conceivable level. It is the story of the God who took a chance on men with a bad past. It is the story of the God who came among human beings in the shape of a human personality, and one after

and were edified; and walking in the fear
of the Lord, and in the comfort of the Holy
Ghost, were multiplied.
32 ¶ And it came to pass, as Peter passed
throughout all *quarters,* he came down also
to the saints which dwelt at Lydda.
33 And there he found a certain man
named Eneas, which had kept his bed eight
years, and was sick of the palsy.

was built up; and walking in the fear of
the Lord and in the comfort of the Holy
Spirit it was multiplied.
32 Now as Peter went here and there
among them all, he came down also to the
saints that lived at Lydda. 33 There he
found a man named Ae-ne'as, who had
been bedridden for eight years and was

---

the action of the accompanying verb is continuous. The sense then would be, "and it was continuously multiplied."

F. The First Missions to Gentiles (9:32–11:30)

1. Peter's Preliminary Mission (9:32-43)

The transition here is abrupt, and the phrase **as Peter went here and there among them all** is even vaguer in the Greek than in the English. According to Harnack, Luke is drawing again upon the Jerusalem-Caesarean source, the interest of the section up to 11:18 being concentrated on Peter's conversion of the Caesarean Cornelius and his defense of his action at Jerusalem. In that case 9:32 ff. may pick up the story of Peter where it was broken off at 8:25, and **among them all** may refer to the "many villages of the Samaritans" mentioned in that verse. A still more attractive suggestion is that the events of ch. 12 have been misplaced, and that chronologically 12:1-17 (also from the Jerusalem-Caesarean source) should precede 9:32 ff. (See on ch. 12.) In 12:17 we read that Peter, after his escape from prison, "departed and went to another place." This would lead up well to the equally vague statement in 9:32 that he **went here and there among them all.** At the moment Peter was a fugitive and had no fixed place of abode.

The narrative, like the story of Peter and John's visit to Samaria (8:14-25), reads like the account of an episcopal tour. "One would say," writes Alfred Loisy, "that the head of the episcopal bench comes to give his recognition and sanction to the results achieved by the zeal of believers whom the persecution of Stephen has scattered towards the coast of Palestine" (*Les Actes des Apôtres* [Paris: Émile Nourry, 1920], p. 428). Again, the miracles in this section have been considered somewhat suspect because they are so obviously parallel with certain prominent miracles both in the Gospels and in the O.T. The healing of Aeneas recalls Jesus' cure of the paralytic (Luke 5:18-26), and the story of Dorcas closely resembles that of the raising of Jairus' daughter (Luke 8:41-42, 49-56), and also awakens echoes of the miracles of Elijah and Elisha (cf. I Kings 17:17 ff.; II Kings 4:32 ff.). Without questioning the general trustworthiness of the narrative, we may admit that it is part of Luke's purpose to show how in the cures of Peter the miraculous activity of Jesus is still being carried on.

32. **Lydda,** between Jerusalem and Joppa, was famous for purple-dyed materials, and after the destruction of Jerusalem it became also a center of rabbinical learning.

---

another got hold of them, got hold not just of their minds or their manners, but got hold of their whole being and made them new men.

32-43. ***More Signs of Resurrection Power.***—The story of Paul the apostle, begun in ch. 9, is interrupted by two stories about Peter. In the first story Peter cures a man named Aeneas of paralysis, and in the second he raises a woman named Tabitha from the dead. Stories like these occur over and over again in the history of early Christianity. They occur too often to allow us to discredit them as fiction. As we now have them, they may be exaggerated, but every one of them has this much truth at the heart of it: wherever the risen Christ is present, there is new power to overcome the handicaps of human existence. Miracles do happen. They happened then and they happen now. A Christian fellowship in which there are no signs of new life, no indications that people are rising above the dead level of their old selves, that they are conquering the fears and anxieties that threaten the smooth operation of their physical organism—in that fellowship there is

34 And Peter said unto him, Eneas, Jesus Christ maketh thee whole: arise, and make thy bed. And he arose immediately.

35 And all that dwelt at Lydda and Saron saw him, and turned to the Lord.

36 ¶ Now there was at Joppa a certain disciple named Tabitha, which by interpretation is called Dorcas: this woman was full of good works and almsdeeds which she did.

37 And it came to pass in those days, that she was sick, and died: whom when they had washed, they laid *her* in an upper chamber.

38 And forasmuch as Lydda was nigh to Joppa, and the disciples had heard that Peter was there, they sent unto him two men, desiring *him* that he would not delay to come to them.

39 Then Peter arose and went with them. When he was come, they brought him into the upper chamber: and all the widows stood by him weeping, and showing the coats and garments which Dorcas made, while she was with them.

40 But Peter put them all forth, and kneeled down, and prayed; and turning *him* to the body said, Tabitha, arise. And she opened her eyes: and when she saw Peter, she sat up.

41 And he gave her *his* hand, and lifted her up; and when he had called the saints and widows, he presented her alive.

42 And it was known throughout all Joppa; and many believed in the Lord.

paralyzed. 34 And Peter said to him,
"Ae-ne'as, Jesus Christ heals you; rise and
make your bed." And immediately he rose.
35 And all the residents of Lydda and
Sharon saw him, and they turned to the
Lord.

36 Now there was at Joppa a disciple
named Tabitha, which means Dorcas or
Gazelle. She was full of good works and
acts of charity. 37 In those days she fell
sick and died; and when they had washed
her, they laid her in an upper room.
38 Since Lydda was near Joppa, the disciples, hearing that Peter was there, sent two
men to him entreating him, "Please come
to us without delay." 39 So Peter rose and
went with them. And when he had come,
they took him to the upper room. All the
widows stood beside him weeping, and
showing coats and garments which Dorcas
made while she was with them. 40 But Peter
put them all outside and knelt down and
prayed; then turning to the body he said,
"Tabitha, rise." And she opened her eyes,
and when she saw Peter she sat up. 41 And
he gave her his hand and lifted her up.
Then calling the saints and widows he presented her alive. 42 And it became known
throughout all Joppa, and many believed

34. **Make your bed:** Cf. Luke 5:24, "take up your bed"; alternatively, "spread your couch," i.e., with a view to eating; for which cf. Luke 8:55 (of Jairus' daughter), "He directed that something should be given her to eat."

35. **Sharon** is a transliteration of a Hebrew word meaning "the coastal plain."

36. **Joppa:** The modern Jaffa and the port of Jerusalem. **Tabitha** is Aramaic for "gazelle," for which the Greek word is "Dorcas." The only way to bring out the point in English translation is to give both the Greek and the English interpretation as in RSV.

39. **Widows:** Possibly there as nurses and as professional mourners—a part they certainly played at a later date—but more probably simply as Dorcas' beneficiaries.

41. **Saints and widows:** Though "saints" is the all-inclusive word for "Christians," we need hardly suppose that the widows were not Christians.

something radically wrong. An observation that one cannot resist making in connection with these two stories about Peter is that they are exactly the same kind of stories that were told about Jesus. In other words there is no indication in the N.T. that the early church believed that the power to perform miracles was confined to Jesus. Jesus promised that his disciples by gift of the Spirit would do greater things, and according to the stories in the Acts, they proceeded to do them. Acts therefore pleads that the miracles of Jesus can still be used as evidence for his divine nature. If to perform a miracle means that a man is divine, then

43 And it came to pass, that he tarried
many days in Joppa with one Simon a
tanner.

10 There was a certain man in Caesarea called Cornelius, a centurion of
the band called the Italian *band,*

in the Lord. 43 And he stayed in Joppa
for many days with one Simon, a tanner.

10 At Caes-a-re'a there was a man
named Cornelius, a centurion of

---

43. A tanner: Hardly a suitable lodging for a scrupulous Jew, but it is not likely that Luke is consciously hinting that Peter was becoming more liberal. "A psychologist might think that lodging in so questionable a house may have turned Peter's mind to the problem of clean and unclean foods, which is raised in the next chapter" (Lake and Cadbury, *Beginnings of Christianity,* IV, 111-12).

2. Conversion of Cornelius (10:1–11:18)

As has already been indicated (p. 129, above), it is possible that the account of Peter's escape from prison (12:1-17) has been chronologically misplaced and ought to precede the story of the conversion of Cornelius. It was only after the revolt which followed Herod Agrippa's death (12:20 ff.) that a Roman garrison was established at Caesarea, where Cornelius appears to have been stationed. A consequence of this rearrangement of the sequence of events would be that Peter's activities at Lydda, Joppa, and Caesarea would be taking place during much the same period as the early mission work of Paul and Barnabas at Antioch, and all three would return to Jerusalem to give account of their missions at approximately the same time. For the whole sequence of events see on 12:17.

Luke evidently regards the conversion of Cornelius as an event of supreme importance. He even adopts the literary device, common in epic writing, of twice reporting every detail in the story. Everything that the narrator tells in 10:9 ff. is repeated by Peter in his defense in 11:4 ff.; while the vision of the centurion in 10:3 ff. is described again by Cornelius himself, on Peter's arrival at Caesarea, in 10:30 ff. Such stress can be put on the incident only because Luke regards it as the first case of the admission to baptism of an uncircumcised pagan; and the initiative in this new departure is ascribed, not to Paul, but to Peter. On this account radical scholars summarily dismiss the incident as unhistorical, and use it as one of the chief arguments against the Lukan authorship of Acts. The visions and angelic appearances, it is alleged, give the whole story a legendary coloring. Had Peter been enlightened in so unmistakable a manner about the lack of distinction between clean and unclean food, he could hardly have been guilty at Antioch of the equivocal conduct described in Gal. 2:11-13. Such a vision and the experience that followed it must have been regarded as conferring on Peter not only the right but the duty to evangelize Gentiles, and Peter, rather than Paul, would have to be considered as God's chosen instrument for the pioneering missionary work among pagans. If the whole question of the legitimacy of admitting Gentiles had already been settled in the case of Cornelius (11:18), the later discussions at Jerusalem (Gal. 2; Acts 15) could never have taken place. On the contrary 11:20 appears to record the first genuine case of preaching to Gentile Greeks, and it cannot have been anticipated by this incident. Finally, a motive for the insertion of this "legend" is ready to hand: From 15:7-9 it is clear that our author actually did think it important to show that it was not Paul but Peter who was the pioneer of Gentile missions. This assumption is the reverse side of his

---

the power of the Spirit in Peter certainly is divine. All this implies that the earthly Jesus had no monopoly on miracles. The miracles as we have them in the N.T. are the signs of the tremendous surplus and overflow of divine energy that had come into the world through Jesus and was being communicated to men through channels chosen by him. It was a sign in the language of its own day. The language of our day may differ, but the sign is the same—new life as the result of resurrection power.

10:1-48. ***The Story of Peter and Cornelius.***—This story at first sight does not look like a fertile field for the modern interpreter, but the

overemphasis upon the Judaistic aspect of Paul (e.g., the circumcision of Timothy in 16:1-3, and his compliance with James in the matter of fulfilling temple vows in 21:17 ff.) —both being due to his desire to gloss over any suggestion of conflict between the Pauline and Petrine parties within the church.

The incident undoubtedly raises difficulties, though they would be lessened by the chronological arrangement suggested above (see again on 12:17). Cornelius was presumably a "God-fearer" (10:2), i.e., an adherent of Judaism who did not accept the conditions of proselytism. But as he was of Gentile birth and not even a proselyte, his admission to baptism without circumcision was a new departure and violated the principles which had hitherto controlled the extension of the church. The question is whether such official action by Peter, and its confirmation by the apostles at Jerusalem, can be reconciled with the future course of events as revealed by Galatians and Acts. Many scholars hold that the proceedings of the "apostolic council" (Gal. 2; Acts 15) imply that the legitimacy of Gentile missions had never been before the mother church, and that it was the arguments of Paul that first induced the apostles to give their sanction to the new development.

In reply it can be argued that the council at Jerusalem took place at least ten years after Paul's conversion; for a large part of that time Paul presumably had been preaching to Gentiles (Gal. 1:16); and it is scarcely credible that the church at Jerusalem can have been unaware of what he was doing, or that the question of the legitimacy of such a Gentile mission did not occur to its leaders. Indeed Gal. 1:24 ("they glorified God because of me") claims that they actually approved. Moreover Galatians suggests that the new factor which precipitated the trouble later at Jerusalem was not the preaching to Gentiles for the first time, but the renewed question of its legitimacy. The "false brethren" (Gal. 2:4) apparently had come only recently into the limelight, and did not represent the hitherto prevailing attitude of the Jerusalem church. Thus the fact that the legitimacy of Gentile Christianity was re-examined at the council is no proof that it was not at least tacitly recognized at an earlier date; and such recognition may well have been given first as a result of just such an event as the conversion of Cornelius.

It is often objected that the incident robs Paul of his originality as the Apostle to the Gentiles, and that his reference to Peter in Gal. 2:8 as the apostle to the circumcision proves that Peter cannot have preached to Gentiles. But even a notable exception does not make Peter the Apostle to the Gentiles. Nor on the other hand does Paul ever claim that he was the first to preach to Gentiles. His sense of independence and originality sprang not from that but from his conviction that he was called directly by Christ to do for the Gentiles what others were doing in the main for the Jews. The fact that Paul calls Peter the apostle to the circumcision no more proves that Peter never preached to Gentiles than does Paul's claim to be the Apostle to the Gentiles prove that he never preached to Jews; we know in fact that he often did so (I Cor. 9:20).

Peter's behavior toward Cornelius is entirely in line with his impulsive nature, and shows the same uncalculating spirit that later led him to throw aside traditional scruples

---

more carefully he reads it, the more he will discover the richness of its meaning for people today. Take first the story as a whole.

The story is one chapter in the growth of Christianity. Christianity grew up in much the same way as an individual grows up, and growing up is never easy. One of the most difficult problems in growing up is the problem of leaving home. One cannot nestle in the shelter of home forever, nor can one ignore the fact that without that sheltering there would have been no life at all. A man must break away from home as a bird leaves the nest, and yet he must not forget the fact that he owes his life to his home.

Christianity was born in a Jewish home. It can never repay its debt of gratitude to that home. There it learned about the moral majesty of God. In that home it learned that religion and morality should go hand in hand in an inseparable union. But like all offspring, it had to leave home. The world-wide implications of Christianity could not be confined within the walls of Judaism. Judaism was the religion of a nation; Christianity was the religion of all nations. The swaddling clothes had to be stripped away; the exclusiveness of Judaism had to be overridden; its provincialism had to be displaced by universalism. The break had to be made; and it was made.

and live in intimate fellowship with Gentiles at Antioch (Gal. 2:12). But if the story of Cornelius is indeed historical, how are we to explain Peter's subsequent change of front when "he drew back and separated himself, fearing the circumcision party"? If the circle around James had sanctioned Peter's conduct with Cornelius at Caesarea, they could, it is argued, hardly have found fault with him for doing the same thing at Antioch; nor could Peter have been so vacillating as thus to disown the crucial step he had taken when he admitted Cornelius to fellowship. This objection rests on a misunderstanding which, it must be confessed, is due partly to Luke himself, who seems throughout to be confusing two distinct questions—social intercourse between Jews and Gentiles, and the admission of Gentiles to the Christian community. In Acts 11:3 the disciples at Jerusalem are represented as criticizing Peter for having held tablefellowship with non-Jews, and it is to this question that Peter's vision on the housetop appears to be related (cf. also 10:28). But the question to which Peter's defense is successfully directed is the admission of Gentiles to Christian baptism—a very different matter. Note too that at 11:18 the church "glorifies God," not because the social barriers between Jew and Gentile have been broken down, but because "to the Gentiles also God has granted repentance unto life." In other words, in the conversion of Cornelius the Jerusalem church recognized what, after renewed criticism by the "false brethren," they reaffirmed at the council—the legitimacy of Gentile Christianity. But they did not yet admit the right of a Jew to disregard the social prohibitions of the Jewish law. Luke may not have clearly realized the distinction between these two steps; hence he too, like modern critics, may have been so puzzled by Peter's vacillation at Antioch that he omitted the incident altogether from his narrative. A clearer perspective may not perhaps excuse Peter's conduct, but it at least makes it understandable.

Our conclusion, then, is that however we may question certain details in Luke's story, there is no reason to doubt that, in the person of Cornelius, Peter admitted the first Gentile, and that the legitimacy of his action was acknowledged by the Jerusalem church. Streeter, after discussing the incident, concludes that "the fundamental fallacy of histories of the Apostolic age inspired by the Tübingen school was the tacit assumption that Gentile Christianity was of one single type, and that that type was the creation of Paul" (*The Primitive Church,* p. 48). One wishes that the editors of *The Beginnings of Christianity* had given more heed to their own admission that "it is one of the mistakes of the Tübingen School that it did not recognize that Peter, not only in Acts but also in the Pauline Epistles, is on the Hellenistic, not on the Hebrew side" (Vol. I, p. 312).

10:1-2. Caesarea was at the time the Roman capital of the province of Judea and as such a garrison town. The **Italian Cohort** is probably the *Cohors II Italica Civium Romanorum,* which was a corps composed of freedmen from Italy and is known to have been stationed in Syria by A.D. 69. The fact that Cornelius' **household** was also at Caesarea

---

The process of growing up is usually punctuated by specific events. An adolescent leaps from stage to stage and each stage is begun by an event: the first trip away from home; the first love affair; a failure in school; the loss of a friend; the first money ever earned. In much the same way Christianity grew up. It was a succession of events, no one of which by and in itself might seem to be of any great significance, but each of which marked a new stage in the growth of the Jewish child. The story of Peter and Cornelius is such an event. It is the story about the first time a Gentile was publicly and officially welcomed into the Christian fellowship without conforming to the requirements of the Jewish law. It marks the point at which Christianity dramatically and decisively asserted its independence of Judaism. Such a declaration had to come, for Christianity by its very nature cannot be secondary to anything else. It cannot play second fiddle to any state or nation, nor can it be true to itself and serve any exclusive ecclesiastical or institutional system.

The leading figures in the story are Peter and Cornelius. They are just about the last people in the world whom you would expect to be drawn together. In the first place Cornelius was a Gentile and Peter was a Jew, and between them there was a great gulf fixed. Furthermore Cornelius was a high-ranking officer in the army of the Roman Empire and Peter had no rank at all, but was a follower of a country carpenter who had been put to death. Cor-

2 A devout *man*, and one that feared God with all his house, which gave much alms to the people, and prayed to God always.

3 He saw in a vision evidently, about the ninth hour of the day, an angel of God coming in to him, and saying unto him, Cornelius.

what was known as the Italian Cohort,
2 a devout man who feared God with all his household, gave alms liberally to the people, and prayed constantly to God.
3 About the ninth hour of the day he saw clearly in a vision an angel of God coming in and

suggests that he may have retired and settled there. **Who feared God** (φοβούμενος τὸν θεόν): A phrase commonly held to be a description of Gentiles who had accepted the truth of the Jewish religion and had become loose adherents of the synagogue, without going the length of being circumcised and becoming full proselytes. That the phrase was often so used is certain—other possible examples in Acts are 13:16, 26. But it is doubtful whether it can be considered a technical designation of a clearly defined group—the non-Jewish fringe attending the synagogues—parallel to Jews and proselytes, or whether it could not also be used on occasion as an honorable epithet of any devout worshiper of God—Jew, proselyte, or Gentile, as the context may decide. An alternative expression is σεβόμενος (τὸν θεόν), usually translated "devout," for which see 13:43, 50; 16:14; 17:4, 17; 18:7. (See note, *Beginnings of Christianity,* V, 84 ff.) **The people,** i.e., "the Jewish people"—almost a technical use of ὁ λαός, in contrast to τὰ ἔθνη, the nations or Gentiles.

nelius was a man of the world; Peter was a country boy with little or no experience outside his own province of Galilee until his position in the Christian movement thrust him onto the larger stage of world-wide activity. Cornelius was a professional man; Peter was a laboring man. One might go further in the contrast between these two men, and the further the contrast goes the more one marvels at the fact that these two men could ever find any basis upon which they might unite their efforts.

What was it then that drew them together? It might all be explained on the basis of guiding circumstances. On the one hand Peter had been turning over and over in his mind the whole question of the relationship of the new Christian movement to the rest of the world. He had been raised within the formidable barriers of Judaism. It was hard for him to think beyond those barriers. And yet the longer he lived in association with Jesus, and the more the spirit of Jesus dwelt in him, the more suspicious he became of the barriers which separated Jews from the rest of the world. This was probably not so much a deliberate act of thought on his part as it was a gradual growth in deeper understanding of the solidarity of the children of God. As time went on, he was more and more impatient with the lines that had been drawn between secular things and sacred things, between clean things and unclean things. If God is the creator of all things, how then could some things be more acceptable to him than others? What right did men have to draw lines beyond which God's care and interest could not and would not pass? In other words, the deeper Peter plunged into the truth that he found in Jesus, the more unwilling he was to confine himself to the artificial boundaries of Judaism. He was in the position of a man who, born and raised within an institution, comes to the point where he finds that the institution cannot contain the Spirit of God; it can only convey it.

Cornelius was in an entirely different situation. As described by the writer of the Acts, he was a religious man. That is, he had all the basic impulses that we associate with religion. He recognized the fact of God and did not hesitate to say his prayers. He was generous in his attitude toward his fellow men. He was regarded by all his associates as a man of integrity. As a Gentile he was not allowed into the inner sanctuary of the Jewish synagogue but he was on the fringe of it. He was something like the people we see today in great numbers who have a religious temperament but who have no church connections. His devout spirit was not committed to any religious institution.

Each of these two men had what the other needed. Peter had all the strength of institutional religion and needed to be set free from the confinements of it; while Cornelius had all the freedom of the religious spirit of the Gentiles and needed the supporting framework of institutional religion which would give that spirit discipline and direction. The circumstances of these two men are dramatized by the writer of the Acts. Peter's growing dissatisfaction with the institutionalism of Judaism and his

4 And when he looked on him, he was afraid, and said, What is it, Lord? And he said unto him, Thy prayers and thine alms are come up for a memorial before God.

5 And now send men to Joppa, and call for *one* Simon, whose surname is Peter:

6 He lodgeth with one Simon a tanner, whose house is by the sea side: he shall tell thee what thou oughtest to do.

7 And when the angel which spake unto Cornelius was departed, he called two of his household servants, and a devout soldier of them that waited on him continually;

8 And when he had declared all *these* things unto them, he sent them to Joppa.

9 ¶ On the morrow, as they went on their journey, and drew nigh unto the city,

saying to him, "Cornelius." 4 And he
stared at him in terror, and said, "What
is it, Lord?" And he said to him, "Your
prayers and your alms have ascended as a
memorial before God. 5 And now send men
to Joppa, and bring one Simon who is
called Peter; 6 he is lodging with Simon, a
tanner, whose house is by the seaside."
7 When the angel who spoke to him
had departed, he called two of his servants
and a devout soldier from among those
that waited on him, 8 and having related
everything to them, he sent them to Joppa.
9 The next day, as they were on their

---

4. As a memorial: Scripture regularly compares prayer and alms with sacrifice (Ps. 141:2; Phil. 4:18). In the LXX this same Greek word is used of the part of the meat offering that was burned (Lev. 2:1).

7. Those that waited on him: As we would say, "his orderlies."

9. About the sixth hour, i.e., noon, and not a usual hour for prayer, as were the third and the ninth (see 2:15; 10:3, 30). But all the hours mentioned in the N.T. are multiples

---

final acknowledgment of God's universal sovereignty are dramatized in the story of the trance in which he saw let down from heaven a sheet that contained all sorts of creatures, clean and unclean. Cornelius' increasing sense of the insufficiency of his own religious life is put in the dramatic form of a vision in which he was directed by an angel to seek out a man named Peter who could show him how to link the energies of his own native religious genius with the life and influence of Jesus. But in using the pictures of the vision and the trance, the writer of the book of the Acts is trying to say that there is something more to it than that. He is trying to say that Peter and Cornelius were brought together not only by natural circumstances, by the attraction of opposites, but also by the hand of God. He is trying to make it clear that these two men were brought together not by their own efforts or by the drift of human events but by the specific intention and will of God. In his rather naïve way he draws a picture of the overarching providence of God within which the apparently trifling events of our day-to-day existence are marshaled by a process beyond our imagining.

The same idea is expressed in a poem that Thomas Hardy wrote when the "Titanic" went down. The iceberg and the ship did not simply happen to come together. In one sense it was all part of a larger plan. Each one was prepared apart from the knowledge of the other, and in the fullness of time they were brought together in an event, in this instance, which was tragic and destructive.

Well: while was fashioning
This creature of cleaving wing,
The Immanent Will that stirs and urges everything

Prepared a sinister mate
For her—so gaily great—
A Shape of Ice, for the time far and dissociate.

And as the smart ship grew
In stature, grace, and hue,
In shadowy silent distance grew the Iceberg too.

Alien they seemed to be:
No mortal eye could see
The intimate welding of their later history.

Or sign that they were bent
By paths coincident
On being anon twin halves of one august event,

Till the Spinner of the Years
Said "Now!" And each one hears,
And consummation comes, and jars two hemispheres.[8]

[8] From "The Convergence of the Twain," *The Collected Poems of Thomas Hardy*. Copyright 1925. By permission of the Trustees of the Hardy Estate, Macmillan & Co., London, and The Macmillan Co., New York.

Peter went up upon the housetop to pray
about the sixth hour:
10 And he became very hungry, and
would have eaten: but while they made
ready, he fell into a trance,
11 And saw heaven opened, and a certain vessel descending unto him, as it had
been a great sheet knit at the four corners,
and let down to the earth:
12 Wherein were all manner of four-
footed beasts of the earth, and wild beasts,
and creeping things, and fowls of the air.
13 And there came a voice to him, Rise,
Peter; kill, and eat.
14 But Peter said, Not so, Lord; for I
have never eaten any thing that is common or unclean.
15 And the voice *spake* unto him again
the second time, What God hath cleansed,
that call not thou common.

journey and coming near the city, Peter
went up on the housetop to pray, about
the sixth hour. 10 And he became hungry
and desired something to eat; but while
they were preparing it, he fell into a trance
11 and saw the heaven opened, and something descending, like a great sheet, let
let down by four corners upon the earth.
12 In it were all kinds of animals and reptiles and birds of the air. 13 And there came
a voice to him, "Rise, Peter; kill and eat."
14 But Peter said, "No, Lord; for I have
never eaten anything that is common or
unclean." 15 And the voice came to him
again a second time, "What God has
cleansed, you must not call common."

---

of three—third, sixth, ninth—and it is possible that the four quarters of the day were used to mark the approximate time.

11. Something descending: The Greek word means any **vessel,** implement, or object; it is used even of the human body (I Pet. 3:7; I Thess. 4:4).

15. What God has cleansed: Presumably by the command to eat. Or have we an echo of Mark 7:14-23, where Mark's comment on Jesus' teaching is that "thus he declared all foods clean" (RSV)?

There are few people who have not had some indication of similar preparation for the great experiences of their lives. When two people come together in love they almost invariably feel that their union is something over and above the chance of circumstance. As their love deepens through the years, they are more and more convinced that God brought them together. So it is with other great events in history. While on the one hand God was preparing the United States for the emancipation of the Negro, arousing the interest of the people up and down the land, so on the other hand he was preparing a log cabin, a boy, a rail splitter, a lawyer; and at the proper moment he brought the two together and in the perfect union of the properly prepared man and the adequately aroused public opinion the great event took place. So also it seems to us in retrospect that God was working from both ends when Christ was born. The Roman Empire meant a breathing spell of peace, a universal language, a system of good roads. The breakdown of traditional religious faiths meant a sincere desire on the part of human beings for something that would give them new power. At the same time God was preparing a young woman to bring into the world a child; a carpenter to train the boy in an honest trade; a young man charged with the destiny of mankind. When the time came, the situation and the man were brought together in a convergence, the result of which has been renewed life for countless human beings ever since. So Peter and Cornelius came together.

When Peter and Cornelius finally met, it was as though a great wall was once and for all removed. Here were a Jew and a Gentile standing face to face with nothing between them. Peter proceeded to tell the story which he had already told many times, the story of how Jesus went about doing good, how God was with him, how he was killed and how God raised him on the third day, how he is now the judge of all people everywhere. That was all Cornelius needed to know. Without any more ado, without any ceremony whatsoever, Cornelius and all his family and friends were filled with the Holy Spirit, and on the basis of that they were baptized.

15. *What God Hath Cleansed, That Call Not Thou Common.*—A warning is here sounded against the tendency to separate things and call some of them sacred and some secular. The Jews had a particularly strong temptation to do just that. The ceremonial law of their religion

16 This was done thrice: and the vessel was received up again into heaven.

17 Now while Peter doubted in himself what this vision which he had seen should mean, behold, the men which were sent from Cornelius had made inquiry for Simon's house, and stood before the gate,

18 And called, and asked whether Simon, which was surnamed Peter, were lodged there.

19 ¶ While Peter thought on the vision, the Spirit said unto him, Behold, three men seek thee.

20 Arise therefore, and get thee down, and go with them, doubting nothing: for I have sent them.

21 Then Peter went down to the men which were sent unto him from Cornelius; and said, Behold, I am he whom ye seek: what *is* the cause wherefore ye are come?

22 And they said, Cornelius the centurion, a just man, and one that feareth God, and of good report among all the nation of the Jews, was warned from God by a holy angel to send for thee into his house, and to hear words of thee.

23 Then called he them in, and lodged *them.* And on the morrow Peter went away with them, and certain brethren from Joppa accompanied him.

24 And the morrow after they entered into Caesarea. And Cornelius waited for them, and had called together his kinsmen and near friends.

16 This happened three times, and the thing
was taken up at once to heaven.
17 Now while Peter was inwardly perplexed as to what the vision which he had
seen might mean, behold, the men that
were sent by Cornelius, having made inquiry for Simon's house, stood before the
gate 18 and called out to ask whether Simon
who was called Peter was lodging there.
19 And while Peter was pondering the
vision, the Spirit said to him, "Behold,
three men are looking for you. 20 Rise and
go down, and accompany them without
hesitation; for I have sent them." 21 And
Peter went down to the men and said, "I
am the one you are looking for; what is
the reason for your coming?" 22 And they
said, "Cornelius, a centurion, an upright
and God-fearing man, who is well spoken
of by the whole Jewish nation, was directed
by a holy angel to send for you to come
to his house, and to hear what you have to
say." 23 So he called them in to be his
guests.
The next day he rose and went off with
them, and some of the brethren from Joppa
accompanied him. 24 And on the following
day they entered Caes-a-re'a. Cornelius was
expecting them and had called together his

---

19. The Spirit becomes "I" in the next verse and is probably thought of as identical with Jesus. Previously (vss. 13-15) Peter has addressed "the voice" as "Lord." And does Luke intend to distinguish between the "angel" who spoke to Cornelius (vs. 3) and the "Spirit" who spoke to Peter? (See on 8:26.)

---

was a dividing line, on the one side of which all things were clean and on the other side of which all things were unclean. The tendency persists right down to our own time.

The modern distinction between "sacred" and "secular" is largely false. The activity carried on in a church is no more sacred than that carried on in a laboratory. One can be profane in either place to the extent to which one directs one's energies to the business of exploiting what is found, rather than to exploring the richness of it and exclaiming at the wonder of it. Hence the true division is between the sacred and the profane—that which is centered upon God and that which is not; and the introspective, self-centered worship found in a church may be as profane in this sense as the materialistic research found in a laboratory. On the other hand the selfless, unflagging persistence of a scientist who has dedicated his life to the fuller understanding of the physical universe may be as sacred a thing as the humble prayer of a saint who finds the fulfillment of life in the adoration of God.

This is not to say that the activity of worship, which is normally listed among the sacred elements of life, is an activity which can be disregarded by men and women who are engaged in other activities less specifically religious and more worldly in their external appearance. It is to say, rather, that any activity which is good is a sacred activity in that the power to en-

25 And as Peter was coming in, Cornelius met him, and fell down at his feet, and worshipped *him*.

26 But Peter took him up, saying, Stand up; I myself also am a man.

27 And as he talked with him, he went in, and found many that were come together.

28 And he said unto them, Ye know how that it is an unlawful thing for a man that is a Jew to keep company, or come unto one of another nation; but God hath showed me that I should not call any man common or unclean.

29 Therefore came I *unto you* without gainsaying, as soon as I was sent for: I ask therefore for what intent ye have sent for me?

30 And Cornelius said, Four days ago I was fasting until this hour; and at the ninth hour I prayed in my house, and, behold, a man stood before me in bright clothing,

31 And said, Cornelius, thy prayer is heard, and thine alms are had in remembrance in the sight of God.

32 Send therefore to Joppa, and call hither Simon, whose surname is Peter; he is lodged in the house of *one* Simon a tanner by the sea side: who, when he cometh, shall speak unto thee.

33 Immediately therefore I sent to thee; and thou hast well done that thou art come. Now therefore are we all here present before God, to hear all things that are commanded thee of God.

kinsmen and close friends. 25 When Peter
entered, Cornelius met him and fell down
at his feet and worshiped him. 26 But Peter
lifted him up, saying, "Stand up; I too am
a man." 27 And as he talked with him, he
went in and found many persons gathered;
28 and he said to them, "You yourselves
know how unlawful it is for a Jew to associate with or to visit any one of another
nation; but God has shown me that I
should not call any man common or unclean. 29 So when I was sent for, I came
without objection. I ask then why you
sent for me."

30 And Cornelius said, "Four days ago,
about this hour, I was keeping the ninth
hour of prayer in my house; and behold,
a man stood before me in bright apparel,
31 saying, 'Cornelius, your prayer has been
heard and your alms have been remembered before God. 32 Send therefore to
Joppa and ask for Simon who is called
Peter; he is lodging in the house of Simon,
a tanner, by the seaside.' 33 So I sent to
you at once, and you have been kind
enough to come. Now therefore we are all
here present in the sight of God, to hear
all that you have been commanded by the
Lord."

---

25. The Western text is very vivid here: "And as Peter was coming near to Caesarea one of the slaves ran ahead and announced that he had arrived. And Cornelius jumped up and met him."

28. Unlawful (ἀθέμιτον); cf. I Pet. 4:3, "lawless idolatry." "The word means contrary to θέμις, the divinely constituted order of things, breaking a taboo" (Lake and Cadbury, *Beginnings of Christianity,* IV, 117). "Something which is not done" gives the feel of the word, though our expression has not the religious nuance of the Greek word.

---

gage in it is God-given and the end toward which it moves is God-centered. A businessman, therefore, is not occupied with sacred things on Sunday and secular things on Monday. He is occupied every day with things sacred, because all things bear the burden of divine life. He may be profane at his desk as well as in his pew, self-seeking in his business as well as in his religion. But wherever he is, his hands touch holy things, things as holy as facts and figures, products of the earth, and the personalities of men and women.

The Bible declares the glory of God—all would admit that, certainly—but so does any good book, in its own way and to its own degree, by its vivid portrayals and by its entertaining interest. A cathedral declares the glory of God; so does the Brooklyn Bridge—in the delicate balance of its stresses and strains, in the dependability of its piers, the sweep of its

34 ¶ Then Peter opened *his* mouth, and said, Of a truth I perceive that God is no respecter of persons:

35 But in every nation he that feareth him, and worketh righteousness, is accepted with him.

36 The word which *God* sent unto the children of Israel, preaching peace by Jesus Christ: (he is Lord of all:)

37 That word, *I say,* ye know, which was published throughout all Judea, and began from Galilee, after the baptism which John preached;

38 How God anointed Jesus of Nazareth with the Holy Ghost and with power: who went about doing good, and healing all that were oppressed of the devil; for God was with him.

34 And Peter opened his mouth and said:
"Truly I perceive that God shows no partiality,
35 but in every nation any one who
fears him and does what is right is acceptable to him.
36 You know the word which
he sent to Israel, preaching good news of
peace by Jesus Christ (he is Lord of all),
37 the word which was proclaimed throughout all Judea, beginning from Galilee after
the baptism which John preached:
38 how
God anointed Jesus of Nazareth with the
Holy Spirit and with power; how he went
about doing good and healing all that
were oppressed by the devil, for God was

---

34. Peter's speech to Cornelius and his associates follows the same lines as do the other Petrine speeches, the emphasis being on the judicial murder of Jesus by the Jews and on the Resurrection, which vindicates his claims. But this message is now, whether by Peter himself or more probably by Luke, skillfully adapted to a Gentile audience. The catholic relationship of God to the righteous of all nations alike is stressed, and Jesus is no longer, as in 2:36, the Jewish "Lord and Christ," but **Lord of all** (vs. 36). The fulfillment of purely national messianic expectation falls into the background, and Jesus is presented not only as "Christ," but as **judge of the living and the dead** (vs. 42). **God shows no partiality:** Literally "God is not an accepter of faces"; cf. I Pet. 1:17, "who judges each one impartially."

36-38. The Greek is very clumsy, but the RSV gives a perfectly satisfactory rendering: ῥῆμα simply picks up λόγον, both being governed by οἴδατε, while Ἰησοῦν . . . θεός must be regarded simply as an awkward periphrasis for ὡς ἔχρισεν Ἰησοῦν ὁ θεός. For the curious adverbial use of ἀρξάμενος, the nominative apparently being outside the construction of the sentence, cf. Luke 24:47; see also Luke 23:5; Acts 1:22. **Anointed,** i.e., "made Christ," "made Messiah"; cf. 4:27. Does this refer to the baptism of Jesus, with the implication that it was only then that he became Messiah? Elsewhere (e.g., 2:36, with which cf. Rom. 1:4) it seems to be suggested that it is in virtue of his resurrection

---

cables, and its "choiring strings." A Christian saint declares the glory of God; so also does any laboring man—in the strength of his body, the co-ordination of his muscles, and his faithfulness to his job.

As our range of vision is thus extended, the whole universe expresses to us its divine significance and our religion becomes an all-inclusive thing.

34-35. ***"Then Peter . . . Said, 'I See Quite Plainly That God Has no Favourites'"*** (Moffatt).—The supernational character of Christianity is suggested. It all began with Jesus. Never setting foot outside of Palestine, he was a supreme example of a man who was so provincial that he became universal. He went so deep into human life that he touched the very core of it. He can be translated into every language on the face of the earth without any serious losses or changes. The Cross can be understood by the most cultured and the most ignorant. His way of life rises above the way of political systems, and loyalty to him stands far above loyalty to any particular nation. It was because of him, therefore, who though he was a Jew yet belonged to all men, that the disciples began to see that the fences they had built had no divine sanction, that God had no favorites, that there were no superior races, that there was no chosen people in the sense of a people who had priority above and beyond all others. Thus Christianity soon became one of the great supernational movements of the world. Never was it needed more than it is now, and in that specific role. Internationalism will never become a reality until someone common to all races is

39 And we are witnesses of all things which he did both in the land of the Jews, and in Jerusalem; whom they slew and hanged on a tree:

40 Him God raised up the third day, and showed him openly;

41 Not to all the people, but unto witnesses chosen before of God, *even* to us, who did eat and drink with him after he rose from the dead.

42 And he commanded us to preach unto the people, and to testify that it is he which was ordained of God *to be* the Judge of quick and dead.

43 To him give all the prophets witness, that through his name whosoever believeth in him shall receive remission of sins.

44 ¶ While Peter yet spake these words, the Holy Ghost fell on all them which heard the word.

45 And they of the circumcision which believed were astonished, as many as came

with him. 39 And we are witnesses to all
that he did both in the country of the
Jews and in Jerusalem. They put him to
death by hanging him on a tree; 40 but
God raised him on the third day and made
him manifest, 41 not to all the people but
to us who were chosen by God as witnesses,
who ate and drank with him after he rose
from the dead. 42 And he commanded us
to preach to the people, and to testify that
he is the one ordained by God to be judge
of the living and the dead. 43 To him all
the prophets bear witness that every one
who believes in him receives forgiveness of
sins through his name."

44 While Peter was still saying this, the
Holy Spirit fell on all who heard the word.
45 And the believers from among the cir-

---

that Jesus is Messiah. But would not Luke himself think of him as Messiah by birth, having been "conceived by the Holy Spirit"? Probably the verse should be taken in a more general sense as an echo of Isa. 60:1, applied by Jesus to himself in Luke 4:18. **Oppressed by the devil:** All Jesus' miracles and mighty works are regarded in the Gospels and Acts as triumphs over the demonic powers; cf. especially Luke 10:18, where, at the return of the seventy, after hearing the report of their cures in his name, Jesus cries out, "I saw Satan fall like lightning from heaven."

39. On a tree: It is interesting that the same word is used for the cross in I Pet. 2:24, "He himself bore our sins in his body on the tree"; cf. also 5:30, again on Peter's lips.

41. Witnesses: The supreme qualification of an apostle; cf. 1:8, 22; Luke 24:48. The reference to eating and drinking is no doubt to meet the objection that the risen Jesus was merely a "ghost"; cf. Luke 24:39 ff.

42. Ordained by God to be judge, i.e., to undertake the supreme function traditionally delegated to him as the "Son of man," whom the book of Enoch, e.g., constantly pictures as judge; cf. I Pet. 4:5, "They will give account to him who is ready to judge the living and the dead," and II Tim. 4:1, "Christ Jesus who is to judge the living and the dead." See 17:31 for another periphrasis for the title "Son of man," which is avoided in Acts—except at 7:56, which is an echo of Luke 22:69—as likely to be unintelligible to Hellenistic readers.

43. Forgiveness of sins, cf. Luke 24:46-47. This idea is greatly emphasized in Acts. Peter's speech in 2:38 claims that the messianic promises are fulfilled by the gift of the Spirit and the forgiveness of sins; and in Paul's speeches the climax to which everything leads up is the forgiveness of sins (see 13:38; 26:18).

44. The word: Not merely Peter's speech, but the gospel message.

---

acknowledged who will be the basis of a supernationalism.

45. ***They . . . Were Astonished . . . That on the Gentiles Also Was Poured Out the Gift of the Holy Ghost.***—"The Gentiles also." Indeed why not? Why should the Jewish people be amazed that God had poured out his spirit upon the Gentiles? It was largely because of their habitual reference to the ceremonial law, according to which the Gentiles were beyond the pale. It was a shock to them to realize that God cared as much about the Gentiles as he did about them. From such a starting point we can go on to consider the place of ceremonial law in re-

with Peter, because that on the Gentiles also was poured out the gift of the Holy Ghost.

46 For they heard them speak with tongues, and magnify God. Then answered Peter,

47 Can any man forbid water, that these should not be baptized, which have received the Holy Ghost as well as we?

48 And he commanded them to be baptized in the name of the Lord. Then prayed they him to tarry certain days.

cumcised who came with Peter were amazed, because the gift of the Holy Spirit had been poured out even on the Gentiles.
46 For they heard them speaking in tongues and extolling God. Then Peter declared,
47 "Can any one forbid water for baptizing these people who have received the Holy Spirit just as we have?"
48 And he commanded them to be baptized in the name of Jesus Christ. Then they asked him to remain for some days.

---

48. To be baptized: Does the passive imply that Peter delegated the act of baptism to an assistant? Also cf. Paul's words, "Christ did not send me to baptize but to preach the gospel" (I Cor. 1:17). **In the name of Jesus Christ:** The most primitive formula (cf. 8:16; 19:5) later displaced by the trinitarian formula (Matt. 28:19).

The account of Cornelius' baptism is interesting as combining the primitive point of view, according to which the gift of the Spirit takes the place of water-baptism, and the intermediate position that baptism is at least a necessary condition of admission to the church (see on 2:37). As at Pentecost, the Spirit is given independently of baptism: "While Peter was still saying this [i.e., before there is any mention of baptism] the Holy Spirit fell on all who heard the word" (10:44). But by the time Luke wrote, baptism was a universally practiced initiatory rite, and so we read here that Peter **commanded them to be baptized in the name of Jesus Christ.** Indeed, Lake suspects that the mention of baptism is due to the writer's preconception that Cornelius *must* have been baptized before admission to the Christian fellowship. Neither in Peter's own account of the incident (11:15-18) nor in his reference to it at the Jerusalem conference (15:7-9) is there any mention of baptism. When replying to the charge of having treated these Gentiles as members of the fellowship (11:3), Peter insists that in the gift of the Spirit they had already received from God all the authentication that was necessary (11:17). More significantly still, he points his argument by quoting the words "John baptized with water, but you shall be baptized with the Holy Spirit" (11:16). As Lake pertinently asks: "What would have been the point of this quotation if the true end of the story had been, 'So I baptized Cornelius in water'?" (*Beginnings of Christianity,* I, 341.)

---

ligion. First, the necessity of it. We cannot have religion without ceremonial law any more than we can have a meal without certain rules of etiquette and ritual of table arrangement and serving. And yet it must be clearly recognized that the ceremonial law is fraught with danger. Those dangers will be considered at greater length in the Expos. of ch. 11. Here it is sufficient to point out that one of the hardest lessons the early Jewish Christians had to learn was that the ceremonial law always took second place to the law of love, and in some instances had to be scrapped altogether. It is still hard for people to exceed the limits of their own ceremonial law. For some it is natural to believe that unless a person is baptized in a certain way, he is not baptized at all; that unless he receives Communion in a certain form and manner, he actually does not receive it at all; that unless he is ordained according to a certain formula and by certain authorized people, he is not ordained of God at all. Jesus made himself unmistakably clear on the issue when he said, "The sabbath was made for man, and not man for the sabbath" (Mark 2:27). In other words, the ceremonial law is entirely secondary to something larger and more inclusive and of greater importance.

The end of this chapter suggests a sequence of events which might well become the pattern of Christian practice at all times. First, the Spirit fell upon Cornelius and all his family and friends. That was the big thing, the real thing. Next, they were baptized, for things of the Spirit crave to become articulate in tangible forms. Finally, **They asked him** [Peter] **to remain for some days.** The supposition is that after the great experience of the Spirit, and after the expression of that Spirit in the outward and visible sign, there still remained the

11 And the apostles and brethren that
were in Judea heard that the Gentiles
had also received the word of God.
2 And when Peter was come up to Jerusalem, they that were of the circumcision
contended with him,
3 Saying, Thou wentest in to men uncircumcised, and didst eat with them.
4 But Peter rehearsed *the matter* from
the beginning, and expounded *it* by order
unto them, saying,
5 I was in the city of Joppa praying: and
in a trance I saw a vision, A certain vessel
descend, as it had been a great sheet, let
down from heaven by four corners; and it
came even to me:

11 Now the apostles and the brethren
who were in Judea heard that the
Gentiles also had received the word of
God. 2 So when Peter went up to Jerusalem, the circumcision party criticized him,
3 saying, "Why did you go to uncircumcised men and eat with them?" 4 But Peter
began and explained to them in order:
5 "I was in the city of Joppa praying; and
in a trance I saw a vision, something descending, like a great sheet, let down from
heaven by four corners; and it came down to

11:1-2. The narrative which follows seems to imply that the church challenged Peter's action and recalled him to Jerusalem to justify it. The Western text, possibly in order to remove this impression, freely rewrites: "So Peter after some time wished to go to Jerusalem . . . and he met them [i.e., the leaders at Jerusalem] and reported to them the grace of God. But the brethren of the circumcision disputed with him. . . ."

3. The same criticism had been leveled at Jesus himself (Luke 15:2; 19:7).

---

day-by-day cultivation and development of it in the routine of human existence.

11:1-18. ***The Protest Against Peter.***—"Gentiles join the Christian church!"—so the news might be flashed around the world by the magic of modern communication. But even though there was no radio or telephone in the first century, it did not take long for the news to reach Jerusalem that Cornelius and his household had become Christians. What a triumph for the new movement! It was reaching out beyond its national and religious frontiers and beginning to embrace the world. Something like a victory rally we should expect to greet such news when it arrived in Jerusalem. But instead of that there was a meeting of protest.

The protest was directed at Peter and the sum and substance of it was that he had eaten a meal with a Gentile—he had violated the ceremonial law. Just how it would be possible for Christ to save a world in which one person was forbidden to eat a meal with another, the objectors had never stopped to figure out. It had always been so: many believe that no man should tamper with traditions. Peter did, and Peter was now being brought to task.

The protest was not from the whole Christian group, but from the "circumcision party." Apparently there was within the group a smaller group that was ultraconservative. They were the tories of early Christianity, the meticulously orthodox, the right wing of the movement. Their platform rested upon the assumption that Christianity was a movement *within* Judaism, and therefore must conform to the life and practice of Judaism as they knew it. A man could not be a Christian unless he were a Jew first; he could not be baptized before he had been circumcised. They had neither the imagination nor the mind to grasp the vision of Christianity as a movement *from* Judaism, beginning where the religion of the prophets left off. It is to Peter's everlasting credit that he did not join the circumcision party. Paul was highly educated and cosmopolitan, and we should not expect him to be found in the ranks of any such party. But Peter was different. He had neither the background nor the worldly experience of Paul. Furthermore he was a Palestinian Jew; he had never been beyond the hills of his own country; he was a fisherman by trade and had none of the broadening influences of education. But he had Jesus, close association with the emancipating mind of his Lord, which more than made up for all the other deficiencies. Through those brief years of deepening intimacy with Jesus, he had learned more than he knew; he had caught the spirit of his Master and that spirit led him to make decisions that the most learned might have been unable to make.

It is interesting to us who are so plagued by parties in the church to observe that they have been there from the beginning. Paul had to struggle with them in Corinth and here, right in Christianity's home town, in the first

6 Upon the which when I had fastened mine eyes, I considered, and saw fourfooted beasts of the earth, and wild beasts, and creepings things, and fowls of the air.

7 And I heard a voice saying unto me, Arise, Peter; slay and eat.

8 But I said, Not so, Lord: for nothing common or unclean hath at any time entered into my mouth.

9 But the voice answered me again from heaven, What God hath cleansed, *that* call not thou common.

10 And this was done three times: and all were drawn up again into heaven.

11 And, behold, immediately there were three men already come unto the house where I was, sent from Caesarea unto me.

12 And the Spirit bade me go with them, nothing doubting. Moreover these six brethren accompanied me, and we entered into the man's house:

me. 6 Looking at it closely I observed animals and beasts of prey and reptiles and
birds of the air. 7 And I heard a voice saying
to me, 'Rise, Peter; kill and eat.' 8 But I said,
'No, Lord: for nothing common or unclean has ever entered my mouth.' 9 But
the voice answered a second time from
heaven, 'What God has cleansed you must
not call common.' 10 This happened three
times, and all was drawn up again into
heaven. 11 At that very moment three men
arrived at the house in which we were,
sent to me from Caes-a-re'a. 12 And the
Spirit told me to go with them without
hesitation. These six brethren also accompanied me, and we entered the man's house.

---

12. **Without hesitation:** The Greek properly means "making no distinction" (i.e., between Jew and Gentile); cf. 15:9, where with reference to this same incident we read, "He [God] made no distinction between us and them." In the parallel passage in 10:20 the Greek verb is in the middle voice and is rightly translated "without hesitation," an idea which is picked up in 10:29, "I came without objection." **Six brethren:** A new detail, not given in ch. 10, but apparently referring to "some of the brethren from Joppa" (10:23) and "the believers from among the circumcised who came with Peter" (10:45).

---

days of its flowering, there was a party. It was inevitable that it should have been so, for wherever there is a large group, there is bound to be a difference of opinion within the group. People do not think alike, and although they may agree upon some fundamental proposition—for example, Jesus is Lord—yet within that agreement there is room for more than one interpretation and for many shades of opinion. As long as people do not think alike there will be parties in politics, in education, in religion.

Parties at their best call attention to something that might otherwise be overlooked. When the weight is all on one side, then a party will restore the balance by throwing its weight on the other side. In the Church of England, when the weight was all on the side of individualism in religion and freedom in faith, the High-Church party helped to restore the balance by throwing its weight on the side of the church, its ministry, and its sacraments. That kind of party influence is valuable. Every good government needs a loyal opposition.

Parties at their worst, however, divide the church and dissipate its energies. For when the party loyalty becomes an ultimate loyalty, then there is nothing but dissension and havoc ahead. When a person is more concerned about Protestantism or Catholicism than he is about Christianity, his party loyalty then amounts to treason. There are parties in the church today; liturgical parties, theological parties, ecclesiastical parties. It is not the party itself that is evil; it is the person who puts the party above the church. So long as party loyalties are all kept subordinate to the higher loyalty to Christ, they may well do more good than harm, for in him there are no parties and in him all the lesser loyalties are transfigured and redeemed from their narrow ways.

The circumcision party made the mistake that most parties sooner or later are bound to make: they failed to distinguish between the spirit and the system and they mistook one for the other. It is upon this rock that most parties come to grief. It is worth further examination.

Consider, by way of illustration, the relationship of the spirit and the system in democracy. Democracy is above everything else a spirit that prevails in a society which believes that

13 And he showed us how he had seen an angel in his house, which stood and said unto him, Send men to Joppa, and call for Simon, whose surname is Peter;

14 Who shall tell thee words, whereby thou and all thy house shall be saved.

15 And as I began to speak, the Holy Ghost fell on them, as on us at the beginning.

16 Then remembered I the word of the Lord, how that he said, John indeed baptized with water; but ye shall be baptized with the Holy Ghost.

17 Forasmuch then as God gave them the like gift as *he did* unto us, who believed on the Lord Jesus Christ, what was I, that I could withstand God?

18 When they heard these things, they held their peace, and glorified God, saying, Then hath God also to the Gentiles granted repentance unto life.

13 And he told us how he had seen the
angel standing in his house and saying,
'Send to Joppa and bring Simon called
Peter; 14 he will declare to you a message
by which you will be saved, you and all
your household.' 15 As I began to speak,
the Holy Spirit fell on them just as on us
at the beginning. 16 And I remembered the
word of the Lord, how he said, 'John baptized with water, but you shall be baptized
with the Holy Spirit.' 17 If then God gave
the same gift to them as he gave to us
when we believed in the Lord Jesus Christ,
who was I that I could withstand God?"
18 When they heard this they were silenced.
And they glorified God, saying, "Then to
the Gentiles also God has granted repentance unto life."

15-16. At the beginning, i.e., at Pentecost. **I remembered:** For the formula cf. 20:35, "remembering the words of the Lord Jesus. . . ." In the Gospels this saying about baptism is regularly attributed, not to Jesus, but to John the Baptist (Mark 1:8 and parallels). In Acts 1:5 also the words are put on Jesus' lips.

18. They glorified God: Probably in the simple sense of praising God for his great works (cf. 21:20). But the phrase may carry the technical Jewish sense of admitting a previous error, for which cf. John 9:24, "Give God the praise; we know that this man is a sinner." Also cf. Josh. 7:19; Rev. 16:9. This would fit in well with the preceding phrase **they were silenced;** and the meaning would be that they withdrew their objections to Peter's conduct.

---

the rights and responsibilities of government can be and must be shared by all the people. It is basically an attitude of mind toward man and his nature; it is a spirit of good will toward men because they are men; it is grounded in a reverence for life. But the spirit by itself is not enough. As the spirit of man must have a body, and the body must have a skeleton, so the spirit of democracy must have a system of government. It must have a legislative body to express the will of the people and make its laws; it must have courts and constitutions, executives and elections. Without such a mechanism the spirit would evaporate. But the essential thing to remember is that the spirit and the system are not identical. The spirit of democracy has prevailed in many different systems. In ancient Greece it was the small city-state and every citizen had a voice in the election. In the United Kingdom there is a parliamentary system; in the United States a constitutional system; in Sweden a democracy in the apparel of a monarchy. In other words, without the system the spirit of democracy would disappear, but the system and the spirit are not the same thing.

In the United States, for example, one of the most important instruments in the democracy is the Supreme Court. Essential as that judicial body is, when people are inclined to raise the court above the level of all criticism and possible change, they run the risk of substituting the system for the spirit itself. The spirit is always and forever the same, but the system must remain flexible and adjustable. New situations may demand new systems in order that the spirit may flow freely and act creatively. It is conceivable that a court such as the Supreme Court might become so fixed and changeless as to be a hindrance to the democratic spirit rather than a help.

Another illustration of the same thing is to be found in the relationship between etiquette and social grace. Social grace is a spirit which dwells in people by which their relationship with their neighbors is governed and directed. A book of etiquette is the system by which and through which social grace most

19 ¶ Now they which were scattered abroad upon the persecution that arose about Stephen traveled as far as Phenice,

19 Now those who were scattered because of the persecution that arose over Stephen

3. Early History of the Church at Antioch (11:19-30)

This section is clearly a continuation of 8:4, the words **those who were scattered** (vs. 19) being intended to pick up "those who were scattered went about preaching the word" (8:4). Luke is presumably basing his narrative again on the Antiochene source, for now he takes up once again the story of the church at Antioch. Just as Philip preached to the Samaritans and had his work confirmed by Peter and John (8:14-17), and the conversion of Cornelius at Caesarea by Peter was approved by the Jerusalem church (11:18), so now at Antioch a larger Gentile mission is undertaken and is subsequently investigated and blessed by Barnabas (11:22-24). Luke is concerned to show that at each stage of the rapidly expanding Christian mission the innovators carried with them the consent of the mother church.

a) Foundation of the Church (11:19-21)

The new developments noted in these verses are of epoch-making importance, and they are described with a sobriety, not to say casualness, that contrasts strongly with the highly dramatized story of Cornelius. As Johannes Weiss well says: "The interesting thing about this statement is that the transition to the Gentile mission does not appear here as the result of conscious deliberations and solemn decisions but as an obvious extension of the work, which must have seemed quite natural to these men who had grown up in a Greek environment. And that is at the same time a genuinely historical conception of the course of events, for the great innovations in the life of the spirit are usually brought about in such a way that their first beginnings arrive quietly and imperceptibly, so that when the world becomes aware of them, it is already face to face with accomplished facts" (*The History of Primitive Christianity* [ed. F. C. Grant; London: Macmillan & Co.; New York: Wilson-Erickson, 1937], I, 171-72).

The chief significance of vs. 20 lies in the assertion that the momentous step of preaching to pagans was taken independently of Paul. Not that we should conclude from this that Paul was forestalled, and that in his Gentile missions he was merely following an example set by Antioch. He was probably already at work himself along similar lines in Syria and Cilicia (Gal. 1:21). It is in fact entirely likely that the initiative was taken in various places by various individuals more or less simultaneously. But the ultimate preponderating importance of Paul's work, the fact that his letters bulk so large in the N.T., while Luke has given to the second part of Acts the form of a history

easily expresses itself. Good manners cannot easily dispense with good books of etiquette, and yet how painful it is to see a person who has learned and observed all the rules of good etiquette but has not in himself the spirit of social grace for which all the rules of etiquette were originally designed. He lacks the one thing needful. He does not know when to suspend the rules of etiquette in order to let the real grace of good manners flow freely. Some people are so painfully polite that they make all their companions ill at ease. It is another example of the system mistakenly substituted for the spirit. It is what we are always unconsciously in danger of doing in government. It is what a group of Christians were in danger of doing in religion. It is a fundamental inability to see the difference between the instrument and the music to be played upon it. Without the instrument, no music. But when the instrument is exalted to the position of the music itself, and more care is spent in tuning and perfecting the instrument than upon the creating of the music, then there is failure ahead. The circumcision party in Palestine and parties of different names in our contemporary Christianity are guilty of putting the instrument in the place where the music ought to be. Some Peter always pays the price of such misdirected party spirit.

19-26. ***The New Church in Antioch.***—First, how did it begin? The first Christian community of any size outside of Jerusalem was the one in Antioch, a large metropolitan center

and Cyprus, and Antioch, preaching the word to none but unto the Jews only.

traveled as far as Phoe-ni'ci-a and Cyprus and Antioch, speaking the word to none

of Pauline Gentile missions—all this has thrown into the shade the early non-Pauline missions to pagans. Yet it is a mistake to regard Paul as the sole founder of Greek Christianity. As Wilhelm Bousset reminds us: "Between Paul and the Palestinian primitive church stand the Hellenistic churches in Antioch, Damascus, Tarsus. . . . In any case the development of the Apostle's life took place on the foundation of the Hellenistic churches" (*Kyrios Christos* [Göttingen: Vandenhoeck & Ruprecht, 1926], pp. 75-76). Quite apart from Paul's pioneering it is impossible to say how soon and how far work among Hellenistic Jews would begin to touch pure Gentile Greeks.

This, of course, is the problem raised by the crucial words in vs. 20, **some of them . . . spoke to the Greeks also.** For the distinction between "Hellenes" and "Hellenists" see on 6:1. Though the best-attested reading here is undoubtedly "Hellenists" (Ἑλληνιστάς with ℵ B), the pointed contrast with **to none except Jews** makes it certain that the reference is to pure Greeks and not to "Grecizing Jews," and accordingly most editors adopt the reading "Hellenes" or "Greeks" (Ἕλληνας with ℵ2 A D). The confusion in the MSS is probably due simply to the fact that the distinctions between various classes within the church were soon forgotten; and after two or three hundred years the difference between a "Hellene" and a "Hellenist," a "Greek" and a "Grecian," became as obscure and as unimportant as it is to the ordinary reader today. But in this particular passage it is just this distinction that gives point to the whole incident.

19. Antioch, on the Orontes, ranked as capital of the East, and was the seat of the imperial legate of the Roman province of Syria and Cilicia. It was, according to Josephus, the third city of the Roman Empire, second only to Rome and Alexandria. The mass of the population would be Syrian, with a large Jewish colony, but its culture was chiefly Greek. It was a very important center of commerce, its port being Seleucia (13:4). Some few miles distant was Daphne, the headquarters of the cult of Apollo and Artemis, and its *Daphnici mores* became so notorious that when Juvenal wishes to sum up in one line the moral degradation of Rome, the worst that he can say is that "the Syrian Orontes has flowed into the Tiber" (*Satires* III. 62). The center of gravity of Christianity rapidly passed from Jerusalem to Antioch. Tradition closely associates Peter with the city, naming him as its first bishop; and later illustrious names among its bishops are Ignatius and John Chrysostom.

where people of all cultures freely mingled. At first it was distinctly outside the pale of Judaism, and the church might never have got a foothold there had there not been a disaster in Jerusalem.

The death of Stephen started trouble in the mother church. The sympathizers with Stephen were not willing to confine Christianity to the narrow limits of Judaism; and, because of the opposition in Jerusalem to a policy of greater inclusiveness, they were scattered abroad. Some of them got as far as Antioch. Christianity in Jerusalem was not destroyed; it was dispersed. The death of Stephen, that looked so much like a tragedy, was the thing that made success. The seed pod burst and, though the incident was a painful one, the fruit of it was incalculable. In times like our own, when so many good things in life seem to be destroyed, it is good to remember that no good thing can ever be destroyed. It can only be dispersed.

The church in Antioch got under way when a few daring men preached the gospel to the Greeks. The swaddling clothes were at last completely stripped off. Christianity had stepped out of its local pasture and taken the fields of the world for its grazing. It has never been free, however, from the temptation to narrow its activity and to set limits upon its field. The action of the Christians in Antioch was confirmed by the immediate growth of the Christian community there. **A great number believed, and turned unto the Lord.** Any nationalistic arguments against the policy of the leaders in Antioch could be completely met and answered by the fact that the church grew by leaps and bounds.

Second, who was the leader of the church in Antioch? You cannot have a Christian community without a Christian leader. It is a proved fact that nine times out of ten where the church is weak it is weak because the leadership

20 And some of them were men of Cyprus and Cyrene, which, when they were come to Antioch, spake unto the Grecians, preaching the Lord Jesus.

21 And the hand of the Lord was with them: and a great number believed, and turned unto the Lord.

22 ¶ Then tidings of these things came unto the ears of the church which was in Jerusalem: and they sent forth Barnabas, that he should go as far as Antioch.

except Jews. **20** But there were some of
them, men of Cyprus and Cy-re'ne, who on
coming to Antioch spoke to the Greeks[h]
also, preaching the Lord Jesus. **21** And the
hand of the Lord was with them, and a
great number that believed turned to the
Lord. **22** News of this came to the ears of
the church in Jerusalem, and they sent

[h] Other ancient authorities read *Hellenists*.

---

20. Men of Cyprus and Cyrene: Note 13:1, where Lucius of Cyrene is mentioned with Barnabas of Cyprus (cf. 4:36) among the leaders of the Antioch church. It would be attractive to think of Barnabas as one of the group of early pioneers; but the fact that he was sent from Jerusalem to investigate tells against this, though he was perhaps sent because he was a compatriot of the missionaries. **Preaching the Lord Jesus:** Or perhaps, "preaching Jesus as the Lord"; for the "gospel" which they preached was in fact the "lordship" of Jesus.

21. The hand of the Lord, being a common O.T. phrase, probably refers to God's assistance, while **turned to the Lord** rather awkwardly gives the same title again to Jesus.

b) Visit of Barnabas (11:22-24)

Barnabas (for whom see on 4:36), though not one of the twelve, here appears to be ranked as an apostle, for he undertakes the same function of confirmation that was previously performed by Peter and John after Philip's mission to Samaria (8:14-17). He was certainly a much more important figure in the early church than we are apt to realize, and was the leader in the movement which virtually resulted in the transference of the headquarters of the church from Jerusalem to Antioch. When he linked up with Paul, the latter occupied for a time a quite subordinate position; and indeed Paul's whole future work may have owed more than is commonly acknowledged to the encouragement of Barnabas, the "Son of encouragement." It is interesting that one who was a "Levite" (4:36), and presumably closely associated with the national cult, could detach himself so far from his Jewish connections as to identify himself so fully with the Hellenistic movement, even though later, on one famous occasion, his early prejudices reasserted themselves (Gal. 2:13).

The present mission of Barnabas to Antioch, as a representative of the Jerusalem church, is suspect to some scholars on the following grounds: (*a*) Barnabas is much more likely himself to have been one of the Cypriote pioneers (cf. 11:20); (*b*) in the sequel he appears, not as a representative of Jerusalem reporting on Antioch, but as a representative of Antioch acting as a delegate of his fellows in a mission to Jerusalem (11:30; 12:25); (*c*) the incident, like the mission of Peter and John to Samaria, merely illustrates the quite artificial "thesis" of our author that every new development must receive apostolic confirmation. But, as will be argued below, one of the main objects of the visit to Jerusalem mentioned in 11:30 was in fact to report back to Jerusalem on the situation at Antioch. Moreover Gal. 2:11-13, and the apostolic decrees mentioned in ch. 15, make it clear that the Jerusalem church did actually claim some oversight over the churches of

---

is poor. Even in times like our own, when so many things work against Christianity, wherever the church is led by able men and women something happens. Limited as they were in their vision, the leaders of the mother church in Jerusalem at least had the wits to send the best man they could lay their hands on to lead the new church in Antioch. The man was Barnabas, generous-hearted, liberal-minded, good-natured, sympathetic, confident, full of faith, just the kind of man who could take hold of a small, almost amorphous group of people and weld it into a strong Christian body.

We have met Barnabas before in the story

23 Who, when he came, and had seen
the grace of God, was glad, and exhorted
them all, that with purpose of heart they
would cleave unto the Lord.
24 For he was a good man, and full of
the Holy Ghost and of faith: and much people was added unto the Lord.
25 Then departed Barnabas to Tarsus,
for to seek Saul:

Barnabas to Antioch. 23 When he came
and saw the grace of God, he was glad; and
he exhorted them all to remain faithful to
the Lord with steadfast purpose; 24 for he
was a good man, full of the Holy Spirit and
of faith. And a large company was added
to the Lord. 25 So Barnabas went to Tarsus

Syria and Cilicia. There is therefore really no difficulty in supposing that Barnabas, who was already a prominent figure at Jerusalem, was sent to investigate the pioneering activities of his fellow Cypriotes.

22. **They sent:** Perhaps Luke is suggesting that Barnabas went in the role of an "apostle"; the wider use of this title is already becoming apparent (see on 1:12).

23-24. **Grace . . . glad** (χάριν . . . ἐχάρη): In the Greek there is a graceful play on the words impossible to reproduce in English (cf. Jas. 1:1-2). But is it intentional? **With steadfast purpose,** literally "with the purpose of their heart," an unusual expression which occurs elsewhere only in Symmachus' Greek translation of Ps. 10:17. Barnabas' personal qualities of goodness and faith are described as due to possession by the Spirit, as was Stephen's eloquence (6:10).

c) Paul Comes to Antioch (11:25-26)

At this point we pick up again the thread of Paul's life. After his first visit to Jerusalem he had gone into the "regions of Syria and Cilicia" (Gal. 1:21); and he himself states that it was only "after fourteen years" (Gal. 2:1) that he again visited Jerusalem—the point which we reach at 11:30. Most of the time may well have been spent at Tarsus, whither Luke tells us he went immediately after his first visit to Jerusalem (9:30). From Acts one certainly does not gain the impression that anything like so long a period as fourteen years has elapsed between 9:30 and 11:30, and the "fourteen years" of Gal. 2:1 may possibly be a primitive scribal error for "four" (see note on p. 152). If the time was indeed as long as Galatians states, Paul may have been engaged in wider missionary activities of which we know nothing, and it may be that some of the events mentioned in the long catalogue of sufferings in II Cor. 11:23-27 must be fitted into this period. Certainly neither Gal. 1:21 nor Acts 9:30 necessarily implies that Paul never moved outside Syria and Cilicia. But all this is only speculation, for the truth is that neither from Acts nor from Paul's letters do we know anything certain about Paul's life during this intervening period before the so-called first missionary journey. But, as Weiss shrewdly points out, this silence of Acts has some bearing upon our judgment of its historical trustworthiness: "This phenomenon is of the highest importance in connection with the origin of the narratives of the Book of Acts. If they were fiction, based perhaps upon Galatians, we should certainly have had some stories about this period. Why could not the imaginative author of the *Acta Pauli* just as well have thought up something about his mission in Tarsus or in Cyrene as about the later period?" (*History of Primitive Christianity* [ed. F. C. Grant; London: Macmillan & Co.; New York: Wilson-Erickson, 1937], I, 205.) However Paul was occupied, these early years, of which we know absolutely nothing, must have been of supreme importance. In them Paul found himself and thought out the gospel which he purposed to proclaim. It was as no mere novice that he set out on his great tours; he was already a missionary of long and varied experience. "It cannot be too much insisted upon that the real development of Paul both as a Christian and as a theologian was completed in this period which is so obscure to us, and that in the letters we have to do with the fully matured man" (*ibid.*, I, 206).

Barnabas now brings Paul from Tarsus to be his colleague at Antioch, where they spend **a whole year** together (vs. 26). In Galatians, Paul says nothing of this time spent

26 And when he had found him, he brought him unto Antioch. And it came to pass, that a whole year they assembled themselves with the church, and taught much people. And the disciples were called Christians first in Antioch.

to look for Saul; 26 and when he had found him, he brought him to Antioch. For a whole year they met with[i] the church, and taught a large company of people; and in Antioch the disciples were for the first time called Christians.

[i] Or *were guests of.*

with Barnabas at Antioch, for the reason no doubt that at the moment he is concerned chiefly with his contacts with the original apostles, and his silence has led to questions as to the historicity of Luke's notice. But we know from Gal. 2:11-13 that some four years later Paul and Barnabas were again at home together at Antioch, whither they had returned from the first missionary tour (14:26); and it is entirely reasonable to suppose that Paul may have first been brought there under the circumstances described in Acts, and may have labored there for a time before starting out on his tour with Barnabas.

25. To look for Saul: The turn of the sentence gives the impression, perhaps quite unintentionally, that our author thinks of Paul as not being at the moment prominently in the public eye.

26. They met with the church, or possibly, "they were entertained by the church"; the Greek word is the same as in Matt. 25:35, "I was a stranger and you welcomed me." **Christians:** In the N.T. the word occurs only here, in 26:28, and in I Pet. 4:16. The word has the usual Latin termination denoting "a partisan of"—as Herodian, Caesarian, Pompeiian—and shows that already the word "Christ" was in common use as a proper name. The intention of the folk of Antioch was doubtless to fasten on the disciples a kind of party designation as a nickname. Within the church the same termination later labeled various heretics—Basilidians, Valentinians, Arians. As the word "Christ," meaning "anointed" or Messiah, must have been unintelligible to Greek pagans, it is possible that the disciples were in fact first called "Chrestians"—Chrestus being a common enough Greek proper name, meaning "good." This seems to have been the view of Suetonius, who tells us that the Jews had made disturbances at Rome "at the instigation of Chrestus" (*Claudius* 25). Paul never uses the adjective, but uses in its place various adaptations of his favorite phrase "in Christ"—e.g., "I know a man in Christ" (II Cor. 12:2).

of the Acts. We found him first selling his farm in order to give the proceeds to the Christian disciples in Jerusalem. We saw him get hold of Paul and pull him out of the pit when it looked as though his future lay behind him. He was the kind of man whose eyes could see the substance of things yet being imperfect. He could see possibilities in Paul and he could see infinite possibilities in the Christian church in Antioch. He is described by F. J. Foakes Jackson in the following terms:

> Barnabas indeed is one of the most attractive characters in the New Testament. He possessed the rare gift of discerning merit in others. Probably inferior in ability to Paul, he was his superior in Christian graces. He seems to have been utterly without jealousy, eager to excuse the faults of others, quick to recognize merit, ready to compromise for the sake of peace. Paul's elevation of character makes him scarcely human, whilst the virtues of Barnabas make him singularly lovable. The Paul of history contributes to the progress of the world, Barnabas and those like him make it endurable to live in. Whilst we admit the greatness of Paul, we cannot forget that Barnabas was the real pioneer of a world-embracing Christianity.[1]

The first thing Barnabas did when he got to Antioch was to remember Paul. He knew that he needed help if he were to make the most of the opportunities that the city of Antioch presented to the Christian church. He went to Tarsus and found Paul and brought him back to Antioch. There they worked together teaching, instructing, and preaching. Within a year they had the church established on firm ground, and by that time the people who belonged to the church were called for the first time Christians. There never has been a better name by which to describe the followers of Christ. We are not Catholic or Protestant, liberal or ortho-

[1] *The Acts of the Apostles* (London: Hodder & Stoughton; New York: Harper & Bros., 1931; "The Moffatt New Testament Commentary"), p. 100.

27 ¶ And in these days came prophets from Jerusalem unto Antioch.

27 Now in these days prophets came

d) Visit to Jerusalem at the Time of the Famine (11:27-30)

This paragraph raises difficult problems both of history and of criticism. Barnabas and Paul are represented as visiting Jerusalem as the bearers of relief from the richer church at Antioch to the presumably poverty-stricken church of Judea—a mission which would mark a significant stage in the transference of the church's center of gravity from Jerusalem to Antioch. Critics doubt the historicity of this visit on the following grounds: (*a*) The alleged motive for the visit is to be dismissed, for no such prophecy as that of Agabus could possibly have been made. The reference to Agabus is itself a mere "doublet" of 21:10-11, where the same prophet intervenes at Caesarea on the eve of Paul's last visit to Jerusalem, when the latter was once again traveling as a "relief agent" and carrying the "collection" from the Gentile churches. (*b*) On the usual critical reconstruction there is no reference in Galatians to this visit, usually called the "famine visit." The visit described by Paul in Gal. 1:18-24 obviously corresponds with that of Acts 9:26-29. The second visit mentioned in Galatians (2:1-10) has been generally considered to be the same as that described at length in Acts 15:2-29—usually called the "council visit"—though the identification results in almost insoluble historical difficulties (see on ch. 15). Accordingly we have in the present passage mention of a visit to Jerusalem falling apparently between the two mentioned by Paul. Now Paul in Galatians is concerned to narrate his every movement, in particular his visits to Jerusalem, in order to prove that at no time did he come into such close contact with the original apostles as might invalidate his claim to have received his own apostolic commission directly from Jesus. His object is to prove that "the gospel which was preached by me is not man's gospel. For I did not receive it from man" (Gal. 1:11-12). Unless he is deliberately deceiving his readers, it is difficult to suppose that he paid another visit in the interval between the first visit and that to the council. In particular would it have been disingenuous to remain silent about an official visit to Jerusalem as a delegate from Antioch. Whether in fact he did or did not see the apostles, here was an opportunity to do so that might have been held up against him. If the visit did take place, then he must have mentioned it.

Various solutions of the puzzle have been propounded: (*a*) The whole incident can be explained as a vague reminiscence, or transposition, of the "great collection" undertaken later by Paul as a result of the demand made at the council that the Gentile churches should "remember the poor" (Gal. 2:10). (*b*) Paul may have been appointed to accompany Barnabas, but for some unexplained reason only Barnabas went. Luke,

dox. We are Christians. And in that descriptive name we find the common basis of our unity.

27-30. ***The First Christian Relief Fund.***—Just about nineteen hundred years ago two men were traveling from Antioch to Jerusalem. They were not on a business trip, neither were they traveling for pleasure. They were on a mission of mercy. The crops failed that year in the southern part of Palestine and the people were suffering from a shortage of food. The new Christian church, begun just a few years before, was in desperate need. The Christian church up north in Antioch, the first offspring of the mother church, heard about the need in Jerusalem and decided that it was their duty to send relief to their fellow Christians down in the stricken part of Palestine. They did not want to send it by post, but by messengers. They chose the two leaders of the church, gave the relief fund to them, and commissioned them to deliver it in person to the Christians in Jerusalem. Those men were Barnabas and Paul, the bearers of the first Christian relief fund.

We might ask why it is that Christians have always been so interested in relieving the needs of others. Some people would be content to account for it by purely practical considerations. For it is a matter of fact that hungry people are not good neighbors; that discontented people are not likely to be peaceful citizens; that people who live on the fringe of existence with just barely enough to get along *on* are not likely to be people who are easy to get along *with*. And in those great areas where more than half the population have not enough to eat or to wear, in those areas we find the

finding the appointment noted in his sources, drew the natural conclusion that Paul did in fact go. (*c*) The account of the "famine visit" here and that of the "council visit" in ch. 15 are "doublet" descriptions of the same visit, derived from different sources and narrated from different viewpoints. The author, it is suggested, found in his sources two independent accounts of the same journey, the one stressing the generosity of the Antioch church, the other concerned with the debate at Jerusalem on the question of the legitimacy of Gentile Christianity. The first may be held to reflect the attitude of Antioch, the second that of Jerusalem. Supposing these two accounts to refer to different events, the author inserted this first one in what seemed to him a convenient place. It might even be suggested that the mutilation of the original order of events has been glossed over by the insertion of the story of the persecution by Herod (ch. 12, which we have already seen to be misplaced), while the notice in 12:25 serves to bring Paul and Barnabas back to Antioch, whence Luke has quite unhistorically taken them. This reconstruction is ingenious and cannot be rejected out of hand. It is adopted by almost all modern radical critics. But against it stands the fact that it does nothing to explain the serious discrepancies between Gal. 2:1-10 and Acts 15. (*d*) Preferable to any of these is the alternative solution, first suggested by Sir William M. Ramsay in 1895, and supported by C. W. Emmet in an essay in *The Beginnings of Christianity* (II, 277 ff.). This solution is that the visit of Gal. 2:1-10 should be identified, not with the "council visit," but with the "famine visit"—these two visits being rightly distinguished by Luke as two separate events. There are clear hints both in Acts and in Galatians that this is the correct solution.

First, then, in Acts: In 11:22 Barnabas had been sent in the name of the Jerusalem church on a mission of investigation into affairs at Antioch. It is natural to assume that he would return to Jerusalem to report. This he did, at the same time taking Paul with him and acting as commissioner for Antioch in the delivery of the famine relief. It is the latter aspect of his mission that at this point interests Luke, as an example of how the center of gravity is passing to the Gentile churches. But at the same time, on the basis of Barnabas' report, the whole Gentile question was bound to come up for discussion; and naturally it is this aspect of the mission that interests Paul as he writes his account in Gal. 2. The idea that this question could not have been raised till the later council is contradicted both by the reference in 11:20 to the mission to Gentiles conducted by the Antioch church, and also by all a priori probabilities. But the discussion indicated in Gal. 2 is still private and informal; the controversy was not yet at the stage of public debate, which it reaches at the council meeting of Acts 15.

In Galatians, too, several minor references seem to confirm this solution. The words "I went up by revelation" (Gal. 2:2) might refer to the inspired warning given by Agabus in 11:28. Again, Paul's words "which very thing I was eager to do," with reference to the injunction that he and Barnabas should "remember the poor" (Gal. 2:10), fit in excellently in connection with a visit made specifically for charitable purposes. The aorist tense ("I was eager") is almost equivalent to a pluperfect, and fits the fact that Paul had indeed just brought alms to Jerusalem; it would be much less natural if Paul was merely anticipating the later "great collection for the saints." Finally, Peter's ambiguous conduct in Antioch, mentioned in Gal. 2:11 ff., is much more understandable

---

seedbed of discontent, violence, and revolution. So on the purely practical grounds of expediency we can say that we protect ourselves by feeding them. As we quiet them and satisfy their basic necessities, we defend our own life against attack. By relieving them we reinforce our own security.

But we can be sure that this was not the motive that sent Paul and Barnabas from Antioch to Jerusalem with relief for the Christians there. Surely it was no consideration of expediency that moved them to make that trip. We must go further in our search for the motives behind Christian relief funds and point out that it is the natural instinct of all human beings to help others in distress. That is neither idealism nor sentimentalism; it is fact. For instance, suppose a small tanker in the North Atlantic should find itself in serious distress and send out an SOS. Every ship within reach, regard-

if it took place *before* the debate at the later council, perhaps during the difficult days referred to in Acts 15:1-2. Indeed, on the supposition that Gal. 2:1-10 is describing the "council visit," so incredible has Peter's action seemed that some scholars have suggested that Paul in Gal. 2 is not treating events in strict chronological order, and that Peter's visit to Antioch was in fact earlier than the council at Jerusalem (so Turner, "Chronology of the New Testament," *Dictionary of the Bible,* ed. James Hastings [New York: Charles Scribner's Sons, 1900]). The proposed solution harmonizes Acts and Galatians without the need for any such adroit manipulation.

Finally, as to chronology: We know from Josephus (*Antiquities* XX. 5. 2) that a famine took place *ca.* A.D. 46, and this may be accepted as the date of the second or "famine visit" of Paul to Jerusalem. According to Gal. 2:1, the first visit was "fourteen years" earlier, which, on the inclusive method of reckoning, would place it in 33. Paul's conversion, being "three years" earlier still (Gal. 1:18), would have to be dated as early as 31, perhaps not quite impossibly early, if the Crucifixion is dated in 29 or 30. But the difficulty of such an early date for the conversion, and of the long period of fourteen years, about which we know nothing, spent in Syria and Cilicia (Gal. 1:21), has led to the surmise that in Gal. 2:1 Paul really wrote "after four years." We would then have two possible series of dates:

The conversion	31 or 39	
The first visit ("after 3 years"—inclusive)	33 or 42	
The "famine visit" ("after 14 years")	46 or 46	("after 4 years")
The "council visit"	49	

Between the second and third visits there took place the first missionary tour (*ca.* 47-48) and probably the writing of Galatians—for the whole problem is intimately bound up with the "South Galatian theory" and the early dating of Galatians. These problems will be discussed later in connection with ch. 15. Alternatively, those who identify the visit of Gal. 2 with the "council visit" must date: the conversion *ca.* 36; first visit ("after three years") 39; "council visit" ("after fourteen years"—dating inclusively not from the last mentioned visit but, surely most unnaturally, from the conversion) 49. Galatians, of course, on this hypothesis was written after the council.

If the "famine visit" is, as we conclude, historical and separate from the "council visit," it marked a real crisis in Paul's career. If the account in Galatians is correct concerning the first visit, this second visit must have been Paul's real introduction to the Jerusalem church. Accompanied by Barnabas, the most honored representative of Hellenistic Christianity, he would receive a welcome and a recognition which he had not formerly enjoyed; and doubtless he and Barnabas would obtain at least provisional sanction for their projected Gentile tour.

27. Prophets are frequently mentioned in the N.T. and are usually ranked next to apostles (I Cor. 12:28; Eph. 2:20; 3:5; 4:11; Rev. 22:9). In Acts they are mentioned in

---

less of the colors it sails under, would give up the normal course of its journey and rush to the aid of that ship in distress, for it is indeed the natural instinct of one man to help another man when he is in trouble. If you saw a small child shivering in the cold, obviously lost, hungry, thinly clad, afraid, your natural instinct would be to help him. You would not ask whether he were a Roman Catholic or a Protestant, a Gentile or a Jew, a Japanese or a German, a Britisher or an American. You would help the child because you would say to yourself, "It might be my child."

And so it is the natural instinct in every human being to relieve distress in others, for distress reduces us to the level of our common humanity where we huddle together to fight our common foes. And it is not until we are reduced to that lowest level of humanity, where our needs are the basic needs and our foes are the primal elements of weather, disease, and death, against which all men everywhere battle relentlessly, it is not until we get down to that level that we realize that we are united with all mankind, and that in one sense their trouble is our trouble, their pain and anxiety are our pain

28 And there stood up one of them
named Agabus, and signified by the Spirit
that there should be great dearth throughout all the world: which came to pass in
the days of Claudius Caesar.
29 Then the disciples, every man according to his ability, determined to send
relief unto the brethren which dwelt in
Judea:

down from Jerusalem to Antioch. 28 And
one of them named Ag'a-bus stood up and
foretold by the Spirit that there would be
a great famine over all the world; and
this took place in the days of Claudius.
29 And the disciples determined, every one
according to his ability, to send relief to

13:1; 15:32; 21:9-10. It is obvious that they exercised their function in virtue of charismatic personal gifts rather than of official standing, and there is no evidence that they were in any way ordained to office. The instructions which Paul lays down concerning them (I Cor. 14:29-39) make it clear that their enthusiasm sometimes outran their sense of order and decency. Hence the injunction to "test the spirits to see whether they are of God" (I John 4:1; cf. I Thess. 5:20-21).

28. Agabus is mentioned also in 21:10, where he warns Paul of the fate that awaits him at Jerusalem. The Western text here reads, "And there was much rejoicing, and when *we* had conversed together. . . ." The verse thus becomes the first of the "we" passages. If the reading is genuine, it suggests that the diary source, here used for the first time, originated in Antioch; if it is not genuine, it at least shows that the "Western" reviser may have connected Acts with Antioch. **The days of Claudius:** Both Tacitus (*Annals* XII. 43) and Suetonius (*Claudius* 18) confirm that there were several famines in Claudius' reign (A.D. 41-54), while Josephus (*Antiquities* XX. 5) mentions one in Judea which was at the worst *ca.* A.D. 46.

---

and anxiety, and their burden is our burden, for it is the burden of humanity, the burden of the race.

But even that is not the real reason for sending relief either in this twentieth century or in the earlier days when Paul and Barnabas went from Antioch to Jerusalem. The real reason is to be found in the fact that Jesus took this natural instinct, refined it into love, and made it the cornerstone of human character. Jesus said to people, "Love is not only one of the important things in a man's life; it is the only important thing." A man can be famous, successful, rich, achieve great things, but if he has not cultivated and refined that natural instinct to help others in distress until it rises above all other instincts and dominates them, is sovereign over them, that man, as a man, is a failure. That is the school in which we as Christians have been trained; and though we recognize the fact that we have often failed to pass the examination and have often let other lesser, baser instincts rule over that supreme one, nevertheless there are signs that we have gained some ground and grown in our capacity to love.

For instance, during World War II we heard over and over again reports like this: American doctors in the Pacific dressed the wounds of a Japanese prisoner. The Japanese could not believe their eyes. Why should an enemy doctor dress the wounds of a prisoner? The American doctors did it because, whether or not they went by the name of Christian, they had been trained and drilled for two thousand years in the quality of compassion, and they dressed the wounds of a man because he was a man and, notwithstanding his national and racial differences, because he breathed the same air and felt the same pain and was loved by the same God.

Jesus is now training and cultivating in us that capacity to care for other people, regardless of the name by which they go. So we as Christians—and this differentiates us from all other people—not only have the capacity to love others in distress; we have the *command* to love. We seldom think of love as a commandment; love to be real must be freely given, unsolicited. Yet Jesus did command that we love one another. We are marching under the orders of one who did not say to us, "Love if it is convenient, love if you find the person congenial, love if you get on with a person and benefit from him, and agree with his politics." We are marching under the orders of one who said, "Love and love; friend, foe, enemy, known and unknown alike, whether you suffer or whether you gain, whether you benefit or whether you lose, for love is of God, and without love there is no life worth talking about."

That is the reason for relief funds. Not only

30 Which also they did, and sent it to the elders by the hands of Barnabas and Saul.

12 Now about that time Herod the king stretched forth *his* hands to vex certain of the church.

the brethren who lived in Judea; 30 and they did so, sending it to the elders by the hand of Barnabas and Saul.

12 About that time Herod the king laid violent hands upon some who be-

---

30. The elders: Mentioned now for the first time as specifically Christian office-bearers. Here they are perhaps the presidents of the house churches of Jerusalem; and in 15:6, 23 they appear with the apostles as a kind of church council. The fact that the alms from Antioch were handed over to them suggests that one of their duties was to act as relief officers. (For their possible relationship to "the seven" see on 6:6.) The fact that on this occasion the alms were handed over to them need not imply that the apostles were absent from Jerusalem, possibly on account of Herod's persecution, as is urged by those who decline to identify this visit with that of Gal. 2. It was not in any case the business of the apostles "to serve tables" (6:2). Whether "elders" would as early as this be officially ordained is doubtful, but 14:23 (where see a fuller discussion) shows that in the Pauline churches the custom quickly arose of so consecrating them to their office, though it may be that Luke's language reflects the usage of a slightly later time.

G. Persecution Under Herod (12:1-25)

This chapter is in the nature of an interlude; as already noted (pp. 151-52), it has been suggested that it was inserted to fill the gap between two accounts of one and the same visit to Jerusalem. But if the story of Peter's escape from imprisonment by Herod is historical, it is one of the few incidents in the first half of Acts that can be dated with relative certainty. It must have happened in A.D. 44, the year Herod died (Josephus *Antiquities* XIX. 8. 2), for it is plain that Peter left Jerusalem just before Herod's death, probably in the spring of 44. It follows that Peter's imprisonment took place before the famine and Paul's visit to Jerusalem, which cannot have been earlier than 45 or 46. Therefore, strictly speaking, ch. 12 ought to come before 11:19 ff. If the two visits of Paul to Jerusalem mentioned in chs. 11 and 15 respectively are still held to be doublet accounts of the same visit, then the present Herod section will be correctly placed in relation to the Jerusalem version (ch. 15), but wrongly placed in relation to the Antioch version (ch. 11). This would be natural enough, for the story about Herod clearly would be part of the Jerusalem tradition.

Our reconstruction of the order of events may be further helped by the curiously vague remark about Peter in vs. 17, **Then he departed and went to another place.** Where did Peter go? We have already remarked that chronologically ch. 12 must come before 11:19 ff. Immediately preceding this is the story about Cornelius, introduced at 9:32 with an equally vague reference to Peter going "here and there among them all." No explanation is given of how he came to be so doing. The placing of 12:17 before 9:32 would give an excellent sequence, and explain both the vagueness of the reference to "another place" and the reason why Peter came thus to be wandering about. At the moment, having fled from the persecution of Herod, he had no fixed place of abode.

---

do we have the natural capacity for it, but we have from our Lord the command to do it; to go into all the world and give cups of cold water, to feed the hungry, to heal the sick, to clothe the naked, to relieve the needs of those in distress.

Out of our surplus and abundance, then, we give to them who are in need, not only because it is the human, decent thing to do, but because it is the Christlike thing to do. And we do it as a demonstration that there is yet in this hard, brutal world of violence, the spirit of lovingkindness and compassion which dwells within Christian men and women who try to follow in the footsteps of two men who traveled from Antioch to Jerusalem to deliver the relief funds to the people there who were starving.

12:1-19. ***Peter's Narrow Escape.***—The story is like a parenthesis inserted in an otherwise uninterrupted narrative. It is another escape

An attractive consequence of this reconstruction would be that Peter's activities in Lydda, Joppa, and Caesarea (the conversion of Cornelius) would be taking place at much the same time as the early mission work of Paul and Barnabas at Antioch. Peter would return to Jerusalem at just about the same time as Paul and Barnabas came there on their "famine visit." Peter's argument with the narrower Jewish faction (11:1 ff.) would take place not far from the time when Paul conferred with the same faction during the "famine visit," as recorded in Gal. 2. Thus the question of the legitimacy of Gentile missions would be very much in the limelight, and the development of the mission of Paul and Barnabas to Jerusalem, which according to Acts 11:29-30 was originally merely charitable, may well have been along the lines indicated in Gal. 2. The chronological order of events would then be as follows:

(*a*) Acts 12:17, Peter's escape from Jerusalem (A.D. 44)
(*b*) Acts 9:32–10:48, Peter's tour through Palestine to Caesarea and the conversion of Cornelius (44-45)
Acts 11:22-26, the work of Barnabas and Paul at Antioch (44-45)
(*c*) Acts 11:28, the famine in Palestine (45-46)
(*d*) Acts 11:2, Peter's return to Jerusalem (early 46)
Acts 11:30, the "famine visit" of Paul and Barnabas (early 46)
Gal. 2:1-10, the discussion at Jerusalem (early 46)

The persecution under Herod was apparently not very general, but was directed mainly against the church's leaders. Some scholars believe that at this time not only James but also his brother John was martyred. It is regarded as strange that the persecution did not touch John, who from the beginning of the narrative appears with Peter as one of the two leading representatives of the Jerusalem church. Moreover he is not again mentioned in Acts. (The best discussion of this possibility is in R. H. Charles, *The Revelation of St. John* [New York: Charles Scribner's Sons, 1920; "International Critical Commentary"], I, xlv ff.) The actual evidence in support of John's early martyrdom is slight enough: (*a*) The prophecy of Mark 10:39 which, it is held, would gain point if, at the time Mark wrote, it was known to have been fulfilled in the case of both brothers. Curiously Luke omits the prophecy from his Gospel. (*b*) A statement of Philip of Side (fifth century) in the "de Boor fragment" that "Papias in his second book says that John the divine and James his brother were killed by the Jews." (*c*) Two early martyrologies which commemorate the martyrdom of James and John on the same day, December 27. (*d*) The silence concerning any later residence of the apostle John in Ephesus both on the part of Acts and also of Ignatius in his Epistle to the Ephesians (A.D. 110-15). Each of these pieces of evidence is disputed and quite inconclusive; but the cumulative effect is considerable, and as Streeter remarks, "The wonder is that any evidence at all should survive of a tradition apologetically so inconvenient as that of John's early death" (*Four Gospels*, p. 435).

Loisy argues that the editor of Acts suppressed not only the death of John but also the account of a judicial process against James. He considers it incredible that the death of James could have been dismissed in a single sentence, when so much space is given to Peter's escape. The motive alleged is that the editor is unwilling to imply that a Christian leader could be guilty of an infraction of the law so grave as to justify a capital sentence

story. Furthermore it is such a narrow escape that to Peter himself and to all its observers it is miraculous. To be sure, there is always the possibility that this story, like the other similar ones in the Acts, has been embroidered by later hands, and that the story as it now stands is the product of fact around which the filaments of fiction have been affectionately woven. Nevertheless there is also the possibility that this story is one of those escapes that is so narrow as to be indubitably miraculous in the eyes of those most intimately concerned.

Life is full of such stories. A sick man, by all the predictions of the medical profession condemned to death, takes a turn for the better and escapes by the skin of his teeth. A man left for lost suddenly hears a voice that breaks the silence of his doom. People caught in situations like animals in traps find themselves suddenly and inexplicably at large. There is hardly a

2 And he killed James the brother of John with the sword.

longed to the church. 2 He killed James the

after formal trial. This surely is sheer perversity! The disproportion between the attention given to James and to Peter is understandable enough if we remember that Peter's story is one that catches the imagination and lends itself to edifying use. Again, the remark that the murder of James "pleased the Jews" (vs. 3) is supposed to imply that there was a formal trial before the Sanhedrin. This too is pure assumption. If the author had found in his sources an account of such a trial, there is no reason whatever why he should have suppressed it; for his tendency is to emphasize the guilty responsibility of the Jewish religious leaders rather than of the civil power as represented here by Herod. If we ask in surprise why so little is said about the first martyrdom—so far as we know—of one of the twelve, the answer perhaps is that the brevity of the notice reflects the true instinct of the early church, which, in its ardent expectation of Jesus' speedy return, regarded bodily death as insignificant. Finally, it is not surprising that Loisy concludes that the whole story of Peter's escape is fiction, based entirely on the known fact that whereas James was martyred, Peter escaped from Jerusalem. But whatever the marvelous coloring of the story, there are circumstantial details (especially vss. 12-17, **the house of Mary; . . . a maid named Rhoda**) which suggest that the story came from one who knew the topography of Jerusalem and was possibly even present in the house when Peter arrived. It seems to be a true story of escape—no doubt with certain miraculous embellishments—preserved in order to explain how it was that Peter, who ought to have been one of the first victims, succeeded in escaping death. A real escape is described in terms of current belief—the unexpected, whatever the true source of rescue, being ascribed to angelic intervention. In so far as the details are true Peter himself may well have been the original source of information; John Mark may have been an eyewitness and may have heard Peter's story; and from Mark, Luke may have had it at first hand.

12:1. Herod the king is Herod Agrippa I, the grandson of Herod the Great (Luke 1:5), and should be distinguished from the Herod Antipas of the Gospels, who was one of Herod the Great's sons and ruler of Galilee and Perea. Agrippa was brought up in Rome in intimate relations with the imperial family, and was a close friend of the young Caligula, who on his accession gave him the title of "king" and bestowed upon him the tetrarchy of Philip (Luke 3:1), to which he shortly afterwards added also the tetrarchy of Herod Antipas. The Emperor Claudius, in whose succession to Caligula Herod had been instrumental, added Judea and Samaria. Agrippa, hitherto still at Rome, then returned to Judea, and in order to win the favor of the people showed great zeal in the practice of the outward rites of Judaism. Another outlet for this religious patriotism he found in this persecution of the "Nazarenes." After his death in A.D. 44 the whole of Palestine became a Roman province. Agrippa II, before whom Paul made his defense (25:13 ff.), was his son.

2. James the brother of John: The son of Zebedee. In the Gospels the order of the names is reversed, "John the brother of James" (Mark 5:37); but by the time Acts was written John was the more prominent, and in 1:13 is mentioned before James, about whom nothing more is known. Some who accept the hypothesis of John's early martyrdom think that the original text here read, "killed James and his brother John"—a tour de force in the interests of a theory!

man or woman alive who cannot recount some incident in his own life which tells the story of an escape that was so unexpected as to be virtually unexplainable in purely natural terms.

Men and women are always getting into trouble, just as Peter was constantly in and out of prison. Sometimes God gets them out of it. The light shines in the cell, the chains fall off. We can never tell when or where something like that may happen, neither can we ever assume that we are lost or that our case is hopeless. At any moment the angel of deliverance may appear. And yet it is also true that God does not always get us out of our trouble: sometimes he sees us through it. He did not get Jesus out of the Cross: he saw him

3 And because he saw it pleased the Jews,
he proceeded further to take Peter also.
(Then were the days of unleavened bread.)
4 And when he had apprehended him, he
put *him* in prison, and delivered *him* to
four quaternions of soldiers to keep him;
intending after Easter to bring him forth
to the people.
5 Peter therefore was kept in prison:
but prayer was made without ceasing of
the church unto God for him.

brother of John with the sword; 3 and when
he saw that it pleased the Jews, he proceeded to arrest Peter also. This was during
the days of Unleavened Bread. 4 And when
he had seized him, he put him in prison,
and delivered him to four squads of soldiers
to guard him, intending after the Passover
to bring him out to the people. 5 So Peter
was kept in prison; but earnest prayer for
him was made to God by the church.

---

3. The days of Unleavened Bread, strictly speaking, came after the **Passover** and not before it, as the somewhat careless writing here would seem to suggest. The "Passover" was on Nisan 14, and "the days" followed from the fourteenth to the twenty-first. But apparently Luke regarded the two terms as synonymous, for in Luke 22:1 he writes that "the feast of Unleavened Bread drew near, which is called the Passover."

4. Four squads, a **quaternion** for each of the four watches of three hours. **Bring him out** (ἀναγάγειν), i.e., for public execution. **After the Passover:** Cf. Mark 14:2, "Not during the feast, lest there be a tumult of the people."

5. Earnest prayer: The same Greek word that is used of Jesus' prayer in Gethsemane (Luke 22:44).

---

through it. Thus when no angel appears, it does not mean that God has forsaken us; it simply means that he has chosen another course.

Within this passage there are several verses that suggest developments of relevant subjects:

5. ***Peter . . . Was Kept in Prison: but Prayer Was Made Without Ceasing . . . unto God for Him.***—What chance has prayer against a prison? You might as well match a smoke ring against a bulldozer, or expect a zephyr to blow down a skyscraper. So it appears. But prayer is an invisible power like electricity. It can get behind walls and around obstacles. It can move men and mountains. Never say when a person is prostrate, that there is nothing that can be done about it. You can pray for him! Who knows the power of the prayers offered for those in danger? Who has measured the influence of prayer over prison walls? Surely the ones who have been behind those walls and who have been miraculously delivered are the ones most likely to say that there is an unseen power stronger than the prison walls which seem to defy both God and man. Luther said that he would rather have an army against him than a hundred men and women praying.

There are a great many people in the world today who say quite frankly that prayer cannot do anything. They believe that the universe is governed by an inflexible and immutable law which does not respond to the personal desires of human beings. They would not expect to see a traffic light change from green to red because someone asked it to change, for the light operates according to certain laws over which the personal desires of pedestrians have no influence whatever. They apply the same principle to the universe. They say that to pray for a man in prison is as futile as it would be for a child to scream at a locomotive going full speed and by his screaming expect to stop it. Things do not work that way. That point of view has at least this much to be said for it: it reckons squarely with the orderliness of the universe and it takes into account all the discoveries that scientists have made about the regular and dependable operation of the laws of life.

And at the other extreme there are those who say that prayer can do everything. If a good man is in prison, all you need to do is to pray for him. No matter what happens or how great the crisis may be, the remedy is always the same: pray about it. We recognize a fundamental truth in this position, and that truth is that the universe is not quite so inflexible as we once thought it was, that behind mechanical contraptions like the traffic light there is the mind that planned the light, operates it, and if it gets out of order, repairs it. There is something in the universe that responds to the expressed desires and longings of the human heart. Like the power of the audience to change the total effect of the play on the stage, so is the power of man to change the total situation by the spiritual response he makes to it. And yet we are not completely at home in this position either, for we know that there are some

6 And when Herod would have brought him forth, the same night Peter was sleeping between two soldiers, bound with two chains: and the keepers before the door kept the prison.

7 And, behold, the angel of the Lord came upon *him,* and a light shined in the prison: and he smote Peter on the side, and raised him up, saying, Arise up quickly. And his chains fell off from *his* hands.

8 And the angel said unto him, Gird thyself, and bind on thy sandals. And so he did. And he saith unto him, Cast thy garment about thee, and follow me.

9 And he went out, and followed him; and wist not that it was true which was done by the angel; but thought he saw a vision.

6 The very night when Herod was about
to bring him out, Peter was sleeping between two soldiers, bound with two chains,
and sentries before the door were guarding
the prison; 7 and behold, an angel of the
Lord appeared, and a light shone in the
cell; and he struck Peter on the side and
woke him, saying, "Get up quickly." And
the chains fell off his hands. 8 And the angel
said to him, "Dress yourself and put on
your sandals." And he did so. And he said
to him, "Wrap your mantle around you
and follow me." 9 And he went out and
followed him; he did not know that what
was done by the angel was real, but thought

---

6. Bring him out (here προάγειν) : Probably with the same meaning as in vs. 4, but possibly (like προσαγάγειν, 16:20) "bring out for trial."

---

things that prayer by itself cannot do. When a blizzard comes, all the prayers in the world cannot by themselves remove the snow. Prayer by itself is not going to unite the broken particles of Christendom. Prayer alone will not reconcile a man and wife who for years have lived a life of wrangling and discord.

Most of us, therefore, are left standing somewhere in between those two extremes—that prayer cannot do anything; that prayer can do everything. On the basis of our own experience we say that prayer can do at least two things: it can bring a man and God closer together, and it can bring to pass some things which otherwise might never come to pass. The first is the more important. When prayer becomes simply an automatic device to get something for nothing, it leaves out the most majestic of all the notes of prayer—that prayer has the power to bring a finite human creature into closer relationship with the infinite God. Speech is the bridge between human beings. So it is the bridge between God and man. We get to know a man by talking with him. We get to know God in the same way. The deeper a man goes in prayer, the more he reduces the gulf that is between himself and his Maker.

But prayer also actually brings things to pass. There are some things God cannot give us until we want them enough to ask for them. God cannot always give us health until we really want it. Surely he cannot give us character until we really want it to the exclusion of everything else. So great is the power of our desire. We get in the long run just about what we want in life. If a man wants money more than anything else, the chances are that he will get it. If he wants goodness more than anything else, the chances are that God will give him that. But first he must learn how to ask for it.

It is harder for us to understand this principle when it is applied to prayer for other people, people who are sometimes on the other side of the globe. How can our prayer do a man in prison any good? And why should it be necessary for us to pray for him? If God wants to save him, is he not able to do it without our asking? God certainly has the power to do it; nevertheless, by the constitution of things, we are often drawn into that act of liberation. If a man's life is in danger, God, who is the source of life and the originator of that particular life, surely has the power to save it, but sometimes he does not save it unless you or I send a pint of our blood. There is a gap in the chain which it is our mighty privilege to fill. Until another human being fills that space and closes the circuit, the life of God does not flow. If it is true that sometimes it means a pint of another man's blood to save the life of a man on the other side of the globe, is it too much to say that in this mysterious universe there may be times when it takes your prayer or mine to make the connecting link between the power of the Almighty and a helpless human being?

At any rate that is what the first Christians believed when they prayed for Peter. Their successors through all the following centuries, in their own way, have continued to pray for those in trouble.

10 When they were past the first and the second ward, they came unto the iron gate that leadeth unto the city; which opened to them of his own accord: and they went out, and passed on through one street; and forthwith the angel departed from him.

11 And when Peter was come to himself, he said, Now I know of a surety, that the Lord hath sent his angel, and hath delivered me out of the hand of Herod, and *from* all the expectation of the people of the Jews.

12 And when he had considered *the thing,* he came to the house of Mary the mother of John, whose surname was Mark; where many were gathered together praying.

13 And as Peter knocked at the door of the gate, a damsel came to hearken, named Rhoda.

he was seeing a vision. **10** When they had
passed the first and the second guard, they
came to the iron gate leading into the city.
It opened to them of its own accord, and
they went out and passed on through one
street; and immediately the angel left him.
11 And Peter came to himself, and said,
"Now I am sure that the Lord has sent his
angel and rescued me from the hand of
Herod and from all that the Jewish people
were expecting."
12 When he realized this, he went to
the house of Mary, the mother of John
whose other name was Mark, where many
were gathered together and were praying.
13 And when he knocked at the door of the
gateway, a maid named Rhoda came to an-

10. **The first and the second guard:** Of the four soldiers on duty (vs. 4) two would be chained to Peter while the other two mounted guard. The Western text adds that when Peter and the angel "went out, they descended the seven steps"—possibly the same steps from which on a later occasion Paul addressed the people (21:40). For though we do not know where Peter's prison was, it may well have been the Tower of Antonia. This had gates **leading** both to the temple and **into the city.**

12. **The house of Mary** was, according to church tradition which can be traced back to the fourth century, the house in which was the upper room, where the Last Supper took place. If, as tradition also holds, it was the headquarters of the Jerusalem church, vs. 17 shows that "James and the brethren" were not resident there at the moment. Were they hiding from persecution? **The mother of John whose other name was Mark:** Have

10*a*. ***They Came unto the Iron Gate That Leadeth unto the City; Which Opened to Them of His Own Accord.***—Gates that opened of their own accord! Let no one spoil the story by asking how it was done. Over and over again it happens in everyday life. The anticipated problem never arises; the dreaded difficulty disappears before it is reached. Let these gates speak to apprehensive people of the trouble that never happens. They remind us of the fact that a hill is never so steep when you begin to climb it as it appears to be from a distance. Burdens are never so heavy once you pick them up as they are when you weigh them in preparation. Troubles that stagger you in anticipation often shrink the moment they are bravely shouldered.

The wise man is the man who takes the days as they come in the calm and simple trust that he will have the strength that he needs when the time comes. Some of the troubles will disappear; some of the gates will open of their own accord. And the others?—God will give him the key when he gets there.

10*b*. ***Forthwith the Angel Departed from Him.***—We must be prepared to encounter angels. Likewise we must be prepared for their departure. The tides of inspiration come and go; the waves of divine energy flood and ebb; the angels appear and disappear. The parent goes so far with the child, and then the child must be prepared to go the rest of the way by himself. So God from time to time gives particular guidance and protection to men and women; and then he withdraws to let them stand on their own feet and make their own way. When the angel departs, some people go to pieces; others keep right on going. Peter was one of those. The angel came like a flash of light in the darkness. Before he knew it, he was through the guard, outside the gates, a free man—and the angel had gone! From there he had to go on by himself.

13. ***When He Knocked at the Door of the Gateway, a Maid Named Rhoda Came to Answer.***—What was the trouble with Rhoda? She was so excited when she saw Peter that instead of letting him in, she ran back to tell

14 And when she knew Peter's voice, she
opened not the gate for gladness, but ran
in, and told how Peter stood before the
gate.
15 And they said unto her, Thou art
mad. But she constantly affirmed that it
was even so. Then said they, It is his angel.
16 But Peter continued knocking: and
when they had opened *the door,* and saw
him, they were astonished.

swer. [14] Recognizing Peter's voice, in her
joy she did not open the gate but ran in
and told that Peter was standing at the
gate. [15] They said to her, "You are mad."
But she insisted that it was so. They said,
"It is his angel!" [16] But Peter continued
knocking; and when they opened, they saw

---

we a hint here that the original source of the story was Mark himself? The latter is again mentioned in vs. 25; 13:5, 13; 15:37-39. Paul mentions him in Col. 4:10 (as a cousin of Barnabas); Philem. 24; II Tim. 4:11; and it is most interesting and significant that on all three occasions Luke's name appears in the same context. The two evangelists evidently had ample opportunity to share their reminiscences.

15. It is his angel. The idea of an accompanying guardian angel may be traced in every stratum of Scripture. In Gen. 48:16 Jacob speaks of "the Angel which redeemed me"; in Dan. 10:20, 21; 12:1 we find guardian angels of nations; and in Rev. 1:20 "the angels of the seven churches." In Tob. 5:21 we are told that "a good angel shall go with him." In Matt. 18:10 the "little ones" have "their angels"; and in Heb. 1:14 we read of "ministering spirits sent forth to serve." Here a distinction is evidently intended between

---

the others that he was there! Her emotion was out of proportion to her intelligence. Some people have too little emotional luster; others have too much. Rhoda was one of those. We see them all the time. There are the people who get so emotionally stirred up about war relief work that they would almost be glad to have a war in order that they might have the opportunity to relieve its distress. There are people who go to church so much that they never have time to ask what relevance the church has to the life they live or the world they live in. Some people get so worked up over the gospel of salvation that they have no strength left to open the door that might save someone. More than one human relationship goes on the rocks because one of the persons involved feels deeply but never finds a way to put that feeling into a demonstration of love. Some men love their wives sincerely but that love is never channeled into the small but expressive actions which more and more become the universal language of love—opening a door for them, carrying a bundle, sharing a family problem, sending a message. It was not that Rhoda was lacking in love. Rather was it that Rhoda was love out of harness. What was needed at the moment was the opening of a door, but Rhoda bathed herself in a shower of emotional stars.

16. ***But Peter Continued Knocking.***—Here is another side of Peter's character. Peter was predominantly fiery, impulsive, passionate, but he was also on occasion plodding and persistent. It is worth remembering that most people have more than one side to their character. Certain traits are likely to predominate over others, but it is always dangerous and unfair to interpret another person's action solely in the terms of any single trait in his character. Napoleon was aggressive and ambitious, but he had another side to his character—he could be as tender as a child. Jesus was gentle and sympathetic beyond the comprehension of ordinary men, but he had another side to his character—he could be so severe as to make men weep. So Peter had another side. It is indicated in this passing reference to his persistence at the door of his friends' house. It is reflected throughout his life. As a fisherman, he kept on fishing even though he toiled all night and caught nothing. As a disciple of Jesus, he kept on following even though he fell down again and again. As a leader of the early church, he kept on preaching even though he was opposed by his friends and often blundered into mistakes. It was passion plus persistence which made Peter the leader that he was.

Persistence is the secret behind every achievement in life. The electric-light bulb was not made in a flash. Edison worked on it, labored over it, despaired of it, experimented with it for months and months. The idea of it no doubt came to him like lightning, but the fulfillment of the idea was the result of months of persistent, plodding labor. It gave Edison the right to say that genius is 1 per cent inspiration, and 99 per cent perspiration.

It is no different with a poet. The poems of John Keats were not plucked like so many

17 But he, beckoning unto them with the hand to hold their peace, declared unto them how the Lord had brought him out of the prison. And he said, Go show these things unto James, and to the brethren. And he departed, and went into another place.

him and were amazed. 17 But motioning to them with his hand to be silent, he described to them how the Lord had brought him out of the prison. And he said, "Tell this to James and to the brethren." Then he departed and went to another place.

the Lord's "angel" (cf. 8:26) in vs. 11, who is the divine agent of the escape, and Peter's "angel," who is in some way Peter's own spiritual representative—as we should say, "his ghost."

17. James is "the Lord's brother" and apparently at the moment the acting head of the church at Jerusalem. Does this mean that the rest of the twelve had fled temporarily from the city? Peter of course reappears at Jerusalem at 11:2 and at the council in ch. 15. Yet even on that formal occasion it is not Peter but James who, after the debate, delivers the judgment. James's prestige as "the Lord's brother," combined perhaps with the respect with which he was regarded by the Jewish community, evidently quickly gave him preeminence at Jerusalem (see also on 21:18).

To another place: Failing the suggestion made above that this phrase links up the narrative with 9:32, the following explanations have been given of this oddly vague note: (*a*) Peter simply went to another house in the city, where he could lie low. In 4:31 "the place" seems to be a house. It may be that in the earliest telling of the story there was still a desire to keep the place of refuge secret. (*b*) Antioch is suggested as a likely place of retreat. But if so, why should the name be suppressed? Loisy thinks the reason is that the name would recall the unfortunate quarrel later at Antioch, when Paul fell out with Peter and Barnabas (Gal. 2:11 ff.)—an incident which Luke ignores in Acts, giving another reason for the estrangement between Paul and Barnabas (15:36 ff.). (*c*) The early apologists, ignoring the necessity of bringing back Peter to Jerusalem for the council, seized on this phrase as marking the point where Peter departed to take up his bishopric at Rome. But the Epistle to the Romans seems to imply that at the time of writing (A.D. 54) no apostle had yet visited the city. It is most improbable that Peter did any missionary work in Rome so early. It is barely possible, but most unlikely, that, as Rackham suggests, he went to Rome as the best of all hiding places (*Acts of the Apostles,* p. 180). The tradition that Peter was in Rome in the days of Claudius is bound up with the legends about Simon Magus. (See p. 111 above and B. H. Streeter, *The Primitive Church,* pp. 15-16.)

polished marbles out of a hat. He labored over them, revising them, rewriting them, considering each word until he found the only one that would fit. There was as much persistence in each poem as there was in the Grecian vase which he chose to celebrate.

It is the same in the realm of character. Few if any characters are born ready made. They are forged by men and women who keep everlastingly at it. Setbacks, reversals, defeats, failures, come what may, they keep on trying. They do not carry their past like weights to hold them down; they keep moving. If they have a bad habit, they try to correct it. When they slip into it again, they do not give up the battle; they attack it from a different angle. To be sure, behind all their effort is the confidence that they have God's support and good will. They are not trying to be good because they are afraid of God; they are trying to be better because God loves them and trusts them.

No one has ever accomplished anything in public life without this quality of persistence. Florence Nightingale did not establish the dignity of nursing overnight. She had to keep at it through months and years, first convincing her own family, then the officials of the government, then the officers of the army, the soldiers themselves, and finally the public. The battle that Jane Addams fought against the slums of Chicago was continual and never ending. No sooner had one area been cleaned up than another appeared. The battle of Frank Nelson of Cincinnati for clean government went on and on through the years. It was not only his passionate concern that brought results; it was his dogged persistence. World gov-

18 Now as soon as it was day, there was no small stir among the soldiers, what was become of Peter.

19 And when Herod had sought for him, and found him not, he examined the keepers, and commanded that *they* should be put to death. And he went down from Judea to Caesarea, and *there* abode.

20 ¶ And Herod was highly displeased with them of Tyre and Sidon: but they came with one accord to him, and, having made Blastus the king's chamberlain their friend, desired peace; because their country was nourished by the king's *country*.

21 And upon a set day Herod, arrayed in royal apparel, sat upon his throne, and made an oration unto them.

18 Now when day came, there was no
small stir among the soldiers over what had
become of Peter. **19** And when Herod had
sought for him and could not find him,
he examined the sentries and ordered that
they should be put to death. Then he went
down from Judea to Caes-a-re'a, and remained there.

20 Now Herod was angry with the people of Tyre and Sidon; and they came to
him in a body, and having persuaded Blastus, the king's chamberlain, they asked for
peace, because their country depended on
the king's country for food. **21** On an appointed day Herod put on his royal robes,
took his seat upon the throne, and made

---

19. Put to death: A common enough penalty for a guard convicted of allowing the escape of a prisoner held on a capital charge (*Codex Justinianus* IX. 4. 4). But the Greek might mean simply "to be led away," i.e., to prison. **From Judea to Caesarea:** Rather a curious expression, for which cf. 21:10, for Caesarea was in fact the Roman capital of Judea.

20-21. We have no information why **Herod was angry** with Tyre and Sidon. But whatever the reason, Herod held the trump card, for Phoenicia still depended for its food on the cornfields of Galilee, just as in the days of Solomon (I Kings 5:9). **Blastus,** of whom we know nothing more, was presumably bribed to obtain favorable terms. The **appointed day** was, according to Josephus, a feast in honor of the emperor. But Luke seems to mean that a special day was fixed for the reception of the Phoenician delegates. Agrippa's **royal robes** were, according to Josephus, on this occasion entirely of silver.

---

ernment will not spring into being in the twinkling of an eye. It will come because some men will keep working at it, trying this course and then that, pleading with the people, correcting misunderstandings, until they finally clear away all obstacles.

Some people have a flair for making great beginnings. They have unbounded enthusiasm, an inexhaustible reserve of ideas, imagination, personality, and charm. They make a spectacular plunge into the ocean of activity while the crowd cheers. But the spray soon begins to fall, and the sea is still again, leaving no trace of their impact. They made a good beginning, but they could not keep going. They had the incentive to start, but not the persistence to continue. It is the day after day that is difficult. It is the everlasting round of duties that do not sparkle that is wearing. Almost anyone can launch an undertaking, but not everyone has the grit to keep it moving.

One of the most surprising anticlimaxes in all literature comes in the last two verses of Isa. 40: "Even the youths shall faint and be weary, and the young men shall utterly fall: but they that wait upon the Lord shall renew their strength; they shall mount up with wings as eagles; they shall run, and not be weary; and they shall walk, and not faint." The final test is not the ability to rise to great heights on great occasions, nor to stretch the nerve and muscle to incredible lengths under pressure; the final test is the ability to keep going, to walk, to plod through the mire and the dust, through the irritations and nuisances of each day's toil, through the disappointments, detours, and delays of each day's travel; and to do it without fretting and without that weariness which is the sign of a worn spirit. Peter rose to great heights on occasions—think of Pentecost. He did exceed his own strength more than once—think of his healing the lame man. But what really counts is the fact that Peter kept going. If he fell down, he got up. If he made a mistake, he tried again. He weathered the storm of opposition from without and dissension from within. He was a rock that no storm could wear down.

21-24. ***The Death of Herod.***—Most expositors will not turn to this passage with any real hope of finding a message in it. Yet even here are some seeds which might possibly sprout into

22 And the people gave a shout, *saying, It is* the voice of a god, and not of a man.
23 And immediately the angel of the Lord smote him, because he gave not God the glory: and he was eaten of worms, and gave up the ghost.
24 ¶ And the word of God grew and multiplied.
25 And Barnabas and Saul returned from Jerusalem, when they had fulfilled *their* ministry, and took with them John, whose surname was Mark.

an oration to them. 22 And the people
shouted, "The voice of a god, and not of
a man!" 23 Immediately an angel of the
Lord smote him, because he did not give God the glory; and he was eaten by worms and died.
24 But the word of God grew and multiplied.
25 And Barnabas and Saul returned from[j] Jerusalem when they had fulfilled their mission, bringing with them John whose other name was Mark.

[j] Other ancient authorities read *to*.

22-23. **The voice of a god:** No very unusual flattery, as Orientals were accustomed to deify their monarchs, and the worship of the "divine" Augustus was rapidly spreading throughout the empire. **An angel of the Lord** is the usual agent of divine retribution, as in the case, e.g., of Sennacherib's army (II Kings 19:35). **Did not give God the glory,** i.e., instead of arrogating it to himself. But possibly—especially if with the Western text we read "glory" for "the glory"—this may be the common Jewish expression meaning "admit oneself in the wrong and ask forgiveness" (see on 11:18).

Josephus (*Antiquities* XIX. 8. 2) gives a vivid account of Herod's death. The superstitious king had been taught to believe that an owl was to be the harbinger of his fate. In the midst of the flattering plaudits of the crowd he saw an owl sitting on the awning of the theater, whereupon he was seized with sudden pains in the belly, was carried to his palace, and died on the fifth day from a loathsome disease.

24-25. These verses are another of the characteristic Lukan "summaries" marking the end of one of the "panels" (see Intro., p. 15). **Returned from Jerusalem:** This meaning seems obviously required. At 11:30 Barnabas and Paul had come to Jerusalem; they now return to Antioch. But curiously the best MSS, including both Codex Vaticanus (B) and Codex Sinaiticus (א), read "returned to Jerusalem"; and on the accepted principles of textual criticism this ought to be preferred as the more difficult reading and the one more likely to be changed to the easier "from Jerusalem." On the other hand a visit to Jerusalem by Paul would not naturally be called a "return." If "to Jerusalem" is accepted as correct, we must suppose either: (*a*) The verse picks up and repeats 11:30—perhaps to indicate that the events of ch. 12 preceded the famine and the visit to Jerusalem, as we have seen to have been almost certainly the case. We would then have to translate,

---

significance. One could begin with the picture of Herod on his throne, **in royal apparel.** There he was, apparently at the peak of his power. The people went so far in their hysterical idolization of him as to call him a god. The fact that his power rested upon graft and cruelty did not concern them. All they saw was his outward splendor. The next day he was dead! It was the suddenness of it that appalled them. It seemed as if an angel of the Lord had struck him down for his vainglory. "How are the mighty fallen!" (II Sam. 1:19.) Herod was dead, and his body eaten by the same worms that devoured the body of his slave.

But the word of God grew and multiplied. With no royal pomp to decorate it, no royal prerogatives to protect it, the little plant continued to grow and spread. The truth will live and grow, no matter what; evil will fall and perish in spite of all its boasted bulwarks. In days like these we do well to recall how the church grew. Everything seemed to be against it, but God was for it and nothing could withstand it. The great alignments of force that now threaten us do their worst when they frighten us. Let not their apparel deceive us. They wear their power as a covering for their weakness, and their fierce displays of authority they substitute for real demonstrations of influence. They will fall by their own weight.

In the meantime what did the Christians do about Herod? He was putting them in prison, killing them, persecuting them. They endured him. They did not attempt to oppose him; they could see the folly of that. They had neither the numbers nor the weapons. They

13 Now there were in the church that was at Antioch certain prophets and teachers; as Barnabas, and Simeon that was called Niger, and Lucius of Cyrene, and

13 Now in the church at Antioch there were prophets and teachers, Barnabas, Symeon who was called Niger, Lucius

"Returned to Jerusalem and fulfilled their mission"—the aorist participle πληρώσαντες being "timeless" and here referring to what took place not before but actually after the action of the main verb. For other possible examples of this construction see 16:6; 23:35; 25:13. (*b*) Translate, by an inversion of the order of the Greek: "Returned [to Antioch] having fulfilled their mission to Jerusalem."

Bringing with them . . . Mark: This is in favor of the reading "from Jerusalem," for Mark's home, we know, was in Jerusalem. He was a relative of Barnabas (Col. 4:10), so that the delegates from Antioch may well have stayed at his home. Possibly "John" now took the Roman praenomen or **other name** of Mark with a view to his coming travels in Gentile districts.

II. From Antioch to Rome (13:1–28:31)

A. First Mission of Barnabas and Paul to the Gentiles (13:1–14:28)

At this point there is a clear break in the narrative, and according to Harnack, Luke picks up again the Antiochene source which he laid aside at 11:30. With Harnack's analysis the main division of the book of Acts would come at 15:35, where the Antiochene source finally ends. But it is at this point that we reach the beginning of what may be called "The Acts of Paul." As soon as Paul becomes the central figure our author appears to possess much fuller and more trustworthy information than he did for the period covered by the first twelve chapters. Thus, though Harnack includes chs. 13–14 among the sections derived from the Antiochene source, there is some evidence that Luke may begin here to draw upon a separate source covering the mission to Cyprus and the rest of the "first journey." In view of the fullness and accuracy of his details it is hard to doubt that he possessed some such written document. And the fact that in 13:1 Barnabas and Saul are mentioned as if for the first time suggests that Luke is writing with the beginning of a new source before him. It is not likely that Luke himself was an eyewitness for this section. But Mark was present during the first part of the tour; and for the remainder there was no lack of likely informants—quite apart from a possible written source. For example, Timothy was a native of Lystra (16:1-2) and in II Tim. 3:11 Paul himself appeals to his recollection of events during this first tour.

just kept on preaching, praying, sharing, hoping. They found a life in Christ that was rich enough and strong enough to sustain them so that Herod's violence was like the raging of a small, impetuous child. And in the end they survived him, magnificently and decisively survived him! While the worms took care of Herod, the word of God grew and multiplied.

How to resist evil and oppression, that is the question that has long plagued the mind of man. The answers have been as varied as men are various in their temperament and disposition. The Christian answer is like a still small voice that is occasionally heard even over the din of life's more furious cries. It is the way of endurance, rather than retaliation; it is the way of standing fast by the growing thing, rather than the way of ruthlessly uprooting the dying thing. It has been tried and tested by individuals and not found wanting. No nation has yet been in a position to attempt it. But the time will come when even the nations will see that the Herods of this world fall by their own weight, that to endure them is better than to fight them, and that in the long run the word of God grows and multiplies.

13:1-4. *The Mission Is Launched.*—The great Mediterranean mission of Paul the apostle is now ready to be launched. There are several things worth noticing and remembering before we proceed to the mission itself.

(*a*) The mission had a long history behind it. It was not planned on paper; it grew out of the soil of events. One thing led to another, though no one could see at the time that anything was leading anywhere, especially in the direction of a Mediterranean mission. Acts 1–12 tells the story: the extraordinary power of the

Manaen, which had been brought up with Herod the tetrarch, and Saul.

of Cy-re'ne, Man'a-en a member of the court of Herod the tetrarch, and Saul.

1. Commissioning of Barnabas and Paul (13:1-3)

Of the five leaders of the Antioch church three are no more than names. It is extremely dangerous to read into this scene (as does, e.g., Rackham) later Catholic ideas of church orders and ordination, as if it was at this moment that Paul was admitted into the "apostolic succession" and received from apostolic hands the apostleship which was his greatest boast. There is no sign that any "apostle" in the narrow sense of the word was present, and the idea that there was an "ordination to the apostolate" is in direct opposition to Paul's persistent claim that he was "an apostle—not from men nor through man, but through Jesus Christ" (Gal. 1:1). That "church order" was already far-developed is contradicted by the whole tone of vss. 1-3. The five are mentioned as if they were the leaders of the church, and no other officers are mentioned; the so-called "ordinands" are on complete equality with those who are to ordain them; the agents of the "laying on of hands" are simply "they," and there is no word whatever of a "bishop" who could be conceived as the only "regular" channel for the transmission of the apostolic grace. Even Rackham confesses that Paul's ordination must have been somewhat irregular: "The fact that he had been ordained not by their [the twelve's] hands but irregularly, by specially inspired prophets, was so to speak of advantage to him: it enabled him to say with truth that he had not been made an apostle by man" (*Acts of the Apostles,* p. 193). Barnabas and Paul are simply being **set apart** formally by the laying on of hands to be the church's representatives in the larger work that lay before them.

13:1. The church at Antioch: For the expression τὴν οὖσαν ἐκκλησίαν see on 5:17. We ought perhaps to translate, "There were at Antioch in the local church prophets. . . ." **Prophets and teachers:** It is suggested that the Greek (by use of the couple τε) classifies the first three names as "prophets" and the last two as "teachers." However, the two are almost identical, the function of the first being hortatory and that of the second didactic, though "prophets" always rank higher in N.T. lists. But surely Paul was as truly a "prophet" as Barnabas. **Manaen** is the Hebrew Menahem. The word σύντροφος, **which had been brought up with** (KJV), was a complimentary title given at court to certain contemporaries of a prince of the imperial family and was retained by adults. Hence a **member of the court of Herod** gives the sense, though it may also be implied that Manaen had been a playfellow of the young Herod at Rome. **Symeon,** if like **Lucius** he came from **Cyrene,** may conceivably be the "Simon" who carried Jesus' cross (Mark 15:21). His surname **Niger,** "black," suggests an African origin. Of **Lucius** we know nothing, though he was probably one of the original evangelists mentioned in 11:20.

disciples, their constant proclamation of the good news, their daily prayers and remembrances of the risen Jesus, the growing interest of the bystanders, the opposition of the government, friction and disagreement within the original band of followers, the branching out of the new faith, its break with Judaism, and finally the flowering of its life in Paul's mission to the Gentile world. It was among other things the natural outcome of events.

Too many movements fail because they are planned on paper and have no roots in the soil of historic events. One example of this is the movement for unity within the Christian church. Too often it fails because it begins at a conference table where a group of leaders try to work out the constitution and bylaws of a united church which has no foundation in the common life and experience of the people who make up the church. Obviously such paper work must be done before the union can take place, but the paper work must come as a result of events which cry out for union, and must have behind it the propelling power of history. Paul did not begin by drawing maps of the Mediterranean. He drew the maps when it became clear to him that everything was working together toward a universal gospel. The maps, therefore, had some chance of being used and not hung on the wall, where most of the plans for church union unfortunately hang.

The same thing is likely to happen in regard to our efforts to bring about world peace. The mechanics of world peace cannot be overlooked, but the mechanics alone can never accomplish it. We will not have world peace, no matter

THE TRAVELS OF PAUL in the BOOK OF ACTS
CHAPTERS 13-28
MILES 0 50 100 200
KILOMETERS 0 50 100 200 300
JEROME S. KATES, Cartographer
CHESTER C. McCOWN, PH.D., Research Editor
COPYRIGHT 1949, THOMAS NELSON AND SONS
BLACK SEA
SEA OF ADRIA
MEDITERRANEAN SEA
ITALIA
MACEDONIA
ACHAIA
MYSIA
BITHYNIA
GALATIA
PHRYGIA
ASIA
LYCAONIA
PISIDIA
PAMPHYLIA
LYCIA
CILICIA
SYRIA
PHOENICIA
SAMARIA
JUDEA
EGYPT
SYRTIS
CRETE
CYPRUS
CAUDA
MALTA
SAMOTHRACE
Rome
Three Taverns
Forum of Appius
Puteoli
Rhegium
Syracuse
Thessalonica
Beroea
Amphipolis
Apollonia
Philippi
Neapolis
Athens
Corinth
Cenchreae
Troas
Assos
Adramyttium
Mitylene
Thyatira
Chios
Samos
Ephesus
Miletus
Cos
Cnidus
Rhodes
Patara
Myra
Attalia
Perga
Antioch
Iconium
Lystra
Derbe
Tarsus
Seleucia
Antioch
Salamis
Paphos
Lasea
Fair Havens?
Pt. Salmone?
Sidon
Tyre
Ptolemais
Caesarea
Antipatris
Jerusalem
Damascus
Cyrene
Alexandria

2 As they ministered to the Lord, and fasted, the Holy Ghost said, Separate me Barnabas and Saul for the work whereunto I have called them.

3 And when they had fasted and prayed, and laid *their* hands on them, they sent *them* away.

2 While they were worshiping the Lord
and fasting, the Holy Spirit said, "Set
apart for me Barnabas and Saul for the
work to which I have called them." 3 Then
after fasting and praying they laid their
hands on them and sent them off.

2-3. Worshiping: The Greek word is that used later of formal liturgical worship, especially sacramental worship; but here the reference is probably simply to the **praying** which, as so often in Luke's writings, is combined with **fasting** (cf. 9:9, 11; 14:23; Luke 2:37; 5:3). **The Holy Spirit said:** Presumably through the inspired utterance of one of the prophets (cf. 15:28, "It has seemed good to the Holy Spirit and to us"). **Laid their hands on them:** See on 6:6.

---

how good the plans for it may be, until the plain man in every land becomes aware that he is dependent in his daily life upon the life of the plain man in every other part of the world. When he feels it in his wages, his diet, his pleasure, his security both economic and spiritual, then he will see to it that the necessary plans are produced. We are nearer that point than we were fifty years ago; but there is still a long way to travel, and the question is whether or not it will take a complete and utterly devastating war to make the plain man realize his actual predicament.

(*b*) The mission had the right man at the head of it. No movement moves entirely by itself. The current of history is not enough to carry it. It needs the direction and leadership of a man. When the right man is leading the right movement, something happens. No wonder the Mediterranean basin began to shake! Paul leading the mission to the Gentiles! The right man in the right place. Someone has said that the greatest miracle in the N.T. is the fact that at the time when the Christian church needed a man like Paul, Paul was there to meet the need. He had the Jewish background and the Christian experience. He had the Roman privilege of culture, education, and citizenship. He had the mind of a philosopher and the heart and spirit of a mystic. He had the courage of a crusader and the humility of a saint. Granted that events had so worked together that all things were ready for the launching of the Christian movement into the high seas of the world, if Paul had not been there to do it the movement would have passed, the opportunity would have been lost, and Christianity buried, at least for the time being, in its own swaddling clothes.

Every movement cries out for the right man. What would the monastic movement in the Middle Ages have been without Francis and Dominic? What would the movement against slavery have amounted to without Lincoln and Wilberforce? What would the ecumenical movement in contemporary Christianity have been without Charles H. Brent, John R. Mott, and William Temple? So there is always an appeal from events to the minds and hearts of great men. The two must work together, in what exact relationship no one can presume to say. Some have thought that the events produced the men; others have maintained that the men brought the events to pass. It is not necessary for us to decide one way or the other. It is necessary for us only to recognize the fact that the movement of God needs the leadership of men, and that when the right men respond to the maneuvers of God in history at the right moment, we need not be surprised if the whole world is turned upside down.

(*c*) Paul had the fellowship of the church behind him. He did not undertake his mission singlehanded and alone. Nor did he do it in the spirit of a prima donna. It was not a spectacular solo flight. He was one of several men ministering to the Christians in Antioch. It was those Christians who, after they had fasted and prayed, laid their hands on him and sent him off. Paul therefore had not only his own experience and strength to count on, but he had also the fellowship of the faithful behind him; he represented them; they prayed for him.

Too many times has the church failed because it has fallen into the hands of prima donnas who insist on going their own way, responsible to no one. Most of the sects were started in just that way, whereas in the historic churches, no matter what their particular form of ecclesiastical polity may be, there has always been the sense that the leaders are sent out by the fellowship; that they are trained by the elders; that they are responsible to their predecessors; that they are not free lances, but that their own individuality flowers as it drinks deep

4 ¶ So they, being sent forth by the Holy Ghost, departed unto Seleucia; and from thence they sailed to Cyprus.

4 So, being sent out by the Holy Spirit, they went down to Se-leu'ci-a; and from

2. Mission to Cyprus (13:4-12)

At this point begins what is usually called Paul's "first missionary journey." Two facts should be noted. First, the tour was not just a private enterprise undertaken by Barnabas and Paul. The church as such was now standing behind their work, had solemnly commissioned them, and was sending them out as its representatives. Second, Barnabas was still the leader of the enterprise. At the outset his name still stands first, as presumably it did in Luke's source (vs. 7; 14:14), though our author quickly shows a tendency to give Paul the prominence (vss. 13, 43-46, 50). At Lystra it is Barnabas who is taken for Zeus (14:12) and Paul for Hermes—"because he was the chief speaker." Doubtless it was largely for that reason that Paul was in fact the virtual leader and the chief target of the opposition (14:19).

It is not clear that Luke intended to divide Paul's travels formally into *three* "missionary journeys" as is customarily done by modern writers. Notice, for example, the rapidity with which he passes from the "second" to the "third" journey (18:22-23). We ought perhaps rather to think of Paul's missionary work as falling into two main periods: (*a*) Before the council at Jerusalem (ch. 15), while his headquarters were still Tarsus and Antioch and his colleague was generally Barnabas. This would include the work already done in "Syria and Cilicia" (Gal. 1:21), and the present "first missionary journey," which was in fact a preliminary survey of part of the field more systematically covered in the second period. (*b*) After the council at Jerusalem, when Paul broke away from Antioch as his headquarters and made use of various bases in Asia Minor and Europe, from which he covered the larger field of Asia Minor, Macedonia, and Achaia; he now had not Barnabas but Silas and Timothy as his chief collaborators. But as most of our maps are still based on the idea of "three missionary journeys," it may be convenient to retain this somewhat artificial terminology.

The missionaries' first objective was **Cyprus**, possibly because it was Barnabas' own homeland. It has been argued (e.g., by F. J. Foakes Jackson, *The Life of St. Paul* [New York: Boni & Liveright, 1926], p. 86) that the evangelization in Cyprus did not deliber-

of the life and practice of the fellowship of the faithful. Along these lines lies the real meaning of apostolic succession.

The application of this truth to contemporary world-wide movements is so obvious that it needs only to be mentioned. Solitary leaders without the people behind them will never make peace in the world. It is only when leaders rise up to express and carry out the will of the people that we can expect any great forward movement. To be sure, the leaders must be in advance of the people, in advance of their thinking and their courage; nevertheless the leaders without the people behind them are helpless. Pray that the time will soon come when the people will say, "Separate us a man, O God, who can lead us in the paths of peace."

(*d*) Paul had Barnabas beside him. God sent them out not only one by one, but in pairs and teams. Paul, with all his brilliance, needed the even-tempered, gracious Barnabas. The two together did what neither could have done by himself, and more than the sum total of what each could have done separately was accomplished by the two working together.

The Christian ministry is always like that. No one man has all the talents. There is no such thing as a perfectly rounded human being. Every single person has a rough or a flat spot somewhere. One of the reasons why the church is not more successful than it is can be found right here. It is not always ready to recognize the different gifts with which the same Spirit endows different men. A man with the gift of preaching is useful no matter where he is, but link him with another devout man who has the gift of administration and you triple the power.

As we look backward at this first Christian team, Paul towers above Barnabas. But we cannot be at all sure that in the sight of God the difference in stature is by any means so great. Paul left the footprints on the pages of history, but nobody knows how much Barnabas contributed to the spirit and strength that kept those feet moving. There is no indication that

ately include Gentiles, but was directed only to Hellenistic Jews. In favor of this view it is pointed out that nothing is said of any converts being baptized or of any church being founded, as if the object of the mission were to proclaim the messiahship of Jesus to the Jews rather than to form a Christian church as a rival to the Jewish synagogues. It has also been surmised that one reason for Mark's defection after the Cyprus mission was over was that he still had a Judaistic bias and that now a purely Gentile mission in the interior was contemplated. It is true that in vs. 5 we read that **they proclaimed the word of God in the synagogues of the Jews.** But the synagogue was the regular starting point even in places where the chief work was ultimately among Gentiles, and it is very difficult to believe that in Cyprus the apostles abstained from preaching to Gentiles, especially as 11:20 proves that certain Cypriote converts had already shown themselves so eager to evangelize pagans that they had gone to Antioch to do so.

In the encounter of Paul with **Bar-Jesus** we have the first of two "popular" stories which our author has introduced into this section, the second being the dramatic scene at Lystra when the apostles were mistaken for gods (14:8-18). The first story has been quite unnecessarily dismissed as a mere doublet of Peter's encounter with Simon Magus, introduced, so it is alleged, in order to bring out the parallelism between Paul's career and Peter's. Bar-Jesus' offense is quite different from Simon's, who, far from opposing Peter, professed conversion; while Bar-Jesus appears as a Jewish rival who tries to prevent Sergius Paulus from being influenced by the Christian gospel. There would be nothing extraordinary in a Roman official having in his household a Jewish teacher if, as was common enough, he was interested in that religion. Bar-Jesus apparently, like Josephus himself when taken captive by Vespasian, may have professed to be a prophet invested with miraculous powers. If he did in fact pose as a "magician," his presence with Sergius is interesting evidence of the superstition of the Roman ruling classes. But probably in the main Bar-Jesus was, as a Jew, combating Paul's new doctrines, and at the same time "protecting his own bread and butter." As for Paul's treatment of him, the account can hardly be taken literally, even though it is true that Paul can elsewhere contemplate handing over a sinner to Satan "for the destruction of the flesh" (I Cor. 5:5). It is natural enough that Luke, finding in his source a reference to a "magician," should paint the scene as a demonstration of the superior power of a Christian prophet in the very field of "magic" in which the sorcerer made his claims. Probably the facts are that Paul denounced Bar-Jesus' spiritual blindness, and this led to the legend that the apostle had inflicted upon him actual physical blindness—perhaps under the influence of the story of Paul's own blindness at the time of his conversion (see on vs. 11).

As for **Sergius Paulus** himself, less is known about him than used to be supposed. His name was formerly believed to be attested by an inscription from Soli in Cyprus, but the reference is now denied by Lake. According to Lightfoot, Pliny the Elder, writing some twenty years later, mentions a Sergius Paulus as one interested in natural history, and if this is the same person, his inquiring mind may well have led him to an interest first in Judaism and then in Christianity. But Lake thinks that this reference too must be eliminated (*Beginnings of Christianity,* V, 455 ff.). The only unimpeachable reference to Sergius Paulus is apparently an inscription from Rome (*Corpus Inscr. Lat.,* VI, No. 31545); unfortunately this does not connect him with Cyprus. But there is no reason

---

Barnabas felt himself in a lower order or in any way secondary to his partner. When Christian leaders can work together in that spirit of joint leadership, the church can expect to move forward.

(*e*) The movement had the Spirit of God within it. **Separate me Barnabas and Saul,** said the Spirit, **for the work whereunto I have called them.** Neither history, nor men, nor fellowship, nor teamwork by themselves alone, make things move. Things begin to move when the Spirit of God broods upon them. The divine action operates through the channels which have already been described, but it is not merely the sum total of all these things lumped together; it is something over and above them all.

One cannot help feeling as one looks back at the history of the early church that the primary mover was God; that God himself had

5 And when they were at Salamis they preached the word of God in the synagogues of the Jews: and they had also John to *their* minister.

there they sailed to Cyprus. 5 When they arrived at Sal'a-mis, they proclaimed the word of God in the synagogues of the Jews. And

whatever to doubt that a man of this name was proconsul of Cyprus at this time. Whether Paul really succeeded in converting him must be confessed to be more doubtful. There is no mention anywhere in the N.T. of his baptism, nor is anything told of the subsequent history of so eminent a convert. It is strange too that even in Christian legend he plays no part, especially when we remember that there does exist an alleged correspondence between Paul and the contemporary statesman and philosopher Seneca. It is possible that Renan is right in his view that Luke, or perhaps even Paul himself, was misled concerning Sergius Paulus' conversion by the fact that he gave a courteous audience to what must have seemed to him, as a cultured man of the world, the preaching of an interesting religious enthusiast.

One last problem remains: Why is it that at this point Luke changes the apostle's name from Saul to Paul? The following reasons have been given: (*a*) Origen, supported later by Jerome, thought that Saul adopted the name of his famous convert, just as a conqueror might take as his title the name of a vanquished nation. The words ὁ καὶ Παῦλος might then mean "who also [as well as Sergius] was a Paul." This is most unlikely. (*b*) The change of name may be due to a change of source, if, as has already been suggested, Luke at 13:1 began to draw upon some special Pauline source. The identity of the apostle's new name with the proconsul's, though interesting, would then be no more than a coincidence. (*c*) Perhaps more probably the change is due not to Luke's sources but to his own instinct as a historian. Paul, as one born a Roman citizen, would have possessed and almost certainly used his cognomen all his life. But Luke is conscious that at this point the apostle is entering on his career as a missionary to the Roman world; possibly the very coincidence of his cognomen with that of the proconsul reminds Luke that "Paulus" is the seal of his hero's Roman citizenship; and it is not as the Jew "Saul" but as the Roman citizen "Paul" that he proposes henceforth to treat him. It is much more likely that Paul derived his name from the Roman family of which his parents may have been clients than that he assumed it as a token of his modesty—so Augustine, quoting I Cor. 15:9, "the least of the apostles"—or that it was given to him as a nickname because of his shortness of stature.

4-7. Seleucia was the port of Antioch; **Salamis** was the eastern port of Cyprus and its largest town, **Paphos** being the official capital, near which was a famous temple of Aphrodite. **Cyprus,** after having been an imperial province, originally incorporated

come into the world; that he was working all things together for good, for Christ. The time was right, the peace of Rome was prevailing, the Greek language was universal, the roads were good, the need and the thirst for righteousness were great, the leaders were ready, and God launched his mighty movement! During the intervening centuries that movement has had its ups and downs; it has its bright pages and its dark ones; it can boast of great achievements and hang its head in shame when it confesses its lamentable failures. Nevertheless, through its history one feels the impelling Spirit of God. He will not let it die; he will not let it give up or cease to be. Neither will he take it over and run it autocratically. He will continue to guide it, spur it on, protect it, hold it responsible to the highest, raise up men to lead it, and when it asks for help, he will give it in good measure, pressed down and running over.

So they, being sent forth by the Holy Ghost, departed unto Seleucia; and from thence they sailed to Cyprus. So quietly, with people scarcely realizing what was happening, the Christian mission was launched. So Christ came, silently, almost unnoticed.

How silently, how silently,
  The wondrous gift is given!
So God imparts to human hearts
  The blessings of his heaven.
No ear may hear his coming,
  But in this world of sin,
Where meek souls will receive him, still
  The dear Christ enters in.[2]

[2] Phillips Brooks, "O little town of Bethlehem."

6 And when they had gone through the isle unto Paphos, they found a certain sorcerer, a false prophet, a Jew, whose name *was* Bar-jesus:

7 Which was with the deputy of the country, Sergius Paulus, a prudent man; who called for Barnabas and Saul, and desired to hear the word of God.

8 But Elymas the sorcerer (for so is his name by interpretation) withstood them, seeking to turn away the deputy from the faith.

they had John to assist them.
6 When they had gone through the whole island as far as Pa'phos, they came upon a certain magician,[k] a Jewish false prophet, named Bar-Jesus.
7 He was with the proconsul, Sergius Paulus, a man of intelligence, who summoned Barnabas and Saul and sought to hear the word of God.
8 But El'y-mas the magician (for that is the meaning of his name) withstood them, seeking to turn

[k] Greek *magus* (as in Matthew 2. 1).

---

with Cilicia, had become in 22 B.C. a senatorial province. Luke therefore, with his usual accuracy in such matters, rightly calls its governor, not a "procurator," but a **proconsul** (cf. 18:12 on Gallio at Corinth).

7. A man of intelligence, i.e., of an inquiring mind and likely to give an audience to missionaries, whom he probably classed with the ubiquitous Stoic and Cynic traveling teachers.

8. Elymas the magician (for that is the meaning of his name): A very puzzling sentence. Does it mean that "Elymas" is a "translation" of Bar-Jesus, or that the meaning of "Elymas"—in this case the man's proper name added to the patronymic Bar-Jesus—is "magician"? (*a*) On the latter assumption the best suggestion is that "Elymas" is related to a similar Arabic word meaning "wise," but this seems very farfetched. (*b*) It is very difficult to see how "Elymas" can be a translation of "Bar-Jesus" ("son of salvation"), unless we accept the even more farfetched suggestion that "Bar-Jesus" is itself a corruption of a transliteration of an Aramaic word meaning "make ready"; this might then be "translated" by the Greek word "Etoimas," which the Western text reads in place of "Elymas" (so Zahn, *Die Apostelgeschichte des Lucas* [Leipzig: A. Deichert, 1922], II, 417-18). This man "Etoimas" might then conceivably be identified with a Cypriote sorcerer whom Josephus calls "Atomus" (*Antiquities* XX. 7. 2). (*c*) Probably the best solution is to take the idea of translation very loosely and suppose that the meaning simply is that the Jew "Bar-Jesus" was commonly known among the Greek-speaking populace as "Elymas"—two names which, as in the case, e.g., of John Mark, were not etymologically related. F. C. Burkitt suggests that "Elymas" may be a corruption of ὁ λοιμός, meaning "the pestilential fellow" ("The Interpretation of Bar-Jesus," *Journal of Theological Studies,* IV [1902], 127-29). **From the faith,** i.e., from Christianity (see on 14:22).

How different are our modern methods and publicity stunts! But is God different? Has he changed his ways? One is more than half inclined to doubt it.

6-12. *The Encounter with Elymas.*—Elymas is one of the many minor characters in the Acts. He was a sorcerer, and sorcerers of one kind or another are always with us. Regardless of the particular bag of tricks that they happen to carry, their line of trade is always the same. They deal in magic, and magic is the attempt to bend the will of God to suit the will of man. Magic presumes to have power to control the laws of God and to exercise that power by secret knowledge in favor of particular persons. It does not worship God; it uses him.

Religion easily degenerates into this kind of sorcery. In our own time one of the most obvious manifestations of it is the rise of cults which promise health and prosperity to those who practice its principles. "Prayer is a cure of insomnia," is a typical trade-mark. Religion then becomes a means to an end, rather than an end in itself. It is offered as a wand which will change geese into swans and lead into gold. In such modern garb Elymas walks the streets of every modern city.

The sadness of it all is that intelligent men like Sergius Paulus are taken in by him. In every individual, deeply buried in some and near the surface in others, is the desire to master the circumstances of his life. He would rather be God, even though a small one, than serve God, even though he is the God of all the

9 Then Saul, (who also *is called* Paul,)
filled with the Holy Ghost, set his eyes on
him,
10 And said, O full of all subtilty and all
mischief, *thou* child of the devil, *thou* enemy of all righteousness, wilt thou not cease
to pervert the right ways of the Lord?
11 And now, behold, the hand of the
Lord *is* upon thee, and thou shalt be blind,
not seeing the sun for a season. And immediately there fell on him a mist and a
darkness; and he went about seeking some
to lead him by the hand.
12 Then the deputy, when he saw what
was done, believed, being astonished at the
doctrine of the Lord.
13 Now when Paul and his company
loosed from Paphos, they came to Perga in

away the proconsul from the faith. 9 But
Saul, who is also called Paul, filled with
the Holy Spirit, looked intently at him
10 and said, "You son of the devil, you
enemy of all righteousness, full of all deceit
and villainy, will you not stop making
crooked the straight paths of the Lord?
11 And now, behold, the hand of the Lord
is upon you, and you shall be blind and
unable to see the sun for a time." Immediately mist and darkness fell upon him and
he went about seeking people to lead him
by the hand. 12 Then the proconsul believed, when he saw what had occurred, for
he was astonished at the teaching of the
Lord.
13 Now Paul and his company set sail

---

10. Son of the devil: Possibly a deliberate antithesis to "Bar-Jesus," "son of salvation." **Making crooked the straight paths:** An echo perhaps of Prov. 10:9; Hos. 14:9.

11. For this vivid description of blindness cf. Deut. 28:28-29. This is another verse quoted by those who believe that our author used technical medical language. There is an obvious reminiscence of Paul's own blindness: "He could see nothing; so they led him by the hand. . . . And immediately something like scales fell from his eyes" (9:8, 18).

12. The correct translation is probably **believed, . . . for he was astonished at the teaching** rather than "believed, in astonishment [at the miracle], on the teaching"; cf. Luke 4:32, where the people "were astonished at his teaching."

3. Mission to Galatia (13:13–14:28)

We shall obtain a clearer understanding of this section if we remind ourselves at the start that the churches founded on this tour are the "churches of Galatia" (Gal. 1:2) to which the letter was written. This view, usually known as the "South Galatian theory,"

---

earth and sky and sea. Always is he ready therefore to listen to people who promise him the secret of control and mastery. How to get something for nothing, that is what he wants to know. And how to be something for nothing, that is what he wants to be. No wonder he is fertile ground for the sorcerer who shows him the short cuts. Faith is hard; force is easy. Elymas travels the easy way and his followers are legion.

When Paul met Elymas, he did not cloak his feeling in fine language. He said, "You son of the devil, you enemy of all good, full of all craft and all cunning, will you never stop diverting the straight paths of the Lord?" (Moffatt.) Jesus did not hesitate to use language like that. "Ye serpents, ye generation of vipers" (Matt. 23:33) he called his opponents. Peter did not hesitate to use strong language when Ananias and Sapphira lied. Some of our Christian leaders today, however, withdraw so completely into the mists of polite and ambiguous language that its true meaning is never guessed. We must not be guilty of unjustified harshness either in our speech or action. But there are times when it is better to speak out than to beat around the bush. A wise pastor once said, "There are times when the best possible thing you can do for a person is to give him a good, stiff rebuke." Too often our pastoral counselors hide behind the shrubbery of soft words, and in their desire not to hurt the feelings of their patient, deceive him into believing that he is better than he really is. The kindest thing that Paul could have done for Elymas was just what he did—to tell him exactly what he was, a fake, a quack; to show him exactly where he stood, namely, under the threat of blindness as a sign of the Lord's judgment.

13. ***John Turns Back.*—And John departing from them returned to Jerusalem.** John joined Barnabas and Paul as an assistant when they started out for Cyprus. He stayed with them through the first weeks of their trip, but when

is increasingly, though not yet universally, accepted by scholars. A full discussion of the problems involved belongs rather to an introduction to Galatians, and here the briefest sketch must suffice. (See also Vol. X, pp. 435-37.)

During the first quarter of the third century B.C. a northern tribe of Gauls had invaded Asia Minor, and had roamed and plundered at will, until finally Attalus of Pergamum succeeded in confining them to a tract of country in the northern part of the central plateau, which henceforth became known as "Galatia" in the stricter and narrower sense, their chief towns being Ancyra, Pessinus, and Tavium. It was to churches in this district that, according to the "North Galatian theory," the Epistle to the Galatians was written.

In the latter half of the first century B.C. the Gaulish King Amyntas, by the favor of Augustus, acquired a large dominion, the "kingdom of Galatia," which included, besides Galatia proper, part of Phrygia, Lycaonia, Pisidia, Pamphylia, and western Cilicia. At the death of Amyntas in 25 B.C. this whole "kingdom" passed into the hands of the Romans. Pamphylia was constituted a province by itself; at the time of the "first tour" western Cilicia with part of Lycaonia formed the "kingdom of Antiochus"; while the remainder became the Roman province of greater "Galatia." Thus the churches of Antioch, Lystra, Derbe, Iconium, though south of Galatia proper, were nevertheless in the province of Galatia, and could be spoken of as "the Galatian churches." Their members, though of differing nationality and living under various political conditions, all had this in common, that they belonged to the Roman province of Galatia and had the right to style themselves "Galatians." To them, according to the South Galatian theory, the epistle was written. But after some three hundred years this grouping of the provinces was abandoned; the name "Galatia" reverted to the northern part of the province; and the wider meaning of the name was apparently forgotten, until it was recovered largely through the researches of Sir William M. Ramsay. Hence it was assumed that Paul's letter must have been written to the Celts of northern Galatia.

The acceptance of the South Galatian theory greatly simplifies the problems raised by Acts. The book obviously sets out to give an account of the main stages of Paul's missionary work. It tells of the foundation of churches in Macedonia, Achaia, and Asia. From the epistles we learn that there was also an important Christian community in Galatia. Paul had visited it at least twice; and the letter reflects an intimate acquaintanceship such as could come only from close intercourse. The Galatian churches evidently ranked as a fourth group alongside the churches of Macedonia, Achaia, and Asia. Yet on the old theory that these churches were in northern Galatia, apart from three possible allusions which are much better explained otherwise (see on 16:6; 18:23; 19:1), Acts makes no reference whatever to Paul's work in Galatia. Conversely, if Antioch, Lystra, Derbe, Iconium are not "the Galatian churches," it is strange indeed that no letter of Paul should have been preserved addressed to these his first Gentile foundations. And finally, it may be remarked that the trouble with "Judaizers" reflected in the epistle is surely much more likely to have arisen in the southern towns with their considerable Jewish population than in the remote northern districts inhabited by Celtic highlanders. If it is asked why Acts gives us no hint that such trouble had arisen with Judaizers in south Galatia, it may be replied that Luke perhaps thought it sufficient to mention how the trouble came to a head shortly afterwards at Antioch (15:1-2), and thus led up to the council where the whole question was settled. Moreover Luke always tends to gloss over trouble within the church. By the time he wrote, these temporary disputes had been settled; and in any case, as Emmet does well to remind us, Luke did not "write with the view of enabling future generations to illustrate the letters of his friend" (*Beginnings of Christianity*, II, 284).

The South Galatian theory makes possible, though not necessary, the acceptance of an early date for the Epistle to the Galatians, perhaps early in 49. It would then be written from Antioch on the return thither from the first tour and *before* the council at Jerusalem. The trouble in Galatia would then be part of the same trouble as, and con-

Pamphylia: and John departing from them returned to Jerusalem.

from Pa'phos, and came to Perga in Pamphyl'i-a. And John left them and returned

current with, the trouble at Antioch described in 15:1-2. Paul, we are told, was in Antioch "no little time" (14:28). While engaged there in the controversy he hears of the defection of the Galatian churches under the influence of similar propaganda (Gal. 1:6). As he is about to go to Jerusalem, he cannot visit them himself (Gal. 4:20). He therefore writes them this urgent letter, following it up on the first opportunity with a visit, during which he explains the decisions of the council (16:1-6). Though, once again, all this belongs properly to the criticism of Galatians, it is of great importance for the study of Acts. For if Galatians was indeed not written till after the council, it is virtually impossible to accept Luke's account in ch. 15 as anything approaching the truth (see on ch. 15).

a) From Paphos to Perga (13:13)

13. Paul and his company: In Luke's mind Paul, and not Barnabas, is already the leader of the party. **Perga:** Apparently they did not land at the seaport town of Attalia (14:25), but sailed eight miles up the river Cestrus, which though not now navigable probably then was. They did not, it appears, preach at Perga at this time, but only on the return journey (14:25). **John left them:** Why? Possibly because he felt that his commission from Antioch was restricted to Cyprus, and as a Jerusalemite he hesitated to embark upon a largely Gentile mission in the interior before it had been sanctioned by the mother church. Possibly because, as Barnabas' kinsman, he was jealous of Paul, who was rapidly taking the leadership. Possibly because he shrank from the rigors of a mountain journey. Loisy and others think that the rift between Paul and Barnabas (which came to a head in the incident reported in Gal. 2:13, and led to the separation in 15:36-41) was already beginning, and that Luke is masking the deeper cause—a difference of opinion as to the limits of Gentile exemption from observance of the law—by stressing both here and in 15:36-41 a quite subordinate cause of disagreement in the person of Mark. That Paul was later reconciled to Mark seems clear from Col. 4:10.

they got to Asia Minor and decided to leave the coast and go up north into the more rural and less cultivated districts, he left the party and went home. His reasons for leaving are not indicated; we can only guess at them, and one man's guess is as good as another's. We can be fairly sure that he had some good reason for doing what he did. Few people do anything for which they have not some reason which at least to them seems to be a good one. In this case John may have felt that the change in itinerary meant a change in the policy of the mission, which he did not approve and was not prepared to accept. He may have felt that the response in the rural areas would not justify the danger and risk undertaken by the missionaries. He may have felt that the key cities were the places to strike first. He may have found it difficult to get along with Paul. At any rate, for some reason he returned to Jerusalem and he stands as a symbol of the man who turns back.

A great many people start out in the right direction with every good intention in the world, but when things go against them, when they cannot have their way, when the way is rough and steep, they turn back. There is a great temptation for men and women who started out toward world peace and world government to give up. They are disappointed by the lack of co-operation that they have received, they are disillusioned about humanity in general, they are disgusted by the ruthlessness of international politics, and they are ready to go home.

In individuals the same characteristic often turns up. We all know people whose attitude is, If you do not play my way, I will not play at all. It is the unmistakable slogan of the spoiled child. It is the undeveloped personality of one who has not yet learned how to adapt himself to circumstances that are not in his favor. Rather than put up with the necessity of adjusting himself to disagreeable conditions, he will go home and have none of it.

It is hardly necessary to point out that we need men and women who, once they have put their hand to the plow, do not turn back. The great battles of the world are won by the people who are able "to see it through." John, the subordinate to Barnabas and Paul, for some reason or other, good or bad, was not able to see it through. And it is worth noting that the

14 ¶ But when they departed from
Perga, they came to Antioch in Pisidia,
and went into the synagogue on the sabbath day, and sat down.

to Jerusalem; 14 but they passed on from
Perga and came to Antioch of Pi-sid'i-a.
And on the sabbath day they went into the

b) At Pisidian Antioch (13:14-52)

Why did Paul, instead of working for a time in Perga and the neighboring towns, at once strike inland? Had a visit to Pisidian Antioch been a part of the original plan, it would have been more natural to approach it by way of Cilicia and Lycaonia, and so to have avoided the passage of the Taurus range, a difficult mountainous route beset by bandits (cf. II Cor. 11:26, "in danger from rivers, danger from robbers"). It would seem, then, that the expedition was undertaken on the spur of the moment, perhaps because Paul's encounter with Sergius Paulus had inspired him with the desire to take the gospel to the Roman colony of Antioch. At the same time he would strike the main road from the east to Ephesus and so onward to Rome. The apostle's eyes may already have been fixed on the west. This seems more likely than Sir William M. Ramsay's theory that Paul's original intention was to preach in the coastal districts of Pamphylia, but the enervating climate brought on malaria (Paul's "thorn in the flesh"? II Cor. 12:7), and compelled him to seek the bracing air of Antioch, which has an altitude of some four thousand feet (*The Church in the Roman Empire* [New York: G. P. Putnam's Sons, 1893], pp. 61 ff.). But a sick man would surely have returned to Cyprus rather than undertake the strenuous Taurus passage. If Paul was in fact ill, it is more likely that the sickness came on at Antioch, and compelled him to stay there longer than he intended, so that it would be literally true that "it was because of a bodily ailment that I preached the gospel to you at first" (Gal. 4:13). And it would be equally true in the case of the other Galatian churches also; for Paul may well have turned back southeastward to Iconium, Lystra, and Derbe, in preference to pressing on toward the west, because he was not yet fully recovered and thought it best to travel in the direction of home.

Arriving at Antioch, the travelers opened their mission in the **synagogue.** Luke consistently pictures Paul as so doing. Indeed he leaves the impression that Paul's first objective was always the Jewish community, and that it was only after his approach to them had failed that he decided to "turn to the Gentiles" (vs. 46). That this to some extent corresponds to Paul's experiences is shown by, e.g., I Thess. 2:15. And that Paul should everywhere have made the synagogue his *point d'appui* is entirely natural; he would there be sure of an interested audience and could look for converts from among the Gentile proselytes and adherents. But it must be confessed that in Luke's account such rejections by the Jews, followed by a turning to the Gentiles, conform to a certain conventional pattern. One would imagine that in 13:46 Luke was describing a radical and final change of policy. Yet in place after place the same crisis is reached, only to be repeated again when Paul moves on (cf. 13:50-51; 14:1-2; 17:1-5; and especially 18:5-6; 19:8-9; 28:25-28). It has been suggested that Luke is deliberately illustrating Paul's own thesis stated in Rom. 1:16, "to the Jew first and also to the Greek." Certainly there is no doubt that he is concerned to show that if the Jews had rejected the gospel, it was through no lack of opportunity to hear it and welcome it. And making a certain allowance for the conventional repetition of the program, there is no need to question the substantial accuracy of Luke's picture on the ground that such persistent preaching to the Jews is inconsistent with Paul's self-confessed role as Apostle to the Gentiles (Gal. 1:16; 2:7-8). There is no evidence whatever that Paul ever discriminated against his own people or confined his attention exclusively or even chiefly to the heathen. His own words in Rom. 9; 10:1; 11:11-16; I Cor. 9:20 make it abundantly plain that he was profoundly concerned about the conversion of the Jews and was doing everything in his power to bring it about.

Paul's address in the synagogue at Antioch can hardly be taken as an exact transcript of the apostle's own words. It must be regarded as a summary or free composition by the

15 And after the reading of the law and the prophets, the rulers of the synagogue sent unto them, saying, *Ye* men *and* brethren, if ye have any word of exhortation for the people, say on.

16 Then Paul stood up, and beckoning with *his* hand said, Men of Israel, and ye that fear God, give audience.

17 The God of this people of Israel chose our fathers, and exalted the people when they dwelt as strangers in the land of Egypt, and with a high arm brought he them out of it.

18 And about the time of forty years suffered he their manners in the wilderness.

synagogue and sat down. **15** After the reading of the law and the prophets, the rulers
of the synagogue sent to them, saying,
"Brethren, if you have any word of exhortation for the people, say it." **16** So Paul
stood up, and motioning with his hand
said:
"Men of Israel, and you that fear God,
listen. **17** The God of this people Israel
chose our fathers and made the people
great during their stay in the land of
Egypt, and with uplifted arm he led them
out of it. **18** And for about forty years he

---

author himself, though as always it is constructed with rare skill and is exactly appropriate to the occasion. Paul's line of argument here is as suitable to a Hellenistic-Jewish synagogue as are his words at Athens to a highly educated Greek audience. Yet there are obvious reminiscences of earlier speeches in Acts, particularly Peter's at Pentecost, and Stephen's. The style throughout is Luke's own; and the speech is most noteworthy, not as an actual Pauline sermon, but as the typical argument of a Christian preacher of Luke's day addressed to a Hellenistic-Jewish audience. For our knowledge of what Paul actually preached in Galatia we must depend not so much on this "sermon" as on Gal. 3:1 ff.—redemption through Christ crucified, salvation by faith and not by works, the indwelling life of the Holy Spirit.

The main ideas of this speech are: (*a*) Jesus is the divinely promised offspring of the house of David. (*b*) Having been rejected by the Jews of Jerusalem, he is now offered as Savior to Paul's audience of Jews of the Dispersion. (*c*) Both his crucifixion and his resurrection were foretold in Scripture and guarantee forgiveness of sins.

14. Antioch of Pisidia: Not in Pisidia (KJV), for the town was actually in Phrygia and was called "Pisidian" to distinguish it from Antioch in Caria, because it lay near the Pisidian border. It was a Roman colony and a military center, and the most important town of south Galatia.

15. The setting is the same as when our Lord himself spoke in the synagogue at Nazareth (Luke 4:16 ff.). The service would consist of the reading of the Shema, a prayer by the "ruler" or "leader," readings from the Law and the Prophets, an address, and the blessing. The use of the plural, **rulers of the synagogue,** seems to imply that more than one could hold office together in a single synagogue; cf. Mark 5:22, where Jairus is "one of the rulers of the synagogue," and 18:8, 17, where both Crispus and Sosthenes are mentioned as "rulers," but possibly of different synagogues.

16-18. You that fear God: See on 10:2 and cf. vss. 26, 46. **With uplifted arm,** i.e., with a display of power; cf. Deut. 4:34; etc. **Bore with them,** literally **suffered . . . their manners** (ἐτροποφόρησεν). Other MSS, with the alteration of one letter, read "nourishing them" (ἐτροφοφόρησεν). The same variant appears in Deut. 1:31, whence no doubt the word is borrowed.

---

reason for his failure, no matter how good it might be, would not be good enough to excuse him in the eyes of posterity for letting down his elder companions.

17-41. ***Paul's First Recorded Sermon.***—Here is a sample of Paul's missionary preaching in its earliest stage. Obviously its contents cannot be copied slavishly by an interpreter in the twentieth century, but a study of the intent and meaning of its contents, together with its general method, can be pursued with great profit by the preacher and teacher of today.

(*a*) Look first at the congregation. It is composed of two groups: the faithful Jews and the fringe of interested spectators. Paul kept both groups in mind as he spoke. Some preachers

19 And when he had destroyed seven nations in the land of Chanaan, he divided their land to them by lot.

20 And after that he gave *unto them* judges about the space of four hundred and fifty years, until Samuel the prophet.

21 And afterward they desired a king: and God gave unto them Saul the son of Cis, a man of the tribe of Benjamin, by the space of forty years.

22 And when he had removed him, he raised up unto them David to be their king; to whom also he gave testimony, and said, I have found David the *son* of Jesse, a man after mine own heart, which shall fulfil all my will.

bore with[l] them in the wilderness. 19 And
when he had destroyed seven nations in the
land of Canaan, he gave them their land
as an inheritance, for about four hundred
and fifty years. 20 And after that he gave
them judges until Samuel the prophet.
21 Then they asked for a king; and God
gave them Saul the son of Kish, a man of
the tribe of Benjamin, for forty years.
22 And when he had removed him, he raised
up David to be their king; of whom he
testified and said, 'I have found in David
the son of Jesse a man after my heart, who

[l] Other ancient authorities read *cared for* (Deut. 1. 31).

19-20. The **seven nations** are enumerated in Deut. 7:1. Our text makes it appear that the **four hundred and fifty years** was the period between God's "choice" of Israel—in the promise made to Abraham—and the actual occupation of the land. The Western text rewrites the sentence to make it clear that the 450 years, in accordance with current Jewish reckoning, covers the period of the judges. This is probably the real intention of our text, the words **after that** referring, not to the end of the 450 years, but to the occupation of the land. **Samuel the prophet:** Cf. 3:24, where also Samuel is regarded as the first of the prophets. Moreover he is regarded as the last of the "judges," and as such the link between the two orders.

21-22. Forty years: Not in the O.T.; but Josephus also gives this as the length of Saul's reign. **Removed him:** The reference is probably rather to Saul's rejection as king (I Sam. 15:23) than to his death. The Greek word (cf. Luke 16:4) almost means "deposed." The quotation is a combination of Ps. 89:20; I Sam. 13:14; and Isa. 44:28—probably another example of the use of *testimonia* (see on 3:21-23).

---

are inclined to speak only to the faithful and therefore feel free to limit themselves to the semisecret jargon of professional religion and theology. Others speak only to the fringe and are afraid of everything that has the aura of tradition about it. They strain to be original and become bizarre. They try to shock and only cheapen their message. The great preacher keeps both groups in mind. Phillips Brooks was once called to be the resident preacher at Harvard University. He was rector of Trinity Church, Boston, at the time, and the pressure from those who wanted him to remain was great. To a man who wanted him to accept the new appointment, and who said that Trinity Church was filled with old people to whom he had preached for years, he replied, "I know that I have not much to say to my senior warden, for he is as far along the way as I am. But every time I get up into the pulpit I think of the person sitting in the last pew who may be hearing the gospel for the first time." Woe to the preacher who forgets that person!

(*b*) Glance now at Paul's general technique. It was a Jewish congregation and Paul preached a thoroughly Jewish sermon. He couched the whole in terms of Jewish history, he founded it upon proof texts from the Jewish scriptures, he appealed to a Jewish mentality and to a Jewish need. When he preached to Greeks in Athens, he preached a Greek sermon which Greeks might be able to comprehend. In other words, Paul took his congregation seriously, and without modifying the content of his message or in any way diluting it, he delivered it in language and imagery which the people not only understood intellectually, but also felt emotionally. A universal message in a local frame; that was Paul's technique. How much preaching falls down at that very point! It is as though the preacher stood in a vacuum, encased in the plate glass of his professional dialect, speaking to people who can see him but cannot hear him, and who can watch his motions but understand none of their meaning. It would be useless, for example, for a preacher to tackle the same subject that Paul tackles in this sermon in the same way that Paul tackles it. The sermon would never leave the

23 Of this man's seed hath God, according to *his* promise, raised unto Israel a Saviour, Jesus:

24 When John had first preached before his coming the baptism of repentance to all the people of Israel.

25 And as John fulfilled his course, he said, Whom think ye that I am? I am not *he*. But, behold, there cometh one after me, whose shoes of *his* feet I am not worthy to loose.

26 Men *and* brethren, children of the stock of Abraham, and whosoever among you feareth God, to you is the word of this salvation sent.

will do all my will.' 23 Of this man's posterity God has brought to Israel a Savior,
Jesus, as he promised. 24 Before his coming
John had preached a baptism of repentance to all the people of Israel. 25 And as
John was finishing his course, he said,
'What do you suppose that I am? I am not
he. No, but after me one is coming, the
sandals of whose feet I am not worthy to
untie.'

26 "Brethren, sons of the family of Abraham, and those among you that fear God, to us has been sent the message of this salva-

---

23-25. His promise: Possibly that quoted in vs. 34; or the reference may be to II Sam. 22:51; Ps. 132:11, 17. **A Savior, Jesus:** Cf. Matt. 1:21, "You shall call his name Jesus, for he will save his people from their sins." The allusion here and in vs. 32 to the "promise" reminds us of Paul's argument in Gal. 3. **Before his coming,** literally "before the face of his coming in"—a very marked Hebraism. For John's words see Luke 3:15-16. **What do you suppose that I am?** echoes the words in Luke, "All men questioned in their hearts concerning John, whether perhaps he were the Christ."

26. This salvation: With special reference to the word "Savior" in vs. 23. At this point Paul makes his direct appeal from the Jews of Jerusalem to those of the Dispersion.

---

ground where, incidentally, most sermons must content themselves to remain. The early history of Israel means little or nothing to the modern man. The proof texts of the O.T. prove nothing to him, and the assumption that David wrote the psalms proves that Paul was unenlightened. It would be hard to find a better illustration of the fatal consequence of preaching a good Jewish sermon to a modern congregation.

(*c*) The heart of the sermon is in vss. 32 and 33: "So we now preach to you the glad news that the promise made to the fathers has been fulfilled by God for us their children, when he raised Jesus" (Moffatt). We can easily distinguish four major points in the sermon, points which, when stated in current thought and language, are as valid now as they were when Paul made them:

(i) What he had to say to them was good news, not good advice. That distinction has been made so often that it has become trite. And yet Christian preachers by the score go on giving good advice in enormous doses, with only a scrap of good news thrown in now and then.

> If a man is overboard in the middle of the Atlantic, it is useless to instruct him in the best methods of swimming ashore. He cannot achieve anything in his own strength. Left to himself, he is doomed; and his only hope is in something or somebody outside himself who can rescue him.[3]

So Paul's sermon was about the rescue of the human race that had recently taken place. It was in the indicative mood, not the imperative. It did not begin by telling people that they ought to be good, but by telling them that God was good enough to do something which would save them from destruction.

(ii) The good news is news of salvation. God had kept his promise and given them a Savior. That is exactly what they wanted and what they needed. They needed a life belt, not a book of swimming rules. So after a long series of disasters, through which God did not desert them, he gave them Jesus. Jesus will save them. Paul does not stop at this point to describe how that rescue will take place. It is as though a man stood up in a prison camp and said: "The enemy has been conquered! You are saved! You are free!" Jesus had been captured by the enemy. He had been held the victim of sin and the prisoner of death. But he conquered both and his enemy has been made his footstool. It is only a matter of time when the multitudes will be released from the prisons and will be rescued under his leadership. The

[3] W. A. Smart, "The Author of Salvation," in *Contemporary Thinking About Jesus*, ed. Thomas S. Kepler (New York & Nashville: Abingdon-Cokesbury Press, 1944), p. 400.

27 For they that dwell at Jerusalem, and their rulers, because they knew him not, nor yet the voices of the prophets which are read every sabbath day, they have fulfilled *them* in condemning *him.*

28 And though they found no cause of death *in him,* yet desired they Pilate that he should be slain.

29 And when they had fulfilled all that was written of him, they took *him* down from the tree, and laid *him* in a sepulchre.

30 But God raised him from the dead:

31 And he was seen many days of them which came up with him from Galilee to Jerusalem, who are his witnesses unto the people.

tion. 27 For those who live in Jerusalem and
their rulers, because they did not recognize
him nor understand the utterances of the
prophets which are read every sabbath,
fulfilled these by condemning him.
28 Though they could charge him with
nothing deserving death, yet they asked
Pilate to have him killed. 29 And when
they had fulfilled all that was written of
him, they took him down from the tree,
and laid him in a tomb. 30 But God raised
him from the dead; 31 and for many days he
appeared to those who came up with him
from Galilee to Jerusalem, who are now his

27-29. Did not recognize him: Cf. Peter's words in 3:17. That the Crucifixion was foretold in prophecy is also a Petrine rather than a characteristically Pauline idea (cf. I Pet. 1:10-11). The Greek of vss. 27-29 is very awkward and involved and the text is almost certainly corrupt. **They could charge him with nothing deserving death:** What Luke 23:4 says of Pilate is here said of the Jews in general. **The tree:** Again a Petrine expression (see on 10:39); but Paul uses the word in Gal. 3:13. **They . . . laid him in a tomb,** i.e., the Jews so did. Perhaps Joseph of Arimathea is thought of as acting on behalf of the Sanhedrin.

31. His witnesses: If the speech was actually Paul's own, he would certainly have claimed himself to be such a witness, for he based his very right to be considered an apostle on the fact that he had "seen Jesus our Lord" (I Cor. 9:1). Yet here he "is virtually telling a Pisidian congregation that if they doubted his statement they could go to Palestine and investigate the matter among the eye-witnesses of the risen Jesus" (Foakes Jackson, *Life of St. Paul,* p. 98).

---

prisons in which people are confined today are the mental prisons of fear and anxiety, the prisons of poverty and want, of sin and guilt. The gospel is first of all the announcement that God has rescued them from their prison houses; God has kept his promise of salvation.

(iii) The proof of the promise of salvation is the resurrection of Jesus. **But God raised him from the dead.** You rejected him; God raised him up. There is the proof that God has fulfilled his promise. Paul traced the promise through the history of Israel. God stood by them in all their trials and tribulations; he promised not to forsake them; he promised to send them a Savior, and he did. If anyone doubted that Jesus was that Savior, the resurrection was the proof that his doubt was mistaken. So the resurrection of Jesus stands here at the heart of the gospel. It was something that God did, and in doing it he confirmed and fulfilled his promise of salvation.

It is not likely that the modern preacher would set forth the resurrection of Jesus in these terms. Its Jewish historical context is not altogether relevant to a contemporary congregation. But the truth will not be altered, simply enlarged, if that national context is stretched until it becomes the human context. There is a promise latent and implicit in humanity, a promise that it will be saved from its failures and frustration; that its transiency will finally be transcended, and that all the intimations dimly felt in the earthly creature will finally be made manifest in the sons of God. In Jesus that promise is fulfilled and in his resurrection the earthly creature becomes the son of God in glory.

(iv) This good news of salvation, sealed by the resurrection, has moral consequences. **Through this man forgiveness of sins is proclaimed to you.** Right from the beginning Christianity was more than a way out of trouble. It was a way out of sin into newness of life. It was more than the promise of peace of mind. It was the challenge of the peace of God.

It is important to point out that this moral consequence is the result of God's rescue, not of man's achievement. Paul knew all too well the futility of rules. He had been brought up on them. He knew them by heart. Try as he did,

32 And we declare unto you glad tidings,
how that the promise which was made unto
the fathers,
33 God hath fulfilled the same unto us
their children, in that he hath raised up
Jesus again; as it is also written in the second psalm, Thou art my Son, this day have
I begotten thee.
34 And as concerning that he raised him
up from the dead, *now* no more to return
to corruption, he said on this wise, I will
give you the sure mercies of David.
35 Wherefore he saith also in another
psalm, Thou shalt not suffer thine Holy
One to see corruption.

witnesses to the people. 32 And we bring
you the good news that what God promised
to the fathers, 33 this he has fulfilled to us
their children by raising Jesus; as also it is
written in the second psalm,
'Thou art my Son,
today I have begotten thee.'
34 And as for the fact that he raised him
from the dead, no more to return to corruption, he spoke in this way,
'I will give you the holy and sure
blessings of David.'
35 Therefore he says also in another psalm,
'Thou wilt not let thy Holy One see
corruption.'

32-33. The good news is that of vs. 23. **Us their children:** The Greek is τοῖς τέκνοις ἡμῶν ("to our children"), and the evidence for this reading seems decisive. Yet the meaning must surely be that given by KJV and RSV, though ERV has "unto our children." This is a case in which we can only suppose some very primitive corruption of the text. **By raising Jesus:** This might conceivably refer to Jesus' ministry rather than to his resurrection. But the immediately following reference to the Resurrection makes it more likely that the latter is in view here also. The "sonship" or "messiahship" of Jesus foretold in the **second psalm,** which is here quoted, was in early Christian thought sealed and authenticated by the Resurrection (cf. Rom. 1:4, "Designated Son of God . . . by his resurrection from the dead"). The same verse from Ps. 2 is spoken by the voice at Jesus' baptism (Luke 3:22), where a Western reading gives, "Today I have begotten thee" instead of "In thee I am well pleased." Some MSS read "in the first psalm"—perhaps because in third-century Psalters the first two psalms were linked together as one.

34-35. The first quotation is from Isa. 55:3. The phrase **the holy and sure blessings** is quite obscure in the Greek unless one reads in, according to true rabbinical fashion, some idea not in the original context; and its very obscurity gives the speaker the opportunity of relating it to the same word (i.e., "holy"; **thy Holy One**) in another quotation, this time from Ps. 16:10, which makes a very much more obvious reference to the Resurrection in the words, **Thou wilt not let thy Holy One see corruption.** The **blessings of David,** promised in vs. 23, are thus shown to have been finally sealed in the Resurrection.

---

he could not keep them all. The harder he tried, the more he broke them. The more he broke them, the more troubled he was in his heart and conscience. Not until he confronted Christ was he on the right track. In that relationship he found his peace; and besides that, he found the power, hitherto lacking, to advance along the way of moral development and perfection.

We are coming to the border of Paul's great doctrine of justification by faith. Put in its simplest terms it is something like this: A book of rules never makes a well-regulated family, no matter how good the rules are or how faithful the family is in its effort to obey them. The conscientious child is on tenterhooks lest he break the rules, and the unruly child is tempted to see how many he can break and get away with it. There is no "justification" in such a family; no one is on right terms with anybody else; everyone is at sixes and sevens with everyone else. It is only right relationships that make a good family. If the relationship is right between the father and mother, and between the parents and the children, then the rules will take care of themselves. The whole structure will be undergirded by confidence and trust; fear and anxiety will disappear. When the rules are broken, as they surely will be by imperfect beings, the relationship of trust and understanding will clear away the guilt and make it possible for a second chance to be undertaken bravely. That kind of a relationship Paul found in Jesus. At last he could rest in confidence. In Jesus he saw and felt the love of the Father beyond the shadow of any doubt. From that point onward the moral rules and regulations became

36 For David, after he had served his
own generation by the will of God, fell on
sleep, and was laid unto his fathers, and
saw corruption:
37 But he, whom God raised again, saw
no corruption.
38 ¶ Be it known unto you therefore,
men *and* brethren, that through this man
is preached unto you the forgiveness of
sins:

36 For David, after he had served the counsel of God in his own generation, fell asleep,
and was laid with his fathers, and saw corruption; 37 but he whom God raised up saw
no corruption. 38 Let it be known to you
therefore, brethren, that through this man
forgiveness of sins is proclaimed to you,

---

36. In his own generation, or possibly **after he had served his own generation by the will of God** (KJV): With either translation the point is that David's life belonged to his own generation only, for he was not raised from the dead (cf. 2:29). One wonders whether exactly the opposite point is not being made in 8:33, where the obscure words of Isa. 53:7-8 are applied to Jesus: "Who can describe his generation? For his life is taken up from the earth"—i.e., Christ belongs not to any one generation, but to all eternity.

38. Forgiveness of sins: The expression itself is Lukan rather than characteristically Pauline. It is used in almost exactly the same way in the speeches ascribed to Peter, both at Pentecost and at Caesarea (cf. on 2:38-40; 10:43). It occurs in the Pauline epistles only in Col. 1:14; Eph. 1:7, in both passages in close conjunction with the word "redemption," which elsewhere, rather than "forgiveness," is the characteristic Pauline word.

---

a joy and not an ordeal. The strain was taken out of life and serenity took its place.

To use another illustration along the same line: The first thing a person who wants to swim has to learn is to trust the water. No matter how perfectly he can make the arm and leg movements, unless he has the confidence to yield himself to the buoyancy of the water and to believe that the water will hold him, all the motions that he can make will be only frantic and futile attempts to do the impossible. Once he can rest upon the water, then his movements will become increasingly effective, and the more skillful he is with his arms and legs, the more surely and swiftly will he move through the water toward his destination. It is when a person is able to rest upon and within God that he is then able to improve his own moral and spiritual movements. Before that his activity is little more than panic that proves nothing. In Christ, Paul at last came to rest upon the tender mercy and love of God. At last he was justified, set right with God. The nervous tension and moral strain were at long last relaxed, and he was free to develop every conceivable stroke that would propel him more effectively through the troubled waters of life. No wonder he wanted to travel around the world to tell the people the good news!

When a preacher gets up into his pulpit today to preach this basic Christian gospel of salvation, there are two or three things that he might well remember. The people who are listening to him are not always aware that they need to be saved. They know that things are not what they ought to be, but they do not consciously identify that inward restlessness and apprehension with the need of salvation. The preacher's first task therefore is to help them see what it is that is imprisoning them. Here are some of the things: the mastery of materialism, the tyranny of the flesh, the waste of war, the injustice of social disorder, the sense of meaninglessness, the fear of the future, the perils of selfishness. Once he has made these articulate for them, he then can proceed to preach the good news of salvation.

It is not enough, however, to tell a modern congregation that Jesus saves them from all these things. They want to know how, and what they should do next. One of the ways by which Jesus saves them is simply by association with them. The more they know of him, the more they begin to feel the love of God. The more they think about his teaching, the more habitually they dwell within the family of God and behave as children of God and brethren of all other men. One of the objects of the preacher is to set forth the figure of Jesus; to make up, ever so imperfectly, for the lack of personal acquaintance with Jesus himself. Let the preacher clear away the mists that have gathered around the incomparable figure; let him remove misunderstandings that linger in the back of people's minds; let him take pleasure in introducing them to the personality

39 And by him all that believe are justified from all things, from which ye could not be justified by the law of Moses.

40 Beware therefore, lest that come upon you, which is spoken of in the prophets;

41 Behold, ye despisers, and wonder, and perish: for I work a work in your days, a work which ye shall in no wise believe, though a man declare it unto you.

42 And when the Jews were gone out of the synagogue, the Gentiles besought that these words might be preached to them the next sabbath.

43 Now when the congregation was broken up, many of the Jews and religious proselytes followed Paul and Barnabas; who, speaking to them, persuaded them to continue in the grace of God.

44 ¶ And the next sabbath day came almost the whole city together to hear the word of God.

45 But when the Jews saw the multitudes, they were filled with envy, and spake against those things which were spoken by Paul, contradicting and blaspheming.

39 and by him every one that believes is
freed from everything from which you
could not be freed by the law of Moses.
40 Beware, therefore, lest there come upon
you what is said in the prophets:
41 'Behold, you scoffers, and wonder, and
perish;
for I do a deed in your days,
a deed you will never believe, if one
declares it to you.'"
42 As they went out, the people begged
that these things might be told them the
next sabbath. 43 And when the meeting of
the synagogue broke up, many Jews and
devout converts to Judaism followed Paul
and Barnabas, who spoke to them and
urged them to continue in the grace of
God.
44 The next sabbath almost the whole
city gathered together to hear the word of
God. 45 But when the Jews saw the multitudes, they were filled with jealousy, and
contradicted what was spoken by Paul, and

---

39. The expression **every one that believes is freed,** and the contrast drawn between the freedom gained through faith in Christ and that ineffectually sought after through the law, appear at least superficially Pauline and may well be a conscious attempt to echo Pauline doctrine. But the verse hardly attains to the full Pauline thought of "justification" as the state of the saved man who is completely "just" or "right" in the sight of God. Moreover the implication here is that the law can free from some things, but not from **everything;** the gospel is thus complementary to the law, whereas according to the authentic Paul, faith is the only way to salvation, the law being totally powerless to save (cf. especially Rom. 7).

40-41. **The prophets,** i.e., in the book of the minor prophets, in this case Hab. 1:5 in the LXX (cf. 15:15). **Perish:** The Hebrew text of Habakkuk reads "be astonished."

43. **Devout converts to Judaism:** Literally "fearing (i.e., worshiping) proselytes." The phrase is found nowhere else and the reference is probably to the same people who are elsewhere called "fearers of God" (see on 10:2).

---

about whom he believes the whole of human history revolves; let him do whatever he can to bring this living figure to life before the very eyes of his congregation. It is hard really to know Jesus and be forever lost.

In addition to that, the preacher must so arouse the interest of his listener, so stimulate him, that he will be willing to let himself go, to make the venture of confidence, and to feel within himself the power which enables him to say, "I can do all things through Christ which strengtheneth me" (Phil. 4:13). And the preacher must also help to provide the social context in which this new life may be lived. In other words the Christian gospel demands the Christian fellowship. The individual must be set in the midst of a society in which he is trusted, where, if he sins, he will be forgiven gladly; if he fails, allowances will be generously made; and if he becomes proud, he will be gently but firmly rebuffed. One of the chief difficulties today is that the Christian fellowship has become so loosely knit that it has lost its power to act as the body of Christ in which a person may practice the freedom and liberty which he has found in Christ.

42-52. ***The People's Response.***—The rest of the chapter suggests thoughts on the responsibility of the congregation. In Paul's case those who listened to him reacted with complete ap-

46 Then Paul and Barnabas waxed bold, and said, It was necessary that the word of God should first have been spoken to you: but seeing ye put it from you, and judge yourselves unworthy of everlasting life, lo, we turn to the Gentiles.

47 For so hath the Lord commanded us, *saying,* I have set thee to be a light of the Gentiles, that thou shouldest be for salvation unto the ends of the earth.

48 And when the Gentiles heard this, they were glad, and glorified the word of the Lord: and as many as were ordained to eternal life believed.

49 And the word of the Lord was published throughout all the region.

reviled him. 46 And Paul and Barnabas
spoke out boldly, saying, "It was necessary
that the word of God should be spoken
first to you. Since you thrust it from you,
and judge yourselves unworthy of eternal
life, behold, we turn to the Gentiles. 47 For
so the Lord has commanded us, saying,

'I have set you to be a light for the
Gentiles,
that you may bring salvation to the
uttermost parts of the earth.' "

48 And when the Gentiles heard this,
they were glad and glorified the word of
God; and as many as were ordained to
eternal life believed. 49 And the word of
the Lord spread throughout all the region.

46: **It was necessary:** Our author—perhaps rather than Paul himself—seems to be trying to answer the question: Why was it that the Apostle to the Gentiles consistently began his work in the Jewish synagogues? The answer is that God's will made it necessary, in order that the Jews might not be able to excuse themselves by a plea of ignorance. Moreover once the Jews had rejected the approach, the preachers were free with a good conscience to **turn to the Gentiles.** The opposition of even the Jews of the Dispersion thus becomes yet another justification for missions to Gentiles. Though, as we have seen, this turning to the Gentiles does not mark the beginning of Gentile missions, and is repeated again and again in accordance with a conventional pattern, yet the present incident does in fact mark a real stage in the development of Christianity. It meant the inauguration of the policy of setting up Christian churches separate from the Jewish community, a step which apparently had not been taken even in Cyprus, and which was destined to produce a Gentile Christianity entirely supplanting the original proclamation of the messiahship of Jesus as an exclusively Jewish gospel. **Eternal life:** Literally "life belonging to the age [to come]"—the glorious messianic age which God would bring in after "the end." The Jews, Paul argues, are renouncing their own most characteristic hope.

47-48. The quotation is from Isa. 49:6, the original reference being to Israel as the servant of Yahweh. **Ordained to eternal life:** The word might mean little more than "disposed," with reference merely to human choice. But it is much more likely that God's predestination is in view; and it seems indeed that this actual phrase is not uncommon in that connection in rabbinical literature (H. L. Strack and Paul Billerbeck, *Kommentar zum Neuen Testament aus Talmud und Midrash* [Munich: C. H. Beck, 1924], II, 726).

---

proval. How could it have been otherwise? They heard the good news with the same relief a drowning man feels when the life belt saves him from the sea. They wanted to hear it again the next sabbath. A few more serious listeners waited for Paul and Barnabas after the service and talked further with them about their own salvation. But by the time the following sabbath came, the crowd was so great that the Jews were jealous and stirred up a few important men and women to make things so difficult for Paul and Barnabas that they finally left Antioch and went to Iconium.

There is always the danger that Christians will try to keep the comfort and power of Christ for themselves. The story is told of a wealthy congregation that deliberately chose its minister because they knew that he would not fill the church and make it uncomfortably crowded. At the other extreme is the attitude of Christians who would rather see their enemy destroyed than saved by the power of the gospel. The hardest thing for the Jews to grasp was the fact that the salvation Paul told them about was for everyone who wanted it. Christians today often have the same difficulty, though they hide it behind respectable garments of righteousness.

The important thing is that Paul and Barnabas went to another town. It reminds us of Jesus in Nazareth, "He did not do many mighty works there, because of their unbelief" (Matt.

50 But the Jews stirred up the devout and honorable women, and the chief men of the city, and raised persecution against Paul and Barnabas, and expelled them out of their coasts.

51 But they shook off the dust of their feet against them, and came unto Iconium.

52 And the disciples were filled with joy, and with the Holy Ghost.

14 And it came to pass in Iconium, that they went both together into the synagogue of the Jews, and so spake, that a great multitude both of the Jews and also of the Greeks believed.

50 But the Jews incited the devout women of high standing and the leading men of the city, and stirred up persecution against Paul and Barnabas, and drove them out of
their district. 51 But they shook off the
dust from their feet against them, and
went to I-co'ni-um. 52 And the disciples
were filled with joy and with the Holy Spirit.

14 Now at I-co'ni-um they entered together into the Jewish synagogue, and so spoke that a great company believed,

---

50. Women: A true touch of local color, for women apparently held a more prominent place in society in Asia Minor than in most parts of the Greco-Roman world. **Of high standing:** The same word that is used in Mark 15:43 of Joseph of Arimathea, the "respected member of the council." **The leading men of the city:** Presumably the magistrates who, probably without actually investigating the merits of the case, would expel the apostles from Antioch as likely disturbers of the peace.

51. Shook off the dust: A literal fulfillment of Jesus' command to his disciples (Luke 9:5; 10:11). A good Jew was careful not to bring into Palestine any dust from pagan territory. To "shake off dust" against anyone was thus equivalent to treating him as a heathen. There is perhaps also the suggestion that the missionaries symbolically cleared themselves of all further responsibility for a self-condemned community.

c) At Iconium and Lystra (14:1-18)

(1) At Iconium (14:1-7)

At this point, instead of pressing onward toward the west, as may well have been the original intention, the apostles turned southeast to Iconium, possibly because Paul was not yet wholly convalescent after his illness and felt that he should be moving in a homeward direction. To reach Iconium they would have to cross a high mountain pass, now known as the Sultan Dagh, which separates Antioch from the main Ephesus highway, off of which a branch road led south to Iconium. This town, the modern Konia, nearly one hundred miles from Antioch, was also within Roman "Galatia," and was the chief town of a group of other smaller towns included in the region known officially as Galatian Lycaonia. Here, in spite of the apparent "burning of their boats" (13:46), the apostles followed the same plan, and once again **they entered . . . into the Jewish synagogue.** Luke tells us little about the results, and indeed vss. 1-7 are peculiarly vague, so much so that they are virtually rewritten by the Western reviser in an endeavor to give greater clarity and concreteness. Evidently the Jews showed the same hostility as at Antioch, but the reference to **signs and wonders** may be taken as evidence that the mission met with some success. Rackham well remarks that such "signs" may be taken to indicate not only what we call "miracles," but, still more, "manifestations of the spiritual

---

13:58). Two things are necessary: the good news must be faithfully and carefully set forth; and the people must respond with willingness to yield themselves to its demands. A powerful preacher with an unresponsive congregation is helpless, and the responsiveness of the congregation cannot always be measured by the power of the preacher. Discouraged preachers, remember Paul!

14:1-7. *The Mission in Iconium.*—The stay in Iconium was a stormy one. Though much more briefly described, it followed essentially the same pattern as the one in Pisidian Antioch. The preaching of Paul and Barnabas was welcomed in the beginning with applause and widespread approval, and ended with mob violence. The town was divided, and the group that was hostile finally succeeded in winning

2 But the unbelieving Jews stirred up
the Gentiles, and made their minds evil
affected against the brethren.
3 Long time therefore abode they speaking boldly in the Lord, which gave testimony unto the word of his grace, and
granted signs and wonders to be done by
their hands.
4 But the multitude of the city was divided: and part held with the Jews, and
part with the apostles.
5 And when there was an assault made
both of the Gentiles, and also of the Jews
with their rulers, to use *them* despitefully,
and to stone them,

both of Jews and of Greeks. 2 But the unbelieving Jews stirred up the Gentiles and
poisoned their minds against the brethren.
3 So they remained for a long time, speaking boldly for the Lord, who bore witness
to the word of his grace, granting signs
and wonders to be done by their hands.
4 But the people of the city were divided;
some sided with the Jews, and some with
the apostles. 5 When an attempt was made
by both Gentiles and Jews, with their rulers,

---

life of the church—a life itself supernatural." But though history is somewhat silent about what happened at Iconium, legend is busy enough. The Acts of Paul tells how a young woman called Thecla hears Paul preach at Iconium and causes him more than a little embarrassment by her determination to be baptized. The two are brought together before the magistrates, Paul being condemned to be scourged and expelled and Thecla to be burned. A miraculous fall of rain saves her, and she then follows Paul back to Antioch and dresses as a boy in the hope of being allowed to accompany him. Finally she is exposed to the wild beasts, but escapes and dies at an advanced old age. But in the midst of all these absurdities there has been preserved what may well be an authentic description of Paul's personal appearance: "A man of small stature, with his eyebrows meeting and a rather large nose, somewhat bald-headed, bandy-legged, strongly built, of gracious presence; for sometimes he looked like a man and sometimes he had the face of an angel."

14:1. Together: Or possibly better "in the same way" as they had done at Antioch.

2. Unbelieving: The Greek word properly means "disobeying," but it is frequently used in the N.T. as the opposite of "believing," thus stressing the active nature of both faith and unbelief; cf. I Pet. 2:7-8, and especially John 3:36, "He who believes in the Son has eternal life; he who does not obey the Son shall not see life." **Jews:** The Western text expands this into "the chiefs of the synagogue and the rulers," perhaps to bring the scene into line with 13:15.

3-5. Vs. 3, particularly the connective **so**, follows very awkwardly after vs. 2, and the passage would read much more naturally if it were either omitted or read before vs. 2. As the text stands, vss. 3-5 appear almost as an enlarged doublet of vss. 1-2. **For the Lord:**

---

the others to its side. The episode ended in an unsuccessful attempt to stone the two missionaries. Though the attackers did not succeed in stoning Paul and Barnabas, they did succeed in driving them out of town.

The short passage describing the stay in Iconium is filled with words expressing violent feeling and action. One is not surprised that there is no record of any outstanding work. How could anyone work under such circumstances as those? Every minister knows how difficult it is to work in an atmosphere where there is dissension, suspicion, and unconcealed antagonism. How many times he excuses his own failures on the ground that the conditions were unfavorable to the work of the Lord! And yet in this instance in Iconium, and in many another, there are signs that the work of the Lord was done in spite of circumstances.

Sometimes a man makes his most lasting impression under circumstances which seem to be completely unfavorable. Sometimes the best sermons are preached when everything seems to be working against them. Let this legend about Paul be a lesson to everyone who is working under difficult circumstances. Thecla, now venerated as a saint in both the Latin and the Orthodox churches, came under the influence of Paul while he was in Iconium, was instructed by him in that city, and now her memory remains as a witness to the fact that no matter how hard the situation may be, how barren it

6 They were ware of *it,* and fled unto
Lystra and Derbe, cities of Lycaonia, and
unto the region that lieth round about:
7 And there they preached the gospel.
8 ¶ And there sat a certain man at Lystra, impotent in his feet, being a cripple
from his mother's womb, who never had
walked:

to molest them and to stone them, 6 they
learned of it and fled to Lystra and Der'be,
cities of Lyc-a-o'ni-a, and to the surrounding country; 7 and there they preached the
gospel.
8 Now at Lystra there was a man sitting,
who could not use his feet; he was a cripple

---

or perhaps better "in reliance on the Lord." **The apostles:** The first time the title has been given to Paul and Barnabas. **With their rulers:** Probably only the "rulers" of the Jews, though the word is sometimes used of city magistrates (16:19). Luke frequently uses it somewhat loosely of Jewish officials (Luke 8:41; Acts 3:17; 13:27). It would have been more difficult for the apostles to return to Iconium (vs. 21) if the civil authorities had also taken action against them.

6. Cities of Lycaonia: If the implication is that Iconium was not a city of Lycaonia, then Luke, though technically inexact, is following local usage perfectly correctly. Officially Iconium had been incorporated with Lycaonia for administrative purposes. But since the days of the Persian dominion it had been in fact the frontier town of Phrygia, and the natives counted themselves Phrygians rather than Lycaonians proper, as were the people of Lystra and Derbe. The system of local government also was different in Lystra and Derbe, so that if in fact the apostles had run foul of the civil magistrates at Iconium, they would now be coming under a different local authority.

(2) At Lystra (14:8-18)

The site of **Lystra,** the modern Zoldera, was discovered only in 1885, when an inscription was also found proving that Augustus had made it a Roman colony. It is nearly twenty miles from Iconium. "Derbe" (vs. 6) has not yet been satisfactorily identified, but it seems to have been only a few miles from Lystra. The story of the healing of the lame man at Lystra has been quite needlessly suspect because of the numerous echoes of other incidents in Acts. It closely resembles Peter's healing of a lame man at the Beautiful Gate (3:2-8), a fact which has been urged in support of the theory that Luke consciously sets himself to stress the parallelism between the careers of Peter and Paul; the expostulation of the apostles in vs. 15 is similar to that of Peter to Cornelius in 10:26; and the speech of Paul closely resembles part of his address at Athens (ch. 17). But though Luke may consciously or unconsciously have been influenced by accounts of other incidents, the whole story of the miracle and its sequel is so vividly told that it must surely be founded on fact. Indeed the whole account of the happenings at Lystra is so much more

---

may appear, there is always the possibility that some good thing may come out of it.

There is a great temptation to use the confusion of the times as an excuse for not achieving any great thing. How can we, we ask? Everything is so upset; no one knows what the future may bring; the ordinary ways are turned upside down; the thunder is already rumbling through the skies; this is no time to expect great things of us! Perhaps not, but out of just such times great things have come. Remember Paul in Iconium; nothing but trouble and strife; nothing else, but two of the most lasting impressions he ever made, one on a young girl named Thecla, and another on the only man we know of who took the trouble to describe his personal appearance.

A short paragraph from an essay by E. M. Forster sets forth the same idea: "Ancient Athens made a mess—but the Antigone stands up. Renaissance Rome made a mess—but the ceiling of the Sistine got painted; Louis XIV made a mess—but there was Phèdre; Louis XV continued it, but Voltaire got his letters written."[4]

8-18. *Paul's Sermon in Lystra.*—Paul's sermon in Lystra is interesting because of the particular framework of circumstances within which it is set. Paul had healed a lame man. There was nothing unusual about that, for wherever the gospel went there were similar signs of God's power to restore the minds and bodies of

[4] Lionel Trilling, *E. M. Forster* (Norfolk, Connecticut: New Directions Books, 1943), p. 180.

9 The same heard Paul speak: who steadfastly beholding him, and perceiving that he had faith to be healed,
10 Said with a loud voice, Stand upright on thy feet. And he leaped and walked.

from birth, who had never walked. 9 He
listened to Paul speaking; and Paul, looking intently at him and seeing that he had faith to be made well, 10 said in a loud
voice, "Stand upright on your feet." And

dramatic than any other part of the story of Paul and Barnabas that it is permissible to suppose that Luke is relying on information supplied by an eyewitness. Timothy was probably a native of Lystra (16:1-2) and may well have been the informant. It is noticeable too that Paul's speech at Lystra contains two of the very few verbal echoes in Acts of Paul's own language in the epistles (cf. vs. 15 with I Thess. 1:9; vs. 17 with Rom. 1:20; and see below).

It is an extraordinarily interesting coincidence that the story of how Barnabas and Paul were hailed as Zeus and Hermes is staged in exactly the same district where twice already popular legend had told how these same two gods had "come down . . . in the likeness of men" (vs. 11). There is the gruesome tale of Lycaon, who entertained the gods by feasting them on human flesh, for which crime he was turned into a wolf; and there is the beautiful legend of Baucis and Philemon, the poor couple who were the only folk who welcomed the gods, and who were rewarded by being allowed to die at the same time, that neither might be left to mourn the other (Ovid *Metamorphoses* VIII. 626 ff.). Whether or not there was a conscious recollection of these legends in the minds of the people of Lystra, or of Luke himself, is, of course, impossible to surmise. Perhaps the best comment on Luke's story, and strong evidence surely of its truth, is contained in Paul's own words in his letter addressed among others to this very community: "You did not scorn or despise me, but received me as an angel of God" (Gal. 4:14).

Paul's speech at Lystra (vss. 15-17), addressed as it is to pagans, is not unlike the speech at Athens, where the same lines of thought are developed more fully. Hitherto Paul's speeches have been addressed to Jews, or at least to sympathetic adherents of the synagogue. He is now confronted by purely pagan hearers. But his main argument is still characteristically Jewish. There is but one God, the evidence of whose existence is clear for all to see in his works of nature and providence; and him only must men worship and serve. As in the speech at Athens, the purely Hebrew gospel is skillfully flavored with widespread Greek ideas which find their fullest expression in Stoicism and will be more fully discussed under ch. 17.

8-10. The very language recalls Peter's miracle (3:2-8). In both stories the patient **is a cripple from birth.** Both Peter and Paul are described as **looking intently at him,** and in both cases the healed man **sprang up and walked.** At Lystra **faith** is stressed as a

the people who heard it. The unusual thing in this case was the response of the people. When they saw Paul heal the lame man, they thought that the gods had come down to earth. That kind of power was the power that only the gods could exercise, so they called Barnabas Zeus, and Paul Hermes. They went farther than that; they began to prepare the animals and the flowers for a sacrifice to the two gods who had descended upon them so unexpectedly. It was upon the threshold of that amazing performance that the sermon was preached.

The first thing to notice about the sermon is the decisiveness with which the two disciples of Jesus rejected and renounced any divine pretensions whatsoever. "We are but human, with natures like your own" (Moffatt). Lesser men have not always been so quick to reject the facile and misguided adulation of the crowd. The matinee idol thrives upon such flattery, and let no one think that all matinee idols are on the stage. They are in business, at the head of armies and navies, in positions of governmental prestige, in professorial chairs, and in pulpits! One of the greatest dangers to which people in public life are exposed is the adulation of people whose minds are too thin to think deeply and who like to think that their heroes are gods. Most men in such positions know the emptiness of the flattery, but at the same time enjoy it enough to accept it and finally lose the ability to thrust it from them as a dangerous and poisonous thing.

Not so Barnabas and Paul. They had the natural, unaffected humility of all great men. The thought that ignorant people might be so

11 And when the people saw what Paul
had done, they lifted up their voices, saying in the speech of Lycaonia, The gods are
come down to us in the likeness of men.
12 And they called Barnabas, Jupiter;
and Paul, Mercurius, because he was the
chief speaker.

he sprang up and walked. 11 And when the
crowds saw what Paul had done, they lifted
up their voices, saying in Lyc-a-o'ni-an,
"The gods have come down to us in the
likeness of men!" 12 Barnabas they called
Zeus, and Paul, because he was the chief

---

necessary condition of healing, while Peter's speech following his miracle also emphasizes that "his name, by faith in his name, has made this man strong" (3:16). The Western text tells the story even more dramatically: "This man listened gladly to Paul's speech, and he was in the fear of God. And Paul . . . said with a loud voice, In the name of the Lord Jesus stand upright on your feet and walk. And immediately that very moment he sprang up and began to walk."

11. In Lycaonian: Most of the people of the district would no doubt be bilingual; they would understand Paul speaking in Greek, but would naturally fall into the native dialect in moments of excitement. It is not suggested that Paul understood what they said, but their actions spoke clearly enough.

12. Barnabas, as the more reserved and imposing, and perhaps as still the nominal leader of the mission, **they called Zeus;** and **Paul . . . they called Hermes,** the patron god of oratory, **because he was the chief speaker** (ὁ ἡγούμενος τοῦ λόγου). There is an interesting parallel in Iamblichus, *The Egyptian Mysteries,* where Hermes is called ὁ τῶν λόγων ἡγεμών.

---

misled as to take them for gods was so repellent to them that before they said anything else, they made it unmistakably clear that they were human beings, no less and certainly no more.

The next interesting thing about the sermon is that it is about God, with no reference to Christ. The heart of the Christian message from the beginning until now is what God has done in Christ. And yet in this sermon there is no mention whatever of Christ, no Crucifixion, no Resurrection. Paul said nothing which any good Jew might not have said. The reason for it is obvious. The people who hailed Barnabas and Paul as gods were people who had no real knowledge of God. Their idea of God was a childlike idea. The thing that impressed them most was the sight of two men who did something that they could not do. In their minds the only explanation was that those two men were themselves gods, and they were prepared to put them on pedestals for public veneration and worship. The man who could do the most tricks was to their way of thinking the most godlike. It was the unusual and extraordinary which was the proof of God's presence and power.

Even in our own sophisticated days religion of that kind is by no means lacking. It is the religion of men and women who take temporal, imperfect things and idolize them as gods. Some people idolize their nation, and whether it is right or wrong, follow it with the complete loyalty and confidence that belong only to the transcendent God. Some people idolize their business and put its claims over and above all other claims of family and duty. Some idolize other people and so completely surrender their lives to them that they have no room left for the higher loyalties that are over and above all our deepest and most sincere human ties and affections. It is religion in its adolescence. It is the religion of hero worship. It is deceived by the passing glory of transient things. It takes imperfect things and exalts them to the place of God, whereas the Christian religion is the service of the God who emptied himself that he might become like us. Adolescent religion wants to make men into gods, whereas the mature religion of Christianity tells of a God so great that he could become man, yet lose nothing of his dignity or power.

So before Paul could tell the people about the revelation of God that was in Jesus, he had to tell them something about God. You cannot preach about a God who became incarnate if you have no real God to become incarnate. Modern preachers find themselves in a similar situation. Because of the materialism of the atmosphere in which we live, most people have little if any sense of God to begin with. The first thing the preacher must do therefore is to begin to arouse in the minds and hearts of the congregation the awe and reverence which the thought of God evokes. He must turn to such fundamental questions as: What do we

13 Then the priest of Jupiter, which
was before their city, brought oxen and
garlands unto the gates, and would have
done sacrifice with the people.
14 *Which* when the apostles, Barnabas
and Paul, heard *of,* they rent their clothes,
and ran in among the people, crying out,

speaker, they called Her′mes. 13 And the
priest of Zeus, whose temple was in front of
the city, brought oxen and garlands to
the gates and wanted to offer sacrifice with
the people. 14 But when the apostles Barnabas and Paul heard of it, they tore their
garments and rushed out among the mul-

---

13. Zeus, whose temple was in front of the city: The Greek means literally "the local [τοῦ ὄντος; see on 5:17] before-the-city Zeus"—πρὸ τῆς πόλεως being practically equivalent to an adjective. Thus an inscription "to Zeus before the city" (Διὶ προαστίῳ) has been found at Claudiopolis, near Lystra (quoted by Ramsay, *Church in the Roman Empire,* p. 51). **Garlands,** or woolen fillets used to decorate the sacrificial victims. **The gates** are either those of the temple or, more probably, of the town, where perhaps the healing of the lame man had taken place, the city gate being a favorite place for crippled beggars to sit. The priests would hasten to do sacrifice at the site of the miracle.

14. Tore their garments: There is evidence from rabbinical literature that this gesture, like that of "shaking off dust" (13:51; and note the mention of blasphemy in vs. 45 [KJV]) was "the prescribed reaction against blasphemy" (*Beginnings of Christianity,* V, 271, where see an interesting essay on the subject)—in this case the suggestion that sacrificial worship should be paid to mere men (cf. Mark 14:63; Acts 18:6; 22:22-23; and possibly 16:22).

---

mean by God? Where is God and how shall I find him? What do we mean by a personal God? Does God hear and answer prayer? So long as people are carried along on the tide of a pseudoscientific philosophy of life, according to which life is only an impersonal process with neither point nor purpose, they are not likely to understand or see the significance of the Christian gospel that God made himself manifest in man.

For this kind of preparatory preaching the O.T. is indispensable. Isa. 6, with its vision of God, the song of the heavenly choir, the response of the impure man to the utterly pure God, the cleansing by fire, the call and its acceptance contains the essential elements of theism without which Christianity falls like a bridge without piers. The same thing is true of the psalms, where the personal relationship between man and God is sung in unforgettable phrases. Even in the narratives of the O.T. you cannot forget the background of God against which they are all set. Take the story of Joseph and see how all the local circumstances of the story are held together by the prevailing purpose of God. "God did send me before you to preserve life" (Gen. 45:5). Such a sense of the overruling wisdom and purpose of God must precede any deep understanding of the act in which God himself became man.

Paul did exactly what has been recommended. He turned to the O.T. not to a specific text or passage but to a doctrine that pervades the whole book, the doctrine of creation. He tried to turn the minds of his listeners away from the false gods whom they were ready to make out of unworthy human beings to the great God who made the heaven and the earth and all that is in them. The great word, of course, is **He did not leave himself without witness.** There is not a spot on the face of the earth, according to Paul, where God has not left some sign of his presence. The rains and the seasons; the sun and the stars; food and the joy of life—these are signs of God's goodness. To be sure, in some places he seems to have given more specific signs. In Galilee he walked the very ways of earth; he spoke the language of mankind and died the death of all men. But to say this is not to say that God has absented himself entirely from the rest of the earth. Not at all! Wherever people have responded to truth as they believed it to be; wherever they have thirsted for goodness and beauty; wherever they have sacrificed themselves on behalf of another—there God has left his footprints.

Christianity is at the same time general and specific. It says in one breath, "There is salvation in no one else" (4:12), and in the next, God **did not leave himself without witness.** Both are true. When God is only the god of everything in general, he is likely to become the god of nothing in particular. When, on the other hand, God is only the god of something in particular, he is likely to become the god of nothing in general. According to the revelation of God in Christ, God is the creator and sustainer of the universe; he is the Father

15 And saying, Sirs, why do ye these
things? We also are men of like passions
with you, and preach unto you that ye
should turn from these vanities unto the
living God, which made heaven, and earth,
and the sea, and all things that are therein:
16 Who in times past suffered all nations
to walk in their own ways.
17 Nevertheless he left not himself without witness, in that he did good, and gave
us rain from heaven, and fruitful seasons,
filling our hearts with food and gladness.
18 And with these sayings scarce restrained they the people, that they had not
done sacrifice unto them.

titude, crying, 15 "Men, why are you doing
this? We also are men, of like nature with
you, and bring you good news, that you
should turn from these vain things to a living God who made the heaven and the
earth and the sea and all that is in them.
16 In past generations he allowed all the
nations to walk in their own ways; 17 yet he
did not leave himself without witness, for
he did good and gave you from heaven
rains and fruitful seasons, satisfying your
hearts with food and gladness." 18 With
these words they scarcely restrained the
people from offering sacrifice to them.

---

15. Of like nature (ὁμοιοπαθεῖς), or "of like feelings," perhaps in contrast to the "impassivity" (ἀπαθεία) conventionally attributed by the philosophers to the gods. **Turn from these vain things;** cf. I Thess. 1:9, "How you turned to God from idols, to serve a living and true God." **A living God,** or perhaps **the living God** (KJV), for with this phrase, a regular description in the O.T. of Yahweh, the definite article is regularly omitted, as also in I Thess. 1:9 quoted above.

16. He allowed: Hitherto God, because of their ignorance, had overlooked the sinfulness of **their own** idolatrous **ways.** The implication is that now, when they can no longer plead ignorance, their only hope is in repentance; cf. 17:30, "The times of ignorance God overlooked, but now he commands all men everywhere to repent"; and Rom. 3:25, "This was to show God's righteousness, because in his divine forbearance he had passed over former sins."

17. He did not leave himself without witness; cf. Paul's words in Rom. 1:20, "Ever since the creation of the world his invisible nature, namely, his eternal power and deity, has been clearly perceived in the things that have been made. So they are without excuse." The argument is admirably adapted to a Hellenistic-pagan audience.

---

of all mankind, regardless of whether men know and believe in him or not; he loves them all; and he has given them all some indication of his presence and power. Yet he has made himself known specifically in Jesus, and apart from that revelation there is no complete knowledge of the divine character and will. Christians can reasonably claim the priority of this revelation and of its central place in the human understanding of God. But Christians cannot reasonably claim that apart from the revelation of God in Christ there is no knowledge of God whatsoever. Friedrich von Hügel often referred to "the unincarnate Christ," and Christians cannot afford to forget the profound implications of that revealing phrase of a great interpreter.

This sermon is another instance of the fact that Paul always kept his congregation in mind. Without changing or diluting his message, he set it forth in terms which the circumstances of his listeners demanded. It is another warning to preachers who are tempted to preach on "The Lord is my shepherd" to people who have never seen a sheep, and who preach on the love of God in Jesus to people who have no God.

It is also another instance of the discouraging fact that the public is likely to prefer the demagogue who pretends to be God to the God who condescends to become man. It is the thirst for the spectacular and miraculous, which lies so deep in the nature of humanity that it is easily satisfied by every cheap and passing show of power. Paul was stoned and left for dead. It is interesting to speculate on how he would have been treated if he had accepted the honor of divinity which the people were eager to bestow upon him. And it is to his everlasting credit that he had both the wits and the grace to see clearly the vanity of any temporary advantage that such an honor might have given him, and to walk steadily in the footsteps of his Lord and Master who set aside his divine prerogatives that he might taste human life even to its dregs and die the death of man, even the death of the Cross.

19 ¶ And there came thither *certain*
Jews from Antioch and Iconium, who persuaded the people, and, having stoned Paul,
drew *him* out of the city, supposing he
had been dead.
20 Howbeit, as the disciples stood round
about him, he rose up, and came into the
city: and the next day he departed with
Barnabas to Derbe.
21 And when they had preached the gospel to that city, and had taught many, they
returned again to Lystra, and *to* Iconium,
and Antioch,

19 But Jews came there from Antioch
and I-co'ni-um; and having persuaded the
people, they stoned Paul and dragged him
out of the city, supposing that he was dead.
20 But when the disciples gathered about
him, he rose up and entered the city; and
on the next day he went on with Barnabas
to Der'be. 21 When they had preached the
gospel to that city and had made many
disciples, they returned to Lystra and to

---

d) Return to Antioch (14:19-28)

19. But Jews came: It has been suggested that this verse seems to continue the narrative of vs. 7, in which case the story about Lystra may have come from another source, possibly, as suggested above, from a special eyewitness account. Notice how, as elsewhere (e.g., 15:1), Luke ascribes Paul's troubles to Jews coming from a distance. **Stoned Paul:** The apostle recalls his experience in II Cor. 11:24-25, "At the hands of the Jews . . . once I was stoned," and in II Tim. 3:11, "What befell me at Antioch, at Iconium, and at Lystra, what persecutions I endured."

20. He rose up and entered the city: A miracle is not implied. Rather does the incident recall Jesus' escape at Nazareth (Luke 4:29-30). **Derbe** is the one place in Galatia at which it is nowhere stated that Paul met with any trouble.

21-28. These verses are considered by some scholars to be merely a vague editorial summary inserted to round off the narrative, and to bring Paul back to Antioch and finally to Jerusalem for a visit which is in fact the same visit as that already mentioned at 11:30. But of this there is no possible proof. Vague the narrative certainly is; and it is a little difficult to understand why the apostles at this point deliberately turned back

---

19. *Paul's Narrow Escape.*—They stoned Paul and dragged him out of the city, supposing that he was dead. There was every reason to believe that Paul was dead; the violence that had been done to him was enough to kill him; he looked dead. But in reality he was not; he was alive. First impressions are often wrong, and the judgments of common sense are frequently in error. For example, for centuries men believed that the earth was flat. It certainly looked flat; it felt flat; and it seemed to stand fixed and stationary like the top of a table. It finally appeared, however, that those first natural suppositions were wrong. The earth was not flat at all; it was round and mobile, revolving like a ball!

Judging by appearances, we might suppose that life began and ended with birth and death. We cannot see anything before or after; the cessation of breath in a man's body looks like the end of his existence. Yet in every age there have been men and women who came to see that their first impression was wrong; that their supposition about death was mistaken. When a man dies, it looks like the end of him, whereas in reality it is the beginning of a new chapter in his spiritual history.

When Mary Magdalene first saw Jesus on Easter morning, she supposed him to be the gardener (John 20:15). Certainly the gardener was the only one she would expect to find in the garden at that hour of the morning, and Jesus was the last one she would expect to find. He had been killed two days before and buried in a sealed tomb. It was only natural that Mary should mistakenly suppose him to be the gardener. But she was wrong! It was Jesus. Over and above the suppositions of our common sense there are the laws that are still wrapped in the midst of God's mysterious ways. A man is unwise, therefore, to count on his common sense alone, for too often in human experience that common sense has been mistaken and men have been shocked out of it into something that at first seemed incredible.

21-28. *Derbe and the Return Trip.*—In this brief account of the mission in Derbe and the return trip through the cities already visited there are two items in which there are real teaching possibilities.

22 Confirming the souls of the disciples, *and* exhorting them to continue in the faith, and that we must through much tribulation enter into the kingdom of God.

23 And when they had ordained them elders in every church, and had prayed with fasting, they commended them to the Lord, on whom they believed.

I-co'ni-um and to Antioch, 22 strengthening
the souls of the disciples, exhorting them
to continue in the faith, and saying that
through many tribulations we must enter
the kingdom of God. 23 And when they had
appointed elders for them in every church,
with prayer and fasting, they committed
them to the Lord in whom they believed.

---

to towns from which they had been expelled. One suggestion is that they may have reached Derbe late in the year and found the passes over the Taurus closed, and that they turned back on their tracks to fill in time. If so, when **they returned to Lystra and to Iconium and to Antioch,** they would probably revisit only actually Christian circles, and the significance of this second visit would be that for the first time little communities or churches of purely or chiefly Gentile Christians were being organized.

22. To continue in the faith, i.e., in "Christianity," a use very common in post-Apostolic Christian literature (cf. 13:8). The **tribulations** are those which are to precede the end (Rev. 1:9), and are identified with the apostles' present persecutions. **We must enter:** The "we" is merely a generalization and must not be taken as the mark of a we-passage or diary extract. The **kingdom of God** here seems to carry its eschatological meaning.

23. Appointed elders: The word "elder" (πρεσβύτερος) does not occur in the Pauline epistles except the Pastorals (I Tim. 5:17-19; Tit. 1:5); and in the light of Galatians in particular, which contains no hint of the existence of any formally appointed church "officers," it seems unlikely that at this time Paul gave his churches a fixed organization and regularly ordained "elders." Rather would he recognize the special respect with which certain of the senior members were regarded and exhort his converts in general "to

---

Through many tribulations we must enter the kingdom of God. Certainly Paul was the man who could speak from that avowal with authority. Since the day of his conversion, his life had been one tribulation after another. Everywhere he went he met opposition. The disciples distrusted him, the circumcision party undid his work wherever it could, John Mark deserted him, the people stoned him. If anybody ever knew what trouble was, Paul certainly knew. Yet he was the one who reassured his converts in Asia Minor that the only way to enter into the fullness of life is by way of trouble.

For one thing, trouble makes us conscious as nothing else ever does that we are dependent creatures. We are dependent upon powers outside ourselves from the beginning to the end, but so long as things go well there is the possibility that our real dependence may be hidden behind the screen of our apparent independence. But when trouble comes, we know exactly where we stand—that our own resources are not adequate, and that we rely constantly on the power of God. A severe illness, a serious shock, an overwhelming grief, a heartbreaking disappointment—to such troubles human beings are the natural heirs. It is not possible to circumvent them or completely avoid them. It is possible, however, to recognize the fact that by way of these very troubles men and women enter into the depths of life where, for the first time perhaps, they become conscious of the mighty undercurrent of which the waves on the surface are but the manifestation and evidence. When a person learns to rest upon the power of the undertow, he has begun to live in the kingdom of God. The kingdom of God is the rule of God; so long as a man thinks he is his own ruler, he is not entirely under God's rule; and there is nothing like trouble to show him who is the real ruler of his life.

Besides that, trouble draws us closer to other human beings as nothing else does. Look at a family that has been through serious troubles and you are more than likely to see a family bound together by ties that are stronger than they would be otherwise. Look at a nation that has been through great tribulation and you see a nation welded together in a unity of spirit of which the nation that knows nothing but prosperity has no conception. The individual who has been through long periods of trouble has an understanding of other people in their troubles that the person who has been spared never has. Since therefore the kingdom of God implies a social rather than a solitary existence, it is easy to see how through tribulations we

24 And after they had passed throughout Pisidia, they came to Pamphylia.
25 And when they had preached the
word in Perga, they went down into Attalia:

24 Then they passed through Pi-sid′i-a,
and came to Pam-phyl′i-a. 25 And when
they had spoken the word in Perga, they

---

be subject to such men" (I Cor. 16:16; cf. I Thess. 5:12-13). The word **appointed** (χειροτονήσαντες) means literally "chose by show of hands" and, strictly speaking, should imply some form of popular voting. But it had come to be used of choice in general without reference to the means (cf. 10:41, men "who were chosen by God"). The duties of such elders were probably at first very varied and would cover alike instruction, administration, and discipline, until finally they emerge—e.g., in the Pastoral epistles—as "presbyter-bishops." Since Paul regarded the church as the true "Israel of God," he may naturally have planned its embryonic organization on the lines of the Jewish church, in which case his elders would be broadly comparable with the "rulers" of the Jewish synagogues. The word elder is also commonly used to describe the third section (*zeqēnîm*) of councilors who, together with the high priests and scribes, composed the Sanhedrin—being, according to some authorities, the nonlegal members of that council. Finally, the same word seems to have been used in Asia Minor as a title for the officers of various guilds, and in Egypt for both civil and religious office-bearers (Deissmann, *Bible Studies*, pp. 154-57; 233-35). See also on 11:30. **The Lord** is here Jesus, rather than God.

25. Attalia was the chief port of Pamphylia.

---

may enter into that kingdom, for by suffering men grow closer and closer to their fellow men.

The second seminal phrase of this section is the last part of vs. 27: **When they arrived, they gathered the church together and declared all that God had done with them, and how he had opened a door of faith to the Gentiles.** The opening of a door is one of the most suggestive figures in the language. Wider horizons, broader vistas, greater visions, further possibilities, release from four walls, fresh air, new life—all these overtones hover around the opening of a door.

Notice first that Paul and Barnabas did not presume to claim that they themselves opened the door. They cleared away the clouds of ignorance and doubt, set forth the true as they had seen it in Jesus, and removed all unnecessary obstacles. In this particular case there was one serious obstacle that had to be removed, namely, the Jewish ceremonial law, and especially the requirement of circumcision for admission into the Christian fellowship. Paul recognized from the very beginning that the Jewish ceremonial law had been superseded by the revelation of God in Christ. He removed that obstacle at once. God then opened the door into faith. Such is the interpreter's role always.

There are two classes of serious obstacles that the modern interpreter must remove. The first is the intellectual obstacle. There are some unbelievers who will always be unbelievers on the ground of intellectual dissent. They are to be honored for their sincerity and independence of thought. There are other unbelievers, however, who are restrained from believing not by any legitimate intellectual obstacle, but by a misunderstanding of the issue, a false notion of what is meant by the terms used, or by a mistaken idea of what the Christian belief requires of them. For example, scores of students have said that they do not believe in the divinity of Christ. You then ask them what they mean by the divinity of Christ, or what they think the church means by it, and they proceed to set forth the doctrine in terms that they might have learned in the fifth grade in school. They are surprised when you say that no intelligent churchman is asked to believe that, and that Christian thought at its highest level, not on the level of popular belief, has never believed that. The interpreter's opportunity is to clear away the clouds of misunderstanding, to correct mistaken ideas, and to set forth the cardinal affirmation of the Christian church in such intelligible terms as to make it clearly visible to the student. If, after that has been done, the student decides against the Christian faith, that is a matter for his own conscience and private judgment. The chances are, however, that once the unnecessary obstacles have been removed, God will open a door into faith for him.

One of the ways by which interpreters most successfully bring about the opening of doors is the way of analogy, that is, to show "a correspondence between things unlike in themselves." A good analogy helps to reduce the

26 And thence sailed to Antioch, from whence they had been recommended to the grace of God for the work which they fulfilled.

27 And when they were come, and had gathered the church together, they rehearsed all that God had done with them, and how he had opened the door of faith unto the Gentiles.

28 And there they abode long time with the disciples.

went down to At-ta-li'a; 26 and from there
they sailed to Antioch, where they had been
commended to the grace of God for the
work which they had fulfilled. 27 And when
they arrived, they gathered the church together and declared all that God had done
with them, and how he had opened a door
of faith to the Gentiles. 28 And they remained no little time with the disciples.

27-28. Besides rounding off the account of the first tour, these verses are perhaps also an editorial summary marking the transition from the "Antioch" narrative of chs. 13–14 to the "Jerusalem" narrative of ch. 15.

---

scale of things to comprehensible limits without changing the nature of it. For instance, the doctrine of the Trinity is often rejected by people, not because they have carefully and accurately considered it and believe it not to be the true interpretation of the nature of God, but because they do not know what it really means; it is all confusion, like a landscape seen through a frosted windowpane. An analogy will often help to clarify the contour of the doctrine, even a simple one like this: An idea is conceived in the mind of a man. It germinates, begins to grow, spread, develop in all directions. It is an invisible, abstract thing; no one can measure it or take a picture of it. It spins around and around in the man's mind until finally he puts the idea down on paper. The invisible idea takes the form and substance of a book, something solid and concrete as stone. One might think that having reduced itself to the limitations of time and space, the idea had lost some of its original power. But such is not the case. Once the book is published, it passes from person to person, and the idea is communicated from mind to mind. In other words, the book has an influence. It becomes part of the life of people whom the author has never seen. Its influence may remain centuries after the author has died. Here, then, are three separate realities: an idea, a book, and the influence of the book. And yet they are not separate at all; they are inseparable. You cannot think of one without the other, and if you want to name the reality in its completeness, you have to say the idea-book-influence, these three, separate yet forever inseparable. So the creative power of God is invisible, like the wind or the current of a river. But it moves, like all invisible things, toward visibility, and finally takes substance in the person of Jesus of Nazareth. Far from being reduced by this act of concretion, from that point of visibility, the influence radiates in all directions, and the Spirit rests upon men and women of every generation, in every quarter of the globe. According to Christian belief, therefore, when we think of God, we cannot think of the creative power only, but of the created substance also, and the consequential influence. And when someone asks us which is more important, or which comes first, we cannot say, for the reality of God is nothing less than all three, Father, Son, and Holy Spirit.

An analogy such as this one will not convince the unbeliever who has carefully investigated the matter and whose judgment leads him in another direction, nor will it convince the unbeliever who sees the issue clearly but who does not wish to assume either the moral or spiritual responsibilities of accepting it. But for the person whose mind is in a state of innocent confusion, it may lead the way to the opening of a door into faith.

The other obstacle to be removed is more difficult to get at. It is the spiritual obstacle, the deep-seated fears which paralyze a man's spirit so that, though he would like to believe, he dare not. One of the basic human desires is the desire for safety. We are all surrounded by innumerable dangers, and we all defend ourselves against them as well as we can. We want to be safe from disease, so we have an annual examination at the doctor's. We want to be safe from financial worries, so we carry insurance and keep a large savings account. We want to be safe from loneliness, so we make ourselves attractive and cultivate our friends.

This desire for safety is a natural thing, but there is always the possibility that it may become an unnatural fear and be inverted into the dread of danger. In that case the things that are normally sought after as defenses against danger are clung to as though they were gods,

15 And certain men which came down from Judea taught the brethren, *and*

15 But some men came down from Judea and were teaching the breth-

B. The Controversy Concerning Gentile Freedom (15:1-41)

1. Trouble at Antioch and Jerusalem (15:1-5)

This chapter has raised more problems than any other in the book of Acts. Every kind of error and confusion has been attributed to the author, perhaps the least culpable being that he has misunderstood completely the nature of the dispute. Thus Kirsopp Lake writes: "Reading Acts xv as a connected narrative, and merely looking for the general meaning of the decrees, it is clear that the meaning of Luke was that they represent the minimum of the Law which was to be required from Gentile Christians in lieu of circumcision. . . . Closer investigation into the wording of the decrees . . . suggests that the decrees were concerned with the problem of social intercourse between Jews and Gentiles in the Christian Church, not with the problem of circumcision" (*Beginnings of Christianity* [London: Macmillan & Co., 1920-33], V, 204-5). But a study of the events leading up to the council, particularly in the light of what has been said about the probable order of events (see on 12:1 ff.), and the relation between the accounts of a conference at Jerusalem in Acts and Galatians respectively (see on 11:27-30), makes it clear that there were in fact *two* matters in dispute; and any obscurity in Luke's narrative is due to the fact that he does not strictly hold them apart. Before the council there had been two sets of developments:

(*a*) As recorded in 15:1-2, representatives of the ultra-Judaistic party, who insisted that the new Gentile converts should be circumcised before admission to the church, had arrived at Antioch from Jerusalem. Hitherto these converts had been treated in much the same way as were the so-called "God-fearing" Gentiles in the Jewish communities of the Dispersion: they were admitted to worship without being circumcised. In addition the Gentile Christians were being baptized, as also were Jewish proselytes. But this baptism was coming to be regarded as a complete substitute for circumcision, as Jewish proselyte-baptism was not. Not unnaturally the Judaistic party, whose members, in spite of Paul's bitterness, may have been quite sincere men, regarded this as an innovation that would denationalize the Jewish gospel, turn the Messiah into a non-Jewish "Savior" or *Kyrios,* and make salvation an individual matter instead of being the privilege of Israel. Hence their challenge: **Unless you are circumcised according to the custom of Moses, you cannot be saved.** On the basis of the South Galatian theory we may suppose that this trouble arose not only at Antioch but extended also to Paul's newly founded Galatian churches.

(*b*) As recorded in Gal. 2:11-14, and probably at approximately the same time, trouble had also arisen in Antioch concerning the question of social intercourse between Jewish and Gentile Christians, a related but essentially different problem. And it had been brought to a head by the inconsistency of Peter himself, who, before the arrival of the delegates from Jerusalem, "before certain men came from James, . . . ate with the

and the more firmly they are grasped, the less able they are to save us in case of danger. The insurance policy, for instance, which began as a normal protection for the future, becomes an idol for the present, and assumes a position of priority to which secondary things have no right, making the person who began as a normal human being wanting safety, a terror-stricken creature serving an insurance policy as though it were a god, and finding in the service no assurance of real safety.

Once again the interpreter's task is to remove the unnecessary obstacles. He can take away the fear of ill-health by showing that, sick or well, men can live useful lives. He can take away the fear of poverty by rerouting the confidence of a man so that it rests in God and not in any intermediate thing. One after another, as the obstacles are removed, self-concern being the source of them all, God opens a door into faith.

15:1-35. ***The Council of Jerusalem.***—The success of Paul and Barnabas in Asia Minor made it clear that Christianity could never be confined within the borders of Palestine and it raised the practical question: If Gentiles are

said, Except ye be circumcised after the manner of Moses, ye cannot be saved.

ren, "Unless you are circumcised according to the custom of Moses, you cannot be

Gentiles; but when they came he drew back and separated himself, fearing the circumcision party." (Gal. 2:12. Note that the identification of the visit of Gal. 2:1-10 with the "famine visit" of Acts 11:30 makes it possible to date Paul's dispute with Peter at Antioch [Gal. 2:11-14] *before* the council of Acts 15; as already noted, some of the scholars—e.g., Zahn, Turner—who identify the visit of Gal. 2 with the "council visit" feel that the trouble with Peter at Antioch must have taken place before it.) This was all the more serious because it was at the common meals that religious fellowship found its deepest expression. It meant the division of the church into two separate groups and rendered futile the vision of one universal church. True, the Judaizers may not have insisted on the Gentiles observing all the food laws, and to that extent could claim that they were not interfering with the liberty of Gentile Christians. But on these terms the only possible way to unity would have been for the Gentiles to come wholly into line, so that Paul was perfectly right in protesting that they were "compelling the Gentiles to live like Jews" (Gal. 2:14). Doubtless Paul's dispute with Peter, as well as the findings of the Judaistic delegation, was among the causes which led to the whole question of the development of Gentile Christianity being referred once again for decision to Jerusalem.

There were thus two issues on which a ruling was required: first, the necessity or otherwise of circumcision, or the question of the legitimacy of a purely Gentile Christianity. This had already been provisionally decided at the earlier conference of Acts 11:30 and Gal. 2:1-10, but was now raised again in an acute form. Second, there was the issue of "foods," or the question of unrestricted social intercourse between Jewish and Gentile Christians, and the abolition of all ritual restrictions between "clean" and "unclean." These two issues were separate, though of course closely related. It is salutary to remind ourselves that even today there are Christians, e.g., in a mixed white and colored community, who will freely admit the equality of their brethren "in Christ," and yet rigidly refuse social intercourse with them.

15:1. Some men: The Western text defines them as belonging to "those of the sect of the Pharisees who had believed," as in vs. 5. **Came down from Judea:** Whatever may be true of the account of the council, these introductory verses are evidently written from the point of view of Antioch. A Jerusalem source would have said, "went down to Antioch," and would have spoken of "**Jerusalem**" rather than "Judea." **The custom of Moses,** i.e., according to the requirements of the law.

to become Christians, must they first become Jews? In other words, must a man be circumcised before he is baptized? The question was not a new one; it had come up many times before, notably in the case of Cornelius (cf. chs. 10–11). But as so often happens, the church did not answer the question until it was forced to. The answer could no longer be postponed. The increasing number of Gentile converts under the leadership of Paul and Barnabas demanded an answer. Hence the council was called.

The leaders of the church must have been well aware of the fact that the question had dynamite in it. To an outsider the discussion may have looked like a dispute over relatively unimportant ceremonial practices. Baptism versus circumcision was a debate the outcome of which was doubtless a matter of indifference to the average intelligent citizen of the Roman Empire. But it was not so much the practice that mattered; it was the issue that was behind it. In its largest terms that issue was: Is Christianity a national religion or a universal one? Is its Jewish setting and frame a context apart from which it has neither meaning nor power, or is it a chrysalis which, once it has served its creative purpose, must be left behind in the interest of growth? If it is the latter, then the Jewish ceremonial law, having served its purpose, must be abandoned if the church is to fulfill its role as a world-wide religion. This issue has already been discussed at some length in the Expos. of chs. 10–11, but it will be worth our while to look a little more carefully at the debate and those who participated in it. The specific question has been answered, but the debate goes on from one generation to another, and in that debate we recognize many familiar features.

2 When therefore Paul and Barnabas had no small dissension and disputation with them, they determined that Paul and Barnabas, and certain other of them, should go up to Jerusalem unto the apostles and elders about this question.

3 And being brought on their way by the church, they passed through Phenice and Samaria, declaring the conversion of the Gentiles: and they caused great joy unto all the brethren.

4 And when they were come to Jerusalem, they were received of the church, and *of* the apostles and elders, and they declared all things that God had done with them.

5 But there rose up certain of the sect of the Pharisees which believed, saying, That is was needful to circumcise them, and to command *them* to keep the law of Moses.

saved." 2 And when Paul and Barnabas
had no small dissension and debate with
them, Paul and Barnabas and some of the
others were appointed to go up to Jerusalem to the apostles and the elders about
this question. 3 So, being sent on their way
by the church, they passed through both
Phoe-ni'ci-a and Sa-ma'ri-a, reporting the
conversion of the Gentiles, and they gave
great joy to all the brethren. 4 When they
came to Jerusalem, they were welcomed by
the church and the apostles and the elders,
and they declared all that God had done
with them. 5 But some believers who belonged to the party of the Pharisees rose
up, and said, "It is necessary to circumcise
them, and to charge them to keep the law
of Moses."

---

2. Were appointed: The Greek is "they appointed Paul and Barnabas . . . to go." But who did the appointing? Grammatically it is the delegation from Jerusalem. This, as in the case of Peter's visit to Samaria (8:14 ff.) and Barnabas' to Antioch (11:22 ff.), would imply that, at least in Luke's view, the church at Jerusalem still had the right of general oversight. But more probably the meaning is that the church at Antioch took the decision to send a deputation to Jerusalem—though even this would be an admission that the last word lay with the mother church. The Western text rewrites the verse to make it clear that it was the delegation from Jerusalem that took the initiative and to add color to the **dissension and debate:** "For Paul said that they should remain as they were . . . and was vehement to this effect. But those who had come from Jerusalem charged them, Paul and Barnabas and some others, to go up to the apostles and elders at Jerusalem to be judged before them." **Some of the others:** Those who think that this is the visit of Gal. 2 would include Titus (Gal. 2:1) who, curiously enough, though so prominent in the epistles, is never mentioned in Acts.

3. So (μὲν οὖν): The usual resumptive particle, perhaps here marking the transition from an Antioch to a Jerusalem narrative (cf. 16:5). **Phoenicia and Samaria** are assumed to possess Christian communities. Samaria was evangelized by Philip (8:4 ff.), but there is no word either in Acts or the epistles as to when converts were won in Tyre and Sidon.

5. Some believers . . . Pharisees: Presumably members of some right-wing section of the church that had sent the deputation to Antioch. But the demand for circumcision, introduced as if it had not been mentioned before, and the abrupt phrase **to circumcise them** without any antecedent to which the "them" refers, suggests again a transition to a new source. It is worth noting too that nothing is here said, as in vs. 1, about the

---

Like most general assemblies, the council was divided into conservatives, liberals, and those who stayed in the middle of the road. The leaders of the conservative group are not named, but let us not pass over their case too lightly. As we look back upon the scene, we are likely to think that there was nothing to say on the side of the conservatives. History has proved that they were mistaken. But there was, and there nearly always is in every debate, something to be said on the conservative side. In the first place the old, established ways of a community have a strong and valid claim upon it. The tried way is the best way until it is proved otherwise. When a system has prevailed for several centuries, it cannot be relegated to the scrap heap without considerable proof on the part of the innovators that it has a worthy

6 ¶ And the apostles and elders came together for to consider of this matter.

6 The apostles and the elders were gathered together to consider this matter.

necessity of circumcision for salvation. Is the argument this time that, if not for salvation, then to make social intercourse possible, the new converts must be circumcised? To explain the meaning of the word **them** some MSS insert in the previous verse words borrowed from 14:27, "And that he had opened a door of faith for the Gentiles." That heathen converts in general are to be circumcised is obviously the intention. Some scholars, identifying this conference with that of Galatians, think that the demand was that Paul's companions ("some of the others," vs. 2) should be circumcised, for Paul hints in Gal. 2:3 that pressure was put on him to circumcise Titus.

2. Council at Jerusalem (15:6-29)

The speeches which Luke puts upon the lips of the chief figures in the debate, whether or not they are an actual report, are admirably in character. Peter recalls his own experience with Cornelius, urges that God has manifestly given **them the Holy Spirit just as he did to us** and has **made no distinction between us and them,** and asks why they should be burdened with the yoke of observance which Jews themselves had found too heavy to bear. Paul and Barnabas bear witness to the evident blessing of God upon their own mission to the Gentiles. James makes a speech of characteristically Jewish flavor, pointing out that Peter's dealing with Cornelius was after all in keeping with the words of Scripture, and then as chairman of the conference gives his **judgment.** This consists of two parts, corresponding to the two problems which had been referred to the conference for settlement: (*a*) As to circumcision, his opinion is **that we should not trouble those of the Gentiles who turn to God** (vs. 19). On this primary issue the decision is definitely against the Judaizers. (*b*) As to the matter of social intercourse, the Gentiles are to be reminded that they are not the only section of the church that deserves consideration. There are still Jews loyal to the law of Moses whose consciences must be respected. Therefore the Gentiles too must be ready to make concessions. Accordingly certain supplementary injunctions are added, which Luke gives both at the close of James's speech (vs. 20), and also in the letter in which the "decrees" are embodied (vss. 28-29).

If Luke's account stood alone, the picture would now be reasonably clear. But nearly all discussion of the council and the decrees has been wont to start from the supposition, which we have rejected, that Gal. 2:1-10 gives a parallel account of the same council visit as that described in Acts 15. Scholars are thus involved in the almost impossible task of reconciling the two accounts. Our identification of the visit of Gal. 2 with the famine visit of Acts 11:30 has largely relieved us of these difficulties. But as this identification is not yet commonly accepted—indeed Hans Windisch dubs it "a clever and convenient exit" which he proceeds to "block" to his own satisfaction in a few sentences (*Beginnings of Christianity,* II, 321-22)—we must face the difficulties and see what alternative solutions there may be.

and more adequate successor. In the dispute which we are considering, the law of Moses had been the spiritual and moral pattern of the people for generations. It was both an ethical and a ceremonial law. Circumcision combined both elements, and was in a sense the cornerstone of the whole system. If circumcision went, the law would go too. The conservatives had the wits to see that. One leak in the dike is enough to destroy the whole thing. No wonder there were serious-minded people who thought twice before they were willing to approve of a move as radical as that. After all, the law of Moses had held the people together in spite of exile and foreign occupation. It had given them the character to resist the moral degeneracy that was all around them. It was their backbone, so to speak, and backbones are not to be removed, nor is it an easy thing to substitute one for another.

What a poor substitute for the law of Moses the love of Christ must have seemed to the leaders of the conservative party! The followers of Christ were just a handful of men and women

In comparing the accounts of Gal. 2 and Acts 15, on the supposition that they must refer to the same visit, certain general considerations may usefully be kept in mind: (*a*) The ease with which discrepancies arise in two parallel and perfectly sincere accounts of the same event. As Lake remarks: "Unless written records are preserved the most extraordinary discrepancies arise in an incredibly short time even among the most careful and trustworthy persons," and "there is no reason to suppose that either account is insincere" (*Beginnings of Christianity,* II, 154). (*b*) If Paul's testimony at first seems preferable as the firsthand account of one who took part, Luke's account, though later, is likely to be much less biased. Paul, indeed, as he writes Galatians is in the midst of a bitter controversy. The people whom Luke calls "some believers who belonged to the party of the Pharisees" (15:5) Paul castigates as "false brethren secretly brought in, who slipped in to spy out our freedom . . . that they might bring us into bondage" (Gal. 2:4). (*c*) Historical narratives will vary according as they are written subjectively or objectively. Luke looks back on events from outside and beyond them; he tells of what the church saw and heard, and puts on record its public deliberations and official decisions. Paul is concerned with the inner side of events, his own motives and emotions, particularly as they are related to his private consultations with the leaders of Jerusalem. Paul is concerned to stress his own independence; Luke to stress the unity which was eventually reached.

But even with these considerations in view, the discrepancies between the two accounts are so flagrant that one is almost compelled to question the historicity of Acts 15. (*a*) The whole setting of the two accounts is completely divergent. Galatians pictures a private discussion between leaders; Acts a public and formal debate with a judgment committed to writing and issued as an encyclical. No doubt a private discussion may have preceded the public debate, and Luke need not necessarily have mentioned it. But Paul could hardly have completely ignored the public discussion and written as if the private conference alone took place: for such is the only possible inference from his words, "privately before those who were of repute" (Gal. 2:2). (*b*) If Paul is indeed describing this conference (i.e., the council in Acts 15) to the Galatians, it is incredible that he should not refer to its main decision, which was to the effect that Gentiles need not be circumcised. According to Acts 15, what the council gave Paul was an authoritative ruling that though there were to be certain minimum requirements, Gentile Christians were exempt from the obligation to keep the great mass of the Jewish ceremonial law. Paul had only to quote the decision of the council to the Galatians in order to clinch his argument with the local Judaizers, who were themselves appealing to the authority of Jerusalem. (*c*) If what has just been said would show up Paul as a singularly ineffective controversialist, another consideration would show him up as hardly an honest one. If, when he writes, he has just been describing the proceedings of the council, how can he honestly ignore the restrictive clauses of the decrees, and state that the "only" obligation imposed was that "they would have us remember the poor" (Gal. 2:10)? On the

---

of whom no one had ever heard. To be sure, they were increasing in number every day, and while men like Paul and Barnabas had no prominence in the world, it was clear to the most casual observer that they were quite definitely men of parts. Nevertheless the way of Christ was new and untried, traveled by ardent but inexperienced men and women. What match was that for the well-worn, proved way of Moses? The burden of proof rested on the followers of the new way.

Not only was the way of Christ a new way, but to the worldly-wise elders who stood by the old way, it was a naïve way innocently trusting in the power of love and renouncing everything that was contrary to love. What chance did a religion like that have in a world in which men could behave like wild beasts? That was the question that must have been in the minds of the conservatives as they tried to see their way through this probem. Men, they argued, need law as well as love, and the law of Moses is the law of God. Let it go, and you leave the people with no moral backbone, like a building without a steel frame.

Furthermore, Jesus himself was circumcised. According to the account of the debate, no one brought it up but it would not have surprised us if they had. According to Matthew's Gospel, Jesus came to fulfill the law, not to destroy it.

supposition that the clauses refer to ceremonial restrictions, it would simply not be honest to suppress evidence telling against his own point of view. If on the other hand they refer to moral offenses, it would actually have been to Paul's advantage to quote them, as evidence that on the authority of those "who were reputed to be pillars" themselves (Gal. 2:9) emphasis was to be placed, not on ritual, but on fundamental ethical principle. It may be noticed in passing that a similar difficulty has been felt concerning Paul's silence about the decrees in I Corinthians, which on any reconstruction of events was written after the council. He is dealing with the question of "food offered to idols" (I Cor. 8:1 ff.; 10:25 ff.), and to quote the decrees might seem to strengthen his case. But the point at issue is quite different in the two letters. In I Corinthians it is the relationship between Gentile Christians and pagan society, not, as in Galatians, the imposition on Gentile Christians of Jewish obligations. In I Corinthians Paul's silence, though perhaps surprising, is at least understandable; in Galatians it is not.

The conclusion is that the visits of Gal. 2 and Acts 15 cannot be identified without laying Paul open to the charge of dishonesty, or Luke to the charge of ignorance of the facts, if not willful distortion of them. Failing the solution of identifying the visit of Gal. 2 with the famine visit of Acts 11:30 and antedating Galatians before the council, there seems no alternative to frankly admitting the discrepancies and confessing that here the narrative of Acts is quite unreliable. It then will be necessary to assume that what really happened is correctly narrated in Gal. 2:1-10. The account of Acts 15 is due to the author's misunderstanding. At a later date, after the writing of Galatians and I Corinthians, a second council was held and the decrees passed, as indicated by Acts 15. We are to suppose that our author, coming on the text of such decrees and being ignorant of its date, inserted it here at what seemed to him the most appropriate place. The truth is that the decrees were adopted only at a later date—probably when Paul was absent on his third missionary journey, for James mentions them to Paul, as if for the first time, on the return of the latter to Jerusalem (21:25). It is argued, by those who hold by the later date of Galatians, that this later passing of decrees restrictive of Gentile liberty was part of a reactionary Judaistic movement which expressed itself both in the trouble with Peter at Antioch and in the trouble with the Judaizers in the Galatian churches. Such a reconstruction is of course possible, and even plausible. But it is useless to deny that it seriously undermines confidence in the reliability of Acts, and renders the Lukan authorship very questionable. One may still prefer the "clever and convenient exit" afforded by the identification of the visit of Gal. 2 with that of 11:30; it is not necessary to consider that this way of escape from a maze of difficulties has yet been adequately "blocked"!

6. For the discrepancy (assuming that they refer to the same occasion) between the picture of a public "debate" (vs. 7) and the picture in Gal. 2 of a private discussion, see the note above. Those who wish to reconcile Acts and Galatians make vs. 6 refer to the private discussion with **the apostles and the elders,** and vss. 7 ff. to the public debate in the presence of "all the assembly" (vs. 12).

He came to point out the full meaning of it; not to relax it, but to raise its standards and to make it a part of the inner life of a man as well as a part of his daily routine. He attended the synagogue as long as he was allowed; he went to the temple when he arrived in Jerusalem; he took part in the Passover meal. Furthermore he was a product of the law of Moses. He came from a home where that law was the law of life. Behind him were the priests and prophets who had enriched the law by the travail of their soul. You can no more uproot Jesus from the soil of his Jewish ancestry than you can uproot a flower from the soil and expect it to live. So the conservatives might well have argued.

It is enough to point out that in the everlasting struggle between the conservative and the liberal the truth is never all on one side. We are likely to dismiss the case of the conservative as reactionary, interested only in preserving the *status quo,* the enemy of progress, the exponent of the small and narrow. Often it is just that. But on other occasions the conservative has a real contribution to make; he forces the innovator to think twice before he throws away something which he thinks he has outgrown.

7 And when there had been much disputing, Peter rose up, and said unto them, Men *and* brethren, ye know how that a good while ago God made choice among us, that the Gentiles by my mouth should hear the word of the gospel, and believe.

8 And God, which knoweth the hearts, bare them witness, giving them the Holy Ghost, even as *he did* unto us;

9 And put no difference between us and them, purifying their hearts by faith.

10 Now therefore why tempt ye God, to put a yoke upon the neck of the disciples, which neither our fathers nor we were able to bear?

11 But we believe that through the grace of the Lord Jesus Christ we shall be saved, even as they.

7 And after there had been much debate,
Peter rose and said to them, "Brethren, you
know that in the early days God made
choice among you, that by my mouth the
Gentiles should hear the word of the gospel
and believe. 8 And God who knows the
heart bore witness to them, giving them the
Holy Spirit just as he did to us; 9 and he
made no distinction between us and them,
but cleansed their hearts by faith. 10 Now
therefore why do you make trial of God by
putting a yoke upon the neck of the disciples which neither our fathers nor we have
been able to bear? 11 But we believe that
we shall be saved through the grace of the
Lord Jesus, just as they will."

7-9. God made choice among you (ἐν ὑμῖν): Or possibly—by a Semitic construction paralleled in the Greek of I Sam. 16:9; Neh. 9:7—"made choice of you, that by my mouth"; i.e., the church is God's chosen instrument; Peter, the church's agent. If Gal. 2:1-10 really refers to the same occasion, it is very odd that there Paul particularly stresses the fact that "Peter had been entrusted with the gospel to the circumcised" (Gal. 2:7), not to **the Gentiles.** If we read "made choice of you," then the words **in the early days** might refer back to Luke 24:47-48. More probably Peter's conversion of Cornelius is in view, for vss. 8-9 clearly refer to that incident, and there are several verbal echoes of chs. 10 and 11—cf. vs. 8 with 11:17 ("God gave the same gift to them as he gave to us") and the use of the verbs καθαρίζειν (**cleansed**) in 10:15 and 11:9; and διακρίνειν (**made no distinction**) in 11:12 (where see Exeg.); 10:20; 11:2—the only passages in Acts where these verbs occur except the present verses. God is called one **who knows the heart** also in 1:24, again in a speech by Peter.

10-11. Though it is put on the lips of Peter, this passage has a true Pauline ring—more so perhaps than any other in Acts. The suggestion that the law is something **which neither our fathers nor we have been able to bear** recalls such passages as Gal. 5:1-3, where Paul warns his readers not to "submit again to a yoke of slavery" and argues that in effect it is impossible for any man "to keep the whole law."

To **make trial of God** means to stretch God's patience to the breaking point, to act contrary to his will and so **tempt** him to vengeance (cf. I Cor. 10:9, "We must not put the Lord to the test, as some of them did and were destroyed"). The Jews commonly used the word **yoke** in the sense of "obligation" and spoke, e.g., of "the yoke of the commandments" or "the yoke of the kingdom of heaven." To many, no doubt, the observance of the law must have been a real burden; but it is equally true that many, like the psalmist, found in it their "delight." Paul in this respect cannot be considered a typical Jew.

The liberal side of the case was ably presented by Peter. Peter's record as far as this particular issue was concerned was not altogether clean. Just as you would expect, Peter's heart was usually in the right place. It does not surprise us to find him the spokesman for the liberal case, even though we know that he did not always succeed in practicing the principles which he believed. In Paul's letter to the Galatians he tells of Peter's disappointing behavior in Antioch. At first Peter did not hesitate to eat with Gentile Christians; as usual, his impulse was a good one, and he acted upon it, generously and wholeheartedly. But when the representatives of the circumcision party arrived from Jerusalem, Peter "drew back and separated himself, fearing the circumcision party" (Gal. 2:12). Paul was not the kind of a person to

12 ¶ Then all the multitude kept silence, and gave audience to Barnabas and Paul, declaring what miracles and wonders God had wrought among the Gentiles by them.

13 ¶ And after they had held their peace, James answered, saying, Men *and* brethren, hearken unto me:

14 Simeon hath declared how God at the first did visit the Gentiles, to take out of them a people for his name.

15 And to this agree the words of the prophets; as it is written,

16 After this I will return, and will build again the tabernacle of David, which is fallen down; and I will build again the ruins thereof, and I will set it up:

17 That the residue of men might seek after the Lord, and all the Gentiles, upon whom my name is called, saith the Lord, who doeth all these things.

18 Known unto God are all his works from the beginning of the world.

12 And all the assembly kept silence; and
they listened to Barnabas and Paul as they
related what signs and wonders God had
done through them among the Gentiles.
13 After they finished speaking, James replied, "Brethren, listen to me. 14 Symeon
has related how God first visited the Gentiles, to take out of them a people for his
name. 15 And with this the words of the
prophets agree, as it is written,

16 'After this I will return,
and I will rebuild the dwelling of David, which has fallen;
I will rebuild its ruins,
and I will set it up,
17 that the rest of men may seek the Lord,
and all the Gentiles who are called by my name,
18 says the Lord, who has made these things known from of old.'

We believe that we shall be saved through the grace of the Lord Jesus. These words again have a Pauline flavor; but the salvation in view is the eschatological salvation of Jewish expectation, rather than the Pauline idea of present salvation "in Christ" through faith. **Just as they will** is ambiguous and might refer either to the Gentiles or to **our fathers.** But the argument is clear enough: both Jew and Gentile are to be saved, not by submitting to the **yoke,** but through **grace.**

12-14. Barnabas and Paul: The former again taking precedence, perhaps as being more influential at Jerusalem. **James** is, of course, "the Lord's brother" (see on 12:17; 21:18). **Symeon,** the Jewish spelling of "Simon," is used of Peter elsewhere only in II Pet. 1:1 (in Codex Sinaiticus and other uncials), and is in keeping with the marked Jewish flavor which Luke characteristically gives to the whole of James's speech. **Has related how** (καθώς, not ὡς): More exactly, "has given a report, as if God . . . ," which would read like a cautious admission on James's part that appearances supported Peter's contention. But possibly this is to overstress strict grammar. James, perhaps significantly, makes no reference to Barnabas' and Paul's report. **Visited:** A word commonly used by Luke of God's providential action (Luke 1:68, 78; 7:16).

15-18. The prophets: Again the Book of the Twelve (minor) Prophets. The quotation is from the Greek of Amos 9:11-12, and its whole point depends upon the variations from the original Hebrew in the LXX which reads **that the rest of men may seek the Lord** in place of the Hebrew "that they may possess the remnant of Edom" (Amos

let a thing like that pass unnoticed. In the presence of them all he said to Peter, "If you, though a Jew, live like a Gentile and not like a Jew, how can you compel the Gentiles to live like Jews?" (Gal. 2:14.) It may well have been Paul's rebuff that prepared and strengthened Peter for the test the next time it came.

How many liberals there are like Peter! Their hearts are in the right place; their intentions are good; they believe the right thing. But when the opposition appears, they disappear in a cloud of subservient acquiescence. It is easy to be a liberal in politics so long as you travel in liberal company, but when you stand a lone liberal in the midst of rabid conservatives, then how easily the pious, conservative platitudes slip off the tongue! Human beings want to be thought well of. It is hard for a man to take the disapproval of his friends or his community. He will do almost anything to win their good

19 Wherefore my sentence is, that we trouble not them, which from among the Gentiles are turned to God:

20 But that we write unto them, that they abstain from pollutions of idols, and *from* fornication, and *from* things strangled, and *from* blood.

19 Therefore my judgment is that we should not trouble those of the Gentiles who turn to God, 20 but should write to them to abstain from the pollutions of idols and from unchastity and from what is

9:12), and so changes a promise that Israel shall possess her inheritance into a prophecy of the conversion of the Gentiles. It must be confessed that a Hebrew Christian like James is not likely thus to have quoted the LXX in defiance of the Hebrew, and still less likely to have chosen an interpretation of Scripture that runs contrary to his original prejudices. But the LXX version suits our author's point of view, and to him rather than to James the details of the speech must almost certainly be ascribed.

19. My judgment is: Almost "I decree," as if James, as president of the council, is giving a personal decision on his own recognized authority. James was obviously at the moment the predominant personality at Jerusalem. **Should not trouble:** Or perhaps, bringing out more accurately the present infinitive in the Greek, "should stop troubling," i.e., insisting that the Jewish law with regard to proselytes, in particular circumcision, should be enforced.

20. Pollutions of idols are defined in vs. 29 as "what has been sacrificed to idols," which makes it likely that a food restriction rather than idolatry in general is in view. Even meat offered publicly for sale had often been previously consecrated at some heathen temple. It was also a common custom to issue invitations to dinner in a temple, the conventional fiction being that the god himself was the host. **Unchastity:** This may mean either sexual vice in general or the licensed prostitution of heathen cults. **What is strangled,** if retained in the text (see next paragraph), refers in fact to the same food restriction as does **blood.** The meat of animals killed by strangling, considered a delicacy in pagan society, would contain the blood which, in accordance with the principle that "the life is in the blood," was strictly prohibited to Jews (cf. Gen. 9:5; Lev. 3:17; etc.; Deut. 12:16, 23-25).

The exact meaning of these prohibitions has been much debated. There are three possibilities: (*a*) The best Greek MSS, followed by our translations, give four prohibitions; in that case the decrees must be regarded as dealing mainly with prohibitions for Christians of particular kinds of "unclean" food forbidden to Jews. The difficulty is the inclusion of "unchastity" in a set of regulations dealing with food. (*b*) Various Western authorities (Codex Bezae, Latin versions, and such fathers as Irenaeus, Cyprian, Tertullian) omit "what is strangled," so that we have a three-clause decree which can be interpreted as a prohibition against three typical sins—idolatry, fornication, and murder ("blood"). In favor of the originality of this reading it is argued that the omission of "what is strangled," if it was in the original text, is difficult to explain, whereas it might easily have been added as an explanation by a scribe who took "blood" to refer to the prohibition against eating meat with the blood in it, as was the case when animals were killed by strangling. The Western text also adds the words, "And whatever you do not wish to happen to yourselves, do not to another." This is hardly likely to

will; he will even go so far at times as to betray the thing he believes and the person he loves. Liberals, beware! Remember Peter.

Fortunately Peter learned his lesson, and according to the account in the Acts, came out for the liberal position in the council of Jerusalem. He could not forget his experience with Cornelius. He saw then and there that Christianity was a far-reaching religion. He had the insight to perceive its universal nature, even though he did not always have the courage to admit it in public. Neither did he forget his encounter with Paul, the outspoken and fearless one. So by the time the Jerusalem council met, he was ready to stand up in public and say that God gives the Holy Spirit to the Gentiles just as he gives it to the Jews, and that no unnecessary obstacles should be placed in the

21 For Moses of old time hath in every city them that preach him, being read in the synagogues every sabbath day.

strangled[m] and from blood. 21 For from early generations Moses has had in every city those who preach him, for he is read every sabbath in the synagogues."

[m] Other early authorities omit *and from what is strangled.*

---

be original, for Tertullian did not read it, but it at least shows that the Western scribes regarded the decrees as dealing with moral rather than with ceremonial prohibitions. Against the originality of the three-clause version it may be argued that the scribe responsible for the Western text was perplexed by the inclusion of "unchastity" in a set of prohibitions dealing presumably with a compromise on the food question. He therefore omitted "what is strangled" and reduced the decrees to a three-clause injunction against crimes of ordinary morality, adding the negative version of the Golden Rule to make his meaning clear. (*c*) The three-clause version might be interpreted as an injunction to avoid heathen worship in its most characteristic features—idolatry, temple prostitution, and the blood baths of the mystery cults.

On the whole it seems rather unlikely that the council thought it necessary to impress upon Gentile Christians, as the condition of free social intercourse with Jewish Christians, the abstention from such obvious sins against Christian morality as idolatry, unchastity, and murder, or from the more blatant forms of heathen worship. In any case "to abstain from blood" is a curious equivalent for "thou shalt not kill." In view of what has been said about the matters under discussion at the council it seems most probable that the decrees, whether in three or four clauses, enjoined abstention from the forms of unclean food most offensive to Jewish scruples—food which had been offered to idols, and the flesh of strangled animals which therefore still contained the blood—and added a reference to "unchastity" as the sin to which former pagans were particularly prone. The decision taken at the council was a compromise. Gentile Christians are to be exempt from circumcision; but for the sake of Jews living among them they too must be prepared to make concessions and abstain from offensive practices, if Gentile and Jew are to enjoy full social intercourse together in a united church.

21. For . . . Moses . . . is read, i.e., the Jewish law is still dear and familiar **in every city,** even in largely Gentile communities, and therefore the majority must make concessions to the scruples of the minority. This seems a much better meaning than to paraphrase: "The claims of Moses are sufficiently safeguarded by the publicity that he receives in the synagogue; therefore there is no need to demand circumcision of the Gentiles." Alternatively we might paraphrase: "From the first God intended, through the teaching of Moses, ultimately to call even the Gentiles to himself, as is prophesied by Amos; and in proof of this is the fact that men **preach him** not only in Jerusalem, the ancient 'dwelling of David' [vs. 16], but **in every city.**"

---

way of the Gentiles who wish to become Christians. As usual, Peter came out on the right side and the Master's confidence in him was not misplaced.

If the truth were known, however, it was not so much the argument of Peter that carried the convention as it was the report of Paul and Barnabas. They did not argue at all; they simply told what had happened as they preached the gospel to the people in Asia Minor. One can imagine how the people at the council began to sit up and take notice as the talk shifted from theoretical and abstract considerations to the vivid accounts of the two men who watched God work miracles through the preaching of the gospel and bring to life those who had long since given up all hope of life. It was as if they had said: "This matter is not simply a matter for you to sit here and discuss in the way you would discuss a mathematical formula. This is a matter of life and death. It is something that is taking place in the lives of human beings. It must be given the freedom to grow. You cannot hamstring it with your ceremonial laws, however useful they once were. This is the life of God come to dwell among us. It is free, like a gift, and it is for all!"

As a matter of fact they did not say even that much. Their story told the tale. In most great movements the events, not the debates, swing

22 Then pleased it the apostles and elders, with the whole church, to send chosen men of their own company to Antioch with Paul and Barnabas; *namely*, Judas surnamed Barsabas, and Silas, chief men among the brethren:

23 And they wrote *letters* by them after this manner; The apostles and elders and brethren *send* greeting unto the brethren which are of the Gentiles in Antioch and Syria and Cilicia:

22 Then it seemed good to the apostles
and the elders, with the whole church, to
choose men from among them and send
them to Antioch with Paul and Barnabas.
They sent Judas called Bar′sab-bas, and
Silas, leading men among the brethren,
23 with the following letter: "The brethren,
both the apostles and the elders, to the
brethren who are of the Gentiles in Antioch

---

22. **It seemed good** (ἔδοξε), "it was voted"—the Greek word being that regularly used for taking a decision in assembly. **Judas called Barsabbas** was presumably a brother of "Joseph called Barsabbas" (1:23), if Barsabbas is a patronymic; but it may mean merely "born on the Sabbath." He probably represented the Judaistic section of the conference. **Silas,** whose name in the epistles is Grecized as Silvanus (I Thess. 1:1; II Thess. 1:1; II Cor. 1:19; I Pet. 5:12), later became Paul's companion, and would be a Hellenist; he was, like Paul, a Roman citizen (16:37).

23. **With the following letter,** literally "writing by their hand," i.e., sending the letter by their hand. The fact that Luke restates the decrees in the form of a letter has made them more suspect than ever in the eyes of the critics who regard the letter as being entirely of Luke's own composition. Contemporary writers were certainly in the habit of inventing letters, just as they did speeches, to set forth the views of their heroes. Dionysius of Halicarnassus, for example, in his study of Thucydides, treats the famous letter of Nicias as though it were one of the speeches and the creation of Thucydides himself (*On Thucydides* 42). The letter here is certainly "Lukan" in style. But some such "encyclical" may well have been actually issued and, whether or not Luke possessed a copy of the text, in a matter of such importance it seems likely that he would follow the outline of the original. **The brethren** is to be connected with **both the apostles and the elders,** not taken with the latter alone, as in the alternative translation "the apostles and the elder brethren" (ERV). If it is asked why the letter is addressed only to **Antioch and Syria and Cilicia,** and not, e.g., to Galatia, where the controversy had been raging, the reply is that the debate had arisen on a report from Antioch "about this question" (vs. 2). In any case Paul himself delivered the decrees in Galatia (16:4).

---

the vote one way or another. Arguments for or against church unity, for example, are not likely to sway the minds or emotions of delegates to a convention, but put before those delegates stories of Christians who have scrapped their differences, combined their efforts, and united in one strong fellowship, and there is a chance that you will win them to your side. Laws and decrees more often than not sanction and systematize something that already exists. It was the fact that God was already at work among the Gentiles that finally determined the decision of the council.

As it often happens, the decision was a compromise. It represented the point of view of those who were in the middle of the road. No one was better suited to express that point of view than James. He was a conservative by nature, but he had a fair and open mind. He and Gamaliel would have understood each other. Neither of them was willing to sponsor unreservedly a new idea, but neither of them wanted to kill it. They were both willing to give it a chance. Many a new movement has been saved by conservatives who have judicious minds. Their sense of fairness saves them from being reactionaries. They would never be the spur or the spirit of a movement, but they might well make it possible for the movement to get under way.

The positive point that Paul gained as a result of the council was that circumcision was not to be required of Gentiles. To that extent the verdict was a victory for the liberals. But the Jews were not exempt from circumcision, and the Gentiles were required to observe the minimum moral law, or to keep the food laws of Judaism out of respect for the feelings of the Jews who might be associated with them. Whether it was a moral or a ceremonial law

24 Forasmuch as we have heard, that certain which went out from us have troubled you with words, subverting your souls, saying, *Ye must* be circumcised, and keep the law; to whom we gave no *such* commandment:

25 It seemed good unto us, being assembled with one accord, to send chosen men unto you with our beloved Barnabas and Paul,

26 Men that have hazarded their lives for the name of our Lord Jesus Christ.

27 We have sent therefore Judas and Silas, who shall also tell *you* the same things by mouth.

and Syria and Ci-li'cia, greeting. 24 Since
we have heard that some persons from us
have troubled you with words, unsettling
your minds, although we gave them no instructions, 25 it has seemed good to us in
assembly to choose men and send them to
you with our beloved Barnabas and Paul,
26 men who have risked their lives for the
sake of our Lord Jesus Christ. 27 We have
therefore sent Judas and Silas, who themselves will tell you the same things by

26. Men who have risked their lives: Or "who have devoted their lives," as translated by Lake and Cadbury, who comment: "The English rendering 'hazarded' for παραδεδωκόσι is indefensible; it means 'given up,' not 'risked'" (*Beginnings of Christianity,* IV, 180). We may compare Gal. 2:20, "The Son of God, who loved me and gave himself for me." Critics who question whether Paul had any part in the issuing of the decrees think that these words referred in the original to Judas and Silas, and that the mention of Barnabas and Paul both in vs. 25 and in vs. 22 is an addition by the editor, who attributed to this council decrees which were really issued on a later occasion. "The recommendation that these are men who hazarded their lives for the name of the Lord Jesus Christ is superfluous in the case of the two who were well known in Antioch, but necessary in the case of Judas and Silas who were unknown there and to whom the recommendation referred in the text of the source" (Weiss, *History of Primitive Christianity* [ed. F. C. Grant; New York: Wilson-Erickson, 1937], I, 262-63).

which they were required to obey depends upon the interpretation which one places upon vss. 23-29. Whichever it may be, the important thing to remember is that the decree was a compromise. History usually moves that way. Conventions and councils lag behind the march of events. This particular council did not declare itself decisively in favor of Paul's point of view. It was enough, however, that they let Paul go ahead. It was his mind that had grasped the immensity of the gospel; he had seen the far-reaching implications of the death and resurrection of Jesus; he had discerned in that life the outpouring of the love of God which eventually would break down every barrier that man had erected between himself and his fellow man and which would wipe out social, racial, and economic differences and distinctions between man and man. The wonder is not that the others did not see it; the wonder is that Paul, with his Jewish background, saw it so completely and so soon! And the glory of it is that the council of the church, while it was not prepared to go as far as Paul went, nevertheless put no insuperable obstacles in his way.

Over and over again the church has had to face the same kind of question. In its simplest terms it is a question of deciding what is essential and what is not, what is the frame and what is the picture, what is the *esse* and what is the *bene esse.* For example, the church's doctrine was originally set in the framework of Ptolemaic astronomy. Along came Copernicus and Galileo, who completely turned things inside out. They put the sun in the center of the universe and retired the earth to an insignificant place among larger and more important planets. At first the church felt that it must keep the old framework; that the Christian picture of life could not exist in a Copernican frame. But fortunately there were some, like Paul, who saw that the astronomical frame was not really a part of the picture itself, and that in fairness to fact the church would have to let the old frame go. So the doctrine of the church was reset in the magnificent and starry grandeur of a Copernican universe. The same thing happened when Darwin told the world about evolution. Here was a new and different time scale, an account of slow growth and development that seemed to make nonsense out of Genesis. There were many conservatives in the church, and there still are, who believed that the framework of Genesis was so much a part of

28 For it seemed good to the Holy Ghost, and to us, to lay upon you no greater burden than these necessary things;

29 That ye abstain from meats offered to idols, and from blood, and from things strangled, and from fornication: from which if ye keep yourselves, ye shall do well. Fare ye well.

30 So when they were dismissed, they came to Antioch: and when they had gathered the multitude together, they delivered the epistle:

31 *Which* when they had read, they rejoiced for the consolation.

32 And Judas and Silas, being prophets also themselves, exhorted the brethren with many words, and confirmed *them.*

word of mouth. 28 For it has seemed good
to the Holy Spirit and to us to lay upon
you no greater burden than these necessary things: 29 that you abstain from what
has been sacrificed to idols and from blood
and from what is strangled[m] and from unchastity. If you keep yourselves from these,
you will do well. Farewell."
30 So when they were sent off, they went
down to Antioch; and having gathered the
congregation together, they delivered the
letter. 31 And when they read it, they rejoiced at the exhortation. 32 And Judas
and Silas, who were themselves prophets,
exhorted the brethren with many words

[m] Other early authorities omit *and from what is strangled.*

---

28. To the Holy Spirit and to us, i.e., the decisions have been inspired by the Spirit (cf. 5:32, "We are witnesses to these things, and so is the Holy Spirit"). **To lay upon you no greater burden:** If Rev. 2:24 ("I do not lay upon you any other burden") is a quotation of this, it may confirm the existence of an actual written encyclical which was widely current; for the author of Revelation is hardly likely to be quoting Acts.

29. You will do well, i.e., either "act rightly," or alternatively "prosper." Εὖ πράττειν is a common closing salutation in the papyri letters. The Western text has the interesting addition, "being carried along by the Holy Spirit."

3. Paul and Barnabas at Antioch (15:30-41)

30-32. They went down to Antioch: The delegation which in vs. 2 had been appointed to go to Jerusalem now returns to report, strengthened by the addition to their number of **Judas and Silas** as delegates from Jerusalem sent expressly to confirm the report of Paul and Barnabas.

---

the real picture that if it were once lost, the picture would soon fade away. But, again, there were enough people like Peter and Paul to see that the Genesis story was a frame and not the picture itself, and that in the interest of truth and growth the church would have to set the doctrine of creation in a new frame. It was not long before most people saw that nothing essential had been lost, and more and more were willing to admit that something had been gained.

The issue is most likely to be raised again over the question of orders in the ministry of the church. Everyone is prepared to acknowledge the fact that the division of the church is a scandal. Most churchmen are frank to admit that the church would be stronger and more effective if it were united. But when actual steps toward reunion are suggested, the same fundamental question comes up: what can we change or let go, and what must we keep? There is always a circumcision party that wants to keep something which, if kept, will obstruct the way of growth. Most are willing to agree that we must keep the Scriptures, the faith of the classic creeds, and the two major sacraments, and on these matters there is likely to be a large amount of agreement and common consent. But when it comes to the ministry, that is another question, and that is the rift which is now largely responsible for keeping churches apart from each other. The question will sometime have to be faced: Is a particular order of the ministry an essential part of the gospel which therefore cannot be altered or given up without betraying the church and its Lord, or is it one of the things that as circumstances change and new demands are made upon the church may conceivably be changed or let go altogether? Those who believe that there can be no real church apart from the historic episcopate are the conservatives; it is possible that in an earlier age they would have said that there can be no real Christian without circumcision. Those, on the other hand, who say that the historic episcopate is one of the things that

33 And after they had tarried *there* a
space, they were let go in peace from the
brethren unto the apostles.
34 Notwithstanding it pleased Silas to
abide there still.
35 Paul also and Barnabas continued in
Antioch, teaching and preaching the word
of the Lord, with many others also.
36 ¶ And some days after, Paul said
unto Barnabas, Let us go again and visit
our brethren in every city where we have
preached the word of the Lord, *and see*
how they do.
37 And Barnabas determined to take
with them John, whose surname was Mark.
38 But Paul thought not good to take
him with them, who departed from them
from Pamphylia, and went not with them
to the work.

and strengthened them. 33 And after they
had spent some time, they were sent off
in peace by the brethren to those who had
sent them.[n] 35 But Paul and Barnabas remained in Antioch, teaching and preaching the word of the Lord, with many others
also.
36 And after some days Paul said to
Barnabas, "Come, let us return and visit
the brethren in every city where we proclaimed the word of the Lord, and see how
they are." 37 And Barnabas wanted to take
with them John called Mark. 38 But Paul
thought best not to take with them one
who had withdrawn from them in Pam-
phyl'i-a, and had not gone with them to

[n] Other ancient authorities insert verse 34, *But it seemed good to Silas to remain there.*

---

33. They were sent off: But in vs. 40 Silas is back in Antioch; to explain this the Western text adds: "Silas decided to stay there, and Judas went alone." Hence vs. 34 in KJV.

35. A vague conclusion, perhaps marking the end of one or other of the Aramaic sources which have been used for the first half of Acts. It is noticeable that from this point onward there are few if any examples of Aramaism in the language or of apparent mistranslation from an original Aramaic source.

36. The paragraph beginning with this verse describes the preparations at Antioch for the "second missionary journey," which started as a revisitation of places formerly evangelized, with the purpose probably both of announcing the decrees and also of following up the Galatian epistle—if this, as we have suggested, was written before the council. The real forward movement begins at 16:6, though one gets the impression that from the first a wider mission is in view.

37-38. To take with them . . . not to take with them. There is an interesting variation in the tense of the Greek verb twice here used; in the first instance it is an aorist, in the second a present infinitive. "Barnabas, with easy forgetfulness of risk, wishes συνπαραλαβεῖν Mark—Paul refuses συνπαραλαμβάνειν, to have with them day by day one who had shown himself unreliable" (J. H. Moulton, *Grammar of New Testament Greek* [Edinburgh: T. & T. Clark, 1906], I, 130. Quoted in *Beginnings of Christianity,* II, 40). **Who had withdrawn:** See on 13:13.

---

may be adapted to meet the present demands of the will of God, and that it is possible to conceive that in the future it may be superseded by some other system of ministry and government which more nearly matches the needs of the church, will be the liberals. The general assemblies of the church will probably steer somewhere between those two views and make a compromise statement which, while it dares no bold advance, may nevertheless open the way for some Charles Brent or William Temple who, making the most of the opening, will take a long step forward, with which in due course the councils of the church will catch up.

Paul and Barnabas left the convention feeling just the way we do when we leave our conventions. How slowly they seem to move! How they seem to resist the Holy Spirit! How afraid they are to take a brave, daring stand! And yet looking back on them all, beginning with this one in Jerusalem, we see that God moves slowly but surely through their cautious and often clumsy movements.

36-41. Paul Goes Back to Asia Minor.—Like every good pastor, Paul wanted to go back over the ground which he had already covered. **Come, let us return and visit the brethren in every city where we proclaimed the word of the Lord,** said Paul to Barnabas. Farmers know that you cannot plant seeds and then forget

39 And the contention was so sharp between them, that they departed asunder one from the other: and so Barnabas took Mark, and sailed unto Cyprus;

40 And Paul chose Silas, and departed, being recommended by the brethren unto the grace of God.

41 And he went through Syria and Cilicia, confirming the churches.

the work. 39 And there arose a sharp contention, so that they separated from each
other; Barnabas took Mark with him and
sailed away to Cyprus, 40 but Paul chose
Silas and departed, being commended by
the brethren to the grace of the Lord.
41 And he went through Syria and Ci-li'cia,
strengthening the churches.

---

39. A sharp contention: Though Luke puts down Paul's estrangement from Barnabas to disagreement concerning Mark, it is certain that the cause must have lain deeper. Their mutual confidence had already been strained by the incident at Antioch when Paul clashed with Peter and "the circumcision party" and "even Barnabas was carried away by their insincerity" (Gal. 2:11-13). His language shows clearly how bitterly Paul felt this defection. The incident proves that Barnabas was not wholly won to Paul's position; and at this juncture he still perhaps felt it imprudent to offend the Jerusalem church by identifying himself unreservedly with Paul's fresh plans for founding Gentile churches wholly emancipated from Jewish legal obligations. It is quite likely that Luke may have glossed over the deeper cause of the break by giving undue prominence to Mark. But that the difference of opinion came to a head at this moment can hardly be doubted. There is no evidence that Paul and Barnabas ever met again, and Barnabas is not mentioned again in Acts. But the bitter feeling evidently did not last. Paul later twice mentions Barnabas, though with no particular warmth (I Cor. 9:6; Col. 4:10), and seems to have regarded Mark with affection (II Tim. 4:11). Indeed the very fact that Mark was welcomed later into Paul's entourage suggests that he was not really the cause of the trouble with Barnabas. **To Cyprus,** which was Barnabas' own country and in the evangelization of which he had shown a special interest (cf. 13:4 ff.).

40. Paul chose Silas, who was with him as far as Corinth and is mentioned along with Timothy at the beginning of both the Thessalonian letters. In I Pet. 5:12 he appears as coauthor with Peter of the epistle.

41. Syria and Cilicia: Though we are told nothing in detail about the founding of Christian churches in these districts, vs. 23 implies their existence, and they may have owed their birth to Paul's work in the period referred to in Gal. 1:21. **Strengthening the churches:** The Western text adds, "and delivering the commands of the elders," evidently to stress the fact that Paul proclaimed the apostolic decrees. But these had already been sent to the district in writing (vs. 23). It is interesting to note that according to Luke, the "second journey" and the "third journey" both alike began with a short preliminary tour of confirmation (see 18:18-23).

---

them; parents know that you cannot have children and then ignore them; doctors know that you cannot have patients and never see them; good pastors know that you cannot convert a man and then let him drift. The follow-up is perhaps even more important than the original contact. Paul wanted to follow up what he had done; he wanted to see "how they are doing." People do not spring into spiritual maturity overnight. Once the seed is planted it must be cultivated; once the life is undertaken it must be encouraged, confirmed, and trained. The faithful pastor, like Paul, goes back again and again to see how his people are doing. Sometimes they are not doing so well and they need his guidance or his warning; sometimes they are doing well and they need his friendly interest in their well-being and happiness. Above all they need to be reminded that the Christian life is not something that can be developed in a two-year course and then dropped. It is something that a person must go over again and again; going back over the same questions, the same affirmations, he can grow in stature and in spiritual wisdom.

The return was a sad one for Paul in one sense, for he went without Barnabas. They disagreed about John Mark, who had left them on the first trip and gone back home. Barnabas characteristically wanted to give him another chance, but Paul was convinced that they needed a man made of finer material. So Bar-

16 Then came he to Derbe and Lystra: and, behold, a certain disciple was there, named Timotheus, the son of a cer-

16 And he came also to Der'be and to Lystra. A disciple was there, named

C. Mission of Paul to Europe (16:1–18:17)

Paul is now launched on what is generally known as his "second missionary journey" though, as we have already noted, it is not clear that Luke intended to divide Paul's travels formally into three parts. Usually the "second" tour is considered to end with the summary account of a journey to Syria in 18:22. But there is no clear dividing line at that point, as there is here at the beginning of the second journey; and the remaining period of missionary travel, right up to the return to Caesarea and the decision to go up to Jerusalem at 21:14, is treated by our author as a single unit, perhaps based on some continuous source. This mission work is centered mainly on two points, Corinth and Ephesus, and its sphere is Greece in the wider sense of the term—first European Greece ("Macedonia" and "Achaia") and then Middle-Eastern Greece ("Asia").

1. Through Galatia and Asia (16:1-10)

Paul's route would lead direct from Cilicia over the Taurus pass through the so-called "Cilician Gates" into the "Galatian" portion of Lycaonia, his eastern limit on the first tour, and would then follow his former route in the reverse direction through **Derbe, Lystra,** Iconium, Pisidian Antioch. The last two are not mentioned but are probably included in **the region of Phrygia and Galatia** (vs. 6). The brevity of the notice of Paul's second visit to Galatia reminds us that Luke is much more interested in the pioneering work that led to the foundation of new churches than in their subsequent development (cf. the similarly brief reference to Paul's final visit to Achaia in 20:2-3).

a) Timothy Joins the Apostle (16:1-5)

The one incident of importance in Galatia was the circumcision of **Timothy,** and great difficulty has been felt at the apparent inconsistency on the part of Paul. The matter is of real importance, as Luke could not fail to know whether his traveling companion Timothy had been circumcised, and if this report of his circumcision is held to be false, the hypothesis of Lukan authorship falls with it. On the other hand it seems very hard to reconcile such an action with Paul's attitude at the council and with the principles

nabas went off to Cyprus with John Mark, and Paul went his own way northward with Silas. One of the saddest spectacles in life is to see great pairs break up. It is never safe to make a final judgment upon the merits of either party concerned. One hesitates to blame either Paul or Barnabas in this particular case, but one cannot refrain from regretting that two men who worked so well together should have been separated in an atmosphere of irritation, or from recalling the fact that there is no human being, no matter how great his stature may be, in whom there is not a flaw to remind him of his imperfect nature. Paul must not have been an easy person to get along with. Few geniuses are. The standard that he set for himself was so high that others less spiritually agile than himself must have found it indeed hard to attain. It is, however, from such implacable human standards of value that the best work proceeds, and the men who expect the most of us, even more than we feel at the time they have the right or the reason to expect, are the ones which later on we may recognize to have drawn us to our greatest heights.

16:1-5. ***Paul Takes Timothy with Him.***—Paul needed an assistant. Even more than that, he needed a companion. No man is entirely self-sufficient, and the greater the man, the more he needs someone with whom he can share the heights and depths of his experience. Paul had found such a man in Barnabas, and now that Barnabas was no longer with him, he selected a young man named Timothy. He lived in Lystra, and Paul undoubtedly met him when he was there the first time; now he met him again. He was in every way an outstanding young man, well suited for the enviable place which he was about to take by the side of Paul.

Piecing together the references to Timothy in other books of the N.T. we have a sufficient picture of Timothy as a young man. He had in the first place the advantage of a good background. Paul knew his grandmother, Lois, and

tain woman, which was a Jewess, and believed; but his father *was* a Greek:

Timothy, the son of a Jewish woman who was a believer; but his father was a Greek.

which he lays down so trenchantly in Galatians. Moreover if Timothy had a pious Jewish mother and grandmother (II Tim. 1:5), it is difficult to believe that Paul would insist on what they had considered unnecessary. Nor can it be denied that there is no time in Paul's career when he would be less likely to circumcise a Gentile convert. The controversy at Antioch and Jerusalem was in the recent past; Paul at the moment must have been peculiarly sensitive on this matter, and much on his guard against any action that might seem to stultify the victory he had won for Gentile freedom; at that very moment Paul was engaged in delivering to the churches **for observance the decisions which had been reached . . . at Jerusalem**; and, above all, Timothy was a Galatian, a member of the very community to which Paul had written, "If you receive circumcision, Christ will be of no advantage to you" (Gal. 5:2). The whole incident has accordingly been dismissed by radical critics as a Judaizing "tendency-tradition" designed to counterbalance Paul's refusal to have Titus circumcised (Gal. 2:3). Less drastically it is suggested that Timothy may have been one of Paul's original converts during his first Galatian mission, that he had been subsequently circumcised at the instigation of Judaizers, and that tradition later grew up that he had received circumcision at Paul's own hands (so A. C. McGiffert, *History of Christianity in the Apostolic Age,* p. 234). On the other hand it may be reasonably urged that Timothy's case is hardly on a par with that of Titus, whose circumcision, if as many hold it did in fact take place, would be much harder to justify. Though Timothy's father was a Gentile, his mother was a Jew. In his case the question of expediency undoubtedly came into consideration. To circumcise him would greatly increase his usefulness to Paul, for it would disarm suspicion among the Jews in the new districts which he was planning to visit. Moreover we have several hints in his letters that Paul would not have considered such action culpably inconsistent if he felt that it would contribute to the success of his gospel. In view of the peculiarly difficult situation that Paul had to face during a time of transition from Jewish to Gentile Christianity, it is impossible to maintain dogmatically that under no circumstances could he have circumcised a half-Jew. We cannot expect rigid consistency from one who could write: "To the Jews I became as a Jew, in order to win Jews; to those under the law I became as one under the law. . . . I have become all things to all men, that I might by all means save some" (I Cor. 9:20, 22).

16:1. There: Where? At Lystra or at Derbe? Traditionally Timothy has always been held to have been a native of Lystra, but an attempt has been made to deduce from 20:4

his mother, Eunice. They were both women in whom religion was a natural and spontaneous thing. From his Greek father Timothy inherited the Greek love of knowledge and beauty, and that, added to the strong Hebrew strain of faith which came from his mother's side of the family, gave him a rich heritage. He was brought up on the Hebrew scriptures (II Tim. 3:15) so that the O.T. was in his blood. He was young (I Tim. 4:12) and had all the enthusiasm of a man who has not been soured by life. He was not only a friend, companion, and assistant to Paul, he was like a son (I Tim. 1:2). Paul took a great interest in him and showered his affection upon him. Apparently Timothy never disappointed him, for he was with him to the end, and there is not the slightest sign of anything but great happiness in the relationship. Some of the great relationships in a man's life are like this one, an older man bound to a younger one by the ties of affection and unselfish interest.

It is an interesting commentary on Paul that he circumcised Timothy before he took him on his missionary tour. A smaller man might have made the most of his victory in Jerusalem and used this situation to flaunt his victory before his opponents. Not so, Paul. He knew that Timothy, who was half Greek, would be in constant contact with Jews. To be circumcised would avoid a great deal of trouble and open for him a great many doors that otherwise would remain closed. A mature person is a person who knows when to stand for a principle and when to compromise. Paul never gave any better indication of his maturity than when he circumcised Timothy. What a great lesson young clergymen might learn from Paul on

2 Which was well reported of by the brethren that were at Lystra and Iconium.

3 Him would Paul have to go forth with him; and took and circumcised him because of the Jews which were in those quarters: for they knew all that his father was a Greek.

4 And as they went through the cities, they delivered them the decrees for to keep, that were ordained of the apostles and elders which were at Jerusalem.

5 And so were the churches established in the faith, and increased in number daily.

6 Now when they had gone throughout Phrygia and the region of Galatia, and were

2 He was well spoken of by the brethren
at Lystra and I-co'ni-um. 3 Paul wanted
Timothy to accompany him; and he took
him and circumcised him because of the
Jews that were in those places, for they
all knew that his father was a Greek. 4 As
they went on their way through the cities,
they delivered to them for observance the
decisions which had been reached by the
apostles and elders who were at Jerusalem.
5 So the churches were strengthened in
the faith, and they increased in numbers
daily.

6 And they went through the region of

(see Exeg.) that he may have belonged to Derbe. **Timothy** is from this point Paul's constant companion, though at the moment he appears to be junior to Silas. There is, however, nothing in Acts or the genuine Pauline epistles (e.g., I Cor. 16:10-11; Phil. 2:22) to indicate for certain that Timothy was a young man—an inference drawn from the Pastoral epistles (I Tim. 4:12), from which also we learn that his mother's name was Eunice and his grandmother's Lois (II Tim. 1:5). Though their names are Greek, they had probably both been Jews by religion. Timothy is associated with Paul in the opening verses of I and II Thessalonians, II Corinthians, Philippians, Colossians, Philemon.

4. The decisions (RSV) or **the decrees** (KJV): The Greek word is the same that is used in Luke 2:1 and Acts 17:7 of an official enactment by the emperor.

5. So: Again the usual particle (cf. 15:3) marking the end of a section and the transition to a new subject, in this case the wider mission to Macedonia and Achaia. If the journey source proper begins at vs. 6, we ought perhaps to consider 15:36 (or vs. 30?)–16:5 as a piece of editorial "connecting narrative" with which our author links up the two halves of the book.

b) To Troas (16:6-10)

The next few verses seem designed to show how "the Apostles, guided in surprising ways by signs from above and contrary to their own plans, conducted no mission at that

---

this particular point. How many congregations are ruined because ardent young clergymen stand for a principle when, without compromising the ultimate principle, they might yield to the natural and well-meaning dispositions of the people! Nothing is worse than a minister who never stands for anything—nothing worse, except one who stands for something with such stubbornness and lack of imagination that he brings down the whole house upon the head and shoulders of himself and his congregation. Like most great men, the older Paul grew, the more sensitive he became to the feelings of others and the more tolerant he became of their eccentricities. The fanatical zeal that he had in the beginning mellowed into strong and affectionate love in his maturity. The change was largely if not entirely due to the gradual molding of his life by the crucified Companion with whom he continually dwelt.

To come back to Timothy, we find in him a man competent in every way for the Christian ministry. He was endowed with extraordinary gifts. Apparently he used those gifts generously and wisely. And yet in spite of all his talents, he did not leave any great mark upon the church of his day. If it were not for his association with Paul, his name would be virtually lost in the Christian memory. He represents thousands of able men and women who leave no particular mark upon the records of their generation, and yet are the very strength and enduring character of their age. It is the destiny of some to play conspicuous parts in the history of their time, and of others to play parts equally important but less spectacular. Timothy played that latter part.

6-10. ***Paul Goes Through Asia to Macedonia.*** —Our chief interest in this passage is not geographical but theological. It is made clear by

forbidden of the Holy Ghost to preach the word in Asia,

Phryg'i-a and Galatia, having been forbidden by the Holy Spirit to speak the word

time in Asia Minor, but were driven on to Troas and beyond into Europe itself" (Weiss, *History of Primitive Christianity,* I, 279-80). Luke's language is somewhat obscure and the route which he indicates somewhat uncertain, but his intention clearly is to explain why it was that the missionaries instead of taking, as might have been expected, the great road through the Lycus and Meander valley past Colossae and Laodicea to Ephesus, by-passed these centers and embarked upon a mission to Europe. The sequence of events seems to have been this: (*a*) Paul had planned to **speak the word in Asia,** but had **been forbidden by the Holy Spirit** to do so. (*b*) He therefore **went through the region of Phrygia and Galatia** till he came **opposite Mysia.** (*c*) His revised plan had then been **to go into Bithynia,** but again **the Spirit of Jesus did not allow them.** (*d*) Accordingly, once more changing their plans, **passing by Mysia, they went down to Troas.** For understanding the route the key words are **they went through the region of Phrygia and Galatia.** On the North Galatian theory this was supposed to refer to separate regions: first, "Phrygia," i.e., the region of which Antioch and Iconium were the chief towns (see on 14:6), and second, "Galatia," which was thought to mean northern Celtic Galatia proper (see on 13:13–14:28). On this view Paul was supposed to have made a great detour into the far northeast and to have founded churches, perhaps at Pessinus, Ancyra, and Tavium. But there is no ground whatever for inserting at this point a visit to northern Galatia, which would have taken Paul far out of his way, and for which no adequate motive can be adduced. Even the proponents of the North Galatian theory admit that it is strange Luke gives no account of the foundation of these "northern" churches. Maurice Goguel explains his silence as due to a deliberate omission of material in his source because he did not wish "to mention the churches of Galatia which in the sequel had been the occasion for Paul of such cruel disillusion"; and Luke "was in a hurry to arrive at the evangelization of Macedonia, which appeared to him to be the principal object of the tour" (*Introduction au N.T.,* III, 261). The feebleness of such arguments needs no comment! It is much more satisfactory to regard "the region of Phrygia and Galatia" as a composite expression referring to a single district—that part of the Roman province of "Galatia" which was still popularly known as "Phrygian." Paul's route thus becomes reasonably clear. As it had become apparent, either through divinely given intuition, or advice which was considered inspired, or the force of circumstances, that meanwhile there were insuperable obstacles in the way of a mission to Asia, Paul turned north through Galatic-Phrygia and so onward till he arrived **opposite Mysia,** perhaps at Kotiaion or Dorylaion. Here he contemplated a sally into Bithynia, a Greek-speaking district which may well have seemed a promising field. Possibly he was aiming in particular at the important town of Nicomedia. But once more **the Spirit of Jesus did not allow them,** and accordingly they turned west and made their way down to the sea at Troas through wild, unfrequented territory where the traveler again would doubtless be "in danger from rivers, danger from robbers, . . . danger in the wilderness" (II Cor. 11:26). The obstructing cause in each case was probably the Jewish opposition, already experienced in Galatia, which spread from town to town and shut the door against Paul everywhere. It is curious that Paul experienced such difficulty in planting the first seeds of Christianity in Asia. Certainly he wrote a letter to Colossae, and perhaps one to Laodicea; but even these communities, it seems, he reckons among those "who have not seen my face" (Col. 2:1). It seems likely, then, that even while he was working at Ephesus, Paul's personal influence did not extend very far afield. The only natural explanation would seem to be the inveterate prejudice raised against him in the Asian Jewish communities by the situation reflected in the Galatian epistle (see also on 19:1-41).

6. The region of Phrygia and Galatia (τὴν Φρυγίαν καὶ Γαλατικὴν χώραν): The Greek is grammatically awkward, and it is not clear whether Φρυγίαν is a substantive or an adjective. The parallel in 18:23, where the order of the words is reversed, favors the

7 After they were come to Mysia, they assayed to go into Bithynia: but the Spirit suffered them not.

in Asia. 7 And when they had come opposite My'si-a, they attempted to go into Bi-
thyn'i-a, but the Spirit of Jesus did not

view that it is a substantive ("Phrygia and the Galatian territory"), but grammatically an adjective would be less awkward ("the Phrygian and Galatian territory"). In either case the phrase is a composite description of a single district. According to Ramsay, **region** (χώραν) is the word officially used to describe the *regiones* into which a Roman province was divided. Part of the old kingdom of Phrygia belonged to the province of Galatia and part to the province of Asia; and the two parts would be known as the *regiones* of *Phrygia Galatica* and *Phrygia Asiana* respectively. The supporters of the North Galatian theory interpret otherwise and find here—in the mention of "the Galatian territory"—a possible point at which to fit in a visit to northern Galatia proper.

Having been forbidden by the Holy Spirit: The aorist tense of the participle indicates that the prohibition was laid upon them *before* they went through the "Phrygian-Galatic" territory, rather than that the obstacle developed after they had left. This would suggest that the guidance of the Spirit was recognized in their experience at Lystra and Iconium, perhaps in renewed Jewish opposition. Luke feels that at all the great turning points of Paul's career he received divine guidance "by revelation" (Gal. 2:2) either through direct vision or through the inspired insight of others (cf. 9:3-5; 11:28; 13:2; 16:9; 19:21; 21:11; 22:17-21; 23:11).

Asia regularly means the Roman province of Asia, consisting originally of Mysia, Lydia, and perhaps Caria. In 116 B.C. part of the ancient Phrygia had been added. But perhaps here the word is used in the narrower sense of the Greek cities of the Aegean coast with their hinterland.

7. Bithynia included the whole of the coastal regions lying north and east along the Propontis and the Black Sea. When Pliny wrote as governor in A.D. 112, Christianity had

three specific statements that Paul's travels were guided by God. The Holy Spirit stopped him from preaching in Asia, the "Spirit of Jesus" prevented him from going into Bithynia, and a "man of Macedonia" in a vision called him to Greece. Paul was not traveling for pleasure or for profit; he was traveling as an ambassador of God. It is not surprising, then, that he turned to God for directions and that he took for granted a divine strategy of which his travels were but a single episode. The guidance apparently took different forms and shapes; the Holy Spirit, the Spirit of Jesus, and the vision of a man. In how literal a fashion Paul himself thought of these directions from God, no one can now know. Whether they were objective experiences by which the Spirit communicated with Paul, or whether the experiences as they are described in the Acts are imaginative and pictorial ways of dramatizing the habitual response of a God-centered mind to the total situation in which opportunity and responsibility meet to do God's will, we cannot say with any certainty. In the light of what we know about the period in general and about Paul in particular, it is safe to assume that what went on inside Paul's consciousness was at least to some extent and in some way incited by events which took place outside his consciousness.

The subject of guidance is one upon which the expositor may well linger. The rank and file of the people do not expect to be guided by God, and groups that have taken guidance most seriously have often reduced it to absurdity and made God in the likeness of a messenger boy to tell us what to do next. The result is that guidance is either discarded as a superstition or scorned as a fad of religious adolescents. A clear and intelligible exposition of the guidance of God is therefore in order.

The belief that God guides us rests upon the assurance that God has an all-embracing plan by which and according to which he guides us. That is what theology means by providence. It is somewhere between fatalism on the one hand and accidentalism on the other. Fatalism says that everything is arranged and planned beforehand. Accidentalism says that nothing is arranged beforehand. Belief in providence says that there is a grand strategy within which there is room for personal freedom and response.

There are three things worth pointing out about this providence of God:

(*a*) The providence of God is flexible enough to include free men. God does not plan what time you get up in the morning or what you put on. He leaves as much as possible to you. Neither does he plan directly for a long spell

8 And they passing by Mysia came down to Troas.

9 And a vision appeared to Paul in the night; There stood a man of Macedonia, and prayed him, saying, Come over into Macedonia, and help us.

allow them; 8 so, passing by My'si-a, they
went down to Tro'as. 9 And a vision appeared to Paul in the night: a man of
Mac-e-do'ni-a was standing beseeching
him and saying, "Come over to Mac-e-

---

already become widespread throughout the province. **The Spirit of Jesus** is the reading of the best MSS. It is an expression not found elsewhere in the N.T. But cf. II Cor. 3:17. Does Luke imply that Paul had a vision of Jesus, as in 23:11?

8. Passing by Mysia: This was the northwestern part of the province of Asia. To reach Troas, Paul would need to pass through it; but he would be "passing by" it in the sense that he did not attempt to "speak the word" in it. **Troas** was a relatively modern city, founded by the successors of Alexander the Great, near the site of ancient "Troy," and had been raised to the rank of a Roman colony. It enjoyed special imperial favor because the Julian family boasted their descent from Iulus the son of Aeneas.

9. A man of Macedonia: How did Paul know that the man was a Macedonian? Because of his request? Or because he recognized him as one with whom he was already familiar? W. M. Ramsay (*St. Paul the Traveller and the Roman Citizen* [London: Hodder & Stoughton, 1896], 200 ff.) attractively conjectures that the man of the vision was Luke himself. He thinks that Luke may have been a native of Philippi, that he met Paul at Troas and instilled into his mind the idea of a mission to Macedonia. But there is no other evidence that Luke belonged to Philippi (but see on 20:5).

---

of illness. He lets some things work themselves out and take their own course. His plan is more like the over-all plan of a parent. A good parent plans for the development of his child. When the child breaks his toy, the parent does not deliberately plan the catastrophe, but because his plan for the child includes a training in handling the losses of life, he therefore exposes the child to the normal risks of existence and lets the toy break, even though momentarily it looks as though the child's heart would break too. God's plan for us is not like an iron glove which he forces upon every hand, upon the sensitive fingers of the artist, as well as upon the strong hands of the workman. His plan is flexible enough to bring out what is most native to each of us. What we do plays a large part in the success of the plan.

(*b*) The providence of God is forceful enough to preclude the possibility of ultimate failure. God's plan has many setbacks, but he never gives it up. Sometimes he can recover it by using the scraps that men and women leave behind, their blunders, their stakes, and their crosses. A foolish family feud like the one in the story of Joseph he can use to carry his purpose forward (Gen. 45). An exile, an imprisonment, a dark night, a miserable failure—all these things he can rearrange and weave back into the pattern. And when persuasion fails, he can use pressure. Human life, according to his plan, must be community life. Society must provide employment for all men. When wealth is so tied up that a large proportion of the people have no work, pressure is brought to bear and men go back to work, even though it may be in a munitions factory. God did not deliberately bring about the war, but he can use its scrap material to carry out his grand strategy.

(*c*) The purpose of the providence of God is to preserve life, not only to preserve the length of life but the quality of it and the richness of it. The purpose does not always make itself plain from day to day. Things often happen which seem to have no point whatever and to contribute nothing to the total plan and purpose of a man's life. But it must always be remembered that there is more to come, that the story is not yet over, that there is another chapter. No one would assume that there is no point to the plot of a novel while he is still in the middle of it. In the same way one cannot say that any single event in his life is purposeless. The truth is that the purpose will be revealed later on. On Good Friday the Cross must have seemed to be the most purposeless event in the history of mankind. Only after the story of redeemed humanity developed, only in the succeeding chapters, did the purpose begin to reveal itself. As time went on it became more and more evident that in the Cross, as in no other event, God went before us to preserve life. It is therefore in retrospect that a man is most often likely to see the purpose of God made unmistakably plain in a pattern which gradually emerges out of the events of his existence.

For example, a young man studying for the

10 And after he had seen the vision, immediately we endeavored to go into Macedonia, assuredly gathering that the Lord had called us for to preach the gospel unto them.

11 Therefore loosing from Troas, we came with a straight course to Samothracia, and the next *day* to Neapolis;

do'ni-a and help us." 10 And when he had seen the vision, immediately we sought to go on into Mac-e-do'ni-a, concluding that God had called us to preach the gospel to them.

11 Setting sail therefore from Tro'as, we made a direct voyage to Sam'o-thrace, and

---

10. We sought to go: Whether or not Luke first joined Paul at this point, this is the first instance of the use of the first person plural, and this first "we" section extends to vs. 17, though Luke, if he is the diarist, possibly remained with Paul at least until vs. 40, if not throughout the journey. Admittedly the limits of these "we" sections are vague.

2. In Macedonia (16:11–17:15)

a) Philippi (16:11-40)

Paul's missionary strategy is shown by the fact that the first place at which he makes a halt in his new field is again, like Pisidian Antioch, a Roman military colony. Whether or not it was his own city, Luke seems to feel a personal interest and pride in **Philippi**

---

ministry was dangerously ill for a year. At the time the illness seemed to be nothing but a miserable interruption and hindrance to the main purpose of his life. After many years in the ministry, however, in retrospect the period of illness was recognized for what it really was —a valuable part of the man's preparation for the pastoral ministry of the church.

Once a man is convinced that there is a divine plan which in turn is the expression of the divine will, and to which he can make an intelligent response, it is then possible to show him in what different ways God guides him to the fulfillment of that plan and will. The manner of the guidance will be different under different circumstances and in the lives of different people.

Whatever the will of God may be, it is not anything that can be communicated by any automatic device or magical means. Christians cannot go to any sacred book and, opening it at random, put their finger upon a sentence and say, "That is the will of God for me." They cannot go to an oracle and expect to receive a direct message from God. They cannot rely upon horoscopes or ouija boards or automatic writers and expect to be given explicit directions from on high. It is not so easy as that! Their knowledge of the will of God will be found somewhere in their interpretation of the events of history, illuminated by God's revelation of himself in the prime event of history, and perceived by the inspired mind and spirit of man.

Here, for example, is the way in which Abraham Lincoln tried to discover the will of God in history. A delegation of clergymen visited Lincoln and talked to him about the Emancipation Proclamation which he signed a week later. In response to their remarks Lincoln made the following reply:

> The subject is one upon which I have thought much for weeks past, and I may even say for months. I am approached with the most opposite opinions and advice, and that by religious men who are equally certain that they represent the divine will. I am sure that either the one or the other class is mistaken in the belief, and perhaps in some respects both. I hope it will not be irreverent for me to say that if it is probable that God would reveal His will to others on a point so connected with my duty, it might be supposed He would reveal it directly to me; for, unless I am more deceived in myself than I often am, it is my earnest desire to know the will of Providence in this matter. And if I can learn what it is, I will do it.
>
> These are not, however, the days of miracles, and I suppose it will be granted that I am not to expect a direct revelation. I must study the plain physical facts of the case, ascertain what is possible, and learn what appears to be wise and right. The subject is difficult, and good men do not agree.[5]

In an article on the Oxford Group Henry P. Van Dusen defined guidance in the following words, "An eager mind, purified by rigorous religious discipline, relaxed yet alert, expectantly open to the most delicate suggestion of the highest." [6] Victor Hugo wrote, "God makes visible to men his will in events, an obscure text written in a mysterious language."

11-40. ***Paul's Ministry in Philippi.***—Two women have prominent places in Paul's min-

[5] *The Practical Cogitator*, ed. Charles P. Curtis and Ferris Greenslet (Boston: Houghton Mifflin Co., 1945), pp. 499-500. Used by permission.

[6] "The Oxford Group Movement," *Atlantic Monthly*, CLIV (1934), 250.

which he styles **the leading city of the district of Macedonia.** Thessalonica was the official capital of the province as a whole, and Amphipolis was at least of equal importance in the neighboring district. But Philippi had a prestige that was all its own. Originally an insignificant town called Krenides, it had been fortified by Philip of Macedon and given his name. After the defeat of Brutus and Cassius in 42 B.C. it was again enlarged and was given the status of a **colony** by Augustus with the title of *Colonia Augusta Iulia Philippensium.* Whatever may be the exact meaning of Luke's description of it as **the leading city** (for which see note below), Philippi evidently gave itself airs. It had organized itself as a miniature Rome. Its magistrates, like those of Rome, styled themselves, not *duoviri,* but *praetores* (see vs. 22), and like Roman magistrates were accompanied by "police" or more literally "lictors." In a word Philippi aped the imperial city!

(1) The Church Is Established (16:11-15)

From Acts one would gather that Paul's stay at Philippi was comparatively brief. Yet he remained long enough to lay the foundation of a strong church, which he always regarded with peculiar affection, and which remained unwaveringly loyal to its founder (Phil. 1:3-5). From Philippi alone did Paul consent to receive financial aid (Phil. 4:10, 15; II Cor. 11:8-9). No other epistle is so filled with expressions of joy as is that to the Philippians. There is no evidence in the letter that Paul was ever troubled at Philippi by Jewish hostility. Indeed Luke gives us the impression that it was as "Jews" that the missionaries were assailed at the instigation of the heathen population (vss. 17, 20). The letter gives no sign that the church suffered from the machinations of Judaizers. Any divisions that Paul deprecates are due, not to doctrinal, but to personal differences (Phil. 2:2 ff.). So far as false doctrine was concerned, the danger was not from Judaistic but from antinomian tendencies—very natural among heathen converts (Phil. 3:18-19). The church's freedom from Jewish opposition was due perhaps to the Jews' small numbers and influence. But as the Thessalonian church enjoyed the same immunity—not, it is true, on the occasion of Paul's first visit, but in its subsequent history, so far as we can gather from the epistles—we may conjecture that Paul was on his guard at both cities, and had forewarned his converts against the danger of subversive Jewish activities.

11. Samothrace is an island halfway between Troas and the Macedonian coast, and being over five thousand feet high is a prominent landmark. The wind must have been favorable as the voyage took only two days compared with five on a later occasion (20:6). **Neapolis,** on the Strymonian Gulf, is the modern Cavalla; it was a port second only to Thessalonica and was the terminus of the *Via Egnatia.*

---

istry in Philippi. The first is Lydia. Paul found her in a small group of women who met on the banks of the river for prayer. It was Paul's first congregation in Philippi. Not a very promising one! All women and no men; no building to meet in; no prestige or influence in the city to count on. Nevertheless it grew into one of the strongest, most generous of all the churches that Paul founded. It can be assumed that Lydia played a large part in its growth and development.

In the first place, she was a businesswoman. Apparently she represented a firm that sold dyes. Furthermore she was a successful businesswoman, otherwise she would not have been sent from Thyatira to represent the firm's interest in Philippi. She was well to do. Above all she was deeply religious. She had been drawn to the Jewish community because she found there an oasis in the midst of the spiritual and moral drought that prevailed elsewhere. The Jewish community in Philippi was small and unimportant; nevertheless Lydia was not reluctant to associate herself with it, and there Paul found her on the bank of the river in prayer.

There has always been a place in the church for women of the world. As women extend the interests and occupations of their world, their influence in the church can increase. Their judgment and experience are valuable to the church as it ministers to all sorts and conditions of men. What a blessing a superintendent of nurses, or a principal of a high school, or a librarian, or a social worker, has been to the women of the church. The fact that they have had greater advantages, that they have superior intelligence, and that they occupy positions of influence in the community should not separate them from those who remain in more obscure places, but draw them even closer so that the benefits with which they are blessed can be distributed throughout the community.

12 And from thence to Philippi, which is the chief city of that part of Macedonia, *and* a colony: and we were in that city abiding certain days.

the following day to Ne-ap′o-lis,
12 and from there to Philippi, which is the leading city of the district of Mac-e-do′ni-a, and a Roman colony. We remained in this city

12. The leading city of the district of Macedonia. Literally the Greek means "a first city," and it is known from inscriptions that certain cities in Asia, Bithynia, and Macedonia enjoyed the honorary title of πρώτη. Lake and Cadbury state, however, that "as a definite title it has been found so far only in the cases of cities which were members of a κοινόν ["union" or "league"] in their particular province, and were not Roman colonies at the time" (*Beginnings of Christianity,* IV, 188). There is no evidence that Philippi was a member of the Macedonian "union," whereas it was a colony. The more general meaning given to the words in RSV is therefore probably here correct. As Ramsay puts it, "Amphipolis was ranked first by general consent, Philippi first by its own consent" (*St. Paul the Traveller,* pp. 206-7).

District (μερίδος) is the word technically used, not of a province as a whole, but of the subdivisions of a province. From a description in Livy (*Annals* XLV. 29) we know that Philippi was in the first "district" of Macedonia; and it is very tempting to read πρώτης μερίδος for πρώτη τῆς μερίδος, as suggested by the old Languedoc Latin version which has *primae partis,* and to translate, "which is the [capital] city of the first district of Macedonia." In the papyri πόλις is quite commonly used of the metropolis of a district—as we say, "town." But the MS evidence is perhaps too slight to justify even such an attractive emendation.

A colony (κολωνία): A transliteration of the Latin instead of the correct Greek word ἀποικία. Here only does Luke so characterize a city, a hint perhaps of his personal interest in Philippi. As a colony Philippi would enjoy *libertas, immunitas,* and *jus Italicum,* i.e., self-government, immunity from imperial tribute and the same rights as Italian citizens.

But perhaps the most notable thing about Lydia was her hospitality. As soon as she was baptized she invited Paul and his friends to her house. Some less fearless woman might have hesitated to take in a Jewish rabbi and his company, especially when there were many indications that he was not the usual kind of rabbi and might get them into an embarrassing situation. But in spite of all these considerations, Lydia insisted that they stay with her, and they did.

Hospitality has always been one of the human graces. To share one's home with other people is to that extent sharing one's life. It has often been said that you never know a man until you live under the same roof with him. To offer a man the hospitality of your home is to offer him an entrance into the sacred precincts of your life. In Christianity hospitality is the expression in action of that brotherhood for which Christ died, a demonstration of the family of God. It is more than a grace; it is a virtue. Together with clothing the naked, feeding the hungry, giving a drink to the thirsty, and visiting the lonely, Jesus makes it one of the basic requirements of life in his kingdom: "I was a stranger, and ye took me in" (Matt. 25:35). Hence Lydia, otherwise obscure and unimportant in comparison with the larger interests and enterprises recorded in the Acts, rises to a place of dignity and honor, for when Paul and his friends were friendless in a hostile city she gave them the hospitality of her home.

The other woman who played a large part in Paul's ministry in Philippi was as different from Lydia as day is from night. She was a slave girl with a disordered mind. Clever men exploited her mental weakness and sold her wares to a superstitious public. The border line between insanity and inspiration is so fine that it is often possible to mislead the public into believing that the ravings of a mad man are in reality the revelations of God. There are always those pitiful human creatures whose minds are so split and divided that they are no match for the real world in which they live, and there are always those shrewd, calculating men who are ready to take the tragic dissolution of a mind and turn it to their own profit. Nature cannot go very far without producing a freak, and human nature cannot resist the temptation to put the pitiable freaks of life into a side show and admit the public for a price.

Unlike Lydia, this poor girl was a nuisance to Paul. Wherever he went, she went. Whenever he spoke, she screamed. It was more than the nerves of Paul could bear. Every preacher who has been surrounded by the mentally sick

13 And on the sabbath we went out of the city by a river side, where prayer was wont to be made; and we sat down, and spake unto the women which resorted *thither*.

14 ¶ And a certain woman named Lydia, a seller of purple, of the city of Thyatira, which worshipped God, heard *us:* whose heart the Lord opened, that she attended unto the things which were spoken of Paul.

15 And when she was baptized, and her household, she besought *us,* saying, If ye have judged me to be faithful to the Lord, come into my house, and abide *there.* And she constrained us.

some days;
13 and on the sabbath day we went outside the gate to the riverside, where we supposed there was a place of prayer; and we sat down and spoke to the women who had come together.
14 One who heard us was a woman named Lydia, from the city of Thy-a-ti'ra, a seller of purple goods, who was a worshiper of God. The Lord opened her heart to give heed to what was said by Paul.
15 And when she was baptized, with her household, she besought us, saying, "If you have judged me to be faithful to the Lord, come to my house and stay." And she prevailed upon us.

---

13. **The riverside** seems to have been a customary place for a Jewish **place of prayer** (προσευχή): The word is commonly used by Philo, Josephus, and in inscriptions as a synonym for "synagogue." Paul adopted his usual approach by way of the synagogue and accordingly **sat down**—the usual posture of the teacher—**and spoke to the women who had come together.** The last words give an accurate touch of local color, for social convention seems to have allowed women singular freedom in Macedonia.

14. **Lydia** may be either a personal name or may mean "the Lydian," as **Thyatira** was a Lydian city famous for its trade in **purple** dyes. If the latter, can her personal name have been Euodia or Syntyche, both of whom are mentioned in the Philippian epistle (Phil. 4:2)? **A worshiper of God:** See on 10:2.

15. Presumably Lydia was a well-to-do woman and **when she was baptized, her household,** i.e., family and slaves alike, would compulsorily follow her into the new faith. This sense of family solidarity, admirable in many ways, must have led to some quite superficial "conversions." **She prevailed:** The same Greek word as in Luke 24:29, "But they constrained him saying, 'Stay with us, for it is toward evening.'"

---

will sympathize with Paul, and so perhaps may be permitted to derive some slight encouragement from the fact that Paul's patience was not equal to the situation. He finally turned to her in annoyance and rebuked the evil spirit, and it came out of her! Would that the impatience of modern preachers and teachers produced such beneficial results! The slave girl was healed. Some pressure had been released by the spiritual authority of Paul and she was no longer a freak. Neither was she any longer valuable to her owners.

That was the beginning of more trouble for Paul. Without an opportunity to defend himself, with no real examination of the case in hand, Paul and Silas were thrown into jail. Nothing was said about the fact that they had healed a girl. They were branded as agitators. Furthermore they were blacklisted as Jews. That was enough to condemn them, and without more ado they were cast into prison.

The story of Paul's miraculous escape from prison follows the pattern of other similar situations which have already been considered at some length. The figure of the jailer, however, deserves special attention inasmuch as he raised a question which has been raised by people before and since, and is one of the most profound questions asked by people today. Men and women who are bewildered by the complicated problems of life, and are honestly seeking to find their way through them, ask the same question that the jailer asked, though not in the same words.

The jailer was a thoroughly frightened man. Even though earthquakes were decidedly more frequent in that part of the world than they are in our Western world, nevertheless one did not take them as a matter of course, nor did one ever become accustomed to them; and, according to the testimony of those who have been through them, they invariably leave a man with a sense of paralyzing helplessness. Not only was the earth shaking, but the prison walls were shaking, and the prospects for any future at all were in serious danger. It is in such a state of insecurity that men begin to think about the basic realities of life. It is no wonder that the jailer asked the question, **Sirs, what must I do to be saved?** It is in such a state of mind that

16 ¶ And it came to pass, as we went to prayer, a certain damsel possessed with a spirit of divination met us, which brought her masters much gain by soothsaying:

16 As we were going to the place of prayer, we were met by a slave girl who had a spirit of divination and brought her own-

(2) Opposition and Imprisonment (16:16-24)

There follows an account of yet another encounter with sorcery (cf. 8:9; 13:6), this time with **a slave girl who had a spirit of divination;** and once again, as in the case of Elymas and later of the silversmiths of Ephesus (19:24-27), the opposition to Paul is motivated by fear of the loss of worldly gain; for the girl **brought her owners much gain by soothsaying.** There is no reason whatever to doubt the historicity of the incident. Paul himself testifies to his own belief in the reality of demons (I Cor. 10:20) and to his own ability to exercise apparently "miraculous" powers (II Cor. 12:12), so that there is nothing in the account which need be held to betray the hand of a later writer. The historicity of the "miracle" is confirmed by the fact that it is quite unedifying. Paul shows no pity for the girl, nor any concern for her spiritual welfare; nor is it suggested that, as was the case at Ephesus, he was protesting against magic by the performance of the cure. In a word there is no "apologetic" reason whatever for the insertion of the incident. Loisy, it is true, considers that the sequel is out of all proportion to the incident, and thinks that the cure has been substituted for an original account of a controversy caused by the apostles' teaching. But in any case the historicity of the arrest and imprisonment is undoubted, for Paul alludes in both Phil. 1:30 and I Thess. 2:2 to the ill treatment he had suffered at Philippi. Nor need we question the connection of the arrest with the incident that precedes it. The very fact that the apostles are represented as being persecuted as **Jews** (vs. 20) confirms the historicity of the setting, for the natural bias of our author is to represent the initiative in all opposition to Paul as coming from the Jews. In this case the trouble had nothing to do with the specifically *Christian* teaching of Paul: the charge is that he is engaged in illegal *Jewish* propaganda, and this is used as a cloak to cover the plaintiffs' own irritation at the loss of private gain. It is worth repeating that it is not as Christians, but as Jews, that Paul and his companions are here molested. Shortly before this the Jews had been expelled from Rome by Claudius; they were no doubt suffering from local hostility all over the empire; and it would be easy therefore to arouse prejudice among pagans who could not distinguish Judaism from Christianity.

16. A spirit of divination, literally, "a spirit, a python"—a name given first to the priestess of Apollo at Delphi, and then to soothsayers in general, with reference to the serpent by which the god was symbolized. Plutarch (*Moralia* 414E) tells us that ventriloquists were called "pythons."

people ask the same question today. They are scared stiff.

In contrast to the frightened jailer was the untroubled confidence of Paul and Silas. They had surprised the prisoners by spending the first part of the evening singing hymns. Different people take their disasters in different ways, and certainly this was a new way to take a jail sentence. Most people would have spent the night protesting the injustice of their punishment. Paul and Silas spent it praising God, for Paul and Silas had something inside themselves which gave them that extraordinary human capacity to rise above any and every situation and to mold the raw material of their lives in such a way as to master it.

Their answer to the jailer's question was straightforward and simple: **Believe on the Lord Jesus Christ, and thou shalt be saved.** To be sure, that is the only answer to the question, and yet for people whose minds are unsettled by contemporary discord and confusion, that answer needs to be amplified and broken down into more explicit directions. Belief in Jesus we take to mean both an intellectual assent to the principles which he made plain in his teaching and in his living, and also a surrender of the will to the love of God as it was made manifest in Jesus. When we say that we believe in a man, we imply not only that we believe what he says to be true but also that we trust him. And even though we do not know in detail exactly how he would behave under every conceivable circumstance, nevertheless we know enough about him to be willing to risk our lives in his hands. So when we say that we believe in

17 The same followed Paul and us, and cried, saying, These men are the servants of the most high God, which show unto us the way of salvation.

18 And this did she many days. But Paul, being grieved, turned and said to the spirit, I command thee in the name of Jesus Christ to come out of her. And he came out the same hour.

19 ¶ And when her masters saw that the hope of their gains was gone, they caught Paul and Silas, and drew *them* into the market place unto the rulers,

20 And brought them to the magistrates, saying, These men, being Jews, do exceedingly trouble our city,

21 And teach customs, which are not lawful for us to receive, neither to observe, being Romans.

ers much gain by soothsaying. 17 She followed Paul and us, crying, "These men are
servants of the Most High God, who proclaim to you the way of salvation." 18 And
this she did for many days. But Paul was
annoyed, and turned and said to the spirit,
"I charge you in the name of Jesus Christ
to come out of her." And it came out that
very hour.
19 But when her owners saw that their
hope of gain was gone, they seized Paul
and Silas and dragged them into the market place before the rulers; 20 and when
they had brought them to the magistrates
they said, "These men are Jews and they
are disturbing our city. 21 They advocate
customs which it is not lawful for us

---

17. Paul and us. The first person plural is after this dropped and not resumed till 20:6 (see also on 21:18). **The Most High God** was a title commonly used of the God of Israel by pagans (see note on 7:48 and cf. Luke 8:28, where the title is used by the Gerasene demoniac in non-Jewish territory). The implication is that Paul and his companions are Jews (vs. 20). **The way of salvation** is also an expression very common in the records of Hellenistic syncretistic religions.

18. I charge you in the name: The common formula of exorcism, here used for the first time in Acts.

19-21. Her owners: The plural has been needlessly thought to imply that the girl was employed by a business syndicate. It may mean simply "master and mistress." **The market place,** literally the agora, which probably here means rather the "place of judgment," "courthouse." **The rulers** is a quite general term for local municipal authorities. In the next verse they are more specifically called "magistrates" (στρατηγοί, which is the common Greek word for the Roman *praetores*). Correctly such magistrates were called *duoviri,* but the Philippians used the more dignified title! Timothy and Luke were evidently not arrested, which indicates that Paul and Silas were the prominent figures.

Customs which it is not lawful: The reference here is not to specifically Christian teaching regarded as a *religio non licita,* or unlicensed cult, in contrast to Judaism, which was licensed. The missionaries are regarded as **Jews** who are **disturbing our city** by engaging in illegal Jewish propaganda; for though Judaism was itself a *religio licita,* active proselytizing was frowned upon as a menace to the national cult of the emperor, which as **Romans,** i.e., citizens of a Roman colony, the Philippians were bound to respect.

Jesus, we mean that we believe what he says and what has been said by the church about him, and that we are willing and ready to trust our lives to him. Having made that initial commitment, most people need to go further and to take specific steps toward the translation of their commitment into action.

They must do at least four things:

(*a*) The person who would be saved must join the Christian church, for no man can be saved apart from the community in which he lives his life. No one can be a Christian in private, for Christianity is a movement and it involves people working together in relationships both private and public. Apart from that movement a person can have no complete knowledge of Christ, for Christ makes himself known not only in the solitariness of a man's inner life, but also and primarily where two or three are gathered together in his name. In the company of those who are drawn together by their common devotion to him, Christ is most vividly known.

Though Communism and Christianity are by

22 And the multitude rose up together
against them; and the magistrates rent off
their clothes, and commanded to beat *them.*
23 And when they had laid many stripes
upon them, they cast *them* into prison,
charging the jailer to keep them safely:
24 Who, having received such a charge,
thrust them into the inner prison, and
made their feet fast in the stocks.
25 ¶ And at midnight Paul and Silas
prayed, and sang praises unto God: and the
prisoners heard them.

Romans to accept or practice." 22 The
crowd joined in attacking them; and the
magistrates tore the garments off them and
gave orders to beat them with rods. 23 And
when they had inflicted many blows upon
them, they threw them into prison, charging the jailer to keep them safely. 24 Having
received this charge, he put them into the
inner prison and fastened their feet in the
stocks.
25 But about midnight Paul and Silas
were praying and singing hymns to God,
and the prisoners were listening to them,

---

22. **Tore the garments off them:** Or more probably perhaps "tore their own garments." It is true that the Philippian magistrates might not be expected to make this characteristically Jewish gesture of horror (for which see on 14:14). But Luke may well have pictured them as doing so. As Ramsay puts it: "The Praetors . . . rent their clothes in loyal horror, with the fussy, consequential airs that Horace satirises in the would-be Praetor of a country town (*Sat.* I. 5, 34): the fabric of the Empire was shaken to its foundations . . . ; but the Praetors of Philippi stood firm, and the populace rose as one man, . . . to defend their country against her insidious enemies" (*St. Paul the Traveller,* p. 219).

23-24. **The jailer** would correspond rather to the governor of the prison and would perhaps be a centurion. The **inner prison** would possibly be underground. **The stocks** would be much after the traditional village pattern and would be fastened to the walls.

(3) The Miraculous Deliverance (16:25-40)

The details of Paul's escape, as of Peter's in ch. 12, have been regarded with much suspicion, and for similar reasons. It is not that the opportune earthquake need cause any difficulty, for earthquakes were very common in the district and, as Ramsay again writes, "any one that has seen a Turkish prison will not wonder that the doors were thrown open" (*ibid.,* p. 221). Nor need much stress be laid upon the parallelism with Peter's escape as evidence for later redaction. But there are certain internal signs that the paragraph may come from a source other than, and inferior to, the "we" source into which it is inserted. Vs. 35 seems to take no account of the earthquake and the escape, and it would follow admirably immediately after vs. 24. The scribe of the Bezan Codex (D) was evidently puzzled by this and tried to clarify the picture by writing: "When it was day, the magistrates assembled together in the courthouse, and remembering the earthquake which had taken place they were afraid, and sent the police. . . ." There are moreover certain improbabilities—that the criminals made no attempt to escape nor the jailer any attempt to secure them. Again the Bezan scribe saw the difficulty and added, "Having secured the rest, he brought them out." We ought perhaps to recognize the probability

---

no means identical, and in many ways as far apart as the poles, they are at least alike in this: They are both movements, and they are both movements which involve a community of persons, and one can be neither a Christian nor a Communist by himself alone, but only in association with other people engaged in the same enterprise. A person can live a good life outside the church but he cannot live a Christian life outside the church, for there is no Christianity without the Christian community.

(*b*) The person who would be saved must learn the fundamental principles which underlie Christian belief and behavior. Just as a Communist must have some basic knowledge of the philosophical principles upon which Communism is constructed, so a Christian must have at least an elementary knowledge of the principles upon which Christianity rests. He must know, for example, what the doctrine of creation means, and how the Christian doctrine of man is different from the humanistic or the

26 And suddenly there was a great earthquake, so that the foundations of the prison were shaken: and immediately all the doors were opened, and every one's bands were loosed.

27 And the keeper of the prison awaking out of his sleep, and seeing the prison doors open, he drew out his sword, and would have killed himself, supposing that the prisoners had been fled.

28 But Paul cried with a loud voice, saying, Do thyself no harm: for we are all here.

29 Then he called for a light, and sprang in, and came trembling, and fell down before Paul and Silas,

30 And brought them out, and said, Sirs, what must I do to be saved?

31 And they said, Believe on the Lord Jesus Christ, and thou shalt be saved, and thy house.

32 And they spake unto him the word of the Lord, and to all that were in his house.

33 And he took them the same hour of the night, and washed *their* stripes; and was baptized, he and all his, straightway.

26 and suddenly there was a great earthquake, so that the foundations of the prison
were shaken; and immediately all the doors
were opened and every one's fetters were
unfastened. 27 When the jailer woke and
saw that the prison doors were open, he
drew his sword and was about to kill himself, supposing that the prisoners had escaped. 28 But Paul cried with a loud voice,
"Do not harm yourself, for we are all here."
29 And he called for lights and rushed in,
and trembling with fear he fell down before
Paul and Silas, 30 and brought them out
and said, "Men, what must I do to be
saved?" 31 And they said, "Believe in the
Lord Jesus, and you will be saved, you and
your household." 32 And they spoke the
word of the Lord to him and to all that
were in his house. 33 And he took them the
same hour of the night, and washed their
wounds, and he was baptized at once, with

---

that both here and in ch. 12 certain features have crept in (some of which occur so often in ancient tales of escape as to become almost conventional—the singing of captives, the intervention of angels, the opening of doors of their own accord) which cannot claim the same historical value as can the "we" narrative as a whole.

26. Fetters were unfastened: Presumably the meaning is that "the chains and stocks were detached from the wall, which was shaken so that space gaped between the stones" (*ibid.*).

27. To kill himself, i.e., to forestall the penalty which Peter's jailers paid (12:19).

30-31. What must I do to be saved? On the lips of the jailer this might mean no more than "How am I to escape the consequences of this?" or "How am I to save my reputation?" But Luke's meaning is of course that the jailer, astonished at the earthquake, seeks the "way of salvation" (vs. 17) which Paul has thus miraculously vindicated. The reply given is the essence of Paulinism in a single sentence—**Believe in the Lord Jesus, and you will be saved.**

33. With all his family: The second case of a household baptism. Doubtless such occasions would eventually lead to infant baptism. Tradition, and even legend, tell us nothing more about the Philippian jailer, save that two minuscule MSS give his name in vs. 27 as "Stephanas"—presumably the same person whose household Paul calls "the first converts in Achaia" (I Cor. 16:15; cf. I Cor. 1:16).

---

materialistic doctrine of man. He must have some understanding of what the church means by the doctrine of the Incarnation and the Atonement. He need not have technical knowledge of these doctrines, but in order to practice his Christian faith he must at least to some degree understand the framework within which the practice of that faith is possible. There is no use in asking a man to love his enemies unless he believes in the kind of God and the kind of universe in which such seemingly unnatural love is conceivable and practicable. One reason why so many Christians come so far short of fulfilling their Christian respon-

34 And when he had brought them into
his house, he set meat before them, and
rejoiced, believing in God with all his
house.
35 And when it was day, the magistrates
sent the sergeants, saying, Let those men
go.
36 And the keeper of the prison told
this saying to Paul, The magistrates have
sent to let you go: now therefore depart,
and go in peace.
37 But Paul said unto them, They have
beaten us openly uncondemned, being
Romans, and have cast *us* into prison; and
now do they thrust us out privily? nay
verily; but let them come themselves and
fetch us out.
38 And the sergeants told these words
unto the magistrates: and they feared, when
they heard that they were Romans.

all his family. 34 Then he brought them up
into his house, and set food before them;
and he rejoiced with all his household
that he had believed in God.
35 But when it was day, the magistrates
sent the police, saying, "Let those men go."
36 And the jailer reported the words to
Paul, saying, "The magistrates have sent
to let you go; now therefore come out and
go in peace." 37 But Paul said to them,
"They have beaten us publicly, uncondemned, men who are Roman citizens, and
have thrown us into prison; and do they
now cast us out secretly? No! let them come
themselves and take us out." 38 The police
reported these words to the magistrates, and
they were afraid when they heard that they

---

35. The police, literally the "rod-carriers" or "lictors," who accompanied the praetors carrying the fasces, a bundle of rods tied together round an ax.

37. Luke recounts with evident relish how Paul and Silas, the **Romans** whose rights had been flagrantly violated, stood on their dignity before the petty provincial officials. The *Lex Valeria* and the *Lex Porcia* made illegal the scourging of **Roman citizens.** It is surprising that Paul had not earlier protested his Roman citizenship and so escaped scourging, as he did later at Jerusalem (22:24-25). Perhaps in the rush and clamor of the crowd he had no chance, and in any case minor police officials may not have concerned themselves much about the niceties of Roman law. It is significant that Paul himself states that he had been three times "beaten with rods" (II Cor. 11:25), presumably by Roman officials, as his five floggings by the Jews are mentioned separately in the previous verse. The word **uncondemned** might seem to suggest that it would have been legal after fair trial to sentence a citizen to flogging. But in no circumstances might a citizen be flogged, and a formal trial would only have aggravated the offense by making it more deliberate, The correct word would have been something corresponding to the Latin phrase *re incognita*—"without due investigation."

38. They were afraid, i.e., because the violation of the protection given by citizenship might result in severe penalties, such as disqualification from holding office.

---

sibility in action is that they are illiterate; they are trying to sustain the lofty ideals of Christianity on the meager diet of a kindergarten.

(*c*) The person who would be saved must do his spiritual exercises daily. Just as a man does his physical exercises in order to preserve his body, so a man who wants to be a Christian must strengthen the muscles of his spiritual nature. A Christian lives in two worlds at one and the same time, the material world of bread and butter and the invisible world of love and loyalty and sacrifice. He cannot live in the invisible world unless he develops those faculties by which he can be in communication with the things that are unseen. He must develop his spiritual eyes and ears. Before he understands the theology of prayer he must begin to pray. He can do it simply; thanking God for his existence and for the wonder of the world in which he is at liberty to live; taking account of his mistakes and blunders, asking God to forgive him and offering his desires to God so that God may be able to give him the things which it is already his will to give.

(*d*) Finally, the person who would be saved must take part in some specifically Christian activity. In one sense all work can be Christian work, but there is another sense in which some activities are more specifically Christian than others. The thing that a man does for the good of someone else, some public service, or some private charity that is over and above the re-

39 And they came and besought them,
and brought *them* out, and desired *them*
to depart out of the city.
40 And they went out of the prison, and
entered into *the house of* Lydia: and when
they had seen the brethren, they comforted
them, and departed.

17 Now when they had passed through
Amphipolis and Apollonia, they
came to Thessalonica, where was a synagogue
of the Jews:

were Roman citizens; 39 so they came and
apologized to them. And they took them
out and asked them to leave the city. 40 So
they went out of the prison, and visited
Lydia; and when they had seen the brethren,
they exhorted them and departed.

17 Now when they had passed through
Am-phip′o-lis and Ap-ol-lo′ni-a, they
came to Thes-sa-lo-ni′ca, where there was

---

39. **Came and apologized:** The Western text again adds lifelike details: "And they came with many friends into the prison and implored them to leave, saying, We did not know the truth about you, that you are righteous men. And they brought them out and implored them saying, Depart from this city, lest they again make a riot and shout against you to us." The magistrates were apprehensive of the mob and evidently distrusted their own ability to keep order; the wronged parties must be induced to submit to the additional injustice of expulsion, in order to save the local authorities from further embarrassment. As Ramsay says, "The Bezan Text hits off admirably the situation. . . . One would gladly think this Lukan" (*St. Paul the Traveller*, p. 224).

b) Thessalonica (17:1-9)

Passing **through Amphipolis and Apollonia,** both cities on the great military road, the *Via Egnatia,* Paul **came to Thessalonica,** which was the capital of the province and, like the modern Salonika, a flourishing commercial city with a good port. Its natural advantages have so conserved its importance that even today it has some 150,000 inhabitants. In Paul's day the *Via Egnatia* gave it direct communication with Rome, and after Ephesus and Corinth it was the busiest city of the Aegean, where streams of humanity from every quarter met—just the type of place which Paul usually selected for his work. The Romans had left it its liberty, so that it was a "free city" with its own Macedonian democratic constitution and its own magistrates, known as "politarchs" (vs. 6).

Luke's account of Paul's mission at Thessalonica is evidently much abbreviated. Our author's chief interest is in Paul's teaching in the synagogue and the inevitable break with the Jews, which is told in the way which has almost become conventional. It looks as if he has considerably shortened the account as originally given in his source, for **Jason** is casually mentioned, as if already known, and the source must have mentioned that the missionaries had found lodging with him. Vss. 8-9 too show signs of drastic abbreviation. Fortunately the Thessalonian epistles provide a most valuable supplement and enable us to fill in the picture.

---

quirement of social decency—it is such an undertaking that incorporates a man into the fullness of the Christian life and service. As a man cannot be a Christian in private, or in complete religious illiteracy, or in spiritual inaction, so he cannot be a Christian in isolation from the needs of humanity.

Some such specific directions as these are essential to the modern man or woman who has a sincere desire to become a Christian. They will be effective, however, only as they are given by Christians who, like Paul and Silas, are able to demonstrate to the world that they have within themselves the power of God by which they are able to master the circumstances of life.

17:1-9. *Paul and Silas in Thessalonica.*—When Paul began to preach to the Jews in Thessalonica, he had to do what he always had to do, and what preachers and teachers have had to do ever since. He had to explain the Cross. The Cross meant not only death; it meant also disgrace. Death on the cross was the equivalent of death in the electric chair, and it would not be easy to convince people today that a man who died in the electric chair was the master of the world. It was no easier then. It took a lot of explaining.

2 And Paul, as his manner was, went in unto them, and three sabbath days reasoned with them out of the Scriptures,

a synagogue of the Jews. 2 And Paul went in, as was his custom, and for three weeks[o] he argued with them from the scriptures,

[o] Or *sabbaths.*

The following facts emerge: (*a*) Clearly the **three weeks** preaching in the synagogue covers only preliminary Jewish work. That the stay was considerably longer appears from the fact that Paul found it worth his while to settle down at his trade in order not to be a burden to the local church (I Thess. 2:9; II Thess. 3:7-12), while the Philippians sent him supplies on at least two occasions (Phil. 4:16). It is possible indeed that from Thessalonica Paul carried through a wider mission, perhaps to Illyricum (Rom. 15:19), for the Christian devotion of the Thessalonian church is said to have been "sounded forth," not only in Macedonia and Achaia, but "everywhere" (I Thess. 1:8). (*b*) Acts implies that the conversion of both Jews and Greeks was due to Paul's preaching in the synagogue. But the epistles make it clear that the Thessalonian church was composed chiefly of converted pagans (I Thess. 1:9). Evidently Luke has recorded what was in fact the least important part of Paul's work, the synagogue preaching probably being followed by a purely Gentile mission. (*c*) As to the main theme of Paul's message, Acts implies that it was the messiahship of Jesus. But this would have been of no particular interest to pagans. The actual subject of Paul's preaching is more likely to have been as indicated in I Thess. 1:10—"To wait for [God's] Son from heaven, whom he raised from the dead, Jesus who delivers us from the wrath to come." Paul evidently laid great stress upon the Resurrection, the Parousia, and the Judgment, for his converts seem to have lost interest in their daily occupations in expectation of Christ's immediate coming (II Thess. 3:10-12). (*d*) I Thess. 2:17-18 confirms Acts' account that Paul was compelled to leave Thessalonica before he wished and in circumstances which made him fear for the permanence of his work. As Paul writes, "Satan hindered" a return visit—a reference perhaps to the diabolic scheme of the officials, who bound over Jason as a security against further trouble from Paul, and thus put an impassable gulf between Paul and his friends.

The accuracy of Luke's picture of Jewish aggression at Thessalonica has been questioned in view of the fact that Paul writes to the Thessalonians that "you suffered the same things from your own countrymen as [the Judean Christians] did from the Jews" (I Thess. 2:14)—i.e., the persecution was at the hands of the heathen populace. But in the very next verse Paul adds that the Jews "displease God . . . by hindering us from speaking to the Gentiles," words which may well have Paul's local experience in view. Moreover in 17:7 the missionaries are accused of **saying that there is another king, Jesus,** a charge which could emanate only from Jews who, regarding the expected Messiah as a "king," would readily give a political turn to the affair by alleging that Paul was setting Jesus up as a rival to Caesar. As the epistles show, it was not as king that Paul preached Jesus but as Savior, and only Jews could have so distorted his message.

17:1-2. They: The "we" is dropped. Possibly Luke did not accompany Paul but remained at Philippi (but see on 16:10). **Three weeks** (RSV), or perhaps more correctly

Though the Cross has gathered to itself the associations of centuries of piety and faith, even now it comes as a shock to people when they stop to think what it really means. How could anyone as good as Jesus meet such an undeserved and bitter end? How can God be the Father of Jesus and let such affliction overtake his glorious Son? How can a man be King and die before he is crowned? Sovereignty and suffering do not go together in the modern mind any more than they did in the ancient mind, and it is a hard matter to make an honest man see that the real sovereignty of Jesus is to be found somewhere in the suffering.

So together with Paul, from generation to generation, interpreters of the Cross explain that **it was necessary for the Christ to suffer;** or according to Moffatt's translation, "the messiah had to suffer." They must realize, however, that they cannot explain the necessity of the Cross to a modern congregation in the same way that Paul explained it. **Paul . . . argued with them from the scriptures, explaining and proving that it was necessary for the Christ to suf-**

3 Opening and alleging, that Christ must needs have suffered, and risen again from the dead; and that this Jesus, whom I preach unto you, is Christ.

4 And some of them believed, and consorted with Paul and Silas; and of the devout Greeks a great multitude, and of the chief women not a few.

5 ¶ But the Jews which believed not, moved with envy, took unto them certain lewd fellows of the baser sort, and gathered a company, and set all the city on an uproar, and assaulted the house of Jason, and sought to bring them out to the people.

3 explaining and proving that it was necessary for the Christ to suffer and to rise
from the dead, and saying, "This Jesus,
whom I proclaim to you, is the Christ."
4 And some of them were persuaded, and
joined Paul and Silas; as did a great many
of the devout Greeks and not a few of the
leading women. 5 But the Jews were jealous,
and taking some wicked fellows of the
rabble, they gathered a crowd, set the city
in an uproar, and attacked the house of
Jason, seeking to bring them out to the

---

three sabbath days (KJV), which, rather than "weeks," is the regular meaning of the Greek word in the LXX. In the N.T. σάββατα means "week" only when used in the genitive case preceded by the number of the day, e.g., "the first day of the week" (Mark 16:2).

3-4. Necessary for the Christ to suffer and to rise: The idea of a "suffering Messiah" was quite alien to the Jews, who had never related the suffering servant passages of Isa. 53, etc., to their Messiah (see on 3:18). The Greeks, though more accustomed to the idea of a suffering God, would find the idea of a bodily resurrection equally hard of belief. Vss. 2-3 give a typical summary of Paul's message to the Jews. As the same theme has been fully developed in the speech in ch. 13, Luke does not elaborate it here. **Devout Greeks:** see on 10:2.

5. Were jealous: Not unnaturally, as these "devout" persons would be looked on as prospective converts to Judaism. **Jason** was probably a sympathetic Jew. It is not necessarily implied that he was yet a convert; nor is there any evidence that he was the Jason mentioned in Rom. 16:21. **Bring them out,** i.e., either to arraign them before the popular assembly, or perhaps simply to subject them to violence.

---

fer. The modern congregation does not find the answer to its questions about the Cross in proof texts from the Bible. The interpreter will have to go deeper than that. He will begin with the story of the Cross as the Gospels set it forth in simple, unadorned narrative, and then let the story probe the depths of human life and scale the heights of the divine Love until, in a mysterious and wonderful way, these meet and blend at the very point where one beam crosses another on a hill outside a city wall.

To help the people understand and appreciate the Cross he may point out to them that the Cross is something done *for* us. In spite of all our best efforts to give ourselves away in love and service, we seldom get beyond the first down payment. Complications arise, responsibilities to friends and family frighten us, self-consideration rules us, fear of death threatens us, until we tighten our grip and try to keep life by holding on. We know that it would be better to let go, but we cannot. We look at the Cross and we know that it is the way of life and that there is no other way, but our legs are paralyzed and we cannot walk in it. At that point the Cross does something for us. It balances every ounce of human evil, crime, and wrongdoing by the weight of its own perfect offering. It restores to us the dignity of the human family and opens the way for a new relationship with the Father. When a man is down and out, someone else has to make his decisions for him and assume the responsibility of them. When humanity was down and out, Jesus made the decision in favor of love. He died for us, and took upon his own shoulders the burden of the world's sin. He had to suffer, for in no other way could he have taken the brunt of man's mischief.

But the Cross also does something *to* us. As human beings we inherit its life. It has entered into the blood stream of humanity. Just as one of our ancestors once stood erect and walked, so one of our brothers gave himself utterly and lived. We inherit both the walking and the living. We can never be the same. We can never be content with the standard of self-preservation. Always will we be haunted by the vision of a better way. Always will we look for-

6 And when they found them not, they
drew Jason and certain brethren unto the
rulers of the city, crying, These that have
turned the world upside down are come
hither also;
7 Whom Jason hath received: and these
all do contrary to the decrees of Caesar,
saying that there is another king, *one* Jesus.

people. 6 And when they could not find
them, they dragged Jason and some of the
brethren before the city authorities, crying,
"These men who have turned the world
upside down have come here also, 7 and
Jason has received them; and they are all
acting against the decrees of Caesar, saying

---

6. City authorities, literally "politarchs," which was the correct title for the native magistrates of a free Macedonian city. The word was previously unknown and was quoted against Luke's accuracy, but it is now confirmed by numerous inscriptions, one of which—a block from a first-century A.D. arch in Thessalonica containing a list of "politarchs"—is in the British Museum.

7. Received them, or "harbored them" (so Lake and Cadbury, who suggest that "possibly Jason provided the work which Paul says he did while in Thessalonica"). **Another king:** The word commonly used of the Roman emperor.

---

ward to the Cross as to the ultimate goal of humanity. When repeated failures dull the edge of our spirit, and we are about ready to settle down for a period of getting and grabbing, the Cross will loom up on every horizon to mark the way to life. The spread of airplane wings signs the cross in the sky, the red badge marks it on a nurse's arm, the prone bodies of the wounded sign the ground with it, and white stones mark the dead with its seal. Everywhere there flashes across our vision the reminder: "There is a better way! Don't be afraid to give." And those reminders do something not only for us but to us. Jesus had to suffer to stir men and women out of their spiritual doldrums.

Greatest of all, the Cross does something *through* us. Almost immediately it started to reproduce itself in miniature. Stephen was the first. The company grew daily. Men who rejoiced in the fact that the Cross had done something for them found that the Cross was doing something through them. It is doing the same today. It builds hospitals and schools; it softens bitter tongues and turns away wrath; it relaxes the grip of possession and releases men from the fear of losing. In places unknown and unnumbered it is saving life. Through people like ourselves it raises from time to time its banner carrying the words "Love at any price."

There it is—the everlasting necessity of the Cross. Sometimes the only way you can make any impression upon a man is to die. Once he sees what his deviltry will do to a good man, once he feels what a good man's innocent suffering will do to his deviltry, there is a good chance that the devil in him will then be mastered. So it is between man and man, and there seems to be no real difference as between man and God. Jesus had to suffer to save men from themselves. God had to give his Son in order to reconcile the world unto himself.

It was in Thessalonica that Paul and Silas were described in words that the world has never forgotten. **These men who have turned the world upside down have come here also.** Or in Moffatt's translation, "These upsetters of the whole world have come here too!" As an upsetter of the world, Paul was in the direct succession of the prophets. They had always been "troublers of Israel." From Elijah, Nathan, Amos, and Jeremiah to John the Baptist, the line was unbroken. Their function was to make those in authority uneasy.

One often wonders who the successors to the prophets are today. Leaders of the church, by and large, do not often upset anyone if they can help it. Too much depends upon satisfied customers. Budgets are not raised from people who have been made extremely uncomfortable. The temptation of the leaders of the church, therefore, is to soothe and never upset. And it must be said that there is a time and place for soothing. The church has in its hands the balm of Gilead. There is healing even in the sound of the name of Jesus: "It soothes our sorrows, heals our wounds, and drives away our fear." Woe to the church that withholds the healing ministry of Jesus! A church in which the minister keeps the people upset all the time is a church that hears only half of the gospel. Paul upset people, but he also established them by setting them firmly upon the great foundations of God's love in Christ. Side by side with the sharp words that pricked the conscience were the tender words of his affection and trust.

Keeping in mind both of these aspects of the ministry, let the leaders of the church

8 And they troubled the people and the rulers of the city, when they heard these things.
9 And when they had taken security of Jason, and of the others, they let them go.
10 ¶ And the brethren immediately sent away Paul and Silas by night unto Berea: who coming *thither* went into the synagogue of the Jews.

that there is another king, Jesus." 8 And the people and the city authorities were disturbed when they heard this. 9 And when they had taken security from Jason and the rest, they let them go.
10 The brethren immediately sent Paul and Silas away by night to Be-roe'a; and when they arrived they went into the Jew-

---

9. Taken security (ἱκανὸν λαβεῖν, a translation of the Latin term *satis accipere*), i.e., a bond would be exacted from Jason which would be forfeited in the event of any further trouble with the Christians.

c) Beroea (17:10-15)

10. Beroea was some forty-five miles west from Thessalonica and is described by Cicero (*Against Piso* 36. 89) as a town "off the road," lying south of the main Egnatian highway. Paul's work here evidently had permanent success, for "Sopater of Beroea" is mentioned in 20:4 as accompanying Paul to Jerusalem with his church's share of the collection. **The Jewish synagogue:** Again Paul is represented as making the synagogue his headquarters, though his most important work must inevitably have been among Gentiles (see on 13:14).

---

go out to upset the world. Upset its lethargic complacency; upset its social and economic *status quo;* upset its conscience; upset its scientifically prejudiced mind; upset its moral indifference; upset its smug self-satisfaction. Let this warning, however, be sounded: the only people who have ever creatively upset the world have been those who dearly loved the people they were trying to upset. Too often the church has failed in its mission because it has secretly despised and scorned the people whom it upset. Not so with Paul. And with Jesus it was the very depth of his love which was the most upsetting thing of all!

It was no wonder that Paul turned the world upside down, for his Lord and Master had already provided all the tools and machinery for such a feat of spiritual engineering. For example, Jesus turned upside down the world's wisdom. The wisdom of the world runs this way: "If you don't look out for yourself, no one else will." Jesus turned that completely upside down and said: "The only way to look out for yourself is to forget yourself, and if you forget yourself, God will look out for you." According to the wisdom of the world, the more carefully you provide for the future, the more insurance you will have against its unpredictable accidents. Jesus turned that upside down and said, "Do not worry about the future. Do the will of God from day to day and the future will take care of itself."

Again, Jesus turned upside down the world's values. According to the world's hierarchy of values, sovereignty ranks above service. The more service a man can command the more sovereignty he has. Jesus turned that upside down and said that real sovereignty means the willingness to serve. In the markets of the world money is worth more than men. In the mind of Jesus men came first, and the value that money might have was derived from the fact that it might help men to be better men. Furthermore, Jesus turned society upside down. In the social registers of the world the well born and the blue bloods come first. In the kingdom of God the twice born have priority over the well born; the poor in spirit come before the proud and successful; sinners take precedence over the self-righteous saints.

As the servant of such a Master, no wonder that Paul turned the world upside down. It is fair to say, however, that Paul did not accomplish such a feat on his Master's example alone. His own penetrating insight and his own colossal grasp of the gospel made it possible for him to turn both the thinking and the living of his world upside down. It is the mind of the Master working in co-operation with the mind of a responsive disciple that brings about such an overwhelming change in the state of affairs.

10-15. *Paul Preaches in Beroea.*—The present expositor finds little pertinence hidden in this section. Others may find treasures as yet not revealed to him. To be sure, one might well take the phrase **they received the word with all readiness of mind** and base an ex-

11 These were more noble than those in Thessalonica, in that they received the word with all readiness of mind, and searched the Scriptures daily, whether those things were so.

12 Therefore many of them believed; also of honorable women which were Greeks, and of men, not a few.

13 But when the Jews of Thessalonica had knowledge that the word of God was preached of Paul at Berea, they came thither also, and stirred up the people.

14 And then immediately the brethren sent away Paul to go as it were to the sea: but Silas and Timotheus abode there still.

15 And they that conducted Paul brought him unto Athens: and receiving a commandment unto Silas and Timotheus for to come to him with all speed, they departed.

ish synagogue. 11 Now these Jews were more
noble than those in Thes-sa-lo-ni'ca, for
they received the word with all eagerness,
examining the scriptures daily to see if
these things were so. 12 Many of them therefore believed, with not a few Greek women
of high standing as well as men. 13 But
when the Jews of Thes-sa-lo-ni'ca learned
that the word of God was proclaimed by
Paul at Be-roe'a also, they came there too,
stirring up and inciting the crowds. 14 Then
the brethren immediately sent Paul off on
his way to the sea, but Silas and Timothy
remained there. 15 Those who conducted
Paul brought him as far as Athens; and
receiving a command for Silas and Timothy to come to him as soon as possible,
they departed.

---

11. More noble: "Perhaps the best English rendering would be 'liberal,' in the sense of free from prejudice, in contrast with the bigotry of the Thessalonian Jews" (F. J. Foakes Jackson, *The Acts of the Apostles* [London: Hodder & Stoughton, 1931; "The Moffatt New Testament Commentary"], pp. 161-62).

14. On his way to the sea: This would appear to mean that Paul's guides took him to some port on the coast whence he would sail to Athens, though it may be that "to the sea" is equivalent to "as far as Athens" in the next verse. This was evidently the view of the Western scribe who adds, "he passed by Thessaly, for he was prevented from speaking the word to them." **Silas and Timothy remained there,** i.e., at Beroea. The Thessalonian epistles show how eager Paul was to return; and it is possible that Silas and Timothy were left to watch the situation there and to bring news to Paul when it appeared more favorable.

15. To come to him as soon as possible: The subsequent movements of Silas and Timothy are slightly obscure. According to 18:5, they both "arrived from Macedonia"—apparently for the first time—only after Paul had gone on from Athens to Corinth. But I Thess. 3:1-6 seems to imply that while Paul was still at Athens, Timothy had come to him, was then sent back on a visit to Thessalonica, and finally rejoined him at Corinth. Luke therefore apparently omits to mention Timothy's first arrival from Macedonia and his return thither. **They departed:** Why did Paul leave Macedonia, obviously prematurely and against his will? He probably found that everywhere the Jews were raising against him the same political charge as at Thessalonica, and he therefore forestalled expulsion by the Romans by voluntarily escaping. It is quite possible that at Beroea also the civil authorities took action against him, though Luke characteristically says nothing of such a development.

---

position on response to the gospel, but there are other passages in the N.T. which introduce the same theme in a more striking and memorable way, e.g., the seed that fell upon good ground (Matt. 13:23). In years gone by preachers and teachers were often guilty of bleeding the Bible. They would wrench sermons out of texts, not hesitating to distort the meaning if necessary in order to produce one three-point sermon. That violation of the sacred Scriptures is avoided as far as possible in this exposition. When ideas do not leap from the pages, crying out to be translated into the language of current experience, it is better to skip to another passage, knowing full well that on another occasion, read against the background of different circumstances, the same passage may fairly burst with meaning for the present day.

16 ¶ Now while Paul waited for them at Athens, his spirit was stirred in him, when he saw the city wholly given to idolatry.

16 Now while Paul was waiting for them at Athens, his spirit was provoked within him as he saw that the city was full of

3. In Achaia (17:16–18:17)

a) Athens (17:16-34)

Athens is the only place where Paul's preaching did not provoke persecution, and, significantly perhaps, the only place also where he met with almost complete failure. The city at the time was of no political importance, nor was it a commercial center comparable with Corinth. But it was still the seat of a famous university and was the world's intellectual mecca. Above all was it famed for the number of religious cults to which it gave hospitality—a piety to which Paul pays a slightly ironical compliment in his opening words, **I perceive that in every way you are very religious.** The citizens were ever ready to listen to the latest philosopher and to engage in dialectical debate—but usually in a purely academic spirit, and with no real desire to discover truth for truth's sake.

The account of Paul's stay in Athens has been vigorously assailed by the critics. Loisy even suggests that the author's imagination has spun the whole story out of the name of Dionysius the Areopagite (vs. 34) ! In particular it is argued: (*a*) The obscurity regarding the movements of Silas and Timothy is suspicious. (*b*) Paul's speech is central and all the rest merely an artificially constructed setting. No doubt the speech reproduces local color successfully; but to ascribe to Paul not only the ideas of Greek philosophy but even its actual formulas demands too much of our credulity. The kernel of the speech—the reference to the "unknown God"—is adequately explained by certain literary allusions. It is introduced by the author merely as a clever starting point for a typical piece of Christian apologetic setting forth the fulfillment in the gospel of all that was best in the speculations of paganism. (*c*) It is impossible to suppose that Paul was really tried formally by the court of the Areopagus. What was the charge and who the prosecutor? Why is there no indication of anything judicial in the proceedings, of any line of defense in Paul's speech, of any formal verdict by the court?

We should agree rather with Lake and Cadbury's judgment that "taken as a whole [the story] commends itself at once as a genuinely historical narrative" (*Beginnings of Christianity*, IV, 208) . In favor of this judgment it can be argued:

(*a*) The suggestion that Paul had not intended to conduct a regular mission at Athens, but was **provoked** (vs. 16) into doing so by the curiosity of the philosophers and the stress of his own emotions, seems quite true to life. That Paul should recognize the probable unresponsiveness of the Athenians is likely enough; that such a view of the matter should have occurred to a later editor is much less probable.

(*b*) Though, as usual, the **synagogue** is mentioned as Paul's starting point, all the emphasis is placed on his argument with the Gentiles. Yet Luke frankly reports the utter meagerness of the results, which is hardly what we should expect if our author were merely romancing.

16-34. ***Paul Preaches in Athens.***—This famous passage falls quite naturally into three parts: (*a*) the congregation; (*b*) the sermon; (*c*) the results.

(*a*) The congregation was unlike any congregation Paul had ever addressed. To begin with, it was made up of people who basked in the afterglow of Athens' intellectual glory. They lived on lectures. They were kept alive by a diet of speculation, argument, and discussion. They dealt in ideas as other people dealt in butter and eggs. In modern society they would be called "intellectuals." Paul was at a distinct disadvantage among them because they listened to him as if he were another professional peddler of ideas. He was on the defensive from the beginning. They had the intellectual curiosity which makes for a good audience, but it was the curiosity that is content to remain in the abstractions of the mind, and is loath to venture into the world where ideas must exist as necessities and not luxuries. By and large, such a congregation is the most difficult that a Christian teacher can face. So long as a man can

17 Therefore disputed he in the synagogue with the Jews, and with the devout persons, and in the market daily with them that met with him.

idols. **17** So he argued in the synagogue with the Jews and the devout persons, and in the market place every day with those

(*c*) The curious note in vs. 18, that in the mention of **Jesus and the resurrection** the pagans imagined that Paul was introducing a new god-and-goddess combination, is singularly lifelike and can hardly have been invented.

(*d*) As for the alleged "formal trial," such is not really in view. The reference to **the Areopagus** is in fact ambiguous (the confusion is increased by the KJV, which in vs. 19 has **Areopagus** and in vs. 22 **Mars' hill** for the same Greek word), and the words **brought him to the Areopagus** may mean either that they took him to the judicial court of that name, or that they led him in friendly fashion to the slopes of the hill, where he might have space and quiet to address the crowd of curious Athenians. On the whole it seems more probable that the court is in view, and vss. 22 (**in the middle**) and 33 (**Paul went out from among them**) fit in better with this view. But even so, there is no question of a formal trial on a definite charge. Rather is it a friendly, but somewhat contemptuous, inquiry into the credentials of a new traveling sophist.

(*e*) Finally as to Paul's speech: though it can hardly be doubted that in detail it is a free literary creation of the author, the main line taken may well be Paul's own. Its general tone and tenor are exactly what might be expected in the circumstances. There can be no doubt that Paul went to great lengths to find points of contact with his hearers' ways of thinking. To the Jews of Pisidian Antioch he traced God's purpose in their history; to ignorant pagans at Lystra he spoke of God revealed in nature; and now to the cultured Athenians he strives to demonstrate philosophically that the new Christian religion of revelation is the perfect fulfillment of the religion of reason common to all mankind. We may at least be quite sure that the speech is an integral part of Acts, for apart from it Luke's set of typical speeches would be incomplete.

17. Devout persons; cf. vs. 4 above.

play with ideas the way a child plays with marbles, he is not likely to be drawn by the "nonsense" of the Cross that throws his neatly constructed systems of philosophy into the contradictions and paradoxes which are the product of life's strange and often incomprehensible ways. So long as he is satisfied with the discussion of religion, and finds neither the need nor the incentive to practice it, he will listen to men like Paul with the critical ears of an impartial investigator.

It is to Paul's everlasting credit that he did not shrink from an audience such as that. There is none more difficult or more likely to be unresponsive to the Christian gospel. Their opposition is not the violent protest of the forthright men of Philippi and Thessalonica. It is the silent scorn of the intellectual snob, the cool indifference of the sermontaster. Nevertheless, Paul never missed an opportunity to tell the world what God did in Christ, and he approached this congregation, as he approached all others, determined to do the best he could. After all, he himself was no intellectual pygmy, and Christianity was not only a way of life; it was also an explanation of life. As a way of life it appealed to a man's moral and religious consciousness, and as an explanation of life it appealed to a man's mind.

The mind of man is as important in religion as it is in mathematics, for religion not only moves a man to feel deeply but it also moves him to make up his mind about the universe and his own place in it. Especially is this true of Christianity. There never was a man who thought more clearly or more vigorously than Jesus. He made observations; he drew conclusions; he revised old ideas; he challenged prejudices—all of which call for mentality of a high order. His followers through the centuries have included some of the greatest thinkers of the world: Paul, Augustine, Thomas Aquinas, Luther, Pascal, Temple. To be sure, there have been times in history when the church has closed its mind. It closed its mind to modern astronomy and tried Galileo for heresy. It closed its mind to modern medicine and held back the great movement for the relief of suffering. It closed its mind to evolution and classed Darwin among the malefactors of the race. But this can be said: Whenever the church closes its mind, it might as well close its doors, for at that moment it ceases to take the mind of man seriously, and man minus mind is animal. Thank

18 Then certain philosophers of the Epicureans, and of the Stoics, encountered him. And some said, What will this babbler say? other some, He seemeth to be a setter forth of strange gods: because he preached unto them Jesus, and the resurrection.

19 And they took him, and brought him unto Areopagus, saying, May we know what this new doctrine, whereof thou speakest, *is?*

20 For thou bringest certain strange things to our ears: we would know therefore what these things mean.

who chanced to be there. 18 Some also of
the Epicurean and Stoic philosophers met
him. And some said, "What would this
babbler say?" Others said, "He seems to be
a preacher of foreign divinities" — because
he preached Jesus and the resurrection.
19 And they took hold of him and brought
him to the Ar-e-op′a-gus, saying, "May we
know what this new teaching is which you
present? 20 For you bring some strange
things to our ears; we wish to know there-

---

18. Epicurean and Stoic philosophers: The two most influential schools of philosophy at the time. The former, founded by Epicurus (*ca.* 300 B.C.), had "happiness" as its main aim. The latter, founded by Zeno (*ca.* 300 B.C.), advocated conduct "according to nature." But "happiness" and "nature" were so interpreted that the practical ethics of the two schools were virtually identical. Vss. 24-26 cleverly summarize the tenets of both schools. **Babbler,** literally "seed-picker," used originally of birds, and then of anyone who picks up odds and ends—Shakespeare's "snapper-up of unconsidered trifles." Finally, it is applied to a charlatan or plagiarist, whose learning is secondhand and undigested, like Browning's "Karshish, the picker-up of learning's crumbs." **A preacher of foreign divinities:** The same court 450 years earlier had charged Socrates with "corrupting the young men and not recognizing the gods whom the city recognized, but other novel deities" (Plato *Apology* 24 B; cf. Xenophon *Memorabilia* I. 1. 1). **Jesus and the resurrection.** In Greek this is "Jesus and *Anastasis,*" which to pagan listeners might well sound like the names of a god and a goddess.

19. The Areopagus, as already noted, may be either the hill of that name, which was behind the agora and northwest of the Acropolis, or more probably the council of the Areopagus, which had its seat in the *Stoa Basileios* or court of the "King Archon." This council had general supervision of religious and educational affairs, and one of its functions might be to examine the credentials of traveling lecturers. But Paul, as a Roman citizen and a Jew professing a religion recognized by law, would not be liable to formal arraignment in the Athenian censor's court.

---

heaven the church's mind has never remained permanently closed! Always someone like Paul has come along to push it wide open. One of the greatest contributions that the intellectual of today can make to the church is to see that the gates of the mind are kept open day and night.

(*b*) The sermon was Paul's sincere effort to reach an unfamiliar congregation of intellectuals. He began by telling them how religious they already were. The city was filled with objects of worship; one might almost say that it was cluttered with altars. Those altars indicated that there was in the people some deep-seated desire to worship something. They were not blind to the mystery of life, nor were they totally deaf to the music of the heavenly spheres. The impulse to adore was still strong in them, and could not be successfully hidden by their intellectual coat of many colors. Paul's technique therefore was to begin by assuming this natural curiosity for religion, and by giving them ample credit for what they already had. He began: **Men of Athens, I perceive that in every way you are very religious.**

There is a great deal to be said for such an approach to intellectuals. It sets out to win them rather than to take them by force. Suppose one of them begins by saying, "Of course, I am not a religious person." Following the technique of Paul on this particular occasion, the Christian might say something like this: "Perhaps you are not religious in the formal sense of the word; perhaps you belong to no church and profess no creed. But have you ever come home late at night and suddenly caught your breath as you looked up at the stars and felt all your earthly ways and movements chastened by the silent glory of the sky? Have you ever planted a garden, and as the dusty seeds

21 (For all the Athenians, and strangers which were there, spent their time in nothing else, but either to tell or to hear some new thing.)

22 ¶ Then Paul stood in the midst of Mars' Hill, and said, *Ye* men of Athens, I perceive that in all things ye are too superstitious.

23 For as I passed by, and beheld your devotions, I found an altar with this inscription, TO THE UNKNOWN GOD. Whom therefore ye ignorantly worship, him declare I unto you.

fore what these things mean." 21 Now all
the Athenians and the foreigners who lived
there spent their time in nothing except
telling or hearing something new.
22 So Paul, standing in the middle of
the Ar-e-op'a-gus, said:
"Men of Athens, I perceive that in every
way you are very religious. 23 For as I passed
along, and observed the objects of your
worship, I found also an altar with this inscription, 'To an unknown god.' What
therefore you worship as unknown, this I

---

21. Something new: Or to bring out the force of the Greek comparative, "the last new idea" (Lake and Cadbury). The curiosity of the Athenians was notorious. As Demosthenes had said to them three hundred years earlier, "Instead of guarding your liberties, you are forever gadding about and looking for news" (*Philippics* I. 43).

22. In the middle obviously suits the council better than the hill. **Very religious** (RSV), rather than **too superstitious** (KJV), is the better translation, though doubtless the word carries a trace of irony.

23. To an unknown god: There is no evidence of the existence of any such inscription in the singular number. Eduard Norden (*Agnostos Theos* [Leipzig and Berlin: B. G. Teubner, 1913]) argues that our author has simply borrowed the idea out of a lost book entitled *Concerning Sacrifices,* which Philostratus attributes to Apollonius of Tyana; in it the religiosity of the Athenians is illustrated by their erection of altars "of unknown demons" (Philostratus *Life of Apollonius of Tyana* VI. 3. 5). This seems most improbable. On the other hand Pausanias bears witness to the existence of altars to "unknown gods" on the road from Phalerum to Athens and also at Olympia (*Description of Greece* I. 1. 4; V. 14. 8), and an altar of the second century has been found at Pergamum, the inscription on which may possibly be reconstructed in the same terms (see Adolf Deissmann, *Paul* [London: Hodder & Stoughton, 1926], pp. 287-91). Though we know of no altar to any one deity specifically called "the unknown god," Diogenes Laertius (I. 110) tells how during a plague Epimenides the Cretan instructed the Athenians to let loose black and white sheep on the Areopagus, and, wherever they lay down, to sacrifice to "the

---

sifted through your fingers, been deeply stirred by the mystery of growth? Have you ever sat by your radio and through the medley of words and music been drawn to the outer fringe of time and space, where the sound waves finally break on the brink of the last horizon? Have you ever stood beside a baby's crib and wondered at the mystery of life, where it comes from and where it goes?"

The answer to questions like these is invariably "Yes." It is then the Christian's pleasure to tell the man or woman how religious he really is. In the ordinary experiences of life he has come very close to the threshold of worship. He has a secret altar somewhere in his life before which he unconsciously yet wistfully worships. It is the altar to an unknown God. Paul found it among the other altars that were more specific and unabashed in their religious allegiances. He began at that altar to make his appeal to the nonreligious intellectuals of Athens. It is always one possible place for the Christian teacher and preacher to begin.

Paul went on to tell them that they were wasting their precious capacity for religion. They were worshiping unworthy gods, small ones that could be contained in an idol or an image. He told them about the God who was the maker and master of the universe, the source of all life, the Lord of all nations, the indwelling Spirit of every single individual. It was as if he had said to them: "If you are going to be religious, be religious in a big way. If you are going to adore something, adore something inconceivably good and great. If you are going to have a god, as you all secretly have, have the real God. If you have the capacity for religion, develop it, make the most of it. Just as a man who has the ability to walk is never satisfied to creep or crawl, do not be satisfied with

24 God that made the world and all things therein, seeing that he is Lord of heaven and earth, dwelleth not in temples made with hands;

25 Neither is worshipped with men's hands, as though he needed any thing, seeing he giveth to all life, and breath, and all things;

26 And hath made of one blood all nations of men for to dwell on all the face of the earth, and hath determined the times before appointed, and the bounds of their habitation;

proclaim to you. 24 The God who made
the world and everything in it, being Lord
of heaven and earth, does not live in
shrines made by man, 25 nor is he served
by human hands, as though he needed anything, since he himself gives to all men life
and breath and everything. 26 And he made
from one every nation of men to live on all
the face of the earth, having determined
allotted periods and the boundaries of their

---

appropriate god," i.e., the unknown god who was concerned in the matter. It is just possible that it was some such altar that Paul observed, and that "to an unknown god" is Luke's not quite accurate paraphrase. But probably Luke has simply given the polytheistic inscription a monotheistic turn to serve the purpose of his argument. **Worship as unknown;** cf. John 4:22, "You worship what you do not know; we worship what we know, for salvation is from the Jews." For the idea that apart from revelation even the pagans are driven by an inward urge to actions which only revelation can make intelligible, cf. Paul's argument in Rom. 2:14-16.

24. Does not live in shrines made by man; cf. 7:48.

26. He made from one: The Western text followed by all later MSS reads **of one blood** (KJV). The unity of human nature was a fundamental doctrine of the Stoics. **Periods:** Probably with reference to the doctrine that each nation has its allotted era of prosperity and predominance (cf. Dan. 8:10; Luke 21:24, "until the times of the Gentiles are fulfilled"). Alternatively we may translate "seasons," and cf. 14:17, "he . . . gave you . . . fruitful seasons."

---

a religion that uses only about one tenth of your religious capacity. Never be satisfied with a gold or silver shrine. The God of the universe is too much alive to dwell in a thing like that. He once dwelt in a person, and that living image of God is the only image that is worthy of your serious devotion. Furthermore, there is a day coming when you will all be judged by him who is the living image of the invisible God."

So Christians are often asked, "If I am already religious in the sense in which you have described it, what more then can I do? If I pray and worship as I go about my daily routine, what more do I need to do?" An analogy may help to answer the question. Every normal person is endowed with a measure of intellectual curiosity. He reaches out with the fingers of his mind to grasp and to investigate the truth of the world around him. Yet no one would be satisfied to leave him so. He is educated. Education assures him that he is an intelligent human being already, and then begins to train and direct those natural curiosities until they develop into the mature thinking man. Thus the child who has the ingenuity to make strange sounds with his vocal chords and queer marks with a stone grows into the man who can speak a magnificent language and write a great drama. So also is a man equipped with the natural impulse to pray and worship. He has a native thirst for God. Religion assures him that he is by nature a praying creature. It then begins to nurture and correlate those natural impulses, eliminating that which is harmful, restraining that which is distracting and diverting, avoiding waste of spiritual energy, and in this way increasing and intensifying the power of those elemental drives. Thus the man who stands awe-struck beneath the stars grows into the man who worships the God in whom **we live, and move, and have our being,** and whose offspring he is. Religion has discovered and developed his highest spiritual capacity.

But beyond that the Christian can point out that if a man has scientific inclinations, he wants to know the truth about science; and if he has artistic talents, he wants to know the best in art. Likewise, given a man who is naturally religious, he wants to know the truth in religion. If the truth about God is to be found in Jesus as it is found in no other person or place, then he wants to know it. If he is going to worship any god at all, he wants to worship the real one,

27 That they should seek the Lord, if
haply they might feel after him, and find
him, though he be not far from every one
of us:
28 For in him we live, and move, and
have our being; as certain also of your
own poets have said, For we are also his
offspring.
29 Forasmuch then as we are the offspring of God, we ought not to think that
the Godhead is like unto gold, or silver,
or stone, graven by art and man's device.

habitation, 27 that they should seek God,
in the hope that they might feel after him
and find him. Yet he is not far from each
one of us, 28 for
In him we live and move and have our
being;'
as even some of your poets have said,
'For we are indeed his offspring.'
29 Being then God's offspring, we ought not
to think that the Deity is like gold, or silver,
or stone, a representation by the art and

27-28. Feel after him and find him; cf. Wisd. Sol. 13:6, "While they are seeking God and desiring to find him." The thought of vss. 27-28 "does not merely border on Stoic pantheism, it is nothing else but that" (Weiss, *History of Primitive Christianity*, I, 241-42). **In him we live and move and have our being:** The words seem to be an echo of a line in a poem attributed, rightly or wrongly, to Epimenides, the semimythical Cretan referred to in the note on vs. 23. The second quotation, **For we are indeed his offspring,** is from the *Phaenomena* of Aratus, who was born *ca.* 310 B.C. and hailed from Soli in Cilicia, Paul's own country (for a full discussion of the two quotations see *Beginnings of Christianity,* V, 246 ff.). No doubt it was a stock quotation in Stoic circles. But is Paul likely to have spoken thus in the terms of Stoic pantheism? Such passages as I Cor. 15:47-50 would rather suggest that he did not think of unredeemed man as being possessed "by nature" of a kinship to God, but rather drew a sharp contrast between man's fleshly nature and the spiritual nature of the divine Being.

29. The Deity is like gold . . . man; cf. Rom. 1:22-23, "Claiming to be wise, they became fools, and exchanged the glory of the immortal God for images resembling mortal man or birds or animals or reptiles"—a passage which, surely significantly, immediately follows Paul's nearest approach to Stoic thinking when he writes, "Ever since the creation of the world his invisible nature, namely, his eternal power and deity, has been clearly perceived in the things that have been made" (Rom. 1:20).

---

and the real God is the God of the universe, who in the fullness of time manifested forth his glory in Jesus. By him we shall be judged; and by none other shall we be saved.

(*c*) The results of this sermon were not the results that usually followed Paul's preaching. There was no persecution, and no strong church was established. Was the sermon then a failure? Many commentators have said, "Yes, it was." One dare not make too hasty judgment. There are several factors to consider.

First, it is never possible to measure accurately the results of a sermon. It is tempting and easy to judge the success of a sermon by the tangible results it produces. The preaching to the Thessalonians, for instance, is judged to be successful because of the strong church it left behind in Thessalonica. And likewise the preaching to the Philippians and the Corinthians. But the tangible results of a sermon are not the only ones. The people whose lives are touched and secretly changed are not always found on the parish lists, and the record of the change is not always written up in the parish calendar. To be sure, Paul left behind him in Athens no church comparable to the ones in the other cities he visited, but no one knows how many intellectuals were shaken out of their intellectual pride by the quiet, humble, yet learned words of Paul. And no one knows how great an influence this particular sermon had as a strong Christian appeal to the world of Greek culture and learning. Many an apologia has been inspired by the sermon on Mars' Hill, and those who now may try to show confused intellectuals the way to God turn to Paul's sermon in Athens and reap the reward of what might have seemed to him to be his failure.

It must also be remembered that part of the failure of a sermon is the failure of the listeners to respond. No matter how powerful a speaker may be, he cannot speak to stones and make them listen. People did not always listen to Jesus, and when they did, they did not always hear or understand what he said. We have already granted that this congregation of intellectuals was a difficult one. Their very lack of passion made their hearts hard to touch, and

30 And the times of this ignorance God winked at; but now commandeth all men every where to repent:

31 Because he hath appointed a day, in the which he will judge the world in righteousness by *that* man whom he hath ordained*; whereof* he hath given assurance unto all *men,* in that he hath raised him from the dead.

32 ¶ And when they heard of the resurrection of the dead, some mocked: and others said, We will hear thee again of this *matter.*

33 So Paul departed from among them.

imagination of man.
30 The times of ignorance God overlooked, but now he commands all men everywhere to repent,
31 because he has fixed a day on which he will judge the world in righteousness by a man whom he has appointed, and of this he has given assurance to all men by raising him from the dead."

32 Now when they heard of the resurrection of the dead, some mocked; but others said, "We will hear you again about this."
33 So Paul went out from among

30. God overlooked: It is questionable whether Paul would have excused idolatry on the ground of **ignorance.** In I Cor. 15:34 to have "no knowledge of God" is supremely a matter of "shame"; and in Rom. 1:18 Paul writes that "the wrath of God is revealed from heaven" against those who will not acknowledge him even though he has manifested himself to them in nature. On the other hand Rom. 3:25 speaks of the "divine forbearance" in which God "passed over former sins"; cf. also 14:16, "In past generations he allowed all the nations to walk in their own ways."

31-32. Judge . . . by a man: This verse reflects the pure Son of man Christology and eschatology of the Synoptic Gospels. The word **man** (ἀνδρί) almost certainly represents the Aramaic *bar-nāshā',* which in the Gospels is regularly translated "the Son of man." Luke for the sake of his Gentile readers modifies this Jewish terminology. **The resurrection of the dead:** More correctly "a resurrection of dead men."

33. From among them, like "in the middle" (vs. 22), suits the council better than the hill.

their intellectual calm was the most difficult thing in the world to trouble. It may fairly be said that given a congregation like that, it is a wonder that Paul converted Dionysius, Damaris, and some others. In other words, the responsibility for Paul's failure in Athens did not rest entirely on the preacher, but rather on the intellectual coolness of the congregation to which he preached.

A great many people have raised the question whether Paul could not have been more effective if he had been less intellectual. Paul changed his approach from a positive declaration of the Cross and the Resurrection to a broad, general affirmation of a universal God who raised a man from the dead. Jesus is not mentioned by name. The Cross is not specified. Paul, according to many of his critics, was in this instance eating too much humble pie. He was making every effort to meet the intellectuals where they were, to use their own language, to lead them from their own assumptions to the Christian gospel. The questions that the critics raise are: Can it be done—ever? Can you ever start from the broad, generally accepted principles of natural theology and work up to the Cross, or must you not always start with the Cross, striking like lightning all the general assumptions and propositions of the mind, and let the glory of the Cross illuminate and redeem the troubled ways of the mind?

It is hard to answer categorically one way or the other. It is true, however, that not many so-called intellectuals are explained into Christianity. That is to say, they are not converted often by intellectual arguments. They are more likely to be converted by an experience in which their moral consciousness has been shocked or their spiritual awareness has been awakened. Philosophers were converted during World War II not by the theologians but by the horror that they witnessed and by the heroism of Christians who were able to transcend it. The intellectuals of our own day are far more likely to be converted by a church that does something sacrificial than by a church that thinks something acceptable and plausible.

Does this mean that the approach Paul made to the people in Athens is always out of order? Not at all. While the kind of apologia Paul made in Athens may not convert intellectuals, it will confirm those in whom there is already the will to believe, and it will articulate their incipient faith by declaring it in words that

34 Howbeit certain men clave unto him,
and believed: among the which *was* Dionysius the Areopagite, and a woman named
Damaris, and others with them.

18 After these things Paul departed
from Athens, and came to Corinth;
2 And found a certain Jew named Aq-

them. 34 But some men joined him and
believed, among them Di-o-nys'i-us the Ar-
e-op'a-gite and a woman named Dam'a-ris
and others with them.

18 After this he left Athens and went
to Corinth. 2 And he found a Jew

34. **Joined him and believed:** That no permanent impression was made is perhaps suggested by the fact that Paul himself calls Stephanas of Corinth, and not these Athenians, "the first converts in Achaia" (I Cor. 16:15). We have no mention in the N.T. of any Athenian church. Of **Damaris** we know nothing. **Dionysius** became famous in later tradition. Eusebius, on no good authority, makes him the first bishop of Athens (*Church History* III. 4. 11; IV. 23. 3). In the Middle Ages his alleged writings, translated into Latin by Johannes Scotus in the ninth century, became, as a popular handbook of mysticism, almost as well known as Paul's own writings.

Athens may be said to be Paul's one significant failure. Critics have urged that I Cor. 2:1-6, where Paul disclaims all "plausible words of wisdom" and professes to preach only "Jesus Christ and him crucified," proves that he can never have adopted methods such as Luke attributes to him at Athens, and have thus entered into competition with Greek philosophy. We should prefer to believe that when Paul reminds the Corinthians how he arrived among them "in weakness and in much fear and trembling," he is recalling the mood in which he left Athens with the sense of failure heavy upon him. Paul had learned his lesson. "He realised, what is as true to-day as then, that mere academic argument on behalf of Christianity seldom converts anybody" (A. H. McNeile, *St Paul* [Cambridge: University Press, 1920], p. 67).

b) Corinth (18:1-17)

Owing to the fullness of Paul's correspondence with the Corinthian church, we know more about it and its problems than about any other of Paul's churches. The information given by Acts is manifestly very incomplete. But from the epistles we know that no other church caused him more trouble and grief and, in the end, more thankfulness. He wrote to it at least four letters; visited it at least three times; and from it he wrote, in addition to the Thessalonian epistles (and possibly Galatians, if it is dated later than we have suggested), the greatest of all his letters, that to the Romans. Corinth, the official title of which was *Laus Iulia Corinthi,* had been refounded by Julius Caesar in 46 B.C. as a Roman colony on the site of the ancient city destroyed by Mummius in 146 B.C. Situated on the isthmus between two seas, with a port on each, it rapidly and inevitably became a prosperous commercial center, and quickly took its place as the capital of the province of Achaia. Its population was extremely cosmopolitan, and accord-

they understand. The writer of the Fourth Gospel did exactly that when he said, "And the Word was made flesh." *Logos* was like the word "reality" in our own day. It did not mean the same thing, but it was a technical word that had become popularly understood and used. Christians in the second century did not hesitate to take those current coins and give them Christian values. It is not likely that the church will make any great advance in our day until it has translated its message into language that is understood in the twentieth century. To do that is not to appease the intellectuals or to curtail the power of the gospel. It is to follow the example not only of Paul the apostle, but also of Jesus the Master, who, when he spoke to the people about the kingdom of God, said that it is *like* a farmer sowing seed, *like* a shepherd, *like* a father, *like* a woman who has lost a coin. He took the old vessels and filled them with new wine. Occasionally, as he himself predicted, the wine was too strong and the vessels broke, but temporarily at least they served their purpose.

18:1-17. ***Paul's Ministry in Corinth.***—Without achieving any great success, Paul left the capital of learning and culture and went to Corinth. **After this he left Athens and went**

uila, born in Pontus, lately come from Italy, with his wife Priscilla, (because that

named Aquila, a native of Pontus, lately come from Italy with his wife Priscilla, be-

ing to Mommsen it was "the least Greek of the Greek cities." Similarly its religion was highly syncretistic; the various mystery cults, especially that of the neighboring sanctuary at Eleusis, won great popularity; and in particular the temple of Aphrodite, with its world-famous cult of unchastity and one thousand (so Strabo) religious prostitutes, attracted innumerable pilgrims. Even in an age which was careless in such matters, "to live like a Corinthian" (κορινθιάζεσθαι) summed up in a phrase every type of debauchery. It is not by chance that, in addition to frequent references in the Corinthian letters, the two passages in which Paul assails most passionately pagan immorality were both written from Corinth (I Thess. 4:3-7; Rom. 1:18-25). The city was not an intellectual center comparable with Athens or Alexandria or even Tarsus. Nevertheless traveling philosophers would be there in abundance, and the city still prided itself on its intellectual heritage. On the road to the port of Cenchreae the tourist would be shown with veneration the tomb of Diogenes, the famous cynic, just next to that of the notorious courtesan Lais—apt commentary perhaps on the ethos of the city!

With Paul's first visit to Corinth we reach the one fixed point for the determination of the chronology of his missionary work. In 1905 there were published four fragments of an inscription found at Delphi (see Deissmann, *Paul,* Appendix I) containing words of a letter of greeting from the Emperor Claudius to the city of Delphi. Enough is preserved to prove that it dates from the year in which the emperor was saluted as such "for the twenty-sixth time," and that at this time Gallio was **proconsul of Achaia.** We can fix the date of his arrival as about the midsummer of either A.D. 51 or 52, probably the former. Paul had already been **a year and six months** (vs. 11) in Corinth before Gallio took office, and therefore must have arrived about the beginning of 50 or 51. Because, after his trial, he stayed on **many days longer** (vs. 18), perhaps over the winter, we may assume that he left early in 52 or 53.

It would appear that, just as at Athens, Paul did not at first contemplate embarking upon a prolonged mission at Corinth. He was probably still hoping for a return to Macedonia, and meanwhile he filled in time by working at his trade (vs. 3) and speaking as opportunity offered at the weekly service at the synagogue. It was only **when Silas and Timothy arrived from Macedonia** (vs. 5), probably with the news that the door there was still closed, that Paul launched out on his own lines by taking independent premises **in the house of a man named Titius Justus** (vs. 7), as later he did in the "school of one Tyrannus" at Ephesus (19:9). Though Luke again repeats his thesis of an inevitable rupture with the synagogue before preaching to the Gentiles began (see on 13:13), it is possible that Paul moved into his own headquarters not so much because he had finally broken with the Jews—in which case to settle down **next door to the synagogue** (vs. 7) was hardly the most tactful course—but rather because he wished to remain in close touch with the many Gentile inquirers who would frequent the synagogue and who

to Corinth. Life in a seaport was likely to be more hospitable to the Christian gospel than life in the sheltered cloisters of the schools and academies. It is often true that a mill town is more fertile ground for Christianity than a college campus. Athens was proud, and Athens was old. There is an intellectual pride that is a more formidable obstacle to the gospel than the most flagrant immorality, and there are some places with a past so glorious that it is an irresistible temptation to linger in its twilight rather than to face the uncertainties of a new dawn. Athens had both the pride and the glory that were rapidly fading, so Paul moved on from a city renowned for its learning to one notorious for its vice. So his Master had moved on, from town to town, from person to person, passing by those who reveled in their past and going on to those who were dissatisfied with their present condition and longed for a new life.

Common sense would tell us that Paul probably arrived in Corinth a disappointed and dejected man. Did the gospel have the power he thought it had? If it did, why did it not stir those who had the best mental equipment to receive it? In such a dispirited mood it would not surprise us to find Paul's physical health

Claudius had commanded all Jews to depart from Rome,) and came unto them.

cause Claudius had commanded all the Jews to leave Rome. And he went to see

always provided him with his first non-Jewish converts. It is true, nevertheless, that the Thessalonian epistles provide confirmation of the hostility of the Corinthian Jews. In I Thess. 2:15-16; 3:7 Paul may well be referring to the situation in which he is writing at Corinth as well as to his treatment by the Jews at Thessalonica.

Concerning Paul's mission to Corinth, the Corinthian epistles do much to supplement Luke's somewhat meager account: (*a*) Humiliated by his failure in Athens, Paul evidently faced his task in a somewhat despondent mood (cf. vs. 9). Never before had he been called upon to face, with his gospel, such a combination of extreme worldliness and intellectual cynicism. As he writes, "I was with you in weakness and in much fear and trembling" (I Cor. 2:3). (*b*) As to the character of his message: again warned by failure he determined not to use the academic method, not to trust to "plausible words of wisdom," but to preach the plain and central gospel of "Jesus Christ and him crucified" (I Cor. 2:1-5). (*c*) The epistles indicate that the extent of Paul's work was wider than Acts would suggest. The household of Stephanas are the "first converts" not only of Corinth but of all "Achaia" (I Cor. 16:15), while we hear of a church at the port of Cenchreae (Rom. 16:1) and of "all the saints who are in the whole of Achaia" (II Cor. 1:1). (*d*) The epistles make it clear that the church was predominantly Gentile and that there were comparatively few Jewish believers. Moreover the moral abuses to which they were prone seem to indicate that Paul's converts had come straight from heathenism rather than from the ranks of the proselytes or "God-fearers." Acts therefore almost certainly gives a false impression in the suggestion that Paul's approach was largely through the Jewish community. In line with this mistaken view Luke mentions only Jewish disciples and converts—Crispus, Aquila and Priscilla, Titius Justus; there is no word of the Gentile names we meet in the epistles—Stephanas, Gaius, Fortunatus, Achaicus, Chloe. (*e*) As to the social rank of the converts, they were mostly from the lower and less educated classes (I Cor. 1:26). Yet there must have been some of superior station—e.g., perhaps Stephanas (I Cor. 16:15). The cleavage between rich and poor was evidently at the root of the trouble in connection with the Lord's Supper (I Cor. 11:18-22), and people who preferred the Alexandrian allegorism of Apollos to the simpler preaching of Paul must have boasted some education. (*f*) Finally, the epistles stress the tendency of the community to schism—Paul, Peter, and Apollos each having their enthusiastic followers, who used the name of their own chosen leader as a party war cry, instead of acknowledging the unity of all in Christ (I Cor. 1:10-13; 3:3-7).

18:2. Aquila and **Priscilla** were evidently folk of some means who traveled widely, for we meet them not only at Corinth but at Ephesus (18:26; I Cor. 16:19) and at Rome (Rom. 16:3-5—unless it is held that this chapter is addressed to Ephesus), where they had a "church in their house." An edict of **Claudius** in A.D. 49 **had commanded all the Jews to leave Rome**—according to Suetonius, because they had been creating disturbances "at

reflecting the strain of his spirit. In this case our common sense is confirmed by a line in a letter which Paul later wrote to the people of Corinth. Recollecting his first days in Corinth, he wrote, "And I was with you in weakness, and in fear, and in much trembling" (I Cor. 2:3). Painful as it was, it was probably for Paul's own good in the end. Uninterrupted success is enough to ruin any man, let alone a preacher of the gospel. It was doubtless in those periods of discouragement that Paul learned the power of the Cross and began to see its full glory. Christian ministers cannot preach about a Cross the suffering of which they have never shared; and the greatest suffering of all is the suffering of one who sees the Lord he loves above all others scorned by the multitude and ignored by the great, while he himself stands by helpless, unable to make others see or feel the love he feels and knows so deeply. The man who goes through that begins to know in a small way what the everlasting Love suffers when the children are not even conscious that he is there.

When a man is in the mood that Paul must have been in when he arrived in Corinth, the best thing that can happen to him is to meet another man with whom he has something in

3 And because he was of the same craft,
he abode with them, and wrought: (for
by their occupation they were tentmakers.)
4 And he reasoned in the synagogue
every sabbath, and persuaded the Jews and
the Greeks.

them; 3 and because he was of the same
trade he stayed with them, and they worked,
for by trade they were tentmakers. 4 And
he argued in the synagogue every sabbath,
and persuaded Jews and Greeks.

---

the instigation of Chrestus" (*"Iudaeos impulsore Chresto assidue tumultuantes Roma expulit"* [*Claudius* XXV])—probably a reference to Jesus, who by a popular misunderstanding was supposed to be still alive, though Chrestus may of course have been quite a different person. **Priscilla** in the epistles is called Prisca (Rom. 16:3; I Cor. 16:19; II Tim. 4:19) where she is twice named before her husband as if the more important of the couple (cf. vss. 18, 26). Harnack has even suggested her as a possible author for the Epistle to the Hebrews! There is no indication whether Aquila and Priscilla were already Christians before they met Paul. If so, a church must have been founded in Rome before A.D. 49, and the reference by Suetonius may well be to disturbances caused by the preaching of the Christian gospel to the Jews of Rome.

3. Tentmakers (σκηνοποιοί): Goat-hair cloth, used for tents, was a notable export from Paul's native province of Cilicia. But Lake and Cadbury argue that the word at this time commonly meant a "leatherworker."

4. The synagogue: An inscription has been found in Corinth datable about Paul's time, which can be reconstructed to read "Synagogue of the Hebrews" ([συνα] γωγη εβρ [αιων]; see Adolf Deissmann, *Light from the Ancient East,* tr. L. R. M. Strachan [London: Hodder & Stoughton, 1910], p. 16).

---

common. That is exactly what happened to Paul. He met Aquila. They had a great deal in common from the start. They were both Jews, and they were both well born. They had both traveled a good deal, Aquila on business and Paul on a mission. They were both in a sense refugees. Aquila and his wife had been driven from Rome in the emperor's frantic attempt to purge the city of Jews. Paul had been driven not out of one city only, but out of many. They were pilgrims, so to speak. They were both Christians; at least there is nothing in the story to indicate that Aquila and Priscilla were not already Christians when they first met Paul. And above all, they both had the same trade, they both knew the same skill and worked at the same craft. No one is quite sure what the trade was, so perhaps it is better to remain content with the traditional belief that it was the trade of tentmaking. It is not so much what the trade was that matters; it is that they both had it, and that in the time of Paul's spiritual depression he found a companion with whom he could work. "And they all worked together" (Moffatt). According to the record in the Acts, Paul was a workman in the city of Corinth before he was an evangelist. It would be brash to guess how many other spiritual leaders have had to find recreation in physical labor, and how blessed they are when they can work in company with people who are sympathetic and congenial. For most people life would be intolerable apart from its close human associations. Those associations warm it as a fire warms a house; they make its burdens bearable and its wounds endurable. No wonder Paul spoke so many times with such affection of the two friends who took him in when he came to Corinth, a sick, discouraged man.

It is interesting to notice how Paul recovered. The old vitality came back. First it was physical labor; he gave his mind a rest. There are times when the most creative minds must lie fallow. No preacher should preach fifty-two Sundays a year, and no teacher should teach all the year round. The greatest thoughts often come when a man is doing something else. So Paul dropped everything for a season. He stopped preaching and turned to manual labor. Then he went back to the synagogue, the place where he always began, his home base, the place he was familiar with. **And he argued in the synagogue every sabbath.** Not spasmodically, when he happened to feel like it, but every sabbath. The old fire was coming back, the intensity, the passion. How wonderful it is to see a man make a comeback! After a long spell, when the tide seems to have ebbed, keeps going out and never turns, suddenly it begins to come in. The water level rises, the beaches are washed once again with the waters from the deeps. That is what happened to Paul, and it happens daily to people who have thought that they were through. Then, marvelously, "by the time Silas

5 And when Silas and Timotheus were come from Macedonia, Paul was pressed in the spirit, and testified to the Jews *that* Jesus *was* Christ.

6 And when they opposed themselves, and blasphemed, he shook *his* raiment, and said unto them, Your blood *be* upon your own heads; I *am* clean: from henceforth I will go unto the Gentiles.

7 ¶ And he departed thence, and entered into a certain *man's* house, named Justus, *one* that worshipped God, whose house joined hard to the synagogue.

8 And Crispus, the chief ruler of the synagogue, believed on the Lord with all his house; and many of the Corinthians hearing believed, and were baptized.

5 When Silas and Timothy arrived from Mac-e-do'ni-a, Paul was occupied with preaching, testifying to the Jews that the Christ was Jesus.
6 And when they opposed and reviled him, he shook out his garments and said to them, "Your blood be upon your heads! I am innocent. From now on I will go to the Gentiles."
7 And he left there and went to the house of a man named Titius[p] Justus, a worshiper of God; his house was next door to the synagogue.
8 Crispus, the ruler of the synagogue, believed in the Lord, together with all his household; and many of the Corinthians hearing Paul believed and were baptized.

[p] Other early authorities read *Titus.*

---

5. For the movements of **Silas and Timothy** see on 17:15. **Paul was occupied with preaching:** Or rather, bringing out the force of the imperfect, "began to be absorbed in preaching"; i.e., after the arrival of his helpers he laid aside his manual labor and devoted all his time to preaching. **That the Christ was Jesus** (RSV), rather than **that Jesus was Christ** (KJV), is the correct translation, for "in the Jewish synagogues 'the Messiah' was the known and Jesus the unknown quantity" (*Beginnings of Christianity,* IV, 225).

6-8. Shook out his garments: See on 13:51. **Your blood . . . heads:** For this Jewish formula cf. II Sam. 1:16; Matt. 27:25. **He left there,** i.e., ceased to preach in the synagogue. But if we suppose that the conventional break with the synagogue has been artificially introduced by our author, the words—if from an earlier source—may have originally meant "left Aquila's house and went to his new headquarters." **Titius** (or Titus) **Justus** was identified by Chrysostom and others with the Titus of the epistles, who otherwise is not mentioned in Acts. But Gal. 2:1 seems to prove that the latter had joined Paul at a much earlier date. **Worshiper of God:** See on 10:2. **Crispus, the ruler of the synagogue:** For the office see on 13:15. Paul mentions Crispus' baptism in I Cor. 1:14. There is a certain humor in the situation. Paul's rival preaching station is **next door** to the synagogue, and his first convert is one of its chief officials!

---

and Timotheus came south from Macedonia, Paul was engrossed in this preaching of the word, arguing to the Jews that the messiah was Jesus" (Moffatt). Paul was once more in full stream. He was *engrossed* in his preaching, absorbed by it. His recovery was complete. Some people live lives in which there are very few ups and downs. Their spiritual and emotional energies stay at a fairly steady level. But there are others whose ups and downs are great. Let them take courage from Paul. He was not always on the crest of the wave. He had his downcast periods. When that happened, he went to work on his tentmaking and gradually the life came back.

It was not long, however, before the Jews began to make trouble for Paul. This time it got under Paul's skin. He was irritated. He washed his hands of them. He moved out, completely and entirely. He even went to live with a Gentile, named Titius Justus. Paul was not a moderate man. He was not the kind of a man to sit on the fence with a leg on each side. He was on either one side or the other. When John Mark wanted to go with him on the second journey, after turning back on the first one, Paul said, "No." There was nothing more to be said. Barnabas could give John another chance if he wanted to, but not Paul. Paul had made up his mind and there were no two ways about it. He was a decisive person. So now, when he sees that the Jews are a stone wall which he can never penetrate, he breaks with them, and the break is a complete one. He even refuses to live with two close friends because they are Jews. So he moves. That kind of decisive movement always has a place of power in the church. Not everyone can do it; perhaps not everyone should do it. There is a place indeed for the reconcilers, the pacifiers, the peo-

9 Then spake the Lord to Paul in the night by a vision, Be not afraid, but speak, and hold not thy peace:

10 For I am with thee, and no man shall set on thee to hurt thee: for I have much people in this city.

11 And he continued *there* a year and six months, teaching the word of God among them.

12 ¶ And when Gallio was the deputy of Achaia, the Jews made insurrection with one accord against Paul, and brought him to the judgment seat,

9 And the Lord said to Paul one night in a
vision, "Do not be afraid, but speak and do
not be silent; 10 for I am with you, and no
man shall attack you to harm you; for I
have many people in this city." 11 And he
stayed a year and six months, teaching the
word of God among them.

12 But when Gallio was proconsul of
A-cha'ia, the Jews made a united attack
upon Paul and brought him before the

9-10. As so often, a vision marks a crisis in Paul's career. The words **I have many people in this city** show how clearly our author realized that at Corinth was to be the most vigorous and perhaps the largest of all Paul's churches.

11. A year and six months: This probably denotes the period before the arrival of Gallio, not the duration of Paul's whole stay at Corinth; for after the trial he still remained "many days longer" (vs. 18).

12. Lucius Junius **Gallio** was the elder brother of the celebrated Seneca and uncle of the poet Lucan. Seneca dedicated to him *Anger* and *The Happy Life* and draws a pleasing picture of his character: "Other vices he knew not, but flattery he hated"; "To love him to the utmost was to love him all too little"; "No mortal was so sweet (*dulcis*) to one as he was to all." The implication of this verse is that Gallio had just come into office, and that the Jews thought a new governor might yield to pressure. **The tribunal** (βῆμα) means first the seat of a magistrate, then the court or even the person of the judge himself—as we say in English, "the bench."

---

ple like Barnabas, who are ready to reconsider, to placate and heal. But there is also a place in the church for people like Paul, who go either one way or the other, who refuse to straddle. Pastors must be both kinds of people. There are times when their role is to bear with patience the stupidity of their people; to understand, make allowances, and be slow to judge. There are other times when their role is to stand for something, to take a side, to refuse to compromise, to confront their people with their stubbornness and stupidity and, if there is no indication of will to improve, move on to another place. It takes the courage of a man like Paul to do that, and it also takes the wisdom and charity of a man like Paul to know when to do it!

About this time Paul received a wonderful message from God. "Have no fear," God told him, "speak on and never stop, for I am with you, and no one shall attack and injure you; I have many people in this city" (Moffatt). That message should be written on every preacher's wall. The order comes first: "Speak on and never stop." No matter how discouraged you may become, no matter how much you may doubt the effectiveness of your speaking, no matter how many other things seem to be more important, nevertheless, speak on and never stop! The news must be told; the word must be spread. How can the people know and believe unless someone tells them? You have told them, you think. Yes, but like children, they have to be told over and over again. Sometimes they are not in the mood to hear what you say; if they do hear it, they may not take it in. The words may have been scrambled in their minds, all mixed up with thoughts about their business or their home. Sometimes they have no way to listen. There is no receiving instrument, and if there is, it may be tuned to another station, at least for the time being. So speak on and never stop! Sunday after Sunday, week in and week out, year after year, and decade after decade.

The order is followed by a promise: **I am with you.** Do not be afraid of anything. Do not let the businessmen or the politicians, the wealthy or the prominent, frighten you into silence. They cannot hurt you, they can only prove you are right. Do not be afraid of running out of material. The reservoirs of God are inexhaustible. You may think that you have said all you have to say. Not at all! There is more; the whole story is never told, and the scenery changes from day to day. So keep on

13 Saying, This *fellow* persuadeth men
to worship God contrary to the law.
14 And when Paul was now about to
open *his* mouth, Gallio said unto the Jews,
If it were a matter of wrong or wicked
lewdness, O *ye* Jews, reason would that I
should bear with you:
15 But if it be a question of words and
names, and *of* your law, look ye *to it;* for
I will be no judge of such *matters.*

tribunal, 13 saying, "This man is persuading men to worship God contrary to the
law." 14 But when Paul was about to open
his mouth, Gallio said to the Jews, "If it
were a matter of wrongdoing or vicious
crime, I should have reason to bear with
you, O Jews; 15 but since it is a matter of
questions about words and names and your
own law, see to it yourselves; I refuse to be

13-15. For the charge cf. 16:20-21; 17:7. If the actual charge was that Paul was **persuading men to worship God contrary to the law,** the meaning probably is that Paul was engaging in propaganda which the Jews themselves disowned. If Gallio had allowed the charge, he must have pronounced Christianity to be contrary to *Roman* law, for it remained a "licensed religion" only so long as it could shelter itself under the aegis of Judaism. But Gallio, as a Roman, can see no distinction between the defenders of Jewish orthodoxy and the leader of a heretical Jewish sect, and declares that his function is to judge criminal offenses and not to mediate in religious squabbles **about words and names and your own law,** i.e., the *Jewish* law. Luke probably intends the reference to be to *Jewish* law throughout, as he would be less likely to hint that Paul could be guilty of an offense against Roman law. Some critics (e.g., Loisy) think that the author has staged the whole scene as a bit of apologetic designed to illustrate the fundamental identity of Judaism and Christianity in the eyes of the Roman authorities and the equality of treatment meted out to each. Luke is no doubt attracted throughout by this idea; but there is no reason to conclude that he invented the incident rather than that he utilized a real episode which was well suited to point his thesis. Gallio's behavior—though hardly perhaps in the character of a *dulcis*—is entirely credible. The defendant was a Roman as well as a Jew; Gallio quickly saw that the charge was a frame-up; and he was not going to be imposed upon.

---

speaking. Keep on telling it, in every form you can think of. If you are tired, God will give you the strength to keep going. If you are spiritually exhausted, God will give you the power. There are times when the more weary you are the more the word of God comes through; your resistances are down, your self-consciousness is gone. You are too tired to resist or to think of yourself and the impression you are making. Then God speaks as he may not have had the chance to speak before. The best sermons often come at the end of the long winter season when the preacher feels that he is dragging bottom. Why? Because God is with him and speaks through him, not only in spite of his weariness, but because of it.

And the promise is followed by a reminder: **I have many people in this city.** You may think that they are all stupid, beyond redemption, lost in their own selfish interests, impervious, untouchable, doomed. Not at all, says God. Among these unattractive, unresponsive-looking people, I have a great many who are ready to hear my word. You may not see them right at the beginning; they may not respond instantly. But they have the desire and the need in their heart. They are fearful and timid, they have been disappointed before; therefore they hold back in the beginning. But go out to find them, woo them, tell them the story. See what lies behind their faces; get to know them where they really live. Do not go at them with hammer and tongs. They may be under judgment, true enough, but do not crush them until you have loved them. If they are proud, do not talk about judgment; tell them about Jesus and make them feel ashamed. Let them see that you are in the same predicament; that you face the same human temptation and danger; that you too cry out for the living God.

One of the great recoveries of our time is the recovery of the judgment of God and the reality of sin. The danger is that some young and inexperienced exponents of this gospel go out as the preachers of doom, with a club in their hand instead of a cross. The people, most of them, are already in the shadows of doom, although they may neither know nor understand it. Show them what the doom really is; show them how it came upon them; show them the glory overhead. For these are God's people. They have the capacity to respond to him. They

16 And he drave them from the judgment seat.

17 Then all the Greeks took Sosthenes,
the chief ruler of the synagogue, and beat
him before the judgment seat. And Gallio
cared for none of those things.

18 ¶ And Paul *after this* tarried *there*
yet a good while, and then took his leave
of the brethren, and sailed thence into
Syria, and with him Priscilla and Aquila;
having shorn *his* head in Cenchrea: for he
had a vow.

a judge of these things." 16 And he drove
them from the tribunal. 17 And they all
seized Sos'the-nes, the ruler of the synagogue, and beat him in front of the tribunal. But Gallio paid no attention to this.

18 After this Paul stayed many days
longer, and then took leave of the brethren and sailed for Syria, and with him Priscilla and Aquila. At Cen'chre-ae he cut his

---

17. They all seized Sosthenes. Who did? Most naturally the meaning is "all the Jews," and a few MSS so read. But the Jews are hardly likely to have beaten their own official, unless it is held that Paul's break with the Jews was not as complete as Luke suggests and Sosthenes was the leader of a pro-Paul minority within the synagogue. Alternatively we may suppose that **they all** means the whole audience, which would be mainly Gentile. Encouraged by Gallio's pointed snub to the Jews, the onlookers vent their spite on the Jewish leader. This is the view of the Western text which reads, "all the Greeks." If **Sosthenes** is the same person who is afterwards associated with Paul in the writing of I Corinthians (1:1), then presumably he was converted after this incident. This would favor the first interpretation. Gallio has often been unfairly criticized, as if Luke's comment that he **cared for none of those things** (KJV) implied an indifference to spiritual issues. The words merely mean that he **paid no attention** (RSV) to the commotion.

D. Mission of Paul to Asia (18:18–19:41)

1. Preliminary Tour of Confirmation (18:18-23)

This account of a flying visit, first to Ephesus and then to Syria and possibly Jerusalem, is curiously brief and vague, and on that account it has been suspected by the critics. It has been treated either (*a*) as a doublet of the journey to Jerusalem in ch. 21, where there is also mention of a **vow** (21:23-24) and the same ominous foreboding of coming disaster (cf. vs. 21, **if God will** with 21:14, "the will of the Lord be done"); or (*b*) as an attempt of the editor to represent Paul as the founder of the Ephesian church, which was in fact founded by others; hence the insertion of a visit by Paul before that of Apollos (vs. 24). Even the visit to Antioch is suspect on the ground that after the trouble there with Peter and Barnabas, Paul must have broken with the local church. The visit is inserted by Luke to maintain the illusion of perfect harmony at Antioch. All this appears to be entirely perverse and fractious criticism. It is wholly probable that on its way to Caesarea Paul's ship called at Ephesus, stopped for a few days to unload and take on cargo, and then took Paul on as a passenger to Caesarea. Nor is it unnatural

---

are not all fools by any means. They are not all money-mad, capitalist tycoons, they are not all vain, proud and self-righteous. They are more like children who have played with fire and been burned. They mean well, but they have not learned how to live. Some of them are hopeless, at least from your point of view; but some of them, many of them, are waiting to be shown. Look over the congregation when you wonder how you can face it another year, and remember the words of the Lord: "I have many people in this congregation."

It was fortunate for Paul that Gallio was proconsul of Achaia at this particular time. Gallio was a man built on a large scale. He was cultivated. His younger brother was Seneca, the philosopher. Gallio was accustomed to deal with big things and not, like many political leaders, to putter about with the trivial and unimportant. Such a man is almost sure to see things from a big point of view. He is not trapped by petty and personal considerations. He can see an issue quite apart from his own relationship to it. His judgment is inflexible but calm.

19 And he came to Ephesus, and left
them there: but he himself entered into the
synagogue, and reasoned with the Jews.
20 When they desired *him* to tarry longer
time with them, he consented not;
21 But bade them farewell, saying, I
must by all means keep this feast that
cometh in Jerusalem: but I will return
again unto you, if God will. And he sailed
from Ephesus.

hair, for he had a vow. 19 And they came to
Ephesus, and he left them there; but he
himself went into the synagogue and argued with the Jews. 20 When they asked
him to stay for a longer period, he declined;
21 but on taking leave of them he said, "I
will return to you if God wills," and he set
sail from Ephesus.

---

that Paul should wish to confer with his fellow leaders at Antioch and Jerusalem before undertaking the next stage of his missionary program. The brevity of the account is easily explained by supposing that the companion to whom we owe the travel narrative did not on this occasion accompany Paul, but had returned perhaps to Philippi, where the "we" narrative is resumed at 20:6.

18. Many days longer. As we have seen, Paul probably left Corinth in the early months of either 52 or 53. If in fact he was heading for Jerusalem, he would be planning to be there in time for the Passover. **Cenchreae** was the eastern port of Corinth. **He cut his hair.** Who? Grammatically it might be Aquila, and this would suit the latter's Jewish outlook. But Luke would hardly think this worth mentioning; and much more probably the reference is to Paul himself. The **vow** would be a Nazarite vow (see Num. 6:5, 18). Normally the cutting of the hair, and the offering of it in sacrifice, marked the completion of the vow. For example, Josephus writes, "Those who suffer from illness or are in some other misfortune are accustomed to make a vow that for thirty days before they offer the sacrifice they will abstain from wine and from shaving their heads" (*Jewish War* II. 15. 1). In that case we must suppose that Paul was redeeming such a vow before setting sail. Alternatively the meaning may be that the cutting of the hair marked the beginning of the period of thirty days during which it was not again to be cut. In that case Paul perhaps intended to redeem his vow and offer the sacrifice, as was prescribed, in the temple at the Passover season; and the purpose of Luke's remark is to explain why Paul was in such haste to reach Jerusalem. This was apparently the view of the scribe of the Western text (see on vs. 21). Some critics think that the vow here mentioned was really taken in connection with the incident described in 21:20-26 and has here been antedated (see on 21:26).

19. Ephesus. It is not suggested that a regular church was founded at this time, though Priscilla and Aquila, who are still there at vs. 26, may well have gathered a small community of Christians before Paul's return; vs. 27 suggests that there were already "brethren" at Ephesus.

21. Set sail from Ephesus: The voyage to Caesarea at that time of year would be a long and risky one. It is quite possible that in the course of it one of Paul's three shipwrecks may have taken place (II Cor. 11:25). The Western text here adds that Paul said, **I must by all means keep this feast that cometh in Jerusalem** (KJV). But curiously the same scribe in 19:1 denies that in fact Paul went to Jerusalem at this time by expanding the text to read, "When Paul wished to follow his own plan and travel to Jerusalem, the Spirit ordered him to return to Asia, and he passed through the upper country. . . ."

He has the wisdom to discriminate between serious disorder in society and juvenile petulance among the brethren.

When Paul was brought to Gallio, the charge was that he was breaking a Roman law. Judaism was permitted in the empire, but not every religion was, and Paul was preaching something that was not Judaism. Therefore he was violating Roman law. Gallio saw through the charge at once. Before Paul had time to defend himself, Gallio said something like this: "The matter you bring before me is not a matter that involves Roman law at all. It involves only your own personal bickerings. As such it does not come within my court, and I refuse to have anything to say about it." Whereupon the

22 And when he had landed at Caesarea,
and gone up, and saluted the church, he
went down to Antioch.
23 And after he had spent some time
there, he departed, and went over *all* the
country of Galatia and Phrygia in order,
strengthening all the disciples.
24 ¶ And a certain Jew named Apollos,

22 When he had landed at Caes-a-re′a,
he went up and greeted the church, and
then went down to Antioch. 23 After spending some time there he departed and went
from place to place through the region of
Galatia and Phryg′i-a, strengthening all the
disciples.
24 Now a Jew named A-pol′los, a native

22. Went up and greeted the church: This can mean either (*a*) that Paul went up from the harbor and greeted the church in the town of Caesarea; or, more probably (*b*) that he went up from Caesarea to Jerusalem and greeted the mother church there. In favor of the first alternative is the fact that we are told nothing about what happened at this presumed visit to Jerusalem, while 21:17 ff. gives the impression that Paul had not been in Jerusalem since the "council visit." But quite apart from the conjecture that Paul was hurrying to the Passover, the language favors the second alternative; **went up** is almost a technical expression for visiting the religious capital; **went down** is natural of a journey from Jerusalem to Antioch, but hardly of one from Caesarea to Antioch. As Antioch was Paul's final goal, there seems no particular reason why he should have **landed at Caesarea** except en route for Jerusalem. It is worth noting that Silas probably left Paul at this point. In I Pet. 5:12 he is closely associated with Peter, and he may well have joined him at Jerusalem. Paul evidently still regarded **Antioch** as his base, whence he now set out afresh; for here traditionally we reach the beginning of the "third missionary journey" (but see on 13:4-12).

23. The region of Galatia and Phrygia: Almost the same descriptive phrase as in 16:6, where see note. Paul first retraces his steps (see above, pp. 172-74) **strengthening all the disciples.** At this point once again the champions of the North Galatian hypothesis suggest that a visit to northern Galatia proper may be indicated. They would treat the phrase "the upper country" (19:1) in the same way. In truth Paul follows much the same route as in ch. 16, but on this occasion he is no longer "forbidden by the Holy Spirit to speak the word in Asia" (16:6). As the Western text adds at 19:1, "The Spirit ordered him to return to Asia." This may explain the slight difference in the description of his route as between this verse and 16:6. There it was "through the region of Phrygia and Galatia," or literally "the Phrygian-Galatic region," i.e., through that part of Phrygia which belonged to the province of Galatia. Here it is **through the region of Galatia** (literally "Galatic region") **and Phrygia.** The prohibition to preach in Asia having now been removed, Paul is able to pass due west through "Phrygia," including that part of it which lay in the province of "Asia," instead of striking north as on the previous occasion.

2. Apollos at Ephesus (18:24-28)

Apollos was **a native of Alexandria . . . an eloquent man,** i.e., trained in rhetoric and philosophy, and **well versed in the scriptures.** Following the Alexandrian method, his teaching was probably some type of "Gnostic" philosophy based on an allegorical inter-

Greeks were so overjoyed that the Jews had been put in their place by the Roman officer that they took the ruler of the synagogue and beat him. And where was Gallio while that was going on? "Gallio took no notice" (Moffatt).

The great people in life are the ones who know what to see and what not to see. It is not that they are indifferent, but that they have learned to discriminate between the important and the unimportant. It is often better to leave the unimportant things as you find them; they will often take care of themselves. A good parent is one who knows what not to notice. A good businessman is one who knows what not to notice. Even God, according to Paul, did not notice too much the ignorance of man before Christ came: He "winked at" it (17:30). He let it go for the time being. So did Gallio let this situation go. He thought it would straighten itself out, and it did.

24-28. *Apollos in Ephesus.*—Apollos is the kind of man whom we might call a Christian, but not quite. He had a great many of the re-

born at Alexandria, an eloquent man, *and* mighty in the Scriptures, came to Ephesus.

of Alexandria, came to Ephesus. He was an eloquent man, well versed in the scriptures.

pretation of scripture. Possibly it would resemble the kind of teaching we have in Hebrews, which indeed has been ascribed to Apollos—a pure conjecture, but one which suits well enough the intellectual genre of its author. But was Apollos at this point already a Christian? Luke certainly implies that thus far his Christian knowledge and experience were incomplete. **He had been instructed in the way of the Lord,** i.e., he knew something about Christian beliefs and the Christian way of life. He also **spoke and taught accurately the things concerning Jesus,** i.e., he was well informed about the story of Jesus and possibly about his teaching. But **he knew only the baptism of John:** This must mean that though he had accepted John's baptism with water as a symbol of cleansing and repentance, he was not yet aware that Christian converts were baptized into the name of Jesus, nor had he any personal knowledge of the specifically Christian experience of the possession of the Holy Spirit, which was normally consequent upon the Christian baptismal confession. This would seem to be exactly the stage reached by the other "disciples" whom Paul finds at Ephesus in 19:1-7, and the question suggests itself whether we can accept these two paragraphs as evidence of the existence of a "John the Baptist sect" apart from and perhaps in rivalry to the Christian church. Even if such a sect did not appear later, that would not disprove its existence at this time, for after the destruction of Jerusalem other sects, such as the Essenes and the Therapeutae, also disappeared. But in fact the Fourth Gospel, with its constant insistence on the subordination of John the Baptist to Jesus, certainly suggests that some time later at Ephesus there may still have been some who acknowledged John rather than Jesus, or at least preferred John's simple baptism of repentance to baptism into the name of Jesus. Even as late as the early third century we have reference to the fact that "some even of the disciples of John, who seemed to be great ones, have separated themselves and proclaimed their own Master as Christ" (*Clementine Recognitions* I. 54). Some scholars have even discovered the remnants of such a sect in the curious community known as the "Mandaeans" (see F. C. Burkitt, "Mandaeans," *Encyclopaedia Britannica,* 14th ed.; also Intro. to John in Vol. VIII). The present paragraph may then be cautiously accepted as indicating the continued existence of an independent, though quite possibly friendly, John the Baptist sect, which the orthodox Christian community was obviously in process of absorbing.

Was Apollos a Christian when Paul met him? Luke apparently regards him as such, though an imperfect one. He is already **fervent in the spirit** (KJV; this, with a reference to the Holy Spirit, is probably the correct translation rather than **fervent in spirit** [RSV]), even though he has not yet received Christian baptism. But since he **knew only the baptism of John,** he was presumably still unaware, or unwilling to confess, that in the experience of the Christian church the baptism by Spirit predicted by John had been realized. Accordingly he cannot yet have acknowledged Jesus as Messiah—the essence of

quirements and many of the electives as well. He had a knowledge of the Scriptures. It is obvious that you cannot be a Christian without that. He had been instructed in the teachings of Jesus. Certainly there is no Christianity without that. Moreover he had the desire to pass on to others what he himself had. He was a missionary. And in addition he had a good background. He had the culture of Alexandria, one of the philosophical centers of the empire. What then did he not have? What was it that Aquila and his wife missed in this fine Christian teacher? The only clue that the Acts gives us is that he did not have the baptism of Jesus; he had only the baptism of John.

If by baptism is meant only a ceremonial or ritual act, then the clue does not lead us far But the chances are that it means more than that. The baptism of John was a baptism into moral improvement; it initiated men into a great reform movement, and let no one underestimate the importance of it. But it was not the baptism of Jesus, for the baptism of Jesus was a baptism into death and resurrection. It was a dying to self. It was a recognition that of your own self you can do nothing and that you are willing to stand as a sinner in the presence of God, claiming nothing, only counting on his love and forgiveness. It changed the center of things from self-directed effort to God-given

25 This man was instructed in the way
of the Lord; and being fervent in the
spirit, he spake and taught diligently the
things of the Lord, knowing only the baptism of John.
26 And he began to speak boldly in the
synagogue: whom when Aquila and Priscilla had heard, they took him unto *them,*
and expounded unto him the way of God
more perfectly.

25 He had been instructed in the way of
the Lord; and being fervent in spirit, he
spoke and taught accurately the things concerning Jesus, though he knew only the
baptism of John. 26 He began to speak
boldly in the synagogue; but when Priscilla and Aquila heard him, they took him
and expounded to him the way of God

---

the confession made at baptism "into the name of Jesus," and that which distinguished it from "the baptism of John." This reading of the situation is confirmed when we are told that after instruction by Priscilla and Aquila, Apollos did in fact proclaim, as presumably he had not previously done, **that the Christ was Jesus.** It may be concluded, then, that when Paul first met him, Apollos had not crossed the line that divided the followers of John from the Christian community. If it is asked why Priscilla and Aquila after instruction did not baptize him, the answer is that almost certainly they did. But Luke, assuming that Apollos was already a Christian, omits to record his baptism, though in truth, as in the case of the "disciples" in 19:1, the completion of baptism is the chief point of the episode. But perhaps the most significant thing about these conversions from the discipleship of John to Christianity is that they show that the emphasis of Christian teaching was still largely on the messiahship of Jesus. To accept this was to become a Christian.

25. The Western text reads, "Who had been instructed in his own country in the word of the Lord"—an interesting indication, if it were reliable, that Christianity had already been preached in Alexandria. **Fervent in spirit** (RSV): Or perhaps better, **fervent in the spirit** (KJV), for the meaning is not that Apollos' own spirit was "fervent," but that he was literally "boiling" with the energy of the Holy Spirit (cf. Rom. 12:11, "aglow with the Spirit"). **The baptism of John:** It has been suggested that this may mean more narrowly "the baptism of Jesus by John" (cf. 1:22); that Apollos knew Jesus had been baptized by John as one of his followers, but had no knowledge of the fuller messianic teaching about Jesus. But this seems ruled out by 19:3, where "into John's baptism" quite clearly has the wider meaning of "baptism as administered by John."

---

grace. It was the difference between a man who tried desperately to be good and a man who admitted that he was a sinner. Once that admission was made, he was raised into a new kind of life in which he had a power over himself that he never had before. Before it, he was like Atlas trying to carry the world on his shoulders; after it, he was like a man carrying the Cross. What a difference! No wonder Aquila and Priscilla took him home and **expounded to him the way of God more accurately,** explained what it really meant. That is what Apollos missed: he missed the meaning of the gospel. He was a Christian, but not quite, and in a case like this a miss is as good as a mile. It is like a man who marries a wife. He does all the good things a good husband ought to do. He provides a home for his wife; he protects her from harm; he is proud of her; he gives her everything she might desire. But he does not surrender himself to the marriage state; he does not give himself, trusting her, reverencing her, always conscious of his union with her, the union in which he finds himself and loses his anxious unrest.

The churches are filled with people who are Christians, but not quite. They know the gospel. They try to live a good Christian life. They have a high sense of moral responsibility; they assume their part in the life of the community. But they have missed what the way of God really means. They have the baptism of John, but not the baptism of Jesus. They have never given up the direction of their own lives. They have never stood in the presence of the mighty God and admitted that of themselves they could do nothing. They have never been the receivers of God's grace; only the givers of God's goods. This is no merely academic distinction. It is the difference between life and death. It is the difference between a man who is frantically trying to hold on to a sinking

27 And when he was disposed to pass
into Achaia, the brethren wrote, exhorting
the disciples to receive him: who, when he
was come, helped them much which had
believed through grace:
28 For he mightily convinced the Jews,
and that publicly, showing by the Scriptures that Jesus was Christ.
19 And it came to pass, that, while
Apollos was at Corinth, Paul having
passed through the upper coasts came to
Ephesus; and finding certain disciples,

more accurately. 27 And when he wished to
cross to A-cha'ia, the brethren encouraged
him, and wrote to the disciples to receive
him. When he arrived, he greatly helped
those who through grace had believed,
28 for he powerfully confuted the Jews in
public, showing by the scriptures that the
Christ was Jesus.
19 While A-pol'los was at Corinth,
Paul passed through the upper country and came to Ephesus. There he found

---

27-28. The brethren: Note the assumption that in spite of the brevity of Paul's earlier visit (vss. 19-20), there was already a Christian community at Ephesus. **That the Christ was Jesus:** The same message as was Paul's in vs. 5, where see note.

3. Paul at Ephesus (19:1-41)

Luke's account of Paul's work at Ephesus is peculiarly tantalizing. It contains some of the most vivid writing in Acts and is obviously in part based on quite firsthand information. Yet a comparison with the epistles shows that Luke has omitted to mention incidents of crucial importance to Paul, and has given a very incomplete picture of the course of his mission. It must be supplemented from the epistles: (*a*) From Ephesians we gain no light, as it is almost certainly a circular letter, not specifically addressed to Ephesus. (*b*) Rom. 16, on the supposition that it is addressed to Ephesus, gives us the names of a number of prominent church members, some of them Jews, and suggests that there were at least three "house churches" in the city. One was in the house of Aquila and Priscilla (Rom. 16:5), and two other similarly constituted congregations are mentioned (Rom. 16:14, 15). (*c*) But the Corinthian correspondence is richest in information. Paul sent at least four letters to Corinth, all written during or immediately after his stay at Ephesus. The first is lost while II Corinthians is made up of at least two letters. (See Vol. X, pp. 265-71.) All show that throughout his Ephesian ministry Paul was troubled by

---

ship and a man who, knowing the seriousness of his plight, reaches out for a life belt that has been thrown down from above. It is the difference between ethics and religion, and the difference between the religion of good works and the religion of faith. In the first you find a man who by all his might and main goes out to slay Goliath. In the second you find a man who has been slain by his own conviction of unworthiness and who has been saved by the love of the Father.

Once again a miss is as good as a mile. To obey the commandments of Jesus, to practice the principles set forth in the Sermon on the Mount is a moral goal to which all Christians aspire. But if a man has nothing more than a moral goal to strive for, he has missed the meaning of Christianity. Of him it may be said that he is a Christian, but not quite, and a miss in this case is as good as a mile!

The church was not, is not, and never can be a society for the improvement of morals. It was at the start, is now, and always must remain a resurrection center, in which men and women see the reality of God, surrender the direction of their lives, die to their own selfish wills, and are raised into a new and different life, a life in which all the old problems will be there, but will be controlled, so that underneath the disquietude of the world will be "the peace of God, which passes all understanding." From a fellowship such as that there streams into the world rivers of life that reclaim the waste spaces and do by indirection what all the conscious striving of our moral effort fails miserably to do.

19:1-41. ***The Ministry in Ephesus.***—This chapter describes all too briefly Paul's long and fruitful ministry in Ephesus. It falls quite naturally into four parts.

1-7. ***The Question of Baptism Comes Up Again.***—Paul had no more than arrived in Ephesus when he met twelve men who had the baptism of John but not the baptism of

developments in Corinth. We learn moreover from II Cor. 12:14 ("Here for the third time I am ready to come to you") that after the writing of I Corinthians, Paul must have paid a hurried visit to Corinth that is not mentioned in Acts—a "painful visit" he calls it (II Cor. 2:1)—in an attempt to deal with an intractable situation. The visit was evidently a failure—it was followed by a letter written "out of much affliction and anguish of heart" (II Cor. 2:4; cf. II Cor. 7:8-9)—and it is passed over in silence by Luke, either because it raised unhappy controversial issues, or because it fell outside the outline of the main tours. It was only after he had left Ephesus that Paul received cheering news from Corinth (II Cor. 2:12-13; 7:5-7) and in consequence wrote the major part of II Corinthians, which strikes a note of rejoicing.

The Corinthian letters also throw much light on the sufferings endured by Paul at Ephesus. Of these, with the exception of the riot from which Paul escaped unscathed, Luke makes no mention, though the speech to the Ephesian elders at Miletus refers to "trials which befell me through the plots of the Jews" (20:19) and in 21:27 fanatical "Jews from Asia" are mentioned. Yet Paul himself writes of "the affliction we experienced in Asia; for we were so utterly, unbearably crushed that we despaired of life itself" (II Cor. 1:8; cf. I Cor. 4:9-13; II Cor. 4:8-12; 6:4-5; 11:23-27). It must have been in Ephesus that Paul endured the imprisonment that he shared with Andronicus and Junias (Rom. 16:7). Finally Paul can write: "If the dead are not raised at all, . . . what do I gain if, humanly speaking, I fought with beasts at Ephesus?" (I Cor. 15:29, 32). If this is to be taken literally, it means that Paul was actually thrown to the beasts in the arena but somehow escaped. Alternatively it may be a metaphorical description of the ferocity of his human adversaries, as when Ignatius calls the soldiers that guard him "leopards" and says, "I am fighting with wild beasts" (Ign. Rom. 5; Ign. Smyrn. 4). Or the sense may be merely hypothetical, "If, as seemed so likely, I had fought with wild beasts, . . . what would I have gained?" But however we understand the words, Paul must have been in some dire peril, from which perhaps he may have been rescued by the courageous intervention of Aquila and Priscilla who, so he says, "risked their necks for my life" (Rom. 16:4). It is hard to believe that Luke can have been familiar with these letters and yet remained silent about these events. Many scholars now believe that it was during an Ephesian imprisonment that Paul wrote Philippians, and perhaps also Colossians, Ephesians, and Philemon.

We have already noticed what difficulty Paul had found in planting the first seeds of Christianity in Asia (see on 16:6). Similarly his personal influence seems soon to have ceased to be predominant in Ephesus. Paul wrote no great letter to the city, and subsequently all the traditions of Ephesus are Johannine rather than Pauline. It is likely that soon after Paul's departure serious defection took place. His speech to the elders warns them that "after my departure fierce wolves will come in among you, not sparing the flock, . . . to draw away the disciples after them" (20:29-30). If the words are Paul's, they show that he already feared for the permanence of his work; if they are Luke's, they testify to the critical condition of the church when the account was written. On a short view Paul himself passes a verdict on his work at Ephesus when he writes to Timothy: "You are aware that all who are in Asia turned away from me" (II Tim. 1:15).

a) Paul's Return and His Ministry in Asia (19:1-10)

19:1. While Apollos was at Corinth: The consequences of the visit appear in I Corinthians. According to Acts (18:28), Apollos' preaching was chiefly to Jews. But from the account in I Corinthians of the "parties" at Corinth (I Cor. 1:10 ff.; 2:3 ff.) we

---

Jesus. We have already met this situation in connection with Apollos (18:24-28) and have considered it at some length. One's first inclination is to think of this controversy over the two baptisms as one of the irrelevant relics of ancient Christianity, and to see nothing comparable to it in the current religious situation. Of one thing let it remind us: from the very beginning there has never been absolute unanimity among Christians. There have always been differences of opinion and practice. While the writer of the Acts draws the picture of a

2 He said unto them, Have ye received
the Holy Ghost since ye believed? And
they said unto him, We have not so much
as heard whether there be any Holy Ghost.
3 And he said unto them, Unto what
then were ye baptized? And they said, Unto
John's baptism.

some disciples. 2 And he said to them, "Did
you receive the Holy Spirit when you believed?" And they said, "No, we have never
even heard that there is a Holy Spirit."
3 And he said, "Into what then were you
baptized?" They said, "Into John's bap-

---

would surmise that it was rather the intellectual Greek section of the community at Corinth that Apollos attracted to himself. His learning, eloquence, and experience in the allegorical teaching methods of Alexandria put Paul at a disadvantage, and caused the unhappy faction-crisis at Corinth. Apollos himself was probably entirely innocent; trouble may have arisen only after he left; and Paul seems to have borne him no grudge nor in any way held him responsible. **Paul passed through the upper country:** Here again supporters of the North Galatian theory (pp. 172-74) find a reference to the northern coasts of Galatia proper. Rather the meaning is that Paul went across the high ground west of Pisidian Antioch instead of along the lower main road through Colossae and Laodicea. **Ephesus** was commonly styled "the Light of Asia." It was the seat of the Roman proconsul and also of the confederation of cities known as the "Asiarchate." The imperial spirit was fostered by the worship of the emperor, and the "Asiarch" was the provincial high priest of the imperial cult. As a busy seaport and the western terminus of the great trade route to the Euphrates, Ephesus enjoyed great commercial prosperity. Her principal glory was the temple of Artemis, one of the Seven Wonders of the World. One cannot but contrast the transitory glory of Ephesus with the permanence of the faith Paul preached. Today the name of Artemis has vanished from memory; on the site of her great temple nothing remains but a few fragments of broken marble; the village built on its precincts is named in memory of St. John; and a prominent tower in the vicinity is called the "Prison of St. Paul."

Some disciples: Again Luke obviously means Christian disciples. But they too, since like Apollos they only knew "John's baptism," cannot in any full sense have been Christians. Just as Luke seems to assume that Apollos was already a Christian, so does he call these twelve (vs. 7) "disciples." The whole account is somewhat obscure, and Luke seems to have had no very clear knowledge as to who these people were. Probably the idea (whether it is Luke's own or that of his authority for this incident) that it was part of the function of the apostles to mediate the gift of the Holy Spirit has transformed the conversion of some disciples of John to Christianity into a story of how imperfect Christians were changed into perfect ones by the laying on of apostolic hands.

2. That there is a Holy Spirit: The Western text reads, "whether any are receiving the Holy Spirit."

3. Into John's baptism: See on 18:24-25. Lake and Cadbury, on the contrary, deny that there is any question of these "disciples" belonging to a "John the Baptist sect." The contrast is merely between baptism with and without the gift of the Spirit: "The 'baptism of John' does not for our author necessarily imply direct or indirect influence from the Baptist, it is his name for Christian water baptism without the Spirit" (*Beginnings of Christianity,* IV, 238).

Christian fellowship welded together in an extraordinarily close and sympathetic unity of spirit, nevertheless there are unmistakable signs that the unity, even in those early days, was not the perfect unity for which Christ prayed. There was always an Apollos, and Apollos always had his following. There were always the nonconformists, those who baptized according to John and not according to Jesus.

To note this fact is not to excuse our own lack of unity or to diminish our efforts to overcome it. It is rather to moderate our justified impatience with the knowledge that in this imperfect world even those closest to the Master himself found it difficult and sometimes impossible to weave all the loose threads of their belief and behavior into a single pattern in which the harmony of design should endure.

4 Then said Paul, John verily baptized with the baptism of repentance, saying unto the people, that they should believe on him which should come after him, that is, on Christ Jesus.

5 When they heard *this,* they were baptized in the name of the Lord Jesus.

6 And when Paul had laid *his* hands upon them, the Holy Ghost came on them; and they spake with tongues, and prophesied.

7 And all the men were about twelve.

8 And he went into the synagogue, and spake boldly for the space of three months, disputing and persuading the things concerning the kingdom of God.

9 But when divers were hardened, and believed not, but spake evil of that way

tism." 4 And Paul said, "John baptized with
the baptism of repentance, telling the people to believe in the one who was to come
after him, that is, Jesus." 5 On hearing this,
they were baptized in the name of the Lord
Jesus. 6 And when Paul had laid his hands
upon them, the Holy Spirit came on them;
and they spoke with tongues and prophesied. 7 There were about twelve of them in
all.

8 And he entered the synagogue and for
three months spoke boldly, arguing and
pleading about the kingdom of God; 9 but
when some were stubborn and disbelieved,

---

4. How far does this correspond with the picture of the Baptist in the Synoptic Gospels? There also he preaches **repentance,** but **the one who was to come after him** is pictured rather as a stern judge who will "gather the wheat into his granary, but the chaff he will burn with unquenchable fire" (Luke 3:17). It is only in the Fourth Gospel that John consciously proclaims Jesus as one in whom men are to **believe** for salvation—"the Lamb of God, who takes away the sin of the world" (John 1:29).

5-6. For the relation between baptism, the laying on of hands, and the bestowal of the Spirit see on 6:6 and 8:16-17. **Spoke with tongues:** See on 2:1-4.

8. As usual, Luke represents Paul as using the synagogue as his first base of operations and then, after the inevitable break, proceeding on his own lines. By stating that his main theme was **the kingdom of God,** Luke possibly implies that he used this characteristically Jewish subject as a prolegomenon to more distinctively Christian teaching. But as we have already seen, the kingdom of God in Acts is sometimes almost a synonym for the church (see on 8:12).

9. Some were stubborn: It is worth noting that at Ephesus it was not the whole body of the Jews, as at Corinth (18:6), who rejected the new gospel, but only a few "die-hards."

The baptism of John has disappeared, but that for which it stood still remains. To be baptized into John meant to reach after something yet to be attained. To be baptized into Jesus meant to rejoice in something already attained, though not yet fully explored or developed. These two points of view are still to be found within Christianity. As Clifford L. Stanley has pointed out, there are those for whom Christianity is like courtship; it is a striving toward a desirable but distant goal. And there are others for whom it is like marriage; it is a resting in something already wonderfully attained, the full and mysterious richness of which is still to be explored and developed. Both lives are active lives, but the activity of courtship has a tension and uncertainty about it of which the activity of marriage at its best knows nothing. Courtship is a struggle to attain something. Marriage is the enjoyment and development of something already attained. Marriage is departure from something. It begins with something given and proceeds to live out the full implications of it.

The great main stream of Christianity has always been in the latter direction. It is not so much the struggle for moral perfection that characterizes the great Christians as it is the framework within which that struggle takes place. They are not relieved of moral responsibility. Far from it. Their responsibility is greater than ever. But they assume it as those who have been taken into the secret of life and who can therefore carry the responsibility with a buoyancy of spirit that the world calls gaiety.

8-10. ***Paul Leaves the Synagogue for the Lecture Hall.***—Paul began in Ephesus where he always began, in the synagogue. Jesus began there. It was the natural place to begin. One

before the multitude, he departed from them, and separated the disciples, disputing daily in the school of one Tyrannus.

10 And this continued by the space of two years; so that all they which dwelt in Asia heard the word of the Lord Jesus, both Jews and Greeks.

speaking evil of the Way before the congregation, he withdrew from them, taking the disciples with him, and argued daily in the
hall of Ty-ran'nus.[q]
10 This continued for two years, so that all the residents of Asia heard the word of the Lord, both Jews and Greeks.

[q] Other ancient authorities add, *from the fifth hour to the tenth.*

The hall of Tyrannus would be a large room owned by one Tyrannus, perhaps himself a rhetorician, who rented it to visiting lecturers. Paul would therefore appear to the public as a traveling sophist such as was a common figure at the time. It might thus be some time before the revolutionary nature of his gospel was appreciated, so that he was able to teach without serious interruption "for two years." The Western text adds that Paul taught "from the fifth to the tenth hour," i.e., from 11 A.M. to 4 P.M. during the heat of the day—after business hours were ended and his own work for a living had been finished.

10. All the residents of Asia: This at first sight might seem an odd exaggeration. But it probably means that from his base at Ephesus Paul endeavored to conduct a more extensive mission. It may, e.g., have been at this time that Christian communities were formed at Colossae, Laodicea, and Hierapolis (Col. 2:1; 4:13) and perhaps in the remainder of the "seven churches" of the Apocalypse (Rev. 1:20). Paul's agent in such work may have been Epaphras (Col. 1:7; 4:12). Vss. 22, 26 also suggest that Paul's work extended beyond Ephesus itself (see also II Cor. 2:12). **Both Jews and Greeks;** cf. Paul's words to the elders of Ephesus in 20:21. That Paul had many Jewish converts in Ephesus is confirmed by the large number of Jewish names in Rom. 16, if that chapter is considered as addressed to Ephesus.

---

would naturally assume that a religious message would have the best chance among religious people. The synagogues were filled with the most religious people of their day and it was natural that both Jesus and Paul should begin there. Religious crusaders in the world today would very likely begin with the churches. They would have every reason to assume that the greatest response would come from the people who already lived the most active religious lives.

Both Jesus and Paul were disappointed. Jesus was driven out of the synagogue and preached out of doors. In town after town Paul left the synagogue in desperation and went to a more responsive group. What is it about religious people, church people, that makes them so blind to new truth, and so unresponsive to new truth, and so unresponsive to new life? Doubtless it is the very strength of their convictions which sometimes becomes the weakness of their understanding. Because they know the truth they need not search for it, nor can they expect it or allow it to change its garments. Whatever the reason may be, let churchmen beware of the fact that they have often been passed by because their religious certainty had degenerated into religious bigotry.

In this case Paul went to a public lecture room. He used the room from eleven to four, the free hours of the midday when business took a rest from its labors. We might almost say that Paul was the first noonday preacher. His intention at least was the same; to reach the people where and when they could be reached. Paul's successors have often been incredibly slow to adjust their schedules to meet the daily routine of the people they minister to. While Christianity cannot put itself in the position of accommodating modern man in his desire for ease and comfort, it surely can make certain concessions in the places and times when its ministry is exercised. The churches in our great cities which have been kept alive are the ones that have adapted themselves to the life that is around them. A church, for example, in a business district of a large city will miss its opportunity if it does not develop a weekday ministry which may eventually overshadow its Sunday ministry. Paul was a good strategist. He went to the synagogue first. When he did not get a hearing there, he went to the place where he had the chance of being heard favorably by the most people. No wonder the gospel spread all over Asia in two years, even without the help of radio!

11 And God wrought special miracles by the hands of Paul:

12 So that from his body were brought unto the sick handkerchiefs or aprons, and the diseases departed from them, and the evil spirits went out of them.

11 And God did extraordinary miracles by the hands of Paul, **12** so that handkerchiefs or aprons were carried away from his body to the sick, and diseases left them and the evil spirits came out of them.

b) Paul and the Exorcists (19:11-20)

These verses leave the impression that they are derived from a less reliable source than the rest of the chapter. There is a suspicious parallelism between the kind of miracles ascribed to Paul here and Peter's miracles in 5:12-16, and Paul's clothes are superstitiously credited with the same healing power as was Peter's shadow. We miss the sobriety with which Jesus' own healing acts are described; the nearest parallel is "the fringe of his garment" (Matt. 9:20; 14:36). Luke seems concerned to emphasize two ideas: (*a*) the power of "the name"; and (*b*) the superiority of Christian exorcism to all its rivals. The real importance of the passage is the light it throws on popular belief in the all-pervading presence and reality of demonic powers, and in the dominant power of "the name." The intensity of the belief in demons, even in Christian circles, is shown by the fact that in every ancient order of baptism exorcism plays an important part. And as for "the name," we have already seen (3:16) that miracles are expressly said to be wrought, not by the apostles' own virtue, but by its power. When Paul declares (Phil. 2:9-11) that God has bestowed on Jesus "the name which is above every name," he adds that at the mention of this name not only mankind must bow the knee but also everything "in heaven and on earth and under the earth"—meaning that "the name" has absolute power over all those unseen powers of evil that inspired so much dread.

11-12. Extraordinary miracles: It is well to remember that Paul himself claims that he had the power to work miracles (see Rom. 15:18-19; II Cor. 12:12). **From his body,** literally "skin."

11-19. ***One of the Early Church's Worst Enemies Appears Again.***—The early church, as one might expect, had many enemies. The Jews, by and large, were against it. Rome was indifferent, if not hostile to it. Caesar and Christ were everlastingly opposed to each other. Yet in many ways its worst enemies, the most subtly dangerous ones, were the invisible ones, the ones that were in the air. And of these one of the most dangerous of all was magic. Now magic and the supernatural go together. One of the reasons why magic is not one of the church's great enemies today is that the supernatural has lost so much of its power over the lives of men and women. Magic is the attempt to control the supernatural in favor of man. It is the brash attempt to bend the will of God. It is a mechanical affair completely divorced from any moral considerations whatsoever. It is an attempt to leave character out of man's dealings with the divine.

Magic always fascinates people and it always tempts them. Short cuts to power always lure human beings. In the world of early Christianity magic was a major temptation because it was a world governed by a multitude of gods in the interests of specially chosen groups of people. The danger of magic to Christianity is nowhere so apparent as where it threatens to invade Christianity itself. In this passage, for example, Paul himself comes very close, at least in the minds of the people, to being a worker of magic. **And God did extraordinary miracles by the hands of Paul, so that handkerchiefs or aprons were carried away from his body to the sick, and diseases left them and the evil spirits came out of them.** That is very near the border line of magic. We recognize, of course, something that is legitimate in the action of the people. Things that are closely associated with great persons become themselves powerful to the degree to which they succeed in suggesting and communicating the power of the person. The power of a personality like Paul's, for example, was so great that it overflowed into the things that were physically associated with him. These things then, charged with the personality of Paul, became transmitters of his power. Once divorce those things, however, from the personality of Paul and they become the devilish instruments of a mechanical magic. For example, a small piece of exquisitely carved Japanese ivory is precious to its owner because for many years it was worn on the watch chain of Phillips Brooks. When he went to call on a family in which there were small children, the first thing

13 ¶ Then certain of the vagabond Jews,
exorcists, took upon them to call over them
which had evil spirits the name of the
Lord Jesus, saying, We adjure you by Jesus
whom Paul preacheth.
14 And there were seven sons of *one*
Sceva, a Jew, *and* chief of the priests, which
did so.

13 Then some of the itinerant Jewish exorcists undertook to pronounce the name
of the Lord Jesus over those who had evil
spirits, saying, "I adjure you by the Jesus
whom Paul preaches." 14 Seven sons of a
Jewish high priest named Sce'va were doing

---

13. Jewish exorcists: The frequent occurrence of Jewish names of God in the magical papyri proves how prominent were Jews in the magic of the ancient world. For a similar competition in magic cf. 8:9-13; 13:6-12. **Pronounce the name of the Lord Jesus:** That the name of Jesus was used in exorcism by non-Christian circles is proved by a line of the great Paris Magical Papyrus which runs, "I adjure thee by Jesus the God of the Hebrews." The point of the extraordinary scene that follows is to show that the name of Jesus cannot be used effectively by those who have no part in him. Rather does the demon actually gain strength by such misuse of the name. This is an unusual point of view, for usually the name was thought to work *ex opere operato.* One cannot but contrast the attitude of Jesus himself when confronted by an exactly similar situation: "Do not forbid him; for no one who does a mighty work in my name will be able soon after to speak evil of me" (Mark 9:39; cf. Luke 9:49-50).

14. Sceva: No such Jewish **high priest** is known. The claim to such parentage may well have been part of the self-advertisement of a gang of impostors. But as Ramsay says, there is a certain "vagueness" and "vulgarity" in the whole story, and "the writer here is rather a picker-up of current gossip, like Herodotus, than a real historian" (*St. Paul the Traveller,* p. 273).

---

he did was to take the Japanese trinket off his chain and give it to the children to play with. Now, as one holds it in one's hands, one can almost feel the presence of the great man who wore it, for material things have a way of absorbing and communicating the power of the persons with whom they are closely associated. But if one were to assume that the piece of ivory, because of its association with Phillips Brooks, had unusual powers to prevail over the normal, natural course of events, then one obviously would be descending into the realms of magic.

Paul resisted the temptation, but the church has not always resisted it. The stories of the relics of the saints are presumably stories of the miracles of God, but as one reads them objectively, one must admit that they are more fairly classed among the feats of human magic. Real miracles are different, for miracles are acts of God and not of man. Whereas magic is a human attempt to control the laws of God, a miracle is a divine act demonstrating divine control over divine laws. Miracles have no ulterior motives behind them; magic always has. That is why Jesus did his best to avoid anything that in the slightest resembled magic. The power of the Cross, as he understood it, was the power of suffering love wherever it was to be found. It was never the power of a splinter of wood that someone claims to have been a piece of the original Cross. That way lies the deceptive and dangerous power of magic. It is a way that both Jesus and Paul avoided as they would poison. Unfortunately the same cannot always be said of the church that followed in their steps.

The fact that magic deprives a man of his personality is vividly illustrated by this passage in the Acts. The sons of the high priest took up magic as they would a trade. They learned the passwords and their fortune was made. When they heard about the power of Jesus, they added his name to their list. Notice the fact that they did not take Jesus into their lives; they simply added his name to their magic stock in trade. They commanded evil spirits in the name of Jesus **whom Paul preaches.** The spirit responded, **Jesus I know, and Paul I know; but who are you?** In other words they had no personal identity at all because they were exploiting the moral power of a life in which they had no share. They were like people today who invoke the name of Jesus over their babies and over their young brides and grooms but who have taken no part in the life of Jesus themselves. They deal in a religion of which they have no personal experience. The name of Jesus has authority on the lips of a man when the spirit of Jesus dwells in that

15 And the evil spirit answered and said, Jesus I know, and Paul I know; but who are ye?

16 And the man in whom the evil spirit was leaped on them, and overcame them, and prevailed against them, so that they fled out of that house naked and wounded.

17 And this was known to all the Jews and Greeks also dwelling at Ephesus; and fear fell on them all, and the name of the Lord Jesus was magnified.

18 And many that believed came, and confessed, and showed their deeds.

19 Many of them also which used curious arts brought their books together, and burned them before all *men:* and they counted the price of them, and found *it* fifty thousand *pieces* of silver.

20 So mightily grew the word of God and prevailed.

this. 15 But the evil spirit answered them,
"Jesus I know, and Paul I know; but who
are you?" 16 And the man in whom the
evil spirit was leaped on them, mastered all
of them, and overpowered them, so that
they fled out of that house naked and
wounded. 17 And this became known to all
the residents of Ephesus, both Jews and
Greeks; and fear fell upon them all; and
the name of the Lord Jesus was extolled.
18 Many also of those who were now believers came, confessing and divulging their
practices. 19 And a number of those who
practiced magic arts brought their books
together and burned them in the sight of
all; and they counted the value of them
and found it came to fifty thousand pieces
of silver. 20 So the word of the Lord grew
and prevailed mightily.

15-16. Jesus I know. . . . The point is that the demon acknowledges the names of both Jesus and Paul, but questions the right of these exorcists to use them. **Mastered all of them** (ἀμφοτέρων), literally "both of them"; but apparently this is a very early example of a usage of the word, later common, which made it equivalent to πάντων ("all").

18-19. Divulging their practices: Or perhaps their "magic spells" (so Lake and Cadbury, *Beginnings of Christianity,* IV, 242), for the word (πράξεις) sometimes has this technical meaning. **Their books,** i.e., documents inscribed with magical spells and charms. Such "Ephesian letters," as they were called, were famous the world over, and were credited with sovereign efficacy in averting ill luck. **Burned them in the sight of all:** Reminiscent of the Florentine "Holocaust of Vanities" in the days of Savonarola. **Fifty thousand pieces of silver:** Calculated to be worth at least $10,000, or £2,500, if the silver drachma is the unit of money—a typical touch of Oriental hyperbole in keeping with the rest of the story.

20. Mightily, or possibly, "According to the might of the Lord the word grew and prevailed."

man's heart. Magic can reach no lower level than when the people of a nation claim the sanction of the name of Jesus without in any serious way attempting to cultivate the character of Jesus.

The sons of the high priest got the worst of it in their attempt to capitalize on the name of Jesus. The evil spirit not only challenged their identity and called their hands, but also **leaped on them, mastered all of them, and overpowered them, so that they fled out of that house naked and wounded.** So Christianity finally won its way against magic. This section ends with a picture of the workers in magic collecting their books to burn them in public. Reflected in the light of that fire might have been the image of him who at the beginning of his life rejected all the temptations to exercise lordship over the laws of God, as in later years he refused to exercise any uninvited lordship over men and women. He was never a wonder-worker, but always God's agent in the working of miracles.

Magic is still one of the enemies of Christianity. There are people who trust horoscopes and others who turn to a fortuneteller when a major decision is to be made. There are some who use prayer as a kind of mechanical device for obtaining the things they want. But magic is not one of the most dangerous enemies of current Christianity. Its counterpart in our time is its opposite—materialism. Magic can thrive only in a world swarming with divinities. It rests on the idea of capricious deities. But without the supernatural it cannot exist. Materialism, on the other hand, thrives only in a world in which there are no divinities, or in a world in which the deity has become so completely re-

21 ¶ After these things were ended, Paul purposed in the spirit, when he had passed through Macedonia and Achaia, to go to Jerusalem, saying, After I have been there, I must also see Rome.

22 So he sent into Macedonia two of them that ministered unto him, Timotheus and Erastus; but he himself stayed in Asia for a season.

21 Now after these events Paul resolved
in the Spirit to pass through Mac-e-do'ni-a
and A-cha'ia and go to Jerusalem, saying,
"After I have been there, I must also see
Rome." 22 And having sent into Mac-e-
do'ni-a two of his helpers, Timothy and
E-ras'tus, he himself stayed in Asia for a
while.

---

c) Paul's Future Plans (19:21-22)

With these verses we return to surer ground. They may be said to stand as a preface to the remainder of Acts, just as the Lord's commission in 1:8 outlines the plan of the whole book. That Paul had plans as presented here, but postponed carrying them out at once, is confirmed by the epistles (II Cor. 1:15-17, 23), as also is the mission of **Timothy** (I Cor. 4:17; 16:10) and **Erastus** (II Tim. 4:20; cf. also Rom. 16:23—but is this the same Erastus?).

21. Resolved in the Spirit, i.e., under divine inspiration and guidance, as is constantly stressed in the last chapters (cf. 20:22). **Through Macedonia and Achaia:** The plan is carried out at 20:1-2. **To Jerusalem:** The primary reason for this visit is not mentioned in Acts—to deliver the collection for the support of the Jerusalem church (see Rom. 15:25). Paul speaks of his intention of visiting **Rome** in Rom. 1:10-15; 15:22-29. The latter passage gives the impression that the visit was to be merely *en passant* on his way to Spain, possibly because some other missionary had already founded a church at Rome, and Paul wished to hold by his principle of not building "on another man's foundation" (Rom. 15:20). According to tradition, Peter had already visited Rome. If so, he may on his way there have sown the seeds of the Cephas party at Corinth (but see on 12:17).

22. Stayed in Asia: In view of what follows, presumably at Ephesus. But vss. 21-22, and particularly the opening phrase (literally, "now after these things were completed") leave the impression of being a conclusion to the whole account about Ephesus. The vague phrases **for a while** and "about that time" (vs. 23) show that Luke has no very clear idea about the chronology, and it is possible that the story of the riot—perhaps from another source—has been misplaced. In that case **Asia** may here mean the province in general, and during the period in question some of Paul's wider missionary work may have been achieved (see on vs. 10).

---

sponsible to scientific law and order that it ceases to be deity. In the world of magic nothing is impossible. In the world of materialism only the obvious is possible. It is a world shorn of its wonder. In such a world it is not surprising to find now and then a charlatan who captivates the crowds simply because he has brought back into a prosaic universe the incomparable thrill of the magician who does the impossible. When scientists reduce life to a formula and destroy every shrine so that there is no place of worship left, we need not be surprised when Hitler comes along and fascinates the crowds by the wonders that he can perform. For Christianity it is neither magic nor materialism, but a universe governed by God according to law in which he is able to do all things toward the fulfillment of his purpose.

20-41. ***A Great Commotion Arose.***—Wherever Paul went he stirred up trouble. In Ephesus it involved the whole city. The clash was between the religion of Diana and the religion of Jesus. Diana was the goddess of fertility. Her temple in Ephesus was one of the wonders of the world, and her worshipers were numbered by thousands and thousands. Images of the goddess could be seen in almost every home, and the making of the images kept scores of silversmiths busy and rich. Jesus, on the other hand, had no temple and only a handful of followers. The only image of him was a mental image, and no business prospered because of him. In the conflict between Jesus and Diana it looked as though Jesus had lost before the battle began. But let us see what happened.

It began with a speech by Demetrius. He was the leader of the silversmiths. Whether or not there are labor unions as such, men who labor for a living find it to their advantage to work together for their common interest, and it is

23 And the same time there arose no small stir about that way.

23 About that time there arose no little

d) The Riot at Ephesus (19:23-41)

This vivid piece of narrative is full of interesting local color, and almost every sentence can be illustrated from inscriptions and the evidence of contemporary writers. Throughout, Luke's accuracy in detail is notably confirmed. It will be well to have the setting before us at the outset: (*a*) As the capital of a Roman province Ephesus was under the supreme governorship of the proconsul. For purposes of justice Ephesus was a chief assize town; accordingly **the courts are open, and there are proconsuls** (vs. 38). (*b*) As a "free city" Ephesus retained its own democratic Greek constitution. Power no doubt gravitated to the boule or senate, but the city was still nominally governed by the demos (**the crowd,** vs. 30) gathered in its **assembly** (vs. 32), which met apparently as a **regular assembly** (vs. 39) three times a month. The executive officer, who called and **dismissed the assembly** (vs. 41) and acted as its chairman, was known as the **town clerk** (vs. 35). As appears from inscriptions, he was a most important personage, events being dated by reference to the term of office of so-and-so as town clerk. (*c*) As a religious center Ephesus was the seat of the "Asiarchate" or religious confederacy of the cities of Asia. The **Asiarchs** (vs. 31) were provincial, not municipal, officials and had special charge of the festival in adoration of the emperor, on which occasion each Asiarch strove to outdo his predecessor in the splendor of his games. One of the titles of the reigning Asiarch was "High Priest of Asia." Acts speaks of "Asiarchs" in the plural. In fact only one held office at a time; but he held it for only four years. Hence there may well have been a body of "ex-Asiarchs" spoken of generally as "Asiarchs," just as the Gospels and Acts mention "high priests." It is not necessary, with Ramsay, to suppose a problematical "council" of Asiarchs representing other cities beside Ephesus.

The ostensible motive of **Demetrius'** attack on Paul was religious zeal for the temple worship of **Artemis** (Latin, **Diana**); the real motive, as at Philippi, was fear of damage to business interests. When devotion to religion and patriotic sentiment can be made to coincide with self-interest, then fanatical intolerance knows no bounds! The whole story is so vivid and so true to life that it is impossible to doubt its historicity. The only point not reasonably clear is the part played by **Alexander.** Probably the Jews feared that the riot would, as so often, result in an attack upon themselves, because of their known hostility to idolatry. Alexander was put up to try to avert this by drawing the crowd's attention back to Paul, and making it clear that the Jews repudiated all responsibility for him and his teaching. That this actually happened is entirely likely. But it also serves to illustrate Luke's thesis that Paul's misfortunes were always due to popular hostility, usually at the instigation of the Jews, and that time and again he was protected by friendly Roman officials.

---

inevitable that out of their ranks should emerge a spokesman, a man who shares their point of view and who knows their lot, yet who, because of his superior intelligence, is destined for a place of leadership. Such a man was Demetrius, by no means the complete scalawag that it is our temptation to believe him to be.

His speech made sense from beginning to end. This is the way it went. The sale of images was the silversmiths' living. There could be no doubt about that. No more shrines, no more wealth for the workers in silver. That is always a good place to begin when you are trying to convince a man that you are right. Let him see that you recognize the basic and practical necessities of life. No business, no bread. Then Demetrius went on to point out that Paul had already slowed down the traffic in images. People were not buying as many replicas of Diana as they had in other years because Paul and his colleagues were telling them that **gods made with hands are not gods.** Incidentally there could be no better evidence for the power of Paul's preaching than the falling off in the silversmith trade. Following upon these two statements, the conclusion would seem to be, "Down with Paul!" But Demetrius was too smart for that. He took another tack and appealed to the great goddess herself. If Paul went on and weakened the faith of the people in Diana, what would become of Diana? Her temple would fall into contempt and she would

24 For a certain *man* named Demetrius, a silversmith, which made silver shrines for Diana, brought no small gain unto the craftsmen;

25 Whom he called together with the workmen of like occupation, and said, Sirs, ye know that by this craft we have our wealth.

26 Moreover ye see and hear, that not alone at Ephesus, but almost throughout all Asia, this Paul hath persuaded and turned away much people, saying that they be no gods, which are made with hands;

27 So that not only this our craft is in danger to be set at nought; but also that the temple of the great goddess Diana should be despised, and her magnificence should be destroyed, whom all Asia and the world worshippeth.

stir concerning the Way. 24 For a man
named De-me'tri-us, a silversmith, who
made silver shrines of Ar'te-mis, brought
no little business to the craftsmen. 25 These
he gathered together, with the workmen
of like occupation, and said, "Men, you
know that from this business we have our
wealth. 26 And you see and hear that not
only at Ephesus but almost throughout all
Asia this Paul has persuaded and turned
away a considerable company of people,
saying that gods made with hands are not
gods. 27 And there is danger not only that
this trade of ours may come into disrepute
but also that the temple of the great goddess
Ar'te-mis may count for nothing, and that
she may even be deposed from her magnificence, she whom all Asia and the world
worship."

---

24. Silver shrines: No such silver models have ever been found, though miniature earthenware temples are vouched for. It has been pointed out (E. L. Hicks, "Demetrius the Silversmith," *The Expositor*, I [1890], 401-22) that νεωποιός (literally "temple maker") is found in inscriptions as the title of a board of "vestrymen" of the temple at Ephesus, and it is suggested that Luke may have mistakenly taken this title literally. Indeed such a "vestryman" with the name of **Demetrius** is actually mentioned in one inscription (*British Museum Inscriptions*, III, 2, 578). It is certainly much more likely that Demetrius would make silver images of Artemis than silver shrines. **Artemis** of Ephesus, though bearing the name of the maiden huntress whose birthplace Ephesus claimed to be, was in fact a divinity of fertility, some form of the great Asiatic mother goddess. **Business:** And consequently "profit," a meaning the Greek word often carries.

27. Come into disrepute: Lake and Cadbury suggest that "the tone of the sentence might be given by 'that our business will be shown up'" (*Beginnings of Christianity*, IV, 247). **The temple** was one of the Seven Wonders of the World. It was octagonal, about 340 by 160 feet. Instead of mortar, gold is reputed to have been used between the joints of the marble blocks. It had 127 pillars 60 feet in height, and each was erected by a king. They had drums 20 feet in circumference and 6 feet high, with 8 life-size figures sculptured on each. The "cella" or "holy of holies" was 70 feet wide and open to the skies. The finding of the foundation deposit of treasure under the great altar by D. G. Hogarth in 1904 ranks as one of the greatest romances of archaeological research (see C. M. Cobern, *The New Archeological Discoveries* [New York: Funk & Wagnalls, 1917], pp. 468 ff.).

---

be deposed from her magnificence. Thus the argument proceeded from finances to faith. It began with the hard facts of making a living and ended in a shower of religious stars. Its logic was implied rather than stated and the inevitable conclusion was never put into words. The men were left to draw their own conclusions, and the case was so carefully worded that it drew from the men not a campaign against Paul but a crusade for Diana. They raised the cry, **Great is Diana of the Ephesians.** It is little wonder that by this time the city was filled with confusion. There is nothing that so stirs people into frenzy as a religious battle cry based upon sound business principles!

What followed was what you would expect—a riot. The people poured into the great amphitheater, shouting and yelling, dragging along with them innocent bystanders who might have some connection with Paul. The story of the riot as it is told by Luke reveals the tragic truth about all riots. **Now some cried one thing, some another; for the assembly was in confusion, and most of them did not know why they had come together.** They were swept along by the crowd, not knowing whither they went

28 And when they heard *these sayings,* they were full of wrath, and cried out, saying, Great *is* Diana of the Ephesians.

29 And the whole city was filled with confusion: and having caught Gaius and Aristarchus, men of Macedonia, Paul's companions in travel, they rushed with one accord into the theatre.

30 And when Paul would have entered in unto the people, the disciples suffered him not.

31 And certain of the chief of Asia, which were his friends, sent unto him, desiring *him* that he would not adventure himself into the theatre.

32 Some therefore cried one thing, and some another: for the assembly was confused; and the more part knew not wherefore they were come together.

33 And they drew Alexander out of the multitude, the Jews putting him forward. And Alexander beckoned with the hand, and would have made his defense unto the people.

28 When they heard this they were enraged, and cried out, "Great is Ar'te-mis
of the Ephesians!" 29 So the city was filled
with the confusion; and they rushed together into the theater, dragging with them
Ga'ius and Ar-is-tar'chus, Mac-e-do'ni-ans
who were Paul's companions in travel.
30 Paul wished to go in among the crowd,
but the disciples would not let him; 31 some
of the A'si-archs also, who were friends of
his, sent to him and begged him not to
venture into the theater. 32 Now some cried
one thing, some another; for the assembly
was in confusion, and most of them did not
know why they had come together. 33 Some
of the crowd prompted Alexander, whom
the Jews had put forward. And Alexander
motioned with his hand, wishing to make

---

29. Modern excavation has laid bare the ruins of the **theater** which was of immense proportions and capable of holding over twenty thousand people.

Gaius and Aristarchus, Macedonians: Aristarchus was from Thessalonica (20:4; 27:2; see also Col. 4:10; Philem. 24). Gaius, according to 20:4, was not a Macedonian but came from Derbe, unless indeed the words "of Derbe" are attached to Timothy, and Gaius grouped with Aristarchus and Secundus as "Thessalonians" (see on 20:4; 16:1).

30-32. The crowd is properly the demos, who would meet in **assembly** to transact their business as a governing body. But it is doubtful whether either of these two words is here used in this technical sense; for the occasion is obviously a popular riot rather than a meeting of the "regular assembly" (vs. 39).

33. Some of the crowd: The Greek is ἐκ δὲ τοῦ ὄχλου, which should probably not be taken as in the KJV translation, **drew Alexander out of the multitude,** but (with RSV) as the subject of the sentence. For this very harsh construction cf. John 7:40; 16:17; Luke 21:16; Acts 21:16. We can then translate συνεβίβασαν by **prompted,** which would be in line with a common usage of the word in the LXX, where it often means to "instruct" (cf. I Cor. 2:16).

---

or why. Race riots in Detroit; lynchings in the South; mob violence in industry; mass murders in war—it is always the same; the emotions of men let loose without reason or restraint until in their fury they can kill without a thought or pity.

This scene in Ephesus reminds us of something that we cannot afford to forget. It is this: If you want to stir people up, there are two ways of doing it. The first is to wave the flag, and the second is to beat the religious drum. If the first fails, the second is sure to succeed. If you cannot keep a man out of office on the basis of his own lack of merit, you can surely do it either by casting doubt on his patriotism or by rousing antagonism against his religion. If you cannot stir up the people by appealing to their national pride, you can almost always do it by appealing to their religious fanaticism. When a spark may ignite the bonfire that will burn up the world, we need to remember what happened in Ephesus. When men ask us if we are not willing to fight for our religion, we would do well to ask in reply whether that question is a question of faith or of finances. No one would deny, it goes without saying, the

34 But when they knew that he was a
Jew, all with one voice about the space of
two hours cried out, Great *is* Diana of the
Ephesians.
35 And when the townclerk had ap-
peased the people, he said, *Ye* men of Ephesus, what man is there that knoweth not
how that the city of the Ephesians is a
worshipper of the great goddess Diana, and
of the *image* which fell down from Jupiter?
36 Seeing then that these things cannot
be spoken against, ye ought to be quiet,
and to do nothing rashly.

a defense to the people. 34 But when they
recognized that he was a Jew, for about
two hours they all with one voice cried
out, "Great is Ar'te-mis of the Ephesians!"
35 And when the town clerk had quieted
the crowd, he said, "Men of Ephesus, what
man is there who does not know that the
city of the Ephesians is temple keeper of
the great Ar'te-mis, and of the sacred stone
that fell from the sky?[r] 36 Seeing then that
these things cannot be contradicted, you
ought to be quiet and do nothing rash.

[r] The meaning of the Greek is uncertain.

Alexander's part in the drama is as obscure as Sosthenes' in 18:17 (but see on 19:23-41, above). Was he the "Alexander the coppersmith" of II Tim. 4:14? **Make a defense,** i.e., to defend the Jews against the suspicion of implication in Paul's alleged misdemeanors. This is more likely than that Alexander was a Jewish Christian and that he was attempting to defend Paul.

35. The **town clerk**'s speech (vss. 35-40) reads so like an apologia for Christianity that we may safely accept it, not as the actual words of the official, but as Luke's presentation of a typical Christian defense against current popular slanders. Certainly Luke records it, not because of its interest for the actual situation, but because of its bearing upon a question with which he is constantly preoccupied—the relation of the Christian church to the Roman civil authority.

Temple keeper, literally "temple sweeper," was an honorific title granted by Rome to certain cities which possessed "league" temples of the imperial cult. In one recently discovered inscription Ephesus is called: "The first and greatest metropolis of Asia and twice temple-keeper of the Emperors . . . and temple-keeper of Artemis" (quoted by Cobern, *New Archeological Discoveries,* p. 467). Thessalonica and Beroea also held the title of "temple keeper." **The sacred stone that fell from the sky** was some symbol of Artemis, possibly a rough image, for which a supernatural origin was claimed. The same Greek word is elsewhere used of meteorites, and it is believed that it was a meteorite that was brought from Pessinus to Rome as a symbol of the Great Mother. Does the word contain a hint that the image of Artemis at any rate could not be despised as a god "made with hands" (vs. 26)?

---

real claim of patriotism or religious loyalty. What can be denied is the right of any man to use those deep-seated human emotions as the fuel to feed the lusts of the flesh. It is possible that a religious war against Communism might be brought about by those whose real interests are more largely financial than religious. Christians who remember Ephesus will be on the alert.

After two hours of shouting, one of the public officials was able to quiet the crowd and make a speech. His voice was the voice of reason and fortunately it prevailed. He advised the people to "keep calm and do nothing reckless" (Moffatt). He pointed out to them the folly of their action and reminded them that there were orderly ways to settle whatever grievances the silversmiths might have. Thank God for the disciplined people who do not lose their heads and who have the power to restore to sanity others who temporarily lose theirs. Gamaliel, Gallio, the town clerk of Ephesus, they all belong to the fellowship of those who reconcile and heal.

The damage was done, however. There was nothing left for Paul to do but to leave the city. The agitators had accomplished their purpose in spite of the fact that the assembly had been peacefully dismissed. So riots always leave their scars. No matter what the official outcome may be, the fact that human beings for the moment became beasts cannot be undone or denied. Try as good men may to blot out the shame, it is there and never completely fades away. The bombing of cities from the air in a kind of frenzied retaliation may be justified by logic and rationalized by common sense, and restitution may be made in abundance. But the

37 For ye have brought hither these men, which are neither robbers of churches, nor yet blasphemers of your goddess.

38 Wherefore if Demetrius, and the craftsmen which are with him, have a matter against any man, the law is open, and there are deputies: let them implead one another.

39 But if ye inquire any thing concerning other matters, it shall be determined in a lawful assembly.

40 For we are in danger to be called in question for this day's uproar, there being no cause whereby we may give an account of this concourse.

41 And when he had thus spoken, he dismissed the assembly.

37 For you have brought these men here
who are neither sacrilegious nor blasphemers of our goddess. 38 If therefore De-me′-
tri-us and the craftsmen with him have a
complaint against any one, the courts are
open, and there are proconsuls; let them
bring charges against one another. 39 But
if you seek anything further,[s] it shall be
settled in the regular assembly. 40 For we
are in danger of being charged with rioting
today, there being no cause that we can
give to justify this commotion." 41 And
when he had said this, he dismissed the
assembly.

[s] Other ancient authorities read *about other matters.*

---

37. Sacrilegious, literally "robbers of temples." Paul's remark in Rom. 2:22 shows that a pious Jew would regard this as a particularly heinous crime: "You who abhor idols, do you rob temples?"

38. The courts are open, literally "court days are held." They may have access to the Roman *conventus* or assizes over which the proconsul presides. As there was of course only one proconsul, the phrase **there are proconsuls** perhaps means "there are such people as proconsuls" (Lake and Cadbury, *Beginnings of Christianity,* IV, 251).

39. The present concourse was presumably not a **regular assembly,** i.e., one of the stated meetings of the *ecclēsia,* of which there were three monthly. At these justice would be administered by the demos according to municipal procedure, in contrast to the provincial procedure of the proconsular assizes. Luke again quite correctly uses the technical terms.

40. We are in danger: Perhaps a sarcastic echo of Demetrius' words (vs. 27). The town clerk points out where the real danger lies—not in loss of trade, but in the risk that the Romans might treat this irregular assembly as **rioting** and punish the city for it. **There being no cause . . . commotion:** The Greek here is very awkward, but RSV quite satisfactorily gives the intended sense.

---

damage has been done. Good men like Paul will suffer because of it, and honest men will no longer be able to walk with a free and untroubled conscience through the cities of the world.

Sometimes as we follow Paul through storm after storm, we wonder what kept him going. Certainly the power that sustained him is quite beyond the reach of our analysis or even of our understanding. But may not one of the things that kept him going be suggested by a line at the very beginning of the passage, **I must also see Rome?** Paul had a supreme ambition; it was to make the gospel travel. Rome was the center of the world, and he would not rest until he reached the city built on seven hills. Through the ups and downs of his missionary work, behind all the failures and disappointments, steadying him and giving him the strength to carry on, was the determination to see Rome. It was the power of attraction of the distant goal that more than once saved the immediate situation.

There are times when we do not ask to see the distant scene, one step is enough. But there are other times when to see the distant scene makes it possible to take the next step toward danger. The people who move through the troubled waters of life without losing either their mind or their disposition are the people who have their eye on some distant goal, while those who have their eyes fixed on the immediate necessities of life lose their nerve and give up the fight. The people who will go through the disorders of a time with the least loss of spirit are the ones whose eyes are set on a new and better order of things, not only in this present world, but also in that world which is invisible and in which the towers of Rome never crumble.

20 And after the uproar was ceased, Paul called unto *him* the disciples, and embraced *them*, and departed for to go into Macedonia.

20 After the uproar ceased, Paul sent for the disciples and having exhorted them took leave of them and departed for

E. Paul's Final Visit to Macedonia and Achaia (20:1-4)

In these four verses, before the beginning of the next "we" section at vs. 5, Luke gives a lightning sketch of Paul's next movements. The extreme brevity of the account of what was in fact a most important journey is noticeable. It reminds us again that Luke is interested, not in the development of communities already founded, but in the onward march of Christianity. Furthermore since 19:21 Paul's eyes have been turned toward Jerusalem, and Luke hurries on to bring him there. We may also suspect that Luke is silent on certain matters contained in his source on the ground that they are better suppressed, e.g., the trouble in the Corinthian church and, it may be, the persecution directed against the Macedonian communities.

Leaving Ephesus in fulfillment of the intention expressed in 19:21, Paul headed for Macedonia and Greece. His route is not stated, but probably he coasted north to Troas, where he had not preached on his first visit but now found "a door . . . opened for me" (II Cor. 2:12), though he was too restless to take advantage of it. He was expecting the return of Titus, who had been sent on a mission to Corinth, and as the latter had not arrived, he "went on to Macedonia" (II Cor. 2:13)—probably first sailing to Neapolis and thence on to Philippi, where Titus finally joined him with good news from Corinth (II Cor. 7:5-16). Out of the fullness of his relief and joy he wrote II Cor. 1–7. One matter still not satisfactorily settled at Corinth was that church's response to the appeal for the "collection," and Paul therefore also wrote II Cor. 8–9 and sent the letter on to Corinth by the hands of Titus and "the brother who is famous among all the churches" (II Cor. 8:18), whom some would identify with Luke himself. Leaving Philippi, Paul meantime passed, we may suppose, along the route taken in the second tour—Apollonia, Thessalonica, Beroea. It is possible that it was at this time that he paid the visit to Illyricum mentioned in Rom. 15:19. And so finally **he came to Greece.** The sketch is so summary that we are not even told at what town he stayed; but it was certainly Corinth. **There he spent three months,** during which he wrote the Epistle to the Romans.

After three months Paul was preparing to start by sea for Syria, still in accordance with the plan of 19:21, when he discovered a Jewish plot. Its nature is not stated; but obviously a pilgrim ship would provide an excellent opportunity for murder on the high seas, and the fact that Paul was carrying the collection would be an added incentive. The Western text characteristically reads that "he wished to sail for Syria but the Holy Spirit told him to return through Macedonia." This route had the additional advantage that it would enable Paul to collect his company of delegates on the way. For the seven disciples whom Luke mentions as Paul's companions were almost certainly local representatives chosen to carry their churches' contributions to Jerusalem—possibly to avoid any appearance of interested motives on the part of Paul. Luke curiously makes no mention here of the collection, though it is alluded to incidentally in 24:17 where Paul says to Felix, "I came to bring to my nation alms and offerings." Luke's silence is rather sur-

20:1-6. ***Paul Returns to Macedonia and Greece.***—No one could guess from this passage alone what was happening to Paul as he traveled about Macedonia and Greece. Nothing is said, for example, of the trouble which was brewing in Corinth and which weighed heavily upon Paul's mind and heart. The fact that he was traveling from city to city to collect money for the less privileged Christians in Jerusalem is not mentioned. Neither is it mentioned that during the three months he spent in Corinth he wrote the Epistle to the Romans. What we have in this passage is not much more than an outline map of his travels. For reasons best known to himself Luke chose to have it so. He reduced this part of the story to a skeleton of geographical fact.

The passage has at least this much value for us in addition to whatever narrative value it may have: It reminds us that outline maps

2 And when he had gone over those parts, and had given them much exhortation, he came into Greece,

3 And *there* abode three months. And when the Jews laid wait for him, as he was about to sail into Syria, he purposed to return through Macedonia.

4 And there accompanied him into Asia Sopater of Berea; and of the Thessalonians, Aristarchus and Secundus; and Gaius of Derbe, and Timotheus; and of Asia, Tychicus and Trophimus.

Mac-e-do′ni-a. 2 When he had gone through
these parts and had given them much encouragement, he came to Greece. 3 There he
spent three months, and when a plot was
made against him by the Jews as he was
about to set sail for Syria, he determined to
return through Mac-e-do′ni-a. 4 Sop′a-ter of
Be-roe′a, the son of Pyr′rhus, accompanied
him; and of the Thes-sa-lo′ni-ans, Ar-is-tar′chus and Se-cun′dus; and Ga′ius of
Der′be, and Timothy; and the Asians,

---

prising as the collection would have been a good illustration of his thesis of the unity of the church. Perhaps he simply takes it for granted as something familiar to all and in which he himself was directly concerned—possibly as the representative of Philippi. It is clear from the epistles that the delivery of the collection was Paul's chief motive for his return at this time to Jerusalem; Rom. 15:25-27—"I am going to Jerusalem with aid for the saints"—was written just before his departure. In I Cor. 16:1-4 he had urged the Corinthians to contribute liberally, and the whole of II Cor. 8–9 deals with the matter and contrasts the liberality of the Macedonians with the reluctance of the wealthier Christians of Corinth. Paul evidently regarded this enterprise as crowning his work in the four provinces, and as soon as it was completed he purposed to go to Rome and the West (Rom. 15:28). The significance of all this is that it proves how anxious Paul was to stand well with the mother church and to emphasize the unity of Jew and Gentile in Christ. As Streeter well says: "It is evident that the carefully organised collection for the impoverished church in Jerusalem, mentioned so often in Paul's epistles, had a political so to speak, as well as a purely philanthropic object. . . . The Gentile churches were to be made to feel the essential unity of the Church by realising their debt to, and their unity with, the Mother Church; the Mother Church was to recognise the Gentile communities as true daughters of Israel" (*The Primitive Church* [New York: The Macmillan Co., 1929], pp. 52-53).

20:2. Through these parts, i.e., Macedonia—probably by the route followed in the second tour.

4. Into Asia (KJV) should certainly be omitted with the best MSS, as the delegates were obviously bound not for Asia but for Jerusalem. **Sopater:** One Sosipater is mentioned in Rom. 16:21 along with Timothy and Lucius. If the two are identified and Lucius is assumed to be Luke, then (assuming that Rom. 16, with the rest of the epistle, was written from Corinth) Romans and Acts agree that Timothy, Luke, and Sopater were all three with Paul at this point. In 19:29 Gaius and Aristarchus are mentioned together as "Macedonians." It may be therefore that the same grouping should be retained here, **Aristarchus, Secundus,** and **Gaius** being classed as **Thessalonians,** while the description **of Derbe** should perhaps be taken with **Timothy** who, though usually considered to be a native of Lystra, is in 16:1 with reference to "Lystra and Derbe" ambiguously stated to

---

never tell the whole story of a man's life. A man might keep a daily record of his engagements and appointments, his comings and goings, and yet leave no indication whatever of the real drama of what was going on inside him. You can watch a person come and go on his regular routine of business and never guess the fears and fancies which are more real to him than the pavements he so regularly treads. Suppose, for example, that the last chapters of the Gospels were reduced to a few lines like these: "And Jesus went from Galilee to Jerusalem; on several occasions he went to a garden called Gethsemane, and finally left Jerusalem and went to a hill called Calvary just outside the city wall." Every detail is accurate and yet all the details together tell virtually nothing about the drama of redemption, the geographical minutiae of which it faithfully reports.

Scientific method and habit of thought has

5 These going before tarried for us at Troas.
6 And we sailed away from Philippi after the days of unleavened bread, and came unto them to Troas in five days; where we abode seven days.

Tych'i-cus and Troph'i-mus.
5 These went on and were waiting for us at Tro'as,
6 but we sailed away from Philippi after the days of Unleavened Bread, and in five days we came to them at Tro'as, where we stayed for seven days.

---

be "there." No delegate is mentioned from Corinth or Philippi. Did Paul represent the first and Luke the second? For **Tychicus** (cf. Col. 4:7) the Western text reads "Eutychus"—the hero of the next paragraph. **Trophimus** is stated in 21:29 to be an "Ephesian" (see also II Tim. 4:20).

F. Return to Jerusalem (20:5–21:26)

1. From Philippi to Miletus (20:5-16)

At this point begins the second of the "we" sections. The first person plural continues until vs. 15, is then dropped, and is resumed again at 21:1. Whether the intervening section, and in particular the address to the Ephesian elders, also formed part of the diary source will be discussed later. Though after 21:18 the "we" does not occur again until 27:1, it can be assumed that Luke was Paul's almost constant companion from this point until his arrival at Rome. Since the first "we" section ended at Philippi during the second tour—the last "we" is at 16:16—and the second begins also at Philippi, a possible inference would be that the author of the diary had remained at Philippi during the intervening period and may himself have been a Philippian. This would tell against the identification of Luke with the Lucius of Romans 16:21 (see on vs. 4 above) who was with Paul at Corinth. At best it is a plausible but precarious hypothesis (see also on 16:9).

5. It is not clear whether the whole party, or only Tychicus and Trophimus, **went on and were waiting for us at Troas;** probably only the latter. But it seems curious that the Asiatic delegates should have come to Paul at Corinth, presumably with their contributions, instead of waiting for him in Asia. Perhaps the meaning—somewhat obscured by vague phraseology and variant readings—is that with the change of plan they were trysted to come north from Ephesus to Troas, where they would meet the rest of the party and all together would take ship for Syria.

6. Paul no doubt observed **the days of Unleavened Bread** at Philippi. As the voyage thence to Troas took **five days,** the wind must have been contrary, for on his first tour he had made the same trip in the reverse direction in two days (16:11).

---

inclined us to reduce all life to an outline map of statistics and analyses, omitting the motives, the satisfactions, the desires which alone make the map significant. Imagine an outline of the life of Paul that leaves out the fact that in the midst of trouble and perplexity he sat down and wrote the Epistle to the Romans! For Luke's purpose the outline is enough, but for our purpose of understanding Paul the outline must be filled in "with tears and with trials," of which Paul speaks later on. Few people would disagree with this point, and yet there are many people who are willing to take a reading of life which is as bare of the things that make life real as this passage is bare of the things that made Paul's life significant.

The first line of the passage is different. There we get a glimpse of the real Paul. "When the tumult had ceased, Paul sent for the disciples and encouraged them" (Moffatt). One might have expected the disciples to have encouraged Paul; Paul was the one who had had a dastardly hard time of it, not only in Ephesus, but in every city all along the line. But it was the other way around. It was Paul, who in spite of all his suffering, was nevertheless the source of encouragement. When a couple who had lived a long and wonderful life were temporarily separated by the death of the wife, it was the husband for whom everyone was immediately concerned. People wondered whether he would be able to endure the great memorial service that was held for his beloved wife. And yet during and after the service, it was the husband who was comforting and strengthening the children and grandchildren and hosts of friends. Moral and spiritual power has a way of increasing as the demand increases, and the more a man has to begin with, the more he has when, by all natural reckoning, his supply should be exhausted.

7 And upon the first *day* of the week, when the disciples came together to break bread, Paul preached unto them, ready to depart on the morrow; and continued his speech until midnight.

8 And there were many lights in the upper chamber, where they were gathered together.

9 And there sat in a window a certain young man named Eutychus, being fallen into a deep sleep: and as Paul was long preaching, he sunk down with sleep, and fell down from the third loft, and was taken up dead.

10 And Paul went down, and fell on him, and embracing *him* said, Trouble not yourselves; for his life is in him.

7 On the first day of the week, when we
were gathered together to break bread,
Paul talked with them, intending to depart
on the morrow; and he prolonged his
speech until midnight. 8 There were many
lights in the upper chamber where we were
gathered. 9 And a young man named Eu'ty-
chus was sitting in the window. He sank
into a deep sleep as Paul talked still longer;
and being overcome by sleep, he fell down
from the third story and was taken up
dead. 10 But Paul went down and bent
over him, and embracing him said, "Do not

---

7. The first day of the week is certainly Sunday. But was the time Saturday evening—the "first day" on Jewish methods of calculation beginning at what we would call 6 P.M. on Saturday—or Sunday evening? Almost certainly the latter, as **the morrow**, when Paul intended to depart, most naturally means the day after that first mentioned, and therefore is presumably Monday.

8. Lights: An improbable suggestion is that these are mentioned in refutation of the calumny that immoral practices took place at Christian gatherings; an alternative suggestion is that the stuffiness caused by the lamps accounted for Eutychus' drowsiness. The Western text reads "small windows" (ὑπολαμπάδες).

7-12. *The All-Night Service at Troas.*—In Troas, Paul and his party were reunited once again. After a week's visit they planned to depart. It was the night before their departure that they met together in an upper room for the breaking of bread. The description of the service is of great interest to the student of early Christian liturgy. Its chief interest to us, however, is in something quite apart from the liturgy. The service apparently began with instruction, and no less a person than the apostle Paul was the instructor. A young man named Eutychus sat in the window as the instruction was given. It would be interesting to know why he chose that particular place; perhaps the room was overcrowded and there was no other place; perhaps his attention was not entirely undivided and the seat in the window gave him an opportunity to divert himself if the talk failed to interest him. At any rate, he sat in the window and Paul's address went on and on. In fact it went on for so long that Eutychus finally fell asleep and, what is more, fell out of the third-floor window in which he was sitting. Preachers may be excused if they find some consolation in the fact that even Paul was not able to hold the attention of everyone in his congregation. They also may be warned by the incident against the danger of talking too long. We have no exact transcription, of course, of any sermon of Jesus, but the impression is unmistakable that he spoke in rather brief, well-defined blocks of speech. The longest of the parables can be told in three minutes. In timing a sermon one must keep in mind not only clock time but psychological time. People can listen for an hour easily if the periods of attention are so arranged according to a pattern or form that they can be easily grasped and understood. Listening to a person improvise for a half hour might seem like eternity, whereas listening to a symphony for an hour might seem like a moment. The difference is that the first is done at random; the second is done according to form. The chances are that Paul, on this last night before leaving, was preaching at random, and even for Paul that was a dangerous thing to do.

More important than the length of the sermon, however, is what happened to the young man. He was picked up for dead. But when Paul reached him, he threw himself upon him as Elijah and Elisha had done on earlier occasions. **Do not be alarmed,** he said, **for his life is in him.** It is quite obvious that Luke thinks that Paul brought the boy back to life. The story itself seems to indicate that, whereas the boy looked dead and the people thought he was dead, Paul could see that he was not really

11 When he therefore was come up
again, and had broken bread, and eaten,
and talked a long while, even till break
of day, so he departed.
12 And they brought the young man
alive, and were not a little comforted.
13 ¶ And we went before to ship, and
sailed unto Assos, there intending to take
in Paul: for so had he appointed, minding
himself to go afoot.
14 And when he met with us at Assos,
we took him in, and came to Mitylene.

be alarmed, for his life is in him." 11 And
when Paul had gone up and had broken
bread and eaten, he conversed with them
a long while, until daybreak, and so departed. 12 And they took the lad away alive,
and were not a little comforted.
13 But going ahead to the ship, we set
sail for As'sos, intending to take Paul
aboard there; for so he had arranged, intending himself to go by land. 14 And when
he met us at As'sos, we took him on board

---

11. It has been needlessly suggested that in the original source the word **eaten** referred not to Paul but to Eutychus, on the ground that eating is a conventional proof of a complete cure (9:19; 10:41; Luke 8:55).

The incident with reference to Eutychus at Troas is suspect by many critics because his restoration to life recalls certain O.T. miracles (cf. Elijah's action in I Kings 17:21 and Elisha's in II Kings 4:34-35). But no miracle is necessarily implied. Luke certainly says that Eutychus was "taken up dead," and the inference may be intended that Paul restored him to life. But equally the wording may mean that all thought him dead (though, if so, it would certainly be more natural to write ὡς νεκρός), but that Paul going down to investigate discovered that he was not (cf. 14:9-10; Mark 9:26-27). Luke's view of the incident may well have been the same as that of Philostratus who, after telling how Apollonius of Tyana restored a girl to life, remarks: "Now whether he detected some spark of life in her, . . . or whether life was really extinct, . . . neither I myself nor those who were present could decide." The "many lights" suggest a solemn religious gathering. The occasion is "the first day of the week" which is already the regular day of observance. The time is evening, perhaps on the analogy of the Last Supper, and because this was the most convenient time for working people. The "breaking of bread" seems to be a specifically liturgical action. Though presumably it took place at a common meal, no mention is made of the meal; for when we are told that Paul **had broken bread and eaten,** the last word means not merely that he partook of food—for this would be prior to, not after, the liturgical "breaking"—but that he "communicated." A common fellowship meal, or agape, is almost certainly assumed; but it is clear that the solemn religious significance of "breaking bread," as distinct from the meal as such, is beginning to assert itself.

13-16. While his companions went ahead by a coasting vessel around the promontory of Lectum to **Assos,** Paul went across **by land** (πεζεύειν, literally "to go by foot," but in contrast to sailing it can mean by any method of land transport). From II Tim. 4:13

---

dead at all. It is almost exactly parallel to the story of Jesus raising the daughter of Jairus. "She is not dead, but sleepeth" (Luke 8:41 ff.). What we find in this story is the willingness, yes, the eager desire of people to attribute to someone they both admire and trust, acts of superhuman power. Whether or not the stories are historically accurate, this much can be said of them: the fact that they were circulated indicates the kind of person about whom such a story could be widely circulated. Granted that Paul did not raise a young man from the dead, the fact that people could easily believe that he did strongly suggests that Paul was a man of such overflowing vitality and spiritual energy that it was not at all impossible for his contemporaries to believe that he actually made a dead man live again. So stories like these bear their indirect yet invaluable testimony to the stature of their heroes.

13-16. ***Paul Moves on Toward Jerusalem.***—This is another passage in which there is not much more than itinerary. In that it resembles vss. 1-6, which we have already considered. One further comment might be made: Luke was not interested in biography. Much as he loved Paul, the purpose of his book was not to write a full-length biography of his hero. In fact, interest in biography is a relatively modern thing. For the last four or five hundred years people have been increasingly curious about the story of other people's lives. It was not so when the

15 And we sailed thence, and came the next *day* over against Chios; and the next *day* we arrived at Samos, and tarried at Trogyllium; and the next *day* we came to Miletus.

16 For Paul had determined to sail by Ephesus, because he would not spend the time in Asia: for he hasted, if it were possible for him, to be at Jerusalem the day of Pentecost.

17 ¶ And from Miletus he sent to Ephesus, and called the elders of the church.

and came to Mit-y-le'ne.
15 And sailing from
there we came the following day opposite
Chi'os; the next day we touched at Sa'mos;
and[t] the day after that we came to Mi-le'tus.
16 For Paul had decided to sail past Ephesus,
so that he might not have to spend time
in Asia; for he was hastening to be at Jerusalem, if possible, on the day of Pentecost.

17 And from Mi-le'tus he sent to Ephesus and called to him the elders of the

[t] Other ancient authorities add *after remaining at Trogyllium.*

---

we learn that Paul lost some of his baggage, which presumably his friends omitted to put on the ship; for he asks Timothy to bring on from Troas a "cloak"—or possibly a "case for books"—some papyrus volumes, and some parchment rolls. From Assos he sailed to **Mitylene,** the chief town of the island of Lesbos, and then on three successive days reached a point on the mainland **opposite Chios,** the eastern coast of **Samos, and Miletus.** Luke remarks that Paul **had decided to sail past Ephesus,** which may imply that he had chartered a ship and could therefore choose his own ports of call, but more probably merely indicates that he had purposely chosen a vessel that did not put in at Ephesus because he did not wish to **have to spend time in Asia,** i.e., the district around Ephesus, where he would inevitably be delayed by friends. Luke does not suggest that Paul feared any hostility at Ephesus—though this may well have been the case—but gives as his reason that **he was hastening to be at Jerusalem, if possible, on the day of Pentecost,** probably because he wished to vindicate his loyalty in the eyes of Jewish Christians who would be attending the feast. Whether he got there in time we are not told. Probably he did so; for the fact that he spent "some days" at Caesarea (21:10) suggests that he found himself with time to spare, perhaps because favorable winds had enabled him to make "a straight course" from Miletus to Patara where they were immediately able to change ship (21:1-2).

2. Paul's Defense to the Elders of Ephesus (20:17-38)

Critics have vigorously assailed the historicity of this whole incident. If Paul was in such haste to reach Jerusalem, how could he spare all this time at Miletus? Even to send a message to Ephesus and bring the elders to Miletus would take some three days. If he had the time on his hands because the ship had to unload and take on at Miletus, why did he not go in person to Ephesus? Loisy thinks that the truth may be that delegates arrived

---

Bible was written. The Gospels are not satisfactory from a modern biographical point of view. They make no attempt to tell the full story of the life of Jesus, but they tell only so much of it as bears upon the mighty act that God was performing in the world. In the same way Luke was primarily interested in the story of the church, its expansion and development, and he was interested in the life of Paul only as it had to do with that expansion.

There is no doubt that we have gained something, and that biography enriches not only our knowledge of life, but also our enjoyment of it. Yet there is this much to be said for our nonbiographical ancestors: they were less likely than we are to miss the forest for the trees. They were more likely to be aware of and to be concerned with great, sweeping movements in which men played their important parts, to be sure, but the total significance of which was greater than any single man and could not be completely appreciated in terms of any one man's life. No one would advocate the elimination of hero worship from life. Some of the best things in life come about when one young person secretly worships another who has lived well. Yet it is well to remember that history is more than its heroes, and that its heroes are understood only as they are seen against the infinitely complex yet magnificent background of history's march through time.

17-38. ***Paul's Farewell Address to the Elders of the Church of Ephesus.***—When the elders of the church of Ephesus met Paul at Miletus, he

18 And when they were come to him, he said unto them, Ye know, from the first day that I came into Asia, after what manner I have been with you at all seasons,

church. 18 And when they came to him, he said to them:

"You yourselves know how I lived among you all the time from the first day that I

from Ephesus with a contribution to the collection, and that the redactor has substituted Paul's summons to them and the address. As for the speech, it is objected that Paul is so sure of the fate that awaits him at Jerusalem that it can only be a prophecy *ex eventu.* Moreover it contradicts what we know from the Epistle to the Romans of Paul's mind at this time. In that letter, so far from expecting an immediate end of his career, he is forming projects for the evangelization of the West (Rom. 15:28). The address must therefore be considered to be an artificial composition of the author which completes Luke's collection of typical speeches. We have already had a speech to Jews at Pisidian Antioch, one to uneducated pagans at Lystra, one to intellectuals at Athens. Here we have a typical exhortation to Christians, with which is combined an apology for Paul's missionary methods.

But on the positive side there are strong counterarguments. The speech has a better claim than any other in the book to be included in the memoirs of the eyewitness; for it lies between 20:5-16 and 21:1-18, both of which passages certainly belong to the diary source. Quite apart from the risk of a hostile reception—a possibility which Luke consistently glosses over—Paul's hesitation to visit Ephesus is understandable enough. If time was short, then it was one thing, even though it cost him three days, to summon the Ephesian elders to meet him; it was quite another thing to allow himself to become involved on the spot with all his friends and all his problems at Ephesus. As for the alleged discrepancy between the speech and Paul's mood as revealed in Romans, it is easy to reply that when he wrote from Corinth the Jewish plot against his life (vs. 3) had not yet been unveiled, and he may still have hoped to complete his mission at Jerusalem without incurring arrest at their hands. But by the time he reached Miletus he may have become convinced that his hopes were vain and that he must be prepared for the worst. Even in Romans he shows signs of grave apprehension and asks for his readers' prayers that he "may be delivered from the unbelievers in Judea" (Rom. 15:31). Leaving aside for the moment the objections to the speech as a prophecy *ex eventu,* we must admit that it reflects the sentiments, and indeed the actual language, of Paul more closely than any other speech in Acts (see *Beginnings of Christianity,* V, 412-13). Very significant too, and arguing strongly against the theory of a free composition by an editor, is the fact that the speech contains references to experiences at Ephesus not mentioned in the account in ch. 19 (e.g., vss. 19, 31, 34-35) and agrees closely with the hints of danger and difficulty which we have traced in the Corinthian letters. The prominence of the personal element and almost complete absence of the doctrinal—apart from vs. 28, where see Exeg.—are also unfavorable to the idea of free composition. We may therefore cautiously conclude that Luke's account of the meeting with the elders, and even his report of Paul's words, is substantially accurate, though admittedly certain details in the speech may be due to Luke's rewriting of it *ex eventu.*

spoke to them as a pastor speaks to his people. What he said could only have been said to those with whom he had had a long and close personal association. The scene is one of the most moving in all the N.T., and the words need hardly any comment at all. This is one of the few points in the Bible at which the expositor might do well to remain silent. Anything that he may presume to say is said more as a meditation upon the words of Paul than as an exposition of them.

First of all Paul reminded the elders of what he had already done. He was no stranger to them; he needed no letters of introduction or reference. He had lived with them for three years or more. They had watched him work and they knew how he lived. All they needed to do was to recall what they themselves had seen. They were not dependent upon any secondary evidence. They themselves had seen him endure the hardships of the gospel. The Jews plotted against him time after time and finally

19 Serving the Lord with all humility of
mind, and with many tears, and temptations, which befell me by the lying in wait
of the Jews:

20 *And* how I kept back nothing that was
profitable *unto you,* but have showed you,
and have taught you publicly, and from
house to house,

set foot in Asia, 19 serving the Lord with
all humility and with tears and with trials
which befell me through the plots of the
Jews; 20 how I did not shrink from declaring to you anything that was profitable,
and teaching you in public and from house

A further important question is how far the passage illustrates church organization at Ephesus. Vss. 17, 28 are often quoted as proof that already there were regular church office-bearers and that Paul, as an apostle, must have ordained them to their office, though no mention is made of this in Acts. But so far as the passage has any bearing on official organization, its chief interest is that while Luke describes the office-bearers as πρεσβύτεροι ("presbyters," **elders,** vs. 17), Paul calls them ἐπίσκοποι (**guardians** [RSV], **overseers** [KJV], vs. 28), the regular Greek word for "bishop." This is a reminder that, as "was pointed out long ago by Jerome and by several of the Greek fathers, there is no passage in the New Testament which compels the assumption that the terms 'Episcopos' and 'Presbyter' are the names of two different offices" (Streeter, *Primitive Church,* p. 114). But it is only fair to add with Streeter that whereas it is "clear that episcopoi could be called 'presbyters,' it does not, however, follow that all presbyters could be called 'episcopoi' " (*ibid.,* p. 85). It is doubtful, however, whether the passage can be used as evidence for any strictly official "orders" at this early stage. It is not clear that the title **elders** (vs. 17) means anything more than the "elder brethren"—those who held leadership in virtue of their personal and religious prestige. Vs. 28 certainly has the flavor of later church consciousness, as reflected, e.g., in the Pastoral epistles, and for that very reason can only doubtfully be accepted as Paul's exact words. But read in the light of, e.g., I Cor. 16:15-18, even this verse may be held to imply little more than the "guardianship" naturally exercised by the older men in virtue of their more mature Christian experience, without any other "official" appointment than that of the Holy Spirit, who equips every Christian for the service he is best fitted to render. "The writer regards inspiration as giving function, not office as conferring inspiration. They were ἐπίσκοποι because they had the Holy Spirit, they did not have the Holy Spirit because they were ἐπίσκοποι" (Lake and Cadbury, *Beginnings of Christianity,* IV, 259).

19-20. Plots of the Jews: Luke does not mention any such plots at Ephesus, where it was Gentiles and not Jews who were responsible for the riot. But it is reasonable to suppose that the Jews were the cause of much of the trouble about which Paul speaks in the Corinthian letters (cf. Rom. 15:30-31). **Shrink from declaring:** Cf. Paul's own words, "I am not ashamed of the gospel" (Rom. 1:16).

---

made it impossible for him to remain in the city. His life was filled with "tears" and "trials," and yet he went about his work teaching and preaching from house to house and in the public lecture hall. They saw in him a man who had mastered his pride and who could take the insults of unworthy opponents without losing heart. Some men are gradually worn down by opposition; their point of view is dulled by it and their energies are exhausted by it; they themselves become imitators of the opponents whom they despise. Not so Paul. The elders did not have to think twice to remember how he went about his ministry in Ephesus unshaken by the constant grilling of criticism.

And then Paul reminded them how he had always told them the truth. He had held nothing back if he thought it was for their good. He told them the pleasant things, but he told them the hard things too. He never held out the hope of resurrection without the suffering of the Cross. He never diluted the truth to make it easy for them or comfortable for himself. The hardest thing a pastor has to do is to tell one of his flock that he has made a mistake, that he is in the wrong, and that he must change the direction of his way. It is easier to approve than to condemn, and only the man who himself stands firm upon the foundations of God will be able to do both.

21 Testifying both to the Jews, and also
to the Greeks, repentance toward God, and
faith toward our Lord Jesus Christ.
22 And now, behold, I go bound in the
spirit unto Jerusalem, not knowing the
things that shall befall me there:
23 Save that the Holy Ghost witnesseth
in every city, saying that bonds and afflictions abide me.
24 But none of these things move me,
neither count I my life dear unto myself,
so that I might finish my course with joy,
and the ministry, which I have received of
the Lord Jesus, to testify the gospel of the
grace of God.

to house, 21 testifying both to Jews and to
Greeks of repentance to God and of faith
in our Lord Jesus Christ. 22 And now, behold, I am going to Jerusalem, bound in the
Spirit, not knowing what shall befall me
there; 23 except that the Holy Spirit testifies to me in every city that imprisonment
and afflictions await me. 24 But I do not
account my life of any value nor as precious to myself, if only I may accomplish
my course and the ministry which I received from the Lord Jesus, to testify to

---

21. Paul had called the **Greeks** to **repentance** and the **Jews** to **faith** in Jesus as Messiah. In form the sentence is what grammarians call a "chiasmus."

22-23. Bound in the Spirit, i.e., under the compulsion of the Holy Spirit. Now as always Paul sees the Holy Spirit's guidance in the force of circumstances. **The Holy Spirit testifies:** No such prophecies have hitherto been mentioned by Luke, who here perhaps writes *ex eventu.* But we have an illustration in the incident of Agabus (21:10-14); for Paul's premonition of coming disaster cf. Rom. 15:30-31.

24. Accomplish my course: Cf. Paul's own words, "I have fought the good fight, I have finished the race, I have kept the faith" (II Tim. 4:7). **The ministry:** Cf. Paul's message to Archippus, "See that you fulfill the ministry which you have received in the Lord" (Col. 4:17). **The gospel of the grace of God:** The word **gospel** (εὐαγγέλιον) occurs in Luke-Acts only here and in 15:7. The phrase is a perfect summary of the Christian message and as such very apposite in this typical address to already confirmed Christians.

Paul, they remembered as their minds flashed back as he talked, not only told the whole truth, but he told it to everyone, Jews and Greeks alike. What he had to say was meant for everyone, for it had to do with the God and Father of all. Repentance before God and faith in the Lord Jesus Christ—those were the two things that Paul kept talking about, and those things embraced everybody. Everybody had fallen short of the glory of God, and Christ died for every single human being. Therefore there were no special groups, no chosen few. Paul took them all into the great orbit of his gospel.

After this brief recollection of the past by which the old fellowship was renewed and strengthened, Paul proceeded to tell them what he was about to do. He was on his way to Jerusalem, "under the binding force of the Spirit" (Moffatt). Paul never traveled like a gypsy, going from place to place as he happened to take a fancy. He moved under the guidance of God; he was traveling for a purpose and his itinerary, as it were, was made up in heaven. Now he was going to Jerusalem, not because he thought it would be pleasant to renew old acquaintances, but because God was sending him there. What would happen when he got there he did not know. He never did know what would happen when he arrived in a city, but he never expected to know. God would reveal his will when the time came, and that was soon enough. Some people require a guarantee of safety before they leave home; at least they want all the arrangements carefully made and accommodations prepared. But that was not the way Paul traveled. He never knew whether he would be met by a group of hospitable women or by a mob of raging madmen.

Two things, however, he did know: he knew that there was trouble ahead and that these people would never see him again. He knew the first on the basis of past experience. In town after town it had been the same story, response from a few, rebuke from the others. He knew well what the inside of a jail looked like, and he knew the sting of the lash on a man's skin. There was no reason to believe that things would be different in Jerusalem. They never have been very different for the men and

25 And now, behold, I know that ye all, among whom I have gone preaching the kingdom of God, shall see my face no more.

26 Wherefore I take you to record this day, that I *am* pure from the blood of all *men*.

27 For I have not shunned to declare unto you all the counsel of God.

28 ¶ Take heed therefore unto yourselves, and to all the flock, over the which the Holy Ghost hath made you overseers, to feed the church of God, which he hath purchased with his own blood.

the gospel of the grace of God. 25 And now,
behold, I know that all you among whom
I have gone about preaching the kingdom
will see my face no more. 26 Therefore I
testify to you this day that I am innocent
of the blood of all of you, 27 for I did not
shrink from declaring to you the whole
counsel of God. 28 Take heed to yourselves
and to all the flock, in which the Holy
Spirit has made you guardians, to feed the
church of the Lord[u] which he obtained

[u] Other ancient authorities read *of God*.

---

25. See my face no more: Was this foreboding fulfilled? If not, Luke is hardly likely to have recorded it. If so, the tradition based on the Pastoral epistles that Paul was released from his Roman imprisonment and did in fact revisit Asia can hardly be accepted as authentic. **The kingdom:** As usual in Acts, it is impossible to be sure whether the reference is eschatological or to the church regarded as the kingdom of God (see on 8:12; 19:8).

26. Innocent, i.e., because he had not shirked the preacher's responsibility.

28. With this charge cf. I Pet. 2:25; 5:2-4, where, as in this passage, the "guardian" is synonymous with a "shepherd." The text of the latter part of the verse is uncertain. If we read with RSV **the church of the Lord** [i.e., Jesus Christ] **which he obtained with his own blood,** the sense is quite clear and natural. But the best MSS (Vaticanus, Sinaiticus) read **the church of God** (KJV), in which case the last phrase **with his own** [i.e., God's] **blood** becomes almost impossibly daring. It is probably for this reason that the Western reviser changed the text to "the church of the Lord." If we adopt the almost certainly correct reading **the church of God** (KJV), then the last clause should probably be translated "with the blood of his Own." It is quite possible that "his Own" (ὁ ἴδιος), with the omission of the word "Son," was an early title of Jesus comparable with "the Beloved," "the Only-begotten." In Rom. 8:32 we have the words "he who did not spare his own Son" in a verse which is obviously an echo of Gen. 22:16, where the LXX has "beloved son."

The word **obtained** is an entirely legitimate translation of the Greek term (περιποιεῖσθαι) and would be suitable if the verse is a conscious echo of Isa. 43:21, where the LXX has the same word. But N.T. usage supports, rather, the stronger translation "save alive," "rescue from destruction" (cf. Luke 17:33*a* with Luke 9:24*a*; Heb. 10:39). Paul's doctrine of redemption through the death of Christ is clearly in view.

---

women who dared to cut across the grain of the world's easy virtue. It followed from this that he would not return to Ephesus. If he should be at liberty to travel, he would head straight for Rome. So this was the last time that he would meet with his friends from Ephesus. There is always a sadness about a last time; even a last class in school has a somber tone about it, especially if there has been a real relationship between teacher and students. How much more poignant must have been this last meeting between pastor and people! How many memories must there have been which were not spoken and how many prayers offered for which there were no words!

Paul, however, did not allow his friends to linger in the deep waves of emotion, but he led them on to think about the future. They are to be the guardians of the flock. Their task will not be easy. Wherever there are sheep there are wolves, and wolves never spare the sheep. They must be on the alert, therefore. The trouble will not always come from outside, as they might expect; it will sometimes come from within. Wherever there is truth, there is the temptation to pervert it, sometimes willfully, and sometimes innocently and unconsciously. As guardians of the truth, they must watch for the enemy outside, like Gnosticism then and Communism now, but they must also be on the watch for

29 For I know this, that after my departing shall grievous wolves enter in among you, not sparing the flock.

30 Also of your own selves shall men arise, speaking perverse things, to draw away disciples after them.

31 Therefore watch, and remember, that by the space of three years I ceased not to warn every one night and day with tears.

32 And now, brethren, I commend you to God, and to the word of his grace, which is able to build you up, and to give you an inheritance among all them which are sanctified.

33 I have coveted no man's silver, or gold, or apparel.

with his own blood.[v] 29 I know that after
my departure fierce wolves will come in
among you, not sparing the flock; 30 and
from among your own selves will arise men
speaking perverse things, to draw away the
disciples after them. 31 Therefore be alert,
remembering that for three years I did not
cease night or day to admonish every one
with tears. 32 And now I commend you to
God and to the word of his grace, which is
able to build you up and to give you the inheritance among all those who are sanctified. 33 I coveted no one's silver or

[v] Or *with the blood of his Own.*

29-30. This prophecy of the growth of heresy at Ephesus finds its fulfillment in I Tim. 1:3-7. Is Luke again writing *ex eventu?* Similar predictions of the coming of false teachers occur in the pseudonymous (?) farewells in I Tim. 6:20-21; Jude 17-23; II Pet. 3:16-17.

32. The word of his grace, i.e., the message of God's grace as preached by the apostle (cf. vs. 24) ; less probably, the sayings of Jesus, of which one example is given us in vs. 35. **The inheritance among all those who are sanctified:** Another echo of the authentic Paul, who elsewhere gives "thanks to the Father, who has qualified us to share in the inheritance of the saints in light" (Col. 1:12).

33-35. Cf. Samuel's self-defense at his farewell in I Sam. 12:3. **These hands ministered:** Similarly Paul writes to the Corinthians, "We labor, working with our hands" (I Cor. 4:12; cf. I Thess. 4:11; II Thess. 3:7-12). **Help the weak:** Cf. Eph. 4:28, "Doing honest work with his hands, so that he may be able to give to those in need." **Remembering the words of the Lord Jesus:** This seems almost to have become a formula when quoting a saying of Jesus (cf. 11:16; Luke 22:61; 24:8; it is used also by Clement and Polycarp). There is no evidence whether this saying of Jesus, not of course recorded in the Gospels, was at this time written in a collection or was only traditional. The fact that Luke does not include it in his Gospel suggests that he was ignorant of it until he

the enemy from within, like the religion of the law then and the shallow faith of moralism now.

When Paul had finished, he commended them to God and left them with an unforgettable sentence of Jesus, **It is more blessed to give than to receive.** It is interesting to see how Paul brings his whole talk to a head by crystallizing it in a few words of the Master. It was like a sermon that leads up to a text. Happier, indeed, is the man who, like Paul, spends his days and nights giving, giving what he has and what he is, than the man who, fearful of what the future may bring, spends his days hoarding what few things he can gather together in anticipation of disaster. As so often happens, the mind of Jesus took a half dozen words and by them set forth the wisdom of God.

Frederick Brooks, a younger brother of Phillips Brooks, was rector of St. Paul's Church, Cleveland. Like his famous brother, he had the power that wins both the confidence and the affection of people. He himself was young and ministered to a young congregation. At the very height of his youthful powers he died. It was the kind of death that stirred a whole city. It was the kind of grief that words only hide and never express. When the people wanted to place a memorial to him in the church, they decided upon a large and noble stained-glass window. In the window is represented the figure of Paul taking leave of the elders of Ephesus. The sails are raised and waiting for the wind. Paul has told them the things that were in his heart. They know that he cares nothing about his own life but only about the mission upon which God has sent him. Underneath are inscribed the words, "Sorrowing most of all for the words which he spake, that they should see his face no more." So the sadness of separation

34 Yea, ye yourselves know, that these
hands have ministered unto my necessities,
and to them that were with me.
35 I have showed you all things, how
that so laboring ye ought to support the
weak, and to remember the words of the
Lord Jesus, how he said, It is more blessed
to give than to receive.
36 ¶ And when he had thus spoken, he
kneeled down, and prayed with them all.
37 And they all wept sore, and fell on
Paul's neck, and kissed him,
38 Sorrowing most of all for the words
which he spake, that they should see his
face no more. And they accompanied him
unto the ship.

21 And it came to pass, that after we
were gotten from them, and had
launched, we came with a straight course
unto Coos, and the *day* following unto
Rhodes, and from thence unto Patara:

gold or apparel. 34 You yourselves know
that these hands ministered to my necessities, and to those who were with me. 35 In
all things I have shown you that by so
toiling one must help the weak, remembering the words of the Lord Jesus, how he
said, 'It is more blessed to give than to receive.' "
36 And when he had spoken thus, he
knelt down and prayed with them all.
37 And they all wept and embraced Paul
and kissed him, 38 sorrowing most of all
because of the word he had spoken, that
they should see his face no more. And they
brought him to the ship.

21 And when we had parted from them
and set sail, we came by a straight
course to Cos, and the next day to Rhodes,

---

discovered it in his source of Paul's speech. Or are the words **It is more blessed to give than to receive** to be taken rather as Paul's (or Luke's?) own summary of the gist of Jesus' teaching? There are several possible echoes of the saying in later Christian literature. In Did. 1:5 we read, "Blessed is he who gives according to the command"; and in *Apostolic Constitutions* IV. 3, "For the Lord also said that he who gives is more blessed than he who receives." There is a parallel in Epicurus: "To do well is not only better than to fare well, but also more pleasant" (Epicurus, in Plutarch *Moralia* 778 C).

37. Fell on Paul's neck, and kissed him: For the language cf. Gen. 33:4; 45:14; 46:29.

3. From Miletus to Caesarea (21:1-14)

It is noticeable with what gusto Luke always recounts the details of a sea voyage. Leaving Miletus, on the first day the voyagers reach **Cos** on the northeast shore of the island of that name; then on two successive nights they anchor at **Rhodes**, again at the northeast point of the island, and at **Patara** on the Lycian mainland. Here, or at Myra (see below on vs. 1), they change from the small coasting boat to the larger ship. With the prevailing west wind they would be able to take the shortest course, southwest of

---

is passed on from generation to generation, and the warmth that has kindled the fires of human relationship continues to heal the wounds of our present grief.

One cannot but wonder whether there must not be an epilogue to the words of Paul, and whether in the case of human relationships which have been so deep and real there must not be another day in another land when those who have been loved and lost awhile smile once again like angel faces.

21:1-16. *The Trip from Miletus to Jerusalem.* —About the journey from Miletus to Jerusalem Luke tells us little. He is not writing a travelogue but a religious tract, and his pace quickens as he moves on to the last great chapter in the development of his thesis. There are two things, however, that we notice as we travel swiftly along toward Jerusalem.

The first is that wherever the party went there were small groups of Christians who took them in. As they went from island to island in the Aegean before they struck out for Tyre, so they went from group to group, islands of hospitality in the sea of strangeness. Even in Tyre there were some Christians, and they welcomed Paul and his party with open arms. Now that the whole world has become more navigable we are more likely to be at home in all parts of it. Nevertheless there are still times when we are glad to meet groups of people otherwise strange to us who, because they are Christians, accept

2 And finding a ship sailing over unto Phenicia, we went aboard, and set forth.

and from there to Pat'a-ra.[w] 2 And having found a ship crossing to Phoe-ni'ci-a, we

[w] Other ancient authorities add *and Myra*.

Cyprus, instead of sailing under the lee of the island around its eastern shore. The distance across the open sea to **Tyre** is about 350 miles. But evidently the weather was very favorable; lost time was made up; and we have the impression that from this point Paul is not pressed for time in order to reach Jerusalem by Pentecost. Seven days are spent at **Tyre,** and the party is now evidently oppressed by grave foreboding, for again Paul is warned not to go to Jerusalem, and, as at Miletus, there is a solemn farewell on the seashore. **One day** is spent at **Ptolemais** and **some days** at **Caesarea** with **Philip the evangelist.** Here a final warning is given to Paul by **Agabus,** but Paul persists in his mission in spite of the affectionate entreaties of his friends.

Once again critics have questioned the credibility of the record. Can Paul, with his supposed haste to reach Jerusalem, really have spent several days both at Tyre and at Caesarea? But we have already seen that by now he may have had time to spare. He may indeed have wished to fill in time, so that he might not have to spend too long in the dangerous environment of Jerusalem before the actual date of the feast. Because Luke does not care to explain all this, Loisy, for example, gratuitously rejects the whole narrative as due to a later redactor. But if we are to cut and carve, and pick and choose, even in what to all appearances is a genuine "we" passage, one wonders where a sane criticism of the book is to begin!

21:1. Patara: The Western text adds the words "and Myra," probably correctly, for from 27:5-6 we learn that Myra was the port of call for larger ships. It was a stage farther along the Lycian coast.

us as members of the same family. It is impossible to say what it meant to American and British soldiers and sailors to be greeted on the shores of an island in the South Pacific by a group of friendly black men singing "Onward, Christian Soldiers." The walls of prison camps must have seemed not quite so impenetrable when prisoners heard their neighbors reading the Gospels aloud.

If the forces of materialism unite to wage war upon the civilization that we have learned to value, we may once again appreciate the meaning of the Christian fellowship; and to know that in all parts of the world there are groups of faithful men and women who believe in the God we believe in, follow the same Lord and Savior, and try to live as sons of their Father in heaven, may make all the difference between defeat and victory. All the more reason, therefore, to keep the local groups strong. If one link in the underground movement had been weak, the result would have been death for scores of men and women. If the local units of the Christian movement are weak, the whole movement will fail. The least we can do in a world like this is to keep our stations strong, so that as men travel about the world they will find the fellowship ready to sustain them and send them on the next lap of their journey fortified for whatever may overtake them.

The second thing we notice is that Paul was warned on more than one occasion not to go to Jerusalem. People seemed to know what was in store for him if he went there. The feeling against him must have been strong and widespread. It was the last gasp of Jewish nationalism. It was even more violent than the opposition to Jesus in that Paul had covered more ground and had made the outcome of the issue even more explicit and unmistakable. If Paul lived, Judaism, as it had been known for centuries, died. The issue was as definite as that. Things could not go on as Paul had begun them and the national cult still survive. The issue was drawn. It was a matter of public knowledge. Paul's friends therefore urged him not to set foot in Jerusalem. Quite naturally and understandably they cared more about his personal safety than they did about the cause which he unfalteringly served.

Paul, on the other hand, would hear none of it. **Then Paul answered, "What are you doing, weeping and breaking my heart? For I am ready not only to be imprisoned but even to die at Jerusalem for the name of the Lord Jesus."** Paul had long since passed that point in life where his own personal safety was of more than secondary interest. When a man comes to that point in life when he says, "This is my course, and to it I am committed; what happens to me in the process is of no account," that man may be said to have reached his spiritual maturity.

3 Now when we had discovered Cyprus, we left it on the left hand, and sailed into Syria, and landed at Tyre: for there the ship was to unlade her burden.

4 And finding disciples, we tarried there seven days: who said to Paul through the Spirit, that he should not go up to Jerusalem.

5 And when we had accomplished those days, we departed and went our way; and they all brought us on our way, with wives and children, till *we were* out of the city: and we kneeled down on the shore, and prayed.

6 And when we had taken our leave one of another, we took ship; and they returned home again.

7 And when we had finished *our* course from Tyre, we came to Ptolemais, and saluted the brethren, and abode with them one day.

went aboard, and set sail. 3 When we had
come in sight of Cyprus, leaving it on the
left we sailed to Syria, and landed at Tyre;
for there the ship was to unload its cargo.
4 And having sought out the disciples, we
stayed there for seven days. Through the
Spirit they told Paul not to go on to Jerusalem. 5 And when our days there were
ended, we departed and went on our journey; and they all, with wives and children,
brought us on our way till we were outside
the city; and kneeling down on the beach
we prayed and bade one another farewell.
6 Then we went on board the ship, and
they returned home.

7 When we had finished the voyage from
Tyre, we arrived at Ptol-e-ma'is; and we
greeted the brethren and stayed with them

3-4. The fact that the ship had to **unload its cargo** explains adequately the length of time spent at **Tyre.** There is no record of the founding of a church at Tyre, but it may well have taken place during the mission described in 11:19. Evidently Paul knew of the presence of Christians, for he is described as **having sought out the disciples** (RSV), not merely as **finding disciples** (KJV). The Greek word is ἀνευρόντες, which is more correctly translated by RSV. **Not to go on:** The tense in the Greek—a present, not an aorist, infinitive—suggests the sense "to stop going on" or "to abandon the idea of going on." Though the warning is said to be **through the Spirit,** Paul ignores it, presumably doubting its inspiration.

5. Days there were ended: The Greek word here (ἐξαρτίζειν, properly to "finish equipping") is most unusual and was possibly suggested by the fact that the days were spent in "fitting out" the ship.

7. The Greek may be translated either (*a*) **When we had finished the voyage from Tyre, we arrived at Ptolemais** (RSV), in which case the journey of some twenty miles from Tyre to Ptolemais was made by boat; or (*b*) "Having completed our voyage, we arrived at Ptolemais from Tyre," in which case the main "voyage" from Lycia to Syria is considered to have ended at Tyre, and the trip to Ptolemais was made either in a coastal boat or possibly by land.

It is easy to see that no man will ever reach such a point unless he has at some point along the way surrendered himself to something so much greater than himself that he is able to view his own losses without anxiety or regret. Such a person will not throw his life away at the first opportunity. Jesus took care not to be pushed off a cliff to his premature death, and Paul took steps to protect himself from the fatal lash of the Roman soldier. Yet he will be ready at any time to do what seems right and necessary without regard to his own welfare. A few men like that in public life would save politics from the scramble for spoils which it usually is and restore the credit of public servants. Groups of people like that in the social order would re-establish the foundations of the family and recover the dignity of morality. People like that in the international world would open the way for a new order in which nationalism would be surrendered to the welfare of humanity. These people have been called "unpurchasable men." They cannot be bought, because they have ceased to live for themselves and have lost their life in something infinitely more interesting and more valuable than anything that they by themselves alone might ever be.

One pauses upon the phrase **for the name of the Lord Jesus.** Of how many heroic deeds has

8 And the next *day* we that were of Paul's company departed, and came unto Caesarea; and we entered into the house of Philip the evangelist, which was *one* of the seven; and abode with him.

9 And the same man had four daughters, virgins, which did prophesy.

10 And as we tarried *there* many days, there came down from Judea a certain prophet, named Agabus.

11 And when he was come unto us, he took Paul's girdle, and bound his own hands and feet, and said, Thus saith the Holy Ghost, So shall the Jews at Jerusalem bind the man that owneth this girdle, and shall deliver *him* into the hands of the Gentiles.

for one day. 8 On the morrow we departed
and came to Caes-a-re'a; and we entered the
house of Philip the evangelist, who was
one of the seven, and stayed with him.
9 And he had four unmarried daughters,
who prophesied. 10 While we were staying
for some days, a prophet named Ag'a-bus
came down from Judea. 11 And coming to
us he took Paul's girdle and bound his
own feet and hands, and said, "Thus says
the Holy Spirit, 'So shall the Jews at Jerusalem bind the man who owns this girdle
and deliver him into the hands of the

---

8. Caesarea is some forty miles from Ptolemais. When **Philip** was last mentioned, we read that he "came to Caesarea" (8:40), which appears to have been his home town. **Evangelist** later became the title of an official order in the church, but here it is probably used merely because earlier in the book Philip's work is described as that of "evangelization" (cf. 8:12, 35, 40). Eusebius seems to regard this Philip as one of the twelve rather than **one of the seven** (*Church History* III. 31. 3; V. 17. 3), and in later tradition the two Philips, like the two Johns (apostle and elder), were constantly confused.

9. Daughters, who prophesied: Lake and Cadbury well remark that "the absence of any statement as to what the daughters of Philip did or said is a sign that here we have the account of an eyewitness. In fiction a new character is introduced only in order to do or say something" (*Beginnings of Christianity,* IV, 268). It is hardly likely at this early date that these women belonged to an order of **virgins** (KJV), or that their power to "prophesy" is related to their virginity. Luke merely remarks that they were **unmarried** (RSV). Was he interested in them as one of his sources of information?

10-11. Agabus is presumably the **prophet** previously mentioned in 11:28. He acts symbolically like some O.T. prophet (cf. Isa. 20; 13:1-11; and for a similar prediction of captivity and death see John 21:18). The prophecy is not exactly fulfilled; for in the sequel the Jews attempt to lynch Paul, and he is actually rescued by Gentile officers. But ultimately Paul was of course delivered **into the hands of the Gentiles** and executed by them, and the primary instigators of his arrest were the Jews. Luke as usual places the major responsibility on the Jews, as he does for Jesus' crucifixion (2:23).

---

that been the motive? How many lives have been changed for the sake of Jesus? It is not in our power to calculate an answer. But it is safe to say that when all the motives for human decency and goodness have been added up, none will be found to have turned more men and women from darkness to light than the desire to do it for the sake of Jesus. Sometimes our sophisticated religious leaders are inclined to think that we have outgrown the power of that motive, and they often seem to lose Jesus in the mists of profound and abstract thought. Their thinking is not to be in any way despised, but we may venture the prediction that if there is still any power in Christianity to transform the life of individuals, it will be, in some form or other, the power of the personal Jesus over the personal lives of men and women. A consistent, systematic structure of theology is indispensable. We cannot live an orderly Christian life without it. But in the last analysis the world will be changed by the people who are willing **not only to be imprisoned but even to die . . . for the name of the Lord Jesus.**

Added to these greater things is the human interest that lies just beneath the surface of the passage, as unmistakable as it is unexpressed. There is, for one thing, the relationship between Luke and Paul. One can almost feel the affection of the older for the younger man as

12 And when we heard these things, both we, and they of that place, besought him not to go up to Jerusalem.

13 Then Paul answered, What mean ye to weep and to break mine heart? for I am ready not to be bound only, but also to die at Jerusalem for the name of the Lord Jesus.

14 And when he would not be persuaded, we ceased, saying, The will of the Lord be done.

15 And after those days we took up our carriages, and went up to Jerusalem.

Gentiles.' " 12 When we heard this, we and
the people there begged him not to go up
to Jerusalem. 13 Then Paul answered,
"What are you doing, weeping and breaking my heart? For I am ready not only to
be imprisoned but even to die at Jerusalem
for the name of the Lord Jesus." 14 And
when he would not be persuaded, we
ceased and said, "The will of the Lord be
done."
15 After these days we made ready and

---

13. For the name of: Or as we should say, "for the sake of" (but cf. 5:41, where the phrase "for the name" is used absolutely; and see on 3:6).

4. Paul with the Jerusalem Church (21:15-26)

Paul showed notable courage in appearing thus openly at Jerusalem for the festival. His Gentile converts would not be there to support him; Jewish Christians present might well include some of his Judaizing opponents from Antioch, Galatia, and Corinth; and there would be crowds of orthodox Jews such as had plotted against him at the various towns he had touched. Curiously Luke does not tell us whether Paul was in time for the feast, though that is probably assumed. Nor does he say anything about the handing over of the collection, which was the chief motive of the visit. But the passage does throw interesting light on the setup of the Jerusalem church. None of the twelve were apparently then in residence, for there is no mention of "apostles," unless indeed they are included in the more general term "elders." Particularly noticeable is the pre-eminent position held by **James** "the Lord's brother." This at first sight seems remarkable in the case of one who in Jesus' own time was not a believer, and may have been partly due to the thoroughly Jewish idea that religious offices were essentially hereditary, so that Jesus' nearest male relative would seem to be marked out by divine right to be his vicegerent until his return. But James seems to have been highly honored in his own right even in orthodox Jewish circles. Josephus tells us that when Ananus the Younger, the high priest, brought "the brother of Jesus the so-called Christ" before the Sanhedrin and had him condemned to be stoned, "the more moderate Jews, who accurately interpreted the law, were much disgusted at this" (*Antiquities* XX. 9. 1). Thus when Paul came to Jerusalem, the Christian community was under a man universally honored as "James the Just"; on this account it was subject to little or no persecution, but was rather respected as a Jewish sect, whose members looked indeed for Jesus' return as Messiah, but otherwise were chiefly remarkable for their scrupulous observance of the Jewish law. This would explain the anxiety of the church's leaders that Paul too should stand well with the Jewish community.

15. We made ready: The word (ἐπισκευασάμενοι) is regularly used of fitting out equipment, sometimes of preparing transport for a journey. Perhaps the idea here is that they "saddled animals." The Textus Receptus reads ἀποσκευασάμενοι which KJV trans-

---

he points out Cyprus to him on the way. The Greek word literally means "having made Cyprus rise up out of the sea," and we can imagine the delight with which Paul told Luke about those early days of his travels for the gospel. This was new country for Luke, and there is nothing that gives an older person more pleasure than to point out for the first time places hitherto unknown to his younger friends.

And then there was the affection shown to Paul by the Christians along the way. The ones who pleaded with him not to go to Jerusalem did so because they loved him and could not bear to see his life sacrificed to the stupidity of

16 There went with us also *certain* of the disciples of Caesarea, and brought with them one Mnason of Cyprus, an old disciple, with whom we should lodge.

17 And when we were come to Jerusalem, the brethren received us gladly.

18 And the *day* following Paul went in with us unto James; and all the elders were present.

went up to Jerusalem. 16 And some of the
disciples from Caes-a-re'a went with us,
bringing us to the house of Mna'son of
Cyprus, an early disciple, with whom we
should lodge.

17 When we had come to Jerusalem,
the brethren received us gladly. 18 On the
following day Paul went in with us to
James; and all the elders were present.

lates with the delightful archaism **took up our carriages,** i.e., "took up our baggage" (ASV).

16. The meaning of the much contracted Greek is probably **bringing us to the house of Mnason . . . , with whom we should lodge** (RSV), rather than **brought with them one Mnason . . . , with whom we should lodge** (KJV)—for to bring the intended host along with them seems odd. The journey from Caesarea to Jerusalem is about sixty-five miles and Mnason may have lived anywhere en route where they might break the journey for the night. If his house was actually in or near Jerusalem, it would seem that the Caesarean Christians were doubtful of the welcome that Paul would receive from the resident Christians at Jerusalem. **Mnason** is called an **early disciple,** possibly as one of the pioneers from **Cyprus** mentioned in 11:20.

18. Paul went in with us: The first person plural is not used again till 27:1, though there is no reason to suppose that the author was not with Paul almost continuously until his arrival at Rome. It is interesting that at 16:17, where also the use of the "we" is dropped, "Paul" is similarly distinguished from the "us," as if perhaps to hint that the writer "proposes at this point to drop out of the story and leave the whole stage to Paul" (Lake and Cadbury, *Beginnings of Christianity,* IV, 193).

the Jerusalem masses. Agabus went so far as to bind his hands and feet with Paul's own girdle, so that no mistake could be made about the seriousness of the situation. People do not do things like that unless they care greatly. There are times when Paul, the scholar and theologian, overshadows the Paul of human affection and tenderness. When that happens, we need to recall the scene on the beach at Tyre. Men, women, and children, all of them were there to see Paul off. Down on the sand they all knelt and said their prayers together. It is a picture of human relationships at their best, when someone greatly beloved never fails to love in return.

Yet Paul did not capitalize upon the affection which the people felt for him. He preserved his amazing human capacity for objectivity. He did not appreciate their solicitation less because he did not accept it or act upon it. Rising above the tallest of them, he took a calm and steady view of the entire scene. There was almost a severity about him as he refused to be deflected from his course. All real love has somewhere within it the element of fear, the fear of the Lord, the impulse to withdraw from something too sacred to touch. So there was in Paul's love enough fear to save it from sentimentality, and as he went on his way toward Jerusalem there was something in his face that reminded them of the face that once was set like a flint.

17-26. ***Paul Arrives in Jerusalem.***—Paul's welcome in Jerusalem was a cordial one. The leaders of the church listened to him tell about the success of his work with the Gentiles. One cannot help wondering, however, how sincere was their applause, for no sooner had he finished the story than they brought up the old subject of the ceremonial law. Paul was being severely criticized, they said, by thousands of Jewish Christians who heard that he permitted Jews who lived among Gentiles to take liberties with the law of Moses. Nothing was said about the relief funds that Paul had collected for the Christians in Jerusalem. If they were accepted as presumably they were, they were soon forgotten, and the conversation returned to exactly the same point where Paul had left it in Jerusalem several years before.

It is hard for us to understand the stubbornness of the Jewish Christians. Our sympathy is entirely with Paul. We must remember, however, that the Law was as much a part of the life of the Jews as the Constitution is a part of the life of Americans, probably a more important part. It is hard to change the customs and prac

19 And when he had saluted them, he declared particularly what things God had wrought among the Gentiles by his ministry.

20 And when they heard *it,* they glorified the Lord, and said unto him, Thou seest, brother, how many thousands of Jews there are which believe; and they are all zealous of the law:

21 And they are informed of thee, that thou teachest all the Jews which are among the Gentiles to forsake Moses, saying that they ought not to circumcise *their* children, neither to walk after the customs.

22 What is it therefore? the multitude must needs come together: for they will hear that thou art come.

19 After greeting them, he related one by
one the things that God had done among
the Gentiles through his ministry. 20 And
when they heard it, they glorified God. And
they said to him, "You see, brother, how
many thousands there are among the Jews
of those who have believed; they are all
zealous for the law, 21 and they have been
told about you that you teach all the Jews
who are among the Gentiles to forsake
Moses, telling them not to circumcise their
children or observe the customs. 22 What
then is to be done? They will certainly

---

20. They glorified God, perhaps implying that their worst fears were disappointed. **And they said . . . :** For this "collective speech"—as Lake and Cadbury call it, "an ecclesiastical propriety rather than a physical possibility"—cf. the collective prayer in 1:24.

The incident that follows (vss. 23 ff.) is somewhat obscure, but the intention of the church leaders is clear enough. Rumors, they say, are current that Paul has been persuading Jews of the Dispersion to be disloyal to their ancestral faith. It would be well therefore that he should do something to prove that he is not so hostile to Judaism as has been reported. Let him therefore show his zeal for traditional customs by associating himself publicly with four Jewish Christians who are about to observe the ritual necessary for the due fulfillment of a vow.

Thousands, literally "tens of thousands." Though the word may be merely a vivid hyperbole, it has suggested to some critics that the original reference was not to Jewish Christians but to Jews in general, with whom James is anxious to maintain good relations (see on vs. 27). **Jews of those who have believed,** i.e., Jewish converts to the Christian faith. The Western text here reads "in Judea" for **among the Jews,** thus indicating, probably correctly, that "Jews" is here used in the narrower geographical sense.

21. Not to circumcise: It was of course precisely to disprove this kind of calumny that Paul had circumcised Timothy (16:3).

---

tices of centuries, especially when the people who observe them are in danger of being completely absorbed by an empire that tolerates but does not understand their traditions. Try, for example, to change the rules of the Supreme Court and see how firmly the people hold their ground. Take Independence Day out of the calendar in the interests of world government and see how little willing the people are to make the change. Try to change the seat of government from Washington to St. Louis in the interest of greater centrality of location and see how the people rally to defend the city on the Potomac. In many ways these comparisons are not fair ones, but they suggest, at least to a slight degree, the sort of feelings that were stirred up when Paul began to relax the law. Wise Jews realized that it was the beginning of the end, and the rank and file of the people knew that something familiar had been changed.

The leaders of the Jerusalem church, therefore, wanted to make one last effort to save the situation. After all, while Paul had been traveling about the world, reaping the harvest of many strange and wonderful cities, they had been at home, living the same life, following the same routine, looking at the same scenery, moving in the same patterns. No wonder they cared more possessively about the cradle of Christianity. They could see that Christianity was too big for Palestine, but they could hardly be expected to see that Judaism was not big enough for Christianity. Their plan was to placate the Jewish Christians, to pour oil on the troubled waters by persuading Paul to do something which would publicly affirm his loyalty to the

23 Do therefore this that we say to thee: We have four men which have a vow on them;

24 Them take, and purify thyself with them, and be at charges with them, that they may shave *their* heads: and all may know that those things, whereof they were informed concerning thee, are nothing; but *that* thou thyself also walkest orderly, and keepest the law.

hear that you have come. 23 Do therefore
what we tell you. We have four men who
are under a vow; 24 take these men and
purify yourself along with them and pay
their expenses, so that they may shave
their heads. Thus all will know that there
is nothing in what they have been told
about you, but that you yourself live in

23-24. Under a vow: The fact that the **four men** were to **shave their heads** suggests that this was a Nazarite vow (see on 18:18). It is suggested that Paul should **pay their expenses,** i.e., pay for the necessary sacrifice which marked the completion of the vow (see Num. 6:13-20). To do this on behalf of a poorer brother was a recognized act of piety. According to Josephus, Herod Agrippa I frequently paid the expenses of Nazarites in order to win popularity with the Jews (*Antiquities* XIX. 6. 1). **Purify yourself:** Apparently it was proposed that Paul should associate himself with the four in their vow, the phrase being the equivalent of the Hebrew words "to separate himself unto the Lord," which in Num. 6:2 define the taking of a Nazarite vow. But Paul can hardly have taken a personal vow, for the minimum period for a Nazarite vow appears to have been thirty days (Josephus *Jewish War* II. 15. 1). A possible alternative is that during the period of their vow the four had incurred some defilement which imposed upon them "seven days" (vs. 27) in a state of ceremonial impurity, followed by the shaving of the head, and on the eighth day the sacrifice of pigeons as a sin offering (see Num. 6:9-11); and that Paul by paying for this sacrifice would associate himself with the purification. This would best explain the reference to the "seven days" (vs. 27). But against it is the fact that "the days of purification" (vs. 26), on the analogy of the phrase "days of his separation" (Num. 6:13), more naturally refers to the whole period of the vow than to an interval of defilement within that period. Probably Luke himself had no very exact idea of the ritual involved. Indeed the key passage in Num. 6:1-12, on which Luke is perhaps dependent, does not very clearly distinguish the ritual involved in the vow itself from that in connection with the temporary defilement.

---

law and the temple. If they could convince Paul's critics of his essential Judaism, they might avert a crisis.

The proposal they made to Paul is not exactly clear in our text, but the sum and substance of it was that he associate himself with four poor men who were under a vow and were about to go to the temple for purification. The point was to get Paul into the temple in the performance of some ceremonial act which was indisputably associated with the law. If, in our own day, it were a question of the patriotism of a man in public life, his advisors might counsel him to take part in a ceremony in a national cemetery, in which the patriots were to be exalted and honored. It may surprise some readers that Paul agreed to the proposal, apparently without any reluctance. But do not forget that Paul was born a Jew. Israel was his homeland and Christianity was in his mind the new Israel. The continuity was unbroken and undisguised. He was perfectly at home in the temple; in fact, if it had not been for the religion of the temple, he would not have been ready for the religion of Jesus. Furthermore he longed to see Jewish and Gentile Christians go forward as a united people. He had not yet given up hope that his own people would finally accept Jesus as the Messiah. Anything that he could do to win their confidence he was willing to do, provided, of course, that it did not violate the essential principles of the new faith in Christ. Surely there could be no harm in his taking part in one of the ancient temple rites, and if it did anything to heal the breach between the Jews and Gentiles, it would be more than justified. So Paul accepted the proposal of the brethren.

There is a deep-seated desire in most human beings to reconcile those who have become estranged. Sensitive people are hurt when they see churches split, communities divided, governments torn asunder, families broken, nations at loggerheads with each other. There are times

25 As touching the Gentiles which believe, we have written *and* concluded that
they observe no such thing, save only that
they keep themselves from *things* offered to
idols, and from blood, and from strangled,
and from fornication.
26 Then Paul took the men, and the
next day purifying himself with them entered into the temple, to signify the accomplishment of the days of purification,
until that an offering should be offered for
every one of them.

observance of the law. 25 But as for the
Gentiles who have believed, we have sent
a letter with our judgment that they should
abstain from what has been sacrificed to
idols and from blood and from what is
strangled[m] and from unchastity." 26 Then
Paul took the men, and the next day he
purified himself with them and went into
the temple, to give notice when the days
of purification would be fulfilled and the
offering presented for every one of them.

[m] Other early authorities omit *and from what is strangled.*

---

25. The point of this verse appears to be that Paul, by taking part in this purely Jewish ceremony, will be doing nothing to compromise himself with his Gentile converts; for the apostolic decrees (15:28-29) have already made it plain that only certain definitely limited obligations have been laid upon Gentiles. It must be admitted that James seems to mention the decrees as a new development of which Paul is being informed for the first time. For the possible problem raised by this see note on p. 200. But this impression is almost certainly due to the fact that the verse contains, not an actual statement by James, but rather a comment by Luke designed, as we have just noted, to exonerate Paul from any suggestion that he is implicating Gentiles in the minutiae of Jewish ceremonial.

26. Went into the temple: The tense is imperfect and may suggest that Paul did this several times, perhaps performing a daily ceremony **for every one of them** in turn. For **days of purification** see on vs. 24 above.

The question remains: Could Paul, the champion of a free Gentile Christianity, really have acted thus without being guilty of gross hypocrisy? Many critics answer "No!" Thus Windisch writes: "The most palpable error seems . . . to be the allegation that Paul on his last visit to Jerusalem was willing to enter into the bargain, which James and the elders proposed, and, in order to give a spectacular example of his fidelity to the Law, consented to join the four men who wished to fulfil their vow with due legal ceremony. Such behaviour, it may be thought, would be hypocrisy in a man who outside of Jerusalem strongly opposed the compulsory observance of the Law, and preached everywhere that it had been done away in Christ. Again, the report of Acts seems incredible, and hardly conceivable as coming from 'Luke' " (*The Beginnings of Christianity,* ed. F. J. Foakes Jackson and Kirsopp Lake [London: Macmillan & Co.; New York: The Macmillan Co., 1920-33], II, 320-21). But no very convincing reason can be given for the invention of such a story. It can of course be ascribed to Luke's "tendency" to overstress the friendly relations between Paul and the Jewish leaders of the church. But strongly against this is the fact that he says nothing about any further support given to Paul by these leaders; indeed, once Paul is arrested they appear to abandon him to his fate.

Loisy goes farther and ingeniously suggests that the vow was not taken at this time as a spectacular object lesson, but was related to the vow taken at Cenchreae (18:18), which, he thinks, has been antedated into the second tour. To fulfill the vow it would

---

when it seems that anything would be worth while if only it would heal the breach, any concession would be justified if only it would bring the two parties together again. Among the benefactors of the human race the conciliators stand in a high place. They have been the ones who have decided how far men could go in compromise without sacrificing their principles. They have been the ones who were willing to take the longest steps in the direction of peace.

Paul took the longest step toward peace that he knew how to take. No one knew better than he how serious was the tension between the old Judaism and the new Christianity, but he was not willing to accept the break until he had done everything within his power to prevent it. If by publicly associating himself with the temple, he could heal the breach between the Jewish and the Gentile Christians, he was ready to do it. Paul is a warning to the firebrands

27 And when the seven days were almost ended, the Jews which were of Asia, when

27 When the seven days were almost

be necessary for Paul to appear publicly in the temple, and in order that he might be less conspicuous and thereby escape danger, it was suggested to him that he should join himself to four others so that his identity might be merged in a group. The maneuver was in order to escape the attention of the Jews, not to attract it to Paul; but our author, with his usual desire to gloss over the anti-Jewish aspect of Paulinism, makes Paul guilty of an act of insincerity, to which he would never in reality have condescended. In reply it must be said that if Acts gives a true picture, then we must admit a certain disingenuousness in Paul's conduct. But is it really behavior of which he would be incapable? Windisch himself reminds us that in accordance with his own watchword, "To the Jews I became as a Jew, in order to win Jews" (I Cor. 9:20), Paul may well have made a point of observing the ceremonial law when among Jews, especially at the feasts; and that, as in the case of Timothy's circumcision, he may sometimes have felt that circumstances, of which we know nothing, justified concession to Jewish scruples. As Weiss well writes: "We should not judge Paul from the point of view of a consistently liberal and enlightened theologian. It would be very hard for us to say from our standpoint what was and what was not possible for him. A genuine historical sense will keep us modest. A nature so many-sided and versatile as Paul's could combine many attitudes that seem to us irreconcilable" (*History of Primitive Christianity* [ed. F. C. Grant; New York: Wilson-Erickson, 1937], I, 371). Thus it is not the performance of the rite in itself that causes difficulty; it is rather the fact that it was done apparently with an ulterior motive—to suggest something that was not strictly true, "that you yourself live in observance of the law" (vs. 24).

Could Paul do this without hypocrisy? Although the reports current in Jerusalem were exaggerated, they were true at least in part; though often among Jews Paul may have lived as a Jew, when working among Gentiles he must often have treated the law as if it no longer existed—as in fact in his view it did not for any Christian (Rom. 10:4). As an honorable man he can hardly have set out to demonstrate that the accusations against him were wholly false—"that there is nothing in what they have been told about you" (vs. 24); but he may well have wished to show that they were not wholly true. As a matter of fact, the action he took was precisely of the kind to show that he was wrongly accused of forbidding Jews ever to "observe the customs" (vs. 21); but it was quite inadequate as a proof that he himself kept the law in every detail and advised his Jewish converts to do likewise. "Luke's object was not so much to show that Paul was a strict Jew, but that he was still so far in sympathy with Judaism as to be able to take his part in a religious rite which did not compromise his principles" (C. W. Emmet, *Beginnings of Christianity*, II, 294).

G. Paul the Prisoner (21:27–28:31)

The account of Paul's arrest and imprisonment seems to fill a quite disproportionately large space in Luke's second volume. Indeed the story of Paul's fortunes from his appearance at Jerusalem to his final arrival at Rome occupies nearly one quarter of the whole book. Moreover the remaining chapters, though they cover nearly five years, give

among us; the ones who are impatient, the ones who are ready to fight at the drop of a hat. Paul was something of a firebrand himself, but before he gave up hope that his people would rise to their glorious opportunity, he made one last effort to pave the way toward peace.

27-40. ***The Riot in the Temple.***—Paul went into the temple, therefore, to make peace, but instead of that he started a riot. No sooner was he recognized by the out-of-town Jews than he was seized by the mob, dragged out of the temple, and first the temple itself and then the whole city was thrown into confusion.

So, look at the charge that was laid against Paul. It was that he had profaned the temple by taking a Gentile into its sacred precincts. This was not the first time that Paul had got into trouble with the law, and this was by no

they saw him in the temple, stirred up all the people, and laid hands on him,

completed, the Jews from Asia, who had seen him in the temple, stirred up all the

us no information about the development of any of Paul's churches or about his relations, epistolary or otherwise, with them. Instead we have a narrative at great length and with many repetitions about Paul's appearances before one tribunal after another, followed by the extraordinarily vivid story of the voyage to Rome. Several reasons may be suggested for this lack of proportion: (*a*) Luke was almost certainly at Paul's side during the whole of the period, and he naturally draws fully and freely from his own personal recollections. (*b*) He seems to be conscious of the parallelism with the story of Jesus' own passion, and to be deliberately elaborating it. Like Jesus, Paul appears before the Sanhedrin, is handed over by his fellow countrymen to the Gentiles, is accused before a Roman governor, and stands before a Herod. His chief accusers are the same, the Sadducean priesthood, and the charge again culminates in an accusation of treason against Caesar. "This resemblance is not due to arbitrary invention. It is the natural working out of a law which had been enunciated by the Lord himself: 'as the master, so shall the servant be' " (Rackham, *Acts of the Apostles,* p. 404). Yet Luke as an artist is certainly concerned to draw out the dramatic significance of the parallelism. (*c*) These concluding chapters contain Luke's final "apology" for Paul. Largely it is put in the apostle's own mouth in four speeches addressed to the Jewish people (22:3-21), the Sanhedrin (23:1-6), the Roman Governor Felix (24:10-21), and the Jewish King Herod Agrippa (26:2-23). In particular Luke's purpose of commending Christianity to official Roman authority comes to a head in these chapters. We have already noticed that wherever in Acts Christianity is brought to the cognizance of the Roman authorities, its innocent character is vindicated to their entire satisfaction. In this concluding section Paul comes into contact with three separate Roman officials. Two—Lysias and Festus—are represented as expressly testifying to his innocence, while Felix shows him considerable favor and only refrains from freeing him in order to conciliate the Jews. Even as a prisoner at Rome, Paul is pictured as free to preach to any who cared to come to him. Luke evidently wished to demonstrate that while the orthodox Jews were consistently hostile, the verdict of Roman authority had been favorable to Paul. May we surmise that he is appealing to the authorities of a later day who, at the time Acts was being written, were not perhaps treating Christianity with a like toleration?

1. Paul's Arrest and Defense (21:27–22:29)

27. The seven days: Cf. on vs. 24. The simplest solution would be that Paul himself had taken a vow for seven days; but there is no evidence that such a short period was permissible. Schwartz cleverly cuts the knot by reading ἑβδομάδες for ἑπτὰ ἡμέραι and obtaining the meaning, "When the weeks [i.e., Pentecost; see on 2:1] were completed."

Jews from Asia: The attempt to conciliate the Jewish Christians only leads to a clash with the orthodox Jews. Probably they were from Ephesus, for they recognized Trophimus, and may have been the same who had put up Alexander to repudiate Paul (19:33).

means the first riot of which Paul had been the center. But this was the most serious trouble in which Paul had been involved, since this charge was one which, if proved, would oblige the Roman government to punish by death. The situation is not easy for us to understand since there is nothing comparable to the temple in our national or religious life, and it is therefore difficult for us to appreciate either the reality or the seriousness of the charge that was made against Paul in Jerusalem.

To understand it at all we must go back to that fundamental human instinct which we call the tribal instinct. Men cluster together in tribes to protect themselves against invaders and to preserve their interests against all who might threaten them. Once the tribe is amalgamated, its unity must be preserved by excluding all who are not a part of it. Doors are closed to the rest of the world and barriers are erected which make it clear that no others will be admitted or tolerated. It is an effort toward self-

28 Crying out, Men of Israel, help: This
is the man, that teacheth all *men* every
where against the people, and the law, and
this place: and further brought Greeks also
into the temple, and hath polluted this
holy place.
29 (For they had seen before with him
in the city Trophimus an Ephesian, whom
they supposed that Paul had brought into
the temple.)
30 And all the city was moved, and the
people ran together: and they took Paul,
and drew him out of the temple: and forthwith the doors were shut.

crowd, and laid hands on him, 28 crying
out, "Men of Israel, help! This is the man
who is teaching men everywhere against
the people and the law and this place;
moreover he also brought Greeks into the
temple, and he has defiled this holy place."
29 For they had previously seen Troph'i-
mus the Ephesian with him in the city, and
they supposed that Paul had brought him
into the temple. 30 Then all the city was
aroused, and the people ran together; they
seized Paul and dragged him out of the
temple, and at once the gates were shut.

28-29. The law and this place: Cf. the accusation against Stephen in 6:13. **Brought Greeks into the temple:** In 24:6 Paul is accused only of trying to profane the temple, not of actually doing so. It was an offense punishable by death to introduce a Gentile within the barrier which separated the Court of the Gentiles from the Court of Israel. A marble block from the barrier has been preserved with the inscription, "Let no foreigner enter within the screen and enclosure surrounding the sanctuary. Whosoever is taken so doing will be the cause that death overtaketh him" (Deissmann, *Light from the Ancient East,* p. 80). Paul's expression "the middle wall of partition" (Eph. 2:14) is probably an allusion to this barrier. **Trophimus:** Cf. 20:4 and II Tim. 4:20.

30. The gates were shut: Presumably by the temple police as a precaution against more rioting within the sacred precincts.

---

defense by way of unity. As the human race has grown, the tribes have grown in size and comprehensiveness, but they still exist, though now they are large enough to include a whole race, or an empire, or the whole of the Western world.

No people in the history of the last three thousand years have counted more heavily upon the power of the tribe to defend it against attack than have the Jews. They not only stood together through thick and thin, but they saw to it that the strength of their ranks was not diluted by the addition of outsiders. They closed every door that opened into the outside world. They forbade intermarriage. They separated themselves from the rest of the world by the requirement of circumcision. They observed a sacred day of rest that others of the world did not observe. They did not eat with those who belonged to a different race, and their daily life was a continual ritual by which they purified themselves from any contact with the Gentile world which they might inadvertently or unavoidably have. It must be admitted that the system worked remarkably well, else how could we account for the fact that though for more than two thousand years the Jews had no national government, no homeland, no flag, nevertheless they maintained their integrity as a people?

It was for all this that the temple stood. It was an oppressed people's defense against a hostile world. It was their assurance of national unity. It preserved their pride when they had little else to be proud of and practically nothing left to hope for. Once the doors of the temple were thrown open to the world, they saw their solidarity as a people evaporate into thin air and their defense against the world disappear overnight. That is the reason why they turned with such fury against anyone who even so much as implied that the temple as it stood was not all that it might be. That is why they crucified Jesus; that is why they stoned Stephen; that is why they arrested Paul.

Modern readers of the story must be careful not to assume too readily an air of superiority. As has been said, our modern tribes are larger, but they are at times no less ruthless. Suppose, for example, that the headmaster of a prominent and exclusive boys' preparatory school, patronized by the wealthy, admitted a Negro to the student body. It is not at all unlikely that the headmaster, if he refused to reconsider his action, would be asked by the board to resign. While the situation is quite different from the one which we meet in the Acts, the motives involved are essentially the same. It is the old, deep-seated desire to preserve the unity and purity of the tribe by excluding all outsiders.

31 And as they went about to kill him, tidings came unto the chief captain of the band, that all Jerusalem was in an uproar:

32 Who immediately took soldiers and centurions, and ran down unto them: and when they saw the chief captain and the soldiers, they left beating of Paul.

33 Then the chief captain came near, and took him, and commanded *him* to be bound with two chains; and demanded who he was, and what he had done.

34 And some cried one thing, some another, among the multitude: and when he could not know the certainty for the tumult, he commanded him to be carried into the castle.

35 And when he came upon the stairs, so it was, that he was borne of the soldiers for the violence of the people.

36 For the multitude of the people followed after, crying, Away with him.

37 And as Paul was to be led into the castle, he said unto the chief captain, May I speak unto thee? Who said, Canst thou speak Greek?

31 And as they were trying to kill him,
word came to the tribune of the cohort that
all Jerusalem was in confusion. 32 He at
once took soldiers and centurions, and ran
down to them; and when they saw the
tribune and the soldiers, they stopped beating Paul. 33 Then the tribune came up and
arrested him, and ordered him to be bound
with two chains. He inquired who he was
and what he had done. 34 Some in the
crowd shouted one thing, some another;
and as he could not learn the facts because
of the uproar, he ordered him to be brought
into the barracks. 35 And when he came
to the steps, he was actually carried by the
soldiers because of the violence of the
crowd; 36 for the mob of the people followed, crying, "Away with him!"
37 As Paul was about to be brought into
the barracks, he said to the tribune, "May
I say something to you?" And he said, "Do

---

31. The tribune of the cohort: The Greek is *chiliarch*—"officer of a thousand"—the garrison consisting of a **cohort**, which numbered on paper 760 infantrymen and 240 cavalrymen. They would probably have their "barracks" (vs. 34) in the Tower of Antonia at the northwest corner of the temple area with which it was connected by "steps" (vs. 40).

32-33. Centurions: From the use of the plural it would seem that at least two hundred soldiers were called out. **Arrested,** i.e., took him into "protective custody." **Two chains:** Possibly he would be chained to a soldier on each side, as was Peter in 12:6.

34-35. The description is so vivid that the writer must surely have been an eyewitness.

37. Know Greek: Perhaps better, **speak Greek** (KJV), for the Greek is an abbreviation for Ἑλληνιστὶ γινώσκεις λέγειν.

It is interesting to notice in this particular case how the charge grew. It began with the fact that the people saw Paul in the company of Trophimus, an Ephesian. They were seen on the street together. The charge then leaped to the conjecture that Paul had taken Trophimus into the temple! No one had seen them together in the temple, at least it was never claimed that they were seen there together, but people were ready to jump from fact to conjecture, even when the conjecture involved a man's life. So rumors grow from scraps of observed fact to imposing fabrics of fiction. Charges against men and women begin with shreds of evidence and grow until they are serious enough to condemn them for life. What a warning there is here for idle tongues and irresponsible talk. More damage may be done by talk than by an army. Listen to the charges made against a man and wife. They begin with the fact that the husband was seen in the company of a woman not his wife. They end with the conjecture that the husband and wife are on the verge of divorce. Harmless seems such talk at the time, and yet what unhappiness can it breed and what havoc can it spread!

So much for the charge. Rooted as it was in one of the most persistent impulses of human nature, it was nevertheless an unjust charge. Allowing for the natural human tendency to move in tribes, understanding as we do the motives that lay behind this particular charge, we cannot escape the fact that the charge was unjust because it was not true. Even if Paul had

38 Art not thou that Egyptian, which
before these days madest an uproar, and
leddest out into the wilderness four thousand men that were murderers?
39 But Paul said, I am a man *which am*
a Jew of Tarsus, *a city* in Cilicia, a citizen
of no mean city: and, I beseech thee, suffer
me to speak unto the people.
40 And when he had given him license,
Paul stood on the stairs, and beckoned with
the hand unto the people. And when there
was made a great silence, he spake unto
them in the Hebrew tongue, saying,

you know Greek? **38** Are you not the Egyptian, then, who recently stirred up a revolt
and led the four thousand men of the Assassins out into the wilderness?" **39** Paul replied, "I am a Jew, from Tarsus in Ci-li'cia,
a citizen of no mean city; I beg you, let me
speak to the people." **40** And when he had
given him leave, Paul, standing on the
steps, motioned with his hand to the people; and when there was a great hush, he
spoke to them in the Hebrew language,
saying:

---

38. The Egyptian was a rebel who **stirred up a revolt** during the procuratorship of Felix. According to Josephus (*Jewish War* II. 13. 5), he led his followers, not **into the wilderness,** but "out of the wilderness" to the Mount of Olives. This has suggested to some critics that Luke had read, but incorrectly remembered, Josephus. But "in the wilderness" was the conventional place for religious leaders to appear (cf. Mark 1:4; Matt. 24:26), and this may well have influenced Luke's language. Josephus says that the Egyptian led out not **four thousand men** merely, but thirty thousand, of whom most were killed or captured, while he himself "disappeared from view." Lysias the tribune evidently thinks now that he has unearthed him. Josephus, a few paragraphs before the mention of **the Egyptian,** states that **the Assassins** (the Greek is a transliteration of the Latin *sicarii:* they were so called because they hid a knife—*sica*—in their clothes and during festivals engaged in "patriotic" assassination) were active in the time of Felix (*Jewish War* II. 13. 3); but he does not connect them with **the Egyptian.** Critics have asked whether this may not be another faulty recollection of Josephus on Luke's part. There is no evidence, as is often alleged, that the revolt of this Egyptian, or indeed any other rising before that of Bar Cochba, was in the full sense of the word "messianic."

39. As a **Jew,** Paul had a right to be in the temple; as a **citizen** of **Tarsus,** he might claim to be able to speak Greek. But though Tarsus may have been **no mean city,** it was only when Paul later asserted his Roman citizenship (22:25) that Lysias showed any sign of being impressed.

40. In the Hebrew language, or more probably in the popular Aramaic, which was commonly but inaccurately called "Hebrew" (cf. 26:14).

---

led Trophimus into the temple, we would question the right of anyone to take exception to his action. But the truth is that in this case Paul did not take a Gentile into the temple. The charge therefore was based upon conjecture which was accepted as a fact.

Not only was the charge unjust, but the treatment of the victim was outrageous. What went on a man of the present might describe as a "brawl." There was nothing about it that suggested the fact that the man at the center of it all was one of the relatively few individuals who has determined the destiny of the world. It was mob violence at its worst. Paul was so badly treated that the commander of the garrison assumed that he was the leader of a band of Egyptian assassins. He was appalled when Paul began to speak in Greek. To such a depth can humanity sink when it allows its emotions to go unbridled and undisciplined. The furnaces at Dachau were the modern equivalent of the cruelty of which humanity is capable when it ceases to think and begins to fight.

Over against the unjust charge and the undignified treatment of the victim there is the magnificent dignity of Paul himself. Beaten by the crowd, arrested by the soldiers, deprived of every dignity to which his humanity alone should have entitled him, Paul rises above the turmoil in all the majesty of Christian nature. He asks permission to speak to the people. His temper, which was not by nature mild, was under control; he did not meet fury with fury; he remembered his Master who, when he was reviled, reviled not again. With a gesture he drew the people to him. **And when there was a great hush, he spoke to them in the Hebrew language.** (So the Lukan account; yet see Exeg.)

22 Men, brethren, and fathers, hear ye my defense *which I make* now unto you.
2 (And when they heard that he spake in the Hebrew tongue to them, they kept the more silence: and he saith,)

22 "Brethren and fathers, hear the defense which I now make before you."
2 And when they heard that he addressed them in the Hebrew language, they were the more quiet. And he said:

The sequence of events at this point is a little difficult of acceptance. It is hard to understand how, in the midst of a riot from which he had to be forcibly rescued, Paul can have succeeded in obtaining permission to address the mob or, having done so, could possibly make himself heard. Moreover the whole interlude adds nothing to the progress of the action. When it is over—or if it is omitted as an embellishment of strict history—we find ourselves at 22:24 in exactly the same position as we were at 21:34: at both points Lysias "ordered him to be brought into the barracks." As for Paul's address to the mob, once we admit that it was spoken at all, there is nothing in the early part of it that might not have been spoken by Paul. But vss. 17-18, which represent him returning to Jerusalem immediately after his conversion with the intention of preaching there, are out of line with Galatians, though in line with Acts, and can hardly be Paul's own words. Indeed the relation of the speech to the parallel accounts of the conversion in chs. 9 and 26 makes it probable that this account, like that of ch. 9, is the work of the author, based possibly on an authentic speech of Paul recorded in ch. 26 (see on 9:1-31). If we find it impossible to believe that Paul can have made a speech at all under the circumstances of the riot, then we must suppose that Luke, knowing Paul to be innocent of the charge which has roused the mob's ire, thinks that the best way to demonstrate his innocence is to allow him in his own words to recount the story of his conversion and his divine commission.

If there is anything in this story for which we may be grateful, it is the hush which fell (but see Exeg.) when Paul began to speak. It is a sign not only of the impressive personality of Paul, but also of the capacity of the crowd still to be impressed by one of Paul's spiritual stature. One might have feared that once the crowd was whipped into such a fury by the lash of its emotional fears and prejudices, nothing could ever restore it to its normal state of reasonableness. And yet when the figure of Paul confronted the wild mob, its fury was subdued, at least for the time being, by the power of one man's dignity and self-control. In the spring of 1948, when Gandhi was killed by a young fanatic, the same kind of a hush fell over the civilized world. It meant the same thing that it meant two thousand years ago; it meant that in spite of the demonic powers that take possession of men and women, those men and women still have the capacity to respond to the ideal when that ideal is incarnate in some suffering servant of humanity. It is in those periods of silence and calm that humanity has a chance to catch its breath and save itself from total destruction.

22:1-22. ***Paul Speaks in Self-Defense.***—When the people had become still, Paul began to speak. He told once again the story of his experience on the way to Damascus. This story has been considered in some detail in the Expos. of ch. 9. There are, however, several things to be noted about the speech itself.

In the first place Paul spoke to the people in their own language. As an educated man, Paul could have spoken Greek, and many people in his audience would have understood him. A lesser man might have thought that it would impress the people to speak the cultivated tongue of the civilized world. But not Paul. He spoke the popular dialect he had learned as a boy, that the simplest person in the crowd might understand. What a lesson there is here for all speakers, especially for teachers and preachers! How often men are tempted to speak a language that has about it the air of academic superiority but has lost the flavor of the market place and the home. No wonder they are not understood. They sacrifice the simplicity of common speech for the artificial and elaborate tongue of learned discourse. They need to be reminded that when the Son of God spoke, he spoke in a language that every farmer and fisherman could understand. He never let affectations in language obscure the burden of his thought. In Paul he had a faithful follower.

Next, there was not the slightest sign of bitterness in anything that Paul said. He might have been excused had he taken the opportunity to lash out against the unfair treatment he

3 I am verily a man *which am* a Jew,
born in Tarsus, *a city* in Cilicia, yet brought
up in this city at the feet of Gamaliel, *and*
taught according to the perfect manner of
the law of the fathers, and was zealous
toward God, as ye all are this day.
4 And I persecuted this way unto the
death, binding and delivering into prisons
both men and women.
5 As also the high priest doth bear me
witness, and all the estate of the elders:
from whom also I received letters unto the
brethren, and went to Damascus, to bring
them which were there bound unto Jerusalem, for to be punished.
6 And it came to pass, that, as I made
my journey, and was come nigh unto
Damascus about noon, suddenly there shone
from heaven a great light round about me.
7 And I fell unto the ground, and heard
a voice saying unto me, Saul, Saul, why
persecutest thou me?

3 "I am a Jew, born at Tarsus in Ci-
li'cia, but brought up in this city at the
feet of Ga-ma'li-el, educated according to
the strict manner of the law of our fathers,
being zealous for God as you all are this
day. 4 I persecuted this Way to the death,
binding and delivering to prison both men
and women, 5 as the high priest and the
whole council of elders bear me witness.
From them I received letters to the brethren, and I journeyed to Damascus to take
those also who were there and bring them
in bonds to Jerusalem to be punished.
6 "As I made my journey and drew near
to Damascus, about noon a great light from
heaven suddenly shone about me. 7 And I
fell to the ground and heard a voice saying to me, 'Saul, Saul, why do you perse-

---

22:3. The phrasing and punctuation of this sentence are uncertain. Perhaps a translation preferable to RSV would be, "brought up in this city, educated at the feet of Gamaliel"; for Paul was **educated** by Gamaliel rather than **brought up,** or more literally "nurtured" by him. Similarly the second part of the verse may be translated either as in RSV or alternatively, "educated strictly [or "accurately"—κατὰ ἀκρίβειαν being taken absolutely as an adverbial phrase] at the feet of Gamaliel, being zealous for the ancestral law of God." In favor of the latter translation are the parallels in 21:20 ("zealous . . . for the law") and particularly Gal. 1:14 ("zealous . . . for the traditions of my fathers"), whereas the phrase **zealous for God** does not occur elsewhere in the N.T., though in Rom. 10:2 we have "zeal for God." For **Gamaliel** see on 5:34. It has been pointed out that Paul's version of what the rabbis commonly taught concerning the law shows little sign of the influence of Gamaliel, who laid much stress on the importance of repentance rather than of "works." Indeed one feels that at times Paul's Christian doctrine is nearer to the mind of the great rabbi than is the type of rabbinical doctrine which he attacks.

4-5. This Way: See on 9:2. The **council of elders** is equivalent to the Sanhedrin, as is clear from Luke 22:66. **Those . . . who were there:** The Greek is ἐκεῖσε (not ἐκεῖ), which, if taken strictly, would imply that those whom Paul persecuted at Damascus had fled "thither" and were not regular residents. This would agree with 9:2, where see note.

6-8. Here begins the second of the three accounts of Paul's conversion. The interrelation of the three and the significance of the variations between them have already been fully discussed on p. 120. **About noon:** This detail is repeated in 26:13, but is absent from ch. 9. **Jesus of Nazareth:** See on 2:22.

---

had received not only in Jerusalem, but in the cities throughout Greece and Asia Minor. But such was not the course of Paul's speech. He spoke quietly and without rancor. He even went so far as to give the people the benefit of the doubt and assume that what they were doing when they arrested him they supposed to be in the interests of their religion. Paul described himself in the days before his conversion as "ardent for God as you all are to-day" (Moffatt). Indeed that was a magnanimous concession for a man who had been beaten by a mad crowd to make. No wonder that the people became more and more quiet. Not only did he speak to them in Hebrew, but he spoke to them generously. It would not have been difficult for Paul to have written a generous speech, but to speak on the spur of the moment, a moment

8 And I answered, Who art thou, Lord? And he said unto me, I am Jesus of Nazareth, whom thou persecutest.

9 And they that were with me saw indeed the light, and were afraid; but they heard not the voice of him that spake to me.

10 And I said, What shall I do, Lord? And the Lord said unto me, Arise, and go into Damascus; and there it shall be told thee of all things which are appointed for thee to do.

11 And when I could not see for the glory of that light, being led by the hand of them that were with me, I came into Damascus.

12 And one Ananias, a devout man according to the law, having a good report of all the Jews which dwelt *there,*

13 Came unto me, and stood, and said unto me, Brother Saul, receive thy sight. And the same hour I looked up upon him.

14 And he said, The God of our fathers hath chosen thee, that thou shouldest know his will, and see that Just One, and shouldest hear the voice of his mouth.

cute me?' 8 And I answered, 'Who are you,
Lord?' And he said to me, 'I am Jesus of
Nazareth whom you are persecuting.' 9 Now
those who were with me saw the light but
did not hear the voice of the one who was
speaking to me. 10 And I said, 'What shall
I do, Lord?' And the Lord said to me,
'Rise, and go into Damascus, and there
you will be told all that is appointed for
you to do.' 11 And when I could not see
because of the brightness of that light, I
was led by the hand by those who were
with me, and came into Damascus.

12 "And one An-a-ni'as, a devout man
according to the law, well spoken of by
all the Jews who lived there, 13 came to
me, and standing by me said to me, 'Brother
Saul, receive your sight.' And in that very
hour I received my sight and saw him.
14 And he said, 'The God of our fathers
appointed you to know his will, to see the
Just One and to hear a voice from his

---

12. **Ananias** is described as **a devout man according to the law** with the implication, useful in an apology before Jews, that Paul after his conversion was ministered to by a good Jew. No mention is made of Ananias' vision described in 9:10-16, but his words to Paul in vss. 13-16 combine the sense of those he himself heard in his vision (9:15-16) and those he afterwards addressed to Paul (9:17).

13. **Received my sight and saw him:** The Greek word (ἀναβλέπειν) means both to "recover sight" and to "look up" (cf. Luke 18:41 with Luke 19:5), and the double force can be brought out in English only by some such translation as RSV.

14. **Know his will:** For the expression cf. Rom. 2:18; Col. 1:9. **Just One:** For the title see on 3:14.

---

that had been ablaze with impassioned fury, and to speak without a trace of resentment was an achievement such as comes only to those who have trained their bodies and kept them in subjection to their mind and spirit.

Another thing to notice is that Paul spoke from his own experience. He did not set forth propositions of faith or belief. He spun no theories or philosophies. He told what had happened to himself. He admitted frankly his first hatred of the Christians. He did not hesitate to identify himself with the best traditions of rabbinical Judaism. And then he went on to tell what happened on the way to Damascus. He had told it a hundred times before. The details were not always exactly the same. Sometimes the emphasis fell in one place and sometimes in another. The details did not matter; the emphasis made little difference. It was the light that mattered, the light that blinded him to everything else. It was the voice that counted, the voice that accused him of persecution. Those were the things that he could never forget; those were the things that changed his life; those were the things to which he returned over and over again, in times of doubt and uncertainty, in times of suffering and mental anxiety. It was in that one brief moment of time that eternity laid its claim upon him. It was in that one decisive experience that he found all the explanations that he needed, all the strength that he required, and all the assurance that his human frailty demanded.

It is the testimony of personal experience that is the irrefutable argument. It is the power of a life which has been changed that no

15 For thou shalt be his witness unto all men of what thou hast seen and heard.

16 And now why tarriest thou? arise, and be baptized, and wash away thy sins, calling on the name of the Lord.

17 And it came to pass, that, when I was come again to Jerusalem, even while I prayed in the temple, I was in a trance;

18 And saw him saying unto me, Make haste, and get thee quickly out of Jerusalem: for they will not receive thy testimony concerning me.

19 And I said, Lord, they know that I imprisoned and beat in every synagogue them that believed on thee:

20 And when the blood of thy martyr Stephen was shed, I also was standing by, and consenting unto his death, and kept the raiment of them that slew him.

21 And he said unto me, Depart: for I will send thee far hence unto the Gentiles.

22 And they gave him audience unto this word, and *then* lifted up their voices, and said, Away with such a *fellow* from the earth: for it is not fit that he should live.

mouth;
15 for you will be a witness for him
to all men of what you have seen and heard.
16 And now why do you wait? Rise and be
baptized, and wash away your sins, calling
on his name.'

17 "When I had returned to Jerusalem
and was praying in the temple, I fell into
a trance 18 and saw him saying to me, 'Make
haste and get quickly out of Jerusalem,
because they will not accept your testimony about me.'
19 And I said, 'Lord, they
themselves know that in every synagogue
I imprisoned and beat those who believed
in thee. 20 And when the blood of Stephen
thy witness was shed, I also was standing
by and approving, and keeping the garments of those who killed him.'
21 And he
said to me, 'Depart; for I will send you far
away to the Gentiles.'"

22 Up to this word they listened to him;
then they lifted up their voices and said,
"Away with such a fellow from the earth!

---

17. Returned to Jerusalem: As in ch. 9, the impression given, that Paul returned to Jerusalem immediately after his conversion, is inconsistent with his own account in Galatians (see on 9:20-31). But whereas here Paul is bidden to leave Jerusalem in a vision whereby he is commissioned, in ch. 9 he is sent away by "the brethren" because of an attempt on his life (9:29-30). The fact that he was **praying in the temple** is mentioned as proof that he was still a loyal Jew. The **trance** is possibly mentioned in II Cor. 12:2-4.

19. Paul's words are apparently intended to be a rejoinder to the warning he has just received that the Jews would reject his testimony. Surely the very fact that he had previously persecuted the Christians will arrest the Jews' attention and convince them of the sincerity of his conversion.

20. Stephen thy witness: Its use in such a context as this makes it easy to see how the word (μάρτυς) soon took on the sense of **martyr** (KJV).

21-23. The mention of the **Gentiles** sets a spark to the mob's wrath, not because it was considered wrong to seek converts to Judaism, but because Paul is claiming a divine commission to preach in the name of Judaism what to them appears rank heresy. This seems tantamount to blasphemy! Hence the violent demonstration with **garments**

---

cynic or unbeliever can withstand. When the world shakes for fear of what may befall it, nothing can steady it so much as the simple, direct statement of a man or a woman who has seen the Lord and whose whole life is illuminated by the light of the vision.

One more thing worth noticing about Paul's speech is that it all went well until he came to the word "Gentiles." All through the first of it, when he told them about his early upbringing in the law, there was intense interest. Even during the brief account of the vision on the road to Damascus there was no sign of unrest. The people accepted it all with interest and curiosity, if not with sympathy and credence, until he came to the point where the Lord told him to leave Jerusalem and go to the Gentiles. That was the word that was like a spark to a fuse. It was the signal to quit reason and resort to bestial irrationality. **Away with such a fellow from the earth,** yelled the crowd. **For he ought not to live.** What a sad comment upon the

23 And as they cried out, and cast off *their* clothes, and threw dust into the air,

24 The chief captain commanded him to be brought into the castle, and bade that he should be examined by scourging; that he might know wherefore they cried so against him.

25 And as they bound him with thongs, Paul said unto the centurion that stood by, Is it lawful for you to scourge a man that is a Roman, and uncondemned?

26 When the centurion heard *that,* he went and told the chief captain, saying, Take heed what thou doest; for this man is a Roman.

27 Then the chief captain came, and said unto him, Tell me, art thou a Roman? He said, Yea.

28 And the chief captain answered, With a great sum obtained I this freedom. And Paul said, But I was *free*-born.

For he ought not to live." 23 And as they
cried out and waved their garments and
threw dust into the air, 24 the tribune commanded him to be brought into the barracks, and ordered him to be examined by
scourging, to find out why they shouted
thus against him. 25 But when they had
tied him up with the thongs, Paul said to
the centurion who was standing by, "Is it
lawful for you to scourge a man who is a
Roman citizen, and uncondemned?"
26 When the centurion heard that, he went
to the tribune and said to him, "What are
you about to do? For this man is a Roman
citizen." 27 So the tribune came and said
to him, "Tell me, are you a Roman citizen?" And he said, "Yes." 28 The tribune
answered, "I bought this citizenship for a
large sum." Paul said, "But I was born a

---

and **dust,** for which see on 14:14 and 16:22. No actual parallel has been quoted for the throwing of dust into the air; perhaps it should simply be understood as a gesture of anger and contempt—as we might speak of "throwing mud."

24-26. Scourging, quite apart from punishment, was the legally recognized method of extorting confession from a slave. **Tied him up with the thongs:** Alternatively the meaning may be "bent him forward for the thongs," i.e., to receive lashes from the whip, or flagellum, consisting of leather thongs. The flagellum was reserved for slaves and might not be used on a free man.

For the dialogue that follows cf. 16:36-39, and for the words, **a Roman citizen, and uncondemned,** see on 16:37. The Greek is ʽΡωμαῖος **(Roman** [KJV]); but at this time it regularly meant, not an inhabitant of Rome, but a citizen of the empire.

28. For a large sum: As it was customary for newly made citizens to adopt the name of the reigning emperor, and the tribune's name was Claudius Lysias (23:26), it is likely that he became a citizen during the reign of Claudius. Significantly Dio Cassius (*Roman History* LX. 17. 5-6) tells us that early in that reign, under the influence of Messalina, citizenship was frequently sold for large sums, though later the merest trifle might purchase it. The Western text reads, "I know how much it cost me to obtain the citizenship,"

---

crowd! Paul not fit to live! One cannot help wondering who then is fit to live. And one cannot help remembering that human beings, endowed with intelligence and compassion, can nevertheless so completely yield themselves to the baser impulses of their nature that they make a judgment not only stupid but immoral and proceed to act upon the basis of that judgment toward the destruction of all that is good and noble. How self-deceived men can be, and how blind to the truth that stares them in the face! Such a story leaves the reader sober and humble. It shows him to what depths his kind may stoop and at the same time to what incredible heights some few chosen ones may gloriously reach.

23-30. *Paul Takes Advantage of His Citizenship.*—The crowd was even more disorderly after Paul's speech than it had been before it. The people **cried out and waved their garments and threw dust into the air.** They behaved the way disorderly crowds always behave, like wild animals. By this time the Roman commander was at the point of exasperation. Not being a Jew, he had absolutely no idea of what it was all about, but he took immediate steps to find out. He had Paul taken into the barracks and proceeded to prepare him for the torture of the lash. The Exeg. explains the lash-custom of extorting confessions. But why torture Paul to find out what the situation really was? It is one of those questions the answer to which is obvious

29 Then straightway they departed from him which should have examined him: and the chief captain also was afraid, after he knew that he was a Roman, and because he had bound him.

30 On the morrow, because he would have known the certainty wherefore he

citizen." 29 So those who were about to examine him withdrew from him instantly; and the tribune also was afraid, for he realized that Paul was a Roman citizen and that he had bound him.

30 But on the morrow, desiring to know the real reason why the Jews accused him,

which might be taken as a sneer—"It does not cost much to buy citizenship nowadays!" This would give much more point to Paul's rejoinder, **I was born a citizen.** We have no knowledge how Paul's parents may have acquired citizenship, though Jerome (*On Philemon* 23; *On Famous Men* 5) preserves a late tradition that they had come from Gischala to Tarsus, in which case they may conceivably have been rewarded by citizenship in return for some service rendered to Mark Antony in Palestine (so Lake and Cadbury, *Beginnings of Christianity,* IV, 284).

2. Paul Before the Sanhedrin (22:30–23:11)

The sequel, as Luke narrates it, raises many difficulties. It might have been expected that Paul's declaration of his citizenship would result, not merely in his escape from scourging, but in the reference of his case directly to the Roman governor over the head of the Sanhedrin. Loisy even argues that Paul must have made such a direct appeal to the governor, but that our author has refrained from mentioning it in order to avoid giving the impression that his hero was unwilling to vindicate himself before a Jewish court. However that may be, it seems probable that Paul must have been forthwith released had not the Sanhedrin at this point formally laid a charge against him. This they almost certainly did, and any further inquiry into the case would therefore be taken on their initiative and not on that of Lysias, as vs. 30 seems to imply. In that case it seems likely that action against Paul was taken at the instigation of the priestly Sadducean hierarchy rather than of the Pharisees, and that they proceeded against him, not as a religious heretic, but as a disturber of the peace who was likely to bring down on the community the wrath of the Romans, and thus rob the Sadducees themselves of their political prestige. The way Luke tells the story shows that he is conscious that the Sadducees were Paul's chief opponents. On the other hand he implies, probably wrongly, that it was Lysias himself who took the initiative in summoning the Sanhedrin. There follows a very vivid piece of writing—whatever our judgment of its historical accuracy. Just as Paul begins his defense, the high priest orders him to be struck on the mouth. Paul makes an angry retort, but then apologizes, saying that he did not know that the speaker was the high priest. Then realizing that Pharisees as well as Sadducees are present, he makes a clever tactical move and declares that he is a Pharisee and is being tried "with respect to the hope and the resurrection of the dead." He thus splits the court, the resurrection being a subject of contention between the two sects. Luke then presents us with the amazing spectacle of that august body transformed into a mob which would have torn Paul in pieces had not Lysias once again rescued him.

Most modern critics vigorously question the historicity of Luke's account of a formal "trial" of Paul by the Sanhedrin. (*a*) It is thought inconceivable that a Roman official

to the military mind and utterly obscure to the civilian mind. At any rate that is what he set about to do. And it was at this moment that Paul took advantage of his Roman citizenship.

Paul never tried to conceal the fact that he was proud of his Roman citizenship. Indeed there was every reason why he should have been proud of it, for it gave him a kind of status that otherwise he would have lacked, for not everyone who happened to live within the boundaries of the empire was a citizen. Some were slaves. Some had bought their citizenship; some, like Paul, had inherited it. It was something to be proud of, for Rome was, in a way, head and shoulders above all the empires that had gone before her, and to be a citizen of Rome not only entitled a person to the protec-

was accused of the Jews, he loosed him from *his* bands, and commanded the chief he unbound him, and commanded the chief priests and all the council to meet,

in the person of Lysias should have handed over a Roman citizen to Jewish jurisdiction merely because he desired "to know the real reason why the Jews accused him" (22:30). The whole account of the "trial" is vague. Why did not Paul recognize the high priest? There is no word of any definite charge against Paul, nor of any verdict being reached. The stage seems to be set merely to give Paul the chance to deliver another apology. Moreover the interlude of the trial adds nothing to the progress of the drama's action, any more than does Paul's defense before the crowd. So purposeless do the proceedings appear that Lysias once again takes the case in hand, and at 23:10 we find ourselves at exactly the same point as at 22:24 and 21:35: for the third time Lysias "commanded the soldiers to . . . bring him into the barracks." This suggests that the trial scene, no less than the address to the crowd, is merely an editorial interlude.

(*b*) It is urged that such a tactical move as that by which Paul split the court is quite unworthy of the apostle. Thus Windisch writes: "The whole picture can hardly be considered historical; for it implies hypocrisy on the part of Paul. . . . If Paul could have behaved as Acts represents him here, and then write the sharp invective (Phil. iii. 2) against Pharisaism, he would have been a hypocrite. For he tells the Philippians that though he had been a zealous Pharisee he had given up all his privileges of birth and race for the sake of Christ, and he denounces the Jewish religion. An effort to harmonise these two passages is an insult to Paul! . . . A personal friend could not possibly have represented Paul as denying his convictions in order to save his life" (*The Beginnings of Christianity,* ed. F. J. Foakes Jackson and Kirsopp Lake [London: Macmillan & Co.; New York: The Macmillan Co., 1920-33], II, 333).

(*c*) Even if Paul is considered capable of such tactics, the result, it is argued, could not have been as Luke describes it. Paul was in fact trying to divert the court's attention from the main question by raising a side issue. According to Luke's account (21:28) it was simply not true that it was "with respect to the hope and the resurrection of the dead" that Paul was "on trial." And in any case such an irrelevant reference to the resurrection would not have won any support even from the Pharisees. If Paul was indeed being charged with "teaching men everywhere against the people and the law and this place" (21:28), the Pharisees themselves must have been bitterly hostile to him. Both sects laid much more stress on practice than on doctrine; and belief in the resurrection, though accepted by one and rejected by the other, was in those days of sophistication and easy tolerance a much less important issue than Luke would have us suppose. Indeed our author's suggestion that the Sadducees' hostility was due mainly to Paul's preaching of the resurrection is an exact parallel to 4:2, where he similarly suggests that the Sadducees were "annoyed" with Peter and John "because they were . . . proclaiming

tion of her law and army, but it gave him a kind of prestige, both social and political, of which any man might well be proud. Paul had learned how to be content with little or nothing in the way of conveniences and comforts, but that did not mean that Paul had lost his human capacity to appreciate the things that make physical life pleasant and agreeable.

From our democratic point of view we regret that there was such a discrimination between those who were citizens and those who were not, and that the same rights and privileges were not granted to all the people who lived under the Roman rule. But due credit must be given to Rome for the fact that it grasped the concept of the state as the protector of the individual, even though it may not have applied that principle as universally as we should like it to have been applied. It is not possible that any political principle will be completely and perfectly applied to any particular situation in the world. The best we can do is to keep the principles clearly formulated and sincerely accepted, and to apply them as well as we can to whatever situation confronts us.

Paul's citizenship gave him, among other things, the protection of Roman law against the violence of the mob. The surprising thing is that Paul took advantage of his privilege so seldom. He never claimed his rights as a Roman citizen merely to make things easier for himself. It was only when his life was in danger that he

priests and all their council to appear, and brought Paul down, and set him before them.

and he brought Paul down and set him before them.

in Jesus the resurrection from the dead." In both cases the enmity of the Sadducees was due rather to motives of political expediency. On this occasion Paul's assertion of his faith in the resurrection would neither have won over the Pharisees to condone his offense against the law, nor would it alone have sufficed to kindle the wrath of the Sadducees.

To these arguments a fairly adequate reply may be made. (*a*) Admittedly Lysias is not likely to have allowed Paul to pass even temporarily out of Roman jurisdiction. But he may quite well have met with representatives of the Sanhedrin in order to hear them present their complaint against Paul for transmission to the Roman court. This would be in line both with 22:30 ("desiring to know the real reason why the Jews accused him") and with 23:28 ("desiring to know the charge"), where see Exeg. As we have seen, the true tradition behind the records is probably that the Sanhedrin did lay such a complaint, and at the preliminary hearing of it Paul may have delivered a defense which in Acts has become the nucleus of what appears to be the story of an official trial before the Sanhedrin. It is not impossible that in certain details (e.g., the striking of Paul) the story has become colored by reminiscences of Jesus' trial.

(*b*) As for Paul's tactical move, his attempt to win over a section of his judges by the plea that he himself is a loyal Pharisee is, to say the least of it, disingenuous. But the very fact that Luke ventures to attribute such conduct to his hero at least suggests that the story is true. And in view of such passages as Phil. 3:4-6; II Cor. 11:21-22, it would be rash to declare that Paul the Christian could not still claim to be a Pharisee. We know from Romans that Paul at this time was particularly concerned to win over to Christianity the best elements in his own nation; and in the stress of the moment he may have been tempted to overemphasize his favorite thesis that all that was best in Judaism had reached its fullest development in the Christian faith, one of the basic doctrines of which, a belief in the resurrection, Paul shared with the Pharisees. As Emmet has pointed out, if the whole story is invented, it "must come from a period and author interested in suggesting a *rapprochement* between Christianity and Pharisaism. There are, however, in later times, few, if any traces of such tendency" (*Beginnings of Christianity,* II, 296). It therefore seems likely that Paul actually did adopt this line of defense. If we feel difficulty in admitting this, it is a moral and not a historical difficulty. Indeed Paul himself may have regretted his action, and on one interpretation of 24:21 he is represented as apologizing for it.

(*c*) As for the argument that the reference to the resurrection is totally irrelevant —technically, and as an answer to the formal charge, that is no doubt the case. But from Paul's point of view the question of the resurrection was always central, and he knew perfectly well that if he had not been preaching that Jesus was risen he would never have been put on trial. And in any case, as Lake well puts it: "It is usual for reformers when arrested not to answer the charge, but to make a speech in favour of the reform they desire. Paul's speech is psychologically correct, and therefore not historically improbable" (*Beginnings of Christianity,* V, 214).

brought up the question of his rights as a citizen. He was willing to take the insults of the crowd, to be accused unjustly, to be put in prison and make no mention of the fact that his persecutors were violating the law of the empire. But when the commander ordered him to be scourged, he knew that it meant permanent injury, if not death, and then he resorted to his rights and privileges as a citizen of the empire.

People do not always use their privileges as carefully as that. Officers in the army and navy are not unknown who have used their rank to make themselves more comfortable and who have exploited those under them to their own advantage. Men in political office are tempted to use their power and influence to get their friends out of difficulties and to save themselves from discredit. It is regrettable, but true, that

23 And Paul, earnestly beholding the
council, said, Men *and* brethren, I
have lived in all good conscience before
God until this day.
2 And the high priest Ananias commanded them that stood by him to smite
him on the mouth.

23 And Paul, looking intently at the
council, said, "Brethren, I have lived
before God in all good conscience up to
this day." 2 And the high priest An-a-ni'as
commanded those who stood by him to

The conclusion is, then, that though Luke's account is in part somewhat misleading, and such as to suggest that he himself was not actually present at the "trial," it is in the main historical. Admittedly Paul is not seen at his best, and we are left with an unhappy sense of contrast between the apostle and his Master. "Where," asks Jerome, "is that patience of the Savior, who, led as a lamb to the slaughter, opened not his mouth, but spoke gently to the smiter? . . . We do not detract from the Apostle, but we proclaim the glory of the Lord who, when he suffered in the flesh, rose superior to the injury and weakness of the flesh" (*Against the Pelagians* III. 4).

30. **Unbound him:** Much better "released him"—presumably from close confinement, for surely Paul must have been relieved of his shackles as soon as he protested his citizenship. But he must still have been kept in some kind of light custody, for in 23:18 he is still "the prisoner." **Commanded . . . the council to meet:** As already noted, it seems more probable that the Sanhedrin itself would take the initiative.

23:1. The "trial" can hardly have begun with the speech of the accused, and it is clear that Luke has given us only the briefest summary of the proceedings. **I have lived** (πεπολίτευμαι), literally "lived as a citizen"; but the word had lost its full force (cf. Phil. 1:27). **Conscience** (συνείδησις) is a favorite Pauline word (Rom. 2:15; I Cor. 8:7; II Cor. 1:12). But it usually stands for the consciousness of having done either right or wrong—and can thus be qualified by an adjective (cf. 24:16; and see II Cor. 1:12)—rather than, as in the more modern usage, for a faculty which acts as an inward guide to moral conduct, though Paul in Rom. 2:15 comes near to this idea.

2. Ananias was high priest from A.D. 48, when he was nominated by Herod Agrippa II, till *ca.* 58, when he was deposed. Josephus tells us that as high priest he had used the most dishonest methods to curry favor with the people. His action in commanding **those who stood by** Paul **to strike him on the mouth** fits Josephus' description of him: "A bold man in his temper, and very insolent; he was also of the sect of the Sadducees, who are very stern in judging offenders above all the rest of the Jews" (*Antiquities* XX. 9. 1, 2). **To strike him:** As Jesus had been struck (John 18:22)—presumably because he persisted in maintaining his innocence. Or did Ananias consider Paul's mode of address —**Brethren**—insufficiently respectful to the chairman?

---

those who are privileged to wear the garb of a Christian minister are sometimes tempted to use their position of respect for their own profit. Indeed one of the signs of a man of mature character is his ability to use his privileges wisely, not in such a way as to relieve him of his legitimate burdens and responsibilities, but to make it possible for him to be of most use to his brethren.

23:1-11. *Paul Appears Before the Sanhedrin.*—All through the ordeal that began in the temple and continued in the privacy of the barracks, Paul had kept himself under perfect control. The more furious the mob became, the more composed he became. Far from being inflamed himself, his bearing grew more and more dignified as the farce continued. When he finally raised the question of his Roman citizenship, he spoke with a quiet courtesy that completely disarmed the officer. But when Paul appeared before the Sanhedrin, things were different.

He began his defense in the same quiet, restrained tone of voice. **Brethren, I have lived before God in all good conscience up to this day.** Suddenly he was interrupted and the high priest ordered him to be struck in the face. It is a sad commentary upon the quality of manhood in which the office of high priest was invested. Leaving aside the standards of the Sermon on the Mount, such behavior was not worthy of the best in Judaism. A people who could produce a Jeremiah who in turn might inspire the Servant poems of Isa. 53 ff., a peo-

3 Then said Paul unto him, God shall smite thee, *thou* whited wall: for sittest thou to judge me after the law, and commandest me to be smitten contrary to the law?

4 And they that stood by said, Revilest thou God's high priest?

5 Then said Paul, I wist not, brethren, that he was the high priest: for it is written, Thou shalt not speak evil of the ruler of thy people.

strike him on the mouth.
3 Then Paul said to him, "God shall strike you, you whitewashed wall! Are you sitting to judge me according to the law, and yet contrary to the law you order me to be struck?"
4 Those who stood by said, "Would you revile God's high priest?"
5 And Paul said, "I did not know, brethren, that he was the high priest; for it is written, 'You shall not speak evil of a ruler of your people.'"

---

3. God shall strike you: Josephus tells us that at the beginning of the Jewish War Ananias was assassinated by "robbers"—possibly the Sicarii or the Zealots (*Jewish War* II. 17. 6, 9). Had Luke this in mind? **Whitewashed wall:** A term of abuse of which the origin is obscure, though we may compare the "whitewashed tombs" to which hypocrites are compared in Matt. 23:27. But why a "wall"? Some recall the "wall . . . daubed with untempered mortar" in Ezek. 13:10-16.

5. I did not know: Why not? No very convincing reason can be given. Because Ananias was a new holder of the office since Paul's earlier visits to Jerusalem, and Paul did not know him by sight? Because someone else was presiding, possibly the tribune, and Paul did not know who had given the order? Because, owing to bad eyesight, Paul had made an honest mistake? Or is Paul being ironical? No one could have imagined that such an order would come from the high priest! **It is written:** In Exod. 22:28, from which Josephus deduces that "he that does not submit to the high priest shall be subject to the same punishment as if he had been guilty of impiety to God himself" (*Against Apion* II. 23).

---

ple who had risen to such heights of spiritual cultivation, had little excuse for such a slump into brutality. It is a warning of the danger to which all hierarchies are continually exposed; it is the danger of becoming so completely formalized that they become hard. A hierarchy in religion is no more exempt from the dangers of professionalism than a hierarchy in politics or military government, and the dangers of professionalism always amount to the same thing—the neglect of the personal element in a situation. Doctors can become so professional that they pronounce their diagnosis of mortality as though their patients had no feelings whatever. Public officers of the state can become so professional that they pursue their course of action regardless of the people whose lives and property they shatter as they go. Indeed even the minister of the church can become so professional that he handles the delicate balances of a person's life with such clumsy and unfeeling hands that he might as well strike the person across the face. It was bad enough when the soldiers struck Paul, but when the order came from the high priest himself, the hardest heart of the most carefree worldling was almost sure to be shocked.

The high priest's action had two results. The first was that Paul lost his temper. He could hold himself in check no longer. **You whitewashed wall!** he called Ananias. It was an epithet expressing unlimited contempt. Things that were contaminating to the Jew were painted white so that they could be clearly seen and avoided. So sepulchers were whitewashed because a corpse was unclean and no Jew wanted to touch one if he could help it. Paul's anger reached such a pitch that he did not hesitate to describe the high priest in terms of contamination, something to be avoided like the plague. A moment later Paul said that he did not know that it was the high priest to whom he had spoken with such uninhibited frankness. Perhaps he did not, but it is interesting to notice that Paul does not, according to Luke's story, explicitly apologize for what he said, and one cannot help wondering whether Paul might not have said the same thing even if he had known whom he had the honor of addressing!

For there is a point beyond which the human spirit cannot be stretched. Paul had a violent temper to begin with. It was the temper of a passionate man. It was controlled only by the most severe training and discipline. People had been teasing it for several days, tantalizing it, trying to see how much it could stand. Finally it exploded. We may wish that Paul had been

6 But when Paul perceived that the one part were Sadducees, and the other Pharisees, he cried out in the council, Men *and* brethren, I am a Pharisee, the son of a Pharisee: of the hope and resurrection of the dead I am called in question.

7 And when he had so said, there arose a dissension between the Pharisees and the Sadducees: and the multitude was divided.

8 For the Sadducees say that there is no resurrection, neither angel, nor spirit: but the Pharisees confess both.

6 But when Paul perceived that one part
were Sad′du-cees and the other Pharisees, he
cried out in the council, "Brethren, I am
a Pharisee, a son of Pharisees; with respect
to the hope and the resurrection of the
dead I am on trial." 7 And when he had
said this, a dissension arose between the
Pharisees and the Sad′du-cees; and the assembly was divided. 8 For the Sad′du-cees
say that there is no resurrection, nor angel,
nor spirit; but the Pharisees acknowledge

---

6. A Pharisee, a son of Pharisees: Cf. 26:5 and Phil. 3:5. As a Christian, Paul can still claim to be a Pharisee (cf. 15:5 for "believers who belonged to the party of the Pharisees") and a champion of the best traditions of Judaism—the best defense he can make against the charge of subversive preaching (21:28). **The hope and the resurrection:** This might be taken to refer to the messianic hope and the resurrection which, according to the Pharisees, was its condition. But the words in the Greek have no definite article and are perhaps best taken as a single expression equivalent to "the hope of the resurrection." Similarly in 24:15 Paul speaks of "having a hope . . . that there will be a resurrection" (cf. also 26:6-8); and in 24:21 it is simply "with respect to the resurrection" that Paul is on trial.

7. The assembly was divided: Josephus tells how once he escaped from a mob by the same ruse of dividing "their opinions" (*Life* 139-44).

8. For the divergent views of the Pharisees and Sadducees on eschatology see Mark 12:18 and parallels and Josephus, who says that the Pharisees maintain that "every soul is imperishable, but the soul of the good alone passes into another body, while the souls of the wicked suffer eternal punishment." Of the Sadducees he writes, "As for the persistence of the soul after death, penalties in the underworld, and rewards,

---

able to stand his trial in silence the way his Master stood silent before Pilate. And yet there is some consolation in the fact that a man of the spiritual power of Paul, self-controlled as he had taught himself to be, came to a point where his human feelings could stand no more. It does not excuse our flights of ill-temper, not in the least; but it does give us the benefit of the company of one who tried his best and to a magnificent degree mastered his temperament but who, when the pressure was too great, let himself go in all the vitriolic spleen of his primitive nature. It may not be the lowest in us that gives a secret cheer when Paul strikes fire with his tongue and describes the contemptible high priest in terms best suited to his degenerate professionalism.

The second result of the high priest's action was that Paul broke up the meeting by breaking it in two. We shall never know, of course, how deliberately Paul chose his strategy. If we knew beyond any doubt that he did deliberately choose it, then the question would be raised, How noble was such a choice? But knowing only what Luke has chosen to tell us, we must content ourselves by observing what Paul did and how it worked out. The Sanhedrin that Paul faced was a divided camp, and he knew that it was divided. It was divided between the Sadducees, who controlled the temple, and the Pharisees, who had the greatest influence over the religious life of the people. The main interest of the Sadducees was to keep the temple going. It was an extremely profitable undertaking. So long as Rome tolerated it, they wanted no trouble with Rome. They wanted no innovations; they were against anything that might upset things as they were. The Pharisees, on the other hand, had a genuine if sometimes misguided interest in the religious life of the people. Their minds were still open to the word of God. If there was such a thing as the resurrection of the dead, they were ready to accept it even though it was such an idea as might cause some embarrassment to the temple hierarchy. Their religion was, to be sure, a legalistic one, but it was not a religion limited by the plaster cast of self-interest and reactionary stupidity.

To be perfectly frank about the situation, Paul's word drove a division between the two groups. He proceeded to ally himself with the Pharisees. He had been born one. In one sense

9 And there arose a great cry: and the
scribes *that were* of the Pharisees' part
arose, and strove, saying, We find no evil
in this man: but if a spirit or an angel hath
spoken to him, let us not fight against God.
10 And when there arose a great dissension, the chief captain, fearing lest Paul
should have been pulled in pieces of them,
commanded the soldiers to go down, and to
take him by force from among them, and to
bring *him* into the castle.

them all. **9** Then a great clamor arose;
and some of the scribes of the Pharisees'
party stood up and contended, "We find
nothing wrong in this man. What if a
spirit or an angel spoke to him?" **10** And
when the dissension became violent, the
tribune, afraid that Paul would be torn in
pieces by them, commanded the soldiers
to go down and take him by force from
among them and bring him into the barracks.

---

they will have none of them" (*Jewish War* II. 8. 14). The Sadducean disbelief in the existence of angels and spirits is not mentioned elsewhere. **Them all:** The Greek is τὰ ἀμφότερα, properly meaning "both" (but see on 19:16). Chrysostom preserves strict grammar by identifying **angel** and **spirit,** for which see on 8:26.

9. Scribes of the Pharisees' party: Cf. Mark 2:16; Luke 5:30. Most, but not necessarily all, of the scribes would be Pharisees. Later copyists were evidently impressed by the parallel presented by Gamaliel in 5:34-39, and the Textus Receptus inserts **let us not fight against God** (KJV)—an echo of Gamaliel's words in 5:39. **A spirit or an angel:** Here at any rate the two are identical, and the reference is obviously either to Paul's vision at his conversion (22:6-11) or to that later in the temple (22:17-21), both of which Paul had described the previous day.

---

he was still a Pharisee. His very bonds were the proof of his Pharisaical association, for he was being tried at that moment because he had preached the hope of Israel—the resurrection from the dead. So he won the good will of the Pharisees. The name of Jesus was not mentioned, intentionally or otherwise, so that the conflict was centered not in anything uniquely associated with the new way of life, but in the old question over which the Jews had argued for so many years. The hearing therefore turned into a row between the two antagonistic groups within the Sanhedrin. The opposing parties became so violent that the commander had to intervene with troops and take Paul back to the barracks.

It would be hard to find a better example of the way the divided opinion of a group can be used to destroy it. The Sanhedrin was split and Paul, at least for the time being, made his escape between the two factions. There lies the danger to which democracy may repeatedly be exposed. If the enemies of democracy can create enough friction between capital and labor so as to set the two groups against each other, their battle will be won. It is the old story of the house divided against itself; it can never stand. That is the reason why Christians are so deeply concerned about the divisions which rend the fellowship and break the unity of the body of Christ. They sap its energy and dilute its strength. When the church should be presenting a united front to the forces of evil, it debates the validity of its orders, disagrees about the source of its authority, wrangles over the creedal statement of its belief. Through such appalling loopholes of dissent and discord the enemy easily escapes, leaving the church to squabble over the crumbs of its own arguments. The differences within the Christian fellowship cannot be passed over carelessly. We have observed the fact that even in the early days when the life of the fellowship was fresh with its first enthusiasm there were differences of opinion and practice. But there was also a unity that bound the body together in one concerted witness to the world that Jesus is Lord. We need that concerted witness now. We want that basic agreement that Jesus is the Lord and Master of life. We want it because the world is rocking on its foundations. We want it because men are hungering and thirsting for something that will fill the emptiness of their barren lives, for a certainty that will restore their balance, and for a faith that will sustain them through a period of possible dissolution and catastrophic change. A debating society will never meet the need. It must be a fellowship knit together in Christ.

The next night Paul heard the Lord speaking to him. This is what he said: **Take courage, for as you have testified about me at Jerusalem, so you must bear witness also at Rome.** No one will ever be able to explain the source from which such unassailable reassurance comes. At a time when the whole sky is dark, when all the

11 And the night following the Lord stood by him, and said, Be of good cheer, Paul: for as thou hast testified of me in Jerusalem, so must thou bear witness also at Rome.

12 And when it was day, certain of the Jews banded together, and bound themselves under a curse, saying that they would neither eat nor drink till they had killed Paul.

11 The following night the Lord stood by him and said, "Take courage, for as you have testified about me at Jerusalem, so you must bear witness also at Rome."

12 When it was day, the Jews made a plot and bound themselves by an oath neither to eat nor drink till they had killed

---

11. The Lord stood by him: Once again a vision marks a crisis in Paul's career (cf. 18:9-10). To visit **Rome** had, according to 19:21, been in Paul's mind for some time. Perhaps now he begins to see in a possible appeal to Caesar a providential means of attaining his end. But such an appeal might to Jews appear an act of apostasy; and Luke perhaps records the vision to show that divine sanction was given to Paul's intended action.

3. Paul's Transference to Caesarea (23:12-35)

Once again critics find grave difficulties in Luke's story of a Jewish plot and the consequent removal of Paul to Caesarea. (*a*) First, as to the alleged motive for Paul's removal. The actual transference is of course historical beyond all question: once Paul had put forward his claim to Roman citizenship, such a transference became automatic. Luke, on the other hand, gives as the reason for Paul's removal the discovery of a plot, first to persuade Lysias to bring Paul once again before the Sanhedrin, and then to murder the apostle on his way to the council. But, it is argued, even admitting the first appearance before the Sanhedrin to be historical, it is inconceivable that there can have been any likelihood of a second similar investigation. The details regarding the plot can therefore hardly be accurate. Indeed the whole story of a plot becomes suspect, for the real reason for Paul's removal to Caesarea was not Lysias' fear of such a plot, but the fact that Paul's claim to citizenship made such transference inevitable. In reply it must be said that Luke's story of a plot seems much too circumstantial to be pure invention, and it must in broad outline be accepted as history. We may admit, however, that

---

reserves have been spent, and every way seems to be blocked, then from some secret, invisible source comes the encouragement that we need to keep us going. Some people are satisfied to call it our "second wind." Others are not satisfied with that naturalistic explanation, for in some inexplicable way it does not do justice to all the facts. They prefer to say what Luke says: **The following night the Lord stood by him and said "Take courage."** The Lord stood by Paul—what a wonderful phrase to describe that miracle of renewed strength. As one reads the story of Paul, one feels increasingly that through all the perils the Lord stood by him, not to save him from danger, but to save him *in* danger. That is the only kind of safety that Paul expected, the safety that saw him through danger. On so many occasions Paul was on the very brink of disaster, and yet somehow or other he came through unscathed. A person who did not know the secret might innocently say that he led a charmed life. There was no charm about it. It was simply that the Lord stood by him. Paul knew it; he accepted it; he literally threw himself upon it. It gave him a kind of daring that was beyond the boldness of a gladiator. He had been taught it from childhood; he learned it by heart in the psalms—"A thousand shall fall at thy side, . . . but it shall not come nigh thee" (Ps. 91:7)—but he felt it, knew it in his heart, when he stood by the Cross and felt the love of God flowing through the sacrificial life of Jesus, poured out indiscriminately upon those who deserved it and those who did not, given extravagantly to men and women who were still sinners.

Any disciple who in some measure shares Paul's experience can do anything; for no matter what happens to him or around him, he knows that the Lord stands by.

12-35. ***Paul Is Sent to Felix.***—When the hearing before the Sanhedrin turned out to be a fiasco, the conspiracy to kill Paul took a more bloody course. It was led by Jews who remain

13 And there were more than forty which had made this conspiracy.

14 And they came to the chief priests and elders, and said, We have bound ourselves under a great curse, that we will eat nothing until we have slain Paul.

15 Now therefore ye with the council signify to the chief captain that he bring him down unto you to-morrow, as though ye would inquire something more perfectly concerning him: and we, or ever he come near, are ready to kill him.

Paul. 13 There were more than forty who
made this conspiracy. 14 And they went to
the chief priests and elders, and said, "We
have strictly bound ourselves by an oath
to taste no food till we have killed Paul.
15 You therefore, along with the council,
give notice now to the tribune to bring
him down to you, as though you were
going to determine his case more exactly.
And we are ready to kill him before he
comes near."

---

there is not likely to have been any suggestion of a second investigation before the Sanhedrin; and it is certainly possible that Luke's story has been colored by his tendency to exonerate the Romans and blame the Jews for all Paul's troubles.

(*b*) Second, it is argued that the size of Paul's escort must have been grossly exaggerated. Two hundred infantrymen with seventy horsemen and two hundred *dexiolaboi* amount to a small army. Yet such precautions can be plausibly enough explained. Paul may well have appeared to Lysias a much more important person than some critics are ready to admit. He was the leader of a numerous body of preachers throughout the Jewish world. He had come to Jerusalem with alms for the poor, and had been welcomed by James, the respected head of a sect reverenced for its strict observance of the law. If Paul had bitter enemies in Jerusalem, then, even discounting the possibility that the Pharisees were supporting him against the Sadducees, he also had many friends; and were he murdered by fanatics, his death might provoke serious factional riots. Lysias doubtless wished to guard not only Paul but his own reputation, as indeed the Western text hints when it adds in vs. 25 that he "was afraid that the Jews would seize him [Paul] and kill him, and meanwhile he would be charged with having taken a bribe" (to allow Paul to be murdered). We also have the evidence of Josephus that while Felix was in office the district was a hotbed of bandits and the whole populace was on the verge of revolt. In this setting Lysias' precautions become quite intelligible.

12. Made a plot (συστροφήν): The word in the LXX is used with the same sense as συνωμοσία ("conspiracy," vs. 13) and ἐνέδρον ("ambush," vs. 16). But in 19:40 it appears to mean a "riotous meeting" ("commotion," RSV), and we might perhaps here translate, as Lake and Cadbury suggest, "held an indignation meeting." **An oath neither to eat nor drink:** Fortunately the rabbis were able to devise means of release from such oaths; so the plot having failed, we need not assume that the plotters starved to death!

14-15. The chief priests and elders: In the light of the sectarian dispute the previous day, is there any significance in the omission of "the scribes," who would be mostly Pharisees? **Determine his case:** The Greek word implies that the court is to reach a verdict as well as to **inquire** more fully into the case.

---

nameless. There were more than forty of them. They supplied the zeal that any conspiracy must have before it can succeed. They went at the matter with all the solemnity of fanatics. They were determined to get rid of Paul, and they vowed not to eat or drink until the deed was done. Notice that it was a relatively small group. Undoubtedly the rank and file of Jews had nothing against Paul. After all, he had just come from abroad with relief funds for suffering Jews, and the Pharisees themselves had refused to condemn him. In most cases it is small groups that stir up the trouble. They build the fire and strike the match. They are the ones to be watched.

In this particular case the small group had prominent colleagues—the high priest, the elders, and the Sanhedrin. In other words they had the officials behind them. Officials are more than likely to be conservative, and the more official they are and the higher their office, the more conservative they become. Even in the church we see this strange transformation taking place almost daily. To make a man a bishop is to make him a conservative, not always, to be sure, but too often. So in Jerusalem the officers

16 And when Paul's sister's son heard of their lying in wait, he went and entered into the castle, and told Paul.

17 Then Paul called one of the centurions unto *him,* and said, Bring this young man unto the chief captain: for he hath a certain thing to tell him.

18 So he took him, and brought *him* to the chief captain, and said, Paul the prisoner called me unto *him,* and prayed me to bring this young man unto thee, who hath something to say unto thee.

19 Then the chief captain took him by the hand, and went *with him* aside privately, and asked *him,* What is that thou hast to tell me?

20 And he said, The Jews have agreed to desire thee that thou wouldest bring down Paul to-morrow into the council, as though they would inquire somewhat of him more perfectly.

16 Now the son of Paul's sister heard of
their ambush; so he went and entered the
barracks and told Paul. 17 And Paul called
one of the centurions and said, "Bring this
young man to the tribune; for he has something to tell him." 18 So he took him and
brought him to the tribune and said, "Paul
the prisoner called me and asked me to
bring this young man to you, as he has
something to say to you." 19 The tribune
took him by the hand, and going aside
asked him privately, "What is it that you
have to tell me?" 20 And he said, "The
Jews have agreed to ask you to bring Paul
down to the council tomorrow, as though
they were going to inquire somewhat more

---

16. The son of Paul's sister: This is the only reference we have to any of Paul's family connections. Does it suggest that his sister was married in high priestly circles, so that the young man got wind of the plot? The Greek may be translated "heard of their lying in wait, having come in upon them, and he entered into the castle" (ASV mg.) —i.e., he stumbled by accident upon the plot and then reported it to the Roman authorities.

18. Paul the prisoner: See on 22:30. The Greek word need not imply that Paul still wore fetters.

20. As though they were going to inquire: Codex Vaticanus (B) here reads ὡς μέλλων . . . πυνθάνεσθαι, which can only give the meaning "as though thou wouldest inquire" (ASV and ERV). The RSV presupposes either μέλλοντες (referring to **the Jews**) which is the reading of the later Greek MSS, or μέλλον (referring to **the council**) which is read by Codex Sinaiticus (א) and agrees better with vs. 15, where μέλλοντας refers to the members of the council.

---

were the conservatives, and they saw in Paul a disturbing influence which they could not tolerate. It was not for the general good, they persuaded themselves, for such an innovator to be at large. It was therefore no more than their official duty to get rid of him. After all, their predecessors had taken the same course with all the disturbing prophets, Elijah, Jeremiah, John the Baptist, and the rest, and they did not have the vision to see that in following them they were reaping the bitter harvest of the Lord's judgment upon those who persecuted the prophets which were before them. It is not out of order, therefore, to say that officials need to be watched. It is easy for them to mistake their own personal gain for the general welfare and to stop progress in an effort to promote it.

The conspiracy to kill Paul, however, was met by a campaign to save him. The leader of the campaign, the person who started it, was Paul's nephew. He appears at no other point in the story of Paul. Out of the blue, it seems, appears a young man who cares enough about his uncle to take steps to save his life. He managed to get into the barracks and tell Paul that there was a group of Jews who planned to kill him as he was being taken from the barracks to the Sanhedrin for further investigation. It was around this young man that the forces of good began to rally. All we know about him is that he discovered an evil plot and was willing to do what he could to stop it. It is in such small and unpretentious ways that all good movements usually begin. Some honest, forthright person takes the first step in the right direction, and other less adventuresome spirits fall in and follow. In this case there was an officer in the barracks who was more than willing to escort the young man to the commander so that he might tell him the story.

21 But do not thou yield unto them: for
there lie in wait for him of them more
than forty men, which have bound themselves with an oath, that they will neither
eat nor drink till they have killed him: and
now are they ready, looking for a promise
from thee.

22 So the chief captain *then* let the young
man depart, and charged *him, See thou* tell
no man that thou hast showed these things
to me.

23 And he called unto *him* two centurions, saying, Make ready two hundred
soldiers to go to Caesarea, and horsemen
threescore and ten, and spearmen two hundred, at the third hour of the night;

24 And provide *them* beasts, that they
may set Paul on, and bring *him* safe unto
Felix the governor.

25 And he wrote a letter after this manner:

closely about him. 21 But do not yield to
them; for more than forty of their men lie
in ambush for him, having bound themselves by an oath neither to eat nor drink
till they have killed him; and now they are
ready, waiting for the promise from you."
22 So the tribune dismissed the young man,
charging him, "Tell no one that you have
informed me of this."

23 Then he called two of the centurions
and said, "At the third hour of the night
get ready two hundred soldiers with seventy horsemen and two hundred spearmen
to go as far as Caes-a-re'a. 24 Also provide
mounts for Paul to ride, and bring him
safely to Felix the governor." 25 And he
wrote a letter to this effect:

---

23. **Third hour of the night:** i.e., about 9 to 10 P.M. **Spearmen** (δεξιολάβους): The word is otherwise unknown and the translation is purely conjectural, though obviously it must have something to do with "holding by the right." The men in question may have been light irregular or native auxiliaries. Lake and Cadbury suggest that the meaning may be "led horses"—and that "Paul was sent with a detachment of 70 cavalry with 200 led horses" (*Beginnings of Christianity,* IV, 293). This would reduce the escort to a reasonable size and would get rid of the infantry which, if haste was necessary to avoid the ambush, would only have been a hindrance. Moreover a march from Jerusalem to Antipatris and back within twenty-four hours (vss. 31-32)—some forty miles in each direction—is a quite impossible feat for infantry. For **Felix** see Exeg. at beginning of ch. 24.

25. **He wrote a letter:** The style of the letter is so characteristic of Luke himself that it is likely to be his own composition rather than an actual copy. The original would be, of course, in Latin, so that Luke can profess to give only its general tenor, remembered perhaps through having heard it read in court. When a prisoner was sent up to a higher court, it was necessary to send with him a written statement called an *elogium.* Whether genuine or not, the letter is exactly what we might expect to be sent to a superior by a subordinate who wished to place his own conduct in the best possible light. No mention is made of Lysias' order to scourge a Roman citizen. So far from revealing that only a last-minute claim by Paul saved Lysias from committing a serious misdemeanor, the letter rather gives the impression that Lysias himself discovered Paul to be a Roman citizen and accordingly rescued him from the Jewish mob.

The commander was ready to join the group to save Paul for two good reasons. First, it was decidedly to his interest to keep peace and quiet in Jerusalem. There were many people in the city to whom the death of Paul would be a shock. Paul had many friends and supporters in the city. If it came to a showdown, the leaders of the Christian community would undoubtedly stand by him. There were others who on general principles would disapprove of an act that could be described only as cold-blooded murder. As a good administrator of the peace, therefore, the commander had every reason to prevent the murder of Paul.

But the commander had another and, it may be suspected, even stronger reason for allying himself with those who wanted to save Paul. A few days before, he had made an embarrassing

26 Claudius Lysias unto the most excellent governor Felix *sendeth* greeting.

27 This man was taken of the Jews, and should have been killed of them: then came I with an army, and rescued him, having understood that he was a Roman.

28 And when I would have known the cause wherefore they accused him, I brought him forth into their council:

29 Whom I perceived to be accused of questions of their law, but to have nothing laid to his charge worthy of death or of bonds.

30 And when it was told me how that the Jews laid wait for the man, I sent straightway to thee, and gave commandment to his accusers also to say before thee what *they had* against him. Farewell.

31 Then the soldiers, as it was commanded them, took Paul, and brought *him* by night to Antipatris.

26 "Claudius Lys'i-as to his Excellency
the governor Felix, greeting. 27 This man
was seized by the Jews, and was about to
be killed by them, when I came upon them
with the soldiers and rescued him, having
learned that he was a Roman citizen. 28 And
desiring to know the charge on which they
accused him, I brought him down to their
council. 29 I found that he was accused
about questions of their law, but charged
with nothing deserving death or imprisonment. 30 And when it was disclosed to me
that there would be a plot against the
man, I sent him to you at once, ordering
his accusers also to state before you what
they have against him."

31 So the soldiers, according to their instructions, took Paul and brought him by

---

26. His Excellency: The same title that is given to Theophilus in Luke 1:3. See on 1:1 and cf. 24:3 (of Felix) and 26:25 (of Festus). **Governor** (ἡγεμόνι): Properly he was procurator of an imperial province, a title which is more correctly rendered into Greek by ἐπίτροπος, though ἡγεμών is very commonly used in the N.T.

28. Desiring to know the charge: This again suggests that the so-called "trial" by the Sanhedrin was rather a preliminary investigation with a view to preparing a charge to lay before the Roman court.

29. Once again Luke insists that Roman authority could find no substance in the charges made against Paul by his countrymen.

31. The distance of **Antipatris** from Jerusalem is supposed to have been about forty miles, although its exact site is not known. If so, it would be about two thirds of the way to Caesarea.

---

mistake about Paul. He had begun to torture Paul on the assumption that he was a Jewish leader of Egyptian bandits. He did not take the time to inquire whether or not he might be a Roman citizen, for it did not seem possible to him that he could be. When he discovered that Paul was not only a Roman citizen, but also that he was one by birth, he was forced to change his tactics and release Paul from the torture chamber. Not only had he endangered the life of a Roman citizen, but he had also endangered his own position as commander of the Roman garrison in Jerusalem. It was a mistake that no commander could afford to make. Self-interest has more than once persuaded a man to choose the better way, and it is not too much to say that in this instance the commander's self-interest was entirely in the interest of Paul.

There is every reason to believe, however, that the commander was an honest servant of Rome; and that in doing as he did, he not only covered himself and his own safety but gave protection to a man whose personality had not failed to impress him and the injustice of whose persecution he had the wit to perceive. Mixed, then, were his motives in protecting Paul? Perhaps they were. So are the motives of most of us when we launch out into the dangerous waters of moral action. We can be thankful when the motives of self-interest support and incite those other less selfish interests which move out toward the things that are good but dangerous.

And then there was the convoy that was sent to accompany Paul on the forty-mile journey to Antipatris and on beyond to Caesarea. We are likely to think of convoys as part of the machinery of war, and war means destruction, and destruction that is evil through and through. Yet it is fair to point out that even in the context of the destructive machinery of war there can be

32 On the morrow they left the horsemen to go with him, and returned to the castle:

33 Who, when they came to Caesarea, and delivered the epistle to the governor, presented Paul also before him.

34 And when the governor had read *the letter,* he asked of what province he was. And when he understood that *he was* of Cilicia;

35 I will hear thee, said he, when thine accusers are also come. And he commanded him to be kept in Herod's judgment hall.

night to An-tip'a-tris. 32 And on the morrow they returned to the barracks, leaving
the horsemen to go on with him. 33 When
they came to Caes-a-re'a and delivered the
letter to the governor, they presented Paul
also before him. 34 On reading the letter,
he asked to what province he belonged.
When he learned that he was from Ci-
li'cia 35 he said, "I will hear you when your
accusers arrive." And he commanded him
to be guarded in Herod's praetorium.

---

34. What province: The Greek (ποίας), as regularly in the Koine, is merely the equivalent of τίνος, and there is no need to suppose that Paul was asked "to what kind of a province" (imperial or senatorial) he belonged. Roman law allowed the accused to be tried either in his own native country or in that in which the crime was alleged to have been committed. The rules of procedure required that this should be the first question asked. Luke can have had no possible reason for recording this detail unless he was himself present, or possibly even had access to the papers in the case (cf. the similar incident in Luke 23:6-7, when Pilate, on learning that Jesus is a Galilean, sends him to Herod).

35. I will hear you: Felix would have jurisdiction over Paul either as procurator of Judea, in which the "crime" had been committed, or as the deputy of the legate of Syria and Cilicia, Paul's native province, who would rank as his administrative superior. Hitherto Paul has been represented as playing merely a passive part. He now appears in the role of one who has presented an appeal for an official "hearing." This would seem to suggest that he had asserted his Roman citizenship, not merely to escape scourging, but to evade the jurisdiction of the Sanhedrin and come under the immediate jurisdiction of Rome; and that his transference to Caesarea may have taken place, not merely to safeguard him from the Jewish plot, but at his own request as a privilege he had the right to claim. **Herod's praetorium** was presumably the palace built by Herod the Great, which we may suppose to have been taken over by the Roman authorities as their administrative premises.

---

elements that in themselves are good because they save life. Think of the convoys that guided the hospital ships through the perilous ways of mine-infested waters. Think of the convoys that guarded the ships that carried troops and supplies. It was such a convoy, small indeed in comparison, which protected Paul from the violence of a group of fanatical men who conspired against his life. As they accompanied him to the palace of Felix, they fulfilled their purpose, which was to protect and save life. The next day they may have been engaged upon errands of a very different nature, and it may be that in the final judgment their salvation will rest upon the fact that they once made it possible for Paul the apostle to travel unmolested from Jerusalem to Caesarea.

Most people will find their earthly salvation in such fragments of good, surrounded often by things of which they are less than proud. We, like the soldiers of the Roman convoy, are set in a context of evil. It is impossible for us to avoid it completely. We cannot escape it any more than we can entirely escape bacteria. Our actions, no matter how innocent they appear to be, are more than likely to be tainted with selfishness from which it is almost impossible for us to disengage ourselves. Yet from time to time there looms out of the context of evil some good, unselfish thing, something that shines with no mist or cloud upon it. It is by those things that our fellow men may judge us, and for those things that they will remember us; and when God looks at us, though he will love us not for what we have done but in spite of what we have done, nevertheless those good things, like the convoy that accompanied Paul, may seem to him to have been of right intention, and will give us some fair introduction to the life of his kingdom.

24 And after five days Ananias the high priest descended with the elders, and *with* a certain orator *named* Tertullus, who informed the governor against Paul.

24 And after five days the high priest An-a-ni'as came down with some elders and a spokesman, one Ter-tul'lus. They laid before the governor their case

4. Paul at Caesarea (24:1–26:32)

a) Paul and Felix (24:1-27)

Antonius **Felix** was procurator of Judea from A.D. 52 till his recall, probably in 58, and was the brother of Pallas, the notorious freedman favorite of Claudius, to whom no doubt he owed his preferment, and backed by whose influence, according to Tacitus, "he thought that he could commit all kinds of enormities with impunity" (*Annals* XII. 54). Tacitus and Josephus agree that he was a thoroughly bad man, and Luke's narrative shows him to have been venal and corrupt. In a famous epigram Tacitus says of him that "with all manner of cruelty and lust he exercised the functions of a prince with the disposition of a slave" (*Histories* V. 9). But few officials emerged with any credit from the almost impossible task of administering Judea, and by fair means or foul Felix seems to have been able for several years to maintain some measure of order. Hence Tertullus' compliment, **through you we enjoy much peace** (vs. 2). According to Josephus, he suppressed the robber chief Eleazar, defeated a formidable rebellion by an Egyptian-Jewish impostor in Jerusalem (see on 21:38), and settled what threatened to be a civil war between Greeks and Jews at Caesarea (*Jewish War* II. 13. 2; *Antiquities* XX. 8. 6, 7).

Some radical critics have questioned the historicity of Paul's "trial" before Felix on the ground that no decision is given and that the case comes up again under Festus as if for the first time. But Luke's account is not of a formal trial, at which a verdict would be given, but merely of an *anakrisis,* or preliminary hearing, at which the Jews would have the opportunity of presenting their complaint and the accused of stating his defense. In the nature of things there could be no verdict in the absence of the witnesses for the prosecution (see vs. 19). There is nothing in Luke's narrative that is either improbable or inconsistent with the sequel.

Tertullus would be a Roman professional counsel for the prosecution, a *causidicus* or advocate. His speech, though probably a free composition by our author, certainly reflects what Luke must have known to be the charge brought against Paul. It begins with a conventional *captatio benevolentiae* designed to win the judge's favor by a personal compliment, and then for the first time charges Paul with a really indictable offense—not merely of attempting to profane the temple, but of being a habitual insurrectionist, the **ringleader** of a revolutionary **sect** called the **Nazarenes,** and a constant disturber of the peace in every quarter of the civilized world. In the eyes of provincial authorities there could be no more serious charge.

Paul's speech also begins with a *captatio.* It falls into two parts, vss. 10-16 and vss. 17-21, which cover almost exactly the same ground and read almost like two alternative versions of the same speech. Note how each part makes the same four points: (*a*) Paul's motive in going to Jerusalem was a religious one, in harmony with, and not opposed to, the rites and interests of the Jewish people: he went up **to worship** (vs. 11), and **to bring**

24:1-9. ***Tertullus Presents the Case Against Paul.***—When Paul's case was presented to the Roman procurator, the Jews hired a lawyer named Tertullus to represent them. Tertullus began with flowery oratory. His compliments to Felix were probably not taken very seriously by either himself or Felix. They were a part of the formality of public address, especially in the courtroom. Why it is that it is so easy for people to say things in public that they do not mean is a question which is not easily answered. Political orations, for instance, can pay the most glowing tributes to candidates who in private life are scorned by the speakers who praise them in public. Insincerity is one of the most grave temptations of people who make a practice of speaking in public.

The best thing that can be said about Tertullus is that he was honest as far as the charge against Paul went. He began with the real charge, that "this man [is] a perfect pest" (Moffatt). That was the charge in a nutshell.

2 And when he was called forth, Tertullus began to accuse *him,* saying, Seeing that by thee we enjoy great quietness, and that very worthy deeds are done unto this nation by thy providence,

3 We accept *it* always, and in all places, most noble Felix, with all thankfulness.

4 Notwithstanding, that I be not further tedious unto thee, I pray thee that thou wouldest hear us of thy clemency a few words.

5 For we have found this man *a* pestilent *fellow,* and a mover of sedition among all the Jews throughout the world, and a ringleader of the sect of the Nazarenes:

against Paul; 2 and when he was called,
Ter-tul'lus began to accuse him, saying:
"Since through you we enjoy much peace, and since by your provision, most excellent Felix, reforms are introduced on behalf of
this nation, 3 in every way and everywhere
we accept this with all gratitude. 4 But, to
detain you no further, I beg you in your
kindness to hear us briefly. 5 For we have
found this man a pestilent fellow, an agitator among all the Jews throughout the world, and a ringleader of the sect of the

---

to my nation alms and offerings (vs. 17). (*b*) He denies that he has been guilty of making any disturbance (vss. 12, 18). (*c*) He challenges his opponents to prove their charge, stating that they cannot adduce any evidence (vs. 13), and that the witnesses to the alleged offense ought to be present (vs. 19). (*d*) He pleads that his only offense is that he belongs to a perfectly law-abiding sect called **the Way** (vs. 14), and that in particular he believes in a **resurrection** (vss. 15, 21). The parallels between the two halves of the speech are certainly striking and strongly suggest a "doublet."

Can this speech be Paul's own? At most, one feels, only partially. There are certain details inconsistent with Paul's own teaching and character. Vs. 15, with its statement of belief in one resurrection for both the just and the unjust, does not agree with Paul's own doctrine. Vs. 17 might be quoted as evidence of authenticity, for if the reference is to the collection, this is something which Paul stresses in his own letters, but Luke elsewhere entirely omits (but see Exeg., *ad loc.*). And if the words are Paul's own, the implication (vs. 18) that the collection was actually offered in the temple would be, to say the least of it, disingenuous. But even if once again the speech is largely a free composition, it almost certainly follows the main lines of a defense to which Luke himself may well have listened.

24:1. After five days: Presumably counting from Paul's arrival at Caesarea, though this raises chronological difficulties when taken in conjunction with vs. 11, where see note.

2. When he was called, i.e., Paul—as in 25:6, 17, 23—rather than Tertullus. **We enjoy much peace:** Though Tertullus has a thoroughly Roman name, does the use of the first person plural pronoun **we** (and the expression "our law" in vs. 6 [KJV]) imply that he was in fact a Jew, or merely that he is identifying himself with his clients? **This nation** (ἔθνει), i.e., the Jews. The more usual word for the Jewish people is λαός (cf. 10:2; 26:17, 23), the plural ἔθνη being regularly used of the Gentiles. But for the usage here and in vs. 10, cf. Luke 7:5; 23:2. Alternatively it is just possible that ἔθνος was technically used to mean a "province"—here Judea, in 26:4 Cilicia.

5. We have found: The exact phrase used in the charge against Jesus in Luke 23:2. **The sect:** The word is αἵρεσις (whence our "heresy") and was commonly used of the various Greek "schools" of philosophy. Josephus too uses it of the Jewish sects. It is only on the lips of opponents that Luke applies it to Christians—apparently with a contemp-

---

Paul was a public nuisance. He made trouble wherever he went. Certainly no one could deny that. Read the accounts of Paul's visits to city after city and you read the story of riot, public disturbance, and disorder. No government can tolerate that, and Tertullus was smart when he began his charges against Paul on those grounds. He went on, of course, to say that he was "a ringleader of the Nazarene sect," and that "he actually tried to desecrate the temple" (Moffatt). These latter charges probably made much less of an impression on Felix than the first one. Felix was almost certain to be more concerned about the political and social life of the people

6 Who also hath gone about to profane the temple: whom we took, and would have judged according to our law.

7 But the chief captain Lysias came *upon us,* and with great violence took *him* away out of our hands,

8 Commanding his accusers to come unto thee: by examining of whom thyself mayest take knowledge of all these things, whereof we accuse him.

Nazarenes. **6** He even tried to profane the
temple, but we seized him.[x] **8** By examining
him yourself you will be able to learn from him about everything of which we accuse him."

[x] Other ancient authorities add *and we would have judged him according to our law.* [7] *But the chief captain Lysias came and with great violence took him out of our hands,* [8] *commanding his accusers to come before you.*

---

tuous nuance, as we might use "heretic" (cf. vs. 14; 28:22). **The Nazarenes:** Or more strictly "Nazoraeans" (see on 2:22). The word is used in the plural only here. George Foote Moore, who concludes that the word is a place name derived from Nazareth, writes: "In Jewish sources . . . Christians are called *noṣrīm* [*noçrîm*]. . . . Ναζωραῖος would seem therefore to be an attempt to represent the Hebrew adjective *noṣrī* [*noçrî*] or its Aramaic equivalent in Greek letters and grammatical pattern" (*Beginnings of Christianity,* I, 426). Less probably other scholars (J. M. Robertson, W. B. Smith, Arthur Drew), putting much weight on Matt. 2:23, derive both the Jewish name *noçrîm* and the Greek Ναζωραῖος from the Hebrew verb *nāçar,* meaning "to observe," "to watch over," and so "to save." They think that the prophets are quoted as saying, "He shall be called a Nazarene" (Matt. 2:23), not merely because Jesus came from Nazareth, but because he was a "savior" (cf. Matt. 1:21). The name, as applied to a sect, might then be roughly translated "the Salvationists." An equally improbable suggestion is that Matthew's reference (in 2:23) to the prophecy that "he shall be called a Nazoraean" is to be explained by deriving the word from, or at least by a play upon, either *nêçer* (Isa. 11:1, "There shall come forth a *shoot* out of the stem of Jesse"), or *nāzîr* (Judg. 13:7, "The child shall be a *Nazarite* to God." For Nazarites see Num. 6:1-21). But the derivation from Nazareth remains much the most probable.

6. To profane the temple: This in itself, if proved, would have been legal ground for Paul's execution by the Romans (see on 21:28). Paul therefore is particularly concerned to disprove this charge (vs. 18). If the additional words in later MSS, **would have judged according to our law** (KJV), should be genuine, this would again raise acutely the question of the competence of the Sanhedrin to deal with the case on its own authority. But the words, together with the continuation in vss. 7 and 8*a,* are not in the best uncials and therefore probably prove no more than that later scribes were not conscious of any difficulty in Paul's being tried by the Sanhedrin. It must, however, be admitted that the longer Western reading improves the sense, and it is defended by many scholars as genuine. Thus Lake and Cadbury: "Many commentators . . . argue that the Jews would not have rested their case on the admissions to be extracted from Paul. . . . The adjournment of the case by Felix has more point if the Jews had already appealed to the evidence of Lysias. . . . The Jewish case was that Paul was their prisoner. He had defiled the Temple, and by a law which was recognized by the Romans he had incurred the death penalty. It was essential to their case to show that Lysias had exceeded his powers in taking him away" (*Beginnings of Christianity,* IV, 299).

8. By examining: The Greek word suits the shorter better than the longer version, for it is properly used of examining the prisoner rather than the witnesses.

---

than about their religious life. He could hardly afford to have Paul at large if the peace of the land was to be continually disturbed by him.

It is the charge that has been made against "the troublers of Israel" from time immemorial. And not only of Israel, but of every people and every nation. People do not like to be disturbed in their thinking; they do not like to be shaken out of the ruts in which they have traveled for generations; they prefer to go on as they are just so long as they are on top. When someone comes along like Socrates, or Jeremiah, or Paul,

9 And the Jews also assented, saying that these things were so.

10 Then Paul, after that the governor had beckoned unto him to speak, answered, Forasmuch as I know that thou hast been of many years a judge unto this nation, I do the more cheerfully answer for myself:

11 Because that thou mayest understand, that there are yet but twelve days since I went up to Jerusalem for to worship.

12 And they neither found me in the temple disputing with any man, neither raising up the people, neither in the synagogues, nor in the city:

13 Neither can they prove the things whereof they now accuse me.

14 But this I confess unto thee, that after the way which they call heresy, so worship I the God of my fathers, believing all things which are written in the law and in the prophets:

9 The Jews also joined in the charge,
affirming that all this was so.

10 And when the governor had motioned
to him to speak, Paul replied:

"Realizing that for many years you have
been judge over this nation, I cheerfully
make my defense. 11 As you may ascertain,
it is not more than twelve days since I went
up to worship at Jerusalem; 12 and they
did not find me disputing with any one or
stirring up a crowd, either in the temple
or in the synagogues, or in the city.
13 Neither can they prove to you what they
now bring up against me. 14 But this I
admit to you, that according to the Way,
which they call a sect, I worship the God
of our fathers, believing everything laid
down by the law or written in the prophets,

---

10. For many years: Felix had been procurator only since A.D. 52; but it seems that he may have acted as military prefect in the province for some time previously.

11. Not more than twelve days: Taken in conjunction with vs. 1 ("after five days") this raises difficulties, for Luke's narrative of events since Paul **went up to worship at Jerusalem** requires more than twelve days. Indeed, if 21:27 means that Paul's arrest took place "seven days" after he associated himself with the vows of the four men, at least sixteen or seventeen days are necessary. Loisy seizes on the discrepancy as a chance to cut out of the diary source those events which he believes to have no basis in history—e.g., Paul's appearance before the Sanhedrin and the plot of the Jews. Others think that the figure twelve is arbitrarily reached by adding together the "seven days" of 21:27 and the "five days" of 24:1. The truth probably is that Paul is simply speaking in round numbers —as we might say "about a fortnight."

12. Stirring up a crowd (ἐπίστασιν ποιοῦντα ὄχλου): The first Greek word occurs elsewhere in the N.T. only in II Cor. 11:28, where it is translated "the daily *pressure* upon me of my anxiety for all the churches."

14. According to the Way: This translation is certainly correct, ἡ ὁδός being used as a name for the Christian community (see on 9:2). The translation **after the way which they call heresy** (KJV) is impossible, for ὁδός never means "manner." **Believing everything laid down by the law:** This can hardly be Paul's own statement in view of such passages as Gal. 3:15-25; Rom. 7; 10:4—which declare the law to be a thing of the past.

---

or Lincoln, who will not let them settle down in the comfort of their preconceived ideas, they call him "a perfect pest" and do their best to get rid of him. In the United States, when the question of civil rights for men and women of every color and creed came to a head, men who dared to trouble the people about it, to demand that they think seriously about it in view of revising their long-established practices, have been treated like public pests, just as Paul was treated like a pest, and their future seemed to have no more earthly certainty about it than had the future of Jesus or Paul.

10-21. ***Paul's Defense.***—The content and manner of Paul's defense was much the same as it had been on other occasions, notably on the steps of the temple in Jerusalem (22:1-21), and there is no need to repeat what has been said about it. One further comment, however, might be made about this particular defense—it was shrewd. Paul had recovered his composure which he had lost temporarily under the provocation of the high priest. His mind never operated in a more orderly fashion than it did on this occasion. Paul knew that his opponent was a lawyer, and he answered his charges in such a

15 And have hope toward God, which they themselves also allow, that there shall be a resurrection of the dead, both of the just and unjust.

16 And herein do I exercise myself, to have always a conscience void of offense toward God, and *toward* men.

17 Now after many years I came to bring alms to my nation, and offerings.

18 Whereupon certain Jews from Asia found me purified in the temple, neither with multitude, nor with tumult.

15 having a hope in God which these themselves accept, that there will be a resurrection of both the just and the unjust. 16 So
I always take pains to have a clear conscience toward God and toward men.
17 Now after some years I came to bring
to my nation alms and offerings. 18 As I
was doing this, they found me purified in
the temple, without any crowd or tumult.

---

15. For the conjunction of the ideas of **hope** and **resurrection** see on 23:6. This verse no more than the last reflects the true mind of Paul. The idea of one single **resurrection of both the just and the unjust** is in line with Jewish eschatological teaching as expressed, e.g., in Dan. 12:2. But Paul himself in I Cor. 15 seems to expect either a resurrection for Christians only, or else one for Christians at Christ's coming and one for others at "the End." In the Revelation too there are two resurrections (Rev. 20:4-15). And in any case Paul's faith centered on the resurrection of Jesus, which the Jews denied, not on some universal resurrection **which these themselves accept.**

17-18. Alms and offerings: Presumably by **alms** is meant the collection which Paul had brought to the Jerusalem Christians from the provincial churches (see on 20:1-4), and which is elsewhere not alluded to in Acts. It is possible that the **offerings** are those in connection with the vow ritual **in the temple** (21:26), and that it is merely the compressed writing which leaves the impression that **alms and offerings** together refer to one project. As the words read, the implication appears to be that Paul made an offering of alms to his nation and that the Jews **found** him **doing this—in the temple.** Paul might quite honestly have represented a collection for Christian brethren as alms for his nation; but it would have been incredibly disingenuous to try to create the impression that it was a temple offering.

Jews from Asia: Presumably the Ephesians who had recognized their fellow townsman Trophimus and "supposed that Paul had brought him into the temple" (21:27-29). The grammatical construction breaks off in an anacoluthon which, it must be confessed, is typically Pauline.

---

way as to outclass the lawyer on his own ground. Paul, like Tertullus, paid a compliment to Felix, but it was more restrained and therefore lacked the suggestion of insincerity. He went on to say that the charges made against him could not be proved and he then proceeded to marshal the facts: he had been in Jerusalem only twelve days; he had had no arguments with anyone either in the temple or in the city itself; he was the cause of no riot. To be sure, he worshiped God after the manner of the way called Christian, but that did not diminish in any way his loyalty to the Jewish scriptures and the Jewish hope. He had been away from the city for several years and had returned only to bring financial relief to his people. The men who made the trouble for him were Asiatic Jews who were not present to press their complaint.

If Paul admitted before the Sanhedrin (but see Exeg.) that he had possibly made a mistake in dividing the group by bringing up the question of the resurrection, he was playing one of his trump cards. We are not at all sure that it was a mistake for Paul to do what he did before the Sanhedrin, but we are sure that if he thought he had made a mistake, he could have done nothing better than to say so frankly, as he did before Felix. Honesty always disarms a man's opponents. The men who claim everything are often suspected of having nothing, whereas the men who are willing to admit their shortages are more often than not granted an allowance of credit. Some of us who live in democratic countries long for a political leader who will promise no more than he knows he can reasonably hope to fulfill, and who will claim no more perfection of performance than the record legitimately allows. It would seem that a man who dared to tell the truth about

19 Who ought to have been here before thee, and object, if they had aught against me.

20 Or else let these same *here* say, if they have found any evildoing in me, while I stood before the council,

21 Except it be for this one voice, that I cried standing among them, Touching the resurrection of the dead I am called in question by you this day.

22 And when Felix heard these things, having more perfect knowledge of *that* way, he deferred them, and said, When Lysias the chief captain shall come down, I will know the uttermost of your matter.

23 And he commanded a centurion to keep Paul, and to let *him* have liberty, and that he should forbid none of his acquaintance to minister or come unto him.

But some Jews from Asia — 19 they ought
to be here before you and to make an
accusation, if they have anything against
me. 20 Or else let these men themselves say
what wrongdoing they found when I stood
before the council, 21 except this one thing
which I cried out while standing among
them, 'With respect to the resurrection of
the dead I am on trial before you this day.' "
22 But Felix, having a rather accurate
knowledge of the Way, put them off, saying,
"When Lys'i-as the tribune comes down, I
will decide your case." 23 Then he gave
orders to the centurion that he should be
kept in custody but should have some
liberty, and that none of his friends should
be prevented from attending to his needs.

---

21. This verse is sometimes taken as an indication that Paul realized the disingenuousness of his attempt to divide the court by invoking the resurrection, and admitted that therein he might perhaps have done wrong. Much more probably the words are ironical: "I have done no wrong, unless it is considered wrong to profess belief in the resurrection!" Incidentally Paul also makes the point that the charge against him is purely doctrinal, and therefore a matter of which a Roman court should take no cognizance.

22. **Having a rather accurate knowledge of the Way:** Possibly because he had been instructed by his Jewish wife Drusilla whom, perhaps for this very reason, Felix associates with himself at the second hearing.

23. **Some liberty** (ἄνεσιν): What the Romans called *custodia liberior.* Paul would be permitted to communicate with his friends and receive certain privileges. Luke again stresses the "indulgence" (a possible translation of ἄνεσις) with which the Roman authorities treated Paul. The **custody** would be military confinement, which would safeguard the accused pending trial without subjecting him to the discomfort of a public jail.

---

himself and his actions would win the confidence of the people in a way that no other man could. But as things go now, the men who tell the tallest tales seem to get the biggest vote.

There was, then, both in the case of Tertullus and Paul a basic honesty. Neither one indulged in that favorite sport of beating around the bush. They both came straight to the point; they wasted no words; they counted upon no ambiguities of thought or speech. The difference between the two was that Tertullus was on the side of a cause that was already lost, and Paul was on the side of a cause against which the gates of hell shall not prevail.

22-27. *Felix and Paul.*—The character of Felix is interesting as a study in contrasts. According to all the secular histories of the time, Felix was not much better than a scoundrel. Tacitus draws a picture of a man who would stoop to almost anything for personal gain. And yet according to Luke, Felix behaves about as well as you could expect a political ruler to behave. He was absolutely fair and courteous to Paul. He refused to make a hasty judgment upon the case, and in the meantime he saw to it that Paul was made comfortable, even though he was kept in custody. The moral life of Felix would not bear too close an investigation, and the wife that he happened to have at this particular time he had taken from another man. This wife, Drusilla, also had an interest in Paul; Felix sent for Paul in order that he and Drusilla might both hear what he had to say about the religion of Jesus. When Paul began to talk about morality, he was promptly though politely dismissed. That was a sore subject for both of them, and they preferred to leave it alone. On other occasions, however, Felix had

24 And after certain days, when Felix came with his wife Drusilla, which was a Jewess, he sent for Paul, and heard him concerning the faith in Christ.

25 And as he reasoned of righteousness, temperance, and judgment to come, Felix trembled, and answered, Go thy way for this time; when I have a convenient season, I will call for thee.

26 He hoped also that money should have been given him of Paul, that he might loose him: wherefore he sent for him the oftener, and communed with him.

27 But after two years Porcius Festus came into Felix' room: and Felix, willing to show the Jews a pleasure, left Paul bound.

24 After some days Felix came with his
wife Dru-sil'la, who was a Jewess; and he
sent for Paul and heard him speak upon
faith in Christ Jesus. 25 And as he argued
about justice and self-control and future
judgment, Felix was alarmed and said, "Go
away for the present; when I have an opportunity I will summon you." 26 At the
same time he hoped that money would be
given him by Paul. So he sent for him often
and conversed with him. 27 But when two
years had elapsed, Felix was succeeded by
Por'cius Festus; and desiring to do the
Jews a favor, Felix left Paul in prison.

---

24. Felix came: Does this imply that after adjourning the hearing he had been absent from Caesarea for **some days? Drusilla,** according to Josephus, was the sister of Herod Agrippa II, whom Felix, with the assistance of the Cypriote magician Atomus (see on 13:8), had seduced from her first husband Aziz, king of Emesa. Tacitus, certainly incorrectly, speaks of her as the granddaughter of Antony and Cleopatra (Josephus *Antiquities* XX. 7. 1-2; Tacitus *History* V. 9). As an explanation of why Drusilla appeared at the hearing with Felix the Western text (here only in the Harclean margin) adds, "And she asked to see Paul and hear the word. So desiring to satisfy her he sent for Paul."

25-26. In view of his corrupt administration and marital irregularities, when Paul lectured him on **justice and self-control and future judgment,** it is little wonder that **Felix was alarmed! When I have an opportunity:** This need not be taken—as is suggested by the translation **convenient season** (KJV)—as a mere pretext for refusing to face up to Paul's moral challenge. Luke is concerned to show that the Roman, like Sergius Paulus (13:12), was genuinely impressed by Paul's preaching—so much so indeed that **he sent for him often and conversed with him.** The taking of **money** from prisoners as a bribe for release was expressly forbidden by law; but it is quite in keeping with what we know of Felix' character. The habit was so common (see, e.g., Josephus *Jewish War* II. 14. 1) that it is rash to conclude that Felix necessarily supposed Paul to be better off than the general run of prisoners.

27. When two years had elapsed: This might be taken as meaning after Felix had been two years in office—an interpretation which fits in better with the little evidence we have concerning the date of Felix' recall, and which would have important results for the dating of the last period of Paul's life (see *Beginnings of Christianity,* V, 471). More commonly the meaning is taken to be that Paul's trial was adjourned for two years until the advent of Festus. For the bearing of this timetable on the chronology of Acts see on 25:1. **Felix was succeeded:** It was the complaints of the Jews which ultimately

---

long conversations with Paul, and over a period of two years saw him frequently.

Felix was in the dilemma which almost all public officials are in. He had certain basic instincts that were good. They had never been completely smothered. On the other hand he lived and worked in a world of ruthless competition where ideals had no chance at all against the strong winds of private and selfish enterprise. The picture is almost a tragic one. Felix, the man, stands upon the edge of Christianity, lingers upon its threshold, cannot resist the curiosity to find out what he can about it, gives to its most ardent and notable exponent every courtesy and consideration which it is within his power to give. Felix, the man in public office, cannot afford to do much more than think about Christianity and discuss it academically;

25 Now when Festus was come into the province, after three days he ascended from Caesarea to Jerusalem.

25 Now when Festus had come into his province, after three days he went

led to Felix' being recalled in disgrace by Nero (Josephus *Antiquities* XX. 8. 9); he therefore had the more reason for **desiring to do the Jews a favor,** or perhaps better, "to ingratiate himself with the Jews" (so Lake and Cadbury, *Beginnings of Christianity,* IV, 306); but he evidently failed to do so. **Left Paul in prison:** The Western text adds "on account of Drusilla"—evidently with the idea that Paul by his lecture had antagonized her. That Paul was kept waiting for a decision in his case for no less than two years has seemed incredible to some recent critics, who accordingly, as already noted, take the reference to be to Felix' tenure of office. But so far as we know, it was left entirely to a magistrate's own discretion to decide when a case should be heard, so that Paul's treatment cannot be considered exceptional. Apart from his account of Paul's appearances before the various authorities, Luke tells us nothing about these two years of captivity at Caesarea—a silence which is the more surprising as he was almost certainly at Paul's side during the whole period. The reason probably is that these years seemed to Luke to contribute nothing to his main theme of the expansion of Christianity. None of Paul's letters was assigned in antiquity to this period, though some modern scholars so assign one or more of the "captivity epistles." But this theory has met with little acceptance, and it would be precarious to use these letters as sources for speculation concerning Paul's activities and experiences while at Caesarea. It is interesting to note that Streeter (*Four Gospels,* p. 218) believes that during these two years at Caesarea Luke not only prepared part of the "travel document" of Acts, but also compiled the notes which went to compose the special Lukan material of his Gospel—the material which, when later combined with Q, made up, according to Streeter, Proto-Luke or the first shorter edition of the Gospel.

b) Paul and Festus (25:1-27)

Paul's appearances before Festus and in particular his appeal to Caesar raise some difficult questions:

(*a*) What exactly did such an appeal involve? *Provocatio,* or the right of a citizen to appeal against the verdict of a magistrate, dated from very early days and was confirmed by the *Lex Valeria* of 509 B.C. The appeal was originally to the people as a whole, then to the "tribunes of the people," and finally to the emperor, who was vested with tribunitian power and thus constituted the supreme court of appeal. Presumably from the moment of appeal all proceedings in the lower courts were stayed. Though originally the right of *provocatio* was limited to the area called *domi*—within the walls of Rome and a mile beyond them—it seems certain that in Paul's time it had been extended to all citizens of the empire.

he cannot commit himself nor can he separate himself from the ways of the world in which he must win his political living. Personally there was a great deal that could be said in his favor. Publicly he belonged to the group of political leaders who rise no higher than the level of their lowest supporters.

How many men in public life today are in the same dilemma! Their personal and their public life are split in two. They do not wish to carry over into their personal life the standards which prevail in their public life, and yet they do not dare carry into the public life the motives and desires which they secretly cherish in their personal life. Like the hummingbird, they hover above the nectar of life, but they never come to rest in the real richness of it. Finally they are undone. Felix was recalled to Rome for mismanagement of the government. "How are the mighty fallen!" And how great their memorial might have been!

25:1-12. ***Paul Appeals to Caesar.***—Felix was replaced by Festus, who, when he arrived in his new province, found among the items of unfinished business the case of the Jews against Paul. He saw through the plot of the high priests who wanted him to have Paul sent down from Caesarea to Jerusalem so that they might kill him en route. He let the matter rest until he himself went to Caesarea, and then he sent for Paul. The charges that the Jews made against him were the same, and as before, Paul

(*b*) What now was the policy of the Jews? Luke hints at a second plot to murder Paul en route to Jerusalem. But this is almost certainly secondary. Their real object was to secure that Paul should once again come under Jewish jurisdiction, and they hoped to take advantage of the new governor's inexperience in order to gain their end. Nor did Festus at first give a definite refusal. He invited Paul's accusers to come and lay their case before him according to regular procedure at his court at Caesarea. There it would be decided whether or not the Sanhedrin was a competent court. As a result of the preliminary hearing, Festus then suggested to Paul that he himself (**before me,** vs. 9) should preside over an investigation at Jerusalem—probably because he felt that it would be possible to obtain more accurate information on the spot.

(*c*) Why then at this particular juncture did Paul appeal? Clearly, in the first instance, to escape the risk of being handed over to Jewish jurisdiction, to which Festus seemed inclined to commit him. As a Roman citizen he has a right to a Roman trial: **I am standing before Caesar's tribunal, where I ought to be tried** (vs. 10). Such a claim Festus could hardly have rejected, as Luke realizes when he somewhat naïvely pictures Festus asking Paul's consent to the transference of the investigation to Jerusalem. Why then does Paul now appeal from the jurisdiction of the procurator to that of Caesar himself? He can hardly have taken the decisive step, as is sometimes suggested, merely because he saw thereby a quick and easy way of achieving his desire to reach Rome—though doubtless Luke traces here as elsewhere the working of Providence. The human reason was almost certainly because he felt that, contrary to the impression left by Luke's narrative, Festus was already taking an unfavorable view of his case.

We may perhaps conjecture that when Felix was recalled, in his desire to "ingratiate himself with the Jews," at whose instigation we know he was subsequently prosecuted at Rome, he not only left Paul a captive but may actually have handed over the affair to Festus with a report hostile to Paul, which caused his case definitely to take a turn for the worse. This would help to explain why it was that, after the case had been in abeyance so long, immediately after Festus' arrival it developed unfavorably for Paul—though Luke as usual lays responsibility for the new offensive on the Jews. Whatever his motive, Festus was clearly contemplating an investigation at Jerusalem. Paul knew that the change of venue to the hostile atmosphere of the Jewish capital must seriously imperil his cause. True, he would still be under Roman jurisdiction, though it is not clear exactly what is the implication of the words **be tried on these charges before me** (vs. 9). Historically it is improbable that a session of the Sanhedrin could have been contemplated at which Festus was to participate or even preside. Paul was now being held, not only on a religious charge, but on the definite political one of being a dangerous insurrectionary. The implication is that Festus expressed willingness to let the Sanhedrin investigate the religious charges, while he reserved to himself the political charge and the pronouncement of the final verdict. That the political charge was the principal one appears from the fact that, though the Jews apparently did not follow up the case, it still went forward to trial at Rome. Paul knew, then, that after inevitable condemnation by the Sanhedrin, he would be remitted back to Festus for final judgment—but with his case irreparably blackened as a result of the Jewish verdict. He therefore appealed, not merely to avoid Jewish jurisdiction, but to escape the governor's unfavorable verdict, with which he feared himself to be faced.

---

pleaded "not guilty." Since the charges against him could not be proved, Festus was left in a difficult position. He wanted to keep in the good graces of the Jews, and yet he could not in clear conscience condemn Paul. He knew that he could not force a Roman citizen to submit to a provincial court, so he asked Paul if he would be willing to go to Jerusalem and be tried by him there.

At that point Paul's patience was exhausted. The prospect of another trial was more than he would face. The case had been in the courts for two years and the hearings had been innumerable. He refused to go through it again. Right then and there he exercised his ultimate right as a citizen of Rome: he appealed to the emperor. If the case had to be tried again, it should be tried before the highest authority in

2 Then the high priest and the chief of the Jews informed him against Paul, and besought him,

up to Jerusalem from Caes-a-re'a.
2 And the chief priests and the principal men of the Jews informed him against Paul; and

It is frequently argued that the privileged treatment received by Paul at Caesarea, and the declaration of his innocence ascribed by Luke to Lysias, Agrippa, and even Festus, prove that they saw no substance in the case against him. Yet the fact remains that Paul would never have appealed to Caesar—with all the trouble, expense, and delay which such an appeal involved—had he not felt that he was faced with a virtually certain conviction. At Jerusalem and Caesarea there would be many fanatical witnesses ranged against him; at a distance his hope of acquittal would be much greater. Luke's narrative, though it approximately follows the facts, is undoubtedly colored by his tendency to insist that Paul was never in danger of conviction by Roman authority. Hence the implication that the appeal was due not to the imminence of conviction by Festus, but to the desire to escape the danger of being handed back to Jewish jurisdiction. Of this danger there can have been no question, but the final verdict in any case must have lain with Festus.

(1) Paul Before Festus (25:1-12)

25:1. From the little that we know of Porcius **Festus** it appears that he was a prudent and honorable man, and in happier circumstances might have proved a successful ruler. But he was charged with an impossible task; after Felix' maladministration the province was a hotbed of bigotry, faction, and intrigue, and before his term of office had expired Festus died in despair. Outside Acts, Festus is mentioned only by Josephus (*Jewish War* II. 14. 1; *Antiquities* XX. 8. 9).

Had come into his province: Or possibly "had entered upon his office." The Greek word (ἐπαρχία) may have either a geographical or an administrative meaning. The date of Festus' accession to office depends upon how we interpret the data relating to the recall of Felix (see Josephus *Antiquities* XX. 8). Lake's conclusion is that "the summer of 55 is the most probable year for the entry of Festus into office and should be regarded as the year in the autumn of which Paul left Caesarea for Rome, which he reached in the spring of 56. But it is possible that Festus did not reach his province until the year after the recall of Felix, so that Paul may have left Caesarea in 56 and reached Rome in 57" (*Beginnings of Christianity,* V, 466-67). Lake's dating greatly contracts the usual estimate of the length of Paul's stay at Caesarea, and it can be reconciled with Luke's account only if the "two years" in 24:27 refer not to Paul's imprisonment but to Felix' term of office. It is possible too only if the "famine visit" and the "council visit" are identified, and both dated as early as A.D. 46, as otherwise the period between the council and Paul's last visit to Jerusalem would be impossibly compressed. Lake also brings Paul to Rome much earlier than is usually supposed—the traditional date being 60 or 61. But the evidence of Josephus is so confused that it would be rash to use the accession of Festus as a key point for the dating of Paul's closing years. **From Caesarea to Jerusalem:** Caesarea was the seat of civil government; Jerusalem, the

the empire. Festus did the only thing he could do; he granted Paul's request, and probably was relieved to have the burden shifted to someone else.

We have not enough facts to say with any certainty what caused the delay in the prosecution of Paul's case. All we can say is there was a delay that seems to us inexcusable. There was no more evidence against Paul at the end of two years than there was the day he was arrested. It was a case of putting off the moment of decision. Perhaps no one wanted to assume the responsibility for it. Whatever the reason, the delay went on, and Paul's life was to that extent limited and bound. Unfortunately not all the victims of legal delay have the inner resources that Paul had which enabled him to live above the harassing circumstances of his life. What he did from day to day we do not know, but we know that imprisonment did not

3 And desired favor against him, that he would send for him to Jerusalem, laying wait in the way to kill him.

4 But Festus answered, that Paul should be kept at Caesarea, and that he himself would depart shortly *thither.*

5 Let them therefore, said he, which among you are able, go down with *me,* and accuse this man, if there be any wickedness in him.

6 And when he had tarried among them more than ten days, he went down unto Caesarea; and the next day sitting on the judgment seat commanded Paul to be brought.

7 And when he was come, the Jews which came down from Jerusalem stood round about, and laid many and grievous complaints against Paul, which they could not prove.

8 While he answered for himself, Neither against the law of the Jews, neither against the temple, nor yet against Caesar, have I offended any thing at all.

they urged him,
3 asking as a favor to have
the man sent to Jerusalem, planning an
ambush to kill him on the way.
4 Festus
replied that Paul was being kept at Caes-a-re′a, and that he himself intended to go
there shortly.
5 "So," said he, "let the men
of authority among you go down with me,
and if there is anything wrong about the
man, let them accuse him."

6 When he had stayed among them not
more than eight or ten days, he went down
to Caes-a-re′a; and the next day he took his
seat on the tribunal and ordered Paul to
be brought.
7 And when he had come, the
Jews who had gone down from Jerusalem
stood about him, bringing against him
many serious charges which they could not
prove.
8 Paul said in his defense, "Neither
against the law of the Jews, nor against
the temple, nor against Caesar have I of-

---

religious capital which Festus, in order to conciliate his unruly subjects, visits at the first opportunity.

3. Asking as a favor: The Greek word is χάριν which seems to be related to the use of χαρίζεσθαι in vs. 16 with the meaning "to give up to judgment." Lake and Cadbury make the attractive suggestion that here "χάρις has a legal meaning such as 'rule' or 'order,'" and compare the Cambridge technical term "a Grace of the Senate." The point would be that the Jews asked Festus to issue an official "order" handing over Paul to their own jurisdiction at Jerusalem.

5. Men of authority (δυνατόι): Or possibly "men of ability," i.e., such as would be competent to take part in the inquiry. The word is frequently used of power in debate (cf. 7:22; Luke 24:19). **If there is anything wrong,** literally "out of place," "amiss"—an obvious euphemism.

8. Against the temple: This was the basic charge (21:27-28) out of which had been developed the more general religious charge of hostility to the law, and the political charge of fomenting insurrection.

---

thwart his spirit; for before, when he and Silas were in jail, they sang hymns; and on other occasions when the days were long, Paul turned them to good effect by writing letters that are still read and treasured by the Christian world.

The fact that there was a higher authority to which he might appeal must have given Paul courage, even though the authority was vested for the moment in a man of no greater stature than Nero. The most sacred right of an individual is the right to be heard again and to have his case reconsidered by an impartial judge. Mistakes are made, new evidence is discovered, differences in judgment are inevitable, so that it is hard to pronounce a final judgment upon the merits of an individual who stands before the law. The fact that he has the right to carry his case to the highest authority in the land gives him the assurance that the gates are not permanently closed against him and that he is not the victim of human malice or mistaken judgment.

It is good to remember that above all the earthly courts there is a higher court, and that over and above all the judges of the world there is the "Judge eternal, throned in splendor." Many men and women have been misjudged in the courts of the world; their motives

9 But Festus, willing to do the Jews a
pleasure, answered Paul, and said, Wilt
thou go up to Jerusalem, and there be
judged of these things before me?
10 Then said Paul, I stand at Caesar's
judgment seat, where I ought to be judged:
to the Jews have I done no wrong, as thou
very well knowest.
11 For if I be an offender, or have committed any thing worthy of death, I refuse
not to die: but if there be none of these
things whereof these accuse me, no man
may deliver me unto them. I appeal unto
Caesar.
12 Then Festus, when he had conferred
with the council, answered, Hast thou appealed unto Caesar? unto Caesar shalt thou
go.
13 And after certain days king Agrippa
and Bernice came unto Caesarea to salute
Festus.

fended at all." 9 But Festus, wishing to do
the Jews a favor, said to Paul, "Do you wish
to go up to Jerusalem, and there be tried
on these charges before me?" 10 But Paul
said, "I am standing before Caesar's tribunal, where I ought to be tried; to the Jews
I have done no wrong, as you know very
well. 11 If then I am a wrongdoer, and
have committed anything for which I deserve to die, I do not seek to escape death;
but if there is nothing in their charges
against me, no one can give me up to
them. I appeal to Caesar." 12 Then Festus,
when he had conferred with his council,
answered, "You have appealed to Caesar;
to Caesar you shall go."
13 Now when some days had passed,
Agrippa the king and Ber-ni'ce arrived at

---

9. Do the Jews a favor: Or "to ingratiate himself with the Jews" (cf. 24:27). But Festus may well have had the more worthy motive also of collecting more accurate information on the spot (cf. vs. 20). **Before me:** See the discussion on pp. 314-15. The point is that Festus guarantees that Paul will still be ultimately under Roman jurisdiction.

10. I am standing before Caesar's tribunal: Paul protests against being handed over even temporarily to Jewish jurisdiction. The provincial tribunal, before which he is already standing, derives its power by delegation from Caesar himself, and as a Roman citizen he **ought to be tried** by Caesar's representative and none other.

11. I do not seek to escape death: Or more literally, "I am not begging myself off from dying." It has been noted that Josephus, on the occasion described in the note on 23:7, is recorded as saying, "I refuse not to die if justice so require" (*Life,* 29). Is this another reminiscence of Josephus on the part of Luke? Surely most improbable! **I appeal to Caesar:** See the full discussion on pp. 314-15.

12. His council: His chief officers who would be acting as assessors at the investigation. Apparently the appeal was not allowed automatically. Festus first consulted his assessors and then "decided" (vs. 25) to grant it.

(2) Festus Consults with Agrippa (25:13-27)

Many critics have found the narrative of Paul's appearance before Festus and Agrippa, for which this section prepares the way, frankly incredible. It is argued that the story is nothing more than an hors d'oeuvre served up after the legal process at Caesarea is in fact complete (so, e.g., Goguel, *Introduction au N.T.,* III, 318). Its only purpose is to introduce a third account of Paul's conversion, to represent the apostle as delivering his

---

have been misunderstood; their actions have been misinterpreted; their lives mistakenly condemned. Let them never forget that there is another Judge, in whose judgments there is no error, and whose justice is moderated by love. It is in that judgment alone that we ultimately stand. It is for the divine approval alone that we daily strive. And when justice as it is administered in the courts of the world goes askew, there is a justice in heaven to which our appeal can be made and before which we stand in the pure light of the truth. In that court how many human verdicts have been reversed!

13-27. ***Festus Calls In Agrippa.***—Agrippa was a royal personage. To begin with, he was a Jew; but he was a Jew with a Roman back-

14 And when they had been there many days, Festus declared Paul's cause unto the king, saying, There is a certain man left in bonds by Felix:

15 About whom, when I was at Jerusalem, the chief priests and the elders of the Jews informed *me*, desiring *to have* judgment against him.

16 To whom I answered, It is not the manner of the Romans to deliver any man to die, before that he which is accused have the accusers face to face, and have

Caes-a-re'a to welcome Festus. 14 And as
they stayed there many days, Festus laid
Paul's case before the king, saying, "There
is a man left prisoner by Felix; 15 and when
I was at Jerusalem, the chief priests and
the elders of the Jews gave information
about him, asking for sentence against him.
16 I answered them that it was not the
custom of the Romans to give up any one
before the accused met the accusers face

---

defense and declaring his innocence before a new authority in the person of Agrippa, who could be considered to be both competent as regards the facts and also impartial. The prediction too that Paul should "carry [Jesus'] name before the Gentiles and kings" (9:15) is now in process of fulfillment. We may admit perhaps the apologetic coloring of the narrative, without however questioning the substantial accuracy of the main facts. Certainly the pretext (vss. 26-27) that Festus desired help in formulating a charge to Caesar appears somewhat lacking in verisimilitude. After all this time the charges must surely have been clearly enough set forth, as must also the lines of Paul's defense. It seems probable too that the private talk between Festus and Agrippa must be Luke's free composition, for it is difficult to see how he can have ascertained what transpired between them. But provided that we assume that this is not a regular trial, but rather a semi-official inquiry, there is no reason why we should doubt that the vivid piece of drama is securely founded on fact.

As elsewhere in Acts—cf. the story of Cornelius—we have in vss. 14-21 a second slightly variant account, put on the lips of one of the actors, of a matter already described by the author himself—in this case Festus' consultation with the Jews about Paul's case (cf. vss. 2-5). Whereas in vs. 3 the Jews ask for Paul to be "sent to Jerusalem," according to Festus in vs. 15 they asked for **sentence against him.** He also adds that his reason for declining the request was that Paul must have a scrupulously fair and legal trial (vs. 16). His reason for suggesting a transference of the case to Jerusalem is to collect more information (vs. 20), not merely "to do the Jews a favor" (vs. 9). Festus naturally puts the best possible complexion on his own actions. His speech should be compared with Lysias' letter to Felix (23:26-30). In both Luke sets forth how he would have his readers believe that Paul's case appeared to the Roman authorities.

13. Agrippa the king is Herod Agrippa II, the son of that other Herod who has gone down in history as the first royal persecutor of the church (ch. 12). Agrippa II, though in high favor at Rome, had not received his father's kingdom of Judea; but in A.D. 53 he had received the former tetrarchies of Philip and Lysanias, to which were later added some towns in Galilee and Perea. He was also entrusted with the custody of the temple treasure and the appointment of the high priest. He might therefore in Jewish affairs be considered a colleague of Festus and one whom the latter might well consult. **Bernice,** his sister, was the daughter of Agrippa I and elder sister of Drusilla (24:24). She was a fascinating but utterly profligate woman, and eventually became the mistress of the Emperor Titus. Yet once she displayed real magnanimity by appearing as a suppliant with bare feet to intercede for the Jews, and narrowly escaped with her life from the brutal procurator Gessius Florus (Josephus *Jewish War* II. 15. 1). **To welcome** (ἀσπασάμενος): This is the reading of the best uncials and is an interesting example of the "timeless" use of the aorist participle, which here practically serves to express purpose.

16. Not the custom of the Romans: This principle is laid down in the Roman *Digest* and is of course the basis of all criminal justice.

license to answer for himself concerning the crime laid against him.

17 Therefore, when they were come hither, without any delay on the morrow I sat on the judgment seat, and commanded the man to be brought forth.

18 Against whom when the accusers stood up, they brought none accusation of such things as I supposed:

19 But had certain questions against him of their own superstition, and of one Jesus, which was dead, whom Paul affirmed to be alive.

20 And because I doubted of such manner of questions, I asked *him* whether he would go to Jerusalem, and there be judged of these matters.

21 But when Paul had appealed to be reserved unto the hearing of Augustus, I commanded him to be kept till I might send him to Caesar.

22 Then Agrippa said unto Festus, I would also hear the man myself. To-morrow, said he, thou shalt hear him.

to face, and had opportunity to make his
defense concerning the charge laid against
him. 17 When therefore they came together
here, I made no delay, but on the next day
took my seat on the tribunal and ordered
the man to be brought in. 18 When the
accusers stood up, they brought no charge
in his case of such evils as I supposed; 19 but
they had certain points of dispute with
him about their own superstition and about
one Jesus, who was dead, but whom Paul
asserted to be alive. 20 Being at a loss how
to investigate these questions, I asked
whether he wished to go to Jerusalem and
be tried there regarding them. 21 But when
Paul had appealed to be kept in custody
for the decision of the emperor, I commanded him to be held until I could send
him to Caesar." 22 And Agrippa said to
Festus, "I should like to hear the man myself." "Tomorrow," said he, "you shall
hear him."

19. Points of dispute (ζητήματα): This is a better translation than **questions** (KJV; cf. 18:15; 26:3). So ζήτησις in 15:2, 7 means not so much an "inquiry" as an "argument" or "debate." **Superstition** (δεισιδαιμονία): The word here probably has a contemptuous flavor (but see on 17:22), which seems a little out of place when addressed to Agrippa, who at least outwardly professed the Jewish religion. Hence it is just possible that τῆς ἰδίας refers to Paul rather than to his accusers, and that we ought to translate "his own superstition."

20. Being at a loss (ἀπορούμενος δὲ ἐγώ): The translation does not do justice to the emphasis on the first person singular "I." Festus insists that he himself took the initiative in suggesting that the case be heard at Jerusalem, because he wished more information, not because of pressure from the Jews. But there is no mention here of the promise that the inquiry is to be "before me" (vs. 9).

21. The decision (διάγνωσιν): As Deissmann has pointed out, this is a good example of the use of "technical terms of contemporary constitutional law which by accident are not known to us from other sources until later. . . . Διάγνωσις is a technical expression for the Latin *cognitio,* but is not found elsewhere until . . . the end of the 2nd cent. A.D. in the title of an official in a Roman inscription" (*Light from the Ancient East,* p. 346 n.). **Send him to Caesar.** This might perhaps better be translated "remand him" (Lake and Cadbury).

22. I should like: If, more literally, we translate "I had a desire," we shall have an interesting parallel with another Herod who "had long desired to see [Jesus]" (Luke 23:8).

ground and a regal setting. When he and his sister arrived in Caesarea, Festus told him about Paul, and asked him to hear the case and give him the benefit of his counsel. Agrippa was glad to hear Paul. He had almost certainly heard about him, and as a cultivated Jew he would naturally be interested in this man who had traveled so widely and stirred up so much trouble. So the hearing was arranged. It had no legal status whatever; it was simply for the benefit of Festus and Agrippa. But it provided a magnificent setting for Paul's final defense

23 And on the morrow, when Agrippa was come, and Bernice, with great pomp, and was entered into the place of hearing, with the chief captains, and principal men of the city, at Festus' commandment Paul was brought forth.

24 And Festus said, King Agrippa, and all men which are here present with us, ye see this man, about whom all the multitude of the Jews have dealt with me, both at Jerusalem, and *also* here, crying that he ought not to live any longer.

25 But when I found that he had committed nothing worthy of death, and that he himself hath appealed to Augustus, I have determined to send him.

26 Of whom I have no certain thing to write unto my lord. Wherefore I have brought him forth before you, and specially before thee, O king Agrippa, that, after examination had, I might have somewhat to write.

27 For it seemeth to me unreasonable to send a prisoner, and not withal to signify the crimes *laid* against him.

23 So on the morrow Agrippa and Ber-
ni'ce came with great pomp, and they entered the audience hall with the military
tribunes and the prominent men of the
city. Then by command of Festus Paul was
brought in. 24 And Festus said, "King
Agrippa and all who are present with us,
you see this man about whom the whole
Jewish people petitioned me, both at Jerusalem and here, shouting that he ought
not to live any longer. 25 But I found that
he had done nothing deserving death; and
as he himself appealed to the emperor, I
decided to send him. 26 But I have nothing
definite to write to my lord about him.
Therefore I have brought him before you,
and especially before you, King Agrippa,
that, after we have examined him, I may
have something to write. 27 For it seems to
me unreasonable, in sending a prisoner, not
to indicate the charges against him."

---

23. Tribunes and the prominent men: These play much the same part as the "council" or "assessors" in vs. 12. They are called in 26:30 "those who were sitting with them." The usual technical Greek term would be σύνεδροι.

24. The whole Jewish people (πλῆθος): Strictly speaking it was only the Jewish leaders who had so **petitioned** (vss. 2, 7, 15) and πλῆθος may be used of the narrower group, as it is of the "assembly" of apostles and elders in 15:12. There is, however, inscriptional evidence that πλῆθος was used as the equivalent of δῆμος of the whole people in the official political sense (Deissmann, *Bible Studies,* p. 232). The Western text here, as represented by the margin of the Harclean Syriac Version, is much fuller and very vivid: "The whole Jewish people petitioned me, both in Jerusalem and here, that I should hand him over to them for torture without defense. But I was not able to hand him over on account of instructions which we have from the Emperor. So I said that if anyone wished to accuse him he should follow me to Caesarea where he was in custody. And when they arrived, they clamored that his life should be taken away. But when I had heard this and that side, I found that in no respect was he worthy of death. But when I said, Do you wish to be tried with them in Jerusalem? he appealed to Caesar. . . ."

26. To write: According to the *Digest* (XLIX.b) such written reports, called *litterae dimissoriae,* had to be sent when cases were remanded to the supreme court. **My lord** (τῷ κυρίῳ): Caligula was the first to style himself *Dominus,* and Domitian improved on this with the title *Dominus deus.* The papyri show that in Egypt from the middle of the first century B.C. κύριος is more and more frequently used of the emperor.

---

and for the summation of his case. The scene was one of pomp and ceremony. Paul appeared not so much a prisoner as a personage. The company to which he was to speak was the most distinguished that could be assembled. No rioting now, no provocations to anger; nothing but the most favorable circumstances for him to rehearse the thrilling story of his life. Agrippa was gracious to him and all the surroundings were eminently suitable.

26 Then Agrippa said unto Paul, Thou art permitted to speak for thyself. Then Paul stretched forth the hand, and answered for himself:

2 I think myself happy, king Agrippa, because I shall answer for myself this day before thee touching all the things whereof I am accused of the Jews:

26 Agrippa said to Paul, "You have permission to speak for yourself." Then Paul stretched out his hand and made his defense:

2 "I think myself fortunate that it is before you, King Agrippa, I am to make my defense today against all the accusations of

c) Paul's Defense Before Agrippa (26:1-32)

Luke evidently intends Paul's speech before Agrippa to be the climax of his defense. In literary form it is so polished and elaborate that it would seem at first sight to be almost entirely an editorial production. Yet there are evident marks of verisimilitude. As has already been noted (p. 120), the story of Paul's conversion in the present chapter is more compact and straightforward than the alternative accounts in chs. 9 and 22, and it can be more easily harmonized with Galatians. It seems to reproduce more accurately Paul's own ultimate conviction when it represents him as receiving his apostolic call directly from the risen Christ at the time of the vision, rather than later through the agency of Ananias. It is therefore extremely probable that Luke either himself heard this address, or at least found an account of it in his sources, and used it as a basis for the other two accounts of the conversion. But if we recognize here an authentic Pauline kernel, it is also clear that Luke has elaborated it, for in places his own viewpoint is clearly reflected. Vs. 20 contains the idea that immediately after his conversion Paul betook himself to aggressive missionary work both at Damascus and Jerusalem (cf. 9:20, 28-29); and vss. 4-9 suggest, as does Luke's description of the scene before the Sanhedrin (23:6-10), that the chief complaint of the Jews against Paul was that he preached the resurrection. For the points at which this account of Paul's conversion differs from the other two accounts see Exeg., p. 120.

26:1. Made his defense: The Western text (in the margin of the Harclean Version) has "confident and consoled by the Holy Spirit"—thus vividly illustrating the fulfillment of the promise of the Holy Spirit's help given in Mark 13:9-11.

2. I think myself fortunate: This is not merely a formal compliment or *captatio benevolentiae*. Herod, true to his family tradition, was always loyal to Rome, and later in the Jewish War was found on the side of the conquerors. But before the outbreak he always did what he could to help his countrymen and to avert the catastrophe. He was thus both pro-Roman and also an understanding champion of his own people's interests,

26:1-23. ***Paul Makes His Defense Before King Agrippa.***—Once again Paul tells his story. It is essentially the same story he has told on many occasions. Like all men whose lives are divided by an event which completely changes them, Paul goes back again and again to that one decisive event. While the outline of the story is always the same, the total impression that it makes varies somewhat according to the circumstances under which it is told. This time, for example, the elegant surroundings in which Paul stands are reflected in what Paul says and the way he says it. His speech has a kind of grandeur about it that it did not have when he spoke on the steps of the temple to the angry crowd. Also the fact that the speech was addressed primarily to King Agrippa inevitably made a difference in the tone of it.

Think of the two men, Paul and Agrippa. Were there ever two men farther apart than those two? Here they were confronting one and the same fact: the resurrection of Jesus. To Agrippa it was preposterous; to Paul it was a foregone conclusion: **Why is it thought incredible by any of you that God raises the dead?** As the two men pondered that question, the contrast between them grew by leaps and bounds.

In the first place Paul and Agrippa lived in two entirely different worlds. Look at the world of Agrippa. He was a Hellenized Jew. He was brought up in Rome with all the luxury and elegance of Roman culture. He was the last of the Herods. He was one of the unfortunate sons of a famous family, born too late to inherit the vitality of the family, reaping only the bitter fruit of its decline. He lived at the end of an era. He was the personification of an age

3 Especially *because I know* thee to be expert in all customs and questions which are among the Jews: wherefore I beseech thee to hear me patiently.
4 My manner of life from my youth, which was at the first among mine own nation at Jerusalem, know all the Jews;
5 Which knew me from the beginning, if they would testify, that after the most straitest sect of our religion I lived a Pharisee.

the Jews, 3 because you are especially fa-
miliar with all customs and controversies of the Jews; therefore I beg you to listen to me patiently.
4 "My manner of life from my youth, spent from the beginning among my own nation and at Jerusalem, is known by all
the Jews. 5 They have known for a long
time, if they are willing to testify, that according to the strictest party of our religion

---

and this double character would make Paul the more ready to make his defense before him.

3. Especially might be placed in the sentence in three ways: (*a*) **Because you are especially familiar.** (*b*) "Especially because you are familiar." (*c*) "That it is especially before you"—which would be in line with the use of the word in 25:26.

4. My own nation: If we translate as RSV **among my own nation and at Jerusalem**—the contrast being between the "nation" and Jerusalem—then the reference is probably to Paul's own province of Cilicia. If we translate, "my manner of life spent from the beginning from my youth among my own nation and at Jerusalem"—the contrast being rather between his boyhood spent among his kinsmen at Tarsus and the more mature years spent at Jerusalem—then "nation" could mean the Jewish community at Tarsus (see on 24:2).

5. Sect: See on 24:5. **Religion:** The Greek word refers to religious practice rather than to creed, to form of worship rather than to system of belief. The good Jew always stressed practice rather than doctrine. "Religion" here includes the "customs" mentioned in vs. 3 (cf. Jas. 1:26-27, where all the stress is on the practical side of religion).

---

that was dying. He lived in a world that looked like a fire after all the flame is gone and nothing is left except smoldering embers that will not be fanned into life.

Paul, on the other hand, lived in a world which had just been born, a world not nearly so safe for him personally, full of risks and hazards, dangers and perils of every imaginable kind, but a world in which things were intensely alive. If Agrippa's world was lighted by the dull glow of dying embers, Paul's world was lighted by the blazing sun that blinded him on the way to Damascus. It was a world re-created by the intrusion of the spirit of Christ, around which gathered a group of people who were vitalized by that spirit. It was a world in which men were looking forward to something which should be revealed, and not backward to a glory that had passed. No wonder Paul thought that the resurrection of Christ was a self-evident fact; he lived in a world that had been made new by that one fact, a world in which anything might happen; whereas Agrippa lived in a world that was dying a slow death, and the thought of resurrection was as foreign to that world as breathing is to a corpse.

Some people are living today in a world that has gone, a world of past elegance, faded glory, forgotten dreams, lost traditions, dwindling dividends, failing enterprises. They make brave efforts to carry on and hold on, but behind the façade there is a resignation that amounts to despair. Their future is behind them. Of course, in a world like that, to people like that, the resurrection of Jesus is incredible. But some people even now live in a world which is continually on the verge of rebirth; its dangers and struggles are the birth pangs of a new era. For them the resurrection of Jesus is not preposterous at all; it is the supreme incident from which all others derive their life and meaning. In a world like that you expect resurrections, and the resurrection of Jesus anticipates and confirms all the others.

The second contrast between the two men is that Paul cared more than Agrippa cared. It made a supreme difference to Paul whether or not God raised Jesus from the dead. It was not the close, personal interest that the other disciples had, the disciples who had known Jesus personally, and who were grief-stricken by his death and by the knowledge that they would never see him again. Paul was not interested merely in prolonging a precious experience; he never had that experience in the first place. But as Paul read the record of his people and

6 And now I stand and am judged for
the hope of the promise made of God unto
our fathers:
7 Unto which *promise* our twelve tribes,
instantly serving *God* day and night, hope
to come. For which hope's sake, king
Agrippa, I am accused of the Jews.
8 Why should it be thought a thing incredible with you, that God should raise
the dead?

I have lived as a Pharisee. 6 And now I
stand here on trial for hope in the promise
made by God to our fathers, 7 to which our
twelve tribes hope to attain, as they earnestly worship night and day. And for this
hope I am accused by Jews, O king! 8 Why
is it thought incredible by any of you that
God raises the dead?

---

6. Hope in the promise: This might seem most naturally to refer to the messianic hope. But the parallel with 23:6 and 24:15, and the words that follow in vs. 8, make it clear that the resurrection hope is in view. At the same time Jesus' claim to be Messiah is validated by his resurrection. **Our fathers,** i.e., the patriarchs, in particular Abraham, Isaac, and Jacob.

7. Twelve tribes: The Greek has a singular archaic sounding word, δωδεκάφυλον, which suggests, as the English does not, that in their hope the twelve tribes are one single community. **By Jews:** The words are emphatic—as we might say, "By Jews, of all people!"

8. God raises the dead: The question is a general one, but Paul of course here has Jesus' own resurrection particularly in view. But for the apostle the resurrection of Jesus and the general resurrection were related in the closest possible manner (see I Cor. 15:12-23).

---

listened to the word of God as it came through the prophets, he knew that God had promised his people that there should come among them one who should bear their transgressions, and in bearing them be transfigured by them, and be the salvation of his people and of the whole world. And it made all the difference in the world to Paul whether or not God had fulfilled that promise. He saw something in Jesus that looked like the promise of God. Jesus had the power to save men from slavery. He had saved Paul himself. Paul saw in Jesus the possibility of a new kingdom, the kingdom of God, and he wanted to know whether God was for him or against him. If God let him die and did nothing about it, the weight of the whole universe was thrown against the kingdom; but when he saw God take that spirit and raise it up for eternity, he knew that the weight of God's universe, in spite of all evidence to the contrary, was on the side of the new kingdom. It was the fulfillment of God's promise, and it made all the difference in the world to Paul to know that.

It probably did not make any real difference to Agrippa one way or the other. Unconsciously, if not consciously, he knew that his world was going; the only thing for him to do was to enjoy it as much as he could while it lasted. He did not really care whether Jesus was alive or dead. The fate of a village carpenter played no significant part in the life of a king, and whether God's universe was on the side of good or evil probably seemed to him little more than academic discussion about something that made little difference to the ordinary routine of life. It is hardly to be wondered at that he did not have the imagination to reach out and see this thing that to Paul was the one, clear, shining reality of life.

Perhaps it is not necessary to point out that there are scores of people today, even within the Christian church, to whom it does not make any real difference whether Jesus is dead or alive. Whether or not God raised him from the dead and thus gave his signature of approval to the character of Christ is a matter of indifference. Where people do not care one way or the other, the resurrection is either a preposterous bit of superstition based upon a legend, or it is a pious belief to be tolerated in those who find it comforting. When Pavlov, the great Russian scientist, at the age of eighty-seven, was giving advice to the academic youth of Russia, he pointed out three things which they must remember in all their academic work. The first was gradualness. Do not be in a hurry, he said. Take each day as it comes, step by step. The second was modesty. Do not be proud; be humble in the presence of fact. The third was passion. Remember, he said, that science demands of a man *all* his life. Be passionate in your work and in your searchings. That was his advice to potential scientists! How much more does Christianity demand *all* of a man's life. To a man who approaches this question of the resurrection without any passion, as though

9 I verily thought with myself, that I ought to do many things contrary to the name of Jesus of Nazareth.

10 Which thing I also did in Jerusalem: and many of the saints did I shut up in prison, having received authority from the chief priests; and when they were put to death, I gave my voice against *them*.

11 And I punished them oft in every synagogue, and compelled *them* to blaspheme; and being exceedingly mad against them, I persecuted *them* even unto strange cities.

9 "I myself was convinced that I ought
to do many things in opposing the name
of Jesus of Nazareth. **10** And I did so in
Jerusalem; I not only shut up many of the
saints in prison, by authority from the
chief priests, but when they were put to
death I cast my vote against them. **11** And
I punished them often in all the synagogues
and tried to make them blaspheme; and in
raging fury against them, I persecuted them
even to foreign cities.

9-11. These verses give the impression of a much more general and systematic persecution than Acts seems to imply in its account of the events after Stephen's death; and the part played by Paul in person is specially stressed—evidently as proof of his fanatical loyalty to Judaism. **Put to death:** In the earlier chapters only the deaths of Stephen and James are recorded, but more obscure Christians may well have perished without mention. **Cast my vote:** This does not necessarily prove that Paul had been an official member of the Sanhedrin, for the expression is often used metaphorically. It may mean little more than 22:20, "I also was standing by and approving" (cf. 8:1).

Tried to make them blaspheme, literally "was forcing them to blaspheme." But the Greek does not necessarily imply that they did so, as does the KJV translation "compelled them to blaspheme." It is, of course, blasphemy of Christ that is in question, which in Jewish eyes would not be blasphemy at all. Lake and Cadbury appositely quote Pliny, who says that while renegade Christians could be forced *maledicere Christo* ("to curse Christ"), true Christians would not yield to any compulsion (Pliny *Letters* X. 96). Indeed the reference to efforts to make Christians blaspheme looks like a reading back into Paul's words of ideas more applicable to later times.

---

nothing great depended on it, without caring much one way or the other, the resurrection will be little more than a relic of a preposterous faith. Jesus appeared to those who cared most. There is not much likelihood that he will ever appear under any other conditions.

There is still a third contrast between Paul and Agrippa. Paul's God was not Agrippa's God. Paul put the whole matter in terms of what God did, not in terms of a spectacular achievement on the part of the man Christ Jesus. One would like to know what went on in the mind of Agrippa when Paul put the question, **Why is it thought incredible by any of you that God raises the dead?** Agrippa more than likely thought to himself, "God, God, what has God to do with it?" For Agrippa, God was probably one of those properties to be brought out on state occasions, for great public ceremonials and celebrations, but had little if anything to do with the thoughts that a man thinks and the life that he lives. Of no great concern was God to Agrippa, and with a lifeless God like that, the resurrection is as empty as a bubble, as inconsequential and as easily dismissed.

How different Paul's God was from that! Paul's God was the creator of the heavens and the earth; he made the sea and the sun, the grass and all the trees; everything that had breath drew that breath from God. He moved the tides and marshaled the seasons in their proper order. He created man in his own image. He was the maker of history and the master of it. What God promised he was able to perform. He was a God of power and action. He did things. When you come up against a God like that, it is not so incredible that he should do what he chooses to do in accordance with his purpose, and if his purpose is to redeem the human race and raise it to a new level of life, it is not surprising that he should raise the dead.

For some people God is so small that he is lost among the stars. He is but the image of a God, something that can be carried about with them from place to place for their own convenience. For others God is locked up in the prison house of his own laws, a slave to his own creation, bound by the very fabric which is the work of his hands, self-bound, self-imprisoned. Of course if God is a God like that, then the universe is a mesh of law and order, cause and effect, in which nothing ever can happen that

12 Whereupon as I went to Damascus with authority and commission from the chief priests,

13 At midday, O king, I saw in the way a light from heaven, above the brightness of the sun, shining round about me and them which journeyed with me.

14 And when we were all fallen to the earth, I heard a voice speaking unto me, and saying in the Hebrew tongue, Saul, Saul, why persecutest thou me? *it is* hard for thee to kick against the pricks.

15 And I said, Who art thou, Lord? And he said, I am Jesus whom thou persecutest.

16 But rise, and stand upon thy feet: for I have appeared unto thee for this purpose, to make thee a minister and a witness both of these things which thou hast seen, and of those things in the which I will appear unto thee;

12 "Thus I journeyed to Damascus with
the authority and commission of the chief
priests. 13 At midday, O king, I saw on the
way a light from heaven, brighter than the
sun, shining round me and those who
journeyed with me. 14 And when we had all
fallen to the ground, I heard a voice saying to me in the Hebrew language, 'Saul,
Saul, why do you persecute me? It hurts
you to kick against the goads.' 15 And I said,
'Who are you, Lord?' And the Lord said,
'I am Jesus whom you are persecuting.
16 But rise and stand upon your feet; for
I have appeared to you for this purpose,
to appoint you to serve and bear witness
to the things in which you have seen me
and to those in which I will appear to you,

14. When we had all fallen: Contrast 9:7. **Hebrew language:** Cf. on 21:40; Aramaic is probably meant. **To kick against the goads:** A proverbial saying, found both in Greek and Latin, usually with reference to fighting against the will of the gods, but not yet paralleled from any Semitic source. The word translated by KJV **hard** (σκλῆρον) means, in this context, not "difficult" but "painful"; hence RSV, **It hurts you to kick. . . .**

16. Rise and stand upon your feet: Cf. Ezek. 2:1, "Son of man, stand upon thy feet, and I will speak unto thee." Like Ezekiel, Saul is to stand to receive his commission directly from the risen Christ. It is here that this account differs most seriously from the other two, and corresponds rather with the impression left by Paul's epistles. No mention is made of the part played by Ananias (see Exeg., p. 120). The highly colored biblical style of the words of the divine commission should be noted. It is God himself who speaks through the lips of the risen Jesus.

To appoint you: The word (προχειρίσασθαι) is the same as when Ananias says in 22:14, "The God of our fathers appointed you." **The things in which . . . I will appear to you:** The Greek is very awkward, but the reference is apparently first to the present vision on the Damascus road, and secondly to the subsequent visions which Paul is later to experience (e.g., 18:9-10; 22:17-21; 23:11).

has not happened before, and in which the unpredictable is impossible. In a universe like that the Resurrection quite obviously is ruled out from the start. Resurrections do not occur in such a universe, only repetitions.

But if there is a God who is not the servant but the master of his laws, who can reach down into the creation which he has made and which he can control from without as well as influence from within, who can turn the tide of events and out of something that looks like pure matter bring a mind, and out of something that is pure brain bring a spirit, it is not difficult to think of that God reaching down to take a spirit that is as pure as sunlight and raise it up to everlasting life. The question is therefore, What kind of a God do men believe in? Agrippa's God had no resurrection power in him and the story about Jesus rising from the dead is a preposterous tale. But Paul's God is a God who raises Jesus from the dead as naturally as he raises the sun in the eastern sky.

There is one final contrast that is the most important of all. Paul knew Jesus and Agrippa did not. Agrippa had undoubtedly heard about Jesus; his uncle, Herod, was the one who tried him on the day before Good Friday, and who had the same kind of curiosity about him that Agrippa manifested when Festus asked him to hear Paul's case. And Agrippa had possibly heard tales of the Resurrection, stories that the women told and which spread like wildfire from village to village. But the stories did not always tally; some of them ended in silence

17 Delivering thee from the people, and *from* the Gentiles, unto whom now I send thee,

18 To open their eyes, *and* to turn *them* from darkness to light, and *from* the power of Satan unto God, that they may receive forgiveness of sins, and inheritance among them which are sanctified by faith that is in me.

17 delivering you from the people and from
the Gentiles — to whom I send you 18 to
open their eyes, that they may turn from
darkness to light and from the power of
Satan to God, that they may receive forgiveness of sins and a place among those
who are sanctified by faith in me.'

---

17. Delivering you: Such visions are always recorded by Luke at critical points in Paul's career, and the promise is of course particularly apposite to the apostle's present predicament. But the word (ἐξαιρούμενος) might alternatively be translated "choosing you out," which would be appropriate enough with reference to the present commission, but somewhat awkward with **from the Gentiles**—unless indeed the point is that Saul as a Greek-speaking Jew is chosen as a missionary representative of Jew and Gentile alike.

18. This verse reminds us of Col. 1:12-14; "Giving thanks to the Father, who has qualified us to share in the inheritance of the saints in light. He has delivered us from the dominion of darkness and transferred us to the kingdom of his beloved Son, in whom we have redemption, the forgiveness of sins." Vss. 17-18 awaken echoes also of Jer. 1:7; Isa. 35:5; 42:7, 16. **Forgiveness of sins** is a Lukan rather than a strictly Pauline expression (see on 13:38).

---

and some in fear, and none of them came to any definite, conclusive proof that Jesus had been seen. It was natural that Agrippa should dismiss the whole matter as one of the things that people like to talk about for a while and then forget as though they had never heard it.

But Paul knew something far above and beyond that. He may not have known Jesus in the flesh, he may never have heard his voice or felt the touch of his hand, but he knew the Lord Christ who, in a blinding light on the road to Damascus, confronted him, laid hold upon him, possessed him, demanded his life completely, changed and re-created his whole character, and set him upon a new and untraveled way. For Paul the Resurrection was no theoretical speculation. When he said that Jesus is alive, he was talking about someone he had met, not casually the way one meets a friend on the street, but catastrophically, dynamically, the way one meets overpowering truth or overwhelming love. And as Paul went on those long, dangerous missionary journeys, in prison and out of prison, in peril of every sort and kind, opposed by people who heard and did not understand or want to understand, seeming often to make no headway, running up against the resistance of humanity with its prejudices and narrowness, he found something strengthening him, empowering him, reviving him, enabling him to do the impossible, steadying him through the hours when there was nothing to do but wait. It was the Christ in him, through whose strength he could do all things. It was no philosophical principle or theological concept; it was a personal relationship, a vivid, undeniable experience. To tell Paul that the Christ he knew was dead was as though a man told him that the sun was dark. He knew otherwise. He felt the power. He had been blinded by the light. He had been saved by the indescribable warmth of it.

One of the reasons why the Resurrection seems so incredible to modern men and women is that many of them have never really encountered this living spirit who is abroad in the universe and whom Paul identified as the spirit of Christ. If a person ever feels that experience, if he sees it in another person, he is never able to say that Jesus is dead. He knows that Jesus is alive because the vitality of Jesus flows through him, because Jesus has touched him, and the touch is not the cold hand of death.

As Agrippa listened to Paul, he listened as one who lived in a different world, who cared only as men care for the spectacle of the passing moment, whose God was more like a piece of stage furniture than the divine dramatist by whom and for whom the stage was made, and whose knowledge of Jesus was like the knowledge of men who know a little about everything and nothing about anything that amounts to very much. What on earth could he say when Paul asked him why it seemed incredible to him that God should raise the dead? There was nothing he could say, for in his world the dead were dead indeed, and God was the last person who could do anything about it.

When contrasted with the charming but

19 Whereupon, O king Agrippa, I was not disobedient unto the heavenly vision:

20 But showed first unto them of Damascus, and at Jerusalem, and throughout all the coasts of Judea, and *then* to the Gentiles, that they should repent and turn to God, and do works meet for repentance.

21 For these causes the Jews caught me in the temple, and went about to kill *me*.

22 Having therefore obtained help of God, I continue unto this day, witnessing both to small and great, saying none other things than those which the prophets and Moses did say should come:

23 That Christ should suffer, *and* that he should be the first that should rise from the dead, and should show light unto the people, and to the Gentiles.

19 "Wherefore, O King Agrippa, I was
not disobedient to the heavenly vision,
20 but declared first to those at Damascus,
then at Jerusalem and throughout all the
country of Judea, and also to the Gentiles,
that they should repent and turn to God
and perform deeds worthy of their repentance. 21 For this reason the Jews seized
me in the temple and tried to kill me. 22 To
this day I have had the help that comes
from God, and so I stand here testifying
both to small and great, saying nothing
but what the prophets and Moses said
would come to pass: 23 that the Christ must
suffer, and that, by being the first to rise
from the dead, he would proclaim light
both to the people and to the Gentiles."

---

20. Throughout all the country of Judea: Unless the verse is intended as a rough summary of Paul's whole missionary career, rather than of his activity immediately after his conversion, these words go farther even than 9:28-29 in suggesting that Paul at once engaged in public preaching; and they contradict Gal. 1:22, where Paul says that he "was still not known by sight to the churches of Christ in Judea." The Greek too is almost impossibly awkward and suggests some primitive corruption. **Repent and turn:** The twofold meaning of the Hebrew word *shûbh* (cf. 3:19).

21. To kill (διαχειρίσασθαι): For the unusual Greek word see on 5:30.

22. Help (ἐπικουρία): The somewhat unusual Greek word is among those quoted as belonging to Luke's medical vocabulary. But though used by Hippocrates and Galen, it also occurs in nonmedical writers like Josephus and Polybius.

23. The Christ must suffer: See on 3:18 and 17:3. The prophets in fact, as understood by Jews, nowhere proclaim that the Messiah must suffer, for Isa. 53 was not interpreted messianically. Possibly Paul, realizing this, is making the point that at least there is nothing in Scripture to forbid the idea of a suffering Messiah. More probably Luke is simply reproducing the regular Christian argument that Jesus is Messiah, not in spite

---

worthless life of King Agrippa, the figure of Paul rises to its most titanic proportions. If any words can give a fair sense of those proportions, they are the words of Paul himself when he said, **Whereupon, O king Agrippa, I was not disobedient unto the heavenly vision.** That was the clue to it all. The chances are that Agrippa never had any great visions, and the ones he may have had were soon lost among the innumerable and competing interests of his life. Paul had a vision which he did nothing to create or deserve, but once he had it, he was obedient to it to the very end. It was in the obedience that the grandeur of Paul was to be found. No one could say of Paul that he was a perfect man. He had a temper that was hard to control and sometimes got out of hand. He had an impatience of lesser people that often made him hard to get along with. He had human prides and vanities which were not always under discipline. He often stumbled over the thoughts he tried so ardently to express, and the truth he saw was not always the whole truth. But to the vision that he had he was obedient. He never turned his back upon it; no trial was too severe for him to endure, no ignominy too humiliating for him to accept. He went on and on, through the converging ranks of opposition, through personal trials and tribulations, through the red tape of exasperating legalism, through nature's stormy and implacable ways. Not perfection could he claim before Agrippa, but obedience.

It is the most that can be asked or expected of a man that he be true to the vision he has seen. He may lapse from time to time into mistakes and failures; he may not always accomplish the thing he has set his heart upon. That is to be expected of a human being whose weaknesses often tempt him and whose imper-

24 And as he thus spake for himself, Festus said with a loud voice, Paul, thou art beside thyself; much learning doth make thee mad.

25 But he said, I am not mad, most noble Festus; but speak forth the words of truth and soberness.

26 For the king knoweth of these things, before whom also I speak freely: for I am persuaded that none of these things are hidden from him; for this thing was not done in a corner.

27 King Agrippa, believest thou the prophets? I know that thou believest.

24 And as he thus made his defense,
Festus said with a loud voice, "Paul, you
are mad; your great learning is turning you
mad." 25 But Paul said, "I am not mad, most
excellent Festus, but I am speaking the sober truth. 26 For the king knows about these
things, and to him I speak freely; for I am
persuaded that none of these things has
escaped his notice, for this was not done in
a corner. 27 King Agrippa, do you believe
the prophets? I know that you believe."

of, but in virtue of, the Cross. **The first to rise:** Christ is "the first fruits of those who have fallen asleep" (I Cor. 15:20), the "first-born from the dead" (Col. 1:18); therefore in virtue of his own resurrection he is qualified to **proclaim light**—to bring "life and immortality to light through the gospel" (II Tim. 1:10).

24. **Paul, you are mad:** Paul has deliberately been using language which while intelligible to Agrippa the Jew, to whom the defense is chiefly directed, might well appear to the sophisticated Roman as the ravings of a demented apocalyptist!

25-26. **The sober truth:** Exactly the right English idiom. Literally the Greek means **words of truth and soberness** (KJV). **The king knows** (ἐπίσταται): Almost "is an expert," for the Greek word is stronger than the English "knows." **Done in a corner** appears to be a Greek proverbial expression for which no Semitic parallel has elsewhere been found (cf. vs. 14).

fections are sometimes more than he can handle. The question that is asked of a man's total life is, Has he been obedient to his vision? When he has fallen behind in the pursuit of it, has he gathered himself together to overtake it once again? Paul stands among the few who were obedient to the end. He knew how to run the race; he knew how to set aside everything that might hold him back; he knew how to keep his eye on the goal and then press toward it with all the energy of his unified being, supplemented by strength the source of which he alone knew and the secret of which he alone could tell. It is not surprising, therefore, that even in the courts of mankind, where judgments are passed upon the achievements of men and women, Paul wears the victor's crown, as a man who turned the world upside down. It can hardly be doubted that in that higher court where the secrets of all men shall finally be disclosed, he wears the crown of life that never fades away. Agrippa had everything and possessed nothing. Paul had nothing and yet possessed all things. Such is the paradox of two personalities, one a king and the other a prisoner, one a judge and the other a condemned man; and yet, one a lost soul draped in the trappings of a king, and the other a hero and a saint bound in the chains of a prisoner.

24-32. ***How Festus and Agrippa Responded to Paul's Speech.***—It was Paul's claim that there was nothing in the new way of life that was not implicit in Moses and the prophets. In Christ the principles which were potentially present in the Jewish scriptures were explicitly applied and completely fulfilled. It was not the principles, therefore, to which the Jews objected, but the specific application of them in the revolutionary and redeeming figure of Jesus. As long as religion is content to remain a matter of abstract principle, not many people will take exception to it; indeed many will clasp it closely, even to the point of fighting for it. It is rather when that religion assumes a cutting edge that goes straight to the center of our most cherished rights and fancied privileges that we set ourselves against it and oppose it as we might oppose the very devil himself.

When Paul came to the climax of his speech, Festus dismissed the whole thing as the extravagant and wild assertions of a man whose enthusiam had run away with his judgment. **Paul, you are mad; your great learning is turning you mad.** So the family of Jesus dismissed what he said as the words of one who was beside himself. So the world dismisses those with whom it does not agree and in whom it detects a potential disturber of its peace. Crack-

28 Then Agrippa said unto Paul, Almost thou persuadest me to be a Christian.
29 And Paul said, I would to God, that not only thou, but also all that hear me this day, were both almost, and altogether such as I am, except these bonds.
30 And when he had thus spoken, the king rose up, and the governor, and Bernice, and they that sat with them:

28 And Agrippa said to Paul, "In a short time you think to make me a Christian!"
29 And Paul said, "Whether short or long, I would to God that not only you but also all who hear me this day might become such as I am — except for these chains."
30 Then the king rose, and the governor and Ber-ni'ce and those who were sitting

---

28. **In a short time you think to make me a Christian:** Agrippa probably resented Paul's appealing to him against Festus, and his reply should almost certainly be understood as a sarcastic retort rather than as the confession of one who is more than half convinced—as suggested by the KJV, **Almost thou persuadest me to be a Christian.** But the exact interpretation of this famous crux is uncertain. Literally the words mean "in a little [ἐν ὀλίγῳ] you are persuading [πείθεις] me to make a Christian," or "in a little you are persuaded [reading πείθῃ with Codex Alexandrinus] to make me a Christian." The alternatives seem to be: (*a*) As RSV above, or alternatively "in a short time you are persuading me to become a Christian" (reading γενέσθαι for ποιῆσαι with some inferior MSS). (*b*) Sarcastically—"With small effort you think to make me a Christian" (reading πείθῃ and ποιῆσαι); or alternatively, "With small effort you are persuading me to become a Christian" (reading πείθεις and γενέσθαι). (*c*) The readings πείθεις and ποιῆσαι certainly have the best MS authority, and taken together they can give only the meaning, "In a short time [or perhaps better "with small effort"] you are persuading me to make a Christian." Unless, as Lake and Cadbury suggest, ποιῆσαι χριστιανόν is colloquial Greek for "play the Christian," this might possibly mean: "You are making short work of persuading me to make Festus a Christian!" Paul has appealed to Agrippa against Festus' charge of madness, and Agrippa sarcastically replies that Paul can hardly expect *him* to play the Christian missionary! No explanation is wholly satisfactory. But as the word "Christian" on Agrippa's lips would certainly be a sneer, his reply cannot imply that Paul is on the verge of converting him, as the KJV suggests.

29. **Whether short or long:** Or "whether by small effort or by great." This translation assumes, probably correctly, that the words pick up ἐν ὀλίγῳ in the previous verse. Alternatively "in small and great" may mean simply "altogether," "wholly"—"I would that you might become wholly as I am!"

---

pots, madmen, fools, lightweights, fanatics, dreamers—to such questionable company have the great innovators of humanity been repeatedly consigned.

Paul expected something better of Agrippa. After all he was a Jew; he knew the Jewish scriptures and it was to be expected that by and large he believed them. What Paul was saying was nothing new to him. It had happened in full view of the public. There was no secret about it. There was nothing hidden or withheld. Surely if Agrippa believed the prophets, as Paul assumed he did, the step from them to the revelation of God in Christ followed as day follows night. But how did Agrippa take that Pauline assumption? He refused to take it seriously, but turned it off with a half-humorous quip, "At this rate, it won't be long before you believe you have made a Christian of me!" (Moffatt.) What sharper rebuke can there be to a man who is in dead earnest than to have his most serious words taken lightly? It is the age-old rebuke of the highly polished and cultivated. If they can get out of a difficult situation in no other way, they can almost always smile their way out, and always, of course, at the terrible expense of him toward whom their smile is superciliously directed.

After Paul had finished his defense, both Festus and Agrippa acquitted him. They could not see that Paul had done anything deserving the death penalty. They acquitted him but they did not appreciate him. They were willing to let him go, but they were not willing to take him in. They passed judgment upon him, at least so they supposed, and they had not the slightest suspicion that throughout the hearing he was passing judgment upon them! Their numbers are legion at this very moment, those who find no fault with Jesus, are willing and glad to let

31 And when they were gone aside, they
talked between themselves, saying, This
man doeth nothing worthy of death or of
bonds.
32 Then said Agrippa unto Festus, This
man might have been set at liberty, if he
had not appealed unto Caesar.

27 And when it was determined that
we should sail into Italy, they delivered Paul and certain other prisoners

with them; 31 and when they had withdrawn, they said to one another, "This man
is doing nothing to deserve death or imprisonment." 32 And Agrippa said to Festus,
"This man could have been set free if he
had not appealed to Caesar."

27 And when it was decided that we
should sail for Italy, they deliv-

31-32. Again Luke insists that the authorities can find no case against Paul. **Could have been set free:** Does this imply that once a prisoner had appealed to the highest court, the power of the lower court to acquit lapsed, as well as its power to condemn? The evidence is obscure; but probably all further proceedings would be automatically stayed. In any case the present scene should not be regarded in any sense as an official trial. The verse has sometimes been taken as suggesting that Caesar's verdict was likely to be less favorable, and has been used as evidence that Luke is leading up to Paul's condemnation at Rome. On the contrary Luke's implication surely is that Festus would report to Caesar that there was no case against Paul. But it would be rash to draw from this verse any conclusion one way or the other regarding the final outcome of Paul's appearance before Caesar.

5. Voyage to Rome (27:1–28:16)

At this point begins the last of the "we" sections and much the most dramatic piece of writing in the whole book. For purposes of historical study the detail is of no great importance and is chiefly of interest for the light it throws upon ancient nautical methods. In 1848 James Smith of Jordanhill published a famous essay, *The Voyage and Shipwreck of St. Paul* (4th ed., London: Longmans, Brown, Green, Longmans & Roberts, 1880), in which he proved conclusively that the scene of the wreck must have been St. Paul's Bay, Malta, rather than the island of Meleda in the Adriatic, and argued that the whole account must have been written by an eyewitness who was not himself a seaman. This essay, together with the discussion by Ramsay in *St. Paul the Traveller and the Roman Citizen,* is still the best study of this section.

Luke's whole account may be assumed to be accurate and entirely trustworthy. The criticism of Wellhausen, e.g., seems quite arbitrary when he suggests that a redactor has embellished his source here with an account of a shipwreck, just as he is supposed to have added the description of the riot to his story of Paul's mission at Ephesus. If the present chapter is not in its entirety an authentic firsthand narrative, then we may well despair of finding anything in Acts that we can trust.

The important features in the account are: first, the light it throws on the dominating personality of Paul who, prisoner though he is, exerts his influence at every crisis;

---

him live, but who never see the greatness of him and never feel his love. They would raise no hand to hurt him or block his way; neither would they lift a hand to extend his healing ministry to a wretched world, or open their heart to receive the matchless power of his grace. They are the silent, self-approving acquitters. They have done no wrong, neither have they stood for anything great. They are embroiled in a civilization which is as ephemeral as the dew, and they have no time for him to whom the ages belong. They never know that they are in the dock and he is on the bench, and they go down among the scores of nameless men and women who have passed by the glory of life and have never known it. It is hard to conceive a tragedy more terrible than theirs.

27:1-8. ***From Caesarea to Crete.***—The trip from Caesarea to Crete was fairly uneventful. Luke makes it clear that Paul, though a prisoner, was treated with consideration and was given the liberty to do just about anything he wanted to do. There is a line in the narrative which, while relatively unimportant in itself, sets the

unto *one* named Julius, a centurion of Augustus' band.

ered Paul and some other prisoners to a centurion of the Augustan Cohort, named

and, second, the sobriety of the narrative in spite of all its vividness. Amidst all the terrors of the tempest nothing more miraculous is attributed to Paul than a vision (vss. 23-24). The incident of the viper does not necessarily imply a miracle (28:3-6); nor do the various acts of healing (28:7-10). In any case it must be insisted that Paul himself testifies to his own performance of "signs and wonders and mighty works" (II Cor. 12:12), that the original author is just as likely to have believed in miracle as any later redactor, and that therefore the presence of the miraculous in a N.T. narrative is no proof that it is not primitive and authentic.

Some critics have suggested that three paragraphs are later interpolations: (*a*) Vss. 9-11 which are regarded as a "surcharge" designed to set the personality of Paul in the limelight. In vs. 9 the phrase **Paul advised them** is very vague, and Paul's objection in vs. 10 to setting sail is thought awkward because the decision to do so is not mentioned till vs. 12. The verses could be omitted without any interruption. (*b*) The same is true of vss. 21-26; and again they seem designed to display Paul as a leader and to give him the chance to say "I told you so." (*c*) Vss. 33-38 could also be omitted without damaging the sequence, and in this paragraph, too, Paul is pictured as taking control of the situation. The Eucharistic coloring of vs. 35 (where see note) also causes suspicion. But the objections to all three paragraphs seem quite arbitrary in view of the fact that to show his hero in the best possible light must have been Luke's chief aim in telling the story. As Lake and Cadbury well say, "Inasmuch as the writer was interested in Paul rather than in the voyage, these passages are surely to be retained" (*Beginnings of Christianity,* IV, 324).

27:1. They delivered Paul: Presumably the Roman authorities, though grammatically the subject is left vague. The tense of the verb (an imperfect) also is difficult to explain. **The Augustan Cohort** (σπείρη Σεβαστή) may be variously explained: (*a*) Most probably it is an auxiliary cohort which we know to have been stationed in Syria about this time. The regular legionary cohorts were not given such honorary *cognomina.* (*b*) It has been ingeniously explained as being an auxiliary cohort drawn from Samaria (Sebaste), such as had formed Herod's garrison at Jerusalem (Josephus *Jewish War* II. 3. 4; II. 4. 2). But quite clearly the Greek is a translation of the Latin *cohors Augusta.* (*c*) Possibly the name was given to a body of imperial couriers, elsewhere called *frumentarii,* who were detailed for such duties as keeping open communications between the emperor and his provincial armies, controlling the commissariat, conducting prisoners to Rome. It seems likely that one entrusted with such responsible duties as was Julius would belong rather to such a select corps than to a Syrian auxiliary cohort. But the question must be left open.

mood of the whole trip. It comes in vs. 4, **The winds were against us.** And later on in vs. 7, **The wind did not allow us to go on.** In other words, the party was progressing toward Rome against great odds and handicaps. Navigators, however, learn how to handle adverse winds and to make some progress in spite of them. In this particular case they knew from long experience that the only thing to do was to sail to the east of Cyprus, keeping well under the lee of the island. Any fool could sail a boat if all the winds were favorable; it took a man of intelligence and ingenuity to sail one when the winds were contrary.

This incident of the contrary winds might serve as a parable for the whole of Paul's life. To be sure, he had many things in his favor: a good family, Roman citizenship, a brilliant mind, and a sensitive spirit. Yet not overlooking these advantages, Paul's life was by and large a struggle against winds that were against him. Before his conversion it was the supersensitiveness of a fastidious conscience. After his conversion the internal storms were quieted, but the winds from without continued to rage. His own people made it difficult for him wherever he went; the primitive conditions of travel placed a heavy tax on one who set out to carry the gospel all over the world; his own personal handicaps and weaknesses were always nagging at him; his friends often disappointed him, and the officials of Rome condemned him

2 And entering into a ship of Adramyttium, we launched, meaning to sail by the coasts of Asia; *one* Aristarchus, a Macedonian of Thessalonica, being with us.

3 And the next *day* we touched at Sidon. And Julius courteously entreated Paul, and gave *him* liberty to go unto his friends to refresh himself.

4 And when we had launched from thence, we sailed under Cyprus, because the winds were contrary.

5 And when we had sailed over the sea of Cilicia and Pamphylia, we came to Myra, *a city* of Lycia.

Julius. 2 And embarking in a ship of Ad-
ra-myt′ti-um, which was about to sail to
the ports along the coast of Asia, we put
to sea, accompanied by Ar-is-tar′chus, a
Mac-e-do′ni-an from Thes-sa-lo-ni′ca. 3 The
next day we put in at Sidon; and Julius
treated Paul kindly, and gave him leave
to go to his friends and be cared for. 4 And
putting to sea from there we sailed under
the lee of Cyprus, because the winds were
against us. 5 And when we had sailed across
the sea which is off Ci-li′cia and Pam-

---

2. **Adramyttium** was a port at the east end of the bay which lies immediately south of Troas and around the promontory of Assos. **Asia,** i.e., along the west coast of what we call Asia Minor. **Aristarchus:** See on 19:29; 20:4. Ramsay suggests that he may have accompanied Paul as his personal servant.

3. **His friends:** This seems the obvious meaning, though it has been suggested that Christians may have spoken of themselves as "the Friends," for which we might compare III John 15, "The friends greet you. Greet the friends, every one of them."

4. **Under the lee of Cyprus:** The prevailing winds in summer being westerly or northwesterly, the ship would sail around the east end of Cyprus, whereas on a former journey (21:3) the course had been to the west. Their present course would bring them to the coast of Cilicia, and they would then have to stay close to land, trusting to offshore breezes to help them westward.

5. **Sailed across:** The word seems to imply that after a time they ceased to hug the coast and cut across from point to point—presumably from the southwest point of **Cilicia** to the promontory of **Lycia** just east of **Myra,** across the great bay made by the coast of **Pamphylia.** The Western text adds that the voyage took "fifteen days," which is probable enough against a headwind. **Myra** (cf. 21:1) was a port of call for larger ships, particularly for the grain ships from Egypt, which usually found it impossible to sail direct to Italy against the prevailing northwest winds.

---

with faint praise. In a very real sense the wind was against him.

In one way or another the same thing is true of everyone. There are long spells of fine weather and there are many fair days when the winds are favorable, but there inevitably comes the time when the weather turns foul and the winds are against us. Sooner or later everyone has to face the fact that he cannot have everything he wants in life. Everyone wants good health, but not everyone will have it. For some there will be spells of illness, and for others the prospect of chronic invalidism. Everyone wants a happy family, but not everyone will have it. Everyone wants economic security, but not everyone will have it all the time. Jobs will be lost, depressions will come, incomes will be deflated. Everyone wants to live in a peaceful world, but not everyone will be able to enjoy that happy privilege. It is well for a man to recognize these things from the very beginning, and know from the outset that the winds will often be against him.

The contrary winds did not prevent Paul and his party from reaching Rome, neither did the contrary winds of life prevent Paul from doing what he set out to do. As sailors learn to take advantage of adverse winds, so men learn to profit by the misfortunes of life. No one is a better example of this than Paul. He did not groan over his infirmities, he gloried in them. Even his physical disability—that "thorn in the flesh" that plagued him to the end—he accepted gladly because it saved him from being a prima donna. He learned early in life that the most important thing is not what happens to a man, but how he meets what happens to him. The most important thing was not that he was sent to prison, but how he behaved when he got there. The most important thing was not that he was shipwrecked, but how he handled himself in the hour of the ship's greatest

6 And there the centurion found a ship
of Alexandria sailing into Italy; and he
put us therein.
7 And when we had sailed slowly many
days, and scarce were come over against
Cnidus, the wind not suffering us, we
sailed under Crete, over against Salmone;
8 And, hardly passing it, came unto a
place which is called the Fair Havens; nigh
whereunto was the city *of* Lasea.
9 Now when much time was spent, and
when sailing was now dangerous, because
the fast was now already past, Paul ad-
monished *them,*
10 And said unto them, Sirs, I perceive
that this voyage will be with hurt and much
damage, not only of the lading and ship,
but also of our lives.

phyl'i-a, we came to Myra in Ly'ci-a. 6 There
the centurion found a ship of Alexandria
sailing for Italy, and put us on board. 7 We
sailed slowly for a number of days, and
arrived with difficulty off Cni'dus, and as
the wind did not allow us to go on, we
sailed under the lee of Crete off Sal-mo'ne.
8 Coasting along it with difficulty, we came
to a place called Fair Havens, near which
was the city of La-se'a.
9 As much time had been lost, and the
voyage was already dangerous because the
fast had already gone by, Paul advised
them, 10 saying, "Sirs, I perceive that the
voyage will be with injury and much loss,
not only of the cargo and the ship, but

6. A ship of Alexandria: As is clear from vs. 38, this was a grain ship, probably a government vessel bringing supplies from Egypt to Rome. Julius would therefore be able to requisition a passage for himself and his prisoners.

7. Arrived . . . off Cnidus: This seems at first sight unnecessarily far north, but it would have been advisable to keep well clear of Rhodes, which would present a dangerous lee shore. For the same reason, bearing sharply to the south and rounding **Salmone** at the east end of the island, they **sailed under the lee of Crete,** i.e., to the south of it.

8. Fair Havens: This is said now to be called Stouskalolimenas (for εἰς τοὺς καλοὺς λιμένας) or Kalolomonia. It lies about halfway along the southern coast of Crete **near . . . the city of Lasea,** the ruins of which have been identified. West of it the coast runs sharply north, so that to proceed would be to meet the full blast of the northwest wind.

9. The fast, i.e., the day of Atonement, which fell at the end of September or beginning of October. Apparently the recognized sailing season ended on November 11, but navigation was reckoned perilous after September 14 (Vegetius *De Re Militari* IV. 39), so that **the voyage was already dangerous.**

10. The voyage: Paul's words ("I told you so!") in vs. 21 seem to imply that the intention was to leave Crete altogether and continue the voyage to Italy; but it appears clear from vs. 12 that the proposal meantime was merely to move along the coast to a harbor more suitable for wintering. Paul's advice may have been asked, as he was an experienced traveler who had already been shipwrecked three times (II Cor. 11:25). **Also of our lives:** Paul's foreboding, in this respect at least, was not fulfilled in the sequel (vs. 44).

danger. The most important thing was not that he was afflicted with a miserable physical weakness, but how he dealt with that weakness.

Paul was one whose transcendent spirit mastered the circumstances of his life. The fact that a man can rise above the vicissitudes of his existence is the thing that makes him human. Every other creature is completely molded by his environment. It is man alone who can master his surroundings. Other creatures go where the winds blow them. But man, when the winds are against him, can still determine the direction of his course and the destiny of his journey.

In the rest of this chapter there are clues to the secret of Paul's mastery of the adverse winds.

9-44. *From Crete to Malta: Storm and Shipwreck.*—In the first place Paul did everything he could to avoid the danger of storm and contrary winds. He was an experienced traveler, and when he was consulted about the matter of sailing so late in the fall, he advised against it. Paul had a mind for practical affairs, and he had traveled enough by land and sea to know the perils of both. As a man acquainted with the sea, he knew that it was courting danger to go to sea at the very time when the storms were likely to be at their worst. His advice was not

11 Nevertheless the centurion believed
the master and the owner of the ship, more
than those things which were spoken by
Paul.

12 And because the haven was not com-
modious to winter in, the more part advised to depart thence also, if by any means
they might attain to Phenice, *and there* to
winter; *which is* a haven of Crete, and lieth
toward the southwest and northwest.

13 And when the south wind blew softly,
supposing that they had obtained *their* purpose, loosing *thence*, they sailed close by
Crete.

14 But not long after there arose against
it a tempestuous wind, called Euroclydon.

also of our lives." 11 But the centurion paid
more attention to the captain and to the
owner of the ship than to what Paul said.
12 And because the harbor was not suitable
to winter in, the majority advised to put
to sea from there, on the chance that somehow they could reach Phoenix, a harbor of
Crete, looking northeast and southeast,[y]
and winter there.

13 And when the south wind blew gently, supposing that they had obtained their
purpose, they weighed anchor and sailed
along Crete, close inshore. 14 But soon a
tempestuous wind, called the northeaster,

[y] Or *southwest and northwest.*

---

11. **The captain** is the sailing master in control of navigation. **The owner** would be either a private contractor engaged in the grain trade, or if this was a state ship, possibly a government representative.

12. **The majority** is a curious expression, as if the whole ship's company were called into consultation. Paul's words in vs. 21 would be more natural if we could assume that a minority had actually urged that they should press on to Italy, while **the majority** favored the more cautious plan of trying to reach **Phoenix** some forty miles farther west. This harbor is traditionally identified with Lutro, which is the safest harbor on the south coast and would fit Luke's description admirably if the translation **looking northeast and southeast** is correct. But the Greek words mean literally "down the southwest and the northwest wind." If this describes, as some hold, a harbor whose shores run southwest and northwest, these conditions would be met better by another harbor just around the promontory to the west of Lutro and still called Phineka, according to the map in James Smith's *Voyage and Shipwreck of St. Paul.*

14. **Called the northeaster:** The name appears to be a Grecized form of *Euraquilo,* so that it is a Latinism, or strictly speaking, a hybrid of which the first half is Greek and the second Latin. Hence perhaps the word **called,** which hints that the name is unusual. Cf. 6:9, "The synagogue of the Freedmen [λιβερτίνων, another Latinism] (as it was called)." **Struck down from the land:** Having passed Cape Matala, after which the coast drops away sharply to the north, they would lose the protection of the shore they had been hugging.

---

accepted. Why, we do not know. It has been suggested that the owner was anxious to get on with the voyage in order to deliver the cargo and get his money. But that is pure conjecture, and we dare not overindulge ourselves in vain imaginings.

We are interested in Paul's advice, not so much from a navigator's point of view, as from the point of view of a person who is trying to make the most out of the raw material of his life. We are interested in the fact that Paul brought to bear upon the situation his common sense. He did not advise that they go brashly out to sea in defiance of the seasonal storms; he advised that they profit by their knowledge of the weather, and avoid the storms if possible. That is the first step that every wise person takes. He does everything he can to avoid poor health. He takes care of himself without being anxious about himself. He does not linger in wards reserved for those with contagious diseases unless he has some reason. Likewise, if his family situation is in serious danger, he does everything he can to prevent that danger; or if the situation is already well advanced toward catastrophe, he does everything he can to change it. If it is an acoholic who is the cause of the trouble, he tries to cure him. If it is the neighborhood which is the cause of unhappiness, he tries to change it or move elsewhere. This business of rising above the circumstances of life, of sailing against the adverse winds, does not begin with endurance; it begins with an intelligent effort to change the circumstances.

15 And when the ship was caught, and could not bear up into the wind, we let *her* drive.

16 And running under a certain island which is called Clauda, we had much work to come by the boat:

17 Which when they had taken up, they used helps, undergirding the ship; and, fearing lest they should fall into the quicksands, struck sail, and so were driven.

struck down from the land; **15** and when
the ship was caught and could not face
the wind, we gave way to it and were
driven. **16** And running under the lee of a
small island called Cau'da,[z] we managed
with difficulty to secure the boat; **17** after
hoisting it up, they took measures[a] to undergird the ship; then, fearing that they should
run on the Syr'tis, they lowered the gear,

[z] Other ancient authorities read *Clauda*.
[a] Greek *helps*.

---

16. Cauda (which some MSS spell Clauda) appears in Pliny (*Natural History* IV. 12. 61) as *Gaudus* and today is called in Italian *Gozzo.* **The boat,** or dinghy, which was evidently being towed, would by this time be waterlogged. Notice that Luke writes **we managed,** as if perhaps he himself had pulled at a rope.

17. Took measures to undergird the ship, literally **used helps** [βοηθείαις ἐχρῶντο], **undergirding the ship** (KJV). The exact nature of this operation is doubtful. The use of ὑποζώματα, or "undertrusses," is well authenticated. But were they (*a*) ropes passed around the outside of the ship under the keel transversely, or less probably longitudinally, to hold the timbers together? Or (*b*) undergirders of rope or chain stretched across the ship's hold under the deck and made fast to one of the stout ribs on each side? Or (*c*), as shown in ancient pictures of Egyptian ships, rope trusses "stretched above decks from stem to stern intended to prevent the boat from breaking its back amidships by binding the stem and stern together" (H. J. Cadbury, *Beginnings of Christianity,* V, 351, where see an interesting essay)? The last suggestion is attractive because such trusses were kept taut by being raised from the deck by props—which might well be the function of the **helps.** Alternatively βοηθείαις might be taken with ἄραντες in the previous clause: "They lifted it [the boat] up by using their tackle" (Lake and Cadbury, *Beginnings of Christianity,* IV, 332).

The Syrtis, i.e., the great **quicksands** (KJV) west of Cyrenaica which with the northeast wind blowing would now be dead to leeward. **They lowered the gear** (χαλάσαντες τὸ σκεῦος): The Greek is as vague as the English and may mean either (*a*) they struck the mainsail (so KJV); (*b*) they dropped a sea anchor, which would drag below the water and so retard the drift to leeward; (*c*) they set storm sails in an attempt to "claw" their way into safety. This was done by the ancients by lowering (χαλάσαντες) the sails from the yard, not by pulling them up. The experts reckon that such a maneuver might well have kept them on a course which would bring them to Malta, whereas to have drifted would have taken them much farther south. Some Greek minuscules actually read ἱστία, "sails," instead of σκεῦος.

Paul did his best to change his and failed. So do we all. By no means are we always successful in changing or controlling the circumstances. After we have done our best and thought our most intelligent thoughts, we are sometimes faced with a bad situation, with strong winds against us. When we reach that point, another technique is called for.

Just as Paul thought, no sooner had they put out to sea than they ran into heavy seas and violent winds. They threw the ship's cargo overboard and finally the gear. Things were so bad that **all hope of our being saved was at last abandoned.** That was when Paul began to show the stuff that the human spirit is made of. No time for calculating common sense now! This was the time for heroic spirit and courage. This was the time for that madness which Festus recognized in Paul, that quality that refused to be confounded by death and defeat. Paul therefore stood up in the ship. How wonderful it is that always in time of great danger some human being rises above the danger and rallies the others around him! In this case it was the prisoner who set the others free, for he had something inside him that the others did not have; he was more than a conqueror. The picture of Paul surrounded by soldiers and sailors, the crew and custodians of the ship, is one not easily forgotten. "And the last shall be first."

18 And we being exceedingly tossed with a tempest, the next *day* they lightened the ship;

19 And the third *day* we cast out with our own hands the tackling of the ship.

20 And when neither sun nor stars in many days appeared, and no small tempest lay on *us*, all hope that we should be saved was then taken away.

21 But after long abstinence, Paul stood forth in the midst of them, and said, Sirs, ye should have hearkened unto me, and not have loosed from Crete, and to have gained this harm and loss.

22 And now I exhort you to be of good cheer: for there shall be no loss of *any man's* life among you, but of the ship.

23 For there stood by me this night the angel of God, whose I am, and whom I serve,

and so were driven. 18 As we were violently
storm-tossed, they began next day to throw
the cargo overboard; 19 and the third day
they cast out with their own hands the
tackle of the ship. 20 And when neither sun
nor stars appeared for many a day, and no
small tempest lay on us, all hope of our
being saved was at last abandoned.
21 As they had been long without food,
Paul then came forward among them and
said, "Men, you should have listened to me,
and should not have set sail from Crete
and incurred this injury and loss. 22 I now
bid you take heart; for there will be no loss
of life among you, but only of the ship.
23 For this very night there stood by me an
angel of the God to whom I belong and

18-19. Throw the cargo overboard (ἐκβολὴν ἐποιοῦντο), literally "they made an ejection." The Greek of Jonah 1:5 has exactly the same phrase. They now **began** (note the imperfect tense) the operation which is completed at vs. 38. **They cast out with their own hands the tackle:** Presumably the spare gear which would be encumbering the deck. Some of the less important Greek MSS read **we cast out** (KJV), the passengers assisting, which would give much more point to αὐτόχειρες—"with our own hands" (cf. vs. 16).

20. Neither sun nor stars: On these they would be entirely dependent for navigation, the ancients—in spite of the delightful archaism in the KJV of 28:13!—not possessing the compass. **Hope . . . was at last abandoned:** The Greek verb is in the imperfect tense, which suggests that they were progressively giving up hope.

21. Without food need not imply that there was a shortage of provisions, but only that they were unable to eat—presumably on account of seasickness (cf. vs. 33). **You should have listened:** see on vs. 10. **Incurred this injury:** The phrase in the Greek is an interesting oxymoron, or contradiction in terms, well brought out in the KJV translation **gained this . . . loss.**

First, he reminded them of his advice not to start out. He could not resist that. It is an almost irresistible human impulse to say "I told you so" when our advice is proved by the eventual outcome of things to have been right. But then Paul took a different tack. **I now bid you take heart; for there will be no loss of life among you, but only of the ship.** What sublime confidence! **There will be no loss of life,** he said, and it was not possible to doubt his word. Great spirits inspire confidence in others to an almost unbelievable degree. When a great doctor says to a patient on the verge of death, "You will get well," the patient believes him, and that confidence is more than half the secret of the patient's recovery.

It is not hard to imagine the condition of those on board. In our colloquial language they were "sunk." They were beyond hope. What colossal nerve it took to stand up and say, **I now bid you take heart.** It was like telling a man with a rope around his neck to rejoice. Nevertheless that is what Paul said, and that is the way transcendent spirits behave when things are at their worst. It cannot be explained; it can only be wondered at. When things are at the breaking point, such men are steady. No matter how they may feel, they act as though there were brightness ahead. Instead of giving up in despair, they go on as though everything would come out all right in the end. Some people call that "whistling in the dark." Whatever it may be called, it is based on the sound psychological principle that many times men can change their feelings by changing their course of action.

24 Saying, Fear not, Paul; thou must be brought before Caesar: and, lo, God hath given thee all them that sail with thee.

25 Wherefore, sirs, be of good cheer: for I believe God, that it shall be even as it was told me.

26 Howbeit we must be cast upon a certain island.

27 But when the fourteenth night was come, as we were driven up and down in Adria, about midnight the shipmen deemed that they drew near to some country;

28 And sounded, and found *it* twenty fathoms: and when they had gone a little further, they sounded again, and found *it* fifteen fathoms.

whom I worship,
24 and he said, 'Do not be afraid, Paul; you must stand before Caesar; and lo, God has granted you all those who sail with you.'
25 So take heart, men, for I have faith in God that it will be exactly as I have been told.
26 But we shall have to run on some island."

27 When the fourteenth night had come, as we were drifting across the sea of A'dri-a, about midnight the sailors suspected that they were nearing land.
28 So they sounded and found twenty fathoms; a little farther on they sounded again and found fifteen

---

24. **Stand before Caesar:** Cf. 23:11.

26. **Run on some island:** Paul's words up to this point have been completely natural and in character, and there is no reason whatever to regard the paragraph as an editorial addition. But Luke may well have added these concluding words in the light of what follows.

27. **The fourteenth night:** Again the experts state that "this is almost exactly the time and the course which a ship would take if she was . . . drifting to leeward, and making a minimum of headway on the starboard tack in a strong northeast gale" (Lake and Cadbury, *Beginnings of Christianity,* IV, 335). **Drifting across** is the correct translation, the drift being all in one direction, not **driven up and down** (KJV), though so it might seem to a landsman. **Sea of Adria:** The name, though properly belonging to the waters farther north lying between Italy and Dalmatia, was commonly applied to the whole of the eastern Mediterranean.

They were nearing land, literally "some land was drawing near to them"—a curious inversion. Possibly they heard the noise of breakers slowly becoming louder. Indeed one Latin version has "land was resounding," which suggests that the reading of Codex Vaticanus—προσαχεῖν (for προσάγειν)—may represent an original προσηχεῖν, "to sound an echo."

The source of Paul's confidence is immediately indicated—a vision in the night. We are used to the fact that Paul lived by visions, and we do not try to explain them away in the manner of modern materialists. We need not commit ourselves to the nature of the vision. No one will ever ask us to draw a picture of it, and no one ever presumed to ask Paul to describe it in detail. It was Paul's way of saying that he was living a two-dimensional life, that he was in communication with plans to which his were always secondary, and that he was guided by a wisdom far greater than his own. He lived under God, and the light that came from God gave him direction.

In this instance the vision told him not to be afraid, that he must stand before Caesar, that nothing would happen to prevent his appearance before the emperor. It was his sense of destiny that gave Paul his incredible confidence. He had completely surrendered his life to God and he believed that God was using it for a purpose and that he would not let it go until that purpose had been accomplished. The ship could not sink because Paul had to get to Rome. "Nonsense!" say the practical-minded men. "What control over the winds and waves has the destiny of a single individual?" We cannot answer that question. We can say only that Paul got to Rome and the ship was not lost. It was a case of a man's confidence accomplishing his destiny and his sense of destiny renewing his confidence.

Edward Wilson was one of the polar party of five who reached the South Pole on January 17, 1912. On the return journey of eight hundred miles one man collapsed and died when more than halfway back; another went out and gallantly accepted death; the other three kept on until they came within eleven miles of safety.

29 Then fearing lest we should have fallen upon rocks, they cast four anchors out of the stern, and wished for the day.

30 And as the shipmen were about to flee out of the ship, when they had let down the boat into the sea, under color as though they would have cast anchors out of the foreship,

31 Paul said to the centurion and to the soldiers, Except these abide in the ship, ye cannot be saved.

32 Then the soldiers cut off the ropes of the boat, and let her fall off.

33 And while the day was coming on, Paul besought *them* all to take meat, saying, This day is the fourteenth day that ye have tarried and continued fasting, having taken nothing.

34 Wherefore I pray you to take *some* meat; for this is for your health: for there shall not a hair fall from the head of any of you.

35 And when he had thus spoken, he took bread, and gave thanks to God in presence of them all; and when he had broken *it,* he began to eat.

fathoms. 29 And fearing that we might run
on the rocks, they let out four anchors from
the stern, and prayed for day to come.
30 And as the sailors were seeking to escape
from the ship, and had lowered the boat
into the sea, under pretense of laying out
anchors from the bow, 31 Paul said to the
centurion and the soldiers, "Unless these
men stay in the ship, you cannot be saved."
32 Then the soldiers cut away the ropes of
the boat, and let it go.
33 As day was about to dawn, Paul
urged them all to take some food, saying,
"Today is the fourteenth day that you have
continued in suspense and without food,
having taken nothing. 34 Therefore I urge
you to take some food; it will give you
strength, since not a hair is to perish from
the head of any of you." 35 And when he
had said this, he took bread, and giving
thanks to God in the presence of all he

---

29. Anchors from the stern: As they were off the north coast of Malta, anchoring from the stern would in the north wind keep the bows facing the beach in readiness for running aground, and would prevent the ship swinging around into the wind, as would happen if she were anchored as usual from the bows.

31-32. Paul said: Once again in a crisis Paul takes the lead. But on this occasion his intervention had unhappy consequences. Whether or not the sailors were in fact trying to escape, once the soldiers had **cut away the ropes of the boat, and let it go,** there was no alternative but to beach the ship, and a wreck became inevitable.

34. Not a hair is to perish: For the proverbial expression, which is borrowed from the O.T., cf. I Sam. 14:45, etc., and Luke 21:18.

35. He took bread: It would be farfetched to see anything more here than a simple meal, though the language undoubtedly suggests the Eucharist. The thanksgiving before the bread is broken is an ordinary act of piety before partaking of food. Some authorities

---

Later their bodies were found, together with their diaries and records. Edward Wilson was one of those three. He was not only an explorer; he was a doctor and a great naturalist. Above everything else he was a man of faith. This is what he wrote:

> So I live, knowing that I am in God's hands, to be used to bring others to Him, if He wills by a long life full of work, or to die tomorrow if He so wills, having done nothing worth mentioning. . . . We must do what we can and leave the rest to Him. . . . My trust is in God, so that it matters not what I do or where I go.[7]

[7] George Seaver, *The Faith of Edward Wilson* (London: John Murray, 1948), p. 44.

When a man has that kind of trust in God he can rise to almost any height in time of danger. He is able to set himself completely aside and let the power of God stream through him. If Paul had been going to Rome solely in his own interests, to satisfy his own ambition, that would have been another matter. But Paul was headed toward Rome because he believed that God was sending him there. No danger could daunt him, no delay could make him believe that he would not finally arrive there.

In the case of Edward Wilson it did not make any difference where he went, so complete was his trust in God. In the case of Paul it made all

36 Then were they all of good cheer, and they also took *some* meat.

37 And we were in all in the ship two hundred threescore and sixteen souls.

38 And when they had eaten enough, they lightened the ship, and cast out the wheat into the sea.

39 And when it was day, they knew not the land: but they discovered a certain creek with a shore, into the which they were minded, if it were possible, to thrust in the ship.

40 And when they had taken up the anchors, they committed *themselves* unto the sea, and loosed the rudder bands, and hoisted up the mainsail to the wind, and made toward shore.

broke it and began to eat. 36 Then they all
were encouraged and ate some food themselves. 37 (We were in all two hundred and
seventy-six[b] persons in the ship.) 38 And
when they had eaten enough, they lightened the ship, throwing out the wheat into
the sea.
39 Now when it was day, they did not
recognize the land, but they noticed a bay
with a beach, on which they planned if
possible to bring the ship ashore. 40 So
they cast off the anchors and left them in
the sea, at the same time loosening the
ropes that tied the rudders; then hoisting
the foresail to the wind they made for the

[b] Other ancient authorities read *seventy-six* or *about seventy-six*.

(e.g., Blass in his "β-text" representing the "Roman form" of Acts), however, following the reading of several minuscules, add the words "distributing it to us also"—thus clearly suggesting a celebration of the Lord's Supper. The variant is interesting if only as a hint that originally there was no such incongruity as would afterwards have been felt between a celebration of the Eucharist and an ordinary, not to say hurried, repast.

37. Two hundred and seventy-six persons: The number seems very high and Codex Vaticanus and the Sahidic Version read **about seventy-six** (RSV mg.), which may well be the original reading, as Luke very commonly thus qualifies numbers (cf. 2:41; 5:36; 19:7). In the Greek there would be a difference between the two readings only of a single letter. The mention of the number at this particular point suggests that the remaining supplies may have had to be carefully doled out.

38. Lightened the ship, presumably that it might run aground well up the beach. The operation begun at vs. 18 is now completed.

39. A bay with a beach: The traditional landing place in Malta is still called St. Paul's Bay, and there is no reason to doubt the identification, though today it no longer has a sandy beach. It is situated on the north coast of the island near the northwest point. **Bring the ship ashore** (ἐξῶσαι): Alternatively two important codices—including Vaticanus—read ἐκσῶσαι, "to save the ship." If the storm was abating, as seems likely from the fact that no one was drowned, there was a fair chance of doing this had they not struck a shoal.

40. The rudders in ancient vessels were large steering oars, usually one on each side. These would be raised and lashed on deck while the ship was at anchor, and it would now be necessary to unlash them and lower them into position for use, meanwhile **hoisting the foresail** in order to give the ship some steerage way. The word for "foresail" is elsewhere unknown in Greek, but common enough in Latin. Ancient vessels carried a foresail on a short mast sloping sharply forward, and the word *artemo* seems to be used for either the mast or the sail.

the difference in the world that he should get to Rome, the center of the civilized world. So complete was his trust in God that he believed nothing could stand in his way. The trust in each case was the same and the heroism was the same. The outcome was different.

In the meantime, however, Paul's difficulties were not over, for the storm was followed by shipwreck. Once again Paul was the one who saved the day. When the sailors were planning to desert the ship, Paul said, **Unless these men stay in the ship, you cannot be saved.** The sailors did not abandon the ship. Would that on other occasions there had been someone of Paul's caliber to warn the people that to desert the ship was to abandon hope. It is not the rats only that leave a sinking ship to its fate.

But Paul did more than give good advice. He

41 And falling into a place where two seas met, they ran the ship aground; and the forepart stuck fast, and remained unmovable, but the hinder part was broken with the violence of the waves.

42 And the soldiers' counsel was to kill the prisoners, lest any of them should swim out, and escape.

43 But the centurion, willing to save Paul, kept them from *their* purpose; and commanded that they which could swim should cast *themselves* first *into the sea,* and get to land:

44 And the rest, some on boards, and some on *broken pieces* of the ship. And so it came to pass, that they escaped all safe to land.

28 And when they were escaped, then they knew that the island was called Melita.

beach.
41 But striking a shoal[c] they ran the
vessel aground; the bow stuck and remained
immovable, and the stern was broken up by
the surf.
42 The soldiers' plan was to kill
the prisoners lest any should swim away
and escape;
43 but the centurion, wishing
to save Paul, kept them from carrying out
their purpose. He ordered those who could
swim to throw themselves overboard first
and make for the land,
44 and the rest on
planks or on pieces of the ship. And so it
was that all escaped to land.

28 After we had escaped, we then learned that the island was called

[c] Greek *place of two seas.*

41. **Striking a shoal,** literally "falling foul of a two-sea place"—presumably a neck of land, perhaps just awash, between two stretches of deeper water. James Smith, on the other hand, thinks that the reference is to the "strait" between the shore and the small island of Salmonetta at the northwest end of St. Paul's Bay.

44. **On pieces of the ship** (ἐπί τινων τῶν ἀπὸ τοῦ πλοίου): To give this meaning, some noun or adjective after τινων would be almost essential. On the other hand τινὲς τῶν ἀπό is a phrase twice used in Acts with reference to persons (12:1; 15:5); and an attractive translation would be "on some of those from the ship," i.e., "on the backs of some of the crew."

28:1. Malta: There can be no reasonable doubt that Malta is the island in question. The only alternative is Meleda, off the Dalmatian coast, which was suggested perhaps by the mention in 27:27 of the "sea of Adria."

knew that they had not had a square meal for fourteen days. He made them eat, and as they gathered around to share their meager rations, the meal seemed almost like a holy meal, so closely are men drawn together in time of common danger, and so complete is their dependence upon a power higher than themselves. The men cheered up, the ship ran aground, the plan to kill the prisoners was exposed, and the whole company landed safely on strange territory, the name or nature of which they did not know.

Through it all the character of Paul was the determining factor. He was the one who knew what to do when the winds were against him. He did everything he could to avoid the situation, but once the situation was upon him, he rose above it and mastered it. It is a testimony to the human spirit at its best. Indeed we are not the masters of our fate or the captains of our souls, but we have such strange and wonderful affinity with the God who made us that in a time of adversity we can do more than dumbly endure it; we can exert our wills and stretch our spirits to such a point that in the eyes of future observers it seems as though by the mastery of our touch we had actually changed the course of events.

28:1-10. *Paul Spends Three Months in Malta.* —The first thing that strikes our attention about the sojourn in Malta is the unexpected warmth of the welcome. **The natives showed us unusual kindness, for they kindled a fire and welcomed us all, because it had begun to rain, and was cold.** These were the last people in the world that Paul might have expected to receive him well. After all, he and his party were strangers to them, spoke a different language, came from unknown parts, and might well have been a band of marauders. It would not have been surprising if the natives had beaten them off as undesirable visitors. But instead of that, they built a fire for them because it was raining and cold.

2 And the barbarous people showed us no little kindness: for they kindled a fire, and received us every one, because of the present rain, and because of the cold.

3 And when Paul had gathered a bundle of sticks, and laid *them* on the fire, there came a viper out of the heat, and fastened on his hand.

Malta. 2 And the natives showed us unusual kindness, for they kindled a fire and welcomed us all, because it had begun to rain
and was cold. 3 Paul had gathered a bundle of sticks and put them on the fire, when a viper came out because of the heat and

2. **The natives:** The Greek word means primarily those who speak a foreign language rather than **barbarous people** (KJV). The inhabitants of Malta were Semites of Phoenician extraction. **Welcomed us all** (προσελάβοντο): Or possibly "brought us all to it" (the fire). The variant reading of Codex Sinaiticus, προσανελάμβανον, would give the attractive meaning, "set about [note the imperfect] bringing us to," i.e., "gave us first aid."

3. **A viper . . . fastened on his hand:** There are today no poisonous snakes on Malta, and it has been suggested that this was the *Coronella Austriaka,* which bites though it has no poison fangs. In any case Luke, and certainly the onlookers, thought that the snake was poisonous and that it had struck Paul, and not merely coiled around his hand. Luke probably sees here a fulfillment of the promise given in Luke 10:19, "I have given you authority to tread upon serpents and scorpions . . . and nothing shall hurt you"; cf. also Mark 16:18 (probably not known to Luke, as it is in the unauthentic "long ending"), "They will pick up serpents, and if they drink any deadly thing, it will not hurt them."

There was a time when the thing Paul needed most was the blinding light of the midday sun on the road to Damascus, but the thing he now needed above everything else was the warm glow of the light upon a friendly hearth. He had been under a mental and physical strain that would have taxed a younger man. He needed not only comfort but companionship. The people gave him both. How he must have blessed them for it!

Human beings can be so brutal to each other that we need to be reminded from time to time how kind they can be. If one man sees another in distress, his natural impulse is to help him. If one small ship is lost at sea, every other ship within reach of it will alter its course to search for the ship in distress. If one town in the country is destroyed by flood, every village and city in the land runs to its rescue. How tragic it is that the basic instinct to help our fellow human beings is so often perverted and debased that nations war against each other and one man sees how cruel he can be to another! We were not made for such brutality and we will not reach our maturity until we learn to overcome it.

One of the things that the world needs most is the kind of friendliness that the Maltese showed to Paul's shipwrecked party. They took a chance that the strangers meant no harm. It was a risk in the interest of good will. What they did might almost be taken as a parable about God himself. When God made the world, he made two great lights, one to shine by day and the other by night. They were splendid in their shining and no man anywhere could be blind to them. But when God wanted to redeem mankind, he kindled a fire on the hearthstone of the world. Its shining was not dazzling like the sun; it was warm, approachable, like the fire on a hearth. It drew men out of the cold and rain and welcomed them into the fellowship of friendliness.

To be sure, that is not the whole story of the gospel. There is the other side that is more terrible, like the blinding sun. But we cannot afford to neglect this aspect of it, this human, friendly side of the gospel. People who are alone in the world, not knowing which way to turn or whether it is worth turning any way at all, more likely will be saved by the warm fires of lovingkindness than by the scorching fires of judgment. There has been in our day a rediscovery of the stern, fearful righteousness of God before which a man stands trembling. That is well and good, for we had diluted the gospel and made it something soft and spineless. At the same time we must be on our guard lest we make God so fearful that men neither dare nor desire to approach him. We have rediscovered also the sinfulness of man and the depravity of his nature, but we would do well not to forget that man has in his nature wells of goodness that are only occasionally drawn upon, and that he has even in his sinful nature the capacity to reflect the goodness of God. Both of these truths Paul grasped firmly, and if he were ever tempted to doubt the second one,

4 And when the barbarians saw the *venomous* beast hang on his hand, they said among themselves, No doubt this man is a murderer, whom, though he hath escaped the sea, yet vengeance suffereth not to live.

5 And he shook off the beast into the fire, and felt no harm.

6 Howbeit they looked when he should have swollen, or fallen down dead suddenly: but after they had looked a great while, and saw no harm come to him, they changed their minds, and said that he was a god.

7 In the same quarters were possessions of the chief man of the island, whose name was Publius; who received us, and lodged us three days courteously.

fastened on his hand. 4 When the natives
saw the creature hanging from his hand,
they said to one another, "No doubt this
man is a murderer. Though he has escaped
from the sea, justice has not allowed him
to live." 5 He, however, shook off the creature into the fire and suffered no harm.
6 They waited, expecting him to swell up
or suddenly fall down dead; but when they
had waited a long time and saw no misfortune come to him, they changed their
minds and said that he was a god.
7 Now in the neighborhood of that place
were lands belonging to the chief man of
the island, named Publius, who received
us and entertained us hospitably for three

---

4. **Justice:** Probably the word should be understood in a personal sense as the name of Dike, the goddess of justice and vengeance. There is extant an interesting epitaph (quoted by Wettstein from *Anthol. Pal.* VII. 290) to a man who, though he came safely through a shipwreck on the sandy shores of Libya, was immediately afterward killed in his sleep by the bite of a viper.

7. **Publius:** The Greek is Πόπλιος which may stand for either Publius or, less probably, Popilius. He is called **the chief man of the island.** The exact word (πρῶτος) has been found in two inscriptions as a title of an official in Malta, so that we may list this with the use of the title "politarch" of the Thessalonian officials (17:6) as an illustration of Luke's accuracy in small details of local color. It is not clear whether the **chief man** was a native official or the representative of the Roman authority on Malta, which at the time was attached to the province of Sicily.

---

surely those doubts were modified, if not dispelled, when the natives took him in out of the rain.

No sooner had the strangers been welcomed than a snake entered the picture. From the earliest experiences of humanity snakes have had a way of spoiling things. In this case everyone assumed that the snake was poisonous. Whether it was or not is beside the point. It probably was not, but we have no way of knowing. There are no poisonous snakes in Malta now, but that does not prove that there were not then. The point of the story that interests us is not the poisonous nature of the snake, but the poisonous nature of the conclusions that the natives drew about the snake.

When they saw the snake bite Paul's hand, they immediately assumed that Paul was a murderer and the snake's fatal bite was his fair punishment. Not only primitive people, but people otherwise sophisticated, have interpreted physical misfortune as a penalty for sin. If a man is struck down with a dread disease, according to their theory, he must have done something to deserve it. If a man is accidentally drowned, his sudden death is the hand of fate reaping the harvest of his faults. It is so clear in this case that the snake bite had nothing to do with the morals of Paul that it might well be used to show people the absurdity of interpreting the crosses of life in terms of punishment.

When Paul did not drop dead the people were amazed, and immediately reversed their previous judgment and said he was a god. They went from one extreme to the other. One moment Paul was a murderer and the next a god. So absurd can human judgments become when they are divorced from reason and common sense. Even if the snake had been poisonous, and even if it had bitten Paul and not killed him, that would have been no sign that Paul was divine. Yet there is something deep in human nature that craves the miraculous and looks for God in the abnormal and unnatural. If Jesus had come down from the Cross, the crowd would have believed him and hailed him as the Son of God. But when Jesus endured the Cross, they mocked him and let him die. They could not see that the godlike thing to do was to carry the Cross, and in carrying it take away its fearful weight.

Oddly enough, people are not very different

8 And it came to pass, that the father of Publius lay sick of a fever and of a bloody flux: to whom Paul entered in, and prayed, and laid his hands on him, and healed him.

9 So when this was done, others also, which had diseases in the island, came, and were healed:

10 Who also honored us with many honors; and when we departed, they laded *us* with such things as were necessary.

11 And after three months we departed in a ship of Alexandria, which had wintered in the isle, whose sign was Castor and Pollux.

days. 8 It happened that the father of
Publius lay sick with fever and dysentery;
and Paul visited him and prayed, and putting his hands on him healed him. 9 And
when this had taken place, the rest of the
people on the island who had diseases also
came and were cured. 10 They presented
many gifts to us;[d] and when we sailed, they
put on board whatever we needed.
11 After three months we set sail in a
ship which had wintered in the island, a
ship of Alexandria, with the Twin Brothers

[d] Or *honored us with many honors.*

8-9. Sick with fever: The incident reminds us of the healing by Jesus of Peter's mother-in-law and others in Luke 4:38-40. Correct medical terminology is used throughout—e.g., πυρετοῖς . . . συνεχόμενον (cf. Luke 4:38) where the plural means "attacks of intermittent fever," always common in Malta; and a distinction is made between Publius' father, whom Paul **healed** (ἰάσατο), and the others who **were cured** (ἐθεραπεύοντο, properly "received medical attention")—perhaps by Luke?

10. Presented many gifts to us: It has been suggested that this is technical medical language for "paid us large fees"! But probably the more obvious rendering is best: **They honored us with many honors** (RSV mg.).

11. After three months: At 27:9 it was already well on into October, and the shipwreck took place more than two weeks later, sometime in the first half of November. They would thus set sail again about the middle of February, which would still be considered dangerously early, if Vegetius is correct in his statement that the seas were closed from November 11 to March 5. Pliny on the other hand states that the sailing season reopened on February 8 (Vegetius *De Re Militari* IV. 39; Pliny *Natural History* II. 47). **With the Twin Brothers as figurehead** (RSV), i.e., **Castor and Pollux** (KJV), who were regarded as patron deities of sailors and whose sign in the zodiac, the Gemini, was thought to bring good luck in danger at sea.

---

today. They look for the miraculous; they ask for the short cuts; they want something for nothing. They want to get around the laws of life instead of obeying them. They want to charm the snakes instead of steering clear of them. If a man should claim to do the impossible, to run a country without taxes, to fight a war without sending men overseas, to stop inflation without controlling prices, many would hail him as a god, and be willing to believe his most fabulous promises. The trouble is, at least as far as the fate of the man is concerned, that the next moment they might reverse their judgment and call him a murderer.

Religion cannot be completely bound by reason; we are sure of that. It cannot be reduced to pure logic; we know that. Yet on the other hand, when religion rides free of reason, and becomes purely a matter of emotion and desire, it degenerates into the basest kind of superstition. Religion goes beyond reason, but it cannot go against reason. When it does, it gets into trouble. The natives of Malta are a perfect example of what the trouble is like. They made two contradictory conclusions about a snake bite within a few minutes. Both were wrong. Paul was neither a murderer nor a god, and to have treated him as either would have been a disastrous mistake. Their conclusions were wrong because they left out the clear, simple observation of the facts. The snake had nothing to do with Paul's sin, and the immunity of Paul to the bite had nothing to do with his nature and did not imply that he was either more or less divine than any other human being.

The governor of the island entertained the party, and apparently was well rewarded for his trouble. His father was sick and Paul cured him, and after that all the sick people on the island came to Paul and were made well. What the facts were we have no way of knowing. How greatly they were amplified we cannot say.

12 And landing at Syracuse, we tarried *there* three days.

13 And from thence we fetched a compass, and came to Rhegium: and after one day the south wind blew, and we came the next day to Puteoli:

14 Where we found brethren, and were desired to tarry with them seven days: and so we went toward Rome.

15 And from thence, when the brethren heard of us, they came to meet us as far as Appii Forum, and the Three Taverns; whom when Paul saw, he thanked God, and took courage.

as figurehead. 12 Putting in at Syracuse, we
stayed there for three days. 13 And from
there we made a circuit and arrived at
Rhe'gi-um; and after one day a south wind
sprang up, and on the second day we came
to Pu-te'o-li. 14 There we found brethren,
and were invited to stay with them for
seven days. And so we came to Rome.
15 And the brethren there, when they heard
of us, came as far as the Forum of Ap'pi-us
and Three Taverns to meet us. On seeing
them Paul thanked God and took courage.

---

12. **Syracuse** was the great port at the easternmost point of Sicily.

13. **Made a circuit:** This is the meaning of the archaic **fetched a compass** (KJV). The Greek is περιελθόντες; but both Vaticanus and Sinaiticus read περιελόντες, which may have the same meaning, though it is not elsewhere found with this sense. It is the word used in 27:40 for casting off, or "slipping," the anchors. **Rhegium** is the modern Reggio di Calabria on the "toe" of Italy, and **Puteoli** is Pozzuoli on the Bay of Naples. It seems to have been at this time the regular port of arrival for the grain ships supplying Rome (see a description in Seneca *Epistle* LXXVII).

14. **The brethren** are of course Christians, probably members of the church which had already been founded in Rome—traditionally, perhaps actually—by Peter. **Were invited to stay:** It is objected that Paul, being a prisoner and not master of his own movements, could hardly have accepted such an invitation. The motive for this "insertion" is alleged by critics to be to allow time for the Christians in Rome to get news of Paul's arrival and come out to meet him. But if Julius allowed Paul to visit his friends at Sidon (27:3), he may well have given him a similar privilege here, all the more so because, after the part he had played in the storm, Paul must have won Julius' respect and favor. The scribes of some lesser MSS, evidently sensing the difficulty, altered the reading to παρακλήθημεν . . . ἐπιμείναντες, which may be translated "we were comforted after staying with them"—the implication being that the whole company had requisitioned quarters with "the brethren." But this seems a most improbable supposition.

14-15. **So we came to Rome:** There seems no need to suppose that **Rome** here means the *ager Romanus,* or Roman territory, as distinct from the city of Rome in vs. 16. The

---

Stories similar to this were told about the Christian church from the beginning. Obviously there was in the new movement such an overflow of vitality and spiritual energy that incredible things happened as a result. People are stronger physically when their whole being is charged with some great excitement and consuming interest. Similar cures are made today and will always be made. Whether or not Paul cured people in any such numbers as is told here (see Exeg.) may be open to question. But the general impression was then and is now that when men and women are filled with the spirit of Christ, they can do things that would otherwise be impossible; and that when the spirit of a man is the ruling influence of his life, his material surroundings almost always show marked traces of their spiritual master.

It is not too much to assume, therefore, that when Paul and his two Christian friends left the island of Malta, they left a wake of happiness and spiritual joy behind them. They were remembered for years. People told stories about them, how they made the sick well, how even the snakes bit them and did not poison them. If we find nothing else in the stories than this, they stand as an indirect witness to the power of men who are the servants of Christ. We could not ask for anything greater than that we leave behind us such an impression of spiritual power over the things that hold life in their thrall.

14-31. ***Paul Finally Arrives in Rome.***—Luke now comes to the climax of his story. Paul arrives in Rome, the capital of the world. The break with Judaism had been made. Christianity was no longer a fledgling. Its wings were

16 And when we came to Rome, the centurion delivered the prisoners to the captain of the guard: but Paul was suffered to dwell by himself with a soldier that kept him.

17 And it came to pass, that after three days Paul called the chief of the Jews together: and when they were come together, he said unto them, Men *and* brethren,

16 And when we came into Rome, Paul was allowed to stay by himself, with the soldier that guarded him.

17 After three days he called together the local leaders of the Jews; and when they

---

point simply is that the next stage in the journey brought them to Rome, and that on the way they were met by deputations of Christians from Rome at the **Forum of Appius,** just over forty miles from Rome, and at **Three Taverns,** some ten miles nearer the city. There would be inns at these two places, the former of which is mentioned by Horace and the latter by Cicero (Horace *Satires* I. 5. 3; Cicero *To Atticus* II. 10). Paul doubtless approached Rome along the old Appian Way and entered the city by what is now the Porta Capena.

16. Paul was allowed: The Western text here reads: "The centurion handed over the prisoners to the *stratopedarch* and allowed Paul. . . ." This official was either the *princeps peregrinorum,* an officer of the praetorian guard in command of the courier troops or *frumentarii* (see on 27:1), or, perhaps more probably, the *praefectus praetorii,* commander of the praetorian guard, who took prisoners into custody on their arrival at Rome. Paul himself was granted the privilege of *custodia libera* and would be permitted to **stay by himself** in his own quarters under the supervision of **the soldier that guarded him.**

6. Paul at Rome (28:17-31)

According to Luke, having arrived at Rome, Paul as usual immediately makes contact with the Jews. As he cannot go to the synagogue he summons **the local leaders** to his presence. He then explains why he is a prisoner: he has committed no offense against the Jewish religion; the Romans had declared him innocent and were prepared to release him; but Jewish opposition had compelled him to appeal to Caesar, not because he has any charge to bring against his own people, but simply to save his own life. He is a prisoner because as a Christian he believes that in Jesus Christ **the hope of Israel** has been fulfilled. The Jews reply that no unfavorable report has been sent from Jerusalem about him, but that they would like more information about this new sect which is provoking such widespread opposition. Paul then tries to prove, as he did before Agrippa, that the whole O.T. points to Christ. When his hearers disagree among themselves, Paul is pictured as delivering a parting shot by quoting the famous passage in which Isaiah describes the obtuseness of those to whom he had been commissioned to preach. He then concludes by announcing that henceforth the salvation of God has been sent to the Gentiles.

How far can this be accepted as reliable history? The "we" source ends apparently at vs. 16, and critics who reject the Lukan authorship assume that the author himself, not being present, has simply appended a finale which once again illustrates his thesis that in each new city Paul always first offered the gospel to the Jews, and only after it had been rejected, then turned to the Gentiles (see on 13:14, 46). It is also pointed out that if the whole of this "editorial" finale were excised, vs. 30 would follow excellently after vs. 16.

There seems no necessity for such drastic treatment. Such an interview with the Jewish leaders is natural enough, as Paul might well hope that thereby he might succeed in disposing them favorably to himself, or at least in disarming their hostility in view of the coming hearing of his appeal. But it must be confessed that the last part of the Jews' reply in vs. 22 is quite out of touch with the known facts. It implies that they

though I have committed nothing against the people, or customs of our fathers, yet was I delivered prisoner from Jerusalem into the hands of the Romans:

18 Who, when they had examined me, would have let *me* go, because there was no cause of death in me.

19 But when the Jews spake against *it,* I was constrained to appeal unto Caesar; not that I had aught to accuse my nation of.

20 For this cause therefore have I called for you, to see *you,* and to speak with *you:* because that for the hope of Israel I am bound with this chain.

had gathered, he said to them, "Brethren, though I had done nothing against the people or the customs of our fathers, yet I was delivered prisoner from Jerusalem into the hands of the Romans.
18 When they had examined me, they wished to set me at liberty, because there was no reason for the death penalty in my case.
19 But when the Jews objected, I was compelled to appeal to Caesar — though I had no charge to bring against my nation.
20 For this reason therefore I have asked to see you and speak with you, since it is because of the hope of Israel

---

knew of Christianity only by unfavorable hearsay, and had not themselves come into contact with Christian believers. Yet we know that a strong Christian congregation must have been in existence in Rome for some time; to it Paul had addressed his greatest epistle, which itself implies that there were Jews in its membership; and Luke himself in vs. 15 above has already stated that there were Christians to welcome Paul on his way to Rome. We recall, too, that the presence of Christians in Rome may have been the cause of the riots which had led to the expulsion of the Jews in A.D. 49 (see on 18:2). It is hardly sufficient explanation of the Jews' professed ignorance to argue that it was the consistent policy of the rabbis to affect to ignore the new religion! Vss. 25-28 also raise some difficulty if taken as strict history. Would Paul, usually so tactful and diplomatic, have summoned the Jewish leaders in order to disarm their prejudice, and then have denounced them for their refusal unanimously to believe, using terms calculated to embitter and enrage them?

We must admit, then, a certain apologetic motive in this final section. At the close of his book, as constantly throughout it, Luke represents Paul as not being to blame for the nonconversion of the Jews, and consequently for the predominantly Gentile character of the Roman church. He had offered them the gospel, as he had done in every other city; but they had persistently rejected it, in spite of the fact that Christianity was the perfect fruit of Judaism to which all their past had been leading up. Our author, no doubt, also wishes to demonstrate and explain the injustice of the Jews' enmity for the Christian church, which was very marked at the time when he was writing, and contributed considerably to the hostile attitude of the Roman authorities toward the church.

17. The local leaders: See on 5:17. **I was delivered prisoner:** The Greek verb, as usual, hints at treachery or betrayal.

19-20. Though I had no charge to bring: Luke is concerned to make it clear that at the appeal court Paul appears solely in the role of an innocent defendant. He is making no countercharge. **The hope of Israel,** i.e., the messianic hope, with which Paul always associates faith in the resurrection (see on 23:6 and 26:6).

---

fully spread and would eventually embrace the whole world. Once more, however, the Jews had their chance. Immediately upon his arrival Paul called them together. He explained his reason for being there and he wanted to tell them the whole story. Their reply was typical of people who try to keep an open mind, but whose mind is three quarters closed from the beginning. **We have received no letters from Judea about you,** they said, **and none of the brethren coming here has reported or spoken any evil about you. But we desire to hear from you what your views are: for with regard to this sect we know that everywhere it is spoken against.** They had no evidence against Paul and they wanted to be fair and open-minded, *but* as a matter of fact their minds were closed before Paul ever began to speak.

21 And they said unto him, We neither received letters out of Judea concerning thee, neither any of the brethren that came showed or spake any harm of thee.

22 But we desire to hear of thee what thou thinkest: for as concerning this sect, we know that every where it is spoken against.

23 And when they had appointed him a day, there came many to him into *his* lodging; to whom he expounded and testified the kingdom of God, persuading them concerning Jesus, both out of the law of Moses, and *out of* the prophets, from morning till evening.

24 And some believed the things which were spoken, and some believed not.

25 And when they agreed not among themselves, they departed, after that Paul had spoken one word, Well spake the Holy Ghost by Esaias the prophet unto our fathers,

26 Saying, Go unto this people, and say, Hearing ye shall hear, and shall not understand; and seeing ye shall see, and not perceive:

27 For the heart of this people is waxed

that I am bound with this chain." 21 And
they said to him, "We have received no letters from Judea about you, and none of
the brethren coming here has reported or
spoken any evil about you. 22 But we desire to hear from you what your views are;
for with regard to this sect we know that
everywhere it is spoken against."
23 When they had appointed a day for
him, they came to him at his lodging in
great numbers. And he expounded the matter to them from morning till evening,
testifying to the kingdom of God and trying to convince them about Jesus both from
the law of Moses and from the prophets.
24 And some were convinced by what he
said, while others disbelieved. 25 So, as they
disagreed among themselves, they departed,
after Paul had made one statement: "The
Holy Spirit was right in saying to your
fathers through Isaiah the prophet:
26 'Go to this people, and say,
You shall indeed hear but never understand,
and you shall indeed see but never perceive.
27 For this people's heart has grown dull,
and their ears are heavy of hearing,

21-22. The brethren here are presumably Jewish visitors from Jerusalem. The reference can hardly be to Christians belonging to the Jewish wing of the church. **This sect:** See on 24:5.

23. At his lodging: The Greek word usually means "hospitality," and the suggestion may be that Paul entertained them at an informal reception. **The kingdom of God:** As elsewhere in Acts, this comes near to being a synonym for the Christian church (see on 1:3; 8:12). **Convince them about Jesus:** Presumably that he was Messiah, as proved by Scripture and confirmed by his resurrection—Paul's regular argument with Jews (e.g., 13:30-39).

25-27. Through Isaiah the prophet: The passage is Isa. 6:9-10, and it is quoted here almost verbatim from the LXX. In Mark's Gospel the same passage is used to explain why Jesus failed to convince all his hearers by his parabolic teaching (Mark 4:11-12; see also Luke 8:9-10). The obduracy of unbelievers is to be explained as itself part of God's providential purpose. With the very difficult theological problem which this doctrine involves Paul tries to deal in Rom. 9–10.

The world is full of people today who boast of the fact that they are willing to give every man a hearing, but of course they are not going to listen as though they did not know that what he is talking about is nonsense. What kind of open-mindedness is that? It is almost better to be completely unresponsive to a person than to appear to be willing to listen to him and yet have your mind made up from the beginning that he is wrong.

Paul was able to convince a few that Jesus was the Messiah, but most of them would not believe. It was the Jews' last chance, according to Luke, and Paul's last words were the words of the prophet Isaiah: "You will hear and hear but never understand" (Moffatt). From henceforth the gospel was for the Gentiles.

Luke ends his story at this point. Paul is a prisoner in Rome, relatively free to go about his way unmolested. How and when he died we are

gross, and their ears are dull of hearing, and their eyes have they closed; lest they should see with *their* eyes, and hear with *their* ears, and understand with *their* heart, and should be converted, and I should heal them.

28 Be it known therefore unto you, that the salvation of God is sent unto the Gentiles, and *that* they will hear it.

29 And when he had said these words, the Jews departed, and had great reasoning among themselves.

30 And Paul dwelt two whole years in his own hired house, and received all that came in unto him,

31 Preaching the kingdom of God, and teaching those things which concern the Lord Jesus Christ, with all confidence, no man forbidding him.

and their eyes they have closed;
lest they should perceive with their eyes,
and hear with their ears,
and understand with their heart,
and turn for me to heal them.'

28 Let it be known to you then that this salvation of God has been sent to the Gentiles; they will listen."[e]

30 And he lived there two whole years at his own expense,[f] and welcomed all who came to him, 31 preaching the kingdom of God and teaching about the Lord Jesus Christ quite openly and unhindered.

[e] Other ancient authorities add verse 29, *And when he had said these words, the Jews departed, holding much dispute among themselves.*
[f] Or *in his own hired dwelling.*

29. This verse (KJV) is an addition present in the Western text, but not in the best MSS. It seems out of place, and spoils the dramatic climax reached with Paul's last words.

30. Two whole years: For the question whether or not Paul was released at the end of this period see the special concluding note below. **At his own expense** (μίσθωμα): No instance can be quoted of the word meaning a **hired house** (KJV). It regularly means either money earned, or money paid out, and is best translated as in RSV.

31. The Lord Jesus Christ: Rarely in Acts is this full title bestowed on our Lord (cf. 11:17; 15:26; 20:21). The Western text expands thus: "Saying that this is the Christ, even Jesus, the Son of God, by whom the whole world will be judged." **Quite openly and unhindered:** Luke at the very end strikes the familiar note. So far as the Roman authorities were concerned, they saw no cause to restrict Christian missionary activities. Paul to the end was a favored prisoner. The "captivity epistles," if indeed they were written from Rome, provide proof that Paul was allowed a large measure of freedom to communicate with his friends, and was able to continue to interest himself in and to supervise the life of his far-distant churches. Here Luke breaks off—with a ring of triumph in his closing words, **with all confidence, no man forbidding him.**

What was the final outcome of Paul's appeal to Caesar? Those who accept the Pastoral epistles as three single wholes, each of which is an authentic letter of Paul, have commonly assumed an acquittal at a first Roman hearing, followed by further extensive missionary travels. If Paul was in fact released, the reason may well have been that the case against him fell by default. The Jews at Rome had admitted that they had "received no letters from Judea" following up the case against the apostle; and there is some evidence that if the prosecution failed to put in an appearance within two years, they lost their case by default (see discussion by Lake, *Beginnings of Christianity,* V, 330-31).

not told. Perhaps it is better so, for in one sense Paul never died. Again and again he has come back, first in Augustine, then in Luther, then in Karl Barth. Not only in these great figures has Paul returned, but in many a lesser light. Indeed it may fairly be said that when a man wants to see Jesus, he is almost sure to see him more clearly if he looks at him through the eyes of Paul. For Paul saw him clearly; not only did he see the outward contour of his life, but he saw also the deep, inexplicable mystery of its meaning. Jesus of Nazareth is drawn by the writers of the Gospels, but the Christ of the universe, though seen by them, shines through the strange and wonderful personality of Paul in a marvelous way.

This indeed may be Luke's meaning when he states that Paul "lived there two whole years," release at the end of that period being automatic. If the Pastoral epistles are authentic, Paul after his release may have visited Ephesus and Macedonia (I Tim. 1:3), Troas (II Tim. 4:13), Crete (Tit. 1:5), perhaps Nicopolis (Tit. 3:12), and possibly Spain. A visit to Spain is thought to be implied in the statement of Clement of Rome (5:5-7) that Paul "having come to the boundary of the West . . . was released from the world and went to the holy place." After this it is assumed that Paul was rearrested, condemned, and executed during the Neronian persecution. In this case I Timothy and Titus were written during the interval of freedom and II Timothy during the second imprisonment. When Paul writes of "my first defense" and states that he "was rescued from the lion's mouth" (II Tim. 4:16-17), he has in view his first trial and the release which resulted from it.

If the Pastoral epistles are not authentic—as is held by most modern scholars, on the ground that their theology and their "church consciousness" reflect a date later than Paul—then no early evidence remains of such renewed missionary activity, except perhaps the words of Clement quoted above; and even here, in a letter addressed to eastern readers, "the boundary of the West" might be used as a description, not of Spain, but of Rome. The earliest explicit reference to a second imprisonment following a period of release is contained in a statement of Eusebius (*Church History* II. 22; and see P. N. Harrison, *The Problem of the Pastoral Epistles* [London: Oxford University Press, 1921], pp. 102-4) written some 260 years later and obviously based on a questionable exegesis of II Tim. 4:18. True, most scholars believe that the Pastorals include certain genuinely Pauline fragments. But provided that the letters are not treated as authentic wholes, the allusions in such fragments to missionary activity can be explained by reference to various situations in Paul's life, as described in the epistles and Acts, before his original Roman imprisonment (see Harrison, *Problem of Pastoral Epistles,* pp. 115 ff., and McNeile, *St Paul,* pp. 257-61). It may be said, moreover, that Paul's whole progress from Corinth to Jerusalem reads in Luke's account like a march to martyrdom. We recall how Luke concluded his story of Paul's farewell to the elders of Ephesus with the words, "They all wept, . . . sorrowing most of all because of the word he had spoken, that they should see his face no more" (20:37-38). It is of course possible that Paul's forebodings may have been mistaken and that after his first imprisonment he did return to Ephesus. But it is difficult to believe that Luke would have given us so solemn and affecting an account of the farewell, had he not known that in fact Paul did not return. All that we can deduce from the closing verses of Acts is that presumably after the "two years" some change took place in the prisoner's condition, and it is fairly safe to assume that it was condemnation and death. Complete silence as to an acquittal, not only by all other sources but above all by Luke himself, seems conclusive evidence of condemnation. For Luke the account of such an acquittal would have provided a magnificent climax to a story throughout which he has been constantly concerned to stress the favorable impression which Paul always made on Roman authority. Had he known that Paul had been triumphantly exonerated, it is inconceivable that he should have omitted to tell us so. Such a triumph, moreover, must have been widely known in the church; yet it is not mentioned by one single early writer. This consideration alone almost compels us to pronounce Paul's alleged acquittal to be a fiction, and to conclude that his two years' captivity ended with conviction and death.

On what charge then was Paul executed? The closing verses of Acts indicate that the Jewish case against him was dropped. Luke would never have deliberately created this impression were it not in accordance with the facts; for throughout he has sought to show how the Jews pursued Paul with inveterate hatred, while the Roman authorities befriended him. Similarly the whole of later tradition and legend agrees that both Peter and Paul perished at the hands of the heathen, and that the Jews played no direct part in their fate. Both died not as renegade Jews but as Christian disturbers of the Roman peace in whom the Jews took no interest whatever. It is therefore wholly probable that Paul was executed as a Roman citizen on a charge of sedition against the state. The charge was not that he was preaching new gods or promulgating a novel and illegal religion. Had he been condemned on such a ground his death must have been the signal for a general persecution directed against the Christians, whereas all the evidence shows that Paul died at least a couple of years before the Neronian persecution broke out. But no doubt the original political charge framed by the Jews still stood, and Paul was executed as "a pestilent fellow, an agitator among all the Jews throughout the world" (24:5). In the years of strict government during the early part of Nero's reign such a crime would be sure to meet with condign punishment. A genuine fragment of II Timothy, probably written at this time, shows what may have happened. The first hearing ("my first defense," II Tim. 4:16) possibly resulted in suspension of judgment. But Paul knew that the case against him was too strong and he evidently looked for a speedy sentence. He is, he says, "already on the point of being sacrificed" (II Tim. 4:6). As a citizen he escaped the arena and so was "rescued from the lion's mouth" (II Tim. 4:17). But he knew that in any case he had "finished the race" (II Tim. 4:7).

One final question remains. How are we to explain the abrupt ending of Acts? Why does Luke leave us in suspense without even a hint of what was the final fate of his hero? Various suggestions have been made, and it must be confessed that none is wholly convincing:

(*a*) The author died before his work was complete. But the ending of Acts, though abrupt, is obviously planned with real artistic skill and does not leave the impression of an unfinished work.

(*b*) Luke wrote his book during the two years at Rome and he had, so to speak, "caught up with the events" before the final issue had become clear. This explanation was given in antiquity, e.g., by Jerome (*On Famous Men* 7); and it is also the hypothesis which is finally adopted by Harnack (*The Date of Acts,* tr. J. R. Wilkinson [New York: G. P. Putnam's Sons, 1908], pp. 90-125). But so early a date for Acts is impossible unless we are prepared radically to revise our views concerning the dating not only of Acts but also of the Synoptic Gospels (see Intro., p. 21).

(*c*) Those who deny the Lukan authorship may suppose that the author's source failed him. The theory would be that the principal source, used by a later editor, broke off at this precise point, either because it was written during the two years, or because at the end of that period its compiler left Rome, leaving the document behind in its unfinished state. Norden, who holds this view, quotes the parallel of the biography of Apollonius of Tyana, in which Philostratus states that the narrative of Damis, on which he has been basing his story, breaks off before his hero's death (Norden, *Agnostos Theos,* p. 332). But Philostratus goes on to recount what tradition says about that death; and the author of Acts must almost certainly have done the same.

(*d*) Theophilus, for whom the book was destined, was a Roman official who already knew all that was to be known about the issue. Even the Christian community as a whole must have been in possession of the facts, and there was no need for Luke to retell them. But this seems hardly an adequate reason why so artistic a writer should leave his work thus truncated. Besides, according to the preface, the author's purpose was not merely to record matters of which Theophilus and others might be ignorant, but to treat of things well known "that you may know the truth concerning the things of which you have been informed" (Luke 1:4).

(*e*) Luke ended his second volume thus abruptly because he intended to write a third volume telling the story of the trial, Paul's defense, possibly other events during the years at Rome, and finally his death. The difficulty is that unless Paul was released and engaged again in missionary activity, which is for other reasons improbable, the third volume would hardly have had the amplitude of the other two. But even if Paul *was* released and there was thus sufficient material for a third volume, any writer with Luke's historical and artistic sense must have included the whole judicial process in our Acts, which would thus have reached a magnificent climax, i.e., Paul's acquittal. Yet this remains a possible hypothesis. But even so, it is probable that the third volume was never actually written, for there is no trace whatever of it in tradition. Still, as a provisional hypothesis for explaining the abrupt end of Acts, it is not necessary to suppose that the third volume was actually written, but only that it should have had a place in the author's plan.

(*f*) The problem is perhaps best approached by recalling the main purpose of the author in writing his book. His chief object has been attained when he has brought Paul to Rome, because he has now completed his account of the triumphant march of Christianity from its birthplace at Jerusalem to the capital city of the Roman Empire. Luke has reached his climax when he can represent Paul at Rome "preaching the kingdom of God and teaching about the Lord Jesus Christ quite openly and unhindered." As McNeile puts it, "The addition of anything further about the apostle of a personal kind, however interesting or important, would have been a literary blemish such as St Luke was too good an artist to commit; having planned a sketch of the expansion of Christianity (cf. Acts i:8), he would not allow it to become a biography, even of St Paul himself" (*St Paul,* pp. 119-20). But taken alone, surely even this is an insufficient explanation. Having given the last half of the book so strong a biographical flavor, would not the author at least have relieved us from our suspense?

(*g*) The book breaks off as it does because Luke can thus best serve another of his apologetic aims—to conciliate official Roman opinion by demonstrating that Roman authority was consistently favorable to Christianity and protected the propaganda of Paul. Such a thesis would in his readers' eyes appear to be wrecked, did he go on to record that after all Paul was finally condemned at Caesar's tribunal. Rather than negative the impression left by his book as a whole, the author preferred to break off at the point where he must have begun to record facts out of harmony with his thesis. Once again this theory is attractive, but not wholly satisfying. Whether recorded by Luke or not, the issue must have been well enough known, and the success of such an artifice would be more apparent than real. We might rather have expected that Luke would follow the precedent of the Gospels with reference to the trial of Jesus. He would then have represented the Roman authorities as declaring the innocence of Paul, but forced against their own best judgment to give way to Jewish pressure and condemn an innocent man.

We shall probably find the solution of our problem in a combination of (*f*) and (*g*). The theory of a third volume remains as an improbable but still possible alternative. In conclusion Chrysostom's quaint explanation is perhaps worth quoting: "At this point the historian stops his account and leaves the reader thirsting so that thereafter he guesses for himself. This also non-Christian writers do. For to know everything makes one sluggish and dull" (*Homilies on Acts* LV; quoted by H. J. Cadbury, *The Making of Luke-Acts* [New York: The Macmillan Co., 1927], p. 322).

The Epistle to the

ROMANS

Introduction and Exegesis by John Knox

Exposition by Gerald R. Cragg

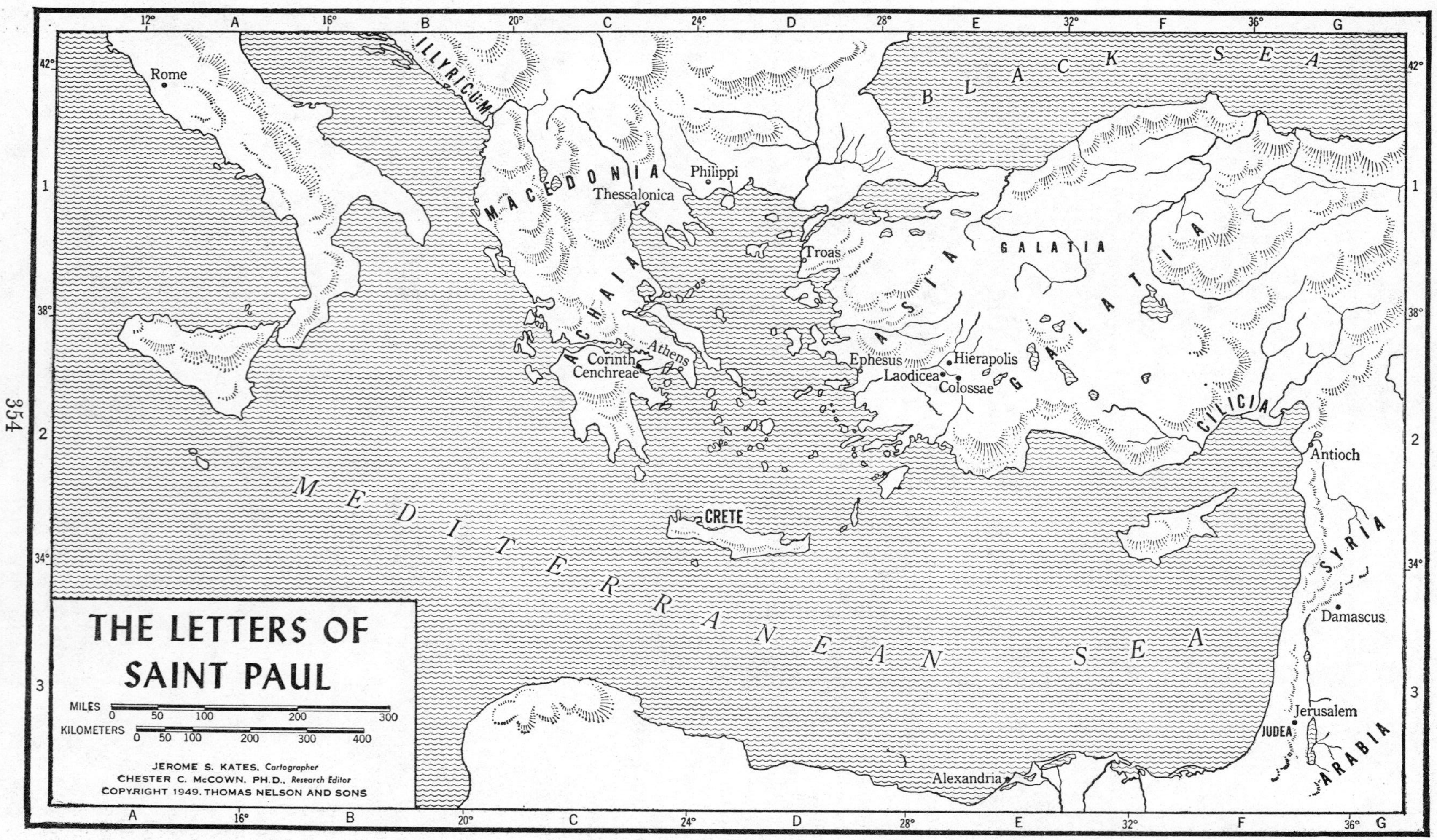
THE LETTERS OF SAINT PAUL
MILES 0 50 100 200 300
KILOMETERS 0 50 100 200 300 400
JEROME S. KATES, Cartographer
CHESTER C. McCOWN, PH.D., Research Editor
COPYRIGHT 1949, THOMAS NELSON AND SONS
BLACK SEA
MEDITERRANEAN SEA
ILLYRICUM
MACEDONIA
ACHAIA
ASIA
GALATIA
CILICIA
SYRIA
JUDEA
ARABIA
CRETE
Rome
Philippi
Thessalonica
Troas
Athens
Corinth
Cenchreae
Ephesus
Hierapolis
Laodicea
Colossae
Antioch
Damascus
Jerusalem
Alexandria

ROMANS

INTRODUCTION

Of the nine letters of Paul which are generally recognized as authentic, the most important are undoubtedly Romans, I and II Corinthians, and Galatians; and of these four the letter to the Romans can lay claim to a certain preeminence. Not only is it the longest letter of Paul which has survived; it is also the weightiest. All of Paul's letters were called forth by the needs of the churches he addresses and have the *ad hoc* character which true letters always have, and Romans is no exception in this regard; but this letter shows signs of having been composed under conditions of greater leisure, and therefore with greater care, than any of the rest, and thus comes nearer to being a systematic and inclusive statement of Paul's faith. It is thus the principal source book for the study of Paul's gospel, and in consequence it is unquestionably the most important theological book ever written. How amazed Paul would have been if he had been told that such a statement would be made twenty centuries afterward about this letter of his!

I. Authorship

Few facts can be surer than that the letter, at least in major part, is from Paul's hand. The evidences of authenticity are so impressive, severally and cumulatively, as to make the case altogether irrefutable. We must not spend much time on a matter so far beyond controversy; but let us look at the most important facts in this case.

We note first that the letter claims to be written by Paul and that absolutely nothing it contains is incompatible with, or even difficult to reconcile with, that claim. The style and vocabulary of the letter are the characteristic style and vocabulary of I and II Corinthians and Galatians, not to mention other indisputable letters, so that to say that Paul wrote any of these letters is really to say that he wrote them all. Style and vocabulary are always exceedingly difficult to imitate, as we recognize when we examine the Pastoral epistles, which also claim to have been written by Paul; and this is particularly true of Paul's style. It is an intensely personal literary style, revealing the man himself in a remarkably striking way. To read Paul's words is to hear his voice, and in a fashion and measure true of few other writers. We cannot doubt the conclusion—or rather the impression—that back of the greater letters stands a single person; and there is not the slightest reason to question that his name is Paul and that he is the same man whose missionary work is described in the Acts of the Apostles, and who was known as an apostle—often *the* apostle—by the later church.

This impression of genuineness is confirmed, so far as Romans is concerned, by every feature of the letter and by almost every word it contains. The teaching of the epistle is engaged with issues which disturbed the churches about the middle of the first century, when Paul was at the height of his career. The stage of development of Christian doctrine which the letter reveals fits the time of Paul. The relation of Paul with the Roman church, reflected in the letter, is what we should on other grounds have regarded as probable. In a word, the internal evidence of the authenticity of Romans is unquestionable, unequivocal, and conclusive.

But the external evidence is equally impressive. Although it is not cited by name—as few epistles were—until nearly the end of the second century, Romans was unmistakably known and used by writers as early as Clement of Rome (A.D. 95), including the writers of some of the New Testament books themselves, especially I Peter (see Exegesis on that epistle, Vol. XII). Both Ignatius of Antioch, who wrote a number of letters to churches when, around A.D. 110, he was making his way under guard from Antioch to Rome and martyrdom, and Polycarp, the bishop of Smyrna, who wrote to the church at Philippi somewhat later, show that they knew this epistle to the Romans as well as other

Pauline letters. Every list or canon of the Pauline letters of which we have any knowledge—orthodox and heretical—has contained it.

II. Place in the Canon

Mention of the place of Romans in the lists of Paul's letters brings up the whole question of the early history of the letters of Paul as a group. Since Romans is the first of these letters to be discussed in this work, it is appropriate to attempt here some summary of that history. Much in the story is obscure, and it is not to be supposed that the writers on the other Pauline letters in this Commentary will agree at every point with the proposed summary. For other references to the subject see the article on the history of the New Testament canon in Vol. I, as well as the Introductions to Ephesians and Philemon in Vols. X and XI of this series.

Many considerations point to the conclusion that the several letters of Paul, though they may have had some limited circulation separately, became widely known only as parts of a published collection. The only title which Romans, for example, is known to have had in the beginning is "To the Romans"—so it is called in the most ancient manuscripts—but such a title for the individual book presupposes a general title for a collection of books, some such title as "The Letters of Paul."

It is not necessary to argue that such a collection was made; the very existence of the Pauline letter corpus in the New Testament bears witness to this development. The only pertinent questions are when and under what circumstances did it occur. There can be no doubt that it had occurred by the middle of the second century, for the great heretical leader, Marcion, who flourished then, possessed such a collection and accorded to it the status of sacred scripture. It is occasionally proposed that Marcion himself made the collection, but there are many indications that he simply appropriated what was already a common possession of the churches, and that the collection was formed and published in the last decade of the first century. The evidence for this view cannot be completely stated here—it can be found in A. Harnack, *Die Briefsammlung des Apostels Paulus* (Leipzig: J. C. Hinrichs, 1926); Edgar J. Goodspeed, *New Solutions of New Testament Problems* (Chicago: University of Chicago Press, 1927), and elsewhere—but the major points can at least be suggested: (*a*) If Marcion had been the original collector of Paul's epistles, they would have suffered a handicap as regards their acceptance among "orthodox" Christians, but of this there is no sufficient indication. Hints can be found that Marcion's *appropriation* of the letters tended to discredit them; if Marcion had *originated* the collection, the signs of orthodox distrust would be unmistakable. (*b*) Marcion's text of Paul's letters differed markedly from what soon became the established text. There is evidence that some of the features of this established text antedated Marcion. (*c*) Writers earlier than Marcion—Clement of Rome (A.D. 95), Ignatius of Antioch (A.D. 110), and Polycarp of Smyrna (*ca.* A.D. 110 and 130)—show a knowledge of several of Paul's letters which can be most naturally explained by the hypothesis of a collection. Ignatius even uses the phrase "Paul in every letter." (*d*) It is known that the letters of Ignatius—six of them addressed to churches and one to Polycarp—survived, not as separate letters, but as a *collection*. The Epistle of Polycarp to the church at Philippi speaks of a request on the part of the Philippian church, soon after Ignatius' martyrdom *ca.* A.D. 110, that such a collection be made. This request is more likely to have been made by the Philippians *after* they had come into possession of a collection of Paul's letters. It is intrinsically unlikely that the idea of a collection of church letters would have occurred *first* in connection with Ignatius, rather than with Paul, who takes precedence both in date and importance, not to mention his long association with the Philippian church. (*e*) The book of Revelation (*ca.* A.D. 95) begins with a collection of letters to churches. Such letters appear oddly in an apocalypse, and their presence can be most readily explained by the prestige which the collection of Paul's letters had given to the letter form.

The contents of this first collection were the letters ascribed to Paul in our New Testament with the exception only of the Pastoral epistles. Such were the contents of Marcion's "Apostle," and many considerations point toward the conclusion that the original collection included these same ten letters. Whether the collection was made by a single individual or by a community we cannot know, nor can we be sure whether it was made as a whole at one time or took place in several stages—the final collection being a uniting of smaller collections or perhaps the completing of a collection which had been growing gradually over several decades. Perhaps the majority of scholars favor the view that the collection was conceived and executed as a whole and was not merely the final phase of a gradual development. But whatever the process may have been by which the collecting of Paul's letters took place, it seems clear that the first formal publication of his letters took the form of the ten-letter corpus which has been described. When the letters of Paul first became widely known, they became known in that form. Romans was a member of that corpus, and needless to say, was always recognized as being one of the most important documents in the collection. It has been from the very beginning one of the most widely quoted of the letters of Paul.

As to its location in the collection, only some plausible surmises may be made. Marcion is known to have had the letters in the following order: Galatians, I and II Corinthians, Romans, I and II Thessalonians, Ephesians, Colossians, Philemon, Philippians. The only question to which this reconstruction of Marcion's list is subject involves the relative position of Philemon and Philippians; some of the evidence points toward the conclusion that Philippians followed immediately upon Colossians, Philemon closing the list. The so-called Muratorian list (see the article on the Canon of the New Testament, Vol. I), *ca.* A.D. 200, arranges the Pauline letters quite differently: I and II Corinthians, Ephesians, Philippians, Colossians, Galatians, I and II Thessalonians, Romans (Philemon appears with the Pastoral epistles); and with this arrangement Tertullian (*ca.* A.D. 200) seems to agree, at least to the extent of placing Corinthians in first place and Romans in last. These are our two earliest lists of the Pauline letters—the Marcionite and the Muratorian—and it is fair to suppose that one of these conforms more nearly than the other to the arrangement of the original collection.

It has been customary to assume that the Muratorian order comes nearer to being the original one. The only grounds for such an assumption are (*a*) the fact that Tertullian has a similar arrangement, which is interpreted to mean that this was the prevailing arrangement at the end of the second century and therefore probably earlier, and (*b*) the fact that Marcion was a "heretic" and therefore by definition iconoclastic. Theodor von Zahn, in discussing this matter of order and in accepting the Muratorian as standard, dismisses Marcion's arrangement as merely whimsical; so others have done. Actually, however, Marcion's order is by and large the order of length, I and II Corinthians being taken as one item and I and II Thessalonians as another. Galatians is an obvious exception, but Marcion placed Galatians in first place for good reasons of his own: it is the letter in which Paul comes nearest to supporting the later Marcionite theological position. The order of length would be a natural one for the original editor of the Pauline corpus to adopt. The fact that this same principle of arrangement has dominated the corpus throughout its later history to our own day would strongly indicate that such was true from the beginning. Besides, why—except for his putting of Galatians in first place—should Marcion have altered the original arrangement? Marcion, it can be shown, usually had good reasons (from his point of view) for whatever alterations he made in the tradition. Why, one may ask again, should he have troubled to rearrange the letters of Paul? Would it not have suited his purpose better simply to appropriate the published corpus and make it his own? It may well be that it was because he so nearly succeeded in doing this that the "orthodox" not only added the Pastoral epistles to the traditional corpus but also rearranged the corpus itself.[1]

We have seen that Marcion had his own reasons for placing Galatians in first place, and it would be unlikely in any case that the original collector and editor would have given so polemical and partisan a letter this dominating position. It is probable, however, that one of the shorter letters (that is, some letter other than Romans) preceded I and II Corinthians in the original collection, for if the collection was published on two papyrus rolls—and it would have been too long for one roll—the two rolls could have been of approximately equal length only if I and II Corinthians and one of the shorter letters occupied one of them, and Romans and the remaining letters, the other. In Marcion's canon it is obvious that such an arrangement on rolls was possible, Galatians and I and II Corinthians comprising, as we would say, "Volume I," and Romans, Thessalonians, Ephesians, Colossians, Philemon, and Philippians comprising "Volume II." It is likely that in the original collection also one of the shorter letters stood with Corinthians in the first roll, and that Marcion simply substituted Galatians for that shorter letter.

There are many reasons for believing that this other letter, the opening epistle of the collection, was Ephesians. Since the collection was meant for the use of all the churches, it might most appropriately begin with a letter addressed to all the churches. Ephesians is the only letter in the collection which has this general character: the words "in Ephesus" in the salutation are not found in the earliest manuscripts. The content of Ephesians fits it to be a preface or introduction to the rest of the letters. Besides, where, if not in first place, could Ephesians have been placed? A letter without a church name, a general letter, at the beginning of the published corpus would be very appropriate—indeed, may well have been deemed necessary—but such a letter in the midst of the church letters would constitute an unthinkable interruption of the pattern.

It may be surmised, therefore, that the original

[1] For further discussion of this subject see John Knox, *Marcion and the New Testament* (Chicago: University of Chicago Press, 1942), pp. 39-76.

collection of Paul's letters was arranged as follows: Ephesians and I and II Corinthians on one roll; and Romans, I and II Thessalonians, Galatians, Colossians-Philemon, and Philippians on the other. It is interesting to note that the order of the Muratorian list is, according to volumes or rolls, the precise opposite of this, and that the Pastoral epistles are also named there in what would seem to be reverse order, Titus before Timothy. Romans would thus have been the third letter in the corpus—I and II Corinthians being considered as one—and would have been the first letter in the second volume. Just as soon as I and II Corinthians came to be thought of as two letters for editorial purposes, and also I and II Thessalonians, the application of the principle of relative length would have different results: Romans, shorter than I and II Corinthians together, is longer than I Corinthians alone, and in lists from the fourth century on this letter tends to move to the head of the corpus. Its place there was soon established, and there it still stands.

III. Destination, Time, and Place

The title "To the Romans" cannot be earlier than the first publication of the Pauline letters, for as the letter left Paul's hand it had no title. There is, however, the address in the salutation, "to all God's beloved in Rome," and everything in the letter—with the exception of ch. 16, which as we shall see constitutes a special problem—confirms that address. The only basis for the slightest doubt at this point is the fact that there is evidence of the absence of the word "Rome" from some manuscripts extant in the early period. This fact, an element in the somewhat complicated problem of the text of Romans, will be discussed later at some length. At the moment it is enough to say that whatever the meaning of this fact may be, Paul undoubtedly sent this letter to the church at Rome. The only alternative is the supposition of a general letter; and 1:13 and 15:22-32 rule out such a possibility. It is conceivable, of course, that Paul sent substantially the same letter to other churches also—the great body of it would be suitable for general use—but the particular letter which has come down to us is unquestionably the letter which went to Rome, with some possible additions as we shall see. The question whether this was or was not the only form of the letter can be discussed more appropriately later.

In the case of none of Paul's other letters are the time and place of the writing so clearly indicated in the letter itself as in the case of Romans. In 15:19 ff. Paul lets us know that he is near the culmination of his career. He has preached the gospel, he says—with some exaggeration perhaps—"from Jerusalem and as far round as Illyricum," and goes on to make the amazing statement that he no longer has any room to work in that vast area. He wishes to go to Spain, since Italy itself is already being evangelized, and to visit the Roman church on the way. But he cannot do so at once; he must first make a visit to Jerusalem. The reason for this visit is both clear and significant. For some time (II Cor. 8:10 would suggest at least a year), he intimates, he has been engaged in taking a collection among the churches of Macedonia and Greece for the help of the poor at Jerusalem. Just now that collection is virtually if not quite complete, and Paul is awaiting an opportunity to deliver it. The only other letters in which this collection is mentioned are Galatians (some would dispute this reference) and I and II Corinthians. Galatians (2:10) alludes to the occasion and the beginning of it; I and II Corinthians (I Cor. 16:1-4; II Cor. 8–9) refer to it as being then in progress; Romans (15:25-28) looks upon it as just completed. Since in I Cor. 16:3-4 Paul indicates that he plans to end his work on the collection in Corinth and to depart from that city for Jerusalem, and since at the time of writing II Corinthians (9:3 ff., etc.) he is manifestly carrying out that intention and is actually on his way to Corinth, it is natural to suppose that he wrote Romans in Corinth. This would have been Paul's last visit to that city, since it was in Jerusalem just afterward that his final imprisonment began (cf. Acts 20:2-3). As to the date of this final visit to Corinth and therefore of the letter to the Romans, it is impossible to speak with any assurance. Everything depends upon one's general conception of the chronology of Paul's life. I would date Romans not later than A.D. 53, but most students would place it about five years later.[2]

IV. Purpose

Consideration of the purpose of this letter involves a twofold question: first, we must ask why Paul wrote to the Roman church at all; and second, why he wrote just as he did. The answer to the first of these questions has been suggested in the preceding paragraphs. The reason for his addressing a letter to Rome appears in 1:8 ff. and 15:19 ff. He has finished his work in Asia Minor and Greece, he says, and wants to push farther west. No statement of the apostle could more eloquently proclaim what he conceives his work to be. He is an evan-

[2] The question of the chronology of Paul's life is too complicated for discussion here and besides does not bear vitally enough upon our understanding of the letter to the Romans. The basis of the opinion referred to above is presented in John Knox, *Chapters in a Life of Paul* (New York and Nashville: Abingdon-Cokesbury Press, 1950), pp. 13-88.

gelist, not a pastor. His calling, as he conceives it, is to plant, not to water. He not only does not wish to build on other men's foundations; he does not really enjoy *building* on his own. He has indicated in II Cor. 11:28 how oppressive he has found the care of the churches. But for an extended period he has been concerned almost entirely with this pastoral care, as Galatians and I and II Corinthians (written within this period) and the travels, anxieties, and activities to which these letters refer bear witness. His major preoccupation during this period—perhaps three or four years—has been the disastrous rift between the conservative Jerusalemite body of Christians and their Gentile brethren. Paul's work has lain almost entirely among Gentiles and he himself has been both misunderstood and opposed by many Jewish Christians. As a consequence of a conference in Jerusalem on this issue (Gal. 2:1-10; Acts has this same conference in mind in 15:1-29, although it probably places it too early in Paul's ministry), Paul sets about raising a sum of money, of undisclosed but obviously large proportions, among the Gentile churches for the relief of poverty at Jerusalem. He hopes that this offering—so important symbolically that in spite of danger to his person he intends to deliver it himself—will heal the breach and bring peace to the church. Such a result will mark a real culmination of that whole phase of his work which had begun perhaps fifteen or sixteen years before, when moving westward from Antioch he embarked on his strenuous missionary labors; and it will open an entirely new phase, enabling him to resume his strictly evangelistic work in some virgin territory. Since Christ has already been preached in Italy, he looks toward Spain as the new field of work; but on the way toward that distant country, on the western rim of the ancient world, he hopes to visit the church at Rome, of which he has often heard. He writes this letter to announce his plan and to appeal for the co-operation of the Roman Christians.

Such considerations make quite clear the occasion of Paul's writing to the church at Rome; but it is more difficult to understand why the letter he wrote on this occasion is the longest and theologically the most weighty of all his letters. One would suppose that a very brief note would have been adequate to announce his plans for visiting Rome and to prepare the way for his being welcomed there by the Roman church. The very fact that he expects to see his readers so soon would, it might be argued, render unnecessary and even inappropriate the extensive statement of his theological position which he actually makes.

It has sometimes been urged that his motive for making the letter to the Romans the occasion for this statement is his rather desperate need of their help in his mission to Spain. According to this view Paul is primarily interested, not in the Romans' welcoming him, but in their giving large financial support to the Spanish mission. Rome must be the base of operations in the territories farther west, just as, according to this same view, Antioch had been in the eastern and earlier phase of his work. Paul must therefore persuade the Roman church of the importance of his mission, and he writes with this purpose primarily in mind. For this reason he emphasizes the universal need of salvation in Christ and the universal availability, as well as the perfection, of that salvation. He is not ashamed of the gospel, and he wants the Romans to share his enthusiasm for it and his pride in it, so that they will support his effort to take it to the "barbarians" in the western parts of the empire.

That Paul will be ready to accept whatever help the Roman Christians will give him as he embarks for Spain would be scarcely doubtful in any case, but that an appeal for this help is the major purpose of this letter is most unlikely. If it had been such, one would expect more explicit and more frequent references to Paul's plans and his needs than this letter does in fact contain. Indeed it is not till ch. 15 that the reader receives even a hint that the apostle plans a mission to Spain. From 1:8-15, the only other passage in the letter mentioning his plans, no one would gather that he is contemplating anything other than a visit to Rome. It is to the *Romans* that Paul hopes to impart "some spiritual gift" (vs. 11) and it is among *them* that he hopes to "reap some harvest." It is in connection with preaching, not in Spain, but in Rome that he thinks of his "obligation both to Greeks and to barbarians" and of his pride in the gospel: "So I am eager to preach the gospel to you also who are in Rome."

It is also doubtful that Paul would have been as dependent upon the assistance of the Roman church as this view assumes. One learns from other letters that Paul was relatively, and could be if necessary entirely, independent of economic assistance. He had a trade which he insisted on practicing wherever he went, and he took pride in supporting himself with his own hands. The good will of the Roman church would have been of the greatest importance to him as he left for Spain, but it is questionable that he would have expected or wanted much if anything more than this (but see on 15:24). In a word, although Paul is undoubtedly interested in commending himself and his "gospel" favorably to the attention of the Roman Christians, there is too little evidence that his primary motive was a desire for their support of the Spanish mission.

We shall be on safer ground if we find the explanation of the character and scope of the letter to the Romans partly in the situation of the apostle as he wrote it, and partly in the particular character of the Roman church. Some attention must now be given to each of these factors.

(*a*) Surely one reason Paul writes a long letter is simply that he has time and leisure to do so. For several years he has been laboring under great pressure—as the letters to the Corinthians and the Galatians amply demonstrate. But now, he has reason to feel, the period of crisis is about to end and his work in Asia Minor and Greece is about done. Only the obligation of taking the offering to Jerusalem prevents his moving immediately toward the west. He is awaiting in Corinth—among old friends now fully restored to him—the opportunity of departing for Palestine. He is in a quieter, more composed mood than he has been for years. It is not surprising that the only extant letter coming out of that brief epoch in his career should contain the most careful and comprehensive statement we have of Paul's theological position. The contents of most of Paul's letters are obviously suggested either by the problems and needs of the churches to which he is writing or else by some development in his own personal relationship with the particular church. This may also be true of Romans: we do not yet know enough about the Roman church to be sure it is not true. And as we shall see under (*b*), some of the features of the letter are best explained in that way. But, taken as a whole, the letter seems to be dictated, not by some peculiar need of the Roman church, but by Paul's own desire to make a fairly complete and somewhat comprehensive statement of the message of salvation he is called to declare. One suspects that much of this letter might have been sent as appropriately to the churches in general as to the church at Rome in particular. It is this fact which gives substance to the suggestion that the peculiarities of the text of the epistle (which already have been referred to and will be discussed later more fully) can be best accounted for by the supposition that Paul sent the same letter, with only slight modifications, to a number of churches. Whether one finds this theory convincing or not—arguments against it will appear later—one can scarcely deny that Romans is less obviously dominated by particular considerations growing out of the conditions of the local church or of Paul's relations with it than are the other letters. Ephesians, the one exception, was almost certainly not written by Paul. Paul's own freedom from tension when he wrote Romans undoubtedly has some part in explaining its systematic doctrinal character.

But not only does the situation of the apostle account partly for the length and the ordered argument of the epistle; it also helps explain its theme. That theme is in general the meaning of the salvation in Christ; but this theme is developed with particular reference to the Jewish law and to the calling and destiny of the Jewish people. Such an orientation of the discussion might in any case be expected from a Jewish Christian such as Paul was, but it is the more easily understandable in the light of the fact that Paul has for months, perhaps for years, been engaged in controversy with Jews, both believers in Jesus Christ and nonbelievers, on the very points which this letter emphasizes. Just at this time he has good reason to hope that the issue is on the way to being settled and that the offering will finally seal the peace. He therefore is in a mood to discuss the problem dispassionately, attempting a more systematic and complete justification of his position than was possible in the heat of controversy.

He is the more ready to do this in his letter to the church at Rome because he has had no earlier contact with that church. Of Paul's other church letters all except Colossians were written to churches which he had established and with which he had kept in constant contact; and the church at Colossae also had been founded indirectly by him through one of his associates, Epaphras, so that its members had some personal knowledge of him and he of them. But Rome lay altogether outside his field of operation. He could count on no authentic understanding of his "gospel" among the Roman Christians. They would have heard of the controversy about the law of which Paul had been the center; but they would not have heard Paul state his own case. He wants to make up this lack.

(*b*) It is hard to escape the impression that he is eager to do this, not only because of his desire for understanding and friendly support from the Roman church, but also because he has reason to fear that some initial misunderstanding and suspicion on its part needs to be overcome. This impression is made not so much by any explicit statement in the letter as by the consistently irenic tone of it all. Still, the paragraph 1:8-15 alone goes far to justify it. After speaking of the wide fame of the Roman church's faith and of his long-time earnest desire to visit that church in order that he might "impart . . . some spiritual gift," he hastens to add, "That is, that we may be mutually encouraged by each other's faith, both yours and mine." Paul is plainly eager to make the most amiable possible approach to his Roman readers. This manifest eagerness, when taken in connection with the length and fullness of his explanation of his "gospel," suggests the possibility—better, the likelihood—that Paul is not too well assured of his welcome. His explanation, almost apology, in 15:14-16 for having written so fully when his readers themselves are "full of goodness, filled with all knowledge, and able to instruct one another" is another indication of this same lack of assurance.

This feeling of insecurity is reflected also, it would appear, in Paul's uncertainty as to how he should state the purpose of his coming visit. He seems to give one explanation in 1:1-15 and another in 15:18-29. It has already been pointed out in this discussion that 1:1-15 gives no hint of a projected visit to Spain. Paul wants to "preach the gospel" at *Rome* (1:15) and "to reap some harvest" among the *Romans* (1:13). He justifies his intention of coming to Rome by appealing to his apostolic call—"to bring about obedience to the faith for the sake of his name among all the Gentiles, including yourselves" (1:5). He is clearly claiming authority as an apostle among all Gentile Christians, whether members of his own churches or not. He makes the same point in 1:13: "I want you to know, brethren, that I have often intended to come to you . . . , in order that I may reap some harvest among you as well as among the rest of the Gentiles." He also intimates in this section of the letter that he is acting in obedience to a more specific command of God. For a long time he has been praying that God would send him to Rome (vss. 9-10); now at last he has received the summons. He is coming "by the will of God," whom he "serves with [his] spirit in the gospel of his Son." So much for Paul's explanation in ch. 1. But as he comes to the end of his letter (15:18-29), he seems to state the case somewhat differently. He explains that he has not been able to come to Rome earlier because of his desire to preach the gospel where it had not been preached before. It is only now, when the gospel has been preached "from Jerusalem and as far round as Illyricum," and he has no longer "any room for work in these regions"—it is only now that he is seriously thinking of Spain as his field of work. Rome appears to be, not (as in ch. 1) a field of evangelistic or pastoral service, but a mere way station on his journey to Spain. He still has no intention of trying to build upon "another man's foundation." The point is not that there is any necessary contradiction between chs. 1 and 15, but only that Paul justifies his coming to Roman territory in somewhat different terms. This fact suggests that he is not sure of the reception he will receive there and is uncertain how he can most tactfully explain his coming.

The basis for this lack of assurance on the apostle's part we do not know and shall probably never know. It almost certainly lies in the history and character of the Roman church; but of these, in the earliest period, we are almost entirely ignorant. As to the origin of the Roman community, there is a persistent tradition that Peter was its founder. But this tradition cannot be traced earlier than the end of the second century, although as early as A.D. 95, I Clem. 5:3 ff. associates both Peter and Paul with the Roman church and intimates that they both suffered martyrdom there. This passage from I Clement is important enough to be quoted entire:

> Let us set before our eyes the good apostles: Peter, who because of unrighteous jealousy suffered not one or two but many trials, and having thus given his testimony went to the glorious place which was his due. Through jealousy and strife Paul showed the way to the prize of endurance; seven times he was in bonds, he was exiled, he was stoned, he was a herald both in the East and in the West, he gained the noble fame of his faith, he taught righteousness to all the world, and when he had reached the limits of the West he gave his testimony before the rulers, and thus passed from the world and was taken up into the Holy Place—the greatest example of endurance.

Rome is indicated as the place of both martyrdoms only because I Clement is a Roman document. This earliest documentary evidence of a connection between Peter and the Roman church is obviously weak and would have no significance whatever if it were not strongly supported by a uniform later tradition.

That Peter as well as Paul visited the church at Rome is, in view of the strength of this tradition, more than possible, and there is no reason to deny the double martyrdom there; but it is next to impossible to suppose that Peter established the Roman church. Paul's letter to the Romans leaves the impression that the church at Rome was a strong and well-established community, not a recent foundation. The same impression is made by the Acts account of Priscilla and Aquila (Acts 18:2), who seem to have been Christians in Rome when the Jews were expelled from that city during Claudius' reign. We know, however, that Peter was at Jerusalem at the time of the conference referred to in Gal. 2:1-10. At that time (probably *ca.* A.D. 51) it was recognized that Paul "had been entrusted with the gospel to the uncircumcised, just as Peter had been entrusted with the gospel to the circumcised." Such a conclusion, although it does not rule out the possibility, certainly renders unlikely that Peter had already been carrying on missionary work far to the west of the field in which Paul had been serving. But if Peter's bringing Christianity to Rome happened *after* the conference, the Roman church was younger than both Romans and Acts suggest. The conference occurred probably in A.D. 51 and certainly not earlier than A.D. 48; the letter to the Romans is being written probably in A.D. 53 and certainly not later than A.D. 58. We have thus at most a period of ten years, and probably a much shorter one, between the conference and the writing of this letter. But Paul leaves the impression that the Roman church is well established and has been for a number of years: "I have longed for many years to come to you" (15:23). In so far as Acts bears any testimony on this point, that also supports the view that the church at Rome had been founded well before A.D. 50. Aquila and Priscilla are said to have come to Corinth from Rome at a date which could not have been later than A.D. 51; and one gains the impression that they had been Christians before leaving Rome. If, then, Peter did not go to Rome until after the conference in Jerusalem, he went too late to be the founder of the Roman church.

The fact is, however, that the decision at Jerusalem hardly prepares us to find Peter at Rome at all—that is, as the pioneer evangelist. All that we learn both from Paul's letters and from Acts suggests that Paul was the boldest pioneer of the primitive church. It was he who among the apostles carried the gospel farther and farther to the West. Peter was established in Jerusalem and Antioch when Paul was living in Corinth and Ephesus. If Peter ever came to Rome, it is much more likely that it was after Paul had reached that city than before.

It may also be pointed out that Paul would almost certainly have made some reference to Peter's connection with the church at Rome if any such connection had existed; indeed it is unlikely that he could have expressed himself as he does in 1:5-15 if the Roman church had been established by another apostle. In this passage he tacitly assumes that Rome lies within his proper province—it is a Gentile church and he is the Apostle to the Gentiles.

The most probable ancient account of the beginnings of Christianity in Rome is given by a fourth-century writer known as "Ambrosiater":

> It is established that there were Jews living in Rome in the times of the apostles, and that those Jews who had believed [in Christ] passed on to the Romans the tradition that they ought to profess Christ but keep the law. . . . One ought not to condemn the Romans, but to praise their faith; because without seeing any signs or miracles and without seeing any of the apostles, they nevertheless accepted faith in Christ, although according to a Jewish rite.[3]

[3] Ambrosii *Works* III. 373.

This account is probable for two reasons: For one thing it fits with what Romans implies—namely, that no apostle had been at Rome before Paul's own visit—at the same time affirming what is antecedently likely, that "lay" Christians reached Rome before "official" missionaries. Travel in the first century was far more extensive than in any previous period, and a very considerable part of it was between Rome and the East. Almost at once after Christianity became established in Antioch, Christians would have appeared in Rome; and as nearer cities like Corinth and Ephesus became centers of Christian evangelization, the number of Christians in Rome would have increased. That these believers would form churches there goes almost without saying. Only if one begins by assuming as a matter of definition that only an apostle can "found" a church, is it possible for one to believe that either Peter or Paul founded the Roman church. Their act of "founding" the church, at the most, could have consisted only in putting an official stamp of approved upon an accomplished fact.

Ambrosiater's account commends itself as being roughly correct for another reason: it asserts that Roman Christianity had an original Jewish cast, and such an assertion is in line with what we know of the Roman church subsequently. Not that the later Roman church was made up of Jews; that certainly was *not* true. Even in Paul's time we may be sure that the church there, as in every pagan city, was almost entirely Gentile. This appears clearly enough in the letter to the Romans itself. Paul devotes chs. 9–11 to an attempt to account for the fact—so obvious as to need no demonstration—that the Jewish nation has apparently rejected Jesus Christ. It is not to be supposed, either, that the Gentile members of the Roman church were all Jewish proselytes, insisting on circumcision and the rest of the Jewish law; this was surely not true in Paul's period or later, and strictly speaking may never have been true. Still there is much to suggest that Roman Christianity had from the beginning a soberer, more conservative cast than Pauline Christianity, and that the difference between synagogue and church was less wide at Rome than, say, at Corinth. A comparison of Justin Martyr's account of a Roman Christian service [4] with Paul's discussion of Christian worship at Corinth would indicate this. Pliny's description of the Christians' services in Pontus-Bithynia [5] in some degree confirms it. The fact that Marcion, the great opponent of the Jewish law, and for all his misunderstanding of his master, the greatest disciple of Paul in the early second century,

[4] *Apology* I. 67.

[5] Pliny *Letters* X. 96.

was "exposed" and withstood first, or at least most vigorously, at Rome is probably not unconnected with the traditional conservative cast of Roman Christianity.

If we are right in suspecting such a cast and in trusting Ambrosiater's account (allowing for some exaggeration) as indicating the source of it, we shall not be surprised that Paul should have been looked on with a certain suspicion at Rome, and that he should have felt the need of stating his "gospel" as fully and clearly as possible. The fact that Justin Martyr, who wrote in Rome around the middle of the second century, nowhere makes mention of Paul in the very considerable portion of his work which has survived may possibly indicate that Paul's letter, and even his later visit, did not succeed entirely in overcoming this suspicion.

V. The Text

Several references have been made in the course of this discussion to the question of the text of Romans as calling for more extended discussion than up to this point could properly be given to it. Even now only a sketchy presentation of what is an exceedingly complicated problem can be attempted. For a more adequate treatment the reader is referred to more technical works.[6]

The textual question is twofold: (*a*) Granted that Paul wrote this letter as a whole (see above, p. 355), is there good reason for distrusting the authenticity of any part of it? and (*b*) Is there reason for believing that any part of the letter, genuinely Pauline in authorship, did not belong originally to this particular epistle? These two aspects of the problem will be dealt with in a single discussion.

Disregarding here a number of minor questions, some of which will be treated or at least mentioned at the appropriate points in this Commentary, we are left with three major questions regarding the authenticity of the text. One of these has already been briefly considered. This is the question raised by the fact that in one extant manuscript, and according to some indications, in other manuscripts circulating in the ancient period but now lost, the word "Rome" is not found in 1:7, 15. There are two possible ways to account for the absence of this important place name. One way already noted is to assume that this letter was originally a general letter, or at any rate a letter intended for several churches, and that the absence of the place name in certain manuscripts is therefore to be traced back to Paul himself. The possibility that Paul sent the substance of this letter to other churches besides Rome is certainly not to be denied, although there is no evidence whatever that he did so except the textual facts we are now considering, and these can be accounted for by other hypotheses; but as we have seen, the form of the letter which contained 1:10-15 and 15:22-32 surely went to Rome, and would naturally contain the name in both vss. 7 and 15. To be sure, as we shall notice in a moment, a form of the epistle existed in ancient times which lacked ch. 15, and Lake argues, not too convincingly, that it was this shorter form of the letter which prevalently lacked the word "Rome" in 1:7, 15; but even so, it is clear that another form of the letter contained ch. 15 and it is this form which has come down to us and with which we are concerned. The word "Rome" would probably have been a part of that form from the beginning.

We must conclude then that Paul—at least in the form of his epistle that has survived—wrote the word "Rome" in 1:7, 15, and that it was later omitted in certain manuscripts. One may explain this omission in several ways. One may explain it as owing simply to the possible fact that in certain other forms of the epistle, or in some other form, the word was known not to appear. Some scribe, knowing the epistle in one of these other forms, therefore omits it from his copy of *this* form, thus introducing the error into the manuscript tradition. Or one may blame Marcion for the omission. This has been done frequently, partly because there is some reason to believe that his form of Romans did omit the word, but more because he is known to have done some cutting of both the Gospel which he accepted and the Pauline letters. Of these two explanations the first is the more plausible, since a motive for Marcion's deliberate excision of the word "Rome" is hard to imagine. The only possible motive would be a desire, for whatever reason, to conceal the destination of the epistle; but all the evidence we have of the contents of Marcion's canon shows that the title of this epistle there was "To the Romans." He would scarcely have removed a word from the text only to leave it more conspicuously in the title.

Still another possible explanation of the omission deserves at least to be noted. Allusion has already been made to the collection and publication of the letters of Paul and to the probability that this original collection appropriately began with Ephesians, a general letter. For various reasons, however, Ephesians did not maintain its place at the beginning of the

[6] See, for example, William Sanday and Arthur C. Headlam, *The Epistle to the Romans* (New York: Charles Scribner's Sons, 1895), pp. lxxxv-xcviii; C. H. Dodd, *The Epistle to the Romans* (London and New York: Harper & Bros., 1932), pp. xiii-xxiv; or Kirsopp Lake, *The Earlier Epistles of Paul* (London: Rivingtons, 1914), pp. 324-79; 414-20.

corpus, and other letters, notably I Corinthians and later Romans, became the opening epistle. There would naturally be a tendency to make this opening letter as general as possible. One sees in the broad address of I Corinthians a manifestation of this tendency. Paul probably wrote simply, "To the church of God which is at Corinth"; a later editor added "together with all those who in every place call on the name of our Lord Jesus Christ, both their Lord and ours." Surely Paul would not have intended this letter—one might almost say especially this letter—to be so widely read; none of his letters is so fully concerned with strictly local and personal problems. And what basis would he have had for supposing that such a wide reading might be possible, even if he had wanted it? He was not *publishing* a letter; he was merely sending it by messenger to the community for which alone it was intended. But at a later time this letter became the opening section of a published work addressed to all Christians, "The Letters of Paul"; and the editor would quite legitimately have wished to make that fact clear in the very first sentences. So much for I Corinthians. Now since at other times and places Romans stood in first place among the published epistles, it is at least conceivable that the word "Rome" was omitted from certain copies of Romans for this same reason.

The second major question touching on the authenticity of the materials of the letter to the Romans concerns the long doxology found in most of the best manuscripts at 16:25-27, in the majority of manuscripts at the end of ch. 14, in one very important manuscript at the end of ch. 15, and in a few manuscripts not appearing at all. There is all but universal agreement among students of this letter that these verses were not originally a part of it. The style is not Paul's and the content, while not un-Pauline, is not adapted to closing the argument of this particular epistle. But on this more will be said at the appropriate place within the Exegesis itself.

The third question has to do with the authenticity of the rest of chs. 15 and 16. There are two principal grounds for raising this question: (*a*) The evidence that some ancient manuscripts of Romans ended with ch. 14; and (*b*) the difficulty of accounting in any plausible way for ch. 16 as the work of Paul. Each of these topics calls for some elaboration.

(*a*) No manuscript ending with ch. 14 has come down to us, but manuscripts in which the doxology appears at the end of ch. 14 rather than—or as well as—at the end of ch. 16 are found in great abundance. It scarcely needs to be argued that the appearance of the doxology at any point indicates conclusively that the document at some time or place ended at that point. These indications, as regards a form of Romans ending with ch. 14, are confirmed by certain statements in the church fathers. It is particularly clear that Marcion had Romans in this short form. Tertullian's comment on Marcion's Romans stops with ch. 14, and Origen tells us explicitly that the Marcionite text ended there. Many signs exist that this short form was not limited to the Marcionites but was current in certain orthodox circles as well. One list of early Latin chapter headings, for example, omits chs. 15–16. For a full discussion of the textual evidence for the existence and wide currency of this short form of Romans the reader is referred to the work of Kirsopp Lake already mentioned.

Now the very fact of the currency of this short form is enough to raise the question of the authenticity of the last two chapters. It may be said at once that the great majority of scholars answer it by affirming Paul's authorship of these chapters; their absence from some manuscripts is explained by the supposition either that they were deliberately eliminated by some editor or scribe; or that they were accidentally lost through some damage to a manuscript, which then became a type; or else that Paul issued the letter in a long and a shorter form, only the long form going to Rome. The affirmation of the authenticity of the two chapters is based upon the fact that the style and contents of chs. 15–16, taken as a whole, are consistent with the hypothesis of Pauline authorship (more consistent than with any other hypothesis); and that in spite of the known existence of the "short form," the longer form is witnessed to quite as early, and was apparently always the prevailing form.

We have been speaking of chs. 15–16 as a unit. As a matter of fact, however, their close association in discussions of the text of Romans is due entirely to the fact that they are both lacking from many manuscripts, and not at all to any internal connection. They are indeed quite separate. Ch. 15 is concerned with Paul's relations with the Roman church and with his plans for visiting it, and it ends with a benediction. Ch. 16 makes a fresh start and deals with other matters entirely. There is absolutely no *internal* reason for supposing in advance that the textual history of ch. 16 is the same as that of ch. 15. And at least one piece of external evidence stands decisively against such a supposition: the oldest manuscript of the epistles of Paul which we have (the so-called Chester Beatty Papyrus, which goes back to the third century if not even earlier) has the long doxology *at the end of ch. 15*. The scribe of that manuscript has, after the doxology, made a diagonal mark to indicate a break, and has then transcribed ch. 16. This incontrovertible evidence—and evidence from a very early period—that some copies of Romans ended with ch. 15 justifies us in dealing separately with these two questionable chapters.

A strong presumption in favor of the authenticity of ch. 15 is created by the fact that it follows so smoothly upon ch. 14. There is no break in thought or style. If the "short form" had ended with 15:6, rather than with 14:23, it would be somewhat more difficult to reject it as having been the original and only authentic form. As it is, the "short form" breaks off in the middle of a paragraph. The vocabulary, style, and content of the chapter are quite consistent with the hypothesis of Pauline authorship, and Paul's discussion of his plans sounds entirely natural and authentic. Such statements as vss. 29 and 32 contain would be especially hard to explain as written by one who knew of what happened to Paul in Jerusalem and of the circumstances in which, according to Acts, he finally actually reached the Imperial City. Besides all this, it is difficult to conceive of any adequate motive for the later composition of this material. The case for the authenticity of ch. 15 is strong indeed, and we may assume its truth.

(*b*) This brings us to the complicated problem of ch. 16. This chapter (and it must always be remembered that "chapters" are a modern device; there are no chapter or verse divisions or numberings in the manuscripts) begins with an introduction of Phoebe, a deaconess of the church at Cenchreae, not far from Corinth, who is either arriving with the letter or will arrive soon afterward (vss. 1-2). This introduction is followed by a long list of persons to whom Paul wants his greetings conveyed (vss. 3-16). Next comes a short paragraph of exhortation and of warning against certain troublemakers. A few final greetings to the church addressed from some of Paul's associates at the time bring the chapter to a close, except for the doxology, which needs and has received separate treatment.

The short paragraph of exhortation and warning is enough to raise a question in the reader's mind as to the relationship of this chapter to the rest of the letter to the Romans, since the local church situation which is reflected in this paragraph has not been referred to in the preceding fifteen chapters. One would normally expect a closing exhortation like this to take up for final emphasis some note already struck in the body of the letter; but such is not the case. The paragraph deals with matters not even alluded to elsewhere. A danger so serious and imminent as to call for the vigorous warning sounded here would appear to have demanded at least mention in the body of the letter. The paragraph also has a polemical tone which the letter as a whole has not given us reason to expect. Indeed, Paul has throughout this letter made an apparent effort to be irenic. This outburst of anger at its very close is, to say the least, surprising.

But once one's suspicions have been aroused, one is bound to be struck by the list of greetings. How does Paul happen to know so many people in the Roman church and to know them so well? No fewer than twenty-five individuals and two families are greeted by name. It may be objected that with travel as frequent as it was, there is nothing improbable in Paul's knowing twenty-five or thirty Christians at Rome; he would have known them earlier at Antioch, Corinth, or Ephesus, but they have now moved to the capital city. He greets them by name in order to strengthen his ties with the Roman church he wants to visit. This objection would be quite plausible if most of the twenty-five or thirty were known only casually; but that is not the case. Aquila and Prisca are his "fellow workers" who "risked their necks" for his life; Epaenetus is his "beloved," the "first convert in Asia for Christ"; Andronicus and Junias are his "kinsmen" and "fellow prisoners," "men of note among the apostles, . . . in Christ before me"; Ampliatus is his "beloved," as is Stachys. Herodion is his "kinsman"; Urbanus is another "fellow worker"; Rufus' mother he is able to refer to as having been a "mother" also to him. Is it really credible that all of these persons, so important in the life of the church in Paul's territory and known to him so intimately, should have moved to Rome?

It should also be noted that Paul seems to know personally not only the individuals and families which are named, but also many, if not all, of the house-church groups into which the congregation addressed was divided. He knows such house churches in the homes of Prisca and Aquila, of Asyncritus, Phlegon, Hermes, Patrobas, Hermas, and of Philologus, Julia, Nereus, and Olympas—certainly, one would say, three house churches, perhaps more. It has been remarked that the words of the apostle would most plausibly suggest that he knew these churches and their unnamed members; but at the very least and without any doubt he knew that churches met with these persons. Even so much acquaintance with the Roman community is decidedly not indicated by the rest of the letter. It is common to say, as has been said in this introduction, that Paul's major purpose in writing this letter to the Romans was to explain his position to a church which had had no previous firsthand knowledge of it; much in the letter supports that view of its purpose. But what occasion would there be for such an explanation if he is addressing a church whose members include so many persons who have been so intimately associated with him? It is hard to regard this chapter as originally addressed to Rome.

A number of subtler signs point in the same direction. Paul has been very careful throughout this letter to avoid assuming the tone of a pastor addressing his own proper congregation. The kind of frank assumption of his own importance to the people he is addressing which is found in other epistles does not appear in this; indeed he has tried to avoid any appearance of presumption. But if vss. 17-21 were a part of the letter, he has now thrown this discretion completely to the winds; the paragraph has an unmistakable pastoral tone. The same tone is more subtly conveyed throughout the chapter.

No writer on Romans denies the great force of these several considerations. The majority of writers find them all but irresistible.

But what are the alternatives? There are two of these, and both of them need to be carefully considered. The alternative view usually adopted is that ch. 16 was originally an independent note, a piece of genuine Pauline correspondence, which at some stage in the process of the editing of the Pauline letters became attached to the letter to Rome. If one asks for the name of the church to which this note was originally sent, the most likely answer is Ephesus. At first sight this theory has much to commend it. Paul had lived at Ephesus longer than anywhere else and would have the knowledge of the church there which the note reveals. Moreover, the "pastoral tone" would be entirely appropriate. In so far as the names indicate any specific locality, that locality is Ephesus: Prisca and Aquila were there when Paul wrote I Cor. 16:19, and it is noteworthy that in this allusion to them (also in Rom. 16:3-5) is included a reference to "the church that meets in their house"; Epaenetus is the "first convert in Asia." The other names have no such connection with Asia or Ephesus but might very appropriately be found there.

On closer examination, however, the theory that this is a note of introduction and greeting addressed to Ephesus becomes almost if not quite as difficult as the Roman hypothesis. One remembers first that Paul does not greet a single person by name in any letter of his addressed to a church he knows. The only letter (except of course Rom. 16) in which a person is singled out for greetings is Colossians, and there only one person is named, Nympha, apparently of Laodicea (Col. 4:15); but Paul is not personally acquainted with either church. And is it really credible that so brief a communication as Rom. 16 should contain so little except personal greetings, and should contain such an abundance of these? C. H. Dodd associates himself with Hans Lietzmann in remarking: "A letter consisting almost entirely of greetings may be intelligible in the age of the picture-postcard; for any earlier period it is a monstrosity." The force of this observation cannot be denied; indeed, the more one reflects on it, the more convincing it becomes.

Even more anomalous than Paul's naming all of these people in so brief a letter is the fact that he describes them just as he does. However the note is dated, Paul could not have been for any long period away from Ephesus. Is it natural then to remind the Ephesians that Prisca and Aquila had risked their lives for him and that he is grateful, or that Epaenetus is the first convert in Asia, or that Junias and Andronicus are men of note among the apostles, etc. etc.? If Paul were reminiscing after a very long absence, reminding his readers of facts which they may have forgotten or the younger of them may not have known, this would be understandable; but hardly otherwise. Such remarks as "all the churches of the Gentiles give thanks" (vs. 4) and "all the churches of Christ greet you" (vs. 16) also miss being quite natural and appropriate in a note to Ephesus, which is one of those churches, no matter how the phrases are interpreted. They fit the Roman hypothesis better, as do also the descriptions of Paul's friends, whose histories the Romans might not know; but as we have seen, that hypothesis is equally if not even more difficult.

An additional complication for the Ephesus conjecture arises when we try to visualize the place which this note (i.e., ch. 16) would have had in the original collection of the Pauline letters. At first sight that conjecture seems to derive some support from what we know of the collection. The collection probably was made in Ephesus, and the inclusion of this note becomes more easily intelligible if it is thought of as having been sent to Ephesus. Not only would it have thus been readily available to the collector, but it would also have had an importance for the Ephesian church (referring as it would to its principal original members) which would explain its being thought worthy of inclusion. Philemon was probably preserved as a part of the collection for the same kind of reason (see discussion of Philemon, Vol. XI). But would the collector have included this note as a part of Romans if it had actually gone to Ephesus? Would not the very motives he had for including it at all have guaranteed its being included under its proper title? But if he had given it a title (as "To the Ephesians"), all trace of that fact would hardly have been lost. Goodspeed quotes F. G. Kenyon (in *Chester Beatty Biblical Papyri* [London: Emery Walker, 1936], Fasc. III, p. xviii) as saying, "The difficulty still remains of understanding how a letter of introduction for Phoebe should have been extant without preface or conclusion, and should have become attached to the great Epistle to the Romans." Goodspeed answers:

> The collectors of the letters would possess in their own church chest [i.e., Ephesus] an unimportant letter of Paul's, which they might well wish to include in the corpus they were forming; they would be reluctant to publish so meager a letter as a separate unit, as the Letter to the Ephesians, to stand beside the massive letters to Rome and Corinth. . . . It would not be unnatural for them to append it to one of the longer letters, especially if they knew from Acts that Priscilla and Aquila had a Roman connection. It is enough to say that it was attached to Romans to insure its preservation and circulation, which is precisely what it has done.[7]

But why should this "unimportant letter" have been included except for its local and personal significance? And is it not obvious that this significance is immediately obscured when it is attached to a letter addressed to a distant church? It is true that Philemon may well have been published originally under a single title with Colossians, but the case involves notable differences: Colossians and Philemon are clearly and intimately related—both being sent to the same church—and besides, the address and salutation of Philemon make quite unmistakable its identity as a separate letter. But both address and salutation are, according to this theory, carefully removed from the "note to Ephesus."

It has occasionally been proposed, in an attempt to meet some of the objections to the Ephesus conjecture, that what we have in Rom. 16 is only the ending of a longer letter to the church at Ephesus which, except for this scrap, was lost. But this suggestion, besides being intrinsically improbable and having no support whatever of either an external or an internal sort, does not answer a number of the stronger objections to the Ephesus hypothesis. This last can be said also of the theory that ch. 16 belonged to the particular copy of a general letter that went to Ephesus. This suggestion mitigates the difficulty created by the presence of so many greetings in so brief a note, but does not touch any of the other objections.

The list of scholars who find it impossible to accept this hypothesis is as long and as distinguished as can be cited in support of it. It is important to note, however, that those who accept the Ephesus conjecture, as well as those who adopt the Roman hypothesis, do so not because they find the case for their own position convincing and satisfying, but because they find the other view quite impossible.

But if we cannot "see" the chapter as a part of Romans, nor yet as a note to Ephesus, what is left? The only other possibility is that Rom. 16 was not a part of the original collection of Pauline letters, under either or any guise, but was added to Romans at some later stage in the evolution of the Pauline letter corpus, just as the three Pastoral epistles were added. Indeed, Rom. 16 has a great deal in common with the Pastorals; vss. 17-21, which fit so poorly in Romans, might have been lifted out of the Pastorals.[8] The greetings, although much more extensive, are like those at the end of II Timothy. Such fulsome expressions as "all the churches of the Gentiles give thanks" and "all the churches of Christ greet you" are more natural in a pseudonymous addition to Romans than in a genuine letter of Paul, whether to Ephesus or Rome. There are other details which, though they do not require this hypothesis, fit quite well with it. These will be considered when we come to the exegetical interpretation of the chapter.

Perhaps the best that can be said for this suggestion is that it is not open to objections as serious as those which stand in the way of the acceptance of either of the other alternatives; but in view of the nature of this particular problem, to say this is not to say a small thing. It should be noted, however, that this hypothesis, alone among the three, takes seriously the fact that in the Beatty Papyrus the benediction follows ch. 15. This fact means that at a very early period the epistle existed *with* ch. 15 but without ch. 16. But how could this have happened if the epistle possessed ch. 16, either originally (the Rome hypothesis) or from the time of the first collection (the Ephesus conjecture)? Are we to say that the text of Romans was *twice* shortened, first losing ch. 16 and later ch. 15 also? Or perhaps that it suffered two separate shortenings, in one of which chs. 15 and 16 were dropped off, and in the other, ch. 16 alone? Is it not more likely that our oldest witness to the text of the letters of Paul, the Beatty Papyrus, tells us how Romans originally ended, both as written and as in the first collection? But if in the first *collection* of Pauline letters Romans ended with ch. 15, then ch. 16 must be thought of as either unknown to the collector or as having been rejected by him. In neither case is it likely to be genuine.

If it is asked what motive could have led to

[7] *An Introduction to the New Testament* (Chicago: University of Chicago Press, 1937), pp. 85-86. Used by permission.

[8] C. H. Dodd implies as much in his *Epistle of Paul to the Romans* (New York: Harper & Bros., 1932), p. xix.

the composition of this chapter and its attachment to Romans, the answer is not hard to give: When Rome took the lead in the fight against the heretics toward the middle of the second century and issued a new edition of the Pauline letters—enlarged to include the Pastoral epistles—as a weapon in that fight, the attaching of this note to the Roman letter would serve to strengthen the position of the Roman church by demonstrating that Paul was really intimately acquainted with its members despite the fact that he had not himself visited the city at that time. It may be added that vss. 17-21, concerning those who "create dissensions and difficulties in opposition to the doctrine which you have been taught," and the phrase "through the prophetic writings" in 16:26, would also have served this church in its struggle with Gnostics and Marcionites. But more will be said on these points in the Exegesis.

A tentative reconstruction of the developments in this story of textual change would be somewhat as follows: Romans, as it left Paul's hand, ended with 15:33 and included the word "Rome" in its address. There is not sufficient evidence that the letter originally had any other form; that is, the hypothesis of a general letter or of a letter addressed in various slightly different forms to several churches is insufficiently supported, although it cannot be conclusively refuted. This letter—Romans ending at 15:33—was included in the first collection of Paul's letters late in the first century. From this form of the letter, in some subsequent edition of the collection or some important manuscript of this edition, one chapter was taken away; and in another edition or manuscript, later still, one chapter was added. Three forms of Romans would thus be extant: (A) the original fifteen-chapter form; (B) the fourteen-chapter form; and (C) the sixteen-chapter form. There is some evidence, by no means conclusive, that in B, when ch. 15 was eliminated, the word "Rome" was also omitted from 1:7, 15. C was the final, and became the sole surviving form.

As to why ch. 15 was omitted by some person or group, the usual answer has been that Marcion would not have liked the opening part of the chapter. An equally plausible explanation would be that if the word "Rome" was omitted in order to give the letter the character of a general epistle, then 15:14-33 might have been eliminated for the same reason. But on either assumption a mystery remains: What objection could Marcion have had to 15:14-33 (unless to vs. 27?), and why should a non-Marcionite editor have omitted 15:1-13, which so obviously belongs with the final sentences of ch. 14? Dodd refers to the "incredible stupidity of editors," and perhaps this is the only possible answer.

It has often been suggested that the doxology, 16:25-27, was composed to bring B to an appropriate close, and that it made its way thence to the end of ch. 15 in A and to the end of ch. 16 in C. An alternative view is that the doxology stood first at the end of C and passed from there to the two shorter forms. One important consideration, not often noted, rather strongly supports the second of these views: We know, from Tertullian and others (see above, p. 357), that in some manuscripts of the letters of Paul in the latter part of the second century Romans stood in last place; it is also clear that this doxology, so long and elaborate, may well have been designed to bring, not only Romans, but the entire corpus, to an impressive end. But the likelihood is that in such manuscripts as had Romans in this position, the letter stood in its long sixteen-chapter form; at any rate, we know that Marcion, who used the B form and is generally credited with having produced it, did *not* have Romans in last place. If ch. 16 as a whole is regarded as pseudonymous, it is natural to regard vss. 25-27 as having been always a part of it. Indeed, the admitted fact that these verses are pseudonymous (or editorial) adds some additional strength to the suggestion that the entire chapter is of the same character.

This reconstruction is presented with the greatest tentativeness and with full awareness that it is not free from serious weaknesses. Unfortunately the same charge can be brought against every other proposed reconstruction.

VI. Leading Ideas in Paul's Preaching

Before trying to outline the Epistle to the Romans or to indicate the course its argument takes, it will be useful to attempt a brief summary of Paul's theological position in general. Materials for this summary will be drawn chiefly from Romans, but to some extent from the other letters also. Such a summary will provide a context for the consideration of Romans, both as a whole and in its several parts.

It is often said that Paul was not a theologian, but rather a preacher and evangelist. What that statement probably means is not that Paul is unconcerned with theology, but that his theology has a practical and realistic, as distinguished from a merely intellectual or speculative, character and orientation. Paul's theology in any distinctive sense is soteriology, a doctrine of salvation. Now it is undoubtedly true that Paul is much more concerned to proclaim the fact of the salvation in Christ than to formulate an adequate doctrine or explanation of it; nevertheless the fact and the doctrine are inseparably connected in his mind, and one cannot understand the meaning of the fact unless one takes the doctrine into account.

The discussion of this doctrine of salvation may well take its start from Paul's way of diagnosing the human situation. Man, created in the image of God and with God's law written across his heart, has fallen under the control of sin. Sin for Paul is more than an act or attitude of rebellion against God or of transgression of his law, although it surely involves this meaning and the word—especially the verb—is often used simply in this sense. In the more characteristic sense, however, sin is an outside demonic power, alien to man's true (created) nature, which has gained entrance to man's life and has reduced him to bondage and made him a transgressor. For us modern men it is difficult if not impossible to think of sin as being a real entity, almost a personal being; "sin" for us is likely to mean merely the act of sinning. Paul thought of it as something substantial, lying far deeper in man's life than this act, or even than the impulse which prompts the act. And yet it was not a part of man's own true nature. It was indeed both foreign and hostile to that nature. "I delight in the law of God, in my inmost self," he writes, "but I see in my members another law at war with the law of my mind and making me captive to the law of sin which dwells in my members" (Rom. 7:22-23). This passage will be discussed later in some detail; it is cited now simply to make as clear as possible the understanding of man's condition which Paul's whole theory presupposes.

This condition of being in essential nature a creature and child of God, made for, capable of, and supremely desiring fellowship with the Creator and Father, but being in actual fact estranged from him and thus divided within one's self and against others—this condition was not merely a fact about particular individual men; it was a universal fact, true of each man because it was true of all mankind. It has just been pointed out that we find it hard to think of sin in the concrete way in which Paul could think of it; we find it just as hard to grasp Paul's conception of the corporate unity of the race although, it should be added, if we are at all sensitive and thoughtful, we are certain to recognize the realities which these ancient conceptions represent. Of this human solidarity Adam was the symbol, and the Genesis story of his creation and fall served admirably to account for man's condition. When God made Adam, he made man; when Adam succumbed to sin, all mankind became enslaved. When Adam transgressed, all men became guilty.

The point where sin made its attack, gained its entrance into human life, and took up its seat was "the flesh," and the use of this term requires that a few words at least be said about Paul's conception of psychology. The subject is complicated and difficult and represents one of the points where students of Paul are most seriously divided. This is true because Paul's "psychological" terms are susceptible of different interpretations in different contexts, and he uses them very loosely, with no apparent attempt at either precision or consistency. The most important of them are flesh (σάρξ), soul (ψυχή), spirit (πνεῦμα), mind (νοῦς), heart (καρδία), and body (σῶμα). "Flesh" means usually the physical stuff of human life, and "body" the organization of that stuff (or some other) in the particular form of any individual person. The "body," we learn from I Cor. 15:35-41, does not need to be "fleshly," but our present bodies are. "Soul" is the animating principle of the fleshly body. "Spirit" is primarily used to designate the divine Spirit, who comes upon and into those who believe in Christ, but there is ample reason to hold that the word also sometimes refers to an element in the natural man—which may also be designated "mind" or "heart"—which distinguishes him from the beast and represents the image of God. This element can also be described loosely as "the inner man." The answer one gives to the question whether Paul finds two or three elements in personality depends upon one's conclusion as to how much of a distinction he makes between "flesh" and "soul." For practical purposes, certainly, they are identified, and the adjectives *sarkikon* and *psychikon* are used interchangeably (cf. I Cor. 2:14; 15:44, 46). This account of the meaning of these terms is woefully inadequate, but will be supplemented as these several words appear in the Exegesis.

The word "flesh" is often used by Paul in a purely conventional and morally neutral sense, meaning simply the physical or the natural. Thus Paul can speak of Jesus as "descended from David according to the flesh" (Rom. 1:3) or of Onesimus as "beloved . . . both in the flesh and in the Lord" (Philem. 16). Usually, however, the term has an evil connotation (as in Rom. 8:7-8, for example) : flesh is "sinful flesh." It has sometimes been argued that Paul was a thoroughgoing dualist, regarding the fleshly and material as evil and the spiritual as good. Although there are evidences that Paul had been influenced by such dualism—everywhere prevalent in the Gentile world of his period—it is more than doubtful that he went so far in this direction as this argument claims. He would have stopped short of saying that flesh was *essentially* sinful. He had no doubt, of course, that it was *actually* sinful, but this was true because sin had taken its seat in the flesh and had corrupted it, not because flesh was sinful in origin. The essentially evil thing is not the flesh, but "sin in the flesh." From the physical base within the personality itself sin has brought the whole of personality under bondage and has destroyed the original balance and harmony of God's creation.

Sin works itself out in decay and death. This consequence, which is God's judgment upon sin, is, according to Paul, already appearing, and the early chapters of Romans indicate the signs he sees of the approaching doom.

Something at least must be said here of the significance of the law in reference to this plight of man. Paul as a good Jew never doubts the divine origin of the law—both what we should call natural law and the written law, the Torah, entrusted to the Hebrew people. At the same time he knows—and one is justified in assuming bitter experience of his own as the source of this knowledge—that no peace is to be found through the law. Indeed, Paul would have said that just the contrary is the case: the law succeeds only in making one miserably aware of one's bondage to sin. In this fact he finds the original divine intention in giving the law; without the law sin would not have been known as sin, and man would have perished without warning. The law awakens him to his condition and thus makes his salvation possible, but it is powerless to release him from slavery or to save him from corruption and death.

This release and salvation have been accomplished, not through the law, but through Christ. "God has done what the law . . . could not do: sending his own Son in the likeness of sinful flesh and for sin, he condemned sin in the flesh [i.e., placed it under sentence of death]" (Rom. 8:3). As to Paul's Christology in the strict sense—that is, his conception of the *nature* of Christ, enough is perhaps said in the comment on Rom. 1:3-4, below, especially as Christology in this sense is not as important an interest of Romans as of some of the other letters. Romans is really concerned with the *work* of Christ, and to this phase of Christology we must give larger attention in this summary.

It is often pointed out that Paul, in trying to set forth the reality and meaning of the salvation which he and others had actually found in Christ, seized on any possible metaphor suggested by his environment and used any terms made available by the thought patterns of his day. Thus he represents Christ as paying for us a ransom or a debt which we could not pay, as offering on our behalf the sufficient sacrifice which we could not offer, or as winning a victory over our demonic adversaries which we could not win. It would be a mistake to suppose that Paul regards these representations as mere figures of speech, although if we had pressed him, he would almost certainly have agreed that some of them were intended more literally and realistically than others. To this question of how literally we are to take these several statements about Christ we shall return in a moment. Meantime it may be proposed that Paul's most important statement about the work of Christ—that is, the statement which gives the essential clue for the interpretation of other statements on the same theme—is that found in Rom. 5:12-21 (cf. I Cor. 15:22, 45 ff.). Here Paul represents Jesus as having become the second Man, the head of a new humanity, a spiritual humanity, just as Adam headed the old, natural humanity. "As in Adam all die, so also in Christ shall all be made alive" (I Cor. 15:22). This new spiritual humanity will be fully in existence only after the present age, already dying, has come to an end; but it already exists in principle, in the church, the fellowship of believers, upon whom the Spirit has come as an "earnest" of their inheritance. To be saved is to be incorporated "in Christ," that is, to belong to this new and heavenly order, primarily eschatological but even now proleptically present, just as the day is present in the dawn.

As to how Christ comes to be the second Man, the saving Man, Paul seems to make two answers. The most important of these might be stated in some such way as this: Adam through his disobedience became the slave of sin, and all men following him have participated in this slavery; Jesus was perfectly obedient, refused to consent to sin, thus defeated sin, and offered the race the opportunity of a fresh start. We *have* belonged to Adam, the defeated; we may *now* belong to Christ, the victorious. The other answer might be stated as follows: Man is not only the slave of sin, but he is also a transgressor of the law of God, guilty before God and therefore under condemnation; but Christ through his death offered a sufficient sacrifice, satisfied the just requirements of God, and thus made possible God's being just and at the same time forgiving sinful men. Some modern writers try hard to make out that Paul did not sincerely believe in the sacrificial significance of Christ's death; but they do not succeed. Rom. 3:24 ff.; 5:6 ff., not to mention many another passage, too definitely reflect just such a belief. It is impossible to take the allusions to Jesus' vicarious satisfaction of God's righteous demands, any more than the references to his defeat of our demonic enemy, as mere metaphor. Sin appears in Paul as both guilt and bondage; the work of the Savior is correspondingly "justifying" and "redeeming." But the point where this work becomes effective is the moment of the Resurrection, when Jesus Christ becomes manifest as the second representative Man, in the results of whose sacrifice and victory all men are invited to share.

This invitation is subject to no limitation of any kind. Because of the gulf between Jew and non-Jew in the ancient world, and because Jesus and his disciples (as well as Paul himself) were Jews, Paul was particularly exercised throughout his career to affirm that Greeks and barbarians were no less in position to accept the good news of God's saving act in Christ than were Jews. Here again the analogy between the first and second Man has meaning: Adam was man, not Jew; so the risen Christ is Man in the most universal and inclusive sense. The only condition of our belonging to him is our belief in the gospel and our trusting ourselves without reservation to the mercy of God which is disclosed and operative within it. This is faith; it is not in any sense an external limitation or arbitrary condition; it is simply the appropriate response of free persons to God's gracious act. Faith is the human act of receiving the love of God offered in Christ.

Much of Romans is concerned with setting forth the nature of the new life. The key term is "Spirit." The new life is *spiritual* life—God's own life imparted to us and therefore our own true life, since in the beginning he made us by breathing his Spirit upon us. This Spirit, who is love, brings reconciliation within and without, or what Paul calls "peace." The Spirit also brings powerful reinforcement to our own "spirit" so that we are able to triumph over the sinful desires of the flesh and to know something of the original order and peace of God's creation. Paul characteristically thinks of the ethical life as the "fruit of the Spirit"—not the achievement of moral effort, but the inevitable expression of the new spiritual life.

This new life is, as we have seen, primarily eschatological. The new life belongs to the new age. But because the new age is about to break in, some foregleams of it have already appeared and some foretaste of its glories has already been given. The *age* of the Spirit is yet to come, but the Spirit itself has been given as an advance installment of our inheritance. The new life is therefore essentially a hope, but it is a hope which has already begun to be fulfilled and is thus more than a mere hope. The church is a "colony of heaven," an anticipation of the kingdom of God and the guarantee of its reality and its nearness.

Such in barest outline is Paul's "gospel" of salvation. We are now in position to consider even more briefly the way in which the letter to the Romans proceeds to state it.

VII. Argument and Outline

After the salutation and some personal remarks about the Roman church and his own hopes and plans, Paul states what is universally recognized as the theme of the epistle in 1:16-17. This theme might be indicated with the phrase "the salvation available in Christ." All the aspects of that salvation which are to be discussed in the letter are adumbrated in these two verses: Its source in God's gracious action, its availability to Jew and Greek (although to the Jew first), faith as the sole condition of our receiving it, forgiveness ("justification") and life as the essential meaning of it.

Paul opens the discussion of his theme with a demonstration of the world's need of salvation (1:18–3:20). The passage is not as coherent as we might wish—very few extensive passages in Paul are—but the meaning of the passage as a whole is quite clear: all men, both Jews and non-Jews, are sinners before God and are subject to the "wrath"—the final wrath or judgment which is even now appearing. The fact that the Jew has been given a special revelation of God in the Torah will not save him, since he has not kept this law. The law thus serves only to increase the Jew's responsibility and to deepen his despair.

Paul proceeds then to set forth a way of salvation which is not the way of obedience to the law. It is the way of justification in response to faith in Jesus Christ. This section of the discussion, beginning at 3:21, proceeds rather smoothly to 4:25.

Chs. 5–8 are concerned with setting forth the meaning and character of the new life to which God's justifying act admits us. It is much the most important section of the letter, if not indeed of all Paul's correspondence, and will receive the largest attention in the Exegesis. The content of Paul's teaching in this and the two preceding sections of the letter has already been dealt with in a general and preliminary way in the summary statement about his preaching.

In chs. 9–11 Paul turns to a special problem of quite poignant concern to him—the problem presented by the fact, already apparent to him, that the Jewish nation was by and large refusing the gospel. This fact caused him the deepest concern, not only because he himself was a Jew and a lover of his people, but also because the Jewish rejection of the Christ seemed to represent the failure of God's own promises to the fathers of Israel. This problem, hinted at as early as 1:16—"to the Jew first and also to the Greek"—and alluded to from time to time in the course of chs. 1–8, is now taken up for more serious and sustained discussion.

The letter concludes with a practical or ethical section (12:1–15:13) and some personal remarks (15:14-33). The latter have already been examined in connection with the occasion and purpose of the epistle. The ethical teachings are somewhat miscellaneous, as these teachings in Paul's letters are always likely to be, since presumably they are addressed to special needs of particular churches. In Romans they can be grouped plausibly enough under some such heading as "The Will of God Is Love." The discussion of this will of God as regards relations within the church and with men generally —especially with enemies and the state—occupies most of chs. 12 and 13; the section 14:1–15:13 is concerned with the special problem created by differences of conscience among believers on such matters as the eating of meat. Ch. 16, as we have seen, did not originally belong to the epistle.

The epistle as a whole can be outlined as follows:

I. Introduction (1:1-17)
  A. The address and salutation (1:1-7)
  B. The thanksgiving (1:8-15)
  C. The theme (1:16-17)
II. The world's need of God's saving act in Christ (1:18–3:20)
  A. Introduction (1:18)
  B. The failure of the Gentiles (1:19-32)
    1. Idolatry (1:19-23)
    2. God's judgment upon idolatry (1:24-32)
  C. The failure of the Jews (2:1-24)
  D. The impotence of the law (2:25–3:20)
III. The saving act: Justification by faith (3:21–4:25)
  A. Justification defined (3:21-30)
  B. This justification a fulfillment of the old covenant (3:31–4:25)
IV. The new life into which this justifying act admits the believer (5:1–8:39)
  A. Summary of the character and qualities of the new life (5:1-5)
  B. Reconciliation, the promise of salvation (5:6-11)
  C. The basis of life in Christ (5:12-21)
  D. The release from sin and the law (6:1–7:25)
    1. Dying with Christ (6:1-14)
    2. An analogy from slavery (6:15-23)
    3. An analogy from marriage (7:1-6)
    4. The function of the law (7:7-13)
    5. The final despair and release (7:14-25)
  E. The life of the Spirit (8:1-27)
    1. God's saving act (8:1-4)
    2. The new righteousness (8:5-13)
    3. The hope in Christ (8:14-25)
    4. The Spirit as helper (8:26-27)
  F. The assurance of salvation (8:28-39)
V. Jew and Gentile in God's purpose (9:1–11:36)
  A. The apostle's appreciation of Israel (9:1-5)
  B. Jewish apostasy, even if final, not a failure of God's purpose (9:6-13)
  C. God's choice, even if arbitrary, not unjust (9:14-29)
  D. God's choice not arbitrary (9:30–10:21)
  E. Jewish apostasy not final (11:1-32)
    1. Remnant now in church (11:1-6)
    2. Apostasy of the rest of the Jews providentially used (11:7-24)
    3. All Israel will be saved (11:25-32)
  F. Conclusion: Praise of God's inscrutable wisdom (11:33-36)
VI. Ethical teaching: God's will is love (12:1–15:13)
  A. The duty of finding and doing the will of God (12:1-2)
  B. Love within the church (12:3-13)
    1. Each must be subordinate to the whole body (12:3-8)
    2. Each must rejoice in the service of others (12:9-13)
  C. Love for men generally (12:14–13:10)
    1. Enemies (12:14-21)
    2. The state (13:1-7)
    3. Love the fulfillment of the law (13:8-10)
  D. Special need of ethical consecration because of the approaching crisis (13:11-14)
  E. Christian love and differences of conscience (14:1-23)
  F. Conclusion of ethical section (15:1-13)
VII. Personal and closing remarks (15:14-33)
  A. Explanation of the letter and the visit (15:14-24)
  B. The collection for the poor at Jerusalem (15:25-33)
VIII. Introduction of Phoebe, exhortation against heretics, and greetings (16:1-23)
IX. The final doxology (16:25-27)

VIII. Selected Bibliography

An exhaustive bibliography on Romans would be almost endless, since books dealing with any phase of Paul's thought would be relevant. I mention below only commentaries on Romans itself, and only six of these. I have depended constantly upon these books and they are referred to often in this work, usually simply under the names of their respective authors.

DODD, C. H. *The Epistle of Paul to the Romans* ("The Moffatt New Testament Commentary"). London: Hodder & Stoughton, 1932.

KIRK, K. E. *The Epistle to the Romans.* Oxford: Clarendon Press, 1937.

KÜHL, ERNST. *Der Brief des Paulus an die Römer.* Leipzig: Quelle & Meyer, 1913.

LIETZMANN, HANS, *Einführung in die Textgeschichte der Paulusbriefe an die Römer* ("Handbuch zum Neuen Testament"). Tübingen: J. C. B. Mohr, 1933.

SANDAY, WILLIAM, and HEADLAM, ARTHUR C. *The Epistle to the Romans.* New York: Charles Scribner's Sons, 1895.

STRACK, HERMANN L., and BILLERBECK, PAUL. *Kommentar zum Neuen Testament aus Talmud und Midrash.* München: C. H. Beck, 1926. Band III.

ROMANS

TEXT, EXEGESIS, AND EXPOSITION

The Epistle to the Romans.—Whoever is interested in Christianity must necessarily be interested in the Epistle to the Romans. History leaves him no alternative. In age after age this letter has aroused the church from lethargy, and given it the power which is inseparable from a vital understanding of its faith. Consequently, no intelligent student of the past can be indifferent to the book which in the hands of a long succession of reformers has fashioned the life and thought of Christendom. But when we have granted this, can we still insist that Romans is important for the modern man? Is it relevant to the world he actually knows, does it speak to the difficulties by which he is beset? The average person is not greatly concerned about Augustine or Luther, or about the influences which shaped their thought. The society they helped to mold has vanished, and presumably the forces at work within it can safely be relegated to the experts and the specialists. When the ordinary person turns to Romans, he will unquestionably find many things hard to understand. On what grounds, then, can we ask him to make the effort to master this brief but important book?

The simplest answer is the one which in practice satisfies a great many readers who in point of fact never really understand the epistle. Its argument eludes them, but they keep returning to its pages because scattered throughout the letter they find glowing passages which always awaken a response. It is true that the verses which are familiar to the average Christian could easily be condensed into very brief compass, and many of them are included in anthologies of one kind or another. Even so, some of the great passages get overlooked simply because most people will not take the time and the trouble which are necessary if we are to make a complete selection of all the verses which have an immediate appeal. But the habit of mind which seeks out and seizes on a few edifying sections is open to a criticism more serious than the charge of incompleteness. Even when found, it is doubtful if such selected passages, wrenched from their context, can achieve any adequate effect. The claim for Romans must rest on something more substantial than the splendor of a few carefully chosen sections.

Christians believe that Romans is always relevant to the human situation because its message is not dependent for its effectiveness on factors which vary from one century to the next. The letter is not addressed to one age but to all ages; it speaks to problems which are common to men at any time and under all conditions. It may be worth noting, as we pass, that a strong case can be made for the modern character of what Paul wrote. His world was not so different from our own as we are tempted to imagine. The nature of its problems, the atmosphere which pervaded its society, and the kind of mentality which it fostered are all strikingly similar to those which mark our day. We are not so remote from our ancestors of the first century as we think, and what Paul wrote to them can be applied to us with very little modification. But the significance of the similarities between Paul's age and ours can easily be exaggerated. The great truths which this letter sets forth are relevant to our situation for reasons other than that certain coincidences unite centuries which are widely separated in point of time. Romans is important because it speaks of realities far more abiding than any set of circumstances, and it speaks to needs characteristic of man in every generation.

Human life must have some meaning—otherwise it rapidly ceases to be tolerable. Those who suspect that their existence has neither point nor purpose cannot hope to escape from a sense of utter futility. If our life has any significance, it must owe that significance either to something within or to something beyond itself. The claim that we cannot—and need not—go outside the limits of human existence in order to establish the worth of human life is certainly not new; but in recent times it has enjoyed a much wider vogue than ever before. The attempt to vindicate man's dignity by restricting ourselves to values inherent in man's life never achieves any conspicuous success. Often enough we talk freely about man's worth and then do what we can to deny it. In extending the range of his claims we only deepen his

Pp. 373-78 include the expositor's introduction; Text and Exegesis begin on p. 379. Editor.

sense of frustration. To affirm that all necessary values are to be found within ourselves is apt to leave us with no values at all. In this respect we confirm the findings of those who have made the experiment before us. If man's life is to have dignity, serenity, and security, it must draw meaning from something greater than itself. Christians have always insisted that our whole existence is devoid of meaning apart from our dependence upon God. But so bold a claim needs to be carefully interpreted. Part of the importance of Romans lies in its attempt to show how human life is related to the creative Power who is its source and who gives it meaning. The sweep of Paul's view extends from the divine purpose which antedates creation to the goal in which all things will find their final consummation. This is the framework within which he sets his discussion of man's religious problems. His language may be unfamiliar, but the main issue is one which we know all too well. The basic presupposition which underlies the whole argument of the letter is that man's life depends on God. Only when we realize the nature of that relationship, and appropriate the consequences which follow from it, can we hope either to understand our life or to deal successfully with its complexities. Whether we like it or not, we are creatures wholly dependent upon God. This may strip from us the unreal autonomy which we sometimes claim, but in the process we discover the true nature of the liberty which is available. Freedom is not the right to do whatever we wish, but the power to become what we were intended to be. To this subject—the religious dependence upon God which is the secret of our moral independence as we deal with life's problems—Paul returns repeatedly in the course of his letter to the Romans. When we understand the fundamental nature of our life—as rooted in God—we begin to understand the true character of our opportunities and responsibilities.

Having recognized our creaturely status, we begin to see our life both in its true nature and in its proper perspective. It is God's high purpose which gives meaning to our life, and this saves us from any sense of triviality or insignificance. We are not merely bubbles on the surface of the stream, ephemeral episodes in a vast and meaningless process. From of old and to eternity there is a divine plan which gathers up our lives within its mighty sweep. At this point Paul's discussion of predestination—especially in ch. 8—assumes its true importance. Primarily his doctrine is an attempt to explain our awareness of having received great and undeserved religious benefits; but it also serves to place our lives in a setting in which their essential dignity appears.

The source of our lives is in God, and the proper perspective for appreciating their nature is provided by his eternal purpose. Having dealt with these general issues, Paul is confronted with certain related matters which are more immediate and even more urgent. Can we so live that our conduct will not belie our convictions? Man's perennial problem is the fact that he recognizes moral and spiritual obligations which he is apparently incapable of translating, in any adequate measure, into action. This is true at almost every level of insight. Even the man who vaguely desires to do what he feels to be right finds that he is continually falling short of his ideal. For the religious man, however, the problem becomes acute. The will of God is the law which he knows should govern his life; if he cannot fulfill the requirements of that law, his plight is desperate. The higher his standard, the more serious is his failure.

Our understanding of God's demand will naturally depend on our conception of God's nature. There had been a time in Israel's past when men toyed with the belief that human sacrifice was a religious duty; the fascination of that foul requirement was broken only by a higher understanding of what God must be. The fight to establish monotheism had been won by the great prophets; but that did not finally decide the exact character of the requirements which the good man must fulfill. Legal and moral elements struggled for supremacy, and in times when spiritual vision grew dim it was natural that legalism should increase its hold. Men believed that God demanded complete obedience to a system of law which tended to grow more and more complex. The burdens which religious observance laid upon men consequently became almost intolerable, and religious belief failed to provide the incentives without which so great a weight could hardly be sustained. But this was a result which inevitably followed from the corrupting effect which legalism had upon men's understanding of the nature of God. They thought he must be interested primarily in the things which law requires; they believed that he was constantly concerned to see that the full measure of demand should be satisfied. He became not only aloof and austere, but petty and exacting. It is against this perverted view that Paul reacted with all the vehemence of his passionate nature. His polemic against Judaism was inspired by his horror at what the law had done to men's conception of God, to their relationship with him, and to their attitude one toward another. In other words, if we are to meet the demands of life successfully, we must know the nature of the God with whom we deal, we must find a relationship with him which will bring our lives to their true fulfillment, and we must create with others the kind of fellowship which should unite those who find that they are the children of God.

In rectifying the evils to which a distorted view of God gave rise, Paul indicates indirectly the main outlines of his own conception of God. He is persuaded that a response to God as holy love must be central to any adequate understanding of the divine. But once we have grasped this insight, we cannot avoid the conviction that God will give us his good gifts, not because we have earned them, but because it is his essential nature to do so. The whole legal system of ordering the religious life, with its tacit assumption that we can deserve God's favor, rests upon a colossal error. This accounts both for the failure of the Jewish system, and for the inadequacy of almost every form of ethical self-culture. Anything that is founded upon so fundamental a misconception cannot lead to true spiritual liberation. The desire to run our own lives and earn our own salvation is almost universal; consequently, Paul's argument in Romans never loses its force and relevance.

This brings us to the threshold of Paul's central theme: the way in which men, so often defeated by their own misguided efforts, can gain entry to a life which will be full and free. His answer is given in terms of his doctrine of justification by faith. God brings us into a relationship with himself in which the impossible things become actual. The old antipathies, which our attempts to earn merit only aggravated, are swept away and are replaced by a spirit of confident trust. What we could never do for ourselves is done for us by God—through Jesus Christ our Lord. We may notice that many of the great theological themes—the doctrine of God, the person of Christ, the nature of the Atonement—are touched on only by implication in this letter. There is never any doubt, however, of the importance of Christ for Paul's thought. We have seen that our whole religious life can be vitiated by a false conception of God, and our truest safeguard against such misunderstanding is the revelation of God in Christ. We know he is not the kind of taskmaster which we are apt to postulate, because we know that he is the God and Father of our Lord Jesus Christ. And in the same way, though Paul gives us no precise explanation of how it is that the eternal nature of God becomes intelligible in human terms through Christ, he leaves us in no doubt of the importance of Christ's life as an authentic revelation of the divine. He suggests the outlines of a theory of salvation, and though at times we are left to infer the way in which our reconciliation is achieved, he declares in the most emphatic terms that the new life is ours because Christ has won it for us.

The meaning of justification by faith is explained elsewhere in this work, and it is not necessary at the moment to consider in detail the form which the doctrine assumed in Paul's hands. It is well to remember, however, that justification—so central an issue in this letter—is not concerned with an academic debate wholly remote from the interests of our contemporary religious life. When Paul contrasts justification by faith with justification by works, he is setting in opposition two fundamental attitudes which persist throughout man's religious experience. He himself illustrated each in turn—and each in an extreme form—but each of us knows something of both alternatives. The Pharisees of the first century furnished a conspicuous example of the spirit which identifies righteousness with the observance of a code; but we see the same attitude widely reflected round about us, and if we look within ourselves we discover that it is often accepted there as well. Its essence is a loyal submission to the code which happens to govern conduct in the circle to which an individual belongs. The requirements of this code are, within its limits, strict and exacting, and there is usually a strong resentment of new light, and a pronounced impatience with new demands. This accounts for the blighting tyranny which social custom usually exercises in the lives of those who submit to it; the evil effects are seen even more clearly in the realm of moral and religious demands. A particular form of ecclesiastical requirement enters in to usurp the place which the will of God should occupy, and it inevitably proves reluctant to modify itself in any way in the light of a new understanding of God's requirements.

The primary aim of justification, either by works or by faith, is to gain a new standing with God. Until we feel that we are not inevitably condemned because of our failure to satisfy his righteous will, there can be no peace for us in his presence. Justification by works assumes that we can earn acceptance by our own efforts, and by virtue of merit possess the right to stand unabashed before him. This attitude rests, of course, on a certain conviction regarding God's nature: it assumes that he desires the kind of service which multiplies observances and so augments our credit; and we have already seen that in Paul's eyes this is a fatal misreading of the divine nature. It misconceives, too, our human situation; it attempts to retain our independence of God, and ignores our creaturely condition (cf. p. 374). Faith, on the other hand, is a loving trust in and willing submission to God. If we respond to him as our Father, righteous in will and loving in purpose, we commit ourselves in humility to a relationship which he makes possible, but which we could never establish by ourselves. He creates what we could not deserve—a standing in which we can be treated as children of God. On theoretical grounds alone we ought to realize that this is the only relationship which can be reconciled both with what Christ teaches us about God and with what our experience discloses to us regarding ourselves. Paul does not rely on abstract considerations. He bases his argument on what has happened. On the one hand he shows that Christ, by his life and death, has created the conditions which make it possible for us to accept what God wants to give us. On the other hand he proves that the attempt to establish our own righteousness, even when pursued with the utmost intensity and under the most favorable circumstances—as in Judaism—has always led to unmitigated failure.

It appears, then, that justification by faith, so far from being a remote and irrelevant speculation, is an accurate appraisal of our situation and an illuminating statement of the only means by which that situation can be transformed for good. Its importance springs in part from the place where it lays the primary emphasis. Justification by works necessarily stresses outward patterns of behavior. Justification by faith probes to the sources from which finally all conduct springs. To suggest that it is indifferent to what we do is manifestly to substitute a travesty of the truth for the truth itself. Faith creates an attitude which cannot help expressing itself in a certain type of conduct; but the conduct is derivative and subsidiary. Man secures as a by-product what must always elude him when he makes it the principal object of his quest.

In the course of his letter Paul refers repeatedly to the unnatural divisions by which we segregate ourselves from one another. The universal element in Paul's gospel—an element which no sane man would be disposed to discount—is also related to his doctrine of justification by faith. The law, which was the notable example of the desire of men to justify themselves by their achievements, was the peculiar glory of the Jewish people; those who submitted to its demands believed that obedience would win for Israel advantages which would be denied to every other race. It became the symbol of religious and national exclusiveness. Faith, on the other hand, is as universal as man's need of God. Anyone who is aware of his insufficiency, and is able to accept what God offers to all, can enter into the abundant life which is available to everyone. More than once in human history men have been obsessed—sometimes in a rather sentimental way—with human brotherhood, and have attempted to establish it by magnifying one man's essential similarity to another. But in Paul this awareness of our common lot springs from an understanding of God's nature and of his method of dealing with men. Brotherhood must have some more adequate basis than vague good will; in Romans it finds its necessary foundation in the doctrine of a divine mercy which embraces all men within its scope.

The person who finds that he is justified by faith stands at the beginning of a new life. Its full range and final quality are still matters of surmise, but he has no doubt of the decisiveness of the change which has taken place. The new life is related, therefore, both to the things that have been and to those that are still to be. On the one hand it is deliverance from the powers which have held us in their thralldom; on the other it is emancipation into a liberty which enables us increasingly to appropriate the full measure of God's gift to us. We are set free from the sin which held us in bondage. Paul does not suggest that we are able merely to effect some measure of reformation in ourselves, nor does he regard sin as consisting of a series of lapses from moral rectitude. Sin is the state in which we find ourselves. It is part of the human predicament that we are involved in a situation in which the power of evil is both widely prevalent and strongly entrenched. We share in greater or less degree in a moral corruption which is universal. Our whole nature is subtly warped from its proper norm. We may advance different explanations to account for this fact; that it actually describes our condition is apparent. We may not find Paul's terminology particularly helpful: to talk of Adam's legacy does not greatly illuminate the problem; but we can see clearly enough what Paul is trying to describe, and we can appreciate its far-reaching importance. We know that our life is bound up with that of the past, and the errors of our ancestors form a heritage which largely determines the character of our lives.

We cannot simply repudiate the evil they have done, and so escape from its consequences. In subtle ways it reaches out and wraps its tentacles around our life, and we discover that without any desire to do so we ourselves are adding to the problems which we bequeath to generations yet unborn. The experience of the first half of the twentieth century emphasized the naïveté of a great deal of the talk about the essential goodness of human nature. There is no simple formula for breaking out of the circle which encloses our lives, and there is no possibility of denying the manifold ways in which that involvement works to overthrow our hopes and plans. It is clear enough, therefore, that the person who tries to dismiss the whole concept of sin merely on the grounds that our individual peccadilloes are of little consequence is guilty of a most unrealistic attempt to evade the crucial problems of life. So far from discussing imaginary difficulties in discredited terms, Paul is dealing in a particularly illuminating way with one of the urgent issues of all time. His treatment of sin is an important contribution to the discussion of the character of our life, and its value lies less in its luminous analysis than in its firm conviction that ultimate cure depends on proper diagnosis.

The intolerable weight which sin lays upon us is lifted by virtue of what God has done for us in Christ. Deliverance from the past is release into a new kind of life. To be set free from the old bondage would have little value unless some new loyalty entered in to replace the servitude which has ended. Simply to remove one evil leaves a vacancy to be filled by another. Paul declares that in saving us from the old life, God has given us a new spiritual power which possesses us and works within us to achieve the ends of righteousness. The nature of this dynamic is not sharply defined. As we read the great passages in which Paul describes the work of the Spirit within us, we may wish that he had been a little more explicit; but experience reminds us that the only explanation which has any value is provided by participation in the new life in which Paul invites us to share. He suggests clearly enough how we enter that life, and he indicates the benefits which will accrue to those who begin to discover what it means. Though language lacks the facilities to describe in detail what happens, Paul has no doubt that he himself has been radically remade; and he knew scores of others of whom he could confidently say the same. Those who responded to God's offer in Christ found that salvation was not a matter of future hope but of present experience. A new loyalty was the beginning of a new life; intellectual belief, emotional response, and personal commitment opened the way to unforeseen possibilities of confident and victorious living. Here again it seems almost superfluous to remark on the surprising relevance of what Paul wrote. He faces the problems to which we have no clear answer, and he provides the kind of solution for which everyone is seeking. He has an explanation of the disconcerting corruption of human life, whether in society or in the individual, and he shows how we can attain precisely those objectives which are uppermost in the mind of our generation. Security, peace of mind, inward assurance, confidence in meeting life's demands—all the things that psychiatrists discuss but do not always make available follow inevitably as the fruits of the kind of life which Paul offers his readers.

We might assume that he would be content to discuss the crucial issues and leave us to work out the inferences for ourselves. If we deal with the nature of God and the character of man's existence, if we show how the divine becomes real and how the human can be radically transformed, we might be pardoned for feeling that the rest could be remitted to the individual who wished to work out for himself the full implications of the new life. In the final chapters of the letter Paul deals in brief but incisive fashion with many of the practical issues which are inseparable from daily experience. Few of them were characteristic of his age alone. The way in which charity and conviction are to be reconciled, the problem of adjusting the rights of the state and the duties of the citizen, the relations of those who are timid with those who have vigorous faith, and the inescapable demands of the law of love—these are not of interest to one generation only, and any discussion which illuminates their essential character in one age will help those who wish to apply them in another.

There is a further factor—and this of the utmost importance—which we are bound to keep in mind. Romans unfolds the significance of the gospel, but it does so in a particular setting. It relates the good news to both past and future—to the past which marks the way by which God led his people, and to the future in which his purposes will not finally fail. The framework of the discussion, in other words, is history. Paul is not stating abstract religious theories, but drawing inferences from the story of his people. A great deal that appears antiquated and irrelevant in Romans—and much of the discussion about Israel is apt to seem so—is actually concerned with that very live issue, the nature of history. The biblical interpretation of man's past is closely linked to the belief that history is the sphere in which God has most clearly been at work. His mighty acts have disclosed his true nature, and consequently in the Christian tradition not only persons but events become the media of revelation. This is in sharp contrast with certain alternative interpretations which compete for acceptance by every generation. For historians of one school, history is merely the record of what happened to take place; it has no particular meaning, and no intelligible purpose can be discerned behind the pattern of events. There are others who contend that history is the product of material forces, working in accordance with the dictates of economic and scientific laws. The differences between these views do not, of course, concern only the nature of history. The record of what man does is related to our understanding of what man is, and our doctrine of man is determined by our view of God. The biblical view of history cannot possibly be regarded as a supplementary matter in which certain specialists happen to be interested. It declares that God has a purpose for human life, and that the disciplines of experience are the best expositors of that purpose and form the truest aids in understanding both ourselves and God.

If history is the stage on which God has disclosed himself, it is clear that history and revelation are terms intimately related to one another. When history becomes a matter of urgent contemporary concern, we need not be surprised to find that revelation is one of the key words in theology. Few works in the N.T. are more directly concerned with this great and comprehensive question than Romans. It deals with the general method by which God has made himself known—through history, especially through the history of the chosen people. It shows the particular manner in which God has disclosed himself—in Jesus Christ. It makes clear the significance of Christ's life and death for our understanding of God's nature and purpose. It defines the new relationship which this revelation makes possible, and indicates the immediate consequences which will follow from it.

For all practical purposes the Epistle to the Romans is often dismissed as an ancient classic of religious literature, venerable in itself and once no doubt of some significance, but now possessing neither relevance nor interest. It can easily be shown that, on the contrary, Romans deals with subjects which never lose their importance; it treats the eternal themes of God and man, of the true nature of each and of the relationships which should unite them, in ways particularly congruent with the needs of every age. Especially in those times when man's plight becomes clearly apparent and desperately urgent, its treatment of sin forms a penetrating and realistic diagnosis of the nature of his ills. Justification by faith appears not as an abstract theological anachronism, but as a practical offer of deliverance. The great themes in Romans are much more "topical" in character than most of the trivialities by means of which we sometimes attempt to speak to our contemporaries. The great needs of the human heart—of God, of forgiveness, of pardon, and of peace—may be described in varying terms, and the language in which the answers are set forth may differ from one age to the next; but the needs themselves never become unimportant so long as they remain unsatisfied. The practical problem which we face is often one of translation. Romans speaks of urgent matters, but we do not realize the fact because ancient terms have obscured their abiding relevance. This is more than a matter of newer as opposed to older versions. There is a certain irreducible vocabulary of religion; and to a people who think little and talk less about the eternal things of the spirit, the necessary language seems uncouth, if not unreal. Righteousness and salvation, justification and faith, grace and atonement—these terms and many others must be explained again if the essential meaning of the N.T. is to emerge. No man anxious to bring the light of truth to bear upon the dark confusions of human history will resent the disciplines of thought and of expression without which the meaning of such a document as Romans cannot be disclosed. Nor will any conscientious person need practical suggestions as to the best means of opening up the subject matter when others are ready to hear. These things a wise learner will discover as he ponders on the essential themes with which Paul deals. Indeed, the inherent power of the letter to the Romans not only teaches those willing to learn, but makes all words of commendation seem superfluous. Calvin wrote:

> With regard to the excellency of this Epistle, I know not whether it would be well for me to dwell long on the subject; for I fear, lest through my recommendations falling far short of what they ought to be, I should do nothing but obscure its merits: besides, the Epistle itself, at its very beginning, explains itself in a much better way than could be done by any words which I can use.[1]

[1] *Commentaries on the Epistle of Paul to the Romans*, tr. John Owen (Grand Rapids: W. B. Eerdmans, 1947), p. xxix, "The Argument."

1 Paul, a servant of Jesus Christ, called *to be* an apostle, separated unto the gospel of God,

1 Paul, a servant[a] of Jesus Christ, called to be an apostle, set apart for the gospel

[a] Or *slave*.

I. Introduction (1:1-17)

A. The Address and Salutation (1:1-7)

An ancient letter ordinarily began with a brief address in three parts: the name of the sender or senders, the name of the recipient or recipients, and a word or two of greeting, usually simply the word "Greeting." This conventional form can be observed in thousands of papyrus letters recovered from the trash piles of Egypt (see Vol. VII, pp. 35, 45, 77) and, in the N.T. itself, in James and the two letters contained in the book of Acts. One of these begins in Acts 15:23: "The brethren, both the apostles and the elders, to the brethren who are of the Gentiles in Antioch and Syria and Cilicia, greeting"; the other, in Acts 23:26: "Claudius Lysias to his Excellency the governor Felix, greeting." Such was the normal, all but invariable way of beginning a letter. The salutations of Paul's letters conform to this basic pattern, but with very important and distinctive variations. He tends to elaborate somewhat—often considerably—each of the three parts; and the extent and character of these elaborations are likely to bear in each case some relation to the purpose of the particular letter he is writing. This fact most clearly appears perhaps in Romans and Galatians (see Exeg. on Gal. 1:1 ff.). Romans, as we have seen, is written to a church with which Paul is not intimately acquainted, and which he has some reason to suspect entertains an erroneous notion of his own position and some doubt of his apostolic authority. He seeks as far as possible to correct this attitude in the first sentence of his letter, and to set forth both his own position and his message in such a way as to gain the initial sympathy and support of his readers.

1:1, 5. As to his own position, he describes himself as a **servant** [better, "slave"] **of Jesus Christ.** The term "slave of God" (δοῦλος) or some equivalent is often found in the

1:1-7. *Salutation.*—The pattern of the opening verses of Romans may have been dictated by the usage of the age, but the content was supplied by the insights of the Christian faith. At the very outset, therefore, we have an arresting example of the way in which new life can modify old forms. The conventional greetings, used without a thought in almost every letter written in the ancient world, are transformed at the touch of a new power, and the hackneyed structure becomes the instrument for conveying a message of profound religious significance. Paul himself has told us that "if any man be in Christ, he is a new creature" (II Cor. 5:17); even at the point where we might least expect it he completely vindicates his claim. In the first century, letters opened with names of the writer and the recipient, a few complimentary phrases, and a word of formal greeting (cf. Exeg.). In Paul's epistles we see an eager mind transforming these familiar (and largely meaningless) patterns until they glow with new vitality. The religious impulse is so strong that it reanimates the forms usually scarcely read because normally so thoughtlessly written. In a few deftly chosen phrases Paul not only greets his correspondents, but indicates (*a*) the character of one commissioned to preach the good tidings, (*b*) the nature of the community fashioned by the power of the message, (*c*) the kind of greeting which such a messenger can send to such a fellowship, and (*d*) the heart of the good news which he commends. Brief though this passage is, it strikes a note which echoes throughout the entire letter. The gospel, as understood and proclaimed by Paul, is not a dangerous innovation, but the true fulfillment of God's immemorial purpose for his people.

1*a*. *The Slave of Christ.*—Paul writes as a **servant.** The word means more than it has come to mean with us. It points to a measure of dependence and obligation which can properly be conveyed only by a much stronger term —slave (cf. Exeg.). The Christian is so completely at the service of his Lord that by the end of the apostolic age the word had passed into common usage as the most appropriate description of those who were wholly devoted to Christ's cause. We may legitimately assume that when the material which ultimately went to the making of the Gospels was circulating in fluid form, men's minds would again and again be arrested by acts recorded of Jesus and sayings attributed to him, all stressing the profound but disconcerting truth that lowliness is the secret of all service and the only foundation of

O.T. as applied to some prophet or hero or to the nation (cf. Pss. 78:70; 89:3; 105:6; Judg. 2:8; Hag. 2:23; Josh. 24:29; Amos 3:7). In certain passages in Isaiah (notably 52:13–53:12) appears the mysterious figure of the "servant of the Lord" (παῖς LXX; but the Hebrew term is the same). The nation was almost certainly intended under this figure, but the early Christians saw in the phrase a messianic title and interpreted Jesus as a fulfillment of Isaiah's prophecy. Paul, who may well have shared such a view, may here be thinking of himself as the servant of this Servant.

Whether that reference is in his mind or not when he uses this phrase, as he does more than once (cf. Gal. 1:10; Phil. 1:1), Paul wants to emphasize the completeness of his commitment to Christ. He belongs to Christ as a slave belongs to his owner. Thus his action in writing to the Romans and his proposal to visit them do not spring from his own initiative, but from Christ's. The same stress upon Christ's initiative appears in the word **called** in the next phrase, **called to be an apostle;** in the term **set apart;** and in the statement in vs. 5 that it is through *Christ* that he has **received grace and apostleship.** And he has received an apostolic commission, not in a general sense only, but with special reference to the church at Rome. Paul has never been to Rome, it is true; but that does not mean that he is venturing beyond the scope of his commission in now making contact with the Roman church.

The meaning of the phrase rendered in both of our texts **obedience to the faith** is somewhat obscure. The objection to this rendering is that it involves an objective, almost external, meaning for the word "faith" which is certainly not characteristic of Paul. This word will be more fully discussed later; at this moment it is enough to say that for Paul it usually designates an attitude of utter trust in God and reliance upon his mercy. The Greek phrase is literally "obedience of faith," and could mean "the obedience [to Christ] which comes from faith," and this meaning is on the whole more congenial to Paul's thought.

---

greatness. At all events, there is sufficient evidence to warrant our believing that **servant** early became the term by which the leaders of the church believed that they could most appropriately be described (cf. Jas. 1:1; Jude 1; II Pet. 1:1), and it is certainly one which strongly appealed to the mind of Paul. The term suggests one who is not his own, because he has been bought with a price. It was quite natural for Paul to declare that "ye are Christ's." A **slave** is one who looks to his master for everything. He is given his task in terms no less abrupt and compelling than the orders of one who says "Do this" with the assured knowledge that it will be done (Matt. 8:9; Luke 7:8). From his master comes his task; from his master, too, comes the reward; and there is no higher satisfaction than to hear the commendation, "Well done, good and faithful servant" (Matt. 25:21). Even for his daily life—for the means of sustaining it and the privilege of prolonging it—the slave looks to his lord. By reading between the lines of Philemon we can infer how completely the slave's life was in his master's hands, and contemporary evidence abundantly confirms our surmise. Consequently, Paul is pointing to a relationship which is marked at every point by obligation and dependence. The emphasis may seem extreme, but it will appear unwarranted only to those who have never known forgiveness and restitution. At the same time, we need to remember that a servant might be more than a menial. Many an Eastern slave was a man entrusted with offices of high responsibility. The servants of an Oriental ruler might be "his courtiers that are in personal attendance upon him." [2] Men holding such positions possessed considerable power and enjoyed a large measure of trust. This doubtless explains the fact that when Paul has declared that we belong utterly and absolutely to Christ, he can immediately add that "all things are yours" (I Cor. 3:21-23). We may assume, then, that the term points to an abiding relationship, marked by complete dependence on the one hand, and by far-reaching responsibility on the other. It is only by means of such a paradox that we can set forth what it means to be **a servant of Jesus Christ.** At the heart of the Christian experience is the recognition that we are not our own, because we have been bought with a price. The neces-

[2] W. Robertson Smith, *Lectures on the Religion of the Semites* (3rd ed.; London: A. & C. Black, 1927), p. 69; note especially the implications latent in the parable of the unforgiving servant (Matt. 18:21-35).

2 (Which he had promised afore by his prophets in the holy Scriptures,)

of God 2 which he promised beforehand through his prophets in the holy scriptures,

---

2-3. If in vs. 1 and again in vs. 5 Paul is emphasizing his own calling as an apostle and therefore his right to approach the Roman church as a commissioned evangelist, in the intervening vss. 2-4 he is concerned with the origin and essential nature of his "gospel"—the gospel which the letter as a whole is to discuss with some fullness. It is "the gospel of God," i.e., it is *from* God and is concerned with an act *of* God. This act of God was **promised beforehand through his prophets in the holy scriptures**—which Paul had been

---

sary response on our part is the surrender of all we are:

> Love so amazing, so divine,
> Demands my soul, my life, my all.[3]

We lose our life and find it; when we are ready to give ourselves without reserve into the hands of God, we discover for the first time that his gift is abundant life.

This is not the only form in which the paradox can be expressed. The servant is one who, having no liberty of his own, discovers that he possesses perfect freedom. Only those are really free who are completely devoted to some worthy cause or some compelling person. We are bound to be the slave of someone or something; as Paul himself remarks elsewhere in this same letter, "If you yield yourselves to any one as obedient slaves, you are slaves of the one whom you obey, either of sin, which leads to death, or of obedience, which leads to righteousness" (6:16). A false freedom is actually the most absolute kind of servitude, but the Christian follows one "whose service is perfect freedom." It is no accident that Paul, who thought and spoke of himself as Christ's servant, could write with such glowing enthusiasm about the glorious liberty of the children of God.

1*b*-2. *Apostleship.*—Called to be an apostle. It is a distinctive kind of service which Paul discharges. The sense of a high constraint is present both in the verb and in the noun he uses. One who is "sent" is not one who casually selects his task, and Paul never forgot that his commission was a command (cf. Acts 22:21). In his awareness that God had called him, he stood in the succession of the patriarchs and prophets. A. B. Davidson could fittingly use the title *The Called of God* for a volume of studies of O.T. characters, and it is only necessary to think of the experience of Isaiah or Jeremiah to realize how decisive a part God's calling can play in the life of his servants. With a directness which forbids evasion, yet with a personal intimacy which for the first time makes us truly conscious of ourselves, God's demand confronts us. It lays our whole being under contribution, and never leaves us unchanged. When God called Jeremiah, the experience opened the wide vista of a new understanding both of God's nature and of the value which he places upon the individual. When Paul speaks of being "called," there lies behind his words the deep assurance—much easier to grasp than to express—that in his own eternal purpose God has laid on us a task which we cannot evade and which we must discharge to our utmost capacity. The compulsion is inescapable. We have not received an invitation; we have been "effectually called." Because of the memory always with him of the mighty constraint of the Damascus road experience, Paul could not doubt that deep in the purposes of God there was a service which he alone could render and which consequently he could not decline. Moreover, because in this fundamental sense an apostle is one who is called and sent, there could be no question of grasping at an office or of aspiring to a dignity not his by right. Paul's enemies might insinuate that he usurped a place to which he was not entitled, but even in the salutation with which he greets this church, to whose members he is for the most part unknown, he defends himself by implication against such a charge.

The man who is called of God finds himself **set apart** for the work with which he is entrusted. He is separated from ordinary interests, responsibilities, and concerns; the demands of his vocation are such that he can say at last with perfect truth, "This one thing I do." Within the Christian community the apostle has a distinctive place because a distinctive task; though one with the general body of believers, he is set apart for a particular work. In one sense it is his fellow Christians who commission him (cf. Acts 13:2), but he never forgets that ultimately he acts under a constraint which is laid on him by God. He "who had set me apart before I was born, and had called me through his grace, was pleased to reveal his Son to me, in order that I might preach him among the Gentiles" (Gal. 1:15). When a man is possessed of the grandeur of God's purpose, he cannot regard the service

[3] Isaac Watts, "When I survey the wondrous cross."

3 Concerning his Son Jesus Christ our Lord, which was made of the seed of David according to the flesh;

3 the gospel concerning his Son, who was descended from David according to the

falsely represented perhaps as disregarding, disparaging, or distorting—and centers in the appearance of **his Son.** This term "Son" was an established messianic title and also for Paul signifies the intimate relationship in which Christ stood to God. The term does not necessarily imply pre-existence but, in view of other indications that Paul thought of Christ as pre-existent, it is natural to take the word here (as in Gal. 4:4) as involving a reference to this, as well as to the earthly part of Jesus' "career"—the historical life—and the resurrection life.

3-4. Many commentators see in Paul's description of Jesus as **descended from David according to the flesh and designated Son of God . . . by his resurrection from the dead** a concession to the supposed "adoptionist" Christology of the Roman church. By "adoptionist" Christology is meant the view that Jesus *became* the Son of God (or the "Christ" or the "Lord") at some point after the beginning of the earthly life; that God chose or "adopted" him to be the Messiah. The earliest Christology was almost certainly of this type, the Resurrection being the moment of adoption. Rom. 1:3 seems to reflect just such a stage of thinking about Christ, whereas it is known that Paul had gone beyond this, firmly believing as he did in Christ's pre-existence. It is therefore often supposed that he is consciously expressing himself here in terms that will not offend his Roman readers.

Such an interpretation, however, overlooks the fact that the primitive "adoptionism" represented by certain statements in early Acts (e.g., 2:36) was not replaced immediately by the full-blown incarnationism which is expressed in such statements of the Fourth Gospel as "The Word became flesh . . . ; we have beheld his glory, . . . as of the only Son from the Father" (John 1:14). There was almost certainly an intermediate stage, repre-

of such holy ends as a task which he himself has selected but which he might possibly have declined. The good news is from God as well as about him; those who proclaim it are men seized with a sense that God's hand has taken hold of them in order that they might serve his righteous ends. From this followed both the intensity with which Paul defended his apostleship and the devotion with which he discharged it.

3-6. ***For All, Yet for Each.***—Religious enthusiasm is continually in danger of yielding to one or other of two temptations: it becomes so vaguely diffused that it has no particular relevance to any specific situation, or it restricts itself so largely to individual demands that it fails to speak to larger issues. We have in Paul's words an illuminating side light on the way in which the Christian gospel combines the general and the particular. His message, he tells us, is of unlimited scope; it is so comprehensive that it includes people of every nation and race (**for obedience to the faith among all nations**). At the same time it is marked by an intimate immediacy which delivers it from the peril of referring to mankind in general without applying to anybody in particular (**among whom are ye**). In his service of the gospel Paul brings down the great and inclusive declarations of faith to the point where they serve the need of ordinary people in the particular situations in which they find themselves. The mighty phrases that we use finally refer to people like ourselves; to you and me, where we actually are. Paul also indicates the motive which inspires his mission, whether in its most extensive form or in its most intensive application (**for the sake of his name**). One final comment completes his description of his office (vs. 5). **Grace and apostleship**, both of which he receives from his Lord, issue in a particular task: it is his mission to proclaim the good news, and by its means to bring the Gentiles (his own immediate responsibility) into the same kind of obedient freedom in which he himself stands.

3-6. ***Epitome of the Gospel.***—In addition to more personal matters, the opening verses of the letter also contain a brief summary of the gospel which Paul is commissioned to preach, and which makes him bold to send greetings to a church which he has never visited. What he proclaims is not a new departure or a rash innovation in religious thought. There have been anticipations: it was "promised beforehand" (vs. 2). The good news was foretold in the O.T., not in specific texts but in the ex-

4 And declared *to be* the Son of God with power, according to the Spirit of holiness, by the resurrection from the dead:
5 By whom we have received grace and apostleship, for obedience to the faith among all nations, for his name:

flesh
4 and designated Son of God in power according to the Spirit of holiness by his resurrection from the dead, Jesus Christ our Lord,
5 through whom we have received grace and apostleship to bring about obedience to the faith for the sake of his

sented by the letters of Paul and to some extent by the Synoptic Gospels. At this stage the pre-existence of Christ is affirmed, but the older "adoptionist" pattern, with its sharp contrast between the humble human life and the final glorious exaltation remains largely intact. A prologue (i.e., the pre-existence) has been added to the story, but the story itself for a while remains much the same. Only gradually was it realized that the addition of the "prologue" entailed a retelling of the entire story. And it is only in the Fourth Gospel, no earlier than the very end of the first century, that the story is thoroughly and consistently retold.

If this conception of Paul's Christology is correct, the ambiguity of the Greek term translated in RSV **designated** is more easily understood. This English word is well chosen because it too is ambiguous. Does it refer to the mere announcement of an already existing status and relationship: He was the Son of God all the while but only at the Resurrection was this fact made known? Or does the term—as in Moffatt's translation—mean "installed," the suggestion being that at the Resurrection Jesus assumed an office and relationship which he had previously not possessed? Since Paul's Christology is of the intermediate type and therefore not as coherent and consistent as either the primitive adoptionism which preceded it or the incarnationism which followed, it is likely that both meanings of the term (ὁρισθέντος) apply: Jesus had been God's Son before the earthly life began and the Resurrection was a "declaration" of that fact; but the pre-existent Son of God had "emptied himself" (Phil. 2:7) to become in very fact a humble man, and the Resurrection thus meant a real change, a change in fact as well as in formal or merely outward status. The words **in power** emphasize the contrast of Christ's present postresurrection status with the weakness and humiliation of the earthly life. Thus the Resurrection has in Paul's understanding a significance *for Christ himself* which it does not have in the Fourth Gospel, where the death and Resurrection are simply the departure of Christ from the flesh in order that as the Spirit he may be more widely and intimately present.

The most difficult phrase in this whole section is that which is rendered literally and accurately by **the Spirit of holiness.** Is this a reference to Jesus' own spirit or to the Holy Spirit? Is the contrast between Jesus' flesh and spirit; or is it between his human nature,

panding disclosure of God as one who will indubitably redeem his people. The gospel is the fulfillment not merely of human hopes and needs, but of God's settled purpose. By their own powers of intuition men could hardly have guessed that purpose, and the biblical conviction—and its consistent message—is that God has taken the initiative; in the events of history and through the discipline of experience he has made himself known. The prophets are those to whom and through whom he has spoken. What they anticipated has come to pass, "Many prophets and righteous men have desired to see those things which ye see" (Matt. 13:17). The fulfillment is in terms of one who stands to God in a unique relationship of trust, obedience, and insight. According to expectation, he comes of royal lineage, and here we have one of Paul's many incidental references to the life of our Lord. We assume too often that he either did not know or did not care about the historic Jesus. The way in which he so often casually mentions details suggests that there was much that he could assume as common knowledge, and use as the presuppositions of his theological interpretations. An example of such interpretation immediately follows. Jesus' true nature and the character of the relationship in which he stood to God were declared by the Resurrection. In addition to his outward historical life, there was within him what Charles Gore has called "a sacred spiritual nature," and this determined the estimation in which he would be held. The emphasis is significantly laid on

6 Among whom are ye also the called
of Jesus Christ:
7 To all that be in Rome, beloved of
God, called *to be* saints: Grace to you, and
peace, from God our Father and the Lord
Jesus Christ.

name among all the nations, 6 including
yourselves who are called to belong to Jesus
Christ;
7 To all God's beloved in Rome, who
are called to be saints:
Grace to you and peace from God our
Father and the Lord Jesus Christ.

---

flesh and spirit on the one hand and, on the other, the divine nature, conferred through, perhaps identical with, the Holy Spirit manifest in the Resurrection? By spelling "Spirit" with a capital the RSV translators show that they favor the latter view, and it is on the whole more probable. But the phrase is difficult in itself and, however interpreted, apparently somewhat awkward in its context. No proposed explanation of its meaning is altogether satisfying.

Jesus Christ our Lord represents a primitive confession which all Christians would gladly make. It corresponds exactly with the statement in Acts 2:36, to which reference has just been made: "God has made him both Lord and Christ, this Jesus." In Phil. 2:11 Paul speaks of the coming time when every tongue will "confess that Jesus Christ is Lord." The name **Jesus** identified, of course, the remembered person—and Paul knew much more about that person than he has occasion to mention in his letter—and the term **Christ** stands for the faith that in him the prophecies of a Savior are fulfilled and that he will return to inaugurate the final judgment and salvation. But he is also **our Lord;** we know him in intimate spiritual fellowship, especially in the breaking of bread. He is the Head of the church and the Master of life (for further discussion of the lordship of Christ see below, on 10:9).

6-7. Thus Paul, who began by calling himself a "slave of Christ," ends his salutation by associating with himself in this relationship all his readers. They too acknowledge Christ as Lord; they too are **called to belong to Jesus Christ.** They are also **God's beloved** and are **called to be saints.** "Saints," as Paul uses the term, means "set apart for God's

---

power; the sense of the mighty deliverance wrought for men by Jesus Christ makes the effective transformation of our human situation one of the continually recurring themes of the N.T. We are not offered intriguing ideas or pleasant hopes; the declaration of the truth concerning Christ is with a power relevant to our situation, and it was in the Resurrection that its full meaning first became apparent.

A moment's thought makes it clear that Paul's argument involves a sequence which invites development. The essential truth with which he is dealing is the fact of Christ. To begin with, we have the proclamation of the fact: Christ is **declared to be the Son of God.** The heart of the gospel is our conviction that God's "grace and truth" have been revealed among us in incarnate form. A human life became the medium through which the nature of the divine could be disclosed. Things that in themselves transcend our power to grasp them are made intelligible in Jesus Christ. This is not a recondite truth, left in an obscurity which only specialists could penetrate. What Christ was, as well as all that he said and did, openly declared the essential and unique relationship to God which made his life the medium through which the divine power could reach us. In the second place we have the characteristic accompaniment of the proclamation—**with power.** From the earliest days of Christ's ministry men noted with wonder and gratitude the sovereign power with which he met every kind of need (cf. Matt. 9:6, 8; Luke 4:32, 35; 5:17, 24); and it is his ability to change for good our human situation which, generation after generation, has taught men to acknowledge him as "a prince and a Savior." In the third place we have the authentication of the proclamation: (*a*) **according to the Spirit of holiness;** (*b*) **by the resurrection from the dead.**

7. ***The Recipients of the Letter.***—The people to whom Paul writes are also briefly described. The letter is addressed to **all . . . in Rome** (not only to those who know him or identify themselves with his work) who are **God's beloved.** Those who are Christ's inevitably feel that the favor and mercy of God are their sure posses-

8 First, I thank my God through Jesus Christ for you all, that your faith is spoken of throughout the whole world.

8 First, I thank my God through Jesus Christ for all of you, because your faith

possession, use, and service," and thus in a way the word answers to "set apart for the gospel of God" in vs. 1. It is one of Paul's favorite ways of alluding to members of the community, the body of Christ.

We have seen that the usual salutation in an ancient Greek letter was simply the word χαίρειν (greetings). Paul substitutes for this word the closely similar χάρις, (grace), which means for him the free, unmerited favor of God, and adds εἰρήνη (peace), which meant primarily reconciliation with God but also the inner serenity and the harmony with others which flowed from this reconciliation. Since "peace" (*shālôm*) was a common Hebrew salutation, Paul's phrase **grace . . . and peace,** the salutation in all his letters, represents a combination of two characteristic forms of greeting; but in both cases the meaning of the original term is deepened and enriched. The new significance of these terms will receive fuller discussion later in this Exeg.

B. The Thanksgiving (1:8-15)

The salutation in a Pauline letter is normally followed by a paragraph or so in which the apostle felicitates his readers, expressing his obligation to them and his gratitude toward them. This section always begins with some such phrase as **I thank my God through Jesus Christ for all of you** or "I always thank God when I mention you in my prayers." The only letter in which no thanksgiving appears is Galatians; in that case the apostle is apparently in no mood for thanksgiving, but after the salutation plunges immediately into the discussion of the urgent and disturbing occasion of that letter. If II Cor. 10–13 is a separate letter, that too is without the thanksgiving and for the same

sion, because they have entered into a relationship which by its very character seals and confirms this conviction. The core of Paul's message was the declaration that Christ sets men on a new footing with God, and consequently they know his love in a way impossible apart from Christ. This conviction explains his estimate of Christ's person, and the whole nature of the experience to which it introduced him accounts for the belief that we are beloved. The description of the recipients of the letter is amplified by a further phrase—**called to be saints.** Here, too, the idea of vocation—of that effectual calling by which God brings us into the redeemed community—is clearly present. **Saints** did not mean for Paul what it has come to mean with us. They are not perfect people; they are those who have responded to a call and are going in the right direction. It is, of course, a part of the gospel message that those who are saints in this sense ultimately become saints in the other also; but meanwhile (as I Corinthians amply proves) they may be very imperfect people who have taken only the first steps in Christian discipleship.

The actual words of greeting are few and simple, but they say much. He wishes them **grace** and **peace**—the knowledge of God's love to us in actual operation, and that inner serenity which is the mark of those who receive God's gift. Both come from a twofold source—from the God whom we have come to know as Father, and from Jesus Christ who has revealed him to us as such. The association is important; the central affirmation of belief in God is modified by all that we learn of him from Jesus Christ, and consequently the characteristic N.T. phrase is "the God and Father of our Lord Jesus Christ." On the other hand, the depth and intimacy of the new relationship with God into which Jesus brought them—and may bring us—make it natural for men to press further the discovery which led them to call the man of Nazareth "Christ," and to speak of him with reverence and devotion as their Lord.

8-15. ***Thanksgiving and Hope.***—It is the beginning that counts. As the proverb reminds us, "Well begun is half done," and Paul invariably opens his letters with a strong and confident affirmation of thanksgiving. This is more than an idiosyncrasy of composition. It springs from the apostle's firm conviction that gratitude, issuing in praise, is one of the primary and necessary elements in the Christian outlook.

reason. On the other hand I Thessalonians is in its entirety little more than a thanksgiving. **I Cor.** 1:4-9 and Col. 1:3-14 may be cited as typical thanksgivings.

Rom. 1:8-15 diverges from this type in that only a single sentence is devoted to thanksgiving and felicitation in the strict sense. The whole paragraph, however, is personal; and examination of the several Pauline thanksgivings will show that any irenic aspect of his personal relations with the churches he addresses may appropriately be mentioned in them.

8. Paul thanks God for all Roman Christians **through Jesus Christ.** Sanday and Headlam paraphrase here, "through Him Who as High Priest presents all our prayer and praises." This reference to Jesus as high priest may be a little too precise; but there can be no doubt that Paul thought of Christ as a mediator and constantly approached God by way of Christ. Not unrelated to this conception is the apostle's frequent designation of the God of the believers as "the God and Father of our Lord Jesus Christ." He offers special thanks for the **faith** of the Roman church, particularly appropriate in a letter which is to deal so largely with the importance of faith.

This is sound elementary psychology; when transferred to the religious sphere, it explains the large part played by thanksgiving in the book of Psalms. Those who have been taught by a real deliverance what God has done for them cannot be silent. Similarly, in Deuteronomy the whole of ch. 8 is concerned to prove that gratitude to God is the very foundation of the ethical life of his people. In much the same way Paul points out (Col. 1:10-12) that thanksgiving is inseparably linked both with right conduct and with any possibility of steady perseverance. It is perfectly natural for him, then, to say, "First I give thanks. . . ."

His gratitude is neither vague nor general, because it is explicitly directed to God. The whole ground of our thanksgiving is in God. Paul is not talking about diffused appreciation of life, but about that response which is the forthgoing of our spirits to "God, who is our home." The intensely personal character of that response is at least implied by the use of the word **my**. But this kind of thanksgiving—at once so intimate and so profound—can neither be understood nor appropriated apart from its true source and its effectual medium. It is our possession purely because of that insight into God's nature and purpose which comes to us in Jesus Christ. He is the means by which our gratitude becomes articulate because he is the source from which comes that knowledge of God which makes it possible for us to enter into a new relationship with God. Moreover, the praise which might remain vague and diffused is made explicit in him, and by him is lifted into God's presence. The N.T. returns again and again to Christ's high priestly role of mediator, and here it is simply and almost casually assumed that the thanksgiving, which might otherwise lie latent and ineffectual in the believer's heart, is by Christ made our acceptable offering to God. "To render thanks to God," said Origen, "is to offer a sacrifice of praise; and therefore he adds, 'through Jesus Christ,' as through the great High Priest."

The immediate occasion of gratitude—for it is well to remember that the letter is never an abstract treatise, written *in vacuo*—is the widely circulated report of the faith of the Christians to whom he writes. The fact that they are Christians is known for good wherever believers can be found. The very existence of a church at the center of the empire was a comfort and encouragement to Christians elsewhere, and the example of the Romans was an incentive to others. **In all the world** may seem hyperbole because the central and predominant position of Rome is hard for us to appreciate. At least we can note that prominence and influence impose their own responsibilities. The fact that the character of the corporate life of the Roman church had been widely observed is, of course, no more than a proof of the Christian quality of the fellowship. "A city that is set on a hill cannot be hid"; Christians are "the light of the world" (Matt. 5:14), and it is their duty so to let their good deeds "shine before men, that they may see . . ." (Matt. 5:16). It is this same capacity for maintaining a positive witness in a hostile environment to which Shakespeare points in his comparison of a good deed with the light thrown by a candle—"So shines a good deed in a naughty world." [4] It is perhaps right to observe also the paradox which is always characteristic of Christian discipleship. On the one hand there is that self-effacing and unpretentious humility which claims no merit and makes no demands; on the other is the inevitable and irrepressible testimony of authentic faith.

[4] *The Merchant of Venice,* Act V, scene 1.

9 For God is my witness, whom I serve with my spirit in the gospel of his Son, that without ceasing I make mention of you always in my prayers;
10 Making request, if by any means now at length I might have a prosperous journey by the will of God to come unto you.

is proclaimed in all the world.
9 For God is my witness, whom I serve with my spirit in the gospel of his Son, that without ceasing I mention you always in my prayers,
10 asking that somehow by God's will I may

9-10. As we have already noted (see above, p. 361), the apostle makes clear that the projected visit to Rome is not being undertaken merely by his own wish (although he does wish it ardently); nor was it enough to say (as he does in vss. 1, 5, 13) that he is

9. ***For God Is My Witness.***—At the moment the apostle can appeal only to his protestations to prove the intensity of his desire to visit the Christians at Rome. His immediate destination —Jerusalem—lies in the opposite direction, and he reaffirms his fixed intention to come eventually to Rome. It may be that the calumnies to which he has been exposed have forced on him the solemn appeal to God to corroborate the sincerity of his statement. But the words also illustrate a religious attitude of cardinal importance. The apostle so lives in the sight of God that it is both easy and natural for him to appeal to God for vindication of the quality and purport of his life. This sense that our life is lived in the presence of God—always open to his scrutiny, always answerable to his demands—has been responsible for much of the most sensitive Christian discipleship. Others besides the great Puritans have felt that they must stand ready to serve, "As ever in my great Taskmaster's eye." [5]

A parenthesis (**whom I serve . . .**) strengthens the force of Paul's appeal to God as his witness. One of the central facts about the apostle's relationship to God is the alert readiness always to do his bidding—the invariable mark of one for whom God's will is the great directive power in all life. Paul indicates, too, both the organ of this service of God and the sphere within which it is exercised. He serves God **with my spirit**, and he probably refers to that combination of intellectual, moral, and spiritual qualities which constitutes our self-conscious life. The whole man is at God's disposition—all he is, not merely selected qualities or attributes. Every thought is brought into subjection to Jesus Christ (II Cor. 10:5); so is every impulse and every desire. There are many ways in which Paul expressed the completeness of the Christian's dedication to God (cf. I Cor. 3:16, where he speaks of the believer as "the temple of God"). This phrase is in keeping with the others, and points to that utter absorption in God's will and unswerving dedication to it which are and must be characteristic of the Christian. The sphere in which he serves is also indicated: **in the gospel of his Son.** The good news supplies the atmosphere and environment in which the abundant life can be lived. It provides at once the setting for and the content of the work of an apostle. It is general—it determines the atmosphere in which his task is done; it is also particular—it gives him the immediate undertaking which absorbs all his energies.

The statement, to corroborate whose truth Paul has appealed to God as his witness, now appears. He declares that in all his prayers the Roman Christians have a place. This is more than an extravagant courtesy. It is true that he had never visited the church at Rome and that many of its members were strangers to him, but unceasing intercession is one of the marks of the apostolic life. Most of us pray sometimes or occasionally; in the most solemn context Paul can claim that prayer for others runs like an unbroken thread through all his days. This doubtless has its own importance as a form of spiritual discipline, but in the present context it is significant because of what it says concerning human relationships. William Law once remarked that to pray for a man is the best possible preparation for doing him any service of courtesy or love which he requires. General Charles Gordon pointed out that it profoundly affects our reaction to a stranger if we have prayed for him before our meeting, and Bishop Charles Gore aptly adds that it is equally likely to affect his response to us if he knows we have been praying for him. A reconciling and unifying factor of incalculable power has been introduced as soon as two parties know that they are bound together thus by intercessory prayers—and even if they do not know.

10. ***Personal Plans, God Willing.***—To the more general prayers for his readers' welfare Paul always adds a specific request. He has wanted to visit Rome; hitherto he has been frustrated, but ahead, like a lodestar, is this

[5] Milton, "On His Having Arrived at the Age of Twenty-three."

11 For I long to see you, that I may impart unto you some spiritual gift, to the end ye may be established;
12 That is, that I may be comforted together with you by the mutual faith both of you and me.

now at last succeed in coming to you. 11 For
I long to see you, that I may impart to you
some spiritual gift to strengthen you, 12 that
is, that we may be mutually encouraged
by each other's faith, both yours and mine.

---

coming in fulfillment of the general call he had received years earlier to be an apostle to the Gentiles; he is coming because God, **whom I serve with my spirit in the gospel of his Son,** has now specifically directed him to proceed to Rome. He is coming **by God's will.**

11-13. For he longs to **impart . . . some spiritual gift.** This phrase reminds one inevitably of the discussion of spiritual gifts in I Corinthians and of Paul's understanding of church order and government as being largely determined by "the gifts of the Spirit": "To one is given through the Spirit the utterance of wisdom and to another . . ." (I Cor. 12:8-11). It is highly probable, as we have seen, that the Roman church was more conservatively administered than some, at least, of the Pauline churches, and that less stress was placed there on "spiritual gifts." Paul knows this and believes that his coming may help to supply a deficiency in the church's life. Having intimated this, however, he hastens to strike a more irenic note: **that we may be mutually encouraged by each other's**

---

unfulfilled desire. Somehow, sometime. . . . And though the date may be uncertain, he trusts it will be before too long. In this matter, as in all else, his hopes and plans are always placed within the framework of God's purpose for him. If it is God's will, he will come; if not, he has already learned that God's plans can reconcile us to the disappointment of deeply cherished hopes. "By the will of God" was the secret of Christ's obedience (Matt. 26:29), and it has always determined the quality of his disciples' service also. Meanwhile, Paul hopes for a **prosperous journey;** when finally he succeeded in reaching Rome, it was in chains. But as Calvin pointed out, any journey is prosperous —whatever its outward circumstances—provided it is within the will of God.

11-12. ***To Give and Receive.***—The intensity at the heart of the apostolic mission speaks in the earnestness of Paul's desire to see the Christians of Rome. Without passion there is no real life, and certainly no adequate achievement. As J. R. Seeley remarked long ago, no virtue is safe that is not enthusiastic. But the passion in this case is much more than that desire for fellowship which breaks down isolation and makes us long for—and finally achieve—community with others. At the root of his longing there is a disinterested impulse; his first thought is of giving to others what he has found to be of such inestimable worth. He wishes to give the Roman Christians **some spiritual gift,** and the phrase even by itself suggests the manifold variety of riches at God's disposal. The famous chapter on spiritual gifts (I Cor. 12) indicates at once their varied character and the high sense of responsibility which they require in those who receive them. They cannot be arbitrarily claimed or assigned. God gives to each according to his need or capacity; and we cannot limit or circumscribe his gift. To each God gives as may be necessary; hence **some spiritual gift**—this to one, that to another. It is impossible, when considering spiritual endowments, to overlook their end and purpose. They are given in order to build up, confirm, strengthen. They are never offered as ornaments but always granted for use. Hence they are not conferred as a privilege, still less as an immunity; they are an added source of strength and so of responsibility. But the very purpose for which they are granted—the building up, the "edifying" of the fellowship—sets them in a context where mutual giving and receiving is inevitable. It is natural for Paul immediately to supplement his desire to give by his eagerness to receive. There is a deep humility and courtesy apparent in his prompt avowal that he, as well as they, will benefit from fellowship one with another. It may have been a wise approach, but it was an attitude dictated more by the nature of the gifts of which he writes than by the strategy which governed his mission. Benefit is never one-sided. There is always a mutuality in faith. Those who give receive, and they receive in proportion to the generosity with which they have given (Luke 6:38). It is impossible to bless without being blessed. It is no poetic fiction that mercy "blesseth him that gives and him that takes." [6] Moreover, as Calvin remarked, "There is no one so void of gifts in the church of Christ who is not able to contribute something to our bene-

[6] Shakespeare, *The Merchant of Venice,* Act IV, scene 1.

13 Now I would not have you ignorant, brethren, that oftentimes I purposed to come unto you, (but was let hitherto,) that I might have some fruit among you also, even as among other Gentiles.

14 I am debtor both to the Greeks, and to the Barbarians; both to the wise, and to the unwise.

15 So, as much as in me is, I am ready to preach the gospel to you that are at Rome also.

13 I want you to know, brethren, that I
have often intended to come to you (but
thus far have been prevented), in order
that I may reap some harvest among you as
well as among the rest of the Gentiles. 14 I
am under obligation both to Greeks
and to barbarians, both to the wise and to
the foolish; 15 so I am eager to preach the
gospel to you also who are in Rome.

---

faith, both yours and mine. The Roman Christians, Paul acknowledges, will have something to give *him* too. We note again the emphasis upon **faith;** and **as among the rest of the Gentiles** will remind his readers not only of his previous successful work, but also of his apostolic commission and of his authority to preach at Rome.

14-15. In all probability he has this same commission in mind when he makes the statement **I am under obligation** or **I am debtor.** Until he has preached the gospel to all the Gentiles, **to Greeks,** i.e., to those who belonged to the Greek-speaking civilized world—as both he and the Romans did—and **to barbarians,** who spoke other languages and lay outside that world or just on its boundaries; **to the wise and to the foolish.** i.e., the educated and the uneducated—till then he was under a debt. Till then the obligation which God's commission had laid on him is unfulfilled. On this account, as well as on others, he can say, **I am eager to preach the gospel to you also who are in Rome.**

---

fit."[7] If we do not benefit by the gifts that others offer, the fault usually lies in us, in our envy or our pride, and consequently we impoverish ourselves. Paul is emphasizing the fact that he can benefit those to whom he comes by sharing the wealth of spiritual gifts with which God has endowed him, but they can help him by giving him that encouragement without which his mission could hardly be sustained. There is wisdom and profound insight in Paul's approach. We receive much from those of whom we require much. They rise to the measure of our expectation. In actual practice, our religious work usually meets with a poorer response than it should because we demand so much less than we might.

13-15. ***Hope Deferred.***—Paul has protested his concern for the present and future welfare of his readers. Why, then, has he been so slow in coming to visit them? It has not been for lack of trying. To encounter obstacles was no new experience for Paul. He knew well enough that "man proposes, but God disposes," and often his plans had been overruled. There had been a time, at Troas, when every road seemed blocked, every door closed against him (Acts 16:6-8). He had discovered that the way which we hope to follow may open only long after we first try to enter it.

[7] *Commentaries on Romans, ad loc.*

Paul's devotion to his original purpose shows that it is no mere whim to which he is responding. "Again, he shows his love another way," remarks Chrysostom. " 'For neither when I was hindered,' says he, 'did I cease from the attempt, but was always attempting and always hindered and never desisting.' "[8] The urge which drives Paul on is the fulfillment of his distinctive mission. He has been set apart as apostle to the Gentiles; elsewhere among the Gentiles he has gathered converts, and as long as there are those who have not heard, he is under obligation to bring them the good news. He is in debt to anyone who might be regarded as his particular responsibility, and this at Rome as much as anywhere. The constraint of the gospel overrides all artificial divisions. Differences of language, degrees of culture—such things are immaterial when a man feels the irresistible constraint of a task which has been laid upon him by God. Elsewhere in his letters Paul has set forth in greater detail the way in which the gift of God breaks down the barriers by which we separate ourselves from others (Col. 3:11; I Cor. 12:13); not often has he so explicitly related the unity created by the gospel to the specific task of making that gospel universally known. He has preached his message wherever the open door of opportunity allowed; he will preach it at Rome too.

[8] *Homilies on the Epistle of Paul to the Romans, ad loc.*

16 For I am not ashamed of the gospel of Christ: for it is the power of God unto

16 For I am not ashamed of the gospel:

C. The Theme (1:16-17)

16. Paul is now prepared to enter upon the discussion of his "gospel" which forms the body of the letter. He makes the transition from personal introduction to this discussion very skillfully. He has already alluded to the "gospel" four times, affirming not only his commission to declare it to all the Gentiles, but also his desire to declare it to the Gentiles at Rome. **For,** he now says, **I am not ashamed of the gospel.** He used this word "ashamed" undoubtedly because he had felt some temptation to shame. The gospel had been subject to disparagement and ridicule. The book of Acts records an incident of this kind in Athens (Acts 17:18, 32). Paul tells us in I Cor. 1:23 that the early Christian preaching, the *kērygma,* besides being a "stumbling-block" to the Jews, was "folly" to the Greeks. To this temptation Paul has not succumbed, and here he strongly asserts as much. In spite of the fact that the gospel had nothing of an impressive worldly kind to recommend it—it was not adapted to appeal to the proud, whether in their power or wealth or in their wisdom or noble traditions—in spite of this Paul makes no apologies for it. Indeed, he finds in the gospel the source of his own pride: it is **the power of God for salvation.** The words "power" and "salvation" (both to be encountered again in this epistle), as well as the word "gospel," call for some definition.

The word "gospel" is originally an old English term used to translate the Greek *evangelion,* which meant "good tidings"—good tidings of any kind. In the N.T. and in Christian literature generally it means always the good news about Christ, the proclamation of the saving event of which Jesus' life, death, and resurrection were the center. This is the "good tidings" par excellence, *the* gospel. The term is most significant in reminding us of the fact that the first Christian evangelists thought of themselves as announcing a fresh event rather than as disclosing an ancient truth. As they saw it, God had *acted* for men's salvation, and they were proclaiming this new fact. This use of the word "gospel" is in the N.T. predominantly characteristic of Paul—so much so that some scholars have attributed its origin to him. The term is not found in Luke or in John (the verb form is found in Luke); it occurs thirteen times in Mark and Matthew, twice in Acts, once each in I Peter and Revelation, and some sixty times in Paul's letters. Certainly if Paul did not originate this way of describing the Christian message, it was he who gave it widest currency.

16. ***A Confidence Undismayed.***—Yet to preach at Rome must have been a prospect to daunt even a missionary as brave and ardent as Paul. **I am not ashamed,** he writes, **of the gospel of Christ.** These are bold words, and easy to repeat, but they are searching enough if taken seriously. Any one of us knows as much. They probe right to the heart of all the hesitancy, all the cowardly silences, all the secular compromises that mark our discipleship. We know enough of the manifold evasions by which we try to sink our Christian witness in the anonymity which passes unnoticed in a sub-Christian environment. It may be hard for us; think how much harder it must have been for Paul. It was not a claim spoken in a vacuum, for Paul has just said that he intends to come to Rome. To Rome! Even now the very ruins of Rome can overawe the imagination of anyone who knows and loves the past. But think of Rome in the days of its imperial splendor! It was the capital not of a country, but of the civilized world. "Once did She hold the gorgeous east in fee," [9] and north, south, and west her legions stood on the farthest frontiers that cultured men would think it worth their while to claim. What could an obscure provincial bring to a city swollen with imperial pride? Into that city, moreover, there poured the odds and ends of humanity from all over the Mediterranean world. Its narrow streets swarmed with "a people proud but with little reason, averse from labour and from thought, shameless in its vices, brutal and bloodthirsty in its pleasures."[1] Paul was going to the Rome of Nero, and what

[9] Wordsworth, "On the Extinction of the Venetian Republic."

[1] W. M. Macgregor, *Some of God's Ministries* (Edinburgh: T. & T. Clark, 1910), p. 182. To this expositor and preacher I am much in debt—as anyone must be who tries to expound this passage.

salvation to every one that believeth; to the Jew first, and also to the Greek.

it is the power of God for salvation to every one who has faith, to the Jew first

Now Paul calls this gospel the **power of God.** The term *"dynamis"* is used throughout the N.T. to designate a miracle, a manifestation of God's omnipotence, a mighty work of God. Just such a work had taken place in and through the event of which we have been speaking and, as we shall soon have occasion to see, is still taking place—for the event is in a very true sense still occurring. The gospel is the proclamation of this *dynamic* event. But Paul does more than call the gospel a *proclamation* of the *dynamis;* it *is* the *dynamis.* He thinks of the message, the preaching, as he calls it in I Cor. 1:21 ff., as being itself a part of the continuing dynamic event. Just as God used the life, death, and resurrection of Jesus, so also, if in a subordinate way, he is using the preaching of that life, death, and resurrection as a medium of his power.

This **power of God** is **for salvation.** The word "salvation" means deliverance to safety, rescue from any danger, but in the N.T. period it had among Jews come to mean pre-eminently the great deliverance which God would bring to pass in the last days. So it is used by Paul; "salvation" is predominantly an eschatological term. A large part of Romans is concerned with the nature of this salvation, and we shall have better occasion later for discussing it in some detail. In general the meaning was rescue from the bondage of sin and death, the overcoming of all fear and hostility within and without, the attainment of reconciliation. What God had done in Christ, and was still doing, was to make available this deliverance—for, as we shall see, Paul believed that the "last days" had already begun to come.

And not only had God made salvation available, he had offered it to all men—**to every one who has faith, to the Jew first and also to the Greek.** There is some question whether the word "first" appeared in the original text; but in any case only the *word* would be missing. Paul had no hesitancy in ascribing to the Jew a certain priority, both of privilege and responsibility. That the gospel was offered *first* to the Jew was a matter of obvious fact. It does not occur to Paul to deny either the fact or the divine purpose expressed in it. He will devote chs. 9–11 to a full discussion of the relation of Jew and Gentile within God's saving purpose. At the moment he is simply affirming the universality of that purpose: it includes Gentile as well as Jew, **every one who has faith.**

The word "faith," which occurs here in its verbal form—note the KJV's more literal rendering—and in the following verse as a noun, holds the key to much of the meaning of the epistle. Paul has already used the term several times, and it occurs no fewer than four times in vss. 16-17, where the theme of the letter is being stated. At least five meanings of this word πίστις can be distinguished in the N.T. It is sometimes used in the quite objective sense suggested by the usual translation of the term in 1:5, *"the* faith." So used, the word means something like "the Christian religion." Such is its meaning often in

was more, he was going as a Jew. He belonged to a race that had spread over the Roman world, and had made its influence felt without making its name respected. Contemporary Latin literature abounds in references to the manifold ways in which the Jews gained wealth but lost good will. To offset the disadvantage of his race Paul could offer few personal qualities that would command respect and gain him a ready hearing. He tells us that he lacked an impressive bearing, and he acknowledges that he was not the kind of orator that could mesmerize his audience by the brilliance of his gifts. Even the cause of his coming, the message which he offered, was hardly of a kind to win a ready or enthusiastic reception. Paul knew the immediate reaction of both Jews and Greeks to the gospel he preached (I Cor. 1:23), and the ordinary person—a specialist neither in the things of the spirit nor in those of the intellect—was not likely to find it plausible at first hearing. He came proclaiming "one who passed for the son of a carpenter . . . and died like a criminal in the company of robbers"; [2] and he knew that the natural man cannot always comprehend the story of the strange ways by which God's mercy reaches out to men. If Paul was confident, it was not because he was ignorant of the odds against him. The difficulties were

[2] Chrysostom, *Homilies on Romans, ad loc.*

the Pastoral letters and in other late books (cf., e.g., Jude 3). "Faith" sometimes is roughly equivalent to our word "loyalty" or "faithfulness"—this meaning is usual when the word is used of God. God's "faith" is his reliability, his steadfastness. Occasionally the word means simply "belief"—i.e., intellectual acceptance of a fact as true although it is not a matter of knowledge in the ordinary sense. This is apparently its meaning for the writer of James (see Jas. 2:14-26); no wonder he finds it insufficient of itself. A fourth use of the word is found in Hebrews, where faith is defined as being "the assurance of things hoped for, the conviction of things not seen" (Heb. 11:1). This sounds at first like mere intellectual belief; but the writer shows that he means more than this. Faith is conviction issuing in action; it is such assurance of things not seen that one is ready to risk everything one has on their reality and to endure suffering, even death, rather than deny them.

That Paul may occasionally use the word (noun or verb) in one or another—or even all—of these ways need not be denied, but none of them represents its characteristic meaning for him. "Faith" for Paul is the attitude or condition of perfect trust in God's mercy or "grace," complete reliance on it—rather than on one's own effort or merit—for one's salvation, and eager receptivity. It is that disposition of spirit toward God which answers to God's loving disposition toward us. It is indeed the act of receiving into ourselves the love of God, and receiving it in the only way love can ever be received—with utter humility, gratitude, and joy. Faith thus includes a negative as well as a positive element. The positive element is trust in God's limitless goodness; the negative element is awareness of one's lack of righteousness and one's despair of being able to achieve it by one's own effort. The Gospels speak often of repentance and faith; Paul says little about repentance perhaps partly because, as he understands it, the word "faith" (or "to believe") includes also the equivalent of repentance. Faith is an attitude toward God which involves an attitude toward self—all trust in one's own deserving is shut out. This attitude of faith, Paul is going to insist in this letter, is the sole condition of salvation, whether for Jew or for Greek.

---

immense, but he would overcome them; on his side he had the one compensating advantage which could overcome the discouragements ahead. He was **not ashamed,** because he brought **the gospel of Christ.** To him was entrusted a word of power—a word of power which saved, a word of power for everyone who believed.

It was a word of **power.** As we read the N.T., we are struck again and again by the recurrent emphasis on the gospel as mediating the power of God. It was a marvelous gift to men—but not because it corresponded with accepted truths or offered an acceptable pattern of belief. Augustus had revived the ancient religious forms of Rome because he saw in them a means of re-establishing the conventional patterns of corporate life. Such expedients may stabilize a community, but they cannot transform a society. People need a dynamic, not a ritual, and it was as a dynamic that Paul knew the gospel of Jesus Christ. He hailed it as the "demonstration of the Spirit and of power" (I Cor. 2:4). He rejoiced because it was true, but the proof of its truth was the effectiveness of its working. He never ceased to marvel as he watched it "casting down imaginations, and every high thing that exalteth itself against the knowledge of God" (II Cor. 10:5). This had been the characteristic note from the very beginning. Jesus had come with the declaration that "the Son of man hath power on earth to forgive sins"; those who saw and heard him marveled that God "had given such power unto men" (Matt. 9:6, 8). Those who listened to him knew that "his word was with power" (Luke 4:32). His promises to those who followed him are punctuated with the assurance that they too will share in the gift which God has made available through him. His disciples have found it true in every age. "He breaks the power of canceled sin."

It was a **power** which saved. It can be argued, as C. A. Anderson Scott has done in *Dominus Noster* [3] and *Christianity According to St. Paul,* [4] that in the early church salvation was primarily conceived as deliverance from various forms of bondage. Men found that the shackles had been struck from their spirits and they were free. They expressed the sense of deliverance in terms dictated by their own experience. They were set free from the tyranny of evil spirits, from the domination of the law, from the merciless grip of sin. Beneath the temporary forms under which Paul describes our plight, there is

[3] Cambridge: W. Heffer & Sons, 1918.

[4] Cambridge: The University Press, 1927.

17 For therein is the righteousness of God revealed from faith to faith: as it is written, The just shall live by faith.

and also to the Greek. 17 For in it the righteousness of God is revealed through faith for faith; as it is written, "He who through faith is righteous shall live."[b]

[b] Or *The righteous shall live by faith.*

17. The explanation of the "power" of the event, and of the "gospel" as both the proclamation of the event and the medium of the power, lies in the fact that in both the event and the gospel—we have seen that the two cannot be separated—**the righteousness of God is revealed.** This clause raises many questions for the interpreter, only a few of which can be dealt with now, and even they only sketchily. The first question perhaps is whether the term "righteousness" (δικαιοσύνη) designates the intrinsic character of God or an outgoing activity of God. If one is disposed to emphasize God's own righteous character as being the primary content of the revelation, one will see vs. 18 is intended simply to confirm vs. 17 and will interpret both in the light of 3:25; i.e., God's own righteousness and his unqualified opposition to all unrighteousness are seen in his "wrath," his judgment against sin (vs. 18), and in the death of Christ (3:25)—both that it was required and that it was suffered. In these ways God's "righteousness" is vindicated. Even so, it may be noted, the term has an active sense: God's righteousness means "God vindicating his righteousness."

It is more probable, however, that the term in this passage, and usually throughout the epistle, designates not so much God's own righteousness as an act of God on behalf of men. The word is often used in this sense in the O.T. Thus we read in Isa. 51:5 (LXX), "My righteousness quickly draws near and my salvation shall come forth like a light," and in Isa. 46:13 (LXX), "I have brought near my righteousness and I do not hold back my salvation." In these passages—and many others might be cited—"righteousness" is obviously a synonym for "salvation," and means God's act of vindicating those whom he approves. Ps. 98:2, "The Lord hath made known his salvation; his righteousness hath he revealed in the sight of the nations," is illuminating not only because it brings together again these same two terms "righteousness" and "salvation," but also because the term "revealed" corresponds exactly with the same term in Rom. 1:17. In this psalm, it is clear,

an abiding sense of universal need. It spoke in various forms in the society Paul knew.[5] Then, as now, they cried out for deliverance from the past and for a new security for the future. There is no salvation unless the bondage woven by the past is broken; nor is there salvation unless we are delivered into the glorious liberty of God's children. But this can happen only if the power is "of God," if we feel that we are really dealing with that final righteousness which alone can justify us and which alone can accomplish that deliverance which we need. This happens in the gospel—in Jesus Christ.

It is a **salvation** to everyone who believes. There is no aristocracy of privilege. The conditions must be such that ordinary people in their need can fulfill them. The gospel does not demand extraordinary grasp of intellect or unusual spiritual endowments. It does not require

[5] Cf., in Walter Pater, *Marius the Epicurean* (New York: The Macmillan Co., 1891), the description of how men looked for deliverance to the ancient deities of field and forest, and to the fantastic Eastern cults.

that we grasp in its fullness an intricate system of belief. We respond to and receive what God has done for us. As Paul elsewhere suggests, we say "Yes" to his great "Amen" (cf. II Cor. 1:20). We enter the community of those who in loyalty follow on that they "may apprehend that for which" they are "apprehended of Christ Jesus" (Phil. 3:12). Historical circumstances may have given the Jew the first chance. Salvation came through the channel provided by his religious heritage, but it was equally available to the Gentile. Just as there can be no privileged position due to native capacity, so there can be no special prerogatives established by religious tradition.

17. *The Gospel Is the Ground of Confidence.* —Confidence springs from knowledge of the gospel: the man who has good news of God need never be ashamed. In the present verse Paul defines with greater exactness the nature of that gospel which is his reassurance, and in doing so he strikes the keynote of the entire letter. **The righteousness of God** is revealed to those who bring to its reception the necessary

reference is being made not to a passive or static appearance, as when an object has light thrown on it, but to an *action* of God, a saving, vindicating action on behalf of righteousness. The word "revelation" always has this active sense in the O.T. and in Paul as well. There can be no doubt that "righteousness" is used with the same dynamic meaning.

It will be noted, however, that, generally speaking, in the O.T. it is those who *are already righteous* whom God vindicates. The meaning is literally "justification"—i.e., the being declared righteous, the being treated as righteous, of those who are in fact righteous. It is at this point that Paul's doctrine of justification diverges from the O.T. conception, for the distinctive thing about the justification made possible by Christ is that it involves the declaring righteous, the treating as righteous, of those who are in fact *not* righteous. Commentators often seek to get around the difficulty here—the apparent validation of a fiction—by insisting that the verb δικαιόω meant "to make righteous," just as τυφλόω meant "to make blind." In both cases the final sigma is dropped from the adjectival form (δίκαιος and τύφλος) and the verbal ending is added. It is argued that by "justification" Paul means God's act of redeeming us from the power of sin and making us worthy of acquittal, as well as the actual acquittal itself. Such an interpretation can be sustained only by rather violent exegesis. Dodd, who is among those who seek to "relieve" Paul of a forensic doctrine of justification, writes: "The vindication of right involves a real righteousness of the people on whose behalf it is wrought. Thus the 'righteousness,' or act of redress, has for its ultimate issue, not only a people delivered from wrongful oppression, but a people delivered from their own sin, a 'righteous' people in our sense." It may be doubted that the "righteousness" or "act of redress" has essentially any such purpose, whether in the O.T. or in Paul. In the O.T. a "real righteousness" is undoubtedly involved, but it is involved as a prerequisite, not as a consequence. God acts to *vindicate* the "really righteous," not to *make* them so. For Paul too the meaning is primarily acquittal—but not of the "really righteous." Justification confers not primarily a new character, but a new status. It admits one to a new relationship with God. God has reconciled us to himself.

This justifying, reconciling act of God takes place on the basis of faith. The difficult phrase, literally rendered **from faith to faith,** is probably only a way of stressing the exclusive importance of faith, as though one said, "faith from start to finish." The quotation from Hab. 2:4 is not too well adapted to Paul's purpose, but he is eager to avail himself of O.T. support (notice below on 4:1-25). The term "faith" in Habakkuk means "loyalty" or "steadfastness," and the passage affirms that the righteous man shall live because of his faithfulness—or perhaps because of God's faithfulness. Paul is using the word "faith" in another sense, as we have seen. It has been suggested, however, with some

---

quality of **faith.** In 3:21 the same conviction is expressed in slightly different form; it recurs again in 5:1, as also at the beginning of ch. 8. In the present verse Paul is not referring to an abstract quality of the divine nature, but to "an act of God on behalf of men" (cf. Exeg.). The result of this act, from the human point of view, is a new relationship with God, which need not (and indeed cannot) be purchased by merit, but can be received only by faith. Most of the central themes of Romans emerge in this verse, and it merits careful study.

First, the gospel declares an activity of God which issues in the deliverance of his people. It proclaims a righteousness which comes from God and is characteristic of God, and which makes possible a new relationship with God.

Second, this righteousness, therefore, is seen as related in the most intimate manner to the salvation of men. At this point Paul is loyal to the position set forth in certain great passages in the O.T. (cf. Exeg.) but to an even greater extent than psalmist or prophet he affirms that what God has done is both consistent with his nature and faithful to his promises.

Third, the gospel proclaims that there is available to men a righteousness which is given by God, but hitherto we could not fully know its character and we were wholly ignorant of the way in which it could become our own. Man's instinctive tendency has determined the agelong character of his quest: he has tried to merit by his own efforts what he can have only as a gift from God. Consequently a certain attitude of mind becomes of decisive importance—the attitude which is willing to wait in humble trust for what God is willing to give and then receive it with gratitude and without pride. This is

18 For the wrath of God is revealed from heaven against all ungodliness and unrighteousness of men, who hold the truth in unrighteousness;

18 For the wrath of God is revealed from heaven against all ungodliness and wickedness of men who by their wicked-

---

plausibility, that both meanings of the term are involved in Paul's phrase **from faith to faith**—that salvation has its source in God's faith (in Habakkuk's sense) and is bestowed in response to our faith (in Paul's sense). The appropriateness of the Habakkuk passage for Paul's purpose is clearer if he thought of it as meaning **those who are righteous by faith shall live** (RSV) than if he adopted the more usual sense represented by KJV, **the righteous shall live by faith.** The LXX text makes either understanding possible.

II. The World's Need of God's Saving Act in Christ (1:18–3:20)

A. Introduction (1:18)

We have noted the importance for Paul's theology of his way of diagnosing the human situation (see p. 369 above); it is not surprising, therefore, that the argument of Romans begins at that point. The conclusion which these opening paragraphs of the body of the letter will try to drive home is that all men are guilty before God and subject to the bondage of sin, and that they are incapable of saving themselves through obedience to God's law. It is impossible to outline this section with precision because the transitions are not clear and there are occasional digressions; but in general it may be said that

---

what Paul calls **faith.** Its importance in this passage is beyond question, whatever the way in which we may interpret the quotation from Hab. 2:4.

Fourth, the nature of the new **righteousness** is such that we could never have discovered it for ourselves. Therefore we can only say that it **is revealed**—by God's disclosing act it is made known to those who otherwise would never have learned it. Left to ourselves, our attitude was such that we were constantly frustrating the very power which purposed our deliverance. Our own efforts could not win righteousness and our own intelligence could not fathom the method by which it could become ours. What the situation requires is that God should do what the biblical writers are persuaded that he does—so act that in our situation we may learn the truth about his nature and his purpose.

18-32. ***Man's Universal Need.***—From the declaration of God's righteousness, Paul turns at once to the disclosure of God's judgment. The one revelation is incomplete without the other. The gospel declares the holy purpose of God as it speaks to us in love in Jesus Christ our Lord; to understand it—in however fragmentary a way—is to realize the abysmal nature of man's need. If the light is now shining clearly in the gospel, it reveals, in the first instance, the darkness in which so much of our human life is actually enveloped. As a matter of fact, man sees himself in true perspective only as he also sees God's holy character and understands his righteous will. That is why so much of our human self-complacency is possible only when men have forgotten God or are indifferent to him. As soon as there begins to dawn some understanding of what righteousness really is, there follows immediately and inevitably an awareness of that unalterable antipathy to and revulsion from evil which must be the mark of perfect goodness. To this simple but basic fact of religious experience the whole Bible bears witness. It may be the psalmist, acutely conscious that God is of too pure eyes to behold iniquity; it may be Isaiah, appalled in the presence of holiness by the extent to which he is involved in evil; it may be Peter, suddenly aware that he is in the presence of more than human powers and consequently smitten by a sense of his own utter unworthiness.

Eternal Light! Eternal Light!
  How pure that soul must be,
When, placed within thy searching sight,
It shrinks not, but with calm delight
  Can live, and look on thee!

. . . .

Oh how shall I, whose native sphere
  Is dark, whose mind is dim,
Before the Ineffable appear,
And on my naked spirit bear
  The uncreated beam? [6]

This is not a morbid obsession with human frailty: it is simply the inevitable response to any kind of understanding of God's righteousness. It is natural, therefore, that the great

[6] Thomas Binney, "Eternal Light! Eternal Light!"

attention is given first to the moral failure of the Gentiles, then to that of the Jews, and finally, more specifically, to the impotence of the Jewish law.

18. Paul begins, however, with a general remark meant in all probability to apply to both Jews and Greeks. **The wrath of God** is being revealed **against all ungodliness.** By the **wrath of God** is meant not the emotion of anger in a simple human sense, but the just and inevitable issue of sin, the death which is God's judgment upon it. Just as salvation is an eschatological term, as we shall see more clearly later, so is "the wrath." The word refers primarily to the Last Judgment; but Paul sees signs on all sides that this judgment is already beginning to take place. Attention should again be called to the active meaning of the term **revealed.** Goodspeed catches this meaning effectively when he speaks of the wrath as "breaking forth from heaven."

---

declaration (vss. 16-17) of the gospel and its redeeming power should lead at once to the consideration of the terrible extent of human need. Even the grammatical construction underlines the sense: "The righteousness of God is revealed" (vs. 17), and **The wrath of God is revealed.**

The passage further lends itself to useful exposition as a treatment of the nature and consequences of our moral failure. Implicit in the whole section is a certain understanding of human wrongdoing, and in a day when sin is sometimes dismissed as a foolish preoccupation with the consequences of natural impulses it is valuable to recover something of the apostolic conception of sin. Sin is not an act nor even a series of acts; it is that state which makes wrong conduct possible, the condition of mind and spirit whose consequences become apparent in action. Its manifestations are many and various, but its essential quality—what makes it sin—is a willful disobedience to God. Sin is our arrogant affirmation of an imaginary autonomy: it is a proud and haughty attempt of the creature to forget the Creator, or even to usurp his prerogatives. This is no new insight on the part of Paul; it is simply a reaffirmation of the consistent biblical view that man, made for fellowship with and dependence on the Spirit of God, destroys the balance of his life when he rebels and tries to pursue his own purposes in complete independence of God. By seeking a liberty which is illusory, he falls into a bondage complete in its range and terrifying in its consequences. The crux of sin is defiant pride; the nemesis of sin lies in this, that, seeking freedom, it leads to the most utter servitude.

The willful disobedience which is the mark of sin shows itself most clearly in man's deliberate refusal to recognize what God has made perfectly apparent to all who are willing to see. Nature itself—all pervasive and inescapable—speaks of God's power and reflects those qualities which we can sum up only by the word "divinity." The evidence is there for anyone who will take the trouble to notice it; to ignore it is consequently the very mark of that arrogant disregard of God which Paul recognizes as one of the crucial marks of sin.

But sin brings its own retribution, and the consequences appear in one area after another. In the realm of the intellect the consequences are the folly and blindness which find expression in the colossal absurdity of idolatry (vss. 22-23). This in turn leads to a disastrous corruption of the emotional life; the passions, freed from the restraints which normally keep them in effective control, run riot in every kind of perversion (vss. 24-27). The contagion spreads farther and farther; the whole fabric of corporate life becomes corrupted, and every kind of antisocial impulse finds free play (vss. 29-31). The final and most fearful stage is reached when all standards have disintegrated, and conscience is impotent to protest. In direct defiance of what they know of God's judgment, men not only do the things which are contrary to his will, but cynically applaud when others do the same (vs. 32). The picture is black enough in itself; we realize fully its true quality when we return in retrospect to the point from which Paul starts. Sin is not man's error or ignorance; it is willful refusal to know God and serve him. The possibilities of knowledge are present, and it is impossible to plead that man did not know. Both nature and conscience would teach man if he were willing to learn. But the pride of sin has turned him aside, and the consequences of sin—terrible as we see them to be—inexorably follow.

18. ***Judgment on Sin.—For***—even the construction is a reminder that the discussion of man's failure is intimately related to the statement of God's purpose. We understand the one only in the light of the other; there can be no doctrine of man's sin that does not start from God's righteousness.

The term **the wrath of God** is important in the thought of Paul, and doubly important in the exposition of the epistle because it lends itself so easily to misinterpretation. It naturally suggests to us those qualities which we associate

We are undoubtedly right in emphasizing, with Dodd, the objective character of "the wrath," and in rejecting "the simple anthropomorphic idea that God is angry with men"; we must avoid going so far, however, as to make the term refer merely to an *automatic effect* of sin and not also to an imposed penalty for sin. "The wrath" is in the last resort *God's* wrath, even though, as Dodd shows, the name of God is often not used in connection with it. We cannot "absolve" God of responsibility for judgment without accepting in effect the Marcionite belief in two Gods—one of judgment and the other of love. Sin, as we have seen, is bondage, but it is also transgression; and the death which follows upon it is not only the result of the bondage; it is also God's judgment upon the transgression. The wrath, Paul says, is breaking forth *from heaven.*

---

with human anger, such as petulant exasperation, vindictive rage, ungovernable passion; and consequently it corrupts, by means of the lower anthropomorphism, our conception of God. But by ignoring what **the wrath of God** really points to, we suffer in equal measure, and our understanding of the divine character and purpose is vitiated by sentimentalism. As C. H. Dodd has pointed out in his exposition of the phrase,[7] Paul never places God as the subject of the verb "to be angry," although parallels with other words (such as "love" and "to love," "grace" and "to be gracious") might lead us to expect that he would. This forms the point of departure for a detailed examination of the history and development of the word, and the conclusion to which the discussion leads is the assertion that Paul retains the word **wrath** "not to describe the attitude of God to man, but to describe an inevitable process of cause and effect in a moral universe."[8] But the reader will notice the warning in the Exeg. against making "the term refer merely to an *automatic effect* of sin." This merely places under contribution the characteristic prophetic conviction that wrath is manifested in the events of history, and is caused by human sin. Mercy, on the other hand, is not a response to human goodness; it is a quality inherent in the character of God, and its distinctive role is the "deliverance of His people from the power and oppression of sin—in fact, from 'the Wrath.'"[9]

The importance of the conception at once becomes apparent. Instead of being a difficult phrase, to be avoided if possible or treated with diffident uncertainty when necessary, it proves a most useful instrument for affirming truths of the greatest contemporary relevance. "Judgment is set" in the earth and is an inescapable part of the discipline of human life. This follows, of course, from any belief that ours is an orderly universe in which moral considerations ultimately prevail. If we are not at the mercy of chance, cause will inexorably lead to effect, and the turbulence of iniquity will in due season bring its own retribution. Consequently, judgment on evil is part of God's moral government of the universe. Evil is ultimately self-destructive because it must always encounter that final will of creative goodness which underlies and sustains all things. This is not merely an intuitive insight. The Bible repeatedly affirms that history is the scene of God's operation; on its stage man can see the forces of the divine-human drama unfolding. Nor is the disclosure fortuitous—it is revealed, because God is the maker and the master of history. Any age which has seen the pomp of insolent evil overthrown, and has watched the fearful retribution which wrongdoing can bring on those who practice it, should be ready to reconsider the significance of **the wrath of God.**

The qualities in human life which bring the wrath in their wake are roughly of two kinds: those which can be classified as religious sins, and consequently against God **(ungodliness),** and those which can be regarded as moral offenses, and consequently against men **(unrighteousness).** Relentless judgment may finally overtake them, as we have already seen, but the terrible thing about human freedom is that in the interim it can be used for such fearful ends. In their day of power, men of ill will can **hold** *down* **the truth:** they can thwart its free exercise and hinder its natural growth. There is given to men an elemental knowledge of the things that are ultimate and abiding; as Paul will presently demonstrate, a basic perception of God is given in and through man's reason, and a similar understanding of goodness is given through the exercise of conscience. But man can so suppress them that they become wholly ineffective, and having repressed what should curb evil, he lives in the meanwhile in unrighteousness. The imagery is vivid and forceful. It suggests a man deliberately holding a living thing in an alien atmosphere until its life is stifled. It says that we can drown the truth in an ocean of evil.

[7] *The Epistle of Paul to the Romans* (London: Hodder & Stoughton, 1932; "The Moffatt New Testament Commentary"), pp. 20-24.

[8] *Ibid.*, p. 23.

[9] *Ibid.*

19 Because that which may be known of God is manifest in them; for God hath showed *it* unto them.

20 For the invisible things of him from the creation of the world are clearly seen, being understood by the things that are made, *even* his eternal power and Godhead; so that they are without excuse:

ness suppress the truth.
19 For what can be known about God is plain to them, because God has shown it to them.
20 Ever since the creation of the world his invisible nature, namely, his eternal power and deity, has been clearly perceived in the things that have been made. So they are without

B. The Failure of the Gentiles (1:19-32)

1. Idolatry (1:19-23)

19-23. It now becomes apparent that Paul is to speak first to the Gentiles, and that the first and most important item in his indictment of the Gentile world is its idolatry. He has already referred to "men who by their wickedness suppress the truth"—the truth about God's righteous nature and the character of his relations and dealings with men. Now he points out that the Gentiles have been given knowledge of God, so that they cannot plead ignorance of the truth they suppress. The term **known** (γνωστόν) does not necessarily mean merely "what *can* be known"; it may mean "what *is* known." Such may well be its meaning here. In that case Paul is not saying—as otherwise he might seem to be saying—that all that can be known of God has been disclosed to the Gentiles, but rather that what they *do* know they know clearly and surely. This knowledge of God is of **his invisible nature, . . . his eternal power and deity,** and has been given through the

19. ***Sin as Defiance of Insight.***—The culpability of such action is clear enough, and we can understand why, in a moral universe, it brings upon itself the consequences of the antipathy of God's righteous will. But the seriousness of the offense is all the greater because what should prevent or at least correct it is available to all. In each man's reason and conscience God has his witness; some things are "knowable" and are known, and this elementary insight is from God and is his gift. To supplement and illuminate this verse we should turn to the section on conscience which Paul introduces in 2:14 ff. Meanwhile we need only note that Paul is here pursuing a line of reasoning which would be familiar enough to his readers. The Greeks had developed "the argument from design," and we find it, e.g., in the writings of Seneca, a philosopher active at this very time in the very city to which Paul is writing.

20. ***"The Heavens Declare. . . ."***—The face of nature itself testifies to what is beyond nature: **For the invisible things. . . .** This is a "sacramental universe" because it is a created world. Its very constitution is such that the fact of God and equally the fact of his "eternal power" are revealed. In appealing to "this instinctive inference from nature up to nature's God," Paul is again using an approach familiar to those of his readers who had studied the poets and prophets of the O.T. "The heavens declare the glory of God," and it is God who "created the heavens, and stretched them out; he that spread forth the earth, and that which cometh out of it" (Isa. 42:5). After enumerating the various forms of natural life which testify to God's wisdom and power, Job can recapitulate with the question, "Who knoweth not in all these that the hand of the Lord hath wrought this?" (Job 12:9.) To the mind at all disposed to religious reverence the witness of nature is extraordinarily strong. We can take the evidence of Philo, or we can cite the eloquent passage from the *Opticks* in which Newton declares that the marvelous ingenuity of nature is unintelligible except in terms of a belief in God:

> Whence is it that nature does nothing in vain; and whence arises all that order and beauty which we see in the world? . . . How came the bodies of animals to be contrived with so much art and for what ends were their several parts? Was the eye contrived without skill in optics, or the ear without knowledge of sounds? . . . And these things being rightly despatched, does it not appear from phenomena that there is a being incorporeal, living, intelligent, omnipresent? [1]

To Paul's mind the evidence is so clear and strong, and points so conclusively to an intelligent purpose which meets us in demand as well as succor, that only willful and perverse disregard can fail to recognize it. Consequently there is no excuse; we cannot plead ignorance. **So that they are . . .** points to a result. As so

[1] Bk. III. Query 25.

21 Because that, when they knew God, they glorified *him* not as God, neither were thankful; but became vain in their imaginations, and their foolish heart was darkened.

22 Professing themselves to be wise, they became fools,

23 And changed the glory of the uncorruptible God into an image made like to corruptible man, and to birds, and four-footed beasts, and creeping things.

excuse; 21 for although they knew God they
did not honor him as God or give thanks
to him, but they became futile in their
thinking and their senseless minds were
darkened. 22 Claiming to be wise, they became fools, 23 and exchanged the glory of
the immortal God for images resembling
mortal man or birds or animals or reptiles.

---

created order of the natural world (cf., e.g., Ps. 19:1). But although they thus knew God, **they did not honor him as God or give thanks to him.** Moffatt renders 21*b*: "They have turned to futile speculations till their ignorant minds grew dark." As Dodd points out, we are not to suppose that Paul here is consciously indicting the higher Greek philosophy —not that he would have hesitated to do this if he had known it; but he would have done it in other terms. "Platonists and Stoics, and even Epicureans, might in their esoteric circles cultivate the most sublime speculations about the nature of the Divine, but at every turn the traveller in the Graeco-Roman world met with frank idolatry and its moral accompaniments." Sanday and Headlam quote from Enoch 99:8-9: "And they will become godless by reason of the foolishness of their hearts, and their eyes will be blinded through the fear of their hearts and through visions in their dreams. Through these they will

---

often in this part of the letter, we are faced with the inexorable way in which the laws of a moral universe operate.

21. ***The Cumulative Consequences Unfold.***—We have seen something of the perversity of godlessness; now we begin to see its consequences. The opening words of the verse recapitulate the argument which Paul has just set forth: men have at hand the means of knowing God. But this instinctive awareness of God and goodness, an awareness with which we are apparently endowed, should have prompted men to glorify God. Praise, then, is the natural consequence of any knowledge of God **as God,** because inseparable from any conception of deity are those attributes (eternity, power, goodness, justice, mercy) which should constrain us to give God the glory. Moreover, this kind of worship has, as its natural counterpart and consequence, the spirit of gratitude. For what he is, for what he has shown us of himself, for what he has done on our behalf, we should be thankful. From this kind of natural human response to life, godlessness is cut off; it is bereft of the impulse to worship and of the instinct to give thanks. But this straitened poverty of spirit is only the first stage in that utter collapse of human dignity which is the sequel to disregarding God. The man who tries to establish his own autonomy pursues his perverse and arrogant speculations until they lead him to complete frustration. Futility is only the prelude to darkness, that hopeless situation in which man has lost all light and sense of leading. Thought, feeling, will (all included in **heart**)—in fact all the aspects of man's inner life—pass into that eclipse which is the nemesis of his proud and ungrateful disregard of God.

22. ***The Nemesis of Sin.***—The man who makes his own thoughts and desires his supreme standard of judgment has in effect abandoned the attempt to know what is the final truth—God's will and nature—and consequently finds himself at last engulfed in mental impotence and confusion. Those who put their trust in human wisdom (and to the Greek type of mind this was and is the highest form of virtue) are misled and end in a morass of folly. Paul has elsewhere (I Cor. 1:18-25) set forth his estimate of wisdom; here we have an unusually terse expression of the fate which overtakes man when he forsakes his true condition. He was made to find his perfect freedom in humble dependence upon God; again and again he rebels against his created status, claims a kind of autonomy which always eludes him, and discovers that his vaunted liberty is only slavery. When he claims a kind of wisdom that he cannot really achieve, he falls into all kinds of darkened but pretentious error.

23. ***The Degradation Represented by Idolatry.***—The full extent of the resultant folly is seen only in the monstrous folly of idolatry. The mordant sarcasm with which Isaiah ridiculed

24 Wherefore God also gave them up to uncleanness, through the lusts of their own hearts, to dishonor their own bodies between themselves: 25 Who changed the truth of God into a lie, and worshipped and served the creature more than the Creator, who is blessed for ever. Amen.	24 Therefore God gave them up in the lusts of their hearts to impurity, to the dishonoring of their bodies among themselves, 25 because they exchanged the truth about God for a lie and worshiped and served the creature rather than the Creator, who is blessed forever! Amen.

become godless and fearful, because they work all their works in a lie and they worship a stone." It is a typical Jew who is speaking there, as also in Rom. 1:19-23. See article "The Greco-Roman World" (Vol. VII, pp. 88-94) for a discussion of the extent of idolatry in the Gentile world of the first century.

2. God's Judgment Upon Idolatry (1:24-32)

24-27. This section of Paul's letter gives a dark picture of pagan morality. As a complete picture it is inadequate, as Paul himself will remind us in the next chapter, but there can be no doubt of its truth in very large part. Paul's description of current corruption is confirmed by many indications. (The article "The Greco-Roman World" [Vol. VII, pp. 80-84] will be helpful here.) The apostle's primary purpose at the moment is to point not to sins, but to judgment. He sees in the moral corruption, especially in the unnatural sexual vices, a sign that "the wrath" has already begun to work. **God gave**

those who use one end of a log for warmth and the other for worship (Isa. 44:18-20) finds further echoes in Wisd. Sol. 9; 13–15, and both passages prove that Paul is using an argument no less effective because familiar. But it is not merely the irrationality of the practice which is serious; idolatry represents a stage in the fearful corruption which has engulfed the Gentile world. It follows from the blindness which overtakes those who ignore God; it leads to the still more terrible abyss of evil to which the apostle is about to point. For the moment, however, the absurdity of idol worship is sufficient to establish the fate which has overtaken the vaunted wisdom of man. They **changed:** The substitution is their own act; they have ignored the witness of reason and conscience to the manifest perfection (**glory**) of God. In himself he abides in the eternal realm beyond those changing and ephemeral aspects of nature in which deluded man is apt to look for his final satisfactions. Being incorruptible, God is above that decay to which all creaturely things are subject, and in him is "no variableness, neither shadow of turning" (Jas. 1:17). The tragedy of man's plight is that it represents so terrible and yet so needless a repudiation of what he might possess. He can recognize, if he will, the power and divinity of God as these are displayed by the created world; instead, he turns not merely to what is inferior in splendor and dignity, but to a folly which brings in its train inescapable corruption. The choice of the lower, which is what worship of created things implies, carries with it moral as well as intellectual consequences.

24-25. ***Man's Life Reflects the Gods He Chooses.***—Men become like the gods they serve. If they practice idolatry, they find it morally corrupting as well as intellectually bankrupt. The disintegrating consequences of idolatry emphasize a tendency which the prophets had always recognized as inherent in the worship of false gods. Implicit in idolatry is polytheism; and where there are many possible objects of worship, man is likely to choose those which minister to his own desires. The result of his service of anything less than the Creator is the steady deterioration of the quality of his own life. Those who turn their backs on the manifest truth can only be left to the terrible consequences of error. The phrase **God gave them up,** so often repeated in this section, emphasizes the judicial nature of the process which the apostle is describing. This is the way in which the laws of a moral universe inevitably work. The punishment of sin lies not in any direct intervention by which God disciplines offenders, but in the consequences which naturally follow from a lawless life. As it has been incisively remarked by Charles Gore, "The wages of sin is also its fruit." [2] But the process is marked by an accelerating tempo. Those who

[2] *St. Paul's Epistle to the Romans* (New York: Charles Scribner's Sons, 1899), I, 72. Note also Joseph Butler, *The Analogy of Religion,* Part I, ch. ii.

26 For this cause God gave them up unto
vile affections: for even their women did
change the natural use into that which is
against nature:
27 And likewise also the men, leaving
the natural use of the woman, burned in
their lust one toward another; men with
men working that which is unseemly, and
receiving in themselves that recompense of
their error which was meet.

26 For this reason God gave them up to
dishonorable passions. Their women exchanged natural relations for unnatural,
27 and the men likewise gave up natural
relations with women and were consumed
with passion for one another, men committing shameless acts with men and receiving
in their own persons the due penalty for
their error.

---

them up . . . to impurity. We have already seen (above, pp. 396-97) that Paul conceived of sin and its consequences as being in the closest possible connection: decay and death followed upon sin as inevitably as life and peace upon the righteousness of faith, and indeed partook of the same character. So here he sees the prevalence of homosexuality, **the dishonoring of their bodies among themselves,** as a manifestation not only of sin, but also of its issue and punishment, i.e., corruption and death. It is normal Jewish doctrine to find the root cause of both the sin and corruption in idolatry. Paul makes this connection clear both by his use of the word **therefore,** and by his repetition and summary in vs. 25. This verse, besides being repetitive, is somewhat interruptive, for vss. 26-27 do nothing except to emphasize and elaborate the meaning of vs. 24. **For this reason** is another reminder that the basic cause of all this corruption is idolatry.

---

sin not only face the immediate results, they find themselves more vulnerable to the next temptation. From the fundamental error of exalting the creature to the place which belongs to the Creator alone, two types of evil follow. There is uncleanness—sexual aberration in its most revolting forms; there is also a widespread social corruption which distorts all human relationship. Both follow from the error of substituting what is made for him who makes it.

The immediate consequence of changing **the truth about God for a lie** is the debasement of man. By an inexorable logic, those who begin by denying their Maker end by degrading themselves. It would be sentimental to ignore human depravity, but it is no pleasant task to study it in any detail. The very consideration of evil brings the apostle back to the thought of God. The only proper corrective to unwholesome preoccupation with evil is that reverent spirit which, while recognizing existing facts in shame and sorrow, reverts at once to the contemplation of God.

26-27. ***The Corruption Spreads.***—The progressive degeneration of evil is apparent in the horrible uncleanness which was a mark of Roman society. There is nothing static in evil; it cannot be arrested at any given point, and the inference which emerges from Paul's whole treatment of the subject is that those who abandon God lack the power to check the spread of corruption in every part of their experience. Whether or not Paul gives an accurate account of the condition of society in the Roman Empire of the first century is not our immediate problem. There is much corroborative evidence in satirists and moralists of that time, though their strictures must be used with some reserve. Such writers do not profess to exercise the objective care which is the ideal of the social historian. No more does Paul. He writes as a prophet, and he found quite enough in his society to awaken the most anxious concern. Moreover, what Paul is actually emphasizing is a truth which applies with far too exact relevance to the urban life of any civilization. If idolatry means exclusive delight in created things, idolatry is the mark of most of our modern life, and the results of idolatry can be seen in any great city of the world. The pursuit of false objects has led to the acceptance of false values. The cults of pleasure and of wealth—with all that follows from them—flourish everywhere, and the studies of moral conditions in the great centers of population reveal conditions essentially similar to those which Paul describes. Two further comments must suffice. Paul was writing from Corinth, a city aptly described as "the capital of Hellenistic vice," and this doubtless colored his outlook. But what he writes does not profess to be a complete picture. Within a few verses we find him admitting that many Gentiles, even without the assistance of a revealed law, achieve a high level of moral excellence. At this point Paul is describing not those who may be in error, but

28 And even as they did not like to retain God in *their* knowledge, God gave
them over to a reprobate mind, to do those
things which are not convenient;
29 Being filled with all unrighteousness,
fornication, wickedness, covetousness, maliciousness; full of envy, murder, debate,
deceit, malignity; whisperers,

28 And since they did not see fit to
acknowledge God, God gave them up to a
base mind and to improper conduct.
29 They were filled with all manner of
wickedness, evil, covetousness, malice. Full
of envy, murder, strife, deceit, malignity,

28-31. Paul stresses the same point yet again as he now proceeds to mention the antisocial (as distinguished from the sensual) sins of Gentile society. These too he sees as manifestations of God's judgment against idolatry: **And since they did not see fit to acknowledge God, God gave them up to a base mind and to improper conduct.** The various terms in this list of vices are variously translated, as a comparison of our two texts (as well as others) will indicate; but the RSV rendering is unquestionably more

---

those who see the light and sin against it. It is with the consequences of a willful repudiation of the truth that he is dealing. Finally, it is well to notice throughout this whole section a marked restraint and reticence. The subject is one which in honesty must be faced, but on which no man of fine feeling would care to linger. It is even a region where no one should be too eager to judge. The conclusion (vs. 27) is that gross offenders receive the condemnation appropriate to their offense. This is surely an example of the only kind of judgment that Christian humility can venture to pronounce.

28. ***The Fate to Which God Abandons Those Who Abandon Him.***—The consequences of a purely secular mind appear in the fate which it involves. Those who refuse to give God any place in their thought, or who do not think him worth keeping in their minds, in the last resort are left alone with the kind of resources which man's isolation finally affords. Again the results of man's choices are seen in the fruits which they yield. The play on words is difficult to convey exactly in another language, but the device simply indicates the intimate connection between our immediate decisions and our final destiny. **Those things which are not convenient** point directly to current ethical standards. The phrase was one in common use among the Stoics to cover the whole range of antisocial offenses. In other words, it is not merely Christian ethical standards that are threatened; even the better pagan insights revolt against the moral consequences of a godless outlook and are endangered by its triumph.

29-31. ***The Harvest of the Godless Mind.***—The "reprobate mind" (vs. 28) promptly expresses itself in action, and its cumulative consequences are a type of conduct which strikes at all the foundations of social well-being. It was a popular practice among moralists of Paul's day to prepare lists of virtues and vices, and Paul himself does so in more than one place in his letters. Here he is intent on expounding and enforcing the manifold and inclusive degradation which the repudiation of God introduces into all our relationships with our fellow men. Every phase of the **malignity** illustrates the result of that proud arrogance which turns its back on God and rides roughshod over the rights of others. In this context **fornication** is serious, not so much because it is an illicit personal gratification, as because it invades the integrity of another at a point where the consequences for personality are particularly disastrous. **Wickedness** sums up that whole disposition which is willing to seek not the good of others but their harm. **Covetousness** ("which is idolatry") is the lust which makes it possible for us to disregard (or even deliberately to injure) another, because our primary concern is with the world of things and not with the world of persons. **Maliciousness** is that spirit which takes delight in compassing mischief to others. Then the whole conscious life becomes marked by an outlook which excludes all goodness, and leads to hatefulness in attitude and action. **Envy** is grieved at the success or happiness of others and is "glad when they go wrong." (Cf. I Cor. 13:6 Moffatt.) The actual killing of our fellows is only the outward and ultimate expression of a spirit which cherishes angry thoughts against others (Matt. 5:21-26). Our relations with those about us become contentious because they are already bitter, and dissimulation is simply the outward manifestation of a spirit which has learned to practice deceit. The whole character of our relationships takes on a sharp edge toward others, which continually cuts away what is best in those around us and in our dealings with them. **Evil,** which openly vaunts itself in so

30 Backbiters, haters of God, despiteful,
proud, boasters, inventors of evil things,
disobedient to parents,
31 Without understanding, covenant-
breakers, without natural affection, implacable, unmerciful:
32 Who, knowing the judgment of God,
that they which commit such things are

they are gossips, 30 slanderers, haters of
God, insolent, haughty, boastful, inventors
of evil, disobedient to parents, 31 foolish,
faithless, heartless, ruthless. 32 Though they
know God's decree that those who do such

---

accurate than the KJV. Lists of vices in the moralists of the period were likely to be divided as between the sensual and the antisocial. It has already been hinted that Paul seems to have had such a division in his mind, vss. 24-27 being concerned with the sensual, and vss. 28-32 with the antisocial. Some commentators prefer to speak of (*a*) sins against nature and (*b*) sins against society. The phrase **improper conduct,** or more literally, "things which are not fitting," makes use of a common Stoic term for "duty." The right thing is the *appropriate* thing, or that which is "according to nature."

32. The idea that death is the working out of sin itself rather than a punishment arbitrarily visited upon it has been more than once suggested. It is intimated in the

---

many ways, also delights secretly to slander and, insidiously or blatantly, speaks ill of our fellows.

30. ***Delineation of Spiritual Collapse.***—**Haters of God** are the defiantly rebellious; they live in wickedness not because they know no better, but because, though aware of God's displeasure, they are wholly undeterred by it. The transition to the **despiteful** is natural and easy. The insolence which it suggests is of that truculent, swashbuckling variety typified by the braggarts of the Elizabethan stage—a shamelessness which is moved to no reverence of outlook, no humility of demeanor, no restraint in conduct because of any awareness of what God is. It follows as a matter of course that they would be haughty in their relations with others because they are insolent in their attitude to God, and by the same token they have no restraint in their self-glorification and praise of themselves.

At first sight we might appear to be in the midst of a catalogue of vices introduced as a literary concession to conventional moral practice. But as a picture of the corruption which overtakes the self-satisfied exaltation of man and his power, it would be difficult to conceive anything more incisive than Paul's enumeration of the consequences which follow from an exclusive reliance on human gifts and capacities. Both for its mordant stripping away of all false pretense, and for its relevance to certain modern attitudes and contemporary situations, few passages lend themselves more readily to effective exposition. There are still those who cry, "Glory to Man in the highest! for Man is the master of things." [3] But man in his pride is not even the master of himself. The character of the godless disposition shows itself not merely in a propensity to evil; it is marked also by that spirit which is inventive in devising as well as eager in accepting evil. Disobedience to parents is an indication of the breakdown of respect for even the simplest and most widely recognized type of authority. It represents a failure both in basic emotional response and in that sense of order—of the most elementary kind—which is the foundation of every other kind of order.

31. ***Crescendo of Obloquy.***—The passage is working toward its inexorable end. The complete bankruptcy of man without God is shown in intellectual failure, in the lack of loyalty to obligation in the realm of will and action, and in the absence of simple, natural emotional attachment. Here again the life of his own age amply illustrated the evils to which Paul refers only in passing. Because **natural affection** was lacking, both divorce and infanticide were common. When the true bond which should unite man and woman is loosened, no other tie suffices to hold them together; when those responsible for the procreation of children do not feel obliged to accept even the simplest responsibility for them, a new life has no security because it has no value. Two further comments complete Paul's delineation of man's life when he tries to cut it off from God. Bitterness and resentment harden into unrelenting obduracy, and the simplest wellsprings of mercy are dried up.

32. ***The Worst at the Last.***—The final verse is the most devastating of all. Ignorance cannot exonerate the men of whom the apostle speaks. They know the declaration of God's righteous sentence; reason and conscience teach them that those who do such things have the

[3] Swinburne, "The Hymn of Man."

worthy of death, not only do the same, but have pleasure in them that do them.

2 Therefore thou art inexcusable, O man, whosoever thou art that judgest: for wherein thou judgest another, thou con-

things deserve to die, they not only do them but approve those who practice them.

2 Therefore you have no excuse, O man, whoever you are, when you judge an-

---

recurrent statement in this section, "God gave them up," as though God merely took his restraining and protecting hand away from them. "The act of God is no more than an abstention from interference with their free choice and its consequences" (Dodd). Nevertheless the reference here to **God's decree,** or "God's righteous judgment," and the statement that those who **commit such things are worthy of death** will prevent our dismissing the conception of God's deliberate judgment upon sin. The reason why "free choice" of evil has such terrible "consequences" is to be found in God's own righteousness and in his will not only to establish righteousness in his created world but also to vindicate it where it is transgressed.

The final clause of the passage suggests that in Paul's view encouraging others to commit such sins is worse than doing them one's self. This may well be his meaning. On the other hand he may be pointing to a general breakdown of principle in the pagan world, as though he would say: "Not only are these terrible things done, but they are done with the tacit if not expressed approval of the whole society." Here again he finds evidence that God has withdrawn himself from that society, leaving it not only in sin, but in the darkness it has perversely chosen. This is the beginning of the "wrath of God."

C. The Failure of the Jews (2:1-24)

2:1-5. So far it is clear that Paul has been thinking exclusively of the Gentiles; now as he addresses **O man, whoever you are,** he includes the Jew in his indictment, and it

---

mark of death upon them, and deserve the final consequences of their sin. They know all this, and yet they act as they do. But far more serious still is the cynical approval with which they regard those who are guilty of like wrongdoing. With manifest sympathy they applaud others who commit the same kind of transgressions. It is bad enough to sin; it is far worse to encourage others in evil. Many a person offends and then suffers the pangs of conscience; many another can apply a moral standard only to others—he exonerates his own lapses, but detects and condemns the failures of his neighbor. But here we have passed beyond both these stages, and contemplate the plight of men who can take delight in the evil which others do. This bespeaks a spirit which has gone so far from God that it can be regarded only as the final denial of all that God is and stands for.

2:1-29. ***Judgment: Its Unrestricted Scope.***—Paul has drawn a fearful picture of the degradation of pagan society, but this only partially describes the universal human need which forms the background of his gospel. What we need is righteousness, with all that it means of forgiveness by God and of renewal for men. Our plight may be most blatantly apparent in the scandalous conduct characteristic of certain sections of the ancient world, but the ease with which we condemn the grosser evils does not make the subtler ones any less invidious. The moralist himself is under condemnation. The man who claims to live a better life than his neighbor must accept the judgment of his own higher standards. Moreover, our human situation is such that whatever may be the measure of our achievement, we all stand condemned in God's sight. Some fail in one way, some in another, but all fail, and this should have far-reaching consequences in our judgment of ourselves and of each other. To emphasize this simple fact—so important but so easily obscured—is Paul's present purpose. In the first century of our era the typical example of the strict religious moralist was the Jew. Beyond all others, he tried to live by an exacting code. To an unparalleled degree he ended by being self-righteous about it. But the temper of mind which the Jew exhibited in an extreme form is one characteristic of good men in all ages, and it is perhaps significant that Paul opens this chapter with a very general phrase about anyone who undertakes to be censorious about his fellow men. Paul speaks explicitly, in due course, to the Jews of his time, but we can always take to heart the sobering fact that not one of us is entitled to judge others, because we are all alike under judgment. To this sub-

demnest thyself; for thou that judgest doest the same things.

2 But we are sure that the judgment of God is according to truth against them which commit such things.

other; for in passing judgment upon him you condemn yourself, because you, the judge, are doing the very same things. 2 We know that the judgment of God rightly

soon becomes apparent that he is thinking primarily of the Jew. That fact becomes explicit, however, only gradually. (Dodd compares the psychology of Paul's method here with that exhibited in the prophecy of Amos 1–2.) The conjunction **therefore** is difficult to interpret, since it does not connect plausibly with the preceding sentence, or indeed with the preceding paragraph as a whole. Perhaps Paul uses it in proleptic fashion, his mind already assuming what is said in vs. 1*b*: *Because* you **are doing the very same things** yourself, **you have no excuse** in **passing judgment** upon another; for **it is upon those who do such things**—whatever the standards to which they pay lip service—that **the judgment of God . . . falls.** The impressive **according to truth** (KJV) is to be preferred to the more casual **rightly** of the RSV as the rendering of the Greek phrase κατὰ ἀλήθειαν. Paul's point is that God's judgment is not according to race or nationality (cf. vss. 10-11), but

ject the N.T. returns again and again, and we can safely assume that there are few things that we need more seriously to lay to heart. There are the words of Jesus himself, with their warning of the inexorable standards we erect for ourselves if we ever dare to sit in judgment on our fellows. There is Paul's saying later in this letter (12:19)—a comment even more emphatic than his present words—that it is arrogant presumption for anyone except God to be judge of other people's lives. Anyone who tries to do so is appropriating to himself divine prerogatives, and must await the consequences of an attitude so impious and so sacrilegious.

1. ***The Vulnerability of the Upright.***—No skill is more easily mastered than the ability to detect the moral failings of our neighbors; certainly none is exercised with such constancy and such delight. To blast the faults of others subtly confirms our estimate of our own integrity. Paul is shrewd enough to know that in all he has said so far he has had the enthusiastic approval of a certain type of self-righteous mind. We may notice the psychological skill of his method. The Exeg. refers to the parallel of Amos' prophetic warning: having carried his hearers with him while he denounces the evils of their neighbors, he confronts them with the equal enormity of their own deeds. An even more dramatic example of the same method (less general in scope, more intensely personal in application) is Nathan's parable to David (II Sam. 12:1-14): the prophet arouses the king's indignation only to direct it against his own sins. In the same way, Paul, who has detected the murmured approval of his denunciation of the pagan world, turns on these self-righteous Jewish critics of Gentile society. Those who think they live lives of reasonable probity may believe that they are safely separated from the scandalous offenders described in the latter part of ch. 1. A sure barrier of moral integrity divides the upright from the sinful. But the important thing is not the quantitative measurement of iniquity. Paul has been emphasizing the simple fact that his Gentile contemporaries have failed because they have not followed such light as they already had for their guidance. No one escapes the thrust of such a charge; even the most exacting moralist comes under condemnation. The inescapable fact is that we all fail at the one point. The manner of our failure, or its flagrancy, may differ from one person to the next, but the essential fact is that we all see more than we are willing or able to put into practice. So by venturing to judge even notorious sinners, we stand self-condemned: we do **the very same things.**

2. ***God's Standard of Judgment.***—One of the elementary insights of religion is that God—who *is* entitled to judge—judges **according to truth.** "My country, right or wrong" is a criterion to which few people appeal in precisely that bald and blatant form, but motives of loyalty are always influencing—often deflecting—our powers of judgment. We allow concessions in the case of our own nation, our own race, class, profession, or denomination that we indignantly repudiate when others make the same plea. Even the best of us fail here, but early in the history of the Hebrew spiritual pilgrimage a discerning man put the penetrating question, "Shall not the Judge of all the earth do right?" (Gen. 18:25.) Religious insight is persuaded that what God should do, he can and does do: he judges **according to truth.** He alone knows all the facts, and he alone can set them in the light of perfect righteousness. So

3 And thinkest thou this, O man, that
judgest them which do such things, and
doest the same, that thou shalt escape the
judgment of God?
4 Or despisest thou the riches of his
goodness and forbearance and longsuffer-
ing; not knowing that the goodness of God
leadeth thee to repentance?

falls upon those who do such things. 3 Do
you suppose, O man, that when you judge
those who do such things and yet do them
yourself, you will escape the judgment of
God? 4 Or do you presume upon the riches
of his kindness and forbearance and patience? Do you not know that God's kindness is meant to lead you to repentance?

---

is based on the moral facts. The fact that the Jew (the idea must be assumed here although the word has not been spoken) has the law, the highest embodiment of God's will, and is thus in position to see how far short the Gentile world is falling—this fact is no guarantee that he **will escape the judgment of God.** Everything depends upon whether the Jew *keeps* the law—and this, Paul is saying, he has not done. Nor can the Jew rely upon the special **kindness and forbearance and patience** of God toward him; for this was **meant to lead** [him] **to repentance,** and this repentance has not taken place. On the contrary his **heart is hard and impenitent.** So long as this is true, God's previous **forbearance and patience** mean only a more terrible ultimate judgment: **You are storing up wrath for yourself on the day of wrath when God's righteous judgment will be revealed.**

This allusion to the **day of wrath** and the revelation of **God's righteous judgment** as being still in the future may appear to be not easily compatible with Paul's statement in 1:18 that the wrath of God *is being revealed.* In the summary of his doctrine of salvation in the Intro. (see above, pp. 368-71), it was observed that although Paul believed the new age was still to come (in the sense of being consummated), he nevertheless conceived of it as having already come (in the sense of being so near as to make its force felt in the present age). The *age* of the Spirit had not, strictly speaking, arrived, but the life of the Spirit had already begun; and this beginning, a fact of experience, was

---

this righteous judgment of God can henceforth be assumed as the foundation of the entire argument. Moreover, it is well for us to remember that in the N.T. "judgment" is a word which always carries serious overtones of meaning. In our age we have lost the keen sense of the "awfulness" of judgment, perhaps because God's righteous purpose and his holy presence are less vividly before our minds. It is hard to read the N.T. without realizing that judgment implies not only the application of a standard of right, but also condemnation (where there is need) and the execution of the sentence which is pronounced.

3. ***The Root of Evil in Things Good.***—The self-complacency which condemns others without any humbling sense of being involved in the miseries and catastrophies of our sinful human situation is castigated in especially emphatic terms. "You, of all people. . . ." The awareness that we fall short of what our knowledge tells us to be right ought to make us humble. Consequently, the kind of pride which is so blindly confident as to judge others is absurd as well as tragic. Indeed, this brings us very close to the view of true tragedy which all the greatest dramatists have held: the very qualities which are the distinguishing mark of a person work in such a way as to bring about his downfall. The devastating feature of the situation with which Paul is dealing lies in this: good men have allowed their goodness to betray them into self-satisfaction and superiority. Consequently they have brought themselves under the awful judgment of God.

4. ***The Incomprehensibility of Pride.***—It is fearful to contemplate; it is also difficult to understand. Even the judgment of God—because it is a part of his whole nature—should remind men of those other qualities which are the assurance of our ultimate deliverance. Obdurate arrogance is possible only if we blind ourselves to the treasures of goodness and patience which are the mark of God's dealing with his people. Even in the stern discipline which the prophet saw in the historical experience of Israel, he recognized also God's presence to heal and to bless. "In his love and in his pity he redeemed them; and he bare them, and carried them all the days of old" (Isa. 63:9). This should have been apparent to all who with confidence appealed to God; not to recognize its meaning would be to brand themselves as ignorant concerning the whole purpose of God's dealing with men. What history teaches is sharpened in individual experience, and then Paul sees only

5 But, after thy hardness and impenitent heart, treasurest up unto thyself wrath against the day of wrath and revelation of the righteous judgment of God;
6 Who will render to every man according to his deeds:

5 But by your hard and impenitent heart
you are storing up wrath for yourself on
the day of wrath when God's righteous judgment will be revealed. 6 For he will render

for Paul the surest evidence of the imminence of the new age itself. On this characteristic of Paul's religious thinking there will be many later occasions to comment; just now it is enough to observe that precisely the same ambiguity exists in his thinking about God's judgment. It also is being revealed (1:18) and is to be revealed (2:5). Judgment, like salvation, is essentially future, but each has already begun to take effect. In the present passage Paul is thinking of judgment under its future aspect, just as in 1:18-32 he is emphasizing its already present manifestations.

The literary style of this passage (vss. 1-5), with its direct address to the reader or hearer, its piling of question on question, is known as the "Stoic diatribe," because it was the characteristic style of the Stoic preachers whom Paul would have heard on the street corners of many Hellenistic cities. It is a very effective style in argument and Paul often resorts to it.

6-9. The passage beginning here and extending to vs. 16 is difficult, not because of any particular obscurity within the text, but because it seems at first to be out of harmony with Paul's position at two very important points. The first of these is suggested by the sentence quoted from Ps. 62:12, **he will render to every man according to his works.** A considerable portion of this very letter is to be devoted to affirming and demonstrating that God *is* ready to deal with us on another basis—i.e., according not to our works but to

two alternatives: the person who is arrogantly self-righteous either trusts that he will escape judgment, or he despises those very qualities which should make him gratefully accept what God does for him. If pride had not blinded his eyes, he would have recognized **the kindness** which is the source from which all gracious and generous actions flow; he would have felt something of that **forbearance** which is slow to press upon us the full consequences of our folly; he would have responded to the **patience** which "waits long before actively intervening." Surely no religiously-minded person can mistake the true character of **God's kindness.** It is not displayed in order to create a false security or to confirm us in our irreverent pride. To possess God's mercy is a privilege, but it carries with it an exacting consequence. We can claim it only if we are willing to use it for its proper purpose, and that is always to effect a complete and radical change. Anyone who truly sees what God's goodness means cannot complacently remain in his old condition. He must repent, and those who refuse to do so declare that they know nothing beyond the conventional moral trappings of religion.

5. ***The Inescapability of Judgment.***—The kind of indifference which Paul has been describing is nothing less than willful insensibility to all that true religion requires. The man who persists in such callous disregard of what his own insight should teach him concerning his duty is adhering to a course whose cumulative results may not yet be apparent, but which will inevitably confront him at last. The mention of God's riches (vs. 4) suggests by contrast the kind of treasure which men sometimes prefer to lay up for themselves. For the present they may seem to do so with impunity, but the religious man's answer to the apparent indifference of the world to moral realities is the firm belief that consequences, slowly accumulated, will inexorably be disclosed. Finally they must be faced. **Judgment** may be postponed but it cannot be evaded, and the O.T. conviction that the day of the Lord will be a **day of wrath** (cf. Amos 5:18) has its N.T. counterpart. The whole process works toward an end because it has a purpose, and ultimately God's plan will be made manifest. **Judgment** is implicit now; then it will be explicit, and evil with its consequences will stand exposed to sight. But the mark of that **judgment** will be its disclosure not simply of the divine indignation with and revulsion from evil, but of that positive rightness which is inseparable from God.

6-11. ***The Basis on Which We Are Judged.***—Paul's great contribution to Christian thought is his exposition of the way in which man's separation from God is overcome and a new relationship established. It sometimes seems, to be sure, that justification by faith stands in

7 To them who by patient continuance in well doing seek for glory and honor and immortality, eternal life:

to every man according to his works: **7** to those who by patience in well-doing seek for glory and honor and immortality, he

our faith—and indeed that God has always been ready to deal so with men. To remove this difficulty by making the word "works" mean in effect "faith" is hardly possible in view of the stricter use of the term which Paul customarily makes; nor will the context support such an interpretation. Vs. 8, for example, conveys the same meaning as vs. 6: **For those who are factious** ["unscrupulously self-seeking" (Kirk)] **and do not obey the truth, but obey wickedness, there will be wrath and fury.** The difficulty yields somewhat when we realize that Paul is by definition speaking of the situation *apart from Christ.* Soon he is to tell us (3:31 ff.) that a way of justification has been revealed other than through our perfect obedience to the law; but at this moment he is trying to convey what our situation was before that new way became available, and indeed what that situation still is if one has not by faith availed one's self of it.

The second and perhaps more serious difficulty in this whole passage (vss. 6-16) is that it seems to assume not only the possibility that one may be justified by one's works, but

opposition to any emphasis on the value of good works. But actually the contrast is more apparent than real. It is quite true that Paul always vehemently repudiates any suggestion that by our own goodness we can establish any claim upon God, or even set ourselves right with him. But when God's forgiveness has become our sure possession, we are still faced with the duty of expressing in conduct of an appropriate kind the new relationship to which it leads. Consequently, it is possible to set faith and works in opposition to each other only if we overlook the necessary stages which mark the development of the spiritual life. Possibly the complementary character of the two terms becomes more apparent if we insist that justification is by faith, but that judgment is according to works. The doctrine of justification deals with the initial stage; it sets forth the conditions on which the Christian finds peace with God and enters upon the new life made possible by Jesus Christ. In the next stage, when the possibilities before us are translated into terms of actual experience, good works become the concrete expression of that new life which faith has made possible. Strictly speaking, good works are not conformity to any external code of legalistic righteousness; they are the spontaneous and inevitable expression of a certain kind of spiritual life. No man can really have the Spirit without bringing forth the fruits of the Spirit. So the contrast between faith and works applies only at that point where we are considering the means by which we receive God's forgiveness and enter into peace with him. Once faith becomes the governing rule of our approach to God, it naturally expresses itself in a pattern of life which is conformable to God's will: it brings forth good works. "Faith," said Luther in his own vigorous way, "is a most vivid, active, and busy thing, which cannot help doing good deeds all the time."

We can therefore see as a natural consequence how inevitable it is that works should form the basis of judgment. This is not an idiosyncrasy of Paul; it is the consistent witness of Scripture (cf. Matt. 16:27; 25:31-46; Rev. 2:23; 20:12; 22:12; as well as II Cor. 5:10; Gal. 6:7; Eph. 6:8; Col. 3:24). We are not judged by the opinions we hold or by the form of words we use. We are judged by what we do and by the kind of lives we live (cf. Jas. 2:14-26). This is true of all men, whatever their background. It holds for the Jew as well as for the Greek. The whole tenor of a person's life, wrought out consistently and with **patience** (i.e., "with active endurance") shows that he is seeking those things which God can crown with **eternal life.** The very things sought are significant. **Glory, honor,** and **immortality** are common objects of human ambition. As usually pursued, they represent goals toward which men are urged by pride and ambition. But in the religious vocabulary these words have quite a different meaning. **Glory** is the splendor of the perfect life, which has been revealed in Christ and by him made available for others. The **honor** which we seek is honor with God, not with men. **Immortality** suggests that the ends at which we aim belong to a more enduring plane than any earthly benefits we might seek. Those who faithfully follow the right objectives will finally receive the appropriate reward. God will give them **eternal life.** It is his gift, not their achievement. Moreover it gathers up all the separate objectives which Paul has just mentioned. It may be that the apostle is simply using a more

8 But unto them that are contentious,
and do not obey the truth, but obey unrighteousness, indignation and wrath,
9 Tribulation and anguish, upon every
soul of man that doeth evil; of the Jew
first, and also of the Gentile;
10 But glory, honor, and peace, to every
man that worketh good; to the Jew first,
and also to the Gentile:
11 For there is no respect of persons with
God.

will give eternal life; 8 but for those who
are factious and do not obey the truth, but
obey wickedness, there will be wrath and
fury. 9 There will be tribulation and distress for every human being who does evil,
the Jew first and also the Greek, 10 but
glory and honor and peace for every one
who does good, the Jew first and also the
Greek. 11 For God shows no partiality.

---

also that some are actually thus justified. Vs. 10 seems to refer to a situation as real as that to which vss. 8 and 9 refer. The suggestion of vs. 13*b* seems to be that there *are* **doers of the law,** who **will be justified** because they are doers. And in vs. 14 some Gentiles are spoken of as doing **by nature what the law requires.** Yet the whole purpose of this section of the epistle is to establish the point explicitly made in its last sentence (3:20): "For no human being will be justified in his sight by works of the law since through the law comes knowledge of sin." We must suppose, therefore, that Paul—in these references to "working good," to being **doers of the law,** and to doing **by nature the things contained in the law**—is speaking largely hypothetically (as also in vss. 26-27). He is setting forth the *terms* of justification by works. This, he says in effect, is how the "law system" is meant to work. The phrase "*largely* hypothetical" was used just above because it can scarcely be doubted that vss. 14-15 do convey Paul's recognition of genuine virtue among Gentiles. This grateful acknowledgment on his part should be permitted to qualify to some degree the dark picture of Gentile life which he has given us in 1:19 ff.

10-11. The most important point in this section is to be found in these verses: **The Jew first and also the Greek. For God shows no partiality.** On the one hand, the Jew will

---

inclusive term in order to avoid redundancy, but it is permissible to suggest that eternal life is one of those things which we do not win because we strive to gain it for ourselves. If we patiently follow the right things, God will give us what appropriately crowns our quest. Certainly in the Fourth Gospel (where the term "eternal life" is most frequently used) we often find that it follows as the consequence of something else, e.g., we know God through Christ, and we discover that we have entered into a new quality of life (John 17:3). It is also worth noting that though Paul's language suggests a discussion of the last things, the whole trend of his argument shows that he did not sharply divide the present and the future in the exclusive way that subsequently became so common. There will, of course, be a day when the thrones will be set for judgment, and the secrets of every heart will be declared. But as is suggested in the Exeg. of vss. 1-5,[4] the powers of the age to come are already at work. The expectation of final judgment does not exclude the experience of present judgment, and indeed Paul's consistent argument in the present section of his letter is that in a moral universe judgment is an immediate and inexorable reality. And it may be added that what is true of judgment is equally true of eternal life. As to the perfect form of the experience, the phrase refers to something still in the future, but it unquestionably has a present relevance as well.

8-10. ***The Retribution Which Evil Brings.***—The judgment which crowns the consistent pursuit of righteousness works equally to manifest the consequences of wrongdoing. In this case, however, Paul slightly alters the grammatical form. God gives eternal life to those who are entitled to receive it, but the results of wrongdoing are more impersonally set forth. **For those who . . . obey wickedness, there will be wrath and fury.** The purpose of Paul's argument has been to show that wrongdoing brings retribution in its wake, with all the remorseless inevitability with which an appropriate effect follows from a given cause. Those who bring upon themselves such terrible consequences are the people of **contentious** spirit who carry into the religious life the bitter arrogance of the partisan attitude. They stubbornly refuse to bow to God's will, for in this context **truth** suggests not correct intellectual conceptions, but a whole

[4] See also Dodd, *Epistle of Paul to Romans, ad loc.*

12 For as many as have sinned without law shall also perish without law; and as many as have sinned in the law shall be judged by the law;
13 (For not the hearers of the law *are* just before God, but the doers of the law shall be justified.

12 All who have sinned without the law will also perish without the law, and all who have sinned under the law will be judged by the law. 13 For it is not the hearers of the law who are righteous before God, but the doers of the law who will be

---

not be excused because he has the law; but on the other, the Gentile will not be excused because he lacks it. For what God requires of the Jew is not that he hear the law only, but that he do it; and what God requires of the Gentile he has written upon his heart and entrusted to his conscience.

14-15. This reference to **conscience** and to the **law . . . written on their hearts** belongs in a passage which contains some reminiscences of Aristotle and undoubtedly indicates some indebtedness of Paul to contemporary Stoic teachers. Allusion has already been made to Paul's frequent use of the diatribe style; here we have evidence that in his *thinking,* too, he stood under some obligation to these popular preachers. It is more than doubtful that Paul ever studied philosophy in any formal sense, but Stoicism was "in the air" and Paul could hardly have escaped contact with it or have failed to respond

---

standard of life in conformity with God's purpose. Consequently they receive what their way of life has prepared for them. The stern solemnity of the working of the moral law is indicated not only by the fearful implications latent in **wrath and fury, tribulation and distress,** but equally in the impartiality with which judgment falls on all who merit it. Here we are in a realm far removed from the easy sentimentalism into which religion often drifts. Over the whole field of life we are faced with the fact that we are fashioning the kind of destiny we shall finally receive. There is no possibility of any tolerant condoning of the error of those who consciously repudiate the truth, and there is no chance of special exemption for favored people. Every one of us is to stand before the bar of judgment, and those who persevere till the end in working evil will receive the recompense which is their due. Because the **Jew** has had greater privileges, he bears a heavier responsibility. It is not possible for those who claim great prerogatives (as the Jews were quick to do) to evade the consequences which follow. But the note which Paul strikes is not simply one of inexorable sternness. The stress is not merely on the consequences of evil. Paul, by returning to the fact that judgment works both ways (for **glory and honor and peace** as well as for **wrath and fury, tribulation and distress**), redresses a balance which Christians have subsequently often allowed to be disturbed. The purpose which Paul detects is not punitive. He is affirming the tremendous significance, for good and ill, of a moral universe. Central to this is the absolute impartiality with which a judgment based on works must operate. Judgment cannot be partial, nor can it be deflected from its course by special pleas. Otherwise it would be corrupt judgment, and so a denial of all that God's righteousness in a moral universe implies.

12-16. ***Our Insight and Our Responsibility.***—The fact of judgment is inseparable from Paul's gospel, but he makes it clear that it is not judgment in general that he is discussing. The moral character of life presupposes some final day when the realities of our situation will be made perfectly clear. This gives a needed element of seriousness and solemnity to the good news, but it remains good news nevertheless. There are many things which most of us would prefer to keep from view; but when they are remorselessly brought to light, they will be judged **by Christ Jesus.** By that fact judgment acquires not so much a new character as a new emphasis. This may determine the quality of the judgment, but it is important to remember the way in which it works. Each man will be judged by what he actually knows. The circumstances by which we have been surrounded and the opportunities we have enjoyed will be taken into account. "For unto whomsoever much is given, of him shall be much required; and to whom men have committed much, of him they will ask the more" (Luke 12:48). Paul is simply translating into his own idiom, and into terms dictated by the problem he is now discussing, the insight of his Master. Those who know **the law** will be judged in the light of that fact. Those who know it not will be judged by such moral insight as they actually possess. Certain basic moral convictions are the possession of the natural man. Paul's attack on the Gentile world (ch. 1) has been

14 For when the Gentiles, which have not the law, do by nature the things contained in the law, these, having not the law, are a law unto themselves:

15 Which show the work of the law written in their hearts, their conscience also bearing witness, and *their* thoughts the mean while accusing or else excusing one another;)

justified. 14 When Gentiles who have not
the law do by nature what the law requires, they are a law to themselves, even
though they do not have the law. 15 They
show that what the law requires is written
on their hearts, while their conscience also
bears witness and their conflicting thoughts

---

positively to some of the nobler elements of Stoic teaching. It was the Stoic doctrine that all of nature is pervaded by a divine principle, the logos; "conscience" is the human awareness or recognition of this principle, and man's true life is life lived in consistency with this principle, or "appropriately," as we have already been reminded in connection with 1:28. Paul as a Jew knows that in the Torah God has made a higher, more complete revelation of his nature and will than he had made in the natural world; but he accepts as true the Stoic teaching as far as it goes and values it as pointing to the fact that God has not left any man without some valid knowledge of the divine character and purpose and of his own obligation as his creature.

---

based on the fact that they suppressed the God-given testimony of conscience and so fell into hideous immorality. To the same subject he now returns. By such moral understanding as they have, the Gentiles will be judged. They may not have shared in the inheritance of the Mosaic law, but when by their conduct they show that they recognize differences of right and wrong, they prove that they have a law, written inwardly, by which they live. And if their actions demonstrate that they are actually observing the same kind of precepts as those which the law lays down, they are approximating, by the light of conscience, to what the Jew regards as his special and distinctive standard of moral excellence. But at the moment Paul's point of attack is not the exclusiveness of the Jew's position but the falsity of his claim to special privilege. In particular, the assumption (so commonly made by Paul's Jewish contemporaries) that even the possession of the law set them apart overlooks an extremely important fact. The law really belongs only to the man who actually practices it. In this respect the danger of the Jew is (with minor modifications) the danger of the Christian also. There were rabbis who warned the Jews that it was a pernicious illusion that those who "heard" the law were benefited by it; only those who fully practiced it could claim the privileges it offered. Paul restates the same truth—only **the doers of the law** shall be accounted righteous (vs. 13). In exactly the same way there are multitudes of Christians who are complacent because they bear the name of Christ, even though they may not bear his image. They have been born into a Christian environment; they may even hear the Christian message proclaimed. What is more, they may approve or even applaud. But this is a totally false security. From the earliest days the emphasis of the Christian community has been on the necessity of being doers and not simply hearers of the Word (cf. Jas. 1:22-25). The disciple—if he is at all sensitive—is continually rebuked by the memory of his Master's words (Matt. 7:24-27). Paul's aim is to shatter the false complacency of one who imagines that honorary membership in an inherited religious tradition has any real effect on his spiritual status. Moreover, the characteristic danger of many nominally religious people is that they both neglect the essence of the truth to which they pay lip service, and scorn those who, though outside the prescribed orbit, actually act according to the insights which they themselves honor in their words alone. Instances of this immediately spring to mind; in Paul's day the conspicuous example was the Jew who imperfectly fulfilled the law but condemned those Gentiles who not only distinguished between right and wrong but chose the right. The more rigid rabbis were emphatic in teaching that nothing a Gentile might do could be accepted as having any moral or religious merit. Only within Israel, and only among those who lived according to the law, was there virtue. In opposition to this narrow and exclusive attitude, Paul adopts a position which must have struck many Jews as dangerously liberal. Paul's debt to Greek thought is here plainly apparent (cf. Exeg.; also Lightfoot[5]). Whatever may be the relationship between these verses and the

[5] *St Paul's Epistle to the Philippians* (London: Macmillan & Co., 1869), pp. 278-80.

16 In the day when God shall judge the secrets of men by Jesus Christ according to my gospel.

accuse or perhaps excuse them 16 on that day when, according to my gospel, God judges the secrets of men by Christ Jesus.

---

16. This verse seems somewhat out of place where it stands, and some commentators suggest that it ought to follow vs. 13 (so Moffatt). The KJV prefers to regard vss. 13-15 as a parenthesis. In any event vs. 16 connects in thought with either vs. 12 or vs. 13, rather than with vs. 15. It is another reminder (like vs. 5) that though Paul thought of judgment as already making its appearance, its culmination was yet to come. The Judgment Day has not yet fully come, although the forces of judgment are already at work.

---

teachings of Aristotle, Seneca, or Plutarch, what Paul is emphasizing is the simple but far-reaching truth that moral insight may come from more than one source, and that devotion to what is right breaks down many of the artificial barriers by means of which we segregate ourselves from one another. The Stoic doctrine of the law of nature and the voice of conscience was therefore something that Paul could easily accept and assimilate. In the record of his sermon on Mars' Hill we have the same assumption that God's spirit can move and work among men—and does so—quite apart from any special revelation that he may give. It is true, of course, that though Paul uses the current philosophical terms, his own thought goes a great deal beyond the range of what the Stoic in the market place might teach. But he does accept the thought of his time as a starting point. He concedes that there are at least two witnesses to God's power and his purpose which are common to all men, viz., nature (cf. 1:32) and conscience. The Mosaic law is more complete and more explicit than any law of conscience, but those who do not share in the Jewish heritage are not therefore bereft of every means of distinguishing between the right and the wrong. Actually the purpose of all law—whether the law of nature, or the law of Moses, or the law of Christ—is to help men to choose the good and repudiate the evil.

Though Paul has given a very gloomy picture of the state of contemporary Gentile society (1:18-32) he concedes that many individuals do make precisely the kind of distinction between right and wrong with which the Jewish law is concerned. It is **conscience** that helps them. **The law written in their hearts** is a useful means of reminding ourselves of what Paul meant by this important term. He is not describing a "legislative faculty." Conscience does not determine what is right or wrong and then act accordingly. It rather recognizes the law, and applies it to the circumstances of daily life. And no doubt he would have asserted that the law was written on men's hearts because God had graven it there (note the implied parallel with the law graven on stones in Exod. 24:12; cf. II Cor. 3:3). In some cases the inscription may be sharper and more incisive than in others. The law of nature is not so much mistaken as it is merely imperfect. Intuitively men see what is right and wrong (after all, they are God's creatures, with the gifts he implanted in them), but their instinctive perceptions may be partial. Calvin pointed out that all societies took action against adultery because a fundamental human insight knew that such conduct was destructive of all organized life and consequently must be wrong. The law of Moses went a great deal farther than this; with meticulous exactitude it indicated at every point what was right and what was wrong. Given such an appraisal of the judicial activity of conscience, we can appreciate Paul's claim that those who accept the distinction between good and bad already possess a faculty which examines their conduct in the light of this inner standard of judgment. What each man does is brought to the bar of conscience; whether or not his conduct conforms to his understanding of what is right will determine the verdict. Paul has not been suggesting, of course, that one law is exactly like another, or that each man's conscience is as sensitive to evil as his neighbor's. Conscience can and must be educated, and the person who has been disciplined under a higher law will possess a real advantage as compared with someone who is prompted only by a sense of natural decency. But this is not the point of the argument at present. Paul is not concerned with the inherent quality of different types of moral law. He is contending that the man who does what is right is observing the essence of the law, whether he has received it from Moses or not. Loyalty to what we know to be good is more important than merely occupying a place in any tradition, however noble it may be; and when the day of final reckoning arrives, we shall be judged by our conduct, not by our heritage.

Paul wrote about the law as one who had lived under it and knew at firsthand what it meant. This explains the searching and personal quality of much that he says, but it also

17 Behold, thou art called a Jew, and restest in the law, and makest thy boast of God,

17 But if you call yourself a Jew and rely upon the law and boast of your rela-

17-20. The apostle, returning to the diatribe, now addresses the Jew more explicitly. His description of the moral claims the Jew could make, while intended to point up the sins of hypocrisy and pride, is not to be taken entirely in that negative or derogatory sense. Paul would probably have allowed that these claims were in some degree justified. Paul's position as regards the place of the Jew in the new situation which had come into existence with and through Christ was not clear or unequivocal, as we shall have occasion to notice a little later (see below, pp. 420-21). In spite of his firm belief that Jew and

accounts for certain limitations in his outlook. He was far too deeply involved to regard the law objectively, and the intense emotions which the subject aroused no doubt explain the partial degree to which he has integrated his twofold emphasis on the value of the law and its limitations. Moreover, Paul, as a former Pharisee, spoke of the law as his training had taught him to do. He saw it mainly as a system of ritual and ceremonial requirement, and (in his treatment of the subject) does not reveal any deep awareness of the varying quality of the demands which the law laid on those who accepted it. Questions of duty and questions of diet do not stand on the same plane of moral importance, but in the rabbinical schools where Paul received his training the distinction was apt to be overlooked. This is, however, a minor circumstance, because the matter of primary importance with Paul is legalism as a method of gaining righteousness. The very fact that it reduced essential differences to a monotonous level of uniform obligation only emphasizes the general falsity of its approach to the central issues of religion. See also on 7:7-25.

17-29. ***The Position of the Jews and the Nature of Their Failure.***—The terrible plight of the Gentile world has led Paul to remind the Jews that they, as well as others, are subject to God's righteous judgment. The law in which they boast gives them no immunity; it means only that they will be judged by the same principles as, but by a more exacting standard than, those who instinctively do what they know to be right. But Paul presses the matter further still. The Jew has inherited religious privileges of which he is justly proud, but how has he used them? The answer is a withering exposure of moral collapse. Precisely in those matters where the law required obedience from its devotees the Jews had brought contempt on religion and even on the name of God (vss. 17-24). Such failure can be explained only by a false sense of security. **Circumcision** was the outward mark of the Jew's devotion to the law, but the sign meant nothing apart from the obedience which the law required. It is consequently possible to reverse the terms; instead of saying circumcision implies obedience, one can say obedience is really circumcision. Those who are not in the historical tradition but actually walk in the ways of God's commandments have far surer grounds of confidence than the Jews who boast of the law but do not live as it requires.

17. ***Direct Warning to the Jew.***—At the beginning of the chapter Paul was speaking but indirectly to the Jews. Verse by verse the relevance of his argument to the distinctive attitudes of Israel has become increasingly apparent. Now he turns directly to the typical Jew—the man who is proudly conscious of his membership in the chosen race. Paul did not question the great value of the Hebrew heritage—he could speak of it in moving terms when occasion required—but here his enumeration of the things on which the Jew prides himself is edged with irony. He notes the self-satisfaction with which the Jew accepts and uses a name which denotes a privileged relationship to God. He points out the danger of leaning on the law with an indolent complacency. (Note the suggestion of a supine assurance in Sanday and Headlam's rendering the word as "repose." [6]) The Jew, like the Pharisee in Jesus' parable, might approach God (and doubtless often did so) with a proud sense of standing on a different footing with him from other men. There is a sense in which we can legitimately **boast of** our **relation to God,** and its nature was indicated long ago by Jeremiah, "Let him that glorieth glory in this, that he understandeth and knoweth me, that I am the LORD" (Jer. 9:24). But the mark of this permissible kind of pride is really a deep humility, as Jeremiah was careful to insist, and the very phrasing that Paul uses would make his sarcasm apparent to any Jew of sensitive mind. The person who arrogantly boasts of his standing with God

[6] *A Critical and Exegetical Commentary on the Epistle to the Romans* (New York: Charles Scribner's Sons, 1895; "International Critical Commentary"), *ad loc.*

18 And knowest *his* will, and approvest the things that are more excellent, being instructed out of the law;

19 And art confident that thou thyself art a guide of the blind, a light of them which are in darkness,

tion to God 18 and know his will and approve what is excellent, because you are instructed in the law, 19 and if you are sure that you are a guide to the blind, a

non-Jew are on the same basis and in equal need of God's gracious act in Christ, he nevertheless is not ready to conclude that the Jew has no advantage. Paul would have agreed that the Jew is in position to **know** [God's] **will** and to **approve what is excellent** (this phrase might mean "to know right from wrong," but the RSV understanding is usually preferred), because he is **instructed in the law;** and that the Jew might well be **a guide to the blind, a light to those who are in darkness,** etc., since he has the law and the law is **the embodiment of knowledge and truth.** But while the possession of the Torah opens to the Jew the possibility of his becoming a **guide** and a **teacher** to the rest of the world, only *obedience* to the Torah can make that possibility a reality—and here, Paul says, the Jew has notoriously failed. For another Jewish view see II Esdras 3:33 ff. The writer of this passage insists that although the Jew has not done perfectly, he has, as a

proves how false is his confidence. As Calvin pointed out, "the glorying of the heart" is very different from "the boasting of the tongue."

18. ***The Source of Moral Discernment.***—The Jew has the **law** to teach him God's **will,** and in the knowledge of that will he has the sure means of gaining moral discernment. As is indicated in the Exeg., the words can be taken in either of two senses: one indicates the power to distinguish between right and wrong; the other suggests the approval of **what is excellent.** The second presumably represents a more advanced stage in the process to which the first refers. Choice of the better rests on the power to distinguish it from the worse. But discrimination alone is not enough, and words which carry all the overtones of praise may subtly underline the failings of religious pride. We can **approve what is excellent** by *choice,* in which case we strive to conform our conduct to what we see is good, or merely by *judgment,* and then it is quite possible to be persuaded of what is right but remain in aloof detachment from it. This noncommittal approval of **what is excellent** usually finds its most congenial outlet in condemning those who lack such subtle powers of discrimination. Here, also, the attitude of the Pharisee in Jesus' parable is illuminating. It is important to remember that the discrimination to which Paul refers is directly due to the training which the Jew has received: he is **instructed in the law.** But the remainder of this passage proves how easy it is to possess the elements of religious knowledge without living a religious life. To have the form of godliness without the power thereof (cf. II Tim. 3:5) is not, however, a limitation confined to the first century, nor to Jews.

19. ***Blind Leaders of the Blind.***—It is impossible not to detect an echo of Jesus' words about the blind who lead the blind (Matt. 15:14; 23:16). Possibly both Paul and his Master are giving point to their teaching by quoting a proverbial saying well known among first-century Jews. In that case, Paul's true meaning would be clear beyond possibility of mistake. To be a leader of **the blind** is a noble as well as a compassionate activity. The Jew had many of the advantages which qualified him for the task. He should have done it, and he could have done it if he would. The point of Jesus' polemic against the Pharisees was that they possessed responsibilities and powers which they were not using: they might have opened the door of the kingdom to others, but instead they stayed outside and prevented others from entering (Luke 11:52). It would be impossible to devise any imagery which better describes the aimless fumbling of obtuse pride directing helpless ignorance than the figure of one blind man guiding another as sightless as himself. Instinctively one smiles at the comic floundering which finally lands both leader and led in the ditch; but the humor is engulfed by a double tragedy. The people who cannot see need direction (and in the most vital of all areas) but do not get it, while the leaders who should be able to see have forfeited the power because they would not use it. A natural transition carries us from those who cannot walk because they have no vision to those who cannot see because they have no light. The scattering of darkness is a favorite biblical metaphor for the illumination which the word of God brings to human minds. "The people that walked in darkness have seen a great light: they that dwelt

20 An instructor of the foolish, a teacher of babes, which hast the form of knowledge and of the truth in the law.

21 Thou therefore which teachest another, teachest thou not thyself? thou that preachest a man should not steal, dost thou steal?

light to those who are in darkness, 20 a corrector of the foolish, a teacher of children, having in the law the embodiment of knowledge and truth — 21 you then who teach others, will you not teach yourself? While you preach against stealing, do you

---

nation, done better than others. Speaking to God, the writer says: "Thou wilt find individual Gentiles who have kept thy commandments, but not nations." (Other parallel proverbs are cited by Strack and Billerbeck, *Kommentar zum Neuen Testament aus Talmud und Midrasch* [Munich: C. H. Beck, 1926], III, 88.)

21-24. It is impossible to **teach others** if one has not one's self learned; and it is both hypocritical and futile to **preach against stealing** and **adultery** if one is committing those same crimes. Acts 19:37 indicates that the robbing of pagan temples was not an infrequent Jewish offense. Both Lietzmann, and Sanday and Headlam (probably rightly) regard vs. 23 as a declarative statement (in line with vs. 25), rather than as a rhetorical question.

---

in the land of the shadow of death, upon them hath the light shined" (Isa. 9:2). Paul himself, in a passage reminiscent of the first miracle of created light, reminds the Corinthians that "God, who commanded the light to shine out of darkness, hath shined in our hearts, to give the light of the knowledge of the glory of God in the face of Jesus Christ" (II Cor. 4:6). To be the means by which such light bursts in on minds that sit paralyzed in darkness is a privilege which the language of his Scriptures and the substance of his faith would teach the Jew to cherish. But if he fails to discharge the task he claims. . . . Had Paul's mind by any chance reverted to the words of Jesus, "If therefore the light that is in thee be darkness, how great is that darkness" (Matt. 6:23)?

20. ***The Responsibility to Teach.***—The enumeration of Jewish claims—faithful as to their substance but slightly ironical in its form—runs on. The **corrector of the foolish** is one who reproves others for moral lapses as well as for intellectual shortcomings; he not only delivers from false views, he also indicates the true way. The objects of his care are those who make mistakes because they do not understand essential matters rightly. **A teacher of children** has a different but related task. In every community there are some who are ignorant in the way children are ignorant. The contrast is with the person of adult mind and understanding. The reference may be chiefly to those who are children in age, but it is not wise to forget that there are many who need the kind of moral and religious teaching that children receive. At all events, we may fairly note the distinction inherent in the words of this verse between two types of uninstructed mind. On the one hand we have the person who is confused and bewildered because he is unaware of fundamental distinctions, and who consequently often makes serious mistakes in matters of great importance. On the other hand there is the person who is untaught and untouched by moral and religious knowledge.

At the end of the detailed résumé of Jewish claims comes a reference to the foundation on which they all rest. The confidence of the Jew is built on the assurance that in the law he has **the embodiment of knowledge and truth.** This was a conviction central to the Jewish faith, and Paul, for one, would not be disposed to deny it. As we have seen, he was quite ready to concede that as regards its substance the law was holy and good. In a true sense it gave concrete expression to the truth about God and to that knowledge of himself which he had granted to men. Paul's fundamental quarrel with the law was that, granting it mediated important truths, it did not provide men with any possible way of living by them. To try and fail was heartbreaking, but to boast about the law and not even attempt to fulfill its demands was utterly contemptible; and this is precisely the charge which Paul brings against the Jews.

21-24. ***Physician Heal Thyself.***—The rhetorical question which Paul uses clearly suggests that the typical Jew has taught others but has not been willing to learn himself. No one, of course, who has tried to instruct and exhort his fellows can fail to realize, often with shame, how far short he falls of the standard which he commends to others. The natural consequence is a heightened sense of insufficiency. The contrast becomes a lesson in humility and, as an inevitable result, in dependence upon God. But it is equally true that the process—especially when it is a continuous one—should train

22 Thou that sayest a man should not commit adultery, dost thou commit adultery? thou that abhorrest idols, dost thou commit sacrilege?

23 Thou that makest thy boast of the law, through breaking the law dishonorest thou God?

24 For the name of God is blasphemed among the Gentiles through you, as it is written.

steal?
22 You who say that one must not commit adultery, do you commit adultery? You who abhor idols, do you rob temples?
23 You who boast in the law, do you dishonor God by breaking the law?
24 For, as it is written, "The name of God is blasphemed among the Gentiles because of you."

The fact that the Jews boasted in the law made their own disregard of it the more flagrant and harmful. Vs. 24 quotes Isa. 52:5 in the form in which that verse appears in the LXX. The phrase **because of you** does not appear in the Hebrew or in our English O.T. texts, which are based on the Hebrew. This is one among many indications that Paul ordinarily used the Bible in its Greek form.

It is important to recognize that Paul is not attributing the crime mentioned in this paragraph to *all* Jews any more than he is meaning to describe every Gentile when he speaks of sexual vices and perversions in 1:24-27. But one must assume that in both cases he regards the sins mentioned as widespread and characteristic.

---

us to bring our own conduct into slightly more perfect harmony with our precept. Not many of us will reach the happy state where others will say of us, as Chaucer said of his poor parson, "That first he wroghte, and afterward he taughte." [7] At least the development should be in that direction, and anyone who acquiesces in flagrant incongruity between his precepts and his practice proves that he does not really regard his teaching with proper seriousness. If it is not good enough for him to live by, it is not appropriate for him to commend it to anybody else. It was this shocking disparity between what they urged on others and what they did themselves that exposed the Pharisees to the merciless attacks of Jesus. Men who were unctuous in quoting the law, but who did not translate its clear intention into personal righteousness, invited the charge of hypocrisy.

It is with the sin of hypocrisy that Paul is chiefly concerned at the moment. He does not say—though it would have followed naturally from his argument—that hypocrisy is the direct result of spiritual pride, but experience proves it beyond a doubt. Only the man who is complacently arrogant is driven to that form of self-defense which hypocrisy supplies. With bitter sarcasm Paul accuses the typical Jew of breaking all the major commandments of the law. If a man counsels others not to steal yet steals himself, has he not brought his words into contempt by his deeds? Paul is speaking about those who preach, who engage in the dangerous activity of telling others what to do. Nor is it in minor matters only that he finds serious discrepancies between official teaching and private practice. To theft he adds **adultery** (vs. 22); to that in turn temple robbery. The proud monotheism which set the Jews apart should have made this particular offense easy to avoid. The word **abhor** suggests a loathing which borders on physical revulsion.[8] But when there is a chance of gain, those who shrink in horror from **idols** will without misgiving come into contact with the system which they ostensibly abominate. The cumulative charge is serious and may seem overdrawn. This is an essay in controversy, however, and Paul was sufficiently experienced to know that nothing so recoils upon a debater as accusations which are proved to be false. On a priori grounds we would assume that Paul is not making irresponsible charges, and from other sources we have corroborative evidence. The Jews had acquired a bad name throughout the Roman Empire for acquisitiveness; we know that private morals had seriously slumped, and we can infer from the words of the town clerk at Ephesus that sacrilege was an offense which could plausibly be attributed to the Jews (Acts 19:37). The facts could no doubt be amplified as well as confirmed.

Paul has now sufficiently prepared for the point toward which he is moving. The contrast between boasting in the law and then breaking it is sharp enough. But the process brings discredit not primarily on the people who are at fault, but on the truth which they attempt to

[7] *Canterbury Tales,* Prologue, l. 497.

[8] Cf. James Denney, "St. Paul's Epistle to the Romans," in W. Robertson Nicoll, ed., *Expositor's Greek Testament, ad loc.*

25 For circumcision verily profiteth, if thou keep the law: but if thou be a breaker of the law, thy circumcision is made uncircumcision.

25 Circumcision indeed is of value if you obey the law; but if you break the law, your circumcision becomes uncircumcision.

D. The Impotence of the Law (2:25–3:20)

There must necessarily be something arbitrary about any division into sections of the passage 1:18–3:20. The general direction and range of the apostle's thought is clear: he begins with an account of the moral failure of the Gentiles, next considers the failure of the Jews, and concludes with the recognition of the inability of the Jewish law to save from sin and death. But as to just where the transitions from theme to theme take place is not clear at all. We have seen that this is true of the transition from the consideration of the Gentile (1:19-32) to that of Jew (2:1-24). Sanday and Headlam indeed make vss. 1-16 a separate division with the title "Transition from Gentile to Jew." The moment of transition to the third theme is even more obscure; 2:25 will do as well as any other to mark this turn.

25. The Jew was likely to rely upon his membership in the Jewish nation, of which **circumcision** was the sign. Paul here affirms that this membership confers special benefits only **if you obey the law.** As to what these benefits are, he does not clearly say here or elsewhere (see above on vss. 17-20 and below on 3:1, 4). But it is presumed that Paul would have allowed that *if one succeeded in keeping the law perfectly,* one would enjoy the favor of God. His point is that this condition is purely hypothetical. *Actually,* **you break the law** and **your circumcision becomes uncircumcision;** i.e., it is as though you were not a Jew at all.

---

commend. Nor is it the law only which is brought into disrepute; as a result of the failure of the Jews, God is dishonored (vs. 23). The Gentiles, who ought to respond to the preaching of the God of Israel, infer what his character must be from what they see of the conduct of his people. Their instinctive reaction is a blasphemous repudiation. We might expect as much, adds Paul; history has come full cycle, and the words of the prophet again apply (Isa. 52:5). There are few stronger statements in the N.T. of the uncomfortable truth that we are living epistles, "known and read of all men" (II Cor. 3:2). The reverence in which God is held is determined not by his holy and righteous nature, but by the way in which by our lives and conversation we commend him to those among whom we live. Often faith in God is weak because the persuasives thereto are so faulty.

It is a serious charge which Paul brings against his fellow Jews, but the consequences of their conduct were much more serious. Even so, a blanket accusation is very likely to defeat its own end. Granting that there were some Jews whose scandalous behavior degraded the very name of their religion, many of them must have avoided the flagrant sins which Paul castigates. In this case, however, it was not easy to plead not guilty. In the Gospels we have an equally trenchant attack on the stricter Jews. Jesus did not single out the grosser sins which brought immediate discredit. He pointed out that earnest men might observe the letter of the law but kill its spirit. They might pay scrupulous respect to regulations about little duties but be wholly indifferent to the great issues of righteousness and judgment. This is the "lower hypocrisy"—less dramatic than the kind which Paul attacks, but much more insidious and far more widely practiced. Indeed, it is so hard wholly to separate it from religious practice that few can safely claim to dissociate themselves completely from the faults with which Paul is here concerned.

25. ***The Outward Mark and Inner Reality of the Jewish Inheritance.***—The Jew stood in a great heritage. **Circumcision** was the proof that he was heir to the promises given to Abraham, that he had his place in the grand tradition. There were advantages in being born a Jew, but these were really irrelevant. The badge of being a true son of Israel was only the outward expression of a loyal adherence to the law. The two went hand in hand, and the external sign lost all meaning if it was once separated from the obedience which the law required. Paul, it is interesting to observe, does not dispute the claim that **circumcision . . . is of value if you obey the law.** He has broken with the system of legalism, but he can still speak as a Jew. The bitter tone which sometimes marks his controversies with the Jews might prepare us

26 Therefore, if the uncircumcision keep the righteousness of the law, shall not his uncircumcision be counted for circumcision?

27 And shall not uncircumcision which is by nature, if it fulfil the law, judge thee, who by the letter and circumcision dost transgress the law?

26 So, if a man who is uncircumcised keeps the precepts of the law, will not his uncircumcision be regarded as circumcision?
27 Then those who are physically uncircumcised but keep the law will condemn you who have the written code and circum-

---

26-27. In the same way, if an uncircumcised Gentile should perfectly keep the law, he would enjoy all the benefits promised to the Jew. Again, as in 2:14-15, one must not take these verses as meaning that Paul regards any Gentile as *actually* fulfilling all of God's requirements. The argument is hypothetical: *if* a Gentile should keep the law, he

---

to expect a less liberal attitude. But we know that he not only conceded the value of the content of the law (7:14), but when it seemed right to do so, he observed it himself (Acts 16:3; 18:18; 21:26). He opposed the tyranny which the law as a way of life had established over men's minds, and he firmly opposed any attempt to extend its domination to those who had not been trained in the tradition of the Jews. Consequently he accepts the suggestion that circumcision may have value (for the Jew, of course), but at present he is not prepared to concede his opponent any benefit from the admission. When obedience is lacking, what is only its outward sign is destitute of all meaning. The man who breaks the law is in the same position as the man who stands completely outside Judaism. Circumcision is of value only to the man who genuinely tries to live as the law demands. The point is simple but important. Certain people are always exposed to the temptation of confusing the incidental externals with the essential realities. They feel confident of a place in the Christian community because they have been baptized or because they are nominally members of a church, and they would be highly incensed if anyone suggested that they were not really Christians at all. In addition to this superficial assumption that outward signs are a sufficient substitute for active participation in the life of faith, it is necessary to note a parallel form which the trust in outward signs often assumes. It is usually the person who trusts in his own religious achievements who feels that the visible tokens of religion are important. This need not be the product of a humanistic pride; it may simply be the result of a limited view which fails to distinguish between essential and inconsequential things.

26. ***External Conformity and Inward Obedience.***—Many of Paul's Jewish contemporaries would not have hesitated to admit the force of his argument thus far, but very few indeed would have been willing to concede that the terms of the argument could be reversed.[9] Paul claims that if the Jew who breaks the law ceases to be a son of Abraham, the Gentile who observes it, even though lacking the outward sign, becomes in all essential respects a true Israelite. As he has already done on previous occasions, Paul is stressing the importance of obedience to the law. We might express the same truth in somewhat different terms—circumcision and the law are not important current issues—but most of us have felt the force of the taunt that those outside the church sometimes act in a more Christian spirit than those who are proud to be its members. The questions "Who is the true Christian?" and "What really constitutes discipleship?" are pressed upon us in awkward ways. Is it true, as we are sometimes told, that those who repudiate any share in the Christian community—e.g., the communists—have usurped our right to stand in the tradition of the prophets? Are those who claim that they are Christians always the most convincing exponents of what the Christlike spirit of unselfish concern for others really means? There is no easy answer to questions like these, but as soon as they are asked we realize how closely they approximate to the point with which Paul is concerned.

27. ***The True Seeker Condemns the Nominal Observer of the Law.***—Paul has pointed to the contrast between the Jew who neglects the law (while trusting that the outward forms will serve his purpose) and the Gentile who lacks the advantages of belonging to Israel but in his conduct really does the things which the law requires. Given the facts, certain inferences are necessarily drawn, and **those who are physically uncircumcised but keep the law will condemn you who have the written code and circumcision but break the law.** They will

[9] For quotations from rabbinical sources see Dodd, *Epistle of Paul to Romans, ad loc.*

28 For he is not a Jew, which is one outwardly; neither *is that* circumcision, which is outward in the flesh:

29 But he *is* a Jew, which is one inwardly; and circumcision *is that* of the heart, in the spirit, *and* not in the letter; whose praise *is* not of men, but of God.

cision but break the law.
28 For he is not a real Jew who is one outwardly, nor is true circumcision something external and physical.
29 He is a Jew who is one inwardly, and real circumcision is a matter of the heart, spiritual and not literal. His praise is not from men but from God.

---

would be in as good case as a Jew who kept it. Paul may also be meaning to imply, however, what he undoubtedly recognized as true—that *some* Gentiles in actual fact come nearer to keeping the law than *some* Jews.

28-29. The meaning of this passage is not clear. Is Paul anticipating what he will later say about justification by faith and about the new life (see Rom. 9:6 ff.; cf. Phil. 3:3: "For we are the true circumcision, who worship God in spirit, and glory in Christ Jesus, and put no confidence in the flesh"), setting the new righteousness, open to Jew and Greek, over against the righteousness of the law? Or is he stressing the inner character of the law's demands, that they are concerned not only with behavior, but also with the thoughts of our hearts? The argument proceeds more coherently if the second of these meanings is adopted as the intended one: Paul would then be saying, "It is easy enough to accept circumcision *in se* and to obey the other external provisions of the law, but the law asks much more than this of us—asks indeed an inner righteousness—and it is this demand which we find so difficult to fulfill." But the reader cannot always be sure that Paul's argument is proceeding coherently; and the other meaning indicated is not impossible.

The word **praise** means also Judah or Jew (cf. Gen. 29:35; 49:8). A play on the word is apparently being made.

---

not necessarily condemn by judging in a superior and censorious spirit. Their contrasting attitude will by itself be sufficient to expose the hollow pretensions of those who pride themselves on precepts which they never practice. The best example of what is meant is provided by the reference to Matt. 12:41-42 (or Luke 11:31-32). With the attitude of his own contemporaries, Christ contrasts that of the queen of the South and of the men of Nineveh. Instead of the complacency which refuses to consider new truth, there is an eagerness which distance cannot deflect from its quest. Instead of the self-satisfaction which sees no need of amendment, there is a humble spirit which repents as soon as a better way is preached. In each case, to see the contrast is to feel the condemnation.

28-29. ***The True Israelite.***—Paul has been contrasting the man who possesses the outward symbol of the law but lacks the true spirit of obedience with the person who is not a Jew but lives as the law demands. This is not the only time when he emphasizes the inwardness without which all service of God is vain. "So you see," he remarks elsewhere, "that it is men of faith who are the sons of Abraham" (Gal. 3:7). "For neither is circumcision anything," he says later in the same letter, "nor uncircumcision, but a new creation" (Gal. 6:15; cf. Phil. 3:3). The course of his argument, with its implied strictures on the false Jew, makes it natural for him to end by describing the true Jew. The distinction between the Jew who is one by race only and the Jew who is a "true Israelite" was not original with Paul. Ever since the Deuteronomic days men had set "heart circumcision" in opposition to circumcision which was merely in the flesh (cf. Deut. 10:16; Jer. 4:4; 9:26; Ezek. 44:7). But the purpose of Paul gives new point to a familiar distinction. He has swept away the arrogance of the Jew who builds his confidence on externals only. He clinches his point by proving how relative the terms "Jew" and "Gentile" really are, and shows that the sincere Gentile takes precedence of the unworthy Jew.

But if the essence of Judaism is a right spirit before God, then how disheartening are the prospects which face an earnest Jew! When he sincerely tries to reach that goal, he will discover what Paul has learned by bitter experience. Paul found that Judaism postulated a certain end and suggested (in the observance of the law) a means of achieving it, but the more faithfully the method was applied, the more hopelessly insufficient it proved to be. Though Paul has not stated the alternatives so

3 What advantage then hath the Jew? or what profit *is there* of circumcision?
2 Much every way: chiefly, because that unto them were committed the oracles of God.

3 Then what advantage has the Jew? Or what is the value of circumcision?
2 Much in every way. To begin with, the Jews were entrusted with the oracles of

---

3:1. Sanday and Headlam entitle this section (3:1-8) "Casuistical Objections Answered," but in doing so they both unduly discount the pertinence and importance of the questions Paul places in the mouth of his imaginary opponent or heckler, and also exaggerate somewhat Paul's success in answering these questions. **Then what advantage has the Jew?** is a thoroughly relevant and appropriate question. If what Paul has been saying is true—if the mere possession of the law and merely outward circumcision have no value, and if at the same time the Jew can claim nothing beyond this—one might well ask, **What is the value of circumcision?** One would expect, of course, a negative reply. But Paul answers with a strong affirmative: **Much in every way.** His explanation of so illogical an answer is, as he gives it here, certainly not very convincing; the case is stated more fully and persuasively in chs. 9–11. **The Jews,** he says, **were entrusted with the oracles of God.** The term for "oracles" is *logia,* and it is probably intended to refer here to the whole Scriptures; but with special regard, as soon appears, to the *promises* of God to Israel which the Scriptures contain. But what advantage, one might ask, is there in merely *possessing* these promises—any more than in merely possessing the law—since the nation, by its failure to obey the law, does not qualify for the fulfillment of them? What value is there in having received promises based on certain conditions if one does not and cannot satisfy the conditions? The negative answer which such questions expect would seem to be demanded by the logic of Paul's position; but as already noted (see on 2:17-20), Paul cannot fully accept this logic. He therefore seems to modify one of his premises: *now* apparently only **some were unfaithful,** and their **faithlessness**—i.e.,

---

sharply, he has really shown that the Jew has two choices before him. He can rest content with the external assurance that his is the favored heritage—in which case, by denying the true genius of his religion, he exposes himself to the kind of withering attack which Paul has just delivered. On the other hand he may attempt to express in conduct the spiritual inwardness which makes the law a revelation from God—but then he progressively discovers the frustration of repeated failure. Actually there is a third alternative. Paul does not state it here but it constitutes the main argument of this letter.

3:1. ***Has the Heritage of Israel Been Superseded?***—Paul's argument, driven along by the force of his attack on the unworthy custodians of a great tradition, has seemed to prove more than he intended that it should. Granted the kind of dilemma implicit in the closing sentences of ch. 2, is there any value in the Jewish heritage? Or is it an apparently impressive thoroughfare that has proved only a blind alley? Many people, beginning at an early period in Christian history and continuing until the present, have been ready to sweep away the whole Jewish background of Christianity and dispense entirely with the O.T. which contains its sacred books. And when this attitude has represented more than the impetuosity of ignorance, it has claimed to find in Paul its prototype. But Paul (see Exeg.) is not for a moment ready to dispense with Judaism. It may be insufficient—and he spent a great deal of time, in this letter and elsewhere, proving that it is—but it is not therefore worthless. He has shown that circumcision, when it is merely an outward sign, has little value; but it is still the symbol of great promises. Though Paul has had no mercy on a false reliance on externals, he has not thereby repudiated the whole spiritual legacy which Judaism enshrined. His last words in the previous chapter stated that "real circumcision is a matter of the heart, spiritual and not literal." Consequently, a logic which sweeps it away altogether is traveling too fast and too far.

2-4. ***The Abiding Value of the Jewish Tradition.***—So Paul answers his own question with a resounding affirmative. As the Exeg. makes plain, he is a good deal more emphatic than the forcefulness of his previous argument entitles him to be. There is some point in the question which the Jewish objector raises; after all, it would be quite easy to answer him with a simple negative. The grounds for Paul's reply have at least been suggested (see above), but

3 For what if some did not believe?
shall their unbelief make the faith of God
without effect?
4 God forbid: yea, let God be true, but
every man a liar; as it is written, That
thou mightest be justified in thy sayings,
and mightest overcome when thou art
judged.

God. 3 What if some were unfaithful? Does
their faithlessness nullify the faithfulness
of God? 4 By no means! Let God be true
though every man be false, as it is written,
"That thou mayest be justified in thy
words,
and prevail when thou art judged."

---

their failure to keep their obligations under the covenant—does not **nullify the faithfulness of God.** He goes further: God is **true though every man be false.** This may mean only that God's truth or faithfulness to the covenant is thoroughly consistent with his *refusing* to fulfill the promises for the reason that Israel has not been loyal to its obligations under that same covenant; indeed, that God's faithfulness could not express itself in any other way, given Israel's failure. But Paul seems to be saying more than this: otherwise he could scarcely attribute any **advantage** to the Jew; for the possession of merely *conditional* promises is of no value if one has failed to meet the conditions. Thus Paul seems to be suggesting that God's promises to Israel are ultimately *not* conditional. Paul's belief in the final salvation of Israel, based simply on the fact of the promises, emerges clearly at the end of ch. 11, and must be in his mind here.

4. The quotation of Ps. 51:4 is again from the text of the Greek Bible, the LXX (cf. 2:24). Again also, the Greek translators had made a significant change in the meaning of the verse. In the Hebrew, which is followed in our English translations of the psalms, the final verb is active: it is God who does the judging, and the psalmist acknowledges the justice of God's judgments. In the Greek text—at any rate as Paul understands and uses it—God seems to be in the position of being judged, that is, judged as to his fidelity to his promises. Paul affirms that God will **prevail** when the evidence is all presented, and that his integrity will be fully vindicated. The way in which the validity of God's promises to Israel and the justice and wisdom of his dealings with her will

---

it is hardly possible to understand this apparently puzzling—but actually most revealing—section unless we remember that Paul knows the full force of his antagonist's questions because he himself has often asked them. When he became a Christian, he did not shed his Pharisaic background as a snake can cast its old skin. The very insistence of the questions asked is due to the fact that they spring from Paul's own experience, and they throng upon him so tumultuously that his answers by comparison seem lame and ineffective. Actually he has a much fuller case than he presents in this section (vss. 1-8), and if we want to know what his complete reply would be, we have to supplement the one point which he here advances with others culled from chs. 9–11 (see Exeg.). The present passage is practically cast in dialogue form, and with very slight modification it can be revised to make this apparent. It is like a good many debates in that it shifts its ground with confusing rapidity. Points are raised, but before they are half exhausted, a particular phrase deflects the discussion to another subject. Most of the questions can be fully answered from material which Paul elsewhere supplies. The vividness of the passage is due to its clear reflection of many a real debate—sometimes of Paul with his Jewish opponents, sometimes, no doubt, of Paul with himself. When the ground is presumably so familiar and so frequently traversed, it is not surprising that Paul is content to reproduce the disjointed character of an argument as it often actually unfolds.

The first point in his defense of the special position of the Jews is that they **were entrusted with the oracles of God.** The promises came through them. It is something to have been the channel through which God revealed himself. The promises stand (and have been most gloriously fulfilled); therefore the process by which they were transmitted cannot be stripped of all significance, nor can the people who had a part in that process be wholly indistinguishable from other races. As soon as he has mentioned the prerogatives inseparable from the promises, Paul opens up a great subject with which he deals more fully elsewhere, but he also immediately invites further objections. Why talk of privileges if Jews and Gentiles alike are simply under God's judgment? This is the question implied in vs. 3, and it is necessary to notice,

5 But if our unrighteousness commend the righteousness of God, what shall we say? *Is* God unrighteous who taketh vengeance? (I speak as a man)
6 God forbid: for then how shall God judge the world?

5 But if our wickedness serves to show the justice of God, what shall we say? That God is unjust to inflict wrath on us? (I speak in a human way.)
6 By no means! For then how could God judge the world?

---

ultimately be vindicated Paul will discuss in chs. 9–11. At this point there is only a hint of that shout of faith with which those chapters are to end: "O the depth of the riches and wisdom and knowledge of God! How unsearchable are his judgments and how inscrutable his ways! . . . For from him and through him and to him are all things."

5-7. Paul has already suggested (vs. 4) that God's fidelity to his promises is not denied by man's failure to keep the law; indeed, that this truth of God is the more vividly set forth by man's failure. But if this is true, Paul's imaginary heckler asks, why should men be condemned for what has the effect of commending God's righteousness? **If** [he goes on] **through my falsehood God's truthfulness abounds to his glory, why am I still being condemned as a sinner? And why not do evil that good may come?** Paul lets us know that he has been accused of saying this in effect; and it is not difficult to see that his doctrine of justification by faith alone, apart from works of the law (see on 3:21 ff.), could

---

before we proceed, the kind of answer which Paul gives (though not here) to the problem of the promise.[1] For the sake of clarity it can be stated in four propositions: (*a*) God gave the promises to Israel. (*b*) The Jews, by rebelling against his will, have forfeited the promises, and this is God's justification for not granting what he had promised them. (*c*) The true Israel, the remnant, will receive the promises, and as the church of Christ actually has done so. (*d*) The unfaithful Jews, by their apostasy, have opened the way for all other peoples to be brought in, and the salvation of the Gentiles will in time make possible the redemption of the Jews as well. This anticipates the argument of chs. 9–11; for the moment Paul takes a simpler line.

The objection of the Jew assumes that if God does not so fulfill his promises as to satisfy the expectations he has raised, his faithfulness is overthrown, and his promises are proved to be false. To Paul this is one of the dangerous oversimplifications which human logic sometimes achieves. God cannot be confined within the limits which man's reason allows him. If our expectations are disappointed or our calculations overthrown, it is wiser to decide that we are wrong than to assume that God has played us false. The point at issue is who is really faithless? The Jew has no right to claim that it is God, simply because the promises have not been ratified in the anticipated way. Actually the Jews have been the faithless ones because they have not obeyed God. Their disobedience makes it impossible for God to fulfill the promises; to treat their disobedience as inconsequential would strike at the whole foundation of that moral order which is sustained by God's faithfulness alone. Paul's purpose is to prove that God cannot be charged with duplicity because of the way in which he has sustained and fulfilled his promises. And the quotation from Ps. 51:4 is merely the formal confirmation of his argument. As generally interpreted, it meant that sin, by virtue of the punishment which it drew upon itself, served to disclose the righteousness of God.

5. *The Voice of Carnal Contention.*—Again the ground shifts. His antagonist, catching at the echo of a perversion of Paul's teaching, suggests that our unrighteousness cannot both vindicate God's righteousness and merit his punishment. If our sin only displays his goodness, that surely gives it a status of its own in the moral world. Then God cannot justly judge it as evil. This is the kind of jugglery which is always possible in debate. It is a method of scoring a point without making any pretense of reaching the truth, and it is prompted purely by a spirit of "carnal contention." That is why Paul, apologetically but with a shudder, interjects the comment, **I speak in a human way.**

6. *The Necessity and Finality of Righteous Judgment.*—The indignation with which Paul repudiates the suggestion latent in the last question is not due to annoyance at unscrupulous methods of debating. His opponent, to score a point, has struck at one of the basic presuppositions of Paul's faith. If God is active righteousness, and if the life of men is set in a moral world, there must be a process of judgment at work, and at length the imperfect and

[1] See Dodd, *Epistle of Paul to Romans, ad loc.;* see also Exeg.

7 For if the truth of God hath more abounded through my lie unto his glory; why yet am I also judged as a sinner?

8 And not *rather,* (as we be slanderously reported, and as some affirm that we say,) Let us do evil, that good may come? whose damnation is just.

7 But if through my falsehood God's truthfulness abounds to his glory, why am I still being condemned as a sinner?
8 And why not do evil that good may come? — as some people slanderously charge us with saying. Their condemnation is just.

---

easily have been made to appear the basis of such an inference by one who did not understand its true meaning. Later in this letter Paul is going to deal at length with the problem raised by this objection (see below on 6:1-23 and 8:1-27); now he merely says the objection is absurd and has the effect of undermining the reality of the whole moral order: **How could God judge the world?** In other words, to take the position of the heckler is to say that evil is good; and *that* is to talk nonsense.

8. The clause **whose damnation** [i.e., **condemnation**] **is just** calls for special comment. The most obvious meaning is that those who make these objections and attribute to Paul such a sentiment as "Let us **do evil that good may come"** deserve to be condemned. It has been argued, however, that the "whose" is subjective rather than objective, and that Paul is meaning here to acknowledge that the *objectors'* condemnation *of him* would

---

approximate results by which cause and effect now declare God's purpose will be gathered up in his final judgment of all things. But to play with words and prove that our wickedness promotes the righteousness of God threatens the whole conception of a world in which God's judgment can operate. A judge must be righteous; if God is not really righteous, he cannot judge. But God is the source of our world and its creator. If he cannot judge, we are left adrift in a moral anarchy. But if he is indeed judge, what he does of necessity provides us with the standard by means of which every kind of judicial rectitude is tested. Paul, of course, would have contended that the whole historic process, and especially its decisive climax in Christ, provides the area in which God's judgments are made manifest. Faith affords an interpretation of history because history unfolds the purpose of God. Concerning this, Paul will have a great deal more to say before he is finished.

7-8. ***But Is It Fair?***—The point was evidently one often pressed, and the objections of the antagonist are still heard. The question is repeated, though in a variant form. Previously the issue was man's sin and God's justice—if my sin promotes his glory, is he not unfair in punishing me? In the present verse the issue is man's status—**if through my falsehood God's truthfulness abounds to his glory,** why am I to blame? By what I do, his fidelity is only more clearly displayed; should I then be punished as an offender? This kind of argument is used only in the unscrupulous anger which controversy produces. Such things are said merely to embarrass or vilify an opponent. They were, however, actually said, and the vividness of this confused wrangle is sharpened by the sarcastic quotation which Paul now introduces. So far the argument, when coldly stated, produces its own refutation; but when the strife was fierce, men went further still. They accused Paul of teaching that we should do wrong without restraint in order that God might have more abundant opportunity of manifesting his free mercy, and so of multiplying the good by overriding our sin. No one can admire such an argument, but there is certainly an element in Paul's teaching which leaves itself open to this kind of attack. His opponents, as we see in this case, were quick to seize on it. He had to warn his less mature disciples against the parallel distortion which said that Christians might do as they pleased, and which claimed that even their sin glorified God. From time to time in Christian history antinomian groups have put forward the same views—and that in spite of Paul's careful refutation of the idea in ch. 6 of this letter. Certainly the answers he himself has given in this compressed debate can be twisted so as to lead without too much difficulty to the conclusion suggested in vs. 8*a*. Paul, however, refuses to meet the argument; he regards it as insincere. It is an attempt to score an advantage, and only an unscrupulous debater will descend to such tactics. All one needs to do is to show the kind of argument it is, and one has already refuted it.

There is, however, one point in the passage which lends itself to development. Paul, we have seen, does not provide a cogent answer to the questions he has raised. This is not because they are beyond his powers, for in every case he returns later to consider them in detail. The

9 What then? are we better *than they?* No, in no wise: for we have before proved both Jews and Gentiles, that they are all under sin;

9 What then? Are we Jews any better off?[c] No, not at all; for I[d] have already charged that all men, both Jews and Greeks,

[c] Or *at any disadvantage?*
[d] Greek *we.*

be just if he actually held the views ascribed to him. Still another possibility is that the "whose" refers not to the objectors as such at all, but to any who do evil, explaining that they do so in order **that good may come;** these, Paul says, will be condemned for their evil deeds as they deserve, in spite of their specious and hypocritical excuse.

9. As the marginal reading of the RSV will indicate, there is some doubt as to the proper translation of the question with which this paragraph begins. The most natural reading is the one preferred by both of our texts; so understood, the sentence is virtually a repetition of the question with which ch. 3 opened. What makes this translation difficult is the fact that within the course of a few lines Paul seems to answer the same question in two exactly opposite ways. This difficulty leads some translators (e.g., Sanday and Headlam, Goodspeed, etc.) to adopt the reading "Are we Jews at a disadvantage?" It is curious that the same Greek words can carry such irreconcilable meanings; but there are a few instances of the same kind of thing in almost any language. Everything depends on the context in such cases; and this time the context is not clear. How Paul's answer to this question should be understood is also somewhat doubtful, and one's judgment here may well depend upon how one understands his question. The Greek phrase οὐ πάντως may mean **not at all** or it may mean "not altogether." Most commentators and translators have adopted the sense of both question and answer on which the KJV and the RSV also agree; and this wide consensus, in spite of

form which the argument has taken has thrown in high relief one particular attitude of mind. Paul has shown us a glimpse of that kind of mentality which is willing to argue in such a way that a defense of God's providence becomes a justification of man's immorality. To score debating points in this way is more than intellectual sleight of hand, for it suggests a dangerous complacency regarding true moral values. As Gore remarked,

> It is an intellectual exercise at the expense of conscience. And St. Paul shows, by the very contempt with which he treats it, that a man who will play false with his conscience, and then proceed to find intellectual justifications, is not to be met in the intellectual region at all. He has been condemned already.[2]

9-18. ***Our Basic Human Equality Established by Our Status as Sinners.***—The somewhat inconclusive dialogue in vss. 1-8 breaks off, and Paul returns to the line of development of his main theme. **What then?** becomes practically a device for resuming his argument, but it is worth bearing in mind that something has been added to the argument. The Jews, in spite of possessing the great privilege of having received the promises, are still subject to judgment.

[2] ***Epistle to Romans,*** **I, 119. Cf. Expos. on 14:1.**

That much remains, and it is distinctly relevant to the theme which Paul now develops. The uncertainty regarding the translation of a key word in vs. 9 is pointed out in the Exeg. The ERV prefers the sense which the RSV mg. gives. Curiously enough, though the two alternative readings appear to be diametrically opposed to each other, the sense in either case remains about the same. If one argues that Jew and Gentile are equal as they stand before God, it does not greatly matter whether one says that the Jews are not better off or not worse off. It remains that they are both the same. Nor does it even greatly matter that within the space of a few verses (on the basis of the preferred reading) Paul apparently answers the same question in opposite ways. The Jew may benefit immeasurably, from the human point of view, from having received the promises, but seen in a different perspective he still stands, in spite of that advantage, in essentially the same position as the Gentile. The crucial affirmation in this passage is that **all men, both Jews and Greeks, are under the power of sin.** It is consequently frivolous to argue that either the one or the other is in a better—or a worse—position. They are both alike involved in moral bankruptcy. This is the

10 As it is written, There is none righteous, no, not one:
11 There is none that understandeth, there is none that seeketh after God.
12 They are all gone out of the way, they are together become unprofitable; there is none that doeth good, no, not one.
13 Their throat *is* an open sepulchre; with their tongues they have used deceit; the poison of asps *is* under their lips:
14 Whose mouth *is* full of cursing and bitterness:

are under the power of sin, **10** as it is
written:
"None is righteous, no, not one;
11 no one understands, no one seeks for God.
12 All have turned aside, together they have gone wrong;
no one does good, not even one."
13 "Their throat is an open grave,
they use their tongues to deceive."
"The venom of asps is under their lips."
14 "Their mouth is full of curses and bitterness."

---

the rather gross inconsistency in which that interpretation appears to involve Paul, bears witness to the fact that these translations are on the whole the more natural; but it is well to note the other possibilities.

This problem of translation is not very important, however, because there can be no doubt of Paul's meaning at the really essential point. He is intending to affirm that the Jew is not better off (and of course not worse off) than others: **All men, both Jews and Greeks, are under the power of sin.** The meaning of this last phrase, **under the power of sin,** has been discussed somewhat in the Intro. (see above, pp. 369-70) and will be discussed again in the Exeg. of chs. 6 and 7. At the moment it is enough to say that Paul sees all men as guilty before God and the slaves of evil impulses—thus under a righteous condemnation which they cannot evade, and held captive by a demonic power of evil which they cannot successfully resist and from whose grasp they cannot escape.

10-18. This conclusion, based on his observations of Gentile and Jewish life (1:18–2:24), and based also—as we are to learn in 7:7-25—on Paul's own experience with himself, is now confirmed by a string of quotations from Scripture (Pss. 14:1-2 [53:1-2]; 5:9; 140:3; 10:7; Isa. 59:7-8; Ps. 36:1). These passages, apparently somewhat loosely quoted from the LXX, are used without reference to their various contexts, although

---

natural conclusion of the argument which opened in ch. 1. The breakdown of Gentile morality was sketched in lurid colors; then in the following chapter Paul showed that the Jews, in spite of their greater advantages, had failed just as disastrously. And so the way is open to the conclusion: all are under sin. To illustrate and enforce his meaning Paul appeals to the words of Holy Scripture. He forges a catena of passages from Isaiah and the Psalms, and quotes them to confirm his point. The catalogue which it provides of human failings is enough to daunt anyone whose mind is not incurably superficial. The denunciation begins with the very charge which Paul has just made—**none is righteous, no, not one.** To utter depravity he adds general obtuseness, and an apathy which, though it lacks God, will not bother to seek him (vs. 11). It is not as though a few, or even most, had missed the way; with the blind impulse of a leaderless herd **all have turned aside,** and they are at one only in this, that **together they have gone wrong.** (The force of this passage, for Paul's purpose, is obvious. Sometimes his quotations do not seem greatly to strengthen his argument; here he has found the most unequivocal support for his basic contention.) From men so utterly bereft of truth, one can expect nothing but falsehood. Within is only corruption—**their throat is an open grave**—and as a natural consequence smooth deception is the mark of all they say (vs. 13). Those who have lost the way are certain to be entangled in falsehood, and bitterness and hatred follow in an inevitable sequence. Men break out into blasphemies against God and into fierce contentions with one another (vs. 14). The path leads downward all the way; violence follows wrath, and murder is the sequel to strife (vs. 15). At length men are surrounded by the wilderness which their sin has created—ruin and misery and the complete absence of peace (vss. 16-17). The final quotation is an explanatory comment which renders

15 Their feet *are* swift to shed blood:
16 Destruction and misery *are* in their
ways:
17 And the way of peace have they not
known:
18 There is no fear of God before their
eyes.
19 Now we know that what things soever the law saith, it saith to them who
are under the law: that every mouth may
be stopped, and all the world may become
guilty before God.

15 "Their feet are swift to shed blood,
16 in their paths are ruin and misery,
17 and the way of peace they do not
know."
18 "There is no fear of God before their
eyes."
19 Now we know that whatever the law
says it speaks to those who are under the
law, so that every mouth may be stopped,
and the whole world may be held account-

---

this time no serious distortions of the original meanings are involved. For a discussion of these passages in their original contexts the reader is referred to the appropriate volumes in this Commentary.

19-20. Although certainly some of the passages just cited are originally addressed to Gentiles—and it would seem to suit Paul's purpose as expressed in vs. 9 ("both Jews and Greeks") that this should be true—he now applies them all to Jews, no doubt

---

man's self-made misery intelligible (vs. 18); men who live without reverence for God are likely to cease even to live as men. Step by step this composite passage builds up a picture of the plight of irreligious men and the bankruptcy of godless society. The critics of religion often suggest that faith is a superfluous luxury: it affirms, they claim, unimportant speculations about an unreal world. Actually the striking feature of the biblical view of life is its uncompromising realism. It rests not on an appeal to theory but on a delineation of fact. Generation after generation, experience proves that the life which is divorced from God is subject to rapid degeneration. With great skill Paul has so arranged his quotations as to illuminate this downward rush of those who have shut themselves off from the true source of their being. Any confused or troubled age provides abundant illustration of this process, but it is equally true to say that only this process, seen in this light, serves to illuminate the basic needs of human life. It provides a realistic means of interpreting the actual character of our problems, but it does so from a standpoint which holds out the hope of some ultimate answer. If it is true that human life has grown corrupt because it has drifted out of touch with God, we may reasonably expect that those who renew their dependence upon him will find that their corporate life is likewise renewed. If we have ceased to live as men because we have ceased to reverence God, we can hope to restore the true dignity of life if we restore true worship to its rightful place. The series of quotations forms a natural whole. There is unity of theme and progression of thought, and this makes intelligible the curious history of the passage.[3] This collection of quotations was added by some scribe to the text of Ps. 14, and so found its way into certain Greek MSS of the O.T. Thus it gained a place in the Vulg., and so, through various of the early English translations, in the Psalter as included in the Book of Common Prayer. Only the unity and coherence of the passage made this process possible. Paul was seeking material to corroborate his claim; he gathered it from various sources, and set it forth in a form so coherent that it accounts for one of the notable corruptions of the text of Scripture.

19. ***No Place for Protests.***—The main force of this passage as used by Paul would be felt by the Jews. **The law** has greatest authority for **those who are under the law,** and to the Jews the Scriptures spoke with unique force. Paul is marshaling the evidence provided by their sacred literature, and from its pages comes startling confirmation of what he has been saying. Yet the Jews would naturally be more reluctant than the Gentiles to admit the truth of Paul's argument, because they claimed to stand in a position different from that of any other people. What Paul has done is not simply to support his denunciation of national failings by appealing to the greatest exponents of the national genius; the quotations he uses have the added force which is inseparable from the fact that to any Jew these words would carry a divine authority. Even those most likely to protest can be regarded as effectually silenced—**every mouth is stopped.** In the case of the Gentiles there was not the same stubborn pride

[3] Cf. Sanday and Headlam, *Epistle to Romans, ad loc.*

20 Therefore by the deeds of the law there shall no flesh be justified in his sight: for by the law *is* the knowledge of sin.

able to God. 20 For no human being will be justified in his sight by works of the law since through the law comes knowledge of sin.

---

presuming that there could be no question, in any case, about the sinfulness of Gentiles. **Whatever the law** [here the whole Scripture, i.e., the O.T.] says **it speaks to those who are under the law, so that every mouth may be stopped, and the whole world may be held accountable to God.** He repeats that **no human being will be justified in** [God's] **sight by works of the law,** adding that the function of the law is not to save from sin, but to give **knowledge of sin** (cf. Apocalypse of Baruch 15:6; 48:40). This conception of

---

to be overcome, and Paul can assume that he has proved that both the Greeks, who trusted in wisdom, and the Jews, whose confidence was in the law, have missed the way. But more important than the sense of failure is the realization of our impotence and need. When man has nothing more to plead, he is likely to see himself in the clear light of what he understands of God; then he knows that he is not only helpless, but has been brought under the judgment of God. This state of humility, in which we recognize our helplessness and our accountability to God, should have come naturally to the Jew. The whole tenor of his Scriptures ought to have created a conviction of guilt, and consequently should have awakened the sense of an impending judgment.

20. ***The Insufficiency of Works.***—The certainty of judgment is not modified by the possession of the law. The kind of deeds which the law commands will not serve our purpose—**For no human being will be justified in his** [God's] **sight by works of the law.** A person is **justified** when he is not accounted guilty; he is acquitted, he is reckoned as righteous before God. The word denotes the verdict which is rendered, and comes from the law courts; after due trial the charges against a man are dismissed, and he is treated as an upright person. It is true, of course, that a term which comes from the courts need not always be restricted to relationships of a strictly legal character. It may also be noted that though a man can be treated as righteous without necessarily being *made* righteous, there must be sufficient grounds for doing so. From this it follows that what he is declared to be, he will more perfectly become.

The law is incapable of justifying men, but that is not its proper function, and it cannot fairly be expected to accomplish more than its given task. **Through the law,** as Paul says in explanation, **comes knowledge of sin.** It may show us our duty, though it does not enable us to do it; in the process it succeeds in teaching us our sinfulness. We become aware of the contrast between what we do and what we ought to do. The proper task of the law is to develop conscience, and it does this by awakening in us the consciousness of sin.

At this point Paul is performing a real service to all who wish to think accurately about moral and religious problems. The place of codes has become confused. Some people have exalted regulations to the point where they have become an insufferable burden. In the process their rules have failed to preserve the values for whose defense they were ostensibly devised. In the consequent reaction other people have repudiated every kind of traditional moral code. Judged by their fruits both "puritanism" (so-called) and its opposite have failed. Paul suggests a different approach: (*a*) Conscience is developed and strengthened as we are taught to discriminate between good and evil. (*b*) A code provides us with a standard by which we can test our own conduct. (*c*) Unless the code is unworthily low, it shows us with disconcerting clarity the contrast between our obligations and our actual performance. (*d*) As soon as religious values enter, we come to understand that our duty is to God, that we have lamentably failed therein, and consequently we come to understand what sin means. (*e*) To expect a code to transform our lives, deliver us from sin, and make us upright men and women is to ask it to do what it cannot rightly be expected to do. (*f*) To choose the right, we need a new motive, sufficiently compelling to enable us to forsake the wrong which our code has taught us to recognize.

Having set the law in its proper and legitimate place, Paul is now prepared to indicate the nature of the new power which makes us right with God. Before leaving this subject, however, we should remind ourselves that the impotence of law will be more fully discussed in ch. 7.

The failure of the law may seem a matter very remote from the modern mind but, once its close connection with a sense of sin is recognized, it becomes a good deal more relevant than at first sight it seems. In religious circles

21 But now the righteousness of God without the law is manifested, being witnessed by the law and the prophets;

21 But now the righteousness of God has been manifested apart from law, although the law and the prophets bear

the positive use of the law Paul is later to discuss at some length (see below on ch. 7). Just now he is concerned only to demonstrate its impotence to secure man's release from guilt and slavery.

III. The Saving Act: Justification by Faith (3:21–4:25)

A. Justification Defined (3:21-30)

Paul is now in position to take up again the theme he so boldly set forth in 1:16-17. We have already observed (see above on 1:17) how ambiguous is the phrase **the righteousness of God.** Is the reference (*a*) to God's own righteousness—just as one might refer to his holiness? Or (*b*) does the term have a more active sense: "God declaring righteous"—the justifying *act* of God? Or yet again (*c*) does the phrase designate the status which this justifying act confers? In our discussion of 1:16-17 it was indicated that the term ordinarily has the active sense (*b*) in Paul. In this crucial section, however, all three meanings seem to be present, as we shall see.

21-22. In these verses **the righteousness of God** is apparently used in the third sense (*c*): it means the status of approvedness, the character of being declared righteous, of being acquitted, which God alone can confer. Not only is this meaning indicated by the whole immediate context (vss. 20-22), but also by the use of the word "manifested" or "made to appear" (πεφανέρωται)—a less dynamic term than "revealed" (ἀποκαλύπτεται)

the tendency to neglect sin or even to minimize it receded sharply after World War II. When faced with catastrophic evil, ignorance or any comparable explanation is far too slight to account for the terrible malevolence of the forces at work in the world. But secularism has no sense of sin, and the prestige of science has taught more and more people to think of our life largely in terms of material progress. If those outside the churches are to regain any awareness of what sin means, it can be only because Christians have taught them. Events may help, but even events must have expositors. And Christians themselves often have a very imperfect sense of sin. The kingdom of evil may have become a reality to them, but that is hardly the same thing; we need to recover far more clearly a realization that our life is set in the clear light of God's immeasurable holiness. The reason the law could create an awareness of sin was not simply because it set forth a standard of righteous conduct. That was important, but behind the code was the felt presence of a holy God. "Thus spake God and said. . . ." In those words the Jew enshrined his conviction that the law reflected the mind and will of the Most High. Sin was not simply a transgression of the literal commandment; it was disobedience of one whose holy will seemed more austere the more perfectly men came to know it. The most sensitive biblical writers were always aware that their wrongdoing took on its distinctive quality of sin because it was a direct flouting of the righteous will of him in whose presence their lives were lived. "Against thee, thee only, have I sinned" (Ps. 51:4). But willful disobedience of a righteousness which met them with such exacting demands must necessarily entail judgment. Certainly it deserved the consequences which ought to follow from moral failure when seen in such a setting. Because we have not understood sin in a profoundly personal way, we have too easily dismissed the severity of divine judgment; and so we have found ourselves unable to grasp the wonder of divine mercy. This does not imply that people will discover what grace means simply because they have learned to fear the consequences of their own sin. People know what sin is only if they have come to understand what manner of perfect personal righteousness confronts them; only those who know the gravity of sin can conceive the severity of judgment, and these alone can understand the joy of the new life.

21-30. ***The Secret of True Righteousness.***—In the new day which has now dawned God provides for men a righteousness which otherwise they could never achieve (vss. 21-26): (*a*) This righteousness is beyond the law and independent of it, but it has the witness of both law and prophets (vs. 21). (*b*) It comes through

in 1:17-18. The suggestion conveyed by this verb that the "righteousness" is a state, rather than an action, points to either (*a*) or (*c*); and (*a*) is eliminated as a possibility by the context—God's own state of being righteous would not be dependent upon our faith. The new status of approvedness is not conferred on the basis of one's obedience to the law; in that case no one could receive it, as the apostle has shown. This new **righteousness of God has been manifested apart from law, although** [Paul hastens to add] **the law and the prophets bear witness to it.** (On the testimony of the Scriptures to the new way of justification see below on 3:31–4:25.) The new way of justification is **through faith in Jesus Christ** (on the meaning of this phrase see above on 1:16). **It** happens that in this place, and not infrequently elsewhere, the Greek is literally the **faith of Jesus Christ** (as in KJV); some scholars have regarded the genitive as subjective so that the meaning becomes "the righteousness of God has been manifested through Jesus Christ's own faithfulness." Almost certainly, however, the RSV translators are correct in understanding the genitive to be objective and rendering it as they do: The **faith of Jesus Christ** is *our* **faith in Jesus Christ.** The makers of the KJV undoubtedly understood the passage so, even though they adhere more rigidly to the Greek idiom.

---

faith in Christ, and is open to all who believe in him (vs. 22*a*). (*c*) It is open to all, impartially, and—since all have sinned—all need it (vss. 22*b*-23). (*d*) The substance of the gift—for a gift it is—is a new standing which God in his mercy grants us, and we have it because Christ has brought us out from under the power of all the forces that held us in bondage (vs. 24). (*e*) Why Christ's death is our redemption—those who believe in him discover that by the Cross the tyranny of sin is swept away, and the righteousness and mercy of God are alike perfectly revealed (vss. 25-26).

This determines the nature of our response, and in vss. 27-30 Paul indicates the qualities which distinguish the new faith by which the Christian lives: (*a*) Humility, because boasting is excluded. We can claim no credit for anything that we ourselves have done; it is faith alone which has brought us deliverance (vss. 27-28). (*b*) Universality, because God is the creator of all men, equally concerned for members of all races. Everyone is capable of the kind of response which is necessary for salvation, and Jew and Gentile alike enter into the new life by faith (vss. 29-30).

21. ***The New Revelation of Righteousness.***—Paul has shown that man's experience affords a record of universal failure and of the judgment which inexorably follows upon sin. The law of nature has not benefited the Gentile, nor the law of Moses the Jew. Man's own powers leave him impotent; even the best resources he has hitherto possessed are incapable of helping him. **But now,** therefore, represents more than merely a return to the main thread of Paul's interrupted argument (1:17). What man needs is a new revelation, and in Christ he has received it. What Christ has done constitutes a decisive event; it divides man's new status of liberation and joy from his previous condition of impotence and servitude. The proclamation of the gospel is the declaration that a new era has come. The power of the new age **has been manifested** altogether **apart from law.** What we ourselves can do is not responsible for the new status which we receive. "Law" is a word with many facets. Here it does not indicate the revelation in the O.T. or the religion which that revelation sustained. It stands for religion as crystallized in statutes and ordinances. The supreme example of legalism in religion might be the system which had grown up in Israel, but Judaism was also a concrete illustration of a certain principle. The heart of the matter was the degree to which men relied on what they themselves could do, and their own achievements, says Paul, are incapable of securing for them what God has freely made available in Jesus Christ. In the following clause we have the word "law" again, this time with an article, and clearly pointing to the religious tradition of the Jews, not simply to one manifestation—a partial and circumscribing manifestation at that—of the insights of the O.T. The gospel tells of a new day, but it is related to what has gone before. The partial perceptions of the old era are gathered up in it; they are now perfected and fulfilled. It is important to note that in this compressed passage—one of the crucial statements of what Paul regarded as the heart of the gospel—he has found room to stress the continuity which unites the new and the old. At times Paul seems to attack the law without restraint; at other times he insists on its value and importance. This is not inconsistency; it is due to his perception that the partial, though dangerous if mistaken for the complete, may within its proper limits be of genuine and permanent worth.

22 Even the righteousness of God *which is* by faith of Jesus Christ unto all and upon all them that believe; for there is no difference:

witness to it, 22 the righteousness of God through faith in Jesus Christ for all who

---

22-23. Since the justification now made available in response to faith is **apart from law, it is for all who believe.** Paul's universalism is essentially bound up with his doctrine of justification, as constantly appears (see below, e.g., on vss. 29-30). He has been saying through two chapters that both Greeks and Jews are the slaves of sin; now he affirms that God offers the same salvation to both. **For there is no distinction. . . . All have sinned;** all **fall short of the glory of God.** The **glory of God** refers to man's original estate as created in the likeness of God. Elsewhere Paul alludes to man as being "the image and glory of God" (I Cor. 11:7)—i.e., in his true character. Because of sin man is falling short of this true character and the destiny which belongs with it (see Intro., p. 369); in the same way—as we shall see—because of justification, man may now hope for its restoration (see on 5:2: "We . . . rejoice in hope of the glory of God"). And since this loss through sin is common to all men, so God's provision of help is made for all men on an absolutely equal basis. God stands ready to justify all **by his grace as a gift.**

---

22. ***The Righteousness of God and Man's Plight.***—This is one of the verses in which Paul seems deliberately to accommodate himself to the needs of his expositors. The subject matter is important and touches the heart of the message; the structure is simple, and the sequence invites orderly expansion. **The righteousness of God** recapitulates the thought of the previous verse, and helps us to identify the sense in which Paul uses this extremely important phrase (see Exeg.). He is describing the new status into which the gospel introduces those who accept it, and its nature is made clear by contrast with man's prior state. In somber colors Paul has painted the picture of man's condition when he tries to live apart from God. If his account seems needlessly pessimistic, we have only to remember that the natural man seems strangely incapable—either in that day or in this—of so organizing his affairs that his life will be marked by dignity and will lead to peace. The righteousness which God gives us must be seen against the chaos created by anger and greed, by undisciplined instincts and uncontrolled passions. Distrust of himself, fear of his fellows, alienation from God—these are finally all that the natural man can set against **the righteousness of God.** But Paul has also glanced at another alternative—that of obedience to a moral law—and in ch. 7 he will show us in vivid detail what fruit it has borne in his own life. He shows us how the knowledge of what is right struggles ineffectually to translate its insights into deeds, and he describes the unrelieved despair created by repeated failure.

By contrast, then, we can see the kind of meaning with which Paul would fill a term like **the righteousness of God.** He would show us a life free from failure and from fear, no longer obsessed with past sins and no longer dominated by unregulated impulse. It is a life in which we have peace with God and know progressively the richness of experience to which his free service introduces us. Since the former alienation from God, created by our apprehension of the reaction of perfect righteousness to the tenor of our lives, has been swept away, we are able in humble trust to learn the meaning of that liberty which our grateful dependence on God's will confers. All this is explained in greater detail as the letter unfolds; it is implicit in **the righteousness of God.**

In the second place, we have the means by which this new status becomes ours. Paul has already shown that it is never won by merit, whether within the framework of the Jewish law or not. It comes **through faith in Jesus Christ.** Only the man who desires God's bounty has any hope of receiving it, but we must be prepared to accept it as a gift. When our pride has been broken, we can abandon our self-reliant efforts to deserve divine favor, and humbly commit ourselves to God, to receive what he is prepared to give. But the faith of which Paul speaks is not an attitude of vague and general trust in and self-surrender to God. We find our new relationship with God through Jesus Christ—indeed, **in Jesus Christ.** Nor do we merely respond to what he is; we gratefully avail ourselves of what he has done. The whole situation has been altered by his life, death, and resurrection; from the results of that change we benefit.

Finally, we have the scope of God's gift—it is **for all who believe.** The only limitation is one imposed by the inherent nature of the new

23 For all have sinned, and come short
of the glory of God;
24 Being justified freely by his grace
through the redemption that is in Christ
Jesus:

believe. For there is no distinction; 23 since
all have sinned and fall short of the glory
of God, 24 they are justified by his grace
as a gift, through the redemption which

24*a*. The word **grace**—to appear again and again in the course of this epistle, and all the epistles of Paul—has occurred so far only twice, both times in the salutation. The most elementary meaning of the word is probably "attractiveness" or "charm"; thus in Eccl. 10:12 (LXX) we find that "the words of the mouth of the wise man are grace," and in Luke 4:22 reference is made to Jesus' "words of grace." From this significance it is only a step to "kindness," "graciousness," "good will." The word was frequently used to designate such an attitude when felt or manifested toward another by a personage whose exalted position put him beyond the range of any mere obligation either to feel it or to show it. Thus throughout the O.T. persons are said to "find favor" with kings or with God. Since such favor would always be not a deserved reward, but a generous gift, it is not strange that Paul's use of "grace"—always in connection with God or Christ—should involve primary emphasis upon its unearned character. "Grace" means God's spontaneous, unmerited kindness toward us, his mercy, his love; but it may be extended to include a reference to the actual benefits—especially the salvation in Christ—which because of this loving disposition he confers on us. In this verse the essential meaning of "grace," as in no sense or measure dependent upon the deserving of the recipient, is accented by the addition of the term δωρεάν, "as a gift," "freely," or as both Moffatt and Goodspeed translate, "for nothing."

24*b*-26. We come now to one of the most difficult, as it is one of the most important, passages in the letter. These words of the apostle have been interpreted in as many diverse ways and have occasioned as much controversy as anything he wrote. We can begin safely and surely enough by asserting that the translation of the RSV is at every point preferable to the KJV rendering: **expiation** is better than **propitiation**; the phrase

---

relationship. Paul has shown that it is conditioned by faith, and there are no other terms on which anyone can enter. The things which usually weigh so heavily with us—merit, achievement, inheritance, precedence—all count for nothing. But granted the possession of the only requisite, faith, there are no barriers by which anyone can be excluded. All the artificial divisions by which we segregate ourselves from one another are broken down. Paul's doctrine of the universality of grace follows from his doctrine of justification (cf. Exeg.); we may state the same truth even more forcibly and claim that the one demands the other as its consequence. For one thing, the uniform nature of our moral failure makes ridiculous our efforts to treat any group, any nation, any race, as having special claims upon God's favor. The distinctions we make have no foundation in fact.

23. *The Universality of Need.*—Paul is not devising a particularly pessimistic theory when he says that **all have sinned;** he is merely interpreting admitted facts in terms of a particular point of reference. Man was made for something different from the kind of life which he has actually achieved, and which Paul has described in chs. 1-2. If God created man he presumably did so with a purpose, and we can interpret that purpose only in terms of a life which would correspond with what we know of God's will. Unless we can contest Paul's facts, we cannot dispute his inference: all **fall short of the glory of God.**

24-26. *Justification, Our New Standing.*—We **are justified by his grace as a gift.** The key word is **justified,** and it is the meaning and consequences of the resultant state that Paul is struggling to make clear. "Justification" is obviously a term which cannot be ignored. The tendency to keep clear of important words which have an intimidating sound helps to explain the theological illiteracy which is the mark of all too many congregations. Certainly there is no better point of departure for a study of justification than the present passage, and the best way to deal with a great theme is to indicate point by point what it means in Pauline thought. First, justification is an act of God. It is initiated by him, and it manifests his essential nature. "It is God who justifies," says Paul elsewhere (8:33). The claim seems obvious

25 Whom God hath set forth *to be* a propitiation through faith in his blood, to declare his righteousness for the remission

is in Christ Jesus, 25 whom God put forward as an expiation by his blood, to be received by faith. This was to show God's

in his blood should be thought of in connection with **expiation**, not with **faith**; "passing over" is more accurate than **remission**; etc. But although the passage reads more clearly in the RSV than in the older English text, nevertheless what precisely Paul is intending to say is by no means plain, even there.

The key terms are **redemption** (ἀπολύτρωσις) and **expiation** (ἱλαστήριον); and each of these calls for some attempt at definition. When Moffatt translates ἀπολύτρωσις as "ransom," he correctly indicates the primary meaning of the term. The form of the word used here, however, is abstract rather than concrete, and suggests rather the act of ransoming than the ransom itself. Paul is thus alluding to God's act of redeeming us from our slavery to sin: in and through Christ he sets us free from both its guilt and power. It is not to be supposed that Paul was intending his readers to accept his term "ransom" with the stark literalism with which certain later interpreters have received it. He certainly does not dream of suggesting that God—or Christ—paid a ransom to Satan to induce him to release man (according to Paul, God in Christ dealt with Satan not by buying him off, but by defeating him and destroying his power). Paul seizes on the metaphor of the ransom both because it was familiar to him in a not dissimilar connection in the O.T. (e.g., Deut. 7:8; Isa. 51:11), and also because in many ways it expresses so admirably the reality of the salvation Christ has brought: we were hopelessly bound, lacking any power or opportunity to escape from our bondage to sin and death, when One came who, out of pure love for us, since he owed us nothing, and at great cost to himself, set us free. The content and implication of this **redemption**, or emancipation, Paul will be discussing throughout most of the rest of this letter. It is, as has been said, emancipation or deliverance both from the guilt of sin and from its power and consequences. Just now he is concerned more immediately with freedom from guilt, i.e., with justification, acquittal, forgiveness. But no sharp distinction can be made even in idea between justification and salvation; and surely Paul did not ever think of them as separated in actual fact (see below on 5:9-10).

If **redemption** suggests slavery and the slave, **expiation** much more unmistakably is associated with the sacrificial cultus. Commentators differ as to precisely how the term ἱλαστήριον is to be understood here. Is it a reference to the "mercy seat," on which blood

enough when stated against a background of Christian thought; but it was by no means so apparent when Paul wrote, and certain inherent human tendencies are always likely to obscure it. Apparently, good men in every age are apt to hope that by conscientious effort they can establish a claim upon God, and by their merit stand confidently in his presence. Paul repeatedly rebukes this stubborn misconception (vs. 20; 4:2), yet his insistence that a man is never justified by works is only a negative way of stating that justification is always the act of God. Moreover, in the constant association of justification with Christ and with his work we have another way of emphasizing the same truth. God takes the initiative and he provides the necessary means. God's act declares his nature. In what he has done we see his grace (vs. 24), the radiant attractiveness, the measureless forbearance, the infinite solicitude of the divine generosity. In Christ's death we also behold God's righteousness; indeed, it was to show this very quality that the drama of redemption unfolded.

Second, justification is related to man's present experience. This is not a complete statement, of course, because there is always an implied reference to the final declaration of a man's status which takes place when he stands before the judgment seat of God. This eschatological emphasis, however, is by no means primary, and again and again Paul makes it perfectly clear that he is describing a state into which we have already entered. The tenses which he uses are often present,[4] and he is obviously speaking of an experience relevant to our present situation when he declares here that **they are justified by his grace as a gift.** The purpose of God's decisive act in Christ **was to prove at the present time that he him-**

[4] Cf. Vincent Taylor, *Forgiveness and Reconciliation* (London: Macmillan & Co., 1946), p. 37.

of sins that are past, through the forbearance of God;

righteousness, because in his divine forbearance he had passed over former sins;

was sprinkled on the day of Atonement? (Cf. Heb. 9:5, where this word is used in that sense; the same use is found in the LXX.) So probably the majority of the interpreters of this passage have believed. Most modern commentators, however, doubt that Paul is making precisely this use of the word. They argue that if the ritual of the day of Atonement had been in Paul's mind, he would have thought of Christ as corresponding either to the sacrificial victim whose blood was sprinkled on the top of the ark, or to the priest who sprinkled it (or as the author of Hebrews did, to both), rather than to the lid of the ark, or "mercy seat" itself. The term has a general sense, designating any cult-means of (*a*) propitiating the deity or (*b*) annulling sin and its effects. Dodd has rendered a significant service in establishing the fact that in the LXX the word rarely if ever occurs in the former of these senses (i.e., as a means of propitiating God, of changing a supposed hostility to favor), and that it is constantly employed in the second sense: "a means of expiation," if man is the agent; "a means of forgiveness," if God is the agent (*Journal of Theological Studies,* XXXII [1931], 352-60; also *The Epistle of Paul to the Romans* [London: Hodder & Stoughton, 1932; "The Moffatt New Testament Commentary"] *ad loc.*).

Obviously the meaning "propitiation" in any literal sense is not intended since it is God himself who **put forward** (or "set forth publicly") the *hilasterion.* At the same time Paul is vividly aware of the need of sacrifice if sin is to be forgiven. His use of the phrase **expiation by his blood** is not mere metaphor. The feeling that there can be no annulling of sin without the shedding of blood was native to Paul. The idea of cult sacrifice was in the air he breathed, whether he was on the soil of Palestine or in a Hellenistic city like Tarsus, Antioch, or Corinth. Some commentators hold that Paul did no more than to make use of the *language* of sacrifice, just as he made use of the *language* of the law court; it is probable, however, that much more than language is involved in both cases. The apostle sees man as actually under righteous judgment because of his sin, and the righteous God, who has imposed that judgment, cannot reverse it by merely wishing to do so; or better, such a God cannot will to reverse it unless the just demands of the law are met. A price must be paid; a penalty must be suffered; a sacrifice must be offered. One gets the impression from Jesus' teaching that he thought of repentance as representing this satisfaction of the law; but Paul, who makes

self is righteous and that he justifies him who has faith in Jesus. Indeed, our present experience of justification is our surest ground of confidence that when the secrets of every heart are disclosed, we shall not stand condemned.

Third, justification, though the act of God, becomes effective only when its offer meets with the response of faith. As we have seen already, a man cannot be justified by anything that he himself can do (vs. 23). Paul is convinced that only a personal commitment to Jesus Christ—a relationship based on trust, resulting in fellowship, bearing fruit in obedience—can supply the requisite condition without which justification remains an elusive dream. Our faith prepares the way for what only God can do; by itself it is as powerless as any other good work to win us acceptance, but it opens the door so that God may do for us what his grace designs. **He justifies him who has faith in Jesus,** says Paul; the deliverance and release which are ours through Christ are **to be received by faith.**

Fourth, justification finally depends on what Christ has done for us. We **are justified by his grace as a gift, through the redemption which is in Christ Jesus. A gift** reminds us that it is not of our doing, and the succeeding words clearly show that Paul is thinking not of general benefits, but of that deliverance which he related to Christ's death upon the cross. The result of his sacrifice, as Paul repeatedly assures us, is that God is able to receive men and treat them as righteous. What has happened can be stated in a number of alternative ways, and in vs. 25 Paul further relates our justification to Christ's death by speaking of him as one **whom God put forward as an expiation by his blood.** What God does to justify us rests on what Christ has done to save us. "We are now justified by his blood" (5:9). (We must bear in mind, of course, that when Paul speaks of "Christ's blood," he means "His life as laid down in self-dedication to God." [5])

[5] Dodd, *Epistle of Paul to Romans, ad loc.*

26 To declare, *I say,* at this time his righteousness: that he might be just, and the justifier of him which believeth in Jesus.

26 it was to prove at the present time that he himself is righteous and that he justifies him who has faith in Jesus.

---

no theological use of the idea of repentance, undoubtedly finds in the life and death of Christ the indispensable atoning sacrifice. To be sure, it is God himself who **in Christ Jesus** provides the necessary sacrifice and pays the necessary price; and there is no way within our human command of making such a fact logically consistent with itself. But to acknowledge this is not to reduce to the status of a mere metaphor the whole conception of a sacrifice vicariously offered or of a penalty vicariously paid. This conception was Paul's way of explaining one element in the Christian experience of forgiveness: we are forgiven, and yet God's judgment upon sin is not compromised.

This meaning of **expiation** is confirmed as Paul goes on to say that in and through Christ (and one feels that he is thinking chiefly about Christ's death: **by his blood) God's righteousness** is shown—and here the word for "show," literally, to "prove" or "demonstrate" (ἔνδειξις), suggests that the reference is primarily to God's own righteous character—**because . . . he had passed over former sins.** This must mean then that God's apparent ignoring of man's previous sinning would have been impossible (because morally inadmissible) if it had not been for the fact that all the time the death of Christ, which was a "sufficient sacrifice for the sins of the whole world" (past, present, future), was present in the purpose and foreknowledge of God. Thus in Christ it is proved **at the present time that** [God] **himself is righteous,** just as it is also established in the experience of the community that he **justifies him who has faith in Jesus.** It is possible that Paul intends to imply no opposition, or even tension, between God's own righteousness and his justifying act, i.e., between his justice and his mercy—God's righteousness includes both—but such an intention is by no means ruled out. In that event the "and" in vs. 26 would have the force of "and yet." This, however, is not the only possible interpretation.

It is important to note, before we leave this crucially significant paragraph, that it is the word "faith" which, in the intention of the apostle, carries the largest part of the meaning of the whole passage (vss. 21-26). The new way of justification is not on the basis of obedience to the law—else no one, he has shown, could claim it—but on the ground of faith only. This is said three times in the course of the paragraph.

In dealing with this crucial passage we must remember that Paul was attempting to explain something that was very real but also unique. It was a part of his experience, but it has no true parallels. This naturally complicates his task. He can suggest analogies, but he knows that they are all partial and consequently defective. It is Dodd who points out that Paul uses three distinct analogies, each taken from a different sphere of human activity,[6] and this fact provides a useful framework around which to develop an exposition of Paul's thought. From the law courts Paul takes the metaphor of justification: the judge acquits the prisoner. For emancipation he turns to slavery: the generous owner frees the slave. The sacrificial practices of ancient religion provide him with his third figure—that of expiation by blood. Each figure emphasizes the reality of what God has done for us. The new experience can be described under various forms, but all declare that God has taken the initiative and has done for us what we could never do for ourselves. Each figure also points to a decisive change in our position. The metaphor from the law points out that we were like condemned men who have been acquitted. The analogy drawn from slavery suggests that we were formerly in bondage to sin, but have been set free. Expiation declares that our guilt has been removed and we are treated as innocent. Each figure is related to what Christ has done for us. He brings us out of our alienation from God into an effective fellowship with him, and provides the means by which his mercy—blocked by our own sin—can achieve in us his miracles of transformation.

[6] *Ibid.*

27 Where *is* boasting then? It is excluded. By what law? of works? Nay; but by the law of faith.
28 Therefore we conclude that a man is justified by faith without the deeds of the law.

27 Then what becomes of our boasting? It is excluded. On what principle? On the principle of works? No, but on the principle of faith. 28 For we hold that a man is justified by faith apart from works of law.

27-28. These verses do little more than repeat the point made in the first part of the chapter—indeed in the whole of the section 1:18–3:20—that no one is in position to boast of his status before God. Paul adds now, however, that this is true not only because of the failure of both Jew and Greek to do the **works of law,** but also because God's way of justifying man is on the basis of **faith,** and such a basis automatically shuts out any boasting. To boast of faith, as though it were a matter of merit, is to show that one does not have it, since faith itself involves complete despair of the adequacy of one's own effort and unreserved reliance upon God's unmerited favor.

27-30. ***Consequences of Justification.***—Paul has just stated, with great brevity but great cogency, the doctrine of our redemption. He now proceeds to draw two important inferences. The first concerns the humility which the gospel inspires; the second the scope within which its power works.

27-28. ***Humility.***—In the light of the foregoing verses, **what becomes of our boasting?** The assumption latent in the words is that there is no longer any room either for pride or for its expression. Paul assumes that there is something radically wrong with any form of religious faith which makes it possible for man to be complacent about himself as he approaches God. Pride was a temptation to which he himself was particularly vulnerable. Many factors in his background and in his own character help to explain this. The nature of Jewish religion combined with the position of Jews in the world to foster a kind of outlook which was fiercely conscious of its privileges, and intensely devoted to fulfilling its duties. In the Gospels we catch repeated glimpses of fanatically earnest men whose religious zeal buttressed an arrogant pride. "God, I thank thee, that I am not as other men" is the prayer of the Pharisee in the parable (Luke 18:11). "This people who knoweth not the law are cursed" (John 7:49) is one of the typical sayings attributed to the Jewish leaders, and it admirably reflects a superiority which expressed itself in contempt of those who could not or would not fulfill every minute requirement of the code. Their delight in the chief places at the feast (Mark 12:39), their efforts to attract attention even by their prayers (Matt. 6:5), their ostentation even when giving alms (Matt. 6:2)—the sidelights from the Gospels show us men in whom self-conscious virtue had stifled all humility. But Paul was a Pharisee before he became an apostle; he himself tells us that he had outstripped most of his contemporaries and had excelled in the disciplines to which the exponents of the law devoted themselves (Gal. 1:14). Moreover, again and again in his letters we catch echoes of the old spirit, and we can understand how deep must have been the experience which prompted him to state his settled conviction, "God forbid that I should glory, save in the cross of our Lord Jesus Christ" (Gal. 6:14). In the present context he has just been speaking about the Cross: he has been explaining that there is no other way to God and to peace save that provided by the death of Christ. This leaves no room for pride in anything that we can do. Boasting is ruled out because we know that **the principle of works** is insufficient. Only the **principle of faith** will suffice here; the only proper response is the surrender of our entire self to Christ in gratitude for what he has done. Such an attitude is inseparable from an overwhelming sense of indebtedness. In the presence of Christ's cross we cannot come pointing to our achievements and claiming our proper deserts. Paul has already established that in Christ God has done for us what we could never have done for ourselves. Where boasting is excluded, there is gratitude as well as humility.

No doubt this is the right response; but who can pretend that for most of us it is either easy or natural? Within most of us the Pharisee is lurking very near the surface. If possible, we like to trust in our own resources, we feel a natural gratification in our own virtue. Imperceptibly we begin to trust in what we are or do. That is why failure often plays so necessary a part in religious discipline. It reminds us of what we ourselves cannot do; it teaches us to receive again what only God can do for us. The natural man's distaste for accepting so great a sense of indebtedness doubtless explains what

29 *Is he* the God of the Jews only? *is he* not also of the Gentiles? Yes, of the Gentiles also:

29 Or is God the God of Jews only? Is he not the God of Gentiles also? Yes, of Gen-

29-30. Paul presents now an additional argument for his claim that justification is by faith (see also above on vss. 22-23). Is not any other view, he asks, a denial of monotheism? To the Jew only have been given circumcision and the law—but if God is

Paul meant when he spoke of the offense of the gospel. To the Greek this way was folly; to the Jew it was a stumbling block: the one trusted in his wisdom, the other in his merit. Paul asked men not to trust in anything they could do, but to accept what God had freely done for them. They were to receive it as children receive what their father does for them—but then Jesus had told his disciples that unless they became as little children they could not enter the kingdom of his father.

The nature of this humility is often misconceived. It is a virtue held in low regard by many people. It is treated as though it were an unreal depreciation of oneself in comparison with one's fellows, and so as the precursor of the hypocrisy of the "humble" Uriah Heep. Actually, true humility is the ability to see ourselves as we really are, without the presence of the distorting medium of pride to twist our vision. It is also, of course, the secret of seeing other people as they are; being free from the need to disparage their qualities and achievements, we can heartily appreciate what they are and do. This happens, however, only when we see ourselves in God's light—as his debtors. When the things we value most are not of our own achieving, but have been given to us by God, we can rejoice in them without pride, we can regard ourselves without unreality, we can associate with others without superiority. Those who are really humble are those who possess the secret of true joy—and the experience both of the past and of the present abundantly confirms it. Their humility is the direct consequence, of course, of what Paul has been saying about the new way in which they find peace with God. But lest there should be any uncertainty, he makes his meaning doubly clear. It is not by any law of human achievement that they acquire this necessary virtue. Indeed, the person who tries to be humble either fails completely, or, insofar as he succeeds, is proud that he is humble. That is one reason why pride is the last root of sin. It also explains why the principle of works is so thoroughly excluded.

29. ***The Universal Scope of the Gospel.***— There is, however, one way in which the force of the foregoing argument can be circumvented. If God's rule is limited to certain people, then the rest are not bound by his will. If he is **the God of Jews only**—or of **Gentiles,** for that matter—something of such general and universal scope as faith does not apply. God's universal mercy is one of those far-reaching affirmations of belief to which we give an easy and uncritical assent. We realize that it must follow from our acceptance of monotheism. If there is only one God, and his interest is limited to certain races alone, the rest are banished beyond the range of his care. Any such belief would be fatal to a high spiritual religion, and would enthrone a monstrous favoritism at the heart of the universe.

In Paul's case the problem was complicated by other facts, just as undeniable, which created problems for some people. God had revealed his purpose through one special race. That might be inexplicable, but it was true: it was the way he chose to work. The most sensitive minds in Jewry came to see that their special favors must be the means by which God would ultimately bring his truth to all men. But it was hard to claim special prerogatives without making them exclusive. That is what many of Paul's Jewish contemporaries had done. He himself asserted that salvation is of the Jews—that was the channel through which it came—but the crowning act of that disclosure was such that no man could claim a special privilege in what God had done for him.

The process of revelation has reached its climax in the Cross, and this is not a special way of dealing with the needs of any single race. It does not appeal to a man because of anything that sets him apart from anybody else. Sin was not a problem of the Jews alone; it is the problem of everyone. Hence Paul claims that the Cross is a way of dealing with sin; but sin, as he has been at great pains to prove, is universal; therefore the message which tells of our deliverance must be universal too. Moreover, the Cross is not intelligible only to certain people. It is not necessary to acquire, as a prerequisite, a grasp of the thought or traditions of any race or people. We apprehend its meaning because its appeal is a universal appeal.

This much most of us are prepared to admit; but common experience teaches us how easily we depart from it as a standard of life and

30 Seeing *it is* one God, which shall justify the circumcision by faith, and uncircumcision through faith.
31 Do we then make void the law through faith? God forbid: yea, we establish the law.

tiles also, 30 since God is one; and he will justify the circumcised on the ground of their faith and the uncircumcised because of their faith. 31 Do we then overthrow the law by this faith? By no means! On the contrary, we uphold the law.

the God of the Gentile as well as of the Jew, the ground of justification can hardly lie in these special possessions of the Jew. That ground must be universal. Thus because **God is one,** we must see that **he will justify the circumcised on the ground of their faith and the uncircumcised because of their faith.**

B. This Justification the Fulfillment of the Old Covenant (3:31–4:25)

This long passage is a digression, but a digression which in some measure advances the argument. The point Paul has just made in vss. 21-30 is too important to be left without additional emphasis, if not also further elaboration and clarification; and these paragraphs about the old covenant and Abraham's faith fill this need. That this excursus is not merely an excursus will be clear if the reader tries to omit it and to move directly from 3:30 to 5:1. The passage serves both as an illustration of what is meant by justification by faith and as a further comment on the perplexing question, so close to Paul's attention throughout this epistle, of the relation of the new covenant to the old, and of the position of the Jew in relation to Christ.

31. It is this second interest which dominates the passage, as Paul's way of launching the discussion indicates: **Do we then overthrow the law by this faith? By no means! On the contrary, we uphold the law.** Here **by no means!** is the RSV way of translating a

thought. Most of us retain some sort of "most favored nation clause" in our minds. Unconsciously we prefer white people to dark (or vice versa), or those who speak English to those who use some other language. The church is dangerously apt to acquiesce in the processes which in many places restrict it to the middle or upper strata of society. Our congregations are full of people who frankly declare that they are in favor of the good news for those in their own land but not for anyone abroad; their religious enthusiasm can be stretched to include home missions but no more. They believe that God is **the God of Jews only**—of the favored group to which they themselves happen to belong.

30. ***God's Unity, the Ground of Hope for Universal Salvation.***—The final ground for Paul's doctrine of grace for all is the conviction that **God is one.** Unless that is true, there is no use arguing from the Cross, because all the beliefs which Christ inspires are valid only if they are a disclosure of the one, eternal, omnipotent God. If there is no unity of meaning and purpose at the heart of things, we may as well abandon any effort to interpret the strange world in which we live. Paul's gospel assumes the unity of God and the universality of his rule; it declares that the purpose behind all things is made apparent in a series of events in time; in these it finds the secret of God's method of dealing with men, to bring them into fellowship with himself. That method is the same for all: Jew and Gentile alike are treated as no longer guilty because they accept in simple gratitude what God has done for them. What faith means, and the truth to which they respond, have been set forth with care in the preceding section of Paul's letter. So the Jew, who might expect his circumcision to count, will be accepted because he believes, and the Gentile will be accepted too, though he can plead nothing except the fact that he believes.

31. ***The New Insight Is the Fulfillment of the Ancient Hope.***—Paul has advanced a revolutionary principle, but he is eager to show that it will not prove destructive in its effect. It is intolerable to suggest that justification by faith repudiates everything that has gone before. It is apparent that here he is speaking not of the law as a principle nor of the content of the legal code of Judaism, but of the whole religious heritage of Israel (cf. Exeg.). The tradition which the Scriptures enshrined and transmitted, the insights and the understanding that had come through centuries of discipline—these were not things to be lightly relinquished. This is not the first time Paul has mentioned this

4 What shall we say then that Abraham our father, as pertaining to the flesh, hath found?

4 What then shall we say about[e] Abraham, our forefather according to the

[e] Other ancient authorities read *was gained by.*

---

phrase Paul frequently uses, μὴ γένοιτο. The phrase literally means "May it not be so!" and it usually conveys not only an emphatically negative answer to the question or suggestion that precedes it, but also Paul's sense of the intolerableness of any other answer.

The word **law** (νόμος) is used by Paul in various ways. It can mean what we would express by some such term as "principle"—i.e., the characteristic structure or constitutive pattern of some reality or experience. The word has this meaning in 3:27 (cf. KJV and RSV). Much more often it refers to the moral law, the commandments of God, known in some degree by the Gentiles, but in a pre-eminent measure disclosed to the Jews in the Pentateuch and the other scriptures and oral teachings based on them, i.e., in the whole Torah (see article "New Testament Times: I. Palestine," Vol. VII, pp. 109-11). In the present passage the word "law" is apparently used of the Torah in the most inclusive sense, implying promises as well as commandments. It means nothing less than the entire covenant of God with Israel. It is this covenant which, Paul says, his teaching about justification by faith upholds.

4:1-2. As the marginal note in the RSV shows, a textual question arises in connection with this verse. Many MSS read εὑρηκέναι, "to have found," before **"Abraham,"** and others place the same word before **according to the flesh.** The RSV, following B and a few other ancient witnesses, omits the word; the KJV includes it. The context makes the essential meaning of the verse unmistakable, and the difference in reading is therefore not important. Paul imagines an objector referring to **Abraham** as being **justified by works** and thus having **something to boast about.** The apostle's brief answer, **but not before God,** is elliptical but clear. Paul denies both that Abraham had anything to boast of before God and that his justification was by works. It would seem that he is

---

subject, and he now stands on the threshold of a long digression whose purpose is to prove the essential continuity of the new and the old.

It is a point which requires emphasis because Paul's position was open to misconstruction. He claimed that the law, even in its most comprehensive form, was not enough. Something else was necessary. His opponents jumped to the conclusion that he was sweeping all the treasures of Israel into the discard, and it took no great skill in dialectics to show that this was arbitrary and highhanded. That is why Paul recurs so often to the subject. To declare that the old is insufficient is not to pronounce it worthless. To supplement it where necessary is not to abrogate everything that has hitherto brought strength and comfort to men.

Circumstances made the point a particularly urgent one with Paul; and in his own characteristic way he emphasized a truth of very wide importance. Man's progress has been repeatedly retarded by his tendency to honor the new by repudiating the old. It is true in politics—most revolutions offset great gains in one direction by serious losses in another. It is true in the life of the spirit—reformations repossess forgotten truths, but ever and again at the cost of forfeiting values whose importance experience has confirmed. It is true in the realm of thought—the excitement of a new discovery many a time blinds men to the sober worth of insights which represented a genuine, though possibly a partial, apprehension of the truth. To preserve the old, while supplementing it where it is incomplete, is wisdom of a kind which far too often we neglect. We need to learn the art of "blending the old and the new, without desecrating the one or blunting the ardor of the other, so that progress may be tempered with wisdom, and tradition may be an object of respect rather than a cause of frustration."[7] Paul claimed that the new way confirmed and completed the traditions of the old way; the advance consolidated all that was best in man's previous gains. It was preposterous to suggest that faith meant the **overthrow of the law. On the contrary, we uphold the law.**

4:1. ***Father of the Chosen People.***—The question with which Paul opens this chapter is one posed by the Jewish objector. Surely, he says, your argument collapses, because you have not made allowance for a crucial case—that of **Abraham, our forefather according to the flesh.** For a Jew this was more than one example among others. He traced his lineage to Abra-

[7] Princess Elizabeth, speaking at Oxford, May 25, 1948.

2 For if Abraham were justified by works, he hath *whereof* to glory; but not before God.
3 For what saith the Scripture? Abraham believed God, and it was counted unto him for righteousness.

flesh? 2 For if Abraham was justified by
works, he has something to boast about,
but not before God. 3 For what does the
scripture say? "Abraham believed God, and
it was reckoned to him as righteousness."

---

not denying either the fact of Abraham's good works or his right to pre-eminence *among men* on account of them, but is asserting that his favor *with God* was on a different basis—the basis of faith.

The pronoun "our" in **our forefather according to the flesh** is not to be taken as requiring the supposition that the Roman readers of this epistle were Jews (cf. I Cor. 10:1, where the apostle is unquestionably addressing Gentiles). The "our" is best explained by the fact that it appears in a question of an imaginary Jewish objector and is thought of as being addressed primarily to Paul, himself also a Jew, rather than to the Romans. Strack and Billerbeck, in commenting on this passage, find two interesting passages in II Esdras where works and faith are mentioned together. In 9:7 we read of those who in the last times will be saved "by reason of their works or their faith," and in 13:23 of those who have "works, and faith in the Almighty." Paul rules out works altogether as a factor in salvation.

3-8. The whole argument that Abraham was justified by his faith is made to hinge on the quotation of Gen. 15:6. Needless to say, "believed" in the original passage is far from including all that Paul meant by "faith"; but the Greek term is the same—in the

---

ham, and it was through Abraham that the promises were transmitted to all who followed him. What was asserted of him had therefore exceptional importance. What was true of the founder of the line was presumably true also of all his descendants. We know how easily the typical Jew shielded himself against the consequences of his failures by taking refuge behind Abraham's authority (Luke 3:8). By setting the career of Abraham in a true light, Paul could overthrow a false confidence and prove the value and necessity of the way of faith.

2. ***How Was Abraham Justified?***—There is no doubt that Abraham found favor with God. The fact that he received the promises and became the father of the chosen people puts it entirely beyond doubt. The question at issue concerns the way in which he **was justified.** There are only two possible alternatives: he might have been justified by his good works—a possibility which Paul's argument has vehemently attacked—or he might have been justified because of his faith—the only way, according to Paul, in which a man *can* find peace with God. The importance which Paul attached to Abraham, and the consequent significance of this appeal to his example, appear in the deferential way in which his case is considered. Paul does not impetuously brush aside the possibility that Abraham's good works may have determined his standing with God—though Paul's natural vehemence and the trend of his argument would encourage us to expect as much. Logic would have insisted that "since all have sinned" (3:23), Abraham had sinned, that since "no human being will be justified in his sight by the works of the law" (3:20), Abraham cannot be an exception. But reverence manifests a deference which logic does not know. So Paul does not push the father of the faithful back into the ruck of sinful humanity. The point is worth noting. Sometimes in the heat of argument Paul can press his antagonists with remorseless insistence, but he does not lose the deference which a great tradition demands. He is prepared to concede as much to Abraham as possible—far more than the trend of his argument would strictly allow. Paul was a man of religious reticence and restraint, and we are misled by the superficial marks of his controversial methods if we mistake him for a logic-chopping Philistine. But he makes clear the limits of the concession he has just granted. Even assuming that **Abraham was justified by works,** the grounds of his confidence do not extend to his relations with God. He might expect honor from men, and he might receive it, but that is a different matter from having **something to boast about . . . before God.** Even the exceptional man, says Paul, cannot claim merit in the presence of God.

3-5. ***A Righteous Man, Because a Man of Faith.***—The claim which Paul has just made strikes at the foundation of the whole Pharisaic

4 Now to him that worketh is the reward not reckoned of grace, but of debt.

5 But to him that worketh not, but believeth on him that justifieth the ungodly, his faith is counted for righteousness.

6 Even as David also describeth the blessedness of the man, unto whom God imputeth righteousness without works,

4 Now to one who works, his wages are no
reckoned as a gift but as his due. 5 And to
one who does not work but trusts him who
justifies the ungodly, his faith is reckoned
as righteousness. 6 So also David pronounces
a blessing upon the man to whom God
reckons righteousness apart from works:

LXX, of course, which Paul customarily used—and Paul's use of the passage involves no major distortion of its significance. It is obvious how perfectly the passage suits his polemical purpose—asserting as it does the virtual equivalence of faith and righteous

---

system of acquired righteousness. With a stroke of real controversial brilliance, therefore, he undertakes to prove his point from the law itself. His quotation (from Gen. 15:6 LXX) admirably serves his purpose (cf. Exeg.) because of its equation of faith with righteousness. **Abraham believed God**—that, and nothing he had done, was the reason why he was accounted a righteous man. The salient point throughout the discussion of Abraham is his faith: against all probability he believed. But the passage, as the commentators all remind us, is one which had received a great deal of attention from Jewish teachers (cf. I Macc. 2:52; Ecclus. 44:19-20; cf. also Apocalypse of Baruch 57:2), and their treatment did not always agree with that of Paul. If the law was of such crucial importance, how could Abraham have kept it when he lived centuries before it was given? The accepted rabbinical explanation was that all the patriarchs kept the law by anticipation (cf. Ecclus. 44:20-21 on Abraham: He "kept the law of the most High, and was taken into covenant with him. . . . Therefore he assured him by an oath, that the nations should be blessed in his seed"). The notable feature of Abraham's life, according to the official Jewish view, was his unswerving obedience to God's will, e.g., in the "sacrifice of Isaac," and the conviction had grown that he had been justified on the ground of good works. But Abraham was the typical example of the justified man. Paul is consequently attacking a point of crucial importance.

The character of the prevalent view, with its assumption that faith amounted to a work of merit, made it insufficient for Paul to equate righteousness with faith, and so he proceeds to labor his point by insisting on the significance of the word **reckoned** (vss. 4-5). The term is one which comes from the counting house. Bookkeeping more than once provides biblical writers with imagery to serve their purposes (cf. Mal. 3:16; Esth. 6:1; Dan. 7:10; Rev. 20:12). Here the metaphor reminds us that a person's account may be credited with an asset which he has not fully earned. Daily experience teaches us how widely a gift differs from a wage. A man is entitled to what he has worked for; he expects his wages as a right, and their payment is not a gift. Grace does not enter into the matter at all. A **gift** is something which has not been earned. So, when righteousness is credited to a man on account of faith, it is not because he has earned it. By refusing to rely on good works, he can wholly trust him who **justifies the ungodly.** For a moment the case of Abraham has slipped into the background and Paul indicates what God is able to do for the person who cannot advance a plea for being justified on the ground of what he has done. Even the ungodly man, if he trusts unreservedly in God, finds that **his faith is reckoned as righteousness.**

6-8. ***Blessed Are the Justified.***—The natural association of ideas leads from the ungodly man whom Paul has assured of justification to the ungodly man whom David has described as blessed. Ps. 31:1-2, which Paul quotes, makes no mention of the sinner's deserving the forgiveness which he receives. This explains Paul's comment about **the man to whom God reckons righteousness apart from works.** The psalmist declares that that man has the highest possible kind of happiness **whose iniquities are forgiven and whose sins are covered.** He has sinned, but **the Lord will not reckon his sin.** The argument can be transposed: to say that a man is sinful but is treated as though he were not is the same as to say that he is not righteous but is treated as though he were. When the terms are thus inverted, the relevance of the quotation becomes clear. The intimate connection between justification and forgiveness is important. The two are distinguishable but closely related.

[8] Cf. Dodd, *Epistle of Paul to Romans, ad loc.*

[9] Cf. the detailed discussion in Taylor, *Forgiveness and Reconciliation*, pp. 1-69. But see also Exeg. 5:1–8:39.

7 *Saying,* Blessed *are* they whose iniqui-
ies are forgiven, and whose sins are cov-
red.

7 "Blessed are those whose iniquities are forgiven, and whose sins are covered;

ess and suggesting that Abraham's righteousness was his faith. Paul presses hard the ıeaning of **was reckoned,** making it convey the idea of one's being credited with omething for which one has not paid. This idea lies back of vss. 4-5; on the other hand n vs. 8 the word **reckon** means "charge," and God's grace is manifested in his willingness *ot* to reckon against us the sins we have actually committed. According to the psalmist 32:1-2), that man is **blessed,** not who has committed no iniquity or sin, but **whose iniquities are forgiven, and whose sins are covered.**

aul has been speaking of the man who cannot stablish his merit, yet by grace is set on a footıg of confidence and trust with God. But the ıan who has sinned, and finds that his **sins are overed,** knows that he does not deserve what od's free grace has given him.

Two points connected with the above section vss. 1-8) require further attention. The phrase hich Paul uses in vs. 5 about God "who justies the ungodly" is not merely central to this articular passage, but it is an epitome of the ospel which Paul preached. There is no good ews which does not proclaim the truth about od. Anything less than that can offer us only ıomentary comfort or a temporary respite. ince there is nothing before God or beyond im, nothing concerns us so much as his attitude oward us. But the more aware we are of his oliness, the more conscious we are of our own nworthiness. If there is any spiritual reality in ur faith, there is no room in our minds for omplacency about our moral state. That is hy a religion which declares that God can roperly pronounce to be just only those who re actually just leaves men face to face with desperate alternative. Those who have keen ısight or a sensitive conscience are thrown into espair because they know they are not just nd realize they never will be; those who ersuade themselves that they can meet the reuired standard of uprightness succumb to the emptations which always beset people who elieve in the sufficiency of their own efforts. harisaism was the form in which the second lternative expressed itself in Paul's day; under different guise it always reappears when Chrisanity is reduced to the status of a movement hose aim is ethical self-culture. The gospel as aul preached it had nothing to do with our laims or pretensions; it leaves us confronting ıe paradox of God's treating the unjust as ıough they were just. That paradox becomes a roblem when we insist on dealing with it in n external and legal way, because law takes ccount only of deeds. Law knows nothing of the secret places of the heart, where penitence is born, where a new loyalty enters to change the future direction of a life, where a new obedience begins to reshape a character. It knows nothing of faith. But even in the light of Paul's declaration in 3:21-30—even in the light of the great affirmations in chs. 5 and 8—this justification of the ungodly remains a miracle. It is something, that is to say, which remains unintelligible unless God's power is recognized as present to perform what by our own resources we could never do.

The apostle is not speaking, of course, of the way in which men are finally accepted by God. The chasm which divides men from God is bridged by faith—there is no other way; but once on the other side, men are expected to prove the quality of their faith by the character of their conduct. This was the matter which James was so deeply concerned to establish, and to prove his point he appealed to the very text which Paul has also used—Gen. 15:6. The apparent contradiction between Rom. 4:2-5 and Jas. 2:21-23 is due to different ways of defining the same words. To James "faith" means orthodox belief, and "works" moral obedience to the holy will of God. "Faith alone," according to James's interpretation, is not very different from "works alone," as Paul understood them. The difference in language is no doubt explained by the different environment in which the two men lived, and it is possible to contend that both were attacking the same thing—a lifeless formalism in religion. Paul, however, carries the question further than James. If an inert orthodoxy, whether of belief or conduct, is excluded, how does obedience to the will of God arise? Paul's answer is clear: the root of the moral life is the new relationship of trust to God; and that is what he calls "faith."

He is not, of course, giving here a complete account of the Christian life. That must be pieced together from many passages, and when we have collected all the evidence, we are left with no shadow of doubt that Paul expected the

8 Blessed *is* the man to whom the Lord will not impute sin.
9 *Cometh* this blessedness then upon the circumsion *only*, or upon the uncircumcision also? for we say that faith was reckoned to Abraham for righteousness.

8 blessed is the man against whom the
Lord will not reckon his sin."
9 Is this blessing pronounced only upon the circumcised, or also upon the uncircumcised? We say that faith was reckoned

9-11*a*. Paul's opponent might urge, however, that this promise of forgiveness and this pronouncement of blessedness upon the forgiven are offered only to those who belong to the Jewish nation—has not Paul himself said (3:19) that "whatever the law says it speaks to those who are under the law"? To meet this objection Paul points out

Christian to bring forth the fruit of a sound moral life. He is here concerned with the prior question of how the Christian life ever begins. If sin is universal, as he has shown, and if sin cuts us off from God, as he knew, how can a man ever achieve that right relationship with God which will make it possible for him to walk uprightly? The new life, says Paul, begins when man, believing God's word of hope, commits himself in self-surrendering trust to all that he has learned of God's mercy. What he himself has done counts for nothing.

Paul was suggesting one outlook and condemning another. We have seen more than once that Pharisaism is not an attitude whose manifestations were restricted to one age or place. It represents a spirit which continually reasserts itself, even in the best-regulated congregations. It suggests to people the sufficiency of conforming to the conventions of their country or their class. When they have done what they believe is expected of them, they rest content with the small measure of their achievement. The results are a dull respectability or a lifeless formalism. People acquiesce in the mores of their denomination or their group, and the consequences are intellectual and spiritual stagnation. There can be no other possible result. "Going about to establish their own righteousness, [they] have not submitted themselves unto the righteousness of God" (10:3). The evil effects of this attitude are clearly seen in the Pharisees whom Jesus rebuked. They had a false attitude toward God. They began by believing that they could win his favor and deserve a reward; they ended by believing in a God who could be dealt with in their way. There crept into all their relations with God a calculating adjustment of their own merit which made it impossible for them to regard him as their father. The value which they placed on the things they themselves had done left them finally with the illusion that they were independent of God. If a man ever deceives himself into believing that he can satisfy God's demands upon him, and so be immune to further claims, he has discarded that creaturely attitude which remembers that he is always and wholly dependent on God. Because legalism induces a false conception of our relationship to God, it fosters a false attitude to ourselves and to others. It hides the seriousness of sin, and persuades people that their ills can be removed by such expedients as they themselves devise. Inevitably it produces a superior attitude toward others. Those who act differently deserve condemnation and contempt, and superiority strangles charity.[1] Moreover, all outside the favored circle are abandoned as beyond hope.

9-12. *Circumcision: Outward Sign and Inner Reality*.—Paul's treatment of circumcision as a . . . **seal of the righteousness which he** [Abraham] **had by faith,** serves admirably to set all external rites in their proper place. The Jews insisted on circumcision with a fierce fanaticism, and it became the distinguishing mark which divided them from all other peoples. Paul, by making it subsidiary to faith, places it in a subordinate position as far as its importance is concerned, and strikes directly at the exclusiveness which debarred others from sharing in the covenant of God. In a world where some things are material and others are spiritual, we need signs or seals if we are to maintain a proper balance between the things which can be seen and handled and those which cannot. Signs prevent religious truths from evaporating into abstract unreality; they keep the things that are of greatest importance firmly rooted in our common life and intimately related to all the elements of our ordinary experience. Signs show forth and maintain an essential relationship between two kinds of reality, and constantly remind us that this relationship exists. They also serve as a visible confirmation of what otherwise is often no more than an intangible hope. In the history of religious development "seal" is an important word because it suggests the

[1] On the pharisaical attitude which Jesus condemned cf. C. A. Scott, *Dominus Noster*, pp. 37-40.

10 How was it then reckoned? when he was in circumcision, or in uncircumcision? Not in circumcision, but in uncircumcision.

11 And he received the sign of circumcision, a seal of the righteousness of the faith which *he had yet* being uncircumcised: that he might be the father of all them that believe, though they be not circumcised; that righteousness might be imputed unto them also:

12 And the father of circumcision to them who are not of the circumcision only, but who also walk in the steps of that faith of our father Abraham, which *he had* being *yet* uncircumcised.

to Abraham as righteousness. 10 How then
was it reckoned to him? Was it before or
after he had been circumcised? It was not
after, but before he was circumcised. 11 He
received circumcision as a sign or seal of
the righteousness which he had by faith
while he was still uncircumcised. The purpose was to make him the father of all who
believe without being circumcised and who
thus have righteousness reckoned to them,
12 and likewise the father of the circumcised who are not merely circumcised but
also follow the example of the faith which
our father Abraham had before he was
circumcised.

that the "reckoning" of Gen. 15:6 took place not after Abraham's circumcision, but before. It is not till Gen. 17:11 that the account of the institution of circumcision and of Abraham's own circumcision is found. Dodd writes appropriately: "The Old Testament critic might put the point differently: the early-prophetic stories of Abraham know nothing of his circumcision, which is mentioned in the late priestly document." Thus the covenant of God with Abraham, described in Gen. 15, cannot be thought of as involving adherence to the Jewish law or to the requirement of circumcision when it actually antedated circumcision and the law. **Circumcision** was given **as a sign or seal of the righteousness which he had by faith while he was still uncircumcised.**

11*b*-12. In this way the door is opened to a fresh interpretation of the "fatherhood" of Abraham. He is the **father of all who believe,** whether Jews or not. The translation of the RSV makes the meaning of the passage (obscure in the KJV) thoroughly clear. After reading it, one cannot help asking again the question of 3:1: "What is the value of circumcision?"

confirmation—in terms that people can see and understand—of what God has promised. Consequently it not only reminds, it establishes. It was therefore natural that words which had been used of the rite which outwardly marked the Jew's inclusion in the heritage of Israel should very early have been applied to baptism—the rite by which the Christian's admission to a fuller inheritance was declared.

At the same time it is necessary to remember that these outward signs, because of their representative character, lend themselves to serious distortion. They invite confusion between what is primary and what is secondary. In the present passage Paul's point is that circumcision derives its true significance from the faith which was prior to it. But the sign became confused with the reality, and finally usurped its place. The paramount importance of faith was forgotten because men had become obsessed with the symbol. The same thing can happen, of course, in the experience of any religious community. The peculiarities which distinguish them—whether in worship or in belief—cease to be one form of expressing truths which all religious people hold in common. They become objects of importance in their own right, revered and defended for their own sake. When that happens they have become barriers against others, and the marks of an irreligious exclusiveness.

This is the fate that had overtaken circumcision; the faith behind it should have brought all men together, but the rite given to confirm that faith became in fact the most unyielding barrier to keep them asunder. We may conclude that all outward symbols in religion are significant only if they are kept in the closest relation to the religious reality which originally created them.

11*b*-12. *The Manner of God's Dealing with Men.*—Behind God's dealing with Abraham, Paul sees a clear indication of **the purpose** which he detects in the unfolding of history. Central to it is a certain method of dealing with men. Those who have faith will be received by

13 For the promise, that he should be the heir of the world, *was* not to Abraham, or to his seed, through the law, but through the righteousness of faith.

14 For if they which are of the law *be* heirs, faith is made void, and the promise made of none effect:

15 Because the law worketh wrath: for where no law is, *there is* no transgression.

13 The promise to Abraham and his descendants, that they should inherit the world, did not come through the law but through the righteousness of faith.
14 If it is the adherents of the law who are to be the heirs, faith is null and the promise is void.
15 For the law brings wrath, but where there is no law there is no transgression.

13-15. Likewise **the promise to Abraham and his descendants** was not conditioned upon obedience to the law (although Paul seems to have been looking at the matter somewhat differently in 2:17-25). **If it is the adherents of the law** who are to **inherit the world, . . . faith is null** (since it is not called for) and **the promise is void** (because no one is able to obey the law). **The law** indeed **brings** only **wrath;** it succeeds only in producing **transgression.** This point, already hinted at in 3:20, Paul will discuss more fully later in ch. 7.

God, irrespective of what may appear incidental defects. To overlook the difference established by circumcision is not to ignore essential distinctions, but merely to go behind them to a deeper unity. All men who humbly put their trust in God belong to the family of the faithful, and trace their descent from one common Father. Paul may use a characteristic method, based on an appeal to the letter of Scripture, to prove this, but the purpose of his argument is clear. There is a true unity which is created by genuine faith, and this is not accidental but corresponds to God's intention. From this it follows, of course, that the divisions in which we acquiesce are not always real divisions, but only appear so because of our preoccupation with secondary issues. There is a vital connection, says Paul, between **all who believe.** The crucial case he cites is that of Abraham, and he proves that he is truly the ancestor of all who have faith, whether they are Jews or Gentiles. This also leads to an important inference: "God's method has been the same through all history." [2]

13-14. ***Originally, and Always, by Faith.***—**The promise to Abraham and his descendants** is therefore not restricted to Jews only (cf. vs. 11), and this can be proved on general principles as well as by the kind of historical argument which Paul has just used. If it had been exclusive in character, it would have come by a restrictive means, i.e., **through the law.** Instead, the promise came **through the righteousness of faith.** Paul has already shown that faith was the distinctive quality of Abraham's career, and that he was accounted worthy to receive the promise because he trusted God. He now undertakes to prove that the two methods—law and faith—are not only different but mutually exclusive. **If . . . the adherents of the law** are the only ones who can qualify as heirs, then obviously those who are not strict Jews have no hope. But the "correlative of the promise" was faith; because of faith the promise was given to a man who was still a Gentile, and who was the true forerunner of those who are Jews and of those who are not. So the conclusion remains that if law is necessary, faith is irrelevant; but if faith is sufficient, the law is superfluous. Both law and faith are methods of dealing with the problem created by man's sin; if the promise is associated with the one way, the other must be a mistaken and ineffectual approach to the question.

15. ***The Witness of Experience.***—What can be proved by logic is confirmed by experience. **The law brings wrath** (cf. 1:18), and the inexorable judgment on sin is the exact opposite of everything that "the promise" suggests. Actually the law is responsible even for the sense of sin: **where there is no law there is no transgression.** When the constraint of the commandment is consciously felt, sin is "provoked to opposition . . . and when sin thus becomes conscious defiance, it incurs guilt and deserves punishment." [3] What began as the logical opposition of two ideas ends as the contrast between two realms of spiritual experience. On the one hand we have the world of law, which provokes to disobedience and ends in punishment; on the other we have the world of grace, declared in the promise which is confirmed in response to faith.

[2] Denney, *Expositor's Greek Testament, ad loc.*

[3] A. E. Garvie, *Romans* (New York: Oxford University Press, 1901), *ad loc.*

16 Therefore *it is* of faith, that *it might be* by grace; to the end the promise might be sure to all the seed; not to that only which is of the law, but to that also which is of the faith of Abraham; who is the father of us all,
17 (As it is written, I have made thee a father of many nations,) before him whom he believed, *even* God, who quickeneth the dead, and calleth those things which be not as though they were:

16 That is why it depends on faith, in order that the promise may rest on grace and be guaranteed to all his descendants — not only to the adherents of the law but also to those who share the faith of Abraham, for he is the father of us all, 17 as it is written, "I have made you the father of many nations" — in the presence of the God in whom he believed, who gives life to the dead and calls into existence the

16-17*a*. Again as in vs. 11 (as well as in Gal. 3:6-9) Paul makes the important point that since Abraham's righteousness consisted in his faith, all who have faith are his true descendants. **He is the father of us all**—of Gentiles no less than of Jews. Indeed, it was just because God intended his promises for men of all the nations that he made the fulfillment conditional simply upon faith, and not upon circumcision, which always has for Paul a predominantly racial and national, rather than religious, significance. The statement in Gen. 17:10, **I have made you the father of many nations,** is interpreted as a divine confirmation of the conception of the meaning and purpose of the covenant with Abraham which Paul is here defending.

17*b*. Paul wishes to conclude his digression by bringing the discussion back a little nearer its starting point as well as nearer the point where the next section of his argu-

16. *A Privilege for All, Not the Prerogative of a Few.*—Paul is now free to develop, without fear of further interruption, his thesis that the kind of justification which Abraham exemplifies is open to all alike. The law by its very nature can work only "wrath"; **that is why** the promise depends on faith, so far as our part is concerned, and on **grace,** as concerns God's contribution. Faith and grace are correlative terms. When from God's side comes a merciful favor which we have done nothing to deserve, the only possible response on our part is a humble trust which accepts in gratitude what God has done for us. So it is natural to conclude that if the promise is to **rest on grace,** the relationship which it envisages **depends on faith.** This particular point is inseparable from Paul's position in the widest sense; he now applies it to the specific illustration which he has been discussing—Abraham. In the true sense Abraham is the father of all the faithful, because any who trust in God as he did can claim a part in the same experience of finding peace with God. Those who are **the adherents of the law** could establish an exclusive claim as his descendants only if he had received the promise by following the methods which their rigorous legalism advocates. But Paul has shown more than once that this had not been so, and he now feels free to develop the suggestion of a universal mercy which is latent in his position. All **who share the faith of Abraham** have a part in the promise. This strikes at the root of the old exclusiveness. Paul does not exclude the Jews, but in the light of vs. 12 we may assume that he is only considering those **adherents of the law** who add faith to their good works; it is necessary that they too should find their place, because otherwise the conviction that Abraham is the father of us all would not be substantiated. Behind Paul's words we sense the enthusiasm of one who was brought up in Judaism and is proud of its great traditions, but sees that the hope of Israel is fulfilled in the new community of faith whose frontiers he is helping to extend. Within that community all find their place, not because of any condescending gesture, but as rightful descendants of the forefather of all true believers. In preaching a gospel which accepted no barrier as final, Paul could claim both that he fulfilled the best elements in the faith of Israel, and that he related to the settled purpose of God his belief in the universality of grace. It is not a sentimental generosity which makes the church a world-wide fellowship. Both our inheritance and our understanding of God's will allow us no alternative.

17. *Confirmation from the Scriptures.*—Paul quotes the words of Scripture to confirm his point. He may not be using **many nations** in the sense originally intended by the ancient writer, but the verse serves his purpose well

18 Who against hope believed in hope, that he might become the father of many nations, according to that which was spoken, So shall thy seed be.

19 And being not weak in faith, he considered not his own body now dead, when he was about a hundred years old, neither yet the deadness of Sarah's womb:

things that do not exist. 18 In hope he believed against hope, that he should become the father of many nations; as he had been told, "So shall your descendants be." 19 He did not weaken in faith when he considered his own body, which was as good as dead because he was about a hundred years old, or when he considered the barrenness

ment (5:1–8:39) must begin. He initiates this transition by alluding to **the God in whom** [Abraham] **believed** as giving **life to the dead** and calling **into existence the things that do not exist.** Such a description is intended to remind the reader not only of Isaac's birth "from one . . . as good as dead" (Heb. 11:12), but also of Christ's resurrection from the dead—as well as, perhaps, the marvel of the new life found within the Christian community.

18-22. Paul now describes the character of Abraham's faith in such a way as to bring it into line with the meaning of faith for Paul himself. **In hope he believed against hope;** i.e., there was no real ground for either faith or hope in himself. He was **about a hundred years old; his own body . . . was as good as dead;** and Sarah his wife was barren. Notice that the RSV reads that *although* he considered these things, he *still* believed, whereas the KJV seems to say that he did *not* consider these things and *therefore* believed. This difference rests upon a difference in the MS texts. The RSV reading, which omits the "not," is preferred; but the real sense of the passage is the same in either case. In spite of the fact that Abraham could have had no confidence in his own powers, he nevertheless trusted God implicitly, who had said, "Look now toward heaven, and tell

enough. But more important than what anyone said about Abraham is the conviction that he holds this standing **in the presence of . . . God** as well as in the judgment of men. The role historically assigned to him is that which eternally he possesses. The growth of a critical understanding of the Bible makes it easy for us to divide its contents sharply into two divisions of whose unity we are imperfectly aware. By implication rather than by explicit statement, Paul indicates that the God of Abraham is the God in whom Christians also believe. Abraham too trusted in a God **who gives life to the dead and calls into existence the things that do not exist.** The verse invites development, and three possible points are suggested in the Exeg.—the direct reference to Isaac and his birth; the indirect suggestion of Christ's resurrection, and the implied transformation of the individual Christian. In each case the final result is in direct opposition to our initial estimate of what is possible; in each case, also, only the power of God could accomplish things that are impossible in the eyes of men; in each case what is achieved is a standing marvel in our sight. Moreover, it is the improbable things which God does that increase man's joy and enrich his life beyond anything that our carefully devised predictions could claim to hold in store for us. It is quite possible, of course, to prove that the God in whom Abraham believed was a very different God from the Father of our Lord Jesus Christ. But when we have dismissed with a superior gesture "the primitive tribal deity of a clan of Semitic nomads," we have overlooked the important fact that though there is a difference, there is continuity, and the secret of the growth in understanding is the fact that God could reveal himself with increasing clarity to men who had precisely this quality of faith —the quality which Paul regards as crucial in Abraham's case.

18-19. ***Examination of the Prototype.***—Since Abraham's faith is so important, Paul describes it in greater detail. It was contrary to **hope,** yet it rested on **hope.** So far as nature could inspire hope, Abraham had none; but because he trusted in God's promise, **he believed.** He had been assured that it was the divine purpose that from him should spring many peoples, that his descendants should be as the stars of heaven in number (Gen. 15:5). But apparently the most important facts in the situation were his own great age and the sterility of his wife. He **considered** these, but **did not weaken in faith.** For many well-disposed people faith means nothing more than a comfortable means of ignoring the unpleasant. They rule out disagree-

20 He staggered not at the promise of God through unbelief; but was strong in faith, giving glory to God;

21 And being fully persuaded, that what he had promised, he was able also to perform.

of Sarah's womb. 20 No distrust made him waver concerning the promise of God, but he grew strong in his faith as he gave glory to God, 21 fully convinced that God was

---

the stars, if thou be able to number them. . . . **So shall thy seed be." No distrust made him waver, . . . but he grew strong in his faith.**

This story of Abraham suits the purpose of the writer to the Hebrews, with his somewhat different idea of faith, better perhaps than the purpose of Paul (see Heb. 11:8-12, and also above on 1:17) ; but obviously both N.T. writers read much more into the story than it was intended to carry. Still, there can be no question that the Pauline emphasis upon humble trust in God's mercy and power, as distinguished from reliance on good works, is in line with the deepest element in Hebrew-Jewish life and thought, and that the attitude of the Pharisee in Jesus' parable (Luke 18:9-14) is as false to the true spirit of Judaism as it is to Christ's own teaching or to the gospel of Paul. Thus, although it

---

able realities, and somehow persuade themselves that they are thereby showing a particularly religious attitude. But real faith neither shrinks from the truth, nor, when it proves unpalatable, permits such unwelcome truth to undermine its constancy. This is something as different from stoic fortitude as it is from escapist sentimentalism. It rests on an assurance that among other relevant facts, God's will counts as one. He is able to work his will by means of either promising or unpromising instruments, and even the things that apparently frustrate his purpose can be made to serve his ends.

20-21. ***Beyond Doubt to Strong Conviction.***— There were times, as the account in Genesis assures us, when **distrust** entered Abraham's mind (Gen. 17:7), but this did not make **him waver concerning the promise of God.** The exemplar of faith is not above doubt, but the constancy of his trust in God remains unshaken. The truest faith is not necessarily the kind which never admits a question. The man who feels the assaults of disbelief but keeps inviolate the citadel of his inner confidence in God has discovered for himself the meaning of the prayer, "Lord, I believe; help thou mine unbelief" (Mark 9:24). This is the kind of strength which grows strong. The clause **he grew strong in his faith** is open, the commentators assure us, to more than one interpretation. Because of the parallel treatment of Abraham's case in Heb. 11:11-12, some have suggested that Paul also is assuring us that it was due to the strength which faith gives that an old man was able to beget a son. The more obvious meaning, and apparently the one favored by the RSV, points to the consequences which follow when faith is tested by the assaults of distrust, but overcomes them. Belief which never questions is not necessarily the strongest kind of faith. "There lives more faith in honest doubt . . . "—but more still in the conviction which has faced uncertainties and triumphed over them. The whole aim of Abraham's life was to give **glory to God.** It was his constancy, even when every ordinary consideration would have prompted him to abandon his faith, which notably reflected his desire in all things to promote only God's glory. Actually, none but those who are guided by such a purpose are likely to find their faith confirmed. A man who seeks some lesser aim—his own interest or advancement, or the establishment of his own reputation—will necessarily forfeit that confirmation which God can give to the faith of those who with singleness of purpose strive to set forth his glory. The foundation of this kind of faith—a faith unshaken by opposing forces, increasing in strength as it pursues its true objectives—is a conviction concerning God and his power. In one sense we might regard a belief **that God was able to do what he had promised** as inseparable from faith in God. If he is what we declare him to be—omnipotent and utterly righteous—his promises will fail neither because he forgets nor because his power falters. But most of us keep at the back of our minds an unexorcised suspicion that all we say about God's power is not literally true. For all our lip service about trust in God, we rely chiefly upon what we can do ourselves. Unfortunately this is not because we have learned that religious dependence has moral independence as its correlative; it is due merely to the fact that we are not **fully convinced.** Usually the cause lies in our unwillingness ever

22 And therefore it was imputed to him for righteousness.

23 Now it was not written for his sake alone, that it was imputed to him;

24 But for us also, to whom it shall be imputed, if we believe on him that raised up Jesus our Lord from the dead;

able to do what he had promised.
22 That is why his faith was "reckoned to him as righteousness."
23 But the words, "it was reckoned to him," were written not for his sake alone,
24 but for ours also. It will be reckoned to us who believe in him that

---

must be agreed that Paul has made a somewhat artificial use of Gen. 15:6, the example of Abraham is not without validity and relevance. More will be said both of Paul's use of scripture and of the continuity of the new covenant with the old when we come to chs. 9–11.

23-24. It is undoubtedly artificial, however, to make a specific connection between Abraham's faith in the God who brought life out of the patriarch's own "dead" body and the Christian community's faith in him who brought again **from the dead Jesus our Lord**—a connection already hinted at in vs. 17.

---

to commit our lives into the hands of God in trust: we have not learned what religious dependence means. Our instinct is to rely on our own powers, and when they show signs of insufficiency, to throw ourselves despairingly upon God. Then we claim the literal fulfillment of the promises in which we never more than half believed. In this respect the contrast with Abraham is complete.

22. *The Life to Which Faith Leads.*—This verse is an epitome of the preceding section (vss. 16-21). Paul has described the kind of attitude on man's part which makes it possible for him to be admitted to "peace with God." He has shown us Abraham, who knew that he himself lacked the strength to assure his line of the glorious future which God had foretold, yet trusted implicitly in God's promise, and refused to question God's power to accomplish what he purposed. But essentially this is the only attitude which is open to a truly religious man. If he realizes his own insufficiency, and sees that neither his own worth nor his own efforts can win him an enduring future, yet trusts in God and casts himself upon his resources, then his relationship with God is what it ought to be. It opens the way for wholly new possibilities in the life of the Spirit. Paul has been pressing on his readers the necessity of a certain attitude toward God. The example he uses is Abraham, but the application is to members of the Christian church.

We can note, then, that Paul is describing a certain method of justification. It is the way in which God deals with all faithful souls. It is applied to those who lived under the old dispensation as well as to those who live under the new. The human problem had become infinitely aggravated since Abraham's day, because law had entered and obscured the necessity of faith. Christ has now made clear to all what legalism had so completely hidden. Paul does not suggest that Abraham had advantages equal to those which belong to the disciple of Christ. What was possible of old for a figure of heroic strength and steadfastness is now possible for ordinary men. What was dimly grasped is now fully declared. But Paul does suggest that there is a continuity in God's dealing with his children. Christ's coming does not abrogate the faith by which Abraham lived; it extends it and confirms it. It makes clear its true grounds and gives it a firmer assurance. But faith remains the attitude of trust by which we commit ourselves to God in dependence on his promises.

23-25. *The Significance of Abraham's Example.*—Consequently, in concluding this digression on Abraham, Paul can apply its meaning directly to the Christians to whom he writes. He quotes the scriptural formula about Abraham's faith which was "reckoned to him as righteousness," and affirms that it speaks not merely of Abraham's situation but of ours. Paul is not attempting the pious expedient of making everything that sounds edifying seem relevant to the reader's own situation. He has carefully proved the nature of the justification which brought the forefather—and so, by inference, those who faithfully follow him—into a new relationship with God. The universal scope of the argument makes its conclusion applicable to everyone who fulfills the one necessary condition: having faith. But by pointing to a further parallel, Paul makes it still more apparent that this is not an arbitrary "sermonic" device. Abraham believed implicitly in God, in a God who showed his power by bringing life out of

25 Who was delivered for our offenses, and was raised again for our justification.

raised from the dead Jesus our Lord, 25 who was put to death for our trespasses and raised for our justification.

25. This statement, with its implied distinction between Jesus as **put to death for our trespasses** and Jesus as **raised for our justification,** is more than a rhetorical way of saying, as Dodd suggests: "He died and rose again in order that we might be delivered from the guilt of our sins." To be sure, Paul thinks of the Death and the Resurrection in the closest possible connection; the Death without the Resurrection would be meaningless, just as the Resurrection without the Death would be inconceivable. Still, almost certainly the Death of Christ would have reminded him more vividly of our sins, and the Resurrection of the forgiveness for which Christ has provided both the means and the way.

death. Abraham knew that his body "was as good as dead" (vs. 19); in spite of that, God gave him a son to inherit the promise. Christians also believe in a God who is able to bring life out of death: he "brought again from the dead our Lord Jesus" (Heb. 13:20). For all the superficial similarity, however (see Exeg.), observe the profound difference. As we noted a moment ago, Paul declares that what is found imperfectly in Abraham is expanded and amplified by what Christ has done. Abraham trusted in a God who showed his power; so do Christians, but that power is now seen directed toward a particular purpose. It is manifested in **Jesus our Lord, who was put to death for our trespasses and raised for our justification.** The appeal to the Resurrection consequently shows God's power active to achieve the redemption of man. Because of what Christ's death and resurrection declare, we believe that there is a new means of deliverance from the sin which held us bound, and a firm assurance of a new relationship with God. In that relationship we shall have the end of the fears and frustrations which mark the lives of those whose understanding always outstrips their performance. Paul has consequently prepared the way for a natural resumption of the main thread of his argument, but before turning to consider the "peace with God," which is the consequence of being justified, we should briefly examine two or three questions arising from ch. 4.

(*a*) Abraham's faith has been given a special prominence, in keeping with Paul's own background and his immediate purpose. He has shown that Abraham possessed the kind of faith that justifies men—and will justify Christians too. In its essence it means forsaking all reliance on what we can do by and for ourselves and taking God at his word. This means the discovery that in obedience to God our life comes more and more nearly into correspondence with what we understand of the divine purpose. Such faith is not perfect in itself. The mark of Abraham's experience was that discipline taught him more and more of what God designed to do for him—and of what God required of him. In Paul too we find that faith is never regarded as a static thing, perfect when once achieved. It lives and grows; it is always "from faith to faith." Though Paul has not developed this thought as fully in the present chapter as elsewhere, it is nevertheless apparent that he had no intention of suggesting that the possession of faith could be reconciled with remaining as we are.

(*b*) The chapter is a study of the way in which things apparently improbable prove more unassailable than the things which come within the scope of our ordinary expectations. We begin with the grounds of despair—enumerated in Abraham's case, clear to each of us as concerns our own situation. In spite of this we have reason for hope—God's purpose has been declared, and we can trust in his ability to perform what he has promised (vs. 21). The substance of the promise is that God can give life to things dead in themselves, and can call into existence the things that do not exist (vs. 17). The guarantee of the promise is the fact that God **raised from the dead Jesus our Lord** (vs. 24). The relevance of Christ's resurrection to our lives is declared in 6:4, "So that as Christ was raised from the dead by the glory of the Father, we too might walk in newness of life." Beyond this amazing fact is yet another: not only was Christ raised from the dead, but the purpose of his death was the forgiveness of our sins. But as his death and resurrection are inseparably linked in N.T. thought, so our forgiveness is always connected with that to which it admits us—**our justification** (vs. 25).

5 Therefore being justified by faith, we have peace with God through our Lord Jesus Christ:

5 Therefore, since we are justified by faith, we[f] have peace with God through

[f] Other ancient authorities read *let us*.

IV. The New Life into Which This Justifying Act Admits the Believer (5:1–8:39)

This section of Romans has already been described as the most important section of the letter, if not of all Paul's correspondence (see above, p. 371). It is doubtful that anyone will wish to take issue with such a statement. Up to this point Paul has been concerned with justification—the need for it (1:18–3:20) and the ground of it in God's action in Christ to be received in faith (3:21–4:25). But justification, for all its importance, is preliminary. It is the door to salvation—the entrance to that new order of relationships, that new community of men and God, in which are life and peace. It may well be true that there is something unreal about this distinction between justification and the new life of love, faith, and hope—certainly many a reader of Paul will feel that there is. Forgiveness, one may well object, *is* this new life, or at any rate an integral feature of it—not just the door to it. One does not receive the new life because, and after, one has been forgiven; rather the meaning of forgiveness itself is the restoration of that fellowship, whether with God or (at a subordinate level) with one another, in which are rest and resource. But though this may be said of "forgiveness," it is less obviously true of "justification." "Forgiveness" is a more inclusive term, and of a different order. "Justification" is abstract; "forgiveness," concrete. "Justification" denotes a status before God; "forgiveness," a relationship with him. Justification is legal, forensic; forgiveness is essentially and richly personal. But "justification" rather than "forgiveness" is, for whatever reason, Paul's characteristic term; and justification is hardly more than the prerequisite or presupposition of that communion, that sharing with and in God, which is the Christian life itself. Thus Paul has been able to discuss justification as separable, at least in idea, from the rich empirical meaning of what he often calls "being in Christ." To the description and interpretation of that meaning he now turns his attention.

This section of four chapters is difficult to outline. It is impossible to discover any consistent logic running through the whole and nicely accounting for the sequences of sentences and paragraphs. The section obviously begins with the fact of justification by faith (5:1) and ends (8:39) with a shout of triumph and invincible hope because of the reality and the presence of "the love of God," and there is a general consistency of direction as the apostle moves from the one point to the other. But the path is not absolutely straight, and there are many digressions. It seems best to consider the material of these four chapters under a series of topics, all clearly belonging to the main theme of the section, but to make no attempt at tracing a coherent logical movement from topic to topic.

A. Summary of the Character and Qualities of the New Life (5:1-5)

5:1. The close connection between the beginning of this section and the end of the previous one is indicated more effectively in the Greek than in the English. The last verse of ch. 4 ends with the phrase "our justification" and 5:1 begins with the participle

5:1-11. ***What Justification Means in Terms of a New Life.***—The section does not merely describe the blessings which follow from justification but states the central theme of the whole passage 5:1–8:39. The man who receives a new standing in God's sight discovers that a new life opens before him, a life marked by an increasing appropriation of what God's mercy offers (vss. 1-5) and inseparably related to what God has done for us in Jesus Christ (vss. 6-11).

1. ***Peace with God.***—**Therefore** suggests an immediate connection with the final verse of the preceding chapter and verbal similarities seem to confirm it (cf. Exeg.), but it is related more

"having been justified." The point is that with the beginning of ch. 5 justification is regarded as an accomplished fact, and we are moving on to a consideration of its implications and consequences.

The first of these is **peace with God through our Lord Jesus Christ.** Something has already been said about the meaning of **peace** in the Exeg. of 1:7, where this word also appears. It means not only a cessation of hostility, or the state following upon a cessation of hostility, but also a positive condition of creative harmony, what is soon (vs. 10) to be called "reconciliation." Because the **peace is with God,** it means harmony also with our total environment—since God is the Creator and Ruler—and therefore inner security and serenity. The word occurs frequently in the O.T., especially in the Psalms, with a meaning not dissimilar to that of Paul (see Pss. 29:11; 85:8, 10; 119:165); but this meaning, essentially the same in the formal sense, now involves all that has come to be known of God's goodness within the Christian community—i.e., **through our Lord Jesus Christ**—and is therefore, in concrete fact, something fresh and new. Paul calls it elsewhere "the peace . . . which passeth all understanding" (Phil. 4:7).

A major problem of text appears at this point. Did Paul write **we have peace** (ἔχομεν) or "let us have peace" (ἔχωμεν)? Both forms of the verb appear in MSS. The decision between them is difficult because what we know of Paul's thought in general, and what is indicated by the context of this verse in particular, would both suggest **we have peace** as the correct reading, whereas the textual evidence is strongly on the side of the alternative. "Peace" or "reconciliation," as Paul thinks of it, would appear to be not something to be achieved or obtained, but something that follows inevitably upon our appropriation through faith of God's justifying act in Christ (see, e.g., vs. 11*b*). But although it is undoubtedly true that the indicative form of the verb (i.e., "we have") seems more natural, if not indeed requisite, nevertheless it cannot be denied that the most ancient and important MSS, as well as the majority of the fathers and versions, agree on the subjunctive.

Modern commentators and translators have been divided—some preferring to give greater weight to the actual textual evidence and therefore reading "let us have"; others relying more on what is believed to be the requirement of the sense of the passage, and reading "we have." In this second group are Lietzmann and the RSV. Sanday and Headlam, Moffatt, and Goodspeed are among the many who feel compelled to

---

closely still to the latter part of ch. 3. It is there that Paul has demonstrated that **we are justified by faith,** and the argument which he developed warrants the inferences which he now proceeds to draw. The real authority for Paul's confident **therefore** is 3:21-31; there he explains precisely what he means when he says that **we are justified by faith.** The immediate result is that **we have peace with God.** This simple phrase is closely related to many of the most important doctrines of N.T. Christianity. The experience which it describes follows from justification, and it is practically indistinguishable from reconciliation. Reconciliation, first clearly introduced in Romans at this point, presupposes a deeper sense of what sin means than that characteristic of much of O.T. thinking on the subject. Justification is a concept which might be intelligible to those who have been accustomed to think of man's failure in terms dictated by the requirements of a law; but reconciliation cannot be understood unless we think of a relationship of personal trust which has been severed because of man's sin. Those who were alienated must be brought together again, and this, says Paul, is exactly what the gospel achieves. Those who are restored to fellowship with God are those who receive the gift of his **peace.** The word, of course, was not newly coined by the disciples of Christ; it has rich O.T. associations. Both in the accounts of Jesus' ministry, and in the sermons by which his followers explained to others his significance, we have echoes of the ancient promise that God would give peace to his people, always with the conviction that that deep yearning of men had now been satisfied. In the letters of the N.T. the word is repeatedly used both in introductory salutations and as a form of final greeting. Again and again peace is used to describe the strong inner serenity which believers receive from God—and from God alone. "The God of hope fill you with all joy and peace in believing," says Paul (15:13), and he tells his readers that the kingdom of God means "righteousness, and peace, and joy in the Holy Ghost"

follow the textual evidence where it seems to lead. These, however, adopt the reading "let us have" fully aware that the other would give the more natural sense, and therefore seek to discount as far as possible the hortatory element. Thus Sanday and Headlam stress the fact that the verb is "have" (rather than "get") and that the tense is present (indicating continuous action) rather than aorist: the meaning is "not 'make peace,' 'get,' or 'obtain peace,' but rather 'keep' or 'enjoy peace.'" In "let us have," the same commentators say, "inference and exhortation are really combined: it is a sort of light exhortation, 'we should have.'" Moffatt seeks to express this shade of meaning when he translates, "Let us enjoy the peace we have." In other words there is universal recognition that the *sense* is indicative, whether Paul wrote it so or not; that peace, as well as joy and hope, follows inevitably upon the fact of justification by faith in Christ and is not to be obtained by our own effort. Lietzmann is so sure of this that he is willing to affirm without reservation that Paul wrote the indicative, even if it must be concluded (in order to account for the textual evidence) that the very first edition of the published Pauline letters carried the other reading or, earlier still, that the scribe or amanuensis to whom Paul was dictating the letter understood him to say ἔχωμεν when in fact he said ἔχομεν. Since there would have been little if any difference in pronunciation, such a mistake at an early stage in the transmission of the text of Romans is easily possible. In this commentary we shall accept the meaning which both our texts favor: **we have peace.**

We have this peace **through our Lord Jesus Christ.** The allusion here may be to the act of Christ—or of God in Christ—which has been referred to in 3:24 ff. and else-

(14:17). The importance which Paul attaches to peace is further suggested by two illuminating metaphors which he uses elsewhere to describe its effect. In Phil. 4:7, peace is a sentinel who "mounts guard" over the hearts and thoughts of believers. The image is that of a citadel beset by foes without, manned within by a garrison often turbulent and unreliable. In these circumstances it is "the peace of God" which both subdues the enemy and disciplines the defenders. In Col. 3:15, men are called into the peace of Christ which rules or "arbitrates" in the heart. Peace is now a judge, above the riotous and unruly instincts which clamor for attention. Both images emphasize that inner peace which is one of God's gifts to those who commit themselves in trust to him. But peace means more than that. It "is the sum of all spiritual blessing that man receives and experiences; it is Grace in its fruit and realisation."[5] Consequently, peace with God points to the removal of the fundamental tension, running through all our life and extending to our relations with all things, which is dealt with only when God reconciles us to himself. This thought of the reconciliation which God effects is clearly present in the passage that is under discussion. We have found a new status with God; therefore the hostility which formerly kept us estranged from him has been removed. The fears which kept alive our antagonism to God have been swept away, and we can enter into fellowship with him. This kind of peace is possible only because justification has created a new relationship, and consequently what Christ has done for us is the condition of finding peace as well as of receiving justification.[6] It is therefore perfectly natural for Paul to add that we have our peace **through our Lord Jesus Christ.** There is no way of achieving that deep and abiding harmony with life with which the apostle is here concerned except through God's redeeming activity in Christ. Paul speaks of a kind of life which is free from frustration and immune to defeat; which has found the integration that comes from resolving inward tensions and from discovering an inclusive unity with the most abiding forces in life; which brings with it a blessedness whose full possibilities we can never exhaust.

Since words have many meanings, and so invite misunderstanding, it is well to remember that **peace with God** does not mean merely a state of inward contentment. Men can have a certain kind of peace without having satisfied any of the conditions which govern the gift of **peace with God.** That is why Jesus so sharply contrasted "my peace" with the peace which "the world giveth" (John 14:27). A man who resolutely ignores God and comes to terms with the society about him can achieve a certain kind of peace. There is a thoroughly secular contentment which finds satisfaction by lowering all its expectations. The man "whose heart is

[5] G. G. Findlay, *The Epistles to the Thessalonians* (Cambridge: Cambridge University Press, 1891; "The Cambridge Bible"), p. 47.

[6] Taylor, *Forgiveness and Reconciliation*, p. 90.

2 By whom also we have access by faith into this grace wherein we stand, and rejoice in hope of the glory of God.

our Lord Jesus Christ. 2 Through him we have obtained access[g] to this grace in which we stand, and we[h] rejoice in our hope of

[g] Other ancient authorities add *by faith.*
[h] Or *let us.*

where as the ground of our justification; i.e., we have peace as a result of the life and work of Jesus. But it is on the whole probable that Paul is now thinking more particularly of the present mediatorial work of the risen Lord. The idea that the believer is in a continuing and sustaining relation to Christ as present in the church has so far not clearly appeared in this epistle, but it lies at the heart of Paul's conception of the Christian life and is the real theme of this whole central section of the letter (for the meaning of the phrase **our Lord Jesus Christ,** see above on 1:4).

2*a.* The emphasis throughout this section is upon the *already realized* meaning of the life in Christ. We *are* justified (literally "have been justified"); we *have* peace. And now **we have obtained access to this grace,** and in it we already **stand.** The tense of the two verbs in the first half of this sentence is in fact the perfect—the tense of already completed action (ἐσχήκαμεν and ἑστήκαμεν; the close similarity in sound, the rhyming character, of the two words is no doubt intentional). The meaning of χάρις, **grace,** has been discussed above (see on 3:24). Here, it is clear, the term designates not merely the loving disposition of God toward us, but a kind of emanation of God's reality, God giving himself to us. In other words, **grace** here, and usually, is not subjective only but objective. It designates not only how God feels toward us, but something he gives us—even if it is a self-giving. God's act in Christ—the justifying act—has given us **access to this grace,** and in that grace, through him as still living and present, **we stand.**

2*b.* The basic meaning of the next verb, rendered **we rejoice** in the RSV, is "we boast" or "we exult." Moffatt renders it "we triumph," and Goodspeed, "we glory." The word is an anticipation of the mood expressed in 8:31-39, and its full meaning here can

asleep through his disregard or forgetfulness of God's judgment," says Calvin,[7] may be undisturbed by his need, but his peace is of a wholly different order from that of which Paul is speaking. Often good men, even when greatly preoccupied with righteousness, are content to achieve peace only with themselves. The shallow type of pharisaic mind (cf. Luke 18:11) can come to terms even with pride, and find nothing incongruous in doing so. Because the world does offer its own kind of peace, Christians need to be particularly careful to accept only that **peace with God** which **we have . . . through our Lord Jesus Christ.**

2. *Entry into Grace.*—Vs. 2 is closely parallel in meaning to vs. 1; but Paul has varied his imagery, and metaphors often provide excellent starting points for exposition. **We have obtained access,** says Paul, **to this grace in which we stand.** The language is suggested by an Eastern court. Into the presence chamber of the king only those entitled to enter can come; the rest are excluded—unless, indeed, they can find someone who will introduce them. We lack the merit which would enable us to stand before God, and we cannot gain it by our own efforts.

[7] *Commentaries on Romans, ad loc.*

What we could not do ourselves, Christ has done for us: it is **through him** that we have our new status with God. The **grace** into which we have access prolongs the metaphor. If it represents something objective, "something he gives us," we may legitimately extend it to include that state in which those stand "who are objects of the Divine favour."[8] But the terminology suggests an area which is "fenced in"—into which, without Christ's aid, we could not hope to make our entry. Once there, we manifest a constancy and assurance which could be ours only because of him who introduces us. We stand firm, without the fear which marks those who have no right to be present, yet without the arrogance of those who court a fall. Note on this point Paul's solemn warning, "Let him that thinketh he standeth take heed lest he fall" (I Cor. 10:12).

Paul has described the new status which is ours; he now shows the change which it effects: **We rejoice.** The emotional atmosphere which characterizes the new life is exultation as well as hope. But **rejoice** is hardly strong enough to convey Paul's true meaning (cf. Exeg.). He has used it elsewhere to describe the kind of "boast-

[8] Sanday and Headlam, *Epistle to Romans, ad loc.*

3 And not only *so,* but we glory in tribulations also; knowing that tribulation worketh patience;
4 And patience, experience; and experience, hope:

sharing the glory of God. 3 More than that, we[h] rejoice in our sufferings, knowing that suffering produces endurance, 4 and endurance produces character, and

[h] Or *let us.*

---

be better understood if one will read that triumphant passage. Again, we note the present tense of the action, "we do now rejoice," even though our joy or triumph is based on hope—**hope of the glory of God.** As we have noted above (see on 3:22-23), the **glory of God** refers to man's true character and destiny as created in God's likeness and for fellowship (**sharing**) with him. This **glory** has been lost through sin; but now we are assured that it will be restored, and in that **hope** we triumph. The restoration belongs ultimately, and therefore essentially, of course, to the new age, the kingdom of God—although Paul rarely uses this phrase—the supernatural age of the Spirit which Paul believed was soon to displace the present world.

3-4. This sentence is something of an interruption of Paul's thought, and the essential meaning of the paragraph would be clearer if it were placed in parentheses. It is as though Paul, having spoken of joy and hope, recalls his sufferings and those of others (see II Cor. 11:23-28; 12:7-10), and feels himself challenged. To this challenge he rises with the assertion that far from being destroyed by these experiences, his hope has been strengthened. Sufferings have resulted in disciplined **endurance,** and the experience of enduring hardship cheerfully and patiently ("like a good soldier") has tested and hardened **character;** this **character** in turn has made possible a more vigorous hope than one might otherwise have had. It is impossible to suppose that Paul is intending to say that character is the *source* of our hope. That source is clearly the **grace in which**

---

ing" which has no legitimate place in the religious life (3:27; 4:2). But it is not so much the exultant attitude which is wrong as the grounds which occasion it. We have no occasion of boasting because of what we are or have done (Paul has developed this point with some care), but Christians do have something about which they can exult—God's gift. The fact that his mercy and goodness are recognized as the consistent support of the new life is the secret of that confident joy which should be one of its marks. Paul will enlarge considerably the grounds for our rejoicing before he is finished; for the moment he specifies **our hope of sharing the glory of God.** The true life for which God made us is no longer hopelessly beyond our reach. Paul's verdict on unaided human endeavor was that "all have sinned, and come short of the glory of God" (3:23). In our present experience, when all things are partial and incomplete, we shall only fitfully and imperfectly appropriate that new life; but the important thing is that we no longer belong to an order utterly irreconcilable and opposed. **The glory of God** remains a hope, but it is a hope of whose fulfillment we have an earnest now.

3-5. ***Rejoicing in Suffering.***—It is easy to assert that hope is a ground of glorying, but it is a daring paradox to affirm that we can also boast because of hardship. Bodily sufferings are not usually an occasion for rejoicing. Paul does not mean that we rejoice when surrounded by affliction (like Mark Tapley, in Dickens' *Martin Chuzzlewit,* who was cheerful amid all discouragements); he declares that **we rejoice** because of **our sufferings.** The explanation is not hard to find. Justification is the prelude to a life of steady progress in spiritual understanding and in moral development. It is possible for a man to recognize that the expectation of future good—the full appropriation of the glory of God—goes hand in hand with the acceptance of present hardship; but surely more than this is involved. Exhilaration amid sufferings is due to a recognition of the value of the discipline which they supply. But this is possible only in a world which we have reason to believe is essentially friendly. In a basically hostile environment, hardship would merely break our spirit; it would be insupportable if we felt that at the end of the day the determining forces in our world were antagonistic or even indifferent. But peace with God involves, among other things, an acceptance of our place in an order which is providentially governed by God. In that case we are able to see the value of what would otherwise seem to be only the assaults of blind adversity: "we know that all things

5 And hope maketh not ashamed; because the love of God is shed abroad in our hearts by the Holy Ghost which is given unto us.

character produces hope, 5 and hope does not disappoint us, because God's love has been poured into our hearts through the Holy Spirit which has been given to us.

we stand. But the experience of **tribulations** properly sustained can serve to fortify the very hope they seem calculated to destroy.

5. Returning now to the main theme, Paul affirms that our **hope does not disappoint us** (literally "does not make us ashamed"; cf. 1:16). We are not ashamed of trusting **our hope of sharing the glory of God**—we have no fear that it will prove illusory—because **God's love has been poured into our hearts through the Holy Spirit which has been given to us.** Again we observe the emphasis Paul is placing upon the *already realized:* the **love of God** has already been **poured into our hearts;** the **Holy Spirit** has already **been given to us.** In other words we hope to receive the *glory* of God, because we have already begun to receive the *love* of God. Hope is thus more than mere hope; it is hope already beginning to be realized.

We have noted in our comment on vs. 3 that "grace" is more than a subjective attitude of God; it is objective and existential. It is something not only felt—by God—but given; not only known about—by us—but experienced. The same thing even more clearly appears in connection with Paul's use of the term love (ἀγάπη: *agapē*) in this passage. **God's love** is **poured** out. Although the Greek says ambiguously "the love of God" (also the KJV), nothing is more certain than that the RSV understanding of its meaning is the correct one, and that the reference is not to our love of God, but to God's love of us. That love is not merely a *fact* about God which is recognized; it is the very *reality* of God conveyed and realized, **poured into our hearts.** It is indeed **the Holy Spirit which has been given to us.** There is in this passage a virtual identification of "this grace," "the love of God," and "the Holy Spirit." The Johannine statement, "God is love" (I John 4:8), goes not at all beyond the implications of this Pauline text.

work together for good to them that love God" (8:28; cf. RSV).

The content and significance of this knowledge can be amplified and set forth point by point. Having stated the general principle, Paul develops in detail the lessons of adversity. Bodily hardship has as its fruit heroic **endurance.** When Paul spoke of physical suffering, he was not dealing with any abstract quality but pointing to what had played a large part in his own experience. He believed that in his age and in our kind of world the Christian must expect hardship, and certainly he had had his own share of it. The incidental and almost casual references to tribulations which we find in his letters suggest a record of unparalleled physical endurance (8:35; I Cor. 4:11-13; 15:30-32; II Cor. 1:3-10; 11:23-28). Suffering in itself does not necessarily strengthen character; it may simply break and embitter a man's spirit. Its results depend entirely on the way in which it is accepted; and Paul, of course, is writing of the hardship which comes to the Christian as a Christian. This, he says, produces a vigorous and masculine **steadfastness.**

One of the characters in John Buchan's *Mr. Standfast* remarks:

> The big courage is the cold-blooded kind, the kind that never lets go when you're feeling empty inside, and your blood's thin, and there's no kind of fun or profit to be had, and the trouble's not over in an hour or two but lasts for months and years. One of the men here was speaking about that kind, and he called it "Fortitude." I reckon fortitude's the biggest thing a man can have—just to go on enduring when there's no guts or heart left in you. Billy had it when he trekked solitary from Garungoze to the Limpopo with fever and a broken arm just to show the Portugooses that he wouldn't be downed by them. But the head man at the job was the Apostle Paul.[9]

Out of his own experience Paul is assuring his readers that the things we usually account deterrents can be transformed into the means of strengthening our constancy. The second lesson of adversity is that **endurance produces character.** Experience is cumulative; one discovery provides the point of departure for the next. A

[9] London: Hodder & Stoughton; Boston: Houghton Mifflin Co., 1919, p. 177. Used by permission of the Tweedsmuir Trustees, A. P. Watt & Son, and the publishers.

A considerable part of the central section of this epistle is devoted to the Spirit (see below on 8:1-30), and no discussion of what Paul means by that term need be attempted now. It is enough to recall what was said about the Spirit in the brief introductory survey of Paul's thought (see above, p. 371). The Spirit is the supernaturally bestowed essential *life* of the community; that life is here described as **God's love . . . poured into our hearts.**

It is interesting to note that we have here a kind of hierarchy of terms. The first and most important is "God's love"—also called "this grace" and, as we have seen, all but identified with the Holy Spirit. This love both manifests itself in God's act of justifying us and offers itself to us as the Spirit—the breath of a new life, God's own life imparted to us. "Faith" is our response to this love, our acceptance in humility and trust of what God offers us. "Peace" is the consequence of the response of faith to God's justifying act, and "hope" is our confident expectation that God, who has begun his good work in us, will complete it. Every one of these terms will appear again and again in the course of this part of Paul's discussion.

---

quality acquired or confirmed is not an end in itself but only a means to further advances. When hardship bravely endured has established fortitude, fortitude in turn creates the kind of character which stands trial without faltering. Paul uses a term which describes the temper of the seasoned veteran in contrast with that of the raw recruit. Various attempts have been made to compress into one word the exact shade of meaning which **character** covers in a rather inclusive way. Both "testedness" and "approvedness" have been suggested, but they are ungainly words and sacrifice as much as they gain. **Character produces hope.** The original ground of rejoicing which Paul specified was hope (vs. 2), and this is not the careless kind of repetition which is caused by hasty composition. What begins as an intellectual belief is strengthened by the experience which life's conflicts bring. The discovery of what God can do for those who trust in him animates to fresh vitality the true but imperfect hope with which we began. Like every other Christian grace, hope grows strong only as it is exercised. As a result of what our probation has taught us, we have new confidence; having been put to the test and not found wanting, we have firmer grounds for hope. So do the disciplines of suffering teach us that **hope does not disappoint us.** There are some hopes to which people cling—often with a desperate intensity—which can prove only illusory. They hope that chance will bring them wealth they have not earned, they hope that in their case the seed which they have sown will never come to harvest, they hope that for those they love cause will not produce effect. The hopes which ignore the nature of the moral world in which we live must eventually put to shame those who trust in them. Anyone who ignores the laws which govern God's universe will eventually find himself covered with confusion. Paul, however, is describing men and women whom suffering leads not to despair, but to an increasing confidence.

The conclusion of the matter is simply stated. Everything that we have learned, all that tribulation and its related experiences have taught us, rests on an assured conviction that **the love of God** supports our lives. What he has already done is the source of our confidence regarding what he will yet do. We know that a God who has given us so much will not abandon us at the last. We may notice two important inferences. Justification, strictly speaking, means that we are treated as righteous. But if that were all, we might be acquitted and yet be left in despair. That it means much more is apparent here (as also in vss. 1-2). Our new confidence is due not simply to the discovery that our outward lives are surrounded by God's mercy and supported by his care. **The love of God is shed abroad in our hearts; it has been poured into** them, and still floods them. Moreover, the joy which this creates is not simply one of satisfaction; it strengthens the will so that we can resist sin and defeat it. **God's love** becomes the central and determining motive of our life. It is the secret of the growth in true goodness which ought to be the normal consequence of finding ourselves in a new relationship to God. Justification becomes the door to further advance; progressive enrichment is the mark of the new life (see Exeg.). Its scope and quality, as well as the means by which it is appropriated, will be set forth in greater detail as the letter unfolds. At present Paul does not develop his doctrine of the Holy Spirit; he merely states that it is **through the Holy Spirit** that **God's love is poured into our hearts.** We may notice, however, that in his thinking the nature of the Spirit is intimately affected by all he knew of Christ and of his risen presence. Our understanding of the love of God is largely determined by what Christ has taught us to expect.

6 For when we were yet without strength, in due time Christ died for the ungodly.
7 For scarcely for a righteous man will one die: yet peradventure for a good man some would even dare to die.

6 While we were yet helpless, at the right time Christ died for the ungodly. 7 Why, one will hardly die for a righteous man—though perhaps for a good man one will

B. Reconciliation, the Promise of Salvation (5:6-11)

6-8. While we were yet helpless, i.e., incapable of either atoning for our guilt or throwing off our bondage, **Christ died for the ungodly.** It is the fact that we are **ungodly** which so movingly **shows** or proves God's **love for us: While we were yet sinners Christ died for us.** This happened **at the right time,** i.e., at the time predetermined in God's

6-11. *The Amazing Gift Which We Have Not Deserved.*—Paul has shown that God's love, which makes our justification possible, is also the motive power which enables us to grow in spiritual understanding and power. Character develops as difficulties are met and overcome, and hope, rooted in love, becomes the mark of the new life. Having supplied in the briefest outline a hint of the material he will subsequently develop, Paul returns to the thought of the divine love which makes possible these marvelous things. There is no adequate way of indicating what are the height and depth and length and breadth of the love of God, because we lack both the necessary knowledge and the satisfactory terms. Even when we most fully grasp what God has disclosed in Christ's death, we are left impotently groping for suitable imagery in which to express what we have discovered. It is with this problem that Paul now struggles, and he illuminates God's love by contrasting Christ's response to our need with our normal reaction to one another.

6. *Help, When Our Need Was Greatest.*—While we were floundering impotently in the morass of our sin and our reliance on our own efforts, Christ came to our aid. **We were yet helpless,** because nothing that we ourselves could do was sufficient to meet our moral need, and none of the remedies so far suggested had been able to improve our situation. It is this state of despairing impotence which Bunyan so vividly describes in the opening pages of *The Pilgrim's Progress.* Our problem was sin, and we were utterly incapable of coping with it. In the moral and spiritual world those who can neither help themselves nor find a helper are certain to be **ungodly:** darkened in mind and degraded in life. What this means in extreme cases Paul has shown in chs. 1–2, but **ungodly** is not properly defined by comparisons with ordinary respectability. It is really understood only in the light of God's holiness and the "glory" which is the status we were meant to occupy. That is a comparison which makes all conventional goodness seem tawdry and worthless. Our best efforts are recognized as what the prophets declared them to be—only "filthy rags." For men like that—for men like us—**Christ died.**

It was an event in time, and the most decisive of all events. Paul cannot think of it as one episode among others, taking place at one point rather than another simply because chance would have it so. To Paul there was a marvelous appropriateness in the timing of the Incarnation. It was according to God's purpose, but it coincided perfectly with man's need. Attempts are sometimes made to prove that contemporary social forces—the Roman peace, the organization of the empire, the collapse of the old religions, the proven insufficiency of man's attempts to achieve moral regeneration—explain what Paul meant when he said that God sent forth his Son "in the fullness of time." Paul himself never explained his meaning, but they are surely nearer to the spirit of Paul who find the clue to his words in his strong sense of the critical juncture in which he lived. In one respect, every age is for religious men a time of crisis. When God confronts men with a demand for decision, it is impossible to ignore the fact that he governs and directs all things according to his purpose and may at any time decisively intervene. But what is true of every period must have seemed especially so to men who were persuaded that in their own experience God had "visited and redeemed his people." The clue to Paul's conviction that **at the right time Christ died** is to be found not so much in our analysis of the human situation as in a keener perception of the divine purpose.

7. *Help, When There Was No Prospect of Aid.*—The stark improbability of what he affirms as good news staggers Paul's mind; his incredulity is conveyed in Moffatt's translation by the device of repeating the last clause as a cry of bewildered astonishment, "For the un-

8 But God commendeth his love toward us, in that, while we were yet sinners, Christ died for us.

dare even to die. 8 But God shows his love for us in that while we were yet sinners

purpose; the event of Christ was not an accident of history, but a purposeful act of God. Paul never works out systematically the relation in which he thinks of Christ as standing to God, but this passage reminds us of how close that relationship is. It is God who, through the death of Christ, has opened to us a way of escape.

godly! Why, a man will hardly die for the just." Some commentators have found Paul's distinction between the good man and the righteous man surprising, but surely it corresponds to one of the most familiar facts in our experience. In every religious community there are people who uphold a high standard of inflexible rectitude. Their ideals are above reproach, and their devotion to them never falters. With grim determination they pursue their self-appointed task of making other people better. They command respect, but they never arouse affection. We almost hate ourselves for admiring the aims they pursue. They are upright, but for some reason—perhaps because they are deficient in charity and forbearance, perhaps because they do not know the meaning of joy, perhaps because they have no sense of humor—they are unlovely. There have always been people devoted to this inflexible and repellent kind of goodness. Paul knew them and evidently felt about them much as we do. It is exceedingly improbable that anyone would lay down his life for such a person. Reluctant admiration, unsupported by affection, never prompts a sacrifice like that. On the other hand, we all know good men for whom, in an impulsive moment, we might conceivably be willing to die. There is a quality in true goodness that awakens a response of love which sets few limits to the sacrifices men will make. Only love can so subdue our concern for our own self-preservation that we would forfeit our life for the sake of someone else. The point is not so much that **perhaps for a good man one will dare even to die** as it is that we must feel persuaded that the person is worthy of the sacrifice we make. For this purpose admirable qualities alone do not suffice; respect must pass over into love before we will venture our lives for another. Because a cursory examination of our own hearts will confirm Paul's contention, he can effectively proceed with his argument. The full wonder of the divine love is apparent only when we compare it with the best that we are willing to do for one another.

8. *The Love of God.*—God shows his love for us in that while we were yet sinners Christ died for us. Our state was such that nothing in us offered any inducement to such a sacrifice. So far from being good, we were sinners. The love of God is not something we had either earned or deserved. Its utterly unmerited quality is one of the things that convinces us that it must be divine. The inferences which we draw from this passage are exceptionally important.

(*a*) By his death Christ did for us what we would never do for one another. Consequently we see in his Cross the manifestation of a goodness which transcends all human standards.

(*b*) If his death declares a love that is more than human, we can only venture to affirm that this is a revelation of what the love of God must be (see Exeg., vs. 5).

(*c*) This is the first step toward that identification of what we know of God and what we see in Christ which makes possible Paul's easy transition from the one to the other. The strength of this passage lies in its simple and natural equation of the values we see in a concrete life with the truths we surmise regarding ultimate reality.

(*d*) Reconciliation, with which Paul will be even more explicitly concerned in subsequent verses, is seen to depend on the amazing goodness of God as this is manifested to us in Christ and especially as it is supremely set forth in the Cross. The fact that **God shows his love for us** is the foundation of our conviction that we "who sometime were far off are made nigh by the blood of Christ" (Eph. 2:13).

(*e*) The problem with which Christ's death deals is our failure—our sin and the alienation from God which it creates. The object which Christ's death achieves is the sanctifying of believers—we are enabled to live a new life, upright and victorious.

(*f*) What Paul declares to be God's nature corresponds exactly with what Jesus teaches regarding his Father. God showed his love, said Paul, **while we were yet sinners;** he is kind, said Jesus, even to the ungrateful and the evil. Even the unjust are not beyond the reach of his bounty. And what Jesus taught by word he demonstrated by conduct. While men and women were yet sinners they learned that they

9 Much more then, being now justified
by his blood, we shall be saved from wrath
through him.
10 For if, when we were enemies, we
were reconciled to God by the death of

Christ died for us. 9 Since, therefore, we
are now justified by his blood, much more
shall we be saved by him from the wrath
of God. 10 For if while we were enemies we

9-10. Christ's death has opened this way by making possible our justification: we **are now justified by his blood.** Again, as in 3:25-26, we are forced to recognize the vicarious sacrificial or expiatory significance of Christ's death, as Paul understood it. Once more, also, we are reminded of the distinction between justification and salvation. In both of these verses that distinction is implicitly made: we are *now* **justified;** it is *now* **that we are reconciled;** but *salvation* is still in the future: we shall **be saved by him from the wrath of God** (for "wrath of God" see on 1:18). It is notable also that again (cf. 4:25) whereas justification is mentioned in connection with the death of Christ—**by his blood, . . . by the death of his Son**—salvation is more closely associated with the Resur-

---

could come to him, and in coming they found forgiveness and a new life. The publicans and harlots heard that they had a better chance of entering God's kingdom than some whose respectability was above suspicion; and the good news was plausible because they heard it from one who taught them by his never-failing friendship and compassion what restoration really meant.

9-11. ***Our New Standing and Our New Life.***—Paul has shown that men need not stand defeated and condemned before God. They have been justified, and this is the beginning of a new life. But the decisive step was taken when our fundamental alienation was removed. If that was possible, there is nothing that we need dismiss as beyond God's power. So Paul is arguing from the greater to the less—from the fact of justification to the assurance of an abundant life. Having proved that the initial problem has been solved, he can show what follows as a consequence. The structure of the argument appears in the arrangement of the clauses: **Since, therefore . . . much more.** The condition of all else is, of course, justification. Paul has proved this already (3:21-31) and he has reverted to it repeatedly since. The form in which he recapitulates his contention serves a useful purpose in that it clearly states the decisive importance of Christ's death in making possible the justification of sinful men. The magnitude of the problem is apparent at once, and Paul never suggests that he is describing a vague or indecisive form of divine activity. Not by such means can the problem of sin be overcome. **We are now,** he says, **justified by his blood.** The sacrificial overtones of his statement are obvious, but at the moment he is intent on emphasizing the fact that this is a divine activity which he is describing. God has acted decisively for our deliverance. But unless much more were intended, God would not have done this much. He would not have brought us to a new status—especially at so great a cost—unless he intended to complete the process, and bring us into fuller fellowship with himself. We shall **be saved . . . from the wrath of God.** The emphasis is on the new state of peace with God, but our former condition of enmity is never far from mind.

10. ***Reconciliation.***—It is the consciousness both of the old and of the new that makes "reconciliation" so inevitable a word in the present context. It is one of the great terms in the Christian vocabulary, but disuse has made it unfamiliar and consequently unintelligible to many of our people. Nothing is more important than that Christians should once more master the elements of the language of our faith, and few terms repay careful study more abundantly than "reconciliation." Moreover, few passages offer a better point of departure than the present one, though it should be carefully compared with II Cor. 5:19-20; Eph. 2:11-17; Col. 1:19-22. Five points of major importance emerge.

(*a*) Reconciliation is the act of God. He takes the initiative, and he carries the work to its appointed end. All the verbs are active in voice. It is not an accidental development; nor does it naturally or automatically take place. The problem with which it deals is a hostility so deep and settled that it would persist indefinitely unless drastic action were taken. Because we are so deeply involved we cannot help ourselves, and there is nothing within the range of our experience that can offer any aid. Our situation proclaims that only God can solve so grave a spiritual problem; the gospel declares that he has done so. God has acted; reconciliation is his work.

his Son; much more, being reconciled, we shall be saved by his life.

were reconciled to God by the death of hi: Son, much more, now that we are recon

rection: we shall **be saved by his life.** Here **his life** is manifestly a reference to the continuing reality of Christ—his living reality as Lord of the church. To be incorporatec into this new supernatural community, the community of grace, of love, of the Holy Spirit, of Christ—it can be described in all of these ways—is to "know . . . the powe of his resurrection" (Phil. 3:10), to "be united with him in a resurrection like his' (Rom. 6:5), to share his new supernatural and endless life, to be a part of the new creation. To be sure, Paul has not so far mentioned the church, but its reality is pre supposed in all he is saying in this whole passage—indeed in all of Romans—and nc statement of his about the meaning of the Christian life can be understood except in the context which that reality provides.

A few words need to be said about **reconciliation** (καταλλαγή), which appear several times in this paragraph and often elsewhere in Paul's writings. It designates wha

(*b*) God's reconciling work has as its chief object man. It is not the material world which has learned to ignore God's laws or disobey them, though at times Paul speaks as though man, by his sin, had infected the whole creation with his own disorder. It is man himself who has rebelled against God, defied the divine purpose for his life, and destroyed the fellowship for which he was intended. He has erected, on a false foundation, a whole series of relationships which constitute a kingdom of evil, and which aggravate the estrangement from God which is the mark of our natural life. It is this estrangement, of course, which is the crux of the matter. In his ignorance man either disregards God or fears him. The whole tenor of his life is such that no word except "hostility" describes the relationship in which he stands to God. The quality of his life is condemned by the standards of righteousness inseparable from God, and even if his mind is not alienated, he knows that he has destroyed the true basis of fellowship. But a relationship is mutual and affects both persons (see Exeg.). To say that **we were enemies** describes not only our outlook but the nature of the relationship to which we were a party. We belonged to a relationship shattered and broken. God is the other party to that relationship, and only by a sphinxlike immobility of spirit could he remain unaffected by that fact. We are cut off from God, and he knows it. Our attitude to God is hostile and that is the character which we have in his sight. This is the amazing thing about reconciliation. Paul never ceases to marvel at the paradox that when we were in that unlikely and unlovely state of hostility to him, God reconciled us to himself. "But God shows his love for us in that while we were yet sinners Christ died for us."

For if while we were enemies we were reconciled to God by the death of his Son. . . .

(*c*) Reconciliation declares that men anc women who were hostile and alienated are sc no longer. But it goes a great deal further. A: the passage in Col. 1 shows conclusively, reconciliation means that our enmity to God ha: been replaced by the closest kind of fellowship We were formerly excluded from communior with his spirit as well as from sharing in hi: purpose. The removal of hostility would have singularly little meaning if it operated on a plane where we were left in aloof neutrality. I would be unreal; and in any case the basic N.T conviction that God loves us even when our sir has broken the relationship between us, make: it utterly impossible. In the present passage Paul's mind moves forward to the thought o the enriching fellowship with God which is the glory of the new life. **Much more, now that we are reconciled, shall we be saved by his life** The complete nature of the change is seen ir the contrast between the sullen hostility which preceded and the loving fellowship which followed our reconciliation.

(*d*) The personal character of Paul's understanding of reconciliation is a feature of every passage in which he discusses the subject. Wha Christ has done by his death is to make "peace through the blood of his cross" (Col. 1:20). Bu peace has no meaning except in a world where personal values predominate. To make peace i: "a moral activity wrought by a person or persons upon persons; it is reconciliation in it: most distinctive aspect."[1] Our fear of falling into the cruder kinds of anthropomorphism often keeps our Christian thinking on a level so barrenly impersonal that we overlook the

[1] Taylor, *Forgiveness and Reconciliation*, p. 80.

is undoubtedly the most important element in the "peace" spoken of in vs. 1. Sanday and Headlam identify "peace" with "reconciliation," presumably thinking of "peace" only in the sense in which the term is used in this passage. Speaking generally, it is fair to say that "peace" is the richer, more inclusive term; but at the base of it, as we have seen (on vs. 1), is the conception of the cessation of hostility and, more positively, reconciliation. Since it is our guilt which has separated and estranged us from God, God's justifying act is also a reconciling act. And in that passage "justification" and "reconciliation" (as here) are used apparently interchangeably.

Is it God or man who needs to be reconciled to the other? This question is frequently debated—but not too relevantly or fruitfully. Where there is estrangement it must necessarily be in some sense mutual. Needless to say, Paul makes very clear that God is never estranged in the sense of ceasing to be loving: not only does he *desire* that the estrangement be overcome, but in Christ he has *at tremendous cost acted* to overcome it (cf. vs. 8). But it is nevertheless true that so long as sin exists, God and man are estranged *from each other.* God has acted to deal with sin and thus to overcome the estrangement, as it affects himself as well as man. Jesus would have said that God deals with sin by moving us to repentance; Paul interprets Jesus' own death as an effective means of annulling sin and thus of reconciliation. Surely **the wrath of God** is not only objective, impersonal punishment; the phrase is meant also to suggest some measure or kind of estrangement from the sinner on God's own part.

---

true nature of the gospel. We forget that "all true life is meeting," as J. H. Oldham puts it, and that our greatest possibilities as well as our gravest problems belong to the world of personal relations. We forget that God himself is only an abstract concept until our experience of his personal dealing with us teaches us that he is our Father. Part of the practical value of a strong emphasis on reconciliation is that it provides the most effective antidote to arid impersonalism in our religious thought. It delivers us from unreality into a world of experience where the decisive fact is that "God shows his love for us" (vs. 8) by reconciling us to himself.

(*e*) There is the most intimate connection between our experience of reconciliation and the fact of Christ's death. Reconciliation is God's great act of mercy, but its effective means is Christ's cross. **We were reconciled to God by the death of his Son.** The context of the great passage on reconciliation in II Cor. 5 makes it plain that Paul regards the reconciling work of God as something which is accomplished in the death and resurrection of Christ, and in Col. 1 and Eph. 2 the wording leaves no room for doubt concerning the intimacy of the connection between God's purpose and the Cross as the means by which he chose to effect it. Christ's death gave full and final expression to all those truths which men's minds must grasp before God's mercy can come home to them. It declares the magnitude of their own sin and the inexhaustible richness of God's love. It shows forth the perfect obedience to God's will and requirement which we cannot achieve but with which, when we see it in Christ, we can identify ourselves. It proclaims the judgment which follows on wrongdoing, the righteousness which sin offends, and the divine patience which never grows weary in doing good. It points to life freely offered to God on behalf of men, and so gathers up all the wealth of sacrificial thought and imagery. And every other element necessary to break down our hostility and bring us back to fellowship with God is present. Even the concrete reality of the historical incident is important. It is "in the body of his flesh" that Christ has reconciled us. It is the human Christ —the Word made flesh—and not an imaginary figure in a mythical dumb show who brings us into the liberty and peace of God's sons. The necessary condition of reconciliation is provided by what Christ has done. Paul is quite convinced that no man by his own efforts can possibly reconcile himself to God. Man's utmost merit is insufficient for that purpose. Man therefore contributes nothing except the willingness to be reconciled, but that much must be forthcoming on his side. God cannot compel us to be his children. Any suggestion of constraint would shatter the personal nature of the relationship in which we stand with God. We can decline to be reconciled, and even of a man too strict to break the commandments it may be said, "He was angry, and would not go in" (Luke 15:28).

11 And not only *so,* but we also joy in God through our Lord Jesus Christ, by whom we have now received the atonement.

12 Wherefore, as by one man sin entered into the world, and death by sin; and so death passed upon all men, for that all have sinned:

ciled, shall we be saved by his life. 11 Not
only so, but we also rejoice in God through our Lord Jesus Christ, through whom we have now received our reconciliation.

12 Therefore as sin came into the world through one man and death through sin, and so death spread to all men because all

---

11. It is because God has taken the initiative in dealing with the mutually estranging sin that **we have now received our reconciliation:** we are reconciled to God (this is the main thing), but it is also true that in a different sense he is reconciled to us. We **rejoice** in the new knowledge of God **through our Lord Jesus Christ**—i.e., within the new community—and in the new assurance of our ultimate salvation which this knowledge makes possible for us.

C. The Basis of Life in Christ (5:12-21)

Paul has just said (vs. 10) that we shall be saved by Christ's life. Now he will set forth his view of how or why the Resurrection has this effect. (In connection with this passage as a whole see Intro., p. 370.)

12. Paul is following good contemporary Jewish doctrine in saying that **sin came into the world through one man and death through sin.** The explanation of the presence of evil in the world, both physical and moral, by reference to Adam's disobedience was quite common. Adam, in virtue of the fact that he was the first man, was not only the symbol of the race, but also its effective representative. When he transgressed God's command, all of his descendants were involved in some way in his transgression and therefore in the suffering of death which was its penalty. It is often pointed out that this consequence of Adam's sin is not mentioned in Genesis itself. There only Adam and Eve are punished; nothing is said of their descendants. Indeed, the idea of the transmission of the penalty to the entire race does not appear explicitly in the entire O.T. although it seems unlikely that the story of Adam's disobedience and punishment was not conceived of from the beginning as throwing some light on the meaning of man's tragic lot. Still, that conception is not clearly stated till a century or so before Paul's own time in some of the so-called

---

11. ***The Joy of the Redeemed.***—Paul has just spoken of that rich life of fellowship with God to which reconciliation opens the door. It is natural, therefore, that he should immediately suggest the characteristic emotional experience which accompanies the new life. **Not only so,** he adds, **but we also rejoice in God through our Lord Jesus Christ.** It was this exultant quality in the early Christians that so much impressed and puzzled their pagan neighbors. It was different from anything that marked ordinary human life. Pleasure is one thing; joy another. Pleasure, when chosen wisely and used in moderation, may do much to mitigate the rigors of experience; but it can never create the atmosphere with which joy surrounds the man who has found it. Pleasure is ephemeral, usually awakened for the moment by some external stimulus, and as transient as the cause which called it forth. Joy has an enduring quality; it is a state sustained by abiding sources of spiritual renewal, and "no man taketh" it from us. Joy is the emotional experience which God has attached to the attainment of the true spiritual life for which we were created. But this means that it is inseparable from a discovery of our proper relationship to God. In dependence on him we discover the secret of creative power and we master the disciplines of humble and happy service. That is why we "rejoice in God"; the religious man is persuaded that only in him can we find the wellsprings of joy. The Christian is equally sure that there is no way of attaining the requisite fellowship with God except through Jesus Christ. Apart from Christ we lack the knowledge of God which enables us to "exult." He has not only shown us the Father, but he has made possible that reconciliation without which there could be no joy.

12-14. ***Sin in the Light of Grace.***—Paul uses sin throughout the present passage as a foil for grace. Actually this is always the best way in which to regard sin. When considered in isola-

13 (For until the law sin was in the world: but sin is not imputed when there is no law.

men sinned — 13 sin indeed was in the world before the law was given, but sin is

apocryphal and pseudepigraphical books (see Wisd. Sol. 2:24; Ecclus. 25:24 ["From woman is the beginning of sin, and through her all die"]; II Baruch 17:3 ["Therefore the long time that he lived did not profit him, but brought death, and cut off the years of those to be born after him"]; II Esdras 7:118 ["O thou Adam, what hast thou done? For though it was thou that sinned, the evil is not fallen on thee alone but upon all of us that come of thee"]).

It will be noticed that in these passages from contemporary—or near-contemporary—Jewish writings nothing is said about the transmission of *sin*; only death is mentioned. Since, however, death is everywhere thought of as the penalty of sin, it is hard to see how it was possible to think of death as "spreading to all men" unless one thought that sin also in the same automatic way became the universal human lot. And indeed Paul sometimes seems to say just this, as, e.g., in vs. 19, "By one man's disobedience many were made sinners." In the present passage, however, he appears to be saying that death became universal not because sinfulness was the universal human inheritance from Adam, but **because all men sinned.** This was the usual rabbinical doctrine. Henry St. John Thackeray explains the view of the rabbis: "Though death since Adam reigns generally throughout the world, yet it only gains power over the individual on account of his own sin" (*The Relation of St. Paul to Contemporary Jewish Thought* [London: Macmillan & Co., 1900], p. 33). But whatever Paul or the rabbis thought about the question of whether actual sinfulness is inherited, they undoubtedly believed that we inherit a *tendency* toward evil. At the very least Paul would have said that the impulse toward righteousness had been so weakened by Adam's transgression that we are no longer able to do the right. Thus, whether death is considered a consequence of an inherited guilt or the penalty of our own individual transgression, it is "because of Adam" that all die (cf. I Cor. 15:22).

13-14. It is clear that we have between vss. 12 and 13 one of those abrupt changes of grammatical construction which are characteristic of Paul's style, as indeed of any colloquial style. When Paul wrote the first half of vs. 12, he obviously intended to conclude it in some such way as this: ". . . so through one man righteousness came into the world and life through righteousness, and so life became available to all men." But having got midway in his sentence, the apostle thinks of a possible difficulty the reader or hearer may find in the statement he has made and therefore breaks off his sentence in order to deal with it. He is soon too far away from the sentence to return to it, although the *thought* he had meant to convey is expressed clearly enough in later sentences.

tion, it produces an unwholesome preoccupation with our shortcomings. It creates a false kind of pessimism. It obscures the important fact that the gospel does not declare that we are sinful, a fact we know already; instead it offers forgiveness and restitution to those who have sinned. Moreover, if sin is not closely related to the thought of God, it subtly ceases to be sin and men persuade themselves that it does not really matter. Religious teaching which ignores the fact of sin suffers in its understanding of both righteousness and mercy. Paul neither minimizes nor exaggerates the gravity of sin. It is serious, both because of its inherent nature and because of its wide diffusion. He regards it as a universal element in human experience. **All men sinned,** he says tersely; and he is but repeating what he has previously said, "All have sinned, and come short of the glory of God" (3:23; cf. 11:32). From his own experience he knew how it stood with a sensitive Jew; observation showed him how urgently the Gentile world needed moral regeneration. He states his conclusion from facts which he regards as incontestable. As the present section proves, he does not think of sin as the transgression of a law, even of a law divine in origin. Coming "short of the glory of God" meant descending to a lower plane than that on which man found true self-realization. The man who sinned was "alienated from the life of God" (Eph. 4:18).

Sin, then, was serious in its nature, universal in its extension, and disastrous in its results.

14 Nevertheless death reigned from Adam to Moses, even over them that had not sinned after the similitude of Adam's transgression, who is the figure of him that was to come.

not counted where there is no law. **14** Yet death reigned from Adam to Moses, even over those whose sins were not like the transgression of Adam, who was a type of the one who was to come.

The difficulty just referred to is that of accounting for death as a penalty of sin in view of the fact that **death reigned from Adam to Moses.** It might be argued that since it was Moses who gave the law, there could have been no transgression and thus no punishment of transgression until after his time; and yet death had actually reigned. Paul's answer is not as persuasive as it would have been if he had made use here of the conception of "natural law" to which he has earlier alluded (2:14-15). His actual answer is to say that although sin was **not counted where there is no law,** it was nevertheless **in the world.** But one might ask, "If it was not counted, why should man have died on account of it?" One wonders why Paul does not reply by appealing to the law "written on the heart" from the "creation of the world." In other words **the law was given** long before Moses, and God was thus in position to "count" and punish sin from the very beginning. The description of those **from Adam to Moses** as those **whose sins were not like the transgression of Adam** may help explain Paul's silence here. Sanday and Headlam understand the phrase **not like the transgression of Adam** as meaning "not in violation of an express command." If that understanding is correct, Paul may be meaning to attribute to men before Moses some vague and general knowledge of God's will, but not such knowledge as conferred responsibility or obligation. But such a supposition is in violation of the clear implications of 1:18 ff. It seems more likely that Paul has for the moment forgotten the natural law and is therefore trying to deal with a logical difficulty which, granted the existence of law, would not exist at all. It has already more than once been pointed out (see, e.g., Intro., p. 369) that Paul thinks of sin not simply as transgression, but as a demonic power which has reduced man to a kind of slavery, and of death therefore as having a double aspect: it is both the "wages" or the inevitable end of the slavery and also the judgment of God upon the transgression. It is clear, therefore, that Paul would have been able to understand the mere fact of the prevalence of death **from Adam to Moses** without reference to transgression at all, but his statement in vs. 12 that "death spread to all men because *all men sinned*" indicates that he is here thinking of death as the punishment of transgression, and it is this aspect of it which gives rise to the logical difficulty we have been considering.

With the words **who was a type of the one who was to come,** Paul returns to the idea of vs. 12, and in them he sums up what he had evidently intended to say in that connection. The sense in which Adam was the **type** of Christ is opened up in vss. 15-21.

So grave a phenomenon required an explanation of some kind. If this is God's world, how did sin find entry; and, once within, how did it gain such power? Paul's explanation of the origin of sin appeals to the story of Adam. To this extent he was justified, that the Genesis story was certainly told to explain how sin found a lodgment in a divinely created world. And if "myth" is a biblical category which explains, as though in terms of history, things that run out beyond the limits of history, his answer is as good as any that our limited knowledge is likely to provide. Ours is a tainted race; we see the consequences though we dimly divine the cause. But in that twilight which surrounds the beginnings of our conscious life, sin and death became inseparably associated—at least so Paul believed. Sin introduced into man's life a principle of decay, and death was its outward result. Whatever we may think of the explanation, we can understand the problem with which he was wrestling. Total death—death both of the body and the soul—is intimately associated with sin, while sin can never appear trivial because of the nature and nearness of man's end. The solemnity which attaches to death is due to the moral context in which, like the rest of man's life, it must be set.

15 But not as the offense, so also *is* the free gift: for if through the offense of one many be dead, much more the grace of God, and the gift by grace, *which is* by one man, Jesus Christ, hath abounded unto many.

15 But the free gift is not like the trespass. For if many died through one man's trespass, much more have the grace of God and the free gift in the grace of that one man Jesus Christ abounded for many.

15-21. That sense as a whole is clear, but the first half of this section (vss. 15-17) is awkwardly constructed and is marked by no little repetition and confusion. The amazing thing is not that Paul's writings contain some such passages, but that, freely dictated letters as they were, they contain so few of them. The general idea is manifest: just as Adam, the head and symbol of the old natural humanity, by his disobedience involved all men in guilt, bondage, and death, so Christ by his obedience qualifies as the head of a new humanity—a "new creation"—in which are justification, redemption from the power of sin, and victory over death. Paul finally manages to say this directly and clearly in vss. 18-21, but the earlier verses are confused.

15-16. This confusion lies in the fact that the paragraph is given the form of an attempt to show the faults of a really perfect analogy! Actually the analogy could hardly have been improved on; there is correspondence at nearly every point. But Paul begins by asserting that **the free gift is not like the trespass.** In the one case, he says, you have a **trespass** and in the other **the grace of God.** These are, to be sure, very different in their concrete character—at opposite poles, in fact—but if **the grace of God** is a reference to God's act in Christ, then these terms are *perfectly analogous* in Paul's formal argument. Still, he repeats: **And the free gift is not like the effect of that one man's sin.** Here he attempts to show that the analogy breaks down in that in one case we have **judgment following one trespass** and in the other **the free gift following many trespasses;** but actually in Paul's argument throughout this passage as a whole **the free gift** follows, not

---

15-16. ***Our Solidarity in Need.***—Whatever the forms taken by Paul's explanation—and we must remember that these do not affect his central point—he is concerned with an important reality which the modern world has no reason to forget. He states, as a fact, man's solidarity in need. The life of one affects many, and no one can really cut himself off from the total life of mankind. No truth has become a more necessary part of our outlook; certainly no single fact has had such bitter expositors to teach us its cogency. When humiliation, disillusionment, and economic insecurity open the way in one nation for rampant nationalism, the consequences are felt around the world. No man lives to himself, and the truth can be amplified to prove that no one is so obscure that his actions do not reach out in ever-widening circles to affect men whose names he does not know and of whose very existence he has been completely unaware.

So far, unfortunately, we have largely allowed our sin and folly to teach us how closely interrelated we are. This is the fact on which Paul seizes. One man's act has done incalculable harm to all who followed him. But Paul is equally persuaded that the same principle works in the opposite way as well. We have taught ourselves—with what sorrow the whole world knows—that we are bound together for ill. The gospel declares it is equally true that we are bound together for good. This is not a theoretical possibility which Paul states. He does not say, "Because this works for evil, we can surely expect that it will work for good." He says that what Christ has done can alter the character of every single person and can transform the nature of the common life which all men share together. The essential condition without which this miracle could not happen is the solidarity of the race—for good as well as evil. But Paul adds that God in his mercy has intervened to use this natural law for our salvation. The principle was always there: we turned it to our own destruction; but the mighty act of God has now used it for our redemption.

The argument can be carried a stage further, and it is actually with this new development that Paul is primarily concerned. The heart of his argument is that grace is mightier than sin. That is doubtless why he felt obliged to disturb the balance of what was in itself an admirable analogy (see Exeg.). He was not willing to suggest that the consequences of Adam's trans-

16 And not as *it was* by one that sinned,
so is the gift: for the judgment *was* by one
to condemnation, but the free gift *is* of
many offenses unto justification.
17 For if by one man's offense death
reigned by one; much more they which

16 And the free gift is not like the effect of
that one man's sin. For the judgment following one trespass brought condemnation,
but the free gift following many trespasses
brings justification. 17 If, because of one
man's trespass, death reigned through that
one man, much more will those who re-

---

many trespasses, but "one act of righteousness" (vs. 18). The true analogue of "one trespass" is not "many trespasses," but this one righteous act. In other words the second sentences in these two verses (i.e., those beginning with "for") in both cases fail to sustain the shorter sentences with which the verses begin.

The word "many" (literally "the many") at the end of vs. 15 is not to be interpreted as implying any limitation: the contrast is not between "many" and "all," but between "many" and "one." Indeed the "many" must mean "all." This is certainly true of the first occurrence of the word in vs. 15, and again in vs. 16. The term rendered **offense** in the KJV means literally "a slip or fall to the side"; the RSV **trespass** is a better translation. Sanday and Headlam point out the similarity in meaning between this term (παράπτωμα) and the more frequent ἁμάρτημα, which is translated "sin" and means literally "missing the mark." These commentators say, "It is however appropriate that παράπτωμα should be used for a 'fall' or first deflection [as here] . . . , just as ἁμάρτημα is used of the failure of efforts toward recovery."

17. The **free gift** of vss. 15 and 16 (three Greek terms are used, but the RSV translators are correct in making no distinction) is referred to in vs. 17 as **the free gift of**

---

gression are perfectly offset by the results that will follow from **the grace of God and the free gift in the grace of that one man Jesus Christ.** That might seem to imply an equality between them which in fact does not exist. **The free gift is not like the effect of that one man's sin.** To declare that a power as great as but no greater than sin has entered human experience would be to proclaim a very hesitant gospel. It would leave us with a dualism which nothing could resolve, and man would have no assurance of deliverance. **Much more** is one of the key phrases of the passage. The contrast is ultimately far more important than the parallel, because it declares the supremacy of grace.

The terms in which Paul sets forth this contrast between sin and grace invite expansion. In vs. 15, the word **abounded** determines the form which the thought assumes. Sin is circumscribing in its effect; all its consequences can be compressed into the single word "death." The working of sin is like a vicious circle, always limiting the scope of its devotees until at last it leaves them no standing room save death. The inheritance which it offers is the negation of all the values that true life provides. But whereas sin is restrictive in its operation, grace enlarges and expands the scope of the recipient's experience. The results of **the free gift . . . of that one man Jesus Christ abounded for many.** Paul clearly means "for all," and he pictures a bounty which overflows without measure for the enrichment of everyone who will accept its benefits. "Abundant life" is not a phrase which he uses, but the idea is one which he continually employs. In vs. 16 we are again reminded of how extreme is the difference between the results of sin on the one hand and of grace on the other. This time the language recalls the processes by which a judicial verdict takes effect. First comes the wrongdoing (the **trespass**), then the sentence which is pronounced upon it (**judgment**), then the disabilities which follow as a result (**condemnation**). The sinner is cut off from fellowship with God; all the dark and unlovely consequences of sin envelop him, until death closes the unhappy chapter. How different is the operation of grace! No matter how widely we have strayed or how often we have fallen, our need is enclosed within the bounds of this offer of mercy. Even when the past has been stained by hideous transgression, God's free gift assures the sinner of acquittal. His new status is not due to his own merit, nor can he himself in any way secure it. That is why the emphasis falls so strongly on **the free gift;** and the standing it confers is marked by full possession of the liberty which sin destroys.

17*a*. *The Heritage of Adam, and of Christ.*— The founder of a race occupied a place in ancient thought for which we usually make insufficient allowance. The nature of a people,

receive abundance of grace and of the gift of righteousness shall reign in life by one, Jesus Christ.)

18 Therefore, as by the offense of one *judgment came* upon all men to condemnation; even so by the righteousness of one *the free gift came* upon all men unto justification of life.

ceive the abundance of grace and the free gift of righteousness reign in life through the one man Jesus Christ.

18 Then as one man's trespass led to condemnation for all men, so one man's act of righteousness leads to acquittal and

---

righteousness. The "righteousness" is undoubtedly the legal righteousness, the **justification,** mentioned at the end of vs. 16. Again we have a distinction implied between this justification and the reigning **in life** which is the final salvation (cf. vs. 10). In this sentence Paul succeeds finally in putting into satisfactory form the analogy he has begun to suggest in vs. 12.

18-19. Having done so, he very effectively repeats and emphasizes his idea in these two sentences. If the words "and death" had been inserted after the word **condemnation,** the analogy would be completely drawn in each sentence. As it is, these words are clearly implied—the term **condemnation** meaning not only the *sentence* of death but also its execution. The context of these verses makes their meaning as a whole perfectly clear; indeed, one feels that Paul has been trying to say just this since he began this passage in vs. 12.

At two points of detail in these verses some comment may be appropriate. One of these involves the translation of the phrases rendered respectively in both of our texts **made sinners** and **made righteous.** The Greek term here is καθίστημι, and it means "make" only in the sense of "appoint," "constitute," "install," or "instate." The conception of a

---

the character of their customs, and the form of their laws were often attributed to their progenitor. It is this thought which Paul is using for his own purposes. Adam was the founder of one race, Christ of another. Unredeemed mankind not only traced its origin to Adam, but bore the qualities which he transmitted to his descendants. In the same way, the new humanity traces its life to a new founder, Christ. All the benefits we enjoy we receive from him, and the very life in which we participate is his gift. Unity is the mark both of the old race and of the new. As Adam's descendants were bound together in sin for evil ends, Christ's people are united in the life of his spirit to promote his purposes. Paul, of course, is not merely developing an interesting parallel. He loves to contrast the new manhood in Christ with the old manhood in Adam because he found that he could thereby illustrate what is his central subject in this section of his letter. The old life throws into clear relief the true marks of the new life. Its slavery to sin makes clear the moral victory which is characteristic of the emancipation in which the Christian shares. We understand our spiritual wealth when we compare it with our former poverty. The main interest centers in the life in Christ. Christ alone is its source. He makes it possible, and his living presence is still at work among his people to create the new manhood which will correspond to the divine intention. As Gore says, he is "perpetuating His life by His Spirit in that society which He has established to be His body." [2]

17*b*-21. *To Reign, in Life.*—To an even greater extent than usual the passage, vss. 12-21, requires to be treated as a whole. The general argument is far more important than any of the details, and cannot be ignored; but there are certain phrases which are likely to start the mind along fruitful avenues of thought.

(*a*) In vs. 17 there is a striking play on the word **reign.** Because of sin, death has broken into human experience and has established its absolute tyranny over our life. The imagery suggests a careless act whereby our first forefather opened the door to a malign external power, and all the race now groans beneath this tyrant's oppression. The mythical nature of the interpretation does not affect the fact which Paul describes, and his phrase awakens in the mind a vivid picture of the lifeless desolation which prevails when death reigns. Paul's thought is moving in the somber world which experience makes painfully familiar to us all. If death means the "disastrous consequence of sin, physical and spiritual," [3] the desolation amid which mankind is wandering is the aptest

[2] *Epistle to Romans*, I, 185.

[3] Dodd, *Epistle of Paul to Romans, ad loc.*

19 For as by one man's disobedience many were made sinners, so by the obedience of one shall many be made righteous.

life for all men. 19 For as by one man's disobedience many were made sinners, so by one man's obedience many will be made

forensic justification is thus in Paul's mind when he says **made righteous.** A more accurate translation would be: "As by one man's disobedience many were constituted sinners, so by one man's obedience many will be constituted righteous" (see on 1:17, etc., above). The other point needing comment is the translation of ἑνὸς δικαιώματος as **one man's act of righteousness** (vs. 18). **Act of righteousness** (RSV) is certainly better than **righteousness** (KJV), since the Greek term is concrete rather than abstract. But is "one" an adjective qualifying "righteous act" so that we should read, with Goodspeed, "one righteous act" (Sanday and Headlam, and Lietzmann also favor this reading), or is it a pronominal substantive, as in both of our texts, "the righteous act of one man"? And what is this "act of righteousness"? Is it God's justifying act, as in vs. 16 (the final word in this verse is this same term), or is it Christ's own act of perfect obedience to God's will? Vs. 19 would suggest the second answer, and the RSV clearly conveys it. Christ's perfect obedience or "act of righteousness," however, is also an "act of redress" (Moffatt), so that the difference in meaning between the possible translations is not so large as it might seem.

Christ by his perfect obedience "unto death, even death on a cross" (Phil. 2:8), sets in reverse, so to speak, the process begun by Adam's disobedience. He gives the race of men the opportunity of a fresh start. He becomes the head of a justified, redeemed, and triumphant community.

commentary on the meaning of **death reigned.** That is the condition we have known; the new possibility which the gospel makes actual is suggested in the marvelous phrase, **reign in life.** The full force of the contrast brings out the regal and victorious quality of the new life. Its emancipated estate, its abundant scope, its satisfying effect are conveyed by the assurance that the sphere in which we reign is "life." The structure of the verse is such that the emphasis falls heavily on the closing words, **through the one man Jesus Christ.** This is what we would expect. It is not simply because Paul has a habit of using some such phrase at the end of an important paragraph (cf. vss. 11, 21). The extreme nature of the contrast requires some cause capable of explaining so decisive a change. If Adam could entail such consequences on his posterity, how infinitely greater must be Christ's power to lift us out of apathetic servitude to be kings in life!

(*b*) In the same verse (vs. 17) **the abundance of grace and the free gift of righteousness** remind us of the boundless liberality which marks God's mercy. It is the unrestricted, overflowing amplitude of grace which arrests Paul's attention in the present section. He "giveth not the Spirit by measure" (John 3:34), and the same undeserved generosity distinguishes all God's treatment of our fallen race. Since it is a gift we cannot claim to have won it by our merit; all we can do is thankfully to receive what God gives us. There is, of course, a condition which governs that reception: only by faith can we lay hold of grace. In vs. 17 Paul does not mention this invariable element in our redemption, but he has written so largely about it elsewhere that he can assume it: we **receive the abundance of grace** only by faith.

(*c*) One of the terrifying features of human life is the wide extension of our influence which the interrelated character of our lives makes possible. The results of sin go on and on, and even repentance has no power to arrest their progress. In vs. 19 it is possible to render one of the key phrases in such a way as to express this fact. **Made sinners** and **made righteous** miss something of the quality of the original (see Exeg.). K. E. Kirk, following Moulton-Milligan's *Vocabulary of the Greek Testament,* suggests that "to be constituted" means "to be given rank as," but it does not mean that the functions attached to that rank are discharged. Consequently, the verse could also perhaps be translated to read, "As by one man's disobedience many will be put in the way of sin, so by one man's obedience many were put in the way of righteousness." We then have two extreme examples—one working for evil, one for good—of what we know to be one of the fundamental laws of the moral life. We cannot make another person either good or bad, but we can "put him in the way" of becoming the one or the other. We can so shape his outlook or influence his conduct that his feet are set either in the paths of peace or in the way that goes down to death. What daily experience teaches us to be true is confirmed by our ex-

20 Moreover the law entered, that the
offense might abound. But where sin
abounded, grace did much more abound:
21 That as sin hath reigned unto death,
even so might grace reign through righteousness unto eternal life by Jesus Christ
our Lord.

6 What shall we say then? Shall we continue in sin, that grace may abound?

righteous. 20 Law came in, to increase the
trespass; but where sin increased, grace
abounded all the more, 21 so that, as sin
reigned in death, grace also might reign
through righteousness to eternal life
through Jesus Christ our Lord.

6 What shall we say then? Are we to continue in sin that grace may abound?

20-21. The same idea is repeated yet again in this final sentence. The way in which the **law came in, to increase the trespass** can more appropriately be discussed in connection with the next chapters (especially ch. 7), but Paul's meaning here has been indicated sufficiently clearly in 3:20; 4:15; and 5:13. The law "increases" the trespass both by making clear its character as trespass and, as we shall see more fully later, by stimulating dormant sinful impulses into new activity.

As sin reigned in death is a striking clause. Sanday and Headlam comment: "Sin reigns, as it were, over a charnel-house; the subjects of its empire are men as good as dead, dead in every sense of the word, dead morally and spiritually, and therefore doomed to die physically."

D. The Release from Sin and the Law (6:1–7:25)

Reference has already been made to the difficulty of outlining the section of the letter to the Romans on which we are now engaged, i.e., chs. 5–8 (see above, p. 450). There was similar difficulty in connection with the section 2:25–3:20 (see above, p. 417). The source of the difficulty in both cases seems to be that Paul often takes up

---

perience of redemption. Even God himself cannot *make* us good unless our wills co-operate; but the example and inspiration of Christ's obedience "put us in the way" of a similar obedience.

(*d*) We have in this passage an interesting study of the various degrees in which we experience abundance. In vs. 20 the KJV translates by **abound** a word rendered in the RSV as **increase.** It may be taken as the first stage which Paul recognizes. But in vs. 15 we have another word, also translated by "abound," which, for the sake of distinction, might be rendered "overflow." Finally, also in vs. 20 we have a much stronger form of the same word, **did much more abound** in the KJV, and **abounded all the more** in the RSV. The distinction may serve to set our minds following after Paul's as he thought about the mysterious manner in which sin multiplied and the providential way in which grace "overflowed exceedingly" in order to achieve our deliverance. There is a serious undertone in vs. 20, as there must be in any realistic appraisal of life, for the grim fact cannot be evaded that as offense is added to offense, sin flourishes with a lavishness which threatens to engulf all goodness. Only the sentimentalist ignores the expansive power of the kingdom of evil; Paul's confidence rests on his conviction that righteousness has a power greater still. Moreover, God's goodness can challenge sin and overthrow it precisely where it has most arrogantly vaunted its might.

21. ***As Sin Reigned.***—The expository possibilities of this verse are brilliantly suggested by Sanday and Headlam, as quoted in the Exeg. The palace of sin is the house of death. No one doubts the reality of sin's kingdom, and no one who submits to it can ignore its final consequences. There may be certain splendors in its domain (one can "enjoy the pleasures of sin"—"for a season"), but its subjects already bear upon themselves the marks of death. The paralysis creeps on from one region of experience to another. The man who silences the voice of conscience finds that his spirit is involved in the death which overtook his moral life, and when the body perishes, this only sets the seal on what has already happened in the soul. **As sin, . . . [so] grace. . . .**

6:1-14. ***Dying with Christ.***—The present section opens with what may seem a wholly factious objection, but as it unfolds it develops an extremely important theme. The new life involves a decisive break with the old—that is why it is fantastic to suggest that we should **continue in sin** because God's grace would thereby find fuller scope. Death itself is not

a new theme before he has quite finished with the old one, so that the first paragraphs of the new section of his argument are marked by a curious mixture or overlapping. He has taken up the fresh theme, but he is not quite ready to lay down the old one; he remembers something about the old theme he had meant to say. If he had known he was writing for eventual publication, or if for any other reason he had been in the habit of revising and copying his letters before dispatching them, these incoherencies and digressions would no doubt have been eliminated; but it is probable that he rarely if ever prepared his letters with such a degree of literary care. After all, who does?

We have seen that Paul begins the section chs. 5–8 in such a way as to indicate that his attention has turned from justification to the concrete meaning of the new life which follows upon it. Nevertheless 5:12-21 are concerned, one feels, quite as much with justification as with its consequences, if not more. They are indeed concerned with both, with "acquittal and life" (5:18). Ch. 5 is thus in a way a transitional chapter, in which the mixture and overlapping of themes to which we have referred are quite noticeable. So true is this that many commentators prefer to regard ch. 5 as the concluding part of the discussion of justification which begins at 3:21, and to place the point of transition from justification to the new life at the beginning of ch. 6. The other and more usual arrangement is here preferred; but the mixed character of ch. 5 must be recognized. There can be no doubt that at 6:1 Paul is fully launched on his discussion of Christian life.

But chs. 6–8 are themselves not easy to outline. The break between 6–7 and 8 is fairly clear—in 6–7 Paul is considering what might be called the negative meaning of the salvation made possible by Christ, i.e., the freedom it involves from sin and law (and always, implicitly at least, from death); in ch. 8 he is speaking of the positive meaning of the new life, possession of and by the Spirit. But although it is possible to say that ch. 6 is concerned largely with sin and ch. 7 with the law, it is not possible to say precisely where the transition from one theme to the other occurs. There is something "rough and ready," therefore, in the division here adopted.

1. Dying with Christ (6:1-14)

6:1-2. The statement in 5:20 that "where sin increased, grace abounded all the more" reminds the apostle of an objection to his doctrine to which in a somewhat different form he has alluded in 3:8: **Are we to continue in sin that grace may abound?** The fact

---

more final than the Christian's severance from the past. Baptism means a union with Christ so intimate that the great crises of his life are reproduced in our own experience. As he died for our deliverance, we die to sin; as he rose to newness of life, so do we.

The second step in the argument is an expansion of the meaning of our identification with Christ. His death is reflected in our death to the things that destroy the life of the spirit; but his death had its sequel in his resurrection, and if our experience is parallel to his in the matter of our death to sin, surely it will be equally so as concerns the new life in righteousness. The practical importance of what Christ has done for us is seen most clearly when we realize that the grip in which sin held us has been irrevocably broken. Moreover, we begin to learn how we ought to regard our own lives: the whole perspective is distorted unless we see ourselves as **alive to God in Christ Jesus.**

The necessary conclusion can now be stated: we cannot be the servants of sin, nor can our bodies be its instruments. We must serve God; our new status demands no less.

1-4. ***Silencing the Insincere.***—The gospel can be misunderstood in various ways and from various motives. Some miss the point because they are uninstructed, others because they are dull of understanding. But some, with a perverse factiousness, distort it to suit their own purposes, even when it is perfectly plain that they ought to know better. It is the murmur of lawlessness, perverting the truth to prolong indulgence, which now arrests Paul's attention. We must remember that he has already given two answers to this kind of suggestion. He has insisted that in a world governed by moral law, wrongdoing inevitably brings retribution; God will finally "render to every man according to his works: . . . for those who are factious and do not obey the truth, but obey wickedness, there will be wrath and fury" (2:6-8). In other words, if we keep moral problems in the right context, certain kinds of casuistic objections cannot be maintained. This is a truth whose

2 God forbid. How shall we, that are dead to sin, live any longer therein?

2 By no means! How can we who died to

that this question is raised twice in the brief compact argument of the first third of this epistle suggests that Paul was often challenged—either seriously or mockingly—on this issue, and perhaps also indicates some sensitiveness on his part to the weakness of his logical position in answering it. In 3:8 the question was not pertinent to the discussion, and Paul was able simply to deny and dismiss the implied charge. Now, however, since he is engaged in describing the new life to which God's justifying act in Christ, received in faith, admits us, the question is altogether relevant, and some attempt to answer it is plainly required.

He begins with a vigorous denial, **God forbid.** He repudiates emphatically and without qualification the alleged antinomian implications of his doctrine of justification —the notion, i.e., that since we are justified by God's free grace and not at all by our merit, there is no reason for or obligation to ethical living. It is not hard to see that such a notion may have seemed to follow as a natural conclusion upon Paul's premises, nor can it be said that Paul ever effectively demonstrated its logical impropriety. He knew that it was not the right conclusion and often says so earnestly and vigorously, but one is not sure that he was clear as to *why* it was not. As a matter of fact, Paul's rejection of "the law" as binding upon the believer leaves no theoretical basis for ethical obligation. There is, of course, ample ground in Paul's theory for the ethical life as a fact, even a necessity, but not as an obligation; i.e., Paul recognized that the believer in Christ *must in the nature of the case* live an ethical life, but that is not the same thing as saying that he *ought to* do so. In vs. 2, e.g., his point is not that we *should* not **continue in sin,** but that we *will not, cannot* do so: **How can we who died to sin still live**

relevance to life never lessens, and many people are able to defend what they secretly know to be wrong only because they strip from the question all the great moral considerations which make every issue more than merely a matter of expediency. But there is another retort to the man who suggests that his sin really gives God a greater chance, and we have an example of it in 3:8. In this instance the question is asked disingenuously, as Paul suspects, in order to score a debating point. But great moral issues are far too important to be twisted for any purpose whatsoever, least of all for the discomfiture of an opponent in an argument. A man who will do this has an essentially frivolous mind; in any case he cannot be met by argument, because without sincerity in seeking the truth, we get no further than futile quibbling. If anyone is willing to subordinate the evidence of his conscience to the requirement of his argument, he has passed beyond the reach of constructive debate. In that case the discussion cannot be usefully prolonged, and the antagonist may be recalled to a better mind by a sharp rebuke. In this chapter we have a third way of dealing with the problem. In one respect certainly it is not—in a formal sense—a complete reply to the question which Paul himself has raised: **Are we to continue in sin that grace may abound?** His immediate answer is a vehement negative: **By no means!** The argument which then unfolds may not strictly be a logical answer to the issue (see Exeg.), but it meets the case by showing that the new life is not capable of the kind of distortion that the questioner suggests. There might be other answers, but this is a perfectly legitimate one. What seems logical when one considers only part of the evidence becomes illogical when one considers all the evidence. One of the commonest difficulties that people create for themselves arises from this tendency to deal with moral questions in too circumscribed a setting.

> There are more things in heaven and earth . . .
> Than are dreamt of in your philosophy

is a rebuke which applies to many besides Horatio.[4] Paul's unexpressed contention is that the nature of man's moral problems becomes clear only when you lift his life into the light of God's purpose as it has been unfolded in the great drama of Christ's death and resurrection. From what is there revealed, we necessarily draw certain inferences as to the nature of our true life. This is logic too, but of a wider and more inclusive kind than that which first prompted the question.

The passage also emphasizes one of those

[4] Shakespeare, *Hamlet,* Act I, scene 5.

3 Know ye not, that so many of us as were baptized into Jesus Christ were baptized into his death?

sin still live in it? 3 Do you not know that all of us who have been baptized into Christ Jesus were baptized into his death?

in it? For the man in Christ the ethical life is not the obligatory life, but rather the only possible life. Such is Paul's doctrine; and a major problem, both for him and for his interpreters, lies in his recognition that in actual fact, believers in Christ were able to live very unethical lives. A little later a suggestion will be made (see on vs. 14*a*) as to how this apparent contradiction between doctrine and fact is to be resolved. Just now the theory itself is under consideration.

3-4. The ground for this theory or doctrine was laid in 5:12-21. Adam was the head of the old humanity in and over which sin has won its victory and established its control; Christ is the head of the new humanity—the new man—from which sin has been excluded in shameful defeat. The essential meaning of the Christian life—although Paul never uses this phrase—is that by way of justification by faith one has been made a member of this new humanity. This new humanity may appropriately be called by Christ's name since it was through his vicarious sacrifice for our guilt and triumph over sin and death that it was created, just as the old humanity was called by Adam's name since it was through his transgression that sin gained entrance into human life: "As in Adam all

simple distinctions which constitute the foundation of all morality. **How can we who died to sin still live in it?** There is a fundamental incompatibility between certain things, and it is as insurmountable as the difference between death and life. In ordinary experience it is common for ingenuity to try to disguise such distinctions. We persuade ourselves that the wrong is nearly right, that what we know is forbidden by our understanding of the truth is actually permissible in view of all the circumstances. The kind of argument latent in the question asked in vs. 1 presupposes some such blurring of the frontiers of good and evil. Whatever logic may do with Paul's argument about sin and grace, any true religious insight knows that the suggested inference is wrong because it obscures the difference between sin and righteousness. Nothing could more aptly illustrate Paul's contention than the absolute breach between life and death. "To live" and "to die" cannot be reconciled. In spite of our loose talk about being "almost dead," there is a decisive break between the two which nothing can obscure. To die is to pass irrevocably out of one world of associations into another. All ties are loosed, all contacts severed, and the normal activities of one kind of life are suspended. One cannot be partly dead; one cannot cease to belong to this world for certain days and yet come back to it for others. Indeed, the poignancy of death is due to its terrible finality. "I shall go to him, *but he shall not return to me*" (II Sam. 12:23). In the new life, says Paul, the breach with sin is no less decisive: you cannot die to it and still live in it.

At this point it may also be noted that in his wider teaching Paul makes effective use of the contrast between the present state of the Christian and that in which he previously lived, and he sets it forth by a play on the words "dead to" and "dead in." The plight of the natural man can be expressed only as a kind of spiritual death—he is "dead in sin" (cf. Col. 2:13, "And you who were dead in trespasses and the uncircumcision of your flesh, God made alive"; cf. also 7:9, 10, 13, 24; 8:6; Eph. 2:1). On the other hand, the state of the redeemed man is truthfully described when he is said to be **dead to sin.** This is the language which Paul uses repeatedly in the present section of the letter (vss. 2, 7, 8, 11; 7:4; also Col. 3:3). Moreover, it will be discovered that the imagery—which evidently appealed to Paul, and which he used with considerable variety—can be unfolded in other ways as well. There is the association between sin and death which we have already noted, and there is the fact that sin, too, is overthrown—"sin lies dead" (7:8). The effectiveness of this contrast is due to the meaning which the N.T. writers (and Paul with them) give to both "life" and "death." The man who is **dead to sin** is the man who knows the meaning of fellowship with God, and it is in this that true life consists. But it is equally true that the man who forfeits that relationship cuts himself off from God, and it is that separation from the divine which is the real source of death's poignancy. So does death become a fit description for the life which is lived without God. It is also worth noting that the feeling that death cuts us off from God ("Shall the dust praise thee?"—Ps. 30:9) is finally and completely dissipated only by our conviction that Christ's resurrection

4 Therefore we are buried with him by
›aptism into death: that like as Christ was

4 We were buried therefore with him by
baptism into death, so that as Christ was

ie, so also in Christ shall all be made alive" (I Cor. 15:22). The phrase "in Christ" is favorite one of Paul's and its significance cannot be too narrowly or rigidly defined, ›ut it may be suggested that this verse from I Corinthians gives the clue to the under-tanding of its meaning in at least half of the instances. To be "in Christ" is to be ncorporated in the newly created humanity, the new supernatural community or order f relationships, the new "body," which has come into existence through and around hrist. The essential fact about the believer is that he is no longer "in Adam"; he is "in hrist." He is no longer a "natural man"; he is a "spiritual man." Thus Paul can speak f members of the church as those **who have been baptized into Christ Jesus.**

The real point of Paul in this passage now clearly emerges: the believer can have o traffic with sin because in the order of life to which he now belongs sin does not xist—he has **died to sin.** Paul can just as well say the same thing in the obverse way, nd sometimes does, as in Gal. 5:24: "Those who belong to Christ Jesus have crucified he flesh with its passions and desires." It matters not at all whether one says that "the eliever has died to sin," or "sin has died to the believer"; both are metaphorical ways f saying that one who is "in Christ . . . is a new creature: old things are passed away;

ffers the answer to our questions about our nal destiny.

It is the core of Paul's argument that a new thical motive and a new spiritual power enter ur lives through our complete self-identifica-on with the risen Christ. The intimacy of this nity will be emphasized in vs. 5, and its nature ill be subsequently explained; here Paul states as a fact and suggests the way in which it omes about. Baptism is the outward act which eclares that our lives are yielded in loyalty nd obedience to Christ. In the first days of ne church baptism was of believers, after re-entance and the acknowledgment of their ith; it can easily be seen therefore how closely ne requisite conditions correspond to the se-uence of thought which Paul has developed in is teaching concerning justification by faith. ut at the moment he is anxious to stress the ntimacy of the relation between the believer nd the Lord, and baptism is consequently set orth as the parallel in our experience to Christ's eath and resurrection. There were three dis-nguishable stages in Christ's passion—his cru-ifixion, his burial, his resurrection. Similarly, nere are three stages in baptism—our descent nto, our burial under, our rising from, the aters which symbolize regeneration. What is nore, Paul infers that the parallel can be ressed a step further: there are in the Chris-an life these three stages which mark our eath to the old and our dedication to the new. he symbolism here, however, is not fully de-eloped, and we are left with this fundamental eclaration—as Christ was crucified, dead, and uried, we share in his experience by dying to n; as Christ rose in the power of a new life, we share in the wonder of the resurrection by entering a life wholly new both in moral quality and in spiritual scope.

The implications both of death and of new life are developed in more ways than one, and the subject is common to the whole section. In vs. 4, however, there is a statement of the wider theme which lends itself admirably to development. Paul begins with a claim which he regards as self-evident and axiomatic. He has no need to prove it by argument, and it justifies the important inferences that he wishes to make. **We were buried therefore with him** [Christ] **by baptism into death,** he says. Under different forms we share an identical experience: we have died—Christ literally through his crucifixion, we sacramentally through baptism. The decisive character of the break involved has already been noted. We have also seen that the significance of Christ's death was closely connected with the overthrow of sin's power. The previous verses have clearly set the discussion in a moral framework. By our self-identification with what Christ has done in his death, we have decisively passed out of the old world where the law of sin held us in its grip; we have died, and so are beyond its power and sway. The next step in Paul's argument is a reaffirmation of the fact of the resurrection. He does not mention it merely as a historical incident; he sees it as a decisive manifestation of God's power: **Christ was raised from the dead by the glory of the Father.** The last phrase is of particular interest; in the Fourth Gospel we have the same expression, again in connection with resurrection from the dead (John 11:40). It seems reasonable to assume that the early church saw in new life be-

raised up from the dead by the glory of the Father, even so we also should walk in newness of life.

raised from the dead by the glory of the Father, we too might walk in newness of life.

. . . all things are become new," and chief among the old things that have passed away is sin.

In the course of chs. 6–8 this essential point is stated and emphasized in various ways, some of them more apt and effective than others. The first of these ways makes use of the analogy of the death of Christ. We **were baptized into his death.** The figure was suggested perhaps by the superficial resemblance of immersion, almost certainly the customary form of baptism in the primitive church, to burial, **We were buried . . . with him by baptism into death;** but the ground of it is deeper. We have seen that Paul thought of the Resurrection as marking the crucial point within both the experience of Jesus and his saving significance (see Intro., p. 370). It was then that the "new humanity" came into being and the "old humanity" came under final judgment. Paul sees the death of Christ as symbolizing the end of the old, and the Resurrection as marking the beginning of the new. The Resurrection presupposes the Death; to belong to Christ the risen one is thus to have died to the world.

On **by the glory of the Father,** Sanday and Headlam remark that "glory" here means "power," but "power viewed externally rather than internally"; not so much "the inward energy" as "the signal and glorious manifestation." They quote an earlier commentator as comparing this statement of Paul with John 11:4, 40 (where "glory" again is associated with a resurrection).

Newness of life probably means simply "new life," i.e., the life in Christ, life in the new community between men and God, and among men, which has come into being through him and of which he is the head and center—life in the new order of the Spirit. In that life sin has no place.

yond death the most striking of all disclosures of the splendor of God's power. Moreover, we are reminded that Paul was never tempted to minimize the significance of the great events of Christ's life. "In Christ God was reconciling the world to himself"; and when Paul affirmed that Christ rose, he never suggested either that this was what we might expect in the case of so exalted a spirit or that it merely symbolized the spark of the divine which is in every man. He saw the resurrection as revelation, and he believed that it ought to be "marvelous in our eyes." He also believed that it had a direct bearing on our life from day to day. We have died, as Christ has died; we have risen, as he has risen. So much he has already suggested. Now comes the important inference. The purpose of the process is that **we too might walk in newness of life. Too**—you will notice. The new life is one which we share with him who also rose. The intimacy of our union with Christ appears even more clearly in subsequent verses, but we can note that our fellowship includes the moral adventure of living a new kind of life. No apostolic writer would have questioned that it was a high adventure, and none would have thought of it as an adventure on which we had embarked alone. Even the verb Paul uses is admirably chosen to make clear the nature of our undertaking. To **walk** requires effort. It is also a means of proceeding from one point to another, and it presupposes that we have a goal before us. It is neither effortless nor pointless. It requires voluntary exertion, and it is something that we must do for ourselves. Christianity, as one of the Cambridge Platonists reminds us, is "a way of walking, not a way of talking." We walk **in newness of life.** No phrase could more fittingly express the exhilarating wonder of "living by dying." We have left behind us the old world of disheartening ineffectiveness. Instead of our shabby record of continued failure, we begin to discover for ourselves the meaning of the gift of God (cf. 2:7). Finally we may note the parallel between **the glory of the Father,** which is the effective cause of our resurrection (as of Christ's), and the **newness of life** in which we are to walk. The gift of God displays the "wonders of his grace," and our lives are touched with a reflection of that same splendor. The new life is radically different from the old. Contrast is the decisive thing, and it can be developed in a number of ways; but among them will certainly be the glory of the new as opposed to the gloom of the old.

5 For if we have been planted together in the likeness of his death, we shall be also *in the likeness* of *his* resurrection:

6 Knowing this, that our old man is crucified with *him*, that the body of sin might be destroyed, that henceforth we should not serve sin.

5 For if we have been united with him in a death like his, we shall certainly be united with him in a resurrection like his.

6 We know that our old self was crucified with him so that the sinful body might be destroyed, and we might no longer be en-

5-8. Vss. 5-10 are somewhat perplexing because one would have expected a different orientation or emphasis in the argument. The main point—the same as in the preceding paragraph—is quite clear, but Paul is now saying, **If we have been united with him in a death like his, we shall certainly be united with him in a resurrection like his,** whereas we should have expected him to say, "If we have been united with him in a resurrection like his, we must already have been united with him in a death like his." The argument apparently called for by the context would seem to be that since we are in fact members "of Christ," i.e., joined with the risen one, we know that we have also been **crucified with him** (cf. Gal. 5:24) and have therefore died to sin and thus are **freed from sin.** Instead of proceeding backward, however, from the fact of the Resurrection to the Death which the Resurrection presupposes (as one would expect in view of the particular point he is trying to make), Paul seems here to be arguing forward from the death with Christ to the hope of resurrection with him. This is true in vs. 5, and again in vs. 8: **But if we have died with Christ, we believe that we shall also live with him.**

The difference in tense which appears in both vss. 5 and 8 is significant. Paul indicates that the believer has *already* **died with Christ** (or **been united with him in a death like his**), but that the *living* with Christ is still in the future: **we shall also live with him** (cf. vs. 5*b*). We have several times noted (see on 5:9-10, 17) this same distinction in tense as between justification (or reconciliation) and salvation (or life). Justification

5-11. ***United with Christ.***—We have been **united with him,** says Paul, **in a death like his.** At first sight the symbolism of baptism might seem too slight a foundation for so strong a claim; but baptism, of course, is intimately linked with faith, and one of the consequences of faith is union with Christ. In heart and will we are united with him because of "the personal attachment to its object" which is a part of the nature of saving faith. It is not a union of personalities which achieves an immediate and static finality. Our loyalty grows stronger and our attachment becomes deeper as we discover more fully what it means to be "in Christ." The intimacy of the identification of our will and purpose with his is more adequately suggested by metaphors than in propositions. When Paul says that **we have been united with** Christ, he suggests a figure familiar enough to readers in a world of olive groves and vineyards. It means that we "have become grafted," we "have grown together." It is a natural development of the imagery which Christ used when he spoke of himself as the vine and of us as the branches (John 15:1-8; cf. also Paul's fuller use of the same figure of speech, 11:17). Unity could scarcely find stronger expression, but a shoot grafted onto the parent stem only grows gradually into complete identity with the vine. What such close identity actually means in the experience of the disciple must be inferred not so much from this single passage as from the whole range of Paul's writings. We can certainly include (*a*) grateful acceptance of the gifts of God which come to us through him; (*b*) a love of Christ and a loyalty to him which mean that our wills are dedicated to serve what we see to be his purpose; (*c*) such a keen awareness of the presence of the living Christ that our spirits can enter into true fellowship with him; and (*d*) an attitude so receptive to his commands that our powers—of heart and mind and will—are constantly directed by his Spirit.

It is not a vague or ill-defined kind of union which Paul describes. In certain kinds of mysticism—especially when a pantheistic element is present—the personality of the individual is engulfed in an impersonal process and so lost. The strongly personal quality which is characteristic of Christian faith not only safeguards all true personal values but strengthens and develops them. "God is a spirit," we are spirits, and our spirits are capable of intimate fellowship with his Spirit. But because God in his omniscient splendor and power is too vast for frail spirits to meet, he has mercifully provided

7 For he that is dead is freed from sin.
8 Now if we be dead with Christ, we believe that we shall also live with him:

slaved to sin. 7 For he who has died is freed
from sin. 8 But if we have died with Christ,
we believe that we shall also live with him.

is an accomplished fact; salvation is promised and assured us, but it is essentially a hope —although a hope already beginning to be fulfilled and thus doubly sure (see on 5:5). This distinction in time between justification and salvation, however, is more convincing than the same kind of distinction between the death to sin and the life to God. Just as the death and resurrection of Christ as objective facts must be considered together if either is to have significance, so they cannot be separated in the experience of the believer. It thus appears that either the death to sin and the life to God are both present, or they are both future. When Paul then asks, "How can we who died to sin still live in it?" (vs. 2), the appropriate answer would seem to be, "But the believer has not yet fully died to sin, just as he has not yet come fully into possession of the new life." The new life is the "life of the world to come." We have received only a foretaste of it; only in that same measure have we actually "died to sin." Both the Crucifixion and the Resurrection are, as applied to the believer, eschatological facts.

But both are also present facts because the present world is not only doomed but is already beginning to die, and the new age is not only surely promised but the first

that our fellowship with the divine Spirit shall be through his son Jesus Christ. The unity is one of aim and outlook; and as Paul suggests, it is extraordinarily close. It is not, however, an identification in which we lose our distinctive quality. Instead, for the first time we fully find ourselves. Moreover, our union with Christ is necessarily governed by the nature of his life and the purposes which it served. **We have been united with him in a death like his,** and Paul explains this by adding (vs. 10) that **the death he died he died to sin.** His life, though surrounded by the forces of sin, was marked by complete moral antipathy to them, and his death was a final expression of that opposition on his part to everything that was evil. It was a conclusive breach with sin, decisive in its nature and its effect—it was **once for all.** This meant that he died from under its jurisdiction, into a realm where sin had no sway. The same thing happens in the believer's case. We too have decisively repudiated the old allegiance which was the mark of our servitude to sin. The language presses as far as possible the identity of our case with Christ's. **Our old self was crucified.** The old personality, organized around a certain set of interests and values, was as truly put to death by association with Christ's crucifixion as were the thieves who died in the same manner as he did and at the same time. As a result our **sinful body** was **destroyed;** and this was purpose as well as consequence. To avoid misunderstanding it is necessary to remember that Paul does not use "body" in the way we would. It is not the physical organism as such to which he refers; rather it is "the self as the organization of the sinful impulses inherent in the flesh."[5] Christ's physical crucifixion has its moral equivalent in our death to sin.

The passage invites treatment in a number of ways. Clearly Paul's purpose is to stress the moral consequences which follow from our union with Christ. His death is not only relevant to our situation; in a true sense our identification with Christ, made possible by faith, is so real that we share in his death. But since it was a death to sin, our risen life will be within an order where sin no longer reigns supreme. Paul's argument is from the one assured experience to what he believes will certainly be its consequence. It is therefore possible to open up the meaning of the passage by developing the relationship between the things which we already possess and those which we have only by anticipation. Paul is absolutely assured of certain things because they are already a part of experience; and he regards it as quite legitimate to draw certain conclusions from them. He does so in both vss. 5 and 6. The way in which the eschatological terms used in the section have both a future and a present reference is explained in the Exeg. This in itself sheds further light on the nature of the things we anticipate. We might reasonably expect them simply because they follow logically from what we already know. But in part they also enter into present experience. **We shall certainly be united with him in a resurrection like his** is a sound inference from the fact that he rose from a death in which we also participate. But the new life is something we already experience—imperfectly, of course, but genuinely enough. The significance of this in the moral struggle

[5] Dodd, *Epistle of Paul to Romans, ad loc.*

9 Knowing that Christ being raised from the dead dieth no more; death hath no more dominion over him.

10 For in that he died, he died unto sin once: but in that he liveth, he liveth unto God.

9 For we know that Christ being raised
from the dead will never die again; death
no longer has dominion over him. 10 The
death he died he died to sin, once for all,

installment has been paid—in the coming of the Spirit. In principle, and in some degree in fact, the believer has died to the world and therefore to sin, and the world has died to him—but this death is by no means actually complete and will not be till the new life also has fully come.

9-10. These verses assert the finality of Christ's death and resurrection and their complete sufficiency. The risen **Christ . . . will never die again; death no longer has dominion over him.** He has **died to sin, once for all.** He is thus in his present risen life entirely and irrevocably free from any bondage to sin; **the life he lives he lives to God,** i.e., in constant communion with God and in uninterrupted obedience. It is God alone who **has dominion over him.**

What does this passage imply as to the "sinlessness of Jesus"? Is it to be inferred that in the earthly or historical life Jesus *was* under the dominion of sin and death? Paul would surely not have expressed himself so. He would have said, however, that Jesus' life was lived in the realm where sin and death had established their dominion and in close contact with them. If "sinlessness" means refusal to consent to sin, then it is fair to suppose that Paul would have regarded Christ as sinless; if it means, as it is often thought of as meaning, virtual separation and aloofness from sin and thus freedom from temptation and struggle, it is highly unlikely that Paul would have ascribed it to Jesus. The writer to the Hebrews (4:15) states quite explicitly the answer which, it is probable, Paul would have given to the question we have raised: "One who in every respect has been tempted as we are, yet without sinning."

of each of us is clear. Because there are some things about which we have no doubt—God's love and mercy declared in the way he has dealt with us in Christ, the power of Christ's cross, and our ability to identify ourselves with what it means—there are other things about which we can be confident—our fuller participation in the victorious and abundant life. And in the moral struggle what is still a hope is also in some measure a fact. To a certain degree we already know what it is to overthrow the power of sin, and victory does not always or wholly elude us. That is why Paul can use both the present and the future tense when speaking about the abundant life which is our counterpart to Christ's resurrection.

The verses in question also usefully remind us that there can be no moral life of high quality unless there is some form of drastic discipline. We cannot expect to drift without effort into the appropriation of a power which overthrows the evil within and about us. "Mortification" (to borrow Gore's suggestive play on words) is a necessary part of Christian experience. When we translate into ordinary language the high phraseology in which Paul talks about sharing Christ's passion, we discover that it means putting to death within us the instincts and impulses which war against God's will. "Mortify therefore your members which are upon the earth" (Col. 3:5).

The final clause in vs. 6 sums up an important aspect of the Christian experience of salvation. The past and what it meant to us is destroyed, that **we might no longer be enslaved to sin.** Our old state was one of servitude; we were bond servants of the powers that held us in thralldom. These were of various sorts—for man's bondage is not always of one kind—and with sin Paul often associates the law and the evil powers of the spirit world. The imagery of the slaveowner fitted well with the highly personalized manner in which Paul spoke of sin—"sin sprang to life," "sin slew me and I died." It was therefore natural for him to refer to it as a malign power which held us in an unrelaxing grip. The form in which we conceive of sin is not here a matter of great importance, though anyone who has struggled ineffectually to escape from its power will not be disposed to quarrel with Paul's language. Salvation as emancipation is important, and it is one of Paul's central themes. No one is saved in a general sense; he is saved from something and to some-

11 Likewise reckon ye also yourselves to
be dead indeed unto sin, but alive unto
God through Jesus Christ our Lord.

but the life he lives he lives to God. **11** So
you also must consider yourselves dead to
sin and alive to God in Christ Jesus.

But according to the logic of Paul's position in this passage, the believer should be free not only from sin but also from temptation. To say that one is "dead to sin" can hardly mean less than this. This Paul would not have asserted even of Jesus during his earthly life. But it is true of Christ in his risen life; and it is with Christ as risen from the dead (and therefore belonging no longer to the realm where sin exists) that the believer is united and identified.

11. This union or identification is expressed in the phrase **in Christ Jesus.** We belong to Christ, "the second Adam," and are members of the newly and divinely created corporate community of which he is the head (see on vss. 3-4). In the realm of that community's life sin and death do not exist; the believer is **dead to sin and alive to God.**

But if this is true, what need is there for Paul to say, **So you also must consider yourselves dead to sin?** If the believers are *in fact* dead to sin, how can they help considering themselves to be so; and, indeed, why should it matter whether they *consider*

---

thing. Unless he is redeemed from the forces which hold him bound, he cannot even begin the new life. And it is useless to tell him he should be free unless he is shown how he can gain his liberty. The present passage contains all the essential elements of Paul's doctrine of salvation. It states the power that holds us bound (in this case sin); it indicates the realm of experience into which we are saved (variously described as newness of life, living with Christ, being alive to God); it is perfectly explicit about the means by which our deliverance is effected (by faith we are identified with Christ, so that we are able to die to sin as he died on the Cross, and to live to righteousness as he rose from the dead).

In reading the paragraph (vss. 5-11) one may be conscious of the incomplete character of our moral advance, but it is impossible to miss Paul's emphasis on the decisiveness of what we already know and the far-reaching consequences it holds for our lives. There is no claim on a dead man; death ends all counts against him (vs. 7). There is nothing one can say that will mitigate the force of the simple words, "He is dead." That particular man has passed beyond our reach, for good or evil. This indicates the kind of answer that we should give to the claim of sin: **We have died with Christ.** Paul strengthens his argument by pointing to the absolute finality of Christ's death. He died once; in so doing he passed completely and forever out of the domain of sin. His death was historical and it was unique. How astonished Paul would have been if he could have read the speculations of ingenious men who try to show that he fathered upon the world a mystery religion! In a mystery cult the death of the deity can be repeated innumerable times. Paul was convinced that he was talking about something that was rooted in our real world. Its very inherent character alone would make it preposterous to suggest that it could be repeated. The death Christ died was a death to sin; he broke its hitherto unchallenged power to hold men's spirits, and he did that once. Once is enough. The way of deliverance is open and is clear. All that remains is life, and **the life he lives he lives to God** (vs. 10). The eternal God is the means by which he lives, the sphere in which he lives, the end for which he lives. All his powers are taken up into God, all his consecration is to God, all his fellowship is with God. This is one of the points at which words fail because our grasp of truth is so imperfect. The full meaning of what it is to live beyond death "by the glory of the Father" we cannot guess, but the little we understand has a direct bearing on what we think of ourselves.

So you also must consider yourselves dead to sin and alive to God in Christ Jesus (vs. 11). "If we have been united with him in a death like his," we are, so far as sin is concerned, to regard ourselves as dead men. We do not respond to its suggestions. We are not answerable to its demands. We live in a world where its writ does not run and where its power is impotent. This, we should notice, is the way we are to **consider** ourselves. Paul does not suggest that the promptings of sin no longer awaken any response in our hearts, because sad experience teaches us that they do. But as a rule our reaction is determined by our estimate of ourselves, and we are often alive to sin's suggestions only because we do not consider ourselves dead to sin's authority. The first step in passing beyond the influence of sin is to know that we have passed out of its kingdom and always to

12 Let not sin therefore reign in your
.ortal body, that ye should obey it in the
ısts thereof.
13 Neither yield ye your members *as*
ıstruments of unrighteousness unto sin:
ut yield yourselves unto God, as those
ıat are alive from the dead, and your
ıembers *as* instruments of righteousness
nto God.

12 Let not sin therefore reign in your
mortal bodies, to make you obey their
passions. 13 Do not yield your members to
sin as instruments of wickedness, but yield
yourselves to God as men who have been
brought from death to life, and your members to God as instruments of righteousness.

ıemselves so or not? Here we are back again with the problem created by the discrepancy etween what the Christian must be—not merely "ought to be"—and what he is (see bove on vss. 1-2).

12-13. This problem continues to appear as Paul now proceeds to explicit exhorta-.on: **Let not sin . . . reign in your mortal bodies. . . . Do not yield your members to sin s instruments of wickedness, but yield yourselves to God . . . and your members to ;od as instruments of righteousness.** One sees, of course, the practical necessity of such xhortations as these; but it is not at first apparent how Paul could have thought of ıis necessity as consistent with his conception of the real character of the believer as eing "in Christ" and therefore "dead to sin."

:gard ourselves in that light. The positive ɔunterpart to seeing ourselves as **dead to sin** to know that we are **alive to God in Christ esus.** Here again intuition may tell us more ıan words can ever express. Clearly, however, ıe sharp antithesis between **dead to sin** and **live to God** gives us a start. In the one case 'e pass from under sin's power and cease to be nswerable to its authority. In the other case, ıerefore, we fully submit to God's reign and nter the realm where his rule is effective. ecause the oppressive tyranny of sin has been roken, we can submit to the beneficent sover-ignty of God. Since the impulses which sin rompts no longer control our actions, we are ree to serve God's purposes and to do his will.

At this point, however, the exact parallel reaks down. Thus far we have been consider-ng the alternative authorities by which our ives are governed; but the kinds of relation-hip created between sovereign and subject are undamentally different. A man may be the lave of sin, and—if he has any moral insight—e becomes increasingly aware that his servitude umiliates and degrades him. (This particular xperience is movingly described in ch. 7.) 3ut the man who is **alive to God** enters a rela-ionship in which his service opens the way to uller fellowship with his Lord. It means more han being conscious of God's presence; as we lo his will we learn to share it, and we delight o discover that it is "good and acceptable and ɔerfect" (12:2). If delight in God's law was ɔne of the noblest features of the old dispensa-ion, much more should it be a mark of the :hildren of the new covenant, who are **alive to 3od in Christ Jesus.** The concluding words are not a conventional addition, like the final clause in too many of our prayers. They point to one of the main subjects in the preceding verses, and recapitulate one of Paul's principal themes. The life of the Christian is **in Christ.** How close that identification ought to be Paul has shown by the imagery he has used. He now suggests that the new life has Christ as the sphere in which it is lived, the atmosphere by which it is surrounded. The extent to which this decides the character of that new life is clear as soon as we reflect on the meaning of Paul's words. Christ provides the laws by which that life is governed, the nourishment by which it is sustained, the ends toward which its ener-gies are directed. No man can be **alive to God** except **in Christ Jesus.** One might as reasonably urge him to breathe freely in a vacuum.

12-14. ***Consequences of the New Outlook.***—From what Paul has said it follows that Chris-tians ought to adopt a new attitude to life. This is the truth that he enforces in vs. 11, and from it he draws now the necessary practical deduc-tions. The first and general consequence of what he has said is the necessity of working out in our ordinary daily life the moral results of being **alive to God in Christ Jesus.** We cannot divorce theology (the truth about God) from ethics (the practical application of what we know to be true), and Paul would have been the last man on earth to permit high doctrine to be separated from common duty.

The first application: Acknowledge only reigning powers. Sin is a tyrant who has been deposed and consequently his authority has been overthrown. In practical affairs we ought to act accordingly. It is possible to give theo-

14 For sin shall not have dominion over you: for ye are not under the law, but under grace.

14 For sin will have no dominion over you, since you are not under law but under grace.

14a. The probable solution of this problem is at least suggested by the future tense of the verb in the sentence **For sin will have no dominion over you,** as was also true of the future tenses noted in vss. 5 and 8. Salvation is, as we have had occasion to note more than once (cf. on 1:16; 5:9, 10; 6:8), essentially eschatological. It belongs to the new age. That new age—the age of Christ, the age of the Spirit—has not yet come, although there are unmistakable signs that it is about to come, indeed is beginning to come. The Spirit has been given; and the Spirit, as we have already hinted, is more than the sign or seal of a promise; it is the very life of the new age manifesting itself among us. The Spirit is, as Paul will say a little later (8:23), the "first fruits," or as it is called in Eph. 1:14, the "earnest of our inheritance." But the "inheritance" itself has not been actually received. We are heirs in principle, but not yet in fact. It is as though the will had been declared legal, we have been pronounced the rightful heirs, a token payment has been actually paid to us, and it is only a matter of a brief time till the bulk of the estate will be in our possession. This figure serves as well as any other to set forth the way in which for Paul the future was already present. Only less apt perhaps would be the analogy of the moment at the beginning of each day when the first signs of dawn appear. Should one then say that the day has come or that it will come? Clearly one might truly speak in either way: in actual fact the day has not come (the darkness is as deep as ever), but in principle it has come and, indeed, in those hints of color and light on the eastern horizon it has begun to come in fact.

Now when Paul speaks of what the believer essentially is—as he does so frequently in this chapter—he is always thinking of what he *will be*. The sureness of that future, its nearness, and the fact that it is, in the way already several times indicated, already

retical assent to sin's deposition and yet submit to his commands. Sin has no longer any right to **reign in** our **mortal bodies,** and we should not allow him to do so. But sin, though actually deposed, can sometimes dupe us into doing his will. The **passions** of our physical being are the means through which he has hitherto achieved his purposes. The material side of our being, through the insistence of its appetites, has brought our higher nature into bondage. What Paul is suggesting is an incongruity as pronounced as that contained in Jesus' story of the evil spirit, ejected from a man's life, who came back and repossessed it with no better claim than squatters' rights could give him. For us to recognize that we have passed from death to life, and yet allow sin to reassert his power, is to deny the reality of the gospel. The redeemed life cannot permit its **members** to be seized by sin and used **as instruments of wickedness**—as weapons on the side of evil in the spiritual war.

The second application: Our duty is to **yield** ourselves **to God,** and our **members . . . as instruments of righteousness.** Our working allegiance should correspond to our theoretical status. It is no use to establish by means of a theological argument that we are **men who have been brought from death to life** if we never demonstrate the truth of our claim by translating it into the substance of our daily conduct. When we do that, our whole being will be used to establish the things in which we profess to be most deeply interested; even our members will be used as weapons with which to fight the battle of **righteousness.** The redeemed man finds that his body is the temple of God's spirit, and evil powers are denied even the rights of temporary entry. (As often happens, Paul himself provides the most illuminating commentary on what he has written. I Cor. 6:9-20 both expands and illustrates what he has here stated in compressed form.)

The third application: **Sin will have no dominion over you, since you are not under law but under grace.** The tense is future. Paul demands that we see ourselves not only as we are but as we shall be. It is the combination of tenses (cf. the treatment of this whole subject in the Exeg.) which makes it possible for Paul to maintain both the present moral reality and the ultimate spiritual truth of his position. This is not an exercise in self-delusion; it is due to the conviction that what is potential is on the way to becoming actual. Paul does not regard the present status as the most important thing about a person or an institution. More signifi-

becoming present—these considerations enable him to refer to it often as though it were an actual present fact. The interim between the present moment and the full dawning of the new age is so brief that for most purposes it can be disregarded. Thus he can say, "We who died to sin" (vs. 2), as though salvation from sin had already been realized; but he can say equally readily, as here, **Sin will have no dominion over you.** But there can be no doubt that strictly speaking the second of these statements is the more accurate.

If we can justifiably make a distinction between the "theological" and the "ethical" in Paul's letters, we might say that in the theological sections Paul tends to disregard the interim and to speak of the believer as though the new age had already fully come; in the ethical sections he cannot do this. He *must* deal with the presence of sin in the believer; but he lacks really adequate theoretical tools or terms for doing so.

14*b*. What does Paul mean by saying, **You are not under law but under grace?** Does he mean that we **are not under law** (*a*) in the sense that all of the commands of the law are now invalid, no longer binding, for the believer; or (*b*) in the sense that the believer, because of the power of the Spirit, now finds himself able to fulfill the law and is therefore not aware of its restrictions and demands; or (*c*) in the sense that the believer does not now have to rely upon his obedience to the law for his acceptance with God? Perhaps all of these three senses are present, but if so, the same ambiguity about tense of which we have been speaking is also present. Senses (*a*) and (*b*) are essentially future, and thus taken, the more accurate statement would be "we *will be* not under law"; only the third sense allows strictly for the present tense. We are (i.e., now) *not* under law only in the sense that our acceptance with God is not conditional upon our obedience to it, but rather upon our faith in Christ.

---

cant is the determining spiritual force at work within the person or the institution. Unless that force is stifled, it will finally achieve the results which correspond to its dynamic power. That is why Paul can—without a trace of flattery or deception—refer to very imperfect men and women as "saints." It explains his ability to see without illusion the congregations that he gathers, and yet to set forth an uncompromising doctrine of the high status of the church of Christ. The practical truth of what he suggests in the present verse is that a man who sees himself as definitely emancipated from sin's power is likely at last to find himself immune to sin's solicitations. A power which we now know has no authority is a power whose demands, however plausible and appealing they may be, we shall finally succeed in completely repudiating. There is more involved than sound psychology. Paul gives a true account, no doubt, of the way the human mind reacts; but he also sees that the assurance of our final deliverance is closely related to the kind of dispensation under which we live. It would be pointless to say to a man who is struggling along under the domination of legalism, "You will eventually be completely free." He will always be bound. There exists so close an interrelation between the principle of legalism and the experience of sin's power that the two prove to be inseparable. Paul has stated this already and will amplify it later on. For the moment it is enough to declare that those who are certain of complete deliverance are those who live in the present assurance that they are dependent only on the good will and mercy of God.

The fourth application: Christians are expected to reach a much more exacting standard than that unheroic acceptance of conventions which passes for morality in the world at large. Paul insists that the believer has passed from one clearly defined jurisdiction into another. Those **who have been brought from death to life** cannot be content with the quality of life which seemed sufficient before "our old self was crucified." This does not merely mean a more rigorous application of certain principles—though since our society still retains certain traditional Christian standards, this sometimes happens. Paul's basic contention is that there is a worldly or secular outlook on life and a Christian one. Our judgments of other people, our estimate of money and of all the other objects of man's perennial pursuit, our scale of objectives and the ambitions we cherish—all these things are decisively affected by the outlook which governs our approach to them. Moreover, the character of our corporate life shows clearly that the forces which Paul recognized as manifestations of a worldly and irreligious spirit are still strong among us. The bitter chaos of international affairs, the open antipathies which divide races and classes, the malice and hatred which flourish among us show clearly that "the world of sin is still what it always was." There are words of peace and comfort in this passage,

15 What then? shall we sin, because we are not under the law, but under grace? God forbid.

15 What then? Are we to sin because we are not under law but under grace? By

2. An Analogy from Slavery (6:15-23)

15. Here Paul returns to the question with which this section of the letter began (cf. vs. 1): **Are we to sin because we are not under law but under grace?** And again he answers with a vigorous denial, **God forbid.** But again his justification of this denial takes the form of a demonstration of the *impossibility* of sin rather than of the *moral wrongness* of sin. As a matter of fact, does it not again appear that having dismissed the law as binding upon the believer, Paul lacks any real basis for establishing ethical *obligation* (see above, p. 471)? If it is the law which produces transgression, and if the believer in Christ is released from the law, is he not freed also from the *possibility* of transgression? One can avoid this conclusion only if one understands Paul to mean by "the law" merely the Jewish law, and indeed even solely the ceremonial requirements of that law; but Paul never makes this distinction between the moral and the ceremonial elements of the law, and the whole nature of Paul's argument here and elsewhere strongly indicates that by "the law" he means any and every commandment of God. The law, he seems often to say, is abrogated in Christ: **We are not under law**—law of any kind.

We now see the basis of the constant association of the law with sin in Paul's thought (he is to deal with this subject more fully in 7:7-13). Both sin and the law belong to "the old man," the situation "in Adam." Paul has reminded us in the first half of this chapter that when we were "baptized into Christ," we "died to sin," i.e., were separated from the realm where sin had established itself. But just as where there is no law, there is no sin (in the sense of transgression), so where there is no sin, Paul argues, there is also no law (in the sense of obligation).

but its general tenor reveals the fact that Paul saw the Christian's moral life as an unremitting struggle with evil forces. The struggle begins with so drastic a breach that "crucifixion" is an appropriate word by which to describe it; while the distinguishable quality of the life itself is that those who share it know that it is a life lived beyond that kind of death.

15-19. ***No Man Can Serve Two Masters.***—Paul returns to the question which opened this chapter, and gives virtually the same answer even though he states it in a slightly different form. Sin, he has told us, belongs to the old life, and those who by death have entered a new realm are no longer subject to its power. A man cannot continue in sin, since it belongs to an entirely different world. He now alters the imagery. We cannot sin, he says, because we are dealing with two kinds of service which are strictly incompatible. **Sin** and **righteousness** are alternative forms of **obedience;** one must choose between them, for it is absolutely impossible to select both. To emphasize this truth slavery was a useful figure of speech. Everyone was familiar with it—ancient society was built upon it—and it was consequently unnecessary to explain his illustration. Everyone knew that the master had complete and exclusive jurisdiction over his slave. In the case of the slave all his skill, all his energy, all his time were wholly at his master's disposal. So that, given the fact of slavery, a man could not serve two masters, even when their requirements were not fundamentally incompatible in character: the demands of the owner excluded all others. In the case of Paul's illustration there is added the further fact that the two masters are utterly opposed in nature. The illustration could be even further expanded: not only does the master require the undivided allegiance of his slave, but he frees that slave from all other claims. The slave is answerable to no one else for what he does, and in every conceivable situation he is responsible to his master only. This, says Paul, is exactly what happens so far as our moral allegiance is concerned. When you were **slaves of sin,** he says, you were entirely free from the claims of righteousness; in the same way, now that you belong **to righteousness,** you are beyond the orbit within which sin can appeal to your obedience.

The passage sets clearly before us the exclusive kind of choice which is part of the moral life and cannot be evaded. We cannot avoid the issue even by procrastination. To each of us comes the demand, "Choose you this day whom ye will serve" (Josh. 24:15), and we cannot halt indefinitely between competing claims.

16 Know ye not, that to whom ye yield yourselves servants to obey, his servants ye are to whom ye obey; whether of sin unto death, or of obedience unto righteousness?

17 But God be thanked, that ye were the servants of sin, but ye have obeyed from the heart that form of doctrine which was delivered you.

18 Being then made free from sin, ye became the servants of righteousness.

no means! 16 Do you not know that if you
yield yourselves to any one as obedient
slaves, you are slaves of the one whom you
obey, either of sin, which leads to death,
or of obedience, which leads to righteousness? 17 But thanks be to God, that you
who were once slaves of sin have become
obedient from the heart to the standard of
teaching to which you were committed,
18 and having been set free from sin, have

16-18. He now attempts a second illustration of the impossibility of the believer's continuing in sin—this time drawn from the institution of slavery. His meaning in general is perfectly clear—essentially the same meaning as throughout this chapter and to 7:6: just as a change in masters makes an utter difference to the slave, since the slave always belongs *entirely* to whoever owns him, so entrance into Christ makes an utter difference for the believer; again "old things are passed away" and "all things are become new." This general sense is unmistakable, but like 5:15-16, this passage would undoubtedly have been changed in details if Paul had reviewed and revised it. **Sin, which leads to death** hardly corresponds with **obedience, which leads to righteousness.** Surely he would have preferred to write, instead of the latter, "righteousness which leads to life" or better still, "God who gives life." He could scarcely have intended to speak of "obeying obedience," but that is precisely what he says. One also can scarcely believe that Paul intended to say that in the believer obedience to sin had been replaced by obedience to what would seem to amount to a new law, **the standard of teaching to which you were committed.**

The character of every life is determined by the kind of loyalty which rules it, and in the moral realm there are really only two possibilities: we are for either "the good or evil side." This may create difficulties for the man who likes to balance one choice against another and hold his decision in reserve, but it has great advantages as well. It really simplifies matters enormously, and in our more honest moments we are ready to admit it.

There is no escaping the appeal of a life which is definitely and finally committed one way or the other. Very few people really want to drift aimlessly without consistent direction or fixed goal. There is no profit in having to decide anew where to stand on every issue that arises. Life does not always correspond to the sharp antithesis which Paul indicates, but the essential truth is beyond dispute. We belong on one side or the other; and the whole trend of our lives confirms the choice we make. It need not be a conscious choice; even the man who hesitates and flatters himself that he is not yet on either side is already on the wrong side. We are making in one direction or the other, and that with cumulative results. If we are on the wrong side, we get worse; if we are on the right side, we get better: the momentum of the moral life carries us in the direction of our choice. The person who has **yielded his members to impurity** finds that it is **to greater and greater iniquity;** but if we **yield** our **members to righteousness,** we can legitimately hope that it will be **for sanctification** (vs. 19).

This hope has already materialized—in part —as far as Paul's correspondents are concerned, and in vs. 17 we have a reminder of the deep gratitude with which we should regard the deliverance of those who were formerly the servants of sin. Such gratitude follows inevitably from the nature of the Christian community. In the previous section, when Paul was speaking of baptism as the means of admission to the new life, we could catch a glimpse of the corporate unity which marks the church. We are not saved into isolated individualism, but into the fellowship of the redeemed. It is only because we are members of the community of grace that the promises of the gospel reach us. The church is the setting of the life beyond death. How natural, then, that we should remember, with thanks to God, that those **who were once slaves of sin have become obedient from the heart** to the substance of the gospel! In such gratitude there is first of all a deep consciousness of the reality of the bondage from

19 I speak after the manner of men because of the infirmity of your flesh: for as
ye have yielded your members servants to
uncleanness and to iniquity unto iniquity;
even so now yield your members servants
to righteousness unto holiness.
20 For when ye were the servants of sin,
ye were free from righteousness.

become slaves of righteousness. **19** I an
speaking in human terms, because of you
natural limitations. For just as you onc
yielded your members to impurity and t
greater and greater iniquity, so now yiel
your members to righteousness for sancti
fication.
20 When you were slaves of sin, you wer

---

19. The truth is that Paul's analogy is not too fortunately chosen—since the natura opposite of slavery to sin is emancipation—and he is having trouble making it work One can hardly avoid being somewhat amused when he shifts the blame to his readers "I use this human analogy to bring the truth home to your weak nature" (Moffatt) Dodd writes: "The apology cannot be called tactful, but it shows that Paul is consciou that his illustration is not going very well."

This section also concludes with exhortation (cf. vss. 12-14). Since you *are* slave of righteousness, cease yielding **your members to impurity and to greater and greate iniquity,** and **yield** them **to righteousness for sanctification.** The term **sanctificatio** (ἁγιασμός) has not thus far occurred in this letter, and indeed occurs rarely in Paul although the closely related "saints" (ἅγιοι) is constantly found. The word basicall means "holy"—in the sense of that which belongs to God. Applying first of all to God' own character, it naturally passes over to objects and persons set apart or consecrated fo God's use. Such is its meaning here. The suggestion is that if we yield ourselves i obedience to righteousness, God will consecrate us to his service. But has not God alread set us thus apart in calling us to be "saints" (1:7)? And in any case can God's act o consecration be conditioned upon any act of ours? This is only another instance of th theoretical difficulties into which Paul falls whenever he resorts to exhortation (se above, p. 479). According to Paul's *theory,* the ethical life is the inevitable "frui of the Spirit," and exhortation is as irrelevant as it is unnecessary.

20. The exhortation is now reinforced (vss. 20-23) with a reminder of the radicall different consequences following upon the two kinds of obedience. What is meant b

---

which the Christian is set free. Our unquestioning acceptance of the modest standards of conventional morality has robbed us of that intense awareness of the bondage to sin which formed part of the early Christian outlook. When our associates were set free from moral servitude, our natural reaction was **Thanks be to God.** Gratitude is also prompted by the reality of the obedience upon which the Christian enters. The new life is not an outward pattern of behavior, thoughtlessly adopted by the convert. The depth of the new allegiance proves how genuine it is; we have become obedient, says Paul, **from the heart.** The Christian is committed to a certain **standard of teaching;** and this too is an occasion for gratitude. Cyril of Jerusalem speaks of the new believer as being handed over to the faith,[6] and the imagery is the same as that which Paul uses. It is not a pattern of doctrine which Paul has in mind, though belief necessarily has its place. He is thinking primarily of the teaching which trains a person in uprightness of life. The contrast is with the demands of sin. The ne service, as well as the old, has its requirements— ethical ones—and the teaching when accepte becomes the moral authority which governs ou lives. The final ground of thanksgiving is th nature of the new allegiance which the Chris tian accepts: **Having been set free from sin we have become slaves of righteousness.** W have noted more than once that Paul is neve content simply with the fact of deliverance; h is always conscious of the new alternativ which is even more important than the ol bondage. We know all too well the futility o releasing a prisoner from jail if we make n provision for his re-establishment in the life o the community. Paul is never guilty of this kin of oversight, and a part of his gratitude for th deliverance of his readers from sin springs fro his assurance that they have entered upon th service of righteousness.

20-23. ***Different Service, Different Satisfac tions.***—A transfer of allegiance has taken place and there is no mistaking the value of the re sults. It is true that in the old days of servitud

[6] *Catechetical Lectures* IV. 3.

21 What fruit had ye then in those things whereof ye are now ashamed? for the end of those things *is* death.

22 But now being made free from sin, and become servants to God, ye have your

free in regard to righteousness. 21 But then
what return did you get from the things of which you are now ashamed? The end of those things is death.
22 But now that
you have been set free from sin and have

"righeousness" in the statement that believers were formerly **free in regard to righteousness?** The same question arises in connection with vs. 18, where believers are spoken of as having now "become slaves of righteousness." At that point, i.e., vss. 17-18, "righteousness" seems to be equated with "the standard of teaching to which you were committed," and thus to be the equivalent of a new and higher law. Such is the most natural way to understand Paul's meaning in vs. 20 also, inconsistent as such a teaching would be with Paul's characteristic view of the relation of sin and the law. In that view slavery to sin is slavery to the law, and freedom from sin is freedom from the law. Perhaps this is another instance of how a somewhat unfortunate analogy has betrayed him.

21-23. What return did you get from the things [i.e., "impurity and . . . greater and greater iniquity" (vs. 19)] **of which you are now ashamed?** The answer is **death.** This **death** is essentially eschatological and therefore—in the full sense—future. But it had already manifested itself within the experience of those who have now "passed from death unto life" (I John 3:14). They had felt themselves already in the grip of a disintegrating power and on the way to spiritual destruction. Paul is thus appealing here

to sin the Christian was not answerable to the demands of righteousness, and these can be exacting enough. But their former immunity was without benefit: **What return did you get from the things of which you are now ashamed?** Throughout his letters Paul is uncompromising in his emphasis on the consequences of wrongdoing. "He who sows to his own flesh will from the flesh reap corruption" (Gal. 6:8). The seeds of evil ripen to a bitter harvest. Besides the other forms of retribution which sin brings, there is the shame which grows more acute as a man looks back from the vantage ground of a new loyalty to the kind of service to which he once submitted. The results of sin, as we have already noted, are cumulative; the man who yields his members to impurity finds that he is involved in "greater and greater iniquity" (vs. 19). A progression of that kind admits of only one conclusion: **The end of those things is death.** The stifling of our higher instincts, the blinding of our truer insights, the atrophy of our finer qualities—these so separate us from the sources of true life that our existence is a foretaste of that final death wherein we are entirely cut off from God. So much for what slavery to sin can offer.

Paul then turns at once, in order to preserve the value of the contrast, to the advantages of the service to which his readers have now submitted. If you **become slaves of God, the return you get is sanctification and its end, eternal life.** The immediate consequence of our new service is a life which begins to bear the marks of holiness; the ultimate consequence is **eternal life.** But eternal life is also in part a present experience. Its strict equivalent is not "life forevermore." It is life of a new quality, life touched into kinship with the life of God. Because it belongs to the realm of reality it is not at the mercy of chances and changes, and is therefore everlasting.

Vs. 23 is more than a striking epitome of the blessings which flow from our new allegiance. In a threefold contrast it gathers up all that Paul has said about two opposing types of service. On the one hand we have **the wages of sin,** on the other, **the free gift of God.** Wages are the outward recognition of something that has been done. They are according to contract, and they are in proportion to our desert. A free gift is not earned, and consequently it need not be restricted to the small measure of our merit. The man who lives under sin can appeal only to the natural law which governs the moral world; but he who accepts God's gift in Christ belongs to the wholly different realm of grace. Equally different are the results which follow. The servant of sin gets the only wages sin can pay. Since these are determined by the inflexible laws of the moral life, he can expect nothing except death. That is the reward sin gives its servants: **The wages of sin is death.** The exact opposite of death, from whatever angle we regard it, is **eternal life.** The two are drastically different as concerns the methods by which they are attained, the qualities which distinguish them, the experiences to which they admit us, and the final prospects which they unfold. In the third place, there is the contrast between

fruit unto holiness, and the end everlasting life.
23 For the wages of sin *is* death; but the gift of God *is* eternal life through Jesus Christ our Lord.

become slaves of God, the return you get is sanctification and its end, eternal life.
23 For the wages of sin is death, but the free gift of God is eternal life in Christ Jesus our Lord.

---

not to a mere eschatological belief, but to an empirical fact (note what is said on this point on 1:18 ff.). The same thing can be said of his reference to **sanctification and its end, eternal life.** This too, although future in fulfillment, was already a present reality.

Paul now sets over against slavery to sin, slavery to God: **You have been set free from sin and have become slaves of God.** This is vastly different from slavery to a "standard of teaching" or to "righteousness," and comes, we may be sure, much nearer to saying what Paul really wanted to say. The believer belongs not to any law, but to God himself. Such slavery is not slavery at all, but freedom. And the **eternal life** is not **the wages** of a servant, but a **free gift** to a son. (Paul has not yet used this term, but only the word is lacking.)

Something should be said about the phrase **eternal life in Christ Jesus our Lord.** The phrase **in Christ Jesus our Lord** is undoubtedly to be interpreted in the light of the contrast of Christ with Adam as representing an entirely new order of relationships, the new community between men and God and among men, essentially eschatological but even now in process of being created. Of this new order perhaps enough has been said (see pp. 472-73). The phrase **eternal life** Paul uses only rarely—nowhere except in Romans (2:7; 5:21; and here) and Galatians (6:8). Paul prefers to speak of the "resurrection" when referring to the ultimate destiny of the believer in Christ. He speaks often, however, of "life"; and "eternal" is always understood. As with the author of the Fourth Gospel, the believer in Christ has become the recipient of a new life, and this life is in its very nature everlasting.

---

sin, the old master who claims the labor of the unredeemed, and **God,** the new master to whose free service Christ admits us. And the parallel can be extended further still, to include the nature of what each offers us as an immediate consequence of the relationship into which we enter. The employment of sin is bitter and frustrating; the gift which God gives is peace and joy.

There are few passages in the N.T. where the problem of human freedom is so explicitly discussed. "Do you not know," asks Paul, "that if you yield yourselves to any one as obedient slaves, you are slaves of the one whom you obey?" (Vs. 16.) But it is also apparent to him that we have only two choices before us; we can be the slaves of sin or the slaves of righteousness. He did not stop to consider the possibility that we might decide to be the servants of no one. To Paul that would have seemed an entirely profitless discussion of a purely hypothetical question. He shared the biblical conviction that man is a created being. Now it is the mark of a creature that he is dependent on his creator, and dependence remains the invariable characteristic of man's life. He may vary his service but, even so, the range of his choice is not really large. The most insidious temptation man could face—and the cause of his most catastrophic fall—was to believe that he could "be like God" (Gen. 3:5). It is consequently nothing but self-delusion to think that we are really independent, or can do exactly as we please. A man always acts under obedience; often when he thinks he has won complete freedom from control, he has merely fallen a prey to license. Our common language (as Gore points out) testifies to the fact. We speak of the drunkard as a slave to drink, of the libertine as a slave to lust; and so one after another of the various impulses to which men submit. But if we are always under obedience, and never completely untrammeled, it behooves us to watch carefully the kind of service which we accept. Some kinds destroy their victims, leading them farther and farther away from the possibility of self-realization. But there is a kind which makes it possible for us to achieve our fullest development and to live in part at least the life we know we ought to live. In this human liberty consists. Those who serve God discover not only that they are set free from every alternative obedience, but that his "service is perfect freedom." We **have been set free from sin,** said Paul, **and have become slaves of God.** In the process we have discovered that **the free gift of God is**

7 Know ye not, brethren, (for I speak to
them that know the law,) how that the
law hath dominion over a man as long as
he liveth?
2 For the woman which hath a husband
is bound by the law to *her* husband so
long as he liveth; but if the husband be
dead, she is loosed from the law of *her*
husband.

7 Do you not know, brethren — for I am
speaking to those who know the law —
that the law is binding on a person only
during his life? 2 Thus a married woman
is bound by law to her husband as long
as he lives; but if her husband dies she is
discharged from the law concerning the

3. An Analogy from Marriage (7:1-6)

Paul feels the need of giving his idea of the believer's necessary separation from sin further emphasis and clarification and decides to try one more analogy. By means of it he succeeds perhaps in emphasizing his idea, but hardly in clarifying it. Indeed, the new illustration from marriage becomes even more awkward than the preceding one from slavery. Again the general intention of the apostle is clear enough: we were formerly married, as it were, to sin; but sin has now died, and we are free to belong to another husband, even Christ, and in fact we do belong to him. We formerly bore "fruit for death"; now we bear "fruit for God." Some such idea as this is apparently in Paul's mind, but his statement in detail is confused.

7:1-3. He begins by citing an axiom—**The law is binding on a person only during his life.** His parenthetical **for I am speaking to those who know the law** is intended as a compliment to his readers; it is the same kind of apologetic remark as we find also in

eternal life in Christ Jesus our Lord. Paul knew no more exhaustive way of describing the only form in which true human liberty can be achieved.

7:1-6. ***An Analogy: Its Problems and Its Point.*** —Analogies are notoriously difficult to control. Even a writer finds that they tend to get out of hand; but his problems are simplicity itself compared with those of a speaker. Take even a simple analogy, and in the course of a few sentences it has revealed the most Protean ability to change its form. Paul, we must remember, was a speaker, with the added difficulties inseparable from being tied to the slow capacities of an ancient amanuensis. Anyone who has read with shame the confused dictation which his secretary has brought back for correction will feel himself quite at home in the opening verses of ch. 7.

The confusion may also be attributed to the fact that two thoughts are present in Paul's mind—there is the old nature, married to sin, which has been put to death, so that our true self can be united to Christ; and there is law, which also belonged to the old order, and whose power has been ended by the death we share with Christ. The ideas are related: they are both intimately connected with death as the decisive breach between the old order and the new; and both are inseparable from any full consideration of what Christ has accomplished for us. So Paul launches out on his analogy, and as the scribe painfully scratches down his words, his active mind, so quick to grasp interrelated thoughts, races ahead, and when the dictation is completed, the result is the confusion before us.

Owing to the method he has chosen and the difficulties inherent in the analogy he uses, this passage does not constitute one of Paul's great statements of his gospel. But it is concerned with great themes, and various useful points emerge.

In vs. 4, Paul reaffirms a principle which he has already enunciated (cf. 6:6) but which he considers sufficiently important to be presented in a different form. The central fact is that we have died to the former life and live a new one. As a result, certain things are past and done with. At times Paul singles out sin as the mark of the old life; but here he fixes on law, and his mind already anticipates that moving demonstration of their inseparable relation which will follow. At all events, both sin and law belong to the old world that lies on the far side of that decisive boundary, death. **You have died to the law,** says he, **through the body of Christ.** It is not an individual experience. It is something we share with all the people of God; together with other members of the church we have died, with Christ, to the power of sin, to the authority of law, to the tyranny of the flesh. Both the purpose and the result of that change are a new allegiance: **so that you may belong**

3 So then if, while *her* husband liveth, she be married to another man, she shall be called an adulteress: but if her husband be dead, she is free from that law; so that she is no adulteress, though she be married to another man.

husband. 3 Accordingly, she will be called an adulteress if she lives with another man while her husband is alive. But if her husband dies she is free from that law, and if she marries another man she is not an adulteress.

15:14-15. **The law** in this sentence may be Roman law, or (barely possibly) Jewish law; more probably Paul is referring to what he conceives to be a principle of any and all law. Having laid down this principle, Paul might have been expected to say: **Thus a married woman is bound by law to her husband as long as** *she* **lives;** but as a matter of fact it is the *husband* who is said to die! It is, of course, true that a woman is freed from obligation to her husband when he dies and that she can then marry another without becoming an **adulteress**—but this is not an instance of the general principle cited in vs. 1. (**The law concerning the husband** is a way of referring to that part of the legal code which states the rights of the husband.)

to another. As is right and natural, we belong **to him who has been raised from the dead.** We are Christ's folk, and the union is one whose intimacy it is impossible to exaggerate. Paul has already used the imagery of marriage, and he presses it into service again. The church is the bride of Christ, and this applies also to each of us individually. Marriage leads naturally to offspring, and the consequence of our relationship to Christ is that our lives are fruitful in all that promotes God's purpose. "And we know," remarks Calvin, "that the fruits which our heavenly father requires from us are those of holiness and righteousness." [7]

Closely related to the above subject is another to which Paul repeatedly returns. It is important, he says, that we should refuse to live in the new life as though we were still bound by the powers of the old. The strange discrepancy to which he refers is too often a characteristic of Christians. We profess to believe in the availability of spiritual resources which nonetheless we neglect to claim. We talk about a liberation whose full freedom we never discover. In particular we are content to be governed by standards which the world may enforce but which ought to be irrelevant to Christians. The incongruity of the situation distresses and bewilders Paul. What was natural before is so no longer: **Now we are discharged from the law, dead to that which held us captive, so that we serve not under the old written code** (vs. 6). The imagery itself offers full scope for expansion. The figure is that of the prisoner set free from his old captivity, granted a discharge which puts him beyond the reach of his former jailer, and freed from the terms of the code under which he served his sentence. He now serves **in the new life of the Spirit.** When Paul attempts a detailed analogy his imagination usually stumbles, but he has an unequaled gift for striking off compressed metaphors which open up the nature of our deliverance.

The figure of the discharged prisoner suggests another way in which the law illustrates Paul's thought. Moral and ceremonial restraints—the oppressive force with which he is concerned at the moment—have no power over us because our way of life puts us beyond their reach. Paul is describing something that happens every day in our relations with the civil law. As he himself points out in 13:3, the man who observes the law has no fear of those who enforce it because he does nothing that gives them any power over him. He may be on excellent terms with the judge and may meet the policeman without a qualm. The scene of their labors is a world to which he does not belong.

In vss. 4-5, Paul is clearly contrasting two kinds of life. We may loosely call the one a spiritual life and the other a life dominated by physical instincts. His use of such a term as **flesh** can lead us into an intricate and highly technical field—one into which not many people would be concerned to follow. But the struggle between the life which is ruled by insight and that which is governed by impulse is a matter of common experience. Many people are content to "live in the flesh," but many others struggle desperately to get free. A complete account of how Paul believed this freedom is attained would be a résumé of his theology; but what he says here provides incidental illumination. As Gore points out, the passions to which Paul refers are "those feelings which we experience without any action of our will." [8]

[7] *Commentaries on Romans, ad loc.*

[8] *Epistle to Romans*, I, 244.

4 Wherefore, my brethren, ye also are become dead to the law by the body of Christ; that ye should be married to another, *even* to him who is raised from the dead, that we should bring forth fruit unto God.

4 Likewise, my brethren, you have died to the law through the body of Christ, so that you may belong to another, to him who has been raised from the dead in order

4. Paul's application of his analogy is as confused as the analogy itself. One would suppose from the whole preceding discussion that the "husband" in vss. 1-3 stands for sin, but now it suddenly appears that he represents the law. And instead of the law's dying, as the husband did, it is the believer who dies! We are back with the same terms as those in which Paul's idea was first expressed at the beginning of this chapter. There it was said that the believer has died to sin; now the death is to the law. We have already noted how closely Paul associates sin and law.

We **have died to the law through the body of Christ.** Paul here may be referring simply to the crucifixion of the body of Jesus (as in 6:6), but more probably **the body of Christ,** as in I Cor. 12:27 and Rom. 12:5, is the church. As members of the new community and sharers of the new spiritual life (i.e., as being "in Christ") we have died to the old order, where both sin and law belong, and have been made alive with **him**

They are the raw material of our moral life. In themselves they may be entirely neutral—like hunger or thirst—but they are among the motives which prompt the will to action. We may yield to them or we may not; if we do, passions are translated into voluntary actions. The way in which this happens largely determines the quality of our moral life. When we have little power to direct our impulses, then our life suffers. We become the slaves of "passions" which are now **sinful passions.** It is the unregulated turbulence of what is natural and morally neutral that makes a man a slave of sin. Deliverance from **living in the flesh** does not come through preoccupation with the sinful passions, but through discovering a power strong enough to make us their masters.

The purpose of an analogy is to illustrate some truth beyond itself, and it is not always wise to concentrate on the particular form, especially when it has become confused. Nevertheless, when Paul refers to marriage, he is concerned with a subject on which the early church held views that our modern society is rapidly forsaking. When he says that **a married woman is bound by law to her husband as long as he lives,** he may have oversimplified the provisions both of Roman and of Jewish law, but he was stating a general principle which he did not expect the Christian conscience would contradict. In the face of modern social practice it seems pointless to argue in detail whether or not Jesus' words in Matthew allow an exception to his general refusal of divorce. Even the more lenient provision belongs to a world wholly different from the "consecutive polygamy" which now claims social sanction. As Jesus reminded the woman at the well, when a person has had a number of partners, it is no longer possible to speak of any new tie as marriage at all. Marriage is a relationship so intimate that it affects personality in a way which must be either unique or utterly destructive. Paul is not developing a doctrine of marriage in this passage; he is assuming it, but often a man's unconscious assumptions are as important as his considered pronouncements.

In the last clause of vs. 6, the rendering of the KJV supplies the kind of contrast which arrests the hearer's mind. Two possible types of service are before us, one **in newness of spirit,** the other **in the oldness of the letter.** The terms tempt us to consider the inner and essential spirit as opposed to the outward and incidental form; but this is plainly not the contrast intended. We serve, as the RSV reminds us, **in the new life of the Spirit,** i.e., a life which is maintained and directed by the Spirit. The alternative is to be ruled by the **old written code**—by the ancient provisions of the law of Moses. For centuries men had tried to regulate their lives by rules, and the result had been consistent failure. The old way has had its chance. But actually the opposition between **old** and **new** is more important because of the fresh hope it introduces than because of any significance which attaches to the chronological contrast, though the old is not necessarily false, nor the new necessarily true. More significant still is the difference between an inward and dynamic control and an external and mechanical one. Regulations have always failed to inspire the

5 For when we were in the flesh, the motions of sins, which were by the law, did work in our members to bring forth fruit unto death.

6 But now we are delivered from the law, that being dead wherein we were held; that we should serve in newness of spirit, and not *in* the oldness of the letter.

that we may bear fruit for God.
5 While we were living in the flesh, our sinful passions, aroused by the law, were at work in our members to bear fruit for death.
6 But now we are discharged from the law, dead to that which held us captive, so that we serve not under the old written code but in the new life of the Spirit.

---

who has been raised from the dead. This union with Christ means the bearing of **fruit for God** (cf. "alive to God" in 6:11), i.e., the living of lives acceptable to God and useful for his purposes.

5-6. The former marriage—now apparently described as with **the flesh**—was also fruitful, but the fruit was **for death. Our sinful passions, aroused by the law** is an anticipation of the point Paul is to discuss more fully in the next section. The earlier figure of slavery seems to replace the marriage analogy as this section ends. **We are discharged from the law, dead to that which held us captive.** Our slavery is no longer to the law, but to God **in the new life of the Spirit,** and is therefore not slavery at all.

---

moral life and they always will. So long as they attempt to govern from outside, they cannot provide the motive power which is capable of translating any ethical ideal into action. The secret of the gospel is that it offers an indwelling Spirit who both directs and inspires.

The passage as a whole declares the freedom which comes from union with Christ. We noted in ch. 6 that Paul sets forth salvation in terms of deliverance—in that case deliverance from the power of sin. He now shows that it also means deliverance from bondage to the law. The domination which is exercised over men's minds by an external system of moral control is too real to be questioned and too persistent to be dismissed as unimportant in our day. The demands of convention and the tyranny of social standards still hold the human spirit, and it is still true that even perfect conformity affords little genuine peace of mind. The peculiar poignancy associated with the service of the law was that it offered so much yet succeeded in giving so little. It promised the assurance of God's favor and in return required the unfaltering obedience of every man who submitted to its demands. Yet the last state of its servants was worse than the first; it awakened the conscience without giving any power to conform to its requirements. Consequently, the more sensitive a man's insight, the closer the law brought him to despair. It could do nothing for the person who tried his utmost and consistently failed. What "the law could not do," the gospel has done. You have been delivered, says Paul: "be not entangled again with the yoke of bondage" (Gal. 5:1). Release is Christ's gift to his people. "God sent forth his Son . . . to redeem those who were under the law" (Gal. 4:4-5); "Christ redeemed us from the curse of the law" (Gal. 3:13). Paul manifestly associated this deliverance with Christ's death. He was born under the law, and he suffered the extreme consequence which the law could impose—he bore the curse which it pronounced on anyone who suffered the death of the cross. But the Resurrection declares that Christ triumphed over death—over the death which involved the curse—and by consequence, over the law which imposed the curse. It is at this point that vs. 4 indicates the way in which Paul believed that Christ's breaking of the curse brought redemption to those who were in bondage to the law. It proved that neither death nor the curse was as decisive as it had seemed. Christ had borne the extreme consequences of both; in breaking their yoke he had passed into the fullness of the risen life. But Paul has shown that we share in his death; if we are identified with his cross, by faith we shall also enter the new life. And one feature of the new life is the knowledge that the law's yoke has been broken. We shall therefore no longer be subject to its circumscribing power. The background of this whole discussion is the Jewish law and Paul's experience of its tyranny. To that degree the matter might seem to have no relevance to the lives of those who were born outside the bounds of the old covenant. But Judaism, as has already been suggested, is one development of a persistent tendency. Men hanker to govern their relationships both with God and with one another by legalistic methods. As a result they make their obedience to God and their fellowship with each other a form of bondage; from that bondage Christ has set us free.

7 What shall we say then? *Is* the law sin? God forbid. Nay, I had not known

7 What then shall we say? That the law is sin? By no means! Yet, if it had not been

4. The Function of the Law (7:7-13)

As early in this epistle as 3:20, Paul has alluded to the close connection he feels to exist between sin and the law. In the present section he is concerned primarily with supporting the claim that no man, Jew or non-Jew, can hope for salvation through obedience to law. But the apostle goes further than to assert the mere insufficiency or impotence of the law as a means of righteousness; he sees it also as in a sense a means of sin. This is no more than hinted at in the opening section of the epistle, especially in the sentence just cited, "Through the law comes knowledge of sin." In 5:20 Paul is more explicit: "Law came in, to increase the trespass." We have just seen that in vss. 1-6, the law has taken the place of sin as the enemy; and there also reference is made to "our sinful passions, aroused by the law."

7. Paul has thus come very close to identifying sin and the law. He sees that he has done so and draws back with a kind of horror—**What then shall we say? That the law**

7-25. ***The Nature of the Law and Its Function in the Spiritual Life.***—By implication Paul has more than once suggested that the imperfections of the law have made it an obstacle in man's pathway. But in the course of a long argument it is difficult to avoid misunderstandings. An unsympathetic critic can seize on a phrase and, by twisting it for his own ends, misrepresent an author's position. Paul knew this by experience, and no doubt he often exposed himself to attack. Certainly he has done so in the preceding verses. He has apparently equated sin and the law; we are bound by neither, and at times the distinction between them is far from clear. Does Paul really mean that the two are virtually the same? The answer is an emphatic "No," but it is necessary for him to explain what his position is.

A discussion of the function of the Mosaic law might seem remote from the interests of the modern mind, but the present passage has a perennial interest and an abiding power which account for its unfailing appeal. This is one of the classic pictures of the plight of man. As Paul wrote he may have had the story of Adam in the background of his mind. Assuredly he drew upon the memory of his own struggles and defeats. But what he has given us is a history of each man's soul. The power and poignancy of the section are due to the faithfulness with which he reproduces the story of his own inner conflict; our answering response is quickened by the exactness of the parallel with things we know all too well. The characteristic of our human experience is the tension set up within a nature divided against itself. Our earthly life is a struggle between insights imperfectly appropriated and instincts only partially controlled. We belong to a physical world, but we feel ourselves to be citizens of a heavenly city; and our carnal impulses are all too often at variance with our spiritual longings. There is no other account which describes with comparable insight this fundamental human dilemma. Man's knowledge of right is invariably greater than his power to perform it. He knows what is good, and he wants to act accordingly; but with monotonous regularity he fails (vss. 16-20). It is his impotence and not his hypocrisy which explains the contrast between his genuine love of the things he ought to do and his inability to translate them consistently into conduct. He is a battleground in the struggle between contending forces, and he himself lacks the power to win the verdict for the higher side. This is a picture with which we are all painfully familiar. We too know of a struggle between our better self and our worse. Often conscience is the voice of God and impulse the prompting of sin; yet again and again conscience protests in vain while impulse carries the day. We know what is right, and reason assures us that it represents our highest good; yet we choose the alternative which we know will work for our destruction.

But the picture is important not merely because it is true and we recognize it as such; it is important too because the cry of despair is answered by an assurance of victory (vs. 25). The profound psychological insight which marks Paul's picture of our need finds its counterpart in the skill with which he draws (in ch. 8) the nature of the new life into which we are released. Seldom has contrast been more effectively used. The sharp literary transition is necessary if the full triumph of God's grace is to be indicated; and yet it is still true that we live a human life in an organism which gives inducements to "serve the law of sin." Whatever may be the experience of an apostle—and even

is sin? By no means!—and undertakes a more careful description of the way in which he thinks of them as related than he has thus far had occasion or opportunity to do.

In I Cor. 15:56 Paul speaks of the law as being "the power of sin." In what sense does he mean that? Apparently he thinks of the law—and we must regard "law" here as meaning primarily the Jewish law, but also the "law written on the heart"; in a word, God's command or law in any form—Paul thinks of this law as being positively related to sin in two ways. The first of these is indicated in his words, **If it had not been for the law, I should not have known sin** (cf. 3:20). The law serves to bring into vivid relief the reality of one's alienation from God. It is impossible to ignore the signs that Paul is speaking here, and throughout this chapter, as we shall see, out of his own experience. He was a Jew and had been "as to the law a Pharisee" (Phil. 3:5). He could not, even as a Christian, have brought himself to question the divine origin and authority of the law: "The law is holy, and the commandment is holy and just and good" (vs. 12). But what had the law actually done for him? As he sees it now, the law had succeeded only

---

the experts disagree—most people know the meaning of the promise long before they experience complete deliverance. Among the men and women with whom we deal, few make any pretense of having entirely passed beyond the stage which Paul describes in ch. 7, and those who do often contradict their claims by the narrow and pharisaical self-righteousness of their lives. In the central part of his letter Paul is discussing sanctification—the process by which we grow in holiness of life—and he makes it clear that saints are not made perfect in a hurry. Anyone of sensitive mind and conscience will recognize his own condition in Paul's description of the human plight; what he needs to know is that the gospel is liberation and not analysis. He needs to learn of a power which will mightily reinforce all his cravings for the good, and he must be taught to find it in the gospel. It will remain true of most of us that we will still know the reality of conflict; but a much more important truth is that we have begun to know the reality of victory. Moreover, victory should increasingly predominate.

The heart of this passage is an experience, first of bondage, finally of freedom, which holds true for those who have never been subject to the law of Moses, and know very little about it. But if Romans is to be intelligently studied, it is necessary to set forth at least in outline Paul's teaching about the law. He refers to it so often that simply to ignore it would leave serious gaps in our understanding of his thought. At first sight he seems to be strangely inconsistent in his attitude. Terms of the highest praise alternate with words of the strongest blame. This is not because the estimate which a strict Jew would form of the law survives to confuse Paul's Christian understanding of its insufficiency. The apparent contradictions are due to the fact that Paul considered the law under three aspects. He saw it, in the first place, as a system of rules, a code of commandments, governing both behavior and worship. But it was also a divinely appointed means whereby those who lived according to its precepts could satisfy God's demands, earn his favor, and by their merit gain salvation. Finally, the law was an outward and abiding symbol of God's favor to his chosen people.[9] The third aspect has little place in Paul's letters, and for present purposes it can be ignored; but he is constantly referring to one or other of the first two, and it is his failure to distinguish between them which causes confusion. As regards its content, Paul was willing to concede the high character of the law, and when occasion required, he was ready to be bound by its precepts (cf. Acts 21:20-26). He could say quite truthfully that **the law is holy, and the commandment is holy and just and good** (vs. 12). But as a method of gaining salvation the law had proved a ghastly failure. It could reveal the nature of sin, but having done so, it was powerless to overcome sin. It made demands which it could not enable men to fulfill. It encouraged an attitude to God which obscured men's highest insights into his nature and purpose, and it deprived them of the creaturely humility which knows that our salvation must be entirely his gift. What Paul attacks so bitterly is the spirit which believes it can win God's favor by multiplying merit. This is the spirit which has led men astray and corrupted them in the process.

At the same time, the law had had a necessary part to play in the discipline of man's inner life; but its role was essentially limited and temporary. Prior to Moses there had been no law, and sin, though admitted to life by Adam's disobedience, slept. With the coming of the law, there emerged a deeper understanding of sin. That, indeed, was the great service which the law performed. It was necessary in order to teach men what God required. In explicit

[9] Cf. C. Anderson Scott, *Footnotes to St. Paul* (Cambridge: The University Press, 1935), p. 43.

sin, but by the law: for I had not known lust, except the law had said, Thou shalt not covet.

for the law, I should not have known sin. I should not have known what it is to covet if the law had not said, "You shall

in making him utterly wretched. It is almost certainly not accidental that the particular commandment of the law which Paul cites as an illustration is **You shall not covet.** This is the one requirement of the Decalogue which directly touches the inner life of thought and motive; and one can readily understand the despair of a man, at one time as self-critical and as self-assertive as Paul, as he finds himself confronted by such a demand. The law made him aware of his real situation as a slave of sin.

One must also bear in mind in this connection the fact that for Paul "sin" is more than "transgression" (see Intro., pp. 369-70 and also on 5:12-14). However sinful one might be, only the law could make one *guilty*. **If the law had not said, "You shall not covet,"** one would still have been subject to the same desires; but not only would one not have *known* that one was guilty of covetousness, but also one would not *in fact* have been guilty of it. Thus in bringing "knowledge of sin" (3:20) the law has more than a merely subjective effect; the objective situation of sinful man is also changed. He becomes a transgressor and thus only now in the fullest sense is a sinner.

and emphatic terms it declared man's duty, but then left him to his own resources in performing it. It sharpened and defined sin, but it also reinforced its appeal. So in time some began to see how harsh and hopeless was the task it imposed while others became aware of the heavy yoke it laid upon them. In a real sense, then, the law was educative; it trained the conscience, it sharpened the sense of sin, and it taught those who were capable of learning the lesson that neither its resources nor their own strength could enable them to fulfill its demands. It was therefore perfectly permissible to describe the law as "our schoolmaster to bring us unto Christ" (Gal. 3:24); but its task was temporary and—except in a subsidiary role—it was destined to inevitable failure.

As we read the present section of Romans, it becomes clear that one of the main tasks of the law was to awaken the conscience. "The happy savage" marks a stage in the life of individuals as well as in the history of societies. **I was once alive apart from the law,** says Paul (vs. 9); i.e., he lived as he pleased; he accepted wants and desires as natural, satisfied them as he was able, and asked no questions about them. Moral problems did not perplex him before he acted, and scruples did not trouble him afterward. But when the law entered, the situation changed. By its command it set limits to the life of instinct, and did so in the name of a higher authority. When the law said, "Thou shalt not . . . ," it crystallized our latent sinfulness into rebellion, and we retorted "I will." But at least we realized what was right, and in our refusal of its authority were enabled to recognize ourselves as sinners. As Paul has expressed it elsewhere in this letter, "Through the law comes knowledge of sin" (3:20). The process may seem negative, but it is very necessary. Paul is not recalling, for the pleasure of reminiscing, an irrelevant episode from what is now a distant past. The commandment always has a part to play. Conscience is always in danger of going to sleep. When we dismiss as irrelevant the role of the law, we assume too easily that we have passed beyond the need of it. Even those who profess that they live above the constraint of rules really mean that they reserve the right to break them whenever they find it convenient to do so. If this is true of individuals, we need not be reminded that it is doubly so of society at large. The soft and flabby morals of our corporate life have not been "tutored" to the threshold of a world governed by grace. "Thou shalt not steal" is still necessary in order to awaken the conscience to the need of honesty, **Thou shalt not covet** is needed to remind us that the acquisitive instinct should not have the final word in life. There are certain elementary requirements which every society forgets to its peril and its loss. We still need to be confronted with the resolute proclamation of what God requires in our common life. There is a standard of mercy, justice, honesty, and integrity which cannot be lowered to suit the "immoral necessities" of an age which finds it too exacting. The law teaches us where we stand vis-à-vis the demands of God. We still need to learn that lesson.

Commandments have their place, but it is strictly limited. They stab us awake when carelessness lulls us asleep; but having done that, they have exhausted their powers. Their real peril appears when they are erected into a moral system, with the professed purpose of

8 But sin, taking occasion by the commandment, wrought in me all manner of concupiscence. For without the law sin *was* dead.

not covet." 8 But sin, finding opportunity in the commandment, wrought in me all kinds of covetousness. Apart from the law

---

8. But Paul thinks of the law as doing more than bringing knowledge of sin. It also stimulates transgression. The law has the effect of stirring sleeping sinful impulses into activity. Not that the law itself does this—the law is only an instrumentality—but sin makes use of the law to produce this greater sinfulness: **Sin, finding opportunity in the**

---

governing our spiritual life and regulating our relations with God. This was precisely what orthodox Pharisaism had done, and because of it man's whole religious outlook had become distorted. It required its adherents to serve partial ends in stultifying ways. Having awakened the conscience (its true function), it could not provide the spiritual power which would satisfy the demands of conscience. Good men were left in a desolating impasse, and bad men were allowed to grow callous in their pride.

The psychological power of this passage is apparent at first sight; but it is appreciated more fully if we understand Paul's characteristic view of man and his nature. We assume that when he speaks of himself as **carnal** (vs. 14), he is using a word which has a depreciatory meaning. With us it *has;* with Paul it simply pointed to the character of our physical constitution. We are made of flesh and blood. The physical side of our life is not inherently evil, but it is peculiarly vulnerable to sin's attack. Temptation appeals to us through our various impulses; by their means it arrests our attention, and it uses their power to subjugate our better judgment. Consequently, Paul believes that our physical nature gives sin its opportunity (see Exeg., vs. 14). When he speaks in this way, he regards sin as an external force, with an independent objective existence of its own. It is a view which raises problems—but then what view of ultimate mysteries does not?—but it corresponds to a type of experience which we all know well enough. Every one of us has struggled with a power which we knew to be evil, from which we vehemently dissociated ourselves, which nevertheless we could not overthrow. Whether we use Paul's metaphorical language or find some alternative terminology, the important thing is to make clear to other people that the experience itself is one in which they have all shared. At the same time Paul reminds us that our physical nature, with its unruly impulses, is only a part of the whole man. There is also what he calls **my inmost self,** that part of him which delights **in the law of God** (vs. 22). But our "higher" nature is subject to the domination of our "lower" selves: our impulses are more powerful than our insights. **I see in my members another law at war with the law of my mind and making me captive to the law of sin which dwells in my members** (vs. 23). This kind of language explains the tendency, still common among Christian people, to set the physical and the spiritual in opposition to one another. But Paul is not thinking in terms of a dualism of that kind. His thought springs from the conviction that God made all things, and to him our whole being, both body and soul, belongs. Sin is man's revolt against God—a rebellion which usually finds its seat in our physical nature, but which emphasizes the distinction between good and evil, not between soul and body. It can be seen at once that an approach of this kind opens up for many people a wholly new understanding of their total being. It gives life a setting commensurate with our intuitive sense of man's inherent dignity, because it declares that our whole life is from God and is his concern. It saves us from a stultifying cleavage between body and soul, because it sees both as part of a life which can be redeemed. Its attitude to evil is realistic, since it recognizes its tremendous power, but also optimistic, since it looks forward to a time when that power will be broken. The individual man discovers progressively the meaning of deliverance as offered by God's grace in Jesus Christ, and gives thanks accordingly (vs. 25*a*). Since God's power is ultimate, and will finally achieve that purpose which explains creation, Paul looks forward to the day when evil will everywhere be overthrown.

7. ***The Clash of Commandment and Desire.***—Paul dates the birth of conscious moral life from the discovery that he wanted something that he should not have. We first learn the meaning of sin when desire and prohibition come into conflict. That, of course, is why the law awakens our sense of sin (vs. 8). By forbidding what appetite craves, it forces us to a scrutiny of what we purposed to do. The commandment which Paul quotes is the one above all others which presses us back to the region where the motives of our conduct are shaped. As such it is most likely to make us aware of the clash

9 For I was alive without the law once:
but when the commandment came, sin
revived, and I died.
10 And the commandment, which *was*
ordained to life, I found *to be* unto death.

sin lies dead. **9** I was once alive apart from
the law, but when the commandment came,
sin revived and I died; **10** the very commandment which promised life proved to

commandment [i.e., against covetousness], **wrought in me all kinds of covetousness. Apart from the law sin lies dead.** Sanday and Headlam point out that the word translated here "opportunity" is used in a military connection to mean "a base of operations." Here it means "a place to start" or perhaps as the same commentators suggest, "something to take hold of." But Paul's whole point in this sentence is not too clear. Does he mean that sin had no way of making guilty sinners of us and thus of destroying us until it was able to make use of the law? This is the meaning most clearly indicated, but if this is what he meant, he is in conflict with what he said, at least equally clearly, in 5:12-14. In that passage sin is represented as not only being "in the world before the law was given," but also as bringing about even then the reign of death. With such a view Paul's statement that **apart from the law sin lies dead** is not easily compatible. But we have already seen that we cannot hold the apostle to strict logical consistency.

9-11. That he is speaking from his own experience appears even more unmistakably as we move from this point to the end of the chapter. Vss. 9-11 represent a further explication of vs. 8. As a background for his statements, one must recognize, first, his memory of his own childhood, and second, the story of Adam in Eden. Paul sees in his own early childhood a reliving of the Eden story. At one time he was carefree, giving expression to his impulses without any fears or scruples of any kind; then he became conscious of the law; at once sin, which had been dormant, became suddenly very much

between conscience and desire. The man who knows that his conduct has been brought to the bar of an explicit standard of right and wrong is the man for whom the moral life has started.

9. ***The Problem of the Happy Pagan.***—But what of the man who has never reached that point? "Never" is too strong a word, of course, but we are surrounded by people whom we can describe only as happy pagans. **I was once alive apart from the law,** says Paul; and multitudes of our contemporaries could use his words, but with reference to their present state. The things which the law forbids they do, apparently with an untroubled conscience. Theft is a venial offense when opportunity invites one to steal; and in any case, "Every one must look after himself first." "But it's perfectly natural!" is another remark which cuts a wide swath through traditional morality. Multitudes of men and women are apparently quite content with the way they meet today and its opportunities; they take no thought for tomorrow, or for any moral reckoning it may bring. They regard religion as harmless but impractical, and they consider its demands as irrelevant. They live very well without its help; they govern their lives without reference to its standards, and they claim that they are perfectly satisfied with the result. For them in any real sense the commandment has not come.

Religious people are often sorely troubled that others should live in serene indifference to things which they themselves consider supremely important. The situation exactly corresponds, however, to Paul's analysis of the awakening of the moral life. He clearly distinguishes three stages. The first is before moral consciousness has been aroused. He does not refer, presumably, to that rudimentary awakening which marks the development of every child. It is possible to reach some measure of maturity without any profound realization of the "augustness" of moral demand. Life is lived as convenience dictates and opportunity allows, and no requirement charged with an ultimate reference disturbs one's peace of mind. The second stage Paul describes with penetrating insight in this chapter. Consciousness of a demand which is reinforced by a divine authority has entered. Confronted with its exacting requirements—and still more with its disconcerting revelations of our own weakness—our state is one in which divided impulse leads through increasing frustration to an admission of our hopeless defeat. In this extreme form the description applies, of course, only to men and women of high mind and serious moral purpose; but to some extent it is true of anyone who realizes that he should conform to a standard of conduct which he admits to be right but

11 For sin, taking occasion by the commandment, deceived me, and by it slew *me.*

be death to me. 11 For sin, finding opportunity in the commandment, deceived me

alive; and his careless, thoughtless existence was at an end. Something like this must be the meaning of vs. 9. It is difficult to suppose that when he says, **I was once alive,** and later, **I died,** he is meaning either term (i.e., "life" or "death") in the full spiritual sense in which he often uses them, indeed has often used them in this very epistle. Perhaps **I died** means "I became aware of my true position as a slave of sin destined for death" (the death itself, as in 5:12-14, not being regarded as a consequence of the law, but only of sin). The **commandment . . . promised life** to anyone who might obey it. Because sin, possessing him, had prevented Paul's obeying it, had indeed led him into disobedience, the same commandment had **proved to be death** to him. Vs. 11 reflects particularly clearly the story of Gen. 3:1-13. There the serpent **finding opportunity in the commandment** of God about "the tree which is in the midst of the garden," **deceived** ("beguiled," Gen. 3:13) Eve and brought about her death.

discovers to be beyond his attainment. The final stage is reached when we have found a means of satisfying those demands whose authority we previously conceded but whose requirements we had been unable to meet.

Paul's principal theme is the means by which we pass from the second stage to the third. He refers to the first only incidentally, but we can infer what he would have said. There are at least two conditions which must be met before the happy pagan is awakened to consciousness of the moral world and of his own poverty when judged by its standards. He must become aware of God as an eternal personal reality by whom he is confronted in his daily life. Familiarity with a vague term, often used but never understood, is not sufficient to awaken a man to a sense of the imponderables which give depth to our experience. In the absence of a keen sense of the actuality of God he is unlikely to be disturbed in his complacent acceptance of conventional standards. The second condition is related to the first. He must recognize that the God whom he has rediscovered meets him with a moral demand which has the authority of a divine purpose behind it. The immediate practical problem is to awaken a sense of God's reality in men and women whom a mechanical and impersonal civilization has robbed both of the gift of awe and of the awareness of need.

11. ***The Subtlety of Sin.***—The religious mind never doubts the gravity of sin, but it often fails to grasp the true character of the problem sin poses. It assumes that we are faced with a trial of strength. So we are; but we are also involved in a test of wits, and this is the more serious aspect of the two. As Jesus remarked, if the strong man had known when to expect an attack, he would have been prepared and would not have allowed his goods to be despoiled. He was taken by surprise; the thief came at a time, perhaps also in a way, that he did not expect. This is always the characteristic of sin. It is the guile of evil which has always been its mark. "The serpent beguiled me," said Eve; and experience prompts us to repeat, "As it was in the beginning, is now. . . ." To this element in religious experience Paul gives clear expression in this verse, **Sin, finding opportunity in the commandment, deceived me and by it killed me.** This is a thought which he has often expressed: "Satan," he says, "disguises himself as an angel of light" (II Cor. 11:14). "The working of Satan," he tells us, is "with all power and signs and lying wonders, and with all deceivableness of unrighteousness" (II Thess. 2:9-10). Our insecurity should make us vigilant, says the writer to the Hebrews, because we are endangered by "the deceitfulness of sin" (Heb. 3:13). The skill and ingenuity with which we rationalize our faults and failings merely proves that old friends reappear even when they have been rechristened with new names. A phrase which Paul used a few verses previously should have prepared us for the ingenuity which sin displays. Sin, quick to grasp an advantage, has seized on the commandment and used it as a base for operations (vs. 8). The same kind of tactical skill is again presupposed; sin has snatched its opportunity, hidden itself behind the fair intention of the commandment, and having lulled its victim into false security has killed him. The vindictiveness as well as the ingenuity of sin finds full expression. It relentlessly pursues a man, misleads and deceives him, and then in an unguarded moment presses home its fatal advantage. It is satisfied with nothing save the complete and utter overthrow of its victim; it is war to the death. No quarter is given; and the decisive finality of the defeat it inflicts is like our final extinction. In this its true nature stands perfectly revealed. We be-

12 Wherefore the law *is* holy, and the commandment holy, and just, and good.

and by it killed me. 12 So the law is holy, and the commandment is holy and just and good.

12-13. The construction of the Greek sentence forming vs. 12 indicates that it was originally intended not as an independent sentence, but as a first clause, to be followed presumably with some such words as "... but sin is the enemy of God and of all that is good." Having said, however, that **the law is holy, and the commandment . . . holy and just and good,** Paul's mind, in characteristic fashion, jumps over the intended but obvious second clause and seizes on the question which he feels may have been suggested by his discussion: **Did that which is good, then, bring death to me?** He has already rejected the identification of the law with sin (vss. 7-11); now he rejects the supposition that the law was the source of death. Sin is the source of death; but sin "worked death" in him **through what is good,** i.e., the law. And if it is asked why God should have put into sin's hand such an effective instrumentality for our destruction, Paul's answer is that this happened **in order that sin might be shown to be sin** [cf. vs. 7], **and through the commandment might become sinful beyond measure** (cf. vs. 8). Thus the two aspects

lieve the specious assurances which tell us that the matter is not serious, until, deceived and overthrown, we know the bitter truth. "It was sin, working death in me through what is good, in order that sin might be shown to be sin, and through the commandment might become sinful beyond measure" (vs. 13). The intolerable burden of it speaks in those last words. And part of the bitterness is due to the mockery with which sin ridicules its victims. It persuades us that we are wise and tolerant; then, when its end is accomplished, reveals us to ourselves as perfect fools.

12-13. ***Sin and the Insufficiency of Regulations.***—Often the meaning of a verse can be restated so that it forms a new point of departure. Paul is satisfied that the law is a reflection of the holy character of God, and that the commandments in which the law is codified are righteous as far as their inherent nature is concerned and beneficent as regards their fundamental aim. But he has already indicated the disastrous results which the law has wrought within his own experience. Are we to assume, then, that man is so constituted that even a high system of moral precepts brings about his downfall? Why is it that even good laws prompt us to break them? The modern man is likely to infer that the law must be wrong because it is apparently unnatural. Restraints which cramp the free expression of our nature should be abolished; to enforce requirements to which men do not respond is manifestly foolish and misguided. Paul's answer brings us back to an interpretation of law in terms of our religious understanding. The law, he says, expresses something that is fundamentally good; but its effect has been to bring into the open the oppressive power which sin possesses. This tyranny is not created by the moral command. It was always present, and we were in the grip of sin even when we were ignorant of the fact. Judged by high standards we were already serving evil ends; but until the canons of moral judgment became clear we remained unconscious of the fact. Our ignorance explains our contentment. We were satisfied with the way we lived because we were untouched by the demands of a worthier standard. Then came the law, and with the law came the beginnings of moral consciousness; suddenly we were involved in mortal struggle. At once sin, our antagonist, seized the commandment (the letter of law) and used it as a weapon with which to kill us. As a result two things clearly emerge: the true character of sin and the real insufficiency of regulations. We see sin as it is because we know that it perverts even what is good in order to use it for its evil ends; and we know that moralism can reveal the nature of evil but cannot cope with its power. In proving and amplifying various aspects of this point, Paul uses some of his most suggestive phrases. In vs. 10, for example, there is the contrast between the high hopes which the commandment arouses and the bitter disappointment to which it leads; it "promised life," it "proved to be death." In vs. 11 and again in vs. 13 we have the law as a weapon of righteousness which is twisted from its proper service and becomes a dagger with which sin stabs our true life to death. Also in vs. 13 we note the cumulative effect of evil; it punishes itself by its own increase—on this point the classical commentary is the speech which Milton puts into the mouth of Sin as she sits at the gates of hell.[1]

12. ***The Limitations of Legalism.***—It is impossible not to admire the honesty with which

[1] *Paradise Lost,* Book II, ll. 790-802.

13 Was then that which is good made death unto me? God forbid. But sin, that it might appear sin, working death in me by that which is good; that sin by the commandment might become exceeding sinful.

14 For we know that the law is spiritual: but I am carnal, sold under sin.

13 Did that which is good, then, bring death to me? By no means! It was sin, working death in me through what is good, in order that sin might be shown to be sin, and through the commandment might become sinful beyond measure. 14 We know that the law is spiritual; but I am carnal,

---

of the law's relationship with sin, mentioned in the Exeg. on vs. 7 at the beginning of this passage, are here referred to again at its close.

We thus see how Paul could think of bondage to sin and bondage to law as being one bondage, and often (as in ch. 6) use the two terms almost interchangeably. Without the law there would have been no awareness of his bondage to sin; and without sin there would have been no awareness of *bondage* to the law, since in that case he would have lived naturally and gladly in accordance with it. In this way it happened that he could think of the law as being an enemy of man comparable in importance with sin and death: "The sting of death is sin; and the strength of sin is the law." A. N. Whitehead in describing religious experience speaks of a movement from "God the void to God the enemy . . . to God the companion" (*Religion in the Making* [New York: The Macmillan Co., 1926], pp. 16-17). The philosopher is not far from the apostle in this analysis. In vs. 9*a* we have something corresponding to "God the void"; and in 9*b*-10, to "God the enemy." Paul seems to be saying that one cannot know the love of God unless one first knows his wrath, and the law is an essential element in this knowledge. In Gal. 3:24 Paul speaks of the law as being "our schoolmaster [custodian, RSV] to bring us unto Christ," but he is not referring to any gradual approach to Christ through obedience to the law. In a way his meaning is just the opposite of this. He means that the law is necessary to produce that utter despair of self which must precede one's acceptance in faith of the salvation which only God's grace can bestow.

5. The Final Despair and Release (7:14-25)

This passage is one of the most important in the letter, and one of the most controversial. The importance consists in the fact that in it—or at least in vss. 14-23—Paul describes the inward, concrete meaning of the human situation formally defined in 3:20: "No human being will be justified in his sight by works of the law since through the law comes knowledge of sin." We have seen that Paul's whole religious and theological

---

Paul refuses to cover his failure by throwing all the blame on the inherent nature of the law. Its working had been disastrous enough in his case, but he knew that the fault lay in the response of his own nature to the kind of suggestion which is inseparable from any commandment. If a prohibition immediately arouses a desire to do what is forbidden, it is an illuminating psychological fact, but it does not make the prohibition wrong. The insight which marks Paul's treatment of the law appears most clearly at this point. He holds firmly to two truths—that the law itself represents a noble and worthy ideal of conduct, but that the principle of legalism is fundamentally unsound. He also realizes why the law fails to achieve its acknowledged purpose: it gives us neither satisfaction at the bar of our own judgment nor conscious rectitude as we stand in the presence of God. It is Paul's keen perception of the essential moral factors in our experience which makes it possible for him to seize the deliverance which the gospel offers. He admits the high character of the law itself, and this saves him from unavailing recriminations; he perceives that the law whets the very appetites within him which it was intended to control, and this reveals to him one of the reasons why moralism is bound to fail; he admits the extent of his own failure, and by refusing to take refuge in excuses, he leaves himself free enough to look about him for help and humble enough to accept it when it comes.

14. ***The Importance of Our Instincts.***—Contrast, as we have already seen, is of the essence of this passage, and Paul again returns to the

position is based upon a certain way of understanding that situation, a certain way of diagnosing the human malady (see Intro., p. 369). No passage in all of his correspondence is comparable in value to this for the light it throws upon this basic part of his thought.

The passage is controversial because of differences of opinion as to its relation to Paul's own experience. Although the contrary view has been argued, it seems all but indubitable that this whole section of the letter (vss. 7-25) is autobiographical. In using the first personal pronoun Paul is not trying merely to give vivid expression to what is imaginary or hypothetical. The passage rings too true and, especially as vs. 24 is reached, strikes too terribly poignant a note to be explained in any such way. This we have been taking for granted (see on vss. 7, 9-11). The real matter of controversy is whether the passage should be taken as representing Paul's *current, present* experience, or the memory of his life before he became a believer in Christ. Probably the majority of commentators have taken the latter view, holding that it would have been quite impossible for Paul the *believer* (the author of 1:16-17; 3:21-26; 5:1-11; 7:4-6; 8:1-39; etc.) to feel as the author represents himself as feeling in this passage. Paul must, then, be describing his inner situation before he became a Christian. It is obvious, however, that the only basis for such a judgment lies in this supposed impossibility; there is nothing in Paul's *language* to suggest that he is remembering the past rather than describing the present.

On the contrary it may be argued that the same considerations which establish the authentic autobiographical nature of this section go far to establish also its contemporaneous character. Although in the light of the vivid way he expresses himself, especially in vs. 24, it is easier to believe that Paul is remembering than that he is inventing, it is easier still to believe that he is simply reporting what he finds true of himself in the very moment of writing. Strong support is given this most natural way of understanding Paul's language here by the position of vs. 25*b*. This sentence is in line with the teaching of other statements in this passage, e.g., vss. 16-17, 22-23; and if the whole passage is taken at face value, i.e., as a description of present experience, its position after vs. 25*a* raises only a minor problem. On the other hand if vss. 7-24 are interpreted as referring to Paul's pre-Christian life, and only vs. 25*a* to his present experience, then the position of 25*b* presents a really serious difficulty. Some who interpret vss. 7-25 in this way seek to avoid or resolve this difficulty by proposing either that 25*b* is a later scribal interpolation or that it has been misplaced—i.e., Paul originally wrote this sentence after vss. 22-23 and only through some accident to the manuscript or a very early copy does it stand where it now does. Moffatt's translation adopts the theory of displacement here and Dodd vigorously defends it (*Epistle of Paul to Romans,* pp. 114-15); so also does Kirk (*Epistle to the Romans,* p. 208). In the absence of the slightest textual evidence to support the hypothesis of either interpolation or displacement, however, one can accept such a theory only as a last resort. Is the difficulty of understanding this whole passage as a transcript of Paul's current experience so clear and so great as to justify a last resort of this kind?

To be sure, one cannot deny the logical incompatibility of all of this passage (except vs. 25*a*), taken thus, with innumerable other passages in Paul's letters where the Christian life is described in terms of reconciliation, peace, and victory. But we have seen and shall see other instances of the same kind of incompatibility which it is quite impossible to explain by referring one of the sets of conflicting statements to Paul's pre-Christian experience. We must, then, in these other instances recognize a paradoxical character in Paul's thought which may well be manifested again in this passage. We have observed that Paul can readily speak of the future as though it were present; if that is true, any discussion of the present is bound to be somewhat paradoxical in view of the fact that the future represents a radically new and different order. The present moment for Paul was made up of a past, doomed and in process of passing, and of a future already beginning to be. Such being his view, although we might reasonably expect his pictures of the past and of the future to be relatively coherent pictures, we shall expect his picture of the present to be decidedly less clear and consistent.

It may also be said that if the question whether Paul is referring here to his experience "before Damascus" or after should be answered, not on the basis of a comparison of one Pauline passage with another, but on the basis of the realities of Christian experience, then we should have to acknowledge the complete plausibility of the view we are defending. What Christian is not aware of the kind of conflict Paul describes so vividly in these verses—aware of it as a present, continuing fact? We do not have to go back to some earlier point in our career in order to find something corresponding to Paul's statement: **I see in my members another law at war with the law of my mind and making me captive to the law of sin which dwells in my members.** Paul's statement may be paradoxical, but it is no more so than our own experience. Why should we suppose that it was more so than his? We shall assume that Paul in this passage is not merely remembering an earlier situation, but is also speaking naturally and sincerely out of his present experience.

So much for general comment on this passage as a whole. We now turn to more detailed comment.

14. When Paul says, **The law is spiritual,** he means only to sum up and repeat what he said in vs. 12. It is **spiritual** in its origin, being God-given; and in its nature, being "holy and just and good." It is not unlikely also that Paul has in mind the fact that the demands of God's law are such that one must be spiritual in order to fulfill them. Such a meaning is indicated by the concluding clause, **but I am carnal, sold under sin.** Here for the first time in the letter the terms "flesh" and "spirit" are brought together, for the Greek term for "carnal" is σάρκινος, or "fleshly." Since the opposition of flesh and spirit is under various aspects one of the important themes of this and the following sections of this letter—i.e., through 8:14—some comment is in order upon the meaning of these terms for Paul. The reader is referred also to several paragraphs in the Intro. (p. 369) dealing with these and other psychological terms.

The word "flesh" refers primarily to the actual material of which human and animal bodies are made (as in I Cor. 15:39), but it easily comes to stand for the whole human being. Thus we read that Jesus was "descended from David according to the flesh" (1:3), that "by the deeds of the law there shall no flesh be justified" (3:20), and of "Abraham, our forefather according to the flesh" (4:1). In such passages the term "flesh" is morally neutral and involves no judgment of value at all. Occasionally Paul uses the word in what is on the whole a favorable or appreciative sense. Thus he alludes to Onesimus as beloved "in the flesh" (Philem. 16), meaning that simply as a human being this slave had been esteemed and loved. This same favorable sense is found more clearly in Phil. 3:4 ff., where Paul speaks of himself as having "reason for confidence in the flesh." To be sure, in both of these passages "the flesh" is being contrasted disadvantageously with other realities, i.e., the "Spirit," the "Lord," "Christ," but it would seem that the contrast is between higher and lower values, not between the bad and the good. In these passages, although the flesh appears as weak and insufficient—as often in the O.T.—it does not appear as evil.

At first sight the ascription of nothing beyond such weakness or insufficiency seems necessarily to be involved in the use of "fleshly" in the present passage: "The law

---

opposition between a law inherently good and a human nature which makes it the instrument of sin. The discussion may seem less remote if we translate it (as Dodd does) into language closer to that to which our generation is accustomed. We would then remember that "instincts" are not an individual characteristic but a racial inheritance. They may not necessarily be bad, and they can be used as the raw material out of which character is built; but by themselves they do not bring us to the kind of life in which "the true ends of personality are attained." Moreover, the whole character of our corporate life tends to strengthen the forces which prevent them from being organized as the foundation of a developed personality. The question is much more fundamental than the quality of our individual choices; forces which

15 For that which I do, I allow not: for what I would, that do I not; but what I hate, that do I.

sold under sin. 15 I do not understand my own actions. For I do not do what I want,

makes demands which only a spiritual man could obey, but I am physical and thus unable to comply." Such might easily be Paul's meaning if it were not for the words **sold under sin.** It is Paul's view that the problem of the impotence of the flesh is enormously increased and complicated because sin has gained entrance to it, has taken up its residence there, and from that base of operations has brought the whole personality into slavery. It seems fairly clear that Paul did not think of the flesh as being *essentially* sinful; but he does regard it as being always or inevitably sinful, i.e., flesh, originally good like all of God's creation, is sinful because sin has in actual fact pervaded and corrupted it. It might be argued that the whole of personality is sinful in the same way; but Paul apparently thought of the flesh as being sinful in a special sense. He seems to think of it as being beyond the reach of redemption. He speaks of the redemption of our "body" (8:23), but not of our "flesh"; and in I Cor. 15:50 he says explicitly that "flesh and blood cannot inherit the kingdom of God." The whole of I Cor. 15 is of the greatest importance for the understanding of Rom. 7 and 8, and the reader will do well to note the comment on that chapter in Vol. X of this Commentary.

15. Paul continues now to make clear the meaning of being **sold under sin**—the meaning of a bondage no less real for being bondage to a power which has established itself within the man himself, i.e., in his flesh. **I do not understand my own actions,** i.e., "I find myself doing what I myself have not willed." **I do not do what I want, . . . I do the very thing I hate.** Every morally sensitive person is aware of what Paul means here. Ovid is often quoted in this connection: "I see and approve the better; I follow the worse" (*Metamorphoses* VII. 19-20). Epictetus uses words even nearer to Paul's: "What he wants he does not do, and what he does not want he does" (*Discourses* II. 26. 4)—although it must be said that Epictetus is pointing to a contribution which he thinks one can recognize and correct. Paul is making almost the opposite point.

we only partly understand and which we imperfectly control also determine the course and character of our life.

15. ***Elucidating the Enigma Which Is Man.***—Perplexity passes through impotence and issues in despair. The bewildered helplessness which pervades the whole chapter finds striking expression in the words **I do not understand my own actions.** Their meaning can be interpreted in various ways, including the literal sense which they carry. If so, they suggest a point of contact with the perplexity which overwhelms the modern man as he considers himself and the life which he shares with others. The old arrogance which could find an answer to every mystery has been severely chastened. We are diffident about forecasting for man the glorious future which humanism so confidently predicted. That is why we hear expressed so often the conviction that it might not be unmitigated disaster if man used his newly discovered powers to destroy himself. Man is an enigma to himself. New sciences spring up continually to try to explain how he thinks or why he acts as he does, but a wider range of information has brought no deeper understanding of the human problem. No issue in contemporary thought has an importance comparable to that of the nature of man. Paul would have taken it for granted that any interpretation which starts from secular or from purely scientific postulates would discover that man remains an enigma to himself. New knowledge touches only the mechanics of his existence and leaves the deeper and more mysterious reaches of his life wholly unexplained. Nor is religion necessarily more successful, as Paul's long struggle as a Pharisee had taught him. Paul writes letters, not treatises; consequently he does not cast his thought in the form of doctrines. Nevertheless, there is implicit in all he wrote a certain view of man's nature and destiny. He believed that this view was not only the true answer to man's problem but the only one which offered any satisfaction to man's mind or any peace to man's conscience. Its essential soundness was confirmed by the quality of the new life which it offered to those who acted as though it were true. He who sees himself as God's child, once alienated by his own sin but now restored to a transforming fellowship, is no longer troubled by the enigma of his own existence.

16 If then I do that which I would not,
I consent unto the law that *it is* good.
17 Now then it is no more I that do it,
but sin that dwelleth in me.
18 For I know that in me (that is, in my
flesh,) dwelleth no good thing: for to will
is present with me; but *how* to perform
that which is good I find not.
19 For the good that I would, I do not:
but the evil which I would not, that I do.
20 Now if I do that I would not, it is no
more I that do it, but sin that dwelleth in
me.
21 I find then a law, that, when I would
do good, evil is present with me.

but I do the very thing I hate. **16** Now if I
do what I do not want, I agree that the law
is good. **17** So then it is no longer I that do
it, but sin which dwells within me. **18** For
I know that nothing good dwells within
me, that is, in my flesh. I can will what is
right, but I cannot do it. **19** For I do not do
the good I want, but the evil I do not
want is what I do. **20** Now if I do what I do
not want, it is no longer I that do it, but
sin which dwells within me.
21 So I find it to be a law that when I
want to do right, evil lies close at hand.

16-20. The apostle draws two inferences from this experience of inner moral struggle and defeat. First, he sees his own aversion to his sinful acts as being tantamount to an acknowledgment of the law of God: **I agree that the law is good.** We probably have no difficulty in following his thought here: our moral struggle, even though we are eventually defeated, does involve an acknowledgment of the authority of the divine law. The second inference is more questionable: **It is no longer I that do it, but sin which dwells within me.** No words could express more forcibly Paul's recognition that sin in the flesh is an external power alien to man's true nature and hostile to him; but these words cannot be taken as literally intended or, at any rate, as representing Paul's whole mind on this subject. At face value they deny man's responsibility for his sinful acts. Such a denial Paul would not have defended as the whole truth; as we have seen, sin for Paul is both thralldom and transgression.

When he says, **Nothing good dwells within me** [better perhaps, "is within my power or reach"], **that is, in my flesh,** he shows that he has in mind primarily the weakness, the powerlessness of the flesh, for he adds, **I can will what is right, but I cannot do it.** Vss. 19-20 only repeat vss. 15-16.

21-24. This tragic division of personality is now described in more poignant terms. **I find it to be a law** [i.e., a rule, a constant pattern] **that when I want to do right, evil lies close at hand** (the same Greek term as in vs. 18 [παράκειται] but with a slightly different meaning). The phrase **the inward man** reminds one of 6:6, where the "old man" is referred to in contrast with the new humanity of which Christ is the head. Here, however, the contrast is between two elements of personality. It is often argued whether Paul thought of personality as having three basic elements—body (σῶμα), soul (ψυχή), spirit (πνεῦμα)—or only two. Probably his thought was not at all clear or consistent at this point, but on the whole it seems likely that he associated "soul" closely with "flesh" and thought of both as set over against what could be called "mind," "conscience," "heart," "spirit," or more vaguely "the inner man" (cf. II Cor. 4:16). The RSV translation **in my inmost self** is excellent, not only because "man" here clearly means "self" (as in 6:6), but also because the phrase seems to suggest Paul's conception that the part of him which assents to, even delights in, **the law of God** is his true, his real self.

16-23. ***Beyond Despair.***—(See Expos. on vss. 7-25). A divided self is a defeated self, and no more poignant expression of this truth has ever been written than Paul's account of his unavailing struggle to satisfy the moral demands of the law. His true self he believed to be on the side of right and so on the side of God; but his physical nature had become a realm in which an alien power exercised its sway, and he was incapable of overthrowing its tyranny. The experience of frustration is the right background for the proclamation of the gospel. The self

22 For I delight in the law of God after the inward man:

23 But I see another law in my members, warring against the law of my mind, and bringing me into captivity to the law of sin which is in my members.

24 O wretched man that I am! who shall deliver me from the body of this death?

25 I thank God through Jesus Christ our Lord. So then with the mind I myself serve the law of God; but with the flesh the law of sin.

22 For I delight in the law of God, in my
inmost self, 23 but I see in my members
another law at war with the law of my
mind and making me captive to the law of
sin which dwells in my members.
24 Wretched man that I am! Who will deliver me from this body of death? 25 Thanks
be to God through Jesus Christ our Lord!
So then, I of myself serve the law of God
with my mind, but with my flesh I serve
the law of sin.

With this true self—now called the **mind**—a foreign principle, with its seat in his flesh (**my members**), is **at war.** This foreign principle is **sin which dwells in my members,** and it has "made captive" the higher, inner, more essential elements of personality, so that Paul is forced to cry, **Wretched man that I am! Who will deliver me from this body of death?** In 6:6 Paul has spoken of the "body of sin," meaning certainly "sinful body" or "body dominated by sin." Here he has the same idea in mind but is thinking especially of sin's awful consequences. The "body of sin" is really a "body of death." It would not be possible to convey his meaning, however, by translating "mortal body." "Doomed body" would be better; but the literal translation cannot be improved on. The order of the words at the beginning of vs. 24 is, in the Greek, "Wretched I man. . . ." The position of "man" is emphatic and suggests that Paul is thinking of his own experience, not as his own simply, but as typical of man's experience in general. He is describing the *human* situation.

25. The difference in the English rendering of this sentence as between the KJV and the RSV reflects a difference in the Greek text in the MSS. The majority of MSS read **I thank God.** Some texts read "the grace of God." A number of the most ancient MSS, however, give **thanks be to God;** this is almost certainly the best reading (see I Cor. 15:57 for a very similar passage). This cry of hope has the same poignant personal character as the cry of distress and despair which immediately precedes it. It *is* a cry of hope, rather than of complete realization, answering as it does to a question in the future tense: **Who will deliver me?** Still, as we have so many occasions to remark, this hope is already beginning to be fulfilled in the experience of the believer, and so it can be voiced with really triumphant assurance.

That this fulfillment is still largely in the future, however, appears unmistakably in vs. 25*b*, where the same division of personality of which the apostle has been speaking throughout most of this chapter is again described (on the position of vs. 25*b* see pp. 499-500 above). The Greek term rendered **of myself** in the RSV is the intensive pronoun in the nominative case, so that, literally rendered, Paul's statement is, "I myself serve the law of God with my mind. . . ." Moffatt takes the "myself" to mean "left to myself,"

---

satisfied man does not know he needs it; but once he has learned that his awakened insight shows him objectives that he cannot reach by his own powers, he is ready to admit that he stands in need of God's help. He is ready also to concede that God as a taskmaster is not a figure of any hope or comfort; and he is prepared to hear with joy of a Father, who, once we have submitted to his will in trust and obedience, will make the failures of the past as though they had never been. He learns that in the moral conflict he is not left to struggle on in his own unaided strength, but that loyalty to and fellowship with a risen Lord supply him with undreamed of resources of power. That is why the cry of desolating despair passes so naturally into the cry of astonished gratitude; and why the analysis of defeat in ch. 7 intro-

8 *There is* therefore now no condemnation to them which are in Christ Jesus, who walk not after the flesh, but after the Spirit.

8 There is therefore now no condemnation for those who are in Christ Jesus.

i.e., apart from God's action in Christ, referred to in vs. 25*a*. The RSV translation indicates the same understanding. This is probably correct, but it is at least worth noting that Paul may again be identifying his essential self (I *myself*) with the **mind,** or "inner man," as in vs. 22.

E. The Life of the Spirit (8:1-27)

Only twice so far in the course of this discussion of the new life in Christ (5:5; 7:6) has Paul referred explicitly to the Spirit, although one of these references ascribes the essential character of that life to the Spirit: "the new life of the Spirit." In this section (vss. 1-27), however, the word occurs no fewer than twenty times. The Spirit is the theme of this culminating section of the argument which began at 6:1 with the question, "Are we to continue in sin that grace may abound?" The apostle, it will be remembered, answered that question with a decisive negative, and went on to show the anomalousness of living in sin when we have in fact "died to sin" (6:2–7:6). It soon appeared, however (7:7-25), that this death to sin could not be thought of as already a fact—certainly not a completed fact—because Paul was able to describe in the most poignant terms his continuing struggle with the demonic enemy which, from its base within his flesh, had brought his whole self into bondage. It became clear that 7:25*a* expressed a *hope,* and such a meaning is confirmed by Paul's words in 5:2 ("We . . . rejoice in hope of the glory of God") and later, in 8:24-25 ("In this hope we were saved").

We were thus reminded again of a fact about Paul's thought to which we first had occasion to refer in connection with 1:16, viz., that salvation for Paul is primarily and essentially eschatological. It will be realized only beyond history. Paul is so sure of the divinely appointed end of history, and so certain that this end is imminent, that he is often able to disregard the interim and to talk as though the new age had come. So he did through 6:2–7:6; so he does quite often. But actually this final fulfillment has not come; and it is "in hope" that "we are saved." To be sure, we *have been* justified; but we *shall be* saved: "If while we were enemies we *were* reconciled to God by the death of his Son, much more, now that we are reconciled, *shall* we be saved by his life" (5:10 RSV. Italics ours).

But what of the immediately present situation? What is our position in the brief interim before the new age fully comes? Do we live only in the *belief* that we have been

duces the description of the victorious life in ch. 8.

8:1-11. ***Theology and the Triumphant Life.***—The opening verses of the chapter contain by implication almost a complete system of Christian belief. God and his purpose, Christ's life and death, the Spirit's presence and power, the seriousness of sin and man's deliverance from its grip, the failure of legal righteousness, the new status which Christ gives to the believer, the reconciliation to God of those who are forgiven, the communication of the Spirit, and the resurrection—even so inclusive a list does not exhaust the subjects to which Paul refers. Yet the primary purpose of ch. 8 is to discuss the nature of the victorious life. We may consequently note that to ignore the great convictions of the faith is evidently not the way to achieve a triumphant quality of life.

1. ***Guilty? Or Not Guilty?***—**Condemnation** is a legal term which describes a spiritual condition. The man who finds himself in God's presence, and there becomes aware of the holiness which confronts and judges him, knows that he cannot abide the searching of so inexorable a righteousness. All that he has done is insufficient, and the utmost that he can do will not materially change the situation; he is convinced that the only verdict he can expect is "guilty." This is the reaction, of course, only of a person of discriminating moral judgment and awakened religious sense. To say that a man of thor-

justified and in the *hope* that we shall be saved? The answer is that both belief and hope are based upon an indubitable reality within the present experience of the believer. And it is at this point that the doctrine of the Spirit becomes relevant.

The background of what Paul has to say about the Spirit lies in the O.T. There the Spirit is the "breath of God"—in the sense of being the presence of God or the power of God as visible or operative in the world. We are told that the Spirit of God brooded over the primeval chaos (Gen. 1:2); that the prophets were enlightened and strengthened by the Spirit (I Sam. 10:10, and often); that no man is able to flee from God's Spirit (Ps. 139:7). The Spirit of God is the self-authenticating presence and power of God. It was believed that the Messiah would be especially endowed by the Spirit; and the new age, which he would inaugurate, was to be an age of the Spirit. Now it was the most certain and intimate fact about the primitive Christian community that it knew within its life a new manifestation of the Spirit. This Spirit validated himself both as the eternal Spirit of God and also as the Spirit of Jesus, who was remembered as companion and Master. The possession of the Spirit was thus the seal of the Resurrection and the sure sign that the new age was already beginning. The Spirit is an advance installment of the future glory, which thus ceases to be altogether future. The Spirit (described in 5:5 as "God's love . . . poured into our hearts") is therefore the empirical ground of faith and hope. He is the guarantee both of the significance of what has happened (i.e., the death and resurrection of Jesus and the justification of the believer) and of the reality of what is still to come (i.e., Christ's return and our full deliverance from the power of sin and death). He binds the whole event, which we call the revelation in Christ, together—bridging the gap between past and future which up to this point has so often appeared as an important feature of Paul's thought.

Throughout this section of the epistle (vss. 1-27), as whenever he speaks about the Spirit, Paul is talking about the present life of the believer. This fact provides the essential clue to the understanding of this chapter. We find here not a piece of theological analysis, but a description of concrete religious experience.

1. God's Saving Act (8:1-4)

8:1. Paul begins with a brief account of the saving act of God in Christ, to which he has been constantly referring and which he has described in essentially the same terms earlier in the letter (e.g., 3:21-26). This little section is by way of being an explanation of 7:25*a*: "Thanks be to God through Jesus Christ our Lord!" The phrase **no condemnation** means not only justification (of a forensic sort) but also deliverance from "this

---

oughly secular outlook has never felt like this is beside the point; a man can be aware of his condemned status only if he has become conscious of God as a holy will which meets him in moral demand. It is equally fallacious to assume—as is sometimes done—that so bitter a sense of spiritual failure must be the counterpart of flagrant moral aberration. It is the man of high standards, not of low ones, who is conscious of condemnation. Paul had accepted exacting requirements and had learned that even his utmost efforts did not suffice to satisfy what his religious understanding demanded. But part of the difficulty lay in his mistaken notion of what God asked him to do. He had completely misunderstood the nature of the relationship which God had intended men to occupy. The emphasis had been entirely misplaced—on what man could achieve, not on what God purposed to give. The extent of that error stood clearly disclosed in the light of Christ's life and death. It was even more important that in Christ was revealed the new way in which men could be justified—given the status of those who are pronounced "not guilty." How faith makes possible the new relationship which God initiates has been Paul's chief theme thus far. He has shown how the verdict which we would naturally expect need never be pronounced, because we have been lifted out of the region where our achievements are decisive, into a new world governed by the mercy of God.

The discovery of this is an event; its appropriation must be a continuing process. But is there no likelihood that the event will have to be endlessly repeated? Those who have sinned are forgiven and brought into a new relationship with God; but they remain imperfect men,

2 For the law of the Spirit of life in Christ Jesus hath made me free from the law of sin and death.

2 For the law of the Spirit of life in Christ Jesus has set me free from the law of sin

---

body of death," i.e., from the doom to which the body of flesh is subject. **Those who are in Christ Jesus** are those who belong to the new community of which Christ Jesus is the head and the center, i.e., to the body of Christ (cf. 7:4).

The words **who walk not after the flesh, but after the Spirit** (KJV) do not occur in the oldest Greek MSS and are properly omitted by the RSV. The clause is obviously borrowed and inserted from vs. 4.

2. The word **law** (νόμος) again means not commandment, but "pattern," or "principle," or "system," or "rule." (The use of the word is certainly approximately if not exactly the same as in 7:21, 23.) The probable meaning of the verse is clearer if commas are placed after "Spirit" and after "Jesus." Paul is saying, "The principle, or rule, of **the Spirit—i.e., of life in Christ Jesus—has set me free,** etc." He is identifying the **Spirit** with the **life in Christ** (i.e., in the community of believers), or with the principle of that life. The Spirit, in other words, is what makes the church the church. The "spirit" of this society—its distinctive quality and possession—is the Holy Spirit. To belong to this community is to know the Spirit; to know the Spirit is to belong to this community. This possession of the Spirit, this participation in the life of the new community, has **set me free from the law of sin and death.** If Paul means here "has already entirely freed me," he is speaking in the eschatological terms of so much of his discourse in this epistle, and really means "has already as good as freed me"—i.e., the thing is so certain and so imminent that it is fair to think of it as having already happened. More probably, however—since the whole context suggests, as we have said, that he is dealing with the actual present experience of the believer—he means to say that the possession by the Spirit has broken the power of sin and death, so that the man in Christ finds himself actually enjoying a partial victory and freedom.

---

who cannot fully do the Father's will. And when they fall, are they not again estranged? Paul answers "No"—in spite of the fact that his letters prove that he knew his correspondents were very far from sinless. How can imperfect folk avoid alienating God? The answer lies in the nature of the new relationship. **There is . . . now no condemnation for those who are in Christ Jesus.** A new era has clearly opened, and what used to be true is no longer relevant. The single word "now" is sufficient to unfold the whole range of incalculable change that has come into our spiritual experience through Jesus Christ. Though not perfect people, we live in a new sphere. Union with Christ is so real and so intimate that he forms the environment which surrounds our lives; his presence is the realm where our days are spent, his will is the power by which our aspirations are directed and confirmed. If Christ is the dynamic of the life lived in union with him, it is impossible for us to remain where we are. Experience becomes the record of progress. But it is not simply growth in grace which puts us beyond condemnation; our life in Christ is such that our true relationship with God is never irrevocably broken. We may fall, but we are less likely utterly to fail. Even if we do, the way of forgiveness has grown familiar, and restitution follows. The atmosphere in which the life is lived and the direction in which it is moving are more important than any of its episodes.

2. ***Liberty Through the Law of the Spirit of Life.***—It was a principle of frustration which formerly worked in Paul's life—and which works within the experience of all who rely upon their own efforts. The dominant authority was exercised by sin and issued in death, and his moral plight was such that he was governed by this principle of evil and obeyed it in his actions. This is the tyranny described in ch. 7; but a higher authority has broken its sway and displaced it. **The law of the Spirit of life,** which becomes effective because of the believer's union with Christ, **has set me free,** says Paul, **from the law of sin and death.** The new principle which is at work in our experience gives life; but only because it is the true source of life. What it does is the reflection of what it is. Paul is describing the overthrow of one authority, lawless and usurping, by another which has both the right and the power to rule our lives.

3 For what the law could not do, in that it was weak through the flesh, God

and death. 3 For God has done what the law, weakened by the flesh, could not do:

3. All of this is possible because God **condemned sin in the flesh.** The word **condemned** in this verse answers to **condemnation** in vs. 1: There is no condemnation *for us* because there was condemnation *for sin.* God has placed sin under sentence of death. This is the meaning of "condemned," and the term is well chosen. Paul does not say that sin has actually been eliminated; but just as the believer is justified but not fully saved, so sin is condemned but not fully destroyed. This defeating and dooming of sin the law had been too weak to accomplish. Paul means, of course, that *man* had been too weak to accomplish this by his obedience to the law. It is man, not the law, which is **weakened by the flesh,** i.e., by sin in the flesh. Paul is using his words loosely—even, as the reader of the Greek will see, ungrammatically—but his meaning is clear. The defeat of sin, which man was not able to bring about, God accomplished by **sending his own Son** (for "Son" see on 1:3; but in the present passage the verb **sending** strongly suggests pre-existence).

Why does Paul say **in the likeness of sinful flesh?** Why not simply "in sinful flesh"? Is he expressing some doubt of the reality of the humanity of Jesus? The same question arises in connection with the equally important christological passage (Phil. 2:7), "was made in the likeness of men: and being found in fashion as a man." (The Greek word for "likeness" in these two passages is the same, ὁμοίωμα.) If it were necessary for us to rely solely upon these two passages for our answer to our question, that answer would almost certainly have to be affirmative, and we can easily imagine with what eagerness later Docetists availed themselves of these texts. Actually, however, for Paul to have doubted the reality of Jesus' humanity (i.e., the reality of his flesh) would have been tantamount to his repudiating his whole conception of why God sent his Son and of what that Son accomplished. God sent his Son to defeat and destroy **sin in the flesh.** This could not have been done, or even attempted, if he had only *appeared* to be in the flesh. The word **sending** in such a case would have no meaning.

It should be pointed out that the Greek word ὁμοίωμα has a somewhat different connotation from "likeness" in English. It does not mean—or at least *may* not mean—mere appearance, but rather the form of manifestation which a concrete thing assumes. Thus Goodspeed renders this, "our sinful human form." Lietzmann says the word in this passage "is almost equal to σῶμα [body]." Kirk has a very interesting discussion of this point (*Epistle to Romans,* pp. 105-6) and concludes: "Thus to say that our Lord came

3-4. ***God's Deed in Christ.***—God has done what we ourselves could never do. Paul declares the fact of the divine intervention; he describes the purpose served by God's action, the necessity which inspired it, the form which it assumed and the method which it employed.

God has done what the law . . . could not do. Christianity is not the conjecture of human speculation but the heralding of what God has done. It begins with his acts, not with our ideas. This gives it at once its concrete character, its positive emphasis, and its immediate relevance. It explains the fact that the voice of the verbs is almost always active. From this also springs the redemptive character of the gospel. It confidently proclaims that human lives can be transformed because it rests its assurance on the evidence of what God has already done.

God has acted **in order that the just requirement of the law might be fulfilled.** It had proved easy to state the demands of the law, but utterly impossible to satisfy them. Men knew that they ought to achieve a certain kind of righteousness and show the fruits of true morality in their lives, but their understanding always outstripped their performance. The dilemma of moralism has been remorselessly exposed in previous chapters. What God has now done is to make possible a life which is not subject to the tyranny of appetite. Because we are now controlled by the Spirit, there is a possibility of fulfilling the demands of the law.

The law had failed because it was **weakened by the flesh.** It could diagnose the moral situation, but lacking the dynamic which could assure us of victory it succeeded only in arousing appetite. It commanded the assent of reason but did not control the power of impulse.

sending his own Son in the likeness of sinful flesh, and for sin, condemned sin in the flesh:

4 That the righteousness of the law might be fulfilled in us, who walk not after the flesh, but after the Spirit.

sending his own Son in the likeness of sinful flesh and for sin,[i] he condemned sin in the flesh, 4 in order that the just requirement of the law might be fulfilled in us, who walk not according to the flesh but

[i] Or *and as a sin-offering.*

---

in the 'likeness' of man would not to a Greek throw any such doubt upon His true manhood as it does in English."

Nevertheless it remains true that Paul here falls short of making as clear and strong an affirmation of Jesus' humanity as the Fourth Gospel does in such a statement as "the Word was made flesh" (KJV), or as Hebrews does in 2:14; 5:7, and elsewhere. The basis of this difference does not lie at all in a more complete acceptance of the genuineness of Jesus' humanity by John than by Paul—the opposite, if anything, is true—but rather in the fact that John has an apologetic interest in asserting Jesus' humanity (i.e., against the Docetists) which Paul does not have—the humanity probably seemed to him to be self-evident and indispensable—as well as in the fact that Paul has a conception of the flesh (as hopelessly corrupted by sin) which makes him shrink from describing Jesus simply as "being in the flesh." But this is what he must mean in fact, such terms as "likeness" and "fashion" (Phil. 2:7) notwithstanding. Perhaps if he had been pressed or challenged, he would have made a distinction between Jesus' flesh and ordinary flesh. The latter is "flesh of sin" (the literal phrasing of the term translated "sinful flesh"); Jesus' flesh was real flesh, but not "flesh of sin." But in that case how could he have been thought of as dealing with **sin in the flesh**? The truth is that Paul had probably not reached a consistent position on this matter (in this connection see also on 6:9-10).

It has been usual to take **and for sin** as a reference to the sin offering (Lev. 4:2 ff.). In that case the death of Christ is being interpreted as a sacrifice for sin, although it would be a mistake to press the analogy too far. At most nothing can be meant beyond what is indicated in the Exeg. on 3:24-26. The exact phrase, however, is "and concerning sin," and may mean, as Moffatt renders it, "to deal with sin." This meaning agrees somewhat better with the verb **condemned** in the following clause.

4. We find here the same difficult term which was discussed in the Exeg. of 5:18, δικαίωμα. There the question was between the meanings "justifying act" and "act of righteousness." In the present verse neither of these meanings is indicated, but rather the simpler sense the term has in 1:32 and 2:26. In both of these passages the word clearly designates the requirement of the law. The RSV translates it with "decree" in one case and "precepts" in the other. Because the meaning is here more generalized, the translation **the just requirement** (RSV) is a good one. **Righteousness** (KJV) is too abstract.

Paul makes in this verse and in the sentences immediately following (vss. 5-17) a somewhat different, and (would one not say?) a somewhat more adequate, answer to the question with which chs. 6 and 7 were largely concerned—the question of the ground of ethical behavior in the believer and especially of the relation in which the believer stands to the law. Up to this point, although he has asserted that "the law is holy, and the commandment is holy and just and good" (7:12), Paul has in effect seemed to deny

---

The true nature of God's act is seen in the result which followed from it: **He condemned sin in the flesh.** This does not suggest that he merely expressed moral disapproval; the law, which could command the assent of reason, had already done that. What God has done in Christ not only exposes sin's basic character, but passes effective sentence upon it. Sin leaves the court—for the imagery is legal—stripped of false pretenses and deprived of powers and prerogatives which it had unjustly usurped.

The method by which this result has been achieved is God's **sending of his own Son.** The doctrines both of the Incarnation and of the Atonement are implicit in what Paul says: Christ came **in the likeness of sinful flesh, and**

5 For they that are after the flesh do
nind the things of the flesh; but they that
ire after the Spirit, the things of the Spirit.

according to the Spirit. 5 For those who
live according to the flesh set their minds
on the things of the flesh, but those who
live according to the Spirit set their minds

---

hat the law has any validity for the believer. There can be no doubt that often Paul ctually saw the matter in that way. But when or in so far as he does so, he destroys, or t any rate seriously weakens, the ground of ethical *obligation* once one is a believer in Christ (on this important point see Exeg. on 6:1-2). One may reasonably believe that n the words **that the just requirement of the law might be fulfilled in us** a needed balance is being restored. The statement in Gal. 5:14, "For the whole law is fulfilled n one word, 'You shall love your neighbor as yourself,' " looks in the same direction, as loes the reference later in that same epistle (6:2) to "the law of Christ." Such passages (including Rom. 8:4) suggest that Paul had in mind the second and third meanings proposed in the Exeg. on 6:14-15, rather than the first. The believer never escapes from obligation to the moral law of God. Paul never distinguishes between "ceremonial" and 'moral" elements in the law, but surely such a distinction is implicit in such a passage as Gal. 5:14. But the believer can be said to be free from the law in two respects: (*a*) he loes not have to depend upon his success in keeping the law for his acceptance with God— ustification is offered on another basis, as we have seen; and (*b*) this justification, or econciliation with God, brings a new power to keep the law which makes the recipient of it less aware of the demands of the law as sheer demands. This new power is that of the indwelling Spirit. Thus in this passage Paul speaks not of our fulfilling **the just equirement of the law,** but of its being **fulfilled in us.**

Again, it must be noted that in so far as Paul is here thinking of a perfect fulfillment, hat fulfillment is in the future. The final clause, however, **who walk** [i.e., who conduct heir lives] **not according to the flesh but according to the Spirit,** indicates that he is not hinking only or even chiefly of the final perfect fulfillment, but of that partial realization, itself the sure guarantee of ultimate perfection (cf. "glory of God" in 5:2), which he Spirit makes possible. Vs. 4 leads immediately into the discussion of the next topic.

2. The New Righteousness (8:5-13)

5. They that are after the flesh (KJV) is probably a more accurate, as it is a more iteral, translation of the Greek than the RSV, **those who live according to the flesh.** Paul is referring simply to "natural" men as contrasted with those who have received he Spirit, i.e., **they that are after the Spirit.** The fact that these two groups of men *live* lifferently is the burden of the second or principal clause in each case: natural men are absorbed in the interests of the flesh **(do mind the things of the flesh);** men who have

---

or sin. It was from within our life that Christ nanifested the perfect obedience to God's will which broke the power of sin. By his life and leath he not only exposed the full measure of our need and pointed the way to our complete leliverance; he also made it impossible thenceorth to hold merely dark and morbid views of our human nature. What can become the appropriate vehicle for so glorious a revelation cannot be wholly corrupt and depraved. The ncarnation is the true charter of our human lignity, as the Atonement is our sufficient assurance of final emancipation.

5-8. ***Carnal and Spiritual.***—Implicit in what Paul has just said is a contrast between two ways of life, and he now exposes the full measure of the difference by setting them side by side. The first comparison which he uses concerns the basic interest which governs each type of life. **Those who live according to the flesh set their minds on the things of the flesh, but those who live according to the Spirit set their minds on the things of the Spirit.** The man whose dominant interests center in physical appetites finds that his whole existence is organized around their satisfaction. In the same way, the man whose life is under the control of the Spirit finds that his conscious interests lie more and more in spiritual things. The second comparison serves to unfold the results to which these contrasting types of life will lead. Preoccupation with impulse and appetite offers only one pros-

6 For to be carnally minded *is* death; but to be spiritually minded *is* life and peace.
7 Because the carnal mind *is* enmity against God: for it is not subject to the law of God, neither indeed can be.

on the things of the Spirit. 6 To set the mind on the flesh is death, but to set the mind on the Spirit is life and peace. 7 For the mind that is set on the flesh is hostile to God; it does not submit to God's law,

received the Spirit are dominated by the interests of the Spirit. The Greek terms here, and in the following verses—φρονεῖν and φρόνημα—refer to a directing of emotion and will, as well as thought, toward an object.

6-7. The close association in Paul's mind of sin and death has already been noted. Death is both the penalty of sin, thought of as transgression, and the final issue of sin, thought of as bondage. But for Paul the relation is closer than either of these terms suggests. Death does not simply follow, however closely and inevitably, upon sin; it is itself present in and with sin. To live in sin is not simply to face the sure doom of death; it is also to be dead in a real sense already. One is aware of the seeds of death in oneself. In the same way, to possess the Spirit and to be dominated by the interests of the Spirit mean more than the *hope* of **life and peace.** One possesses them already, although not perfectly. Vs. 7 gives the ground, assumed in the Exeg. on 6*a*, for the statement made in that verse: **to set the mind on the flesh** means **death** for the reason that such an attitude or state of mind constitutes **enmity against God**—an enmity which issues in death. **The mind that is set on the flesh . . . does not submit to God's law, indeed it cannot.**

pect: **To set the mind on the flesh is death.** We are becoming more and more engrossed in interests which are of necessity ephemeral; when death overtakes us, what is left that can be called life? Besides, we must always remember that in addition to the final consequence of so limited an aim, we face the fact that its immediate results partake of the nature of death. Not only do such interests contain within themselves the seeds of their destruction, but they already infect with their own blight everything with which they come in contact. Alternative interests atrophy; competing claims lose their appeal. On the other hand, **to set the mind on the Spirit is life and peace.** Like **death, life** describes both an immediate experience and an ultimate destiny. In its crowning intensity it is of course a deferred experience; but in part we know already something of its nature and its possibilities. In the Bible we find "life" regularly used to describe that experience of communion with God to which faith and obedience admit the believer,[2] and in the N.T. the word is often a synonym for "salvation." This consequence follows naturally from what Paul has already said about the Spirit. "The Spirit of life" will naturally communicate life to those whose interests are centered in the realm which the Spirit controls. "Peace" also is one of the fruits which we would expect to find in those **who live according to the Spirit** (cf. Gal. 5:22). To achieve the new status made possible by faith is to have "peace with God" (5:1), and this reconciled relation "diffuses a feeling of harmony and tranquillity over the whole man."[3]

To state the contrast might seem sufficient, but Paul underlines the enmity which enters in to separate from God the man whose life is dominated by physical appetite. **For the mind that is set on the flesh is hostile to God** (vss. 7-8). Paul is stating a basic incompatibility; the life which limits its interests to the satisfactions of the flesh cannot **submit to God's law,** and those who chose that kind of life **cannot please God.** The uncompromising character of such a position is apt to appear a little grim to a generation that remembers the struggle to gain for the body its rightful place in God's dispensation. The attitude which frowns on every form of physical satisfaction is derived from the Pauline position, but is a distortion of it. Paul repeatedly implies that the flesh, as the material basis of man's life, is not in itself an evil thing. By its nature it is neutral: it may be good or it may be bad, and which it is depends on the choice made by man's spirit. It is this fact which creates the problem. Once evil enters, the delicate balance of man's life is disturbed, and physical impulse acquires a power which wins for it a role which it should not have. Instead of being a servant, it becomes a master, and the whole personality is changed for the worse. Even the mind is affected, and its interests are imprisoned within the narrow circle which appetite permits. The picture shows us the steady

[2] Cf. F. J. A. Hort, *The Way, the Truth, the Life* (London: Macmillan & Co., 1893), p. 98.

[3] Sanday and Headlam, *Epistle to Romans,* p. 196.

8 So then they that are in the flesh cannot please God.
9 But ye are not in the flesh, but in the Spirit, if so be that the Spirit of God dwell in you. Now if any man have not the Spirit of Christ, he is none of his.

indeed it cannot; [8] and those who are in the flesh cannot please God.
9 But you are not in the flesh, you are in the Spirit, if the Spirit of God really dwells in you. Any one who does not have the Spirit of Christ does not belong to

8-9. Vs. 8 reminds one of 3:20. **Those who are in the flesh** are those who belong merely to the natural order. "But," Paul says, "you do not belong to this natural order of **the flesh;** you belong to the new, supernatural, eschatological order of **the Spirit, if** [or perhaps "since"—see on vs. 17, below] **the Spirit of God really dwells in you."** The possession of the Spirit constitutes, as we have several times observed (see especially p. 505, above), an anticipatory enjoyment of the life of the new age. If we have the Spirit, we belong, most intimately and truly, not to this world, which is doomed and soon to pass away, but to the new world, which is promised and indeed already appearing. Vs. 9*b* states this same truth in obverse fashion: **Any one who does not have the Spirit . . . does not belong.** In this latter case the Spirit is referred to as the **Spirit of Christ,** and belonging to the new order is referred to as "belonging to him"; but the meaning is the same. We have already noted the fact that for Paul, Christ has given his name to the newly created divine order of life which, because of God's act in and through him, is rapidly replacing the natural world; and also the fact that the Spirit can be alluded to as "the Holy Spirit," "the Spirit of God," simply as the "Spirit," or as "the Spirit of Christ." To know Christ, to be in Christ, to be in the Spirit, to have the Spirit, to belong

corruption of a life in which the proper equipoise of body and mind is destroyed and the whole nature becomes gross. To recognize what is happening and to describe it faithfully is not pessimism; it is realism; and in this case, moreover, realism declares that redemption is a process by which the proper balance of man's nature is restored. The "spiritual" life is not an immaterial existence, nor one in which the body is denied its proper part. The decisive question really concerns the source of the motives which actually govern life. Where we start from will determine where we end; our interests will decide the kind of persons we will be. This seems reasonably obvious as long as we restrict our discussion to "the spiritual" and "the carnal"; but the whole trend of Paul's argument is to show that the gospel sets our life in a different order, not merely on a different plane. As Gore says, "What was managed from below is now controlled from above." [4] If we start from human standards and trust in human resources, we end by trying to achieve our own righteousness, and the method we have chosen involves us in the hopeless tensions created by pride on the one hand and failure on the other. Because we rely on human resources, we never break out of an order in which we are limited to human factors. But if we start from God, the values which derive from him and the power of which he is the source will bring us progressively into that liberation of spirit which is his gift. This difference determines the character of our moral and spiritual life. It decides whether we are free men or slaves, and it profoundly affects the quality which we impart to things which are neutral in themselves. It is here that we often mistake the significance of the distinction between the things of the flesh and those of the spirit. We have confused "carnal" with "material." Consequently, we have allowed "the spiritual" to be divorced from the concerns of actual life; by restricting it to "the immaterial" we have equated it with the unreal. It is wholly a matter of the kind of impulses which rule our lives. If we are under the tyranny of physical appetite, we shall live in the flesh; if we are governed by the purposes of God, we shall live in the Spirit. The setting is the same in both cases. The heart of the gospel is a conviction that God has used the concreteness of our human life as the medium for the revelation of his love. As a result, we are only drawing inevitable inferences from the Incarnation if we declare that industry and commerce, politics and statecraft, are areas in which the life of the Spirit can—and must—be lived.

9-11. ***The Spirit of God.***—Paul has described two kinds of life, the one "carnal" the other "spiritual"; and the two are set before us as alternatives. The outward pattern which marks our life will depend upon the inner dynamic which animates it. If we are at the mercy of

[4] *Epistle to Romans,* I, 281.

10 And if Christ *be* in you, the body *is* dead because of sin; but the Spirit *is* life because of righteousness.

him. 10 But if Christ is in you, although your bodies are dead because of sin, your spirits are alive because of righteousness.

---

to the body of Christ—these are all ways of alluding to the meaning of the same experience; and Paul uses them almost if not quite interchangeably. This experience is the experience of being actually incorporated in the living fellowship of the church, of knowing, i.e., the love of God (see on 5:5).

10-11. This fluidity of terminology is further illustrated in the apostle's words, **if Christ is in you.** Here "Christ" is clearly identified with **the Spirit of Christ** of vs. 9*b* and therefore also with **the Spirit of God** of vs. 9*a*. The rest of vs. 10 is somewhat obscure. The Greek is literally rendered in the KJV: **the body is dead because of sin; but the Spirit is life because of righteousness.** Each of these clauses must be separately considered.

Interpreters are divided as to whether, when Paul says **the body is dead,** he is thinking in terms of the ideas expressed in 6:2 ff. or of those found in 5:12 ff. Does he mean (*a*) "The body [i.e., the flesh] is dead to you," just as in 6:2 ff. he describes the "sinful body" as being "destroyed"? Or does he mean (*b*) "The body [i.e., the natural man] is subject to death," just as in 5:12 he speaks of "death" as spreading to "all men"? Those who favor (*a*) point out that the second meaning—i.e., (*b*)—is not consistent with the way the sentence begins (**if Christ is in you**), whereas (*a*) is consistent with that meaning; besides, they say, the adjective **dead** is not appropriate to (*b*)—one would expect "mortal" instead. But both of these objections can be answered: the first of them, by pointing out that if "although" is supplied (as in the RSV, and as the Greek certainly permits) the connection of **if Christ is in you** is with the second of the following clauses rather than with the first. As to the objection to the adjective "dead," one can refer to Paul's habit of vivid speech—a "mortal" body is as good as "dead." On the other hand, against (*a*) stands the phrase **because of sin.** Those who adopt that interpretation have to understand that phrase to mean "with a view to the conquest of sin" (Kirk). But such is surely not the natural way to take the phrase. If (*b*) is adopted, the reference to sin fits nicely into place, the whole clause corresponding exactly and entirely with "death spread to all men because all men sinned" (5:12). This second interpretation—i.e., (*b*)—is probably preferable. Moffatt makes this meaning quite explicit in his translation when he writes, "If Christ is within you, though the body is a dead thing owing to Adam's sin. . . ."

---

impulse, if instinct is the highest power we obey, we are **in the flesh.** But with the Christian the aimlessness of appetite is replaced by **the Spirit of God.** Notice the permanence and the intimacy of the relationship which is presupposed. The Christian's life becomes the dwelling place of God's Spirit. This is a thought which Paul has put forward elsewhere (cf. I Cor. 3:16, where he speaks of us as the temples of the Holy Spirit); but though the imagery suggests that God has come to dwell with his people, it fails to express the central marvel of the Christian experience. The fault lies with the language Paul uses, not with the insight he possesses. There is no fellowship between a temple and the deity which is found and worshiped there; a dwelling place conveys a greater sense of intimacy, but it is still simply the outer shell within which something significant takes place. But when our life becomes God's dwelling place, the central fact is the creation of a certain type of fellowship. Christianity parts company with all forms of pantheism because of its insistence that the individual never becomes a mere instrument of the divine Spirit. The believer remains a person, and a person can never be used as a tool. So long as he retains his true character it is impossible for God to dwell in him without his entering into a distinctive relationship with God. Because of what God is, his Spirit transforms and energizes. He becomes the motive power of a new quality of life, life **in the Spirit.**

It is this new quality of life which makes it possible, if not to distinguish in fact, at least to differentiate in principle between those who are Christ's and those who are not. Vs. 9*b* suggests a test quite difficult to apply but decisive in its results. One is either a Christian

11 But if the Spirit of him that raised up Jesus from the dead dwell in you, he that raised up Christ from the dead shall also quicken your mortal bodies by his Spirit that dwelleth in you.

11 If the Spirit of him who raised Jesus from the dead dwells in you, he who raised Christ Jesus from the dead will give life to your mortal bodies also through his Spirit which dwells in you.

The second clause, **the Spirit is life because of righteousness,** is almost equally ambiguous. It is usual to take the word "spirit" here as a reference to "your spirits" (so the RSV, Sanday and Headlam, Kirk, Moffatt, Gaugler, etc.). This word, however, has heretofore throughout this whole passage undoubtedly referred to the Spirit of God (or of Christ), and this continues to be true until we reach the very end (vs. 16), where the full phrase "our spirit" is used and the reference is unmistakable. It seems best (with Lietzmann) to take **Spirit** here (as in the KJV) to mean the divine Spirit. That **Spirit** means **life** to us **because of righteousness.** Lietzmann writes: "The emphasis is laid on the ethical side of the 'life': it is given 'because of righteousness.' " This seems hardly characteristic of Paul, whom one would expect to make righteousness conditional upon life, rather than life upon righteousness, if "righteousness" means ethical character and conduct. Perhaps here Paul is referring not to our righteousness, but to God's act of justification; or more probably to the state of being justified. Or perhaps the "righteousness" is a real, as distinguished from a merely forensic, righteousness, but it is being thought of as God's gift to us. If that is the proper way to understand the word, Paul means to say here something like: "The Spirit, because he gives righteousness, also gives life"; or "Because he brings a new righteousness to the believer, the Spirit brings life"; cf. vs. 6: "To set the mind on the Spirit [this is the "new righteousness"] is life and peace."

Vs. 11 confirms this general way of understanding vs. 10. The "Spirit" is now unmistakably the divine Spirit—**the Spirit of him who raised Jesus from the dead,** i.e., the life-giving Spirit (cf. "the Spirit is life"). If that **Spirit . . . dwells in you** (cf. 9*a*), you have the assurance that God, **who raised Christ Jesus from the dead will give life to your mortal bodies also**—here the word "mortal" is actually used (cf. on vs. 10*a*). This making alive of our bodies, subject to death because of Adam's sin, belongs to the future consummation of which the indwelling of the Spirit is the guarantee—but note Lietzmann, who doubts the eschatological reference. We note that it is our **bodies** which will be made alive, not our "flesh" (see above, pp. 501, 507-8; see also on I Cor. 15:44 ff. and II Cor.

---

or one is not. One is either for Christ or against him (cf. Matt. 12:30; Luke 11:23). We are always tempted to define the difference in irrelevant terms. We make it dependent on forms of belief: those who uphold the proper kind of orthodoxy surely satisfy requirements. Or again, we accept a standard of good works: the proper people must surely be those who do the proper things. As concerns both classes, Christ himself was quite explicit in stating that they might find themselves entirely outside his kingdom (cf. Matt. 7:21-23). It is a much more searching test that Paul provides, but it can be very simply stated. It is the possession of Christ's Spirit that makes us Christ's folk. We have at the center of our lives that Spirit who was present in full measure in him. We know that what animates our physical body is the spirit which dwells within it. In the same way, what animates the Christian is Christ's Spirit dwelling within him.

Obviously we have moved into a region where language and imagery both reveal their limitations. The ease and rapidity with which Paul passes from **the Spirit of God** to **the Spirit of Christ** have provoked endless argument, but show that the divine dynamic can more easily be recognized than defined. In fellowship with Christ, Paul knew more intensely than at any other time the meaning of God's living presence; the power which made him live in a new way and at a new level was God's Spirit, and he interpreted the nature of that Spirit in the light of what he had learned of Christ. What it would mean in our own experience we can only hope to know as we seek to understand the Spirit which Christ's life fully manifested. We remember the completeness of his obedience to his Father's will; all his powers were surrendered to the single task of fulfilling the Father's purpose. We recall, too, the boundless love with which he responded to men's need.

12 Therefore, brethren, we are debtors,
not to the flesh, to live after the flesh.
13 For if ye live after the flesh, ye shall
die: but if ye through the Spirit do mortify
the deeds of the body, ye shall live.

12 So then, brethren, we are debtors, not
to the flesh, to live according to the flesh —
13 for if you live according to the flesh you
will die, but if by the Spirit you put to
death the deeds of the body you will live.

5:1-5 in Vol. X). God will give us immortal bodies **through his Spirit which dwells in you.** Some ancient texts read here "because of his indwelling Spirit," but there can be little doubt that the reading adopted by both of our English versions is preferable. It will be by the *agency* of the Spirit, not *because* of the Spirit, that God will give life to our mortal bodies. This would be true even if the textual evidence supported "because" (which it does not); even in that case Paul would be finding the source of our *assurance* in the indwelling Spirit, not the motive of God's action.

12-13. The consequence of this is that **we are debtors,** i.e., we owe an obligation, a duty. But our duty is not owed **to the flesh,** so that we should **live according to** its demands, but is rather owed to the Spirit. But this latter remark, although obviously implied, is not actually made by Paul. As so often (cf. 5:5), he breaks off in the middle of his sentence, leaving the obvious unsaid. This time he does so in order to emphasize again the consequences of death or life which hang upon the issue here (cf. vs. 6). There may well be conscious rhetorical purpose in the way the verbs are put together in this sentence (vs. 13): **if you live . . . , you will die; . . . if . . . you put to death . . . , you will live. Body** in this verse must have the same meaning as **flesh.** The idea of putting to death the *deeds* of the body is somewhat strange: why not the desires? Perhaps Kirk's

---

If our lives are recognizably ruled by a spirit of a different kind, it is pointless for us to claim Christ's name.

We will not expect, of course, that our lives will correspond in any adequate measure to his standard; but it is the quality of the dynamic which counts. **If Christ is in you,** the forces which will finally accomplish your physical death are relatively unimportant; **your spirits are alive because of righteousness.** The arresting thing about the passage is the way in which, given the fact of Christ's indwelling presence, the consequences keep enlarging their scope. First our spirits participate in the vitality which comes through him; then, though at first the death of the body may seem irrelevant, it is clear that even our physical being can share in that mighty power of which Christ's resurrection is both the pattern and the proof. We cannot set limits to what can happen: but it is perfectly clear that it will be **through his Spirit which dwells in you.**

12-13. ***Debtors.***—It can be disastrous to submit to mistaken obligations. Those who allow physical appetite to determine the pattern of their experience threaten every force that works for their true well-being. Life as it ought to be represents a delicate equipoise between body and spirit, in which the former serves the latter in a relationship of fruitful subordination. To imagine that our physical nature is entitled to dictate the terms on which life shall be accepted and the manner in which it shall be lived is a modern delusion as well as an ancient error, and it is no less pernicious because recently revived. Since the proper relation between body and spirit leads to liberation and to fullness of life, the falsity of the view which exalts the prerogatives of our physical nature stands clearly exposed: we are not **debtors . . . to the flesh, to live according to the flesh.** Mistakes, however, have their consequences. Much of the poignancy of human life springs from the fact that error, even when sincerely adopted and conscientiously maintained, inevitably leads to tragedy. To be well-meaning never exempts us from the consequences of being wrong. In the present case Paul has already shown that a life disordered by the ascendancy of what should be the subordinate partner must end in death. But the mistaken obligation is matched by a real one, implied though not stated. From what has been said in previous verses it follows that we are bound to give to the spirit the controlling position which belongs to it by right. Then the unruly turbulence which marks the life controlled by passion is subdued, and the proper result follows: **you will live.** It is worth noting that in vs. 13 there is a double play on "life" and "death." Both words are used in the Bible in more than one sense. Life is not only physical existence, but that quality of experience which belongs to those who dwell in God. In the same way death is the cessation of bodily existence,

14 For as many as are led by the Spirit of God, they are the sons of God.

14 For all who are led by the Spirit of God

explanation is right: "The first stage in conquering the 'flesh' is to refuse to put its solicitations into effect by *deeds;* S. Paul has therefore modified the strictly doctrinal form of his statement by reference to practical experience" (*Epistle to Romans,* p. 212).

When Paul says **you will live,** he has already moved into the next section of his argument.

3. The Hope in Christ (8:14-25)

14. This hope of life is based upon the fact that we are **sons of God**—this is the force of the **for** with which the sentence begins. The Greek word "son" (υἱός) suggests status and privilege as well as the natural relationship of a child (τέκνον [vs. 16]). Paul is preparing to make the point that since we are sons of God, we can count on our inheritance; our hope will not disappoint us (cf. 5:5). The expression **all who are led by the Spirit of God** is found also, in only slightly different form, in Gal. 5:18. There the truth being emphasized is that those who are led by the Spirit "are not under the law"; but neither are they subject to the desires of the flesh (Gal. 5:16). Ernest DeWitt Burton writes: "Clearly, therefore, life by the Spirit constitutes for the apostle a third way of life distinct both on the one hand from legalism and on the other from that which is characterised by a yielding to the impulses of the flesh. It is by no means a middle course between them, but a highway above them both, a life of freedom from statutes, of faith and love" (*The Epistle to the Galatians* [New York: Charles Scribner's Sons, 1920; "The International Critical Commentary"], p. 302). "A highway above them both"—a wonderful way to sum up Paul's conception of the new righteousness described both in 8:4-13 and Gal. 5:13-25. The term **are led** suggests "the voluntary subjection of the will to the Spirit" (*ibid.,* p. 303).

but it is also the destruction of that true life which is God's gift to his children. What gave its peculiar poignancy to the early Hebrew conception of death (in the first sense) was the fear that it might endanger life (in the second sense). It might jeopardize man's fellowship with God. But what really undermines that communion with God which forms our true life is the love of evil. Those who choose sin are "those that are perishing"; when the process has continued long enough, they are "dead in trespasses and sins" (Eph. 2:1). What Paul emphasizes in the present passage is the simple but far-reaching fact that those who live on one plane die on another. To live in the fullest sense on the higher level of experience requires unceasing discipline at the lower level. He is not insisting on a repudiation of the body; he merely demands the maintenance of the kind of control which keeps it in its proper place.

14-17. ***Sons and Heirs.***—Some people are so strongly constrained by God's Spirit that they are manifestly brought by that control into a distinctive relationship to God himself. What it means to be **led by the Spirit of God** Paul has already indicated (vss. 1-11); the consequences he now describes by stating that all such **are sons of God.**

The evidence of sonship is a new attitude to God, and that attitude finds expression in words which indicate the peculiar intimacy of our relationship. We easily overlook the suggestion, conveyed by the word "son," of a kinship beyond that of mere descent. The background of Jewish patriarchal society made Paul and his readers familiar with the kind of contrast which Isaac and Ishmael presented—the one was a son, the other only a child in the household. Those who are led by the Spirit have gone beyond formal membership in an ecclesiastical body to claim the standing to which they are entitled, a standing which they can appropriate only if they possess the insight and understanding and devotion which kinship presupposes.

The nature of this relationship is clarified when it is contrasted with another. Some are sons, others are slaves. In the religious life it is a matter of choice which we shall be. The Holy Spirit, as one of the fathers reminds us, is a glad Spirit, and those who relapse into servile fear declare that they have not grasped the deliverance which the gospel offers. The spirit of nervous apprehension, which makes all duties burdens, and finds in discipleship only a heavy responsibility, is common enough among earnest people; but it should be out of place in a

15 For ye have not received the spirit
of bondage again to fear; but ye have received the Spirit of adoption, whereby we
cry, Abba, Father.
16 The Spirit itself beareth witness with
our spirit, that we are the children of God:

are sons of God. **15** For you did not receive
the spirit of slavery to fall back into fear,
but you have received the spirit of sonship.
When we cry, "Abba! Father!" **16** it is the
Spirit himself bearing witness with our

15-16. The **for** here, again, connects with the immediately preceding words: I say that you are **sons of God, for** the Spirit you have received is **the Spirit of adoption.** In thus describing the Spirit Paul is thinking of him both as the seal and guarantee of our new status as sons (a status not possessed by the natural man or by a natural right, but to be conferred on us as a result of God's act in Christ; hence **adoption**), and also as constituting a partial realization of that status, a kind of foretaste of the life of sonship (cf. above, p. 505). The RSV takes the word "spirit" here to mean "attitude" or "state of mind," and therefore renders the phrase **the spirit of sonship.** But although the word "spirit" is susceptible of such an interpretation, it is certainly not the normal meaning of the term for Paul. Throughout this whole discussion, up to this verse, the "spirit" has been the divine Spirit. It is likely that this is true also in this verse, as regards both occurrences of the word. Paul's meaning would be: "The Spirit you have received is not the Spirit of slavery so that you should **fall back into fear** [cf. Heb. 2:15], but is rather **the Spirit of adoption."** The term rendered "sonship" in the RSV is the same word translated "adoption" in vs. 23. It is only because of the supposed meaning of "spirit" in this verse that the translators have not rendered υἱοθεσία in the usual way in vs. 15. The reader should consult the Exeg. on vs. 23 in this connection.

It will be noticed that our two texts deal differently with the next clause. The KJV sees it as the conclusion of the sentence we have just been examining and speaks of **the Spirit of adoption, whereby** [literally "in which"] **we cry, Abba, Father;** the RSV makes this clause the beginning of the next sentence (vs. 16). Since the Greek MSS were unpunctuated, either reading is possible. It seems best on the whole to adopt the KJV arrangement, although no real difference in sense is involved. Either way we look at it this clause is an eloquent reminder of the fact that when Paul speaks of the Spirit, he is speaking of something concretely known in the experience of the believer as a member of the body of Christ. We know we have received **the Spirit** and that the Spirit is **the Spirit of adoption** because we actually find ourselves saying, **Abba, Father.** How could we do this if we were not in fact sons? Indeed, in the moment when we utter this ecstatic cry, it seems that it is not ourselves who utter it, but something divine which has entered into us and possessed us. It is the Spirit who draws, almost forces, this cry from us. It is

---

church. **You did not receive the spirit of slavery to fall back into fear.** Each relationship, we may notice, has its appropriate emotional atmosphere. In slavery it is fear; in sonship it is confidence and grateful joy.

Sonship is a many-sided experience, but the heart of the matter is quite simply described. When we are vividly aware of the intimate fellowship into which God has brought us, a simple but far-reaching exclamation—**Abba! Father!**—epitomizes what we have discovered. So intimate a word points to a correspondingly intense awareness of what we have discovered God to be. This is not a reasoned discovery of our intelligence, though it is certainly not irrational in character; it represents an intuition in which our whole personality responds to what we have learned of God. But it is more than this. **The Spirit himself** bears **witness with our spirit that we are children of God,** i.e., we have the confirmation of the divine Spirit to verify the insight of our fallible human spirits. There is much here that invites further development; e.g., the conviction based on experience of the peculiar intimacy of fellowship between God's Spirit and ours; the awareness which this creates of a dimension of spiritual experience in which we remain ourselves but discover more fully what God is; the understanding of the kind of assurance which is possible in the religious life, and the nature of the evidence on which it is founded.

The quality of the experience marks sonship as the greatest of all privileges, and Paul speci-

17 And if children, then heirs; heirs of God, and joint-heirs with Christ; if so be that we suffer with *him,* that we may be also glorified together.

spirit that we are children of God, 17 and if children, then heirs, heirs of God and fellow heirs with Christ, provided we suffer with him in order that we may also be glorified with him.

---

the Spirit bearing **witness with our spirit that we are children of God.** All of Paul's theology, as we have seen (see above, pp. 504-5), rests back upon this experience of the Spirit.

The word **Abba** is, of course, the Aramaic word for "father." The term recalls to us the fact that the earliest believers were speakers of that language. Paul himself, although a Jew of the Dispersion, knew this language, and it may well have been the language of his prayers. But not all believers said "Abba"; Greek-speaking Christians said Πατήρ **(Father);** and so Paul uses both terms here. It should be added that the Greek allows for either **the Spirit itself** (with KJV) or **the Spirit himself** (with RSV). There is not a clear, consistent doctrine of the "personality" of the Spirit in Paul's letters.

17. Paul is now in position to draw the conclusion which has been in his mind since he wrote in vs. 13: "If by the Spirit you put to death the deeds of the body you will live." **If children,** we are also **heirs**—i.e., we *shall* come into possession of the privileges of sonship when the new age fully arrives. On the pre-Pauline Jewish and Christian use of the word "inheritance," we cannot do better than to quote from Sanday and Headlam (*Epistle to Romans,* p. 204): "Meaning originally (i) the simple possession of the Holy Land, it came to mean (ii) its permanent and assured possession (Ps. xxv [xxiv]. 13; xxxvi [xxxvii]. 9, 11; etc.); hence (iii) specially the secure possession won by the Messiah (Is. lx. 21; lxi. 7); and so it became (iv) a symbol of all Messianic blessings (Matt. v. 5; xix. 29; xxv. 34; etc.)."

It is likely that **provided** is too strong a conditional particle to stand for εἴπερ. The same Greek word at the beginning of 3:30 is rendered "since" in the RSV—and quite properly, because Paul is certainly not expressing any doubt as to the unity of God. "Since" might well be a better translation here also (the same might be said of the same Greek particle in vs. 9). As believers, Paul is saying, we *do* share in Christ's suffering, both in the sense of mystically participating in his death (6:4) and in the sense of suffering trials and persecutions for his sake (cf. vs. 35 below). It is possible also that Paul would have regarded all the "tribulations" of this life, *when suffered by a believer and with the appropriate attitude,* as being "sufferings with Christ," whether they are specifically

---

fies the prerogatives which are attached to it. As a consequence of being **children of God,** we discover that we are **heirs** also. The two belong together. The inference follows naturally from the imagery which Paul is using, and it is confirmed both by insight and by experience. The child of the household can look forward confidently to receiving his due share of all the resources that his father possesses. The prophets saw in God's dealing with their race a process by which he ceaselessly tried to give them more than they were ready or willing to receive. What the Jews lacked the insight to perceive, Christians should understand without difficulty, because it is an easy inference from the whole tenor of Jesus' life and teaching. "Your heavenly Father knoweth that ye have need" (Matt. 6: 32), and it requires only the receptive spirit on our part to open the treasures of his bounty. It is well to recall the extent to which our Puritan ancestors dwelt on the mercies of God which are our proper heritage. All things are ours if we are Christ's—but that follows only from the belief that Christ himself is the greatest of God's mercies and the supreme embodiment of all that God designs to give us. It is therefore natural that Paul should amplify his meaning by adding that we are **fellow heirs with Christ.** The whole sense of triumphant exultation which marks the N.T. references to Christ's appropriation of the glorified life through his conquest of death is not something that we observe as spectators. "If ye then be risen with Christ"—but we *are* risen with Christ, and so partake in all that his resurrection implies.

Such benefits can be gained only by those who are prepared to satisfy the requisite conditions. (Yet see Exeg.) We are **fellow heirs with**

18 For I reckon that the sufferings of this present time *are* not worthy *to be compared* with the glory which shall be revealed in us.

18 I consider that the sufferings of this present time are not worth comparing with the glory that is to be revealed to us.

incurred "for his sake" or not (cf. 5:3-4). But we shall **also be glorified with him.** Does this, taken with **fellow heirs,** mean that Christ also is *yet* to be glorified? Probably not; Christ has already entered into the inheritance and the glory for which we still must wait. This whole passage (i.e., vss. 15-17) should be compared with Gal. 4:5-7.

18-21. Mention of suffering with Christ and of the glory we shall share with him (vs. 17) leads Paul to reflect further upon the contrast between the present order and the new age so soon to come. Our sufferings **of this present time** are as nothing compared **with the glory that is to be revealed to us.** The force of the conjunction **for** at the beginning of vs. 19 is not altogether clear. Kirk suggests that the connection between vss. 19 and 18 seems to be: "If, as we believe, the redemption of the entire universe depends upon the *revelation of the sons of God,* how certain it is that that revelation will take place! The issues involved are too great for God's plans in this direction to be changed" (*Epistle to Romans,* p. 214). This is certainly possible; but the context indicates that Paul is reflecting just here not upon how *certain* the future glory is, but upon how *great* it will be, so that it is better to understand him to be saying: "We do not grasp how great this **glory** will be until we recognize that the whole cosmic order—all things animate and inanimate—are waiting for it **with eager longing.**"

The idea that when Adam disobeyed God's command and fell into bondage to sin the whole natural universe, and not only man, suffered a "fall" was a familiar one in Paul's Jewish environment; e.g., note Gen. 3:17-18, "Because thou . . . hast eaten of the

Christ, provided we suffer with him in order that we may also be glorified with him. Daily experience should have taught us that nothing worth having is ever got until we have paid the appropriate price, and we should consequently expect to find that the same inevitable sequence holds good in the spiritual world. A characteristic feature of the gospel is the uncompromising way in which it insists that the required price is high. Those who desire great spiritual gifts can expect to receive them—but only if they are prepared to meet exacting requirements. Jesus never offered his disciples a smooth path or an easy journey. As his own ministry moved toward its appointed end, he foresaw that he "must suffer many things," and he always insisted that it was enough for the disciple that he should be as his Lord. And so for his followers too he predicted sufferings—though always with the reminder that they might expect benefits in more than compensating measure. Paul is therefore reproducing the gist of Jesus' teaching; the only difference is that he insists more strongly on a sequence which he believes to be rooted in the laws of the spiritual world. The parallel between the believer's experience and his Lord's example is much more than a coincidence of outward pattern. It goes to the heart of the matter, and brings to light the most fundamental affirmations of the gospel. The good news is what it is because the revelation of God's love in the Cross is followed by the declaration of God's power in the Resurrection. To state the matter so boldly is, of course, to lose something of the many-sided wonder of the central sequence in the revelation of God's nature and purpose: the disclosure of the divine leads through crucifixion to the triumphant resurrection life. It is nothing less than a reflection of this crucial truth which Paul expects to see reproduced in the Christian's life. There will be suffering; beyond it there will be a new quality of experience, a new measure of power, a new awareness of our partnership in God's purpose, and a new consciousness of the splendor which surrounds even the daily lives of those who are "risen with Christ."

18-27. *The Experience of Suffering and the Expectation of the Glorified Life.*—No one disputes the reality of the sufferings which we encounter. They are too real a part of experience for anyone to dismiss them altogether; even when they are endured for a high purpose, we can rise to meet them only when sustained by a new assurance. We gain the necessary confidence when we see our sufferings in the proper perspective. Just as real and of far greater significance is **the glory that is to be revealed to us.** But at this point Paul is dealing with something which runs out beyond the limits of

19 For the earnest expectation of the creature waiteth for the manifestation of the sons of God.

20 For the creature was made subject to vanity, not willingly, but by reason of him who hath subjected *the same* in hope;

19 For the creation waits with eager longing
for the revealing of the sons of God; 20 for
the creation was subjected to futility, not
of its own will but by the will of him who

---

tree, . . . cursed is the ground for thy sake, . . . thorns also and thistles shall it bring forth to thee"; and II Esdras 7:11-12: "I made the world for their sakes [Israel's], and when Adam transgressed my statutes, what has now happened was decreed; and the ways of entering this world were made narrow, grievous, and toilsome, and few and evil, full of dangers and burdened with great hardships" (Goodspeed). Lietzmann quotes one of the later rabbis as saying: "Although things had been created in their fullness, they were spoiled after the first man sinned" (p. 85). That nature will be restored to its primeval character when the new age dawns was also a common view. II Esdras 7:75 speaks of the times when God shall "begin to renew his creation," and II Esdras 13:26 describes the Messiah as one through whom God will "liberate his creation." Isa. 65:17 (as well as Rev. 21:1) tells of the "new heavens and a new earth," and it is impossible to suppose that all the innumerable references, scattered through the prophets, to the renewal of nature represent mere metaphor, e.g., Isa. 55:12-13.

Many of the apocalypses emphasize this restoration of nature, often interpreting it in the crudest terms of mere material abundance. A famous passage cited in Irenaeus (*Against Heresies* V. 33. 3) as derived from Papias (found also in considerable part in II Baruch 29:5) is worth quoting because it is typical: "The days will come in which vines shall grow, each having ten thousand shoots, and on each shoot ten

---

our present experience. The intuitions of faith may be unassailably firm, yet they are not reached by logic or defended by reason alone. A poet's insights, however, are no less important because they conform to a pattern different from that of the philosopher's deductions. It is as a poet that Paul is now speaking.

We are heirs of a greater destiny than we normally realize. Though its full splendor may elude our minds, there are avaliable even now testimonies to both its nature and its character.[5]

The first testimony: The unsatisfied yearning of the created order (vss. 19-22). The thoughtful observer needs no convincing that we live in a world which has gone mysteriously but radically wrong. The ills of human life are apparent enough: we have chosen paths which have led us disastrously astray; man's folly and sin have brought upon him their own inevitable consequences. But in some strange fashion the contagion of our own evil has spread beyond the confines of our own life, and the whole of creation seems involved. "Nature, red in tooth and claw" is a problem to any sensitive spirit, especially when the facts we observe seemingly conflict with the faith we hold. Paul offers a bold and imaginative answer to the difficulty. You cannot divide the created order into distinct and independent sections. What happens in one area will have repercussions on all. If there is any unity in the universe, a disaster in one realm will affect conditions in other realms. If man in his pride repudiates his true status, the ground will be cursed for his sake (Gen. 3:17); he cannot isolate the consequences of his sin. The interdependence of the different parts of God's world is so real that man's recklessness and folly result in **the creation** being **subjected to futility.**

But though the confusion in which God's order appears at times to be involved may seem like complete frustration, the relationship which has consequences for evil has also potentialities for good. Judgment is not to futility only: it offers equally a ground of hope. The rest of creation was bound up with man's destiny, not of its own choice, but by God's will, **who subjected it in hope:** the purpose behind this dispensation is one which looks toward the realization of a beneficent plan. When mankind finds deliverance from bondage and enters into **the glorious liberty of the children of God,** nature will experience in her own way a parallel emancipation. As she was involved for evil in man's fall, so she will be involved for good in his redemption. There is implied in Paul's argument a vision of the new world which will match man's redeemed condition. This is a

[5] Lipsius. Quoted by Denney, *Expositor's Greek Testament, ad loc.*

21 Because the creature itself also shall be delivered from the bondage of corruption into the glorious liberty of the children of God.

subjected it in hope; 21 because the creation itself will be set free from its bondage to decay and obtain the glorious liberty of the

thousand branches, and on each branch ten thousand twigs, and on each twig ten thousand clusters, and on each cluster ten thousand grapes, and each grape when pressed will yield twenty-five measures of wine. . . . Likewise also a grain of wheat shall produce ten thousand heads, and every head shall have ten thousand grains, and every grain ten pounds of fine flour. . . ."

Needless to say, Paul is not thinking in any such terms. He is not thinking of what either the original "fall" of nature or its ultimate redemption means to *man* in the way of denied or restored goods or comforts. His words show rather a very marvelous and somewhat surprising sympathy with nature itself for its own sake. It is often said that Paul has no interest in or understanding of nature. There is ground for this view. Surely one cannot attribute to Paul the *appreciation* of nature which is so manifest in Jesus' teaching. Only very occasionally does Paul draw an illustration from nature and, as we shall see even in this epistle (see on 11:17-24), the few illustrations he draws are not very successfully managed. There is no evidence that he was vividly aware of the beauty of nature, found joy in it, or saw in it the continuing work of God. This failure of Paul's has left its mark upon his theology and suggests perhaps more than one way in which his theology needs to be corrected by his Master's. It is probable, e.g., that Paul's attitude toward sex and marriage (as in I Cor. 7) is not unconnected with this failure of appreciation. When all of this is said, however, it must be added that this passage reveals unmistakably that he was not without a certain true feeling for nature. He feels the *pathos* of nature—and must one not recognize that this pathos is as real as the joyousness? He is aware of the **futility**, the meaninglessness, of nature, as felt, as it were, from within nature herself—the ceaseless round, the dreary circle, the endless repetition of existence. The whole universe around him seems to Paul to be waiting restlessly—waiting for that which will fulfill it and give it meaning. This fulfillment will take place when the final "revelation" takes place and we finally secure our sonship—this is the meaning of the words **the revealing of the sons of God.**

Paul insists that **creation was subjected to futility, not of its own will.** This is in contrast, perhaps, but not certainly, to man, who did transgress and therefore suffered subjection by his own fault. The ground for doubt of this meaning lies in the fact that

dream which others shared. The prophet was convinced that God would "create new heavens and a new earth" (Isa. 65:17); and to a writer later than Paul this re-created universe was to be the dwelling place of righteousness (II Pet. 3:13). A new order does not come painlessly to birth; the confusion which we witness and in which we share is the travail out of which a new world will come (vs. 22).

The second testimony: The hope which Christians themselves entertain (vss. 23-25). What we observe in nature we experience in ourselves. As the created order is straining toward a new birth, so **we ourselves . . . groan inwardly as we wait for adoption as sons.** In a world like ours hope must have sufficient warrant; without adequate grounds it would be overwhelmed by despair. We are bold to look forward to a glorious destiny because we have within ourselves its **first fruits.** The living Spirit of God, at work within us, has already begun to produce results which point to what lies in store for us. Our experience of sonship is genuine but incomplete. On the strength of what we know already we can anticipate something of what full sonship will mean, and we are confirmed in the hopes which we already entertain. But what we are given is still hope. Though hope must have sufficient ground if it is to survive, its very character requires that it belong to the realm of the unrealized. There is no virtue in hoping for something that we have within our grasp. Religious hope, as Paul defines it, fixes its expectation on the things that are unseen, not on those that are seen.

The third testimony: The intercession of the Spirit, who helps us in our prayers and finds words for desires that would otherwise remain

22 For we know that the whole creation groaneth and travaileth in pain together until now.

23 And not only *they,* but ourselves also, which have the firstfruits of the Spirit, even we ourselves groan within ourselves, waiting for the adoption, *to wit,* the redemption of our body.

children of God.
22 We know that the whole creation has been groaning in travail together until now;
23 and not only the creation, but we ourselves, who have the first fruits of the Spirit, groan inwardly as we wait for adoption as sons, the redemption

---

Paul seems to be setting over against nature's **own will,** not man's, but God's: **by the will of him who subjected it.** Efforts have been made to interpret this otherwise than as a reference to God, but these have not succeeded; Gen. 3:17 must be in Paul's mind. He does not seek to give any explanation of why God should visit upon all of nature a penalty which only man deserved; he simply observes the fact. If challenged, he would very likely have answered along the lines suggested in 9:19 ff. But nature, although **subjected,** is nevertheless not without **hope.** Having shared in the **bondage to decay**—constant and certain dissolution, a symbol of **futility**—which God decreed after man's disobedience, all of nature will share also in **the glorious liberty of the children of God,** won for us by Christ's obedience. The final redemption will be a cosmic redemption—God's whole creation, despoiled by sin and death, will be **set free.**

22. We observed above Paul's sensitiveness to the pathos of nature's plight of subjection to futility; here he alludes more particularly to the *sorrow* of nature. He thinks of the sufferings of animals—the weak devoured by the strong—of the ruthless destruction of plant life, of natural catastrophes of all kinds; he listens, it is not too fanciful to suggest, to the cryings of the wind and the sea; and he receives an impression that all of nature is **groaning in travail together,** i.e., in all its parts. The whole created world is crying for release from pain, as a woman cries in childbirth; but it does so with hope for that which will give meaning to all the pain and turn it into joy. (On this passage, cf. II Esdras 7:62 ff. and 10:9 ff.)

23. **And not only the creation, but we ourselves . . . groan inwardly as we wait.** We have here a confirmation of the interpretation of "Spirit of adoption" offered in the Exeg. of vss. 15-16 above. We **have the first fruits** [ἀπαρχήν, "first installment"] **of the Spirit,** but even so we groan as we **wait for adoption as sons.** But has Paul not said in vs. 15 that we have already received our adoption? No, only the Spirit of adoption. So here we have received **the Spirit,** who is the seal of our adoption, but we wait still for our

---

unexpressed (vss. 26-27). Though we have the first fruits of the Spirit—the evidence that the divine dynamic is at work within us—we are intensely conscious of **our weakness.** The new standard by which we judge makes us more acutely aware of our failure. This is true of the life of action, but it applies also to the life of prayer. What we should pray for is more apparent than how we ought to pray for it. The general objective is clear: that God's purpose may be so fully realized in us that we may share in the redeemed life. At any particular point, however, we may easily be bewildered, and even our prayers may be confused. There may cease to be the proper correspondence between what we need and what we desire. The Spirit who searches the human heart and works within it directs our uncertain prayers and brings them into conformity with the will of God. The scene is the experience of the believer. The result is a growing understanding of God's purpose, and so a fuller persuasion concerning the hopes we entertain. The cause is the presence of God's Spirit, and his power to bring our inarticulate yearnings into conscious and effective harmony with the divine purpose.

Apart from the general theme, certain phrases deserve more particular attention. The hope of the created order is bound up, says Paul, with **the revealing of the sons of God** (vs. 19). The redeemed humanity for which we wait is present as the growing edge of the future. The gospel declares that a new relationship is open to all men; all are potentially God's sons. In the case of some this possibility has begun to be an actuality; but there is nothing automatic or inevitable about the process. Some who might become sons of God decline the opportunity; they

24 For we are saved by hope: but hope that is seen is not hope: for what a man seeth, why doth he yet hope for?

25 But if we hope for that we see not, *then* do we with patience wait for *it*.

26 Likewise the Spirit also helpeth our infirmities: for we know not what we should pray for as we ought: but the Spirit

of our bodies. 24 For in this hope we were saved. Now hope that is seen is not hope. For who hopes for what he sees? 25 But if we hope for what we do not see, we wait for it with patience.

26 Likewise the Spirit helps us in our weakness; for we do not know how to pray

---

adoption itself. Many commentators (e.g., Kirk, Sanday and Headlam, etc.) try to bring vs. 23 into line with vs. 15 by making vs. 23 refer only to "the public and final recognition" of our adoption; but is it likely that Paul would speak of our "groaning within ourselves" as we wait only for such a "public recognition"? Such ways of relating vss. 15 and 23 overlook the meaning and importance of "Spirit" in both passages.

Our **adoption as sons,** when actual and complete, will mean the **redemption of our bodies** (see on vs. 11, where the meaning is the same).

24-25. The exact bearing of this passage on the argument is not clear—which explains, no doubt, why the MSS contain many variant readings here. The importance of hope has been commented on frequently (e.g., on 5:1-5) and has been the major theme of this section (vss. 14-25). Here the general idea seems to be that *since* we hope, we must realize that something greater than anything we know is in store for us, for **who hopes for what he sees?** Since we have such a great and confident expectation, we must **wait for it with patience.**

4. The Spirit as Helper (8:26-27)

26-27. The word **likewise** indicates a close connection in Paul's mind between the foregoing section and this brief passage. Perhaps he is thinking of the fact that just as the "whole creation" and "we ourselves" groan (vss. 22-23), so also the Spirit groans on our behalf; perhaps his thought has moved back to the point he was making in vss. 15-16, and he means to say here: "Just as the Spirit says, 'Father,' within us, so also he intercedes before God for us." A simpler explanation of the connection, however, seems available: in the whole preceding section (vss. 14-25) Paul has been thinking of the believer's hope and of the possession of the Spirit as the ground of it; now he adds, **Likewise** [i.e., just as he gives us hope] **the Spirit helps** ["gives support to"] **us in our** [present] **weakness.**

---

do not fulfill the requisite conditions: "But to all who received him, who believed in his name, he gave power to become children of God" (John 1:12). It is also important to remember that the N.T. is not discussing an optional form of self-improvement. Our volition is necessary, but more is involved than merely our effort. The "new creation" which becomes a reality in the life of the believer is in a true sense the work of God; only a divine power is sufficient to explain it. But beyond the individual, here and there transformed by the love of Christ, Paul looks for that unrealized system of relationships of which we have a true anticipation in the fellowship of the church. The redeemed community as we already know it is not the expression of man's gregarious instincts; it is the product of God's creative act in Christ. In the church we have an instrument through which Christ works and by means of which he expresses himself (cf. Eph. 1:23); the redeemed humanity which we await will yet more perfectly manifest his purpose and his power. Well may the creation wait **with eager longing!**

The limited **revealing of the sons of God** is in part related to the intractable material with which we are now compelled to deal. We do indeed "wrestle . . . with flesh and blood"—even though that is not the crux of our moral struggle. Our present physical existence is bound up with the created order which is agonizing in birth pangs that foretell the coming of a better day. Paul does not say that our present bodily existence is evil, but he insists that it involves certain limitations. At our present level of existence it provides the appropriate medium through which our spirits can work. The full destiny of the children of God does not postulate a completely disembodied form of existence—though we sometimes use the

itself maketh intercession for us with groanings which cannot be uttered.
27 And he that searcheth the hearts knoweth what *is* the mind of the Spirit, because he maketh intercession for the saints according to *the will of* God.

as we ought, but the Spirit himself intercedes for us with sighs too deep for words.
27 And he who searches the hearts of men knows what is the mind of the Spirit, because[j] the Spirit intercedes for the saints according to the will of God.

[j] Or *that*.

This **weakness** is not analyzed or further described: is it our moral weakness in general (cf. 7:21-23), or is it our weakness in prayer? Probably our weakness in general, which forces us to seek God's help. But of ourselves we cannot even pray—**we do not know how to pray as we ought.** Translated more literally this sentence reads, "We do not know what to pray [i.e., what words to use] as is necessary"; in other words, prayer (because of our **weakness)** is a necessity, but our needs go far beyond the power of our speech to express them. We do not know of ourselves how to pray, just as we do not know of ourselves how to say "Abba, Father." **The Spirit helps us** by making our prayers **for us.** He does so **with sighs too deep for words.** Again, we see how closely Paul's teaching about the Spirit is related to the *experience* of the believer and to what was actually happening in the church, for this reference to **sighs too deep for words** is an allusion to the actual **groanings** of the Christian as he "agonized" in prayer. The meaning is not that the **sighs** are inaudible, but that they *are* sighs, and not words. No doubt the services of the churches, at least of the Pauline churches, were often marked by these groanings on the part of individuals; they were undoubtedly much more often a feature of private prayer (I Cor. 14:13-19 is very important in this connection). Just as the ecstatic cry, "Abba," is interpreted as the cry of the Spirit, and not our own cry, so here, these deep groanings are the Spirit's praying, not ours. He is praying on our behalf, putting our whole need of help into his own unearthly speech, which alone is adequate to express it.

This speech God can understand because he **searches the hearts of men.** He **knows,** therefore, **what is the mind of the Spirit,** i.e., what the Spirit is saying. He knows **that** [RSV mg.] **the Spirit intercedes for the saints according to the will of God** (for **saints** see on 1:7). Translators are divided as to whether the ὅτι of this sentence is "because" or "that": if "because," the clause following gives the *ground* of God's knowing; if "that," the clause indicates the *content* of **the mind of the Spirit.** The latter is on the whole the more likely. This intercession is always **according to the will of God** because the Spirit is indeed the Spirit of God (cf. I Cor. 2:10). As has already been noted about other parts of this chapter, such a passage as this "makes sense" only when we think of it not as a piece of theoretical analysis, but as an account of religious experience.

word "spiritual" as if it did. Paul clearly believed that the Spirit finds at every level of existence the appropriate forms through which he can express himself. What those forms would be in any future life Paul did not know, but he clearly believed that they would be completely different from but not wholly unrelated to the bodies we now use. This suggestion of continuity implies that our physical existence has a status different both from that assigned to it by those who insist on its resurrection in its present form—a most un-Pauline doctrine—and from that allowed it by those who dismiss it as of wholly temporary significance. It is important not because it will continue or because it will cease, but because it can be transformed. What that will mean, we do not know (cf. I Cor. 15), but it is clearly related to a fuller realization of what we now experience partially but in principle: our **adoption as sons** (vs. 23).

The glory that is to be revealed to us points to the visible manifestation of God. From many partial hints we infer what the true splendor of the divine must be; but we know that man has fallen short of that reflection of God to which he might rise, and which would be the fulfillment of his true destiny (cf. 3:23). The manner in which God's glory will be made apparent raises a difficulty as to the proper preposition. Neither **to us** (RSV) nor **in us** (KJV) seems wholly satisfactory, since both seem to be indicated. "To and in us" is what K. E. Kirk suggests. "The final revelation of God's greatness will not merely engross our vision, but

28 And we know that all things work together for good to them that love God, to them who are the called according to *his* purpose.

28 We know that in everything God works for good[k] with those who love him,[l] who are called according to his purpose.

[k] Other ancient authorities read *in everything he works for good,* or *everything works for good.*
[l] Greek *God.*

F. The Assurance of Salvation (8:28-39)

The grand section of the epistle, of which this is the closing part (5:1–8:39), began with an emphasis upon the believer's hope and upon the ground of his assurance that this hope would not disappoint him (5:2-5). That ground was "God's love . . . poured into our hearts." As we have seen, that same hope and its sureness is the theme of vss. 14-25. Indeed, if it were not for the little section, vss. 26-27, this entire chapter, after vs. 13, might be regarded as a discussion of hope and of its basis in the presence of the Spirit. When the theme is so described, it appears that even vss. 26-27 are not altogether an interruption, for the help of the Spirit in "our weakness" and his intercessions for us are precisely this empirical basis of the Christian's confidence. But whether vss. 26-27 are considered an interruption or a brief excursus, there can be no doubt that with vs. 28 the theme of the believer's hope is fully resumed and that it is carried through to the chapter's end.

28. The connection between this verse and the preceding is obvious and close. Paul has said that the Spirit helps us in our prayers and intercedes for us and that God understands and hears the Spirit. Now he goes on to say that **in everything God works** with us **for good.** A notable difference in translation as between the KJV and the RSV occurs here. This difference is partly—but only partly—a reflection of a difference in text. In some of the best ancient MSS and fathers (A B, the Beatty Papyrus, Origen) the word "God" appears as the *subject* of the verb "works with" (συνεργεῖ). If that is the correct

transform our characters . . . so that we ourselves become a part of the manifestation of His true nature." [6]

28-30. ***Everything . . . for Good?***—The grounds of encouragement multiply. Paul has mentioned certain things that we know (vs. 22) —truths forced on our attention by the travail of the created order. He has mentioned other things that we do not know (vs. 26)—duties which outstrip our powers and throw us back in utter dependence upon the Spirit. But the general drift of the argument has led to a constant expansion of the grounds of our certainty, and the note of authoritative confidence is boldly struck. **We know**—not this time the truths emphasized by the pain and suffering in our life, but the presence of a power which changes all evil so that it becomes a source of good. Paul's assurance presumably rests on something much more assured than the bold surmisings even of a deeply religious spirit. This is manifestly a lesson that he had learned through experience. He had had ample opportunity to verify in the school of life the kind of claim he is making. In this we have an explanation of the casual and incidental way in which he occasionally mentions the hardships he had endured. Those who suffer much are too often obsessed with what they have undergone. The secret of deliverance from this painfully general preoccupation with our own misfortunes is the discovery that they can be a source of blessing. Paul states this confidently as a fact—presumably because he had it on the best possible authority.

It is not a happy coincidence in the working of things which Paul declares. There is nothing in the constitution of the universe to encourage the easy optimism that everything will automatically work out to the satisfaction of good people. What Paul affirms is that God co-operates in all things for good with those who love him. This leads to the discovery that even "the sufferings of this present time" become a source of blessing. There is no sentimental attempt to persuade ourselves that evil things are actually good. They remain what they are; but though bad in themselves, they have lost the power to defeat us. No matter how bitter circumstances may be, we can learn to discover in them God's co-operation. Actually, it is in the things which seem most to deny his goodness that we often

[6] *The Epistle to the Romans* (Oxford: Clarendon Press, 1937; "The Clarendon Bible"), p. 213.

29 For whom he did foreknow, he also did predestinate *to be* conformed to the

29 For those whom he foreknew he also

text, the KJV phrasing is obviously mistaken. But even if the word "God" did not appear in the original text (i.e., as subject of the verb), it is far better—even though it is not in the same sense necessary—to take the verb as meaning "he works with" rather than "things work together." In other words, whatever the answer to the technical textual question, the RSV translation can be relied on as correct.

The difference in meaning involved in the two translations is not great: in both cases the emphasis is being laid upon God's effective help. The phrasing "God works with us in everything" makes this help seem more personal (i.e., less automatic or mechanical) than the KJV translation, but not less constant or sure. Those who receive this help are first described as **those who love him,** but because our love of God is not in any sense a meritorious act, or even an act of our own initiation at all, but is simply our response to God's love of us (cf. I John 4:10, 19), Paul immediately adds, **who are called according to his purpose.** The meaning of this clause is opened up more fully in the following verses.

29. The word translated "purpose" in vs. 28 is πρόθεσις and means "plan" or "scheme," as well as "intention." The structure of this plan of God is indicated by the terms, **foreknew, predestined, called, justified, glorified.** These add up to a strong affirmation of predestination, and there is no way of interpreting the terms to avoid such a conclusion. The only possible doubt attaches to the meaning of **foreknew.** The word here has been interpreted (e.g., by Origen) as meaning simple foreknowledge of who would be qualified by faith for justification, etc.; but in the light of the O.T. and N.T. use of the verb "to know" (when God is its subject and men its object), it is impossible thus to construe it (cf. Amos 3:2; Matt. 7:23). The term connotes choice on God's part, or at any rate, approval. Some element of selection is therefore involved

find him most indubitably present. "This I know is God's own Truth," wrote Dr. Edward Wilson, antarctic explorer, "that pain and trouble and trials and sorrows and disappointments are either one thing or another. To all who love God they are love tokens from Him. To all who do not love God and do not want to love Him they are merely a nuisance." [7]

This is a truth of wide application, but not everyone is qualified to profit by it. The power to transform evil events into beneficent influences is given to **those who love God, who are called according to his purpose.** There is a wisdom which draws much of the sting from adversity. Katherine Mansfield once recorded her "belief that suffering can be overcome. . . . Everything in life that we really accept undergoes a change. So suffering must become love." [8] This is nobly stated; but Paul would add that the alchemy by which darkness is changed to light requires more than the grace of acquiescence. When left to our own resources, suffering is more likely to harden and embitter than it is to ennoble and dignify. We need to have a new relationship to God if we are to achieve a new attitude to adversity. But a relationship is always reciprocal, and because it concerns two persons it can be described in two ways. Those who have the power to transform evil circumstances to good uses can be defined—as seen from the human side of the relationship—as **those who love** God. This is our response to what he is and what he has done; it epitomizes that new loyalty which is the secret of our new life. But our love is a response to God's prior act, and the relationship is therefore incompletely described unless defined from the Godward side as well. Those of whom Paul is speaking are therefore those who are **called** of God as truly as they are those who love him. We have noted again and again the apostle's emphasis on the divine initiative. It is impossible to understand the N.T. so long as we think merely in terms of human efforts to achieve human betterment, even when we appeal to religious insights as the effective motive. The decisive fact in Paul's world is the existence of God, and belief in God is saved from the danger

[7] George Seaver, *Edward Wilson of the Antarctic* (London: John Murray, 1933), p. 71.

[8] *Journal of Katherine Mansfield,* ed. J. Middleton Murry (London: Constable & Co., 1927), pp. 163-64.

image of his Son, that he might be the firstborn among many brethren.

predestined to be conformed to the image of his Son, in order that he might be the

in the statement that **he foreknew**—the term looks in the direction of the next, **he also predestined,** and indeed is already halfway toward it.

Paul would not have been a true Jew of his period if the kindred conceptions of foreknowledge and predestination had not had for him a validity which they do not have for many moderns. On the other hand it is clear that Paul had no such carefully worked out doctrine as Calvin or even Augustine attempted to formulate, nor does Paul place much emphasis upon this element in his thought. Henry St. John Thackeray points out that the rabbinical schools of Paul's day taught predestination, but with no denial of individual responsibility. He cites Josephus as saying (*Jewish War* II. 8. 14): "They [i.e., the Pharisees] taught that everything is dependent upon Fate and God, but yet the choice of right and wrong lay for the most part with the individual" (*Relation of St. Paul to Contemporary Jewish Thought,* p. 252). The same inconsistency can be found in Paul. A not dissimilar inconsistency was commented on in connection with 5:12.

Perhaps we go a little distance toward removing this inconsistency when we remember that Paul thought in large social terms much more naturally and thoroughgoingly than we do. The fundamental conviction of the Jew was that God had foreknown (and predestined, called) *Israel*—the nation as a whole. Perhaps Paul is thinking primarily of the church, rather than of the individuals as such who compose it. We must also remember that this whole chapter is written from the standpoint of Christian religious experience. Now one who has received the grace of God finds himself ascribing the whole process of his salvation to God's action; he himself has had nothing to do with it whatever. Even his faith appears to be God's gift. Some doctrine of predestination is the only possible rationalization of this experience, just as some doctrine of freedom is the only possible

of becoming academic by his insistence that God has a purpose which is operative in the world he has made. This it is that gives meaning to the process of which we form a part. We can enter into and work with that purpose, and so rise to such a measure of mastery over life's circumstances that evil turns to good. But always it is response, not independent achievement; not our act, but our answer to God's act. The purpose was prior to our discovery of it; the only accurate way of stating what happens is to say that we respond to God's call.

This becomes more apparent as we grow in awareness of "the long perspective of divine care and protection" (vss. 29-30). Before the beginning of time, God marked as his own those **who are called according to his purpose.** What this foreknowledge means, Paul does not state in detail; but from the general trend of his argument we may be sure that he regards it as the cause which is necessary to explain a certain result, viz., the experience of God's mercy and the discovery that we can co-operate with him in achieving his purpose. Paul's primary interest is not in those aspects of the subject which intrigue and bewilder our minds. Predestination in its various forms is much less a theory of the relation between the divine initiative and the human will than an attempt to state the results of an indubitable experience. The man who has discovered that his life is surrounded by God's love and transformed by God's grace is not content to regard this as an accidental benefit on which he has happened to stumble. It is the manifestation, within the limits of his life, of a purpose which lies behind all things and is older than creation itself. The heart of Paul's faith, so far as "foreknowledge" can express it, is the conviction that our salvation springs from an unceasing activity of God and in its origins antedates all events which unfold upon the plane of time.

In eternity, too, God **predestined** [us] **to be conformed to the image of his Son.** Foreknowledge represents the first step in our salvation, foreordination looks forward to the final stage. We may hope, as we grow in likeness to Christ, that we shall in some small measure share his holiness; but Paul looks beyond the gradual transformations of which we now are capable to the more decisive changes which will mark the finished purpose of God. He foresees the day when we shall share the glorified being of the risen Lord.

30 Moreover, whom he did predestinate, them he also called: and whom he called, them he also justified: and whom he justified, them he also glorified.

first-born among many brethren. 30 And those whom he predestined he also called; and those whom he called he also justified; and those whom he justified he also glorified.

---

rationalization of the sense of responsibility we also find within ourselves. More will be said on this difficult theme in the Exeg. of chs. 9–11.

The chosen ones are **predestined to be conformed to the image of his Son,** i.e., they are predestined to share his resurrection body (cf. Phil. 3:21; II Cor. 3:18). This same idea has appeared several times in the course of this epistle (e.g., 6:5; 8:11). Christ is the **first-born** *from the dead* (cf. Col. 1:18); the reference here is not to the pre-existence status or nature of Christ, but to his human nature as transformed and renewed by the resurrection from the dead (cf. on vs. 17). That nature we shall share as his **brethren** (cf. John 20:17). Heb. 2:11, 12, 17 emphasize Christ's becoming like his "brethren"—i.e., sharing fully in our human lot—here the thought is somewhat different: it is we who are made Christ's **brethren** by the gift of the new life. The writer to the Hebrews is nearer to Paul's thought in this passage when in Heb. 2:10 he speaks of God as "bringing many sons to glory," and of Christ as the "pioneer of their salvation." The stress in the present verse is not upon the pre-eminence of **his Son** (this would be assumed), but upon the dignity of his **brethren.**

30. When Paul speaks of being **glorified,** he is referring to that sharing of the "image of his Son" of which he has already spoken. Now he names two intervening steps—**those whom he predestined he also called** [i.e., "invited," "summoned"]; **and those whom he called he also justified.** Justification, as well as calling, is, from Paul's own point of view, already past, while glorification is still in the future; but since all of these steps are being thought of from the point of view established by God's foreknowledge, they are all alluded to in the past tense.

The end of the process (at which Paul has glanced) naturally emphasizes the purpose which has governed it throughout. What justifies the tedious and often agonizing journey of our race is the fashioning of a spiritual family. The common understanding, the unity of aim, the intimacy of fellowship—all the things that are inseparable from a true family will mark the community in which God intends us to share. Our life is touched with dignity as well as meaning if we can see it as a stage in the discipline by which God is fashioning this household of faith. In the process Christ occupies a decisive place. The family of God ceases to be a dream and begins to be a reality because of him. He has opened the way that others might follow—or to modify the imagery, he was **the first-born among many brethren.** "For it was fitting that he, for whom and by whom all things exist, in bringing many sons to glory, should make the pioneer of their salvation perfect through suffering" (Heb. 2:10).

Having glanced at the beginning and the end of our salvation, Paul notes the intermediary stages. In the eternal order the believer is **predestined;** in the temporal order he is **called.** He is faced with a constraint which compels him to turn from the distracting and unsatisfying claims of the world about him to serve the will of God. Those who yield to this constraint and obey are also **justified.** The whole argument of the letter has aimed to show that God can forgive sinners, that unrighteous men can be treated as though they were righteous and admitted to a new relationship to God. We have seen already that the new standing to which we are admitted is one stage in the Christian's life of progressive sanctification; it therefore naturally finds a place in this rapid résumé of the unfolding history of our salvation.

Those who are admitted to this new standing with God discover that they share in the wonder of the divine life: **those whom he justified he also glorified.** To a limited extent they already know what it means to enter into the splendor of the world to come. The fact that their life has been lifted to a new plane points to the far fuller measure in which they will finally participate in the divine perfection.[9]

[9] Cf. Sanday and Headlam, *Epistle to Romans, ad loc.*

31 What shall we then say to these things? If God *be* for us, who *can be* against us?
32 He that spared not his own Son, but delivered him up for us all, how shall he not with him also freely give us all things?

31 What then shall we say to this? If God is for us, who is against us? 32 He who did not spare his own Son but gave him up for us all, will he not also give us all

31-32. What then shall we say to this? This is a favorite formula of Paul's (cf. 3:5; 4:1; 6:1; 7:7; 9:14, 30). It is characteristic of the diatribe style (see above, p. 407) and in Paul is usually followed by a suggested conclusion which he vigorously rejects (but note as exceptions at this point, this passage and 9:30). This time the formula is used to introduce the final conclusion of Paul's argument: since **God is for us** [cf. especially vss. 28-30], **who is against** [i.e., successfully against] **us?** Thus Paul would silence all opposition. The reference to God in vs. 32 as not "sparing" **his own Son** is almost certainly a reminiscence of Gen. 22:16; and the intense and personal character of Paul's feeling about the love of God will be realized more clearly if one remembers with him the

31. ***No Foe Can Fright. . . .***—**What then shall we say to this?** One little word—**this**—sums up Paul's survey of the elements so strangely mingled in the believer's life. For a moment both the suffering to which we are subject and the glory by which it is transformed pass in retrospect before our minds. Those who would be partners in Christ's purpose cannot expect immunity from the cost such service is certain to exact (vs. 17), but they will be upheld by the assurance that present suffering bears no comparison with the glory in which we shall participate (vs. 18). The interpretation which Paul places on our share in the anguish of the present world order points forward to the fuller realization of what this glory will mean (vss. 19-27). But this is not surmise only; even within our immediate experience we can detect the evidences of a purpose of love which is ceaselessly and creatively at work. What is rooted in the eternal order will come to its victorious conclusion when the broken lights of our present service are gathered up in the full splendor of God's accomplished will. This is the background of Paul's question. If these things are so, what can you say about the life you now know? Certain queries, when properly put, prompt their own answers, even when the conviction that emerges is expressed as a further question. **If God is for us, who is against us?** The full significance of God's co-operation with us in all things (vs. 28) becomes clearer. There will still be difficulties, but they will lose their power to defeat our spirits because of the sustaining assurance that our resources will always exceed the demands upon them. The gist of the passage can therefore be set forth in terms of the evidence which life affords and the inferences we draw from it. The evidence: Good and evil are so mingled in our experience that we know the reality of both; but we discover a divine power reinforcing the good in such ways that we confidently anticipate its ultimate triumph. The inferences: Since God's power is supreme, and all other forces challenge it in vain, (*a*) we note the inestimable comfort of God's support: whether faced by the record of our past, or confronted with the difficulties of the present, we have no need to fear the outcome; (*b*) we note the incomparable encouragement of God's succor: for all that lies ahead, we can be sure that his help will be decisive; and (*c*) we note the importance of the power to evaluate correctly the forces which surround us: we shall not be free from opposition, but we shall escape the depression of spirit which comes from anticipating defeat.

32. ***Having Christ, We Have All.***—An assurance of God's providential care requires some firmer foundation than intuition. Our conviction that God's merciful goodness will not fail his children rests on our experience of redemption. We know that all spiritual powers opposed to our true well-being will be unable to prevail against us because Christ's death has already proved that nothing can keep us in its servitude if we accept the liberation which he offers. The general form of the argument is familiar: because we have received the greater, we shall not be denied the less. If God has already gone beyond the utmost conceivable limits of generosity, is there any necessary gift that he will now withhold? But the benefits of so rich a blessing can be expressed in a variety of ways. We can claim with equal truth that when God has given us his Son, he has in effect given us the world. Beyond what we already have there is nothing that we can need or properly desire. Moreover, God's whole nature as the sole source of every good and perfect gift stands disclosed by the supreme gift he has now given. Consequently, the verse can legitimately be taken as

33 Who shall lay any thing to the charge of God's elect? *It is* God that justifieth.

things with him? 33 Who shall bring any charge against God's elect? It is God who

poignant story of Abraham's sacrifice: "Thou . . . hast not withheld thy son, thine only son." This whole verse (i.e., vs. 32) reminds one of 5:8-10. We note again that far from setting "the love of Christ" over against "the justice of God," Paul speaks of God's love more often even than of Christ's. As a matter of fact he identifies the two and uses the terms interchangeably, just as he can speak of Christ as giving himself or, as here, of God as giving him. The "love of Christ" is God's love moving in and through Christ—God's love expressed and embodied in the whole event of which the life of Jesus is the center. For the meaning of **all things** see I Cor. 3:21-23.

33-35*a*. Just as Paul meant in vs. 31, "Who has any chance of succeeding against us?" so here he means "Who can bring any *effective* **charge against God's elect?** Likewise, **condemn** means to establish or prove guilt, not merely to affirm it. It is difficult to see why the RSV has made a question of the next sentence (vs. 34*b*); there is no linguistic

a reminder of the unexamined blessings which we already possess. God has given us everything; with casual disregard we slight his gifts, and eagerly pursue objects which are not necessary and cannot satisfy. Or again, we may treat the words as a lesson in the comparative value of what God gives and what we sometimes choose in preference. But probably we are nearest, both to Paul's immediate meaning and to the heart of the gospel he preached, if we grasp the intimate relationship between three facts—Christ's death; God's love, which is revealed in that death; our assurance of God's care for us, which is sustained by that death. This helps to integrate our religious thought; what is more important, it maintains the essential unity which is the mark of all true religious experience.

33-34. *Our Impregnable Assurance of Salvation.*—With a mighty sweep and with unfaltering confidence Paul has unfolded the working of God's purpose of salvation. But it is natural for the question to persist whether all the opposing forces will actually be powerless to interrupt this process, and Paul never attempts to evade disconcerting facts. We may have no doubt about God's power; but we may have serious reservations about our own worthiness.

Consequently, sin is the first of the threats to our salvation which Paul considers. **Who shall bring any charge against God's elect?** We may note, as illuminating the cast of Paul's mind, his instinctive choice of a metaphor taken from the courts of law. It has the advantage of being familiar to his readers; it is vivid in itself, it is in an area where issues of right and wrong are at stake, and the consequences are of far-reaching importance to the persons most immediately concerned. At the bar of conscience we know that we have failed to meet the standards of integrity, we have offended against God's holy law. The answer that our apprehensions might reasonably prompt would therefore be, "Sin will bring a charge even against God's elect." This is not a remote or unreal issue with which Paul is dealing. The awakened moral insight is conscious of unworthiness; it knows the impossibility of disparaging moral failure, and it is aware how seriously such failure jeopardizes our spiritual life. But the problem is one with which Paul has dealt at length in earlier chapters, and the present verse merely recapitulates his previous argument. **It is God who justifies; who is to condemn?** The first challenge to our assurance of salvation has already been met; though we are sinners we have been acquitted. We have a new standing with God, and this gives us our security.

The prosecutor's case has collapsed, but may we not be condemned by our Lord himself? We are his servants, but admittedly most unprofitable ones. We are always tempted to prove that we are accepted because of what we have actually done—this is due to the incurable strain of legalism in the human mind; if, however, the claims we so readily make on our own behalf were seriously pressed against us, where would we be? Were this a normal law suit our position would be hopeless; but the imagery itself is sufficient to show how radically the situation differs from any parallel which the affairs of the secular world can afford. To recapitulate the faith is to realize that Christ cannot be against us. The confidence which the Resurrection inspires leads to the assurance that he who might legitimately condemn us is ceaselessly active in our behalf: **indeed he intercedes for us.** The creedal form in which Paul's statements are cast has led to the assumption that he may be quoting from an early confession of faith. Certainly the points which he enumerates are essential elements in the belief of the N.T. church: Christ died, rose again, is at the right

34 Who *is* he that condemneth? *It is* Christ that died, yea rather, that is risen again, who is even at the right hand of God, who also maketh intercession for us.

35 Who shall separate us from the love of Christ? *shall* tribulation, or distress, or persecution, or famine, or nakedness, or peril, or sword?

justifies; 34 who is to condemn? Is it Christ
Jesus, who died, yes, who was raised from
the dead, who is at the right hand of God,
who indeed intercedes for us?[m] 35 Who shall
separate us from the love of Christ? Shall
tribulation, or distress, or persecution, or
famine, or nakedness, or peril, or sword?

[m] Or *It is Christ Jesus . . . for us.*

---

objection, but the context seems more naturally to suggest an affirmation, as in KJV. Beginning with 33*b* we seem to have two affirmations, each followed by a question appropriate to it: "It is God who justifies; who is in position to condemn? It is Christ who died . . . **intercedes for us;** who **shall separate us** from his **love?"**

But this "love of Christ" is manifested not alone in Jesus' death and in his present intercession—note the implied identity of the risen Christ and the Spirit of vss. 26-27—but also in his being **raised from the dead** to the **right hand of God;** in other words, it is manifested not only in what Christ *did,* but also in what happened to him, or in what God did through him, i.e., in and through the entire event out of which the church was created. Thus we see again that the "love of Christ" is the "love of God." Some ancient MSS actually contain the latter rather than the former reading, but the meaning is the same whatever the reading. The full and exact statement is found at the very end of this passage (vs. 39): "the love of God in Christ Jesus our Lord."

35*b*-37. Paul all but began this central section of his letter with a reference to our "tribulations" (5:3; the Greek term is the same as here, although the RSV prefers "sufferings" at that point); now, for emphasis, he adds **distress** (note the same combination of terms in 2:9), and follows with the more specific words: **persecution, famine, nakedness, peril, sword.** "Sword" is the only one of these terms which does not appear

---

hand of God, and intercedes for us. We have therefore a particularly telling example of the way in which theology ought to be related to Christian experience. In this crowning passage of the whole epistle, where the discipline of present discipleship gives force to faith and to our farthest hopes, our assurance of peace with God is associated in the closest way possible with the forms in which the church expressed its beliefs. Paul is speaking about the Christ on whom we rely, and he is probably using the creedal structure familiar in his day; but notice the telling personal relevance of what he says. Our complete dependence is upon Christ: (*a*) on a Christ who is not dead, but who lives; (*b*) on a Christ who is not impotent to save, but who is throned in power; (*c*) on a Christ who is not indifferent to our needs, but who in unfailing and effective sympathy makes known our concerns to God.[1]

It is worth noting that we have here a valuable lesson in the "transmutation of futility." To be conscious of our unworthiness is a necessary corrective of spiritual pride, but to be constantly and hopelessly aware of the reality of sin, and of nothing else, is the way to despair. It is wrong to ignore our spiritual failures, since that leads to unreality; it is wrong to be obsessed with them, since that leads to inevitable defeat. Paul points to a method which at once makes us honest with ourselves about sin but saves us from an unhealthy preoccupation with it. When he remarks, **It is God who justifies; who is to condemn?** he is showing us how to acknowledge the reality of evil even while we escape from its tyranny. Justification takes account of the seriousness of our wrongdoing, but our whole life is taken up into a new relationship with God. Because of the liberty which our new standing confers, we are free from the twin temptations of ignoring sin and of dwelling upon it. This is the simplest way—indeed it is the only way—of finding mental peace and spiritual health.

35. ***Disasters Cannot Intervene.***—Sin cannot condemn us since we are justified; Christ's holiness will not condemn us, since it expresses itself in love, and he who might be our judge stands to plead our cause. We already have strong proofs of God's redemptive purpose, and these are all intimately related to the divine love disclosed in Christ. But have we any final assurance that we shall not be cut off from this love which forms the ultimate security of our souls? May not the blows of adverse circum-

[1] Cf. Sanday and Headlam, *Epistle to Romans*, p. 221.

36 As it is written, For thy sake we are killed all the day long; we are accounted as sheep for the slaughter.
37 Nay, in all these things we are more than conquerors through him that loved us.

36 As it is written,
"For thy sake we are being killed all the day long;
we are regarded as sheep to be slaughtered."
37 No, in all these things we are more than conquerors through him who loved us.

elsewhere in Paul in some similar connection; see especially II Cor. 11:23–12:10, but there are other passages also. The "sword" is not mentioned in these catalogues of or references to the apostle's sufferings because quite obviously he has not yet suffered it. But it was a genuine possibility and a constant threat (cf. II Cor. 11:26). Persecution in Paul's time had not gone so far as to kill—certainly not often—but it might do so at any moment. That Paul is thinking in this verse primarily of sufferings inflicted by others because of the believer's attachment to Christ appears from the quotation from Ps. 44:22. **For thy sake,** as Paul understands it, means "for Christ's sake." But the reference to "tribulations" in this passage must not be limited to such persecutions. Note what was said above on "suffering with him" (vs. 17).

stances achieve what even sin was powerless to effect? To many people this is a more pressing question than those which Paul has already answered. They feel that pain and persecution are evils more insistent and more likely to bend the will than the intangible menace posed by merely "spiritual" temptations. Paul answers with the authority which firsthand experience confers, that nothing can **separate us from the love of Christ.** Even the forces which we admit to be mighty are powerless to cut us off from the true source of our security. All the things which might threaten our well-being—**tribulation, or distress, or persecution, or famine, or nakedness, or peril, or sword**—are incapable of interfering with our highest good. Among injuries caused by the malice of men Paul no doubt would be willing to include misfortunes due to capricious circumstances. It is not hard to dismiss such things if we have never had to endure them; much easy optimism is based on nothing more profound than immunity. Paul knew the power of adversity to embitter and to defeat; all the things he mentions here formed recurring elements in the pattern of his life (cf. II Cor. 11:23-33); moreover, he knew well enough how easily some of them might mark the journey to Jerusalem on which he intended to embark (cf. Acts 20:22-23; 21:4, 10-14). A testimony such as this carries weight only when it comes from someone qualified to give it; then it is impressive indeed.

36. ***An Appeal to Scripture.***—The experience of those who suffer can be illustrated by an appeal to the words of Scripture; but the difference in atmosphere, commonly noted by exegetes, provides the kind of contrast so useful in pressing home the truth. Outwardly the pattern may be identical, whether the words are used by the psalmist under the old dispensation or by the apostle under the new: **For thy sake we are being killed all the day long.** But in the former times these words were a cry of perplexity, an expression of the mystery of seemingly pointless suffering; in the new day they are the prelude to a shout of triumph. This is the transformation wrought in our understanding of the difficulties that beset us. The gospel does not deliver us from misfortunes; it enables us to find in them a blessing, not a curse.

37. ***Victory in the Superlative Degree.***—If the evils which confront us are incapable of separating us from Christ's love, it is because a spiritual vitality of the utmost importance has come into play. There are three distinguishable steps in Paul's thought: we are **conquerors; we are more than conquerors; we are more than conquerors through him who loved us.**

(*a*) It is an important truth that the human spirit can rise above the threat of all opposing forces. We might expect as much, for this is God's world, and throughout its entire range we find that the greatest beauty emerges in the most unlikely places. The pine which grows securely on the edge of the forest is often less graceful than the tree which has caught a precarious foothold in a cleft of the rock and rears its height above the abyss. We see it again and again in nature, and if we are observant, we shall see it also in human life. Courage, gallantry, gaiety, unselfishness—how often we find these virtues flourishing in the most unlikely places, maintaining themselves not because of encouraging circumstances, but in the face of every obstacle that their environment can offer. We find it in the life of faith, and we

38 For I am persuaded, that neither death, nor life, nor angels, nor principalities, nor powers, nor things present, nor things to come,

38 For I am sure that neither death, nor life, nor angels, nor principalities, nor things present, nor things to come, nor pow-

38-39. This sentence, which marks both the end and the climax of this great section of the letter, is a further answer to the question asked in 35*a*: "Who shall separate us . . . ?" In 35*b* Paul has denied that any suffering, actual or conceivable, can do so. Now his answer becomes more universal, including every possible factor, earthly or cosmic. **Neither death, nor life**—i.e., "nothing in death or life" or "nothing whether we live or die." **Angels, principalities, powers** are supernatural and superhuman beings—both good and bad, and of all grades between (see Exeg. on Col. 1:15-20 in Vol. XI). **Things present, nor things to come** (like **death, nor life**) again emphasizes the universality of Paul's denial: nothing which now exists or will exist shall separate us from God's love. One would expect this phrase to follow **powers,** which clearly belongs with **angels** and **principalities.** The only possible explanation of this lack of order is the spontaneous eloquence of the passage. Paul is uttering words as they occur to him in an inspired

gratefully note the courage with which difficulties are encountered, the constancy with which temptation is overcome. The truth of religion finds its authentication in the victorious quality which it imparts to lives which otherwise are wholly undistinguished. It is no small thing that in a world where moral struggle is inevitably our lot, we can claim to have the victory.

(*b*) It is much that we can come through, hard pressed but triumphant: that in itself is cause for gratitude and reassurance. Paul claims, however, that we are **more than conquerors.** We not only defeat the powers of evil, but we snatch a blessing from their onslaught. Sorrow becomes the expositor of mysteries which joy leaves unexplained. Defeats teach us humility when success would leave us insensitive and proud. The tragedies which threaten to blight our joy become the source of our deepest understanding. These things are not merely overcome and rendered harmless; by the alchemy of the spirit they are changed into positive good.

(*c*) Such miracles do not unfold without sufficient cause. The power which robs misfortune of its sting and transforms it into a blessing is the power of love. We would expect as much. In human relationships only love can overcome bitterness and bring about reconciliation.

> And blessings on the falling out
> That all the more endears,
> When we fall out with those we love
> And kiss again with tears! [2]

Human love provides an analogy, but of necessity it is limited and imperfect. Paul is speaking of the transforming power of divine love: **we are more than conquerors through him who loved us.** We know that he regarded his love for Christ as an answering response to Christ's love for him. It was the transforming power of this love which explained all the good which he was able to achieve; the same power accounts for the ability to change evil into a source of good. This is not a complete answer to the problem of suffering, but it sets forth the working philosophy of the man of faith. We may not know why pain has so large a place in human life, but we have discovered a way of turning it into a blessing. We can do this if we have the resources requisite to the task, and they are found only in "the love of God in Christ" (vs. 39).

[2] Tennyson, *The Princess*, Part II.

38-39. ***The Gift Which No Created Thing Can Take Away.***—Confidence is based on experience, and experience is concerned with things which are either past or present. But the discovery of what victory means has relevance to the future as well. Our knowledge that we possess a power capable of transforming the onslaughts of evil into the ministrations of good justifies the assurance that nothing yet to come can bring us to defeat. So long as we remain fixed in our loyalty to Christ, there is nothing in heaven or earth, in time or in eternity, that can separate us from God's merciful care. Paul's outlook therefore reaches beyond the present into the future, beyond the things known to the things merely imagined; but nowhere can he find any conceivable power sufficiently malign to shake his confidence. Opinions differ about the character of the catalogue which follows; some authorities treat it as a carefully constructed series of contrasting forces, others regard it as a product of the

39 Nor height, nor depth, nor any other creature, shall be able to separate us from the love of God, which is in Christ Jesus our Lord.

ers, 39 nor height, nor depth, nor anything else in all creation, will be able to separate us from the love of God in Christ Jesus our Lord.

moment, and without much concern for details of logical order. **Height** and **depth** are astrological terms—"height" (ὕψωμα) meaning the highest position a given star attains and "depth" (βάθος) the abyss below the horizon out of which the stars rise. Stars—depending upon their position—were popularly supposed to exercise certain effects upon the course of human events. It is not necessary to suppose that Paul is manifesting any acceptance of such notions. Again he is emphasizing the inclusiveness of his affirmation that nothing can "separate us from the love of Christ." Whatever the stars may be able to do, they cannot do *this.* The last phrase in this series, **anything else in all creation** (literally "any other creation"), serves quite admirably to end it. Does Paul mean "any other order of creation than that we know" or "anything of which we are not aware in this order of creation"? The difference is negligible, and the RSV translation properly preserves the ambiguity of Paul's own statement.

uncalculating yet inclusive sweep of an eager mind. Whatever Paul's purpose, the result provides us with an unequaled opportunity to emphasize the full scope of the security which our Christian heritage confers.

Neither death, nor life can overthrow the good which God designs for us. There is nothing in this life or in the life to come that has any power to defeat us. Even the haunting fear of that foe from which none of us escapes is removed. Both the mystery and the finality of death have been destroyed. But if Christ can deliver us from apprehension and sorrow when we come to that last ordeal, there is nothing either before or after that we need to dread.

There is no dimension, either of space or time, that can hold any real terror for us. **Things present** and **things to come** may mean the forces at work in this age and those which will belong to the era which lies beyond the end of this present order. They may simply indicate the difference between the things we know because they are a part of experience and those we do not know because they are as yet ahead. But neither the passage of time nor the changes it brings with it can materially affect our confidence. The assurance of God's love is not dependent upon circumstances or chronology.

There are no created beings who can intervene to separate us from the love of God. **Angels, principalities, powers** are supernatural creatures, elements in that hierarchy of spirits which was so real to Paul and his contemporaries. How we define them is relatively unimportant; the terrors which they were capable of arousing were due to the fact that our essential well-being and the course which our lives would follow might be placed at the mercy of forces external to ourselves. That is a fear which is still undispelled, and strange cults like astrology owe any plausibility they may possess to man's ancient dread that powers outside himself may seize control of his destiny.

It might seem that Paul has taken account of everything, of any order of being, here or elsewhere, now or hereafter, that might intervene to cut us off from God. But to silence any lurking apprehensions he adds one final word—**nor anything else in all creation.** If God is supreme, and if his creation is responsive to his will, nothing he has made can obstruct his merciful purpose. Our final security cannot be shaken, but we may pause to notice that it rests on none of the things in which man is always tempted to place his confidence. The ultimate power for good—a power indestructible and undefeated—is love. Its constraint is mightier than any of the coercive agencies in which we usually trust. And its final victory is assured because it is the active expression of the essential nature of God himself. But if God is indeed the creator and sustainer of all things, we can imagine nothing so abiding and unconquerable as the love which declares his purpose. What that love is we can only guess until we see it fully declared in Jesus Christ. Consequently, the only possible and yet the perfectly sufficient way of defining our grounds of hope is to declare that nothing **will be able to separate us from the love of God in Christ Jesus our Lord.** Only such a revelation can inspire an assurance so triumphant.

We may respond to the glory of this passage and at the same time despair of communicating any of its wonder through our own faltering words. With such succinct finality it sums up the confidence created by our faith that any com-

9 I say the truth in Christ, I lie not, my conscience also bearing me witness in the Holy Ghost,

9 I am speaking the truth in Christ, I am not lying; my conscience bears me wit-

The **love of God in Christ Jesus our Lord** is, as we have already noted (under vs. 35), the exact and full way of stating Paul's conception. The **love,** which is the whole meaning of the Christian life, is primarily the **love of God,** i.e., God's love. This love was poured out (5:5) in and through the event of which the life, death, and resurrection of Jesus were the center, and it abides with us as the Spirit of the new community which came into being with that event and in which the event is perpetuated (see on 6:3-4).

V. Jew and Gentile in God's Purpose (9:1–11:36)

Very early in this discussion 1:16-17 was identified as containing the theme of the letter to the Romans—at least of its doctrinal section (the ethical teachings of 12:1–15:13, while not unrelated to this theme, are probably more closely and immediately related to what Paul considers to be the practical needs of the Roman church). By the end of ch. 8 Paul has dealt with this theme in every major part: the world's need of the gospel, the meaning of justification by faith and of the new life (the promise and foretaste of the final salvation) which God through Christ has made available to guilty and sin-enslaved men. One element in this theme, however, has not been adequately discussed—the element suggested by the phrase, "to the Jew first and also to the Greek" (1:16). There has been no lack of discussion of the Jew—2:1–3:20 was devoted to urging that the Jew as well as the Greek was in need of God's new saving act; and the whole of ch. 4 was concerned with demonstrating that the gospel was anticipated in the O.T., and that

mentary on it seems both superfluous and ineffective. Yet the truth which Paul so magnificently sets forth is the message which we are commissioned to convey. To evade our duty is no solution to our problem, and we are less likely to fail if we have the support of a great passage than if we are content with platitudes prompted by our own limited insight. But as we struggle to reduce Paul's glowing affirmations to language natural to ourselves and familiar to our time, it is well to remember that this great passage does not stand alone. There are those who may gravitate to this chapter, and ignore the earlier part of the letter; but Paul did not write what he wrote here as a tour de force. His greatest passages always grow out of his ongoing argument. He did not compose I Cor. 13 as a detached hymn to love; it is part of his discussion of spiritual gifts and of how they should be used. In the same way, his tremendous declaration of assurance follows naturally from the entire course of his argument hitherto. It is the climax of all that goes before, and it cannot be detached. We have this confidence because the nature of our new life warrants it; but our new life is possible only because God's mercy has provided a method by which we find a new standing with God and so enter into the glorious liberty of his children. "Line upon line, precept upon precept," Paul has built up his case; its conclusion is the hymn of triumph which the whole sweep of his argument has inspired.

9:1–11:36. ***The Role of Experience in the Christian Faith.***—Those who read the Scriptures on a selective principle usually confine themselves to the passages which they have learned to love, and for the most part ignore the rest. Sections which are unfamiliar—often simply because they are virtually unknown—seem unattractive and remote, and no attempt is made to wrest from them their full wealth of meaning. Probably Rom. 9–11 is more largely ignored than any other part of the letter. At first sight, of course, the argument appears to lack both relevance and interest: the debate about Israel's hopes and destiny seems of slight importance to Christians of our century. Actually Paul is discussing—in his own terms, no doubt—a subject of intense contemporary concern. Christian people have rediscovered that their faith rests not on a system of ideas, but on a series of events. God has revealed himself in the experience of his people, and they know his nature by what he has done. But if history is the realm of God's self-disclosure, it must occupy in our thought a position of importance comparable to the significance it has acquired in our experience. This explains the prominence which the interpretation of history assumes in theology. In the present section Paul is dealing with precisely this subject, even

all along God has dealt with the Jewish nation on the basis of the requirement of faith—but the particular point ("the Jew first") has not been handled. To be sure, even that point has not been entirely ignored: at 3:1, 9 Paul raised the question, "What advantage has the Jew?" but at that juncture in his argument he was unable to deal adequately with the question. Now having come to the end of his argument as a whole, he takes up the question again and devotes what we know as chs. 9–11 to answering it.

At least three queries concerning this passage in general need to be considered briefly before it is taken up for more detailed comment. One of these is a question concerning the relationship the passage sustains to the rest of the epistle; a second is concerned with the reasons for its inclusion; and the third has to do with its internal structure and the general drift of its argument.

Nothing could be clearer than the fact that with 8:39 Paul brings one part of his work to an end and with 9:1 embarks upon a new and structurally quite distinct section of his letter, which in turn ends quite as decisively at 11:36. Chs. 9–11, in fact, could be lifted out of this epistle without leaving any apparent gap. The ethical section, 12:1–15:13, would follow upon ch. 8 as naturally as upon ch. 11, if indeed not more so; and ch. 9 begins without any explicit reference to the preceding argument. Thus, chs. 9–11 constitute a more or less independent element in the epistle and can be considered not only as a unit, but also with less reference to the rest of the letter than can any earlier section. There is not the slightest reason for supposing that the letter to the Romans ever existed without these chapters; but it has been proposed (e.g., by Dodd, *Epistle of Paul to Romans,* pp. 148-50) that they comprise an earlier composition of Paul (Dodd calls it a "sermon") which he merely incorporated in this epistle. No conclusive objection to this theory can be brought, although one wonders if Paul wrote out his sermons so carefully and kept them by him for future use; and it may also be noted that 9:1-2 would seem even more abrupt as the beginning of a sermon than it does as the sequel of 8:39.

Indeed, when one looks more closely, one recognizes that this passage does not break so completely with what precedes as it seems at first to do. From 8:28 to the end of that chapter Paul is discussing the "election" of the Christians and therefore the certainty of their salvation. The chapter concludes with a shout of triumphant assurance. But what more natural than that the apostle's mind should then turn to those whose rejection of the gospel seems to place them outside the number of the elect—especially as they are not only his own people but also the people to whom the promise of salvation was first given? In other words, for all its structural autonomy, the section, chs. 9–11, does follow not inappropriately upon the discussion of election in ch. 8.

The grounds for Paul's giving so much attention in this letter to the significance of the Jews' apparent rejection of the gospel are not difficult to surmise. One ground undoubtedly lay within the apostle himself, or in his own personal situation. It was pointed out (Intro., pp. 358-59) that at the moment when Romans was being written, Paul was about to embark for Palestine with an offering which the largely Gentile churches in his area of work had raised for the help of their Jewish brethren in Jerusalem. This offering, he hopes, will bring an end to controversy in which he has been engaged for years—controversy concerning the relation of the Christian to the Jewish law and concerning the calling and the destiny of the Jewish people. Because he himself is a Jew, this problem has for him a special poignancy. Not unnaturally, therefore, in this letter written in somewhat relaxed mood, but after much bitter fighting, within himself and with other men of his own nation, he seeks to think through and to state as clearly as possible his position on this issue—this issue so critical for the church and so overwhelmingly and painfully important to him personally.

But another ground for his giving this theme special attention lies almost certainly in the character of the Roman church and in the impression which Paul fears its members have of himself. It has been pointed out more than once that the apostle exhibits signs of uncertainty as to how he will be received at Rome. Although it was recognized that we are not in position to know why this should have been true, attention was called to evidences that Roman Christianity was more Jewish in cast, and therefore soberer, more conservative, than Pauline Christianity (see above, Intro., pp. 360-63). It is not hard to believe that Paul had been represented at Rome as despising the religious heritage which the church at Rome treasured as fully Christian. (Marcion, two generations later, claimed Paul's support in actually doing just this.) But if this is true, the Roman Christians misunderstood Paul, just as Marcion later did; and the apostle feels under the necessity of setting them right by explaining his own attitude toward the Jewish nation and his own conception of their place in God's purpose more fully than there has been any opportunity for doing up to this point in the letter.

As to the structure of this section, it is usual to think of it as falling into three main parts (not counting 9:1-5, which is obviously introductory, and 11:33-36, which is just as manifestly a concluding apostrophe and doxology); these are 9:6-29; 9:30–10:21; and 11:1-32 (so Sanday and Headlam, Dodd, Kühl, and others). If, however, the first of these sections is divided after vs. 13, we recognize that the argument proceeds through four steps which can be represented somewhat as follows: (*a*) The failure of the Jewish nation as a whole to accept the gospel, even if it were final, would not mean a failure of God's promise, because all along that promise has not applied to the nation as a whole, simply as such, but to selected groups or individuals within the nation, e.g., Isaac rather than Ishmael, and Jacob rather than Esau. And these persons (and their descendants) God selected, be it noted, *in advance,* before they had done anything "either good or bad." Thus it is conceivable that in the present time "God's purpose of election" might include only a few Jews by nationality among those who have faith in Christ and thus become heirs of the promise. If that should happen, it would not be true to say that his "word . . . had failed" (9:6-13). (*b*) But this selection of a mere remnant to be the heirs of the promise would seem to be arbitrary. What if it should be so? Even if arbitrary, God's election of some and rejection of others is not unjust. Does he not have the right to do what he will with his own (9:14-29)? (*c*) Both of the two preceding steps have been based on premises which are now, in reverse order, denied—a kind of chiasmus is involved here. In 9:14-29, Paul has said that even if God's choice of a remnant be entirely arbitrary, it is not unjust; *now* he denies that it is in fact arbitrary. Rather it is based on the failure of the Jewish nation as a whole to call upon the Lord *in faith* (9:30–10:21). And (*d*) whereas 9:6-13 proceeded on the assumption that Israel's apostasy was final, Paul now denies that it is such at all. God has not finally rejected his people. He has rejected them only temporarily in order that the Gentiles might have an opportunity to hear and accept the gospel; afterward, or in the end, "all Israel will be saved" (11:1-32).

It would be too much to claim that such a way of analyzing and interpreting this difficult section of the epistle removes all of its contradictions and obscurities. This is surely not true, but it may well serve to mitigate them.

One further remark of a general character is appropriate. These chapters show conclusively that at the time they were written, shortly after the middle of the first century, the Christian churches were already predominantly non-Jewish in membership. It was clear that the future of the movement—at any rate its immediate future—lay not

---

though his approach is determined both by his own background and by the circumstances which dictated the form which his letter took. But Paul might have been surprised to have his discussion labeled an interpretation of history. He was doubtless dealing with specific problems, some of them common to his work wherever he might be, others distinctive of the church at Rome. Moreover, he was thinking of an immediate religious issue—God's faithfulness in dealing with the Jewish race, and this in turn led him to consider the entire manner in which God's favor and mercy operate. In addition, this section of the letter provides us with illuminating glimpses of Paul himself—of the matters near to his heart, of his hopes and fears, of the way in which he thought, and possibly even of the manner in which he spoke. Consequently, we may approach it with three types of expectation. The first is theological:

2 That I have great heaviness and continual sorrow in my heart.
3 For I could wish that myself were accursed from Christ for my brethren, my kinsmen according to the flesh:

ness in the Holy Spirit, 2 that I have great sorrow and unceasing anguish in my heart.
3 For I could wish that I myself were accursed and cut off from Christ for the sake

among the Jews but among the Gentiles. It is this fact, so well established at the time that Paul simply takes it for granted, which constitutes the poignant personal and theological problem with which these chapters deal.

A. The Apostle's Appreciation of Israel (9:1-5)

9:1-3. Paul begins with an assertion of the devotion he feels to his **kinsmen by race.** To the reality and sincerity of this devotion he takes a most solemn oath. A comparison of vs. 1 with Gal. 1:20; II Cor. 1:23 and 11:31 will suggest that his assertion takes this emphatic and solemn form because he had been falsely accused of disloyalty or indifference. He insists he is **not lying** because he knows there are some who are ready to say that he *is* lying. Here, as in Gal. 1:20 and the other passages, we see signs of the deep suspicion and real hostility of which Paul was undoubtedly the object within certain circles of primitive Christianity. This fact is obscured in the book of Acts, written in a later period when the controversies of Paul's own time had been largely forgotten and when there was a strong contemporary motive for emphasizing the unity of the more primitive church; but it appears unmistakably in the letters of Paul. It is not necessary to suppose that the Roman church was actively hostile to Paul, but we have already seen some reason for believing that it suspected him—suspected him of the very fault which he is now so vigorously denying, viz., indifference to his own people and his own religious tradition.

Paul's insistence upon the truth of his statement is here particularly strong, even as compared with the other passages cited. Not only does he affirm that he is not lying, but also he calls, as it were, **Christ,** the **Holy Spirit,** and his own **conscience** to witness to his sincerity. **In Christ** and **in the Holy Spirit** are essentially equivalent phrases: he means that he is speaking as a member of the body of Christ and therefore as possessed by the Spirit.

The fact which Paul affirms so solemnly is that he has **great sorrow and unceasing anguish in** [his] **heart.** Such a statement is all the more impressive and moving, following

---

we shall follow one of the most acute of Christian minds as it deals with a problem of great concern to all our systematic thought about God. The second is religious: we shall listen as a soul of deep earnestness considers God's dealings with mankind. The third is biographical: we shall discover that we know a good deal more about the apostle Paul at the end of the passage than we did at the beginning. (Also see Exeg.)

9:1-5. ***Paul's Loyalty to His Heritage.***—Paul must have laid himself open to constant misunderstanding. The profound character of the subjects he discusses would lead us to expect as much. Many people can grasp only the simplest ideas, and even when they have grasped them, they cannot repeat them accurately. Paul's views doubtless circulated in many garbled forms, and we know that he was often fantastically misquoted. His own style and manner invited misapprehension, and his record gave malicious people, anxious to misrepresent his position, an added advantage. Any man who has served two opposing sides with such complete devotion has given hostages to both his opponents. Paul's letters contain abundant evidence that he was often involved in controversy, and he repeatedly has to correct false interpretations of his position or to deny views unjustly attributed to him. His long debate with the Judaizing section of the early church made it easy for his antagonists to insinuate that he despised the whole heritage of Israel. At the very outset of this passage he pauses to state in the most uncompromising terms his devotion to his racial and religious inheritance. There is a moving poignancy about the earnestness with which he declares his position. The fanaticism of his earlier days has been broken by his discovery that the defects of the law are made good

4 Who are Israelites; to whom *pertaineth* the adoption, and the glory, and the covenants, and the giving of the law, and the service *of God,* and the promises;

of my brethren, my kinsmen by race. 4 They are Israelites, and to them belong the sonship, the glory, the covenants, the giving of the law, the worship, and the promises;

---

as it does immediately upon the triumphant shout with which the previous chapter ends. It has already been pointed out that consideration of election in 8:28-29 leads not unnaturally to a consideration of the problem of why Israel, the originally elect nation, has apparently rejected its salvation. In the same way, perhaps, the thought of how glorious is the privilege of knowing the love of God in Christ reminds Paul of those so near to him who do not know it. This connection appears even more clearly in vs. 3, where Paul goes so far as to say that he finds it possible to wish that he himself might be **accursed** (ἀνάθεμα, literally "delivered up to God for destruction") and **cut off** [this verb is not in the Greek, but the preposition plainly suggests it] **from Christ** (cf. 8:35*a*, 39*b*), if such a sacrifice on his part could save his people. We note again that Paul does not need to explain *why* he is unhappy over his people; the fact that they have by and large rejected the gospel is only too patent.

4-5*a*. So far Paul has been affirming his own personal unhappiness over this apostasy; now he goes on to indicate the theological problem which it creates. For **they are Israelites**—i.e., they are heirs of the covenant made with Jacob when his name was changed to "Israel" ("Israelite" means more than "Jew," indicating not mere nationality, but membership in a chosen people; cf. 11:1). **To them** belongs **the sonship**—i.e., the "adoption" (cf. 8:15, 23), the status of legal sons of God; Paul here has in mind such

---

in the new covenant in Christ; but its place has been taken by an abiding gratitude for the positive benefits which his training had conferred. Though he has broken with Judaism as a system, he finds himself all the more closely identified with Jewry as a race. That is why he feels with such acute intensity the tragedy of Israel's repudiation of the final stage in an inheritance they had prized so highly. He has accepted what his friends have rejected, but his wonder at the marvels of God's grace in Christ, so rapturously set forth in the closing verses of ch. 8, does not for a moment tempt him to complacency because he has found what others have missed. **Great sorrow and unceasing anguish** is his first attempt to convey the personal disappointment involved in the attitude of the great body of his people; but the words are too unimpassioned for his purpose. **For I could wish,** he adds, **that I myself were accursed . . . for the sake of my brethren.** The ASV mg. hints that **wish** is too weak a word for Paul's meaning, and suggests "pray" instead. The parallel with Moses' appeal on behalf of his apostate people then becomes even clearer: "Yet now, if thou wilt forgive their sin—; and if not, blot me, I pray thee, out of thy book which thou hast written" (Exod. 32:32). But Moses asks that if they cannot be saved with him, he may be allowed at least to perish with them; whereas Paul prays that he may lose what he has but what they lack, provided his loss will mean their gain. We know no higher form of love than that "a man lay down his life for his friends" (John 15:13), and the drastic character of what Paul desires is shown by his wish that he could be **cut off from Christ for the sake of my brethren, my kinsmen by race.** He would forgo not only life but abundant life in order that they might discover what he knows. What that would mean is clear if we remember all that he has just said about the wonder of God's gift to those that are in Christ.

The depth of emotion in Paul's words strikes us at once; we realize the passionate devotion of which this man was capable. But more is involved than merely an understanding of the apostle. He has acknowledged his debt to his race and heritage, because these form the channel by means of which God's merciful purpose has entered his life. In the great catalogue of the treasures of Israel (vs. 4) he gives some indication of his profound indebtedness to the inheritance into which as a Jew he had been born. He no longer adhered to the system of thought and practice in which he had been reared, but he did not cease to be a Jew; and to his death he bore the stamp of the school through which he had come. We all know how largely we are influenced by the institutions through which we pass, and even when we react against them we still remain their product. This elementary fact has important religious conse

passages as Exod. 4:22: "Thus saith the Lord, Israel is my son, even my firstborn," or Jer. 31:9: "I am a father to Israel, and Ephraim is my firstborn"; cf. also Deut. 32:6 and Hos. 11:1. To the Jews also belongs **the glory**—i.e., the *Kābhôdh,* the glorious presence of God (cf. Exod. 16:10; 24:16; etc.); **the covenants** are not the two covenants, Jewish and Christian; the word is plural either because, as Sanday and Headlam say, "the original covenant of God with Israel was again and again renewed" (Gen. 15:18; 17:2, 7, 9; Exod. 2:24; etc.), or because several covenants are mentioned in the O.T. (e.g., Gen. 6:18; 9:9; II Sam. 7:11-16; Ps. 89:28; etc.); **the giving of the law**—Paul has never denied the majesty and significance of the Jewish law, although he has defined its intention and function in an unorthodox way (cf. on 7:7 ff.): **the worship**—i.e., the services, the sacrifices, the liturgy of the temple (cf. Heb. 9:1, 6); **the promises,** already discussed in 4:13-20; **the patriarchs**—Paul would not have shared a frequently held Jewish view that the merits of the great fathers of the nation (Abraham, Isaac, Jacob, etc.) could be pleaded in extenuation of failure by their descendants, but he is nevertheless both proud of his ancestry (cf. 11:1; Phil. 3:5) and also aware of the richness of the cultural inheritance which that ancestry has bequeathed (see also on 11:28 and 15:8); and finally, **of their race, according to the flesh,** i.e., "so far as nationality is concerned," **is the Christ.** This last term may mean "the Messiah" (i.e., whoever he might have been; so Sanday and Headlam and apparently the RSV); but more probably Paul means to refer to Jesus himself specifically and personally. He does not mean merely that to Israel belonged all along the hope of a Messiah and the promise of a Messiah, but that the Messiah, who has actually appeared, was of that nation (on **according to the flesh** see also on 1:3).

---

quences. These human institutions, imperfect though they may be, are the means by which most of the great things in our intellectual and spiritual experience become our own. They are, under God, the way in which we learn most about his good gifts. History proves conclusively the strength of any system which develops by drawing on the best elements in its tradition. As individuals, however, we oscillate between undue deference for the past and complete indifference to or even repudiation of its values. Paul points to the only way of wisdom. With a deep gratitude which cherishes the best in his inheritance, he combines awareness of its imperfections and a willingness to modify—or even to abandon—those features of it which had proved their insufficiency.

With admirable precision he states the nature of the heritage of Israel. In our day this heritage is not so much impugned as ignored. There is little tendency among Christians to dispute its right to reverent respect, but the actual content of Judaism, positively regarded, is so little understood that in effect we relegate the O.T. to a position of inferior and often of negligible importance. Point by point Paul enumerates the great elements in Israel's past (vs. 4). He begins by referring to the spiritual prerogative of the Jewish people: **Israelites** was not so much a national or racial designation as an indication of their place in the divine purpose. Because of the distinctive position they held in God's plan, other gifts of priceless worth were added. Some of these (for their precise character, cf. Exeg.) were more temporary than others. The **law** was no longer binding in the way the Jews believed, but Paul was quite prepared to concede that as regards its substance and intention it was holy, just, and good. The **worship** of the temple would be superseded (cf. John 4:21-24), but it had been an instrument for the training of God's people. **The glory** (God's presence among his people); **the sonship** (the consciousness of a relationship with God—of trust, favor, and obedience); **the promises** (the conviction that our faith and hope rest on a declared and unalterable purpose of love and mercy)—these are abiding elements in any high form of religious experience, and must be conserved within the Christian community. It is not, however, merely an enumeration of spiritual gifts which Paul sets forth. Their true significance appears at the end of the catalogue: Paul is showing the way by which Messiah came. Here we have the steps by which God led his people to the point where they might be ready to accept his greatest gift. It is the fulfillment of the O.T. in the N.T. which gives it for Christians its abiding significance; but it is also this which for Paul constitutes the tragic irony of Israel's position. He sees that all the experience of his people presupposes a certain kind of climax; without it the entire process would remain incomplete. The fulfillment they looked for has actually taken place: **of their race, according to the flesh, is the Christ.** The poignancy of the situation is due to the failure of the Jews to recog-

5 Whose *are* the fathers, and of whom as concerning the flesh Christ *came,* who is over all, God blessed for ever. Amen.

5 to them belong the patriarchs, and of their race, according to the flesh, is the Christ. God who is over all be blessed for ever.[n] Amen.

[n] Or *Christ, who is God over all, blessed for ever.*

5*b*. This half verse has been the center of interminable controversy. The issue appears from a comparison of our two English texts. Is **God over all, blessed for ever** (or the one **who is over all, God blessed for ever**) a phrase in apposition with "Christ" and belonging in the same sentence as the rest of vs. 5 (so the KJV and the RSV mg.), or is this phrase grammatically separate, a doxology to God at the end of the recital of the privileges of Israel (so the RSV and most modern translators)? The question cannot be answered on the basis of the Greek since it is a matter almost entirely of punctuation, and Greek MSS in the early period were not punctuated. There is even one additional possibility, viz., ". . . flesh, who is over all. God be blessed forever"; but the choice is probably to be made between the KJV and the RSV translations. The majority of modern commentators favor the latter because of the unlikelihood of Paul's having here referred to Christ as "God" (θεός). Although Paul goes so far as to suggest for Christ "equality with God" (Phil. 2:5-11) and is willing to apply to Jesus passages in the O.T. in which God is alluded to under the name "the Lord," he apparently shrinks from actually calling Christ "God"—i.e., he stops short of doing this unless he does so here. But if he does so here, would he not have done it elsewhere and often? This seems rather conclusive; but Sanday and Headlam argue effectively for the alternative way (i.e., KJV) of taking this passage. Lietzmann, although he adopts the same view as the RSV translators, insists that he does so on neither linguistic nor theological grounds, but because the parallels of other doxologies (e.g., Pss. 41:13; 66:20; 72:18; 89:52; 106:48; Eph. 4:6), especially including the Pauline ones (Rom. 1:25; 11:36; II Cor. 11:31; Gal. 1:5; Phil. 4:20), seem to preclude the reference of this doxology to Christ.

nize what they have waited to see. It is disastrous to be blind, but to be blind to the crowning glory of one's own heritage is a tragedy which words alone cannot convey.

5b. God's Blessings Quicken Our Praise.—Paul has set forth the catalogue of Israel's blessings. In so doing he has mentioned one by one the signal mercies of God, and he has concluded with God's supreme self-disclosure and his crowning gift to men. To all this there is only one appropriate response: an exclamation of gratitude. Those who recognize God's favor must react by ascribing to him all praise. This brief doxology fixes first on the absolute supremacy of God, then on our duty—unending because never discharged—of blessing him for his goodness.

Before leaving this introductory section it is worth noting a point which, though incidental to Paul's main purpose, has an importance of its own. It is natural for a man who is pressed by an opponent to protest his sincerity, but the form which Paul gives to his affirmation of integrity (vs. 1) is plainly more than formal. "I am speaking the truth in Christ, I am not lying; my conscience bears me witness in the Holy Spirit." In the course of his letters Paul repeatedly declares that Christ provides the spiritual atmosphere in which he lives. Within that same inclusive sphere every significant activity of his life is carried on: it is in Christ that he speaks the truth. What he says is confirmed by conscience—by the faculty of moral judgment which assesses every phase of our conduct. But conscience needs continual discipline and enlightenment, and its witness is reliable only when God's Spirit has quickened it. The implications of what he is saying reach out to include every aspect of the life lived in Christ and guided by the Holy Spirit; but they are immediately addressed to the problems of honesty in thought and speech. Truthfulness is not always an easy virtue to practice; on every side it is beset by temptations to casuistry and deception. No system of rules can carry us very far. In a situation in which every code declares its insufficiency, Paul points to the only solution. The kind of affirmation with which he opens the chapter is possible when our life is lived in Christ and our conduct is controlled by the Holy Spirit.

6 Not as though the word of God hath taken none effect. For they *are* not all Israel, which are of Israel:

7 Neither, because they are the seed of Abraham, *are they* all children: but, In Isaac shall thy seed be called.

8 That is, They which are the children of the flesh, these *are* not the children of God: but the children of the promise are counted for the seed.

9 For this *is* the word of promise, At this time will I come, and Sarah shall have a son.

6 But it is not as though the word of
God had failed. For not all who are descended from Israel belong to Israel, 7 and
not all are children of Abraham because
they are his descendants; but, "Through
Isaac shall your descendants be named."
8 This means that it is not the children of
the flesh who are the children of God, but
the children of the promise are reckoned as
descendants. 9 For this is what the promise
said, "About this time I will return and

B. Jewish Apostasy, Even if Final, Not a Failure of God's Purpose (9:6-13)

The meaning of this passage as a whole and its place in Paul's argument in chs. 9–11 have already been briefly and perhaps sufficiently discussed (see above, p. 536).

6-7. Paul has just suggested that the Jews' rejection of Christ and therefore of their salvation not only is the source of the keenest personal anguish but also poses a most serious theological problem, since it was to the Jews that the promise of the Christ and of salvation was first made and has been frequently renewed. **But,** he now says, whatever happens one must not suppose that **the word of God**—i.e., God's promise to the patriarchs—has **failed.** For a promise made to Israel does not necessarily mean a promise made to all Jews. The history of the nation demonstrates this. Although the covenant was made with Abraham and his offspring (Gen. 12:7), it soon became apparent that only some of his descendants were involved, viz., the sons of Isaac (Gen. 21:12-14).

8-9. This means, Paul explains, that it is not the natural children, simply as such, who are **children of God**—i.e., heirs of the promise—but a certain selected number of them. Vs. 8*b* is awkward and seems to be a statement in a circle, but what Paul means to say is clear enough. On vs. 9 see Gen. 18:10, 14. The point is that Isaac was not born in the course of nature, but in fulfillment of a promise of God; and thus it happened that only Isaac's descendants (not Ishmael's) were children of the promise.

6-29. ***God's Sovereignty and His Freedom of Choice.***—God is absolutely sovereign, and is free to choose whom he will as the recipients of his favor. It is impossible to exaggerate the importance of the affirmation which is central to this passage. Because we are little concerned with Israel's exclusive claims, we forget that they give Paul an opportunity of stating a principle of crucial significance. There is no limit to the sovereignty of God. He is maker of his world, and master of all that takes place in it. Control has not passed out of his hands, and our failure to understand the development of his plan does not mean that his power has slackened or his purpose faltered. The declaration of God's absolute supremacy is here related to a particular problem—his choice of the recipients of his favor—but the question of Israel's status is clearly subsidiary to the essential fact that God is Lord of all. Paul uses the main point to answer the special question with which he happens to be wrestling; but this should not disguise the fact that the issue is much wider than the occasion which has served to raise it.

An uncompromising statement of God's sovereign power saves us from a danger which constantly besets us. While giving lip service to the idea of God, we actually relegate him to a remote and insignificant place in our minds. We accept any explanation of life and its development which makes it possible for us in effect to ignore God. He is not central in our thought; we acknowledge him only by a courtesy gesture or as a final resource when every alternative has failed. We make him a kind of honorary president of his universe; but as a reality with whom we must reckon, we have little place for him in our minds. We tacitly agree to disregard him. For this practical neglect there is no better corrective than Paul's strong insistence on the absolute sovereignty of God.

10 And not only *this;* but when Rebecca also had conceived by one, *even* by our father Isaac,

11 (For *the children* being not yet born, neither having done any good or evil, that the purpose of God according to election might stand, not of works, but of him that calleth;)

Sarah shall have a son." **10** And not only
so, but also when Rebecca had conceived
children by one man, our forefather Isaac,
11 though they were not yet born and had
done nothing either good or bad, in order
that God's purpose of election might continue, not because of works but because

---

10-13. But not even all of these were children in this sense, for before Rebecca, Isaac's wife, gave birth to her twin sons, God chose Jacob as the one whose descendants should receive the promise (Gen. 25:23). In vs. 13 Paul means to say that **God loved** Jacob and **hated** Esau, not as a consequence of the character of their lives but before their lives began—that the course of their lives and of the fortunes of their posterity was in each case itself the consequence of God's previously conceived attitude of "hatred"

In the present passage he assumes rather than states God's rule over the world of creation. It has a necessary place, however, in his thought. A pious Jew would take for granted the belief that God controls the world he has made. Theoretically, modern Christians would admit it too; but we are constantly tempted to regard natural law not as the method by which God works, but as a practical substitute for God. Inseparable from any effective belief in divine sovereignty is the conviction that we live in a world which God has made and from whose rule he has not abdicated. But the sphere with which Paul is directly concerned is human history; and he claims that here too God reigns unchallenged. This presupposes, of course, his rule in the world of creation; if he has no effective control over the stage, how can he influence the action that takes place upon it? But many people who acknowledge God's power in the world of nature ignore it in the world of men. Yet the biblical writers declare with one voice that history is the area beyond all others in which the religious man can detect the activity of God. There, at all events, his will is effective in such a fashion as to disclose his character.

We can interpret the story of our race in any one of three ways. We can say that history is the product of impersonal process: man's experience is shaped by forces (e.g., of an economic kind, as in Marxism) which inevitably issue in certain results. Or we can say that history is simply the record of events that happened to fall out that way: chance is the only explanation that we have. This has been the working philosophy of historians as far apart as Thucydides and H. A. L. Fisher. Or with all the biblical writers we can say that history reflects the working of a personal will directed toward certain moral ends. It is this view which determines the nature of Paul's approach to the question of Israel. History is the stage on which God has disclosed himself, and he has selected the experience of his chosen people as the particular means through which to declare his purpose.

But at this point the question of freedom inevitably arises. We can see that man's freedom is involved (and to this question we shall return); but we usually forget that God's freedom is involved as well. If his personal will is really an effective force in human experience, it cannot be restricted within the limits which past events provide. Cause will still lead to effect; but not in any exclusive or mechanical way, because personal purpose must be free to initiate new developments. Moreover, it is intolerable that men should think that they can limit God's freedom by the expectations which they themselves have formed. This is a phase of the subject with which Paul is here especially concerned. There is something particularly irreligious in the suggestion that our wishes could circumscribe the liberty of God or that we should try to use our desires in order to dictate his decisions, as Paul's Jewish critics attempted to do, not because they were particularly arrogant or bigoted; they had merely adopted an attitude all too common in every generation.

Once we begin to discuss election, predestination, foreknowledge, and free will, we are in an area where it is easy for man to bewilder himself. In passing, it may be noted that when the problem is posed as an exercise in logic it is far more confusing than it is when set forth in moral terms. This can be amplified at a later stage; for the moment it is necessary to remember that Paul is directly concerned with the practical religious problem created by man's determination to impose his own wishes on God. That happens only when we have forgotten our true status. For Paul the basic fact

12 It was said unto her, The elder shall serve the younger.
13 As it is written, Jacob have I loved, but Esau have I hated.

of his call, 12 she was told, "The elder will
serve the younger." 13 As it is written, "Jacob I loved, but Esau I hated."

or "love." There is no point in trying to soften these terms. They were intended quite literally by Malachi (1:2, 3) and accepted quite literally by Paul. (But it should be remembered that, as will soon appear, Paul is speaking, at least to some degree, hypothetically.) This act of choosing Jacob was thus an act of pure grace and was not conditional upon either the merit of Jacob or the moral failure of Esau. "Now," Paul must imply as a conclusion of this part of his argument, "what is to prevent God's making a further decision as to just who shall belong to the Israel which receives the fulfillment of the promises? Indeed [as he says in 4:16] such recipients of the promises need not be Jews at all." In other words, God's covenant with Israel could not be regarded as having become invalid even if all Jews rejected the gospel and missed the fulfillment of the promise, because "Israel" means not Jews by natural descent, but the elect, of whatever nation (on the significance of Paul's saying **our forefather** see on 4:1-2).

about man is that he is a creature. From this follow three important consequences: (*a*) we are under obligation to recognize God as the creative source of our life; (*b*) we are dependent—not independent—beings, and our true life is lived in grateful acknowledgment of this fact; (*c*) our proper attitude toward God is one in which we learn humbly to co-operate with him instead of attempting to dictate what he shall do.

Paul's discussion of divine sovereignty has been directed against presumption on the part of the creature; but toward the end of the section we have a glimpse of that moral world in which divine freedom and power are related to issues of right and wrong, of obedience and rebellion. This fact will be developed at greater length; here it is enough to notice that disobedience cuts us off from favor, while faith prepares the way for greater and greater blessings.

It is, however, the emergence of the moral aspect which serves to place the whole question of election in its proper setting. That God chooses some—and by consequence does not choose others—was a commonplace of Jewish thought. A great many of the assumptions which gave the Jewish outlook its distinctive slant could be regarded as the direct consequence of a belief in God's selective action. Among all the races of the world he had chosen the children of Abraham to receive his favor and to bear witness to his truth. Given the general biblical approach to human history, it may have been natural to expect that some would prove better qualified than others to receive God's revelation, and would consequently be chosen as the instruments by means of which he would achieve his purposes. This view emerged, but it lent itself to certain distortions; because these appear and reappear in Jewish thought, it was natural that Paul should attempt to correct them. In the first place there was a belief in the inevitable, almost in the mechanical, transmission of divine favor. The inheritance passed from father to son; it was only necessary, therefore, to stand in the right line and one would receive the blessing of God. We know that the attitude was widespread, otherwise it would not have been worth the prophets' while to protest against it. Those who shielded themselves behind the fact that they had "Abraham for their father" believed in the inviolable privileges which were automatically transmitted to all Jews. John the Baptist might counter their claims by pointing out that God could make the stones of the riverbank into children of Abraham if he so desired, but Paul prefers to argue the case by appealing to the very Scriptures from which the Jews professed to draw their assurance of God's special favor. The whole process is selective, not simply the first act. Of Abraham's children he chose Isaac, not Ishmael (vs. 7). In the next generation he did the same thing; he chose Jacob, not Esau (vss. 10-13). At no point does the process become fixed and automatic. Moreover, we lack the capacity to discern the reasons which govern God's choice. The case of Isaac's sons admirably illustrates this fact (vs. 11); we are left with no explanation except the inference that God must have had his own reasons. At this point we cease to deal with ancient history and face a fact of general experience. We look around us and we find that some are more highly gifted than others, and that certain people are born with advantages which their neighbors lack. Why natural endowments

14 What shall we say then? *Is there* unrighteousness with God? God forbid.

15 For he saith to Moses, I will have mercy on whom I will have mercy, and I will have compassion on whom I will have compassion.

16 So then *it is* not of him that willeth, nor of him that runneth, but of God that showeth mercy.

14 What shall we say then? Is there injustice on God's part? By no means! **15** For
he says to Moses, "I will have mercy on
whom I have mercy, and I will have compassion on whom I have compassion." **16** So
it depends not upon man's will or exertion,

C. God's Choice, Even if Arbitrary, Not Unjust (9:14-29)

14-18. "But," says an imaginary opponent, "you are making out God's choice of who comprises the real Israel to be a merely arbitrary choice. Isaac is chosen, not for any merit of his or for any merit of his descendants which God was able to foresee; and Jacob was preferred to Esau in the same arbitrary way." Paul answers: "Well, suppose I am; suppose the choice is purely arbitrary. Even so, God is not unjust. Does he not have the right to have **mercy upon whomever he wills?"** God's mercy, Paul suggests, quoting from Exod. 33:19, would not be *mercy* if it were not in this way arbitrary—i.e.,

---

are distributed as they are, we cannot say. One man has high intelligence, imagination, and executive capacity; another lacks all these things, and the lives of the two are shaped accordingly. One man is born into a home where he is carefully trained and properly educated, and given the advantages which go with a certain kind of background; another is handicapped all his life because he had no part in these things. Or again, the resources of the world are inequitably distributed; the vast majority of the people in India are undernourished, while many in North America are overfed. We do not know why we belong to the one group rather than the other. The religious person can only bow in the presence of a mystery which God has not unveiled.

But it is this fact which makes it possible for Paul to shift in a profoundly significant way the emphasis of the doctrine of election. The Jews not only inferred that favor was transmitted automatically, they had come to regard their inheritance as election to special privilege. Paul shows that their own Scriptures prove that God's choice has always operated freely and is never bound; but he also claims that election is to responsibility, not to privilege. If this is so—and the subsequent course of the argument of chs. 9–11 aims to prove that it is—then the inscrutable character of election becomes a less insistent problem. We cannot fathom the motives and purposes which lie behind God's choice, but we can at least make sure that we use with a high sense of obligation the advantages which we possess. Though we cannot explain, we can be scrupulous in our stewardship.

Paul has proved with patient emphasis that election is not the result of anything we can do to deserve it. It is due solely to the free choice of God—but (and this is the serious aspect of the question) what cannot be won by merit can be forfeited by negligence. Again the Scriptures demonstrate the point. Judgment operates without regard to any plea of special immunity. If election is to responsibility, a disregard of the necessary moral requirements must mean the loss of the treasured inheritance. **Though the number of the sons of Israel be as the sand of the sea, only a remnant of them will be saved; for the Lord will execute his sentence upon the earth with rigor and dispatch** (vss. 27-28). If the Jews have not **fared like Sodom and been made like Gomorrah** (vs. 29) it is only because of the **children** which **the Lord of hosts** has **left.** But the mark of the remnant is its faithfulness to those requirements which other Israelites, trusting in their exclusive privileges, have ignored. Election not only can be forfeited, it has been forfeited; and to Paul the actual position of the Jews was merely a crowning instance of a moral law whose operation the prophets had described.

In the course of the discussion Paul raises the question as to what constitutes a true Israelite. Certain Jews would promptly answer that physical descent was enough: Israelites were the sons of Israel. **But not all who are descended from Israel belong to Israel, and not all are children of Abraham because they are his descendants** (vss. 6-7). We have already noticed that Paul proves his point by appealing to the scriptural record of a process of selection which differentiates between those who

17 For the Scripture saith unto Pharaoh, Even for this same purpose have I raised thee up, that I might show my power in thee, and that my name might be declared throughout all the earth.

18 Therefore hath he mercy on whom he will *have mercy,* and whom he will he hardeneth.

but upon God's mercy. 17 For the scripture
says to Pharaoh, "I have raised you up for
the very purpose of showing my power in
you, so that my name may be proclaimed
in all the earth." 18 So then he has mercy
upon whomever he wills, and he hardens
the heart of whomever he wills.

---

if it were dependent **upon man's will or exertion.** Likewise, Paul does not hesitate to say, referring to Pharaoh and Exod. 9:16, that God **hardens the heart of whomever he wills.** Paul accepts, apparently with no question or scruple, the statement of Exodus that God kept Pharaoh alive only in order that he might compel him to disobey the divine command and thus to incur the divine anger, **so that my name may be proclaimed in all the earth.**

---

as regards descent have equal claims. This did not happen only in the first and second generation; it was a mark of the whole history of Israel. And it leads to the conviction—already noticed in passing—that the true Israel is a small minority. External considerations are never enough to enroll anyone in a spiritual community. A man may belong to the outward but not to the inward Israel; he may be a nominal but not a real Israelite. To Paul this conclusion is simply a reading of what began far back in history, but is a mark at all times of God's dealing with men. To those who have pondered the message of the prophets it may be a commonplace; it is nevertheless a disconcerting fact which we face too seldom. People belong to an institution, yet never understand its essential genius. They share in the organized life but know nothing of the true spirit. Men may accept the responsibilities of religious office, yet lack the qualifications which alone fit them to discharge its duties. It is true, of course, that we cannot command God's spirit at will, nor by merit make sure that he will choose to work through us; we must remember that it is **not because of works but because of his call** (vs. 11) that we belong to the company of the elect. But carelessness can block God's purpose, and the whole tenor of Paul's argument suggests that the complacent can find no place in his plan. Again we are faced with the fact of moral responsibility: what we cannot win by our efforts we can lose by our negligence. If we are unfaithful, God can and will choose other instruments through which to work his will.

> **Those who were not my people**
> **I will call "my people,"**
> **and her who was not beloved**
> **I will call "my beloved"** (vs. 25).

We have already noticed that the assertion of God's supremacy raised the question of man's freedom. The doctrine of predestination has inspired endless debate, and most of it has been unprofitable. It has usually been treated as an abstract philosophical problem; whereupon it creates insoluble difficulties and leads to destructive or blasphemous conclusions. With Paul it was not a philosophical question at all. He was dealing with a religious issue, and his particular point of departure was the omnipotence of God. To suggest that man can determine his own destiny either by merit or demerit seemed to him to call in question God's effective supremacy. As Anderson Scott has pointed out, the Hebrew mind showed little interest in secondary causes. Every event was traced directly to the final cause, God. If something happened, God was responsible. "This took place" and "God did this" were alternative ways of saying the same thing. An excellent example (and again I am indebted to Scott) is supplied by the Exodus account of an incident to which Paul refers in the present chapter (vss. 17-18). The hardening of Pharaoh's heart is described in three ways: "The LORD hardened the heart of Pharaoh" (Exod. 7:13; 9:12); "The heart of Pharaoh was hardened" (Exod. 7:22; 9:7); and "Pharaoh hardened his heart" (Exod. 8:15, 32). The meaning is the same in every case. Moreover, to trace the effect to God as its final cause by no means relieved Pharaoh of responsibility. On this point of human responsibility the views of the Pharisees were clearly defined. The classic expression of their attitude comes to us through Josephus: "All things are governed by Fate, yet they [the Pharisees] do not take away from men the freedom of acting as they think fit. For they think that it has pleased God to mix up the decrees of Fate and man's will so that man can act virtuously or

19 Thou wilt say then unto me, Why doth he yet find fault? For who hath resisted his will?

19 You will say to me then, "Why does he still find fault? For who can resist his

19-21. "But," again interposes the hypothetical objector, "in that case how can you talk of judgment, as you have done often in this epistle? How can God **find fault** if one

viciously."[3] This simply affirms two facts, God's supremacy and man's responsibility, leaving undecided the philosophical question of their relation; and no one who is more concerned to live his faith than to reflect upon it has ever found the two views incompatible. The man of deep religious insight is persuaded that God's supremacy is unchallenged and that his own moral responsibility is unquestioned. That is why Paul is not deeply troubled by the question **Why does he still find fault? For who can resist his will?** (Vs. 19.) The answer to this problem—a very genuine one philosophically—is wholly in terms of religious intuition: **Who are you, a man, to answer back to God?** (Vs. 20.) Paul would not have felt that this was an unworthy or insufficient reply, and in terms of direct religious persuasion it is not—however inadequate it may appear as a philosophical solution. Because he was not aware of shifting the problem from one sphere to another, he felt no incongruity. And it is worth noting that the same is true of the Calvinists, who believed in absolute predestination but spent their lives in an earnest effort to do God's will. The fact remains that in theory the doctrine is beset with unanswerable problems, while in practice the ordinary religious man is persuaded that under God he has genuine freedom to make decisive moral choices. In Paul's case this was the more so because of his characteristic approach to such questions. He always thought of predestination only as a means of explaining some known fact in past or present experience. He never entangled himself amid the theoretical complexities of a theory of predestination. Men and races forfeited God's favor. Others found mercy and the gift of new life. Judgment and mercy were both great realities in Paul's thought because they were both inescapable facts in his experience. If undeserved favor was due to God, the mysteries of retribution must equally be his work. Predestination is the means by which Paul tries to express this conviction; but it is well to remember that he started not from the realm of theory, but from the world of actual religious experience.

19-29. ***The Potter and His Clay.***—In the paragraph which begins with vs. 19, he elaborates his conception of predestination by means of the analogy of the potter. The imagery would be familiar to anyone acquainted with Jewish religious thought and would immediately recall the use which Isaiah and Jeremiah had made of the same figure. With this background constantly in mind, we observe that Paul's treatment of the potter serves to emphasize three important truths.

First, man's creaturely status is the necessary point of departure. Any discussion of profound religious problems is vitiated if it overlooks this simple but far-reaching fact. We have already seen that Paul's strong insistence on the absolute sovereignty of God carries with it, as a necessary consequence, an admission of man's utter dependence on God. From this it follows that at certain points we have no choice but to admit that God's actions cannot be modified by our wishes. They are not even subject to our scrutiny. We can only acknowledge that his power and wisdom demand our acquiescence. **But who are you, a man, to answer back to God? Will what is molded say to its molder, "Why have you made me thus?"** (Vs. 20.) The requirement is stated in its extreme form: when we do not understand the purposes which govern God's plan, we must submit in faith. Because of the nature of our relation to God, we have to trust even when we cannot see. Nevertheless, Paul is not suggesting that blind submission must always be our role. Throughout the present passage he insists not only that God has a plan, but that man can, in part at least, understand what it is. There is some justification even for the most mysterious of dispensations: God's sovereign right to use his instruments for such purposes as seem good to him is in itself a kind of answer to our questionings. But Paul goes a great deal further than this. He begins to put forward, one by one, considerations which lead us far beyond the acquiescence which submits because it has no choice. In due course, before this present section of the epistle (chs. 9–11) is complete, he will claim that what may momentarily perplex us is only a part of God's purpose to bring all men to the knowledge of grace. For the present, however, he insists that we are as clay in the potter's hand; and the clay cannot dictate the uses to which it will be put.

Second, the basic fact which always marks the

[3] Cf. *Jewish War* II. 8. 14; *Antiquities* XIII. 5. 9.

20 Nay but, O man, who art thou that repliest against God? Shall the thing

will?" 20 But, who are you, a man, to an-

is predestined to disobedience by God himself? **Who can resist his will?"** Paul makes the same kind of reply he made to a not dissimilar question in 3:5-6. He does not so much

potter's work is that out of one lump he fashions many vessels. The original material may be the same, but the completed articles are different and serve varied ends. Some are designed for honorable purposes, others merely for menial use; yet the substance out of which they are all made remains one. In the same way, there is one humanity but there are many races. In God's providence some serve one purpose, some another. All are necessary, and each has its appointed place; but there is nothing fixed or unalterable about the disposition which God makes of his resources. If one race fails to meet its responsibility, its service may pass to another people; and this is true even of those who are set apart for a particularly honorable place in God's plan. If the Jews do not rise to the opportunity which is given them, some other people, more faithful in discharging their appointed duties, will become the instrument through which God works—a possibility based on two considerations: (*a*) God's purpose, while unchanging as regards its ends, allows him flexibility and perfect freedom as regards the means by which he will pursue it; (*b*) the fact that the basic material is the same makes the substitution of one race for another relatively simple. In other words, the Jews occupy their special place not because of any inherent virtue, but solely because God selected them from among the peoples of the earth to make them his "chosen vessels."

Third, there are certain inalienable rights which the potter possesses. As Jeremiah watched the potter at work, he observed that when the material in the potter's hands proved intractable, "he made it again another vessel, as seemed good to the potter to make it" (Jer. 18:4). What the craftsman can do, God can do also. He can determine the destinies of the nations on moral principles. He so deals with Pharaoh that the divine majesty and power "may be proclaimed in all the earth" (vs. 17; cf. also vs. 22). When men fail to fulfill his purpose, they fall under judgment and become **vessels of wrath.** Having disappointed the maker's expectations, they are put into the discard—vessels **made for destruction** (vs. 22). But the rights of the potter extend farther. He can substitute for the defective vessel one which will be suitable for his purpose. Who can object if God, finding that the race which he first chose has failed him, selects a new people gathered from many races? The striking thing about the process is the inexhaustible patience with which God has endured the disloyalty and disobedience of those who have forfeited their privileges (vs. 22). But even more marvelous is the way in which he has made **known the riches of his glory for the vessels of mercy, . . . even us whom he has called, not from the Jews only but also from the Gentiles** (vss. 23-24). As a consequence, Paul places the Christian church in its proper setting. He relates it both to the eternal purpose of God and to the historical process through which God has worked. The new community has its ancestry in the redemptive activity which the Scriptures describe, and it is possible to appeal to the prophets to prove that what seems a fresh development is actually the working out of an immemorial plan (vss. 25-29). Hosea (as Paul interprets—or rather misinterprets—him) pointed out that a people would be chosen who had no visible part in the heritage; the very ones of whom God could say **You are not my people,** would **be called "sons of the living God"** (vss. 25, 26). In the same way Isaiah expected that **only a remnant of the sons of Israel** (vs. 27) would **be saved,** because of the **rigor and dispatch** with which God's judgment would go abroad in the earth (vs. 28). The new household of faith, therefore, has its roots firmly planted in the history of a redemptive process; and it can cite the words of Scripture to vindicate its claims. At the same time, we can already sense that its favored position has direct reference to a yet wider manifestation of God's mercy. In the later passages of this particular section Paul will demonstrate that Israel's temporary repudiation by God is only the necessary prelude to a much fuller manifestation of his all-inclusive goodness. The particular historical process which Paul has described may seem to reflect the element of inexorable judgment which the story of Israel so fully illustrates; but he speaks of **vessels of mercy** as well as of **vessels of wrath,** and declares that God's purpose is **to make known the riches of his glory.**

19-29. ***Mercy and Judgment.***—One final comment on the chapter is required. In this section we have mercy and judgment brought together in such a way that each illuminates the other and both declare the nature of God's dealing

formed say to him that formed *it,* Why hast thou made me thus?

21 Hath not the potter power over the clay, of the same lump to make one vessel unto honor, and another unto dishonor?

22 *What* if God, willing to show *his* wrath, and to make his power known, endured with much long-suffering the vessels of wrath fitted to destruction:

23 And that he might make known the riches of his glory on the vessels of mercy, which he had afore prepared unto glory,

swer back to God? Will what is molded say to its molder, "Why have you made me thus?" 21 Has the potter no right over the clay, to make out of the same lump one vessel for beauty and another for menial use? 22 What if God, desiring to show his wrath and to make known his power, has endured with much patience the vessels of wrath made for destruction, 23 in order to make known the riches of his glory for the vessels of mercy, which he has pre-

---

answer as deny the propriety of the question—"How can you, a man, presume to question the morality of an action of God?"—and then proceeds to use the analogy of **the potter** and **the clay.** This analogy is familiar in the O.T. (cf. Isa. 64:8; Jer. 18:6; etc.) ; indeed Paul's idea is found entire in Isa. 45:8-10.

22-23. Only a few passages in Paul are more obscure than this one, and no certainty is possible as to how it ought to be translated. It is possible that some early textual corruption is responsible for the obscurity, although there is no MS evidence of this; indeed, the only important difference between MSS involves the presence or absence of **and** (καί) at the beginning of vs. 23. The difficulty more probably springs from an original lack of clarity in Paul's style. Dodd may be right when he remarks: "When Paul, normally a clear thinker, becomes obscure, it usually means that he is embarrassed by the position he has taken up." It is obvious at once that we have here a conditional sentence which is not completed—only the protasis is found. Apparently when he began the sentence, Paul intended to end it with some such apodosis as "What is that to you?" or "What legitimate objection can anyone bring?" or "Who is in position to judge him?" Instead of completing his sentence in that way, however, Paul permits his reference to **vessels of mercy** in vs. 23 to lead him immediately to affirm what he has said in 4:16 and has had in mind throughout this chapter also, viz., that Gentiles as well as Jews are among the number of the elect. Having made this statement, he follows with a scripture proof (vss. 25-26) —and the intended apodosis of his first sentence is forgotten.

But the obscurity of vss. 22-23 remains even after the intended apodosis is supplied. A part of the difficulty consists in a question as to the force of the participle **desiring** (or **willing**) early in vs. 22. Does Paul mean *"because* he desired" or *"although* he desired"? Both Moffatt and Goodspeed, among modern translators, and Sanday and Headlam, Kirk, and Dodd, among commentators, adopt the second of these alternatives. Sanday and Headlam paraphrase vs. 22, when taken in this way: "God, although His righteous anger might naturally lead to His making His power known, has through His kindness delayed and borne with those who had become objects that deserved His wrath." This way of interpreting the passage has the religiously valuable effect of softening the

---

with men. Part of the value of the passage is that it sets these two essential qualities in the midst of a historical process. This is natural in view of Paul's religious background; but it contrasts sharply with our tendency to treat both mercy and judgment as abstractions. In the Scriptures these are qualities which are supremely illustrated by the way in which God has actually dealt with his people. History is their only expositor; the discipline of events teaches us what they mean. The deliverance from Egypt was the supreme example of what the divine mercy can do for a nation, and the psalms repeatedly express what individuals have learned concerning the active benevolence of God. In the same way, the misfortunes which apostasy brought down upon the chosen people taught them that judgment is not an abstract postulate but a stern and inescapable moral reality. This had an important bearing on their understanding of the character of God. Mercy and judgment reflect his nature, not because it is plausible for us to think so, but because his dealings with men permit them to hold no

24 Even us, whom he hath called, not
of the Jews only, but also of the Gentiles?
25 As he saith also in Osee, I will call
them my people, which were not my people;
and her beloved, which was not beloved.
26 And it shall come to pass, *that* in the
place where it was said unto them, Ye *are*
not my people; there shall they be called
the children of the living God.

pared beforehand for glory, 24 even us
whom he has called, not from the Jews only
but also from the Gentiles? 25 As indeed he
says in Ho-se'a,

"Those who were not my people
I will call 'my people,'
and her who was not beloved
I will call 'my beloved.'"

26 "And in the very place where it was said to them, 'You are not my people,'
they will be called 'sons of the living God.'"

---

harsh doctrine Paul has been engaged in stating. The principal difficulty with it, however, is that it does not readily allow for the connection of vs. 22 with vs. 23: according to the proposed paraphrase of vs. 22, God **has endured with much patience the vessels of wrath made for destruction** out of his kindness, although he felt an almost irresistible impulse to destroy them; but according to vs. 23, the motive of God's delay and **patience** was **in order to make known the riches of his glory for the vessels of mercy.** It seems best to take **desiring** to mean "because he desired." When one does this, the whole passage (vss. 22-23) comes exactly into line with vs. 17, and two parallel reasons appear for God's "enduring" for a while **the vessels of wrath:** because he wants **to show his wrath** (vs. 22) and **in order to make known the riches of his glory** (vs. 23). An incidental confirmation of this way of taking the passage lies in the presence of **and** (καί) in the majority of ancient MSS (followed in KJV, but not in RSV). If the principle is applied here of preferring the more difficult reading, this **and** should be kept, since it is easier to understand why the word should have been dropped out in some MSS than added in others. But if kept, it cannot easily be construed except as joining the two "parallel reasons" we have noted. Lietzmann construes Paul's sense: "If God in his patience tolerates the condemned sinners [for a while] in order that he may show on the one hand his wrath, and on the other his kindness—that is his own affair and you have nothing to say against it." This may be harsh doctrine, and Paul is going to show soon that he is by no means content with it; but it seems to be what he is saying just here.

24. The grammatical connections of this verse also are not clear. Literally translated, the opening words are: "Whom he has called, even us, **not from the Jews only but. . . .**" There is no grammatical antecedent of **whom** (οὕς), but that pronoun must refer in idea to the **vessels of mercy** of vs. 23. As was said in comment on that verse, Paul makes explicit here the point which has been implicit in his argument from the beginning: not only do some "who are descended from Israel" not "belong to Israel" (vs. 6, RSV), but also some who are *not* descendants *do* belong (cf. 4:16-17).

25-26. This last point, brought in thus incidentally, is further emphasized by two quotations from Hosea. The first of these is from Hos. 2:23 (25), with the clauses reversed and with the verb "love" replacing "have mercy" (but one important MS of the LXX [B] also reads "love"). In Hosea the passage is applied to Israel herself, whom the

---

alternative view. Consequently, biblical belief never withdraws into the realm of theory: it remains intimately associated with what daily life teaches ordinary people; and since experience compels us to recognize that both mercy and judgment are essential attributes of God, the biblical view of life helps us to keep them properly related one to the other. When unreality creeps into religious thought, one is often separated from the other, and always with disastrous results. Judgment, when divorced from mercy, degenerates into an unlovely harshness, while mercy by itself is easily corrupted into supine complacence. The necessary interrelation between the two is clearly suggested in vss. 22-23. The **vessels of mercy**

27 Esaias also crieth concerning Israel, Though the number of the children of Israel be as the sand of the sea, a remnant shall be saved:

28 For he will finish the work, and cut *it* short in righteousness: because a short work will the Lord make upon the earth.

29 And as Esaias said before, Except the Lord of Sabaoth had left us a seed, we had been as Sodoma, and been made like unto Gomorrah.

30 What shall we say then? That the Gentiles, which followed not after righteousness, have attained to righteousness, even the righteousness which is of faith.

27 And Isaiah cries out concerning Israel: "Though the number of the sons of Israel be as the sand of the sea, only a remnant of them will be saved;
28 for the Lord will execute his sentence upon the earth with rigor and dispatch."
29 And as Isaiah predicted,

"If the Lord of hosts had not left us
children,
we would have fared like Sodom and
been made like Go-mor'rah."

30 What shall we say, then? That Gentiles who did not pursue righteousness have attained it, that is, righteousness through

---

prophet thinks of as having surrendered through her infidelity her claim to be the people or the "beloved" of God. Paul applies this to the Gentiles, as later does I Pet. 2:10. The second quotation, from Hos. 1:10, has the same force and application in the original (as Hos. 2:23) and is adapted by Paul in the same way. For Hosea **in the very place** means Palestine; it is not clear what meaning Paul has in mind. Does he think that Christ's Parousia will take place in Palestine and that all the believers will be gathered there to witness it and to participate in the kingdom which will follow upon it? This is possible; but more probably he quotes these words merely because they are in the O.T. text and without much thought about their meaning in the new context in which he is placing them.

27-29. The final quotations in this section, this time from Isa. 10:22-23 and 1:9, bring the argument back to the point Paul began to make at vs. 6, viz., that it is not necessary to suppose the promise to Israel was ever intended to include all Israelites. Isa. 10:22-23 is difficult in the original, as the English attempts to translate this passage will indicate. The makers of the LXX also were not sure as to how it ought to be rendered into Greek. Paul usually quotes from the LXX and is probably doing so here, somewhat freely, although Lietzmann suggests the possibility of his using here another translation. The RSV represents clearly the meaning Paul undoubtedly found in this passage.

D. God's Choice Not Arbitrary (9:30–10:21)

It soon becomes unmistakable that a major change in point of view has occurred between 9:29 and this new section of Paul's argument. Throughout 9:6-29 Paul has been

---

are the natural counterpart to the **vessels of wrath,** and we can profitably observe the combination of qualities which Paul sets forth. From the judgment which manifests God's power we pass to the patience which is forbearing even in the face of continued disobedience; and from this in turn to **the riches of his glory** displayed in his acts of mercy. But though judgment and mercy belong together and each preserves the other from corruption, they do not occupy a position of strict equality. In a moral world judgment is too vital a factor to be minimized or eliminated; but mercy is a more fundamental attribute of God, and more perfectly discloses the splendor of the divine nature. Indeed, as we read this particular section of Romans (chs. 9–11) it becomes increasingly clear that Paul sees in God's judgment a means by which his mercy will finally triumph. The retribution which follows in the wake of disobedience opens the door by which peoples hitherto remote are brought within the circle of God's purpose; but it also prepares the way for the restitution of those who had forfeited their ancient privileges. Paul is quite clearly persuaded that at the last mercy "will triumph over judgment."

30-33. ***The Way to Righteousness.***—Experience has apparently left us face to face with an inexplicable paradox. That it is baffling at first

assuming the final, all but complete, apostasy of Israel (i.e., the nation) and also the ground of that apostasy in what can be described only as the arbitrary decree of God. But from this point on to the end of ch. 11 that assumption, in this complete, consistent, and rigid form, appears to have been abandoned. In the present section the assumption of arbitrariness is apparently being denied, or at any rate its force is being weakened; and in the final section, ch. 11, the whole original presupposition of final, large-scale apostasy is surrendered. The only way in which the earlier passage (i.e., 9:6-29) can be conceived of as possessing some measure of logical coherence with what follows it is the way suggested on p. 536 above: a large "if" is in Paul's mind, consciously or unconsciously, throughout that passage. He now proceeds to show that he does not think the two

---

sight Paul admits: **What shall we say, then?** It might seem that the **Gentiles who did not pursue righteousness have attained it,** whereas **Israel who pursued . . . righteousness** has missed it altogether. There is, however, an explanation; and it lifts the whole problem out of the realm where it is a source of religious perplexity into a region where it gives moral significance to all our endeavors. The key to this transformation is the word **righteousness.** It is clearly central to this passage, but only because it is central both to Paul's faith and the point at which he took issue most sharply with the Jews. The nature of his controversy with those with whom he shares the heritage of Israel is underlined by the different meanings which "righteousness" can bear. It may stand either for a certain pattern of behavior or for a certain kind of relationship with God. The Jews were apt to use it in the former sense; Paul insists that it must be used in the latter. Righteousness is not the kind of life we succeed in living, but the status which God is able to confer on such as are willing humbly to receive it as his gift. **Righteousness through faith** consequently stands in sharp contrast to **the righteousness which is based on law.**

Because the Jews have misconceived the nature of righteousness, they have pursued it in a way which inevitably involved failure. This failure is the problem with which Paul is wrestling; but he is concerned to show that it is not really the stumbling block which at first sight it seems. If we choose a road which cannot possibly lead us to the desired goal it should not surprise us if we never reach our objective. The Jews have followed a path which can end only in failure and futility. A legalistic religion can never bring men to the experience of salvation. It is here that the real tragedy of the situation becomes clear. Paul never challenges the high seriousness of purpose which inspired the Jews' quest for righteousness. There is no question that they have **pursued the righteousness which is based on law.** But good men often defeat their own purposes and bring about their own undoing. There is a strain in all human endeavor which proves self-defeating. Earnestness carries within itself vices which are the seeds of spiritual death. Earnestness is a virtue; its defect is that we take ourselves too seriously and set too high a value on what we ourselves can do. The Jews were a conspicuous example both of the good qualities and of the disastrous consequences of seriousness; but any group of religious people furnishes innumerable examples. That is why Paul is so sure that the gospel is for the respectable as well as for the disreputable members of society. Its unremitting insistence on the things that only God can do strikes at the characteristic fault of those who rely chiefly upon themselves. Moreover, the tragedy of good people is not to be measured simply in terms of achievement. The extent of their failure is seen in the degree to which zeal crushes out charity, love, forbearance, and tolerance. There is an inevitable sequence in religious self-reliance which leads from trust in our own achievements through pride in our powers to blindness to all other values. We not only fail and lose all pity for those who fail with us; we wantonly persist in our errors and repulse even the divine mercy which would help us. This is an arrogance which puts itself beyond the reach even of God's power. We have here a striking illustration of the fact that what is good can be the enemy of what is better. The Jews had failed to grasp the greater truth because they clung so desperately to the partial one. It was not carelessness, it was the whole approach to religion that had proved to be so disastrous. Israel's tragic failure follows from Israel's mistaken course. The perversity which made the Jews cling to their initial error merely aggravates the situation. The essential element in the whole sequence of futility and disappointment is the fact that their entire religious outlook is based on their choice of works instead of faith as the method by which to win God's favor. Dependence upon God means that we are able to receive what he is willing to give; the attempt to work out our own salvation without reference to him can have only one result: it condemns us to the futility of building upon an illusion.

31 But Israel, which followed after the
law of righteousness, hath not attained to
the law of righteousness.
32 Wherefore? Because *they sought it*
not by faith, but as it were by the works
of the law. For they stumbled at that
stumblingstone;
33 As it is written, Behold, I lay in Sion
a stumblingstone and rock of offense: and
whosoever believeth on him shall not be
ashamed.

faith; 31 but that Israel who pursued the
righteousness which is based on law did not
succeed in fulfilling that law. 32 Why? Because they did not pursue it through faith,
but as if it were based on works. They have
stumbled over the stumbling-stone, 33 as it
is written,

"Behold I am laying in Zion a stone
that will make men stumble,
a rock that will make them fall;
and he who believes in him will not
be put to shame."

---

conditions represented by that "if" are true. He deals with these conditions in reverse order: first, the arbitrariness, then the finality of the apostasy.

30-32. When he alludes to the Gentiles as those **who did not pursue righteousness,** Paul is not meaning to deny what he said in 2:14. There were certainly many Gentiles who were concerned about righteousness, just as there were many Jews who were not concerned. Still, by and large, Jews were more serious about the ethical life, about finding and doing the will of God, than Gentiles. Yet, Paul notes, the situation seems to be that Jews apparently find themselves less ready and able than Gentiles to accept the only **righteousness** that is really available or possible, the **righteousness through faith. Why** should this be true? Paul may not be giving up the view he has been defending, that ultimately the reason is the foreknowledge and decree of God; but he makes that decree seem less arbitrary by giving another reason also: the very devotion of the Jews to the law has proved a handicap—they have sought righteousness **as if it were based on works,** and, as Paul has been at pains to show earlier in this epistle (2:25–3:20), no such righteousness is possible. The **stumbling-stone** is Christ—i.e., they have not been able to accept the new way of justification, the "righteousness of God through faith in Jesus Christ for all who believe" (3:22). They have **stumbled over** (or perhaps better **at**) Christ, being unable to accept what he offered, indeed repudiating and turning from him.

33. We have here a combination of two passages from Isaiah, cited somewhat freely from the LXX (Isa. 28:16; 8:14-15). The same two passages are used in approximately the same way in I Pet. 2:6, 8, but are quoted there more accurately. The word "stone" in each of the Isaiah passages appears to be used by the prophet as a symbol of God's help, which will mean the salvation of those who trust themselves to it, but which, especially according to Isa. 8:14-15, can be neglected only at great peril. For Paul this "stone" is Christ. If one believes in Christ, one will be saved; if one does not believe, one will stumble and fall. The fact that I Pet. 2:6-8 also takes these two passages together

---

31. *Straining Toward the Goal.*—The language which Paul uses in this verse and in the one immediately preceding is taken from the racecourse. When he speaks of "pursuing" and "attaining," he is thinking of the eager effort with which the runner speeds down the track and reaches his appointed goal (for similar echoes cf. I Cor. 9:24; Phil. 3:12-14). The imagery has defects, of course. It is a strange race in which those who have made no effort find themselves at the winning post, while earnest contenders either lose the way or find that the goal keeps receding from them irrespective of how earnestly they try. This is something entirely different from the fascination of

> . . . that untravell'd world whose margin fades
> For ever and for ever when I move.[5]

It is not the exhilaration of a mind which searches but remains unsatisfied. Paul is speaking of the pursuing of a moral objective which for all our effort grows more remote. The vehemence with which he dissociates himself from this self-defeating method of serving God springs from his own bitter discovery that legalism is a road which provides no outlet and never reaches any goal.

32-33. *Failure in Spite of Warning.*—The tragedy of the Jews' failure lies partly in the

[5] Tennyson, "Ulysses."

10 Brethren, my heart's desire and prayer to God for Israel is, that they might be saved.

10 Brethren, my heart's desire and prayer to God for them is that they

(along with Ps. 118:22) and interprets them similarly (see also Matt. 21:42; Luke 2:34; and Barn. 6:2 ff.) suggests that both writers were making use of some common collection of O.T. texts which had proved valuable in the presentation of the Christian message, especially to Hellenistic-Jewish hearers. That such collections, books of so-called "testimonies," were early in existence has been demonstrated by Rendel Harris (*Testimonies* [Cambridge: University Press, 1916-20]).

In view of the amount of quotation from the O.T. found in these three chapters, a few general remarks about Paul's way of using Scripture are called for and can be made as appropriately here as elsewhere (this matter has been touched on also in the Exeg. of 3:10-18 and 4:3-22). It will have appeared that customarily Paul used the LXX, rather than the Hebrew original, and that often he quotes that version very freely—perhaps because he is quoting from memory. It has also been noted that he quotes texts often without any regard for the original context. This is certainly true of many of the passages quoted in chs. 9–11 (e.g., Hos. 2:23 and 1:10, as cited in 9:25-26). Such texts thus quoted—what we call proof texts—clearly had indisputable authority for Paul and he evidently expects them to carry conviction to his opponents. Apparently no empirical datum had so much authority in establishing a fact as some scripture text which could plausibly be interpreted as affirming it. Thus in 10:18 Paul proves that the gospel has been preached to the Jews, not by citing the current facts of the Christian mission, but by citing, incidentally with complete and flagrant disregard of its manifest meaning, Ps. 19:4. And yet for all of this resort to dubious or obviously faulty exegesis in detail, it must be said that Paul does not misrepresent the meaning of the O.T. in the large. He recognized the presence in the Scriptures, in the religious life and tradition of Israel, of elements which truly anticipated Christ and of which the gospel was the fulfillment. This was true as regards justification by faith (see on 4:18-22); likewise, although Paul is mistaken in having Hos. 2:23 and 1:10 refer to God's accepting Gentiles, he is not wrong in seeing that the greater prophets stand for such a conception.

10:1-4. Vs. 1 serves not only to remind Paul's readers of his loyalty to the nation (cf. 9:2-5), but also to lighten somewhat the dark impression of the future of the Jews which ch. 9 alone would leave: apparently there is a possibility (at least) **that they may be saved.** Soon (ch. 11) he is going to affirm that they *shall* be saved, but he is not yet

fact that they have been so adequately warned. This gives to their defection a peculiarly wanton quality. They should have been willing to receive the Messiah, and he would have delivered them from shame. He is the foundation stone of God's kingdom, but he became to them nothing more than an occasion of stumbling. The scriptural imagery which Paul uses evidently had a favorite place in early Christian thought (cf. Exeg.; also Sanday and Headlam, Dodd, etc.). The play on the word **stone** suggests possibilities worth exploring. God offers us his mercy and his truth; in the case of one man they are built into the structure of a divine purpose—as they were intended to be—but to another they are as unregarded as the stones which lie in the roadway. But the man who ignores the stone often does so to his own undoing; the man who pays no attention to the truth will discover that when disregarded it can wreak its own revenge.

10:1-4. *Controversy, but with Charity.*—Paul is in the midst of a very serious charge against his fellow countrymen and their religious leaders. The Jews, he claims, have accused God of failing to fulfill his promise; but they are at fault, not he. They have willfully and wantonly pursued righteousness in their own way rather than in God's, and they have brought upon themselves the results inseparable from such perversity. These are facts which cannot be evaded and should not be ignored; but Paul makes his charge against the Jews without any of the resentment which so easily embitters debate. It is hard to exaggerate either the importance or the difficulty of this achievement. Controversy confronts us with a twofold temptation: we either yield to superiority and become

2 For I bear them record that they have a zeal of God, but not according to knowledge.

may be saved. 2 I bear them witness that they have a zeal for God, but it is not

ready for that assertion. Now his point is that in so far as they have forfeited this original election to salvation, they have done so because of failure to understand and accept the "righteousness through faith" (9:30). They are not without **zeal for God,** but they have missed seeing both that God requires a **righteousness** which they can never attain or achieve by their own effort, and also that God is ready freely to give them this righteousness—simply in response to **faith. Christ,** Paul says, **is the end of the law**—meaning probably that in Christ the law is superseded (cf. 3:21; Gal. 3:25), rather than that the goal of the law is reached, although that too is a perfectly congenial Pauline idea. The primary meaning of "righteousness" in this passage is forensic, as is indicated by the RSV translation of the same word (δικαιοσύνην) in vs. 4 with the phrase **may be justified. Their own** righteousness, if such a thing were possible, would be an acquittal deserved on

contemptuous of our opponents, or we succumb to pique which issues in bitterness. This explains why religious disputes are so perilous for those who embark upon them, and are usually so disastrous in their results. We have implicit in this passage a psychological study which invites fuller development, and which makes plain the lines along which that study should unfold.

Controversy may at times be quite unavoidable; but Paul's words emphasize the alternative approach which preserves it from corruption. It is possible to differ without resentment. His heart yearns for the well-being of his opponents: **my heart's desire and prayer . . . for them is that they may be saved.** This is good will which has passed beyond the vagueness that so often condemns generous feeling to mere impotence. An intense desire issues in prayer to God for the salvation of his kinsmen. In Paul's attitude we consequently have a combination of qualities which are necessary for any profound understanding of man's religious situation. On the one hand we have insight which sees clearly and without illusions; on the other we have charitable understanding which, while discerning the cause of spiritual defeat, expresses itself in passionate prayer for those who fail.

2. ***The Importance of Zeal and Its Limitations.***—In his testimony to the Jews' sincerity Paul is generous enough, and it is important to remember that his tribute is not that of a detached observer. It comes from within, out of the heart of their experience. He knows that they have not failed for lack of earnestness, because he once stood exactly where they stand. **I bear them witness that they have a zeal for God, but it is not enlightened.** Paul grants their good qualities, but their enthusiasm is not regulated by adequate knowledge.

We may notice in passing both the importance of **zeal** and its insufficiency. Where it is lacking, all religious effort grows ineffective and subsides into flabby ineptitude. As a rule, we do not suffer from the effects of excessive enthusiasm. Our danger rather is a tepid Laodiceanism. But we know how easily undirected zeal degenerates into fanaticism. Paul is here concerned with a particular application of this general law. It is good to be full of **zeal for God;** but when we begin to assume that we must do for him, by being zealous for his cause, what only he can do for us, then indeed zeal defeats itself and turns into an irreligious solicitude about him, quite incompatible with humble trust and grateful dependence.

Paul suggests—though he does not here develop—the qualities which we actually need. What is necessary is zeal guided by the true knowledge which is a result of genuine religious insight. We can therefore distinguish three stages.

First, we need spiritual insight—the perception which is able to distinguish between the true and the false. We must be able to see religious values as they really are, without confusing them with specious substitutes. We must recognize what is genuinely important, and avoid confusing it with what is plausible but of secondary significance. Genuine spiritual insight must be distinguished both from a pious sentimentalism which lulls all our higher faculties in an emotional Turkish bath, and from a preoccupation with religious forms and phrases which extends no farther than a professional enthusiasm for externals.

Second, true knowledge is the result of genuine spiritual insight. It consolidates all that comes to us through the flashes of perception which open up the nature of the spiritual world. It is consequently a firm and ordered understanding of the realities of our life. It is the appropriation of all the insights that we

3 For they, being ignorant of God's righteousness, and going about to establish their own righteousness, have not submitted themselves unto the righteousness of God.

4 For Christ *is* the end of the law for righteousness to every one that believeth.

enlightened. 3 For, being ignorant of the
righteousness that comes from God, and
seeking to establish their own, they did not
submit to God's righteousness. 4 For Christ
is the end of the law, that every one who
has faith may be justified.

the basis of merit; **God's righteousness** is an acquittal bestowed by grace in response to faith. But although the primary meaning is forensic, the more spiritual and ethical meaning of "righteousness" discussed in 8:4-14 is not excluded.

have gained, and their use in fashioning an interpretation of life that will be adequate to all our needs.

Third, knowledge of this kind provides the only satisfactory basis for zeal. It gives enthusiasm consistency and saves it from fanaticism. It provides it with a reasonable foundation, a comprehensive outlook, a firm grasp of the relevant facts, and the secret of unflagging endurance.

3. ***Good Ends, but False Means.***—Paul is acutely conscious of the tragedy of the man who seeks good ends but pursues them by false means. The purpose of such a person is above criticism, but he condemns himself to defeat. This points to the real explanation of Israel's failure, and in the present verse the apostle goes to the root of the matter. Righteousness is man's greatest need, and in seeking it he finds that two methods are open to him. The one has been indicated by God, the other is suggested by his own desires. The Jews, **being ignorant of the righteousness that comes from God, and seeking to establish their own,** have refused to receive God's gift on the only terms on which it is really available. Kirk [6] claims that the phrase **being ignorant of** fails to convey the right shade of meaning, and suggests "ignoring" as a better rendering. In that case we have an interesting study of the spiritual consequences of willful blindness. Paul's consistent claim is that the Jews had all the knowledge that was necessary; in the law and the prophets they had had a preparation that should have trained them to recognize what God was doing for them in Christ. The key to the whole situation lies in the phrase **seeking to establish their own** righteousness. They were determined, in Denney's words, to "be good men without becoming God's debtors." This proves that they have refused to admit the essential character of the relationship in which men stand to God. When we ignore fundamental laws of the spiritual world, the inevitable result is a fatal disruption of our whole life. Moreover, this stubborn preference of our own way to God's amounts to a refusal of God's offer of salvation. He can give us his greatest gift only in a way that corresponds to its essential nature. The refusal to perceive what that true nature is consequently involves a refusal to accept the gift itself. The particular case with which Paul is dealing is that of Israel's failure; the gospel challenged their cherished prejudices, and they repudiated it. The historical example illuminates a persistent human problem. Man's pride is always prompting him to substitute for God's method some alternative of his own devising. The results are always the same. History is the impartial expositor of man's willfulness.

[6] *Epistle to Romans, ad loc.*

4. ***The End of the Law.***—Paul's chief concern at the moment is to place in sharp contrast these two ways in which righteousness can be sought. The Jews have trusted in a meticulous observance of the requirements of the law; the gospel points to faith as the only means by which we can find favor with God. Legalism is fundamentally a mistake. Its results should make us surmise as much; but with Christ's coming, all doubt about the matter should disappear. He **is the end of the law**—that particular method of attaining righteousness is seen to be bankrupt. This, of course, is a fact which is apparent only to those who have the discernment to see it. Legalism is a way of serving God so congenial to man's pride that even Christians are continually reverting to it. Anyone who trusts in customs or conventions, in forms or observances, in individual effort or corporate achievement is in all essentials relying on a method whose insufficiencies have been exposed. As soon as a person really sees what Christ was and what he did for us, it is impossible to believe that by observing statutes we can please God. To yield ourselves to the searching holiness and the redeeming love disclosed in Christ is the only way of achieving a proper footing with God, and that is precisely what faith makes possible. The first characteristic of the better method of obtaining righteousness is that it is

5 For Moses describeth the righteousness
which is of the law, That the man which
doeth those things shall live by them.
6 But the righteousness which is of
faith speaketh on this wise, Say not in thine
heart, Who shall ascend into heaven? (that
is, to bring Christ down *from above*:)
7 Or, Who shall descend into the deep?
(that is, to bring up Christ again from the
dead.)

5 Moses writes that the man who practices the righteousness which is based on
the law shall live by it. 6 But the righteousness based on faith says, Do not say in
your heart, "Who will ascend into heaven?"
(that is, to bring Christ down) 7 or "Who
will descend into the abyss?" (that is, to

5-8. The reference in vs. 5 is to Lev. 18:5 (the same passage is cited again in Gal. 3:12), although the passage is not quoted exactly. **Shall live by it** means "shall find life in it" or "shall be justified or saved by it." The emphasis needs to fall upon **practices,** i.e., one who is to be saved by the law must *practice* the **righteousness which is based on the law.** Understood between vss. 5 and 6 is some such clause as "and I have already pointed out how impossibly difficult that practice is" (cf. above on 3:20; 7:7 ff.; etc.). Over against this impossible way of finding life Paul sets the way of faith—**the righteousness based on faith**—as simple and available, open to anyone who will enter it. In thus presenting it he uses a passage from Deut. 30:11-14 in the LXX text. Since that text differs somewhat from the Hebrew—and therefore from English texts based on the Hebrew—it will be appropriate to translate the passage from the LXX: "For this commandment, which I command thee this day, it is not too great nor too far from thee. It is not in heaven, saying, Who shall go up for us to heaven and take it for us? And having heard we shall do it. Nor is it beyond the sea, saying, Who will cross for us beyond the sea and receive it for us? And it shall make it heard by us and we shall do it. But the word is near to thee, in thy mouth and in thy heart and in thy hands to do it." It will be observed that Paul makes use of only parts of this material, and that he makes some changes in what he uses (e.g., for "saying" he substitutes **do not say in your heart;** and **the abyss** replaces "the sea"). What makes the passage most difficult, however, is the fact that Paul applies the phrases he selects from it to Christ (or to the new righteousness apart from the law), whereas originally the passage clearly is about the law itself. **Moses writes** this too (i.e., Deuteronomy as well as Leviticus), and he writes it about the law, but Paul applies it to what is to him the very opposite of the law, viz., **the righteousness based on faith.** (The personalization of this righteousness [it "says"] is rhetorical, not like the personalization of Wisdom in certain Jewish writings, e.g., Prov. 1:20; Wisd. Sol. 7:22 ff.) To be sure, the law is conceived in terms more spiritual and vital—less external

based on faith, and the second is that it is available to all: **every one who has faith may be justified.** We have thus been presented with (*a*) the failure and bankruptcy of legalism; (*b*) the characteristic marks of the gospel alternative, as (i) founded on faith, and (ii) universal in scope. Both these latter subjects will be expanded in succeeding verses.

5-10. ***Availability of the True Way, Difficulty of the False.***—The true nature of the new way is appreciated only when it is contrasted with the old. The method which the Jews have been pursuing is so difficult that it is virtually impossible; the approach which the gospel offers is easy and is open to all. Judaism demanded the precise fulfillment of the whole law; it made the complete life contingent upon obeying every rule and regulation. (Note how often good people treat some particular requirement in precisely the same way.) How different, then, is the kind of offer that righteousness by faith holds forth. No impossible feats are required of us. We do not need to scale the heights; the divine has come down and appeared among us in Christ. Neither do we have to search the depths; Christ has risen, and our preoccupation need not be with the dark strongholds of death. It is not with mysteries that we are concerned. What righteousness by faith declares to men is a message intelligible to all and delivered through familiar words. **But what does it say? The word is near you, on your lips and in your heart.** Certain important inferences regarding evangelical

8 But what saith it? The word is nigh thee, *even* in thy mouth, and in thy heart: that is, the word of faith, which we preach;
9 That if thou shalt confess with thy mouth the Lord Jesus, and shalt believe in thine heart that God hath raised him from the dead, thou shalt be saved.

bring Christ up from the dead). 8 But what does it say? The word is near you, on your lips and in your heart (that is, the word of faith which we preach); 9 because, if you confess with your lips that Jesus is Lord and believe in your heart that God raised him from the dead, you will be

and mechanical—in Deuteronomy than in Leviticus, and, as Dodd points out, Paul may be revealing his feeling for this distinction and his preference for Deuteronomy. Still, it is hard to see why Paul should have chosen for use a passage for whose clear original meaning he must substitute a meaning almost the exact opposite. We have already seen more than once that Paul has no hesitancy in quoting Scripture out of its context, but this is a particularly flagrant case. Kirk suggests: "No doubt the original passage was quoted against him in defence of the *righteousness which is by the law,* and he had to make shift to dispose of it somehow." The "shift" he makes, if that suggestion is true, is to give it an altogether different sense. Of course it is possible, as Sanday and Headlam hold, that Paul is not here meaning to represent his teaching as being *based* on Deut. 30:11-14 or as deriving any authority from that passage. He is familiar with these biblical phrases and finds it congenial to express his thoughts in terms of them. This is barely possible, especially in view of the evidence presented by Sanday and Headlam that some of the phrases had become almost proverbial and were used in many connections.

Whatever we may conclude as to Paul's motives in choosing and using these phrases from Deuteronomy, there can be no doubt of his own meaning. He is emphasizing the availability of the salvation in Christ and the fact that this salvation cannot be and does not need to be achieved by human effort. We do not need to **ascend into heaven** or **descend into the abyss** to find the Messiah—i.e., our justification and salvation. We do not need to go or send for him, either above or below (as though one could!). The words **from the dead** probably mean, however, that Paul is thinking not of the Messiah in general, but of Jesus Christ particularly and concretely—of his coming into the world from heaven (cf. Phil. 2:6-7) and of his resurrection. **The word** (originally the "commandment") now becomes **the word of faith which we preach,** i.e., the gospel.

9-10. That **word** is **on your lips and in your heart** in the sense that you have only **to confess with your lips . . . and believe in your heart . . .** [and] **you will be saved.** The particular form of vs. 10 must be thought of as determined by rhetorical considerations. Paul surely does not mean to separate in this way justification and salvation, making one of them dependent upon "believing" and the other upon "confessing." He does want

truth emerge. (*a*) The substance of the gospel is simple and near at hand. It is not remote from anyone who needs it. (*b*) It can easily be grasped by those who are willing to receive it. It is not the preserve of specialists or learned men. It opens up illimitable possibilities, and even apostles admit that they have not "already attained" (Phil. 3:12); but anyone can make a start. (*c*) Sometimes we do not receive the truth in the measure that God's mercy makes available simply because familiarity has blunted our perceptions. In the present case Paul is not exclusively concerned with the Jews who knew the Scriptures yet failed to profit from that knowledge; the problem is a great deal wider than that, and is one which everyone has to face. (*d*) Since the truth is easily available to all, painful effort on our part is not the primary condition of attaining it. Because of God's mercy and grace, the truth is near at hand. It is open to us if we will only receive it. The word has been proclaimed, and all that we have to do is to receive it.

9. ***Salvation.***—The core of the message—what makes it good news and declares its relevance to our situation—is the assurance of salvation. **You will be saved,** says Paul. We have already noticed more than once the quality of life which the N.T. associates with liberation from the tyranny of sin. When the shackles of moral and spiritual bondage are broken, we enter into the freedom which Christ makes possible for his people. We are emancipated from the evils in whose grip we were helpless

10 For with the heart man believeth unto righteousness; and with the mouth confession is made unto salvation.

saved. 10 For man believes with his heart and so is justified, and he confesses with

---

to emphasize, however, that confessing Christ is as truly indispensable as believing in him. One who believes **that God raised him from the dead** will also confess **that Jesus is Lord.** But what is believed and what is confessed is one thing: to believe and confess the Resurrection is to believe and confess the lordship.

The supreme importance of the resurrection of Christ appears over and over again in this letter (e.g., 1:4; 4:24; 5:10; 5:17; 6:4-5, 9-10; 8:11), but it is more fully discussed elsewhere (see especially Exeg. on I Cor. 15). Acknowledgment of the Resurrection meant more than holding an intellectual belief (perhaps this is suggested here by **in your heart);** it was a sign of sharing in the *life* of the Christian community, for that community was in essence the community of the Spirit, and the Spirit was the risen Christ. "God's raising of Jesus" and "God's sending the Spirit" come very close to being two ways of referring to the same event. Thus for one to deny the Resurrection meant that one had not received the Spirit and was therefore not a member of the redeemed community.

In the same way the confession that **Jesus is Lord** is more than the expression of an intellectual conviction. Thus Paul can say—in I Cor. 12:3—that "no one can say 'Jesus is Lord' except by the Holy Spirit"—the same Holy Spirit whose presence alone, as we have just seen, makes the Resurrection also a real thing. Paul certainly does not mean in this Corinthians passage that the words could not be uttered at all except by the Spirit, but rather that they could not be uttered with any understanding of their meaning or with any power to convey their significance to others. Here, too, in vs. 9, some such qualification of his expressed meaning must be understood. The "confessing" as well as the "believing" must be **in thine heart;** it presupposes actual participation in the community in which Jesus is known as Lord.

(i.e., we are redeemed); we are reconciled to God ("we have the Atonement"); we enter into the experience of abundant life, and discover that in Christ we have the secret of a power which enables us to rise above the trials and temptations which beset us into the victorious peace of spiritual freedom. We are delivered from bondage, from guilt, and from moral impotence.

The new life is the result of a new power. Everyone who has taken seriously the demands of the moral struggle knows the terrible strength of the forces which oppose us; only a spiritual power which is mightier still can break their sway. That power is available in Christ, and Paul shows us why it is that Christ is able to redeem us. He points to his divine nature, and his triumph over death. **Jesus is Lord,** and the Incarnation declares that God has "visited and redeemed his people." Eternal love has become concrete and intelligible; in a life lived among us we see the nature of the transforming goodness with which we have to deal. We no longer place our trust in intuitions and aspirations, because we respond to "the Word made flesh." That **God raised him from the dead** is our warrant for believing that the purpose of love revealed in Christ is strong enough to effect our complete deliverance. Even death, man's final foe, could not hold him in its power, and we gratefully acknowledge in his Resurrection the seal of a divine approval on all he was and did.

Paul also points to the means by which we appropriate the power which assures us of salvation. There are certain conditions which must be fulfilled on our part, and he specifies two. First, he mentions outward confession: **You confess with your lips that Jesus is Lord.** Second, there is inward belief: **You . . . believe in your heart that God raised him from the dead.**

10. ***The Pattern of the New Life.***—The point which Paul has just made is amplified and enforced. The Christian life has a clearly defined beginning, and from its earliest moments corresponds to a certain pattern. At the outset there must be the act of faith which places a man in a new relationship to God. Then there is the outward avowal of this inward conviction. It may be (as Sanday and Headlam imply) that Paul is thinking of the kind of confession involved in baptism, which sets the believer's feet in the path which leads to salvation. In any case, the faith which remains undisclosed is not of the kind which brings any sort of spiritual liberation. A genuine belief cannot be suppressed, and the inward conviction will find

11 For the Scripture saith, Whosoever believeth on him shall not be ashamed.
12 For there is no difference between the Jew and the Greek: for the same Lord over all is rich unto all that call upon him.

his lips and so is saved. 11 The scripture
says, "No one who believes in him will be
put to shame." 12 For there is no distinction
between Jew and Greek; the same Lord
is Lord of all and bestows his riches upon

As early as the Exeg. of 1:4 note was taken of the fact that **Jesus is Lord,** or some closely similar formula, served as the first embodiment of what was regarded as essential Christian belief. The Greek term "lord" (κύριος), as well as its Aramaic equivalents, referred to anyone in authority, from the master of a slave, to the head of a family, to the object of worship in a religious cult—thus we have "our Lord Osiris" or "our Lord Caesar." So common was this religious use of the title in the Hellenistic world in which Paul moved that it has often been argued (e.g., by Wilhelm Bousset, *Kyrios Christos* [Göttingen: Vandenhoeck & Ruprecht, 1926]) that the application of the term to Jesus originated there. The fact, however, that we find in I Cor. 16:22 and also in Did. 10 the transliterated Aramaic term *māránā' thā'* ("Our Lord, come") points clearly to the application of the title to Jesus before the Christian movement emerged from its primitive Palestinian setting. Indeed, it is quite likely that the disciples of Jesus were calling him "Lord" (in the sense of "Master") even during the time of the earthly ministry; the Resurrection would at once have transformed the significance of that title, and later Gentile influence would have affected it in only minor ways.

11-13. The aim here seems to be to deny any supposition that there is one way of salvation for the Jew and another for the Greek. The contention is in a way the obverse side of Paul's contention in 2:1-24. Quotations in vss. 11 and 13 are from Isa. 28:16 and Joel 2:32. Once the divine title "Lord" for Jesus had become established—and we have

outward expression. The two belong together, and are as inseparable as the sides of a coin. **For man believes with his heart and so is justified, and he confesses with his lips and so is saved.**

11-13. ***The Gift Is for All.***—The quotation in vs. 11 serves both to recapitulate what Paul has already said about the righteousness which comes by faith and to introduce the next theme: the proclamation of a universal grace which is inherent in the gospel. The emphasis clearly falls on the words **no one.** Salvation is for all. Once the simple conditions already outlined have been observed, everyone can hope for the great gift from God. The results of that gift can be expressed in many ways, and it is worth remembering that included among the rest is the fact that we will not **be put to shame.** The quotation has the further advantage of reminding us that a belief in the universal scope of salvation must inevitably follow from the conviction that there is one true God. Monotheism requires as its natural consequence the recognition that God's mercy cannot be restricted on national or racial grounds.

12. ***The Irrelevance of Man-Made Distinctions.***—Our central religious beliefs make most of our generally accepted distinctions seem utterly irrelevant. The example which Paul puts forward has the advantage that in the eyes of most of his contemporaries the Jew and the Greek were divided at every significant point. Racially, culturally, and religiously there were distinctions between the two. Moreover, both were proud races, and the differences between them provided pretexts for recrimination. Actually, arrogant trust in their own heritage and contempt for the achievements of others are both beside the point. The reason is twofold. (*a*) It can be stated in general or theoretical terms: **The same Lord is Lord of all.** This provides the theological justification of the conviction that God's love reaches out to encompass all his children. (*b*) It can be stated in practical terms: He **bestows his riches upon all who call upon him.** This is the evidence provided by the devotional experience of mankind. The person who sees that mercy and goodness are not restricted to the bounds of his own conventicle is on the way to the discovery of the universal scope of God's salvation.

The principle which Paul lays down applies anywhere, but it had special relevance to the particular example which he cites. The Jews were loath to admit that as concerns either need or opportunity they stood on the same footing as the Greeks. The characteristic exclusiveness of Israel protested against the suggestion that there was no place of special privilege. To the Jews, therefore, Paul's words

13 For whosoever shall call upon the name of the Lord shall be saved.

14 How then shall they call on him in whom they have not believed? and how shall they believe in him of whom they have not heard? and how shall they hear without a preacher?

15 And how shall they preach, except they be sent? as it is written, How beautiful are the feet of them that preach the gospel of peace, and bring glad tidings of good things!

all who call upon him. 13 For, "every one
who calls upon the name of the Lord will
be saved."
14 But how are men to call upon him in
whom they have not believed? And how are
they to believe in him of whom they have
never heard? And how are they to hear without a preacher? 15 And how can men preach
unless they are sent? As it is written, "How
beautiful are the feet of those who preach

---

seen that this happened soon after the Resurrection—those believers who used the LXX were likely to see in the many appearances of the same term in their Scriptures (where it was employed to translate God's name, Yahweh) anticipatory allusions to Christ. Paul has no hesitancy in interpreting the O.T. term in that way, and does so here. The exalted character of Jesus' present lordship appears in Phil. 2:9-11.

14-21. If the general purpose of this third section of Paul's argument is remembered—viz., to insist that responsibility for the failure of the Jews to receive the gospel lies with the Jews themselves—the intention of these verses becomes fairly clear. Paul has just said that the new righteousness which is by faith is offered to all, Jew and Greek alike (vss. 12-13), and is available to **every one who calls upon the name of the Lord.** The Jews, generally speaking, have not called upon his name (i.e., Christ's name). But why? It is of course because **they have not believed.** But why have they not believed? Is it because

---

are both a warning and a reassurance. There is the danger of ignoring the gospel and putting their trust in their own painful method of gaining righteousness; there is the promised consolation that if they turn from their dependence on the law, they will be released from the intolerable burden it imposes.

13. ***The Way of Deliverance.***—The full scope and inclusiveness of the message are emphasized by another quotation: **Every one who calls upon the name of the Lord will be saved.** In their original context the words referred to the Jewish conviction that when the end of the world came, those who called upon the name of the Lord would find safety in the kingdom of Messiah. To first-century Christians the text invited the kind of use Paul makes of it. Messianic expectations have been fulfilled in Christ, and the salvation which he brings is the true satisfaction of the hopes aroused by prophecy (note the use made of this verse in Peter's sermon on the day of Pentecost, Acts 2:21). In their present setting the words suggest four comments about the salvation which Paul has proclaimed. It is universal in scope, but it becomes practically effective for those who are aware of their need and are shaken out of their complacency; who do something about the plight in which they find themselves, and make the kind of effort without which there is no way of receiving God's gift; who turn to the proper source; and who gratefully receive what comes from it.

14-15. ***To Call and Be Heard.***—Those who wish salvation can have it; all they need to do is to call upon God with sincere and humble expectancy. But the stark simplicity of Paul's statement is deceptive. There are certain conditions which must be fulfilled if a man is to call upon God and be heard. No one can approach God as he should if he lacks the requisite faith. **How are men to call upon him in whom they have not believed?** This response of glad acceptance and willing self-dedication is possible only for those who have the necessary knowledge, and knowledge is possible only if men have the means of knowing—i.e., if they have **heard.** If they are to hear, there must be someone who proclaims the truth—they must have **a preacher.** And if men are to preach, they must be **sent:** in an undertaking of this kind no one commissions himself; he is given his message and his task by God.

The context and the general character of the passage make Paul's immediate purpose clear. He is intent on proving that the Jews have missed their opportunity in spite of the fact that they have had every chance. They cannot plead that they had not heard, because God had sent them his messengers, and the quotation

16 But they have not all obeyed the gospel. For Esaias saith, Lord, who hath believed our report?
17 So then faith *cometh* by hearing, and hearing by the word of God.

good news!" 16 But they have not all heeded
the gospel; for Isaiah says, "Lord, who has
believed what he has heard from us?" 17 So
faith comes from what is heard, and what
is heard comes by the preaching of Christ.

---

they have never heard? And have they failed to hear because perhaps no preacher has been **sent** to them? Paul answers these last questions with a clearly implied negative, and proceeds to prove his point, not by citing the work of recent or current evangelists, but by quoting Isa. 52:7: **How beautiful are the feet of those who preach good news!** No, it is not because they have not **heard,** but because they have not **heeded the gospel;** and this in turn is "proved" by another text, Isa. 53:1: **Who has believed what he has heard from us?** Putting the two texts together, Paul sees that the questions in the elaborate series at the beginning of this paragraph (vss. 14-15*a*) are justified by the scripture he has quoted, if indeed they were not suggested in the first place by this scripture. **So,** he

---

from Isa. 52:7—**How beautiful are the feet of those who preach good news!**—is an attempt conclusively to establish the point. But when we have admitted this, it is permissible to note how clearly the passage sets out the conditions which must be fulfilled if the gospel is to be persuasively presented to a pagan age. Paul has begun with the final result toward which all religious effort is directed: he has described the attitude of humble trust which confidently turns to God to receive the gift of a new kind of life; then step by step he has traced the process back, beyond the man himself, to those who have the message and who experience the constraint which compels them to declare it. As a result, the whole passage steps out of the context of an ancient controversy into the very situation where we find ourselves at present.

16. ***The Penalties Attached to Heedlessness.***—The tragedy of heedlessness has never been played out more poignantly than in the history of Israel. Their failure cannot be blamed on an inflexible providence, nor even on their own ignorance. They had the key to salvation and they had the means of knowing what it was; but they declined to give it the requisite attention: **They have not . . . heeded the gospel.** The quotation from Isaiah effectively emphasizes the feeling of helpless despair awakened by such deliberate neglect. For Paul the words of the prophet may have proved that the message, though proclaimed, had been ignored; but it is impossible to consider the words in this particular context without sensing the pathos of the situation. And that situation is commonly repeated among us. In a "Christian" community unnumbered people grow up with nothing more than a nodding acquaintance with the Christian faith. They know its essential vocabulary only well enough to misunderstand its central affirmations. They have enough familiarity with its teachings to concede them a vague respect, but not enough to permit its truths to modify their lives. The message is available; if they wanted it they could have it, but apparently they do not want it. We are inclined to regard this misfortune exclusively from our own point of view. We are chagrined that others should be so indifferent to matters which we consider of vital importance. We are conscious that our corporate witness is weakened by their failure to participate. Paul suggests that it might be studied with greater profit from another angle. What will happen to a civilization which disregards its essential spiritual heritage? How long can a society remain even nominally Christian if its members are cut off from the true sources of their higher life? And what of the tragedy of the impoverished lives about us? Their nonparticipation may inconvenience us; but if there is any truth at all in what we say, the alarming thing is that so many people are deliberately sacrificing their share in the most important thing in all experience. Perhaps part of the trouble lies in the loss of insistent conviction, which is due to our own failure to grasp the urgency of the truths to which we profess allegiance.

17. ***The Work Which Awakens Faith.***—Throughout the whole epistle Paul's argument has rested on the paramount importance of faith. Without faith there is no justification; without justification there is no chance of an abundant life. Usually he assumes that we are familiar both with the nature of faith and with the means by which it is awakened; here he indicates a little more explicitly the way in which we can expect to achieve it. **Faith,** he tells us, **comes from what is heard.** A certain kind of religious belief may be intuitively grasped, but the distinctive kind of faith which is character-

18 But I say, Have they not heard? Yes verily, their sound went into all the earth, and their words unto the ends of the world.

18 But I ask, have they not heard? Indeed they have; for

"Their voice has gone out to all the earth,
and their words to the ends of the world."

summarizes again, **faith comes from what is heard, and what is heard comes by the preaching of Christ.** This repetition in substance of vs. 14 leads to the repetition in vs. 18 of the question, **Have they not heard?** This time the question is answered with a quotation from Ps. 19:4—the psalmist's lines about the sun and the other heavenly bodies are made to refer to the Christian evangelists of Paul's own day. But perhaps, it might be objected finally, they did not **understand** what they heard (vs. 19). Paul answers this objection with three further quotations: the point of the first two (Deut. 32:21; Isa. 65:1) seems to be that since the Gentiles have been able, without previous acquaintance with the God of Israel, to hear and understand, lack of knowledge can hardly be Israel's excuse. Besides, does not Isaiah (65:2) call the nation **a disobedient and contrary people?** He could not do this if their fault were simply a matter of ignorance or misunderstanding.

istic of Christianity is far too sharply defined to be reached by so vague a method. It is our response to something that has happened in the world of men. It recalls to mind the manner of God's self-disclosure and the importance of history as the sphere in which he has declared his righteousness and revealed his mercy. It is this objective quality which makes the role of the witness so important. Those who have seen and understood the mighty acts of God are charged with the responsibility of telling others: unless they do so, those within their reach may never come to the truth. Christianity can be defended by reason; but reason alone is unable to lead men to it, because our belief is our response to something which gathers up the whole range of our experience. The material on which faith seizes is made available by preaching: for **what is heard comes by the preaching of Christ.** This provides the proper justification of all preaching. Unless it bears certain marks and is directed toward certain ends, it is nothing more than the most arrogant posturing before God and one another. It may seem trite to remark that Christian preaching is **the preaching of Christ;** but the fact needs constant emphasis. What sets preaching apart from all other kinds of speech—from lectures on matters of intellectual interest, from moral exhortation on issues of contemporary concern, from comments on the unfolding pattern of events—is that it proclaims Christ and sets forth his abiding significance. "We preach always him," declared Martin Luther; "this may seem a limited and monotonous subject, likely to be soon exhausted, but we are never at the end of it." The aim of preaching is the awakening of faith. The preacher prostitutes his calling when he is content to arouse the momentary interest of his people, or to amuse them merely when they have no more urgent matters in hand. It is true that unless they pause to listen they will never hear; but the purpose of preaching is so to set forth Christ that he will win men's allegiance, and lead them to that act of self-commitment which is our right response to what we see of God's love in Christ.

18. ***The Majesty of the Evangel.***—As the Exeg. points out, Paul had his own methods of expounding Scripture; and to us they often seem arbitrary and far-fetched. Even if it remains true that while doing violence to the meaning of a particular verse he is faithful to the essential purport of Scripture, it is often impossible for us to use passages from the O.T. as he does. When he applies Ps. 19:4 as a proof that the gospel of Christ has been widely proclaimed, we may protest that this is irresponsible exegesis; but it is still true that he has selected a verse which admirably indicates the grandeur of the outreach of truth. We usually think about God's dealings with us in terms that are far too pedestrian. In the spread of the evangel there is a splendor which is fittingly suggested by the majesty of the stars in their courses.

Sun, moon, and stars convey thy praise
Round the whole earth, and never stand;
So when thy truth began its race,
It touched and glanced on every land.

Nor shall thy spreading gospel rest
Till through the world thy truth has run;
Till Christ has all the nations blessed,
That see the light or feel the sun.[7]

[7] Isaac Watts, "The heavens declare thy glory, Lord."

19 But I say, Did not Israel know? First Moses saith, I will provoke you to jealousy by *them that are* no people, *and* by a foolish nation I will anger you.

20 But Esaias is very bold, and saith, I was found of them that sought me not; I was made manifest unto them that asked not after me.

21 But to Israel he saith, All day long I have stretched forth my hands unto a disobedient and gainsaying people.

19 Again I ask, did Israel not understand? First Moses says,
"I will make you jealous of those who are not a nation;
with a foolish nation I will make you angry."

20 Then Isaiah is so bold as to say,
"I have been found by those who did not seek me;
I have shown myself to those who did not ask for me."

21 But of Israel he says, "All day long I have held out my hands to a disobedient and contrary people."

Such a way of interpreting scripture may be, according to our standards, faulty to the point of being absurd, but it conforms to typical rabbinical exegesis in Paul's time (on the use of scripture in Paul see above, p. 553).

---

19. ***Godly Competition.***—The people who should have given heed, but have failed to do so, obviously create a problem. Are they beyond hope? Can they still be reached? The universal note in Paul's gospel—a note often struck in the course of chs. 9–11—presupposes that they will be brought to a better mind; but how is this to happen? The quotation from Deuteronomy suggests the importance of "godly competition." People may remain blind to the value of what they might possess until they are startled by discovering that others have appropriated what they themselves have hitherto declined. It is an elementary psychological fact that we often want something simply because others have it. We observe this reaction at work in the nursery and try to discipline it. Paul suggests that at much more significant levels it can be laid under contribution for our spiritual advantage. He will develop this subject more fully in 11:11, 14, but certain points are worth stressing. (*a*) Our interrelated state makes it possible for us to learn from one another; if we are properly humble, we can learn directly; if not, God's mercy allows us to learn through emulation. (*b*) This fact has some bearing on our doctrine of providence. We do not understand why gifts are distributed as they are, but the problem is less perplexing if we can believe that treasures are so given that some may contribute of what they have, and others may benefit by what they receive. (*c*) Our own heritage assumes therefore a wider significance. It is ours, but we are custodians. If we can share it with others by direct gift, so much the better; if not, we must appropriate it so fully ourselves, and set it forth so persuasively, that those who observe us will grow eager to receive it. (*d*) The person who fails to set forth his Christianity in some clearly recognizable form is not only impoverishing himself, but is depriving others of what they are entitled to expect from him.

20-21. ***Love So Amazing, So Divine.***—Paul is arguing in favor of a certain interpretation of history, and he is using texts from the O.T. to fortify his case. We may not think in the terms which he happens to employ, but it is impossible to read these verses without an intensified awareness of truths which are not dependent on the kind of exegesis Paul uses. On the one hand, there is the unceasing wonder which the contemplation of God's mercy must awaken in every sensitive mind. Beyond all our deserving he is good to us. Paul's immediate concern is with the failure of Israel to appropriate their heritage, and with their replacement by the Gentiles; but the parallel is close enough to the experience of any religious person for us to enter imaginatively into the apostle's thought. None of us can claim that he really deserves the blessings which life brings him. He may say that everything is governed by chance, and that he is fortunate; or he may claim that everything is ruled by a divine purpose, and that God is merciful. He may be forced to admit that he has been blessed not only beyond his deserving but even beyond his desiring. At all events, if he is in any sense a religious man, wonder will contend with gratitude for supremacy in his mind. On the other hand, there is the indescribable tragedy of those who might receive much, but who exclude themselves from their own heritage. It is not merely their loss which makes their position so poignant. The wanton willfulness with which they turn their backs on so much enrichment would be serious enough;

11 I say then, Hath God cast away his
people? God forbid. For I also am
an Israelite, of the seed of Abraham, *of*
the tribe of Benjamin.
2 God hath not cast away his people
which he foreknew. Wot ye not what the
Scripture saith of Elias? how he maketh
intercession to God against Israel, saying,

11 I ask, then, has God rejected his
people? By no means! I myself am
an Israelite, a descendant of Abraham, a
member of the tribe of Benjamin. 2 God has
not rejected his people whom he foreknew.
Do you not know what the scripture says of
Elijah, how he pleads with God against

E. Jewish Apostasy Not Final (11:1-32)

We have seen that the contention of 9:14-29, viz., that God has the right to be arbitrary in his judgments, is considerably qualified by 9:30–10:21, where Paul seems to be adding, "Yes, but as a matter of fact his judgment in this case is *not* arbitrary." An even more striking shift in point of view seems to be involved in the contrast between the opening section of the whole argument (i.e., 9:6-13) and this, the closing section. The fact of this shift cannot be denied: either one can account for it by saying, with many modern commentators, that Paul, even as he was writing, became convinced of the fallacy (or at least of the inadequacy) of his earlier position and decided to change it, or one can explain it in the way suggested on p. 536, above: viz., ch. 9 (i.e., through vs. 29) is dominated by an "if," or rather by two "ifs," which are, in reverse order, denied by chs. 10 and 11. In ch. 11 this denial applies to what at the beginning of ch. 9 appeared to be the major premise of this whole section.

1. Remnant Now in Church (11:1-6)

11:1-6. Paul begins this chapter, however, by making essentially the same point he made in 9:6-13—one cannot say that God has **rejected his people** so long as there is a remnant in the church. It is not altogther clear in precisely what connection Paul mentions (vs. 1) his own authentic membership in the Jewish nation (cf. Phil. 3:5; II Cor. 11:22). Does he mean to be citing his own case as proof, or at least a reminder, that not all Jews have rejected Christ? If so, the reference to Elijah has special point:

---

but they do this in the face of all God's patient endeavor to bring them to the truth. They have both forfeited the blessing and rebuffed him who offered it to them. They have devised the disaster and not simply been overwhelmed by it. The particular example which Paul uses is now a matter of ancient history; the tragedy is re-enacted whenever people ignore and repudiate their spiritual inheritance.

11:1-36. ***Things Yet to Come.***—The difficulties which belief encounters can be met in various ways. Some can be solved with the help of evidence now available, others only by a surmise prompted by faith. The final answer to the problem with which Paul has been struggling lies in a development which God's mercy will yet bring to pass. To take refuge in future possibilities may seem like an admission of defeat, but the argument which anticipates things yet to come is stronger than at first sight might appear. What we expect is based on what we have already experienced, and the whole position ultimately rests on the self-consistency of God. The difficulty created by the apparent rejection of Israel is overcome when we realize that it is a stage—possibly a necessary one—in the process by which God will finally bring everyone to the knowledge of his grace. Consequently, Paul's answer to what seemed at first sight a serious obstacle to faith is the affirmation of a more comprehensive faith—a faith sufficiently inclusive to take up and assimilate the threat involved in the disappointment of ancient hopes.

1-6. ***Man Forfeits, God Does Not Reject.***—The general tenor of the argument thus far might leave the reader—or the hearer, as the case may be—with a suspicion that God has really rejected Israel and that Paul has proved that he was perfectly right in doing so. But it is one thing to prove that man's expectations cannot bind God, or that the Jews in particular had forfeited any claims they might have had, and quite another to acquiesce in the apparent overthrow of the ancient hopes which the divine promises had aroused. Consequently, the question **Has God rejected his people?** is answered with an emphatic "No!" As Paul suggests (cf.

3 Lord, they have killed thy prophets, and digged down thine altars; and I am left alone, and they seek my life.

4 But what saith the answer of God unto him? I have reserved to myself seven thousand men, who have not bowed the knee to *the image* of Baal.

5 Even so then at this present time also there is a remnant according to the election of grace.

Israel? 3 "Lord, they have killed thy prophets, they have demolished thy altars, and
I alone am left, and they seek my life."
4 But what is God's reply to him? "I have
kept for myself seven thousand men who
have not bowed the knee to Ba'al." 5 So too
at the present time there is a remnant,

---

just as Elijah was one of many, so Paul is not alone. But this would seem to involve too much presumption on the apostle's part to be likely, especially as he is writing to an unknown church. It is more probable that he mentions his own Jewish nationality in order to suggest something like this: "How can anyone think that I could believe that God has **rejected his people**? No Jew could believe such a thing; and I am a Jew." To be sure, Elijah (I Kings 19:9-18) once thought that such a complete failure of God's promise had occurred, but God soon showed him his mistake. And so long as this failure is not complete, it is not failure at all (for reasons given in 9:6-13). The saved **remnant**

Exeg.), no Jew could acquiesce in any other conclusion; how much less can he, who is able to claim a share in the purest strain of Hebrew descent: **I myself am an Israelite, a descendant of Abraham, a member of the tribe of Benjamin.** There is a manifest incompatibility in certain suggestions. It is impossible to be a Jew and yet believe that God has cast off his people. The mark of the true Israelite is his awareness of the call of God. He is satisfied that the promises are not illusory and will not fail. Any other attitude would be a contradiction in terms. The justice of Paul's initial premise is beyond question; and it can be extended to other situations and applied in other ways. To belong to any group which is united by common convictions is to accept certain responsibilities. Actions or attitudes which are in manifest opposition to the tenets of the group are—or should be—sufficient to disqualify from further membership. There are many forms of faithlessness which call in question the reality of a Christian's profession. The alarming thing is that so many people are so little troubled by any sense of the incongruity which is involved.

5-6. *The Redemption of the Many Through the Faithfulness of the Few.*—Paul's claim that God has not cast off his chosen people is buttressed by his appeal to the prophetic concept of the remnant. The specific example he quotes is from the story of Elijah. Dispirited and apparently defeated, this man of God was convinced that he was the sole supporter of a cause now irretrievably overthrown. Actually he was only one among a multitude of faithful souls who still stood firm. Paul might have chosen other illustrations, but the story of Elijah had certain advantages over even the great passages in Isaiah. It is the classic example of the folly of a pessimism which rests on judgments based upon appearances. Even when the outlook might seem to justify an unrelieved despair, there are actually signs, for those who will recognize them, of an unfaltering purpose. Pique and self-importance are factors always prompting us to exaggerate the significance of our own contribution; and a false estimate of what we have done makes us despise the role of others. The claim that God had forsaken the Jews, and had abandoned the plans in which they had a part, involved a distorted view of the importance of one race and a blindness to the contribution which other peoples could bring. Moreover, the illustration made it possible for Paul to indicate the part played by the Christian church as an element of hope in any judgment on the outlook before us. That church, he suggests, might be small; but provided it were faithful to its vocation, it could not be insignificant.

This confidence is founded on the conviction that the redemption of the many will come through the service of the few. The promise had come to the people of Israel, but the whole nation had never risen to the full height of its privilege and responsibility. At every period only a devoted minority had accepted the appointed task and faithfully served God. It was this nucleus which was always the saving element: in spite of the apostasy of the many, the sacrifice of the few had availed to keep alive in the community a devotion to the will of God. It served also to increase and clarify the understanding of what God offered to his people and

6 And if by grace, then *is it* no more of
works: otherwise grace is no more grace.
But if *it be* of works, then is it no more
grace: otherwise work is no more work.
7 What then? Israel hath not obtained
that which he seeketh for; but the election
hath obtained it, and the rest were blinded
8 (According as it is written, God hath
given them the spirit of slumber, eyes that
they should not see, and ears that they
should not hear;) unto this day.

chosen by grace. 6 But if it is by grace, it is
no longer on the basis of works; otherwise
grace would no longer be grace.
7 What then? Israel failed to obtain
what it sought. The elect obtained it, but
the rest were hardened, 8 as it is written,
"God gave them a spirit of stupor,
eyes that should not see and ears that
should not hear,
down to this very day."

---

actually exists, **chosen by grace.** Having thus mentioned **grace,** Paul cannot refrain in vs. 6 from emphasizing again the failure of the law, and of works based on the law, and the autonomy of grace. **No longer** means simply "not"; in so far as there is any temporal significance here, it applies not to the fact itself, but to our thinking about it: "we can **no longer** *think* of membership in the redeemed community as being won by our own **works.**"

2. Apostasy of the Rest of the Jews Providentially Used (11:7-24)

7-10. But what about the great mass of Jews who do not belong to this community? Far from appearing to be of **the elect** these seem to have been **hardened.** Paul does not

---

of what he asked from them in return. In actual experience the process had proved to be one by which the extent of the redemptive element within the nation was steadily circumscribed till in a moment of prophetic inspiration it was delineated in the figure of the suffering Servant, and still further restricted till it found perfect expression in the figure of the Son of man.[8]

But having narrowed to a single personality perfectly obedient to the will of God, the remnant was capable of indefinite expansion in the body—i.e., the church—through which the will of the risen Christ expressed itself. It is with this creative and transforming remnant in mind that Paul writes. Not all Israel has missed the way; some—a few—have seen the truth and accepted their place in a redemptive mission. The necessity of a remnant and the possibilities inherent in their devotion are illustrated by a comment of H. G. Wells:

> I am building my expectation of a new phase in human affairs upon the belief that there is a profoundly serious minority in the mass of our generally indifferent species. I cannot understand the existence of any of the great religions, I cannot explain any fine constructive process in history unless there is such a serious minority amidst our confusions. They are the salt of the earth, these people capable of devotion and of living for remote and mighty ends.[9]

[8] Cf. T. W. Manson, *The Teaching of Jesus* (Cambridge: The University Press, 1931), pp. 227-36.

[9] Quoted in Scott, *Footnotes to St. Paul,* p. 55.

The doctrine of the remnant is so true a reading of the forces at work in human history that it can be held in a general form quite apart from any particular kind of faith; but for the religious man it derives its profound solemnity from the fact that it is a manifestation of the way in which God works. He selects his special instruments from the mass, and he chooses them without regard to their merit. This does not mean that he takes no account of the suitability of those who will bear his name before the nations; but they never earn the right by any previous virtue. They are **chosen by grace.** Paul is merely reaffirming what he has already declared in the most emphatic terms. He pauses to point out, as it were, that his doctrine of God's redemptive activity maintains its consistency at every point. So, to underline his central thesis he adds, **If it is by grace, it is no longer on the basis of works.** This is common sense as well as high theology. If grace could be earned, it **would no longer be grace.** As Augustine expressed it, "If grace were not free ["gratuitous" would preserve the play on words in the Latin] it would not be grace."

7-10. ***Failure: Whence It Comes, What It Means.***—God had chosen Israel—"recognized or marked them out beforehand"—as his special instrument. They were his people, as Paul has just shown, because he had freely chosen them; they had not been chosen, as the Jew was apt to think, because they were his people. But the disobedience of the majority has limited to the

9 And David said, Let their table be made a snare, and a trap, and a stumbling-block, and a recompense unto them:
10 Let their eyes be darkened, that they may not see, and bow down their back alway.

9 And David says,
"Let their feast become a snare and a trap,
a pitfall and a retribution for them;
10 let their eyes be darkened so that they cannot see,
and bend their backs for ever."

---

appeal here to the harsh example of Pharaoh (cf. 9:17-18), but cites Ps. 69:22-23 and a conflation of Isa. 29:10 and Deut. 29:4. The latter (cited in vs. 8) is more appropriate for Paul's purpose than the former (cited in vss. 9-10), and much less distortion of the original sense is involved. Paul's meaning in general is clear: How can men and women fail to accept what is so *obviously* God's gracious act on their behalf unless they have been blinded? The old prophets felt the same kind of question in their day. Paul answers it as they did: God has made men blind so that they **should not see** and deaf so that they **should not hear; their eyes** [are] **darkened so that they cannot see.** Insensitiveness on so wide a scale, and with consequences so catastrophic, to values and truths so manifest, could be explained only as supernaturally induced and as having meaning only in God's inscrutable purpose.

---

faithful remnant the efficacy of this call. **What then of the rest?** They **were hardened,** even as the Scripture said they would be. It is important to note, however, that "they have not failed because they have been hardened, but they have hardened because they have failed." [1] This is the inevitable consequence of the misuse of their privilege. Light becomes darkness for those who abuse it. Consequently, the people who should see find that they are blind, and those who should hear discover that they are deaf. But this is what we should expect; gifts which are given for use are forfeited by neglect. Judgment always follows the misuse of privilege. The apostasy of those who had great opportunities is more tragic in itself and more serious in its consequences than the failure of less favored people.

Repeated refusal becomes a habit, and so failure grows to be the unbroken record of a people's life. Complete spiritual insensibility—**a spirit of stupor**—settles down upon them, and the darkest statements concerning those who merit God's judgments can fittingly be applied to their case. This view of Israel's consistent repudiation of God's will for his people must have been commonly accepted in early Christian circles. We have the same interpretation of Jewish history in Stephen's defense before the Sanhedrin, "Ye stiffnecked and uncircumcised in heart and ears, ye do always resist the Holy Ghost: as your fathers did, so do ye" (Acts 7:51). We read that those who stoned Stephen "laid down their clothes at a young man's feet, whose name was Saul" (Acts 7:58), and it is tempting to surmise that Paul first heard this reading of his nation's history and of its present plight from the lips of the man whom he helped to martyr.

The somber bitterness of the "cursing psalms" (it is Ps. 69:22-23 which Paul quotes here) seems out of place in any interpretation of the gospel of God's mercy. Even when we grant that they are not so much an outburst of personal anger as a condemnation of those who persecute the people of God, their spirit still seems dark and narrow. But at least their use underlines an important truth. There is an inexorable process of judgment which works out its consequences in the spiritual world. Those who ignore the truth lose all power of seeing it, and their blindness is no less terrible because they have brought it on themselves. It is not tolerance but only a flabby spiritual sloth which persuades us that willful wrongdoing does not matter. If righteousness is a reality its demands must be exacting, and those who ignore its requirements cannot expect to evade the consequences of their acts. Retribution is not the final word because transgression is not the final factor; but to believe in the ultimate victory of mercy does not detract from the deep solemnity of judgment. Judgment is inseparable from the rule of law in a moral world; to ignore it is not a proof of our emancipation, but merely an indication that indifference is bordering on folly.

[1] Sanday and Headlam, *Epistle to Romans, ad loc.*

11 I say then, Have they stumbled that
they should fall? God forbid: but *rather*
through their fall salvation *is come* unto
the Gentiles, for to provoke them to jealousy.
12 Now if the fall of them *be* the riches
of the world, and the diminishing of them
the riches of the Gentiles; how much more
their fulness?

11 So I ask, have they stumbled so as to
fall? By no means! But through their trespass salvation has come to the Gentiles,
so as to make Israel jealous. **12** Now if their
trespass means riches for the world,
and if their failure means riches for the
Gentiles, how much more will their full inclusion mean!

---

11. But is this blindness and failure *final* in this case? Have the Jews **stumbled so as to fall** (cf. 9:32-33)? Here is the real turning point in the whole discussion of this problem, for Paul answers this question with a vigorous "No," and goes on to adumbrate in a single sentence (11*b*) the amazing doctrine with which the entire argument is to end: **through their trespass salvation has come to the Gentiles, so as to make Israel jealous.** Three steps are taken in this compact sentence: in the providence of God (*a*) Israel has rejected the gospel, in order that (*b*) this gospel might be brought to and accepted by the Gentiles, in order that (*c*) Israel might be moved by such jealousy at seeing its own possession in the hands of the Gentiles as to accept what it now rejects. One can understand Paul's defending such a thesis only if one recognizes that he begins with certain premises, viz., the fact that Jews have by and large actually rejected the gospel; the conviction that this rejection cannot be final (that "all Israel will be saved"—vs. 26); and the belief that a divine providence overrules the whole development in every part. Step (*a*) is actually a fact; and step (*b*) has a factual basis in the sense that, so far as one can see, it was the Jews' prompt repudiation of the gospel which explained its early availability to the Gentiles and also (again so far as we can see) explained its being permitted to assume the form—i.e., nonnationalistic and nonlegalistic—which made it possible of acceptance by Gentiles. One wonders if Paul also found about him actual signs of the **jealousy** upon which he counts as the providential means of bringing Israel back to Christ and its own true destiny, or whether this is entirely the product of his own attempt at rationalization. Signs of hostility he would undoubtedly have found on every hand; but hostility is not necessarily jealousy.

12, 15. The meaning of vs. 12 and the immediately following verses is clear enough when they are taken separately, but the connection of the verses is difficult and awkward. Vs. 12 needs to be interpreted in the light of vs. 15, which largely repeats it. (Vss. 13-14 are an interruption; see below.) The word **failure** is an acceptable translation of the Greek word (ἥττημα), which also—and, it might be argued, more basically—means

---

11-12. ***Temporary Loss and Final Gain.***—There is no question in Paul's mind that the Jews have **stumbled;** he is not willing to concede that it is to such a degree **as to fall.** The first statement says something about man's sin and its consequences; the second would say something about God's ultimate purpose. As the discussion proceeds, it becomes increasingly clear that Paul is relying on God's power to use even our failures as a means of perfecting his plans. With a slightly different emphasis, he is reaffirming his belief that in all things God can co-operate for good with those who love him. But a purpose of universal mercy cannot achieve its goal at a single step, and Paul suggests the stages by which an ever-extending activity of love will accomplish its ends. The apparent forfeiture by the Jews of their spiritual privileges cannot be final; it has already proved to be a necessary part of a wider plan. **Through their trespass salvation has come to the Gentiles.** The next stage will be the dawning realization by the Jews of what they forfeited by their negligence; they will appreciate what they have lost when they see its value demonstrated in the experience of other races. What they learn to desire, they will begin to seek; and what they seek, they will assuredly find. What seemed their loss may thus conceivably accomplish a far wider measure of good than even consistent loyalty could have achieved. Exactly what it will mean for all concerned is still a matter only of wondering surmise. **If their trespass means riches for the world, and**

13 For I speak to you Gentiles, inasmuch as I am the apostle of the Gentiles, I magnify mine office:

13 Now I am speaking to you Gentiles. Inasmuch then as I am an apostle to the

"defeat" (so RSV renders the term in I Cor. 6:7). In view of Paul's tendency to think of man's situation as being, not only one of **trespass,** but also of slavery to sin, something can well be said for the meaning "defeat" in this passage (so Goodspeed renders it; also Sanday and Headlam; Moffatt prefers "defection"). In vs. 15 this same failure of the Jews is designated **rejection,** i.e., of course, God's **rejection** of them. These three terms, "trespass," "defeat," and "rejection," serve really to indicate the three focuses of Paul's doctrine of sin—a doctrine which cannot be reduced to terms of logical consistency but which could not, as he saw it, be defined more simply without the ignoring of some significant aspect of the empirical reality involved. "Trespass" puts the responsibility on the human being; "defeat," on "sin in the flesh," i.e., on the sinful situation into which one is born and by which one is held captive; "rejection," on God's inscrutable purpose.

Paul's feeling, expressed in vs. 12, that if the failure of Israel has resulted in so much good for the Gentiles, its **full inclusion** will mean **much more,** is expressed with greater clarity and specificity in vs. 15. The **riches for the Gentiles** (vs. 12), which have already accrued, are now defined as **reconciliation** (vs. 15), and the **much more** (vs. 12) is **life from the dead** (vs. 15), i.e., the final salvation. (See on 5:10, where the same two terms, "reconciliation" and "life" appear in somewhat the same relationship to each other.) Paul believes that the final consummation of history and the full inauguration of the age to come waits upon the **acceptance** of the Jews (again, of course, God's acceptance of them).

13-14. These verses, as we have seen, are somewhat parenthetical, and their exact meaning is not clear. Paul seems to be saying in effect to his Gentile readers: "Do not

if their failure means riches for the Gentiles, how much more will their full inclusion mean!

13-15. ***The Salvation of the Gentiles and the Ultimate Redemption of the Jews.***—What Paul has been stating with reference to the Jews has also a direct significance for his work among the Gentiles. He allowed no one to call in question the reality of his apostolate to the non-Jewish world; but his preaching is not consequently without reference to the members of his own race. By the very fact that he is creating a Gentile church he is promoting the cause of a still wider fellowship. His **fellow Jews,** seeing the evidences of a divine power in the Christian community, will desire for themselves the same benefits. Moved by jealousy (see vs. 11; 10:19), some of them will turn and be saved. We may notice, in passing, the persuasive power which Paul expects the Christian church to possess. Its witness to the truth will be so clear, the testimony of its corporate life so unmistakable, that those who are without will steadily be drawn within its borders. This was not a hope unrelated to actual experience. In the book of Acts we have the reaction of a stranger visiting a newly organized church, "Who, when he came, and had seen the grace of God, was glad" (Acts 11:23). It was therefore reasonable for Paul to believe that the constraining goodness of God, working through lives dedicated to his service, would bring increasing numbers to an acceptance of the church's faith. His hope for Israel has not been realized. To an amazing degree the Jews have retained not only their corporate unity and their ancestral faith, but also their opposition to Christianity. We might dismiss our failure to touch the Jews as simply the natural result of their notable tenacity in clinging to established ways; but we have every reason to be disturbed when the church does not **make . . . jealous** even those of the same race and background as ourselves. When people who are outside are neither interested in nor attracted by the life of the Christian community, then it is high time to abandon our complacency and seriously to ask ourselves why we have fallen so far short of apostolic expectations.

The clause **I magnify my ministry** gives terse and arresting expression to a conviction which clearly played a large part in shaping Paul's attitude to his work. It is possible to exalt our calling in more ways than one. It may be done by word of mouth, in setting before others a high doctrine of our task, or in declaring the world's need of a redemptive activity like that

14 If by any means I may provoke to
emulation *them which are* my flesh, and
might save some of them.
15 For if the casting away of them *be*
the reconciling of the world, what *shall*
the receiving *of them be,* but life from the
dead?
16 For if the firstfruit *be* holy, the lump
is also *holy:* and if the root *be* holy, so *are*
the branches.

Gentiles, I magnify my ministry **14** in order
to make my fellow Jews jealous, and thus
save some of them. **15** For if their rejection
means the reconciliation of the world, what
will their acceptance mean but life from
the dead? **16** If the dough offered as first
fruits is holy, so is the whole lump; and if
the root is holy, so are the branches.

---

suppose that I am devoting myself to my ministry as **an apostle to the Gentiles** merely because I am concerned about Gentiles [or better perhaps, "because I am indifferent to the salvation of my own people"]. That is far from being the case. **I magnify my ministry** to the Gentiles because [must he not have meant "partly because"?] I see in it a way of bringing about the final salvation of Jews also, by making them **jealous"** (cf. vs. 11). The little word **then** (οὖν) in vs. 13—which cannot be got rid of, though some MSS lack it—makes this passage more difficult. Without that word one might read more simply: "And I say to you Gentiles: in so far as I am an apostle to the Gentiles, I magnify my ministry in order. . . ." Paul wants to dissociate himself from a type of apostleship to Gentiles which involved contempt toward Jews. We have seen that Paul had been accused perhaps of being such an apostle himself (cf. on 9:1-2). It is possible that Paul knows of Gentile Christians at Rome who take this position (vss. 17-32 might suggest this); but it is more likely that he is thinking of this attitude as he has actually met with it in some Gentile Christians in his own churches.

16. Much could be said for placing the paragraph division before, rather than after, this verse—as in RSV and most modern translations. For the sentence really introduces a

---

on which we are engaged; or again, it may be done by putting forth every effort to make our task successful.[2] But even more important than the method is the actual attitude itself. Too much religious work is vitiated by the apologetic, hangdog spirit which marks it. He is an ineffective ambassador whose manner discloses a suspicion that others will think poorly of him because of his appointed task. To **magnify** his **ministry** is possible only if a man holds firmly to certain convictions which disarm the world's jibe about "the foolishness of preaching" (I Cor. 1:21). He must believe that his task is from God; that it fulfills a divine purpose and advances a redemptive plan. This is the source of his authority and his defense against all doubts as to the significance of what he does. Moreover, he must believe that what he says is of decisive importance to men, that it concerns their widest good, and that it relates to their immediate situation. Both the general welfare of all and the particular benefit of each is affected. The man who is persuaded that he is a messenger of good tidings which embrace both God's eternal, redemptive purpose and man's immediate need can do no other than to magnify his ministry.

In vs. 15, Paul is recapitulating what he has already said in vs. 12; but the form in which he has recast his thought offers an excellent starting place for development. To begin with, there is the striking paradox that the **rejection** of the chosen people **means the reconciliation of the world.** The familiar Pauline conviction reappears that our failures can be used to advance God's will, and consequently what seems to be a disaster for one race becomes the means of fuller life for other people. But in addition to the contrast between rejection and reconciliation, there is the wealth of positive meaning in the latter term: beyond the paradox—by which at present we are still confronted—is the splendor of the prospect that God will finally bring in his full salvation.

This particular passage is indirectly of great assistance to us in understanding other parts of the N.T. The selection of documents which have come down to us from the life of the primitive church is such that the conflict with the Jews, whether outside the church or within it, inevitably looms very large. Sometimes in the

[2] Cf. Sanday and Headlam, *Epistle to Romans, ad loc.*

17 And if some of the branches be broken off, and thou, being a wild olive tree, wert graffed in among them, and with them partakest of the root and fatness of the olive tree;

18 Boast not against the branches. But if thou boast, thou bearest not the root, but the root thee.

17 But if some of the branches were broken off, and you, a wild olive shoot, were grafted in their place to share the richness[o] of the olive tree, 18 do not boast over the branches. If you do boast, remember it is not you that support the root,

[o] Other ancient authorities read *rich root*.

new and very important idea. The words **If the dough offered as first fruits is holy, so is the whole lump** is a somewhat awkward translation of the Greek, which rendered literally reads: "If the first fruits (ἀπαρχή) are holy, so also the dough." The original reader was expected to remember Num. 15:19-20 where, in the LXX, reference is made to the "first of the dough" (ἀπαρχὴν φυράματος). Goodspeed translates: "If the first handful of dough is consecrated, the whole mass is. . . ." If this part of the sentence stood alone, one would necessarily be very uncertain of its meaning. Is the "first of the dough" Christ, or is it perhaps the remnant of the saved? As a matter of fact, the context shows that it is neither: **the root** (cf. Jer. 11:16-17) can refer only to the patriarchs in the covenant-making period in the life of the Hebrew nation (cf. 9:5 and 11:28), and this is the idea developed in vss. 17-24; we can hardly interpret the "dough" metaphor, therefore, in any other way. The "first dough," like the "root," is the fathers of Israel, through whom the whole nation is consecrated. Thus it appears that the argument of 9:6-29 was almost entirely hypothetical, since the origins of Israel and God's promises to the fathers are now represented as assuring in fact the eventual salvation of the entire nation.

17. Paul's meaning in the paragraph, vss. 17-24, is clearer than the figure he uses is accurate. At more than one point his ignorance of husbandry is disclosed: branches from a *wild* olive would not be grafted on a cultivated olive stock (if anything, the reverse would be done), and if they were, the grafted branches would not bear the fruit of the cultivated tree. But though his figure is inaccurate—we have seen that Paul's interest in nature is limited; apparently his knowledge of it was no more extensive—nevertheless the views Paul is seeking to illustrate are quite clear: the temporarily discarded branches are, of course, the Jews, and the shoots from the wild olive are the Gentile Christians, who thus **share the richness** [better **rich root**] of the olive tree.

18-22. Paul proceeds to make two points. The first is that since it is **the root that supports** the branches—not the branches, the root—the Gentile Christians have no right

heat of battle Paul says things that sound bitter and vindictive. Here we see for a moment the hopes by which, in the midst of the struggle, he was sustained. Beyond the time when a narrow, arrogant, inflexible Judaism clings to the form of its heritage but forfeits the heart of the matter, he looks forward to the day when an Israel, chastened in mind and humbled in spirit, will turn unto him whom they rejected and in his worship will find their peace.

17-24. ***The Olive: A Study of Pruning and Grafting.***—Though a wild olive shoot would not normally be grafted onto a cultivated olive tree (cf. Exeg.), Paul has found a way—though admittedly an artificial one—of describing the deep debt of men and women who enter into a rich heritage which is not their own. They have not helped to fashion it; hitherto they have contributed nothing to it: but it shares with them its abundant wealth. We have seen how this can happen in the realm of culture. People from a different background discover the resources of another type of civilization, and with delight and gratitude explore its riches. It can happen too in the spiritual realm; those nurtured in another faith can be brought to appreciate and appropriate the blessings God gives us in Christ. Sometimes, indeed, they recognize values to which familiarity or indifference has blinded us; then the phrase **to share the richness of the olive tree** becomes particularly apt. Though Paul probably chose his metaphor without any attempt to suggest subtle overtones of meaning, it is worth noticing that a fruit tree,

19 Thou wilt say then, The branches were broken off, that I might be graffed in.

20 Well; because of unbelief they were broken off, and thou standest by faith. Be not high-minded, but fear:

21 For if God spared not the natural branches, *take heed* lest he also spare not thee.

22 Behold therefore the goodness and severity of God: on them which fell, severity; but toward thee, goodness, if thou continue in *his* goodness: otherwise thou also shalt be cut off.

but the root that supports you. 19 You will
say, "Branches were broken off so that I
might be grafted in." 20 That is true. They
were broken off because of their unbelief,
but you stand fast only through faith. So
do not become proud, but stand in awe.
21 For if God did not spare the natural
branches, neither will he spare you. 22 Note
then the kindness and the severity of God:
severity toward those who have fallen, but
God's kindness to you, provided you continue in his kindness; otherwise you too

---

to despise the Jews, to **boast over the** [discarded] **branches.** It is true that the Jews were **broken off** so that the Gentiles **might be grafted in,** but the Gentiles are warned against taking any credit for this and becoming **proud;** for the Jews were broken off not because they *deserved* less than the Gentiles—as a matter of fact they probably deserved more—but because of their lack of faith; and the Gentiles have been grafted in not because of any merit, but **only through faith.** Vs. 22 contains a warning against overconfidence and carelessness: God's kindness, exemplified in his dealings with the Gentiles, may easily turn to the severity which is manifest thus far in his dealings with the Jews—**you too** may **be cut off. If God did not spare the natural branches, neither will he spare you,** if you renounce the way of faith and begin to rely on your own deserts.

---

drawing wealth from the deep soil and making it available for man's support, is especially appropriate to a religious tradition embedded in the accumulation of past insights and discoveries. Whatever we may think of Paul's effort at a sustained comparison, it is impossible to deny that he has coined a phrase which expresses with unusual felicity the experience of drawing on the resources of a rich tradition which is not our own.

Humility is a virtue necessary in the religious life, but very difficult to cultivate. Pride is the last and strongest citadel of sin. Paul consequently returns again and again to the dangers of spiritual arrogance. The engrafted shoots must **not boast over the branches** (vs. 18). The quaint husbandry of the image at least makes the essential points in the argument clear. The things we value most are not of our own gaining, and to possess them entitles us to no special credit. Those who stand in a certain tradition may feel that they are maintaining its continuity; but the situation is much more accurately described if we admit that the tradition is sustaining them. If the Gentiles have become the heirs of Israel, it is not because they won the right or did anything to deserve the privilege. It is this that makes pride—especially the kind that "boasts over" others—so inappropriate. What we receive is a gift from God; all gifts can be revoked, and those who prove unworthy will certainly forfeit what they now possess. That is the inescapable inference which events force upon us. The Gentiles occupy a favored position because the Jews lost it; the Jews lost it because pride and self-reliance blinded them. Others who allow themselves to fall into the same fault will be overtaken by the same fate. When God has reversed his declared intention once already, may he not do so again if faced with similar provocation? Religious privileges, therefore, are never the ground for pride. They are to be accepted with gratitude; but they can be safeguarded only by undeviating humility.

22. *Love, Without Weakness.*—**Note then the kindness and the severity of God.** In an arresting sentence Paul provides a perfect antidote to two common misconceptions. History shows how often religious people invest God with a severity which is always severe or with a kindness which is only kind. By combining the two —by giving us a severity which is kind and a kindness which is severe—Paul delivers us from harshness on the one hand and from softness on the other. He reminds us that justice and mercy belong together. The gospel offers forgiveness, but it demands repentance. The fate of **those who have fallen** reflects the inexorable element

23 And they also, if they abide not still
in unbelief, shall be graffed in: for God is
able to graff them in again.
24 For if thou wert cut out of the olive
tree which is wild by nature, and wert
graffed contrary to nature into a good olive
tree; how much more shall these, which
be the natural *branches,* be graffed into
their own olive tree?

will be cut off. 23 And even the others, if
they do not persist in their unbelief, will
be grafted in, for God has the power to
graft them in again. 24 For if you have been
cut from what is by nature a wild olive
tree, and grafted, contrary to nature, into
a cultivated olive tree, how much more
will these natural branches be grafted back
into their own olive tree.

23-24. The second point made in this paragraph is that God **has the power to graft** the broken branches **in again,** and that he will do so **if they** [i.e., the Jews] **do not persist in their unbelief.** Paul strongly suggests that they will not persist. He argues that if God was willing and able to graft in unnatural branches, surely he will not fail to graft in again the branches which truly belong to the tree.

of judgment which cannot be eliminated from the moral life. If those who have had the means of knowing ignore what they have been told and dissipate their opportunity, only a cosmic lawlessness could forestall the inevitable consequence and only a culpably weak indulgence would try to do so. **Severity toward those who have fallen** is consequently an epitome of Paul's whole treatment of Israel and its apostasy. This follows naturally from the fact that the gospel, while it offers much, demands much. It requires that the lower be sacrificed for the higher, what is plausible for what is true, what is momentarily appealing for what is permanently satisfying. It asks that the good be subordinated to the better, and it defines the best in terms of rigorous requirements which will finally yield unparalleled rewards. Without the goodness of God there would be no gospel at all; without the severity of God that gospel would be neither plausible nor persuasive. It is the severity of God, the note of demand, which gives the gospel its challenge. In a day like ours merely to speak of comfort would convince few and win none. If the good news is to be a call to high endeavor, it must be equal to the gravity of our plight and the seriousness of our times. Moreover, even the announcement of God's kindness is edged with a warning of what happens to the careless and unworthy recipients of divine favor. It is a contingent gift that men are offered; you can look for God's mercy **provided you continue in his kindness; otherwise you too will be cut off.** Favors are never unconditional, and a person who has been given much may forfeit all.

23-24. ***Sin, Repentance, Final Hope.***—Those who have gained admission to a state of grace need to be vigilant lest they court ejection. But what of those whom their own folly has driven forth? Is their judgment an irrevocable doom? It depends entirely on the attitude which they adopt. If pride hardens them in their error, they themselves sustain the judgment which was first pronounced. But **if they do not persist in their unbelief,** they **will be grafted in.** Beyond their original failure there is always the possibility of reincorporation in the heritage which they repudiated. This is not simply because they have reconsidered the matter. When any far-reaching spiritual issues are at stake, restitution requires more than a better mind on our part. Forgiveness is something that we can never achieve for ourselves, and without it there is no chance of repossessing the place we have forfeited in God's purpose. But God can do what we cannot; he not only makes forgiveness a reality, but he crowns our repentance with the restitution which he alone can offer. **For God has the power to graft . . . in again** those who for faithlessness have been cut away. This is not only possible; it is altogether right and desirable. It corresponds to what should be, and satisfies our sense of what is appropriate. Here (as the Exeg. points out) Paul's imagery clearly stumbles. One does not as a rule graft wild shoots onto a cultivated tree, nor is one very likely to reintroduce branches which were formerly cut off. Jesus expressed the same truth in a variety of ways, each of them far more felicitous than the metaphor which Paul strains so grievously. When the shepherd recovers his lost sheep, there is joy among all his friends; when the woman finds her lost coin, her neighbors share in her rejoicing; when the wayward son comes home, the father restores him to the place which he had deserted, and the household makes merry at his return. This takes account of the emotional overtones of restitution; it is therefore a more appropriate way of expressing what Paul means when he says that **if you have been cut from what is by nature a wild olive tree, and grafted, contrary to nature, into a**

25 For I would not, brethren, that ye should be ignorant of this mystery, lest ye should be wise in your own conceits, that blindness in part is happened to Israel, until the fulness of the Gentiles be come in.

26 And so all Israel shall be saved: as it is written, There shall come out of Sion the Deliverer, and shall turn away ungodliness from Jacob:

25 Lest you be wise in your own conceits, I want you to understand this mystery, brethren: a hardening has come upon
part of Israel, until the full number of the
Gentiles come in, 26 and so all Israel will
be saved; as it is written,
"The Deliverer will come from Zion,
he will banish ungodliness from Jacob";

3. All Israel Will Be Saved (11:25-32)

25-27. What is thus (i.e., in vss. 23-24) strongly suggested is now explicitly asserted: **all Israel will be saved.** But first Paul repeats his warning to Gentiles against claiming any credit for their salvation, against being **wise in** [their] **own conceits.** The word **mystery** was an important one in the religious vocabulary of the Hellenistic world. Indeed, a great class of religious cults, which enjoyed wide popularity at the time, is known by that word—"mystery cults" (see article "N.T. Times: I. Greco-Roman World," Vol. VII, pp. 88-94). Paul's way of formulating the meaning of the Christian life was undoubtedly affected in some degree by the prevalence of these religions, although this fact appears more clearly in other letters, notably I Corinthians, than in Romans. His use of the word **mystery** here may be an instance of this influence, although we should recognize that the word has a quite distinctive sense in Paul. He uses the term rather frequently (I Cor. 2:7; 4:1; 13:2; 15:51; Col. 1:26; etc.), and always to designate "the

cultivated olive tree, how much more will these natural branches be grafted back into their own olive tree.

25. ***The Ceaseless Conflict with Complacency.*** —**Lest you be wise in your own conceits.** This is a fear which finds recurrent expression in Paul's letters. Men are always in danger of trusting in their own powers. They imagine that in some way or other they are preferred before others because they are essentially superior people. Against the arrogance of our complacency the apostle wages ceaseless warfare. Exceptional privileges—especially in the spiritual world—can be received only as gifts, prompted by God's mercy and finally resting on his eternal purpose. The only true wisdom is consequently to cultivate an attitude of grateful humility. This is our protection against the "vain imaginings" on which human pride so often builds. The surest defense against overweening arrogance is to grasp **this mystery . . . : a hardening has come upon part of Israel, until the full number of the Gentiles come in, and so all Israel will be saved.** Some truths are not reached by argument; they are disclosed to us. They form a special revelation. By revelation, as Dodd reminds us, Paul "means . . . a truth divined by religious intuition in the facts of the Gospel—the life, death, and resurrection of Christ and the emergence of the Church." [3] Behind the whole passage lies a profound insight of the kind that men are not likely to achieve by their unaided understanding. That God has dealt with Israel in judgment in order that he may finally deal with them in mercy would itself be too daring a leap in the dark for man's credulity. But that the whole course of history, with its strange distribution of favors, is all part of a coherent process by which these very alternations of favor will bring all men to an enjoyment of what God has designed—this is the kind of conviction which can be inspired only by some clear declaration of mercy. The exact limits that we should set to Paul's universal grace—whether **all Israel** means every Jew, whether **the full number of the Gentiles** includes all men—are surely less important than the source of Paul's conviction and its general scope. The spirit which breaks down every barrier and admits all alike to the fellowship of God's family is a spirit which only God's revelation in Christ can inspire. And unless our faith leads to this kind of comprehensive good will, it is manifestly failing to rise to its full measure. The detailed implications of such a conviction need not be pressed too far—indeed, since Paul is stating an expectation based on faith, it cannot be pressed too far: "the evidence of things not seen" may not be scrutinized minutely. But the essential point is clear. Belief in Christ leads inevitably to the conviction that God's goodness does not stop at any barriers we erect.

[3] *Epistle of Paul to Romans, ad loc.*

27 For this *is* my covenant unto them, when I shall take away their sins.
28 As concerning the gospel, *they are* enemies for your sakes: but as touching the election, *they are* beloved for the fathers' sakes.

27 "and this will be my covenant with
them
when I take away their sins."
28 As regards the gospel they are enemies of God, for your sake; but as regards election they are beloved for the sake of

secret knowledge of some decree of God hidden from men generally" (Lietzmann). In this passage the "decree" was that **a hardening** should **come upon part of Israel** [or perhaps "a partial hardening should come upon Israel"] **until the full number of the Gentiles come in.** Does **full number** (πλήρωμα) mean all the Gentiles or all those Gentiles whom God has foreknown and has predestined to salvation? The answer one gives here will depend upon how unqualified one understands the universalism of this passage as a whole to be. If Paul means, strictly and fully, **all Israel will be saved**—i.e., every Israelite—presumably he is thinking of the Gentiles in the same inclusive terms. (On this point more will be said below on vs. 32.)

The assurance of Israel's eventual salvation is now justified and supported by two quotations from Isaiah (Isa. 59:20-21 is cited in vss. 26-27*a*; Isa. 27:9, in vs. 27*b*). Is this particular combination of passages from some early book of "testimonies" (see above, on 9:33)? One cannot be sure. The passages are quoted accurately from the LXX, except that instead of "from Zion" that version reads "on account of Zion"; also, "his sins" (in the LXX) have become "their sins." Lietzmann quotes the Babylonian Talmud (Sanh. 98*a*) to show that Isa. 59:19-20 was read as a prophecy of the new age: "R. Jochanan [*ca.* A.D. 250] said: When thou shalt see the time in which many troubles shall come like a river upon Israel, then expect the Messiah himself, as it is said, 'For it comes like a river . . .' and then follows, 'And there comes for Zion a Savior.' " It hardly needs to be pointed out again that this is precisely the kind of passage which Paul in 9:6 ff. was insisting did not need to be taken in this inclusive sense at all—i.e., to mean that *all* Israel would be saved.

28-31. Here is another of those sentences whose meaning as a whole is clear enough, but which is hard to interpret in detail. This is true because the several elements in the two clauses *appear* to be parallel, but, except for **enemies** and **beloved,** prove on examination not to be really parallel at all. Thus, **as regards the gospel** means "as regards the way they have responded to the gospel," but **as regards election** means "because they belong to an elect people"; **for your sake** means "with a view to your gain" (cf. vs. 11),

Two important inferences follow from this central conviction. The one declares our intimate interdependence as far as receiving mercy is concerned. "Just as you were once disobedient to God but now have received mercy because of their disobedience, so they have now been disobedient" (vss. 30-31). In neither case does mercy reach men except because of other people. If it does not come through the positive effort of our fellows, it can come negatively as a result of their failures. But it is always mediated; we are so bound together in the bundle of life that at every point and in every way we influence one another. This says much regarding both our own responsibility and the ways in which we receive the good gifts of life.

The second inference concerns the meaning of life's disciplines. "For God," says Paul, "has consigned all men to disobedience that he may have mercy upon all" (vs. 32). In the early chapters of the epistle we saw the nature and extent of human failure. Both Jew and Gentile have missed life's opportunities and perverted its gifts. "All have sinned and come short of the glory of God" is the only epitome of human life that the careful student can offer. The cumulative results of human failure seem so disastrous that at times it is difficult for hope to find any grounds on which to rest. Paul, however, builds his confidence on precisely those facts which threaten to destroy it. He presupposes God's purpose of redemption, and his power to turn evil to good ends; he assumes our involvement one with another and the way in which we affect each other for good and evil. If any group had escaped the common lot and retained its record unsoiled by sin and failure, then its distinctively meritorious position might make it

29 For the gifts and calling of God *are*
without repentance.
30 For as ye in times past have not believed God, yet have now obtained mercy
through their unbelief:
31 Even so have these also now not believed, that through your mercy they also
may obtain mercy.
32 For God hath concluded them all in
unbelief, that he might have mercy upon
all.

their forefathers. **29** For the gifts and the
call of God are irrevocable. **30** Just as you
were once disobedient to God but now
have received mercy because of their disobedience, **31** so they have now been disobedient in order that by the mercy shown
to you they also may[p] receive mercy. **32** For
God has consigned all men to disobedience,
that he may have mercy upon all.

[p] Other ancient authorities add *now*.

---

but **for the sake of their forefathers** means "because of the merit [i.e., faith] of their forefathers." Vs. 29 is rendered by Goodspeed: "God does not change his mind about those to whom he gives his blessings or sends his call." **The gifts** (or "blessings") are enumerated in 9:4-5, and **the call** is the election which has been the presupposition of these three chapters. Vss. 30-31 repeat the idea of vs. 11 (see comment above).

32. The conclusion of the whole argument is: **God has consigned all men to disobedience, that he may have mercy upon all.** The first clause is only a terse summary of the content of 1:18–3:20. In that section, it will be recalled, Paul shows that God "gave . . . up to a base mind and to improper conduct" (1:28) not only the idolatrous pagan world, but also the "impenitent" Jew, "for God shows no partiality" (2:11). In somewhat the same way the second clause of this vs. 32 sums up the content of 3:21–8:39, for there Paul is talking about God's **"mercy"** in justification and salvation. But whereas he discussed the **disobedience** and failure of the Jew along with the Gentile in 1:18–3:20, he did not deal in the same specific way with the Jews' *salvation* in 3:21–8:39. That deficiency chs. 9–11 have attempted to supply. In 3:21–8:39 Paul has spoken of God's **mercy** (although the terms used have been "grace" and "love"); the purpose of 9–11 is to say that this mercy is **upon all.** It is interesting to note that—in spite of "the Jew first and also to the Greek" in 1:16—the argument proceeds from Gentile to Jew in both cases. It is the Gentile who *most obviously* stood in need of salvation; and it is to the Gentile that it has *most obviously* come. In both cases Paul warns against regarding the obvious as the real, or the only real; but the warning is differently directed. In 1:18–3:20 he is concerned to make the *Jew* see that he is in as desperate need of Christ as the Gentile; in 9–11 he wants the *Gentile* to see that he is no surer of ultimate salvation than is the Jew.

Does Paul then believe in a final universal salvation? When he says "all" (vss. 26, 32), is he thinking only of the corporate unities of the Greek and the Jew? Is he saying in effect, "Neither the Greek world nor the Jewish world shall be excluded"? Or is he thinking of every individual? It must be answered that if we had only ch. 11 on which to base our answer, we could hardly avoid interpreting Paul as intending to proclaim

---

difficult to bring together all the broken ranks of mankind in one common experience of deliverance. But since we all fall together, it must be that God can and will use even our common plight to achieve his purpose.

29. ***Faith's Foundation: The Final Rationality of the Order God Has Fashioned.***—The whole argument, of course, would be invalidated at a stroke if we challenged one of Paul's essential postulates. He assumes that we live in an ordered world, whose spiritual laws are as dependable as its physical ones. The basis of this dependability he finds in the character of God. The creation takes its character from its creator. This initial conviction affects the discussion at every point, though it is seldom explicitly stated. **The gifts and the call of God are irrevocable,** says Paul; and in these words he restates his belief in the absolute consistency of God. Life may be puzzling, and our spiritual pilgrimage difficult, but they are not complicated by an unpredictable power behind all things. Both faith and the conduct of life rest on the belief that God's purposes do not vary.

33 O the depth of the riches both of the
wisdom and knowledge of God! how unsearchable *are* his judgments, and his ways
past finding out!
34 For who hath known the mind of the
Lord? or who hath been his counselor?
35 Or who hath first given to him, and
it shall be recompensed unto him again?
36 For of him, and through him, and to
him, *are* all things: to whom *be* glory for
ever. Amen.

33 O the depth of the riches and wisdom and knowledge of God! How unsearchable are his judgments and how inscrutable his ways!
34 "For who has known the mind of the
Lord,
or who has been his counselor?"
35 "Or who has given a gift to him
that he might be repaid?"
36 For from him and through him and to
him are all things. To him be glory forever.
Amen.

an unqualified universalism. Such a conception, it may be added, fits well with certain other elements in his theology. We have seen how naturally a doctrine of salvation by pure grace may lead to a doctrine of predestination (see above, p. 526); but a doctrine of predestination (given that God loves all men) leads at least equally naturally to a doctrine of universal salvation. If love has complete control, although it may for some reason (cf. 11:25*b*) delay, it is bound eventually to save. Such is the logic of predestinarianism when it is saturated with the love of God. The obstacle to our believing that Paul means all this—or just this—in ch. 11 is the fact that he shows himself elsewhere so acutely conscious of the reality of sin and judgment. The issue of faith or unbelief seems to matter too much to him for us easily to suppose that he accepted the "logic" of predestinarianism as being completely adequate. Commentators often support the case for Paul's "universalism" by citing his belief that even the hostile spiritual powers will finally be "reconciled," but the evidence for such a belief on his part is to be found almost entirely in Col. 1:16-20 and in Ephesians—both sources of doubtful authenticity. The other Pauline letters would lead us to suppose that Paul expected Christ not to *reconcile* the demonic powers, but to *judge* and *destroy* them (e.g., I Cor. 15:24-26). Certainly many passages suggest that he thought of the same fate as awaiting unbelieving men.

F. Conclusion: Praise of God's Inscrutable Wisdom (11:33-36)

33-36. This great passage should probably be taken as prompted primarily by Paul's recognition that there was no way of making neat sense out of the realities evidenced in the believer's experience of the grace of God in Christ. These realities far outrun

33-36. ***Lost in Wonder, Love, and Praise.***—Paul has struggled manfully with a vast and very difficult subject. Even his boldest supporter would not claim that he has solved every problem or met every objection. Again and again the great issues with which he has been dealing run out into the mysteries before which we can only be silent. We do not know—and yet silence is not quite the right reaction, because we believe that the inscrutable mysteries are taken up into something yet greater and more comprehensive: the eternal purpose of the Most High. As a result, the final verses of this section are more than a conventional ejaculation of praise. Though strictly speaking they do not provide a conclusion for the argument which has gone before, they do set forth again the convictions without which the whole of the preceding discussion would have been impossible. We cannot propound a philosophy of history if history has no meaning. But if we can assume that there is a God, and that absolute power and infinite love are among his attributes, the discussion can proceed. It becomes possible to speak of the purpose which is unfolded by a sequence of events. What is true at the beginning of the argument is true also at its conclusion. If God is wisdom, power, and love, then we can await with hope the outcome of that process in which we are now inextricably involved. We are swept along by the tide of time, but we can believe that we shall finally reach that haven where human hopes will no longer even seem to be belied. We can marvel at **the depth of the riches and wisdom and knowledge of God,** satisfied that though every

12 I beseech you therefore, brethren, by the mercies of God, that ye present your bodies a living sacrifice, holy, ac-

12 I appeal to you therefore, brethren, by the mercies of God, to present

any logic—as indeed reality always does. Paul has done his best—and when he writes these final sentences, he is probably thinking not of 9–11 only, but of the entire argument from 1:16 on—to explain the meaning of the revelation of God in Christ; but he recognizes, doubtless more acutely than any modern critical reader, how full of gaps and of unassimilable, incompatible elements his argument has been. But this is true not because he has not done well what he has tried, but because the thing he has tried can never be done well, although we can never cease trying to do it. **For who has known the mind of the Lord?** (Isa. 40:13; the quotations in vs. 35 from Job 35:7 and 41:11 seem less apt.) God's being is the *ground* of our life. He is the source, the sustainer, and the end of all that exists: **From him and through him and to him are all things.** How can we hope to *comprehend* him who holds us and all things in *his* hand? **O the depth of the riches and wisdom and knowledge of God! . . . To him be glory forever.** The problem is not solved; but the perplexity is overcome in an act of worship (cf. Ps. 73:17).

VI. Ethical Teaching: God's Will Is Love (12:1–15:13)

With 11:36 Paul has brought the theological argument of his letter to an end; he turns now to practical exhortations. Since in Galatians and Colossians, and also, though less markedly, in I and II Thessalonians, doctrinal discussion is followed by ethical teaching, we are justified in regarding such an arrangement, even though I and II Corinthians and Philippians do not conform, as typical for Paul. But nowhere else, not

attribute of the Eternal One runs out beyond the limits of the human mind, yet these things are the sole foundation of any hopeful effort to understand life. We can begin with what we know of God, even though we must admit the partial and fragmentary nature of our farthest knowledge; such an admission will instill that spirit of reverent diffidence which ought to characterize our search.

For who has known the mind of the Lord,
or who has been his counselor?

The petty arrogance which talks as though it had access to the ultimate treasures of wisdom has exposed its own shallow presumption. Yet while humbly admitting the limits of our knowledge, we can return to certain determinative convictions. If it is true that **from him and through him and to him are all things,** we have found the secret of intelligibility in life; then, and only then, can we confidently end with an ascription of praise: **To him be glory forever. Amen.**

12:1-21. ***Unity of Thought and Action.***—The things we believe and the things we do fall apart with perilous ease. Too often doctrine belongs to a theoretical world, remote from life and powerless to affect our daily conduct. Paul knows nothing of any such divorce. It is true, of course, that his letters reveal a twofold division: there is a theological section which leads in due course to the discussion of practical issues, but the distinction is formal rather than real. Belief is sterile if it does not issue in a new quality of life, and the pattern which should mark the Christian's conduct derives from and can be preserved only by the closest association with the fundamentals of his faith. The essential unity of the Christian experience is consequently a central feature of the apostolic witness. Paul's letters are not simply doctrinal dissertations. They contain much doctrine—because doctrine is necessary, and no full Christian life is possible where it is not adequately grasped—but the doctrine is only one aspect of life. Creeds lose all vitality unless they are intimately linked with emotion and will. Similarly, Christian conduct becomes a platitudinous moralism if it is not always related to distinctive convictions and beliefs. The plea for a Christian ethic independent of Christian theology would have been unintelligible to Paul. The results which have always followed any attempt to keep the Christian standard of conduct while discarding its basis in Christian faith show that Paul had correctly grasped the essential relationship between them.

Because the two are inseparably linked, each reacts upon the other. By relating ethics so closely to faith, Paul emphasizes the connection between holiness and morality in a way that

even in Galatians and Colossians, is the transition from doctrine to exhortation so definite and, one might almost say, so abrupt as here.

In general it may be said that the ethical teachings of Paul's letters, like their other contents, are occasioned by what Paul knows of the needs of the several churches he addresses. This is *obviously* true of I Corinthians—since the letter as a whole enables us to see quite clearly the practical situation with which Paul is dealing—and is true of the other letters in so far as we have any means for testing the matter. In the case of Romans this means is almost entirely lacking. It is a fair guess that whereas some of the materials in this hortatory section reflect Paul's knowledge of conditions in the Roman church, most of them do not. Some of the exhortations undoubtedly occur to Paul as he reflects upon the meaning of what he has been saying through the rest of the letters about the Christian life. Some of them are suggested no doubt by certain common needs which he has encountered in his own churches: he assumes that the same occasions for counsel and exhortation exist also at Rome. A more specific suggestion will be made at a later point (see below, pp. 614-15) as to the reason for Paul's choice of topics.

It is impossible to outline this section neatly, logically, and exhaustively. Many proposals have been made, and the one adopted here is probably no better than several others.

A. The Duty of Finding and Doing the Will of God (12:1-2)

12:1. The passage begins without inner connection with what precedes—**therefore** (οὖν) serving only to mark the transition, and not pointing back to any specific basis of the **appeal** in the earlier part of the letter. In so far as there is an inner connection of a definite kind, that connection is with ch. 8, especially vss. 5-13. This fact lends some weight to the suggestion already noted that chs. 9–11 constitute a kind of insert. The use of the term **mercies of God**—rather than "love of God," which is the term used throughout the earlier part of the epistle and especially at the end of ch. 8—seems to some to connect 12:1 clearly with the end of ch. 11, where the "mercy" of God is being described and extolled; but the force of this claim is considerably weakened when it is observed that the Greek terms for "mercy" are quite different at the end of ch. 11 and the beginning of ch. 12. It is more probable that Paul is not consciously connecting his

---

profoundly affects both. Holiness is delivered from the perils both of remoteness and superstition; morality is saved from slipping into a prudential superficiality. It is important to notice that all the profound associations which gather around the concept of holiness are present to reinforce the demands of ethical insight. At this point Paul is conserving and developing the great tradition of the prophets; he is proving himself a true disciple of Jesus Christ.

1. *Paul's Appeal.*—I beseech you therefore, brethren. The note of appeal reflects the constraint which is the invariable mark of the apostolic mission. It is the quality which should distinguish every Christian ministry. We are "pleading with men." We do not offer good advice or prudential counsel. There is an urgency here which cannot be gainsaid. But this sense of constraint is only quickened by an understanding of the unfathomable love and mercy in which the gospel is rooted. "Line upon line, precept upon precept," Paul has been unfolding for his readers the marvels of God's dealing with his children. He has expounded the new relationship into which by faith men may enter with God, and he has boldly declared that in the new life which it makes possible there is nothing that can separate us from the divine love which is revealed in Jesus Christ. Though the word **therefore** merely marks a transition, it seems reasonable to detect "an inner connection of a definite kind" with ch. 8 (cf. Exeg.), and that chapter is itself the epitome and crown of the first part of the epistle. The link is not with particular words or even clauses, but with a certain inclusive view of the birth and growth of the religious life. A certain inner unity therefore unites the section which sets forth the nature and basis of righteousness with that which interprets it in the light of our actual situation and applies it to our pressing problems. It suggests that all subsequent counsel about conduct springs from the previous declaration of doctrine.

Paul states the character and source of his appeal—**by the mercies of God**—and adds the scope within which he can expect it to operate. Not everyone will feel its constraint. To many

ceptable unto God, *which is* your reasonable service.

your bodies as a living sacrifice, holy and acceptable to God, which is your spiritual

exhortation here with anything specific in the preceding discussion, but with all of it in general: "And now," he is saying in effect, "having reminded you of the meaning of God's gracious act in Christ, may I go on to **appeal to you . . . by** [i.e, by pointing to] **the mercies of God."**

The term for **mercies** (οἰκτιρμοί) is found also in Paul at II Cor. 1:3 and Phil. 2:1 (the singular is found in Col. 3:12). The meaning is probably singular even when the form is plural (so Lietzmann, Moffatt, Goodspeed, etc.). Although the word used here for **present** is not found in the LXX in connection with the offering of sacrifice, there is ample evidence in Greek sources (cited by Lietzmann) of its being so used. This fact makes it likely that Paul has this technical meaning in mind here, although such a connection with sacrifice is not indicated on any of the other occasions when he employs the word (see 6:13, 16, 19; I Cor. 8:8; II Cor. 4:14; 11:2; Col. 1:22, 28).

In the Greek the adjectives **living, holy,** and **acceptable** are co-ordinate adjectives, all in the predicate position, so that literally rendered the phrase runs, "your bodies a sacrifice, living, holy, acceptable to God." It is usually supposed that Paul has especially in mind here the idea of our offering our *living* **bodies,** i.e., our *lives,* as a sacrifice, in contrast to the cult sacrifices of slain animals. Kirk: "The essence of sacrifice, even in O.T. times, lay not in the death of the victim, but in the 'offering of the life' to God. With animal sacrifices, this could only be achieved by slaying the beast and presenting its blood. But S. Paul sees that the truest *sacrifice* that man can offer to God is that of *living* according to His will." Such a meaning is undoubtedly present; but the words "life" and "living" have for Paul a special significance derived from the Resurrection,

people, as we see in our own day, the claims of Christian morality will seem impractical and farfetched. But those who do respond to its demands are bound to each other in a relationship so intimate and distinctive that only the word **brethren,** the language of closest kinship, can convey its meaning.

This appeal, resting on **the mercies of God,** on all that he has done for us, ought to awaken an appropriate response: **present your bodies as a living sacrifice.** The only right reaction to such boundless grace is the consecration of ourselves to God's service. We cease to live to ourselves in order that we may live to him. Paul describes the substance of our offering as our **bodies,** but he means much more than our physical organism; for the "members of the body," as Calvin pointed out, "are the instruments by which we execute our purposes." [4] It is as "the organ of all moral activity" that the body can and must be offered to God as a sacrifice. It is the outward concrete expression of what we really are; it represents our aims and purposes made visible and effective in ordinary life.

1. ***Meaning and Results of Sacrifice.***—The form which our self-offering should take is suggested by an appeal to that other kind of sacrifice through which men had for so long outwardly expressed their response to God's demands. At one point after another, the symbolism of sacrifice serves to illustrate Paul's meaning. It was the outward expression of complete self-devotion to God. The worshiper offered a portion of his own life—a living creature, the fruit of his labors, fit for the support of his life—as the expression of his own dedication to God. It was "not in the death of the victim" that the heart of the sacrificial rite was expressed; the central and decisive thing was "the offering of the life" to God (see Exeg.). When the sacrifice took the form of an animal, this could be achieved only through its death; then the blood, the visible sign of life, could be poured forth as the expression of the believer's devotion. But though the essence of sacrifice remains unaltered, its form is changed. The altar of the old dispensation only suggests a parallel; the offering with which Paul is here concerned is the offering of human lives. It is no new thing for him to set in contrast the dead form and the living reality. He has already urged his readers to yield themselves to God "as men who have been brought from death to life" (6:13). The smoking, lifeless offerings of the old regime are set over against the service of living men, possessed of a new dynamic and instinct with a new vitality (hence the importance of the "resurrection" imagery; cf. Exeg.).

[4] *Romans,* p. 452.

and it is not unlikely that this significance is present here also. This is especially true if he is carrying in mind at all the argument of 8:5-13, and particularly vs. 11: "If the Spirit of him who raised Jesus from the dead dwells in you, he who raised Christ Jesus from the dead will give life to your mortal bodies also through his Spirit which dwells in you." It is these bodies, thus made alive, which we are to **present** to God as a sacrifice. What is offered is **holy** because God has in Christ redeemed it, and by his Spirit possessed it.

Your spiritual worship is in apposition not with **sacrifice** only, but with all of the rest of the sentence. The offering of our **bodies**—i.e., ourselves—as a **sacrifice** is the true Christian cult; Moffatt renders this phrase with a separate clause which both sets forth the meaning of **worship** in this passage and also indicates the relationship in which this clause stands to the rest of the sentence: "That is your cult, a spiritual rite." Both pagans and Jews had their sacrificial rites; this, Paul says, is *your* rite: the presenting of **your bodies as a living sacrifice.** This rite is not external or ceremonial, but is *logikē.* This Greek word obviously suggests the English "reasonable" (so KJV) or "rational" (Goodspeed). Lietzmann has shown, however, that the special significance of the word in this connection is revealed in the use made of it in certain pagan mystical circles in Paul's period; e.g., one of these mystics writes: "Thy word (λόγος) through me praises thee; through me receive all things as a λογικὴν θυσίαν (sacrifice) to the word." The adjective has been left untranslated because of the difficulty of conveying in English the manifest connection between it and the noun (λόγος) with which the sentence both begins and ends. Lietzmann himself interprets: "It is clear that this λογικὴ θυσία is the prayer of the divine Logos dwelling in the mystic." This Logos is more than an abstract principle of rationality; he is the very Spirit of God. The term **spiritual** is therefore a better translation than "rational." The meaning may be, "This worship is appropriate to your new spiritual life"; or it may be, "This worship is really God's Spirit offering your worship for you" (cf. 8:26-27).

Certain important consequences inevitably follow. The new life is the life which has been sacrificed—offered to God. We cease to live to or for ourselves; we are under obligation to serve God in all we are and do. The truest sacrifice therefore is to live according to God's will. It might seem—when seen from one point of view—that the new life is lived under rigorous constraint; but Paul is never weary of repeating that the truest freedom is found only in the most unquestioning service of God. We may be under obligation, but this is the secret of liberty. Certainly the kind of sacrifice about which the apostle speaks has nothing in common with that grim asceticism which finds virtue in gloom. The freedom of the dedicated life is the secret of self-fulfillment; barren self-discipline is its denial.

We can claim, then, that the highest privilege of the new life of discipleship is to use all our powers in God's service; yet there are demands which we cannot evade. Under the old dispensation it was decreed that "no maimed and worthless sacrifice" could be offered to God; we must accept a standard equally exacting. Under the Jewish law all ritual requirements had to be fulfilled; under the Christian gospel it is sacrilege complacently to bring to God lives whose stains have not been cleansed by repentance and renewal. How can we come before him who is "of purer eyes than to behold evil" (Hab. 1:13) if "our sins are still fresh upon us"? From what Paul has said it follows that we are the Lord's; on this account we should be holy: to be careless in God's service is more grievous sacrilege than it ever was to offer unclean beasts upon the altar. Moreover, that holiness which is to be the mark of the life devoted to God is not expressed in esoteric ritual observances, but in the disciplines of ordinary experience. Not apart from daily life, but in its midst, we serve God "without fear, in holiness and righteousness before him, all the days of our life" (Luke 1:74-75). This is the true worship of God; it is the "service" appropriate to beings in whom intellectual and moral qualities unite.[5] Good people are always tempted to believe that God is pleased with them if they multiply outward acts of religious observance. To worship God rightly is to dedicate ourselves to him without reserve, in order that the moral quality of our life may correspond to what we see to be his will.

[5] Cf. Denney, *Expositor's Greek Testament,* II, 687.

2 And be not conformed to this world: but be ye transformed by the renewing of your mind, that ye may prove what *is* that good, and acceptable, and perfect will of God.

worship. 2 Do not be conformed to this world[q] but be transformed by the renewal of your mind, that you may prove what is the will of God, what is good and acceptable and perfect.[r]

[q] Greek *age.*
[r] Or *what is the good and acceptable and perfect will of God.*

2. We are not to conform ourselves to this **age** (RSV mg.) but are to **be transformed,** so as to be true members of the coming age. The contrast between this age and the age to come is obviously in Paul's mind when he uses these contrasting verbs. Here is the same point as that made in ch. 6; and reference to Paul's discussion there of the ethical life of the Christian is necessary for the interpretation of the present passage (see above, pp. 471-74). One must not live appropriately to the present age, but must live as though the new age had already come. To do this involves a complete reorientation, which only the Spirit—who represents that new age—can bring about. He does this by "renewing" our **mind**—i.e., by giving a new life and power to our mind (on the meaning of **mind** here see on 7:21-24; cf. also 6:4). Paul has said in 7:25, and its context, that he serves the law of God with his mind or "inmost self," but that this "mind" is too weak to resist the tendencies to sin in his flesh. But, he reminds us here, our minds can be "renewed." Paul makes little use of the word "repentance" in his discussion of the Christian life, but he comes close to using that term here, for "repentance" means change of mind (μετανοία); and as Lietzmann points out, the verb "transform," associated as it is here with "mind," suggests the idea. But the emphasis as always is not upon the human act, but upon the Spirit's gift.

Prove here means "know surely," "have trustworthy knowledge of." One cannot have such knowledge of God's will unless one's **mind** has been renewed and one's life reoriented. The choice as between the RSV text and margin at the end of vs. 2 cannot be made with assurance. One reading defines the *content* of the **will of God;** the other characterizes the will itself. But it is doubtful that Paul would have felt any significant

2. *Conformed or Transformed.*—One of the persistent threats to the dedicated life is the pull of the environment in which it must be lived. All around us men organize their common life in ways which presuppose that God is dead, or at least can be ignored with safety. The very word **conformed** suggests the gradual process by which our alertness to evil is disarmed; by imperceptible stages we drift into acquiescence in the things the world demands. Society as it organizes itself apart from God imposes its own standards, and gradually we come both to judge and to act as it dictates. There is no greater weakness in the Christianity of our day than the fact that so many church members accept without question the dominant intellectual and social atmosphere of the age. The corrosives of secularism have eaten away the imprint of grace. We ought to live in the new age with the power of a risen life; instead we are content to conform to conventions which our society dictates. That fact would be sufficiently melancholy in itself; but the fleeting and transitory nature of **this world** makes it doubly so. We are faced with the danger of being gradually modified into conformity with something which cannot last. In sharp antithesis to the evanescent character of our secular society (cf. I John 2:17) is the abiding stability of the life into which God brings us. But it is his act. We are **transformed,** and the vivid and unmistakable character of the new experience speaks through even the language which the apostle uses. Those intellectual and moral qualities summed up in the word **mind** ("the practical reason, or moral consciousness," as Denney interpreted them[6]) have become paralyzed in men of worldly outlook; the keen decisive power of God's Spirit must come with transforming effect if the proper service of their lives is to be maintained. The result of this transformation is the ability to **prove,** to discern in actual experience, **what is the will of God.** With a new sensitiveness of insight we discover in our actual situation what God would have us do, and in the process we learn more fully the nature of his purpose for us. We realize that it is the sum of all that men have

[6] *Ibid.,* p. 688.

3 For I say, through the grace given unto me, to every man that is among you, not to think *of himself* more highly than he ought to think; but to think soberly,

3 For by the grace given to me I bid every one among you not to think of himself more highly than he ought to think,

difference. On the whole the RSV text is preferable; the terms **good** and **acceptable** can more readily be understood as defining what God's will is than as describing his will—of course his will is "good" and "acceptable"! The final term **perfect**, or "complete," fits either sense.

B. Love Within the Church (12:3-13)

1. Each Must Be Subordinate to the Whole Body (12:3-8)

3. Becoming more specific, Paul speaks first of the problem created by the diversity of what are called in I Corinthians "spiritual gifts," and here simply "gifts." The nature of this problem can best be seen in I Cor. 12:1–14:40. Does Paul have reason to know that the same disorder exists at Rome as at Corinth because persons with certain gifts despised others and sought to monopolize, or at least to dominate, the church's life? It is extremely unlikely that such was the case. All we know of the Roman church would indicate the presence there of a soberer, better ordered Christianity than at Corinth. It is noteworthy that whereas the "gift of tongues" comes in for largest consideration in I Corinthians, that gift is not even mentioned in Romans. (Is it significant that the

understood by the good life. The semitechnical terms which Paul uses cover the perception that whatever the moral principle can postulate, whatever the fitness of things can require, is satisfied in God's will for us.

3-21. ***Finding Our Place and Discharging Our Responsibility in the Christian Community.***—It is a personal obligation to discover and explore the possibilities of the new life, but it is certainly not an individual achievement. Of that preoccupation with the Christian virtuoso so characteristic of some religious movements, Paul shows no trace. There can be no religious peace except in a new relationship to God: similarly, there can be no religious satisfaction except in a new relationship to others. There is deep understanding of the apostolic outlook in the comment made to John Wesley by an unknown person of whom he asked advice: "Sir, you wish to serve God and go to heaven? Remember that you cannot serve Him alone. You must therefore find companions or make them; the Bible knows nothing of solitary religion."[7] Consequently, the new life is immediately related to the community and our responsibilities in it.

3. ***Avoidance of Pride the Essential Preliminary.***—The initial injunction—not this time a personal plea, but a command backed by all the authority of his office—is to avoid the perils of pride. No one in the Christian fellowship is exempt from the duty of cultivating humility. There is no greater threat to a true understanding of ourselves than a false estimate of our worth. Anyone possessed of an inflated notion of his own importance is certain to see himself through a distorting medium of arrogance or complacency. He will misconceive his own function, and he will jeopardize his proper relationship to others. He will be wrong in his estimate of himself and of his proper contribution to the common life; and his mistake, because it is both insidious in character and inclusive in scope, will be particularly difficult to rectify.

To correct other people's faults is always a difficult and delicate task. If possible, we evade it; when we attempt it, we usually approach it in the wrong spirit and apply methods which are utterly inappropriate. In dealing with the problem the point of departure must be the proper outlook and attitude. What is it that entitles one person to correct another regarding the sin of pride? Obviously it cannot be superior merit, since the reliance on achievement would merely confirm in us the fault which we try to overthrow in others. Only **grace** can authorize a warning against the temptation to pride. Grace is always **given**; consequently, it is never something we achieve by our unaided efforts and so it cannot be a pretext for pride. Nothing can correct pride except true humility—otherwise Satan attempts to cast out Satan—and true humility is a consequence which follows from the gift of God.

The entire treatment of the problem is unusually suggestive. (*a*) In the first place we have the error of thinking of ourselves **more highly**

[7] *Journal of John Wesley* (New York: Eaton & Mains, n.d.), I, 469.

according as God hath dealt to every man the measure of faith.
4 For as we have many members in one body, and all members have not the same office:

but to think with sober judgment, each
according to the measure of faith which
God has assigned him. 4 For as in one body
we have many members, and all the mem-

---

term "spiritual" is not used here in this connection? The word "faith" seems to take the place of "Spirit.") It is possible, of course, that Paul has been informed of some friction at Rome on account of these various gifts. On the other hand he may be assuming (scarcely mistakenly!) that such friction is bound to exist there in some measure. There is always someone, somewhere, who thinks **of himself more highly than he ought to think** because of the office he holds or the function he performs. Paul appeals to the authority of his apostleship—the highest office and function in the church, but one for which he deserves no credit, since it is a **grace given** (cf. 1:5: "grace and apostleship")—in bidding such a one to "take a sane view of himself" (Moffatt). A play on words is involved here, but it appears only in the Greek (ὑπερφρονεῖν . . . φρονεῖν . . . φρονεῖν . . . σωφρονεῖν). The **measure of faith** must mean in this context "the measure of grace" or "the measure of the Spirit" which one's faith—itself a gift of God—has enabled one to receive (cf. I Cor. 12:11).

4-5. The meaning of these verses is fully opened up in I Cor. 12:12-30. Note that the community referred to here as **one body in Christ** is in I Cor. 12:12 called simply "Christ" (see above, p. 473). We are **individually members one of another** because we share together in a common life. Each needs the other and is indispensable to the other.

---

than we **ought to think,** which is the very root of all pride. (*b*) In contrast, we are shown the ideal toward which we should strive—modesty and humility, which are based on **sober judgment** and true insight. (*c*) We are then directed to the means by which we can achieve this standard—**faith.** (*d*) We are reminded of the part which God must play in our deliverance from pride. Faith is God's gift: we possess it **according to the measure . . . which God has assigned** us. Insofar as he gives us faith, we are able to achieve some degree of true self-evaluation.

It is natural that Paul should so promptly follow his plea for a sacrificial spirit with this injunction against pride. The ideas are closely related, partly because arrogance is fundamentally incongruous in one who truly serves God, partly because only complete self-dedication can deliver us from the perils of an unreal and exaggerated estimate of our own worth. Our obligation is to regard ourselves and our position in the community with that **sober judgment** which springs from a constant sense that any gifts we have are not ours through merit or desert. Whatever our opinion of ourselves may be, it will be governed by a humility which remembers that God's grace grants, and our faith receives, anything of spiritual value that we possess.

4-5. ***Interdependence and Its Appropriate Symbol.***—Humility, which is dependent on a proper grasp of the way in which we are related to God, is equally necessary if we are to maintain effective relationships with other people. In developing his conception of the corporate life and its nature, Paul appeals to a parallel so obvious that it could not appear novel, yet so apt that familiarity never lessens its force. The characteristics of the true community and of the living organism are the same. In both we have infinite diversity of parts and wide differentiation of function within an overriding unity of life and purpose. Each part in contributing to the life of the whole contributes also to the well-being of every other member. The unity is due to the principle of life which animates the entire body—in the case of the church, to Christ as the head. In him we are made one. All the diversity, which at first sight promises only disagreement, is gathered up into a unity in which each part supplements the others. Instead of resulting in weakness, our differences contribute to the effective working of the whole. Each supplies capacities which the others lack. But the complementary character of our gifts would not make for harmonious working unless the prior condition had been fulfilled. Without life, the various members of the body cannot minister to the well-being of each other or of the whole organism. In the same way, diversity in the human community breeds dissension and strife unless there is present some power strong enough to bring

5 So we, *being* many, are one body in Christ, and every one members one of another.

6 Having then gifts differing according to the grace that is given to us, whether prophecy, *let us prophesy* according to the proportion of faith;

7 Or ministry, *let us wait* on *our* ministering; or he that teacheth, on teaching;

8 Or he that exhorteth, on exhortation: he that giveth, *let him do it* with simplicity; he that ruleth, with diligence; he that showeth mercy, with cheerfulness.

bers do not have the same function, 5 so
we, though many, are one body in Christ,
and individually members one of another.
6 Having gifts that differ according to the
grace given to us, let us use them: if
prophecy, in proportion to our faith; 7 if
service, in our serving; he who teaches, in
his teaching; 8 he who exhorts, in his exhortation; he who contributes, in liberality; he who gives aid, with zeal; he who does acts of mercy, with cheerfulness.

6-8. But just as it is important that no one overemphasize the importance of one's own gift, it is also necessary that each prize and use one's gift. The health of the body depends as much upon the full functioning of each part as upon its proper subordination to the whole. **Having gifts,** therefore, **let us use them** (this clause is not in the Greek but is obviously implied in all that follows). Some are inspired preachers ("prophets"); let them then preach—being careful only to say no more than the Spirit gives them to say, i.e., **in proportion to our faith.** Some are helpers, serving the church in various practical ways; let them then be active in their service. Others are gifted as teachers and exhorters; let them fulfill their calling. In the same way let the contributor to the church be simple and sincere in his **liberality;** this noun (ἁπλότης) means primarily "simplicity" or "singleness of purpose," but this passage and II Cor. 9:11, 13 strongly suggest that Paul

---

unity to those who would otherwise fall apart in resentful antagonism. In Christ is found the secret of agreement for which men had looked in vain so long. As each person discovers that he is lifted into that fuller life which Christ offers, he learns that in a true sense—though not in a manner easily described—he actually lives in Christ. He is related to Christ as the members of the body are related to the head, and in that experience he discovers that he is involved in a new unity with others. Because each is related to Christ, all are related one to another.

6-8. ***Unity and Diversity.***—All that has gone before prepares us for a proper understanding of our responsibilities within the Christian community. Humility will teach us to recognize what is our true contribution; it will keep us from claiming gifts we lack, and will save us from pride in those we actually possess. Our sense of interdependence with others will teach us to use the aptitudes committed to us by God for the welfare of the whole body. Whatever our special role may be, our service will be marked by concentration on the task committed to us, by zeal in discharging it adequately, and by that gladness of spirit which comes from accepting our proper place in the service of God. We realize that anything we can do is owing to the fact that God has qualified us to do it; we see, moreover, that the various tasks which illustrate the range of our possible labors are all of such a kind as to minister to the well-being, in spirit or in body, of our fellows. Gifts are not for selfish enjoyment, but for the upbuilding of the community. When he discussed this same issue with his Corinthian converts, Paul made it very clear that he had no sympathy with a spectacular exhibition of religious gifts which left the hearers puzzled and uninstructed. A man who could not speak to the profit of others had better remain silent (cf. I Cor. 14). It is worth remembering that to "edify" the church is to build it up (cf. Eph. 4:16). This is most likely to happen when each person accepts his distinctive task as a ministry and is faithful in his allotted sphere.

Each person has his special gift, and each gift has its characteristic quality. **Prophecy,** when exercised **in proportion to our faith,** is a noble activity, and one which contributes greatly to the strengthening of the Christian fellowship; when divorced from its proper religious sources, the gift of speech, however eloquently employed, may have a significance no greater than that which "a noisy gong or a clanging cymbal" might claim (I Cor. 13:1). The same thing may be said of each of the gifts which Paul cites—**serving, teaching, exhortation,** all have their distinctive marks, and our

9 *Let* love be without dissimulation. Abhor that which is evil; cleave to that which is good.

9 Let love be genuine; hate what is

used the word in the sense of "generosity." **He who gives aid** is ὁ προϊστάμενος, and ordinarily means "administrator" or "superintendent." Paul may here be referring to persons with administrative gifts (so Sanday and Headlam, Lietzmann, Kirk); the Greek term can have the meaning given it in the RSV, however. Kühl argues that its position here, between the "contributor" and the performer of "acts of mercy," requires this understanding of it. Let the giver of aid (or the administrator) discharge his task **with zeal** or earnestness. (On the last clause see Prov. 22:8 [LXX] and II Cor. 9:7.)

2. Each Must Rejoice in the Service of Others (12:9-13)

9-12. Consideration of the nature of the community and of the way in which each member is related to it leads easily to consideration of the meaning of love. It is striking that the longer passage in I Corinthians about spiritual gifts concludes in the same way.

exercise of them must be such that each gift will actually achieve the purpose for which it is intended. It is perhaps accidental—but nonetheless suggestive—that when the catalogue reaches the qualities which express themselves in practical helpfulness, the emphasis on the appropriate spirit becomes particularly insistent. It is possible that **he who contributes** may do so in such a way as to make his gifts a mockery. The person who **gives aid**, especially if it is, as the Exeg. suggests, through administrative channels, can soon lose all the interest and urgency which save it from degenerating into lifeless routine. **Acts of mercy**, even though they spring from a true impulse of charity, can be done in a spirit which suggests a necessary but disagreeable duty, and when so performed lose all their power to comfort and encourage the human soul. In coveting the best gifts we must not forget the spirit in which they should be exercised.

9-21. ***The Effect of Love.***—The nature of love is revealed by its power to transform every type of human relationship. It takes up and enriches natural affection, so that the warm emotion characteristic of the family relationship at its best is brought into the family of God. It expands and enlarges that narrow circle to which we usually restrict the action of our love, and brings an ever-wider area of human life within the scope of its power. But it also achieves the transmutation of a force which often works to destroy our peace and to poison human relationships. One of the marked features of our life is the drive provided by the natural desire to excel. We crave superiority. In seeking to achieve pre-eminence we often embitter our own lives and those of others. The way in which this drive can find a new outlet is seen in the desire of parents that their children should gain the successes that they themselves failed to win. But in the Christian fellowship the same redirection of our craving to excel is manifested. We **outdo one another in showing honor;** each is quicker to recognize worth in and give recognition to others than he is to make claims on his own behalf.

More by illustration than through systematic development, Paul fills in the picture of our relationships with each other. Love, as he has shown, is the motive power of the new ethic, but its implications must be made explicit. The principle which shapes the new life will operate in every area of experience, and the way in which it works will be affected by the differing circumstances which prevail in various spheres. Love will govern our dealings both with those within the Christian community and with those outside it. The basic principle will remain the same; of necessity its application will vary. Because of the informality appropriate to a letter, Paul does not draw a sharp distinction between the two regions in which love will work. There is a certain amount of interpenetration, and phrases which might apply to one situation are embedded in the discussion of another. For purposes of exposition it will be convenient to divide the material as follows: (*a*) the basic quality which love manifests, and the immediate reactions which it prompts, vs. 9; (*b*) the meaning of love in the Christian society, vss. 10-13, 15-16; (*c*) the meaning of love as it affects the attitude of Christians toward others, vss. 14, 17-21.

9. ***Love as the Secret of Christian Conduct.***—It is simple to compare the life of a society with the unity of an organism, but it is perilously easy to lose precisely the quality that gives the simile its aptness. We all know societies that have forfeited all claim to homogeneity; it is

Indeed, vss. 9-12 bear about the same relation to I Cor. 13 as vss. 3-8 bear to I Cor. 12. In both cases we have brief summaries of the longer and more adequate statements. On Paul's view of the meaning of love in general and of its relation to the Spirit and the life of the community, see above, pp. 455-56. Love must be **genuine** (literally "nonhypo-

not that their members could not work together if they wished, but that they have lost the motive which made it possible for them to do so. Unity must spring from some principle strong enough to bring together, and hold in one, persons who would otherwise fall apart into selfish and competitive individuality. We have seen the various expedients by which national unity can be created, and the spectacle—alarming though it has often been—has proved that strong and effective corporate action must appeal to some motive sufficiently powerful to weld a nation into unity. Many of the modern appeals have been to false and disastrous principles; the necessary task is to find the true foundations on which constructive unity can be built. Paul has no doubt as to the principle which creates and maintains the church: it is **love.** Concerning love and its meaning he has much to say; and it is scattered throughout all his letters. He has made it perfectly clear that he finds in love that characteristic quality which underlies the whole of God's redemptive activity. It is the secret of all that God has done for us, and it awakens in us an answering response. "We love because he first loved us"; the words may not be the words of Paul but they could easily have been borrowed by the man who explained all his ceaseless endeavor by saying, "The life which I now live in the flesh I live by the faith of the Son of God, who loved me, and gave himself for me" (Gal. 2:20).

It is natural, then, that he should regard love as the quality which more than any other must mark the community of Christians. By its very nature, however, it must be absolutely sincere; pretense is so antithetical to the nature of love that the two could never exist together. But an even greater danger than hypocrisy is sentimentalism. We often relegate love to an unreal world of false emotion, and are amazed that it loses all its power and dynamic. It is one of the mighty forces in the moral world; it remains such only when it is kept in the closest possible relation to moral realities. In its pure form it requires a clear-sighted discernment which discriminates between the basic moral forces of good and evil; as a consequence, it is closely related to the abiding values—the right and the true. Love therefore must be brought out of the murky regions into which novelists and film producers have dragged it: it must be rescued from the misty realm where even religious people often leave it. It must be related to the things which are most real in the realm of moral living: in that clear, bracing atmosphere we must let it work its marvels of regeneration.

What the gospel demands of us, then, is love, but we easily delude ourselves and offer sentimentalism instead. Since we are so prone to disregard its essential nature, Paul gives us, in this verse and the next, a useful reminder of the true character of love. Love is discriminating. The familiar proverb declares that love is blind, and up to a point it doubtless is. Most of us have benefited by this blindness; someone has been persuaded that our modest abilities bear all the marks of genius, and has been willing, with even greater generosity, to draw a veil over our unquestioned failures and shortcomings. But it can be claimed with greater cogency that only love can really see. Certainly it has the power to discern potentialities which hard realism never perceives, and can bring to actuality the things which it detects while they are merely possibilities. This is continuously exemplified in the Gospels. Jesus had no illusions about many of the people with whom he dealt, but he had no doubt as to what they might become. Like others, he saw that Mary Magdalene was a woman wholly in the grasp of evil forces, but he detected in her what they missed—the makings of a saint. He recognized in Zacchaeus the brazenly successful publican whom everyone in Jericho knew, but he also saw a man to whom salvation might come. Love alone possesses the power of discerning what is good and what is evil because love alone has the secret of the necessary insight. So far from being naïve and gullible, only love is free from the deceptions which mislead us in our judgments about men and movements.

In addition to the ability to see, love has the power to act. It is able to reach out and embrace others within the range of its practical good will. In one of his plays Sheridan describes a squire who possessed "as much speculative benevolence as any private gentleman in the kingdom, though he is seldom so sensual as to indulge himself in the exercise of it." [8] Nothing could be farther removed from the spirit which love inspires, or from the standard which the N.T. sets before us.

The practical results of love are many, but among them we must not forget the spirit which strives to excel in treating others with

[8] *School for Scandal*, Act V, scene 1.

10 *Be* kindly affectioned one to another with brotherly love; in honor preferring one another;

11 Not slothful in business; fervent in spirit; serving the Lord;

evil, hold fast to what is good; 10 love one
another with brotherly affection; outdo
one another in showing honor. 11 Never
flag in zeal, be aglow with the Spirit, serve

---

critical"). The suggestion is that it is *not* genuine if it fails to discriminate between the **good** and the **evil;** love is not at war with truth (cf. I Cor. 13:6). This love will manifest itself in warm **affection,** in courtesy **(outdo one another in showing honor),**

---

the deference they deserve. True humility delivers us from a false estimate of ourselves, but it also sets us free to place a proper valuation on the worth of others. What is possible is also desirable, and the result is emulation "in showing honor" (vs. 10).

10-13, 15-16. ***Love Within the Christian Society.***—One of the basic requisites in all right relationships is the readiness to enter sympathetically into the experiences of other people. We are far too apt to be "glad when others go wrong" (I Cor. 13:6 Moffatt), and the ability genuinely to share the joys even of our associates is often painfully circumscribed. The root of envy in us makes us bitter when good fortune comes to others: we prove to our own satisfaction that they did not deserve it or that it is really not as desirable as it seems. This tendency to minimize the successes of others and to dissipate their joy has become proverbial, and only love's transforming influence teaches us to **rejoice with those who rejoice** (vs. 15). We are usually more seemly about sorrow. At least we know the conventional phrases of sympathy, and are ready to make the accustomed gestures. But this is a very different matter from entering profoundly into the experience of other people's grief. Here is one of the places at which by bearing one another's burdens we might more often "fulfill the law of Christ" (Gal. 6:2). It is easier, of course, to sympathize with those in sorrow than it is to rejoice with those who have found great joy. As Chrysostom pointed out, a fellow feeling with grief comes to us naturally, while appreciation of other people's success demands real nobility of soul. It may be that in the one case our instinctive response is not distorted by selfishness or jealousy. We are apt to envy the good fortune of our friends; we have no desire to displace them in their grief. But it is only when we are really prepared to share that grief and lift part of the weight it lays on others that we redeem our sympathy from the reproach of conventionality. (See Expos. on 13:8.)

11-12. ***Characteristics of the Christian.***—The apostle has been describing the outward manifestations of a certain type of character. He has set forth the various relationships which the Christian will fashion with other members of the Christian community; but he also indicates the pervasive atmosphere which will mark this kind of life. The first characteristic is **zeal.** The concern of the Christian for his responsibilities does not blow hot or cold according to the dictates of mood or circumstance. A keen sense of vocation is one of the normal qualities in a Christian's outlook; he gives himself to his work with the realization that any task, however humble, may be the vehicle by which he can serve God (I Cor. 10:31); and the unflagging moral earnestness which marks all he does helps to set the tone which pervades his whole life. But zeal of this kind is never sustained simply by the natural resources of persistence which each of us can bring to the disciplines of daily life. It is related to love as its inspiration; but it must also be continually supported by contact **with the Spirit**—"The Lord, and Giver of Life." It is God's Holy Spirit that inspires and sustains our zeal. Man's spirit catches fire from God's Spirit, and glows with the intensity he awakens. As the writer of Proverbs finely expressed it, "The spirit of man is the candle of the LORD" (Prov. 20:27), and the flame is lighted when our spirits are touched by the Spirit of God. Persevering zeal and quickened intensity are gathered together in one inclusive kind of service—the service of God. All the gifts given for the support of the community, all the activities inspired by the basic principle of love are taken up in this comprehensive requirement: that all our varying tasks and functions must find their proper place within the one all-embracing demand. Whatever may be our particular role, we "serve the Lord Christ" (Col. 3:24).

Paul was not composing a formal treatise, and doubtless he presented his ideas as they occurred to him rather than because a strictly logical sequence demanded that they should stand in a certain order. But though the structure may be loose, the ideas are closely related. We have seen that zeal is inspired and supported by spiritual intensity, and that both inevitably issue in devoted service of God (vs.

and in ardent devotion to Christ (vs. 11). The phrases **rejoicing in hope** and **patient in tribulation** remind one not only of I Cor. 13:7 ("love . . . hopes all things, endures all things"), but also of Rom. 5:2-3, where Paul speaks of "rejoicing in hope" (although the Greek word for "rejoice" is a different term from that used here) and reminds his readers

---

11). In the same way (vs. 12), joy and perseverance grow out of the unresting discipline of prayer, and at the same time strengthen and maintain it. But joy too has a new soil in which it can flourish. Before considering in greater detail the meaning of the terms Paul uses, we may profitably note that he gives us an illuminating study of a particular aspect of the new life. Many people are at the mercy of moods, and their emotional reactions are erratic and uncontrolled. The effective discipline of our life is not a matter merely of right response; it requires also appropriate expression. To set forth Paul's contention is to recognize its relevance and its force. We are (*a*) to **rejoice in . . . hope;** (*b*) to **be patient in tribulation;** (*c*) to **be constant in prayer.**

The old world knew little of the kind of experience into which the gospel initiated men and women, and consequently a new vocabulary had to be devised to express the wonder of the new life. Some words were invented, others were transformed and given fresh meaning. When Paul speaks of the fruits of the Spirit, and includes hope among them, he is clearly contrasting the quality of the new life with that familiar in the pagan world. "Having no hope and without God in the world" (Eph. 2:12) is the way in which Christians saw in retrospect the kind of life they had lived before the light of the gospel burst upon them. Hope is a peculiarly Christian virtue, and in the N.T. one writer after another illustrates or emphasizes its distinctive quality. For Paul it is one of the three abiding elements in experience which survive the disappearance of ephemeral things (I Cor. 13:13); for the author of I John it is the motive of that moral discipline which keeps the Christian pure (I John 3:3). In I Peter, Christ's resurrection from the dead is the means whereby God himself has quickened our dispirited apathy into living hope (I Pet. 1:3). The Epistle to the Hebrews shows us hope as faith which projects itself into the future and provides the constancy which Christians need. It is perfectly clear that the word must mean a great deal more than that diffused optimism with which we are often willing to equate it. It is an outlook on life—its opportunities, its possibilities, its demands—which is possible only to those who see their own experience in the light of a divine purpose. What God has done illuminates what God will yet do, and the perspective of eternity rectifies our vision of the things in time. In this same letter Paul has already spoken of the joy inspired by the "hope of sharing the glory of God" (5:2), but it is obvious that he is speaking of something much more profound than the mere expectation of rewards to come. Hope is the attitude which should be natural to those who know that a great destiny is theirs, who realize that they are meanwhile under discipline, but who are conscious that even now they are encompassed by the proofs of God's goodness. They are persuaded that he loves them, that Jesus Christ has opened to them a wider and richer life, and that spiritual victory is of the substance of their immediate experience. This kind of hope inevitably leads to joy—to that deep and pervading sense that our lives are established in their proper medium and are fulfilling their true purpose. Joy is the counterpart of inner growth; it is the emotional accompaniment of a creative process. Where there is true life, there is joy; and it is well to ponder the fact that the periods of the church's greatest vitality have been the times of her greatest radiance. When she was growing in insight, in understanding, in unity within her borders and in the power to reach those outside her ranks, her constant mark, as the N.T. conclusively demonstrates, was a triumphant and infectious joy. Since then Christians have often learned that they can aptly say of powerful ecclesiastical bodies, "Thou hast multiplied the nation, and not increased the joy" (Isa. 9:3).

There is no incongruity in following a plea for the spirit of rejoicing with an exhortation to **be patient in tribulation.** In 5:3 Paul has boldly claimed that our sufferings are the occasion of our rejoicing, because he knew that even adversity can work for the spiritual good of those who in all things co-operate with God. But this high mood of exhilaration does not always last. We may at times mount up with wings as eagles; at other times we must be content to run, and not be weary—or even to walk, and not faint. So though we may not rejoice at suffering, we can be patient in it. The frankly realistic outlook of the N.T. constantly strikes anyone who contrasts its attitude with the promises of every kind of advantage which Christians have sometimes offered to those who would join them. The faith is not a guarantee that we shall be delivered from misfortune; it is the promise that in the midst of misfortune we shall be sustained, through its discipline

12 Rejoicing in hope; patient in tribulation; continuing instant in prayer;
13 Distributing to the necessity of saints; given to hospitality.

the Lord. 12 Rejoice in your hope, be patient in tribulation, be constant in prayer.
13 Contribute to the needs of the saints, practice hospitality.

that "tribulation worketh patience" (in both cases "patience" means "steadfastness" or "endurance"). The need for endurance in suffering not unnaturally suggests the injunction: **Be constant in prayer.** Sanday and Headlam see in **tribulation** (θλίψις) an allusion to persecution. This is not required, but is surely possible (see comment on 8:35*b*-37).

13. Contribute to the needs of the saints is literally "share in" or "participate in" their needs (κοινωνοῦντες)—sympathetically feeling with them as well as generously serving them. "Sharing" is more than "contributing." Underlying the verb here is the realization of the church as a community (κοινωνία) in which the necessities of one are to be suffered by all, and the privileges of one are to be enjoyed by all.

Hospitality was one of the most important manifestations of the κοινωνία (community) of the primitive church. Christians scattered throughout the world could count on finding in every large center a Christian church which would welcome them, make

---

strengthened, and by its ministries made fit for what God will yet give us. But suffering can teach only those who accept its discipline in the proper spirit. Those who are restive or rebellious learn nothing, and yield their souls a prey to bitterness. Those who are patient can discover that there is comfort even in the darkest valley.

12. *Prayer: The Ground of Christian Graces.*—Paul has been commending Christian graces, not natural virtues. Neither joy nor patience is the expression merely of a happy disposition; both are rooted in and growing from prayer. The qualities which he trusts will be the distinguishing mark of the Christian can be sustained only by means of constant and conscious dependence on God. Apart from his presence, we may cultivate cheerfulness, but will not know the meaning of joy; we may submit with stoic fortitude to the blows of fate, but will not understand the patience which uses adversity for the discipline of our spirits. In all his ethical precepts Paul is inculcating not a pattern of virtuous conduct such as pagan treatises often supplied, but a kind of relationship which springs from and issues in a transformed life. In this relationship prayer is of crucial significance. Halfhearted and intermittent experiments in practicing the presence of God achieve little that is of any permanent value. Continuance in prayer is necessary—we must "pray without ceasing," as Paul elsewhere reminds us (I Thess. 5:17)—but behind such sustained effort there must lie the unflagging discipline without which it cannot be maintained. In reading the letters of Paul—and for that matter all the N.T. writings—it is impossible to avoid being impressed by the reiterated demand for sustained and strenuous effort. In a day when personal religion has generally become slack and slothful, it is sobering to recall how often Jesus confronts his disciples with the exacting claims of the new life. "*When* you fast," he said—not "*if* you fast." Whoever will not accept the rigorous demands implicit in following him need not begin at all (Matt. 10:37-38). Paul turns instinctively to metaphors supplied by the stern life of the soldier on campaign or by the hard training to which the athlete submits (cf. I Cor. 9:26; Phil. 3:14; also II Tim. 2:3-5), and the writer to the Hebrews thinks naturally of the runner in the stadium who presses toward his prize (Heb. 12:1).

13. *Active Charity Is the Touchstone of Good Will.*—Good will is barren if it extends no further than protestations of a common mind and purpose. There come times when charity has no meaning unless it shows some proper recognition of our duty to give appropriate help to those who need it. The story of the Last Judgment (Matt. 25:31-46) underlines with powerful emphasis the futility of a good will which ignores human need. Is it not absurd, asks Jas. 2:16, to say to a needy brother or sister, "Go in peace, be warmed and filled," if you offer only empty words? To recognize need and refuse to respond is to prove yourself destitute of the love of God (I John 3:17). Unanimity of thought and feeling has as its counterpart a keen responsibility for any members of the community who are in need or distress. There are certain forms which, as circumstances of time or place may dictate, it is particularly important that practical aid should assume. We know that in the first century traveling Christians were often in need of hospitality. We read again and again of how Paul himself was taken into the homes of new converts and given enter-

14 Bless them which persecute you: bless, and curse not.

14 Bless those who persecute you; bless

them at home, and give any immediately needed service (cf. Heb. 13:2). Although this feature of ancient church life had its greatest significance in a later period, it was present from the beginning. Rom. 16:1-2 (whether originally a part of Romans or not) is a reminder of this practice of hospitality (cf. II Cor. 3:1), and in some degree the whole letter of Paul to the Romans is an appeal for hospitality on his own behalf (see Intro., pp. 358-63).

C. Love for Men Generally (12:14–13:10)

1. Enemies (12:14-21)

14-16. There can be little doubt that Paul is thinking of persons outside the church itself when he speaks of **those who persecute you** (cf. II Thess. 1:4; Rom. 8:35), although it is not necessary to suppose that he is alluding to legal prosecution. **Bless** means "to

tainment. To those who receive it such hospitality is a boon; for those who can offer it, it is both a duty and a privilege. To withhold it is to stand on God's left hand.

14, 17-21. ***Love as the Regulating Principle in Our Relations with Others.***— (Cf. Expos. on vss. 9, 10-13, 15-16.) Love, which lays its claims upon us within the community, must govern our behavior toward those without as well. Though the line of division is not always sharply drawn, it is clear that Paul has distinguished—in his own mind at least—between what we would naturally do in our dealings with fellow Christians and what our relations with pagan neighbors should be. The minimum that can be demanded is that we refrain from scandalizing the outsider (vs. 17*b*). From the very beginning Paul had recognized the need "to live quietly, to mind your own affairs . . . so that you may command the respect of outsiders" (I Thess. 4:11-12). When urging the Corinthians to "give no offense," he mentions Jews and Greeks before adding "the church of God" (I Cor. 10:32). "Conduct yourselves wisely," he says, "toward outsiders" (Col. 4:5). Evidently he feared, and with good reason, that immature Christians might confuse liberty with license, and fall below even that standard which the good pagan honored in his conduct. This has been a persistent problem in Christian history, and the writings of the sixteenth and seventeenth centuries illustrate how anxious sober Christian leaders always are lest a new emphasis on the glorious liberty of the Christian should lead only to an inglorious evasion of the requirements of elementary morality. In a less dramatic form the problem is with us all the time. The upright pagan is continually scandalized by the Christian who finds it easier to believe the abstruse affirmations of Christian dogma than to practice the obvious precepts of Christian ethics. It is true, of course, that the imperfect Christian is often judged by a standard supplied by the insights of his own faith; it is equally true that his neighbors are often eager to detect and quick to expose any lapses on his part. At the same time, he has implicitly accepted a higher standard, and cannot object if he is held to its requirements. Moreover, charity lays on him an obligation which he cannot escape—to avoid giving offense to any who may suffer because he fails to commend the faith by his conduct. Jesus spoke stern words to those who cause weaker ones to stumble (Mark 9:42), and the Christian church has no greater liability than the lives of those among its members who give offense to others.

But while the Christian cannot claim exemption from the standards which his neighbors accept, he is not at liberty, when he rises above those standards, to treat his neighbors with superiority or condescension. Paul is pointing to an attitude which will make it easier to maintain harmonious relations all around. Clearly he understands that to **live peaceably with all** is a duty of so exacting a kind that its claims must be doubly stressed. There are no easy exemptions for the quarrelsome or contentious spirit. Insofar as it is possible at all, peace must be preserved. Provocation, in other words, must not come from the side of the Christian. The man who had appealed to his readers "by the meekness and gentleness of Christ" (II Cor. 10:1) was not prepared to acquiesce in excuses for contentious behavior. There come times, of course, when it no longer lies with the Christian to determine whether or not peaceful relations shall be maintained. Before his patience is exhausted, the limits set by his own standards may be reached. He may be placed in a position where he cannot be silent; what others do, either as individuals or collectively in society,

15 Rejoice with them that do rejoice, and weep with them that weep.

and do not curse them. 15 Rejoice with those who rejoice, weep with those who

speak well of," "to praise," but also connotes (especially when used as the antonym of **curse**) "to pray for." Vs. 14 closely resembles Matt. 5:44 and may depend upon a saying of Jesus known to Paul. Vs. 15 is not so clearly concerned with extrachurch relations, and **live in harmony with one another** (vs. 16) definitely suggests life within the church.

may be such that in the interests of uprightness he must protest. It is not always easy indeed to know when the limits of acquiescence have been exceeded. The problem is as old as the history of the church and as modern as contemporary experience. There is such a thing as inviting persecution by being needlessly provocative, and the early church found it necessary to check the zeal of some of its members for martyrdom. Christians are not now thrown to the lions, but the mentality which feels that it is praising God when it is merely exasperating other people has by no means disappeared. Yet it is possible to justify what is really apostasy by appealing to our love of peace. If the world praises us too easily, or if we fail to disturb its complacency, it may mean that we have lost contact with the forces of evil. There are times and situations when the world ought to hate us, and there are forms of organized iniquity with which we should be in ceaseless conflict. As so often proves the case, there is a delicate balance between conflicting claims, and no formal rules can ever resolve the dilemma we face. We are to **live peaceably with all**—but only if it is **possible**, and only so far as we can control the situation. If others insist on creating a breach, and still more if their attitudes and actions force us to protest, we may have to maintain our standards in defiance of the demands of our society. The modern history of the church in many parts of the world provides as eloquent a commentary on this truth as anything offered by the story of the early persecutions.

It is desirable to avoid dissension, but it is necessary to go far beyond such modest requirements. Again and again in the latter part of this chapter we are conscious of a demand to do positive good to those with whom we are brought into contact. In one sense a true Christian witness will do this inevitably. Yeast will by its very presence leaven the lump, and Christian standards will influence for good those who come within the orbit of their influence. But something much more direct and personal is involved. Paul is describing an attitude which is so aware of other people's needs and so eager to supply them that every kind of service is joyfully accepted. When Jesus told the story of the good Samaritan, he defined the relationship which ought to exist between the man of good will and his neighbors. Beyond the rather negative requirement of avoiding unnecessary friction we have, then, the positive demands of an outreaching good will.

14. ***The Practical Alternative: To Bless.***—The initial form in which a different spirit shows itself is suggested here: **Bless those who persecute you; bless and do not curse them.** But the key word in this sentence is one which much familiarity has robbed of its freshness and its incisive force; to most of us it suggests little more than vague beneficence. It is possible, however, to distinguish at least three stages in blessing. The first is the fixed and settled wish for the good of another, the steady and unfaltering desire to see those things come to pass which will most genuinely promote his true advantage. In a religious context this desire will naturally pass into prayer for him, and the wish which is not transmuted into intercession remains at that ineffectual level where futility must be its final fate. But to bless means more even than to bring together human need and the divine resources. Genuine prayer leads naturally to a settled endeavor to serve as the channel through which the good things which we have asked in prayer may reach those who need them most. It may seem arbitrary to distinguish between the various phases of what in the last resort must be a unified and coherent expression of our good will, but we usually make this kind of division, if not in reflection then in conduct; we are content to let our blessing remain in areas where it is an ineffectual emotional impulse, never lifted into God's presence, and never translated into concrete terms. It may be noted that Paul says that blessing is the right attitude for us to adopt, but he does not suggest that it is either natural or easy. We ought to bless, but actually instinct might prompt us to curse—to let ill will run out in imprecation and express itself in malignant deeds. The suggested contrast between what we might do if left to ourselves and what we can and should do when prompted by the love of Christ is a theme which emerges repeatedly in this section, and could very profitably be developed. It sets the characteristic Pauline emphasis on the insufficiency

16 *Be* of the same mind one toward another. Mind not high things, but condescend to men of low estate. Be not wise in your own conceits.

weep.
16 Live in harmony with one another; do not be haughty, but associate

We have already had several occasions to observe the fact that Paul is likely to take up a new subject before he is quite ready to leave the old (see on 6:1). As a matter of fact

of the natural man over against our contemporary acquiescence in a very complacent view of man's potentialities, and yet outlines the difference in a way easier for many readers to grasp than the stark Pauline affirmations of sin and grace.

16. *The Secret of Unanimity.*—We are most likely to learn the difficult lesson of unanimity if we first acquire the right attitude to others over the whole range of our intercourse with them. Because love is the guiding principle of the Christian community (see Expos. on vss. 10-13, 15-16), one of its distinguishing features is a strong impulse toward unanimity. This is not the product merely of natural compatibility of temperament and outlook; it is created among people of wide diversity of character by the unifying force of love at work within the fellowship. It shows itself in that unanimity of thought which prevents misunderstandings and in that harmony of feeling which teaches the secret of the true sympathy about which Paul has just been speaking. It will be reflected in all the relationships in which Christians stand one to another, and it is strengthened and extended by so entering into the desires of others and so appreciating their situation that we come to be of one mind with them.

Unanimity is not an accidental discovery and it can be maintained only by resolutely avoiding the things that endanger it. There is nothing more certain to destroy mutual respect than a haughty spirit. Those who are snared into thinking more highly of themselves than they have any right to do will cut themselves off from their fellows, and there is nothing to which people react more promptly or which they resent more deeply than a superior attitude toward themselves. Some will be tempted to pride because they have greater gifts than others; some because they have greater advantages and a more commanding position. "It is not the part of a Christian," remarked Calvin, "ambitiously to aspire to those things by which he may excel others, nor to assume a lofty appearance, but on the contrary to exercise humility and meekness." [9] Whatever the exact manifestation of arrogance may be—whether in selfish ambition or in the haughty superiority to which it leads—pride destroys the harmony of the community. It also fatally circumscribes the sympathies of anyone who becomes obsessed with his own importance. It cuts him off from association with those who need him, and who might be able to help him in their turn, and persuades him to decline tasks which he could usefully perform. Commentators are not agreed as to whether **the lowly** refers to persons or to things, and high authority can be quoted on both sides. This at least is certain, that a man of proud spirit will suffer at both points: He will renounce all dealings with those whom he regards as undeserving of his attention, and he will consequently deprive himself both of the joy which comes from helping those who stand in need of his assistance and the unexpected delight that comes from gaining new insights in places where he did not think to acquire them. Wisdom is not confined to those who think they possess it, and often humble folk have much clearer discernment and sharper insight than many who account themselves far better qualified to make pronouncements about the truth. "Has not God chosen those who are poor in the world to be rich in faith and heirs of the kingdom which he has promised to those who love him?" How superficial, then, is that snobbery which dishonors the poor man (Jas. 2:5-6). Equally real is the loss suffered by those who regard certain tasks as beneath their dignity. Some lessons are better taught by accepting the disciplines of menial work than in any other way. The Christian society should never be subjected to the humiliation of discovering that some duties are regarded as degrading by its members, and in the community at large Christians should prove that self-respect is perfectly compatible with serving one another in places for which others may not compete.

If we are to avoid the absurd incongruities to which conceit gives rise within the Christian fellowship, we must be willing to test our opinions by those of others and, if necessary, subordinate our judgment to theirs. "Here then is condemned all ambition and that elation of mind which insinuates itself under the name of magnanimity; for the chief virtue of the faithful is moderation, or rather lowliness of mind,

[9] *Romans, ad loc.*

17 Recompense to no man evil for evil. Provide things honest in the sight of all men.

18 If it be possible, as much as lieth in you, live peaceably with all men.

19 Dearly beloved, avenge not yourselves, but *rather* give place unto wrath: for it is written, Vengeance *is* mine; I will repay, saith the Lord.

with the lowly;[s] never be conceited. 17 Repay no one evil for evil, but take thought
for what is noble in the sight of all. 18 If
possible, so far as it depends upon you,
live peaceably with all. 19 Beloved, never
avenge yourselves, but leave it[t] to the wrath
of God; for it is written, "Vengeance is

[s] Or *give yourselves to humble tasks.*
[t] Greek *give place.*

Paul in this section of Romans never gets far from the theme with which the section opened, i.e., love within the church, and returns to it fully at the beginning of ch. 14. (On 16*b* see Jas. 2:1-7.)

17-21. Repay no one evil for evil reminds one again of I Cor. 13 ("love does not take account of evil," vs. 5), but even more of Matt. 5:43-44. Vs. 17*b* involves an adaptation of Prov. 3:4 and is to be understood as making the same point as Paul more explicitly makes in II Cor. 8:21, where the same proverb is quoted (cf. also Luke 2:52

---

which ever prefers to give honour to others, rather than to take it away from them."[1]

17. ***The Right Answer to Wrong.***—There are times when the initiative (cf. Expos. on vss. 14, 17-21) seems to pass out of our hands, and when it is peculiarly easy to justify a resentful spirit. What happens if we suffer evil? At least we are not to repay the transgressor in kind. There is a low level to which human relationships sometimes descend: when we do no good to those who do no good to us. Even in its more positive form of being helpful only to those who are helpful to us, we have a standard of conduct which Jesus regarded as the mark of the worldly and irreligious man (Matt. 5:46-47). It was therefore clearly beneath what he expected of his disciples, and love as the governing motive in human affairs will save us from that dreary plane of sullen incivility where we exchange discourtesies simply because they have become the current coin of ordinary intercourse (cf. I Thess. 5:15 for a parallel warning). But love will also do a great deal more, because Paul has elsewhere shown that love—which throughout the present section is regarded as the governing power in human relationships—will consistently transcend evil and manifest itself in the good that transforms (I Cor. 13:5-7).

19. ***To Judge Belongs to God.***—At all events, reprisals have no place among the alternatives that we are free to consider. He does not argue from the corrupting effect which they have on our dealings one with another, but he lifts the whole problem of our relationships with our fellows into the light of God's relationships with all of us. If we resort to reprisals, we are encroaching on the prerogatives of God. We are rudely seizing powers which do not belong to us. It is dangerous for us to sit in judgment at any time or for any reason; that superiority of spirit which exalts itself above others always brings its own nemesis, and the self-appointed judge inevitably finds himself under judgment (cf. Matt. 7:1-2). This attitude, so superior and censorious, springs from that self-regarding pride in which love of self drives out love of others; by making us indulgent to ourselves it makes us inexorable toward our neighbors. But if it is wrong for us even to condemn, how much worse is it for us to act as executioner as well: whereupon the argument moves at once into a much wider sphere, and we see our arrogance in the perspective of the divine prerogative of judging. Reverence and humility alone should compel us to abdicate the rights we had been claiming; but it also becomes clear that our presumptuous irruption into an area where we have neither rights nor status defeats even our immediate purpose. To **leave it to the wrath of God** can legitimately be interpreted as allowing room or scope for the exercise of God's righteous judgments.[2] By intruding we get in the way; by taking matters into our own hands we interrupt the inexorable process by which wrongdoing brings upon itself its final retribution. We are inept bunglers in a region where we do not belong, and we can safely abdicate the rights we have usurped because actually they belong to God. **Vengeance is mine:** retributive justice—the ultimate overthrow of evil because it is evil—is in God's hands. We might express the same truth differently—more abstractly, more impersonally, therefore less truly, and certainly less vividly—by claiming that this is a moral universe, and that cause and effect maintain their unalterable

[1] *Ibid.*

[2] Cf. Sanday and Headlam, *Epistle to Romans, ad loc.*

20 Therefore if thine enemy hunger, feed him; if he thirst, give him drink: for

mine, I will repay, says the Lord." 20 No, "if your enemy is hungry, feed him; if he

---

and II Cor. 4:2). Paul has a good deal of respect for the capacity for moral judgments which ordinary men possess (despite his severe strictures upon the natural man), and does not despise the good opinion of mankind. The Christian must not gratuitously outrage the sincerely held convictions and standards of others. He must, indeed, **as far as it depends upon** [him], **live peaceably with all.** Not only does this mean that one must do one's utmost to avoid arousing another's anger or resentment, but also that one must

---

sequence. Moreover, the process is one on which we can rely. **I will repay, says the Lord.** Our eager impulse to give our enemies their due deserts should be held in check by a solemn realization of the majestic character of God's ordering of the world he has made. Our workaday minds are too often satisfied with a wholly impersonal universe. We are usually content with mechanical regularity and seldom get beyond it to an order in which finally all things serve a personal purpose of righteousness. The religious man's approach can claim to be both simpler and more profound; it gives us a world in which man's dignity and the significance of his conduct are preserved because his life is set in a universe where moral and spiritual as well as physical and material laws pursue their appointed course. It is this sense of the majesty of God's righteous and beneficent purpose which delivers both our thought and our conduct from the blight of religious triviality. It preserves us from the flippant irreverence of approaching the Almighty as though he were a kindly and benevolent grandfather. It guards us against the temptation to use great and mighty phrases in a sense which makes them seem commonplace or even absurd. It introduces that touch of high austerity which saves us from an unbecoming familiarity in the presence of the Most High. It is worth remembering that Paul has brought these things within our purview, not when arguing about the nature of God, but when discussing our relationships with our fellows—with those who ought to be our brothers but actually are not. The high truths of Christian doctrine are of direct and immediate relevance to the ordinary duties of Christian discipleship.

Our most elementary objective, then, must be to avoid a bitter and revengeful spirit in our dealings with those from whom enmity threatens to divide us. We can refuse to descend to the level which others may attempt to dictate; we can decline to be coerced into accepting the standards they may try to impose upon us. But to resist the temptation to retaliate is only the simplest step toward discharging our Christian duty. Instead of countering animosity with ill will, we must go out to meet those who differ from us in a spirit so positive and constructive that the final result will be the creation of harmonious relations. From the Christian point of view to do less than this is actually to be guilty of revenge, "For it is a kind of an indirect retaliation when we turn aside our kindness from those by whom we have been injured." [8]

20. ***True Blessing Means Active Aid.***— "Bless" is one of those dangerous religious words which prompt good resolutions, but which often do not indicate any practical way in which good will can find expression. Paul was too wise to leave the matter suspended in unreal isolation from concrete issues. It is no use advocating a positive alternative to the spirit of reprisals and revenge if it is not set to work in relation to actual situations and real needs. If you bless a man, you will help him; and what is more, you will help him at the point where his need is most acute. If he is **hungry,** you will **feed him;** if he is **thirsty,** you will **give him drink.** The N.T. never forgets the practical truth that spiritual fare is poor sustenance for an empty stomach. What we offer may be of unquestioned value, but an undernourished man needs something else. Consequently, at the point where he is most acutely aware of his lack, we must meet him with good will expressed in terms that he can understand. To a hungry person blessing means bread, whatever else it may ultimately come to include. But though the issue is expressed in its simplest terms, it can legitimately be extended to include much else. Bread is stipulated because we so easily forget our brother's lack of it; but the real point is his need and our ability to satisfy it. The essential mark of love as the motive power of conduct is its ability to translate into terms of practical assistance our insight into the necessities of others. The **enemy,** it is worth remembering, is not one whom we hate. Natural instinct might prompt us to do so, but Paul has already indicated that the primitive urges of

[8] Calvin, *Romans*, p. 475.

in so doing thou shalt heap coals of fire on his head.

is thirsty, give him drink; for by so doing you will heap burning coals upon his head."

not be angry in return, even when one could not avoid giving offense. To try to **avenge** ourselves is to usurp God's prerogative of judgment. Lev. 19:18 forbids vengeance "against the children of thy people"; Paul probably has this passage in mind, but he applies it without any limitation. **Vengeance is mine** is from Deut. 32:35. Paul quotes it not primarily in order to give assurance that vengeance will eventually take place, but to declare that only God can appropriately exercise it. The appropriate *human*

unregenerate passion have been transformed into a steady disposition of good will. An enemy is one who may regard us with bitterness and who is conscious of barriers between us which he is unable or unwilling to transcend; but the whole force of Paul's plea lies in the fact that we are under no obligation to reciprocate like for like. Part of the liberty of the Christian is his deliverance from that dreary sequence of cause and effect in which injury breeds resentment, which leads in turn to alienation and settled hatred. That kind of vicious circle is broken, and the ability to repay evil with good is not so much an oppressive duty as it is the mark of our true freedom.

Whatever may be our enemy's response, we must meet him in good will; even if he remains obdurately hostile, we ourselves have the satisfactions inseparable from accepting our Christian duty—which proves to be our Christian privilege as well. But Paul is satisfied that our enemy will not remain untouched. The effect of our response—which must of course be as free from superiority as from bitterness—is to quicken conscience. Our attempt to show forth the Christian law of love will **heap coals of fire on his head.** The imagery suggests something that cannot be borne without producing the strongest effects. The conviction that Paul is pointing to the pangs of remorse runs back, in the history of interpretation, to Augustine's comment on "the burning shame" which goodness as the response to evil will naturally produce. Because of its forceful and vivid quality, it is perhaps natural that the phrase should have acquired malicious overtones; in current speech it has become the equivalent of a refined and ingenious type of retaliation. Any such usage ignores, of course, the primary fact that Paul is describing the aims and attitudes of the religious man. Actually we are debarred even from the instinctive satisfaction of noting that "our enemy" has recognized his errors and turned from his mistaken ways. We are by definition dealing in love with our brother—it is only *his* animosity which makes him our enemy —and our only possible reaction must be one of delight that we have gained our brother (cf. Matt. 18:15). As to the efficacy of his suggested method, Paul has no doubts. After all, he had given a thorough trial to the chief alternative in the days before his proud will bent to the claims of Christ, and in his varied dealings with all types and conditions of men he must have repeatedly put to the test the method which he is advocating here; moreover, all our insight into religious psychology suggests that this approach is the only one on which we can rely if we hope to restore our broken fellowship with our brother.

If hatred is sin, part of the problem will inevitably consist in the ingenious insincerity with which evil protects itself against the light. With infinite skill it discovers ways of deflecting the disconcerting shafts of the truth, and by subtle rationalization persuades itself that the wrong it has done is really as close to the right as it could reasonably be expected to come. It is impervious to the force of reason or logic, since its characteristic method is designed to neutralize their impact, and any suggestion of superiority puts it instantly on its guard. The only power which can cut through its devious entanglements is love. Love, making no claim to judge, is free from all affectations of greater virtue. Because of its inherent character, it allows the sinner to see himself, yet with hope. Though it involves judgment, it also promises mercy. It is the one way in which the tangled skein of human relationships can be unraveled so that sin appears as it is and the offender is not emotionally committed to its defense. Consequently, what Paul offers is not an idealistic or impractical approach to an intractable problem; he is setting forth the one hopeful and effective answer to the alienations which embitter human life.

The **coals of fire** suggest a further comment. The phrase presumably points to the effect of an awakened conscience, and it has beyond its vivid quality the advantage of pressing home certain truths inherent in what Paul has been saying. It contains a hint of the bitterness which is inseparable from sin. To see love is to recognize for the first time what hatred means; in the light of goodness evil stands exposed,

21 Be not overcome of evil, but overcome evil with good.

21 Do not be overcome by evil, but overcome evil with good.

way to "punish" an enemy is to **heap burning coals upon his head**—i.e., to make him ashamed by meeting his hostility with active kindness and good will. (Vs. 20 is a quotation of Prov. 25:21-22 in the LXX; see Strack and Billerbeck for rabbinical comments, III, 302.) Still, it is doubtful that Paul would have been able thus to define the human responsibility for dealing with evil if he had not entertained vivid expectations of the "wrath of God." The view that God was soon to judge the world and that meantime (to anticipate 13:1-7) the state was acting in God's place made it easier to regard the individual as having no responsibility for judgment. The whole strategy of dealing with evil is summed up in vs. 21: we are not to allow ourselves to hate the enemy—to do so

and "burning shame" must be our reaction when confronted with what we have been and done. The phrase also suggests a process drastic in its character and remorseless in its method. The sentimentalism which often marks our approach to great religious problems is utterly insufficient to the demands of sin and righteousness. If "our God is a consuming fire," it is no simple thing to be confronted with his holy will. To the ancient mind the distinctive operation of fire was to cleanse and purify. It purged away all dross and eliminated all impurities. The method might be drastic, but it was necessary; and the results, while not guaranteed, might well prove promising.

21. ***Victory Remains with Love.*—Do not be overcome by evil, but overcome evil with good.** Everything that Paul has been saying suggests the need of retaining the initiative on behalf of the good. What happens in human affairs usually depends on who is allowed to set the pace which others are required to follow. If hatred is the decisive force, it drags goodness to its own level; if goodness predominates, it tends to lift others to its plane. Goodness can **be overcome by evil;** whenever we allow the forces of darkness to take control and dictate to us the terms on which human relations will be conducted, we abdicate the power of shaping life to better ends. The real defeat of good occurs when it is subordinated to evil. Then the clamor of hatred drowns the counsels of love. When this happens the tragedy is all the greater because so often it is unnecessary and could have been avoided. The one element of hope in our tangled and difficult human situation is that goodness, besides being desirable in itself, can prove redemptive. This is the point where the cleavage between the Christian and the humanist becomes most clearly defined. We are not creatures endowed with more ingenuity than wisdom, struggling to evade the disasters we threaten to bring down upon our own heads. We are not dependent on our own skills to win a precarious progress. We are rather the children of God; we can apprehend and appropriate spiritual powers which are mighty to transform our situation, and we are able to discover—if we will—that in all things God co-operates for good with those who love him. Our problem, of course, arises from the fact that many Christians, though they admit these things to be true, live in a predominantly secular world, and so for a great deal of the time think in a purely secular way. We concede the truth of what the N.T. says even when we are not prepared to practice it.

Two final comments must suffice. Paul has been dealing with a particular range of problems, and his closing counsel here sums up all that he wishes to say regarding our relationships with those who for any reason are opposed to us. Its range of application, however, is a great deal wider, and can aptly be taken as an epitome of the characteristic N.T. attitude to all problems of human conduct. This is because it so faithfully expresses all that was most distinctive in the life and teaching of him who was the inspiration of all Paul's thought and conduct. At the same time, it affirms a general principle and leaves the solution of difficult issues in the realm of practical conduct to the insight of each of us. This often presents us with painful uncertainties regarding the right decision in a given situation, and it confronts us with the disconcerting fact that Christians sometimes interpret their duty in different and even in opposing ways. Yet the essence of Christian discipleship is loyalty to that which our insight convinces us is the will of God. Unless it is our own insight, it has little value as a personal commitment to truth; because it is our own insight, it is continually liable to error and constantly in need of being verified by reference to what we see of God's will in Jesus Christ. In any event, it precludes all simple ready-made solutions which we can automatically apply to any given situation. It

13 Let every soul be subject unto the higher powers. For there is no power

13 Let every person be subject to the governing authorities. For there is

is to be **overcome** by the very evil which has conquered *him;* rather we are to meet his hatred with good will and thus **overcome evil** for us both. (In interesting contrast to Paul's teaching here stands Mattathias' exhortation to his sons in I Macc. 2:67-68: "And you must gather about you all who observe the Law and avenge the wrongs of your people. Pay back the heathen for what they have done . . ." [Goodspeed].)

2. The State (13:1-7)

This short section has an importance out of all proportion to its length because of the influence it has exerted. Several general considerations deserve attention before we examine the passage in detail. One wonders first why this brief account of the proper Christian attitude toward the state appears in this particular letter. Paul nowhere else

may be inconvenient, but the truth does not make us free in order that we may again become entangled in regulations.

13:1-7. *The Christian as Citizen.*—The Christian's duty is specific as well as general, and Paul turns abruptly to consider one particular aspect of our obligation. The law of love, so comprehensive in its outreach, can be expected to confront us with extremely exacting demands. So much emerges from the general treatment which Paul has given the subject in ch. 12, but he has not yet considered any of the concrete situations in which a decision is often so hard to make.

From among these practical problems he now selects the relation of the Christian to the state. It is interesting to note that within less than a generation of the founding of the church this had become an urgent problem. It has remained so ever since, but in most ages Christians have tended to ignore it until circumstances have suddenly made it crucially important. A crisis seldom finds the church forearmed with an adequate interpretation of the prerogatives of the state. Under pressure Christians have either granted the ruler too much latitude, or else have refused to concede him what he is fully entitled to claim. As a result they have been unduly subservient in some periods, while in others they have allowed no satisfactory place in their thought for the necessary functions of the state.

Paul provides us with the earliest study on record of the problem of church and state. Presumably he turned to the question because he found it typical and urgent. There must have been particular reasons which prompted him to give this issue precedence over others. We do not know in detail what they were, but we can reasonably infer their character (cf. Exeg.). In addition to factors whose presence we can easily surmise it may be that other considerations—considerations apt to re-emerge in every generation—had already begun to influence the attitude of certain members of the church. There has always been a strain in Christian thought which needs little provocation to repudiate the authority of the temporal rulers and claim that Christians owe their sole allegiance to "King Jesus." Moreover, the expectation that their Lord would soon return must have fortified the slightly anarchistic element in the church, and doubtless made it difficult for some of the early Christians to settle down as loyal subjects of the state. When even their own affairs were allowed to suffer—and elsewhere Paul hints that this was so—their duties to the state were certain to be neglected.

The problem was complicated by the fact that the Christian always belongs to two communities, and has loyalties to both. Sometimes the one, sometimes the other, claims to be predominant, and to declare their separation certainly does not settle all the problems involved. The intense and eager discussion which has centered around Paul's treatment here in ch. 13 merely illustrates the perennial interest in this subject throughout Christian history.

As the early church approached the problem of the state, it was inevitably influenced by its own background of experience. At the moment the state appeared to be a beneficent power—a bulwark of order and, on the whole, a minister of justice (cf. Exeg.). In due time, however, the church was to find that Rome could persecute as well as protect. One possible reaction to this change is the strident opposition with which the writer of Revelation denounces the civil power. But clearly the predominant Christian attitude was based on something worthier and more enduring than expediency. Most of our evidence points to the conclusion that the early church decided that in those

even touches on the subject unless II Thess. 2:6 is such a reference. Is it because Paul knows of rebellious tendencies among the Christians at Rome? Or does it occur to him to discuss this matter because he is writing to Rome, the seat of the empire, and the very name suggested this topic? Does he write to influence the attitude of the Roman Christians toward the government, or to correct an impression they may have (or he fears they may have) of his own attitude? Or—and this is perhaps the most likely explanation—does he take up the subject at this point because he has been led to think of it by what he has just said about the duty of forgoing private vengeance? We cannot definitely or surely exclude any of these possibilities. We can be certain, however, that whatever the reason for the particular location of this teaching, it reflects an important concern of the apostle, was a frequent topic of discussion between him and his churches, and only by accident is so meagerly noticed in his extant letters.

We can be sure of this because the Roman government was so important, so ubiquitous, and so permanent a feature of Paul's world, and because it had bearing upon the fortunes of the developing Christian movement at so many points. We cannot doubt that Paul, the traveler, found himself often thanking God for the unification of

---

situations where the rights of conscience were invaded the state must be resisted, but in all other matters the Christian must accept and discharge the obligations of his citizenship.

Paul, then, was setting forth a principle which many besides himself were quite prepared to honor in practice. At the same time we must remember that this section of Romans has had an extraordinary history. Paul probably wrote with the purpose of restraining a tendency to turbulence which, after all, was present in the religious background of many Christians, was aggravated by contemporary influences, and held within it immense potentialities for evil. By guarding against one tendency—the one particularly insistent when he wrote—he did not sufficiently protect himself against misconstruction in the opposing sense. He hurled his anathemas against anarchy; he did not foresee that they would be quoted in defense of tyranny. Those who contend for the "divine right" of existing institutions have always found their strongest support in ch. 13, and it could reasonably be claimed that no other part of Scripture has afforded such solace to unscrupulous men. But before condemning Paul too harshly, it is well to remember how often statements that we ourselves have made—and made with complete assurance that they adequately covered a given subject—have been distorted or misinterpreted simply because they were silent on phases of the theme which we assumed were perfectly self-evident.

The general principle which Paul states so unequivocally is the duty of being good citizens. He argues from the nature of organized society, the purpose of God which it is designed to promote, and the right and proper service which ought to constitute the individual's recognition of these facts. He has not guarded himself by including exceptions or discussing difficult cases, and his plea has nothing to do with the beneficence or the oppressiveness of the ruling power. In this respect the parallel with Jer. 29:7 is instructive; the prophet was certainly not resting his appeal on the nature of the state by which his fellow countrymen had been taken captive.

At the same time it is only fair to admit that Paul appeals to men and women whose citizenship possesses certain wholly distinctive marks. While subject to the secular empire, they look for the coming of another kingdom—the kingdom of God on earth. To what extent this becomes an issue of immediate practical politics is a question on which Christians have always differed widely; but there is no doubt that it introduces a new element of tension into our loyalty to the state. We may not be inclined to propose any immediate practical alternative to the existing form of government, but all decisions and policies are subject to careful scrutiny in the light of the insights which the kingdom of God inspires. Inevitably the Christian becomes involved in a conflict of loyalties. He may not work out the meaning of this tension —as Augustine did—in the form of a comprehensive interpretation of history and experience; but he cannot wholly escape the problems which it poses. There are times when he must declare that it is his duty to serve God rather than men; but normally it will be his responsibility faithfully to accept his obligations and conscientiously to discharge them. Since it is the danger of failing at the latter point which causes Paul concern, it is with this that he is exclusively preoccupied.

1. *Let Every Person. . . .* —The emphasis is clear. No one can claim that special privilege gives him exemption from civil obedience, nor

the world which Rome had brought about and for the comparative safety of the seas and the roads for which Roman action against pirates and robbers had been responsible. He would also be grateful often for the protection which Roman magistrates gave him when he was threatened by mob violence. At the same time, the Roman government was already a potential persecutor. That Paul recognized this possibility appears unmistakably in 8:35-38. Christianity, if it was a *new* religion, was *ipso facto* an illegal religion. To be sure, Paul did not regard it as a new religion—it was the true and final form of the ancient faith, the true Israel—but such a position, although it could continue to be maintained theologically, was, especially in view of growing Jewish opposition, increasingly difficult to make convincing practically; and eventually, of course, it became quite impossible. Even in Paul's own time there could be no assurance that every Roman magistrate would take the view which Gallio is said to have taken in Corinth when some Jews brought Paul before him (Acts 18:14-15). Still, in spite of all this it is unquestionably true that the Roman government appeared to Paul, at any rate up to the time when he wrote this letter, as a friend rather than as an enemy.

This fact may well have had a part in determining the character of the teaching in vss. 1-7. It is possible, however, to exaggerate its effect. Certainly one cannot say that Paul's doctrine here is attributable only to the accident of his having found the government on the whole helpful and protective. That doctrine has a deep and firm basis in his tradition. Although there was no little anti-Roman feeling among Jews in his period—witness the great rebellion only a few years after the death of Paul—yet there were many, as there always had been, to affirm the authority of government and the duty of obedience. Such persons may have believed that God would eventually or soon *change* the government; but until he did so, one's obligation was to obey it. One must not take

can he insist that special insight puts him beyond the reach of the state's demands. Paul doubtless speaks against a contemporary background which we know only by surmise; but it was not in the first century alone that men have been tempted to plead a religious right in order to evade their duties as citizens. When times of tension occur, the Christian must settle as best he can the vexed question as to which of the loyalties he recognizes has the higher claim; but under all ordinary circumstances it is his responsibility to serve the commonweal. It would perhaps be well if Christians asked themselves whether in their dealings with the civil power they are not more concerned to claim immunities than to accept responsibilities. It is possible to be too preoccupied with the exemptions which a deserving group can expect to receive. Certainly the church can profitably ask itself whether it has encouraged among its members a proper sense of the privilege of citizenship. Among the values in this temporal order which the Christian can legitimately seek to safeguard, Augustine singles out for special mention our "membership in a state which is venerated as a parent." [4]

The nature of the subjection which Paul requires is not specified; but he himself had repeatedly had occasion to remark that his work was possible only within the framework of established order. The liberty of the citizen to pursue his legitimate interests is always contingent on his accepting the potential restraint which the organized life of the community imposes. The man who is not "in subjection" has not achieved freedom; he has only relapsed into the anarchy of license.

One of the crucial passages in this section is Paul's bold assertion that **there is no authority except from God, and those that exist have been instituted by God.** The background of such a statement must be a strong assurance of God's providential ordering of the world. Nothing can exist apart from his good will and pleasure; all things trace their being to him, and all are held in life by the working of his spirit. It does not follow, of course, that if all being is derived from the fountain of being, it retains intact the evidences of its origin. Still, order even when imperfect and defective is a religious concern of the first importance. It has always been the work of God's spirit to banish chaos and to bring order out of disorder (cf. Gen. 1). This is true in every sphere, and certainly not least in the corporate life of men. The place of the state in a religious dispensation is apparent; but what are we to make of Paul's contention that *all* states exist because God has established them? Is not this the kind of predestination which cloaks evil governments with the sanction of divine right? It all depends, of course, on what is meant by predestination. Man's incurable tendency to think

[4] *The Free Choice of the Will* I. 15.

but of God: the powers that be are ordained of God.

no authority except from God, and those that exist have been instituted by God.

into one's own hand the responsibility of changing the government. In view of this it is possible to see a real connection in thought between 12:19-21 and 13:1-7. This attitude of loyalty to the government was maintained by the great mass of Christians even after persecutions of Christians became frequent and severe, as witness I Pet. 2:13-17, where essentially the same view of the Christian's proper attitude toward the government is expressed as Paul had expressed a generation or two earlier, even though now the Roman government's attitude is certainly less friendly. It is probable, however, that I Pet. 2:13-17 does not come out of a situation of actual persecution. F. W. Beare goes far to demonstrate that I Peter is composite, a second document beginning at 4:12. I Pet. 1:3–4:11 reflects a situation of some danger, but not the "fiery ordeal" referred to in

of God in anthropomorphic terms of the lower order has meant that far too often we have equated God's providential care with the principle of philosophical determinism, and have then equated man's freedom with indeterminism.[5] But neither in Paul nor in Augustine is this kind of opposition envisaged. God's will does not bind and circumscribe his children. It is possible, therefore, to recognize an order which is providential but not determinative; we can acknowledge that government is of divine institution without reducing man to the status of a slave. The meaning of this apparent paradox is much clearer if we approach it in the light of religious experience than if we insist on dealing with it by means of the categories provided by strict logic. The religious man is aware of what can be described only as a new dimension; he comes to know that parallel to the chronological plane on which he is normally content to live his life is another plane—that in which he is aware of a living God who deals with him in and through the events which unfold on the chronological plane. It remains true, for example, that Joseph's history is molded by the fond indulgence of his father, the envy of his brothers, the evil passion of Potiphar's wife, the needs of Pharaoh, and the atmospheric conditions of the Nile Valley; yet Joseph can quite truthfully see in the whole of the natural sequence the providential guiding of God's hand.[6] A new dimension has been added to what otherwise was only a story of shabby intrigue overruled by startling good fortune; but this new dimension transforms the entire narrative into a moving record of religious experience. Something of the same quality enters into our relations with the state if we see in civil order a manifestation of God's purpose for his children, a method of dealing with us which can speak to our condition even through the manifold human imperfections which seem to be inseparable from all governments, good as well as bad.

Inherent in such a point of view is another inference of great importance for understanding the role which this passage has played in Christian history. If the state is a part of God's providential governing of the world, we can justly claim that order in human society must be God's wise provision for the safeguarding of his children's lives. In certain traditions this conviction has been more strongly cherished than in others, and often it is associated with a certain type of background in thought and experience. In the first century a citizen of the Roman Empire never forgot that it was Augustus' great achievement to rescue his world from what threatened to be endemic disorder. The memory of what chaos actually means was still fresh in many parts of the Roman world; the necessity and value of disciplined and regulated public life were consequently never overlooked. A somewhat similar background—in this case provided by the disorders of the later Middle Ages, the violence of the Peasants' Revolt, the chaos created by the struggles of the seventeenth century—no doubt helps to explain the intense concern of German Lutheranism with order as an integral aspect of the divine dispensation. The disorganization and the uncertainties which World War I and World War II left in their wake intensified in certain quarters a new preoccupation with this subject. As long as man persists in making his own future unpredictable, Paul's words will not lack a certain relevance. Those who feel that the crust of civilization is perilously thin, and that the foul turbulence of social dissolution may break through at any moment, are not apt to dismiss lightly the apostolic claim that

[5] Cf. C. N. Cochrane, *Christianity and Classical Culture* (Oxford: Clarendon Press, 1940), p. 481.

[6] Cf. Herbert H. Farmer, *The World and God* (New York: Harper & Bros., 1935), p. 106.

2 Whosoever therefore resisteth the power, resisteth the ordinance of God: and they that resist shall receive to themselves damnation.

2 Therefore he who resists the authorities resists what God has appointed, and those

---

4:12–5:6. Still, there is nothing in the last section of the letter to suggest a basically different attitude to the authority of the state (see F. W. Beare, *The First Epistle of Peter* [Oxford: Blackwell & Mott, 1947]).

13:1-2. Reference is often made in this connection to Wisd. Sol. 6:1-5. This passage, written at some time between 50 B.C. and A.D. 40, is important enough to be quoted:

> Listen therefore, kings, and understand:
> Learn this, judges of the ends of the earth:
> . . . .
> For your dominion was given you from the Lord,
> And your sovereignty from the Most High.
> He will examine your works and inquire into your plans;
> For though you are servants of his kingdom, you have not judged rightly,
> Or kept the Law,
> Or followed the will of God.
> He will come upon you terribly and swiftly,
> For a stern judgment overtakes those in high places (Goodspeed).

This writer is obviously making the same point as Paul's: **there is no authority except from God;** but he makes it in warning rulers of their duties to their subjects, not—as Paul does—in warning subjects of their duties to their rulers. The conception that established rulers are divinely ordained has both implications (i.e., they should discharge their responsibilities worthily, and others should reverence and obey them); and which

---

the maintenance of organized life is of divine ordinance.

2. ***The Individual and the State.***—If public order is part of a divine purpose, it is an exceedingly serious thing to set ourselves against it. It means that we have willfully preferred our private aims to the well-being of society; we have exalted our own preferences above the needs of the collective whole. This kind of gratuitous individualism is destructive of all the values which a community exists to serve; and in a tradition where its virtues have been praised and its dangers overlooked, it is well to ponder the seriousness with which Paul regarded irresponsible opposition to the state. It is only fair to assume that this is not a complete statement of his attitude to constituted power; he himself was ready to affirm, and if need be to act on, the right of conscience to protest against the actions of the state. But that is very different from the perverse and irresponsible defiance of public authority. There is nothing to suggest that Paul intended his counsel to cover the question of opposition to evil and oppressive governments. After all, he was not composing a treatise on political science. He was writing to people in a given situation, confronted by one particular kind of ruling power. We have noticed that he regarded the empire as an agent of order, and disorder was manifestly bad. He was not considering the question whether successful revolt against a bad government could be justified; as Dodd has suggestively remarked, the Roman citizen of the first century knew nothing about successful revolts, and to discuss the possibility would have seemed an academic exercise in an unreal realm. Actually Paul was writing a letter to men and women who lived within sight of Caesar's palace.

The penalties attaching to resistance are simple and can be simply stated: those responsible for insubordination can expect only condign punishment. This is a bald affirmation of an inescapable fact. Unfortunately, for one reason or another people are often disposed to ignore it. Those caught up in the enthusiasm of what they consider a worthy cause forget the possibility of retribution, or hope that in their case it will not operate. It is this which makes the ultimate fate of earnest but often misguided saboteurs so poignant. Paul may have had in mind the Zealots of his own day; but their name has become an adjective, and it aptly fits many an agitator who forgets that **those who resist will incur judgment.** Others, with less

3 For rulers are not a terror to good works, but to the evil. Wilt thou then not be afraid of the power? do that which is good, and thou shalt have praise of the same:

4 For he is the minister of God to thee for good. But if thou do that which is evil, be afraid; for he beareth not the sword in vain: for he is the minister of God, a revenger to *execute* wrath upon him that doeth evil.

who resist will incur judgment. 3 For rulers
are not a terror to good conduct, but to
bad. Would you have no fear of him who
is in authority? Then do what is good, and
you will receive his approval, 4 for he is
God's servant for your good. But if you do
wrong, be afraid, for he does not bear the
sword in vain; he is the servant of God to
execute his wrath on the wrong-doer.

---

of the implications a given writer will emphasize will depend partly upon whether on the whole he approves or disapproves of the rulers, and partly on his own particular purpose in writing. Thus we find Paul writing here: **He who resists the authorities resists what God has appointed, and . . . will incur judgment**—i.e., presumably human punishment, or God's judgment expressing itself through human punishment. But in Enoch 46:5, we read: "And he shall put down the kings from their thrones and kingdoms because they do not extol and praise him, nor humbly acknowledge whence the kingdom was bestowed upon them." See other passages cited in Strack and Billerbeck (III, 303-4).

3-5. Paul's experiences with the Roman government and with its local representatives had on the whole been reassuring; but as we have seen, that fact bears only slightly on the understanding of such a passage as this. Paul's whole manner here suggests the loyal subject—i.e., the subject, loyal by conviction (**conscience**) and therefore loyal whether he happens to be justly treated on a particular occasion or not. The same is

---

worthy motives and more cynical realism, trust that they can evade both the law and its penalties. It is with the punishments which the state inflicts that Paul is primarily concerned; but it is surely not disloyal to the text to recall that the penalties which follow wrongdoing are not merely those administered by the policeman and the judge: even the successful culprit incurs judgment of a kind more serious than he knows. On one score there is no ground for doubt. The inference that can most legitimately be drawn from Paul's words concerns the solemnity with which the law should be invested and its high claims to our respect.

3. ***Due Subjection Without Fear.***—The simple facts of the case cannot be stated too clearly or too often. The upright man should respect the law but he need not fear it. Under good government—and the proviso is always present—the decent citizen will have no fear of what the officers of the state can do to him. If he is afraid, something is wrong—either with the state itself, or with his understanding of his proper role. But since the soundness of the state is taken for granted, one can assume that the fearful man is also the bad man. And he is apprehensive with good cause. Between him and the community there inevitably exists an ineradicable antagonism. His kind of life cannot be reconciled with the principles of public order. On the strength of this the apostle offers a simple piece of practical advice. If you want to be beyond fear of authority, be above suspicion of wrongdoing. But in addition to holding forth negative restraints, the state can offer positive encouragements. The approval of those in authority is more than an alternative to fear, and Paul mentions it as a worthy sequel to our well-doing.

4. ***The Role of the Magistrate.***—This twofold reaction on the part of the state—of aversion to the evil citizen on the one hand and of approval of the good subject on the other—helps to make clear what are the real place and purpose of the civil power in Paul's judgment. The vital word appears to be **servant.** The magistrate's proper task is to uphold the right and suppress the wrong. He can appropriately be described as the agent by which a higher power dispenses the fitting rewards which human conduct has merited. At this point we catch a further glimpse of that moral order which lies behind our organized life, and at every point determines its true character. Paul has referred in ch. 1 to the way in which moral retribution overtakes wrongdoing, and it is another aspect of the same inevitable sequence with which he is at present occupied. Moral law has the same inexorable quality as natural causation. Do what is right, and you will find

5 Wherefore *ye* must needs be subject, not only for wrath, but also for conscience' sake.

6 For, for this cause pay ye tribute also: for they are God's ministers, attending continually upon this very thing.

5 Therefore one must be subject, not only to avoid God's wrath but also for the sake of conscience. 6 For the same reason you also pay taxes, for the authorities are ministers of God, attending to this very thing.

---

true of I Peter (note especially 3:13). The contrasting attitude is found in the book of Revelation, so far as N.T. literature is concerned. If Paul was not merely a loyal *subject* but also, as Acts says, a *citizen,* the attitude toward the state embodied in these verses is even more readily understandable. Lietzmann paraphrases vs. 5: **One must be subject** "not only out of fear but out of conviction." The fear is of God's **wrath** against those who disobey his "ministers" (vs. 4). This **wrath** is not the final judgment (as in 1:18; etc.), but is not on that account less truly **God's wrath.** For God's judgment, although it will be fully executed only in the approaching "day of the Lord," is in a measure executed now by those whom God has appointed to **bear the sword.**

6-7. For the same reason may be parallel to **therefore** at the beginning of vs. 5, or it may refer back no farther than to **conscience** at the end of that verse. **This very thing,** to which **the authorities** are **attending,** is not **taxes,** of course, but the general function of rewarding the good and punishing the evil which is described in the preceding verses. Various ways of defining the distinction between **taxes** (φορος) and **revenue** (τέλος) have been suggested. Lietzmann and Kühl define it as the distinction between direct and indirect taxes respectively. Sanday and Headlam assert that φόρος designates the tribute

---

that the magistrate is God's agent for good; do what is wrong, and he will prove to be the servant by which moral retribution overtakes you. Under such circumstances even the outward evidences of power become significant. The **sword** is never merely a decorative appurtenance, because it is always the symbol of that retribution which wrongdoing brings upon itself. Paul has been describing the results of good and bad citizenship, but he has indirectly indicated a theory of the state which it would be profitable to develop. A certain kind of heritage in Western Christendom makes it easy for many people to regard the state as nothing more than a necessary nuisance or a useful convenience (as the needs of the moment may dictate); at least it has little religious significance. Paul places it firmly in the natural order, with all that this implies of a place in God's dealing with men. The distinctive type of divine activity—that which the gospel proclaims—is redemptive grace; but even when it is not operative God still has other ways of working. He has not "left himself without witness," and the natural order also serves divine ends. Its testimony may be more equivocal and its effects less perfect, but it cannot be ignored. To this natural order the state belongs; in such ways as its more limited scope permits, it works God's purpose in the lives of men.

5-6. *Conscience and Our Civil Obedience.*—Such an interpretation of temporal power places the citizen's proper obedience in a new light. The fact that the rulers "bear the sword" may still make it prudent to obey their commands; but it is much more than a matter of expediency. There is a real duty of Christian obedience, and good citizenship takes its place among the virtues which can properly be associated with the new life. This is the constructive aspect of Paul's approach to the question, and it becomes a matter of **conscience** to accept the duties of membership in the community. Among these is the commonly neglected virtue of paying taxes (vs. 6). There is more than one indication in the Gospels (cf. Matt. 17:25-27) that Jesus expected his disciples to meet the demands which the state laid upon them, and commentators have been quick to recognize in this passage echoes of the command to give to Caesar the things that rightfully belong to him (Matt. 22:21). In some respects Paul's words, though possessing less authority, have even greater interest. Jesus spoke to people who with little difficulty made their objection to taxes appear a religious virtue, and the Palestinian situation had certain unique features. Paul's readers were mainly Gentiles; for them the problem was the simple one which we all know, and it is salutary to recall that the apostle found a place for paying taxes in his

7 Render therefore to all their dues: tribute to whom tribute *is due;* custom to whom custom; fear to whom fear; honor to whom honor.
8 Owe no man any thing, but to love one another: for he that loveth another hath fulfilled the law.

7 Pay all of them their dues, taxes to whom taxes are due, revenue to whom revenue is due, respect to whom respect is due, honor to whom honor is due.
8 Owe no one anything, except to love one another; for he who loves his neigh-

exacted by a foreign master-nation, and τέλος, ordinary taxation (so also Kirk). Perhaps Paul has no particular distinction in mind; certainly he does not think of **respect** and **honor** as separately due to two distinct classes of men. The form of this sentence is in large part determined by rhetorical considerations. The point is that whatever one truly owes another (i.e., **their dues**), whether it is money or respect, one must fully pay.

3. Love the Fulfillment of the Law (13:8-10)

8a. This same idea is expressed in the first clause of this section: **Owe no one anything** —i.e., do not *continue* in a state of owing any of the obligations referred to in vs. 7 (or for that matter, any others); rather fulfill and discharge them. Get rid of all debts, not by denying, ignoring, or evading them, but by paying them; there is only one debt of which one can never get rid—the debt of love. The phrase **love one another** ordinarily suggests a relationship within the church (so in John 13:34); perhaps Paul has the community primarily in mind here, but certainly he is thinking also of all of the Chris-

picture of the state as a part of God's dispensation. We do not often think of the revenue officer as exercising a distinctive ministry to which God has appointed him. Paul evidently did.

7. *The Outreach of Good Citizenship.*—The subject of taxes naturally prompts Paul to consider the much wider question of discharging all the responsibilities by which the citizen is faced. There are many forms of obligation, and we should fulfill them all. **Taxes** reappear, perhaps because they form the natural transition to a more comprehensive treatment of the subject, perhaps because they are a duty which most citizens are particularly willing to evade; but Paul has also explicitly included even those more galling kinds of levy (**revenue**) to which subject peoples have to submit. (Yet see Exeg.) And there is more than that. The stability of the state rests on many things besides the ability to levy taxes and collect them. A government which does not command the **respect** of its people is condemned to impotence and will finally fall. Loyalty has more than sentimental value. If there is no respect for those who ought to receive it, and no **honor** and reverence for the rulers of the people, the public welfare stands in jeopardy. It may be difficult to feel respect for men whose standards and achievements do not deserve it; but it will always be hard to secure worthy public servants unless the community is prepared to regard the holders of public office as entitled to honor and esteem. A country usually gets the kind of government it deserves, and it may be that one of the determining factors is the attitude of the average citizen toward those whom he selects to serve him.

Perhaps it would be of value briefly to recapitulate what Paul has been affirming about the state and the obedience we owe it. (*a*) Civil government, he says, is a provision of God for our good. Willful defiance is therefore disobedience to God, and this inevitably brings us under judgment (vss. 1-2). (*b*) The state exists to uphold the right and overthrow the wrong, and this will determine the attitude of the citizen to the power it wields. The man who faithfully does his duty need have no fear of the rulers; the evildoer naturally is afraid—and should be (vss. 3-4). (*c*) Our acceptance of the role of citizen, with the subordination it involves, is partly a result of prudence; but to a much greater extent it has the force of principle behind it (vs. 5). (*d*) In discharging our duties we shall pay the taxes without which the government cannot function; and we shall also concede it that honor and respect which are equally its due (vss. 6-7).

8. *The Only Permissible Debt.*—The horizon of obligation has been steadily extended from the payment of taxes to the conceding of everything that can be expected of the citizen. But it is not of "citizens" only that Paul is thinking; he is writing to men whose lives comprise many types of activity but should be governed

9 For this, Thou shalt not commit adultery, Thou shalt not kill, Thou shalt not steal, Thou shalt not bear false witness, Thou shalt not covet; and if *there be* any other commandment, it is briefly comprehended in this saying, namely, Thou shalt love thy neighbor as thyself.

bor has fulfilled the law. 9 The commandments, "You shall not commit adultery, You shall not kill, You shall not steal, You shall not covet," and any other commandment, are summed up in this sentence, "You shall love your neighbor as your-

---

tian's relationships. Having paid all of one's obligations to one's neighbor, according to every human standard, one still, as a Christian, owes him love—the meaning of which no conceivable list of our obligations or of other people's "dues" can possibly exhaust. Such is plainly the implication of vs. 8*a*; but the subsequent discussion takes a slightly different turn.

8*b*-10. Paul goes on to point out that love of neighbor covers all the separate requirements of the Decalogue—i.e., those touching on our behavior toward our neighbor (Jesus' summation in *two* "great commandments" [Mark 12:29 ff. and parallels] is more adequate).

---

by one basic principle. This can be stated negatively—we should **owe no man any thing** which he can rightfully claim from us. Here is a moral law which we are quick enough to ask others to obey. Suggestively enough, the unforgiving servant, when claiming the money which is due him, frames his unreasonable demand in the form of a general ethical principle: "Pay what you owe," he says (Matt. 18:28). If we discharge our obligations faithfully and fully, we may not have made great progress, but we have made a very necessary start. But the basic principle can be stated positively, and then it appears as a paradox: we must owe everyone more than we can hope to pay. Paul has previously been speaking of people in authority, and of the distinctive service we owe them; now he speaks of all men, high and low, and of the universal service we owe them. He is both extending and intensifying the conception of obligation. We must be more scrupulous within the limits governed by customary ideas of indebtedness; and we must infinitely widen the range within which they operate. But Paul is also doing more. The paradox is apparent rather than real, because **love** is not merely one duty added to others we may happen to accept. It provides the only inclusive framework within which all duties can find a creative place. It is the motive power which in every situation frees us from the constraint of an external compulsion and enables us to do with the largeness of a liberated spirit the things we could never hope to do simply because we were told that they were our duty.

As a matter of fact, Paul is giving an entirely new significance to the idea of obligation. It does not occupy a conspicuous place in his ethical thought because it has been transformed by its association with a much more comprehensive idea—love. It has become derivative, and every phase of duty is adequately covered if we make sure that love will have its proper place. Consequently, it is the complete fulfillment of the moral law to love the person with whom we come in contact. The definition of our **neighbor** in terms of the person whom we can help is mandatory for Christians in the light of Jesus' story of the good Samaritan. We are to treat everyone we meet with at least as scrupulous a regard for his personal interests as we normally show for our own; if we do so, we may rest assured that we shall have fulfilled all the requirements that even an exacting code of religious commandments could lay upon us. Paul illustrates this fact by an appeal to that code by which all his own earlier efforts had been judged. One by one he enumerates (vs. 9) the commandments from the "second table of laws"; and it is sufficient for him to quote them to prove his point. If we really love another person we cannot possibly injure him in any of the suggested ways. Love would stifle at birth the thoughts which lead to adultery, murder, theft, or any form of covetousness. Because love cannot hurt others, it cannot break the laws designed for their protection (vs. 10); and Paul is satisfied that every other conceivable requirement would be covered by the principle which he lays down.

The importance of these verses for Christian discipleship is obvious, and their manifest dependence on Jesus' teaching makes their claim on our attention all the greater. It is therefore wise to notice certain general comments which they naturally prompt.

Paul has set forth an extremely comprehensive principle which he expects to operate in concrete and particular cases. In its scope love is wide enough to include every demand, yet it

10 Love worketh no ill to his neighbor: therefore love *is* the fulfilling of the law.

self." 10 Love does no wrong to a neighbor; therefore love is the fulfilling of the law.

Paul asserts again the summary character of the "law of love" in Gal. 5:14 (cf. also Jas. 2:8, where this law is called the "royal law"). It is likely that some of the rabbis had arrived at the same insight (see Strack and Billerbeck, I, 907). Vs. 10, literally translated, reads, "The fullness of the law, therefore, is love." This "fullness of the law" probably means not merely the aggregate of its explicit demands, but rather the whole of God's will for us, much of which cannot be defined in legalistic terms. At many points in this Commentary the N.T. meaning of "love" (ἀγάπη) has been observed (see Vol. VII, p. 58; Vol. VIII, p. 694). It will be recalled that Paul uses the term primarily to designate God's love of us—that giving of himself to us, which may also be referred to as the Spirit (see on 5:5). It is therefore—at least for Paul—neither ordinary human affection (φιλία) nor ordinary human moral good will, but is a divine gift. God's "love"=his "grace"=his "Spirit." In Christ (i.e., in the "new creation," the new community) this "love" is poured

is relevant to any situation that may arise. But what is inclusive is apt to appear general and end by becoming slightly abstract. After centuries of lip service to love, the relationships of race to race, of class to class, of group to group, of man to man—and this within Christendom—are still marked by hatred and antagonism. One of the salutary disciplines which Christians need to practice is the habit of continually illuminating their relationships, both individual and communal, by an imaginative attempt to bring them to the bar of love as the N.T. defines it.

Law represents one approach to life, faith and love another. Earlier in this letter Paul set forth in detail a profound statement of how man finds peace with God. On the one hand he exposed the insufficiency of legalism, and showed how even the most meticulous satisfaction of injunctions laid upon man's will could never save us from moral defeat. On the other hand he proclaimed that a new attitude—an attitude of grateful trust in God and of humble acceptance of what he has done for us in Jesus Christ—would bring us into a new relationship and would issue in a new life. The counterpart of this theological position is now set forth in terms of our duty toward others. The same basic premise holds true both in thought and in conduct: law by itself cannot provide an adequate foundation for the good life. What faith does for theology, love does for ethics. It provides a practical alternative to the self-defeating claims of legalism.

The weakness of the law is that it multiplies requirements without providing a sufficient motive to enable us to satisfy them. For innumerable demands with no adequate enabling power, Paul substitutes one inclusive motive. Love gathers up all the diverse requirements of the good life and fuses them into the perfect unity of one comprehensive claim. While supplying the simplicity which shows us our duty and helps us to understand it, love also provides the power without which we cannot do the things we should.

Reiteration has made us so familiar with love as a formative influence in molding the good life that we assume it as a necessary part of any system of religious ethics. Consequently we overlook the profound originality of the N.T. approach. In other forms of religious faith we also have injunctions to love our fellow men; the distinctive quality of Christianity does not lie in the discovery of something that others had completely overlooked. But elsewhere we find the duty of love stated incidentally—perhaps in a high form, but not with regulative force. In the N.T. it is given a central and decisive place. Love does not supply the content of one counsel among many others; it is an inclusive motive which governs the whole of life. The idea itself was not original, but the role assigned to it certainly was. Consequently it is fitting that even the word the N.T. uses was not taken from the normal vocabulary of current ethics. As a distinctive religious term it was as new as the place assigned to it in Christian conduct.

The nature and scope of love is but briefly indicated in the verses under study; the important place it occupies in Paul's thought, however, warrants a glance at the development it receives elsewhere in his teaching. Love as a religious motive is never confused with an emotional response to those who appeal to our affections. If you are to "love your enemies," the word must have some connotation other than the appreciative reaction which your friends awaken within you. Love must mean the settled will to seek the good of those who come within the range of our influence, what-

11 And that, knowing the time, that now *it is* high time to awake out of sleep: for now

11 Besides this you know what hour it is, how it is full time now for you to wake

out upon us and possesses us, so that the love in us is not our own but God's. Thus in I Cor. 13, "love" is treated in the midst of a discussion of gifts of the Spirit. Love is the supreme gift because it is the very presence of the Spirit himself. On the bearing of this passage on Paul's discussion of "the law" earlier in the epistle something is said in the Exeg. of 8:4.

D. Special Need of Ethical Consecration Because of the Approaching Crisis (13:11-14)

11. At many points there has been occasion for comment on the importance for Paul of his eschatological expectations (e.g., Intro., p. 371; 2:1-5; 6:14*a*; etc.) Salvation is primarily and essentially future, but is even now in a secondary or derived sense available,

ever may be their attitude toward us. By the grace of God we will treat even those who do us wrong in the way which natural impulse would teach us to treat only those to whom we respond emotionally. What this involves can best be illustrated by referring to Paul's great hymn of love (I Cor. 13). Paul, it is clear, is describing something over which we have a measure of control, e.g., a kind of control which we have in very limited degree over our emotions and affections. That is why it can mark our relations with a circle far wider than that in which we normally move. Love is not merely a parochial virtue, and Paul regards all men as coming within its scope. Our will to do good to others can recognize no limitations. "May the Lord make you increase and abound in love to one another and to all men" (I Thess. 3:12). Love, though universal, does not cease to be particular: it may be as wide as humanity in its outreach; but it must include the specific individuals with whom we live and work. We are bound to note, however, that the particular often becomes selfish and the general often becomes nebulous. Those who love humanity can be "horrid" to the men and women whom they actually meet, while those who love their families and their friends can be quite deaf to the cry of those beyond their circle. The twofold character of N.T. love saves it from both the vices to which our human affections often succumb. The distinctive quality of love is further apparent in the uniform way in which it expresses itself in self-sacrificing deeds. Insight prompts it to sympathy, and sympathy stirs it to appropriate action; while its inherent nature and its characteristic expression are both the result of the power which calls it forth and sustains it. Love of this order is not our achievement but our response. It does not express human goodness but reflects divine mercy. We would never love one another in this way if we had been left to our own devices. The idea of love is always closely related to its inspiration, Jesus Christ. Paul is never weary of appealing to Christ's love for us as the incentive for our love of others. But in Christ's giving of himself for us the N.T. recognizes the very love of God. "God so loved the world that he gave . . ." (John 3:16), and when, according to our measure, we show a comparable spirit, it is because "the love of God is shed abroad in our hearts by the Holy Ghost" (5:5).

11-14. *Present Duty and Final Destiny.*—The doctrine of the last things occupied a great deal of the thought of early Christians. During the first half of the twentieth century the complacent attitude which formerly had looked forward to an endless prospect of assured and largely automatic progress was rudely shaken by the disclosure of what man is and what he can do. Eschatology no longer seemed to be an antique from the lumber room of theology; it became instead a living issue of tremendous urgency. When it ceased to be a figure of speech to write of the elements melting with fervent heat, the essential religious message of N.T. eschatology became unexpectedly relevant.

There is no doubt that Jesus expected his disciples to live in anticipation of "the end," though he expressly said that they would not know when the end would be. On the whole, Paul is consistently loyal to both these emphases. In his earlier letters he not only accepted the view that the present age would terminate in the return of Christ, but he also believed that the day of the Lord was close at hand. It was near enough to affect the decisions people made and the way they lived; but even so, he stoutly withstood any suggestion that this relaxed the duties they had to discharge. Though the end might come soon, Christians must still accept the responsibilities inseparable

is our salvation nearer than when we believed.

from sleep. For salvation is nearer to

since the future age is already beginning to break in on us. It is this fact which gives the present **time** (καιρός) its crucial importance and imparts to the ethical exhortations

from their part in the present dispensation. In his later letters we find him much more concerned with the new life in Christ than with the new age of Christ—or, to put it with somewhat greater exactness, more concerned with that new age which Christ has inaugurated in the life of the Christian than with hopes whose fulfillment lay hidden in an unpredictable future. In fact, we have in Paul an interesting example of the way in which the early Christians must have solved one of their great but silent crises: they expected Christ to come again, but he did not. This might have shattered the confidence of the new movement; since it did not do so, we must assume that they found an answer which satisfied the doubts that must have risen in their minds. It may be that in John's account of the promise of the Paraclete we find one answer: in the gift of the Spirit, Christ has already returned to his disciples in the form which most fully meets their needs. A similar answer is possibly found in Paul. His growing emphasis on the fact that Christ comes to live in his disciples, and that they find their own lives taken up into his, places in its true perspective the whole doctrine of the final things. At the same time, it leaves untouched those moral values which a proper emphasis on eschatology should safeguard. Since these are true in every age, they deserve a moment's consideration.

The conviction that our civilization is moving toward the goal of God's purpose helps to set our life in the light of eternal values. Our experience is more than a series of casual episodes unrelated to any significant end. Eschatology declares—among other things—that God will finally bring all of history to that conclusion which he has designed; as a consequence, we find our lives lifted out of the region of the accidental and the contingent. Divine judgment becomes a serious reality, and our lives are seen in its light.

In this process the standards which we accept are subject to drastic modification. Secular society surrounds us so completely that we are always tempted to accept its purely relative ways of judging life and its issues. Eschatology means that ultimate justice becomes our absolute standard. We may not know how to apply it in daily experience, but it proves to be a bracing and invigorating force. Our own canons of judgment are constantly subject to its scrutiny, and as they are sifted, they are also strengthened and purified.

When human life lacks a goal it becomes inconsequential, and all its serious issues are subject to postponement. The sense of a divinely appointed end introduces an element of urgency which delivers us from aimless drifting. In a much simpler setting Jesus emphasized the need of settling important matters while time permitted and the opportunity was still present. If we procrastinated the chance might pass, and it would be too late to set things right (Matt. 5:25). Christian history suggests innumerable examples of the way in which an awareness that all things move toward God's appointed end has given Christ's followers the necessary incentive to deal with issues, both large and small, in the same decisive spirit.

Nor is there any doubt that living in the light of an absolute standard exercises a cleansing and astringent effect on the conscience. The irrelevant and the distracting drop out of sight. Things which becloud our insight are removed; factors which distort our vision are swept away. The awareness of divine judgment as a reality makes us conscious of eternal values, and even amid ordinary circumstances we see our duty in a clearer light.

In the awareness of living under imminent divine judgment the N.T. found one of the most effective of all incentives to vigilant self-discipline. Though Christians had been told to watch and pray, they found that even a willing spirit could be depressed by the weakness of the flesh. But a slack and careless attitude could never hope to attain that quality of moral earnestness which the demands of discipleship manifestly required. The realization that the interval before the end might be limited made time precious. Yet it was not primarily the near approach of the consummation that made the matter important. The nature of the end—all it declared about God's purposes and their fulfillment, all it proclaimed about God's judgment and its searching quality—made it much easier for men and women to realize that discipline must be the mark of those who walk by such a light. In all the issues of daily living a person must be alert and ready to serve. Everything becomes a stew-

12 The night is far spent, the day is at hand: let us therefore cast off the works of darkness, and let us put on the armor of light.

us now than when we first believed; **12** the night is far gone, the day is at hand. Let us then cast off the works of darkness and put

---

Paul has given a supreme urgency. It is noteworthy that Paul has not made any of his injunctions *conditional* upon the fact of the rapidly approaching consummation; he has not mentioned the crisis at all in the ethical section until this point, and he mentions it here only to provide an additional incentive for allegiance to standards which have been set up and defined without any reference to it. The near approach of the final salvation and judgment does not make these practical teachings more *true;* but as Paul sees it, the coming event does make them more relevant and compelling. On "waking from sleep" see also I Thess. 5:4-8.

12-14. The Christian belongs not to the old order, the **night,** which is so soon to pass, but to the new order, the **day,** which is already showing signs of breaking. His

---

ardship for which we must finally render an account. The attitude of mind which expresses itself in the aphorism that "he who kills time mortgages eternity" became a characteristic mark of men aware that their lives, being lived in prospect of judgment, must be regulated by watchful self-discipline.

The sense of crisis was inseparable from the outlook of the early church. Christians were faced with fateful decisions, pregnant with future good or ill. This present age was passing away, the new age was standing on the threshold. The new life formed so decisive a breach with the old that only the imagery of a new birth could convey its meaning. The cleavage between the order of nature and the realm of grace was clear, and men were being called to relinquish the old that they might appropriate the new. The sharpness of this kind of demarcation has become obscured with time. One of its sources was in the conviction that men were faced with the fact of God's judgment. Because they believed it was near at hand, it was impossible for them to temporize or delay. What gave them such a vivid sense of the critical character of their decisions was the conviction that they had been brought face to face with God's ultimate purposes.

11. *No Time for Sleep.*—Paul has been outlining the nature of that great constraint which ought to mold the Christian's conduct. Love is the inclusive motive which finally gathers up all others into itself; but its very gentleness may leave us unaware of the pressing immediacy of our duty. Consequently, Paul quotes that added incentive whose general nature we have just considered: **Besides this. . . .** He assumes their awareness of what was an integral part of the early Christian outlook. The end was near and they knew it. Certainly it was no time for a "little folding of the hands to sleep" (Prov. 24:33). A drugged and heavy-headed unawareness of developments around us can have no part in the Christian's attitude to life. An inert, listless indifference to what is happening and what will soon take place is inappropriate at any time, but especially so in days when critical events are on the threshold. The new life presupposes the new age; when Christ first came, in a real, but incomplete, sense the kingdom of God came too. It was an earnest of the day when the kingly rule of God would be fully established, and he would be all in all. That day had seemed imminent when they first believed in Christ; but time had hurried on since then. Therefore it must now be nearer still.

12. *The New Day and the Armor of Light.*—The imagery by which the approach of that great day can most aptly be suggested is the daily miracle of returning light. It points to something that will inevitably come to pass—nothing can prevent tomorrow from dawning. If we postulate that **the night is far spent,** the figure conveys the idea of something already near at hand; implicitly it carries the proper suggestion of a contrast as sharp as that between darkness and day. Moreover, the parallel had the advantage of lending itself quite naturally to further development. The darkness was the shelter beneath which wicked men were likely to perpetrate their evil deeds. Day and night consequently had their moral counterpart, and Paul could call on his readers to abandon **the works of darkness** and perform the works of light. The kind of practice which marks a man's life becomes so habitual a part of him that it is like the clothes he normally wears; but like those clothes it can be changed. The soiled and filthy garments of undisciplined behavior can be laid aside. Instead of such apparel—so shabby and so vulnerable—he can

13 Let us walk honestly, as in the day; not in rioting and drunkenness, not in chambering and wantonness, not in strife and envying:
14 But put ye on the Lord Jesus Christ, and make not provision for the flesh, to *fulfil* the lusts *thereof.*

on the armor of light; 13 let us conduct ourselves becomingly as in the day, not in reveling and drunkenness, not in debauchery and licentiousness, not in quarreling and jealousy. 14 But put on the Lord Jesus Christ, and make no provision for the flesh, to gratify its desires.

ethical life must conform to that fact. He must act as being what he *is*—i.e., to use Paul's figure in Phil. 3:20, as a citizen of heaven. He must act appropriately, or **becomingly,** as belonging to **the day.** On Paul's use of the metaphor of **armor** see I Thess. 5:8; II Cor. 6:7; 10:4. Vs. 13*b* is reminiscent of 1:24-31. To **put on the Lord Jesus Christ** is to enter truly and fully into the realization of our membership in Christ. In connection with this

have **the armor of light,** and be clothed with the deeds which are appropriate to the new day. The phrase invites expansion. It indicates that Paul is thinking not only of the cataclysmic "last day," but of the "new day" which can dawn for anyone in the experience of conversion. It suggests that the nakedness of our haphazard lives can be covered with garments which make it possible for us to face the day without dismay and shame. A new kind of conduct is within our reach, even though it may not be our achievement; and it proves to be the kind of ordered life which is answerable to the demands of God's new day. It has the further advantage that it makes us invulnerable to attack, and the overtones of the phrase suggest its resplendent qualities. Those who wear it can rest assured that they are letting "light so shine before men that they will see [their] good works."

13. *Living in the Light.*—N.T. ethics has little use for conventions; but it does set considerable store by what can be called, in the best sense, good form. There is a certain kind of conduct which is worthy of the Christian, and we should try to accommodate ourselves to that pattern. Paul hints at its quality when he uses the word **becomingly.** There is to be a certain congruity between our lives and the clear daylight in which they should be lived. Our behavior is to be marked by a native dignity and a transparent integrity. It is to have the free restraint which is the result of inward discipline, and all those positive qualities which are placed in such sharp relief by the contrasting vices which Paul enumerates. Loveless passion is shown in all its selfish and undisciplined repulsiveness. The self-indulgence of the individual, intent upon his own gratification without regard to the consequences in other people's lives; the turbulent refusal, whether in anger or jealousy, to accommodate our plans or activities to the needs of those about us—both attitudes are suggested in the words Paul uses.

14. *Finding the Adequate Incentive.*—At first sight the one kind of life might seem to be set in motion by natural impulses of tremendous power, while the other is reinforced only by solemn exhortation. Much wise moral counsel fails because it has no resources stronger than good advice. It builds a wall of straw against the spread of a raging fire. But Paul's consistent theme throughout this letter is that a man must have a new and transforming incentive before he can live a victorious life. He has one sovereign remedy to suggest: **Put on the Lord Jesus Christ.** He has been talking about armor, and the phrase is a natural echo of the imagery he has just used. Christ is more than an example we follow. He is taken into our lives, and our lives are taken up into his in such a way that his fullness makes good all our shortcomings and failures. Paul uses various phrases to suggest that peculiar intimacy of relationship which is at the heart of all Christian experience. In every case he is trying to describe the amazing paradox that by losing ourselves in Christ we completely discover our own personal life. Christ dwells within us, but not to cramp or dwarf our individual qualities and gifts. Indeed, life in its fullest extension can be quite simply described by saying, "For me to live is Christ"; and it can be adequately described in no other way. In the particular passage before us the context suggests that by becoming members of Christ's body we find that we are strengthened at precisely those points where previously our weaknesses prevented us from playing our proper part in the new day. This is natural enough if we remember what has already been said in this letter about those who belong to Christ. They have his Spirit (8:9); and to have his Spirit means that they are saved from bondage to the flesh, and released into the fullness of a new life

14 Him that is weak in the faith receive ye, *but* not to doubtful disputations.

14 As for the man who is weak in faith, welcome him, but not for dis-

passage it is important to consider 6:1–7:6 and 8:4-13; note especially the Exeg. on 6:1-4 and 8:8-9.

E. Christian Love and Differences of Conscience (14:1-23)

So far Paul's exhortations have been of a general sort, unless the paragraph about the duty of allegiance to the state and the payment of taxes should be regarded as an exception. This general teaching was followed by the warning (in 13:11-14) concerning the nearness of the end and the exceptional urgency, therefore, of all our moral duties. This brief paragraph of warning would have prepared the original reader of Romans to expect the letter to come quickly to an end. Note that although different in form and

(8:4-9). Paul there states with but slightly different emphasis the truth which he is developing in the final verses of ch. 13. As Dodd has effectively expressed it: "The life which is appropriate to the New Day is the life of Him who is its Lord, and this life He imparts to those who are 'in Him.'"[7] This in itself is the complete answer to the problems created by the turbulence of physical passions. We no longer find it necessary so to order our plans as to **make . . . provision** for satisfying the clamors of unregenerate instincts. It does not follow, of course, that physical passions are ruthlessly suppressed. That kind of attempted solution usually wreaks its own revenge. The essential thing is that the proper balance of life is restored, and the fierce tyranny of lawless instinct is overthrown.

The classical commentary on these last two verses of the chapter is the famous passage in Augustine's *Confessions,* where he describes how the reading of this section of Romans meant a complete revolution in his life. For months he had struggled helplessly against the power of passions which he could not control, and the continued failure of his attempt to live a decent life had brought him to the verge of despair. He felt bound by the chain of his past sins.

> And I continued my miserable complaining; "How long, how long, shall I go on saying tomorrow and again tomorrow? Why not now, why not have an end to my uncleanness this very hour?"
>
> Such things I said, weeping in the most bitter sorrow of my heart. And suddenly I heard a voice from some nearby house . . . , "Take and read, take and read." . . . Damming back the flood of my tears I arose, interpreting the incident as quite certainly a divine command to open my book of Scripture and read the passage at which I should open. . . . So I was moved to return to the place where Alypius was sitting, for I had put down the Apostle's book there when I arose. I snatched it up, opened it and in silence read the passage on which my eyes first fell: *Not in rioting and drunkenness, not in chambering and impurities, not in contention and envy, but put ye on the Lord Jesus Christ and make not provision for the flesh in its concupiscences.* I had no wish to read further, and no need. For in that instant, with the very ending of the sentence, it was as though a light of utter confidence shone in all my heart, and all the darkness of uncertainty vanished away. Then leaving my finger in the place or marking it by some other sign, I closed the book and in complete calm told the whole thing to Alypius.[8]

14:1-23. *Reconciling Conflicts of Conviction.* —So far the discussion has been pertinent to real life, but not always closely related to concrete problems. Though general principles are necessary, conduct is always concerned with actual situations. The real difficulty is to know how our ultimate motive finds expression in our immediate setting. Even if we acknowledge that love is the decisive factor in Christian living, how do we decide what love actually requires us to do? The pressing problem for most people is to know how to deal with the particular cases which perplex them in daily life. It is all very well to say that love is the only means by which we can construct a harmonious society; but if conscience compels me to do one thing and at the same time apparently prompts you to do another, how does love reconcile the conflict of conviction? One of the commonest discoveries in a fellowship marked by intense enthusiasm is that opinions begin sharply to diverge: you approve what I abhor. What happens then?

To this problem Paul turns in ch. 14; but it is not the first time that the difficulty had de-

[7] *Epistle of Paul to Romans, ad loc.*

[8] *The Confessions of St. Augustine,* tr. F. J. Sheed, pp. 141-42. Copyright 1943. Used by permission of Sheed & Ward, New York and London.

content this paragraph is identical in function with the passage with which the Sermon on the Mount ends in both Luke 6:46-49 and Matt. 7:24-27. What we have, therefore, in 14:1–15:13 has something of the aspect of a postscript. If the textual data (see Intro., pp. 364-65) indicated the early prevalence of a form of the letter which broke off at the end of ch. 13 (instead of ch. 14), the textual problem would be considerably easier of solution; but such is not the case. One must see in 14:1–15:13 a part of Paul's original letter, although one cannot deny the indications that it has something of the character of an appendix to the ethical section.

At first sight it appears to deal with a matter more specific than has so far engaged Paul's attention in this section, and one is likely to conclude that his motive for adding it lay in some information he had about a particular problem of the Roman church. Many efforts have been made to identify the "party" or "sect" at Rome which had created this problem. Who is this man **who is weak in faith** (vs. 1)? Is he a Jew who is not yet entirely free from the requirements of the law and is trying to force his practices on others and in turn is being "despised" by more emancipated Christians? Vss. 5 and 14 seem to say so. But, on the other hand, vs. 2, which refers to the **weak man** [who] **eats only vegetables,** and vs. 21, with its allusion to those who neither **eat meat** nor **drink wine,** point rather to some ascetic sect like the Essenes, who are known to have been vegetarians; vegetarianism was a feature of many religious movements in this period (see Lietzmann for references to sources). Yet another possibility is suggested by the known fact (see especially I Cor. 8:1 ff.) that many Christians—probably Gentiles as well as Jews—in Paul's time were troubled by the problem of whether it was right for them to eat meat

---

manded attention. In I Corinthians he had dealt at some length with the question of clean and unclean meats. In a great city of the Roman Empire much of the meat offered for sale had probably been sacrificed to idols. Could a Christian eat it with a clean conscience, or had evil associations contaminated the food? The discussion in I Cor. 8–10 provides an illuminating commentary on the present verses; and the same is true of Jesus' teaching about the things which defile a man (Mark 7:14-23). The close parallel between the attitude of Jesus and the advice of Paul has already appeared more than once, and indicates the essential unity which marks the N.T. It suggests that the recorded sayings of Jesus are intimately related to a tradition widely diffused in the years before the Gospels were written; it points also to a faithful effort on the part of the early church to be loyal in thought and action to the teaching of its Lord. Moreover, it invests the ethical instruction which Paul gives his readers with much more authority than would belong to the detached comments even of a distinguished apostle. There are occasions in his letters when Paul remarks that on this or that point he has no word from the Lord and consequently offers merely his private judgment. It cannot be assumed that whenever such a phrase is lacking Paul is basing his teaching directly on the tradition of Christ's words; but it entitles us to expect a large measure of conformity between the teaching of the Master and that of the disciple. In the latter part of Romans verbal echoes, repeatedly detected, indicate how close and how conscious Paul's dependence on Jesus' teaching must have been.

Here he singles out two particular problems for discussion: the observance of special days, and the acceptance of regulations regarding food. Both created the same kind of tensions within the Christian community. Both raised the issue of scrupulosity, and set those with stricter views in opposition to those whose approach was marked by a greater measure of freedom. Paul's solution falls naturally into three stages. (*a*) Each man must be fully satisfied in his own mind that his approach to the problem is right, i.e., the claims of conscience are sovereign. Vague suspicions are no substitute for a clear understanding of the issue, and secondhand convictions are of very little help. It is important for each member of the community to follow that measure of insight which he possesses. (*b*) The second principle lays a constraint on each individual. We are to refrain from judging, and must not be quick to condemn those who differ from us. They are not answerable to us for the standards which their conscience lays upon them. In that respect they are responsible to God, who gives an increasing insight into truth to those who ask it. We have no right to sit in judgment on them. To this point the N.T. returns so often that we would do well to lay the warning seriously to heart. (*c*) The third stage sets forth our duty in more positive terms. The strong are

which had been consecrated to pagan deities before it was put on the market. Since this was true of virtually all meat, the decision not to eat meat thus consecrated might well amount to deciding not to eat meat at all.

The very fact that these several possibilities exist, each not without some support in the words of the letter, suggests yet another, viz., that these words of exhortation are prompted not by any particular situation about which Paul knows in the Roman church, but, like most of the rest of this section, by more general considerations. Paul has been concerned up to this point with the practical implications of Christian love. He began (at 12:3) by considering the meaning of this love within the church itself and, although he seemed to leave it with 12:13, has recurred to that specific topic in 12:16 and probably also in 13:8. Now he returns to it again and for a sustained period. When he first dealt with this theme (12:3-8), he discussed the threat to the harmony and unity of the church which was created by divergences of gifts; now he deals with that same threat as arising from differences of opinion of a certain general class. The practices he cites, therefore, in vss. 2, 5, 21 are to be understood not as the characteristics of some one particular party or sect in the Roman church of which Paul has been informed, but merely as examples of a kind of difficulty which might and often did put the reality of love to a test in the several churches. We have noted the close correspondence of Rom. 12:3-8 with I Cor. 12:1-31; 14:1-40, and of Rom. 12:9-21 (with which Rom. 13:8-10 clearly belongs) with I Cor. 13. It is striking that Rom. 14:1–15:13 stands in a similar relation to I Cor. 8–10, where the problem of meat offered to idols is treated. Thus we find that two of the major sources of the disorder at Corinth are taken up for discussion in Romans,

---

not to place temptation in the way of the weak. Some are relatively free from circumscribing scruples; but they must not use their liberty for the undoing of the weaker brethren. Religious freedom is related at every point to conscience; it is not an outward pattern of behavior, but a proper correspondence between our insight and our actions. Unless conviction points the way, we may easily sustain spiritual injury by acting in exactly the same manner as someone else. It may be all right for him but entirely wrong for us. Consequently, an obligation rests on those who feel that they are emancipated not to induce someone else to act as they do unless they are sure that his conscience will approve.

Throughout the practical section of the letter Paul has returned again and again to the controlling motive in all Christian conduct: love. In this chapter also he makes it perfectly clear that a standard of behavior which will consistently be marked by discerning forbearance toward others can be inspired and sustained only by true charity. As an external pattern, an ideal such as he sets forth would be doomed to inevitable failure; even when clearly and imaginatively grasped, it must have the constant support of a motive profound enough to transform our daily human relationships. Only love is sufficient for this purpose, and it proves its adequacy in one situation after another. Having declared that it is the key to all distinctively Christian living, Paul shows how it actually applies to the ordinary problems that perplex us—and, among others, to those created by standards of varying strictness.

1. ***The Way to Welcome the Weak.***—The N.T. assumes that the church is a fellowship marked by a common spirit and a single aim. But unity does not presuppose unanimity, and the strength of the community can be jeopardized by differences in point of view. Christians may be brothers, but some of them will be weaker than others. Those who are diffident in attitude will represent a more hesitant approach to many practical problems, and their diffidence—if regarded with impatience by others—may easily create tensions within the fellowship. Paul certainly expected that diversity would be not only one of the marks of the church but also a test of its charity. **Faith** bears many meanings in the N.T., and here it manifestly suggests something different from that faith by which, as we saw earlier in this letter, men are justified. For practical purposes we may assume that when Paul speaks of **the man who is weak in faith** he is pointing to someone who has not grasped what Christianity means. He does not understand the true nature of salvation, and is consequently unable or unwilling to accept it in its fullness as the gift of God. Natural instinct prompts him to supplement what God offers with what he himself can do, and particularly to make certain, by the scrupulous fulfillment of specific regulations, that he will find grace and favor with God. It therefore becomes apparent that

and taken up in connection with a discussion of love which bears many resemblances to the treatment of that *same theme* in that *same connection* in the Corinthian letter. Is it not fair to infer that Paul deals with these themes because of difficulties he has actually had at Corinth rather than because of any specific knowledge he may have of Rome? Two special considerations make this suggestion plausible: (*a*) Paul was at Corinth when he wrote Romans and would thus have been reminded constantly of these particular difficulties; and (*b*) the treatment in Romans differs from that in I Corinthians precisely in being more generalized and less specific and concrete: as to spiritual gifts, one is not left in doubt that at Corinth it was those who possessed the gift of tongues who were largely responsible for the trouble, whereas Rom. 12:3-8 exhibits no such marks of a particular situation; and as to the "weak brethren," whereas I Corinthians is concerned primarily with those who have scruples about meat offered to idols, the reference of Rom. 14:1–15:13 is, as we have seen, more diffused and vague.

14:1. Lietzmann (p. 57) in listing the uses of the word "faith" in Paul points out that in many passages it seems to designate the whole reality of the new life of the Spirit. He cites a larger number of instances of this usage than is probably justified, but Rom. 1:12; II Cor. 1:24; 4:13 seem good examples of such a use of the term; and we have already interpreted the word as it occurs in 12:3, 6 in that same broad way. In other words, "faith" in these passages seems, by metonymy, to equal "Spirit" or perhaps "grace." Lietzmann also cites Phil. 1:25 and Col. 2:7 as passages in which "in faith" seems to mean "in Christ." Something like this use of "faith" seems to be involved in the words: **the man who is weak in faith,** i.e., nothing more specific is meant than that the man

---

the man of weak faith is moving toward—or has scarcely escaped from—that position which Paul has so vigorously attacked in the earlier part of Romans. He accepts certain rules as obligatory; the observance of them becomes a part of his religious life; and at two points he is in peril of forfeiting the fullness of discipleship. He submits to the servitude of regulation when he might know the glorious liberty of God's children; and he is likely to regard his unduly scrupulous attitude as a necessary part of the Christian life—in which case he is at once restoring merit as a condition of salvation and opening the door to all uncharitableness toward his neighbor.

Though Paul clearly considers that those who set great store by special rules have made limited progress in the Christian life, he is convinced that they have a real place in the Christian community. They are therefore to be received—or (with the more definite overtones that the word conveys) welcomed. One of the marks of the church should be cordial relations even between groups of distinctly different character. Segregation has no place within the life of the fellowship; least of all should it follow the lines of special interest or limited concern. The phrase Paul uses presupposes a community sufficiently inclusive to have a place within it for those who differ widely in insight and in attainment. There is more here, however, than the comprehensiveness which can give shelter to all types of believer. Differences may impose a strain, but they also lay down certain requirements. The strong have to be forbearing in their attitude, and the weak must not try to bind others by their own dogmatisms. As is right, the obligations are most clearly laid on the strong: "The ampler the grace which they had received from the Lord," remarked Calvin, "the more bound they were to help their neighbours."[9] The weak must be received, but in the right spirit and the right way. **Doubtful disputations** is a phrase which can carry a variety of meanings. "Not for altercations or disputings" is Beza's rendering. "Not to debate about matters in doubt" is how Doddridge translates it. Sanday and Headlam suggest "not to pass judgment on their thoughts." In a wide variety of possible renderings two important facts emerge, and both are closely in keeping with the general tenor of Paul's argument. On the one hand, the strong are not entitled to adopt a superior or censorious attitude toward the weak; nor, on the other hand, are they to seize the chance to argue, merely for the sake of the debate, about questions on which there is legitimate difference of opinion. The reasons for Paul's injunction emerge as we study the passage as a whole. The discussion of doubts is essentially irrelevant. As a method of solving problems it is of very questionable efficacy. Paul is not thinking of the patient and earnest search for the truth about matters in dispute; he is talking about the attitude which delights to overthrow an antagonist in debate, and which works toward the triumphant dem-

[9] *Romans, ad loc.*

2 For one believeth that he may eat all things: another, who is weak, eateth herbs.

putes over opinions. 2 One believes he may eat anything, while the weak man eats

is not mature in his Christian character and experience; he has not gone far in appropriating the spiritual meaning of being in Christ. Gal. 4:9-10 is interesting and important in this connection. Note the words "faith" and "spirits." "Faith" in Rom. 14:1 corresponds with "knowing God and being known of him" in Gal. 4:9. The weak brother is to be made **welcome,** i.e., he is to be received into and held in full fellowship with the church. In view of vs. *3b* ("God has welcomed him"), where the same word is used (προσλαμβάνω), it is doubtful that one can (with Kirk) understand the term in vs. 1 to mean "admit to baptism." The allusion is to persons who are already members of the community, but are in danger of being excluded from full fellowship. The word would also have a limited application to members of the church from other areas seeking admittance to the Roman church. **Not for disputes over opinions** is one possible translation of a Greek phrase which may mean "not in order to condemn him for his opinions." This understanding is preferred by most commentators and is probably correct.

2. Literally translated, this sentence begins: "One has faith to **eat anything . . . ,**" i.e., one is sufficiently advanced in the life of the Spirit to be free from scruples about such unimportant external matters as this. (See what was said about the meaning of "faith" just above.)

onstration that the other person is hopelessly wrong. This achieves no useful purpose. Nor can it claim to be a Christian approach to the issue, because it is essentially unkind both in intention and in result. It causes the weaker brother an infinite amount of pain and anguish. It proceeds from an uncharitable spirit on the part of the stronger person. It is prompted by and usually reflects that arrogance which is the failing of men who believe that they are both emancipated and right. But the effect on the weaker is the serious aspect of the matter. "Contentious questions," as Calvin pointed out, always "disturb a mind not yet sufficiently established."[1] It is, moreover, an attitude which has repeatedly demonstrated its essentially unprofitable character. It dissipates energies better conserved for more constructive purposes. It distracts the mind from matters which really require attention. It leads to division and animosity among Christians. It is noteworthy that Bunyan—who lived in an age when men loved to argue about doubtful matters, and whom much experience had made wise in the practical affairs of religious fellowship—invariably seizes on the tendency to "dispute over opinions" as the mark of a frivolous mind, chiefly anxious to avoid the prime responsibilities of Christian discipleship (see on 3:8). Finally, the atmosphere which controversy engenders is always harmful to the Christian society. A difference of opinion imperceptibly leads to the contentious spirit which does not recoil from quarreling, and finally hardens into the antagonism which breaks the bond of peace.

2. *Dealing with Differences of Diet.*—As a specific example of the kind of difference which he has in mind, Paul mentions vegetarianism. Some members of the church regarded the nature and antecedents of their food as completely irrelevant matters; the hesitant disciple scrupulously avoided meat. Paul does not debate the prior issue whether or not **the weak man** is right. He assumes that he is wrong because his restrictive practices reflect an imperfect grasp of what the gospel is and does. He might have pointed out that certain instinctive tendencies apparently prompt many good men to seek added security by submitting to specific requirements. He might also have added that many factors in the contemporary scene made it easy for vegetarianism to become a major issue. Some members of the church came from a Jewish background, and had grown up with the thought of clean and unclean foods always present in their minds. This must have been an important question in the early church. It is possible to argue that the rather ambiguous decree of the Jerusalem Council (Acts 15:29) suggested that even in the new day of freedom from righteousness by ritual observance, Christians would be wise to accept the Jewish customs regarding the slaughtering of meat. At all events, in a predominantly pagan society (the Gentile world for which Paul felt himself specially responsible) the question was complicated by the fact that much of the meat in the shambles came

[1] *Ibid.*

3 Let not him that eateth despise him that eateth not; and let not him which eateth not judge him that eateth: for God hath received him.

only vegetables. 3 Let not him who eats despise him who abstains, and let not him who abstains pass judgment on him who

3-4. Paul now repeats the injunction implied in vs. 1*b*: the one **who eats** must not **despise him who abstains;** and then he goes on to warn the "abstainer" that he too has a duty in love: he must not **pass judgment on him who eats.** And the ground for this tolerance is the fact that **God has welcomed him.** The proof that God has done so, although this is not mentioned, is that this brother also has received the Spirit, and is

from heathen sacrifices. In addition, there was a strain of asceticism, both among Jews and Gentiles, which advocated vegetarianism as a useful form of moral discipline.

It is not surprising that the question arose. The basic inference—the governing principle which underlies all that Paul says on the issue—is that Christianity has lifted the believer into a realm where matters of diet can never be of more than secondary importance. It was the consequence of Jesus' teaching that things from without cannot defile a man (Mark 7:18-19). It followed also from Jesus' comment that to the man whose heart was right, all external things would be clean (Luke 11:41). It was implicit in the form of Peter's vision at Joppa. In that case, the immediate question might concern distinctions between man and man; but it was impossible to ponder the incident without reaching the conclusion that it swept away distinctions between one kind of food and another (Acts 10:9-48).

The particular issue may seem rather remote to us, but Paul is not primarily concerned with what a man may or may not eat. It is well for us to understand the background of the illustration he uses; but it is still only an illustration. The excessive concern about diet is an example of the kind of cleavage which can develop in a community, and Paul does not regard the distinction that it raises as an inconsequential question. The strong Christian is one who sees what is important, morally and spiritually, and what is not. Moreover, he is prepared to ignore the things that do not really matter, or at least to treat them as immaterial. The weak believer is preoccupied with matters which are actually indifferent, but magnifies them till they assume the proportions of really important religious issues. This is an attitude which must be treated with all charity and forbearance, but it remains a weakness all the same; and Christian tolerance, though it must be patient, does not need to be blind. It is not a sign of virtue to believe that your salvation is affected by the things you eat. We might note with profit that as a rule we are dangerously oblivious to the need of cultivating a sense of where to draw the line between what is important and what is not. One of the decisive tests of strength or weakness in the faith is the ability to see clearly in the light of truth where the real issues lie and to act accordingly.

3. ***The Proper Approach to Differences of Conviction.***—The weakness of the man of little faith is a weakness because the matter involved is essentially secondary in nature. This makes it all the more serious when the issue is permitted to become an occasion of violent controversy. Each party to the dispute reacts in a characteristic way, and in the process illustrates the failings to which its members are peculiarly prone. The man who is free from scruples is likely to be arrogantly conscious of his greater emancipation; he despises his weaker brother and regards him with contempt. The stickler for propriety retorts by censuring the freedom of the libertarian. He succumbs to the temptation querulously to condemn the other for accepting a measure of freedom which his own scruples will not allow him to appropriate. This is the inevitable result of controversy. It aggravates all the less amiable qualities in human nature, and places a premium on the defects of our virtues. It is demoralizing to the individual and destructive of the community. Those who are really brothers, and ought to act toward each other as such, become antagonists. The unity of the fellowship is broken. It is often only after indulging in controversy that we are wise enough to recognize the damage that it does. Wrote John Wesley:

> Being faint in the evening, I called at Altringham, and there lit upon a Quaker, well skilled in, and therefore (as I soon found) sufficiently fond of, controversy. After an hour spent therein, (perhaps not in vain,) I advised him to dispute as little as possible; but rather to follow after holiness; and walk humbly with his God.[2]

[2] *Journal,* March 15, 1738.

4 Who art thou that judgest another man's servant? to his own master he standeth or falleth. Yea, he shall be holden up: for God is able to make him stand.

eats; for God has welcomed him. 4 Who are you to pass judgment on the servant of another? It is before his own master that he stands or falls. And he will be upheld, for the Master is able to make him stand.

---

unmistakably and in actual fact a member of the community (cf. Acts 10:46-47). Vs. 4 is obviously addressed to the "weak," but it applies, of course, also to the "strong." It is not likely that Paul thought of one group as being more censorious than the other. It is possible, but doubtful, that he used the word κύριος in the second sentence of this verse in the general sense of **master;** here, as well as in vs. 4*c,* the Lord (i.e., Christ) is probably intended. The Lord will **make him stand,** i.e., "Do not take too gloomy or ominous a view of your brother's chances of salvation." Since he is Christ's **servant,** such matters as to whether he eats this or that lie between Christ and him; others should let these matters remain there and not feel that they are responsible for making a judgment themselves.

The results of controversy are serious enough in themselves, but in religious matters an inherent absurdity attaches to it as well. Both parties are within the community, and neither can excommunicate the other because God has received both alike. In vs. 1 Paul has reminded the strong that the weak have a place in the fellowship; he now points out to the overscrupulous that his brother of more liberal outlook also has a position of his own in the church. The rigorist cannot eject him or impose his own standards upon him. Each has to accept the other because **God has welcomed** both.

4. ***The Arrogance of Those Who Presume to Judge.***—There is a further incongruity inherent in wrangling about religious matters. We act as though we had a right to **pass judgment** on other people. When we take it on ourselves to censure our brethren, we are usurping prerogatives that are not ours. We cannot arrogate to ourselves the rights of someone else. It is an obvious fact that everybody, on the merely human level, is responsible only to his employer for the way in which he discharges the duties assigned to him. For anyone else to step in and correct his ways would be sheer presumption. If his master is satisfied, nothing further can be said; if he is displeased, he will take such steps as seem appropriate. Every one of us, on the highest of all levels, is Christ's servant. To that emphasis, with all it means—as to obligation, direction, succor, and dependence—Paul continually returns. At the very beginning of the letter he reminded his readers that he is Christ's slave; now he recalls them to the recognition that each one of them occupies the same status. They can claim for themselves the privileges involved, but they must also concede to others the rights which are inseparable from discipleship. One of these concerns **judgment.** We are answerable to God for what we do, and we can decline the officious assistance of those who wish to usurp the prerogatives of God. This means that we are faced in a particularly stringent form with the duty of following our conscience. In the course of the present chapter Paul repeatedly infers that one of the primary demands which we as disciples must accept is that of giving the most careful heed to what our sense of right and wrong requires of us. Our moral perceptions, of course, are constantly subject to the chastening discipline of testing our standards by the will of God. More and more we ought to recognize that we are answerable to God—and to God alone—both for the obligations which we accept and for those which we repudiate. This might make us more scrupulous in discharging the duties of our discipleship, but it would also make us more charitable in conceding that our brother too is answerable to God alone. The secret of a respectful tolerance of his practice is to recognize that he does not stand or fall at the bar of our judgment. And here a new element of tremendous significance enters the situation to transform it. There is always the possibility in any state of affairs that a man may stand or fall. Judgment operates, but not much else. Paul, however, is confident that when the Master of all men tests his servants, they will stand. The possibility that they will fall becomes increasingly remote as they grow in awareness of that succor with which God comes to their assistance.

5 One man esteemeth one day above another: another esteemeth every day *alike.* Let every man be fully persuaded in his own mind.

5 One man esteems one day as better than another, while another man esteems all days alike. Let every one be fully con-

5a. The point is further enforced by another example. Here is a man who believes in the observance of the sabbath according to orthodox Jewish usage; or perhaps it is the feast days or regular fast days or some other "days"; it does not matter—the principle is the same and that is all Paul is concerned about here. In Gal. 4:10—as we saw on vs. 1—Paul refers to the observance of "days, and months, and seasons, and years"; and there he deprecates, even opposes, these observances because an effort was evidently being made by a strong party in the Galatian churches to make them normative for all believers. In the same way he writes in Col. 2:16: "Let no one pass judgment on you in questions of food and drink or with regard to a festival or a new moon or a Sabbath." Paul's position in the present passage seems to be that the "strong" are not, on the one hand,

5. ***Differences of Days.***—Various influences might combine to convince Paul's contemporaries that **one day** was **better than another.** Those who had come under Jewish influence would be prepared to set the sabbath apart; widely diffused in pagan society was the belief that certain times and seasons were more auspicious than others. A good deal of this preoccupation would be no more profound than the manifestations of a similar spirit known to us: hesitancy about starting new ventures on Friday, apprehension as to what will happen on the thirteenth day of the month. This is mere superstition; but though its crasser forms may be exorcised, it may find a refuge in professedly religious circles. Once people overlook the true values at stake, a conventional regard for one day as against another may have little spiritual value—indeed, it may have none at all.

From the general tenor of the argument it is quite apparent that Paul is not concerned to overthrow the regular observance of religious duties, nor is he disposed to combat the establishment of recognized times at which we may most suitably discharge these obligations. Elsewhere in his letters he tacitly admits that certain things will be done regularly—e.g., on the first day of the week—and early in the history of the church (as we can see when we read Clement or Hippolytus or the Didache) the religious significance of Sunday became firmly established. After all, some regularity is necessary if our common life is not to disappear in a morass of undisciplined impulse. Paul is not defending chaos in the name of freedom; he is declaring with all possible emphasis that religious conduct must be related to insight. It must have the authority of conscience behind it. The fact that it conforms to a certain pattern does not make it religious in any sense; the object of his attack is the tendency to substitute for a true understanding of the spiritual life, and the things that promote its vitality, a superstitious veneration for particular times. For that reason **every one** must **be fully convinced in his own mind.** Insight never comes secondhand. Derivative convictions are of no value in religious experience. Paul regards genuine conviction as of far greater importance than unanimity. Loyalty to the truth will finally bring sincere people closer to agreement; but nothing can galvanize a lifeless conventionality into vigor or vitality.

It is difficult to exaggerate the significance which the apostle attaches to conscience. We are responsible to God for the standards we accept. When we see his will—even if it is imperfectly—and take it as our rule, we have begun to live the truly religious life, and more perfect understanding will be the reward of honesty and perseverance. The place at which a man actually stands is relatively inconsequential. At present he may very dimly grasp the implications of Christian liberty, but if he faithfully follows the light God gives him, it will finally bring him to the full day of perfect understanding. Only he who superstitiously accepts certain external patterns is beyond hope. Hence Paul lays less store by men's opinions than by their attitudes. At the same time, there is no evading the fact that his sympathies manifestly lie with the man who **esteems all days alike.** With the rigors of sabbatarianism he would have had very little sympathy; but he would certainly have bestowed nothing but contempt on the attitude which reduces everything to a monotonous secularism—and does so in the name of religious freedom. The N.T. may look toward a far greater uniformity regarding special days than much of our ecclesiastical practice would

6 He that regardeth the day, regardeth *it* unto the Lord; and he that regardeth not the day, to the Lord he doth not regard *it*. He that eateth, eateth to the Lord, for he giveth God thanks; and he that eateth not, to the Lord he eateth not, and giveth God thanks.

vinced in his own mind. 6 He who observes the day, observes it in honor of the Lord. He also who eats, eats in honor of the Lord, since he gives thanks to God; while he who abstains, abstains in honor of the

to allow themselves to be coerced in such matters, but, on the other, they are not to try to coerce the "weak." This sort of thing, Paul is saying again, is a private matter—in the sense of being simply and only between the individual and the Lord. It is only when one tries to enforce one's views on others that one violates the Spirit of the community.

5*b*-9. The important thing is that **every one be fully convinced in his own mind** that his behavior in such disputable matters as sabbathkeeping or meat eating is fully in keeping with his relationship to the Lord and is indeed sanctified by that relationship.

accept; but it minimizes differences by making all days holy. When all our lives are entirely lived in the presence of God, no times will be more sacred than others, because all alike will be dedicated to God's glory. The present tendency is to make all days common; Christians struggle to maintain islands of sanctity in this secular sea. The N.T. hallows everything by lifting it into God's presence and keeping it there.

6. ***The Chief End of Man Is to Glorify God.*** —From this it naturally follows that the conscious effort to promote God's honor is more important than the forms by which we try to do so. Some will use one method, some another; but in either case it is the Godward intention that matters. And whatever means we adopt, the test of our genuineness will be the measure in which gratitude and praise are the distinguishing marks of our lives. In this respect both **he . . . who eats** and **he who abstains** can find a level of agreement deeper than the external differences which divide them. Though the special problem which Paul cites is one which has ceased to be of pressing importance, the experience to which he points has been repeated in every century of Christian history. We may not all confess our faith in the same terms, or worship according to the same rites, or govern ourselves according to the same discipline; we may not find it easy to co-operate in common tasks: but age after age men who could not agree in other things have united to praise God with a single voice. Our hymnbooks are still the greatest manuals of Christian unity.

The meaning of this verse is simple and straightforward; but it is perhaps legitimate to point out (with Charles Gore) that there is a play on words which, though not intentional, may prove suggestive to us. "Giving thanks" recalls that simple gesture in which we pause and remember that the food on our tables is a sign that God's mercy underlies all our lives; but in the original it is related to the word which gives us "Eucharist." At all events, whether at the Lord's Supper or at our daily meals, we are reminded that the sacred and the secular are intimately bound together. Actually they are not so much distinguishable objects as different ways of looking at the same things. We rightly abhor a religion which forgets real men and their actual needs, and allows itself to become the hobby of people whose minds are always in church. Faith is concerned with exactly the same objects and relationships with which any other approach to life must deal; but it sees them in a new light. It sets them in a certain perspective and interprets them in terms of a central principle—God. This is why our common meals are sacred and our holiest symbolism uses simple articles of daily use. The heart of every sacramental act is that we use ordinary things to declare extraordinary truths. We set forth common bread, and learn with wonder that God can use it to convey to us the meaning of the self-sacrifice which is at the heart of divine love. We relate the eternal and the temporal; we affirm that the transcendent so enters the world of ordinary affairs that situations in which we happen to be placed are wholly transformed.

But if the sacred meal is related to ordinary things, the common meal should equally be related to sacred things. Paul is telling his readers that when they thankfully receive their daily bread as from God and accept it as a gift of his mercy, they discover that the simple ritual of a common meal is touched with "something of the glory of divine communion." This is a true emphasis of Reformation teaching. The holy table stands not only in the sanctuary, but in each believer's home. In his own

7 For none of us liveth to himself, and no man dieth to himself.

8 For whether we live, we live unto the Lord; and whether we die, we die unto the Lord: whether we live therefore, or die, we are the Lord's.

9 For to this end Christ both died, and rose, and revived, that he might be Lord both of the dead and living.

Lord and gives thanks to God. 7 None of us
lives to himself, and none of us dies to
himself. 8 If we live, we live to the Lord,
and if we die, we die to the Lord; so then,
whether we live or whether we die, we are
the Lord's. 9 For to this end Christ died
and lived again, that he might be Lord
both of the dead and of the living.

The believer does not **live** or **die** to himself. **We are the Lord's**—i.e., we are members of this supernatural community of the Spirit—**whether we live or whether we die.** The point of vs. 7 is obviously not that we belong to one another (i.e., as slaves or servants; in a way, the point is the precise opposite of this), but to Christ only, who by his death and resurrection became the **Lord both of the dead and of the living.** This stress upon

---

household every man is a priest unto God; as such it is his duty and privilege to give thanks. Moreover, that attitude of consistent gratitude is a much more decisive force in determining the religious quality of a life than any pattern to which that life may conform. It is more important to give thanks than it is to eat or to abstain from eating. "It is only the name of God, when invoked, that sanctifies us and all we have." It remains true, of course, that both parties—the man **who eats** and the man **who abstains,** the man who esteems one day above another and the man who esteems all days alike—can promote a common end (the advancement of God's glory) only because the issue at stake is essentially indifferent in character. If some fundamental moral divergence were involved, those who held opposite views could not alike give thanks to God.

7-8. ***United Under God.***—Paul has been dealing with two specific problems, the observance of special days and abstention from certain foods; but both are merely illustrations of a principle which ought to govern our attitude to all issues of this kind. **None of us,** he remarks, **lives to himself.** It is tempting to treat what he says here as an affirmation of our mutual interdependence: for good or ill we and our fellows are inextricably bound together. This would be entirely in keeping with Paul's conviction that we are related to one another in such a way as to lay upon each one of us obligations which prove to be privileges in disguise. Later in this chapter he actually turns to that aspect of the question; but at the moment he is emphasizing something more fundamental still. We are bound one to another in mutual dependence because we are—each of us—related to God. The peculiar quality of our Christian duty to each other springs from the fact that everyone is a child of God. This affects our attitude to others; it also transforms our attitude to ourselves. We become aware that no Christian can rule his life according to the dictates of his own interests. He must allow for other purposes besides his own. Because we belong to a created order, we are dependent at every point upon God's sustaining power. What is true in the realm of nature is equally true in the region of grace. The victorious life is a possibility only because we do not trust in our own resources, but look to receive from God the succor that he is able to give us. Unless we are constantly aware that disaster attends any attempt to claim complete independence for ourselves, we are living in a world of fantastic illusion. The only true framework within which our experience makes sense is the acceptance of God's creative purpose as the decisive factor in our lives. The life of a Christian never corresponds to its proper pattern till the will of God is its controlling object. The heart of secularism is the intention to live in utter disregard of God and in complete reliance on the resources of human ingenuity. We **live to the Lord** when we consciously attempt to conform to his will and in all things seek to promote his glory. This is not true of some phases of our experience only; if it is relevant to the daily tenor of our existence, it applies with equal force to that final crisis beyond which only the insights of faith can take us. In death as much as in life we are dependent on God. Whatever our state may be, we cannot divorce it from him. If nothing can separate us from God's love, nothing can limit his authority over the lives of his children.

9. ***The Purpose of the Drama of Redemption.***—A conviction of this kind must have some more solid basis than intuition, and Paul appeals to the death and resurrection of Jesus Christ. These central events—always in the

10 But why dost thou judge thy brother? or why dost thou set at nought thy brother? for we shall all stand before the judgment seat of Christ.

11 For it is written, *As* I live, saith the Lord, every knee shall bow to me, and every tongue shall confess to God.

10 Why do you pass judgment on your brother? Or you, why do you despise your brother? For we shall all stand before the judgment seat of God; **11** for it is written,

"As I live, says the Lord, every knee shall bow to me,
and every tongue shall give praise[u] to God."

[u] Or *confess.*

"life" and "death" is Paul's way of making more emphatic the unique claim of Christ upon the believer. He is with us in death, as well as in life; indeed, in death who else is with us?

10-12. On what ground, therefore, can the weak **pass judgment** or can the strong **despise?** That Paul addresses the two classes in that order in vs. 10 appears from the

---

most intimate association—are the heart of the apostolic message. They are the source of its power; here they become the ground for claiming that nothing lies outside the scope of Christ's authority. Our Lord himself had declared that God was the God both of the living and of the dead (cf. Matt. 22:32); now his apostle sharpens the same conviction by translating it into the new forms of expression which Christ's passion and his living presence had made natural for his disciples.

Two comments suggest themselves. It was Paul's belief that the tremendous relevance of Christ's passion and of his risen presence—such that no part of our lives can ever pass beyond the scope of his enveloping concern—was not an accidental development. It followed from the mighty crisis of Christ's earthly life because that crisis was rooted in God's eternal purpose for his children. **For to this end Christ died and lived again.** Inherent in our faith is the assurance that it is God's will that we should never fall out of his care and keeping. In the second place, we have an illuminating glimpse into the way in which N.T. theology took shape. It is not a new insight which Paul propounds. Jesus Christ had already taught essentially the same truth, but the form in which it was expressed was different. The divine concern which continually surrounds us is now the love of Christ. God is the God of the dead and of the living; but Christ is the **Lord both of the dead and of the living.** We have a somewhat similar statement in Peter's sermon on the day of Pentecost. The prophet had promised that God would send forth his Spirit; this, said Peter, has now happened, but it has happened only through Jesus Christ and because of him. In both cases the parallel convictions are allowed to lie side by side and the final inferences of faith are not explicitly drawn. But the disciplines of religious experience are already fashioning the ultimates of Christian faith. The life of active discipleship was the sphere in which they took shape—and that is still the only region in which a vivid and intelligent theology can grow.

10-12. ***Those Under Judgment Must Not Judge.***—We never pass beyond our responsibility to Jesus Christ as Lord. Living or dead, we are his; and at certain points this drastically curtails our liberty of action. There are some things incompatible with his lordship which we cannot do. One of them is to exercise the right of sitting in **judgment** on others. Paul has already pointed out (12:19) that we cannot invade God's prerogatives. Now, with the inclusive lordship of Christ as his point of departure, he reverts to the same subject; but in the present instance, by the use of the word **brother,** he makes the anomaly of our venturing to censure one another appear all the more pronounced. When the matter in hand concerns the bearing of Christians toward other Christians, it should not be necessary to point out that what is inappropriate among men at large becomes intolerable within the fellowship of the church.

But the presumption that sits in judgment on our fellows is here closely related to another attitude which is equally reprehensible. Indeed, the confidence which condemns is often only the final expression of the superiority which despises. The serious thing is the haughty arrogance of spirit that exalts itself above our brother. Pride is the source of all sin, the final evil to be eradicated. It is the absolute denial of that humility which ought to be our human response as we stand together in the presence of God.

Whereupon a natural sequence of ideas makes it possible for Paul to lay even greater

12 So then every one of us shall give account of himself to God.

13 Let us not therefore judge one another any more: but judge this rather, that no man put a stumblingblock or an occasion to fall in *his* brother's way.

12 So each of us shall give account of himself to God.

13 Then let us no more pass judgment on one another, but rather decide never to put a stumbling-block or hindrance in the

---

use of the same two verbs as in vs. 3, κρίνω (judge) and ἐξουθενέω (despise); besides, the two terms exactly fit the characteristic temptations of the strong and free on the one hand (to despise) and the weak and bound on the other (to judge). We do not belong to one another but to Christ. It is before God's judgment seat that we shall *all*—"strong" and "weak"—be finally judged and it is to him, and to him only, that we must finally **give account.** The quotation in vs. 11 is from Isa. 45:23 (cf. Phil. 2:10-11).

13-15. Paul's argument now takes a somewhat different direction. Thus far his exhortations have been addressed equally to the "strong" (that they be not contemptuous)

---

emphasis on the position he has taken. Ultimately we shall all appear at the bar of God's **judgment,** and we shall stand there together. That solemn thought of the culmination of a process already at work—for God's judgments are abroad in the world even now—throws into high relief the incongruity of the attitudes we so commonly adopt toward one another. We cannot invade the prerogatives of God; and in any case, when faced with his righteousness, the differences among ourselves are too slight to justify any one of us in exalting himself above his fellows. The judgment of God is the inevitable consequence of his universal sovereignty. He rules over all, and man must acknowledge his rule. The prophet Isaiah, whom Paul quotes somewhat loosely, regards the full recognition of God's reign as the mark of the messianic era. Certainly the words serve to set our lives firmly in the perspective of God's all-embracing rule. It follows naturally that worship is the proper response of those who are aware that a divine kingdom embraces all their lives. **Praise** becomes the instinctive reaction of everyone who knows that "God's greatness [flows] around our incompleteness."[8]

It is perhaps appropriate that a certain ambiguity attaches to one of the key words in vs. 11. Whether we prefer **confess** or **praise,** the alternative remains a complementary necessity. If confession is uppermost, it is still with gratitude as its accompanying overtone; if praise predominates, it is thanksgiving of such a kind as only those who have much to be forgiven can offer. The consciousness of God's sovereignty and judgment prevents us from forgetting that his mercy and our need are constant and inseparable elements in Christian experience. But if this affects our estimate of ourselves, it should equally influence our attitude to others. If we are acutely conscious that the right to judge belongs to God, we will be slow to censure our brothers; if we know that we need to be forgiven, we shall be more charitable toward those who stand in similar need of pardon. Each one of us is accountable to God, and to God alone (vs. 12). While this disciplines our impulse to condemn others, it should sharpen our sense of responsibility to God. If we do not feel obliged to set others right, we may have a better chance of giving a proper **account** of ourselves to God.

13. ***Avoiding Occasions of Offense.***—In the first part of the chapter Paul has dwelt upon the need of mutual tolerance. The strong must not despise the weak; the weak must not censure the strong. But this is only the beginning of a satisfactory solution of the problem created by "indifferent things." What we do exerts considerable influence on those about us; our conduct may profoundly affect for good or ill our fellow men. A special responsibility therefore rests upon the strong. It is to them that questions of taboo—sacred or auspicious days, clean or unclean food—are indifferent. It does not matter to them whether they observe restrictions or ignore them. But the weak are in a different position. So, when we have agreed not to **pass judgment on one another,** we have not settled the question because the excessive scrupulosity of the hesitant man remains. The attitude of the weak may amuse or annoy the strong, but it cannot cause him serious harm; whereas the liberty of the emancipated man may easily do his brother irreparable injury. The two cases are consequently not really parallel, and beyond forbearance of each other must be the concern of the strong not to bring the weak to moral shipwreck. More important than the tolerance which does not judge is

[8] Elizabeth Barrett Browning, "Rhyme of the Duchess May," st. xi.

14 I know, and am persuaded by the Lord Jesus, that *there is* nothing unclean of itself: but to him that esteemeth any thing to be unclean, to him *it is* unclean.

way of a brother. 14 I know and am persuaded in the Lord Jesus that nothing is unclean in itself; but it is unclean for any

---

and to the "weak" (that they be not censorious); now he turns definitely to the "strong" and lays on them a special obligation. The emancipated Christian is to be sure that he is not putting **a stumbling-block or hindrance in the way of** [his weaker] **brother.** Paul explains at once what he means: he is quite certain in his own mind that such things as he is discussing in this chapter do not really matter—and here the reference to **unclean** definitely suggests the Jewish food laws. He is **persuaded** of this **in the Lord Jesus**—i.e., he knows it as a member of the body of Christ and therefore by the illumination of the Spirit. At the same time he recognizes that one cannot violate one's own conscientious scruples without sin, even when one's scruples are really mistaken and unnecessary. A food, however "clean," is in fact unclean **for any one who thinks it**

---

the true charity which is eager to help. It must therefore be a matter of fixed resolve not to cause offense to anyone who is our brother. This is a duty which the trend of Paul's argument makes it natural for him to inculcate; but it also closely reproduces the teaching of Christ. To put hindrances in the way of a man's vocation is devilish work (Matt. 16:23); in our kind of world it may not be possible to avoid offenses, but how wretched is the lot of that man through whom they come (Matt. 18:7)! (Note also the parallels in Rom. 16:17; Rev. 2:14.) It has sometimes been suggested that the two words Paul uses—**stumbling-block or hindrance**—point to the different kinds of obstacles which we put in the way of others. The **stumbling-block** is often carelessly left in the path; we may not regard it, but those who follow may easily trip and fall. The **hindrance** is the snare or trap which is deliberately laid and in which others find their feet entangled. Whether or not a letter writer consciously draws such exact distinctions is hard to say. Certainly in ordinary religious experience we discover that the welfare of our fellow men is overthrown in one or other of these ways—by the heedlessness which leaves unnecessary obstacles in our brother's way, or by the calculating malice which contrives his ruin. Since Paul's experience in Near Eastern cities had taught him much about the moral life, it may well be that exact observation underlies what might appear to be only a slightly repetitious phrase.

14. ***Unclean?***—In principle Paul explicitly takes his stand with the strong. This is not an opinion to which he inclines; it is a basic conviction to which his Christian faith commits him. He is firmly **persuaded** that regulations about food and observances are not of fundamental importance. The language he uses is that of absolute certainty, and is all the more impressive because in his Pharisaic days he held with equal emphasis to the opposite view. This kind of revolution—a complete change of outlook as to what constitutes matters of religious importance—comes to pass only when there is a sufficient motive. Paul found it in Jesus Christ, and the liberty which he now enjoys is part of the great deliverance which Christ wrought for him. He was made free from the dead hand of a tradition which regulates our religious life in terms of outward forms and observances; but he also discovered that all things can be consecrated to a religious use. Nothing is by its nature unclean or taboo. Inanimate things are morally neutral; if accepted in the right spirit and used according to a Christian purpose, they can serve the high ends of God's kingdom. It is perfectly apparent that Paul, though a believer in the disciplined religious life, was not an advocate of what is usually called asceticism. He did not have the ascetic's settled suspicion of natural enjoyments, and he believed that to live in constant fear that some evil power was inherent in material things was to be weak in the faith. Elsewhere he declared emphatically that a man can even eat and drink to the glory of God (I Cor. 10:31).

It is hardly necessary to remark that he is not discussing acts which have an ethical significance. He does not suggest that moral distinctions are unreal or unimportant. Even in his own day his emphasis on freedom from taboo was misunderstood and distorted into a defense of moral license, and the antinomian thread has run right through the course of Christian history. Paul merely insists that things are only things, and the disposition to invest them with moral qualities is a denial of

15 But if thy brother be grieved with *thy* meat, now walkest thou not charitably. Destroy not him with thy meat, for whom Christ died.

one who thinks it unclean. 15 If your brother is being injured by what you eat, you are no longer walking in love. Do not let what you eat cause the ruin of one for

---

unclean. Now if your eating certain foods—although so far as you alone are concerned, you can do so in all innocence—places an irresistible temptation in the path of your brother who *does* have scruples, so that he violates his conscience and falls into sin—if this happens, you have not acted **in love,** i.e., you have denied the Spirit of the fellowship. You have let a mere whim of yours about food **cause the ruin of one for whom Christ died.** The implied rebuke—to be repeated in 15:3—is that if Christ was willing to die because of love of such a one, surely we can deny ourselves so small and temporary a satisfaction as eating a certain food.

That this is what Paul means by putting a **stumbling-block** does not appear very clearly in this passage (vss. 20-22 come somewhat nearer to saying it), but I Cor. 8:7-13

---

the spiritual freedom which Christ has won for us.

But liberty belongs only to those who have actually accepted it. A man can attribute to things a moral significance which in themselves they do not possess. If he thinks that a certain food is defiling, he will feel himself defiled if he eats it. For him **it is unclean,** however neutral it may be to a person of greater emancipation. If a man has a scrupulous conscience, he must obey it; he dare not ignore its verdict. As long as there are different degrees of religious insight and different standards of enlightenment, there is inevitably a subjective element in many of our moral judgments. Training may bring us to a better understanding; but meanwhile we must be prepared to accept the fact that a man's conscience ought to be respected even when it persuades him to accept unnecessary limitations.

15. *Consideration for the Weak.*—This weakness may not deserve respect; certainly it cannot impose its scruples as the standard of another's conduct, but it does merit patient consideration. The strong may hold stoutly to his liberty, and up to a point he is entitled to do so; but when his freer outlook brings his brother into jeopardy, that point has already been passed. The stronger members of the fellowship must consequently submit to the disciplines of charity. This is the more necessary because the liberty that the free man claims is in this instance concerned with inconsequential things. There is a contemptuous note in the phrase **by what you eat:** as much as to say, "For the sake of gratifying your stomach you are willing to destroy your brother's soul." The disparity of values is further heightened when we remember that it is a redeemed soul whom we are endangering on such trifling grounds. Even the most abjectly timid brother is someone for whom Christ was content to die. If he could sacrifice so much, we can surely accept so small a self-denial as charity requires. Paul has just finished emphasizing the freedom from regulations about food which the Christian can legitimately claim. Now he adds, in effect: Having established the right to be free, forgo it for your brother's sake. In the interests of charity waive your unquestioned rights. Do not insist on your privileges—and if you find it hard to renounce them, remember how strong is the motive that bids you do so. "The brother for whom Christ died" (I Cor. 8:11) can claim something from you in virtue of the esteem in which Christ must have held him. Those who meet at the foot of the Cross find that they are brothers, and must act toward each other as such. The aptest commentary on this passage is found in *The Vision of Piers Plowman,* when Langland refers to Calvary and its effect:

> Blood-brothers we became there,
> And gentlemen each one.

We have here in an emphatic form a rule which the N.T. states in various ways: Let what you might claim always exceed what you actually ask; demand less than your acknowledged right; be slow to insist on your prerogatives. The most compelling illustration of the principle is found in the life and teaching of Jesus Christ himself (cf. among many possible examples, Matt. 3:15; 17:24-27). More than once Paul mentions his own consistent practice. "Nor did we seek glory from men," he says, ". . . though we might have made demands as apostles of Christ" (I Thess. 2:6). "What then is my reward?" he asks. "Just this: that in my preaching I may make the gospel free of charge, not making full use of my right in the

16 Let not then your good be evil spoken of:

17 For the kingdom of God is not meat and drink; but righteousness, and peace, and joy in the Holy Ghost.

whom Christ died. 16 So do not let what is good to you be spoken of as evil. 17 For the kingdom of God does not mean food and drink but righteousness and peace and joy

places this meaning beyond doubt. Paul does not mean that the "strong" must abstain from any practice which the "weak" does not like or of which the "weak" does not approve. He has already insisted that neither party should be censorious toward the other; he would certainly also say that neither party should allow itself to be merely tyrannized over by the other. But when a "weak" brother is in danger of death because he is too weak (in another sense) to resist the influence of his "strong" brother's example, love will lead the latter to abstain.

16. This verse is difficult, and one cannot be sure of its precise meaning. Rendered quite literally the Greek says, "Therefore let not your good be blasphemed." The usual way to take "good" is as a reference to the freedom in Christ of which the spiritually mature and strong are able to take advantage, but which must not give occasion for another to fall (cf. I Cor. 8:9, 13). So Sanday and Headlam; Goodspeed translates, "The thing you have a right to do must not become a cause of reproach"; and Moffatt, "Your rights must not get a bad name." On the other hand, in 15:2 the same term **good** (τὸ ἀγαθόν) occurs again—only this time it is "his good" rather than **your** [or according to some MSS "our"] **good.** In other words, in 15:2, the meaning "Christian freedom" does not apply; something like "the worth of the life in Christ" seems indicated. It is possible, of course, that Paul is thinking of one aspect of that "worth" in vs. 16 (i.e., the "freedom" it involves) and of the "worth" in general in 15:2; and the meaning "freedom" (in vs. 16) does have the advantage of fitting more easily into the context. Still, Kirk prefers "the ends that you may legitimately pursue"; Lietzmann, "the Christian ideal"; and Kühl, who sees vs. 16 in close association with vs. 17, "the Christian salvation belonging to the Kingdom of God in so far as it is a present possession." One must also be uncertain as to whether the being **spoken of as evil** refers to an effect outside the church (so Kühl and others) or within the community (so Sanday and Headlam). If one interprets **what is good to you** to mean "the freedom you enjoy in Christ," one will think of the **evil** as being **spoken** within the church, for the issue of freedom is not an issue between the church and the world, but between two groups within the church itself.

17-18. The term **kingdom of God,** so prevalent in Jesus' teaching, seldom occurs in Paul (see I Cor. 4:20; 6:9-10; 15:50; Gal. 5:21; Col. 4:11; II Thess. 1:5; cf. Col. 1:13). The phrase means basically "the kingship of God" or "the kingly rule of God" and

gospel" (I Cor. 9:18). We may claim absolute liberty as a right which the gospel has given us; but we should not use it if a brother is **injured** by our conduct. In the first instance it may only cause him pain—that distress of mind which is occasioned by what seem to be the laxer ways of others; but the inference is that he will finally be tempted to imitate what at first he merely deplores. That will be his **ruin,** and love should intervene to defend him. So the use of things good in themselves may be vitiated by the damage it does a brother.

16. ***The Danger of Discrediting Our Liberty.***—A further consideration should make us careful. The liberty we claim is a good thing because Christ has won it for us. But if we abuse it by selfishly insisting on it as our right, we shall bring it into discredit. If we exercise it in a hard and inconsiderate way, the lovelessness of our conduct will give our freedom a bad name, and men will recoil from what apparently brings harm to others. The tragedy of good things falling into contempt because they are so unworthily represented is repeated generation after generation. The outward pattern may vary, but in every age the Christian message suffers most from those who think they are commending it to their contemporaries.

17. ***The Kingdom of God: What It Is, and What It Is Not.***—Regard both for our brother's welfare and for our own good name should prevent any undue insistence on our rights. We may be quite at liberty to eat or drink whatever we wish, but to cling to this freedom

18 For he that in these things serveth Christ *is* acceptable to God, and approved of men.

in the Holy Spirit; 18 he who thus serves Christ is acceptable to God and approved

usually has an eschatological orientation. This is true in most if not all of the passages just cited. A number of them have to do with what one must do or be in order to "inherit the kingdom of God." The kingly rule, however, was already manifest among men of faith and was not simply or only a future reality. All that has been said about the relation of present and future in Paul is relevant here (see pp. 406-7). Thus in I Cor. 4:20, when Paul says, "The kingdom of God does not consist in talk but in power," he must mean: "It is not by one's own claims that the fact of one's belonging to the kingdom of God [i.e., to the new order in Christ] is demonstrated, but by the spiritual powers that work in and through one." So here also the term is used to refer to the new order, which is the final reality, but into which as even now partly actualized the Christian has been incorporated. The mark of membership in that order is not that one can eat or drink anything one wants to—that is trivial and incidental—but is **righteousness and peace and joy,** the particular "righteousness, peace, and joy" which are known within the

when other and more important matters are jeopardized by it is to lose all sense of proportion. In fact, we fall into an error comparable with that of the weaker brother—we exalt an inconsequential option to the status of a necessary religious principle. The particular example which Paul consistently uses is that of eating and drinking; but the core of the matter is our treatment of indifferent things. The only person who is really free is the one who is able to act in whichever way seems wisest. He can eat if there is nothing to hinder; he can abstain if charity demands. Actually, the man who feels that he must demonstrate his emancipation on every possible occasion is a slave in spite of his apparent freedom. The need to prove his liberty has become a tyranny. The incongruity of the situation becomes even clearer when we realize how completely such conduct ignores the real issues of the religious life. There are certain blessings which Christianity offers to those who accept it; but a militant attitude toward indifferent things forfeits all of them. Preoccupation with a benefit of relatively negligible importance obscures the real purpose of the spiritual life. The kingdom of God has nothing to do with trivial matters like eating and drinking; it does not consist in liberty to satisfy physical needs in any particular manner. In a very real sense Paul strips from our conception of the kingdom everything that would circumscribe it in terms of national or ecclesiastical background. The limitations which our particular heritage might tend to impose upon us are seen as the irrelevant considerations they actually are. Whether we respect the taboos of our past or not is by no means the vital question; liberty in minor matters must be of comparative unimportance because the true acceptance of God's kingly rule involves wholly different things. It offers us the full satisfaction of the deepest needs of the human heart. It gives us a new relationship to God which finds expression in a new quality of upright living; it gives us peace with God which proves to be the secret of peace with one another; it gives us that profound inner satisfaction which only God's presence can create and which the world is incapable of destroying. Obviously Paul is describing neither religious graces nor ethical virtues, because both are fused in one. The whole bent of his mind made that kind of artificial distinction distasteful to him. The root of faith and the flower of conduct cannot be separated. Each needs the other. To exalt either is to forget that uprightness and serenity are only the outward expression of an inward religious experience. If isolated from each other, both belief and conduct lose their vitality. An inherent necessity requires an inseparable union.

18. ***Earning the Truest Approbation.***—Paul has intimated the principles which underlie upright and conciliatory conduct. Whoever adheres to these principles in his daily discipleship will be certain to find favor both with God, who sees the heart, and with men, who observe our outward actions. The verse is brief, and the meaning clear; but certain inferences are worth noting.

(*a*) The apostle has contrasted that preoccupation with ceremonial regulation, which is apt to be the mark of religious people, with the awareness of spiritual realities, which is the gift of true faith. He has pointed out that we can serve Christ either by observing or by disregarding the rules which govern marginal issues;

19 Let us therefore follow after the things which make for peace, and things wherewith one may edify another.

by men. 19 Let us then pursue what makes

community and are imparted by the Spirit (cf. 5:1-5; also Gal. 5:22). It is doubtful that Paul has in mind here the opposition of a spiritual conception of the kingdom to the crassly material conception which was held by many (see above, pp. 519-20). He means simply what he says more clearly in I Cor. 8:8: "Food will not commend us to God," adding, "We are no worse off if we do not eat, and no better off if we do." The phrase **in the Holy Spirit** goes not only with **joy,** but with the whole preceding phrase and means nothing other than Paul would have meant if he had said "in Christ" or "in the Lord." **He who thus serves Christ** is he who, in the way Paul has indicated, is considerate of his brethren. The words **approved by men** rather support, it must be acknowledged, the meaning of **be spoken of as evil** (vs. 16) which Kühl and others have favored, i.e., as designating an effect *outside of* the church.

19-21. The words **peace** and **mutual upbuilding** serve to remind his readers of the two emphases Paul has been making—the need for tolerance and charity (vss. 1-12) and

but we cannot be indifferent to the essential qualities of the triumphant life. We do not have the option of ignoring righteousness, peace, and joy in the Holy Spirit.

(*b*) The inwardness of true discipleship stands in opposition to any formal pattern of behavior. The spiritual quality of a life is determined largely by its controlling motives. There is a vast difference between "serving Christ" by doing certain things and conforming to what seems a desirable standard of behavior. The man who pursues righteousness and peace because of his loyalty to Christ is the man who is aware of God's approval and the good will of his fellow men.

(*c*) There is a type of life which is respectable because of a calculating conviction that decency pays: it is a matter of ancient observation that if we love those who love us, we will reap the appropriate reward. Some people are honest only because "honesty is the best policy." When Paul says that God's approval rests on those whom loyalty to Christ makes upright and peaceable, he is describing not a motive but a result. The spiritual world is so constituted that certain blessings are always derivative. Happiness is not found by pursuing it; it is one of the by-products of an unselfish life. In the same way, the approval of God follows not from the deliberate effort to win it, but from the faithful discharge of those duties which loyalty to Christ lays upon us.

(*d*) The Christian does not seek the applause of his fellow men. Indeed, when we recall Jesus' uncompromising assurance that men will revile and persecute us, we may well be suspicious of the world's praise. At the same time, though it may not be our aim to win the approval of others, a certain kind of life will finally commend itself to those of open mind. Adherence to principle, regard for what is right, consideration for others, and an unruffled serenity—these finally win the respect of our fellows.

19. ***Pursuing the Proper Objectives.***—Paul has stated the nature of the kingdom, and indicated the tenor of life which should be the mark of its citizens. He now comes to the practical inferences which we ought to draw from these things. He has clearly shown that he does not challenge our Christian freedom in the use of things morally indifferent, but he insists that our liberty must always be exercised with proper reference to its effect on others. Granted that a given type of conduct is permissible to me, before I act on that conviction I must pause to consider its consequences for my neighbor. In particular, I must make sure that what I do promotes the **peace** of the fellowship and results in the **upbuilding** of the religious community. The history of Christianity abounds in examples of people, intensely earnest about nonessentials, who have felt at liberty to shatter the unity of the church for the sake of their particular fetish. To divide the church, said the old Puritan, John Howe, "is devil's work," and the remark faithfully reflects an indispensable N.T. emphasis. The parallel translations of this verse serve admirably to remind us of the original meaning of **edify.** Time and carelessness have corrupted the word until it suggests little more than the diffusion of a pious emotional glow; it points to a vague feeling of sentimental goodness. If we bear in mind that edify and edifice come from the same root, we are more likely to grasp the true meaning of what Paul says. The "edifying of itself in love" (Eph.

20 For meat destroy not the work of
God. All things indeed *are* pure; but *it is*
evil for that man who eateth with offense.
21 *It is* good neither to eat flesh, nor to
drink wine, nor *any thing* whereby thy
brother stumbleth, or is offended, or is
made weak.

for peace and for mutual upbuilding. 20 Do
not, for the sake of food, destroy the work
of God. Everything is indeed clean, but it is
wrong for any one to make others fall by
what he eats; 21 it is right not to eat meat
or drink wine or do anything that makes

---

the need for considerateness on the part of the strong toward the weak (vss. 18-21). On vss. 20 and 21 see Exeg. on vss. 13-15.

4:16) points to that constructive upbuilding of the community which is the natural consequence of the chief motive power of Christian conduct. On the verse as a whole there are few apter comments than that of Calvin: "We must indeed eat, that we may live; we ought to live, that we may serve the Lord; and he serves the Lord, who by benevolence and kindness edifies his neighbour; for in order to promote these two things, concord and edification, all the duties of love ought to be exercised." [4]

20. ***The Iniquity of Destroying the Work of God.***—The plea for a constructive attitude retains its force in any situation; but it is not merely as an important general principle that Paul has put it forward. The discussion started from a particular point, and constantly returns to it. In this verse Paul repeats the requirement advanced a little earlier (vs. 15), but the demand has acquired added force from the wider background which he has meanwhile supplied. The wantonly destructive effect of a liberty selfishly pursued stands out starkly against the insistence that it is a Christian's duty to work for the things which build up both the fellowship and those who compose it. **To destroy** is to pull down; it is the direct antithesis to **the work of God.** What God has wrought may mean either the Christian church or the Christian character of the individual. The community of faith can be shattered by the callous indifference which exalts secondary issues but ignores the central obligations of love; in the same way, the man for whom Christ died can be brought to ruin by a wanton disregard of his susceptibilities. To the enlightened man questions of food can never claim a place of great importance; but it is not right, because of them, to **destroy the work of God,** in whichever sense we choose to interpret it. We may believe that ritually all things are pure; but this freedom degenerates into selfish pride if we prefer it to the spiritual welfare of our brother. It is then wrong in almost every respect. It is arrogant—because we believe we are infallibly right; it is selfish—because we decline to mitigate our claims in the interest of our brother's welfare; it is unwarranted—because it rests on a defective sense of proportion and does not recognize secondary issues for what they really are.

Paul has tacitly conceded that "the strong" are right as far as principle is concerned; but this is far from solving the difficulties with which in practice we are faced. Most of us assume that to establish the proper principle is to settle all the problems to which our relationships with other people give rise. But the principle is often abstract, and the situations which demand attention are concrete. In addition to conceding the general principle, the Christian must discover how it can be specifically applied in the spirit of love and for the welfare of others. It is much easier to state a general proposition than it is to translate it into action without doing violence to the claims of charity. To be satisfied that nothing is ritually defiling is one thing; to know what to do in a given situation is quite a different matter. Our theories always need to be interpreted by love.

21. ***The Christian Duty of Self-Restraint.***—Paul has advanced a negative principle: it is wrong so to exercise our freedom that someone else suffers in consequence. Our neighbor may be upset by observing that his brothers do what he has been taught to regard as wrong; he may be tempted to act as they do, in spite of the fact that his conscience is not emancipated to the same degree as theirs. In either case he suffers injury, and it must be our care to avoid whatever imperils his well-being. Now Paul puts forward the corresponding positive principle: it is right to claim less than our due. Even if we can eat and drink whatever we like, we should be ready to forgo the exercise of that liberty if the welfare of our brother should demand it. And this requirement holds good in every area where disagreement may exist. Paul has cited the regulations which govern food and drink, in part because they arise from the subject immediately under discussion, in part because they form an area where men

[4] *Romans, ad loc.*

22 Hast thou faith? have *it* to thyself before God. Happy *is* he that condemneth not himself in that thing which he alloweth.

23 And he that doubteth is damned if he eat, because *he eateth* not of faith: for whatsoever *is* not of faith is sin.

your brother stumble.[v] 22 The faith that you have, keep between yourself and God; happy is he who has no reason to judge himself for what he approves. 23 But he who has doubts is condemned, if he eats, because he does not act from faith; for whatever does not proceed from faith is sin.[w]

[v] Other ancient authorities add *or be upset or be weakened.*
[w] Other authorities, some ancient, insert here ch. 16. 25-27.

22-23. Here Paul returns to the basic idea of the whole passage: opinions on such matters as sabbathkeeping and foods are private matters between a believer and God. **Happy is he** who does not find himself divided as between what he approves and what he knows as a Christian he ought to be able to approve; or perhaps the meaning is, as Moffatt renders it, "He is a fortunate man who has no misgivings about what he allows

are very prone to lay obligations on one another. People still quarrel bitterly about what they can or cannot eat—still more about what they should or should not drink. Paul decisively places all matters of regulation in a position subsidiary to the demands of love, and adds that what is true in one area is true in all. The sovereign law of Christian conduct is always to subordinate our own privilege to our brother's need. It is not spiritual liberty so to walk that others stumble in consequence. This is more than the substance of an exhortation; it is the pattern to which Paul himself conformed. What he urged on others was what he practiced himself (I Cor. 10:31-33).

22. ***Freedom with a Clear Conscience.***—A man is not free because he parades his liberty. We may feel entitled to repudiate ritual regulations without feeling that we must flaunt the fact before those who are less emancipated than we are. After all, the crux of the whole matter is a certain awareness of a new relationship to God. If we are sons of his grace, we are confident that no legalism can bind us; but it is this very sense of his liberating favor, and nothing else, that constitutes the free life. Our freedom really consists in knowing that we are sons of God, not in permission to act toward others as we like. Indeed, if we are children in the Father's house, we are more likely to act toward one another as brothers; and that may easily entail accepting a restriction of our liberty. So, emancipation is linked with the fullest sense of responsibility to God, and we may possess a freedom that we do not practice. The blessedness of the strong man does not lie in the fact that he can do what others cannot. The important thing is to have a conscience which does not condemn us. We can congratulate ourselves if we so assert our Christian liberty that we have no need of subsequent self-recrimination because of our disregard of others. We are fortunate if we so maintain our convictions that we do not injure anybody else. But a clear conscience has a more directly personal significance. For our convictions we are answerable—as Paul has just shown—to God; if at the inner bar of judgment we are satisfied that we are right in the things which we "approve" or "allow," we have every reason to be reassured.

23. ***Their Fate Who Act, but Not from Faith.*** The man of enlightened conscience can eat or forbear as charity dictates; but the man of many scruples cannot claim the same alternative: and it is this simple, basic fact which has determined the character of Paul's whole approach to the problem of mutual tolerance. Having shown wherein the strong man is favored, he now indicates wherein the weak man is vulnerable. Though not inwardly convinced, the diffident person may suppress his fears and try to act in the same way as those who are delivered from the tyranny of scruples. But it is not the pattern of conduct that finally matters; what counts is the witness of each man's conscience that his actions correspond with his insight. It is not reprehensible to have doubts, but to override them invites moral disaster. "He who is undecided is condemned already if he eats, because his action is not based on conviction." "Conviction" is the key word: the only way to preserve our integrity is to adhere strictly to what conscience sanctions. **Whatever does not proceed from faith** [conviction—Goodspeed] **is sin.** In this concluding pronouncement Paul epitomizes his teaching on the subject. He has shown that his sympathies lie with the strong, but he has charged them to deal charitably with the weak. He has indi-

15 We then that are strong ought to bear the infirmities of the weak, and not to please ourselves.

15 We who are strong ought to bear with the failings of the weak, and

himself to eat." **Faith** in these verses seems to mean something like "assurance as to the leading of the Spirit." Vs. 23 amplifies what is said more succinctly in vs. 14*b*. Vs. 23*b* conveys a true idea only when it is seen in the particular context of this passage.

F. Conclusion of Ethical Section (15:1-13)

15:1-2. It will be remembered that some ancient MSS of this epistle (see Intro., pp. 364-65) apparently ended with 14:23, except possibly for the long benediction now found at 16:25-27. It is obvious, however, that the opening verses of this chapter continue without any break the previous discussion. Paul repeats that the **strong** must not be

cated that the weak can be overthrown if they are encouraged to practice a freedom which their conscience does not sanction. The duty of the Christian is to recognize the inwardness of all morality. "The right" is what an enlightened conscience approves; Christian behavior translates into action what commends itself to Christian conviction. From this it follows inevitably that our conduct will not always conform to a given pattern. What is right for one person will be wrong for another, and there is no fixed external measure which can be uniformly applied. Some things, of course, will always be wrong; but there is a considerable marginal range where decisions will differ. This seemingly relative standard, however, is the condition of growth. Loyalty to conviction makes it possible for a man to retain his integrity; and, granted such basic moral honesty, it is possible for the Spirit to lead him more and more fully into all the truth.

It is worth recalling two scriptural parallels which illuminate this passage. Both have often been noted, but both are too relevant to be omitted. (*a*) Jas. 1:6 refers to the man "who doubts" and who is "like a wave of the sea that is driven and tossed by the wind" (RSV). The KJV rendering, "he that wavereth," admirably suggests that "double-minded" uncertainty which is always in doubt about a given course of action, and the imagery of the wave brilliantly indicates the moral instability of the man devoid of clear conviction. (*b*) In the Codex Bezae (Luke 6:4) a saying is attributed to Jesus which indicates how closely Paul is following the teaching of his Lord: "On the same day he saw a man working on the sabbath, and said to him, 'Man, if thou knowest what thou doest, it is well with thee; but if thou knowest not, thou hast incurred a curse and art a transgressor of the law.'"

15:1-33. ***The Measure of Christian Maturity.***—Mutual forbearance was implied in all that Paul said in ch. 14; it is now explicitly discussed in this chapter. Whatever may have been the original relation of this passage to the letter as a whole (cf. Exeg.), the subject matter unfolds without violent dislocation of the theme. The section invites consideration as a whole and readily lends itself to such treatment. The general principle which shapes Paul's thinking can be simply stated: the measure of our strength and Christian maturity is our ability to subordinate our own desires and our own preferences to the actual necessities of those who are weaker than we are. At all points where natural impulse might prompt us to do as we please, Christian insight will teach us to regard with patient sympathy the limitations of other people. The principle, thus stated in general terms, was convincingly demonstrated by Christ in his own life; he is the supreme example of the attitude which we ought to manifest, and he himself is our chief inducement to conform to the pattern which he provides. The illustrative testimony of Scripture provides a natural transition to the apostle's prayer: may the believers achieve such unity that their essential agreement, in spite of differences in outlook, will show forth God's praise and confirm them in the charity which Christ's life exemplified.

1. ***The Obligations of the Strong.***—We find ourselves at once on familiar ground. Paul has already pointed out that those who have entered in larger measure into the liberty which Christ bestows must treat their more hesitant brethren with generous forbearance. Strength is a privilege, but it creates problems both for those who possess it and for those who do not. Paul, it will be observed, associates himself with the strong, but only to emphasize the duties which those who share his position must be willing to accept. Freedom may confer privilege, but it also entails obligation. It is with the responsibilities that Paul is here

2 Let every one of us please *his* neighbor for *his* good to edification.

not to please ourselves; 2 let each of us please his neighbor for his good, to edify

set simply on pleasing themselves. It is not enough for them to **bear with the . . . weak; each** must **please his neighbor**—but please him, Paul quickly adds, **for his good, to edify him** (cf. what was said about being tyrannized over in connection with 14:13-15; and on **good** see on 14:16). The word translated **bear with** is βαστάζειν, which means primarily "to bear." It is used of Jesus' bearing his cross in John 19:17, and of the Christian's bearing his cross in Luke 14:27. The readers of Galatians are enjoined to "bear one another's burdens." It is likely, therefore, that here the word does not mean merely to "tolerate," but also to be ready to suffer deprivation, if need be, rather than to become the occasion of sin on the part of another. The Greek terms which Paul uses here to

chiefly concerned—perhaps because they are so easily overlooked—and he consequently gives us a study in conscious strength and what it entails. Implicit in what Paul writes is a reminder of the characteristic dangers to which the strong are always exposed. They are apt to let their immunity from weakness circumscribe the range of their sympathy. Because they are free from hesitancy and excessive scrupulosity, because they are less often tempted and are less likely to fall, they are apt to dismiss abruptly the claims of their less fortunate brethren. The strong are often deficient in imaginative insight, and their weakness passes over into more serious faults. Since they do not understand the problems of others, their own virtues are apt to minister to their pride, and too often issue in arrogant contempt of those who need their help.

The dangers to which the strong are exposed make it the more necessary to accept the obligations which the mature Christian should be ready to assume. Consideration for others must occupy an important position among our responsibilities, and this presupposes an ability to set our privileges in their proper place. It is quite true that strength emancipates us from conventions and teaches us to treat all human ordinances with a flexibility to which the weak are strangers, but this does not entitle us to disregard the plight of the man who is less fortunate than we are. Because someone insists on retaining burdens which we are able to discard, we are not entitled to disregard his plight. Indeed, one of the weaknesses to which the strong are exposed is the inability to forget their privileges; but Christian freedom emancipates us even from this constraint. The liberty of the Christian man also has its "second mile," and we come to see that the heart of our freedom does not consist in our right to ignore the needless burdens which others insist on bearing. Consequently, though we may be free ourselves, we are willing to treat with patient forbearance **the failings of the weak.** At times this may be galling for us, but we must remember that it is scarcely pleasant for them. Moffatt's free rendering of this verse ("We . . . ought to bear the burdens that the weak make for themselves and us") has at least the merit of reminding us that we are only sharing our weaker brother's burden, and relates the passage to the apostolic definition of the law of Christ (Gal. 6:2).

We can therefore see a little more clearly the nature of our proper attitude to those whose liberty is circumscribed. Instead of receiving only our contempt, the weak man is entitled to expect our sympathy. The fact that he cannot free himself from the encumbrance of a restricted outlook is the mark of his ailment and the measure of his need. We do not censure a man because he is sick; it is unreasonable to blame him merely because he is weak. Christian maturity, therefore, is the willingness to meet him where he is, and to help him with his problems. That will demand of us patience in the face of his exasperating limitations, as well as freedom from resentment on account of the restrictions which he proposes to lay on us as well as on himself. It will involve sympathy if we are to understand his plight and help him to rise above it; meanwhile, it will require a willingness to share the actual discomfort which his burden imposes on us both. This is epitomized in the simple rule by which we are to govern our behavior: we are **not to please ourselves.** The mark of all egotism is solicitude for our own rights, comforts, and concerns; this is precisely what we must subdue.

2. ***Our Duty: To Seek Our Neighbor's Good.***—The negative command, though perhaps sufficient for our own restraint, is inadequate as a means of creating right relationships with others. The injunction "not to please ourselves" must therefore be expanded and expressed in positive form. We are under the

3 For even Christ pleased not himself; but, as it is written, The reproaches of them that reproached thee fell on me.

him. 3 For Christ did not please himself; but, as it is written, "The reproaches of those who reproached thee fell on me."

---

represent the strong and the weak mean "those who are able" and "those who are not able," the "capable" and the "incapable."

3. **For Christ did not please himself.** Almost certainly involved in this statement, as in II Cor. 8:9, is an incidental allusion to Christ's divine pre-existence, the prerogatives of which he was willing to surrender for our sake. Phil. 2:6-8 makes this meaning quite explicit: Christ was not thinking of his own satisfaction or comfort or rights when he "emptied" himself and took "the form of a servant"; he was adapting himself—in the most radical and costly sense conceivable—to our need. How small in comparison the sacrifice asked of the more mature, "capable" Christian for the sake of harmony in the church and the welfare of his brother!

The quotation from Ps. 69:9 fits very loosely to the sense. The original passage means that the godly man **(me)** has to bear the reproaches which the ungodly intend for God **(thee)**. Sanday and Headlam interpret: "St. Paul transfers the words to Christ, who

---

primary obligation of seeking the things that really benefit our neighbor. To please him does not mean that we accommodate ourselves to him in all respects. Simply to accept his limitations would be the end of all progress in Christian understanding. If the weak man could establish his deficiencies as a standard mandatory for the whole fellowship, the life of the church would be petrified at his level and all growth would cease. Our customary behavior toward "difficult" associates assumes that we have only two alternatives: either to ignore and override their susceptibilities, or to give way and yield to their demands. Paul points out that there is a third possibility. We please our neighbor—but **for his good, to edify him.** Our concessions are not for his convenience, or even for the tranquillity of the fellowship; if we bear his burdens, it is in order that he may learn to leave them behind. **To edify,** as we have seen, is to build up. The guiding principle in all we do must be so to act as to secure our brother's growth in Christian understanding. A considerate and conciliatory attitude ceases under these circumstances to be a pliable self-adjustment to the unreasonable demands of a difficult person; it becomes, instead, the outward expression of a constructive purpose.

From what Paul says we may draw several important inferences: (*a*) We learn to accommodate ourselves to our neighbor's tastes when it is for his good; at other points our liberty can rightfully be expressed. In a conflict of claims the prerogatives of liberty may yield to the demands of charity; but only for constructive ends. (*b*) If we yield **for his good,** it is assumed that our compliance represents a temporary adjustment. Paul is not describing a final and irrevocable situation. The weak man, when "edified," will no longer be so weak; constructive treatment of the problem will bring him to a more adequate understanding of what Christian liberty really means. The spirit of the concession, and the end toward which it is directed, will finally make the concession itself unnecessary. (*c*) This presupposes that both the weak and the strong share common principles, though they have appropriated them in differing degrees. Growth in unity is impossible unless divergent standards can be subjected to the discipline of a single ideal. (*d*) It is always necessary to bear in mind that Paul is not establishing rigid rules for the regulation of the church. He is discussing the duty of having a proper regard for the well-being of others. No one is exempt from its demands; but it does not constitute a system of discipline.

3. ***The Power of Christ's Example.***—An example is more forceful than an exhortation; but even more important than the example is the inspiration which enables us to follow it. Paul finds both in Jesus Christ. The disciple can tell what he ought to do by remembering his Master. We are "not to please ourselves," said Paul; and he knew no better way of making that general injunction concrete and particular than by pointing to the figure of **Christ.** This is consistent with his whole approach to ethical problems. The moral standard was epitomized in a life, not in a series of propositions. Paul never lost sight of concrete realities because he never allowed abstract terms to engross his attention. Holiness was not a quality, but the attribute of a man. And that man was one whom we are pledged to follow. What he did was relevant to our prob-

4 For whatsoever things were written aforetime were written for our learning, that we through patience and comfort of the Scriptures might have hope.

4 For whatever was written in former days was written for our instruction, that by steadfastness and by the encouragement of

is represented as addressing a man. Christ declares that in suffering it was the reproaches or sufferings of others that He bore." This is barely possible; but it is more likely that the word **thee** still is thought of as referring to God and that Christ is representing himself as bearing the reproaches which we intended for God. This means that Paul has in mind not only the self-emptying involved in Christ's coming, but also, and perhaps more particularly, the passion of the Cross.

4. It is impossible to know why Paul chooses this particular occasion to justify his use of scripture by an appeal to the general principle that all the scriptures were **written for our instruction,** when he has had already so many occasions exactly like this for making the same explanation. It sounds like an answer to later Gnostics and especially

lems, and nowhere did his example come home with such directness and force as in those areas of conduct where we are most apt to claim our own rights. To a man like Paul, naturally proud and self-assertive, the self-effacing humility of Christ was a ceaseless source of amazement. He appeals to his readers by "the gentleness and consideration of Christ" (II Cor. 10:1 Moffatt); he reminds them of the humility of Jesus and of his selfless obedience to God's will (Phil. 2:5-8). So he recalls the example of Christ when he wishes the Romans to cultivate the forbearance which builds up the weaker members of the community. In each case he cites those qualities which he naturally associates with the redemptive purpose of Christ's ministry on earth. From beginning to end he saw in Christ's life a deliberate process of self-limitation in the interests of our fallen race. If the Lord could do so much for us, we can hardly complain if our brother's need occasionally circumscribes our freedom. But Paul never treats Christ merely as an example; that would lead to despair. Christ at once provides our pattern and gives us the power to conform to it. He is the source of that spiritual strength without which the best example in the world would be only an exasperation. "I can do all things through Christ which strengtheneth me" (Phil. 4:13).

We might have expected Paul to enforce the appeal to Christ's example by citing a number of specific cases in which this attitude was conspicuously apparent. It may have seemed unnecessary to remind his readers of words and deeds they already knew; he may have felt that when his appeal was to the whole tenor of the Incarnation, particular instances would confuse rather than clarify the issue. It is more likely still that at this point Paul's mind worked in ways quite different from those with which we are familiar. He drives home his point not by giving specific illustrations, but by quoting from the Hebrew Scriptures. Ps. 69, which he uses, seems to have been generally accepted in the early Christian church as having a messianic application. The words, when applied to Christ, illuminate the utterly disinterested character of his dealings with men; he bore the reproaches of the ungodly because he refused to confine his mission to those who were conventionally righteous. His utter disregard both of conventions and of consequences forms the supreme example of indifference to personal well-being in the interests of a redemptive task. To us the connection between the words of the psalm and the example of Christ may seem remote. But given the habit of mind which turned to the O.T. for confirmation of new truth, the quotation would recall everything most characteristic of Christ's work. It would recall all he had done more completely than isolated instances could possibly do, and it would carry all the authority of an appeal to sacred scripture.

4. ***The Scriptures and Their Use.***—The method may seem artificial to us. It is indirect at best, and it involves what might appear to be a highly arbitrary use of the O.T. Paul does not usually pause to justify his treatment of scripture; here he does so. As his other letters make apparent, he was apprehensive lest the Gentiles should unwittingly cut themselves off from what was still their religious heritage, even though it might form no part of their racial background. Because they regarded the O.T. as a Jewish work written for Jews, they were likely to ignore or even to disclaim it. But the religious life which does not draw sustenance from scripture is bound to be impoverished. Paul's basic premise is that the usefulness of the Scriptures was not limited either to

Marcionites, who rejected the scriptures, and, in so far, gives support to the view of some older scholars that this chapter was not originally a part of the letter (see Intro., pp. 364-65). But although one does not easily see why Paul should have made this remark just here, it is a perfectly possible remark for him to make. Presumably the connection among the terms of vs. 4*b* is loosely somewhat like this: The **scriptures** give us **encouragement** (a much better translation of παράκλησις than **comfort**) to **steadfastness,** and on that ground we can **hope** for God's final victory (cf. 5:4, where "steadfastness" and "hope" are again related in this same way, but with a middle term added, "character").

---

the times in which they were written or to the people to whom they were originally addressed. Beyond the immediate purpose they served was a far wider one, according to which they were able to bring light and leading to many subsequent generations. Conviction born of faith and confirmed by experience made it possible to declare that they were intended for a much broader and a much more permanent use than that for which they were first written. It is legitimate, then, to claim that they serve the needs of Christians who require instruction and encouragement no less than they served the needs of those who originally heard the inspired words. This of course is true in a general sense; but Paul was most fully convinced of their value in regard to one particular point—that of Christ and his redemptive mission. All the N.T. writers quote scriptural anticipations of Jesus' work in a way that seems to us arbitrary and unconvincing; but behind it is a view of the biblical material which at least makes their attitude intelligible. Scripture contained the record of how God dealt with his people in order to accomplish through them his eternal purpose. That purpose unfolded age by age, and found completion only in Christ. Hence he is the fulfillment of the partial insights of those who went before him. The imperfect can be regarded as anticipating the complete, and it is therefore legitimate to apply the words of psalmists and prophets to Christ. Probably some such argument as this is presupposed at many points in the N.T. However vehemently we may dissent from the particular applications which are made, the method can claim the merit of recognizing and insisting on the unity of God's purpose and the essential coherence of the truth that comes from him.

There are, however, further practical values to be derived from the proper use of scripture, and we ignore them to our serious impoverishment. The ancient writings can educate the Christian and equip him for his task because they clearly bear the imprint of a divine inspiration. Moreover, they are unexpectedly relevant to the situation in which most Christians find themselves. This explains the claim, so startling at first sight, that **whatsoever was written in former days was written for our instruction.** The demands of daily life are varied and insistent; it is difficult to stand firm and easy to give way to discouragement. The scriptures not only speak to our condition, but fortify in us the qualities most necessary for perseverance. **Steadfastness** is that unrelaxing constancy which refuses to give up. It is the quality exemplified by the trained wrestler who, refusing to relax his grip, holds on long after he might plausibly let go. When we might lose heart and relinquish the struggle, the scriptures resuscitate our hope. What we need, however, is not merely the persistence which sees us through a particular crisis, nor even the dogged determination which grimly continues to struggle forward. **Encouragement** provides the proper emotional counterpart to the resolute fixity of purpose which is the mark of steadfastness. Even our English versions suggest something of the constructive comfort which the scriptures are able to supply. They point to an attitude of mind not only continually delivered from discouragement, but also steadily built up in the assured possession of new strength and insight. It is perhaps especially significant that the word Paul uses is the one from which we have taken the name Paraclete. At once it brings to mind all that Jesus said about the Comforter whom he would send (John 14:16-31).

Steadfastness and encouragement become a part of the present experience of the Christian, but they are also gathered together and projected into the future in a new assurance concerning the things to come: **we . . . have hope.** Hope, as we have already seen, is one of the distinctive qualities of the new life, and as a result we must carefully distinguish it alike from secular optimism and from wishful thinking. It is neither the conviction that inevitable progress will produce its automatic results nor the fond persuasion that our dreams will materialize merely because we desire that they should. True hope is grounded in God, and it is of this religious assurance that Paul writes. Since God's Word reveals his nature and

5 Now the God of patience and consolation grant you to be likeminded one toward another according to Christ Jesus:
6 That we may with one mind *and* one mouth glorify God, even the Father of our Lord Jesus Christ.

the scriptures we might have hope. 5 May the God of steadfastness and encouragement grant you to live in such harmony with one another, in accord with Christ Jesus, 6 that together you may with one voice glorify the God and Father of our Lord Jesus Christ.

---

5. God is now described as the ultimate source of both the **steadfastness** and the **encouragement** (cf. 15:13; 15:33; II Cor. 1:3), and in a beautiful benediction the note of love within the church—the major theme of the ethical section now nearing its close—is struck twice again: in the words **to live in such harmony with one another** and **together you may with one voice.** This unity of the church consists essentially in the shared knowledge of **the God and Father of our Lord Jesus Christ.** This phrase is a characteristic N.T. way of referring to God as he is known within the Christian fellowship, and it may

---

teaches us to trust in his purpose, it is the surest means of training us to place our confidence in him.

5. ***The Secret of Agreement.***—If the Scriptures develop in us the qualities we need—qualities of **steadfastness and encouragement**—it will be because the God to whom they witness is the fountainhead and source of precisely these attributes. All the virtues of the religious life are derivative; they are always less our own achievement than God's gift. We often strive to achieve a tenuous spiritual independence; Paul, while preserving a keen sense of our responsibilities, relates our endeavors to an eternal personal reality. Our deepest satisfactions are more assured and more profound because they are our response to what we see in God. Our response is to appropriate them; but this is possible only because God is waiting to bestow upon us his gift. It is therefore natural for Paul to return to his central theme by means of a prayer. Unity has been his concern. It is created by love and preserved by forbearance; but our selfish arrogance continually threatens to destroy it. Men discover the secret of agreement one with another when the spirit of God has taught them what it means. Therefore we rightly look to God for what he can grant us and what we are not likely to gain in any other way. Unity is a grace which is taught by example. When we live in **harmony with one another,** we do so because we have learned the secret from the only source from which it can come. Agreement of this kind is in accordance with the character and example of Christ. This is another variant of Paul's constant theme, "Let this mind be in you, which was also in Christ Jesus" (Phil. 2:5).

6. ***United in Life, United in Praise.***—Unity of life perfects unity in worship. The harmony which Paul has so earnestly commended finds its fullest expression in united praise of God. To **glorify** God is not merely the result of more perfect agreement among ourselves; it is the ultimate aim of that unanimity which the apostle has described. We are less likely to regard our divisions with complacency if we realize that they starve our common worship. Because of them we offer to God a poorer, thinner quality of praise; and we deprive ourselves of all the benefits and satisfactions which come from a wider participation in our rightful response to him. Our earliest accounts of the life of the Christian community suggest that from the very outset corporate agreement went hand in hand with fuller worship. The Holy Spirit burst upon the fellowship when they were gathered "with one accord in one place" (Acts 2:1), and even the casual reader will note how closely the phrases parallel the words of the present verse. "With one accord" appears again and again in Acts in connection with the praise and thanksgiving of the church (cf. Acts 1:14; 2:46; 4:24; 5:12; etc.). This is what we would expect. We cannot hope to glorify God as we should if we are not in agreement with others. Where the hearts of God's worshipers are divided, there is no true harmony in what their voices say. Nor is it enough for us to claim that our private worship corresponds to the proper pattern: unless we are carried beyond our own devotions into a wider fellowship, we forfeit an essential part of the religious experience; for as Calvin aptly put it, "The unity of his servants is so much esteemed by God, that he will not have his glory sounded forth amidst discords and contentions."[5] The quality of praise which we achieve is bound up with the kind of God whom we serve. Those who follow a stern God will accept a harsh form of worship; those who

[5] *Romans, ad loc.*

7 Wherefore receive ye one another, as Christ also received us, to the glory of God.

7 Welcome one another, therefore, as Christ has welcomed you, for the glory of

well have been originated by Paul. (Cf. II Cor. 1:3; 11:31; Eph. 1:3; I Pet. 1:3. Col. 1:3 uses a very similar phrase.) **In accord with Christ Jesus** looks backward to vs. *3a* and also forward to vss. 7-12, in which the example of Christ is to be more elaborately used to bring this whole section to an end.

7-9*a*. The words **welcome one another, therefore, as Christ has welcomed you,** serve to bring us back again to the specific topic with which this section began at 14:1. The Greek word for "welcome" is the same. The general intention of vss. 7-12 is to say: "Just as Christ came under the law in order that he might bring about the fulfillment of God's purpose of salvation for both Jew and Gentile [which has been set forth in chs. 9–11], you Gentiles should be willing to bear with the scruples of some of your less

bowed down to Molech passed their children to him through the fire (cf. II Kings 16:3; 21:6; Jer. 7:31; 32:35; Ezek. 16:21; 20:26, 31; cf. Milton, *Paradise Lost,* Book I, ll. 392-405). The history of mankind is a sad demonstration that religion does not necessarily promote fellowship. If we are to find unity, it must be through the worship of a God who makes unity possible. One of the characteristic ways in which Paul refers to the deity is **the God and Father of our Lord Jesus Christ.** He who taught us to say "Our Father" pointed us to a God in whose worship we can recover our long-lost sense of brotherhood. He who has broken down "the middle wall of partition" which separates us from one another has also shown us that the God whom he worshiped—and revealed—both seeks our united praise and makes it possible. At the same time, we do well to remember that here, as so often in the N.T., the qualities we need the most are not those that we are likely to achieve by our own effort. Paul has written not an exhortation but a prayer. The religious man, as he progressively discovers the unsuspected possibilities of the new life, is increasingly ready to concede that they are more likely to be received from God than won by himself. On the human side the heart of the matter is epitomized in a twofold declaration: harmony is the precondition of true praise; true praise confirms and establishes unanimity.

7. *The Wider Fellowship Which Christ Creates.*—Paul repeatedly introduces a new subject by recapitulating what he has already said on a related theme. He now widens the discussion to include the rift between Jews and Gentiles; but he prepares the way by summarizing his argument about tolerance and forbearance. **Therefore** points back immediately to the prayer of the preceding verse; but it also gathers up all that he has said since 14:1. In order that the kind of praise for which he has just prayed may ascend to God, it is necessary for people of differing points of view to **welcome one another.** This in itself reminds us that mere tolerance does not meet the case. Paul has already suggested that he expects more than a willingness to differ without mutual recrimination. To **welcome one another** is to go beyond polite forbearance to the creation of fellowship and good will among those who hold opposing views. This may seem to make heavy demands on us; but Paul does not forget that we are subject to the constraint of a divine example. As the passage unfolds, his theme is the faithfulness and mercy of God: in active love the heavenly Father overcomes the perverseness of his wayward children. For the moment, however, he concentrates on what Christ has done for us. When he asks us to be forbearing to others, he is not putting forth a claim for which he cannot quote the authority of Christ. If he bids his readers to welcome one another, it is because **Christ has welcomed you**—both parties alike. Anyone whom our Lord receives as a follower we must accept as a fellow disciple. **For the glory of God** has been interpreted in a variety of ways. Some have pointed out—and truly—that genuine charity among Christians proclaims God's glory among men. Others claim that Christ's reception of those whom human differences would keep apart is the means by which God's glory is made known; and they point to the way in which this section subsequently unfolds. These interpretations do not seem to be mutually exclusive, and when the authorities differ among themselves, the expositor may well claim as wide a range as the truth of the passage permits. It is also useful to pause over a third interpretation suggested by Anderson Scott. He renders the verse as follows: "Wherefore welcome one another, even as Christ has welcomed us (or you) into the glory of God"; and adds the comment: "The 'glory of God'

8 Now I say that Jesus Christ was a minister of the circumcision for the truth of God, to confirm the promises *made* unto the fathers:
9 And that the Gentiles might glorify

God. 8 For I tell you that Christ became a servant to the circumcised to show God's truthfulness, in order to confirm the promises given to the patriarchs, 9 and in order that the Gentiles might glorify God for his mercy. As it is written,

mature and less fully emancipated brethren." **A servant to the circumcised** is only one way of rendering a phrase which is literally "servant of circumcision"—and many would say not the best way. In Gal. 4:4, 5 Paul speaks of Christ as "born under the law, to redeem those who were under the law." It is questionable that he means anything else than this here. The Messiah had to be a Jew, accepting the whole Jewish law, in order to **show God's truthfulness,** by bringing to fulfillment **the promises given to the patriarchs;** and since the salvation of the Gentiles was an essential part of that same purpose and plan of God, in order to bring to *them* **his mercy.** One must doubt that Paul means to suggest that the Jews are saved by an act of **truthfulness** and only the Gentiles by an act of **mercy** (so Sanday and Headlam seem to say). Paul may have had something like this

into which Christians are welcomed is the moral splendour of the divine nature, that of which sinners know nothing (iii. 23)." [6]

8. *Christ and the Hope of Israel.*—Apparently Paul is apprehensive that he has not really made his meaning clear. So in order to give further emphasis to his point, he elaborates what he has already said. How has Christ showed forth God's glory except by the way in which he has brought men of opposing traditions into the unity and fullness of a redeemed community? He came to his own people, and he came as one of themselves. Directly he exercised no ministry except among the Jews, and this he could do only by conforming to the pattern of their life. Like all his race, he was "made of a woman, made under the law"; but the purpose of this gesture of humility, as Paul immediately adds, was "to redeem them that were under the law, that we might receive the adoption of sons" (Gal. 4:4-5). What he did looked backward on the history of his people as well as forward to the fulfillment of their hopes. One of the glories of the O.T. story is the unshaken confidence of the "fathers" in the truth of a conviction which they never saw confirmed. Their highest insights pointed to something that (within their experience) was not fulfilled. "These all died in faith, not having received the promises, but having seen them afar off, and were persuaded of them, and embraced them" (Heb. 11:13). But if they had seen only "the cloud-capp'd towers" of a dream city, they would have been of all men most miserable; if God inspired their insights, his faithfulness required that their hopes should not remain forever in abeyance. As men had been gradually taught of God to know his nature and his will, they had cherished with increasing eagerness the expectation of a disclosure fuller still. To the men who wrote the books of the N.T. Christ was God's fullest revelation; but he was also the fulfillment of the hopes that God had hitherto inspired. In him God's nature was disclosed, and by him **God's truthfulness** was confirmed. This is what provides so firm a unity between the O.T. and the N.T. The hope and the discovery which satisfied it were inseparably related. One had not spoken the full truth about Christ until one had set him in his true relation to the process which his coming crowned. The first disciples could never have treated him, as we sometimes do, as though he were an isolated spiritual phenomenon. His good deeds, his wise words, his shining example, his redemptive death, his risen power—all these were the glorious culmination of a divine self-disclosure which for centuries had been unfolding in the history of the chosen people. "Revelation" is one of the great words in the religious vocabulary; but in Christian experience its necessary correlative has been "fulfillment."

9. *The Wider Purpose that Christ Fulfilled.*—The promise was to "the circumcision," and its fulfillment vindicated the truthfulness of God; but the scope of its ultimate purpose was vastly wider. God had originally disclosed his will within a narrow orbit to bring one people to submit to its constraint; but always his providence saw beyond Israel's perfect obedience. This was where many of Paul's Jewish contemporaries failed so lamentably. They believed that if all Israel could perfectly keep the entire law for even a single day, the promised kingdom would come; but they were overlook-

[6] *Footnotes to St. Paul,* p. 66.

God for *his* mercy; as it is written, For this cause I will confess to thee among the Gentiles, and sing unto thy name.

10 And again he saith, Rejoice, ye Gentiles, with his people.

11 And again, Praise the Lord, all ye Gentiles; and laud him, all ye people.

"Therefore I will praise thee among the
Gentiles,
and sing to thy name";
10 and again it is said,
"Rejoice, O Gentiles, with his people";
11 and again,
"Praise the Lord, all Gentiles,
and let all the peoples praise him";

---

in mind momentarily—or the suggested distinction may be only a matter of rhetoric—but when his language is so understood, it comes too directly into conflict with other statements in the epistle, even in chs. 9–11 (e.g., 11:32), for us to be able to regard it as representing Paul's real conviction. Both Jew and Greek must rely on God's mercy.

9*b*-12. That Christ has brought salvation to both Jew and Gentile seems to Paul an appropriate idea with which to bring the entire argument of the epistle to a close. He emphasizes it by a characteristic "string" of quotations—this time from Ps. 18:49; Deut. 32:43; Ps. 117:1; and Isa. 11:10. Differences in wording between the quotations and the familiar texts in Hebrew or English are accounted for by Paul's use of the LXX, which is here closely followed. The context of all of these passages by no means supports Paul's interpretation of them. Isa. 11:10 certainly looks in the direction of Paul's meaning, and Ps. 117:1 is not inconsistent with it; but in Ps. 18:49 the writer is celebrating the triumph of Israel over the Gentiles, and in Deut. 32:43 Moses calls on the nations to rejoice with (i.e., in sympathy with) Israel, whom Yahweh is saving. Paul

---

ing the plain evidence even of their own cherished scriptures. Having been freed from that narrow religious nationalism, Paul, like Second Isaiah, and others too, was always eager to prove that it was as unnecessary as it was mistaken. He believed that the inner logic of the process of God's self-disclosure was to prepare within the orbit of the chosen people something that could never be confined to such limits, but would of inherent necessity break forth to bless all mankind. Other races might not have the same claims and expectation; but that would only manifest more perfectly the goodness of God. Even where men could establish no rights, his bounty would extend. This is a favorite theme with Paul, and we need only pause to notice the aptness of the terms he uses. The exactitude which is characteristic of the law requires that what God should declare in the coming of his son is his faithfulness—the undeviating "truthfulness" (vs. 8) which confirms the ancient promise. But in the extension of the gospel where no claim existed, God declared his free mercy—that love which goes out to meet us even when we dare not regard it as our right. The two, though set in apparent contrast, are of course correlative. Faithfulness and mercy belong together in any profound understanding of God. We need to remember that he is bound by the inherent necessity of his own righteousness, that the stability of the moral order rests on his unalterable truthfulness; but at the same time, the dependability which is our safeguard against spiritual chaos includes within itself a creative love which triumphs over any kind of legalism. To declare that "the law was given by Moses, but grace and truth came by Jesus Christ" (John 1:17) seems to set the two in opposition; but both have their place in God's purpose. The Gentiles enter into an inheritance in which originally they seemed to have no share. Their reaction, as Paul has remarked elsewhere, should be one of humble gratitude, but it should also be one of wondering praise. It is right that they should **glorify God for his mercy.**

There were some in the church who challenged the right of the Gentiles to expect a place in the new dispensation, as there were some who denied to the Jews even that measure of consideration to which their role in God's redeeming activity entitled them. The quotations which Paul now uses would serve, in his thinking, to clarify for both groups their distinctive obligations. He has set forth the general principle that Christ's ministry is the fulfillment of the legitimate hopes of both Jew and Gentile; the purpose of his quotations is to make each aware that the place of the other is not accidental or fortuitous. To the Jew he quotes the Hebrew scriptures—the final court of appeal—to show that the Gentiles are entitled to membership in the church. To ad-

12 And again, Esaias saith, There shall be a root of Jesse, and he that shall rise to reign over the Gentiles; in him shall the Gentiles trust.
13 Now the God of hope fill you with all joy and peace in believing, that ye

12 and further Isaiah says,
"The root of Jesse shall come,
he who rises to rule the Gentiles;
in him shall the Gentiles hope."
13 May the God of hope fill you with all joy and peace in believing, so that by the

reads into these passages the universalism of which he is so strongly persuaded. Still, as we have seen, this universalism is implicit in the profounder parts of the O.T., and Paul is not misrepresenting that literature as a whole, even though, as often, he may misinterpret it in detail (see above, p. 553). It might be added that the LXX had itself gone some distance toward adapting the O.T. text for the uses of a Gentile mission.

13. The word "hope" in the last quotation sets the tone for the benediction. "Steadfastness" and "encouragement" and "hope" were placed together in vs. 4, and in vs. 5 God was called the "God of steadfastness and encouragement"; now he is called **the God of hope. Joy** and **peace** are regarded as the fruit of faith (**believing**), and one may **abound in hope** because of the **power of the Holy Spirit.** This benediction must be interpreted in the light of 5:1-5, of which it is indeed a brief summary. Only the word "love" is missing, and the substance of that is implied in the gift of **the Holy Spirit.** Note the close connection of "love" and "the Holy Spirit" in 5:5, and also what was said above, pp. 511-12. Besides, love, as we have seen, is the theme of the whole practical section of this epistle from 12:3 on, and therefore can be taken for granted in this final sentence.

Of these terms, "hope," "joy," "peace," "faith," "power," "Holy Spirit," only **hope** appears more than once in 15:13; the same is true in 5:1-5. We are thus reminded again of the importance of this idea for Paul. Although the statement of his theme in 1:16-17 did not contain the word, the idea was present and pervasive in that statement: Paul is not "ashamed of the gospel" because it is "the power of God for *salvation*"—and salvation, as we have seen over and over again, is primarily eschatological, an object of

mit them is neither a needless concession nor an act of expediency; prophecy itself assumes that God's purpose will remain incomplete until they are brought within its scope. At the same time, no thoughtful Gentile could hear his cause vindicated by those scriptures without remembering how deeply he is indebted to the Jew. The chosen people have been the channel through which across the centuries God's mercy has been brought into his life. The necessary inferences are clear: the Jews cannot be superior and exclusive because of their prior place; nor can the Gentiles be contemptuous because of their greater freedom.

13. ***Climax of the Argument: In Blessing.***—With vs. 13 we reach one of the major dividing points in the epistle. This, in fact, marks the end of the great theme which began to unfold in ch. 1; through one area after another it has pursued its way, and what now follows is in the nature of a personal postscript. One might therefore expect the apostle to conclude his argument with some appropriate form of blessing, and he does. The key word in his benediction is suggested both by the phrasing of the last quotation he has used, and by the trend of his thought in the earlier verses of the chapter (cf. vs. 5). It is not the first time in this letter that he has seized on hope as one of God's great gifts to those who believe on him (cf. 5:2). **The God of hope,** consequently, reminds us of the vast difference that the gospel makes in our outlook on life. It delivers us from the somber gloom which gradually enfolds our minds when we allow for human factors only and limit our view to our immediate experience. With difficulty we evade the clutches of despair if we do not look beyond what man can do for man; the record of man's thought is darkened by the shadows cast by such pessimism. But the heart of Paul's message is the declaration that we need not consider the limits merely of our human capacity. In Christ we see what God has done for man: to redeem the life of the individual; to transform the nature of his society; to open up, beyond all the bounds of our present experience, limitless possibilities which our thought can

may abound in hope, through the power of the Holy Ghost.

power of the Holy Spirit you may abound in hope.

hope and patient waiting: "In this hope we were saved" (8:24). The central section of the letter (chs. 5–8) began with a summary paragraph about the meaning of the life in Christ (5:1-5) which, as we have just noted, is dominated by this idea—and again we read: "Hope maketh not ashamed." The larger part of ch. 8—probably the most important single chapter in the letter—is also concerned with hope; and this chapter, as well as the great middle section of the epistle, ends with a shout of indomitable assurance as to the coming triumph. The discussion of the place of the Jew in God's purpose in Christ (chs. 9–11) concludes with an almost equally fervent expression of hope, the more remarkable because there was so little of an external sort to encourage it. And now the entire argument of the letter is brought to an end with a benediction in which God is addressed as the **God of hope,** and the prayer is voiced that the believers in Rome may **abound in hope.** What an answer to those who speak of Paul's message as "gloomy" or "forbidding"! To be sure, Paul's joy is in **hope,** not in achievement; he takes a rather dark view of man's present or natural state; perhaps he did not allow sufficiently for the grace of God in creation, although who can deny that his picture of man's condition (1:18–3:20) is on the whole realistic? On the other hand one must recognize that for Paul hope is not merely a future expectation; it is based on the actual, present experience of the love of God in Christ (which *is* the Holy Spirit). We can "rejoice in hope" because the hope is already in process of being realized. We are not "ashamed of the gospel"—or of our hope—because God will surely finish what he has begun. Love, having come to us in our great need, will not forsake us there. "Since we are justified by faith . . . we have peace, . . . we have obtained access to this grace, . . . we rejoice in our hope of sharing the glory of God. . . . Hope does not disappoint us, because God's love has been poured into our hearts through the Holy Spirit which has been given to us" (5:1-5) This is the

explore but can never hope to exhaust. All the resources of God's mercy are offered to us in Christ. This is the ground of our belief that whatever happens we are saved from ultimate disaster.

. . . Safe shall be my going,
Secretly armed against all death's endeavour;
Safe though all safety's lost; safe where men fall;
And if these poor limbs die, safest of all.[7]

But that states our confidence in too negative and limited a way. Here and hereafter God showers upon us the positive gifts which enrich as well as fortify. Two of them which naturally suggest themselves to the apostle's mind are **joy and peace.** In a world so ominous and threatening as ours, both are qualities which can be sustained only by some deep confidence in a final and sovereign purpose of creative good will. In other words, anything which transcends the instinctive optimism of complacency must rest on faith; but faith (and what it does for men) has been the substance of Paul's argument throughout the greater part of this epistle. He does not say, though we can quite properly assume it, that the joy and peace with which he prays God to bless his readers are the emotional consequence of that new relationship with God into which faith has brought us. Without fear for the past, with assurance for all that lies ahead, we are lifted out of sorrow and carried beyond the reach of fear. All the enemies that can threaten our peace of mind are overthrown. The more fully we enter into the heritage of faith, the more assured will be our joy and peace; and hope itself will steadily enlarge its frontiers. Paul has apparently returned to the point from which his benediction started—the God of hope will cause our hope to abound—but he has introduced an idea which saves his blessing from redundancy. The horizons of our hope expand only when God is creatively at work within us. The early Christians knew the divine presence as the secret of power. To this the book of Acts bears constant witness. It is the working of the **Holy Spirit** that saves all our virtues from lifeless formalism. So it is that the **God of hope** can give us an enlarging hope only when his own presence is with us to make his gifts the dynamic of a new quality of life.

[7] Rupert Brooke, "Safety," from *Collected Poems.* Copyright 1915. Used by permission of Dodd, Mead & Co., Inc., Sidgwick & Jackson, and McClelland & Stewart.

14 And I myself also am persuaded of you, my brethren, that ye also are full of goodness, filled with all knowledge, able also to admonish one another.

14 I myself am satisfied about you, my brethren, that you yourselves are full of goodness, filled with all knowledge, and

---

heart of the epistle and this benediction, so near its close, cannot help but remind us of it. Perhaps Paul intended that it should.

VII. Personal and Closing Remarks (15:14-33)

The personal remarks now to be discussed have already come in for some comment in the course of our examination of the occasion and purpose of this letter (see Intro., pp. 358-63).

A. Explanation of the Letter and the Visit (15:14-24)

14-16. Those who see Paul as a dour and grim fanatic overlook such passages as vs. 14—for this pleasant compliment does not stand alone (cf. e.g., II Cor. 8:7; 9:2-3; Phil. 4:15). Indeed, the "thanksgiving" in every Pauline letter is a model of courtesy and charm (see 1:8-12; I Cor. 1:4-9; II Cor. 1:3-7; Phil. 1:3-11; Col. 2:3-8; II Thess. 1:3-4). I Thessalonians as a whole exemplifies this trait of the apostle, as also does Philemon. In 1:12 Paul very delicately indicated his appreciation of the Romans' "faith," and in

---

14. *The Marks of a Living Church.*—As Paul pauses, with his letter virtually ended, the fear possesses him that it may seem arrogant and presumptuous to send words of such strong counsel to a church to whose members he is virtually unknown. We may note, as a rebuke to the assumptions into which we often fall, the marked humility of the apostolic approach. For the moment he does not press his claim to superior knowledge; there is no assertion of the right to teach his brethren. He who above all others might seem entitled to demand a hearing adopts an attitude which is a model of courteous restraint. He does not write because they do not know the essence of the gospel. He assumes that they are familiar with the things he has set forth; perhaps, however, they have momentarily forgotten them. To write Romans and then assure its readers that he has only ventured to remind them of things they doubtless knew already is the epitome of pastoral humility.

If this verse indicates something of Paul's attitude to himself, it also illustrates the nature of his appeal to his fellow Christians. He never made the mistake of asking them to think too meanly of themselves. Even when he holds strong words of condemnation in reserve, as in I Corinthians, he so greets his readers that they know at once how high his expectations are. Unreal self-depreciation holds no place among the legitimate disciplines of the Christian life. If we ought not to think of ourselves more highly than we should, we are not required to pretend that we regard ourselves more meanly than we do. The marks of a strong church which Paul here specifies are three: (*a*) Its members **are full of goodness**—marked by that inward spirit of charity and that outward activity of love which produce the quality of life to which others will be drawn by virtue of its authentic spiritual persuasiveness. They will not only be zealous in all that we usually associate with goodness, but will also naturally display the intuitive concern for others that delivers a community from the uncharitable and acrimonious self-righteousness which sets factions in opposition to each other. (*b*) **All knowledge** is likewise a characteristic virtue of the mature members of a strong church. The term sounds alarmingly comprehensive; but probably Paul has in mind that the Christian will have a firm grasp of what his faith really means. He will understand its content as an intelligible interpretation of life, and will not make the mistake of regarding emotional fervor as an adequate substitute for the light God gives our minds. Paul was not discussing the great themes of righteousness and justification because he naturally delighted in theological niceties. He wrote about the great themes because he considered them supremely necessary. A strong faith is not built on a weak understanding; those who will not struggle with the mysteries of their life are scarcely likely to discover the power which unravels their bewildering tangles. In a day when any easy panacea serves as a substitute for honest thought, it is sobering to remember that Paul did not expect to build strong churches out of people who

15 Nevertheless, brethren, I have written the more boldly unto you in some sort,
as putting you in mind, because of the
grace that is given to me of God,
16 That I should be the minister of Jesus
Christ to the Gentiles, ministering the gospel of God, that the offering up of the
Gentiles might be acceptable, being sanctified by the Holy Ghost.

able to instruct one another. **15** But on some
points I have written to you very boldly
by way of reminder, because of the grace
given me by God **16** to be a minister of
Christ Jesus to the Gentiles in the priestly
service of the gospel of God, so that the
offering of the Gentiles may be acceptable,

---

that connection, too, they are addressed as "brethren." Now he speaks more plainly and with the exaggeration which courtesy both prompts and justifies: **You yourselves are full of goodness, filled with all knowledge.** Having written at great length—perhaps at much greater length than he intended—he now apologizes for his boldness. He has written so fully not because he thought his readers were unable **to instruct one another** and therefore needed instruction from him, but only **by way of reminder** of what they already knew. The phrase "instruct one another" confirms other indications that no

---

were too lazy to think. Closely associated with the two qualities which he has already specified there is a third: (*c*) the ability **to instruct one another.** This presupposes that the members of the church will have a sufficient knowledge of the faith to communicate it to others, and the disposition gladly to undertake the task. Anyone devoid of the necessary knowledge cannot teach; anyone destitute of the goodness which Paul has mentioned will not even try. The impulse to help others will be lacking; and even if the effort is made, only a spirit marked by active love will win the response without which no education is possible.

15-16. ***The Sources of Apostolic Boldness.***—Paul does not claim to have written anything with which a mature Christian would be unfamiliar. He has been reminding his readers of truths they already knew; but he has done so with a measure of authority which requires justification. To some churches he could speak **very boldly** because he had founded them and was responsible for their well-being. In Romans he falls back on a more general plea. His mission entitles him to show the kind of concern which has prompted this letter. God has graciously given him a specific task; and spiritual responsibilities are always given us to be exercised, not merely to be enjoyed. The nature of his commission is developed in vs. 16, and the striking feature of his development of it is his strong insistence on the **priestly** function he discharges. He uses language which has the closest associations with sacrificial customs, and some of his words are technical phrases in the religious vocabulary which the LXX had made current. The priestly task is evidently one which Paul received as a high favor and discharged as a deep responsibility. It is therefore one which we should seriously consider and be ready to accept. The abuses to which priesthood falls a prey, and the violent reaction which was necessary in order to deliver the service of God from corruption, have often led us to repudiate a conception which we should highly esteem. The **minister of Jesus Christ** is one who renders **priestly service.** The sphere within which this sacrificial function is performed is **the gospel of God;** the scope of his task is determined by the particular mission he has received. That mission is **to the Gentiles,** and means much more than sharing with them what he has received, even though these benefits are the blessings which the gospel offers. It is true that the minister is among his people as one who serves; but the apostle sees him also as one who sacrifices. He always stands at the altar, and in Paul's case what he offers to God is the Gentile world.

We should expect no less than this in view of what has already been said about sacrifice. The same general conception has been amplified in "the epistle of priesthood" (Hebrews) where Christ's sacrificial activity is the pattern after which our own service of God should be modeled. We can see how natural and necessary such a conception is if we remember that "the true Christian idea of sacrifice makes the substance of it to be always persons returning to God the life He gave them."[8] All other offerings are but the outward symbol of this central truth. That is why the writer of Hebrews could make such effective use of Christ's offering of himself. That is also why each one of us is called to offer himself a living sacrifice. But certain tasks carry this duty a stage further, and the commission which Paul has received

8 Gore, *Epistle to Romans,* II, 177.

17 I have therefore whereof I may glory through Jesus Christ in those things which pertain to God.

sanctified by the Holy Spirit. 17 In Christ Jesus, then, I have reason to be proud of

---

particular apostle (like Peter) was "in charge" of the Roman church; if that had been the case, it would have been more natural for Paul to have said, "I know that you have been well instructed." Paul has written only **on some points**—as though to say, "I know there is much which you could teach me about the Christian life"—points on which the special **grace given** him as the Apostle to the Gentiles both requires and qualifies him to write (cf. 1:5). He now calls his service of the gospel (cf. 1:9) a **priestly service.** He is the mediator of the love of God in Christ to the Gentiles and the one through whom the Gentile church offers itself to God as a sacrifice (cf. 12:1-2). God has placed him in this crucial mediatorial position, and it is this fact which gives him the right to speak as he has done—at least **on some points**—even to a church he does not know.

17-19. Paul has **reason to be proud** of the **work** he has done **for God.** And he does not feel guilty in acknowledging this pride because it is really not pride in himself but

---

involves the duty of continually offering before God those for whom he is in special measure responsible. Moreover, this ministry, though laid with special constraint on those whose obligations make them particularly conscious of their duty, is a task in which all Christians share. The prayer of intercession is necessarily sacrificial in character. We do not so much call down God's blessing on others as we lift them up into his presence. Then every heart should be an altar, and every other needy soul an offering set forth before God that his quickening fire may fall upon the sacrifice. And it is Paul's conviction that this is precisely what will happen. God will receive the sacrifice because it will be **sanctified by the Holy Spirit.**

This, of course, is true over the whole range of our giving. In the course of a few verses Paul will be discussing the gifts which the Gentiles have given for the support of the needy in the mother church; but it is his constant emphasis that material gifts are lifted to a higher plane when God's Spirit takes their givers, and so the gifts themselves, into his service. Certainly if this is true of the material things men offer, it is doubly so of the sacrifice of ourselves. The deadness of our hearts is touched to life by the gift of God's Spirit. And what happens to us happens also to those for whom we pray. What the laws are which govern intercessory prayer we do not know. We cannot say how it is that our petitions lift others into God's presence where his peace can still their spirits and his power remake their lives. The indubitable evidence of Christian experience affirms that it happens, our ignorance and our skepticism notwithstanding. It would happen a great deal oftener than it does if Christians would take more seriously than they do their priestly ministry of prayer for others.

The whole church is faint and ineffective because we so seldom bother to lift it—and all our brethren within its wide confines—into the presence of God. In our Protestant tradition we profess to set high store upon the priesthood of all believers. We would do well to practice as well as praise it.

17. ***Where Pride Is Proper.***—There are few tasks more exacting than the proper assessment of ourselves. We tend to swing between unreasonable pride and unwarranted self-abasement. Paul, in spite of ceaseless polemic against man's arrogance, knows that there is a quite legitimate pride in which we can properly indulge. If a man is honestly trying to do God's will, he is entitled to feel a certain kind of confidence in his position. He will not be likely to take the credit to himself—after all, it is of a religious man that we are speaking—because he will know that proper pride is not related to personal merit. Paul is **proud of** his **work,** not of himself. But the emphasis does not lie even upon the work. He himself has said that there are strict limits set to the kind of glorying in which he can indulge (Gal. 6:14); his confidence does not arise from anything that he himself can accomplish, but from what Christ enables him to do. **In Christ Jesus** are the crucial words in this verse; what they imply and involve is what makes possible that other important phrase: **my work for God.** A man does not serve God in the spirit Paul desiderates except through intimacy with and dependence upon Christ.

The distinction between legitimate and illegitimate pride is therefore clearly drawn; but it is not always easy to maintain. We may know that we ought to have a high regard for our office and a humble estimate of ourselves. We may concede with Paul that boasting is ex-

18 For I will not dare to speak of any of those things which Christ hath not wrought by me, to make the Gentiles obedient, by word and deed,

19 Through mighty signs and wonders, by the power of the Spirit of God; so that

my work for God. 18 For I will not venture to speak of anything except what Christ has wrought through me to win obedience from the Gentiles, by word and deed, 19 by the power of signs and wonders, by the

in Christ Jesus (literally rendered, the Greek of vs. 17 reads: "Therefore I am boasting in Christ Jesus as regards God's service"), for it is Christ who **has wrought through me to win obedience from the Gentiles.** This result has been achieved by **the power of the Holy Spirit** (another way of referring to this same Christ), manifested in the apostle's **word and deed** as well as in **signs and wonders.** We do not know what any of these were, but the phrase reminds us that Paul believed in miracles as a phase of the new supernatural order of the Spirit which was beginning.

Vs. 19*b* presents two problems. One of these appears in Paul's statement that he has **preached the gospel of Christ . . . from Jerusalem and as far round as Illyricum.** Illyricum was the Roman province on the Adriatic Sea across from Italy, just north of Macedonia and west of Thrace. Does Paul mean by his statement that he has actually preached in Illyricum, or does he mean that his work has taken him as far as the eastern and southern boundaries of that country? The Greek allows equally well for both of these alternatives. Paul is naturally eager in this passage to describe the range of his work in the widest possible terms, and not improperly might name its outside limits. If he had preached in Illyricum, one might have expected him to say, "from

cluded; anyone who wants to glory can hope legitimately to glory only in that he knows the Lord (I Cor. 1:31; cf. Jer. 9:24). Sometimes Paul's language is clearly touched with irony (cf. II Cor. 11:21-30); for he understands how easily we are self-deceived in these matters. The secret of humility is not to be found in any set of rules by which we can govern our attitudes. With Paul, humility is a by-product of his theology. He so thought of God that in his presence he himself could have no possible pretext for pride. By seeing himself in the light of a redemptive holiness which had done everything for him, he knew that confidence in his human powers was ridiculous and irrelevant. Only by keeping the central issues clearly defined can we hope successfully to preserve the distinction between our task, about which we are justly proud, and ourselves, concerning whom we are rightly humble.

18. ***Paul as Christ's Agent.***—Having said so much, Paul can hardly do less than describe more fully the mission which is his occasion for rejoicing; but he pauses to emphasize once more the fact that if he seems to speak about himself, it is only because Christ has used him as an agent for accomplishing his purpose. On other subjects reticence would make him silent; but in the mission to the Gentiles he sees an expression of a divine purpose. If we remember the terms in which he described his call (Acts 26:12-23), we can understand why he is convinced that both his words and his deeds are simply the instruments by means of which the great objective of bringing the **Gentiles** to the **obedience** of Christ is advanced. High reasons of doctrine would prevent him from speaking of anything else, but actually, on any other basis he would be left with nothing to say. His mission was his life. He was so completely devoted to his task that beyond his work among the Gentiles there was nothing about which he could profitably talk. The exact correspondence between his life and his mission resulted in the distinctive quality which his life reflected. He felt that he was serving a great purpose, and there is no comparable source of dignity and courage. He had an objective, a high and worthy one; and he had received the power to do what was necessary, the required drive to bring it to its proper end. In a day when futility is the consequence of the pointlessness of many lives, it is worth remembering that the record of effective action to which Paul now refers is the direct result of placing his life without reservation at Christ's disposal.

19. ***The Evidences of Power.***—One means by which Paul has accomplished his appointed task is **by the power of signs and wonders.** Even the most casual reader of the N.T. knows that mighty deeds were one of the characteristic marks of the apostolic age. Many are disposed heavily to discount the records. They attribute the stories to exaggeration, to imperfect under-

from Jerusalem, and round about unto Illyricum, I have fully preached the gospel of Christ.

power of the Holy Spirit, so that from Jerusalem and as far round as Il-lyr'i-cum I have fully preached the gospel of Christ,

Jerusalem to the Adriatic Sea." As a matter of fact, is it not clear that he is naming Jerusalem as just such an outside limit? For certainly Paul did not begin his work by preaching in that city, or even in Judea at all, as he tells us very plainly in Gal. 1:18–2:1. It may be added that "Illyricum," like "Galatia," had a double meaning—it was the name of a Roman province, but it also designated a people or nationality. Some of the Illyrians actually resided within the borders of Macedonia, and the Illyrian Mountains would have been seen to the west by Paul as he traveled in that country. On the whole, therefore, it seems likely that Paul is not meaning to claim that he has worked in Illyricum; but it is quite possible that he had done so. The silence of Acts on this matter is not significant one way or the other. It is possible also to account for Paul's statement with the supposition that although he has not himself been in Illyricum, he knows that the work he began in Macedonia has extended into that country.

The second problem presented by this verse lies in the phrase πεπληρωκέναι τὸ εὐαγγέλιον—**I have fully preached the gospel.** How could Paul have claimed so much? The same claim is made even more emphatically in vs. 23*a.* He does not mean, of course,

standing of what happened, to the credulity of a prescientific time, to the unreliable reporting of partisan enthusiasts—to anything that will mitigate their embarrassment in the presence of the miraculous. What actually happened in many instances we can never know with accuracy or in detail; but it is certain that the N.T. writers believed that something both notable and unusual took place and became in their experience a powerful medium for conveying a sense of God's power and purpose. What should make us pause before dismissing their testimony with highhanded confidence is not merely the fact that powers similar to those exercised by our Lord were attributed to the apostles. This again might be due to prejudiced reporting. But Paul not only regards the power to perform signs as an apostolic quality, he unequivocally asserts that he possessed that power. He not only could work wonders, he did work wonders. Such is his claim. In II Cor. 12:12, we have an even more striking instance of the same attitude. In that case the apostle was writing to a community with which his relations had been strained, and an unsubstantiated claim—especially about a matter so important as the apostolic office—would certainly be challenged. Paul was too practiced a controversialist wittingly to place himself in so vulnerable a position. He must have felt that what he claimed everyone would concede. Here again we soon run out beyond the limits of our knowledge. This much at least is clear—that the complacent arrogance of scientific dogmatisms has shown very little understanding in its attempts to settle the boundaries beyond which faith is powerless. A more chastened age may conceivably recognize that many things which we are apt to dismiss as impossible are actually true. Similarly, a chastened church will not easily assume that we know how much—or how little—God can do through those who serve him.

The distinguishing mark of a "sign" is not, of course, the fact that it is bewildering to our human understanding, but the fact that it is wholly unintelligible except in the light of what God is and what we believe he is able to do. Not the startling character of what happens, so much as the claim that it happens only because of the felt presence of God, sets miracles apart from events which merely defy the canons of ordinary expectation. It is natural, therefore, for Paul to add at once **by the power of the Holy Spirit.** An apostle is not someone who does phenomenal things, but a man whom God can use in striking ways to accomplish his purposes; and what is particularly true at certain points of his ministry he sees as equally true throughout the entire range of it. So, though **the power of the Holy Spirit** may have been suggested by the foregoing reference to signs, the phrase naturally leads on to a more detailed account of the work which Paul has accomplished hitherto. The mention of two names indicates the expanding scope of his mission. He started from Jerusalem, which was not merely the birthplace of the church, but the center to which some of its members would have been content to see its influence limited. Against that circumscribing tendency his whole career had been a sustained protest. He claims that he has

20 Yea, so have I strived to preach the
gospel, not where Christ was named, lest
I should build upon another man's foundation:
21 But as it is written, To whom he
was not spoken of, they shall see: and they
that have not heard shall understand.
22 For which cause also I have been
much hindered from coming to you.

20 thus making it my ambition to preach
the gospel, not where Christ has already
been named, lest I build on another man's
foundation, 21 but as it is written,
"They shall see who have never been told of him,
and they shall understand who have never heard of him."
22 This is the reason why I have so
often been hindered from coming to you.

---

that he has personally reached every individual, or even every community, with the gospel, but rather that he has touched all the countries of Asia Minor and Greece, and that in each the work of evangelization has been started and is going forward.

20-21. In doing all of this Paul's ambition has been not to preach where (i.e., in lands where) **Christ has already been named** and not to **build** upon a **foundation** other than his own. Isa. 52:15 tells how the nations will be startled by the appearance of God's (suffering) servant and will be amazed to see and contemplate what they had been given no reason to expect. Paul turns this passage to a quite different use, throwing the emphasis not upon the wonder and strangeness of the thing seen, but upon the mere fact of its not having been seen before.

22-24. Paul does not mean to say in vs. 22 that he has **so often been hindered from coming** to Rome because he has been unwilling to build on foundations laid by others; the reason is rather that he has been so busy covering the large field he has just defined that he has had no real opportunity. **But now, since I no longer have any room for work**

---

fully preached the gospel of Christ; but this must be understood in the light of his particular task. Presumably he means that he had sufficiently set forth the essentials of the faith to gather a community of believers and establish a church. When that was done, he moved on to new and untouched areas. His words consequently cannot point to that prolonged and patient effort, continued year after year, to build the new truth into the fabric of men's lives which must be the substance of most nonapostolic ministries. The important thing is that everyone should do fully that measure of work which the nature of his ministry requires, and that the work itself should genuinely be comprehended within the orbit of making known the gospel of Christ. With those who fitfully discharge useful but peripheral and irrelevant good works, Paul (it may be suspected) would have shown very little patience.

20. ***No Trespassing.***—Paul's ministry has not been governed by chance. He has accepted the discipline of "a self-denying ordinance," and has not appropriated to the ends of his mission the preliminary work that other men had done. Behind it there is the drive of a great **ambition** —to bring those who do not know Christ "to confess Him to be what He is to the faith of His people" [9]—but it is controlled by a scrupulous respect for the rights of others. It is not unreasonable to regard Paul's attitude as the earliest attempt to define the professional ethics of the ministry. Charity and efficiency, to say nothing of etiquette, demand that those in the same work should co-operate and not compete. When engaged in a common task, rivalry is iniquitous as well as irrelevant and absurd. The distinctive work of apostles is laying foundations. Each man should therefore be allowed to do it in his own way; moreover, there are special compensations attached to such a task. The worker may not see his cause grow and prosper under his care, and he may not have the satisfaction of an increasing intimacy with those among whom he works; but he has the immense joy of bringing good news to men who have never heard it. The wonder of this experience is suggested (vs. 21) by the quotation from Isa. 52:15.

22-25. ***Hopes and Plans.***—The pressure of other work has always hindered Paul from coming to Rome. Hitherto there have been the claims of cities where the gospel was unknown, and where he felt he must proclaim it; but all the while he had dreamed of reaching Rome and going beyond that great city to the far boundaries of the western empire. Necessity, not indifference, has prevented him from visiting the Imperial City. **But now**—at last the

[9] Denney, *Expositor's Greek Testament, ad loc.*

23 But now having no more place in these parts, and having a great desire these many years to come unto you;

24 Whensoever I take my journey into Spain, I will come to you: for I trust to see you in my journey, and to be brought on my way thitherward by you, if first I be somewhat filled with your *company*.

25 But now I go unto Jerusalem to minister unto the saints.

23 But now, since I no longer have any
room for work in these regions, and since I
have longed for many years to come to you,
24 I hope to see you in passing as I go to
Spain, and to be sped on my journey there
by you, once I have enjoyed your company for a little. 25 At present, however, I
am going to Jerusalem with aid for the

---

in these regions—in some ways the most remarkable statement in the entire letter (on its implications see Intro., p. 358) —**I hope to see you in passing as I go to Spain.** This is Paul's first mention of Spain (see Intro., pp. 358-59). When he expresses the hope that he may **be sped on** [his] **journey there** by the Roman church, he may well mean some material assistance as well as good will (cf. Intro., p. 359; see also I Cor. 16:6, 11; II Cor. 1:16; Acts 15:3; III John 6).

B. The Collection for the Poor at Jerusalem (15:25-33)

It is clear that Paul wishes he could now take ship for Rome. He has just said that he has "longed for many years" to do so (vs. 23)—and for most of this time one may be sure he was actively engaged in the evangelistic work to which he felt called. Now, however, that this work has been completed in Greece and Asia Minor, this longing would naturally have become particularly acute. But for several years he has been engaged

---

way seems clear. In the East there are no great strategic centers still clamoring for his attention. He has exhausted the possibilities for his kind of work in the area for which he had felt particularly responsible, and after one further unavoidable delay he will surely come to Rome.

The poignancy of his statement is due to the unexpected way in which his purpose was actually fulfilled. It is true that after the interruption caused by his journey to Jerusalem he came to Rome; but it was also after the delays and frustrations of a vexatious imprisonment, and it was in chains. Whether he ever succeeded in going beyond Rome to the provinces of the far west we do not know. It may be that he did, and Clement of Rome uses a phrase which at least suggests that Paul had preached in Spain; but certainly in the first instance his purpose was accomplished in a way entirely different from his expectations. Yet it is impossible to feel that this would surprise or seriously disappoint a man like Paul. Experience had taught him that God can accomplish his purposes in ways we do not like and would not choose. He may upset our cherished plans, yet use our disappointments and our limitations. When we plead for what seems to us a better way, we may get no answer save the assurance that "my grace is sufficient for thee" (II Cor. 12:9). Paul was to discover what another of the apostles had been told to expect: that in his old age he would not go where and how he chose, but would find his freedom overruled by those who had the power to bind and carry him wherever they wished (John 21:18).

But though he did not come as and when he hoped, he did reach Rome. One of the striking features of his ministry was the way in which it combined fixity of purpose with flexibility of plan. His final goal never changed, but again and again he had to modify his immediate objective because conditions compelled him to do so. The combination of the two—unvarying loyalty to a central aim, and adjustability in meeting emergent difficulties—helps to explain the versatility of Paul's missionary labors. It may be remarked that many people respond to life in exactly the opposite way. They are diffident and uncertain about any ultimate purpose, but arbitrary and unyielding in their approach to immediate problems. The result is confusion and frustration.

25-29. ***Aid for the Needy of Jerusalem.***—The scheme which now engages Paul's attention was not simply a benevolent effort intended to relieve the necessities of poorer Christians in the mother city of the faith. Paul was willing to postpone cherished plans and expose himself to physical harm because the offering, as the Exeg. shows, was primarily a gesture designed to promote reconciliation between Jewish and Gentile Christians. The im-

in taking an offering for the poor at Jerusalem (cf. I Cor. 16:1-4; II Cor. 8:1–9:15); and now that money must be delivered. Paul greatly regretted the necessity of this trip to Palestine; only a little reading between the lines is required for us to see in I Cor. 16:3-4 (written at least a year and a half, perhaps better two years, earlier than Romans) indications that Paul was eager to avoid the journey and the consequent postponement of his departure for the West. He speaks there of sending "those whom you accredit by letter to carry your gift to Jerusalem." The possibility, however, that he himself may need to go is recognized even then: "If it seems advisable that I should go also, they will accompany me." Now Rom. 15:25 lets us know that it did finally seem "advisable"; Paul decided that much as he would have liked to go to Rome at once, he could not avoid **going to Jerusalem** first. Vss. 31-32 show that Paul's reluctance to make this trip was based not only upon his desire to carry out his major plan, but also upon his recognition of the presence of real danger to his person in Jerusalem. He asks that the Roman Christians **strive together with me in your prayers to God on my behalf, that I may be delivered from the unbelievers in Judea.** The story in Acts of what happened when Paul reached Jerusalem shows that Paul's apprehensions were justified (Acts 21: 27 ff.). He had genuine reason to expect trouble. No wonder, then, he had sought to avoid this trip.

Why could he not avoid it? Almost the only possible answer to the question is this: the great symbolic significance of this **aid for the saints** at Jerusalem which has been raised by the Gentile churches in Paul's area. Paul partly explains that significance in this passage (vs. 27): **They** [i.e., the Gentile churches] **were pleased to do it, and indeed they are in debt to them, for if the Gentiles have come to share in their spiritual blessings, they ought also to be of service to them in material blessings.** Paul thus insists upon the appropriateness of this offering in order to emphasize its voluntary character: they *wanted* to do it because it was so obviously the appropriate thing to do. The contribution had not been exacted from the Gentiles. That it was not, however, a simple act of charity on the part of one group of Christians toward others more needy is at least hinted in vs. 31*b*, where the Romans are asked to pray that Paul's **service for Jerusalem may be acceptable** [εὐπρόσδεκτος] **to the saints.** This indicates Paul's fear that it might not be "acceptable"—i.e., that it might not be received in the way Paul hoped—and such an indication by itself is enough to tell us that the offering had important symbolic meaning. From Paul's point of view it mattered tremendously that the offering should not only be accepted but also that it be accepted as having a certain significance.

There can be no doubt at all as to what that significance was. Paul hopes the gift will have the effect of closing the serious and disastrous rift between Jerusalem and the Gentile churches (or at any rate between Jerusalem and his own Gentile churches). Only if the collection is so received as to have this effect will he be able to **come to** [Rome] **with joy** (see Intro., p. 358).

It is necessary now to consider Gal. 2:10, the only passage in Paul's letters, besides the passages in Romans and Corinthians already cited, where a collection for Jerusalem is referred to. In Gal. 2:1-10 Paul tells of a trip to Jerusalem (he does not say from

---

portance of the objective is perhaps responsible for the illuminating way in which the apostle touches on the duty of giving.

(*a*) The undertaking is essentially sane and sound. Since the Gentiles have received **spiritual blessings** through the Jews, it is right that the Jewish Christians should receive **material blessings** from the Gentiles (vs. 27*b*). In other words, we ought to recognize that the assets of the whole Christian community are indivisible. Admittedly they may be of different kinds and they may be unequally distributed, but common decency will compel us to share our superfluity with those who are in need. We will share our faith as well as our funds, and in all our giving we will remember that brotherhood, and not pity, is our motive. And we will also bear in mind that our generosity seldom exceeds the measure of obligation: we **are in debt to** the other members of the brotherhood.

where), some fourteen years or more after the beginning of his evangelistic work, in order to try to settle this problem of Jew-Gentile relations within the church (see Intro. to Galatians, Vol. X). He tells us that he consulted there with James, Cephas, and John, who were the heads of the community in Jerusalem, and that this conference ended in their fully recognizing the authenticity of Paul's call as the Apostle to the Gentiles. They gave him, Paul says, "the right hand of fellowship," and "added nothing to me . . . only they would have us remember the poor, which very thing I was eager [ἐσπούδασα, literally "made haste"] to do." Now there are only three possible ways of taking this last sentence: (*a*) the reference is to some other earlier collection which Paul raised for the saints at Jerusalem, of which there is no record in his letters, or for that matter, in Acts; (*b*) the reference is to a regular, more or less constant, effort on Paul's part to raise and send money to Jerusalem, which Paul here assures the Jerusalem leaders he has every intention to continue; but again, there is absolutely no indication in either the Acts or in Paul's letters of any such custom (*c*) the reference is to the offering which is in process of being taken in I and II Corinthians and is just complete when Romans was written. It is difficult to avoid the third of these alternatives. The references to the offering in I and II Corinthians and in Romans are not such as to suggest that this matter of sending funds to Jerusalem is a recognized custom. It is quite manifestly a unique undertaking. To say this is not to say that Paul's churches did not accept responsibility for their poor. II Thess. 3:10 reflects the practice of assisting the destitute from a common fund; and other passages in Paul's letters indicate the same practice. But such passages cannot be cited to prove the existence of a custom of sending money *to Jerusalem*. Indeed, Paul has in this very letter (Rom. 12:13) referred to such a practice at Rome—he probably is simply taking for granted that it exists there—and yet he not only has to inform the Roman church of this collection for the Jerusalem church, but must even explain why it has been deemed appropriate to raise it. No, whatever may have been previously done by churches in Syria or elsewhere, the probabilities are strong that when the Jerusalem leaders suggested that the Gentile churches in Paul's territory send financial help, they suggested a new thing. Paul saw in their suggestion a real opportunity and immediately set out to raise as large a sum as possible. It is this collection which is now raised; he feels that he must at all costs take it himself to dramatize its significance as a peace offering by the Gentile churches of whom he is the head and the symbol.

If the reference in Gal. 2:10 is understood in this way, it means that the visit to Jerusalem of Gal. 2:1-10, which took place "after fourteen years," also took place only two or three years before Romans was written, and one cannot avoid the necessity of revising the conventional chronology of Paul's career; but to this necessity we can no more than refer here. Dodd (see pp. 231-32) and many other writers want to make the collection in Corinthians-Romans the sequel of Gal. 2:10, but one cannot do so without making the required chronological adjustment. Paul would hardly have been getting around to responding to the "eagerly" accepted suggestion of the Jerusalem leaders *after some ten years!* Readers who may wish to explore this matter further are referred to the book cited in the Intro., p. 358.

(*b*) The response which Paul's appeal has awakened points to the spirit which ought to mark our giving. When he asked for aid for the poor of Jerusalem, his Gentile converts **were pleased to do** what they could. "God loves a cheerful giver" (II Cor. 9:7), and the willing spirit which should characterize our giving arises from the ready acknowledgment that this is a duty which we are privileged to discharge. (*c*) Generosity always produces appropriate results. In the passage under study Paul shows himself vitally interested in the consequences which he hopes will follow from the presentation of the fund which he is raising. He trusts that the gift which he intends to take to Jerusalem will be accepted by the Jewish Christians as a reconciling gesture. There had been hard feeling and bitter words between the Apostle to the Gentiles and the Christians who clung to Jewish ways of thought (cf.

26 For it hath pleased them of Macedonia and Achaia to make a certain contribution for the poor saints which are at Jerusalem.

27 It hath pleased them verily; and their debtors they are. For if the Gentiles have been made partakers of their spiritual things, their duty is also to minister unto them in carnal things.

saints. 26 For Mac-e-do'ni-a and A-cha'ia have been pleased to make some contribution for the poor among the saints at Jerusalem; 27 they were pleased to do it, and indeed they are in debt to them, for if the Gentiles have come to share in their spiritual blessings, they ought also to be of service to them in material blessings.

According to every indication we have (esp. Acts 21:17 ff.) Paul's fears, expressed in vs. 31, were realized. We do not know whether or not his **service for Jerusalem** was **acceptable to the saints**—there are some reasons for doubting that it had the effect Paul hoped for—but we *are* told that his desire to be **delivered from the unbelievers in Judea** was not fulfilled. If he reached Rome at all, it was as a prisoner on his way to martyrdom. His coming, even so, may well have been **in the fullness of the blessing of Christ** (vs. 29), but it was not with the **joy** which he had anticipated (vs. 32).

So much for discussion of this passage as a whole; we turn now to comment on a few points of detail.

26. Only **Macedonia and Achaia** (i.e., Greece) are mentioned here, but I Cor. 16:1 lets us know that Galatia also was involved in this collection. Probably all of the churches participated. We can only guess at why Paul does not include them in this reference. The best surmise is that he has now in hand only the contributions of the Greek and Macedonian churches; funds from other churches will be brought by others later. They will join Paul at Corinth before his departure for Jerusalem or will join him en route (cf. Acts 20:4; but note that Acts nowhere mentions the fact that the purpose of this trip was to convey money, except quite casually in 24:17, and the fund is there described as "alms and offerings to my nation"). The "saints" is a characteristic early Christian way of referring to members of the new community of faith (cf. e.g., 1:7; Heb. 3:1; Acts 9:13; I Pet. 1:15; Rev. 5:8; etc.). For an important note on the significance of this term and the extensiveness of its use in the ancient church, along with many bibliographical references, see Lietzmann (pp. 121 ff.).

Exeg.). Paul's hopes illustrate a principle of wide application. Practical interest in other people is ineffectual unless it finds some outlet, and in most cases the only way in which it can express itself is through giving. Generosity proves the genuineness of our concern for others, and experience shows that a disinterested eagerness to help is the most effective way of breaking down the barriers that misunderstanding has created. (*d*) The correlative of generous giving is careful administration of what is offered. Having undertaken to raise a fund for the relief of the needy brethren at Jerusalem, Paul watched over it with the strictest care. In his letters we find repeated references to the subject (cf. I Cor. 16:1-4; II Cor. 8–9). The gift was not a levy, but the fact that it was voluntarily offered did not lessen the obligation to see that it was systematically raised and scrupulously administered. He was insistent that his handling of the funds must be recognized as above suspicion. Partly on this account—though partly, of course, to demonstrate the unanimity of the Gentiles in their gesture of sympathy—he was not going to Jerusalem alone. This warning against the maladministration of charity never loses its importance. The temptation to be careless continually besets those who handle the sums that others give.

The journey to Jerusalem represents one more delay in a deeply cherished plan. Only duty could postpone his intention to push on to Spain, but since Paul is persuaded that he is doing his duty, he is satisfied that the results must finally be for the best. Having done what is right, there will be no cloud of remorse to diminish the effectiveness of what he can do among the Roman Christians. We know that he looked forward to bringing them some spiritual gift (1:11-12); only a man whose conscience commends his present course of action can con-

28 When therefore I have performed this, and have sealed to them this fruit, I will come by you into Spain.

29 And I am sure that, when I come unto you, I shall come in the fulness of the blessing of the gospel of Christ.

30 Now I beseech you, brethren, for the Lord Jesus Christ's sake, and for the love of the Spirit, that ye strive together with me in *your* prayers to God for me;

28 When therefore I have completed this, and have delivered to them what has been raised,[x] I shall go on by way of you to
Spain; 29 and I know that when I come to you I shall come in the fullness of the blessing[y] of Christ.

30 I appeal to you, brethren, by our Lord Jesus Christ and by the love of the Spirit, to strive together with me in your prayers

[x] Greek *sealed to them this fruit.*
[y] Other ancient authorities insert *of the gospel.*

---

28. The words **when . . . I . . . have delivered to them what has been raised** stand for a Greek text which, literally translated, would read, **when I . . . have sealed to them this fruit.** The expression is admittedly strange. Moffatt translates: ". . . putting the proceeds of the collection safely in their hands"; and Goodspeed: ". . . seen this contribution safely into their possession." Lietzmann indicates the difficulty: "The sense generally is clear, 'after I have safely delivered the collection to them'; but how is this sense got out of the wording? To 'seal fruit' calls up a familiar image: the sack of grain is sealed for safety; but the collection is not merely to be 'secured' but to be 'securely delivered'; a severe straining of the expression seems to be involved; one word is used where two would seem to be required" (p. 123). Is it possible that Paul's use of this expression is connected with the *significance* of the offering? If so, the verb "finish" **(completed)** also would take on a special sense. When he has delivered this fund in Jerusalem and it has been received there in the hoped for spirit, Paul will have ended his divinely appointed work in Asia Minor and Greece; the "fruit" of his mission will have been "sealed."

30. The solemnity of Paul's appeal for the church's prayers (**by our Lord Jesus Christ and by the love of the Spirit** [i.e., the love the Spirit brings into your hearts]) and

---

fidently declare that he will come to his correspondents **in the fullness of the blessing of Christ.** We recognize immediately the note of certainty which rings in his words. **I know . . . ,** he says. Faithful devotion to what we are convinced is right delivers us from the hesitancy which so often undermines the effectiveness of our actions. He knows that he will **come to** Rome—and therein he will fulfill a hope long and deeply cherished. But the manner of his coming is more important than the mere fact that he will come. **I shall come in the fullness of the blessing [of the gospel] of Christ.** The rendering in the KJV emphasizes the cumulative heaping up of spiritual benefits which follows when a man allows his life to be the instrument by means of which Christ works. The briefer form in which the verse appears in the RSV actually says almost as much. There is no blessing that the gospel offers which Christ's presence does not confer. **The fullness of the blessing of Christ** is a singularly happy phrase. It suggests, for one thing, the many-sided completeness of the gift that Christ brings to men. What area of our life does he not touch into richer vitality? Is there any region where he disappoints our hopes? Only when men bring us a thin and attenuated gospel is there any inconsistency between Paul's words and our actual experience. Again, the phrase points to the distinctive quality as well as to the comprehensive sufficiency of what Christ does for us. To enrich, but with satisfaction that passes into triumphant joy, is the characteristic work of the gospel. Moreover, this kind of experience has its sole source in Christ. To the N.T. writers Christ was not one among a number of alternative sources of such a blessing; there was "none other name under heaven given among men, whereby we must be saved" (Acts 4:12).

30-33. ***Appeal for Prayer.***—The concluding words of the chapter clearly reflect the conflict of emotions in the apostle's mind. Hope and fear contend together, and it is natural for him to appeal to his fellow Christians to watch with him. There is a verbal parallel with the account of Christ's agony in Gethsemane; but the similarity of situation is closer still. Paul is going to Jerusalem because his sense of duty compels

31 That I may be delivered from them
that do not believe in Judea; and that my
service which *I have* for Jerusalem may be
accepted of the saints;
32 That I may come unto you with joy
by the will of God, and may with you be
refreshed.
33 Now the God of peace *be* with you
all. Amen.
16 I commend unto you Phebe our
sister, which is a servant of the church
which is at Cenchrea:

to God on my behalf, 31 that I may be
delivered from the unbelievers in Judea,
and that my service for Jerusalem may be
acceptable to the saints, 32 so that by God's
will I may come to you with joy and be
refreshed in your company. 33 The God of
peace be with you all. Amen.
16 I commend to you our sister Phoebe,
a deaconess of the church at Cen'-

---

the terms he uses to describe the prayer that is needed (**to strive together** ["an intense energy of prayer, wrestling as it were," as quoted by Sanday and Headlam from Hort])—both are eloquent of how much risk Paul thinks of himself as running when he goes to Jerusalem. Obviously there was intense opposition to him among the **unbelievers,** and he cannot count very confidently upon support even from the Christians there.

33. The letter (i.e., chs. 1–15) concludes with a brief and characteristic benediction, emphasizing again the theme which has been so much in the apostle's mind since 5:1, and especially as he approached the end of the epistle: **The God of peace be with you all. Amen.**

VIII. The Introduction of Phoebe, Exhortation Against Heretics, and Greetings (16:1-23)

See the Intro., pp. 365-68, for a discussion of the problem presented by this chapter. There are three possible views: (*a*) that the chapter was, as it purports to be, the conclusion of Paul's letter to the Romans; (*b*) that it is a note addressed originally to

---

him to go, but he knows that his life is in jeopardy. In such a moment the companionship and support of kindred spirits is a sheer necessity. This is no common request for basic human sympathy. He appeals to his readers by the most powerful constraint he can lay upon them—by the Master whom they all serve, and by the love which is created by the spirit of God. What he asks is that they will join with him in an almost convulsive energy of supplication. There is a place for importunity in our prayers (cf. Luke 11:5-13), and the docile respectability of most of our intercessions seems curiously weak when judged by the standard implicit in Christ's words. The grounds of Paul's apprehension are clear (cf. Exeg.). He is fearful of what the non-Christian Jews will do to one whom they regard as an inveterate foe, and he is doubtful whether the Jewish Christians will receive his gesture of fellowship in the spirit which has prompted it. He may lose his life and fail of his purpose. Events proved how well founded were his fears (Acts 21:27; 23:24). The prayers which he requests are not simply for his personal security; **my service** is uppermost in his mind, and brings his thoughts back to his settled purpose of pushing his mission farther to the west. After the danger which he will encounter and the strain through which he will pass, he looks forward to the joy of coming to Rome, and the refreshment he will find when he arrives. In opening the letter he had mentioned that the blessings of a visit would be mutual (1:12), and vs. 32 proves that he looked for more than material support in his mission to Spain. Even the strongest Christians need the sympathy which heals past wounds and refreshes them for future labors. Unknown people can do much simply by reviving the joy of God's greater servants. And for all its difficulties and its dangers, Paul's service was a source of endless joy. So that finally, in spite of apprehensions, his mind comes back to a favorite theme. He has asked for their prayers; he now prays for them, that the God whose presence is the secret of peace may be with them all.

16:1-27. ***A Letter Within a Letter.***—Scholars are not in agreement about the closing chapter of Romans. There are various alternative theories as to the circumstances under which it was written, and the destination for which it

2 That ye receive her in the Lord, as becometh saints, and that ye assist her in whatsoever business she hath need of you:

chre-ae, 2 that you may receive her in the Lord as befits the saints, and help her in whatever she may require from you, for

the church at Ephesus which has become attached to Romans; (*c*) that it represents a pseudonymous addition to the Letter to the Romans designed to bind the apostle more closely to Rome and to strengthen the hands of that church in its battle with the Gnostics in the second century. Weighty objections can be brought against every one of these views; and it is safe to say that when any of them is accepted, it is only because the other two seem even more improbable. Under these circumstances, comment on the chapter is difficult. Reasons were given in the Intro. for regarding (*c*) as the least difficult of the three views and therefore the most likely to be true. Comment will proceed on that assumption, but so far as possible without neglecting the fact that neither of the two alternative theories can be conclusively dismissed.

16:1-2. The few lines of introduction for Phoebe resemble in form many recovered papyrus letters from the period (see Adolf Deissmann, *Light from the Ancient East* [New York: George H. Doran Co., 1927], p. 235). The writing of such letters of introduction, or "commendation," is also specifically known to have been a Christian practice. The obligation of hospitality has already been referred to as one of the most important Christian duties (see on 12:13); but there was always the danger that impostors would take advantage of this generosity. A second-century satire by the pagan writer Lucian, *The Passing of Peregrinus,* has as its theme the way such an impostor played on the sympathies of credulous Christian groups. The Christian traveler, therefore, needed credentials; and what would be better than a letter from a responsible Christian leader? Note Paul's phrase in II Cor. 3:1, "letters of recommendation"; if ch. 16 is pseudonymous,

was intended (cf. Exeg.). Nor is any single theory free of difficulties. Even if not actually written by Paul, this chapter at least represents an attempt to speak in his name; if not his own work, it is by someone relatively close in time and surely near him in spirit. When so much uncertainty attaches to the origin of the chapter, it seems permissible for purposes of exposition to adhere to the view that this chapter can be regarded as Paul's work. This does not necessarily prejudge the validity of any of the alternative theories, nor exclude them as possibilities. It merely eliminates the need to qualify each statement with provisos irrelevant to an expositor's task.

Whatever view we select, however, it is possible to regard this concluding chapter of the epistle as in itself a brief "letter" consisting of five parts. There is a note of commendation to introduce Phoebe. Then follows a list of greetings—an unusually long list, as it happens—and this in turn leads to a solemn warning against a factious spirit, and against false teaching. Next we have salutations from the writer's associates, and in conclusion an extended doxology.

1-2. ***A Letter of Introduction.***—Here is a sample of a kind of document which must have been common in the early church (cf. Exeg.). Hospitality was a duty which Christians were expected to accept gladly and without grudging (cf. I Tim. 3:2; Tit. 1:8; I Pet. 4:9), but it obviously lent itself to abuse. Informers, as well as impostors, might insinuate themselves into the life of the worshiping community and do considerable harm. Hospitality was a virtue whose exercise presupposed watchful care; but more important than the necessary safeguards is the assumption that it will be a consistent feature of the life of the church. This follows inevitably from the character of the Christian fellowship. Those who are "members one of another" and who are taught to "bear one another's burdens" will not be unmindful of the particular needs of those who travel. Though hospitality grows out of an awareness of the necessities of others, it issues in the enriching of the lives of those who practice it. It increases fellowship; it promotes a wider understanding; it cements the ties which bind one group to another. The consciousness of belonging to one church scattered throughout the empire but united in a common faith must have been greatly strengthened by every personal tie with members from other congregations. If "the saints" in one center felt anxious to "salute" their brethren in another (cf. II Cor. 13:13; Phil. 4:22), we can imagine

for she hath been a succorer of many, and of myself also.	she has been a helper of many and of myself as well.

this verse may well have suggested the idea of such a letter as a part of this addition to Romans. That Paul should actually have written such a letter to Rome or Ephesus is perfectly natural and credible, as are the terms of his request that Phoebe be received **in the Lord** and assisted **in whatever she may require.** She is described as **a deaconess of the church at Cenchreae,** the port city of Corinth on the Soronic Gulf (see map, p. 354). Paul is in Corinth when he writes Romans, and it is therefore natural for him to know of Phoebe's plan. Although the term **deaconess** is not incompatible with the assumption of authenticity, it does fit, perhaps slightly better, the theory of pseudonymity. For while we read of "deaconesses" in Pliny's letter to Trajan concerning the trials of the Christians (*ca.* A.D. 112), and later Christian literature contains many references to them, there is no other allusion to a deaconess in the N.T., not even in the Pastoral epistles, where church orders and officers are often specifically discussed. Paul does speak, however, of "bishops and deacons" in Phil. 1:1, and comes very close to making a similar reference in Col. 4:7—and where there are "deacons" we cannot rule out the possibility of "deaconesses." On the other hand, what Paul has to say concerning the behavior of the church at Corinth would lead us to suppose that any movement toward an ordered ministry which may have been taking place in his churches and in his period was not in an advanced stage at Corinth; and one would not expect the situation at Cenchreae to be very different. On the whole, one may say that "deaconess" rather suggests a later period, but gives no clear indication. The word **helper** (προστάτις; cf. on 12:8) properly means "patroness," but if this passage is genuine, it is used here in the broad sense of giving hospitality or other help.

how much more firmly the ties were cemented by actual intercourse.

We have no information about Phoebe beyond what Paul gives us; who she was and what she did are matters of inference. We gather that she was a woman of wealth and of higher social position than many of the early disciples. She consequently had the opportunity of helping others and the means to do so. Among the **many** whom she had aided was Paul himself. We may take it, then, that we have in her case another example of the acceptance by early Christians of the obligations which wealth imposed. The claims of sensitive stewardship are of long standing. Barnabas and Joseph of Arimathea might also be cited, though the status of the latter is more doubtful. Most of the Christians were doubtless poor; consequently, more would be expected of—and apparently more was forthcoming from—those who had greater means. Moreover, Phoebe is said here to have been a **deaconess.** Whatever this term may have meant, it would certainly cover a life marked by constant acts of charity and hospitality. Whether these practical ministries had as yet crystallized into clearly defined office, we do not know. Those interested in the development of the Christian community will be content to notice certain facts: (*a*) The life of the church gave ample opportunity for sustained activity in the succor and encouragement of strangers and the needy; (*b*) the spirit of fellowship from the first expressed itself in practical helpfulness; (*c*) women from the earliest days found scope for usefulness in the church, and they were permitted to perform all such ministries as opportunity provided and the state of public opinion allowed; (*d*) as need required, ministries which had proved their value took more permanent shape. This last point is aptly illustrated by what we know of the development of the diaconate. By the end of the N.T. period it is apparently a more integral part of church life than it had been in the earlier days. Organization was in a flexible state, and took firmer shape as the church responded to the needs by which it was faced. Paul appeals, on Phoebe's behalf, for the kind of reception to which she is entitled. Any practical help that she needs she should receive. She may have been traveling in order to attend to business matters; at all events, the recipients of the letter are to **help her in whatever she may require** from them. This, however, is not enough, and Paul suggests a prior duty. They are not simply to welcome her as a guest in their homes, but they are to **receive her in the Lord as befits the saints.** She is a member of

3 Greet Priscilla and Aquila, my helpers in Christ Jesus:

3 Greet Pris'ca and Aquila, my fellow

3-5. We first hear mention of Prisca and Aquila in I Cor. 16:19. Paul there associates them with himself in sending greetings to the church at Corinth. Since it is clear that Paul was in Ephesus at the time (I Cor. 16:8, 19*a*), it is natural to conclude that Prisca and Aquila were there also. And from the fact that mention is made of "the church that meets in their house" one may infer both the relatively settled character of their residence in Ephesus and their prominence in the Ephesian church. There are no other references to them in the Pauline letters except in Rom. 16:3 and II Tim. 4:19 (both times, as also in I Cor. 16:19, in connection with greetings). Indeed, Prisca and Aquila would be only names to us if we could not read of them also in the book of Acts (18:1-3, 18, 26). We are told that when Paul first came to Corinth, he found them there and "because he was of the same trade he stayed with them." The author of Acts tells us that they had only recently arrived in Corinth from Rome, having been forced to leave that city because of Claudius' edict (*ca.* A.D. 41?) expelling Jews—for Aquila, at least, was a Jew. We are not informed by Acts whether or not they had been Christians in Rome (see Intro., p. 361), but they had certainly become such when Paul left Corinth after some two years (Acts 18:11, 18), for they accompanied him to Ephesus and are described as initiating Apollos into some of the deeper meanings of the Christian life. Although there is no full confirmation of this Acts story in Paul's letters, such indications as we have in I Cor. 16:19 give it support: the couple are at Ephesus when he writes, and his sending their greetings to Corinth would be more natural if, as Acts says, they had

the church and must be taken into the life of the fellowship. A Christian is obviously entitled to more than the courtesies of ordinary hospitality; those who claim a deeper kinship should be admitted to a distinctive intimacy. Phoebe, who has so generously helped others, has earned the recompense of a cordial reception wherever she goes in the Christian community.

3-5a. Prisca and Aquila.—There follows an unusually long list of personal greetings. We have already met **Prisca and Aquila** (Acts 18:2-3, 26), and the close relationship which Paul had established with them prepares us for the marked cordiality with which he speaks of them. He had worked with them at his trade, as well as in the task of spreading the gospel. In a life shared so completely and at so many points, understanding would naturally develop into intimacy of an unusual kind. We are grateful for this fleeting glimpse into that world of personal relationships which forms so important a part of life, but concerning which most historical documents are largely silent. Great movements are not made up of events; they owe their quality to the kind of personal fellowship which they fashion. We would assume that spreading the evangel was a task which would create a deep sense of kinship and unity among those engaged in it. From casual references of this kind we know that our surmise is correct.

In this particular case, however, more is involved than the usual camaraderie established among those who live and work together. Paul feels that he is indebted to these friends for his very life. What the incident was, we do not know; but it was sufficiently recent that their very names prompt him to an expression of gratitude, and it was a matter of such general knowledge that he assumes an oblique reference sufficient: **all the churches of the Gentiles** will immediately grasp his meaning; all who are thankful for his ministry will join with him in gratitude for this act of courageous devotion. He knew what danger meant (cf. II Cor. 11:23-28), and he was not likely to underestimate its cost to others. The church of our fathers was not built easily, or without great risk to those who founded it. We who live so securely should also be grateful to those who went in peril of their lives.

In addition to Prisca and Aquila, Paul greets **the church in their house.** They possessed the qualities of understanding and initiative which fitted them for leadership in the church (cf. their relations with Apollos, Acts 18:26). They evidently also had the material means to promote the cause to which they were committed. They had a house large enough to serve as a center for the common life of the community. Here the brethren could gather for worship and for "the breaking of bread." The arrange-

4 Who have for my life laid down their own necks: unto whom not only I give thanks, but also all the churches of the Gentiles.

5 Likewise *greet* the church that is in their house. Salute my well-beloved Epenetus, who is the firstfruits of Achaia unto Christ.

workers in Christ Jesus, 4 who risked their necks for my life, to whom not only I but also all the churches of the Gentiles give thanks; 5 greet also the church in their house. Greet my beloved E-pae'ne-tus, who was the first convert in Asia for Christ.

---

previously lived in Corinth. The fact that Prisca—in Acts she is called Priscilla—is usually named before Aquila has led to the not improbable conclusion that, at least from the point of view of the Christian community, she was the more important of the two.

As we have seen, one of the major objections to the traditional acceptance of ch. 16 as a part of Romans is that such a view requires that Prisca and Aquila be at Rome so soon after they are known to have been established at Ephesus—and at both places with a **church in their house.** When I Corinthians was written, the collection was already under way; it had just been completed when Romans was written. Scarcely more than two years can separate these two letters. There is, of course, nothing impossible about the supposition that this man and his wife have returned to the city where they had lived earlier; and one can better understand Paul's saying what he does about them (i.e., they **risked their necks**) to the Romans, who might not have known this, than to the Ephesians, who undoubtedly would; likewise the comprehensive **all the churches of the Gentiles** comes perhaps less strangely in a letter addressed to Rome than to Ephesus. There is also some archaeological evidence connecting the names of Prisca and Aquila with Rome (see Sanday and Headlam, pp. 418 ff.). Still, especially when the following

---

ment may have been dictated by the circumstances of the fellowship—by its comparatively small numbers and by the meager economic resources of most of its members—but it had manifest advantages as well. When the city crowds were unpredictable and often hostile, small groups meeting in private households were less likely to attract the unfavorable attention of the mob. The setting, too, must have favored the growth of intimacy and understanding—an important factor in an organization which drew its members from various strata of society—and it must have greatly facilitated the task of instructing converts in the meaning of the faith. Probably for groups like this the N.T. letters were first written; and it requires little imagination to reconstruct the scene, as the little company, no doubt mainly of humble folk, gathered in the home of one of the few more affluent members and listened with earnest concentration to the reading of the latest communication from a distinguished leader of the church. It might be a letter actually addressed to them; it might be one originally written to another community, and received in exchange for one of their own (cf. Col. 4:16). It would have to be read slowly, for it demanded close attention; and since it contained far more than could be appropriated on a first hearing, it would be read again, perhaps repeatedly.

5*b*-16. ***Salutation to Friends.***—The greetings to friends expand into a long and varied roster. Where these people lived is open to doubt. But to whatever center the letter was addressed, it remains true that those to whom Paul wrote had probably come together from widely scattered places. As the apostle remembers this person or that, we catch momentary but intriguing glimpses of the life of the early church. **Epaenetus** is singled out as **the first convert in Asia,** and many have assumed that Paul was recalling with satisfaction the first person whom he himself had brought to Christ in that province. Several are mentioned who have worked hard to advance the common cause. The intimate ties which bound together the community are suggested again and again by the affectionate terms which are used. Concerning many of them we can make conjectures, e.g., that **Rufus** is the son of Simon of Cyrene, who bore for our Lord the burden of the Cross (Mark 15:21)—but we can see only faintly through the veil of time. As we read the roll, however, certain deductions can legitimately be drawn:

It is apparent at a glance—and reflection confirms the inference—that Paul's missionary

6 Greet Mary, who bestowed much labor on us.
7 Salute Andronicus and Junia, my kinsmen, and my fellow prisoners, who are of note among the apostles, who also were in Christ before me.

6 Greet Mary, who has worked hard among you.
7 Greet An-dron'i-cus and Ju'ni-as, my kinsmen and my fellow prisoners; they are men of note among the apostles, and they

reference to Epaenetus as **the first convert in Asia** is taken into account, Ephesus is strongly suggested. At the same time all of the facts cited are quite compatible with the hypothesis of pseudonymity. II Timothy is admittedly pseudonymous; and Prisca and Aquila are mentioned there also, again in first place among a number of persons being greeted by the apostle (II Tim. 4:19). If Prisca and Aquila did return to Rome eventually and become important in the tradition of the Roman church, as the archaeological evidence referred to is sometimes held to indicate, a basis in fact would exist for the pseudepigrapher's allusion here.

Of **Epaenetus** we know nothing. If ch. 16 is not genuine, I Cor. 16:15 provides the obvious pattern for this description of him; and it is interesting to note that some MSS read here (as in I Cor. 16:15): **the firstfruits of Achaia** (so KJV).

6-7. Of **Mary** we know nothing from any source. **Andronicus and Junias**—or, possibly "Junia," in which case they may have been man and wife, or brother and sister, and the following description becomes *"persons* of note"—are described as having been Christians before Paul, as being **men of note among the apostles,** and as having been in prison with Paul at some unidentified time. The allusion to the **apostles** will remind us that the usual meaning of this term in the early period was an authorized evangelist—so also in the Didache, a half century or so after Paul. Apparently, however, the word also often had the narrower meaning which later became its only meaning: one who had been directly "sent" by Christ himself. In this sense Paul applies the term to himself, insisting that Christ had called him into his service as definitely as he had called the original disciples (cf. Gal. 1:1; I Cor. 9:1; 15:8-9). Some MSS and fathers read "who

labors supplied him with an immense number of personal contacts. After all, his primary task was to bring people to the knowledge of God's love in Christ, and itineraries and organization were merely the outer framework for his actual work among men and women. In the story of his travels we necessarily lose sight of the individuals with whom he was constantly in contact. A compressed account, like that in Acts, of labors carried out in many places and continued over many years inevitably becomes slightly depersonalized. But Paul never allowed new names and faces to drive old friends from his memory. A list of greetings such as this shows how often his mind turned back to those with whom he had formerly worked. It suggests the gratitude with which he recalled the favors he had received, the concern with which he watched over his converts' growth in grace, the solicitude with which he remembered his friends as he lifted them into God's presence. All this is the very antithesis of the impersonal professionalism which efficiently discharges necessary obligations and yet permits the personal equation to drop from sight. We forget people whom we should remember simply because we have allowed them to be strangers to our thoughts. A. J. Gossip, in the memoir with which he prefaced W. M. Macgregor's *The Making of a Preacher,* reminds his readers of Macgregor's phenomenal memory for people whom he had met, often only casually, many years before. We assume that this is a gift with which nature has endowed some of us but not others; we might be nearer the truth if we admitted that all of us would remember other people better if we really cared about them more. Paul recalled all sorts of men and women because he found room for them in his thoughts and made a place for them in his prayers. Earlier in this letter he has pointed out the way in which love works when it is the dominant motive in our conduct (12:9-21; 13:8-10); here he unconsciously indicates the way in which it affects the pastoral psychology of an apostle.

The list of names, each with its appropriate greeting, gives us a faint conception of the close

8 Greet Amplias, my beloved in the Lord.

9 Salute Urbane, our helper in Christ, and Stachys my beloved.

10 Salute Apelles approved in Christ. Salute them which are of Aristobulus' *household.*

11 Salute Herodion my kinsman. Greet them that be of the *household* of Narcissus, which are in the Lord.

were in Christ before me. 8 Greet Am-pli-
a'tus, my beloved in the Lord. 9 Greet Ur-
ba'nus, our fellow worker in Christ, and
my beloved Sta'chys. 10 Greet A-pel'les, who
is approved in Christ. Greet those who belong to the family of A-ris-tob'u-lus. 11 Greet
my kinsman He-ro'di-on. Greet those in the
Lord who belong to the family of Nar-

---

were in Christ before me" as a description of "the apostles" rather than of Andronicus and Junias. If that reading should be correct, the reference would probably be to "apostles" in the narrower sense, and Paul's idea would be not that Andronicus and Junias were apostles themselves, but that they were highly regarded by the apostles. But the present reading is preferred. Concerning **kinsmen** see Exeg. on vs. 21.

8-15. Nothing whatever is known from any other source about the twenty individuals and two families named in these verses. Only one of the names is mentioned elsewhere in the N.T., that of **Rufus** (vs. 13), mentioned in Mark 15:21. There we are told that the Simon of Cyrene, who was forced into service to bear Jesus' cross to Golgotha, was the father of Alexander and Rufus. It is often argued that since Mark's reference indicates that these two sons were well known, it is not unlikely that this Rufus is the one referred to by Paul as **eminent in the Lord.** If this identification could be established, it would tend to confirm the Roman destination of this chapter, since Mark is generally believed to be writing primarily for the Roman church. But the identification is hardly

---

and affectionate relations which existed between Paul and his converts. We unconsciously assume that the apostle may have been a great man but that he was probably a forbidding companion. Having read through Romans, some of us might view with alarm the prospect of spending an informal evening in Paul's company. We may study his letters for the good of our souls, but we would not instinctively choose him as a friend. There is plenty of evidence, however, to prove that he not only felt a deep affection for his converts, but aroused in them an answering regard. He reminds the Galatians that at one time they would gladly have plucked out their own eyes and given them to him if the gift could have helped him (Gal. 14:15), and the whole tenor of the letter to the Philippians is intelligible only if we assume a relation of the deepest mutual regard. Here, from beginning to end, the word **beloved** recurs again and again, and his references to his former colleagues and his friends reflect a genuine love that could not but have been mutual. There is not a touch of condescension in the apostle's tone; there is no suggestion that he is commending those who have made worthy progress but are still in an elementary stage of Christian nurture. He is writing to those whom he held dear, and the warmth of his greeting shows how intimate was the tie which bound them to him.

The words of commendation which Paul uses are in themselves illuminating. Those who have **worked hard** are singled out for praise more than once. With most of us the words may not have acquired high religious associations; but Paul evidently considered unremitting effort a quality of great importance in the Christian community. A moment's reflection is enough, of course, to convince us that in a hostile world, already devoted to innumerable other cults, the faith of Christ could make progress only if those who accepted it gave unsparingly of their time and effort to win others. There may have been various circumstances which inclined men to respond to the message once they heard it persuasively presented, but "how are they to believe in him of whom they have never heard? And how are they to hear without a preacher?" (10:14.) There was no illusion in the apostolic church that the good news would spread even if its members remained inert and apathetic. Paul also mentions those who, like himself, had been **prisoners** for their faith. A revolutionary creed like Christianity was certain to shake a large number of vested interests whose beneficiaries could gain the ear of magistrates and governors. We see the results at Philippi,

12 Salute Tryphena and Tryphosa, who
labor in the Lord. Salute the beloved Persis, which labored much in the Lord.
13 Salute Rufus chosen in the Lord, and
his mother and mine.
14 Salute Asyncritus, Phlegon, Hermas,
Patrobas, Hermes, and the brethren which
are with them.
15 Salute Philologus, and Julia, Nereus,
and his sister, and Olympas, and all the
saints which are with them.

cis'sus. 12 Greet those workers in the Lord,
Try-phae'na and Try-pho'sa. Greet the beloved Persis, who has worked hard in the
Lord. 13 Greet Rufus, eminent in the Lord,
also his mother and mine. 14 Greet A-syn'-
cri-tus, Phle'gon, Her'mes, Pat'ro-bas,
Her'mas, and the brethren who are with
them. 15 Greet Phi-lol'o-gus, Julia, Ne'reus
and his sister, and O-lym'pas, and all the

better than a guess. A warm touch is imparted by Paul's statement that Rufus' **mother** has also been a "mother" to him—the allusion certainly suggests a long and intimate acquaintance. We notice also the rather lavish use of the word "beloved" (ἀγαπητός). It is used four times (vss. 5, 8, 9, 12), of Epaenetus, Ampliatus (Amplius), Stachys, and Persis (a woman, as the Greek shows). One cannot fail to be slightly amused by the allusion (in vs. 12) to those hard **workers in the Lord,** "Dainty" and "Delicate"—for that is what the names Tryphaena and Tryphosa mean. It is usually surmised that they were twin sisters. It is sometimes said that the five persons named in vs. 14 form a single family (with which a church meets), and that the same is true of the five persons named in vs. 15. But this interpretation is not necessary at all; conceivably as many as ten "house churches" are represented in the two verses, although such an intention is highly unlikely.

A great deal of research has been devoted to the matter of the geographical distribution of these names (see Lietzmann, and Sanday and Headlam for bibliographical

where Paul and Silas were thrown into prison (Acts 16:19-24), and at Ephesus, where the silversmiths whipped up a tumult that might have led to results more serious still (Acts 19:23-41). Many nameless sufferers paid for their witness with the loss of their liberty, and Paul's greeting rescues two of them **(Andronicus and Junias)** from oblivion. This particular pair had other grounds of commendation: they were **men of note among the apostles, and they were in Christ before me.** The term "apostle" was certainly not restricted to the twelve, even when Paul is added to their number, "as of one born out of due time" (I Cor. 15:8). Again we realize how pitifully fragmentary is our knowledge of the early church. Men holding a distinguished place in the life of the expanding fellowship are known to us only by name, and that by what is virtually an accident. They must have been Jews—Paul refers to them as **my kinsmen**—and they had shared with Paul in the wider mission to the Gentile world. The fact that they were Christians of longer standing than Paul himself showed that their faith had been proved and tested by the years. Persistence is also a virtue not to be despised, and occasional hints in the N.T. show how poignantly the church was conscious of the danger and the tragedy of apostasy. Paul also singles out for commendation those who bear a firmly established name for conspicuously Christian character. **Rufus is eminent in the Lord; Apelles** is a disciple whose constancy has been vindicated under trial. The silent witness of proven worth deserves and receives the apostle's commendation. Whereupon to all of it, as an established part of Christian worship, he adds his salutation: **Greet one another with a holy kiss** (vs. 16). The **holy kiss** stood as an outward symbol of the love and good will which ought to unite the members of the church. Hence in due course it came to represent the peace which is created only by affection one for another. The need of some visible expression of the unanimity which rests on a deep respect for and response to one another still remains; unfortunately we have not discovered the modern counterpart to the **holy kiss.** Then, having remembered so many individuals by name, he finally sends a comprehensive greeting from all the other Christian communities to the church to which he writes. One who works for all is entitled to speak for all. If this part of the letter was really addressed to the Christians at Rome, the unusual form of the greeting—without exact parallel in **Paul's**

16 Salute one another with a holy kiss. The churches of Christ salute you.
17 Now I beseech you, brethren, mark them which cause divisions and offenses contrary to the doctrine which ye have learned; and avoid them.

saints who are with them. 16 Greet one another with a holy kiss. All the churches of Christ greet you.
17 I appeal to you, brethren, to take note of those who create dissensions and difficulties, in opposition to the doctrine which you have been taught; avoid them.

---

references). The most important result of this research is to establish the fact that all of these are names which would have been found at Rome in the first century, but would also have been found in any other large center in the empire. Many of them are frequently found as names of slaves or freedmen. In spite of occasional arguments to the contrary, it may be said that these names, simply as such, give us no clear clue as to the destination of this chapter. They are perfectly compatible with any of the three possible views of its original character which were mentioned at the beginning of our discussion of it.

16. In three other letters Paul mentions the "holy kiss" (I Thess. 5:26; I Cor. 16:20; II Cor. 13:12), and it is probably implied in Phil. 4:21. We find it also mentioned in I Pet. 5:14. Justin Martyr lets us know that it was a regular part of the liturgy at Rome *ca.* A.D. 150 (I *Apology* 65), and there are many later allusions to it. On the significance of **all the churches of Christ** comment has been made (see Intro., p. 367). It is more easily explicable if the chapter went to Rome than if it was addressed originally to Ephesus; but it fits best perhaps into a later period altogether.

17-20. On this passage see Intro., p. 365. This paragraph, in view of the newness of the subject matter and the abrupt change of tone, raises as serious a question as to the original connection of this chapter with the letter to the Romans as does the preceding paragraph of greetings. Indeed, some scholars who affirm that connection have less difficulty working out a satisfactory explanation of the names than of this paragraph of warning. The tone is that of a pastor addressing one of his own churches threatened by schism owing to the activities within it of teachers who are **in opposition to the doctrine** he has taught them. For **the doctrine which you have been taught** would most naturally mean "the doctrine I [or representatives of mine] have taught you." **I rejoice over you**—indeed the whole of vs. 19—also strongly suggests the pastoral relationship. But the letter up to this point not only shows clearly that no such relationship actually existed between Paul and Rome, but also represents Paul as eager to let the Roman Christians know that *he is quite well aware* that no such relationship exists. He has

---

epistles—may reflect the respect with which other Christian communities regarded the church which stood so strategically at the heart of the Roman Empire. But actually, every church possesses opportunities and responsibilities which are unique. The Christians at Ephesus no less than those at Rome require the support of all who share the faith with them.

17-20. ***Beware of Deceivers.***—Experience has taught Paul that those who stand are in danger of falling, and need to take heed accordingly. He therefore now appeals to his readers with the earnestness which is characteristic of his writing whenever he feels that the safety of his fellow Christians is in jeopardy. One of the invaluable safeguards against deception is a keen awareness of the forces which are actually at work around us. One who has the discernment to recognize what is happening will be neither indifferent nor naïve. The somnolence which does not bother, the uncritical carelessness which does not see—these are the qualities which give evil men their opportunity. The watchful Christian will therefore **take note** —but with practical results: he will **avoid** those who might encompass his overthrow. The enemies against whom Paul gives warning are **those who create dissensions and difficulties:** these are the men against whom we need to be constantly on our guard. All the N.T. writers, and certainly Paul not least among them, regard with horror the partisan spirit which breaks up the church into warring factions. From what Paul says elsewhere (e.g., Gal.

18 For they that are such serve not our Lord Jesus Christ, but their own belly; and by good words and fair speeches deceive the hearts of the simple.

18 For such persons do not serve our Lord Christ, but their own appetites,[z] and by fair and flattering words they deceive the

[z] Greek *their own belly* (Phil. 3. 19).

carefully avoided any appearance of presumption. Such reticence is the more striking because Paul *can* take a very "high" view of his authority over his own churches and can express it without apology. This careful restraint through fifteen chapters hardly prepares us for what sounds like a frank assuming of a pastor's responsibilities *and prerogatives* at the very end of the last chapter. Surely, if the chapter is genuine at all, this is a strong argument for Ephesus as against Rome, especially as no reference was made to these schismatics in Rom. 1–15.

If the passage is regarded as authentic, the most natural way to understand the reference to **those who create dissensions and difficulties** is as pointing to the Judaizers (see Gal. 1:7 and throughout; Phil. 3:2-21). So it is taken by Kühl, Sanday and Headlam, Lietzmann, Kirk, etc. Dodd questions this identification, suggesting with a great deal of plausibility that the source of the difficulty was some teacher or group with "quasi-gnostic speculations." A number of sentences and phrases confirm this suggestion: vs. 18 (especially **by fair and flattering words they deceive the hearts of the simple-minded**) reminds one of what is known otherwise of the approach and methods of the Gnostics (cf. e.g., II Tim. 3:6-7; II Pet. 2:3; 3:16). Also the injunction to be **wise** (σοφός) **as to what is good and guileless as to what is evil** (a reminiscence of a saying of Jesus? cf. Matt. 10:16) sounds more like a warning against Gnostics with their "wisdom" than against Judaizers with their "law." Although the reference in vs. 20 to the "enemy" as **Satan** recalls II Cor. 11:12-15, it also recalls such terms as "antichrist" (I John 2:22) and "the firstborn of Satan" (Polyc. Phil. 7:1; Irenaeus *Against Heresies* III. 3. 4). The phrase **their own belly** (vs. 18) might be taken as a reference to the licentiousness of some Gnostics if a similar phrase were not used in Phil. 3:18-19 in connection with a warning about the Judaizers. The meaning in both places is probably something like: "They are motivated by the crassest self-interest." The God who is invoked (vs. 20) to **crush** the

5:20), we know that he regarded the destruction of unity as one of the characteristic "works of the flesh." **Dissensions** are the outward result of strife and jealousy; Paul knew that there were few greater obstacles to the well-being of the Christian community. The whole tenor of his mission had been to encourage the works of the spirit and expose the works of the flesh. This was not a distinctive contribution which he brought to the evangelizing of the Gentiles; he believed it to be a necessary part of the gospel. **The doctrine** which Christians **have been taught** leaves no room for the hateful activities of those who sow division. Here is no variant which Paul has imported into the Christian message, but plainly an emphasis which he considered common to all the recognized leaders of the church. He does not identify the men whose subversive work he so much dreads. Whoever they are, he is sure that they **do not serve our Lord Christ.** So much their activities proclaim; anyone whose work breaks down the church and sows division among its members cannot truly be the servant of the church's master. Those who do not serve Christ usually end by serving themselves. The two are plainly opposites, and usually they prove to be alternatives. There is something essentially selfish and irreligious in the outlook of the man who creates dissension in the Christian fellowship. Since he is not seeking the well-being of all, he must be intent upon promoting his own advantage, and by an inevitable declension his ambitions are increasingly concentrated on his lower **appetites.** The fundamental incompatibility between serving Christ and serving self recalls the mutually exclusive objectives which Christ himself so firmly placed in opposition to each other. It is as possible to serve God and mammon as it is to serve Christ and self. But those who seek false ends usually find specious reasons for doing so. To deceive **by fair and flattering words** may point to the *deliberate* confusing of the minds of simple folk; on the other hand, those who deceive others are often self-deceived. The human

19 For your obedience is come abroad unto all *men*. I am glad therefore on your behalf: but yet I would have you wise unto that which is good, and simple concerning evil.

hearts of the simple-minded. 19 For while your obedience is known to all, so that I rejoice over you, I would have you wise as to what is good and guileless as to what is

heretic is **the God of peace** because it is the peace of the church which has been disturbed (cf. vs. 17).

But if it is a group with Gnostic leanings against which the apostle is warning the church, the paragraph fits more easily into an early second-century period than into Paul's own time. Dodd cites, as evidence that Paul was troubled by schismatics of this variety, Phil. 3:18-19; I Cor. 5:1-13; 6:12-20; Colossians (presumably 2:8-23); and Acts 20:29-30. But what justification is there for regarding Phil. 3:18-19 as dealing with others than are being discussed in the preceding part of the same chapter, viz., the Judaizers? As for the two passages in I Corinthians, they do not need to be taken—indeed they cannot easily be taken—as aimed at sectarian teachers. Paul is warning against *immorality,* not against a *heresy* which permits of, or encourages, immorality. The speech of Paul in Acts 20 is obviously a source for the end of the first century, at the earliest; certainly not for Paul's own time. We are left with some references in Colossians (2:8-23) to what appears to be incipient Gnostic teaching. Disregarding legitimate questions as to the authenticity of the text of Colossians, we may still say that there is

mind apparently recoils from the conscious and considered choice of what it sees to be evil and unprincipled ways. The tribute which vice pays to virtue is as much the blurring of its own insight as the hoodwinking of its neighbor's perception. In any case, it learns the art of offering false but specious reasons for what it does. Therefore, again, **take note.** The N.T. never commends the simple-mindedness of those who are merely gullible. It expects that Christians will be alert to what is happening, shrewd to assess the forces actually at work, and quick to support the good and resist the evil. The seemingly fair outward forms of wickedness will not then mislead the Christian. It is, of course, a discovery renewed age by age that vice does not meet us clothed in its appropriate garments. The word pictures painted by the writer of Proverbs, the imagery in which *The Faerie Queene* abounds, Hamlet's bitter discovery "that one may smile, and smile, and be a villain"—each of these is only another variant of the ancient theme that virtue must be vigilant if it is to avoid deception. Those who are so **simple-minded** that they suspect no evil will certainly be deceived, for the agents of destruction insinuate their poison with such specious suavity that the guileless are often overthrown before they are even aware of the menace that confronts them.

19. *Wise as Serpents, Harmless as Doves.*—Paul is writing to warn those who are exposed to danger rather than to rescue those who have already succumbed. He is confident—though not without a touch of anxiety—because the faithfulness and stability of his correspondents have made them known throughout the Christian world. Still, those who are forewarned are forearmed, and once again there creeps into Paul's writing a touch of the pastoral concern which is so strongly marked in so many of his letters. The tone of restrained propriety which has characterized the epistle hitherto breaks down in the face of his anxiety about them (cf. Exeg.). Constancy of the kind he desires to find in them, as in all the churches, is due to the combination of at least three qualities. He has mentioned **obedience** as an attribute his readers already possess, and he has used the term more than once. We can assume that it implies an adequate understanding of what Christianity is and a faithful acceptance of the demands such knowledge lays upon us. It would include both insight and discipline, the perception of the true nature of the faith and the unswerving loyalty which submits to its requirements. Neither by itself is sufficient. Without understanding, our discipleship is only a conventional conformity to a pattern externally imposed; without the conscientious discharge of what faith demands, our knowledge is only a theoretical scheme of ideas never brought to the test of ordinary life. Beyond this, it is necessary for the Christian to be **wise as to what is good and guileless as to what is evil.** Moral integrity is always based on the ability to dis-

20 And the God of peace shall bruise Satan under your feet shortly. The grace of our Lord Jesus Christ *be* with you. Amen.

evil; 20 then the God of peace will soon crush Satan under your feet. The grace of our Lord Jesus Christ be with you.[a]

[a] Other ancient authorities omit this sentence.

no indication, even as the text stands, that Paul has a very definite enemy in mind or that he feels toward him the bitter hostility which he regularly displays toward the Judaizers and which also is exhibited in the present passage. On the other hand, vss. 17-21 cannot fail to remind one of such passages as Acts 20:29-30; II Pet. 2:1-3; II John 4-11; and II Tim. 3:1-17. On the whole, one may best sum up the situation by saying that this paragraph of warning against heretics is most difficult to explain as a part of Romans; is less difficult in a note to Ephesus; but is accounted for with least difficulty when thought of as reflecting the situation in the period of the Pastoral and the Catholic epistles, i.e., the first half of the second century.

If this chapter as a whole is taken as an authentic part of Romans, no better way of explaining its peculiar features can be proposed than that of Lietzmann: "Up to this point Paul has set forth his position without direct reference to particular incidents in the community; one gets the impression that now at the end of the letter the apostle quite suddenly and impulsively breaks through the restraint he has so far imposed on himself, clearly identifies the enemy, praises and warns the Romans and expresses his hope of the victory of the good. He may have suddenly taken the pen from Tertius the

tinguish clearly and exactly between what is really right and what is actually wrong. In a world where wolves often wear sheep's clothing we need alertness and discernment if we are to avoid being deceived. The wisdom which Paul commends is a practical quality, shrewd to discriminate between what is really good and what is so in appearance only. "All that glisters is not gold"—the proverb has a moral as well as a material application. It is easy to be content with a standard of goodness which a more penetrating insight would perceive to be insufficient or even positively harmful. But unfortunately shrewdness of insight often degenerates into nothing higher than cynicism. Because we can pierce the false front of specious goodness, we dismiss even authentic virtue as a sham. When that happens, we have fallen prey to the guile of evil. Paul is not discussing the innocence which is ignorant of evil; he is concerned with the outlook which knows what is wrong and remains uncontaminated by it. And this is a virtue even harder to acquire than the wisdom which he has just commended. It is easier to recognize the good and remain untouched than it is to know the wrong and remain unchanged. One cannot read his words without calling to mind the parallel saying of Jesus (Matt. 10:16). The cynic has remarked that in practice Christians are often as wise as doves and as harmless as serpents. It is to avoid that kind of perversion of our values that Paul is appealing to his readers.

20. *Assurance of Victory.*—The appropriate results will speedily follow. Evil men create dissensions; Christians who are firm in their essential obedience, and aware of the moral realities by which they are surrounded, will discover that on their side they have the resources of the God who creates and maintains true peace. **The God of peace** is a phrase which repeated use has made familiar to Paul's readers. It is not only apt in this context because of the implied contrast with the difficulties which mischief-makers can create, but it also carries the reminder that victory over disruptive forces is not achieved by human means alone. Whenever we find the power of Satan overthrown, we can rightly be wary of believing that our own strength or skill should get the credit. The language which the apostle uses is skillfully chosen to kindle the imagination of men and women who face the hard battles of the daily moral struggle. On the one hand, it suggests an echo of Gen. 3:15: and anyone nurtured in the early church would be familiar with the biblical interpretation which found in what Christ had done for us the fulfillment of that ancient promise. It was not a vague hope, ill-defined and unconfirmed by experience, that Paul held forth. It was related to the very substance of his message. It recalled the great deliverance which Christ had wrought for men. Moreover, to find your antagonist **under your feet** was the imagery for a complete and unquestioned triumph. The day of final victory to which the

21 Timotheus my workfellow, and Lucius, and Jason, and Sosipater, my kinsmen, salute you.
22 I Tertius, who wrote *this* epistle, salute you in the Lord.

21 Timothy, my fellow worker, greets you; so do Lucius and Jason and So-sip′a-ter, my kinsmen.
22 I Ter′tius, the writer of this letter, greet you in the Lord.

---

scribe to write these forceful words—then he gives it back and begins (with vs. 21) quietly to go on, dictating additional items, slowly and with pauses. In such a pause vs. 22 was written."

21-23. Little needs or can be said about these greetings. **Timothy** is well known—at least as a name. He is mentioned by Paul many times as one of his associates; and Acts 16:1-3 gives us an account of how this association began. Nothing is known of the rest. **Lucius** is sometimes identified with the Lucius of Acts 13:1, **Jason** with the Jason of Acts 17:5-9, and **Sosipater** with the Sopater of Acts 20:4. If Rom. 16 is genuine, these identifications are possible, but not in the least necessary, since all the names are common ones. If Rom. 16 is pseudonymous, it is, of course, possible, even probable, that Acts is the source of these names, but this supposition also is not necessary. **Tertius,** the scribe or amanuensis, is nowhere else referred to, nor is **Quartus.** A **Gaius** is mentioned in I Cor. 1:14, and again the name is found in Acts 20:4. An **Erastus** is mentioned in Acts 19:22 (again along with Timothy), and also in II Tim. 4:20. Is it by any chance significant that of these eight names the only ones not mentioned in Acts are "Tertius" and "Quartus" and that Acts 20:4 does mention a "Secundus"? All four of the last names mentioned in these verses are Latin names.

Gaius is described as Paul's **host** and host **to the whole church.** If this passage is not genuine, the intended meaning is probably that the whole church in Corinth meets in Gaius' house. Actually, however, the church at Corinth would almost certainly have been too large to assemble in one person's residence. And so, if the passage is genuine,

---

writer to the Hebrews refers is a day when all things shall be put "in subjection under his feet" (Heb. 2:8). It is a moral victory of this dramatic finality to which Paul looks forward. He has pointed out the danger which threatens his readers (vss. 17-18); he has shown the qualities which are necessary if it is to be successfully resisted (vs. 19); now he indicates that the appropriate victory will be granted in resounding completeness by the God from whom come all the resources needful for our moral warfare.

It remains only to add the blessing which appropriately crowns this final word of assurance and hope. **The grace of our Lord Jesus Christ** is Paul's favorite benediction. Sometimes he expands and embellishes it, but in one form or another his concluding word always comes back to the quality which, more than any other, seems to him to epitomize all that Christ means to his disciples and all that he does for them. He prays that they may consciously be surrounded by that winning constraint in which attractiveness and transforming power are so amazingly combined, and which has its source in Jesus Christ. But grace is with us not simply as an enveloping aura; it is Christ's gift to us in such fashion that we finally possess within us what at first we only sense about us.

21-23. ***Paul's Companions.***—Dodd[1] suggests that the brief section, vss. 17-20, is the concluding note, written with Paul's own hand, which is a characteristic feature of most of his letters. Such a view would explain the difference of tone which marks it, and the suitability of the benediction with which he concludes the autograph verses. But an equally distinctive mark of Paul's writing is the care with which he associates others—his companions and his fellow workers—with himself. Some of the men whom he mentions are well known to us; others we can conjecturally identify; others still are only names. **Timothy** was more than a traveling companion; he was a friend who occupied a relationship of unusual intimacy. It may be that some of the others are the representatives of the churches of Macedonia, already assembling to accompany Paul to Jerusalem with the offering for the poorer members of the mother church. In that case we can easily imagine something of the eager preparations already afoot

[1] *Epistle of Paul to Romans, ad loc.*

23 Gaius mine host, and of the whole church, saluteth you. Erastus the chamberlain of the city saluteth you, and Quartus a brother.
24 The grace of our Lord Jesus Christ *be* with you all. Amen.
25 Now to him that is of power to stablish you according to my gospel, and the

23 Ga'ius, who is host to me and to the whole church, greets you. E-ras'tus, the city treasurer, and our brother Quartus, greet you.[b]
25 Now to him who is able to strengthen

[b] Other ancient authorities insert verse 24, *The grace of our Lord Jesus Christ be with you all. Amen.*

---

one must suppose that Paul intends to say only that Gaius always stood ready to welcome and entertain Christians in need of hospitality. He kept "open house" for the church.

Something must be said about the word **kinsmen** in vss. 7, 11, and 21. Paul is represented as mentioning six **kinsmen**; there are three at Rome, Andronicus, Junias, and Herodion; and there are three with him as he writes, Lucius, Jason, and Sosipater. The primary meaning of "kinsman" is a blood relative in the ordinary sense. Such is its sense everywhere else in the N.T. (Mark 6:4; Luke 1:36; 2:44; 14:12; 21:16; John 18:26; Acts 10:24) except at Rom. 9:3, where Paul explains that he is using the term in the broadest sense to mean his fellow Jews. It is commonly assumed that such is also its meaning in ch. 16. This may well be true, and if the chapter is genuine, *must* be true, since it is in the highest degree unlikely that Paul has as many as three relatives either within the membership of the Roman church or with him as companions. Still, it is well to remember that the word "kinsmen" most easily means "relatives"; and that the meaning "fellow countrymen" is preferred by most translators and commentators only because of the improbability just referred to. If the chapter is pseudonymous, the more natural meaning is almost certainly intended, the references to Paul's relatives serving the later writer's purpose in strengthening Paul's ties with the Roman church. (See Intro., pp. 367-68.)

Vs. 24 is missing in the best MSS.

IX. The Final Doxology (16:25-27)

See the Intro. as to the various places in the letter to the Romans which this doxology has occupied in the MS tradition. There is a common recognition that Paul

---

for the journey eastward. It would be only right that his immediate associates should join in greetings to other Christians closely identified with his labors, past or yet to come. **Gaius**—perhaps one of the few whom Paul himself had baptized at Corinth (cf. I Cor. 1:14)—was obviously a man with whom the apostle had special ties. It was natural that he should entertain Paul when he revisited Corinth, but he was also **host . . . to the whole church.** Whichever meaning we accept—that he kept open house for Christian travelers, or that the local church gathered in his home—we are left with the mental image of a man with both the inclination and the means to make his own house one of the centers of the whole Christian community. **Erastus, the city treasurer,** would be a man of considerable importance in a society composed mainly of humble folk, and his name is possibly included because he, more than most of the other members, might have contacts in another city. Who was **our brother Quartus?** We do not know. **Tertius,** however, who acted as Paul's amanuensis, has a chance to interject his own word of salutation. This in itself entitles us to draw certain inferences regarding Paul's relations with those on whose labors he depended. If he had treated his scribe merely as "a hand," he might have ignored him altogether. A perfunctory courtesy would have included his name among those of others whose greetings are conveyed in the letter. Tertius, however, has had a distinctive responsibility in the writing; moreover, he is a Christian. On both grounds it is fitting that he should send his own word of greeting to those who will read what he has written.

25-27. *Praise at the End.*—The problem of the last chapters of Romans makes the status of some of the benedictions a little uncertain. But whoever may have been the author of the final verses of the letter, we can accept

preaching of Jesus Christ, according to the revelation of the mystery, which was kept secret since the world began,

26 But now is made manifest, and by the Scriptures of the prophets, according to the commandment of the everlasting God, made known to all nations for the obedience of faith:

you according to my gospel and the preaching of Jesus Christ, according to the revelation of the mystery which was kept secret
for long ages 26 but is now disclosed and
through the prophetic writings is made
known to all nations, according to the command of the eternal God, to bring about

---

probably did not write it, but that it was composed at some stage in the evolution of the Pauline corpus in order to bring this letter to an impressive close. It is held by some to have stood first after ch. 14, in the form of the letter which ended with that chapter, and then to have been moved to the end of ch. 16 in other MSS and to the end of ch. 15 in still others. If it was created in the first place to close the short fourteen-chapter form of Romans, it is possible that—except for parts of vs. 26—it was created by Marcionites, as some scholars have held; in that case the alterations in vs. 26, including the addition of **the prophetic writings** (i.e., the O.T.) was made when the doxology was adopted for use at the end of the longer forms. But it is just as likely that the doxology was composed in its present form for use at the end of ch. 16. This would obviously be most likely if the chapter as a whole is regarded as pseudonymous.

The verb **strengthen** doubtless refers to the need for help in overcoming the opposition of the heretics referred to in vss. 17-21. The **preaching** is referred to in this epistle only here, but it is a good Pauline term (cf. I Cor. 1:21 ff.), and has a meaning substantially equivalent to **gospel.** The idea that the Christian message is a **mystery which was kept secret for long ages** but which God has now revealed is also not strange to Paul (see I Cor. 2:6-7; Col. 1:24-29; 2:2-3; also Rom. 11:25). The reason for distrusting the doxology is its un-Pauline style and the unlikelihood that Paul would, in giving

---

them as the ending which to some primitive Christian—whether Paul or not—seemed appropriate to this great epistle. The fitting climax must be one of praise, but appropriately it gathers together many of the leading ideas of the letter as a whole. With deep gratitude the writer recalls what God can do for his hearers. The weak are made strong, the unstable are established. When the miracle of regeneration happens, it takes place according to a method which God has supplied. The only appropriate way in which men can be redeemed into new and vigorous life is by entering into God's purpose. When they understand what is his will, its power can work in and through them. But the **gospel and the preaching of Jesus Christ** are the means which God has provided for enlightening our understanding. When the truth is so set before us that we can grasp and appropriate it, we are on the threshold of the glorious liberty of the children of God—delivered from the power of evil and set free by God's gift, but in such a way that our religious indebtedness is the guarantee of our moral independence. That is why preaching the gospel—a procedure so slow and apparently so precarious —takes precedence of any direct method which would override man's freedom. Actually, God has always dealt patiently with his children, bringing them gradually to a fuller understanding of the truth. The process is one in which the initiative remains with him—that is why it can and must be called **revelation;** but only in "the fullness of time" has the full truth been declared. In Jesus Christ God has **disclosed** what men did not know and for themselves could not discover. **For long ages** even those who were nearest to the truth did not grasp **the mystery,** did not know of "God's world-embracing purpose of redemption." But once it has been disclosed, **the prophetic writings,** with their intuitions and their flashes of foresight, provide the confirmatory evidence that is needed to make men recognize that God's purpose knows no bounds. To bring **all nations** to walk in the light of the gospel—to understand its truth and to accept its demands—is not an optional interest which some Christians accept but others are free to ignore. Behind the substance of this whole letter, with its disclosure of how God's purpose has unfolded, of what the gospel gives us of spiritual liberty, of what

27 To God only wise, *be* glory through Jesus Christ for ever. Amen.

¶ Written to the Romans from Corinthus, *and sent* by Phebe servant of the church at Cenchrea.

obedience to the faith — **27** to the only wise God be glory for evermore through Jesus Christ! Amen.

so impressive a close to the epistle, strike a note which has not once been struck in the epistle as a whole. The Epistle to the Romans is known to have been in final place in some MSS of the Pauline letters (so Tertullian, etc.); it is an attractive suggestion that the original purpose of this doxology was to bring the whole Pauline collection to a suitable close. The doxology reminds one somewhat of Eph. 3:20-21 and perhaps was based on that model.

it asks from us in moral service, lies the conviction that our response must correspond to **the command of the eternal God.** A strong phrase is needed to suggest a mandatory requirement. It is not a temporary duty laid upon us. But the blessing, so comprehensive in its scope, has by this time become complicated in its structure, and the writer breaks off abruptly and returns to his ascription of praise. The unsearchable wisdom of God is manifest in the gospel, whose nature and terms the preceding verses have declared. In our confused and bewildered world this is the only true wisdom we are ever likely to achieve. In gratitude we return to him what is most due—**glory**—and we are able to offer it only **through Jesus Christ.** He who makes known the depths of the divine purpose, he it is, and not another, who makes possible our approach to God in thankfulness and praise. **Amen.**

Joppa
Bethlehem
2550'
Jerusalem
2593'
Jericho
820 FEET BELOW SEA LEVEL
DEAD
SEA
1292 FEET BELOW SEA LEVEL
Jord
PALESTINE
in New Testament Times
© PIERCE & SMITH